The Culture of Critique

Third Edition

The
Culture
of
Critique

An Evolutionary Analysis of Jewish
Involvement in Twentieth-Century
Intellectual and Political Movements

Kevin MacDonald

ANTELOPE HILL PUBLISHING

Acknowledgements

I acknowledge the contributions of several colleagues whose work I have benefited from greatly. All have been contributors to *The Occidental Quarterly* and *The Occidental Observer*.

Andrew Joyce is a scholar with a Ph.D. in Jewish Studies whose work is cited throughout this revision. I call your attention especially to his important essay "'Modify the Standards of the In-Group': On Jews and Mass Communication" which appeared in the Summer, 2019 issue of *The Occidental Quarterly* and is an important contribution on the Frankfurt School's influence on mass communication in the United States. He has also written on various other topics, including how riots in late nineteenth- and early twentieth-century Russia were exaggerated by Jewish activists to gain sympathy for Jewish suffering and to promote immigration of Jews to the West, and he has written important essays on how Jewish activists have promoted the work of Jewish intellectuals, such as Baruch Spinoza, by grossly exaggerating their contributions to Western intellectual history.

Brenton Sanderson has revealed through his work that ethnic networking among Jewish artists and critics has resulted in exalted reputations for Jewish artists such as Mark Rothko and the Dadaist and Abstract Expressionist movements, while denigrating the reputation of Richard Wagner who had negative attitudes on Jewish influence in music. He has also written extensively on Jewish influence on Australian culture and politics, including advocacy for Israel, promoting immigration and multiculturalism in Australia, ending the White Australia policy, and promoting Aboriginal causes.

Szilárd Csonthegyi is a Hungarian scholar who has performed exhaustive research on the long history of ethnic conflict between Jews and non-Jews, with a particular emphasis on Hungary. He called my attention to a great deal of material that is now online, such as the correspondence of Franz Boas and Frankfurt School intellectuals. This material was not available in earlier editions of this book and has been invaluable in fleshing out the Jewish connections of these scholars, such as their connections to wealthy Jewish donors and their close relationships with the organized Jewish community. His work was also the basis for my section on psychoanalysis in Hungary, particularly on the work of Sandor Ferenczi, in Chapter 5.

Contents

Preface to the 2025 Edition

The Culture of Critique (hereafter *CofC*) was originally published in 1998 by Praeger, an academic publisher. The thesis of the book is a difficult one indeed—difficult not only because it is difficult to establish, but also because it challenges many fundamental assumptions about our contemporary intellectual and political existence.

CofC describes how Jewish intellectuals initiated and advanced a number of important intellectual and political movements during the twentieth century. I argue that these movements are attempts to alter Western societies in a manner that would neutralize or end anti-Semitism and enhance the prospects for Jewish group continuity and upward mobility either in an overt or in a semi-cryptic manner. Several of these Jewish movements (e.g., Jewish activism promoting the shift in immigration policy favoring non-European peoples) have attempted to weaken the power of their perceived competitors—the European peoples who early in the twentieth century had assumed a dominant position not only in their traditional homelands in Europe, but also in the United States and the wider Anglosphere. At a theoretical level, these movements are viewed as the outcome of conflicts of interest between Jews and non-Jews in the construction of culture and in various public policy issues. Ultimately, these movements are viewed as the expression of a group evolutionary strategy by Jews in their competition for social, political, and cultural dominance with non-Jews.

Here I attempt to answer some typical criticisms that have been leveled against *CofC*.[1] I also discuss issues raised by several books that have appeared since the publication of *CofC*.

There have been criticisms that I am viewing Judaism as a monolithic entity. This is definitely not the case. Rather, with all the movements that I discuss, my methodology has been as follows:

(1) Find influential movements dominated by Jews, with no implication that all or most Jews are involved in these movements and no restrictions on what the movements are. For example, I touch on Jewish neoconservatism (Ch. 4), which is a departure in some ways from the other movements I discuss. In general, relatively few Jews were involved in most of these movements, and significant numbers of Jews may have been unaware of their existence. Even Jewish leftist radicalism—surely the most widespread and influential Jewish subculture of the twentieth century—may have been a minority movement within Jewish communities in the United States and other Western societies for most periods. As a result, when I criticize these movements, I am not necessarily criticizing most Jews. Nevertheless, these movements were influential, and they were Jewishly motivated.

(2) Determine whether the Jewish participants in these movements both identified as Jews *and* thought of their involvement in the movement as advancing specific Jewish interests. Motivations for involvement may be unconscious or involve self-deception, but for the most part it was quite easy and straightforward to find evidence for both these propositions. If I thought that self-deception was important (as in the case of many Jewish radicals), I provided evidence that in fact they did identify as Jews and were deeply concerned about Jewish issues, despite surface appearances to the contrary.

Thus it does not stand or fall on whether Jews in a particular movement constitute more than their percentage of the population as a whole, whether Jews in general are ethnocentric, the rate of Jewish intermarriage, or whether most Jews were even aware of particular movements—criticisms that have been leveled at CofC by Nathan Cofnas.[2] The focus is on describing the Jewish identities of the main figures of influential movements and their concern with specific Jewish issues, such as combating anti-Semitism, as well as the dynamics of these movements—ethnic networking, centering around charismatic figures, connections with prestigious universities and media, involvement of the organized Jewish community, and non-Jews who participated in the movements and their motivations.

---

[1] See also my website: http://www.kevinmacdonald.net/replies.htm.
[2] See my article in *Philosophia* (MacDonald, 2022b), which was then retracted and republished in *The Occidental Quarterly* (MacDonald, 2022a) along with a discussion of the retraction.

(3) Attempt to gauge the influence of these movements on gentile society. Keep in mind that the influence of an intellectual or political movement dominated by Jews is independent of the percentage of the Jewish community that is involved in or supports the movement.

(4) Try to show how non-Jews responded to these movements—for example, were they a source of anti-Semitism?

Several of the movements I discuss have been very influential in the social sciences. However, I do not argue that there are no Jews who do good social science, and in fact I provide a list of prominent Jewish social scientists who in my opinion do not meet the conditions outlined under (2) above (see Ch. 2). If there was evidence that these social scientists identified as Jews and had a Jewish agenda in doing social science (definitely not for most of those listed, but possibly true in the case of Richard J. Herrnstein—see below), then they would have been candidates for inclusion in the book. The people I cite as contributing to evolutionary or biological perspectives are indeed ethnically Jewish, but for most of them I have no idea whether they either have a strong Jewish identity or if they have a Jewish agenda in pursuing their research simply because there is no evidence to be found in their work or elsewhere. If there is evidence that a prominent evolutionary biologist identifies as a Jew and views his work in sociobiology or evolutionary psychology as advancing his perception of Jewish interests, then he or she could have been in *CofC* as an example of the phenomenon under study rather than as simply a scientist working in the area of evolutionary studies.

Interestingly, in the case of one of those I mention, Richard J. Herrnstein, Alan Ryan (1994) writes, "Herrnstein essentially wants the world in which clever Jewish kids or their equivalent make their way out of their humble backgrounds and end up running Goldman Sachs or the Harvard physics department." This is a stance that is typical, I suppose, of neoconservatism, a Jewish intellectual and political movement I discuss in Chapter 4, and it is the sort of thing that, if true, would suggest that Herrnstein did perceive the issues discussed in *The Bell Curve* as affecting Jewish interests in a way that Charles Murray, his co-author, did not. (Ryan contrasts Murray's and Herrnstein's worldviews: "Murray wants the Midwest in which he grew up—a world in which the local mechanic didn't care two cents whether he was or wasn't brighter than the local math teacher.") Similarly, twentieth-century theoretical physics does not qualify as a Jewish intellectual movement precisely because there are no signs that Jewish identification and pursuit of Jewish interests were important to the content of the theories or to the conduct of the intellectual movement. Yet Jews have been heavily overrepresented among the ranks of theoretical physicists.

This conclusion remains true even though Albert Einstein, a leading figure among theoretical physicists, was a strongly motivated Zionist (Fölsing,

1993/1997, pp. 494–505), opposed assimilation as a contemptible form of "mimicry" (p. 490), preferred to mix with other Jews whom he referred to as his "tribal companions" (p. 489), embraced the uncritical support for the Bolshevik regime in Russia that was entirely mainstream in the American Jewish community during the 1920s and 1930s, including persistent apology for the Moscow show trials in the 1930s (pp. 644–645), and switched from a high-minded pacifism during World War I to advocating for the development of atomic bombs to defeat Hitler. From his teenage years he disliked the Germans and in later life criticized Jewish colleagues for converting to Christianity and acting like Prussians. He especially disliked Prussians, who were the elite ethnic group in Germany. Reviewing his life at age seventy-three, Einstein declared his ethnic affiliation in no uncertain terms: "My relationship with Jewry had become my strongest human tie once I achieved complete clarity about our precarious position among the nations" (in p. 488). According to Fölsing (p. 488), Einstein had begun developing this clarity from an early age, but did not acknowledge it until much later, a form of self-deception: "As a young man with bourgeois-liberal views and a belief in enlightenment, he had refused to acknowledge [his Jewish identity]."

In other words, the issues of the ethnic identification and even ethnic activism on the part of people like Einstein are entirely separate from the issue of whether such people viewed the content of the theories themselves as furthering Jewish ethnic interests, and, in the case of Einstein, there is no evidence that he did so. The same cannot be said for Jewish movements covered here in which "scientific" theories were fashioned and deployed to advance ethnic group interests. This ideological purpose becomes clear when the unscientific nature of these movements is understood. Much of the discussion in *CofC* documented the intellectual dishonesty, the lack of empirical rigor, the obvious political and ethnic motivation, the expulsion of dissenters, the collusion among co-ethnics to dominate intellectual and academic discourse, and the general lack of scientific spirit that pervaded them. In my view, the scientific weakness of these movements is evidence of their group-strategic function.

Frank Salter's (2000) review in *Human Ethology Bulletin* discussed some of the controversy surrounding my work, particularly an acrimonious session at the 2000 conference of the Human Behavior and Evolution Society where I was accused of anti-Semitism by several participants. For me the only issue is whether I have been honest in my treatment of sources and whether my conclusions meet the usual standards of scholarly research in the social sciences. Salter notes that I based my research on mainstream sources and that the assertions that have infuriated some colleagues, are not only true but truisms to those acquainted with the diverse literatures involved. Apart from the political sensitivity of the subject, much of the problem facing MacDonald is that his knowledge is often too far ahead of his detractors to allow easy communication; there are not enough shared premises for constructive dialog. Unfortunately the knowledge gap is closing slowly because some of his most hostile critics, including colleagues who make serious ad hominem accusations, have not bothered to read MacDonald's books.

Salter also notes that those, such as John Tooby and Steven Pinker, who have denigrated my competence as a scholar in the media, have failed to provide anything approaching a scholarly critique or refutation of my work.

For twenty years there were no academic critiques of *CofC* despite its being published by an academic publisher. Then, beginning in 2018, Nathan Cofnas published several critiques in academic journals.[3] With the exception of *Philosophia*, an Israeli philosophy journal, those journals did not allow me to reply, but I wrote lengthy responses and posted them on my website. My reply to Cofnas was published by *Philosophia* (MacDonald, 2022b), but as I noted in recounting this episode, this "resulted almost immediately in hostile comments from Jewish academic activists, calls for retraction, and condemnation of the journal's editor for allowing such a horrifying breach of academic sensibilities to happen" (MacDonald, 2022a). The editor of the journal was eventually replaced and the article retracted after a back-and-forth with three new reviewers.

WHY ARE JEWS SO INFLUENTIAL?

Jewish populations have always had enormous effects on the societies in which they reside because of several qualities that are central to the Jewish group evolutionary strategy and likely have been under genetic selection in Ashkenazi Jewish groups. First and foremost, Jews are ethnocentric and able to cooperate in highly organized, cohesive, and effective groups. Also important is high intelligence, including the usefulness of intelligence in attaining wealth, prominence in the media, and eminence in the academic world and the legal profession. I will also discuss two other qualities that have received less attention, psychological intensity and aggressiveness, and finally mention the Jewish guru phenomenon.

The background traits of ethnocentrism, intelligence and wealth, psychological intensity, aggressiveness, and strong charismatic leadership result in

---

[3] In the most recent of these critiques, Cofnas (2021) abandons many of the criticisms he previously leveled at my work.

Jews being able to produce formidable, effective groups—groups able to have powerful, transformative effects on the peoples they live among. In the post-Enlightenment world, these traits influence the academic world and the world of popular and elite media, thus amplifying Jewish effectiveness compared with traditional societies. However, even before the Enlightenment Jews have repeatedly become an elite and powerful group in societies in which they reside in sufficient numbers.

It is remarkable that Jews, usually as a tiny minority, have been central to a long list of historical events. Jews were much on the mind of the Church Fathers in the fourth century during the formative years of Christian dominance in the West. Indeed, I have proposed that the powerful anti-Jewish attitudes and legislation of the fourth-century Church must be understood as a defensive reaction against Jewish economic power and enslavement of non-Jews (see *Separation and Its Discontents*, hereafter SAID, MacDonald, 1998/2004a, Ch. 3). Jews who had nominally converted to Christianity but maintained their ethnic ties in marriage and commerce were the focus of the 250-year Inquisition in Spain, Portugal, and the Spanish colonies in the New World. Fundamentally, the Inquisition should be seen as a defensive reaction to the economic and political domination of these "New Christians" (see SAID, Ch. 4).

Nineteenth-century critics of Jews typically complained about Jewish influence in the media and Jewish wealth that often made traditional Western aristocratic elites subservient to them, and, as Richard Wagner famously did, they complained about Jewish influence on culture (MacDonald, 2023c). Jews have also been central to all the important events of the twentieth century. Jews were a necessary component of the Bolshevik revolution that created the Soviet Union and willing participants of horrendous mass murders of its early decades; they remained an elite group in the Soviet Union until well after World War II (Ch. 3). They were a central focus of National Socialism in Germany, in part because of the Jewish role in Bolshevism but also because of their influence in the media and culture in general. Jews have been prime movers of the post-1965 cultural and multicultural/multiethnic revolution in the United States and the West generally, including the encouragement of massive non-White immigration to countries of European origin (see Ch. 8). In the contemporary world, organized American Jewish lobbying groups and deeply committed neoconservative Jews in the George W. Bush administration and the media had a critical role in fomenting wars that benefit Israel (Ch. 4), and neoconservative Jews in the Biden administration encouraged the all-out support for Ukraine against Russia and for Israel against Hamas. The Anti-Defamation League (ADL) is leading the campaign to dilute the First Amendment in order to expunge social media of ideas they don't like, particularly on X (Twitter), and Jewish billionaires are blacklisting students and withholding funds from universities if they don't express enthusiastic support for Israel (MacDonald,

2023e). Indeed, I would say that we are once again witnessing an incredible display of Jewish power in the United States.

How can such a tiny minority have such huge effects on the history of the West? Part of the story is the individualism of Westerners. In *Individualism and the Western Liberal Tradition* (hereafter *Individualism*, MacDonald, 2019a), I develop the view that Europeans are relatively less ethnocentric than other peoples and relatively more prone to individualism, as opposed to the ethnocentric, kinship-based, collectivist social structures which are historically far more characteristic of other human groups, including—relevant to this discussion—Jewish groups (see also Henrich, 2020).

Individualist cultures show relatively little emotional attachment to ingroups. Personal goals are paramount, and socialization emphasizes the importance of self-reliance, independence, individual responsibility, and "finding yourself" (Triandis, 1991, p. 82). Individualists have more positive attitudes toward strangers and outgroup members and are more likely to behave in a prosocial, altruistic manner to strangers. People in individualist cultures are less aware of ingroup outgroup boundaries and thus are less likely to have negative attitudes toward outgroup members. They often disagree with ingroup policy, show little emotional commitment or loyalty to ingroups, and do not have a sense of common fate with other ingroup members. Opposition to outgroups occurs in individualist societies, but the opposition is more "rational" in the sense that there is less of a tendency to suppose that all of the outgroup members are culpable. Individualists form mild attachments to many groups, while collectivists have an intense attachment to and identification with a few ingroups (Triandis, 1990, p. 61). We tend to see people as individuals, as in the ideology of colorblind meritocracy so common among mainstream conservatives.

Western individualism is unique among the cultures of the world and is largely responsible for the success of the West (Henrich, 2020; *Individualism*). Whereas other cultures are based on extended families and strong kinship relations (e.g., clan-based cultures), Western cultures deemphasize kinship as the basis of society. Rather than one's status in a kinship group, individual reputation as being honest and trustworthy is paramount. This leads to lower levels of corruption which plague kinship-based cultures where one's first duty is to help relatives. Individualists are more prone to trust non-relatives based on their reputation, resulting in the high-trust cultures of the West.

But in the contemporary world, individualism's weaknesses have become apparent. All societies must have something that holds them together, even the individualist culture of the West. The problem is that the social glue of Western societies is membership in a moral community rather than a kinship group. In the traditional West, the moral community was defined by Christian religious authority. In prehistoric Europe, people who rejected the moral strictures of the community were expelled from the community (a certain death sentence); in historic times, such individuals were ostracized and subjected to other penalties.

However, with the rise of a Jewish elite hostile to traditional Christian authority, the moral community of the West has been fashioned by a media and academic culture that is hostile to the people and culture of the West—with disastrous consequences. People who violate the established norms of political correctness, such as being proud of their White identity and believing that Whites have legitimate interests in opposing their demographic replacement and disempowerment, are shunned by friends and family, and they may well lose their jobs. And, as discussed below, Jewish organizations are leading the campaign to establish legal penalties for speech that contravenes the boundaries of political correctness as defined by these organizations.

Background Traits for Jewish Influence

Ethnocentrism. Elsewhere I have argued that Jewish ethnocentrism can be traced back to their Middle Eastern origins (see *A People That Shall Dwell Alone*, hereafter PTSDA, MacDonald, 1994/2002b). Traditional Jewish culture has a number of features identifying Jews with the ancestral cultures of the area. The most important of these is that Jews and other Middle Eastern cultures evolved under circumstances that favored large groups dominated by males (Burton et al., 1996). These groups were basically extended families with high levels of endogamy (i.e., marriage within the kinship group) and consanguineous marriage (i.e., marriage to blood relatives), including the uncle-niece marriage sanctioned in the Old Testament. These features are exactly the opposite of Western European tendencies.

Whereas Western societies tend toward individualism, the basic Jewish cultural form is collectivism, in which there is a strong sense of group identity and group boundaries, and moral particularism represented by the phrase "Is it good for the Jews." In Jewish religious writings, non-Jews had no moral standing and could be exploited at will as long as doing so didn't harm the entire group. Middle Eastern societies are characterized by anthropologists as "segmentary societies" organized into relatively impermeable, kinship-based groups. Group boundaries are often reinforced through external markers such as hairstyle or clothing, as Jews have often done throughout their history. Different groups settle in different areas where they retain their homogeneity alongside other homogeneous groups, as illustrated by the following account from Carleton Coon (1951, p. 153):

There the ideal was to emphasize not the uniformity of the citizens of a country as a whole but a uniformity within each special segment, and the

greatest possible contrast between segments. The members of each ethnic unit feel the need to identify themselves by some configuration of
symbols. If by virtue of their history they possess some racial peculiarity,
this they will enhance by special haircuts and the like; in any case they will
wear distinctive garments and behave in a distinctive fashion.

Jews are at the extreme of this Middle Eastern tendency toward collectivism and ethnocentrism. I give many examples of Jewish ethnocentrism in my
trilogy on Judaism—perhaps most notably the ethnic networking that is so important to *CofC*—and have argued in several places that Jewish ethnocentrism
is biologically based (see MacDonald, 2001; SAID, Ch. 1).

A good start for thinking about Jewish ethnocentrism is the work of Israel
Shahak (1994), most notably his co-authored *Jewish Fundamentalism in Israel*
(Shahak & Mezvinsky, 1999). Present-day fundamentalists attempt to re-create
the life of Jewish communities before the Enlightenment (i.e., prior to about
1750). During this period the great majority of Jews believed in the Kabbala—
the Jewish mystical tradition. Influential Jewish scholars like Gershom Scholem ignored the obvious racialist and exclusivist material in the Kabbalistic literature by using words like "men," "human beings," and "cosmic" to suggest the
Kabbala has a universalist message. The actual texts say salvation is only for
Jews, while non-Jews have "Satanic souls" (Shahak & Mezvinsky, 1999, p. 58).

The ethnocentrism apparent in such statements was not only the norm in
traditional Jewish society, but remains a powerful current of contemporary
Jewish fundamentalism, with important implications for Israeli politics. For
example, the Lubavitcher Rebbe, Rabbi Menachem Mendel Schneerson, describing the difference between Jews and non-Jews:

> We do not have a case of profound change in which a person is merely on
> a superior level. Rather we have a case of . . . a totally different species. . . .
> The body of a Jewish person is of a totally different quality from the body
> of [members] of all nations of the world. . . . The difference of the inner
> quality [of the body] . . . is so great that the bodies would be considered as
> completely different species. This is the reason why the Talmud states
> that there is an halachic difference in attitude about the bodies of non-
> Jews [as opposed to the bodies of Jews]: "their bodies are in vain." . . . An
> even greater difference exists in regard to the soul. Two contrary types of
> soul exist, a non-Jewish soul comes from three satanic spheres, while the
> Jewish soul stems from holiness. (Shahak & Mezvinsky, 1999, pp. 59–60)

These people and secular ethnonationalists, who have basically the same
ideas, are firmly in charge in Israel, leading to a long series of protests by liberal Jews in Israel and the U.S. There are many more examples, but in the interest of brevity I'll leave it at that. Even a prominent Israel apologist like

Thomas Friedman (2023) of *The New York Times* wrote that the present government is a "far-right coalition of Jewish supremacists and ultra-Orthodox Jews." But the Israel Lobby still dominates Congress and the Executive branch, so there won't be any changes soon. According to Mitchell Plitnick (2023) writing for *Mondoweiss*:

> When Rep. Jayapal called Israel a racist state in July, Democrats and Republicans leaped on her in a political feeding frenzy. They fell over each other to cash in on the defense of Israel, a state whose racism is not just obvious but a point of pride for many in its government. They immediately and overwhelmingly passed a resolution stating that "the State of Israel is not a racist or apartheid state." Jayapal, of course, voted with the majority. The nine who voted against were all progressives who are atop the list of AIPAC's most hated. It breezed through the Senate by unanimous consent.

Similar overwhelming support for Israel in the Gaza war passed in the House of Representatives and was unanimous in the Senate. Republicans and conservatives generally are especially supportive of Israel.

It's the same with conservative media. Though I am not entirely sure why this is, it is probably partly because a significant portion of their audiences are Evangelical Protestants who think Israel's success will inaugurate the Second Coming of Jesus and the end times. It may also be their desire to gain legitimacy in a cultural environment that is completely dominated by the left which accuses anyone to the right of Mitt Romney of being a raving Nazi.

Ethnocentrism is responsive to particular environmental triggers, what evolutionists term "facultative mechanisms," that is, mechanisms that can be triggered by external circumstances such as perceived threat. The phenomena of a feeling of permanent threat and a siege mentality have been noted by many authors as typical of Jewish culture throughout history (PTSDA, Ch. 7).

A permanent sense of imminent threat appears to be common among Jews. Writing on the clinical profile of Jewish families, E. J. Rosen and Weltman (1982, p. 671) note:

> Jews have traditionally believed that they are God's "chosen people." In Jewish folklore, this notion of "chosenness" has had a double meaning: Although God may have chosen the Jews, they have undergone great travail; their status means that suffering is a basic part of life. A well-known Yiddish saying, "Shver zu zein a yid" ("It's tough to be a Jew"), while often accompanied by a resigned sigh, may even reinforce the notion of superiority by virtue of the burden of oppression and suggests that one wears the burden of that suffering with pride.

Zborowski and Herzog (1952, p. 153) note that the homes of wealthy Jews in traditional Eastern European shtetl communities sometimes had secret passages for use in times of anti-Semitic pogroms, and that their existence was "part of the imagery of the children who played around them, just as the half-effaced memory was part of every Jew's mental equipment."

A good example is how American Jews reacted to the 1967 war. Silberman (1985, p. 184) notes that around the time of the 1967 Arab-Israeli War, many Jews could identify with the statement of Rabbi Abraham Joshua Heschel that "*I had not known how Jewish I was.*" Silberman comments that "This was the response, not of some newcomer to Judaism or casual devotee but of the man whom many, myself included, consider the greatest Jewish spiritual leader of our time." Many others made the same surprising discovery about themselves: Arthur Hertzberg (1979, p. 210) wrote:

> The immediate reaction of American Jewry to the crisis was far more intense and widespread than anyone could have foreseen. Many Jews would never have believed that grave danger to Israel could dominate their thoughts and emotions to the exclusion of everything else.

The Israel-Hamas war of 2023–present is no exception. As Chana Hughes (2023) reports:

> Our lives have changed forever. We have had to change not just the way we think of Israel but how we think of Britain. The past month has exposed an ugly underside. We once thought we lived in a tolerant society. Now we are asking: 'Can we safely share our Jewishness here?', and 'do we belong?'
>
> As Jews we are familiar with tragedy, threat and betrayal. 'Always make sure you have your passport in date', my mother used to tell me. Fortunately, today we are still very far from escape. But the recent rise in anti-Semitism makes us feel like we have moved another step closer.
>
> In the darkest times, however, is when the embers of the Jewish spirit burn brightest. Amidst the tragic loss of life and bloodshed, there are revolutions starting. There is a revolution of Jewish identity and unity.
>
> Although security threats are at their highest, the synagogues have never been fuller. 'We've not seen our synagogue this full since the Pittsburg shooting', noticed a friend, with a sad laugh. Charities distribute thousands of shabbat candles every Friday, WhatsApp groups encourage psalms to be recited around the clock and hundreds of women gather each week to bake ceremonial *challa* bread and pray. One local barber, for the first time ever, vowed to close his shop on Shabbat as a sign of solidarity. Members of the community vow to support his business in return.
>
> 'I have never felt my Jewishness the way I do right now', said a lady, at the kosher butcher, buying chicken soup: 'Ironically just when we're under

attack.' Another ex-colleague reached out to me. She had never embraced her Jewish heritage before but now she feels she has to 'pick a side'. She feels the pain of being vilified and misunderstood but feels that it is worth it. . . .

Pressure builds daily as Israel loses global sympathy and the bloody conflict unfolds. Friends in Israel feel supported there and weirdly they feel safer, even when they run into their bomb shelters. Their sense of connection makes them feel alive. The Jewish community's unity now feels even stronger in contrast to the splintered in-fighting about Israel's judicial reform that was rampant prior to the attack. This month, these differences have been put on hold. Faith and togetherness are our community's protection against threat and we have to cling to them with all our might.

There is also an outpouring of Jewish financial support for Israel in response to the war (Silow-Carroll, 2023). While there are still organizations like Jewish Voice for Peace and *Mondoweiss* that have long condemned Israeli policies toward the Palestinians, they definitely do not represent the vast majority of the power and money of the Jewish community in America.

As the examples from Israel's wars show, Jewish ethnocentrism is often manipulated by Jewish authorities attempting to inculcate a stronger sense of group identification—for example, the messages of ever-increasing threat of anti-Semitism promulgated by the ADL—accompanied by highly successful pleas for donations.

Bar-Tal and Antebi (1992, p. 643) note:

[N]ot surprisingly, Siege Mentality is related to Ethnocentrism. The belief that the world has negative intentions towards the group indicates its evil, malice, and aggressiveness. In this context, the group not only feels victimized and self-righteous, but also superior to the out-group.

Intelligence (and Wealth). The vast majority of American Jews are Ashkenazi Jews. This is a very intelligent group, with an average IQ of approximately 111 with a particular strength in verbal IQ (Lynn, 2011). Since verbal IQ is the best predictor of occupational success and upward mobility in contemporary societies, it is not surprising that Jews are an elite group in the United States. Intelligence, as well as the other traits discussed here, were likely under genetic selection in traditional Ashkenazi societies because scholars were given marriages to the daughters of wealthy Jews, as well as good business opportunities (PTSDA, Ch. 7). Wealth and reproductive success were strongly linked at least prior to the nineteenth century.

Nevertheless, because of the demographic differences between Jews and White Americans, there are many more White Americans at any level of IQ required for upward mobility and leadership positions in American society

(MacDonald, 2022a). For example, at IQ of 140, there are five times as many White Americans as Jews. Contrary to Cofnas (2021), IQ *is thus an insufficient explanation for Jewish influence.*

Intelligence and ethnic networking are important for academic success, and in Chapter 2 I show that Jews and Jewish organizations led the intellectual effort to deny the importance of racial and ethnic differences in human affairs and to pathologize any sense of White identity or White interests (see also Chs. 5, 8). The Jewish role in creating the intellectual context of the Immigration and Nationality Act of 1965 relied on the success of the Boasian movement in anthropology in shaping academic views on race by dominating the American Anthropological Association since the 1920s. This theoretical perspective subverted the strong sense of race and racial interests that were prominent trends in academia and the mainstream media during that period. Science is the *lingua franca* of the West, so the prestige of the Boasians was critical for their success.

Intelligence is also linked to wealth. Based on past results, Jews are probably around 35 percent of the wealthiest Americans, and in a democracy, that translates into a well-funded infrastructure of Jewish causes—such as neoconservative think tanks, the American-Israel Public Affairs Committee, and the ADL—and political parties; the Democratic Party is basically funded by wealthy Jews, and the Republican Jewish Coalition probably provides 40 percent of Republican donations aimed at supporting Israel and moving the party to the left on social issues. ADL (2022) assets in 2021 were listed at $238,000,000, with $62,000,000 in contributions. The national ADL, like the ACLU, the SPLC, the NAACP, and other so-called civil rights groups, is now merely a tax-exempt cadre of the Democratic Party and is active on behalf of anti-White Critical Race Theory, the transgender revolution, and opposition to any talk about the Great Replacement, claiming that the very idea of a Great Replacement is racist and anti-Semitic (T. Moore, 2021)—while stating that Israel must retain its Jewish majority by controlling immigration and preventing Palestinians on the West Bank from voting.

Intelligence is also evident in Jewish activism. Jewish activism is like a full court press in basketball: intense pressure from every possible angle. But in addition to the intensity, Jewish efforts are very well organized, well-funded, and backed up by sophisticated, scholarly intellectual rationales.

Intelligence and organization are also apparent in Jewish lobbying on behalf of Israel. Over thirty years ago a U.S. Defense Department official, noted that, "On all kinds of foreign policy issues the American people just don't make their voices heard. Jewish groups are the exceptions. They are prepared, superbly briefed. They have their act together. It is hard for bureaucrats not to respond" (Findley, 1989, p. 164). At the time there was concern that the State Department had remained a bastion of old school WASPs. This is not a problem any longer, with neoconservative Jews Antony Blinken, Victoria Nuland, and Wendy Sherman firmly in charge of State, during the Biden administration.

Conscientiousness and Emotional Intensity. In my 1994 book on Judaism, I highlighted two personality traits of Jews, conscientiousness and emotional intensity (PTSDA, Ch. 7). Both are heritable and quite likely under selection in traditional Jewish communities. Conscientiousness, which involves attention to detail, neatness, orderliness, striving for achievement, persistence toward goals in the face of difficulty, and the ability to focus attention and delay gratification, is, along with IQ, linked to upward mobility. Social conscientiousness appears to be a sort of "don't let down the group" trait, originally proposed by Darwin (1871) as the basis of group allegiance. Individuals high on this trait would be expected to feel intense guilt for having failed to fulfill their obligations to the group. Moreover, given the importance of conformity to group norms for Judaism, it would be expected that individuals who were low on this trait would be disproportionately inclined to abandon Judaism, while successful Jews who were the pillars of the community and thus epitomized the group ethic of Judaism would be disproportionately likely to be high on group conformity—and also likely to be reproductively successful in traditional societies. The result is that there would be strong selection pressures toward high levels of social conscientiousness within the Jewish community.

Conscientiousness was strongly emphasized in Jewish socialization. Thus, a child reared in a traditional Jewish home would have been socialized to continually monitor his/her behavior to ensure compliance with a vast number of restrictions—the numerous commandments of Ashkenazi religious writing. These are exactly the sorts of environmental influences expected to strengthen the conscientiousness system, what I call "system-specific environmental influences" (MacDonald, 2005a).

Jews also tend to be high on the personality trait of affect intensity; i.e., they are prone to intense emotional experience of both positive and negative emotions (Larsen & Diener, 1992). Individuals high on affect intensity have more complex social networks and more complex lives, including multiple and even conflicting goals. They are prone to fast and frequent mood changes and lead varied and variable emotional lives. Clinically, affect intensity is related to cyclothymia (i.e., alternate periods of elation and depression), bipolar affective disorder (i.e., manic depressive psychosis), neurotic symptoms, and somatic complaints (nervousness, feeling uneasy, shortness of breath).

The common perception of Jewish and non-Jewish psychiatric workers from the late nineteenth century until at least the end of the 1920s was that, compared to gentiles, Ashkenazi Jews (and especially male Jews), had relatively sensitive, highly reactive nervous systems, thus making them more prone to the diagnoses of hysteria, manic depression, neurasthenia (Gershon & Liebowitz, 1975; Gilman, 1993 pp. 92ff), and depression, in men only (Levav et al.,

1997). Gershon and Liebowitz note that 45 percent of 22 patients had bipolar affective disorder—about the same as in an Iraqi population—compared to 19 percent in a study of northern European populations. Within Israel, they cite an Israeli study (in Hebrew) that found that affective disorders were "much more prevalent" among Ashkenazi Jews than Sephardic Jews (Kalman et al., 1970). Additionally, a "preliminary" study found significantly more patients with affective psychoses and fewer with schizophrenia than among non-Jews (Cooklin et al., 1983). A study from 2000 found that in a sample of Israelis with bipolar disorder, the manic phase was "much more common in Israeli bipolar patients" than European and American populations: 55 percent of the patients have illnesses characterized primarily by manias, 28 percent have approximately equal numbers of manias and depressions, and 17 percent suffer predominantly from depressions, but with no difference between Ashkenazi and Sephardic populations (Osher et al., 2000, p. 187).

I emphasize here that affect intensity is also linked to creativity and the manic phase of bipolar affective disorder which seems to be more common among Jews and a more robust component of manic-depressive illness among Jews (D. M. Tucker et al., 1990). During episodes of mania the person has a grandiose self-image ("I am brilliant and can save the world if only people would listen to me"), goal-directed activity such as obsessively working on a project all night, excessive involvement in pleasurable activity like buying sprees and sexual gratification, and racing thoughts which the manic person thinks are brilliant. The depressive part is just the opposite.

Many people may be high on emotionality but not meet the criteria for psychopathology. It's easy to see that people moderately high on positive emotionality—hypomanic or normal but close to the manic range—would be high achievers; they would work persistently toward goals, and they would be very self-confident and have high self-esteem. Such people gravitate to leadership positions in whatever organization they are in, and it's easy to see that they might become gurus, establishing a devoted following, like charismatic rabbis in traditional Jewish communities—Jewish gurus like Freud, Boas, Trotsky, et al. discussed in the following chapters.

For example, Albert Lindemann (1997, p. 448) notes that many of Trotsky's personality traits are stereotypically Jewish:

> If one accepts that anti-Semitism was most potently driven by anxiety and fear, as distinguished from contempt, then the extent to which Trotsky became a source of preoccupation for anti-Semites is significant. Here, too, [Paul] Johnson's words are suggestive: He writes of Trotsky's "demonic power" [in A *History of the Jews*, 1987]—the same term, revealingly, used repeatedly by others in referring to Zinoviev's oratory or Uritsky's ruthlessness [Zinoviev and Uritsky were two other prominent early

Bolsheviks]. Trotsky's boundless self-confidence, his notorious arrogance, and sense of superiority were other traits often associated with Jews. Fantasies there were about Trotsky and other Bolsheviks, but there were also realities around which the fantasies grew.

This emotional intensity extends to Jewish academics writing about Jewish history. Lindemann (1997, p. 12) writes:

[E]specially in popular history, a strong tendency exists to favor an emotionally laden description and narrative, especially of colorful, dramatic, or violent episodes, over explanation that employs calm analysis or a searching attention to historical context. Pogroms, famous anti-Semitic affairs, and the description of the ideas of anti-Semitic authors and agitators are described with moral fervor, rhetorical flair, and considerable attention to the details of murder, arson, and rape. Background, context, and motives are often slighted or dealt with in a remarkably thin and tendentious fashion.

Lindemann comments on the impassioned, moralistic rhetoric and simplistic analyses to be found in Robert Wistrich's *Anti-Semitism: The Longest Hatred* and in the writings of Holocaust historians Lucy Dawidowicz and Daniel J. Goldhagen. "In order to write 'genuine' German history, [Dawidowicz] seems to think, hatred and resentment rather than sympathy or love constitute the appropriate state of mind. She makes precious little effort to understand the motivations of nineteenth-century nationalistic Germans. They are simply contemptible 'other people.'" He describes Howard Morley Sachar's chapter on Romanian anti-Semitism as "a tirade, without the slightest effort at balance" (Lindemann, 1997, p. 509).

Affect intensity influences the tone and intensity of Jewish activism. Among Jews there is a critical mass that is intensely committed to Jewish causes—a sort of 24/7, "pull out all the stops" commitment that produces instant, massive responses on Jewish issues. Jewish activism has a relentless, never-say-die quality. This intensity goes hand in hand with the "slippery slope" style of arguing: Jewish activism is an intense response because even the most trivial manifestation of anti-Jewish attitudes or behavior is seen as inevitably leading to mass murder of Jews if allowed to continue.

Ashkenazi Jews Are Aggressive. Much of the previous is also about Jewish aggressiveness. Jews have always behaved aggressively toward those they have lived among, and they have been perceived as aggressive by their critics. Aggressive behavior by Jews can be found in the ancient world. Bachrach suggests that the Jews were so wealthy, powerful, and aggressive that until around the middle of the fifth century the Roman government viewed a strong anti-

Jewish policy as not politically viable, even though it was continually being pressured in this direction by the Church (Bachrach, 1985). The rather limited anti-Jewish actions of the government during the 150 years following the Edict of Toleration of 313 are interpreted "as attempts to protect Christians from a vigorous, powerful, and often aggressive Jewish *gens*" (p. 408). The Jews themselves were perceived by the emperors, the government, and the Church fathers as "an aggressive, well-organized, wealthy, and powerful minority" (p. 408). Particularly revealing are the suggestion that the solvency of the municipalities depended on Jews paying their taxes and the fear that offending the Jews could set off widespread and costly revolts, such as the one led by Patricius in 351.

E. Horowitz (1998, p. 5) recounts the historiography surrounding Jewish violence and aggressiveness, noting, for example, what a nineteenth-century British historian Rev. George Williams had written:

[The Jews] had followed the Persians from Galilee, to gratify their vengeance by the massacre of the believers, and the demolition of their most sacred churches. They were amply gutted with blood. In a few days 90,000 Christians of both sexes, and of all ages and conditions, fell victims to their indiscriminating hatred.

Commenting on this assertion, E. Horowitz (1998, p. 5–6) notes:

As we shall see, Jewish contemporaries of Williams described the events of 614 rather similarly. A century later, however, in the years following the Holocaust, memories of Jews gratifying their vengeance and giving vent to their "indiscriminating hatred" began to fade, being displaced increasingly by the Sartrean Jew, "passionately hostile to violence" [a reference Jean Paul Sartre's philo-Semitic *Anti-Semite and Jew*]. This was especially true in works dealing with the Holocaust itself. In *The Informed Heart* (1960), Bruno Bettelheim wondered aloud whether the Nazi notion "that millions of Jews . . . would submit to extermination did not also result from seeing how much degradation they would accept without fighting back." . . . [Historians] present a monolithic view of a mythic Jewish past in which abhorrence of violence was deeply ingrained in the Jewish self-image. . . . Yet a reexamination of the record of Jewish religious violence against Christians and the external manifestations of their religion during the millennium after the Christianization of the Roman empire under Constantine . . . would reveal patterns of behavior very much at variance with the alleged historic self-image of the Jews "as a people abhorring violence in any form."

Being aggressive and "pushy" is part of the stereotype of Jews in Western societies, and the behavior of Israeli West Bank settlers—who routinely attack Palestinians with impunity (Bergman & Mazzetti, 2024)—and Israel itself in ethnically cleansing and murdering at least 60,000 Palestinians in Gaza in the war that began on October 7th, 2023 and expanding their territory in Syria after the fall of the Assad regime also fits the stereotype.

In early twentieth-century America, the sociologist Edward A. Ross (1914) commented on a greater tendency among Jewish immigrants to maximize their advantage in all transactions, ranging from Jewish students badgering teachers for higher grades to poor Jews attempting to get more than the usual charitable allotment. For Ross (p. 144–145), while not involving physical violence, "No other immigrants are so noisy, pushing and disdainful of the rights of others as the Hebrews," and:

> The authorities complain that the East European Hebrews feel no reverence for law as such and are willing to break any ordinance they find in their way. . . . The insurance companies scan a Jewish fire risk more closely than any other. [During this period, arson aimed at collecting insurance payouts was often termed "Jewish lightening."] Credit men say the Jewish merchant is often "slippery" and will "fail" in order to get rid of his debts. For lying the immigrant has a very bad reputation. In the North End of Boston "the readiness of the Jews to commit perjury has passed into a proverb."

Ross (1914, p. 150) also reported:

> [Immigration officials had] become very sore over the incessant fire of false accusations to which they are subjected by the Jewish press and societies. United States senators complain that during the close of the struggle over the immigration bill they were overwhelmed with a torrent of crooked statistics and misrepresentations by the Hebrews fighting the literacy test.

Jews were unique as an American immigrant group in their hostility toward American Christian culture and in their energetic, aggressive efforts to change that culture. From the perspective of Henry Ford's *The International Jew*, the United States had imported around 3.5 million mainly Yiddish-speaking, intensely ethnocentric Jewish immigrants over the previous forty years. In that very short period and long prior to achieving anything like the power they obtained after World War II and the 1960s counter-cultural revolution, Jews had had enormous effects on American society, particularly in their attempts to remove expressions of Christianity from public life beginning with an attempt in 1899–1900 to remove the word "Christian" from the Virginia Bill of Rights. Ford (1920) stated in his outlet, *The Dearborn Independent*: "The Jews' determination to wipe out of public life every sign of the predominant Christian character of the US is the only active form of religious intolerance in the country today."

However, the epitome of Jewish aggression is their long crusade as a tiny minority to alter the ethnic balance of the U.S. in order to prevent the sort of mass movement that occurred in Germany in the 1930s (see Ch. 8).

Charges of anti-Semitism and guilt over the Holocaust are not the only instruments of Jewish aggressiveness. Jewish groups intimidate their enemies by a variety of means. People who oppose policies on Israel advocated by Jewish activist organizations have been fired and blacklisted from their jobs, harassed with letters, subjected to intrusive surveillance, and threatened with death. Although there is a great deal of self-censorship in the media on Israel as a result of the major role of Jews in the ownership and production of the media, gaps in this armor are aggressively closed. Paul Findley (1989, p. 296) noted over thirty years ago that there are "threats to editors and advertising departments, orchestrated boycotts, slanders, campaigns of character assassination, and personal vendettas"—a phenomenon that, as noted above, is ongoing.

Incidentally, not all Jewish groups have behaved as aggressively toward the surrounding society as have the Ashkenazi groups that make up the great bulk of American Jewry. For example, a community of Syrian Jews called the SY (pronounced "ess-why") arrived in New York around the same time as the huge influx of Ostjuden (Eastern European Jews). The SY have become wealthy, but they haven't entered into the power centers of American society. They eschew higher education and have no role in the elite media. They are not involved in the legal profession, politics, or academic departments of the social sciences or humanities. Although they tend to be hawkish on matters related to Israel, they have not been involved in creating the edifice that is the Israel Lobby. One gets the impression that they want to make money and stay under the radar by not making waves—the antithesis of the aggressive posture of the Ostjuden.

This is probably how they survived for centuries in the Middle East. In fact, Jews in traditional societies often hid their wealth and controlled the behavior of other Jews so as not to arouse hostility from the surrounding peoples (SAID, Ch. 6). In other words, unlike the Ashkenazim, they have not developed an adversarial, competitive stance toward the people and culture of America. One can't imagine them developing a lobby that would harness the power of the United States on behalf of a foreign government, nor can one imagine them becoming a hostile elite, as Ashkenazi Jews became in the Soviet Union (MacDonald, 2005b). They have shown no tendencies toward developing a culture of critique that subjected Western culture to what John Murray Cuddihy (1974, p. 68) termed "punitive objectivity" and "the vindictive objectivity of the marginal nonmember." Unlike their Ashkenazi brethren, they had no impact on Western societies in the twentieth century. In this regard, they are much more like the Overseas Chinese than their Jewish brothers from Eastern Europe.

To understand the origins and the power of the Israel Lobby, one has to understand the Ostjuden—the *fons et origo* of the two most potent and aggressive twentieth-century Jewish movements: political radicalism and Zionism. It is not that the Ostjuden are particularly ethnocentric compared to other Jews. They are, if anything, less ethnocentric than the SYs with their hyperxenophobia and obsession with blood purity (Chafets, 2007). Indeed, it is obvious that the Ostjuden could never have been so successful in creating the Israel Lobby or in altering the culture and demography of the West had they remained as a hermetically sealed community, shut off from the power centers of the society.

Finally, I have proposed that the most radical, most ethnocentric Jews tend to provide the direction for the entire Jewish community in the long run (MacDonald, 2003b). This has happened once again in contemporary Israel and is supported enthusiastically by the mainstream Jewish community in the U.S. as epitomized by the ADL, the American Israel Public Affairs Council, etc. For example, "With its overwhelming victory in the Arab-Israeli War of 1967, Israel more than doubled the amount of land it controlled, seizing new territory in the West Bank, the Gaza Strip, the Sinai Peninsula, the Golan Heights and East Jerusalem." Israel could have used this land to bargain for a future Palestinian state, but "the acquisition of the territories animated a religious political movement—Gush Emunim, or 'Bloc of the Faithful'—that was determined to settle the newly conquered lands" (Bergman & Mazzetti, 2024).

Settling newly conquered land reflects the attitudes of many prominent Zionists and Israelis. Theodor Herzl (1960, p. 711), the founder of Zionism, maintained that the area of the Jewish state stretches: "From the Brook of Egypt to the Euphrates." This reflects God's covenant with Abraham in Genesis 15: 18–20 and Joshua 1: 3–4: "To your descendants I give this land, from the river of Egypt to the great river, the river Euphrates, the land of the Kenites, the Kenizzites, the Kadmonites, the Hittites, the Perizzites, the Rephaim, the Amorites, the Canaanites, the Girgashites, and the Jebusites."

The flexibility of the ultimate aims of Zionism can also be seen in this 1956 comment by David Ben-Gurion, Israel's first Prime Minister:

> The acceptance of partition [of the Palestinian Mandate] does not commit us to renounce Transjordan [i.e., the modern state of Jordan]; one does not demand from anybody to give up his vision. We shall accept a state in the boundaries fixed today. But the boundaries of Zionist aspirations are the concern of the Jewish people and no external factor will be able to limit them. (in Chomsky, 1999, p. 161)

Ben-Gurion's vision of "the boundaries of Zionist aspirations" included southern Lebanon, southern Syria, all of Jordan, and the Sinai, much of which has already been achieved (in Chomsky, 1999, p. 161). Or consider Israeli Prime Minister Golda Meir's statement that the borders of Israel "are where Jews live, not where there is a line on the map" (p. 50).

These views are common among the more extreme Zionists today—especially the fundamentalists and the settler movement, and notably Gush Emunim—who now set the tone in Israel. Indeed, in the opinion of Israel Shahak and Norton Mezvinsky (1999, p. 73), "It is not unreasonable to assume that Gush Emunim, if it possessed the power and control, would use nuclear weapons in warfare to attempt to achieve its purpose."

Conclusion. The current situation in the United States is the result of an awesome deployment of Jewish power and influence. One must contemplate the fact that American Jews have managed to maintain unquestioned support for Israel since the 1967 war despite Israel's seizing land and engaging in a brutal occupation of the Palestinians in the occupied territories—an apartheid occupation that will most likely end with expulsion or complete subjugation and degradation of the Palestinians. During this same period Jewish organizations in America have been a principal force—in my view the main force—for erecting a state dedicated to suppressing ethnic identification among European-derived peoples, for encouraging massive multi-ethnic immigration into the U.S., and for erecting a legal system and cultural ideology that is obsessively sensitive to the complaints and interests of ethnic minorities (the culture of the Holocaust). All this is done without a whisper of double standards in the aboveground media.

The American Jewish community is well organized and lavishly funded. It has achieved a great deal of power, and it has been successful in achieving its interests. One of the great myths often promulgated by Jewish apologists is that Jews have no consensus and therefore cannot wield any real power. Yet there is in fact a great deal of consensus on broad Jewish issues, particularly in the areas of Israel and the welfare of other foreign Jewries, immigration and refugee policy, church-state separation, and abortion rights.

Nevertheless, while civil liberties were championed by Jewish organizations during the anti-communist wave of the 1950s—when sympathy with communism was mainstream within the American Jewish community at a time when many Jewish communists were being hauled before Congressional committees and universities sometimes required loyalty oaths (MacDonald, 2019b)—Jewish organizations like the ADL are now prominently involved in censoring speech, especially on social media. Jewish consensus changes depending on Jewish interests. As always, interests trump principles.

Massive changes in public policy on these issues, beginning with the counter-cultural revolution of the 1960s, coincide with the period of increasing

Jewish power and influence in the United States. Indeed, one is hard-pressed to find any significant area where public policy conflicts with the attitudes of mainstream Jewish organizations.

WERE NON-JEWISH THEORISTS CRITICAL TO THE SUCCESS OF THE MOVEMENTS DESCRIBED IN CofC?

Anti-biologism is now pervasive in the social sciences and a common thread in the intellectual movements discussed here—e.g., race is interpreted as nothing more than a social construct, so that racial differences in mental ability are completely explained by environmental influences, especially White racism; anti-Semitism is explained by envy or irrational hatred untethered from any consideration of Jewish behavior. An important contemporary example is that biological explanations are completely ruled out in mainstream feminist theory, so that college graduates, especially those with gender studies degrees, emerge as radical environmentalists. For example, Judith Butler, a strongly identified Jewish lesbian whose work has been seen as subversive of traditional sexual norms (J. Bennett, 2024; Butler, 2017), has been highly influential in gender studies for her theory that sexual behavior is "performative"— that people enact their sexual behavior as a choice dictated by cultural norms and constrained by various punishments if one deviates from those norms. As Butler (1988, p. 520) states, "What is called gender identity is a performative accomplishment compelled by social sanction and taboo." Genetic and hormonal influences on gender are thus completely ignored. Butler's (p. 531) theory is self-consciously subversive of traditional gender norms:

> Gender is not passively scripted on the body, and neither is it determined by nature, language, the symbolic, or the overwhelming history of patriarchy. Gender is what is put on, invariably, under constraint, daily and incessantly, with anxiety and pleasure, but if this continuous act is mistaken for a natural or linguistic given, power is relinquished to expand the cultural field bodily through subversive performances of various kinds.

Thus for example, one could become transgender by intentionally overcoming the constraints on gender imposed by culture (thus rejecting any biological constraints) and become a different gender.

Butler's argument is not based on any of the theories discussed in later chapters of this book, but on those of French philosophers, particularly Maurice Merleau-Ponty, Simone de Beauvoir, and Michel Foucault. For example: "In Merleau-Ponty's reflections in *The Phenomenology of Perception* on 'the body in its sexual being,' he takes issue with [naturalistic] accounts of bodily experience and claims that the body is 'an historical idea' rather than a 'natural species'" (Butler, 1988, p. 520).

There is no claim here that the Jewish intellectual movements reviewed in *CofC* are the only influential anti-biological or non-biological movements for understanding human behavior. For example, behaviorism is an offshoot of the British empiricist tradition in philosophy and was highly influential in psychology, eventually being subsumed within cognitive theories, neither of which owes anything to the movements reviewed here. Far more important for the movements reviewed here were Marxism (Ch. 3) and other perspectives essentially developed in service of specific Jewish interests, such as combating anti-Semitism and opposing the racialist theories based on Darwinism (Ch. 2) that were mainstream in the 1920s and in which the success of Western societies was explained at least partly in racial terms.

It was only after the ascent of Jews in American universities (see below) and the decisive influence of the Jewish movements discussed here that French philosophy had a significant impact on Anglosphere intellectuals. However, the movements discussed here are the movements that fundamentally transformed the intellectual landscape in the United States, other Anglosphere countries, and much of the West. Prior to around 1970, philosophy departments emphasized the British empiricist tradition, with almost no coverage of continental philosophy after Kant; in my experience as a graduate student at the University of Wisconsin in the 1960s, one could easily obtain a Ph.D. in philosophy without even a passing acquaintance with continental philosophy. And psychology was still mired in behaviorism. Indeed, one could perhaps argue that it was only the leftward shift resulting from the ascent of the Jewish left that intellectuals looking for anti-biological perspectives discovered the utility of these continental movements in their attacks on the Western tradition.

CHANGE AND CONTINUITY: THE DECLINE OF ETHNIC CONSCIOUSNESS
AMONG EUROPEAN-DERIVED PEOPLE IN THE UNITED STATES AND
THE CONTINUITY OF ETHNOCENTRISM AMONG JEWS

Fundamental to this transformation was the decline of ethnic consciousness among European peoples. It is fascinating to contrast the immigration debates of the 1920s with those of the 1950s and 1960s. The immigration restrictionists of the 1920s unabashedly asserted the right of European-derived peoples to the land they had conquered and settled. There were many assertions of ethnic interest—that the people who colonized and created the political and economic culture of the country had a right to maintain it as their possession.

By the 1940s and certainly by the 1960s it was impossible to make such assertions without being deemed not only a racist but also an intellectual Neanderthal. Indeed, Bendersky (2000) shows that such rhetoric was increasingly taboo in the 1930s. One can see the shift in the career of racial theorist Lothrop Stoddard, author of books such as *The Rising Tide of Color Against White World-Supremacy* and numerous articles for the popular media, such as *Collier's*, *Forum*, and *The Saturday Evening Post*. Stoddard viewed Jews as highly intelligent and as racially different from Europeans. He also believed that Jews were critical to the success of Bolshevism. However, he stopped referring to Jews completely in his lectures to the U.S. Army War College in the late 1930s. The Boasian revolution in anthropology had triumphed, and theorists who believed that race was important for explaining human behavior became fringe figures. Stoddard himself went from being a popular and influential writer to being viewed as a security risk as the Roosevelt administration prepared the country for war with National Socialist Germany.

Another marker of the change in attitude toward Jews was the response to Charles Lindbergh's remarks in Des Moines, Iowa, on the eve of U.S. entry into World War II. Lindbergh's advocacy of non-intervention was shaped not only by his horror at the destructiveness of modern warfare—what he viewed as the suicide of European culture—but also by his belief that a second European war would be suicidal for the White race. In an article published in 1939 in *Reader's Digest*, a popular magazine, shortly after the outbreak of World War II, he stated:

> [It was a war] among a dominant people for power—blind, insatiable, suicidal. Western nations are again at war, a war likely to be more prostrating than any in the past, a war in which the White race is bound to lose, and the others bound to gain, a war which may easily lead our civilization through more Dark Ages if it survives at all. (Lindbergh, 1939, p. 65)

In order for Whites to maintain their dominance over other races, Lindbergh believed that they should join together to fend off the teeming legions of non-Whites who were the real long-term threat.

Lindbergh was not a Nordicist. He took a long-term view that Russia would be a White bulwark against the Chinese in the East. He advocated a racial alliance among Whites based "on a Western Wall of race and arms which can hold back either a Genghis Khan or the infiltration of inferior blood; on an English fleet, a German air force, a French army, [and] an American nation" (Lindbergh, 1939, p. 66). However, he believed the Soviet Union under communism was abhorrent:

I tell you that I would a hundred times rather see my country ally herself with England, or even with Germany with all of her faults, than with the cruelty, the godlessness, and the barbarism that exist in Soviet Russia. An alliance between the United States and Russia should be opposed by every American, by every Christian, and by every humanitarian in this country. (in Berg, 1998/1999, p. 422)

Writing in 1939, Lindbergh clearly viewed the atrocities perpetrated by the Soviet Union to be far worse than anything perpetrated by National Socialist Germany.

In his famous speech on September 11th, 1941, Lindbergh stated that Jews were one of the principal forces attempting to lead the United States into the war, along with the Roosevelt administration and the British. Lindbergh noted that Jewish opposition to Germany was understandable given persecution "sufficient to make bitter enemies of any race." He stated that the Jews' "greatest danger to this country lies in their large ownership and influence in our motion pictures, our press, our radio, and our Government." And, most controversially, he stated, "I am saying that the leaders of both the British and Jewish races, for reasons which are understandable from their viewpoint as they are inadvisable from ours, for reasons which are not American, wish to involve us in the war" (in Berg, 1998/1999, p. 427).

Lindbergh's speech was greeted with a torrent of abuse and hatred unparalleled for a mainstream public figure in American history. Overnight Lindbergh went from cultural hero to moral pariah. Jewish influence in the media and government would be difficult to measure then as it is now, but it was certainly considerable and a common concern of anti-Jewish sentiment of the time. In a booklet published in 1936, the editors of *Fortune* magazine concluded that the main sources of Jewish influence on the media were their control of the two major radio networks and the Hollywood movie studios. They suggested that "at the very most, half the opinion-making and taste-influencing paraphernalia in America is in Jewish hands" (Editors of *Fortune*, 1936, p. 62)—a rather remarkable figure considering that Jews constituted approximately 2–3 percent of the population and that most of the Jewish population were first- or second-generation immigrants.[4] A short list of Jewish ownership or management of the media during this period would include *The New York Times* (the most influential newspaper, owned by the Sulzberger family), the *New York Post* (George Backer), *The Washington Post* (Eugene Meyer), *The Philadelphia*

---

[4] A 1945 report on anti-Semitism by the American Jewish Committee included a section from the 1936 report by the editors of *Fortune* where Jewish media influence is phrased somewhat differently: "Approximately half of opinion-making in the United States is Jewish. Jewish influence in radio, theatre, and motion pictures is considerable while it is less marked in journalism and advertising" (American Jewish Committee, 1945, p. 21).

Inquirer (M. L. Annenberg), *The Philadelphia Record* and the Camden *Courier-Post* (J. David Stern), the Newark *Star-Ledger* (S. I. Newhouse), the *Pittsburgh Post-Gazette* (Paul Block), CBS (the dominant radio network, owned by William Paley), NBC (headed by David Sarnoff), all of the major Hollywood movie studios, Random House (the most important book publisher, owned by Bennett Cerf), and a dominant position in popular music.[5] Walter Winchell, who had an audience of tens of millions and was tied with Bob Hope for the highest-rated program on radio, believed that Lindbergh's opposition to intervention "was unconscionable, a form of treason" (Gabler, 1994/1995, p. 294). Winchell, "the standard bearer for interventionism," was Jewish. He had close ties during this period to the ADL, which provided him with information on the activities of isolationists and Nazi sympathizers which he used in his broadcasts and newspaper columns (pp. 294–298).

There is no question that the movie industry did indeed propagandize against Germany and in favor of intervention. In May 1940, the Warner Bros. studio wired Roosevelt that "personally we would like to do all in our power within the motion picture industry and by use of the talking screen to show the American people the worthiness of the cause for which the free peoples of Europe are making such tremendous sacrifices" (in Gabler, 1988, p. 343). Later in 1940 Joseph P. Kennedy lectured the Hollywood movie elite that they should stop promoting war and stop making anti-German movies or risk a rise in anti-Semitism. Immediately prior to Lindbergh's Des Moines speech, Senator Gerald Nye asserted that foreign-born owners of the Hollywood studios had "violent animosities toward certain causes abroad" (pp. 344–345). Representatives of the movie industry, realizing that they had the support of the Roosevelt administration, aggressively defended making "America conscious of the national peril."[6]

---

[5] This listing is based on several sources: Editors of *Fortune*, 1936; Philadelphia Anti-Defamation Council & The American Jewish Committee, 1941; Gabler, 1988; Kantor, 1982.

[6] Ben Hecht, who was a prominent Hollywood screenwriter and staunch Zionist, included pro-interventionist ideas in movies at this time (Liukkonen, 2008). For example, in *Angels Over Broadway* (1940), Hecht has the Douglas Fairbanks, Jr. character ask, "What happened to the Poles, the Finns, the Dutch? They're little guys. They didn't win. . . ." Rita Hayworth replies, "They will, some day." Hecht also made some uncredited additions to Alfred Hitchcock's *Foreign Correspondent* (1940). When Hitchcock was asked about the anti-Nazi and pro-Britain message of the film, he said that it was all the doing of Walter Wanger and Ben Hecht. (Wanger was also Jewish; his birth name was Walter Feuchtwanger.) In the film a character says, "Keep those lights burning, cover them with steel, build them in with guns, build a canopy of battleships and bombing planes around them and, hello, America, hang on to your lights, they're the only lights in the world." Hecht's strong Jewish consciousness, including his support for the Jewish terrorist group Irgun, which combated the British in the lead-up to Israel becoming a state, can be seen in the following: "In April 1941, [Hecht] wrote a piece titled 'My Tribe Is Called Israel' in his column for P.M., the liberal New York newspaper, defending his efforts to 'increase generally the Jew consciousness of the world,' and castigated 'Americanized Jews' for failing to join him out of fear that they would appear to value Jewish lives more than American ones. It

Harvard historian William Langer stated in a lecture to the U.S. Army War College that the rising dislike of Nazi Germany in the United States was due to "Jewish influence" in the media:

> You have to face the fact that some of our most important American newspapers are Jewish-controlled, and I suppose if I were a Jew I would feel about Nazi Germany as most Jews feel and it would be most inevitable that the coloring of the news takes on that tinge. As I read the *New York Times*, for example, it is perfectly clear that every little upset that occurs (and after all, many upsets occur in a country of 70 million people) is given a great deal of prominence. The other part of it is soft-pedaled or put off with a sneer. So that in a rather subtle way, the picture you get is that there is no good in the Germans whatever. (in Bendersky, 2000, p. 273)

It is also interesting that the *Chicago Tribune* was "circumspect on the Jewish question" despite the personal sentiments of Robert McCormick, the *Tribune's* non-Jewish publisher, that Jews were an important reason behind America's anti-German policy (Bendersky, 2000, p. 284). This suggests that concern with Jewish power—quite possibly concern about negative influences on advertising revenue (see Editors of *Fortune*, 1936, p. 57)—was an issue for McCormick. On balance, it would seem reasonable to agree with Lindbergh that Jewish influence in the media was significant during this period. Of course, this is not to say that Jews dominated the media at this time, or that no other influences were important.

It is also noteworthy that U.S. military officers often worried that Roosevelt was influenced to be anti-German by his Jewish advisors, Samuel I. Rosenman, Felix Frankfurter, and Henry Morgenthau, Jr. (Bendersky, 2000, p. 274), and they worried that Jewish interests and the British would push the United States into a war with Germany. Both Frankfurter and Morgenthau were strongly identified Jews and effective advocates for Jewish interests. Morgenthau actively promoted Zionism and the welfare of Jewish refugees (e.g., pp. 333ff, 354ff). Both supported U.S. involvement in the war against Germany, and Morgenthau became well known as an advocate of the Morgenthau Plan entailing extremely harsh treatment of the Germans during and after World War II.

---

was lucid and strident invective that teetered on the vituperative—a typical Hecht opinion piece—and it caught the attention of the so-called Bergson Group, a small network within the U.S. who sought to advance the agenda of Irgun, a paramilitary organization fighting to establish a free Jewish state across the entirety of the historical land of Israel. The group was led by Peter Bergson (born Hillel Kook), a charismatic twenty-five-year-old Palestinian who sensed in Hecht a potential ally. Bergson reached out and arranged a meeting at the Twenty One Club, Hecht's favorite Manhattan hangout" (E. White, 2017).

Moreover, there is no question that Jews were able to exert a great deal of influence on specific issues during this period. For example, Zionist organizations exerted enormous pressure on the government (e.g., Bendersky, 2000, p. 325). During World War II they engaged in "loud diplomacy" (p. 326) with thousands of rallies, dinners with celebrity speakers, letter campaigns, meetings, lobbying, threats to newspapers for publishing unfavorable items, insertion of propaganda as news items in newspapers, and giving money to non-Jewish politicians and celebrities like Will Rogers in return for their support. (Because Jews are a small minority, this "loud diplomacy" included prominent roles for sympathetic non-Jews—a common theme for Jewish movements aiming to influence non-Jews, as noted in several chapters here.) By 1944, "thousands of non-Jewish associations would pass pro-Zionist resolutions" (p. 326). In 1944 both Republican and Democratic platforms included strong pro-Zionist planks even though the creation of a Jewish state was strongly opposed by the Department of State and the Department of War (p. 328).

Nevertheless, whatever the level of Jewish influence on the media during this period, commentators generally focused on denouncing the seeming implication in Lindbergh's speech that Jewish interests were "not American." I suppose that Lindbergh's statement could have been amended by a public relations-minded editor without distorting Lindbergh's intentions to read something like "Jewish interests are not the same as the interests of other Americans" or "Jewish interests are not the same as those of the country as a whole." However, I rather doubt that this alteration would have assuaged the outpouring of hatred that ensued. The simple facts that the vast majority of U.S. Jews were indeed in favor of intervention and that Jews did have a significant effect on public attitudes and public policy had become irrelevant. As Lindbergh himself said, the choice was "whether or not you are going to let your country go into a completely disastrous war for lack of courage to name the groups leading that country to war—at the risk of being called 'anti-Semitic' simply by *naming* them" (as paraphrased by Anne Morrow Lindbergh, 1980, p. 224; emphasis in original). America had entered into an era when it had become morally unacceptable to discuss Jewish interests at all. We are still in that era.

An exception that proves the rule was Pat Buchanan's 1990 column that referred to Israel's "amen corner" in the United States advocating war with Iraq—indeed, the American Israel Public Affairs Committee had been lobbying Congress behind the scenes to declare war on Iraq (Sobran, 1999). Writing in *The Wall Street Journal*, Norman Podhoretz, former editor of *Commentary*, promptly labeled Buchanan an "anti-Semite" without feeling the need to address the question of whether or not American Jews were indeed pressing for war with Iraq in order to benefit Israel. As in the case of Lindbergh's remarks a half century earlier, truth was irrelevant. While this incident has not altered the taboo on discussing Jewish interests in the same way that it is common to discuss the interests of other ethnic groups, it has resulted in a long-term problem for Buchanan's political career. When Buchanan ran for president in 2000, a hostile columnist writing in a prominent Jewish publication stated, "Out of the slime of the sewers and into the filth of the gutter a desperate Patrick J. Buchanan, the neo-Nazi, has crawled into the political arena using anti-Semitism as his principal device to secure a future for himself" (H. L. Adelson, 1999). The columnist went on to claim that Buchanan "always was a neo-Nazi" and that he "reveals the shallow quality of his tortured, sick, defective mind." Not to be outdone, Alan Dershowitz (1999) wrote, "Let there be no mistake about it. Pat Buchanan is a classic anti-Semite with fascist leanings who hates Israel and loves Nazi war criminals." The example illustrates that Jews continue to exert immense pressure, including smear tactics, to keep Jewish interests off-limits in American political discussion. As with Lindbergh in an earlier generation, Buchanan's experience is a grim reminder to politicians who dare raise the issue of Jewish interests in public debate. Buchanan became completely marginalized within the Republican Party and eventually left it for an unsuccessful run as the Reform Party presidential candidate in 2000.

It is instructive to review in some detail the "Niagara of invective" experienced by Lindbergh (Berg, 1998/1999, p. 428). He was denounced by virtually all the leading media, by Democrats and Republicans, Protestants and Catholics, and, of course, Jewish groups. Many accused him of being a Nazi, including President Roosevelt's Secretary of the Interior, Harold L. Ickes, who labeled Lindbergh "the No. 1 United States Nazi fellow traveler" (p. 428). Reinhold Niebuhr, the prominent Protestant leader (see below), called on Lindbergh's organization, the America First Committee, to "divorce itself from the stand taken by Lindbergh and clean its ranks of those who would incite to racial and religious strife in this country" (p. 428). The committee released a statement saying that neither Lindbergh nor the organization were anti-Semitic.

The reaction of Lindbergh's wife, Anne Morrow Lindbergh, is particularly interesting because it illustrates both the power of moral revulsion combined with hypocrisy that had enveloped any public discussion of Jewish interests, and the power of moral communities as a phenomenon unique to the individualist, non-kinship-oriented cultures of the West (see above). Women, even more than men, are especially prone to avoid being ostracized from a group for violating the moral basis of the community (see below). From Anne Morrow Lindbergh (1980, pp. 220–230, emphasis in original):

> September 11, 1941: Then [he gave] his speech—throwing me into black gloom. He names the "war agitators"—chiefly the British, the Jews, and the Administration. He does it truthfully, moderately, and with no bitterness or rancor—but I hate to have him touch the Jews at all. For I dread the reaction on him. No one else mentions this subject out loud (though many

seethe bitterly and intolerantly underneath). C. [Charles], as usual, must bear the brunt of being frank and open. What he is saying in public is not intolerant or inciting or bitter and it is just what he says in private, while the other soft-spoken cautious people who say terrible things in private would never dare be as frank in public as he. They do not want to pay the price. And the price will be terrible. Headlines will flame "Lindbergh attacks Jews." He will be branded anti-Semitic, Nazi, Führer-seeking, etc. I *can hardly bear it. For he is a moderate*. . . .

September 13, 1941: He is attacked on all sides—Administration, pressure groups, and Jews, as now openly a Nazi, following Nazi doctrine.

September 14, 1941: I cannot explain my revulsion of feeling by logic. Is it my lack of courage to face the problem? Is it my lack of vision and seeing the thing through? Or is my intuition founded on something profound and valid?

I do not know and am only very disturbed, which is upsetting for him. I have the greatest faith in him as a person—in his integrity, his courage, and his essential *goodness*, fairness, and kindness—his nobility really. . . . How then explain my profound feeling of grief about what he is doing? If what he said is the truth (and I am inclined to think it is), why was it wrong to state it? He was naming the groups that were pro-war. No one minds his naming the British or the Administration. But to name "Jew" is un-American—even if it is done without hate or even criticism. Why?

Because it is segregating them as a group, setting the ground for anti-Semitism. . . .

I say that I would prefer to see this country at war than shaken by violent anti-Semitism. (Because it seems to me that the kind of person the human being is turned into when the instinct of Jew-baiting is let loose is worse than the kind of person he becomes on the battlefield.)

September 15, 1941: The storm is beginning to blow up hard. America First is in a turmoil. . . . He is universally condemned by all moderates. . . . The Jews demand a retraction. . . . I sense that this is the beginning of a fight and consequent loneliness and isolation that we have not known before. . . . For I am really much more attached to the worldly things than he is, mind more giving up friends, popularity, etc., mind much more criticism and coldness and loneliness.

September 18, 1941: Will I be able to shop in New York at all now? I am always stared at—but now to be stared at with hate, to walk through aisles of hate![7]

---

[7] Further, in a conversation with his wife on November 24th, 1941, Charles Lindbergh was pessimistic about establishing a Jewish state: "C. and I get into an argument *à propos* of an article in the paper, a speech of a rabbi at a Jewish conference in which he said that the first thing that would have to be done at the peace table after the war was that a large indemnity would have to be paid to the Jews for their sufferings. Also speaks about having a piece of land of their own—which I am sympathetic with. . . . [C.] says it isn't as simple as all that. Whose land

Several issues stand out in these comments. Anne Morrow Lindbergh is horrified at having to walk through "aisles of hate," horrified at having to give up her friends, horrified at being a pariah where once she was idolized as the wife of the most popular man in the country. While she accepts the truth of what her husband said and its good intentions, she thinks it better left unsaid and does not dwell on the unfairness of the charges against her husband, in particular the charge that he is a Nazi. Truth is no defense if it leads to what are regarded as morally unacceptable actions, and slander and smear tactics are warranted and understandable if the goals are morally praiseworthy. She supposes that even a disastrous war that might kill hundreds of thousands of Americans (and, as her husband believed, might result in the destruction of European culture and the White race) is preferable to the possibility of an outbreak of violent anti-Semitism. The moral demeanor of Americans is more important than their survival as a nation or people. And all of this because Lindbergh simply stated that Jews had interests as a group that differed from those of other Americans. Their lesson learned, American politicians presumably realized that even rational, intelligent, and humane discussions of Jewish interests were beyond the boundaries of acceptable discussion. Jews had no interests as Jews that could be said to conflict with the interests of any other group of Americans.

Her reaction fits well with a major point of my 2019 book, *Individualism and the Western Liberal Tradition: Evolutionary Origins, History, and Prospects for the Future*, that the social glue of the unique individualist cultures of the West is based on moral communities rather than on kinship as is true for the other cultures of the world. Individualists, and especially women (because of evolved sex differences in personality—see *Individualism*, Ch. 8), are loath to violate the moral norms of their communities for fear of being ostracized or worse. As noted above, in the contemporary age, the moral norms of Western societies are established by elites in the media and academia, both of which have a strong Jewish presence and influence (see below for a discussion of Jewish influence in the media and academia). Anne Morrow Lindbergh was clearly horrified to realize that her husband's speech had resulted in both of them becoming moral pariahs: "I . . . mind more [than Charles] giving up friends, popularity, etc., mind much more criticism and coldness and loneliness."

By the time of Lindbergh's speech, Jews not only had a prominent position in the U.S. media, but had also seized the intellectual and moral high ground via their control of the intellectual and political movements discussed in *CofC*. Not only were Jewish interests beyond the bounds of civilized political

---

are you going to take? . . . He is very pessimistic of its being solved without great suffering" (A. M. Lindbergh, 1980, p. 239).

discussion, but assertions of European ethnic interests became impermissible as well. Such assertions conflicted with the Boasian dogma that genetic differences between peoples were trivial and in any case irrelevant. They conflicted with the Marxist belief in the equality of all peoples and the Marxist belief that nationalism and assertions of ethnic interests were reactionary. Such assertions were deemed a sure sign of psychopathology within the frameworks of psychoanalysis and the Frankfurt School, and they would be regarded as the babblings of country bumpkins by the New York Intellectuals and by the neo-conservatives who spouted variants of all of these ideologies from the most prestigious academic and media institutions in the society. There may indeed have been other forces that relegated a nativist mindset to the political and intellectual fringe—Gottfried (2000) points a finger at liberal Protestantism and the rise of the managerial state—but it is impossible to understand the effectiveness of either of these influences in ending mainstream assertions of the ethnic interests of Europeans in the absence of the Jewish movements I describe.

The rise of a de-ethnicized non-Jewish managerial elite that rejects traditional cultural institutions—as exemplified by President Bill and Hillary Clinton as well as most Democrats and Republicans—and is interwoven with a critical mass of ethnically conscious Jews and other ethnic minorities is an enormously important fact of our current political life. My claim that Jewish intellectual and political activities were a necessary condition for the rise of such an elite, while obviously difficult to verify conclusively (as any other causal hypothesis would be), is also compatible with the work of others, most notably David A. Hollinger's (1996) *Science, Jews, and Secular Culture: Studies in Mid-Twentieth-Century American Intellectual History* and Carl Degler's (1991) *In Search of Human Nature: The Decline and Revival of Darwinism in American Social Thought*.

The rise of such a de-ethnicized elite of White Americans is hardly an inevitable consequence of modernization or any other force of which I am aware. Such de-ethnicized managerial elites are unique to Western European and Western European-derived societies (see *Individualism*). Such elites are not found elsewhere in the world, either in highly developed nations, such as Japan and Israel, or in the undeveloped nations of Africa and elsewhere. Moreover, the cultural shifts under consideration have also occurred in traditionally Catholic countries like France and Italy, where Protestantism has not been a factor. France in particular has been very open to non-European immigration, and its intellectual life has been deeply influenced by the movements discussed in *CofC* as well as the movements of the left cited above with respect to Judith Butler's work. Conversely, there are many examples where Protestantism has peacefully coexisted with or even rationalized nationalism and ethnocentrism.

HOW AMERICANS SAW THEMSELVES UP THROUGH THE 1920S

Developing theories of why Western cultures have provided such fertile ground for the movements and theories discussed in *CofC* is an important area for research that I have explored in *Individualism and the Western Liberal Tradition*. In this context, it is instructive to look at the way Europeans in the United States saw themselves a century ago.[8] Americans of European descent thought of themselves as part of an ethnic and cultural heritage extending backward in time to the founding of the country. The Anglo-Saxon heritage of the British Isles was at the center of this self-conception, but Americans of German and Scandinavian descent also viewed themselves as part of this ethnic and cultural heritage. They had a great deal of pride in their accomplishments. They had conquered a vast territory and had achieved a high degree of economic progress. They saw themselves as having created a civilization with a strong moral fabric—a country of farmers and small businessmen that had become a world economic power. They believed that their civilization was a product of their own unique ingenuity and skills, and they believed that it would not survive if other peoples were allowed to play too large a role in it. They saw themselves as exhibiting positive personality traits such as courage in the face of adversity, self-reliance, inventiveness, originality, and fair play—the very virtues that allowed them to conquer the wilderness and turn it into an advanced civilization.

Americans at the dawn of the twentieth century looked out on the world and saw their own society as superior to others. They saw themselves and other European societies as reaping the rewards of political and economic freedom while the rest of the world suffered as it had from time immemorial—the despotism of Asia, the barbarity and primitivism of Africa, and the economic and political backwardness of Russia and Eastern Europe.

They saw themselves as Christian, and they thought of Christianity as an essential part of the social fabric and their way of life. Christianity was seen as basic to the moral foundations of the society, and any threat to Christianity was seen as a threat to the society as a whole. When these people looked back on their own childhood, they saw "a simple, secure world of commonly accepted values and behavior" (Bendersky, 2000, p. 6)—a world of ethnic and cultural homogeneity. They had a strong sense of family pride and regional identification, having deep roots in the areas in which they grew up. They did not think of the United States as a Marxist hell of war between the social classes. Instead, they thought of it as a world of harmony between the social classes in

---

[8] The following is based on Bendersky's (2000, pp. 2–46) study of U.S. military officers but is representative of commonly held attitudes in the early twentieth century.

which people at the top of society earned their positions but felt a certain sense of social obligation to the lower social classes.

The early part of the twentieth century was also the high-water mark of Darwinism in the social sciences. It was common at that time to think that there were important differences between the races—that races differed in intelligence and in moral qualities. Not only did races differ, but they were in competition with each other for supremacy. As I described in SAID Chapter 5, such ideas were part of the furniture of intellectual life—commonplace among Jews as well as non-Jews.

That world has vanished. The rise of Jewish power and the disestablishment of the specifically European nature of the United States—a war fought on several fronts—are the real topics of *CofC*. The main thrusts of Jewish activism against European ethnic and cultural hegemony have focused on three critical power centers in the United States: (1) the academic world of information in the social sciences and humanities and its influence on the lower levels of the educational system; (2) the political world where public policy on immigration and other ethnic issues are decided; and (3) the mass media where "ways of seeing" are presented to the public.

At the academic level, Jewish intellectuals led the battle against the ideas that races even exist and that there are differences in intelligence or cultural level between the races that are rooted in biology (Ch. 2). At the level of politics, Jewish organizations spearheaded the drive to open up immigration to all of the peoples of the world. Jewish organizations, media companies, and media personalities also played a key role in furthering the interests of other racial and ethnic minorities, and they led the legal and legislative effort to remove Christianity from the public square (Ch. 8).

THE RISE OF THE JEWS IN AMERICAN UNIVERSITIES

Concurrent with the rise of Jewish influence in the media was the Jewish rise in elite academic institutions and especially the Ivy League universities. The transformation of the faculty in the social sciences and humanities was well underway in the 1950s, and by the late 1960s it was largely complete. The new elite was very different from the old elite it displaced. The difference was that the old Protestant elite was not at war with the country it dominated. The old Protestant elite was wealthier and better educated than the public at large, but they approached life on basically the same terms. They saw themselves as Christians and as Europeans, and they didn't see the need for radically changing the society.

Things are very different now. Since the 1960s a hostile, adversarial elite has emerged to dominate intellectual and political discourse. It is an elite that almost instinctively loathes the traditional institutions of European-American culture: its religion, its customs, its manners, and its sexual attitudes. In the words of one commentator, "today's elite loathes the nation it rules" (Gelernter, 1997).

This "hostile elite" is fundamentally a Jewish-dominated elite whose origins and main lines of influence are described in *CofC*. (By "Jewish-dominated elite," I mean that policies disfavored by the mainstream Jewish community— e.g., policies regarding Israel or multicultural immigration—are highly unlikely to become official policy even if supported by most Americans.) The emergence of this hostile elite is an aspect of ethnic competition between Jews and non-Jews, and its effect will be a long-term decline in the hegemony of European peoples in the United States and elsewhere in the world.

Academia is an important locus of power. As Gross and Fosse (2012, p. 128) point out, the occupation of being a professor is of great sociological significance:

> [Professors] play pivotal social roles producing new knowledge and technology; teaching and credentialing growing numbers of students; advising government, industry, and non-governmental organizations; and shaping social narratives in . . . the "civil sphere." Politics do not bear directly on all work professors do, but higher education institutions as loci of knowledge production and dissemination may be influenced in important ways by their political views.

At least since the nineteenth century, the way we see ourselves has been vitally shaped by the academic community. Contemporary views on issues like race, gender, immigration, and a host of vital issues are manufactured in the academy (especially elite universities), disseminated throughout the media and the lower levels of the educational system, and ultimately consumed by the educated and not-so-educated public. Newspaper articles and television programs on these issues routinely include quotes from academic experts—especially professors from elite institutions.

Hollinger (1996, p. 4) notes "the transformation of the ethnoreligious demography of American academic life by Jews" in the period from the 1930s to the 1960s, as well as the Jewish influence on trends toward the secularization of American society and in advancing an ideal of cosmopolitanism (p. 11). As early as the early 1940s, this transformation resulted in "a secular, increasingly Jewish, decidedly left-of-center intelligentsia based largely but not exclusively in the disciplinary communities of philosophy and the social sciences" (p. 160). By 1968, Jews constituted 20 percent of the faculty of elite American colleges and universities and 30 percent of the "most liberal" faculty. At this time, Jews, representing less than 3 percent of the population, constituted 25 percent of the social sciences faculty at elite universities and 40 percent of liberal faculty who published most (see Rothman & Lichter, 1982/1996, p. 103). Jewish academics were also far more likely to support "progressive" or communist parties from the 1930s to the 1950s. In 1948 30 percent of Jewish faculty voted for the Progressive Party, compared to less than 5 percent of gentile faculty (p. 101).

Using survey data of 60,000 academics from 1969, Lipset and Ladd (1971) show that the 1960s were a critical period for the rise of a Jewish academic culture well to the left of non-Jewish professors. Jews represented around 12 percent of faculty in general, but around 25 percent of the younger faculty (less than age fifty) at Ivy League universities—percentages that were much higher than in previous decades. Jews were heavily represented on the faculties of other elite public and private universities as well, particularly in the politically relevant fields of the law and the social sciences.

Moreover, Jewish faculty were more heavily published than non-Jewish faculty, indicating greater influence. This is important because the academic world is a top-down system: those at the top train the next generation of scholars and police the recruitment of new faculty. For example, a professor at Harvard places his Ph.D. students at the flagship state universities, such as the University of Wisconsin, the University of Michigan, or the University of California-Berkeley, and they in turn place their students at lower-tier colleges and universities—the University of Wisconsin-Oshkosh, etc. They therefore have more influence on the future of the field than less-published scholars. As indicated below, liberal faculty are perfectly willing to discriminate on the basis of political views, and I think it's quite likely that this also occurred in the 1960s.

Importantly, Lipset and Ladd also found that Jewish faculty were well to the left of non-Jewish faculty. Thus, a considerably larger percentage of Jewish faculty rated themselves as liberal or left (74.5 percent) compared to less than 40 percent of non-Jewish faculty. In the social sciences, 84.9 percent of Jewish faculty compared to 76 percent of Protestants and 65.2 percent of Catholics described themselves as liberal or left. Among the Jewish faculty, 59.1 percent approved of 1960s student radical activism, compared to around 40 percent for non-Jewish faculty. Jewish faculty were also more likely to approve relaxing standards in order to recruit more minority faculty and students.

Within the Jewish segment, the least religious Jews were the most liberal. This is important because, as documented in *CofC*, in general liberal-left Jews were not religious but were strongly identified as Jews and saw their politics as advancing specifically Jewish interests. The leftist politics of the new academic elite was thus closely related to Jewish identification, and it was broadly reflective of the political views of the mainstream Jewish community.

In a work published in 1977, Harriet Zuckerman also found high levels of Jewish overrepresentation among elite, high-achieving academics, as indicated in Table 1 below.

Faculty	Percent Jews	Achievement Quotient
Law	36	13.3
Sociology	34	12.6
Economics	28	10.4
Physics	26	9.6
Political Science	24	8.9
History	22	8.1
Philosophy	20	7.4
Mathematics	20	7.4

Table 1: *Jewish Percentage of Faculty at Elite Universities by Department. Achievement Quotient is the percentage of Jewish faculty divided by the percentage of Jews in the population, set at 2.7 percent. (Zuckerman, 1977/1996)*

These findings regarding Jewish overrepresentation replicate similar findings based on surveys cited elsewhere in this volume. In the 1970s, Charles Kadushin's 1974 sample of authors who were published in the top twenty academic journals in America indicated that Jews accounted for 56 percent of social scientists and 61 percent of humanity scholars.

The leftward bias of the social sciences continues today. Social psychologist Jonathan Haidt (2011) conducted an informal survey at a convention of social psychologists (reputedly the most left-leaning academic area of psychology), finding that only 3 in a crowd of 1,000 (0.3 percent) were willing to publicly label themselves as "conservative" compared to around 40 percent of the American public. Haidt sees social psychology as a "tribal moral community" that shuns and ostracizes political conservatives, with the result that research conflicting with core political attitudes is either not performed or is likely to be excluded from peer-reviewed journals because such research faces much more daunting scrutiny and higher methodological standards in the peer review process.

Sociology is another hotbed of leftist academics. Emil Kierkegaard (2024) concluded that "Surveys of sociologists from the 1950s to 2020s show that it is an extremely left-wing field even by comparison with other academic social science fields."

As noted by Zuckerman (1977; see above) and in Chapter 2, Jews are highly overrepresented in sociology. In examining why this might be, Gross and Fosse (2012) found that the most powerful variable was simply having a graduate degree—results they argue are not due to IQ. That is, college professors are liberals because they went to graduate school, and they did so not because they were smarter, but for some other reason. The second strongest predictor was "intellectualism"—the extent of tolerance for controversial ideas. (Based on my experience in contemporary academia, such tolerance would seem to be entirely in the self-conceptions of the professors.) The next most powerful predictor was religious affiliation or lack thereof: people with no religious affiliation, or Jewish affiliation, or non-conservative Protestant affiliation were more likely to be liberal (in that order). Since it's likely that a considerable percentage of professors who declare themselves as having no religious affiliation are Jews, this doubtless underrepresents the importance of Jewishness in accounting for professorial liberalism. (In general, the study would have been far better if race and Jewish ethnic background—not simply religious affiliation—were included as variables.)

Gross and Fosse (2012, p. 154) acknowledge that their data can be interpreted in a number of ways. However, they argue that "the liberalism of professors ... is a function ... of the systematic sorting of young adults who are already liberally—or conservatively—inclined into and out of the academic profession, respectively." Just as a profession like nursing becomes typecast as appropriate for women, becoming a professor is seen as appropriate for liberals: "We argue that the professoriate, along with a number of other knowledge work fields, has been 'politically typed' as appropriate for and welcoming of people with broadly liberal political sensibilities, and as inappropriate for conservatives" (p. 155).

A study completed after Gross and Fosse's paper indicated that liberal faculty members acknowledge being willing to discriminate against conservative job candidates, and that this tendency became stronger among the most liberal faculty (Inbar & Lammers, 2012). Such discrimination is a powerful reinforcement for self-sorting processes—effectively ensuring that the next generation of faculty will be liberal as well.

Gross and Fosse have some ideas on how academia became dominated by the left. Disciplines construct images of the ideal person in their respective fields, and these images are ultimately the result of conflict among competing images. When it comes to understanding the history of how the academy became a bastion of the left, they emphasize the 1960s and the conservative reaction against it. It was during this period that the image of the radical leftist professor replaced the image of the ivory tower professor—the unworldly person of letters and sophistication, at home with his books, his pipe, and his tweed jacket, and totally immersed in discussions of Renaissance poetry or the art of classical antiquity.

Universities were relatively liberal before the 1960s—at least since the decline of Darwinism in the social sciences by 1930. As I have argued, the decline of Darwinian social science (perhaps "eradication" is a better word) resulted in an intellectual gap that was quickly filled by several Jewish-dominated intellectual movements of the left (MacDonald, 2015). Nevertheless, there was a major shift in the 1960s that resulted in the activist left becoming dominant at American universities.

Perhaps the most important aspect of this shift was that before the 1960s liberalism was identified with supporting labor unions and other institutions aimed at improving the lot of the (predominantly White) working class. The intellectual movements that came to dominate the left—perhaps most notably the Frankfurt School, whose members were clearly influenced by their Jewish identities and sense of Jewish interests (Ch. 6)—abandoned the working class because it was insufficiently radical and had succumbed to fascism in Germany and Italy during the 1930s. This caused the Frankfurt School intellectuals and many other leftist intellectuals to reject orthodox Marxism, replacing it by advocating multiracial immigration and multiculturalism, as well as recruiting those who had complaints against the traditional culture of America, particularly feminists and racial, ethnic, and sexual minorities—what is now often called the grievance industry. As discussed below, complaints against the current system are a critical motivating feature of successful intellectual movements. The groups recruited into the coalition of the left then formed the core of the "tribal moral community" described by Haidt (2011)—the community that has come to define the academic culture of the left that now dominates universities, particularly in the social sciences, the humanities, and the law).

As Gross and Fosse (2012, pp. 158–159) note, it was during the 1960s when the universities became strongly associated with the political left in the eyes of friends and foes alike—enough to result in self-selection processes in which conservatives would feel unwelcome in the university:

> Higher education was a crucial micromobilization context for a number of left social movements in the 1960s and 1970s, which further enhanced the institution's liberal reputation; with concerted cultural efforts by American conservatives, especially from the 1950s on, to build a collective identity for their movement around differentiation from various categories of "liberal elites," not least liberal professors; with restricted opportunities for Americans on the far left to enter other institutional spheres; and with self-reinforcing processes by which self-selection into the academic profession by liberals resulted in a more liberal professoriate whose reputation for liberalism was thereby maintained or enhanced.

Further, because departments at elite universities attempt to best represent the *zeitgeist* of their particular academic fields, Gross and Fosse point out they will offer positions to scholars they see as exemplary, and political attitudes are a major part of being exemplary. Imagine the extreme improbability of being hired in a gender studies department as an openly declared conservative heterosexual male—especially at an elite institution (MacDonald, 2008c).

I would also add that not only are liberal attitudes a key component of being seen as a viable job candidate at an elite institution, but also group membership is critical. Being non-White or a member of a sexual minority definitely gives one an advantage in the hiring process, as well as promotion and the prospect of becoming an administrator.

Since the contemporary *zeitgeist* celebrates the multicultural left (as opposed to the pro-White working-class left of the pre-1960s), hiring is biased toward those who espouse the most liberal attitudes, and especially those from aggrieved groups as imagined by the multicultural left. And, as Gross and Fosse point out, this in turn leads to elite institutions being to the left of lesser institutions. In the academic food chain, the result is that graduate students coming from elite institutions are most representative of the leftist academic culture, either because of their socialization in the academic environment or simply because of their perceived self-interest as a victimized group championed by the left. This becomes progressively diluted as one goes to the second- and third-tier schools and eventually down to K–12 education.

This creates a liberal social environment at all levels of the academic pecking order. Public opinion surveys carried out since the 1960s show that going to college results in attitude change in a liberal direction compared to parents. If education level remained the same, there was little change in attitudes (Kaufmann, 2004, p. 191).

Thus, for all its supposed openness to new ideas and espousal of egalitarianism, the academic world is a top-down system in which the highest levels are rigorously policed to ensure ideological conformity, not only for the reasons suggested by Gross and Fosse, but also because any leak in the system would mean that dissidents would benefit from institutional prestige. Thus John J. Mearsheimer and Stephen M. Walt (2007) caused a panic in the ranks of the Israel Lobby with their work on the lobby and its effects on U.S. foreign policy. Mearsheimer and Walt weren't just two easy-to-ignore professors from a third-tier university, nor were they members of an easily marginalized group, such as Arabs. They were well-known and academically productive professors at prestigious institutions—the University of Chicago and Harvard respectively.

This resulted in a full-fledged smear campaign emphasizing "shoddy scholarship"—improbable given their long history of publishing their research in major academic journals (MacDonald, 2007a). This charge was typically made by Jewish activist organizations or others without the slightest experience in scholarship. Mearsheimer and Walt were also charged with the thought crime of anti-Semitism, and their work was likened to *The Protocols of the Elders of Zion*—also improbable given that they are political liberals who have bent over backwards not to offend Jews (MacDonald, 2007b).

Nevertheless, despite their lack of credibility, these efforts have been at least somewhat successful. At the time of this writing in 2024, politicians are loath to cite Mearsheimer and Walt, and it is unthinkable that they could attain positions in the government where they could directly influence U.S. foreign policy. This shows that even elite academics can be marginalized if they come up against powerful interests. But the energy expended by the Jewish activist community against Mearsheimer and Walt shows the danger that elite academics pose to those who disagree with the implications of their ideas. Other examples are E. O. Wilson, the Harvard biologist (see Ch. 2), and Nobel Laureate James Watson, co-discoverer of the structure of DNA.

IS GROSS AND FOSSE'S THEORY COMPATIBLE WITH CofC?

The major question for me is whether the theory of Gross and Fosse (2012) is compatible with my proposal in *CofC* that Jewish intellectual movements were a critical force in producing the leftist political culture in the academic world and beyond. I think the answer is a resounding "yes."

Gross and Fosse propose a conflict theory of successful intellectual movements. In particular, they cite sociological research indicating that successful intellectual movements have three key ingredients: (1) they originate with people with high-status positions having complaints against the current environment, resulting in conflict with the status quo; (2) these intellectuals form cohesive and cooperative networks; and (3) this network has access to prestigious institutions and publication outlets (Frickel & Gross, 2005).

This is precisely the perspective developed in *CofC*. In the following, I provide evidence that Jewish-dominated intellectual movements were a critical factor (necessary condition) for the triumph of the intellectual left in late twentieth-century Western societies, with a focus on the creation of an academic culture of the left. But before embarking on that, it is noteworthy that Gross and Fosse are at least somewhat cognizant of the importance of Jewish influence. They deem it relevant to point out that Jews entered the academic world in large numbers after World War II and became overrepresented among professors, especially in elite academic departments in the social sciences— that is, in the decade immediately prior to the triumph of the multicultural left in the academic world. They cite survey data indicating that 25 percent of the faculty at research universities are Jewish compared to 10 percent overall; these percentages are even higher in departments of social science at research universities (Schuster & Finkelstein, 2006). Correspondingly, conservative Protestants are underrepresented, especially among faculty at elite research universities. Further, and importantly, as noted above, the most liberal professors work at the most elite institutions. These findings also fit well with the views of other social scientists noted above (Hollinger, 1996; Rothman & Lichter, 1982/1996) and regarding sociology as discussed in Chapter 2.

WHY ARE JEWS LIBERAL?

Gross and Fosse also correctly point out that Jews in general are politically liberal. Indeed, Norman Podhoretz (2009, Ch. 31) in his *Why Are Jews Liberals?* noted that over 80 percent of Jews voted for Barack Obama—far higher than any other religious or ethnic group, except Blacks. In the 2024 election, while religious Jews voted around 40 percent for Trump, non-religious Jews (the vast majority of American Jews) voted around 25 percent for Trump (A. Rosen, 2024), in line with previous patterns despite increasing criticism of Israel on the left, especially after the Gaza war of 2023–present. Moreover, the Jewish voting profile in terms of income and occupation is completely different from other liberal voters—reflected in the old saw that Jews "earn like Episcopalians and vote like Puerto Ricans." Whereas the views of Jewish professors are quite in line with the views of the wider Jewish community, the views of non-Jewish White professors are quite out of step with the wider White community.

Thus the liberalism of Jewish professors is entirely in line with the attitudes of other Jews, and it is at least doubtful that the reasons why Jewish professors are liberal are any different from why most Jews are liberal—that is, the liberal proclivities of Jews are a fundamental facet of Jewish identity in the diaspora in twentieth-century Western societies. This means that the deeper motivation for the liberalism of a very significant percentage of faculty at elite universities, especially in departments of social sciences and humanities, is not really addressed in Gross and Fosse's study.

The following, therefore, assumes that Jewish professors are motivated by the same forces that motivate liberalism and radicalism as Jewish ideologies in the Western diaspora—thus the same as the motivations of the principal figures in the Jewish intellectual movements covered in other chapters of this volume.

(1) Jewish intellectuals have a complaint. Gross and Fosse propose that successful intellectual movements begin with a complaint, and there can be little doubt that Jews in general have a complaint, or rather, two related complaints: the long history of anti-Semitism, and the predominance of White Christian culture.

Podhoretz's book is typical of a very large literature that points to the lachrymose view of Jewish history as influencing how Jews see themselves politically in diaspora societies in the West. This view of Jewish history proposes that, beginning with an unfortunate theological belief (that Jews killed God), Jews in Western societies have repeatedly been passive, innocent victims of marauding non-Jews. As I noted in SAID (p. 215):

> Jewish religious consciousness centers to a remarkable extent around the memory of persecution. Persecution is a central theme of the holidays of Passover, Hanukkah, Purim, and Yom Kippur.... Jews learn about the Middle Ages as a period of persecution in Christian Europe, culminating in the expulsions and the Inquisitions. The violence perpetrated by the Crusaders in 1096 in Germany became a central event in Jewish consciousness. ... Detailed lists of martyrs were composed and recited in synagogue ritual for hundreds of years after the event; chronicles of the event were written and a literature on the status of forced converts was developed. ... There is also a strong awareness of the nineteenth-century pogroms in Eastern Europe, especially in Russia. Indeed, the historian Sir Louis B. Namier went so far as to say that there was no Jewish history, "only a Jewish martyrology" (in Berlin 1980, 72). ... [And] when prominent social scientist Michael Walzer (1994, 4) states that "I was taught Jewish history as a long tale of exile and persecution—Holocaust history read backwards," he is expressing not only the predominant perception of Jews of their own history but also a powerful strand of academic Jewish historiography, the so-called "lachrymose" tradition of Jewish historiography.

The lesson that Jews learned from the Middle Ages carries down to today, as Podhoretz (2009, p. 29) notes:

> [The Jews] emerged from the Middle Ages knowing for a certainty that— individual exceptions duly noted—the worst enemy they had in the world was Christianity: the churches in which it was embodied—whether Roman Catholic or Russian Orthodox or Protestant—and the people who prayed in and were shaped by them. It was a knowledge that Jewish experience in the ages to come would do very little, if indeed anything at all, to help future generations to forget.

It is common, therefore, for Jews to hate all manifestations of Christianity. But the decline of Christianity as the central intellectual paradigm didn't improve things for Jews. During the Enlightenment, anti-Jewish ideologies smoothly morphed into non-theological views in which Judaism was a superstitious relic that prevented Jews from shedding their attachment to their people—"giving up their sense of themselves as a people whose members were bound together across national boundaries and wherever they might live" (Podhoretz, 2009, p. 43).

The Enlightenment critique of Judaism implied that Jews should give up their tribal allegiances and economic and political networks and that they should accept the atomized individualism implied by the modern nation-state. As Count Clermont-Tonnerre expressed it when addressing the French National Assembly in 1789, "The Jews should be denied everything as a nation, but granted everything as individuals. . . . The existence of a nation within a nation is unacceptable to our country" (in Podhoretz, 2009, p. 51).

In the nineteenth century, Jews began to be seen by their enemies as an economically successful alien race intent on subverting national cultures wherever they lived. Podhoretz (2009, p. 111) points to "the new racist rationale [that] manifested itself in the portrayal of a war between Aryans and Semites as the central drama of history." For example, Ivan Aksakov, a leader of the Slavophiles in Russia, viewed Jews as a mortal enemy intent on destroying Christianity: "The Western European Christian world will be faced in the future, in one form or another, with a life-and-death struggle with Jewry, which is striving to replace the universal Christian ideal by another, Semitic ideal, also universal, but negative and anti-Christian" (in p. 108).

Even in the United States—the "golden land" as seen by Jewish immigrants—there was exclusion and antipathy from "the upper echelons of the Wasp patriciate" (Podhoretz, 2009, p. 90), and quotas on Jews were established at elite universities. In America, Jews were excluded by WASP elites, and Christian forms of anti-Semitism (e.g., Father Charles Coughlin) remained strong through the 1930s. As discussed above, isolationists such as Charles Lindbergh also tended to see Jews as an interest group aiming at getting America involved in war with Germany.

Jews concluded, as they had ever since the political left and right came to be defined, that their enemies were on the right. But the main lesson Podhoretz and a legion of other Jewish intellectuals have drawn is that over the centuries Western intellectuals have produced a variety of Christian and non-Christian anti-Jewish ideologies, each with the same result: irrational hatred toward Jews. So it's not just Christianity, but European civilization itself that is the problem for Jews.

And, although Podhoretz doesn't explicitly make this move, it's a very short jump from blaming the culture created and sustained by Europeans to the idea that Europeans as a people or group of peoples are the problem—the ultimate conclusion of the Frankfurt School (see Ch. 6). This explicit or implicit sense that Europeans themselves are the problem is the crux of the Jewish complaint.

This Jewish complaint has resonated powerfully among Jewish intellectuals who rose to the heights of the academic world. As John Murray Cuddihy (1974, p. 68) notes, Jewish intellectuals were generally estranged from and hostile toward Western culture and institutions:

From Solomon Maimon to Norman Podhoretz, from Rahel Varnhagen to
Cynthia Ozick, from Marx and Lassalle to Erving Goffman and Harold Gar-
finkel, from Herzl and Freud to Harold Laski and Lionel Trilling, from Moses Mendelssohn to J. Robert Oppenheimer and Ayn Rand, Gertrude Stein,
and Reich I and II (Wilhelm and Charles), one dominating structure of an
identical predicament and a shared fate imposes itself upon the consciousness and behavior of the Jewish intellectual in *Galut* [exile]: with the
advent of Jewish Emancipation, when ghetto walls crumble and the *sht-
etlach* [small Jewish towns] begin to dissolve, Jewry—like some wide-eyed
anthropologist—enters upon a strange world, to explore a strange people
observing a strange *halakah* (law code). They examine this world in dismay,
with wonder, anger, and punitive objectivity. This wonder, this anger, and
the vindictive objectivity of the marginal nonmember are recidivist; they
continue unabated into our own time because Jewish Emancipation continues into our own time.

The various chapters of *CofC* show that hostility to the people and culture
of the West was characteristic of all the Jewish intellectual and political movements of the left that came to be ensconced in the academic world of the
United States and other Western societies. For example, Franz Boas's cultural
relativism, which implied that Western societies were in no way more advanced or superior to other societies, came to dominate academic anthropology at a time when Western societies were far more scientifically and techno-
logically advanced and dominated the world politically and militarily. Boas had
a strong sense that anti-Semitism pervaded non-Jewish society, leading him
to despise non-Jewish culture, particularly the culture of the Prussian aristocracy in his native Germany (see Ch. 2; Degler, 1991, p. 200; Stocking, 1968, p.
150).

Charles S. Liebman's (1973, pp. 153ff) theory of Jewish involvement in the
left emphasizes the idea that leftist universalist ideology allows Jews to subvert traditional social categorizations in which Jews are viewed in negative
terms. The adoption of such ideologies by Jews is an attempt to overcome Jewish feelings of alienation "from the roots and the traditions of [non-Jewish] society" (p. 153).

Many neoconservatives, particularly those centered around Senator
Henry Jackson (e.g., Richard Perle and Paul Wolfowitz), were also motivated by
perceived anti-Semitism in the Soviet Union (see Ch. 4). Estrangement from
and hostility toward non-Jews and their culture were typical of Freud and
other prominent Jewish psychoanalysts—motivated at least partly by their
perception of anti-Semitism (see Ch. 5). Given the complaint that so many of
Freud's followers had about Western society, it is not surprising that psychoanalysis was used to produce theories in which anti-Semitism is attributed to
intrapsychic   conflict,   sexual   repression,   or   troubled   parent-child

relationships, while also denying the importance of cultural separatism and the reality of group-based competition for resources; the Frankfurt School's theory is an outstanding example of this (see Ch. 6). The New York Intellectuals were also motivated by the complaints of anti-Semitism in the Soviet Union (see Ch. 7), and similarly, Jewish involvement in shaping U.S. immigration policy, in the direction of lessening the power of Whites via non-White immigration and multiculturalism, was also motivated by two different complaints about non-Jewish society: the familiar complaint of anti-Semitism, but also the complaint that models of the United States as a homogeneous White, Christian civilization excluded Jews and were dangerous for Jews in the long run given what happened in Germany in the 1930s (see Ch. 8).

In summary, there is good evidence that Jewish intellectuals involved in important intellectual movements of the left that came to dominate academic discourse were motivated by complaints—mainly complaints of anti-Semitism but also complaints of cultural exclusion from White, Christian society.

Finally, it should also be noted that Gross and Fosse point out that studies of professorial politics show that, while professors do have more liberal economic attitudes than other Americans, it is their social attitudes—their views of gender, homosexuality, abortion, etc.—that make them truly distinctive.

This is also the case with Jews generally. For example, the difference between the largely Jewish Hollywood elite and both traditional American elites and the general public is clearest on "expressive individualism"—a dimension tapping ideas of sexual liberation (including approval of homosexuality), moral relativism, and a disdain for religious institutions (Powers et al., 1996). The Hollywood elite is also more tolerant of unusual or deviant lifestyles as well as ethnic and religious minorities. Survey data repeatedly show that the Jewish community in general has more liberal attitudes on issues related to sexuality and church-state separation (S. M. Cohen & C. S. Liebman, 1997).

(2) **Jewish intellectuals formed cohesive, effective networks.** The following is a passage from Chapter 7 summarizing the cohesion of Jewish intellectual networks apparent through the book:

> An important thread apparent in the discussions of psychoanalysis, Boasian anthropology, the Frankfurt School, and radical intellectual and political circles has been that Jewish intellectuals have formed highly cohesive groups whose influence derives to great extent from the solidarity and cohesiveness of the group. . . . Intellectual activity is like any other human endeavor: cohesive groups outcompete individualist strategies. Indeed, the fundamental truth of this axiom has been central to the success of Judaism throughout its history.

Among this self-described alienated and marginalized group there was also an atmosphere of social support that undoubtedly functioned as had traditional Jewish ingroup solidarity arrayed against an outside world seen as morally and intellectually inferior. They perceived themselves as people with a complaint who must cling together against the forces of evil—"rebel intellectuals defending a minority position and upholding the best traditions of radicalism" (Cooney, 1986, p. 265). *Partisan Review*, the flagship journal of the New York Intellectuals (discussed in Ch. 7), provided "a haven and support" and a sense of social identity; it "served to assure many of its members that they were not alone in the world, that sympathetic intellectuals existed in sufficient number to provide them with social and professional moorings" (p. 249). There was thus a great deal of continuity to this "coherent, distinguishable group" of intellectuals "who mainly began their careers as revolutionary communists in the 1930s [to] become an institutionalized and even hegemonic component of American culture during the conservative 1950s while maintaining a high degree of collective continuity" (Wald, 1987, p. 12, 10). The cohesiveness of academic Jews is also indicated by their citation patterns, as mentioned in Chapter 7, citing Greenwald and Schuh (1994).

Finally, contributing to cohesion has been the tendency to center around charismatic leaders—e.g., Boas (Ch. 2), Freud (Ch. 5), Max Horkheimer (Ch. 6), Leo Strauss (Ch. 4), and Trotsky (Ch. 3)—with a powerful moral, intellectual, and social vision. The followers of these leaders had an intense devotion toward them, often mimicking their idiosyncrasies and promoting them as intellectual gods to their students and colleagues.

The strong ingroup biases and high cohesiveness of these Jewish intellectual movements doubtless account for the success of some of the more egregious, politically inspired social science of the last decades. For example, historian John Higham (1984, p. 154) pointed out that the incredible success of *The Authoritarian Personality* studies (i.e., the studies that claimed the group allegiances of non-Jews were the result of psychiatric disorder) was facilitated by the "extraordinary ascent" of Jews concerned with anti-Semitism in academic social science departments in the post-World War II era.

(3) Jewish intellectuals had access to the most prestigious academic institutions. The Jewish-dominated movements that transformed the academic world became ensconced in the most prestigious academic institutions. The New York Intellectuals, for example, developed ties with elite universities, particularly Harvard, Columbia, the University of Chicago, and the University of California–Berkeley, while psychoanalysis and Boasian anthropology became well entrenched throughout academia. The Frankfurt School intellectuals were associated with Columbia and the University of California–Berkeley, and their intellectual descendants are dispersed through the academic world. The neoconservatives are mainly associated with the University of Chicago and

Johns Hopkins University, and they were able to get their material published by the academic presses at these universities as well as Cornell University.

The moral and intellectual elite established by these movements dominated intellectual discourse during a critical period after World War II and through the transformations of the 1960s. College students during this period were powerfully socialized to adopt liberal-radical cultural and political beliefs.

As Eric P. Kaufmann (2004, p. 247) points out in his account of the decline of WASP America, once the new value set was institutionalized, it became the focus of status competition within the boundaries set by these movements. Kaufmann's account is also useful because, in basic agreement with Gross and Fosse, he cites sociologist Mario Diani (1997) who emphasizes that social movements tend to succeed to the extent that leaders of a movement possess "social capital" in the form of social ties to the mass media, corporate cultural intermediaries, and the state intelligentsia—where dominant interpretations of reality are generated. The same applies to understanding the creation of dominant moral communities that are so critical for understanding how popular attitudes toward immigration and multiculturalism are influenced by the elite media and the educational system (see *Individualism*).

The cosmopolitan revolution was not confined to academia. It came to dominate all the high ground in American society, including the mass media, the lower levels of the educational system, and the rhetoric and voting behavior of politicians, the latter influenced by the newly established boundaries of the moral community created by this new elite and via donations to political candidates who lean liberal or left on social issues (see, e.g., Weiss, 2016). In the case of the mass media, there is excellent evidence for a very strong Jewish influence (see below) and for the idea that the mass media provided very positive portrayals of the leftist worldview. Indeed, a major theme of *CofC* is that Jewish influence in the popular media was an important source of favorable coverage of Jewish intellectual movements, particularly psychoanalysis and 1960s political radicalism.

Moreover, as implied by Gross and Fosse, once an organization becomes dominated by a particular intellectual perspective, there is enormous inertia created by the fact that the informal networks dominating elite universities serve as gatekeepers for the next generation of scholars. Aspiring academics are subjected to a high level of indoctrination at the undergraduate and graduate levels; there is tremendous psychological pressure to adopt the fundamental intellectual assumptions that lie at the center of the power hierarchy of the discipline. Once such a movement attains intellectual predominance, it is not surprising that people would be attracted to these movements because of the prestige associated with them. And, as Gross and Fosse argue, conservatives who do not subscribe to these ideas simply self-select to go into a different career.

THE FINAL STEP IN THE RADICALIZATION OF THE UNIVERSITY

The final step in the transformation of the university into a stronghold of the anti-White multicultural left was the establishment of academic departments staffed by the various aggrieved parties championed by the multicultural left after it abandoned the White working class. The 1970s saw the emergence of departments of ethnic studies and women's and gender studies. My former university (California State University–Long Beach) is typical of academia generally in having departments or programs in American Indian Studies, Africana Studies (formerly Black Studies), American Studies (whose subject matter emphasizes "How do diverse groups within the Americas imagine their identities and their relation to the United States?"), Asian and Asian-American Studies, Chicano and Latino Studies, Jewish Studies, and Women's, Gender, and Sexuality Studies.

All of these departments and programs exemplify the leftist academic culture. All are politically committed to advancing the interests and worldviews of their special grievances against Whites and their culture. Often they are avowedly and explicitly on the left.

A critical force in establishing such departments was the Jewish left that came to influence the academic world after World War II, reaching a commanding position by the late 1960s. As noted above, these Jewish intellectual movements, particularly the Frankfurt School and the New York Intellectuals, had developed an explicit ideology that promoting the interests of the working class was a poor strategy given that the working class in Europe had not risen up in communist revolution but had joined fascist movements instead. Moreover, as noted above for the New York Intellectuals, they were well aware that race rather than social class was a far more powerful variable for explaining the deeply embedded attitudes of rural America, particularly in the South—attitudes they regarded as abhorrent, at least partly because anti-Jewish attitudes were common among these groups. Finally, along with the entire Jewish community, they had adopted a cultural and ethnic pluralist model for America in which America would cease to be defined as either White or Christian (see Ch. 8). White Christians were the problem.

As a result, the next step was to broaden the basis of the left and consolidate their power by promoting other groups that had grievances against White, Christian America. Because of the history of European conquest and colonialism, the multiracial immigrants of the post-1960s have been highly susceptible to anti-White attitudes, and thus, like the Jews, prone to having grievances against White America—views that are common among professors of ethnic and gender studies. Although it is difficult to specify the exact linkages here, it is certainly the case that the triumph of the Jewish-dominated intellectual movements in the academic world was followed in short order by the establishment of these other pillars of the cultural left within the university.

Indeed, as noted throughout this volume, a common pattern for Jewish intellectual and political movements has been to reach out and make alliances with non-Jews, many of whom often attain highly visible positions in the movement. This is necessary because Jews are a relatively small percentage of the population, and it is in their interest, whether in influencing academic discourse or the political process, to ally themselves with other groups with grievances against Whites. The culture of the left became solidified within the university when it was able to recruit people who, like so many Jewish intellectuals, perceived themselves to be sexual, racial, and ethnic victims. These people are a large and committed portion of the leftist culture of the university, and in the currently dominant culture of the left, they are highly incentivized to claim victim status as a route to professional success.

Since women have been framed by the regnant cultural left as victims of the previously dominant patriarchy, it's not surprising that women are a large part of the post-1960s grievance coalition in academia. Noah Carl (2021) notes that women are granted around 60 percent of Ph.D. degrees and around 80 percent of bachelor's degrees in departments of ethnic, gender, and cultural studies. These departments are often made up of leftist activists. Moreover, a study of the voting behavior of academics showed that 10 percent of men voted Republican, while only 4 percent of women did (Langbert et al., 2016). In departments of sociology, 81 percent of women agreed with the statement that sociology "should be both a scientific and moral enterprise" compared to 58 percent of men; in anthropology 49 percent of women agreed that "traditional indigenous knowledge is not less 'true,'" compared to 19 percent of men; 36 percent of women agreed that "science is just one way of knowing," compared to 12 percent of men (M. Horowitz et al., 2018). Overall, compared to men, women are more in favor of the leftist programs to end free speech and censor speech they disagree with. They are more inclined toward activism, and less inclined toward dispassionate inquiry; they are more likely to agree that hate speech is violence, that it's acceptable to shout down a speaker, that controversial scientific findings should be censored, and that it should be illegal to say offensive things about minorities.

These sex differences are likely due ultimately to women's greater tendencies toward empathy for putative victims, harm avoidance, and conformity. As I noted in *Individualism and the Western Liberal Tradition* (Ch. 8), there are strong sex differences in the empathy and fear systems, with women being more prone to empathic concern for others and to fear:

> Being high on fear leads to conformity because in the contemporary West there is much to fear if one fails to conform to the attitudes of the main-stream moral community—loss of job, loss of friends and family, and general ostracism. It's much safer to remain within the confines of the moral community.

Within the evolutionary/biological perspective, such differences are importantly influenced by different selection pressures on males and females, as influenced by hormonal differences; for example, greater average muscle mass among men is influenced by testosterone prenatally and during adolescence.

Further, the Jewish movements that came to dominate the academy are not at all different from the wider Jewish community in making alliances with ethnic and sexual minorities. The organized Jewish community has made alliances with non-White ethnic groups and has championed the cause of public visibility for sexual minorities (MacDonald, 2006, 2009a). Charles E. Silberman (1985, p. 350) notes:

> American Jews are committed to cultural tolerance because of their be-lief—one firmly rooted in history—that Jews are safe only in a society ac-ceptant of a wide range of attitudes and behaviors, as well as a diversity of religious and ethnic groups. It is this belief, for example, not approval of homosexuality, that leads an overwhelming majority of U.S. Jews to en-dorse 'gay rights' and to take a liberal stance on most other so-called "so-cial" issues.

This concern for Jewish safety in the more or less homogeneous pre-1965 White society is also at the root of Jewish promotion for multiracial immigration and in particular the Immigration and Nationality Act of 1965 (Ch. 8).

Conspicuously missing from the list of Jewish allies are lower- and middle-class Whites. These are the groups that were most vilified by the New York Intellectuals and the Frankfurt School, and they have suffered the most from the multicultural revolution. These people are being pushed out economically and politically. They are the enraged participants in the Tea Party movement and the supporters of Donald Trump that have been so visible in recent years. They can't move to gated communities or send their children to all-White pri-vate schools. Their unions have been destroyed and their jobs either shipped overseas or performed by recent immigrants, legal and illegal. Their fortunes will continue to decline as millions more non-Whites crowd our shores.

The result of this revolution is the American university as we see it now. Conservatives need not apply, and heterosexual White males should be prepared to exhibit effusive demonstrations of guilt and sympathy with their oppressed co-workers—and expect to be passed over for high-profile, high-paying administrative positions in favor of the many aggrieved ethnic and sexual minorities who now dominate the university.

JEWISH OVERREPRESENTATION AT ELITE UNIVERSITIES

Beginning in the early twentieth century, there has been an ethnic war between Jews and WASPs over admission to Ivy League universities, ranging from quotas against Jews in the 1920s (e.g., Harvard's Jewish enrollment dropped from 30 percent to 15 percent between 1925 and 1926) to the ultimate victory of Jewish activist groups after World War II. The result is that, when controlling for their academic qualifications, Jews have been greatly overrepresented at elite universities for several decades (Unz, 2018c 2012, 2024b). Because elite universities are a critical pipeline into the American elite, admission policies of Ivy League universities are of vital importance. The following is based on figures supplied by Hillel, the campus Jewish organization:

> Jewish students were roughly 1,000% more likely to be enrolled at Harvard and the rest of the Ivy League than white Gentiles of similar ability. This was an absolutely astonishing result given that under-representation in the range of 20% or 30% is often treated by courts as powerful *prima facie* evidence of racial discrimination. (Unz, 2018c)

> [Sociologist Jerome] Karabel [2005] opens the final chapter of his book [*The Chosen: The Hidden History of Admission and Exclusion at Harvard, Yale, and Princeton*] by . . . noting the extreme irony that the WASP demographic group which had once so completely dominated America's elite universities and "virtually all the major institutions of American life" had by 2000 become "a small and beleaguered minority at Harvard," being actually fewer in number than the Jews whose presence they had once sought to restrict. Very similar results seem to apply all across the Ivy League, with the disproportion often being even greater than the particular example emphasized by Karabel. (Unz, 2012)

Unz (2024b) also notes that Claudine Gay, a Black woman, resigned after only six months as president of Harvard due to accusations of plagiarism and anti-Semitism, and that the four previous presidents of Harvard dating to 1991 were either Jewish or married to a Jewish spouse (with three in the former category); the interim replacement for Gay is also Jewish. Further, from Unz (2024b):

> [S]ix of the eight Ivy League university presidents are currently Jewish, including Harvard, Yale, Princeton, Cornell, Brown, and Dartmouth, as are those of other elite colleges such as Caltech and MIT. This ethnic ratio of top academic leadership has remained roughly unchanged for several decades.

Any sign that the enrollment of Jews at elite universities is less than about 20 percent is seen as indicative of anti-Semitism. A 2009 article in *The Daily Princetonian* cited data from Hillel indicating that, with the exception of Princeton and Dartmouth, on average Jews made up 24 percent of Ivy League undergraduates. Princeton had only 13 percent Jews, leading to much anxiety and a drive to recruit more Jewish students. The rabbi leading the campaign said she "would love 20 percent"—an increase from over six times the Jewish percentage in the population to around ten times (Martins, 2009).

The result was extensive national coverage, including articles in *The New York Times* and *The Chronicle of Higher Education*. According to Unz (2012):

> These articles included denunciations of Princeton's long historical legacy of anti-Semitism and quickly led to official apologies, followed by an immediate 30 percent rebound in Jewish numbers. During these same years, non-Jewish white enrollment across the entire Ivy League had dropped by roughly 50 percent, reducing those numbers to far below parity, but this was met with media silence or even occasional congratulations on the further "multicultural" progress of America's elite education system.

Unz (2023a) also cites data indicating a very large drop in Jewish academic performance based on National Merit Scholarship data and competition for academic prizes:

> Harvard's white enrollment dropped by nearly 10 percentage points, steadily falling from 45.1% in 2012 to just 35.4% in 2021. And if, as seems likely, ethnically Jewish students are in the approximate range of 25%, the unavoidable conclusion is that although white Gentiles are nearly 60% of the American population and probably at least 60% of our highest-performing students, they are now approaching a single digit presence at our most elite college.

JEWISH INFLUENCE ON OTHER RELIGIONS IN THE U.S.

Influencing U.S. Protestantism. Given the general rise in Jewish influence after World War II, it is not surprising to find evidence for Jewish involvement in the dramatic changes in Protestant sensibilities in a pro-Jewish direction at that time. John Murray Cuddihy's (1978) book, *No Offense: Civil Religion and Protestant Taste*, focuses on the elevation of Judaism to the status of one of the "big three" U.S. religions, to the point that a rabbi officiates at the presidential inauguration even though Jews constitute approximately 2–3 percent of the population. Cuddihy argues that this religious surface served as a protective coloring and led to a sort of crypto-Judaism in which Jewish ethnic identities were submerged in order to make them appear civilized to non-Jews. As part of this contract, the prominent Protestant theologian Reinhold Niebuhr acknowledged "the stubborn will of the Jews to live as a peculiar people"—meaning that the Jews could remain a people with a thin veneer of religion.

Both sides gave up something in this bargain. The Jews' posturing as a religion left them open to large-scale defection via intermarriage to the extent that they took seriously the idea that Judaism was akin to Protestantism, and in fact this did occur, but without noticeably affecting the power of the organized Jewish community.

What the Protestants gave up was far more important because it has been a contributing factor to the more or less irreversible ethnic changes (barring a cataclysm) in the United States and elsewhere in the Western world. Judaism became unconditionally accepted as a modern religion co-equal with other dominant U.S. religions even while retaining a commitment to its ethnic core. It conformed outwardly to the religious norms of the United States, but it also continued to energetically pursue its ethnic interests, especially with regard to issues where there is a substantial consensus among Jews: support for Israel and the welfare of other foreign Jewries, immigration and refugee policy, church-state separation, and abortion rights (J. J. Goldberg, 1996, p. 5).[9] What is remarkable is that a wealthy, powerful, and highly talented ethnic group was able to pursue its interests without those interests ever being the subject of open political discussion by mainstream political figures, for over eighty years—at least since Lindbergh's ill-fated Des Moines speech of 1941.

I suppose that Niebuhr thought that he was only giving up the prospect of converting Jews to Christianity, but the implicit downgrading of the ethnic character of Judaism provided an invaluable tool in furthering Jewish ethnic

---

[9] J. J. Goldberg also included civil liberties as a common Jewish interest, but, as indicated below, Jewish organizations have led the charge to severely limit free speech related to racial and ethnic interests.

aims in the United States, essentially allowing Jews to win the ethnic war without anyone even being able to acknowledge that it was an ethnic war. For example, during the immigration debates of the 1940s–1960s Jews were described by themselves and others as "people of the Jewish faith." They were simply practicing another religion in an officially pluralistic religious society, and part of Jewish posturing was a claim to a unique, universalistic, moral-religious vision that could only be achieved by enacting legislation that in fact furthered their particularistic ethnic aims. The universalistic, moral-religious vision promoted by Jewish activists really amounted to taking the Protestants at their own word—by insisting that every last shred of ethnic identity among Protestants be given up while Jews were implicitly allowed to keep theirs, if only they would frame their actions within religious context and behave civilly.

The evidence provided by Cuddihy suggests that Niebuhr was socialized by the Jewish milieu of New York into taking the positions that he did—that his position as a major Protestant spokesperson was facilitated by alliances he formed with Jews and because his writings fit well within the Jewish milieu of New York intellectual circles. Niebuhr's behavior is therefore as much an indication of Jewish power and the ability of Jews to recruit gentiles sympathetic to their causes as it is an indication of Protestant self-destruction. One cannot underestimate the importance of Jewish power in intellectual circles in New York at the time of Niebuhr's pronouncements—most notably the New York Intellectuals (Ch. 7). For example, Leslie Fiedler (1948, p. 873) noted that "the writer drawn to New York from the provinces feels ... the Rube, attempts to conform; and the almost parody of Jewishness achieved by the gentile writer in New York is a strange and crucial testimony of our time."

Influencing Christian Zionism. Christian Zionism is a very powerful force for philo-Semitism and pro-Israel attitudes in the United States. There is a fascinating history that suggests that Jewish activist Samuel Untermyer, a committed Zionist, was important in promoting and publicizing the work of C. I. Scofield, whose annotated Bible, first published by Oxford University Press in 1909, is the basis of Christian Zionism. Scofield had a "criminal history, a deserted wife, a wrecked family, and a penchant for self-serving lies." Untermyer also likely provided Scofield with money necessary for his "lavish lifestyle." Footnotes to the Scofield Bible were added in 1967 that placed even greater emphasis on Zionist aims, and some of Scofield's less Zionist footnotes were removed (Carlson, 2002).

For example, the following were added: "For a nation to commit the sin of anti-Semitism brings inevitable judgment"; "God made an unconditional promise of blessing through Abram's seed to the nation of Israel to inherit a specific territory forever;" and "It has invariably fared ill with the people who have persecuted the Jew, well with those who have protected him. The future will still more remarkably prove this principle" (in Carlson, 2002).

Jews have actively supported the Christian Zionist movement. Beginning in 1978, the Likud Party in Israel has taken the lead in organizing this force for Israel, and they have been joined by the neoconservatives. For example, in 2002 the Israeli embassy organized a prayer breakfast with the major Christian Zionists. Jews have founded or funded organizations aimed at Christians, such as Christians United for Israel (founded by John Hagee), which has ten million members and is closely associated with the Zionist Organization of America and the Israeli government (Joyce, 2014). Further, former Jews who converted to Christianity have been leaders in Christian Zionism (see, e.g., Niño, 2025).

Influencing Catholicism. Jewish pressure for altering traditional Roman Catholic attitudes on Jewish responsibility for deicide are recounted in Lacouture (1995, pp. 440–458) and Roddy (1966). Pope John XXIII deleted the "perfidious Jews" reference from the Holy Week liturgy (Lacouture, p. 448). He then solicited the opinions of the world's 2,594 bishops on the Church's relations with the Jews. Virtually all of the respondents wished to maintain the status quo. The Pope was "bitterly disappointed by the response of the episcopate" (p. 449).

Converted Jews were instrumental in creating the Vatican II document *Nostra Aetate* (1965) which changed the historic position of the Catholic Church toward Jews (MacDonald, 2012a). The technique was to find passages of Scripture that conformed to their ethnic interests in raising the status of Judaism while remaining within the intellectual confines of Catholicism:

> *Nostra Aetate* confirmed that Christ, his mother and the apostles were Jews, and that the church had its origin in the Old Testament. It denied that the Jews may be held collectively responsible for Jesus Christ's death, and decried all forms of hatred, including anti-Semitism. Citing the Letter of St. Paul to the Romans, *Nostra Aetate* called the Jews "most beloved" by God. These words . . . staged a revolution in Catholic teaching. (Connelly, 2012)

From the Jewish point of view, a revolution was highly desirable. For example, the comments on Judaism in *The Catholic Encyclopedia* from 1910—during the papacy of Pius X, who is highly regarded by traditionalist Catholics—are instructive. Jews in the time of Jesus are described as a "race" that rejected the call of Jesus for repentance, showing no sorrow for sin, unfit for salvation, and rejecting the true kingdom of God in favor of earthly power: "Jesus justly treated as vain the hopes of His Jewish contemporaries that they should become masters of the world in the event of a conflict with Rome" (Gigot, 1910).

These views, including the view that Jews are a race, can be traced back to Christian intellectuals such as Eusebius in the fourth century (SAID, Ch. 3).[10]

In the post-World War II lead-up to Vatican II, the most influential activist was Jules Isaac, who started several organizations dedicated to furthering Jewish interests within the Church (Held, 2013). Andrew Joyce (2019b) also discusses Isaac's role in changing the attitudes of the Church of England vis-à-vis the Jews, citing a statement by the Church of England Faith and Order Commission (2019, pp. 14–15):

> Jules Isaac, who wrote on Jewish-Christian relations in the aftermath of the Second World War, saw a profound link between historic Christian anti-Judaism and the eruption of antisemitism in the twentieth century. If the first premise of antisemitism is the perception that "there is something inherently wrong with the Jews as a people," then traditional Christian teaching that the Jewish people are collectively responsible throughout time for the death of the divine Christ, and therefore guilty together of deicide, imbues it with a terrible power. Isaac coined the phrase "the teaching of contempt" (*enseignement du mépris*) to describe what he saw as key features of Christianity's sustained hostility to Judaism from earliest times.

FROM THE CULTURE OF CRITIQUE TO THE CULTURE OF THE HOLOCAUST

While *CofC* describes the "culture of critique" dominated by Jewish intellectual and political movements, perhaps insufficient attention was given to the critical elements of the new culture that have replaced the traditional European cultural forms that dominated a century ago. Central to the new culture is the elevation of Jewish experiences of suffering during World War II, collectively referred to as "the Holocaust," to the level of a pivotal historical-cultural icon in Western societies. Here I discuss two books focused on the political and cultural functions of the Holocaust in contemporary life—Peter Novick's *The Holocaust in American Life* (1999), and Norman Finkelstein's *The Holocaust Industry* (2000, 2001). Novick's book, the more scholarly of the two, notes that the Holocaust has assumed a preeminent status as a symbol of the

---

[10] *The Occidental Observer* and *The Occidental Quarterly* have posted several articles on Jewish influence on the Catholic Church: George F. Held's (2013) translations of Léon de Poncins: *The Problem with the Jews at the Council* in four parts; Jimmy Moglia's (2018) "Quo Vadis Vatican? Jewish involvement in the radical changes of the Second Vatican Council"; and my (MacDonald, 2012a) "The role of Jewish converts to Catholicism in changing traditional Catholic teachings on Jews." Andrew Joyce's (2019b) "Jews, White Guilt, and the Death of the Church of England" shows how some of these same figures (e.g., Jules Isaac) have influenced the Church of England.

consequences of ethnic conflict. He argues that the importance of the Holocaust is not a spontaneous phenomenon but stems from highly focused, well-funded efforts of Jewish organizations and individual Jews with access to the major media:

> We are not just "the people of the book," but the people of the Hollywood film and the television miniseries, of the magazine article and the newspaper column, of the comic book and the academic symposium. When a high level of concern with the Holocaust became widespread in American Jewry, it was, given the important role that Jews play in American media and opinion-making elites, not only natural, but virtually inevitable that it would spread throughout the culture at large. (Novick, 1999, p. 12)

The Holocaust was originally promoted to rally support for Israel following the 1967 and 1973 Arab-Israeli wars:

> Jewish organizations . . . [portrayed] Israel's difficulties as stemming from the world's having forgotten the Holocaust. The Holocaust framework allowed one to put aside as irrelevant any legitimate ground for criticizing Israel, to avoid even considering the possibility that the rights and wrongs were complex. (Novick, 1999, p. 155)

As the threat to Israel subsided, the Holocaust was promoted as the main source of Jewish identity and in the effort to combat assimilation and intermarriage among Jews. During this period, the Holocaust was also promoted among gentiles as an antidote to anti-Semitism. In recent years this has involved a large-scale educational effort (including mandated courses in the public schools of many U.S. states) spearheaded by Jewish organizations and staffed by thousands of Holocaust professionals aimed at conveying the lesson that "tolerance and diversity [are] good; hate [is] bad, the overall rubric [being] 'man's inhumanity to man'" (Novick, 1999, pp. 258–259). The Holocaust has thus become an instrument of Jewish ethnic interests, not only as a symbol intended to create moral revulsion at violence directed at minority ethnic groups—prototypically the Jews—but also as an instrument to silence opponents of multiethnic immigration into Western societies. As described in Chapter 8, promoting high levels of multiethnic immigration has been a goal of Jewish groups since the late nineteenth century.

Jewish Holocaust activists insisted on the "incomprehensibility and inexplicability of the Holocaust" (Novick, 1999, p. 178)—an attempt to remove all rational discussion of its causes and to prevent comparisons to numerous other examples of ethnic violence.

Even many observant Jews are often willing to discuss the founding myths
of Judaism naturalistically—subject them to rational, scholarly analysis.
But they're unwilling to adopt this mode of thought when it comes to the
"inexplicable mystery" of the Holocaust, where rational analysis is seen as
inappropriate or sacrilegious [and hence precludes any serious investigations of what actually happened]. (Novick, 1999, p. 200)

Holocaust activist Elie Wiesel "sees the Holocaust as 'equal to the revelation at Sinai' in its religious significance; attempts to 'desanctify' or 'demystify'
the Holocaust are, he says, a subtle form of anti-Semitism" (Novick, 1999, p.
201). Because the Holocaust is regarded as a unique, inexplicable event, Jewish
organizations and Israeli diplomats cooperated to block the U.S. Congress
from commemorating the Armenian genocide. "Since Jews recognized the
Holocaust's uniqueness—that it was 'incomparable,' beyond any analogy—they
had no occasion to compete with others; there could be no contest over the
incontestable" (p. 195). Abraham Foxman, head of the ADL, claimed that the
Holocaust is "not simply one example of genocide but a near successful attempt on the life of God's chosen children and, thus, on God himself" (p. 199)—
a comment that illustrates well the intimate connection between Holocaust
promotion and the more extreme forms of Jewish ethnocentrism.

A result was that American Jews were able to define themselves "as the
quintessential victim community" (Novick, 1999, p. 194). As an expression of
this tendency, Holocaust activist Simon Wiesenthal compiled a calendar showing when, where, and by whom Jews were persecuted on every day of the year.
Holocaust consciousness was the ultimate expression of a victim mentality.
The Holocaust came to symbolize the natural and inevitable terminus of anti-
Semitism.

There could be no such thing as overreaction to an anti-Semitic incident,
no such thing as exaggerating the omnipresent danger. Anyone who
scoffed at the idea that there were dangerous portents in American society hadn't learned "the lesson of the Holocaust." (Novick, 1999, p. 178).

While Jews are portrayed as the quintessential victim in Holocaust icono-
graphy, the vast majority of non-Jews are portrayed as potential or actual anti-
Semites. "Righteous Gentiles" are acknowledged, but the criteria are strict.
They must have risked their lives, and often the lives of the members of their
families as well, to save a Jew. "Righteous Gentiles" must have displayed "self-
sacrificing heroism of the highest and rarest order" (Novick, 1999, pp. 179-180).
Such people are extremely rare, and any Jew who discusses "Righteous Gentiles" for any other reason comes under heavy criticism. The point is to shore
up the fortress mentality of Jews—"promoting a wary suspicion of gentiles" (p.

180). A prominent Jewish feminist exemplifies this attitude: "Every conscious Jew longs to ask her or his non-Jewish friends, 'Would you hide me?'—and suppresses the question for fear of hearing the sounds of silence" (p. 181).

Consciousness of the Holocaust is very high among Jews. A 1998 survey found that "remembrance of the Holocaust" was listed as "extremely important" or "very important" to Jewish identity—far more often than anything else, such as synagogue attendance or travel to Israel (Novick, 1999, p. 202). Indeed, Jewish identity is far more important than American identity for many American Jews: "In recent years it has become not just permissible but, in some circles, laudable for American Jews to assert the primacy of Jewish over American loyalty" (p. 34).

Consciousness of the Holocaust is not confined to Jews but has become institutionalized as an American cultural icon. Besides the many Holocaust memorial museums that dot the country and the mushrooming of mandated courses about the Holocaust in public schools, a growing number of colleges and universities now have endowed chairs in Holocaust studies. "Considering all the Holocaust institutions of one kind or another in the United States, there are by now thousands of full-time Holocaust professionals dedicated to keeping its memory alive" (Novick, 1999, p. 277).

This effort has been very successful. In a 1990 survey, a substantial majority agreed that the Holocaust "was *the* worst tragedy in history" (Novick, 1999, p. 232; emphasis original). Recently, the main thrust of the Holocaust as cultural icon is the ratification of multiculturalism. Between 80 and 90 percent of those surveyed agreed that the need to protect the rights of minorities, and not "going along with everybody else" were lessons to be drawn from the Holocaust. Respondents agreed in similar proportions that "it is important that people keep hearing about the Holocaust so that it will not happen again."

The effort has perhaps been even more effective in Germany:

[C]ritical discussion of Jews in Germany today is virtually impossible. Whether conservative or liberal, a contemporary German intellectual who says anything outside a narrowly defined spectrum of codified pieties about Jews, the Holocaust, and its postwar effects on German society runs the risk of professional and social suicide. (M. M. Anderson, 2001)

Discussions of the work of Jewish intellectuals have come to dominate German intellectual life to the almost complete exclusion of non-Jewish Germans. Many of these intellectuals are discussed in *CofC*, including Walter Benjamin, Theodor Adorno, Herbert Marcuse, and Sigmund Freud.

"Shoah business" has become a staple of contemporary German cultural and political life. Germans thrive on debates about the Holocaust and their ongoing responsibility to preserve its memory, campaigning to erect a gigantic memorial to the Jewish dead in the historic center of Berlin or flocking to hear the American scholar Daniel Goldhagen's crude and unhistorical diatribes against the German national character. (M. M. Anderson, 2001)

Scholars have lost all sense of normal standards of intellectual criticism and have come to identify more or less completely with the Jewish victims of National Socialism.

For example, Holocaust poet Paul Celan has become a central cultural figure, surpassing all other twentieth-century poets. His works are now beyond rational criticism, to the point that they have become enveloped in a sort of stultifying mysticism: "Frankly, I find troubling the sacred, untouchable aura that surrounds Celan's name in Germany; troubling also the way in which his name functions like a trump card in intellectual discussions, closing off debate and excluding other subjects" (M. M. Anderson, 2001). Jewish writers like Kafka are seen as intellectual giants who are above criticism; discussions of Kafka's work focus on his Jewish identity and are imbued by consciousness of the Holocaust despite the fact that he died in 1924.

Like Novick, Finkelstein (2000) takes a functionalist view of the "Holocaust industry," arguing that it serves as a vehicle for extorting money for Jewish organizations from European governments and corporations, and for justifying the policies of Israel and U.S. support for Israeli policy (pp. 7–8). Finkelstein also argues that embracing the Holocaust allows the wealthiest and most powerful group in the United States to claim victim status—a status that is wearing thin and is now often seen as hypocritical because of the Israeli genocide of Palestinians in Gaza beginning in 2023.

The ideology of the Holocaust states that it is unique and inexplicable—as noted by Novick as well—but Finkelstein also emphasizes how the Holocaust industry promotes the idea that anti-Jewish attitudes and behavior stem completely from irrational loathing by non-Jews and have nothing to do with conflicts of interest. For example, Elie Wiesel states, "For two thousand years . . . we were always threatened. . . . For what? For no reason" (in Finkelstein, 2000, p. 53). (By contrast, the basic premise of my book SAID is precisely that anti-Jewish attitudes and behavior throughout history are firmly rooted in conflicts of interest, certainly including the conflict between Israel and the Palestinians.) Finkelstein approvingly quotes Boas Evron, an Israeli writer: "Holocaust awareness [is] an official, propagandistic indoctrination, a churning out of slogans and a false view of the world, the real aim of which is not at all an understanding of the past, but a manipulation of the present" (in Finkelstein, 2000, p. 41).

Finkelstein (2000, p. 8) notes the role of the media in supporting the Holocaust industry, quoting Elie Wiesel: "When I want to feel better, I turn to the Israeli items in *The New York Times*." *The New York Times*, which is owned by the Sulzberger family (see below),

> serves as the main promotional vehicle of the Holocaust industry. It is primarily responsible for advancing the careers of Jerzy Kosinski, Daniel Goldhagen, and Elie Wiesel. For frequency of coverage, the Holocaust places a close second to the daily weather report. Typically, *The New York Times Index* 1999 listed fully 273 entries for the Holocaust. By comparison, the whole of Africa rated 32 entries. (Finkelstein, 2001)

Besides a receptive media, the Holocaust industry takes advantage of its power over the U.S. government to apply pressure to foreign governments, particularly the governments of Eastern Europe (Finkelstein, 2000, pp. 133ff).

In a poignant allusion to the pervasive double standard of contemporary Jewish ethical attitudes (and reflecting a similar ethical double standard that pervades Jewish religious writing throughout history), Finkelstein describes a January 2000 Holocaust education conference attended by representatives of fifty countries, including Prime Minister Ehud Barak of Israel. The conference declared that the international community had a "solemn responsibility" to oppose genocide, ethnic cleansing, racism, and xenophobia. A reporter afterward asked Barak about the Palestinian refugees: "On principle, Barak replied, he was against even one refugee coming to Israel: 'We cannot accept moral, legal, or other responsibility for refugees'" (Finkelstein, 2000, p. 137).

JEWS AND THE MEDIA: SHAPING "WAYS OF SEEING"

The Psychology of Media Influence. Psychological research indicates two types of cognitive processing: implicit and explicit. These modes of processing may be contrasted on a number of dimensions (see, e.g., Geary, 2005; MacDonald, 2008a; Stanovich, 1999, 2004). Implicit processing is automatic, effortless, relatively fast, and involves parallel processing (i.e., processing going on independently in different parts of the brain) of large amounts of information; it characterizes the modules described by evolutionary psychologists designed by natural selection to perform specific functions. Explicit processing is the opposite of implicit processing: conscious, controllable, effortful, relatively slow, and involves serial processing of relatively small amounts of information in a sequential manner (e.g., performing the steps of solving a math problem). Explicit processing is involved in the operation of the mechanisms of general intelligence (Chiappe & MacDonald, 2005) as well as controlling emotional states and action tendencies, such as anger or frustration tending to lead to aggression (MacDonald, 2008a).

The conscious, explicitly processing parts of the brain are thus able to control the lower parts of the brain that utilize implicit processing, for example, emotional states and action tendencies resulting from evolved modules like those underlying ethnocentrism. These work via automatic, implicit processing, but they are controllable by higher brain centers located in the cortex (MacDonald, 2010a, 2009b). Hence the evolved mechanisms underlying ethnocentrism can be controlled by the higher brain centers processing the information they obtain via the media.

Being able to control impulses of any kind taps into the personality system of conscientiousness, often labelled "*effortful control*" because it involves explicit, conscious effort to control impulses. Simply put, conscientious people are relatively better able to regulate the more evolutionarily ancient parts of our brain that are responsible for many of our passions and desires. The critical point is that cultural information is of vital importance for motivating people to inhibit their ethnocentric tendencies—e.g., being aware that explicit assertions critical of Jews would result in ostracism or other penalties. This cultural information relies on explicit processing and provides the basis for prefrontal, top-down inhibitory control of ethnocentrism, so that the control of ethnocentrism and other evolved tendencies (e.g., lust, jealousy, love) is a direct consequence of the control of cultural information. For example, the rise of a new, substantially Jewish elite meant that explicit messages about race (e.g., "there's no such thing as race") and ethnocentrism (e.g., "White ethnocentrism is a sure sign of psychopathology and disturbed parent-child relationships") were being disseminated by the mass media and throughout the educational system. Especially since World War II, these messages have been consistently hostile to White ethnocentrism and the very idea that race exists, and that in turn has meant that Whites have been encouraged to inhibit their natural ethnocentrism.

Moreover, since White people tend to be more individualistic than other peoples, they are less likely than other peoples to make invidious distinctions between ingroups and outgroups and are more likely to be open to strangers and people who don't look like them. They are relatively unlikely to assume, say, that all or most Jews are dishonest because of a particular example of a dishonest Jew. And because Whites are relatively low in ethnocentrism and relatively high in conscientiousness, controlling ethnocentrism is easier for them on average. Their subcortical mechanisms responsible for ethnocentrism are weaker to start with and hence easier to control. They are thus more susceptible to media messages.

Finally, as emphasized throughout my *Individualism and the Western Liberal Tradition*, moral communities are the social glue of Western societies, whereas kinship relationships are the social glue of the other culture areas of the world. Moral communities based on a reputation as capable, honest, trustworthy, and fair are a fundamental aspect of Western individualism and have been a big reason for the historical trajectory that led to Western dominance of the planet. Since the rise of a substantially Jewish elite with major influence in the media, reputation has typically been influenced by the media environment, resulting in conformity to the messages emanating from the media in order to maintain or enhance reputation as a morally upright, trustworthy person.

In the environments that Western peoples evolved in, if individuals acted in defiance of the moral strictures of the community, they would be ostracized. Whereas in the contemporary West, people can survive such ostracism by finding a new niche of like-minded friends, in prehistoric Europe ostracism would have certainly resulted in death. Thus, to a considerable extent, the ability to control media messages facilitates control over Western peoples by penalizing non-conformists and rewarding conformists. This is a major source of Jewish power and influence.

Jewish Ownership of American Media. I noted above that the Jewish attack on European domination of the United States focused on three critical areas of power: (1) the academic world of information in the social sciences and humanities; (2) the political world where public policy on immigration and other ethnic issues, such as policy toward the Middle East, are decided; and (3) the mass media where "ways of seeing" (see W. Kerr, 1968) are presented to the public. The first edition of *CofC* focused on the first two of these areas of power, but little attention was given to the mass media, except where it served to promote Jewish intellectual or political movements, as in the case of psychoanalysis. This lack of attention to the cultural influence of the mass media is a major gap.

It has often been noted that Jews have long been dominant in the Hollywood entertainment industry since its inception. At present it plays a major role in American culture and politics, as it has been "long known as the 'ATM of the Democratic Party'" (Perman et al., 2024). By all accounts, ethnic Jews have a powerful influence in the American media—far larger than any other identifiable group. The extent of Jewish ownership and influence on the popular media in the United States is remarkable given the relatively small proportion of the population that is Jewish.[11] In a survey performed in the 1980s, 60 percent of a representative sample of the movie elite were of Jewish background (Powers et al., 1996, p. 79n13). Michael Medved (1996, p. 37) notes:

---

[11] Discussions of Jewish ownership of the media include: Ginsberg, 1993, p. 1; Kotkin, 1993, p. 61; Silberman, 1985, p. 147.

[I]t makes no sense at all to try to deny the reality of Jewish power and prominence in popular culture. Any list of the most influential production executives at each of the major movie studios will produce a heavy majority of recognizably Jewish names. This prominent Jewish role is obvious to anyone who follows news reports from Tinsel Town or even bothers to read the credits on major movies or television shows.

As of this writing (February 2024), Comcast, controlled by the Roberts family (Jewish), is the largest telecommunications and multimedia conglomerate. It owns assets in television broadcasting (e.g., NBC, Telemundo), cable television (e.g., MSNBC, CNBC, USA Network, E!), Xfinity (cable television, broadband internet, and home telephone service), a film studio (e.g., Universal Pictures), the video-on-demand network Peacock, animation studios (e.g., DreamWorks Animation, Universal Animation Studios), and theme parks. It also owns the Sky Group, Europe's largest media and cable network, which operates in the United Kingdom, Ireland, Germany, Austria, Switzerland, and Italy ("Sky Group," 2024).

David Zaslav is the head of Warner Bros. Discovery, which owns an array of streaming networks (e.g., HBO, Cinemax), cable television networks (e.g., CNN, CNN International, Discovery+), film studios (e.g., Warner Bros. Pictures, New Line Cinema), and video game publishers ("List of assets owned by Warner Bros. Discovery," 2024).

Another dominant media company is the Walt Disney Company, headed by Bob Iger. Disney has a vast array of holdings, mainly in movies (e.g., Walt Disney Pictures, Pixar, Marvel Studios), network and streaming television (e.g., ABC Signature, ESPN, FX), music recording and publishing (e.g., Hollywood Records, which includes country music label DMG Nashville), and theme parks dotted around the world ("List of assets owned by the Walt Disney Company," 2024).

National Amusements is a media empire whose president, Shari Redstone, is the daughter of Sumner Redstone (born Rothstein). National Amusements owns 1,500 screens in the United States, the United Kingdom, and Latin America. It has a controlling interest in Paramount Global, which owns Paramount Pictures film and television studio, CBS television, and a variety of cable television networks (e.g., Black Entertainment Television, MTV, Nickelodeon, Comedy Central, Showtime). Its international division manages international versions of its pay TV networks, as well as region-specific assets, including television channels in Argentina, Chile, India, and the United Kingdom ("Paramount Global," 2024).

Other major television companies owned by Jews include DreamWorks SKG (founded in 1994 by film director Steven Spielberg, former Disney Pictures chairman Jeffrey Katzenberg, and recording industry mogul David Geffen).

DreamWorks has gone through several distribution deals, most recently with Universal Pictures, and the animation studio was spun off in 2004 into NBCUniversal ("DreamWorks Pictures," 2024). Spielberg remains chairman and is also a Jewish ethnic activist. After making the Holocaust film *Schindler's List*, Spielberg established the Survivors of the Shoah Foundation with the aid of a grant from the U.S. Congress. He also helped fund Professor Deborah Lipstadt's defense against a libel suit brought by British World War II historian and Holocaust revisionist David Irving.

In the world of print media, Advance Publications, owned by the descendants of founder Samuel Irving Newhouse, Sr. (born Solomon Isadore Neuhaus), owns twenty-six newspapers (e.g., the Cleveland *Plain Dealer* and Newark *Star-Ledger*) and mass media company Condé Nast, which publishes *Vogue*, *The New Yorker*, and *Vanity Fair*. Advance Publications also has substantial stakes in Warner Bros. Discovery, Charter Communications, and the social news site Reddit, which went public on March 27, 2024.

The newsmagazine *U.S. News & World Report*, which has a weekly circulation of 2.3 million, has been owned and published by Mortimer B. Zuckerman since 1984. Zuckerman has also owned New York's liberal-oriented tabloid newspaper, the *Daily News*, the sixth-largest newspaper in the country, and *The Atlantic Monthly*. Zuckerman is a Jewish ethnic activist. He was head of the Conference of Presidents of Major American Jewish Organizations (2001–2003), an umbrella organization for major Jewish organizations in the United States (*The Forward*, April 27th, 2001, pp. 1, 9). Zuckerman uses his column in *U.S. News & World Report* to promote Israel and is considered to be a media member of the Israel Lobby by John J. Mearsheimer and Stephen M. Walt (2007), authors of *The Israel Lobby and U.S. Foreign Policy*.

Another Jewish activist who had a prominent position in the U.S. media is Martin Peretz, owner of *The New Republic* (TNR) since 1974; he ended his role as editor and regular blogger in 2010. Throughout his career Peretz has been devoted to Jewish causes, particularly Israel. During the 1967 Arab-Israeli war, he told Henry Kissinger that his "dovishness stopped at the delicatessen door," and many among his staff feared that all issues would be decided on the basis of what was "good for the Jews" (Alterman, 1992, pp. 185, 186). Indeed, a staffer stated, "Aside from Israel, he has no meaningful policy views at all" (Wallace-Wells, 2010). One editor was instructed to obtain material from the Israeli embassy for use in TNR editorials.

> It is not enough to say that TNR's owner is merely obsessed with Israel; he says so himself. But more importantly, Peretz is obsessed with Israel's critics, Israel's would-be critics, and people who never heard of Israel, but might one day know someone who might someday become a critic. (Alterman, 1992, p. 195).

The Sulzberger family owns The New York Times Company which, after selling its radio and television stations, mainly in 2007, has focused on print media, including *The New York Times* (the largest-circulation newspaper in the United States), *The New York Times International Edition*, and thirteen regional newspapers located mainly in the South.

Jewish ownership of *The New York Times* is particularly interesting because it has been the most influential newspaper in the United States since the start of the twentieth century. As noted in a book on the Sulzberger family (Tifft & Jones, 1999), even at that time, there were several Jewish-owned newspapers, including the *New York World* (controlled by Joseph Pulitzer), the *Chicago Times-Herald* and the *Chicago Evening Post* (controlled by H. H. Kohlsaat), and the *New York Post* (controlled by the family of Jacob Schiff). In 1896 Adolph Ochs purchased *The New York Times* with the critical backing of several Jewish businessmen, including Isidor Straus (co-owner of Macy's department stores) and Jacob Schiff (a successful investment banker who was also a pro-Bolshevik Jewish ethnic activist). "Schiff and other prominent Jews like ... Straus had made it clear they wanted Adolph to succeed because they believed he 'could be of great service to the Jews generally'" (Tifft & Jones, pp. 37–38). Ochs's father-in-law was the influential Rabbi Stephen S. Wise, president of the American Jewish Congress and the World Jewish Congress, and the founder of Reform Judaism in the United States.

There are some exceptions to this pattern of media ownership, but even in such cases ethnic Jews often have a major managerial role.[12] For example, Rupert Murdoch controls dozens of media companies in the United States, the United Kingdom, and Australia, including television networks, newspapers, film studios, and book publishing. In the United States the Murdoch empire has positioned itself as a gatekeeper for mainstream conservative viewpoints via the Fox News Channel (the most watched cable news network), *The Wall Street Journal* (the largest print circulation newspaper, second largest overall when counting digital subscriptions), and the tabloid conservative-oriented *New York Post* (fourth largest print circulation newspaper). Murdoch is a philo-

---

[12] A partial exception is the Washington Post Company. Until her death in 2001, *The Washington Post* was run by Katharine Meyer Graham, daughter of Eugene Meyer, who purchased the paper in the 1930s. Ms. Graham had a Jewish father and a Christian mother and was raised as an Episcopalian. Katharine's husband, the former publisher of the *Post*, Phil Graham, was not Jewish. The *Post*'s publisher, since 1991, is Donald Graham, the son of Katharine and Phil Graham. This influential publishing group is thus less ethnically Jewish than the others mentioned here. The Washington Post Company has a number of other media holdings in newspapers (The Gazette Newspapers, including eleven military publications), television stations, and magazines, most notably the nation's number-two weekly newsmagazine, *Newsweek*. The Washington Post Company's various television ventures reach a total of about 7 million homes, and its cable TV service, Cable One, has 635,000 subscribers. In a joint venture with *The New York Times*, the *Post* publishes the *International Herald Tribune*, the most widely distributed English-language daily in the world.

Semite. He was the publisher of *The Weekly Standard*, the premier neoconservative magazine edited by neoconservative Jewish ethnic activist William Kristol (see Ch. 4).

> [M]ost of Murdoch's closest friends and business advisers were wealthy, influential New York Jews intensely active in pro-Israel causes. And he himself still retained a strong independent sympathy for Israel, a personal identification with the Jewish state that went back to his Oxford days. (Kiernan, 1986, p. 261)

So it's not surprising that Fox News is strongly pro-Israel.

Media and the Creation of Culture. As many academics have pointed out, the media have become more and more important in creating culture (e.g., Powers et al., 1996, p. 2). Before the twentieth century, the main creators of culture were religious, military, and business institutions. In the course of the twentieth century these institutions became less important while the media have increased in importance (for an account of this transformation in the military, see Bendersky, 2000). And there is little doubt that the media attempt to shape the attitudes and opinions of the audience (Powers et al., pp. 2–3). Part of the continuing culture of critique is that the media elite tend to be very critical of Western culture and civilization, portraying it as failing, dying, and, at worst, sick and evil compared to other cultures (p. 211). These views were common in Hollywood long before the cultural revolution of the 1960s, but they were not often expressed in the media because of the influence of non-Jewish cultural conservatives—e.g., the National Catholic Legion of Decency (1934–1980) and the Hays Commission's Motion Picture Production Code (1934–1968).

Perhaps the most important issue Jews and Jewish organizations have championed is cultural pluralism—the idea that the United States ought not to be ethnically and culturally homogeneous. As described in *CofC*, Jewish organizations and Jewish intellectual movements have championed cultural pluralism in many ways, especially as powerful and effective advocates of an open immigration policy (Ch. 8). The media have supported this perspective by portraying cultural pluralism almost exclusively in positive terms—that cultural pluralism is easily achieved, beneficial to everyone, and is morally superior to a homogeneous Christian culture made up mainly of White non-Jews. People who oppose cultural pluralism are portrayed as stupid and bigoted (Lichter et al., 1994, p. 251), the classic being the Archie Bunker character in Norman Lear's *All in the Family* television series from the 1970s. Departures from racial and ethnic harmony are portrayed as entirely the result of White racism (Powers et al., 1996, p. 173).

Since Jews have a decisive influence on television and movies, it is not surprising that Jews are portrayed positively in the movies. There have been a great many explicitly Jewish movies and television shows with recognizable Jewish themes. Hollywood has an important role in promoting the "Holocaust industry," with movies like Spielberg's *Schindler's List* (1993) and the four-part television miniseries *Holocaust* (1978), written by Gerald Green, directed by Marvin Chomsky, and produced by Herbert Brodkin and Robert Berger. Both of these ventures were lavishly promoted by Jewish groups. The promotion for *Holocaust* in 1978 was remarkable (Novick, 1999, p. 210). The ADL distributed ten million copies of its sixteen-page tabloid *The Record* for this purpose. Jewish organizations pressured major newspapers to serialize a novel based on the script and to publish special inserts on the Holocaust. *The Chicago Sun-Times* distributed hundreds of thousands of copies of its insert to local schools. The American Jewish Committee, in cooperation with NBC, distributed millions of copies of a study guide for viewers; teachers' magazines carried other teaching material tied to the program so that teachers could easily discuss the miniseries in class. Jewish organizations worked with the National Council of Churches to prepare other promotional and educational materials, and they organized advance viewings for religious leaders. The day the series began was designated "Holocaust Sunday," and various activities were scheduled in cities across the country; the National Conference of Christians and Jews distributed yellow stars to be worn on that day. Study guides for Jewish children depicted the Holocaust as the result of Christian anti-Semitism. The material given to Jewish children also condemned Jews who did not have a strong Jewish identity.

This massive promotion succeeded in many of its goals. These included the introduction of Holocaust education programs in many states and municipalities, beginning the process that led to the National Holocaust Memorial Museum and a major upsurge of support for Israel.

In general, television portrays Jewish issues "with respect, relative depth, affection and good intentions, and the Jewish characters who appear in these shows have, without any doubt, been Jewish—often depicted as deeply involved in their Judaism" (Pearl & Pearl, 1999, p. 5). For example, *All in the Family* (and its sequel, *Archie Bunker's Place*) not only portrayed working-class Whites as stupid and bigoted, but it also portrayed Jewish themes very positively. By the end of its twelve-year run, the Archie Bunker character had raised a Jewish child in his home, befriended a Black Jew (implication: Judaism has no ethnic connotations), gone into business with a Jewish partner, enrolled as a member of a synagogue, praised his close friend at a Jewish funeral, hosted a Sabbath dinner, participated in a *bat mitzvah* ceremony, and joined a group to fight synagogue vandalism. These shows, produced by Jewish liberal political activist Norman Lear, thus exemplify the general trend for television to portray non-Jews as participating in Jewish ritual and "respecting, enjoying, and learning from it. Their frequent presence and active involvement underscore the message that these things are a normal part of American life" (p. 16). Jewish rituals are portrayed as "pleasant and ennobling, and they bestow strength, harmony, fulfillment, and sense of identity upon those who observe them" (p. 62).

Television presents images of Jewish issues that conform to the views of mainstream Jewish organizations, and it "invariably depicts anti-Semitism as an ugly, abhorrent trait that must be fought at every turn" (Pearl & Pearl, 1999, p. 103). There is never any rational explanation for anti-Semitism; anti-Semitism is portrayed as an absolute and incomprehensible evil. Positive, well-liked, non-Jewish characters, such as Mary Tyler Moore, are often recruited to lead the fight against anti-Semitism—a pattern reminiscent of that noted in later chapters in which non-Jews become high-profile spokespersons for Jewish-dominated movements. There is also the implication that anti-Semitism is a proper concern of the entire community. Regarding Israel:

> [O]n the whole, popular TV has conveyed the fact that Israel is the Jewish homeland with a strong emotional pull upon Diaspora Jews, that it lives in perpetual danger surrounded by foes, and that as a result of the constant and vital fight for its survival, it often takes extraordinary (sometimes rogue) measures in the fields of security and intelligence. (Pearl & Pearl, 1999, p. 173)

Non-Jews are portrayed as having deep admiration and respect for Israel, its heroism, and achievements. Israel is seen as a haven for Holocaust survivors, and Christians are sometimes portrayed as having an obligation to Israel because of the Holocaust.

In the movies, a common theme is Jews coming to the rescue of non-Jews, as in *Independence Day* (1996), where Jeff Goldblum plays a "brainy Jew" who rescues the world, and in *Ordinary People* (1980), where Judd Hirsch plays a Jewish psychiatrist who rescues an uptight WASP family (Bernheimer, 1998, pp. 125–126). The movie *Addams Family Values* (1993), discussed in Chapter 1 (footnote 26), is another example of this genre. Bernheimer (p. 162) notes that "in many films, the Jew is the moral exemplar who uplifts and edifies a gentile, serving as a humanizing influence by embodying culturally ingrained values." This "Jews to the Rescue" theme also characterizes Jewish leftist radicalism (Ch. 3) and psychoanalysis (Ch. 5): radical Jews save the world from the evils of capitalism, and promoters of psychoanalysis save non-Jews from their neuroses.

On the other hand, Christianity is often portrayed as evil and Christians as psychopaths. Michael Medved (1992, p. 50) describes Hollywood's cumulative attacks in recent years on the traditional family, patriotism, and traditional sexual mores—the Hollywood version of the culture of critique—but the most obvious focus of attack is on the Christian religion:

> In the ongoing war on traditional values, the assault on organized faith represents the front to which the entertainment industry has most clearly committed itself. On no other issue do the perspectives of the show business elites and those of the public at large differ more dramatically. Time and again, the producers have gone out of their way to affront the religious sensibilities of ordinary Americans.[13]

Medved fails to find even one film made since the mid-1970s where Christianity is portrayed positively, apart from a few films where it is portrayed as an historical relic—a museum piece. Examples where Christianity is portrayed negatively abound. For example, in the film *Monsignor* (1982), a Catholic priest commits every imaginable sin, including the seduction of a glamorous nun and then is involved in her death. In *Agnes of God* (1985), a disturbed young nun gives birth in a convent, murders her baby, and then flushes the tiny, bloody corpse down the toilet. There are also many subtle anti-Christian scenes in Hollywood films, such as when the director Rob Reiner repeatedly focuses on the tiny gold crosses worn by Kathy Bates, the sadistic villain in *Misery* (1990).

Another media tendency is to portray small towns as filled with bigots and anti-Semites. Media commentator Ben Stein (1976, p. 22) records the hostility of the media toward rural America:

> The typical Hollywood writer . . . is of an ethnic background from a large Eastern city—usually from Brooklyn [i.e., they have a Jewish background]. He grew up being taught that people in small towns hated him, were different from him, and were out to get him [i.e., small town people are anti-Semites]. As a result, when he gets the chance, he attacks the small town on television or the movies. . . .
>
> The television shows and movies are not telling it "like it is"; instead they are giving us the point of view of a small and extremely powerful section of the American intellectual community—those who write for the mass visual media. . . . What is happening, as a consequence, is something

---

[13] Cones (1997) provides a similar analysis: "This analysis of Hollywood films with religious themes or characters reveals that in the last four decades Hollywood has portrayed Christians as sexually rigid, devil-worshipping cultists, talking to God, disturbed, hypocritical, fanatical, psychotic, dishonest, murder suspects, Bible-quoting Nazis, slick hucksters, fake spiritualists, Bible pushers, deranged preachers, obsessed, Catholic schoolboys running amok, Adam and Eve as pawns in a game between God and Satan, an unbalanced nun accused of killing her newborn infant, dumb, manipulative, phony, outlaws, neurotic, mentally unbalanced, unscrupulous, destructive, foul-mouthed, fraudulent and as miracle fabricators. Few, if any, positive portrayals of Christians were found in Hollywood films released in the last four decades."

unusual and remarkable. A national culture is making war upon a way of life that is still powerfully attractive and widely practiced in the same country. . . . Feelings of affection for small towns run deep in America, and small-town life is treasured by millions of people. But in the mass culture of the country, a hatred for the small town is spewed out on television screens and movie screens every day. . . . Television and the movies are America's folk culture, and they have nothing but contempt for the way of life of a very large part of the folk. . . . People are told that their culture is, at its root, sick, violent, and depraved, and this message gives them little confidence in the future of that culture. It also leads them to feel ashamed of their country and to believe that if their society is in decline, it deserves to be.

This is a good example of social identity processes so important in both Jewish attitudes toward non-Jews and non-Jewish attitudes toward Jews: outgroups are portrayed negatively and ingroups are portrayed positively (see CofC, *passim*, and SAID, Ch. 1).

Jewish influence on the media undoubtedly has a major effect on how Israel is portrayed—a major theme of Finkelstein's (2000) *The Holocaust Industry*. Ari Shavit (1996), an Israeli columnist, described his feelings on the killings of a hundred civilians in a military skirmish in southern Lebanon in 1996: "We killed them out of a certain naive hubris. Believing with absolute certitude that now, with the White House, the Senate, and much of the American media in our hands, the lives of others do not count as much as our own." (Much the same could be said about the Israel-Hamas war of 2023–present, except that the toll of civilian casualties is orders of magnitude higher.)

Ariel Sharon, Prime Minister of Israel (2001–2006), provides another study in contrast. There was a huge difference in the media reaction to Sharon and the response to the situation in Austria in 2000 when Jörg Haider's Freedom Party won enough seats in parliament to have a role in the Austrian government. Several countries, including Israel, recalled their ambassadors in response to the election of Haider. Politicians around the world condemned Austria and announced that they would not tolerate Haider's participation in any Austrian government. Trade embargoes against Austria were threatened. The cause of these actions was that Haider had said that there had been many decent people fighting on the German side during World War II, including some in the SS. He had also said that some of Hitler's economic policies in the 1930s had made good sense, and he had called for a cutoff of immigration into Austria. Haider apologized for these statements, but the electoral success of his party still resulted in the ostracism of Austria and a continuous barrage of alarmist media attacks against him personally.

Contrast this with the treatment of Ariel Sharon's election as prime minister of Israel in 2001. As Israel's Minister of Defense in September 1982, Sharon was in command during the slaughter of 700–2,000 Palestinians, including women and children, in the Sabra and Shatila refugee camps just outside Beirut, Lebanon. *New York Times* journalist Thomas Friedman saw "groups of young men in their twenties and thirties who had been lined up against walls, tied by their hands and feet, and then mowed down gangland style" (Ron, 2001). Radio communications among Israeli military commanders were monitored in which they talked about carrying out "purging operations" in the refugee camps. While the actual killing was done by Lebanese Christians supported by Israel, the Israeli army kept the camps sealed for two days while the slaughter went on. The Kahan Commission, an Israeli commission formed to investigate the incident, concluded that Sharon was indirectly responsible for the massacre, and it went on to say that Sharon bore personal responsibility.[14]

The reaction to the election of Sharon in the U.S. media was subdued to say the least. No trade embargoes were threatened; no ambassadors were recalled. The *Los Angeles Times* dutifully printed a column by a Jewish writer in which Sharon was portrayed as having "learned from his mistakes" (Klein Halevi, 2001). In June 2001, Sharon was indicted as a war criminal in Belgium on the basis of affidavits provided by survivors of the slaughter. It is also noteworthy that Rehavam Zeevi, a close associate of Sharon and Israel's Minister of Tourism as well as a member of the powerful Security Cabinet until his assassination in October 2001, described Palestinians as "lice" and advocated the expulsion of Palestinians from Israeli-controlled areas. Zeevi said Palestinians were living illegally in Israel and "We should get rid of the ones who are not Israeli citizens the same way you get rid of lice. We have to stop this cancer from spreading within us" (Associated Press, 2001).

This has continued into the present (Bergman & Mazzetti, 2024). Israeli settlers have not only continued to build settlements on the West Bank but have repeatedly attacked and intimidated Palestinians, with little or no consequences. And because of the fertility of the religious and ethnonationalist Jews, they have been able to take over the government. The Gaza war beginning in 2023 has led to widespread charges of genocide against the Israelis (e.g.,

---

[14] From the Kahan Commission (1983, p. 73) Report: "We shall remark here that it is ostensibly puzzling that the Defense Minister [Ariel Sharon] did not in any way make the Prime Minister [Menachem Begin] privy to the decision on having the Phalangists enter the camps. It is our view that responsibility is to be imputed to the Minister of Defense for having disregarded the danger of acts of vengeance and bloodshed by the Phalangists against the population of the refugee camps, and having failed to take this danger into account when he decided to have the Phalangists enter the camps. In addition, responsibility is to be imputed to the Minister of Defense for not ordering appropriate measures for preventing or reducing the danger of massacre as a condition for the Phalangists' entry into the camps. These blunders constitute the non-fulfillment of a duty with which the Defense Minister was charged."

Amnesty International), and Benjamin Netanyahu has been charged with war crimes and crimes against humanity by the International Criminal Court.

As noted above, the most radical, most ethnocentric Jews tend to provide the direction for the entire Jewish community in the long run (MacDonald, 2003b). In contemporary Israel the ethnonationalist right is politically dominant and is supported enthusiastically by the mainstream Jewish community in the United States, as epitomized by the ADL, AIPAC, etc. Indeed, the Gaza war has seen an upsurge in Jewish identification, synagogue attendance, and donations to Jewish causes.

> With its overwhelming victory in the Arab-Israeli War of 1967, Israel more than doubled the amount of land it controlled, seizing new territory in the West Bank, the Gaza Strip, the Sinai Peninsula, the Golan Heights and East Jerusalem. Now it faced a choice: Would the new land become part of Israel or be bargained away as part of a future Palestinian state? To a cadre of young Israelis imbued with messianic zeal, the answer was obvious. The acquisition of the territories animated a religious political movement— Gush Emunim, or "Bloc of the Faithful"—that was determined to settle the newly conquered lands. (Bergman & Mazzetti, 2024)

The psychological intensity apparent in this effort is also characteristic of the activist Jewish community in the United States in pursuing its interests, whether directed toward supporting Israel or promoting Third World immigration and multiculturalism in the United States (see above).[15]

JEWISH ORGANIZATIONS, CANCEL CULTURE, AND CENSORSHIP OF THE INTERNET

Too often Whites neglect the activism of Jews in the sphere of speech legislation until it is too late, and Jews have been instrumental throughout the West in orchestrating legal restrictions on speech.[16] In my 2002 Preface I wrote, "One may expect that as ethnic conflict continues to escalate in the United States, increasingly desperate attempts will be made to prop up the

---

[15] At the extreme of ethnocentrism is altruistic self-sacrifice, several examples of which are discussed in *The New York Times Magazine* article cited above. I discuss Jewish martyrdom as an example of extreme Jewish ethnocentrism briefly in MacDonald, 2001. An example is Baruch Goldstein, who in 1994 murdered twenty-nine Palestinians and was beaten to death by the Palestinian survivors. Of course, in many Israeli cases of altruistic self-sacrifice, the perpetrator was not killed and knew that he had a lot of support in the government and would have his sentence shortened to basically a slap on the wrist.

[16] See, for example, the cases of Australia (Sanderson, 2014), Canada (Fraser, 2022), and Britain (Joyce, 2009). I note also a recent journal article on the origin of speech laws in Norway (Ben David, 2024) in which the earliest drafts of the legislation were discovered in the head-quarters of a Jewish group (Yeats, 2024).

ideology of multiculturalism ... with the erection of police state controls on nonconforming thought and behavior." As noted above, there has been a shift from "the culture of critique" to what one might term "the culture of the Holocaust" as Jews have moved from being outsiders to the consummate insiders in American life. Whereas in the 1950s Jewish organizations championed free speech at a time when many Jewish communists were being brought up before Congressional committees on charges of subversion (MacDonald, 2019b), coinciding with their status as an established elite, Jewish organizations are now in the forefront of movements to censor free speech and thought crimes.

The internet has been a major gap in Jewish influence over the major media, but Jewish organizations have taken the lead in attempting to censor the internet. Jewish organizations have also been strong advocates of "hate crime" legislation in all European and European-derived countries. For example, in 1997 the ADL published *Hate Crimes: ADL Blueprint for Action*, which provides recommendations on prevention and response strategies to crimes of ethnic violence, such as penalty enhancement laws, training for law enforcement and the military, security for community institutions, and community anti-bias awareness initiatives. In June 2001 the ADL announced a program designed to assist law enforcement in the battle against "extremists and hate groups." A major component of the Law Enforcement Initiative is the development of specialized hate crime, extremism, and anti-bias curricula for training programs designed for law enforcement personnel.

This has continued. In 2023 the Biden administration unveiled "The U.S. National Strategy to Counter Antisemitism," which although emphasizing violence (which is already illegal) includes provisions to combat online statements:

> DHS [Department of Homeland Security] will conduct a series of regional and online workshops on countering antisemitism, Islamophobia, and related forms of hate-motivated violence, such as online misogyny and gender-based violence, and violence against LGBTQI+, AANHPI [Asian-American, Native Hawaiian, and Pacific Islander], or Black communities. These workshops will provide direct assistance and help DHS identify additional ways to assist the Jewish community and other communities that have been targeted with violence. (ADL, n.d.)

Further, the Countering Antisemitism Act of 2024, as developed by the ADL, contained a provision requiring "the National Coordinator to conduct an annual analysis of online antisemitic content, including Holocaust denial and distortion, and prepare recommendations for Congress on how to counter the spread of antisemitism online" (ADL, 2024)—the beginning of an attempt to bar all criticism of Jews from the internet. As passed by the House (Antisemitism

Awareness Act, 2023), a similar bill provides that penalties would apply to "programs and activities receiving Federal financial assistance" and could thus include defunding universities that allow protests against Israel and its support by the Jewish community, since criticism of or opposition to Israel has been conflated with anti-Semitism.[17] This version of the bill includes a provision that the U.S. government define anti-Semitism as defined by the International Holocaust Remembrance Alliance (n.d.)—a definition that the American Civil Liberties Union opposes because it would likely infringe on the First Amendment by precluding criticism of Israel (Foran et al., 2024). For example, "[h]olding Jews collectively responsible for actions of the state of Israel" would presumably make illegal any claim that, despite the existence of relatively powerless anti-Israel Jews, the Israel Lobby and its power in American politics is a project of the mainstream Jewish community with the support of all of the major American Jewish organizations. The Jewish community thus bears considerable responsibility for the actions of Israel given its influence on U.S. diplomatic and military support for Israel—and U.S. power in international politics. It would also make illegal "[d]rawing comparisons of contemporary Israeli policy to that of the Nazis"—when at least some such comparisons are eminently rational (Cook, 2016; see also Mearsheimer, 2025a).

Moreover, the above section on Jewish influence in the media (or the Israel Lobby) could also run afoul of the provision that would proscribe "[m]aking mendacious, dehumanizing, demonizing, or stereotypical allegations about Jews as such or the power of Jews as a collective—such as, especially but not exclusively, the myth about a world Jewish conspiracy or of Jews controlling the media, economy, government or other societal institutions." And it would appear to claim that no Jews could ever be reasonably claimed to be more loyal to Israel than to the country they reside in: "Accusing Jewish citizens of being more loyal to Israel, or to the alleged priorities of Jews worldwide, than to the interests of their own nations" (for likely examples, see Ch. 4 and MacDonald, 2009d). Finally, two members of the House of Representatives claimed it would infringe on some Christian beliefs, such as the view that Jews were responsible for killing Christ (Kilgore, 2024).

These efforts to end public criticism of Jews or Israel have ramped up since the Israel-Hamas war of 2023–present. University presidents have been removed because they defended the free speech of protesters, and peaceful protesters have been removed by police, blackballed in the job market, penalized by their universities, and physically attacked by pro-Israel groups, without consequences for the attackers—a huge contrast with the Black Lives Matter protests of 2020 and the antiwar protests of the 1960s that were

---

[17] The Conference of Presidents of Major Jewish Organizations also "commend[ed] the passage of the bill": https://tinyurl.com/2ew9j76f.

enthusiastically backed by Jewish groups (see Ch. 3; Unz, 2024a). It should be becoming clear to most Americans just who runs their country.

These censorship efforts are thus far more pervasive and effective than when I wrote about this topic in the 2002 preface—at a time when the internet was nowhere near as developed as it is in 2025. As noted in the 2002 preface, both the Simon Wiesenthal Center and the ADL had already attempted to pressure internet service providers such as AOL and popular websites such as Yahoo! into restricting access to disapproved websites. Yahoo! banned thirty-nine internet clubs originally labeled as "hate sites" by the Simon Wiesenthal Center, and internet auction sites were subjected to protests for selling National Socialist memorabilia.[18] Amazon and Barnes and Noble banned my books *CofC*, *SAID*, and a 2008 compilation of my essays titled *Cultural Insurrections*. These online retailers also came under fire for selling Hitler's *Mein Kampf*, a book that is certainly of historical importance. The ADL also published a report, *Poisoning the Web: Hatred Online*, and urged the U.S. Congress to initiate a comprehensive study of "hate speech" on the internet (Kessler, 1999).

This censorship is much more pervasive because the internet—particularly social media—is now a much more pervasive part of people's lives. When I was growing up, there was no social media, and Jews had more or less pervasive influence on the public conversation via ownership of the three national television networks (ABC, CBS, and NBC), influential newspapers, and the Hollywood studios. However, the rise of social media has allowed ordinary citizens to broadcast their opinions to a wide audience—which Jewish organizations clearly perceive as a danger to Jewish interests. In my case, I was shadow-banned on Twitter (now X) for several years after getting around 33,000 followers; then, after Elon Musk took over in late October 2022, my followers increased dramatically to around 43,000 before I was banned permanently in the spring of 2023 without any explanation of which tweets violated their terms of service. My research, including my research in personality and child development, has been banned by ResearchGate (researchgate.net), the main website for academics to present their research to a wide audience (before being banned, I ranked in the top ten percent in citations by other academics). Another website, *The Occidental Observer* (theoccidentalobserver.net), and the journal I edit, *The Occidental Quarterly* (toqonline.com), have been prevented from processing credit card payments, making recurrent donations and subscriptions difficult. And beginning in 2018, Nathan Cofnas, an academic philosopher, began publishing critiques of my work in academic journals—critiques that I was not allowed to reply to in those journals, resulting in me being forced to reply on my personal website (kevinmacdonald.net), *The Occidental Observer*, and *The Occidental Quarterly*. As noted above, the exception was that

---

[18] See their press releases from July 15th, 1999, November 29th, 1999, and January 26th, 2001.

Philosophia, a peer-reviewed Israeli journal of philosophy, allowed me to reply, publishing it online on January 1, 2022. However, my reply caused a firestorm and was quickly retracted by Springer Nature, a major academic publisher. The editor was fired and the paper sent out for three new reviews, which were uniformly negative.[19] Of course, I am far from the only person who has been treated in this manner. Virtually anyone who stands up for the interests of White people (e.g., Jared Taylor and James Edwards) have been treated similarly.

An important marker of this campaign for censorship has been the conflict between Elon Musk and the ADL beginning after Musk bought Twitter in October 2022. Musk is a self-described "free speech absolutist" (despite the above-mentioned censorship of accounts like mine after he bought Twitter), and the ADL engaged in a campaign to pressure advertisers to boycott X because of an alleged increase in "hate speech" on the platform. Musk denied that there had been an increase in "hate speech" and claimed that the boycott campaign had resulted in a 60 percent decline in advertising revenue, later reduced to 10 percent; Musk then threatened to sue the ADL for 10 percent of the value of X.

Musk went on the offensive:

> A tweet posted by @breakingbaht . . . read: "Jewish communties [*sic*] have been pushing the exact kind of dialectical hatred against whites that they claim to want people to stop using against them."
>
> The billionaire owner and CTO of X, formerly Twitter, responded the same evening: "You have said the actual truth." In another reply, he wrote: "I am deeply offended by ADL's messaging and any other groups who push de facto anti-white racism or anti-Asian racism or racism of any kind." Musk has feuded with the Anti-Defamation League (ADL) before, threatening to sue over its accounting of hate speech on his social media network.
>
> Musk continued on the same tear about the white race. He approved of a tweet reading: "Everyone is allowed to be proud of their race, except for white people, because we've been brainwashed into believing that our history was somehow 'worse' than other races. This false narrative must die."
>
> Musk wrote: "Yeah, this is super messed up. Time for this nonsense to end and shame ANYONE who perpetuates these lies!" (Montgomery, 2023)

Musk took pains to avoid being called an anti-Semite, claiming that he had visited Israel twice and that "I don't know if I am genetically Jewish . . . but I

---

[19] See MacDonald, 2022a (includes a discussion of the retraction, etc.)

am aspirationally Jewish" and "pro-Semitic." After this tweet, he visited Israel again, met with Prime Minister Benjamin Netanyahu after the Israel-Hamas war broke out on October 7, 2023, and later visited Auschwitz-Birkenau. It should also be noted that Musk has had many Jewish business associates over the years (Isaacson, 2023).

Social media companies based in the United States are also under pressure from foreign governments, including France, Germany, Austria, and Canada, where anti-free speech laws are common and there are no constitutional guarantees of free speech.

In my 2002 preface, I wrote:

> Government-imposed censorship is effective in countries like France and Germany, but is not likely to succeed in the United States with its strong tradition of constitutionally protected free speech. As a result, the major focus of the Jewish effort to censor the Internet in the United States has been to pressure private companies like AOL and Yahoo! to use software that blocks access to sites that are disapproved by Jewish organizations. The ADL developed voluntary filter software (ADL HateFilter) that allows users to screen out certain websites. However, while AOL—the largest ISP [internet service provider] by far—has proved to be compliant in setting standards in line with ADL guidelines, the ADL notes that other ISPs, such as Earthlink, have not cooperated with the ADL, and independent web hosting sites have sprung up to serve websites rejected by AOL.[20]
>
> The ADL and the SWC have an uphill road because the Internet has long been touted as a haven for free speech by the high-tech community. ... Clearly Jewish organizations are making every effort to censor anti-Jewish content on the Internet. They are far from reaching their goal of removing anti-Jewish material from the Internet, but in the long run the very high political stakes involved mean that great effort will be expended.

However, since that time, leftist authoritarianism has replaced the libertarian culture of the early years of the internet, and most American technology companies have entirely gone along with the censorship advocated by the ADL. American corporations in general have also gotten in line with leftist positions, often controversially over issues such as: endorsing Black Lives Matter protests; Diversity, Equity, and Inclusion initiatives; endorsing LGBTQ+ issues; and producing "woke" media content. For example, the Walt Disney Company has been labeled "Woke Disney" by conservatives (Jiménez & Barnes, 2023), and Florida governor Ron DeSantis has fought with the company over a bill opposing teaching LGBTQ+ issues in kindergarten through the third grade.

---

[20] The article previously linked has disappeared. However, this material has been updated, see Foxman & Wolf, 2013.

Corporations have been pressured by large asset-management firms that invest in public companies to adopt Environmental, Social, and Governance (ESG) policies to promote diversity and other policies advocated by the left. The most well-known of the companies promoting ESG has been BlackRock Inc., headed by Larry Fink, a Jew. However, after a period of growth in 2020 and 2021, the funds dedicated to ESG investing began to close down due to poor performance and opposition by conservatives, and BlackRock has retreated from the ESG label (Brewster, 2023). There has been wide publicity of the huge costs to brands like Bud Light that used a transgender activist as a spokesperson. Nevertheless, there can be little doubt that the great majority of American corporations remain on the left as seen in their pattern of political donations (Amoros, 2018).

Finally, the generally liberal culture of another pillar of American elite culture, the universities with their traditional support for academic freedom, has been replaced by an authoritarian censorship regime dominated by the left. Mainstream conservatives invited to speak have been greeted with rioting or threats of rioting, often with the support of the university administration. As a result, it's rare to find any universities where there is any significant conservative voice.

Musk's position on free speech is thus out of step with the other elite institutions of American culture and has therefore stirred a hornet's nest of hostility. This is likely one reason why he switched from being a Democrat to supporting Donald Trump in the 2024 election.

THE QUESTION OF BIAS

I have several times been called an "anti-Semite" for the tone of some of my writings, both in *CofC*, on various internet discussion lists, and featured in one of Nathan Cofnas's (2023) critiques. To be perfectly frank, I did not have a general animus for organized Jewry when I got into this project. I was a former New Leftist turned moderate Republican fan of George Will, but I did not advocate for racial interests, nor did I have anything but a cursory knowledge of Judaism and certainly no hostility toward Jews. Before even looking at Judaism, I had applied the same evolutionary group strategy perspective to the ancient Spartans (MacDonald, 1988a). There are quite a few statements in my books that attempt to soften the tone and deflect charges of anti-Jewish bias. My first book on Judaism, *A People That Shall Dwell Alone* (PTSDA, 1994/2002b), has a statement on the first page stating that the traits I ascribe to Judaism (self-interest, ethnocentrism, and competition for resources and reproductive success) are by no means exclusive to Jews. I also write about the extraordinarily high Jewish IQ and about Jewish accomplishments (e.g., Nobel prizes) in that book. In the second book, *Separation and Its Discontents* (SAID, 1998/2004a), I discuss the tendency for anti-Semites to exaggerate their complaints, to develop fantastic and unverifiable theories of Jewish behavior, to exaggerate the extent of Jewish cohesion and unanimity, to claim that all Jews share stereotypically Jewish traits or attitudes, especially in cases where in fact Jews are overrepresented among people having certain attitudes (e.g., political radicalism during most of the twentieth century). And I describe the tendency of some anti-Semites to develop grand conspiracy theories in which all historical events of major or imagined importance, from the French Revolution to the Trilateral Commission, are linked together in one grand plot and blamed on the Jews. All of this is hardly surprising on the basis of what we know about the psychology of ethnic conflict. But that doesn't detract in the least from supposing that real conflicts of interest are at the heart of all of the important historical examples of anti-Semitism. Most of this is in the first chapter of SAID—front and center as it were, just as my other disclaimers are in the first chapter of PTSDA.

It must be kept in mind that group evolutionary strategies are not benign, at least in general and especially in the case of Judaism, which has often been very powerful and has had such extraordinary effects on the history of the West. I think there is a noticeable shift in my tone from the first book to the last simply because I knew a lot more and had read a lot more. People often say after reading the first book that they think I really admire Jews, but they are unlikely to say that about the last two and especially about *CofC*. That is because by the time I wrote *CofC* I had changed greatly from the person who wrote the first book. The first book is really only a documentation of theoretically interesting aspects of Judaism (how Jews solved the free-rider problem that plagued theories of group selection, how they managed to erect and enforce barriers between themselves and other peoples, the genetic cohesion of Judaism, how some groups of Jews came to have such high IQs, how Judaism developed in antiquity). Resource competition and other conflicts of interest with other groups are more or less an afterthought, but these issues move to the foreground in SAID, and in *CofC* I look exclusively at the twentieth century in the West. Jews have indeed made important contributions to Western culture in the last two hundred years. But whatever one might think are the unique and irreplaceable Jewish contributions to the post-Enlightenment world, it is naive to suppose that Jewish activism in Western societies has been intended to benefit Europeans in general; and in any case, I am hard-pressed to think of any area of science and technology that would not have developed without Jewish input, although in some cases perhaps not quite as quickly. In general, positive impacts of Jews have been quantitative rather than qualitative. They have accelerated some developments, for example in finance and some areas of science, rather than made them possible.

On the other hand, I am persuaded that Jews have had some important negative influences. I am morally certain that Jewish involvement in the radical left in the early to middle part of the last century was a necessary but not sufficient condition for many of the horrific events in the Soviet Union and elsewhere. (About this, of course, one can disagree. I am simply saying that I find the evidence compelling.) But the main point is that I came to see Jewish groups as competitors with the European majority of the United States and as powerful facilitators of the enormous changes that have been unleashed in this country, particularly via the successful advocacy of massive non-European immigration into the United States. I found that I was being transformed in this process from a mainstream conservative who had little or no identification with his own people into an ethnically conscious actor—exactly as predicted by the theory of social identity processes that forms the basis of my theory of anti-Semitism (see SAID). In fact, if one wants to date when I dared cross the line into what some see as proof that I am an "anti-Semite," the best guess would probably be when I started reading on the involvement of all the powerful Jewish organizations in advocating massive non-European immigration. My awareness began with my reading a short section in a standard history of American Jews well after the first book was published. Some of the other influences that I attributed to Jewish activism had become more or less irrelevant (e.g., psychoanalysis) or reversible—even radical leftism—so they didn't much bother me. I could perhaps even ignore the towering hypocrisy of Jewish ethnocentrism coinciding as it does with Jewish activism against the ethnocentrism of non-Jewish Europeans. But immigration and its effects on diluting White voting power are essentially irreversible, barring an enormous cataclysm.

I started to realize that my interests are quite different from prototypical Jewish interests—as emphasized in Chapter 8, Jews see non-White immigration as preventing an essentially homogeneous White society from turning on the Jews as happened in 1930s' Germany. We need ways of talking about people who oppose policies recommended by the various Jewish establishments without simply being tarred as "anti-Semites." Immigration is only one example where there are profound conflicts of interest. Writing in November 2001, I noted in my 2002 preface, "we are bogged down in a war with no realizable endgame largely because of influence of the Jewish community over one area of our foreign policy and because of how effectively any mention of the role of Israel and the Israel Lobby in creating friction between the United States, the Arab world, and Iran is muzzled simply by the cry of anti-Semitism." As noted above, such ideas have been greatly elaborated in Mearsheimer and Walt's (2007) *The Israel Lobby and U.S. Foreign Policy.*

At home we have entered into an incalculably dangerous experiment in creating a multiethnic, multicultural society in which the intellectual elite has developed the idea that the formerly dominant European majority has a moral obligation to allow itself to be eclipsed demographically and culturally—the result, at least at its inception and to a considerable degree thereafter, of the influence of Jewish interest groups on immigration policy and the influence of Jewish intellectual movements on our intellectual and cultural life generally, including the media with its very large Jewish influence. As noted above, the rise of Jewish power and the disestablishment of the specifically European nature of the United States are the real topics of *CofC*.

I agree that there is bias in the social sciences and I certainly don't exempt myself from this tendency. It is perhaps true that by the time I finished *CofC* I should have stated my attitudes in the first chapter. Instead, they are placed in the last chapter—rather forthrightly, I think. In a sense, stating them at the end was appropriate because my attitudes about Jewish issues marked a cumulative, gradual change from a very different worldview.

It is annoying that such disclaimers never appear in writing by strongly identified Jews, even when they see their work as advancing Jewish interests. A major theme of *CofC* is that Jewish social scientists with a strong Jewish identity have seen their work as advancing Jewish interests. It is always amazing to me that media figures like the Kristols and Podhoretzes and foreign policy experts like Paul Wolfowitz, Richard Perle, Ben Shapiro, and Mark Levin do not feel an obligation to precede their remarks on issues affected by their solicitude for Israel by saying, "You should be wary of what I say because I have a vested ethnic interest in advancing the interests of Israel." But the same thing goes for vast areas of anthropology (the Boasian school's role in essentially eradicating racial differences research), history (e.g., blatantly apologetic accounts of the history and causes of anti-Semitism, or the role of Jews in the early decades of the Soviet Union), psychology (the Frankfurt School, psychoanalysis), and contemporary issues (immigration, church-state relations). The point of *CofC* that really galls people is the idea that we should simply acknowledge this bias in (some) Jewish researchers as we do in non-Jewish researchers. There are a great many books on how Darwin and Galton were influenced by the general atmosphere of Victorian England, but writing of a Jewish bias immediately results in charges of "anti-Semitism."

The deeper point is that, whatever my motivations and biases, I would like to suppose that my work on Judaism at least meets the criteria of good social science, even if I have come to the point of seeing my subjects in a less than flattering light. Isn't the only question whether I am right? But the real question that concerns my critics is, of course, "Is it good for the Jews?"

CONCLUSION

CofC is really an attempt to understand the twentieth century as what Yuri Slezkine (2004) has termed a "Jewish century"—a century in which Jews and Jewish organizations were deeply involved in all the pivotal events. From the Jewish viewpoint it has been a period of great progress. In the late nineteenth century, the great bulk of the Jewish population lived in Eastern Europe, with many Jews mired in poverty and all surrounded by hostile populations and unsympathetic governments. A century later, Israel is firmly established in the Middle East, Jews have become a hugely powerful group in the United States (the most powerful country in the world) and have achieved elite status throughout the West. The critical Jewish role in murderous communist regimes has been sanitized, while Jewish victimization during World War II has achieved the status of a moral touchstone and is a prime weapon in the push for large-scale non-White immigration, multiculturalism, and the promotion of other Jewish causes. Opponents have been relegated to the fringe of intellectual and political discourse, and there are powerful movements afoot that would silence them entirely.

None of this should be surprising. Jewish populations have always had enormously outsized effects on the societies where they reside because of several qualities that are central to Judaism as a group evolutionary strategy, as noted above: high intelligence (including the usefulness of intelligence in attaining wealth); the ability to cooperate in highly organized, cohesive groups; and personality traits like affect intensity and aggressiveness. This has led repeatedly to Jews becoming an elite and powerful group in societies where they reside in sufficient numbers—as much in the twentieth-century United States and the Soviet Union as in fifteenth-century Spain or ancient Alexandria. History often repeats itself after all. This has particularly been the case in the post-Enlightenment individualistic societies of the West where Jews had unfettered access to the most prestigious media, academic, and political institutions of these societies.

Indeed, recent data indicate that Jewish per capita income is almost double that of non-Jews, a bigger difference than the White-Black income gap. Although Jews make up less than 3 percent of the population, they constitute 11 percent of the richest twenty-five Americans[21] and more than a quarter of the richest four hundred Americans according to the *Forbes* 400 list (LaFranco & Peterson-Withorn, 2023). A remarkable 87 percent of college-age Jews are currently enrolled in institutions of higher education, as compared with 40

[21] This includes non-Jew Kenneth C. Griffin who is at least very sympathetic to Jewish causes (see Haidar & Kettles, 2024).

percent for the population as a whole (Thernstrom & Thernstrom, 1997). Jews are indeed an elite group in American society (see also Ch. 9).

My perception is that the Jewish community in the United States is moving aggressively ahead, ignoring the huge disruptions Jewish organizations have caused in the West (now mainly via successful advocacy of massive non-European immigration) and in the Islamic world (via the treatment of Palestinians by Israel). Whatever the justification for such beliefs, U.S. support for Israel is by all accounts an emotionally compelling issue in Iran and the Arab world. A true test of Jewish power in the United States will be whether support for Israel is maintained even in the face of the enormous costs that have already been paid by the United States in terms of: loss of life; economic disruption; hatred and distrust throughout the Muslim world; loss of civil liberties at home; and now the shame of giving virtually unconditional support to Israel's genocidal policies against the Palestinians, when Jewish organizations are a main support for immigration, multiculturalism, and propaganda promoting inter-ethnic harmony in the West.

In the 2002 preface I noted, "As of this writing, while Jewish organizations are bracing for a backlash against Jews in the United States and while there is considerable concern among Jews about the Bush administration's pressure on Israel to make concessions to the Palestinians in order to placate the Muslim world (e.g., Rosenblatt, 2001), all signs point to no basic changes in the political culture of the United States vis-à-vis Israel as a result of the events of September 11, 2001." The same will likely be said about the current Gaza war and the Iran-Israel confrontations of 2024 and 2025, despite the worldwide pressure on Israel to curb its slaughter of Palestinian civilians. Indeed, under the Trump administration the Israel Lobby achieved its long-term goal of dragging the United States into a war with Iran.

Jews and the Radical Critique of Gentile Culture: Introduction and Theory

For 1,500 years Jewish society had been designed to produce intellectuals. . . . Jewish society was geared to support them. . . . Rich merchants married sages' daughters; . . . Quite suddenly, around the year 1800, this ancient and highly efficient social machine for the production of intellectuals began to shift its output. Instead of pouring all its products into the closed circuit of rabbinical studies, . . . it unleashed a significant and ever-growing proportion of them into secular life. This was an event of shattering importance in world history.

— P. Johnson, 1987/1988, pp. 340–341

An important theme of SAID was the manipulation of ideology in the service of rationalizing specific forms of Judaism, interpreting history, and combating anti-Semitism. The present volume is in many ways an extension of these phenomena. However, the intellectual movements and political activity discussed in this volume have typically occurred in the post-Enlightenment intellectual and political world where Jews were addressing issues in the wider society and attempting to influence the culture of the wider society; they have not been designed to rationalize specific forms of Judaism. Rather, they may be characterized in the broadest sense as efforts at cultural critique and at times as attempts to influence the wider culture of the society in a manner that conforms to specific Jewish interests.

INTELLECTUAL FRAMEWORK

In general, this area of scholarship stands or falls depending on whether certain *specific*, influential intellectual and political movements of the twentieth century were *originated* and *dominated* by Jews who were attempting to advance Jewish interests. Thus it does not stand or fall on whether Jews in a particular movement constitute more than their percentage of the population as a whole, whether Jews in general are ethnocentric, the rate of Jewish intermarriage, or whether most Jews were even aware of particular movements. The focus is on describing the Jewish identities of the main figures of influential movements and their concern with specific Jewish issues, such as combatting anti-Semitism, as well as the dynamics of these movements—ethnic networking, centering around charismatic figures, connections with prestigious universities and media, involvement of the organized Jewish community, and non-Jews who participated in the movements and their motivations.

The Jewish community is clearly not monolithic, although at particular historical periods there has been substantial consensus on particular issues. Individual influential Jews or a separate influential Jewish intellectual movement may be critical of another specific Jewish intellectual movement. For example, the split beginning in the 1930s between the Stalinist left (Ch. 3) and the Trotskyist left (Ch. 4) comes to mind. It is possible that some components of the opposition to the pro-Israel Lobby in the United States, such as the internet journal *Mondoweiss* or Jewish Voice for Peace, may also be reasonably analyzed as Jewish movements. But in order to establish that organizations critical of Israel constitute a Jewish movement, one would have to discuss whether the originators and dominant figures have a Jewish identity and whether they see their activities as furthering Jewish interests. For example, the Jewish critics of Israel may regard a powerful Jewish influence on U.S. policy toward Israel as feeding into perceptions that Jews are disloyal—a very mainstream view among American Jews until well after the establishment of Israel; or Israeli actions vis-à-vis the Palestinians may be seen as hurting Israel in the long run (e.g., Mearsheimer & Walt, 2007)—a 2013 Pew Research Center survey found 44 percent of U.S. Jews believe Israeli settlements hurt Israel. On the other hand, they may oppose what they see as Jewish interests in maintaining a Jewish state for moral reasons or because they see U.S. support for Israel as not in the interests of the United States.

Such a project would thus go well beyond what Nathan Cofnas (2021) labels the "default hypothesis": high average Jewish IQ and urban residency explain Jewish involvement in intellectual and political movements. This default hypothesis is irrelevant to the movements discussed in previous editions of *The Culture of Critique* (hereafter *CofC*) and to another proposed Jewish movement, neoconservatism (Ch. 4). Even when Jews are overrepresented in a particular movement compared to their percentage of the population as a whole—e.g., in 2005 Jews comprised around 12 percent of the board of the National Rifle Association (NRA) (Richman, 2005)—it does not necessarily follow that the movement should be considered a Jewish movement. The movements analyzed in *CofC* were originated and dominated by Jews with a strong Jewish identity and a strong sense of Jewish interests; they exhibited a great deal of ethnic networking and mutual citation patterns, with non-Jews often relegated to subordinate roles that really amounted to window dressing. These movements have been influential, and the Jews at the center of these movements were critical to their influence. Thus, by focusing solely on percentages of Jewish involvement in various areas and deeming any Jewish representation above 3 percent (the approximate percentage of Jews in the U.S. population) as confirming the default hypothesis, the central aspects of the movements considered in *CofC* are ignored.

Rather than attempting to determine percentages of Jews in non-anti-Semitic movements, the methodology of *CofC* analyzes where Jewish power has been directed during specific historical eras. The contrast between these two perspectives can be illustrated as follows: imagine a scenario in which the major Jewish activist organizations, Jewish donors, and Jewish activists are on one side of an issue, but on the other side of the issue are Jews who collectively represent more than 3 percent of the membership but without any major Jewish financial, organizational, media, and activist networks behind them. This would satisfy Cofnas's (2021) default hypothesis, but it would be utterly insufficient as an analysis of Jewish influence on the issue. As will be apparent throughout, *CofC* takes the view that it is critical to establish where the power of the Jewish community is being directed.

There is thus no implication here of a unified Jewish "conspiracy" to undermine the people and culture of the West—the sort of conspiracy portrayed in *The Protocols of the Elders of Zion*. Since the Enlightenment, Judaism has never been a unified, monolithic movement, and there has clearly been a great deal of disagreement among Jews as to how to protect themselves and attain their interests during this period. The movements discussed in this volume were advanced by relatively few individuals whose views may not have been known or understood by the majority of the Jewish community. The argument is that Jews dominated these intellectual movements, that a strong sense of Jewish identity was characteristic of the great majority of these individuals, and that these individuals were pursuing their perception of Jewish interests in establishing and participating in these movements.

Thus there is no implication that Judaism constitutes a unified movement or that all segments of the Jewish community participated in these movements. Jews may constitute a predominant or necessary element in radical political movements or movements in the social sciences, and Jewish identification may be highly compatible with or even facilitate these movements without most Jews being involved in these movements. As a result, the question of the overall effects of Jewish influences on gentile culture is independent of the question of whether most or all Jews supported the movements to alter gentile culture. Indeed, despite my disavowals dating from the original edition of this book (1998), a common tactic of my critics has been to find Jews who disagree with the ideas of the movement or to find examples where Jews constitute more than their percentage of the population in a particular movement. But the point here is to find the locus of Jewish money and power (MacDonald, 2022a). For example, there are certainly Jews who are opposed to Zionism and oppose U.S. funding and diplomatic support of Israel, but the overwhelming power and influence of Jewish involvement with Zionism is on the side of Israel.

On one hand anti-Semites have often implicitly or explicitly assumed that Jewish involvement in radical political movements was part of an overarching Jewish strategy that also included wealthy Jewish capitalists, as well as Jewish involvement in the media, the academy, and other areas of public life. On the other hand, Jews attempting to defuse the anti-Semitism resulting from the fact that Jews have played a predominant role in many radical political movements have often pointed to the fact that only a minority of Jews are involved and that gentiles are also involved in the movements. Thus, for example, the standard response of the American Jewish Committee (AJCommittee) during the 1920s–40s to the predominance of Jews in radical political movements was to emphasize that most Jews were not radicals. Nevertheless, during this same period the AJCommittee undertook efforts to combat radicalism in the Jewish community (e.g., N. W. Cohen, 1972).[22] The AJCommittee was implicitly recognizing that statements that only a minority of Jews are radicals may indeed have been true but were irrelevant to whether (1) Jewish identification is compatible with or facilitates involvement in radical political movements; (2) Jews constitute a predominant or necessary element in radical political movements; or (3) influences on gentile society resulting from Jewish predominance in radical movements (or the other Jewish intellectual movements reviewed in this volume) may be conceptualized as a consequence of Judaism as a group evolutionary strategy.

---

[22] As indicated in SAID (p. 261), the AJCommittee's endeavor to portray Jews as not overrepresented in radical movements involved deception and perhaps self-deception. The AJCommittee engaged in intensive efforts to change opinion within the Jewish community to attempt to show that Jewish interests were more compatible with advocating American democracy than Soviet communism (e.g., emphasizing Soviet anti-Semitism and Soviet support of nations opposed to Israel in the period after World War II) (N. W. Cohen, 1972, pp. 347ff).

Similarly, the fact that most Jews prior to the 1930s were not Zionists, at least overtly, surely does not imply that Jewish identification was irrelevant to Zionism, or that Jews did not in fact constitute a predominant influence on Zionism, or that Zionism did not have effects on gentile societies, or that some gentiles did not become ardent Zionists. Political radicalism has been one choice among many available to Jews in the post-Enlightenment world, and there is no implication here that Judaism constitutes a monolithic unified group in the post-Enlightenment world. That Jews have been more likely than gentiles to choose radical political alternatives and that Jews have been a predominant influence in some radical political movements are therefore facts highly relevant to the present project.

ESTABLISHING JEWISH IDENTITY AND SENSE OF JEWISH INTERESTS

Gelya Frank's (1997, p. 731) statement that cultural pluralism has been the "invisible subject" of American anthropology raises an important question. Why should such a prominent concern of an academic discipline be "invisible"? The empirical program of *CofC* is to examine putative Jewish intellectual and political movements and determine whether the main figures identified as Jews and saw their intellectual and political work as advancing Jewish interests. A basic problem arises from the fact that Jewish intellectuals and political activists may be well advised not to advertise their Jewish identity and commitment to Jewish interests. This is especially the case during times of heightened anti-Semitism and prior to the time when Jewish social scientists had a critical mass at the most elite academic institutions. For example, anti-Semitism was much more common during the 1920s and 1930s, declining to a marginal phenomenon after World War II. During this period, Jews were well advised to be circumspect about their Jewish identities and Jewish commitments. For example, the Zionist movement began in the late nineteenth century but was a minority viewpoint within the Jewish community until the establishment of Israel because of fears of charges of "dual loyalty"—the idea that Jews would be at least as loyal to Israel as to the United States, and perhaps even more loyal to Israel (see MacDonald, 2003b). Even in the twenty-first century, neoconservative Jews with strong emotional and family connections to Israel are careful to frame their proposals for war in the Middle East as serving U.S. interests (see Ch. 4).

This is a general point. Jews, as a relatively small minority in the West, must attempt to appeal to non-Jews and avoid framing their theories and policy proposals in terms of their Jewish identity and Jewish interests. Thus one searches in vain for public pronouncements and framing of theories explicitly in terms of advancing Jewish interests.

Boas's anthropology was strikingly apolitical in terms of explicit theory, but in message and purpose, it was an explicitly antiracist science. Boas's career, rooted in his position as an ambiguously white European Jewish intellectual transplanted to America, continues to offer a model for infusing the science of anthropology with an activist agenda for inclusion, empowerment, and alliance across boundaries. (Frank, 1997, p. 741)

These scholars [i.e., Jewish anthropologists from the 1930s–50s], at least to a significant extent in their strictly professional contributions, effaced their own Jewish backgrounds, possible biases, and investments in the Jewish predicaments of contemporaneous American life. They rarely talked about Jewish matters in their professional print lives. For the most part, they sought to elaborate upon and argue for the need to respect American Indian difference, to maintain, preserve, and foster it. At the same time, they minimized their Jewish difference, irrespective of the degree to which they publicly identified as Jews. (Koffman, 2019, p. 177)

This explains the lucrative and elaborate infrastructure that Jews have created in support of their causes, such as the network of neoconservative think tanks, positions at universities, and opportunities in the media that undoubtedly attract many non-Jews (Ch. 4). But typically, in the absence of evidence of explicit Jewish activism (e.g., being a member of the ADL or AIPAC)—or, as in the case of the Frankfurt School (Ch. 6), having your central academic work, *The Authoritarian Personality* (1950), published by the AJCommittee which funded its research—one must pore over detailed biographies that include, e.g., accounts of private conversations and letters. Freud, for example, left behind a great deal of evidence of his Jewish identity and his sense of Jewish interests (Ch. 5). Others did not, so one is forced to piece together an account on relatively scant evidence.

Again, this is especially the case in periods when Jews have been regarded with suspicion or dislike because of their ethnic background. Science by its very nature is supposed to be conducted without ethnic or religious biases. Thus in anthropology, "there has . . . been a whitewashing of Jewish ethnicity, reflecting fears of anti-Semitic reactions that could discredit the discipline of anthropology and individual anthropologists, either because Jews were considered dangerous due to their presumed racial differences or because they were associated with radical causes" (Frank, 1997, p. 733). Jewish identities and interests were thus forced to be submerged in the language of objectivity and science.

Science is the gold standard of public discourse in the West. Real science is an individualistic endeavor in which individual scientists may defect from a particular movement depending on empirical advances, as opposed to adopting the cohesive, ingroup-outgroup perspective that pervades this volume.

Any movement with ambitions to influence the public via academic culture must present itself as scientifically based and empirically grounded. It must appeal to a Western audience of empirically-oriented social scientists—e.g., the "Protestant bean counters" who dominated American sociology prior to the rise of Jewish Marxist-oriented sociologists (Sennett, 1995, p. 43). As noted in Chapter 7, scientific progress depends on an individualistic, atomistic universe of discourse in which each individual sees himself or herself not as a member of a larger political or cultural entity advancing a particular point of view, but as an independent agent endeavoring to evaluate evidence and discover the structure of reality. Thus it should not be at all surprising that Boas would not proclaim his ethnic commitments, and thus one must examine the evidence with the understanding that the principal figures may well not be forthright about their Jewish commitments.

Recruiting Non-Jews. The involvement of non-Jews in various Jewish intellectual and political movements is a recurrent theme in this volume. As indicated in SAID (Chs. 5–6), the rhetoric of universalism and the recruitment of gentiles as advocates of Jewish interests have been recurrent themes in combating anti-Semitism in both the ancient and modern world.

Since movements parading as scientific in a Western cultural context must not be seen as ethnically motivated and must be at least to some extent appealing to non-Jews (given that Jews have always been a small minority in Western societies), it is certainly a good strategy for Jewish academics and activists to recruit sympathetic non-Jews as graduate students or as political operatives. Again, the paradigm is the neoconservative program of establishing think tanks and activist organizations which resulted in high-profile positions for non-Jews.

Congruence with the Jewish Activist Community. A consideration helpful in understanding the non-coincidental nature of Jewish involvement in various intellectual and political movements is whether the attitudes of a particular Jew are congruent with mainstream Jewish opinion as explicitly stated by prominent Jewish activist organizations like the AJCommittee, the premier Jewish activist organization during the 1920s. This is particularly the case on issues where the attitudes of the Jewish community are out of step with those of the society as a whole. As discussed above, Jewish intellectuals intent on establishing scientific credibility in the wider scientific community are well advised not to explicitly state their Jewish identity or discuss how their Jewish identity informs their attitudes and opinions. Such considerations are anathema to the scientific spirit. On the other hand, Jewish activist organizations are typically not reticent, as for example, in the 1920s immigration debates during which the AJCommittee played by far the greatest role in opposing restriction (Okrent, 2019; see Ch. 8). As discussed in Chapter 2, Franz Boas, motivated by his opposition to restriction, published his study of the skull shapes of immigrants, the conclusions of which were entirely congruent with the activism of the AJCommittee and quite divergent from the attitudes of the great majority of Americans.

Indeed, Boas was greatly motivated by the immigration issue as it occurred early in the century. Carl Degler (1991, p. 74) notes that Boas's professional correspondence "reveals that an important motive behind his famous head-measuring project in 1910 was his strong personal interest in keeping the United States diverse in population." Degler makes the following comment regarding one of Boas's environmentalist explanations for mental differences between immigrant and native children: "Why Boas chose to advance such an ad hoc interpretation is hard to understand until one recognizes his desire to explain in a favorable way the apparent mental backwardness of the immigrant children" (p. 75; see also Ch. 8). Boas's skull shape study was thus likely an example of ethnic activism posing as science—and fraudulent science as well (see Ch. 2).

As discussed in Chapter 8, keeping America diverse has been a clear goal of the American Jewish activist community from the early twentieth century (when facilitating Jewish immigration was a prime goal and Jewish activism was the prime mover of the anti-restrictionist movement) down to the present (when Jewish activists and organizations have championed liberal immigration policies aimed at importing all racial and ethnic groups, the extreme being the Biden administration's "open border" policy administered by Jewish Secretary of Homeland Security, Alejandro Mayorkas). Jewish attitudes conflicted with the American majority at least by 1905 (Neuringer, 1971/1980, p. 83), and restrictionists were clearly in the driver's seat when the restrictive Immigration Act of 1924 finally became law despite intense Jewish opposition.

GENTILE INVOLVEMENT IN JEWISH MOVEMENTS

That some gentiles were involved in these movements is not surprising. At a theoretical level, my thinking is based once again on an evolutionary interpretation of social identity theory (see SAID, Ch. 1). Gentiles may be attracted to the political and intellectual movements that attract Jews, and for many of the same reasons—i.e., reasons related to social identification and ingroup-outgroup competition. For example, African American intellectuals have often been attracted to leftist intellectual movements and environmentalist explanations of racial group differences in IQ at least partly as a reaction to their perceptions of White animosity and the consequent implications of genetic inferiority. In the same way, I argue that anti-Semitism has been a motivating force for many Jewish intellectuals. Recall the motivating role of self-esteem as a theoretical primitive in social identity theory. A great many people who, for whatever reason, feel victimized by a particular sociopolitical system are attracted to movements that criticize the system, blame others for their problems, and generally vindicate their own positive perceptions of themselves and their ingroup as well as their negative perceptions of outgroups. In each of the intellectual and political movements I review, Jewish identification and a concern to combat anti-Semitism were clearly involved.

Moreover, once Jews have attained intellectual predominance, it is not surprising that gentiles would be attracted to Jewish intellectuals as members of a socially dominant and prestigious group and as dispensers of valued resources. Such a perspective fits well with an evolutionary perspective on group dynamics: gentiles negotiating the intellectual status hierarchy would be attracted to the characteristics of the most dominant members of the hierarchy, especially if they viewed the hierarchy as permeable. For example, William Barrett, a gentile editor of *Partisan Review*, describes his "awe and admiration" of the New York Intellectuals (a group of predominantly Jewish intellectuals discussed in Ch. 7) early in his career. "They were beings invested in my eyes with a strange and mysterious glamour" (in Cooney, 1986, p. 227).

Partisan Review was a flagship journal of this very influential intellectual movement and had a decisive influence on success or failure in the literary world. Leslie Fiedler (1948, pp. 872, 873), himself a New York Intellectual, described a whole generation of American Jewish writers (including Delmore Schwartz, Alfred Kazin, Karl Shapiro, Isaac Rosenfeld, Paul Goodman, Saul Bellow, and H. J. Kaplan) as "typically urban, second-generation Jews." The works of these writers appeared regularly in *Partisan Review*, and Fiedler goes on to say that "the writer drawn to New York from the provinces feels . . . the Rube, attempts to conform; and the almost parody of Jewishness achieved by the gentile writer in New York is a strange and crucial testimony of our time."

Almost one-half of Kadushin's (1974, p. 23) sample of elite post-World War II American intellectuals was Jewish. The sample was based on the most frequent contributors to leading intellectual journals, followed by interviews in which the intellectuals "voted" for another intellectual they considered most influential in their thinking. Over 40 percent of the Jews in the sample received six or more votes as being most influential, compared to only 15 percent of non-Jews (p. 32). It is therefore not surprising that Joseph Epstein (1997, p. 7) finds that during the 1950s and early 1960s being Jewish was "honorific" among intellectuals generally; gentile intellectuals "scoured their genealog[ies] for Jewish ancestors." By 1968 Walter Kerr could write:

> What has happened since World War II is that the American sensibility has become part Jewish, perhaps as much Jewish as it is anything else. . . . The literate American mind has come in some measure to think Jewishly. It has been taught to, and it was ready to. After the entertainers and novelists

came the Jewish critics, politicians, theologians. Critics and politicians and theologians are by profession molders; they form ways of seeing.

In my personal experience, this honorific status of Jewish intellectuals remains common among my colleagues and is apparent, for example, in Hollinger's (1996, p. 4) work on the "transformation of the ethnoreligious demography of American academic life by Jews" in the period from the 1930s to the 1960s.[23]

Finally, a major theme is that gentiles have often been actively recruited to the movements discussed here and given highly visible roles within these movements in order to lessen the appearance that the movements are indeed Jewish-dominated or aimed only at narrow Jewish sectarian interests. From the standpoint of social identity theory, such a strategy aims at making gentiles perceive the intellectual or political movement as permeable to non-Jews and as satisfying gentile interests. As indicated above, the rhetoric of universalism and the recruitment of gentiles as advocates of Jewish interests have been recurrent themes in combating anti-Semitism in both the ancient and modern world.

CULTURAL CRITIQUE

Another major theme of this volume is that Jewish intellectuals have developed intellectual movements that have subjected the institutions of gentile society to radical forms of criticism. The converse of this is that gentile-dominated societies have often developed hegemonic ideologies intended to explain and rationalize the current institutions of society. This presumably has been the case for the major religions of the world, and, more recently, ideologies such as communism, fascism, and liberal democracy appear to perform a similar function. Judaism, because of its position as a diaspora minority group committed to its own worldview, has tended to adopt ideologies in which the institutions and ideologies of the surrounding society are viewed negatively.

Social Identity Theory. Such a result follows directly from social identity theory. Particularly striking are the negative views of gentiles apparent in Jewish religious writings. The Law of Cleanness regards gentiles and their land as intrinsically unclean. Gentiles are typically likened to beasts capable of the worst debaucheries, as in the writings of Maimonides where heathen women are suspected of whoredom and heathen men of bestiality (The Code of Maimonides, Book V: The Book of Holiness, XXII, 142). Jews conceptualize

---

[23] A similar phenomenon is apparent in the American movie industry, where anecdotal evidence indicates that gentiles sometimes attempt to present themselves as Jews in order to advance their careers in a Jewish-dominated environment (see Cash, 1994).

themselves as descendants of Jacob, represented in Genesis as smooth-skinned, delicate, and contemplative. Gentiles are represented by Esau, Jacob's twin brother, the opposite of Jacob—hirsute, coarse, and brutal. Whereas Esau lives as a hunter and warrior, Jacob lives by intelligence and guile and is the proper master of Esau, who has been commanded by God to serve Jacob. Lindemann (1997, p. 5) shows that these stereotypes remain salient to Jews in contemporary times.

Social Critique and Aspirations for Upward Mobility and Dominance. For Jews as an upwardly mobile group, social criticism leads naturally to viewing current power structures prior to Jews attaining elite status as morally corrupt, illegitimate, and therefore change-worthy. Discussing Jewish neoconservatives, Jacob Heilbrunn (2008, pp. 11–2) repeatedly states that a major target of hatred for the Jewish neocons was White Anglo-Saxon Protestant (WASP) political power and cultural influence. He finds that the neocons were motivated partly by antipathy to the "social exclusion and WASP snobbery that their fathers experienced in the early part of the twentieth century—an attitude they carried with them through the debates of the cold war and into the halls of power after 9/11." They sought,

> to overturn the old order in America. . . . After all, no matter how hard they worked, there were still quotas at the Ivy League universities. Then there were the fancy clubs, the legal and financial firms that saw Jews as interlopers who would soil their proud escutcheons and were to be kept at bay. Smarting with unsurpassed social resentment, the young Jews viewed themselves as liberators, proclaiming a new faith. (Heilbrunn, 2008, p. 28)

Heilbrunn (2008, p. 73) mentions "the snobbery of the Columbia English department, where Jews were seen as cultural interlopers. This attitude, which also prevailed on Wall Street and at the State Department, produced a lifelong antipathy toward the patrician class among the neocons and prompted them to create their own parallel establishment." The result, as Norman Podhoretz phrased it, was to proclaim a war against the "WASP patriciate" (p. 83).

Given their interest in supporting Israel, it is not surprising that a particular focus of their ire was the U.S. State Department. Influential neocon Douglas Feith (see Ch. 4) told Heilbrunn (2008, p. 12) in an interview that "because of his family history [i.e., decimated by the Holocaust] he understands the true nature of foreign policy, unlike the 'WASPs' in the State Department." Feith sees foreign policy from a Jewish, Holocaust-centric perspective that the WASPs can never understand.

A similar example is from Mark Rudd (2005, p. 58), a radical during the 1960s at Columbia University: "What outraged me and my comrades so much about Columbia, along with its hypocrisy, was the air of genteel civility. Or should I say gentile? Despite the presence of so many Jews in the faculty and among the students . . . the place was dripping with goyishness."

The displacement of the genteel White Protestant culture at Columbia that the neocons and Rudd hated has become part of the general displacement of a non-Jewish White elite in America, especially White men. There is no doubt that neoconservatism and the New Left in general were bent on a similar displacement of WASP elites which, after all, would naturally remove their much-hated genteel culture and their control over foreign policy. (For most of the Biden administration, Jewish neocons held the top positions at the State Department—Antony Blinken as Secretary of State, Victoria Nuland as Under Secretary of State for Political Affairs, and Wendy Sherman as Deputy Secretary of State.) All of their policies have led inexorably in that direction.

To a considerable extent, the current malaise of Whites in the U.S. can be directly traced to the triumph of a new, substantially Jewish elite. Neoconservatives remain highly influential in foreign policy, and the attitudes of the New Left counterculture of the 1960s are pervasive in American political culture—especially regarding non-White immigration, the rise of multiculturalism, and the steady erosion of Whites as a percentage of the electorate. (The last Democratic president to get a majority of White votes was Lyndon B. Johnson in 1964.) Jewish involvement in the New Left and neoconservatism is discussed in Chapters 3 and 4, respectively.

Cultural Criticism and Anti-Semitism. Judaism may come to be viewed as subversive when Jews attempt to inculcate negative perceptions of gentile culture among gentiles. The association of Judaism with subversive ideologies has a long history. Noting the association between Jews and subversive ideas in Muslim countries, B. Lewis (1984, p. 104) states that the theme of Jewish subversion is also familiar in "other times and places." P. Johnson (1987/1988, pp. 214–215) finds that beginning in the Middle Ages converted Jews, especially those forced to convert, were "a critical, questing, disturbing element within the intelligentsia. . . . [Thus] the claim that they were intellectually subversive had an element of truth." The title of a book on Jewish art in the Middle Ages expresses this theme well: *Dreams of Subversion in Medieval Jewish Art and Literature* (M. M. Epstein, 1997). M. M. Epstein comments, "One can sense the anger Jews of the late Middle Ages must have felt when they called for the destruction of Christendom" (p. 115), and it's no accident that Talmudic writings disparaging Jesus and Christianity became a focus of anti-Semitism, as in the Disputation of Paris in 1240.

In the ancient world through the Middle Ages, negative views of gentile institutions were relatively confined to internal consumption within the Jewish community. However, beginning with the converso turmoil in fifteenth-century Spain and as eloquently expressed by Paul Johnson in the epigraph to this chapter, these negative views often appeared in the most prestigious intellectual circles and in the mass media. These views generally subjected the institutions of gentile society to radical criticism or they led to the development of intellectual structures that rationalized Jewish identification in a post-religious intellectual environment.

Faur (1992, pp. 31ff) shows that conversos (ethnic Jews who supposedly converted to Christianity in fifteenth- and sixteenth-century Spain but remained a Jewish group; SAID, Ch. 4) were vastly overrepresented among the humanist thinkers who opposed the corporate nature of Spanish society centered around Christianity. In describing the general thrust of these writers, Faur notes:

> Although the strategy varied—from the creation of highly sophisticated literary works to the writing of scholarly and philosophical compositions—the goal was one: to present ideas and methodologies that would displace the values and institutions of the "old Christian." . . . The urgency of reviewing the values and institutions of Christian Spain became more evident with the first massacre of *conversos* perpetrated by the old Christians in Toledo, in 1449. (Faur, 1992, p. 31)

Similarly, Castro (1954, pp. 557–558) notes that works of "violent social criticism" and "antisocial rancor," especially including social satire, were originated during the fifteenth century by converso writers.

A prime example is *The Celestina* (first edition dating from 1499) by Fernando de Rojas, who wrote "with all the anguish, pessimism, and nihilism of a *converso* who has lost the religion of his fathers but has been unable to integrate himself within the compass of Christian belief." Rojas subjected the Castilian society of his time to,

> a corrosive analysis, destroying with a spirit that has been called "destructive" all the traditional values and mental schemes of the new intolerant system. Beginning with literature and proceeding to religion, passing through all the "values" of institutionalized caste-ism—honor, valor, love—everything is perversely pulverized. (Rodríguez-Puértolas, 1976, p. 127)

This association of Jews with subversive ideologies continued during and after the Enlightenment as Jews were able to participate in public intellectual debate in Western Europe. Paul Johnson (1987/1988, pp. 291–292), writing of Baruch Spinoza, identifies him as "the first major example of the sheer destructive power of Jewish rationalism once it escaped the restraints of the traditional community." Similarly, Heinrich Heine is "both the prototype and the archetype of a new figure in European literature: the Jewish radical man of letters, using his skill, reputation and popularity to undermine the intellectual confidence of the established order" (P. Johnson, p. 345).

As Moritz Goldstein famously noted in a 1912 article, "We Jews manage the intellectual property of a people [Germans] that denies us the right and the ability to do so." Throughout Eastern Europe, Austria, and Germany, Jews came to dominate the culture, often expressing admiration for national icons in various countries while at the same time opposing national cultures: "The secular Jews' love of Goethe, Schiller, and other Pushkins—as well as the various northern forests they represented—was sincere and tender" (Slezkine, 2004, p. 68; see MacDonald, 2005b, pp. 73–74). However, their love of cultural icons transcended national and ethnic boundaries in an age of popular nationalism—for example, their promotion of German culture among the Czechs, Latvians, and Romanians.

Moreover, Jews were not simply lovers of Pushkin and Goethe. A major theme of anti-Jewish attitudes was that Jews were deeply involved in creating a "culture of critique"—that Jewish cultural influence was entirely negative and shattered the social bonds of the peoples among whom they lived—an important tradition among German intellectuals and politicians, such as Richard Wagner, Heinrich von Treitschke, Houston Stewart Chamberlain, and Hitler. For example, von Treitschke, a prominent nineteenth-century German professor and public intellectual, complained of Heine's "mocking German humiliation and disgrace following the Napoleonic wars" and his having "no sense of shame, loyalty, truthfulness, or reverence" (in G. L. Mosse, 1970, pp. 52–53). Von Treitschke also commented that "what Jewish journalists write in mockery and satirical remarks against Christianity is downright revolting," and "about the shortcomings of the Germans [or] French, everybody could freely say the worst things; but if somebody dared to speak in just and moderate terms about some undeniable weakness of the Jewish character, he was immediately branded as a barbarian and religious persecutor by nearly all of the newspapers" (in Lindemann, 1997, pp. 138–139). Such attitudes were prominent among anti-Jewish writers and activists, reaching a crescendo with the National Socialists in Germany.

This "sheer destructive power" of the Jewish intellect was an important aspect of the pre-National Socialist era in Germany. As indicated in SAID (Chs. 2, 5), a prominent feature of anti-Semitism among the social conservatives and racial anti-Semites in Germany from 1870 to 1933 was their belief that Jews were instrumental in developing ideas that subverted traditional German attitudes and beliefs. Jews were vastly overrepresented as editors and writers during the Weimar period in Germany, and "a more general cause of increased anti-Semitism was the very strong and unfortunate propensity of dissident Jews to attack national institutions and customs in both socialist and non-socialist publications" (Gordon, 1984, p. 51).[24] This "media violence" directed at German culture by Jewish writers—most notably Kurt Tucholsky, who "wore his subversive heart on his sleeve" (Pulzer, 1979, p. 97)—was publicized widely by the anti-Semitic press (P. Johnson, 1987/1988, pp. 476–477).

Jews were not simply overrepresented among radical journalists, intellectuals, and "producers of culture" in Weimar Germany; they essentially created the phenomenon of radical critique of German culture. "They violently attacked everything about German society. They despised the military, the judiciary, and the middle class in general" (Rothman & Lichter, 1982/1996, p. 85). P. W. Massing (1949, p. 84) notes the perception of the anti-Semite Adolf Stoecker of Jewish "lack of reverence for the Christian-conservative world."

Anti-Semitism among university professors during the Weimar period was partially fueled by the perception that "the Jew represented the critical or 'negative' aspects of modern thought, the acids of analysis and skepticism that helped to dissolve the moral certainties, patriotic commitment, and social cohesion of modern states" (F. K. Ringer, 1983, p. 7). Reflecting this perception, National Socialist propaganda during the period claimed that Jews attempted to undermine the social cohesion of gentile society while remaining committed to a highly cohesive group themselves—an intellectual double standard in which the basis of social cohesion among gentiles was subjected to intense criticism while the Jews "would retain their international cohesiveness, blood ties, and spiritual unity" (Aschheim, 1985, p. 239). Viewed from this perspective, an important goal of Jewish intellectual effort may be understood as attempting to undermine cohesive gentile group strategies while continuing to engage in their own highly cohesive group strategy. This issue reemerges in the discussion of Jewish involvement in radical political movements in Chapter 3 and the Frankfurt School of Social Research in Chapter 6.

This phenomenon could also be found in France. Gilson (1962, pp. 31–32), in discussing his Jewish professors in fin de siècle France, states:

> The doctrines of these university professors were really quite different from one another. Even the personal philosophy of Lévy-Bruhl did not coincide exactly with that of Durkheim, while Frédéric Rauh was going his own way. . . . The only element common to their doctrines is a negative one, but nonetheless real and very active in its own order. One might describe it as a radical defiance of all that which is social conceived as a constraint from which to be liberated. Spinoza and Brunschvicg achieved this

---

[24] As anti-Semitism increased during the Weimar period, Jewish-owned liberal newspapers began to suffer economic hardship because of public hostility to the ethnic composition of the editorial boards and staffs (W. E. Mosse, 1987, p. 371). The response of Hans Lachman-Mosse was to "depoliticize" his newspapers by firing large numbers of Jewish editors and correspondents. Eksteins (1975, p. 229) suggests that the response was an attempt to deflect right-wing categorizations of his newspapers as part of the *Judenpresse*.

liberation through metaphysics, Durkheim and Lévy-Bruhl through science and sociology, Bergson through intuition.

Just below cultural criticism often lurked pure hatred of non-Jews and their culture. Slezkine (2004, p. 216) describes Walter Benjamin, an icon of the Frankfurt School and darling of the current crop of postmodernist intellectuals, "with glasses on his nose, autumn in his soul, and vicarious murder in his heart," a comment that illustrates the fine line between murder and cultural criticism, especially when engaged in by ethnic outsiders—a theme of the discussion in Chapter 3 of Jews as an elite in the early decades of the Soviet Union. Indeed, Benjamin (1968, p. 229) stated, "Hatred and [the] spirit of sacrifice . . . are nourished by the image of enslaved ancestors rather than that of liberated grandchildren." Jews' lachrymose perceptions of their history—their images of enslaved ancestors—have been potent motivators of the hatred unleashed by the upheavals of the twentieth century and beyond.

Jews and Cultural Critique Since the 1960s. Jews have also been at the forefront of the adversary culture in the United States, England, and France since the mid-1960s, especially as promoters and defenders of the adversary culture in the media and the academic world (Ginsberg, 1993, pp. 125ff; Rothman & Isenberg, 1974b, pp. 66–67).[25] B. Stein (1979, p. 28; see also Lichter et al., 1994) shows that his sample of predominantly Jewish writers and producers of television shows in the 1970s had very negative attitudes toward what they viewed as a gentile-dominated cultural establishment, although their most negative comments were elicited in informal conversation rather than during formal interviews. Television portrayals of gentile establishment figures in business and the military tended to be very negative. For example:

---

[25] An example of this type of intellectual ethnic warfare is the popular movie *Addams Family Values* (released in November 1993), produced by Scott Rudin, directed by Barry Sonnenfeld, and written by Paul Rudnick. The bad guys in the movie are virtually anyone with blond hair (the exception being an overweight child), and the good guys include two Jewish children wearing yarmulkes. (Indeed, having blond hair is viewed as a pathology, so that when the dark-haired Addams baby temporarily becomes blond, there is a family crisis.) The featured Jewish child has dark hair, wears glasses, and is physically frail and nonathletic. He often makes precociously intelligent comments, and he is severely punished by the blond-haired counselors for reading a highly intellectual book. The evil gentile children are the opposite: blond, athletic, and unintellectual. Together with other assorted dark-haired children from a variety of ethnic backgrounds and White gentile children rejected by their peers (for being overweight, etc.), the Jewish boy and the Addams family children lead a very violent movement that succeeds in destroying the blond enemy. The movie is a parable illustrating the general thrust of Jewish intellectual and political activity relating to immigration and multiculturalism in Western societies (see Ch. 8). It is also consistent with the general thrust of Hollywood movies as cultural critique. The Preface reviews data indicating Jewish domination of the entertainment industry in the United States. Powers et al. (1996, p. 207) characterize television as promoting liberal, cosmopolitan values, and Lichter et al. (1994, p. 251) find that television portrays cultural pluralism in positive terms and as easily achieved apart from the activities of a few ignorant or bigoted miscreants.

The writers clearly thought of military men as clean-shaven, blond, and of completely WASP background. In the minds of a few of the people I interviewed, these blond officers were always a hair's breadth away from becoming National Socialists. They were thought of as part of an Aryan ruling class that actually or potentially repressed those of different ethnic backgrounds. (B. Stein, 1979, pp. 55–56)

Indeed, Glazer and Moynihan (1963/1970) credit the emergence of the adversary culture in the United States as a triumph of the New York Jewish cultural-political perspective. Jewish writers and visual artists (including E. L. Doctorow, Norman Mailer, Joseph Heller,[26] Frederick Wiseman, and Norman Lear) were disproportionately involved in attempts to portray American society as "sick," and a common technique of cultural subversion,

involves an attack upon genuine inequities or irrationalities. Since all societies abound in both, there is never an absence of targets. However, the attack is generally not directed at the particular inequity or irrationality per se. Rather, such inequities or irrationalities are used as a means for achieving a larger purpose: the general weakening of the social order itself. (Rothman & Lichter, 1982/1996, p. 120)

The discussion throughout this volume reflects Sorkin's (1985, p. 102) description of nineteenth-century German-Jewish intellectuals as constituting an "invisible community of acculturating German Jews who perpetuated distinct cultural forms within the majority culture." The Jewish cultural contribution to the wider gentile culture was therefore accomplished from a highly particularistic perspective in which Jewish group identity continued to be of paramount importance despite its "invisibility." Even Berthold Auerbach (1812–1882), an exemplar of the assimilated Jewish intellectual, "manipulate[d] elements of the majority culture in a way peculiar to the German-Jewish minority" (p. 107). For secular Jewish intellectuals, Auerbach was a model of the assimilated Jew who did not renounce his Judaism. For the most part, these secular Jewish intellectuals socialized exclusively with other secular Jews and viewed their contribution to German culture as a secular form of Judaism—thus the "invisible community" of strongly identified Jewish intellectuals. This manipulation of culture in the service of group interests was a common theme of anti-Semitic writings. Thus, Heinrich Heine's critique of German culture was viewed as directed at the pursuit of power for his group at the expense of the cohesiveness of gentile society (see G. L. Mosse, 1970, p. 52).

---

[26] Heller combines social criticism with a strong Jewish identity. In a talk described in *The Economist* (March 18th, 1995, p. 92), Heller is quoted as saying that "being Jewish informs everything I do. My books are getting more and more Jewish."

As noted above, in several of the movements discussed in the following chapters it is of considerable importance that their propagators have attempted to clothe their rhetoric in the garb of science—the modern arbiter of truth and intellectual respectability. As L. White (1966, p. 2) notes with respect to the Boasian school of anthropology, the aura of science is deceptive: "They would make it appear and would have everyone believe that their choice of premises and goals has been determined by scientific considerations. This is definitely not the case. ... They are obviously sincere. Their sincerity and group loyalty tend, however, to persuade and consequently to deceive."

The comment is an excellent illustration of Robert Trivers's (1985) evolutionary theory of self-deception: the best deceivers are those who are self-deceived. At times the deception becomes conscious. Charles Liebman (1973, p. 213) describes his unselfconscious acceptance of universalist ideologies (behaviorism and liberalism) in his work as a social scientist and suggests that he was engaged in self-deception regarding the role of Jewish identification in his beliefs: "As a behaviorist (and a liberal) I can testify to having been quite unselfconscious about my academic methodology, but I suspect that this would have to be the case. Otherwise I would be defeating the very universalism I espouse."

CONCEPTUALIZING THE JEWISH RADICAL CRITICISM OF GENTILE SOCIETY

The foregoing has documented a general tendency for Jewish intellectuals in a variety of periods to be involved with social critique, and I have hinted at an analysis in terms of social identity theory. More formally, two quite different types of reasons explain why Jews might be expected to advocate ideologies and political movements aimed at undermining the existing gentile social order.

First, such ideologies and movements may be directed at benefiting Jews economically or socially. Clearly one of the themes of post-Enlightenment Judaism has been the rapid upward mobility of Jews and attempts by gentile power structures to limit Jewish access to power and social status. Given this rather conspicuous reality, practical reasons of economic and political self-interest would result in Jews being attracted to movements that criticized the gentile power structure or even advocated overthrowing it entirely.

Thus the czarist government of Russia enforced restrictions on Jews mainly out of fear that Jews would overwhelm gentile Russians in free economic competition (Lindemann, 1991; SAID, Ch. 2). These czarist restrictions on Jews were a prominent rallying point for Jews around the world, and it is not at all unreasonable to suppose that Jewish participation in radical movements in Russia was motivated by perceived Jewish interest in overthrowing the czarist regime. Indeed, Arthur Liebman (1979, pp. 29ff) notes that Jewish political radicalism in czarist Russia must be understood as resulting from economic restrictions on Jews that were enforced by the government in the context of considerable Jewish poverty and a very rapid Jewish demographic increase. Similarly, well into the 1930s the Jewish socialist labor movement in the United States aimed at bettering the working conditions of its predominantly Jewish membership (p. 267).

Another practical goal of Jewish political and intellectual movements has been to combat anti-Semitism. For example, Jewish attraction to socialism in many countries in the 1930s was motivated partly by communist opposition to fascism and anti-Semitism (Lipset, 1968/1988, p. 383; Marcus, 1983). The general association between anti-Semitism and conservative political views has often been advanced as an explanation for Jewish involvement with the left, including the leftist tendencies of many wealthy Jews (e.g., Lipset, pp. 375ff). Combating anti-Semitism also became a prime goal of Jewish radicals in the United States after Jews had predominantly moved into the middle class (Levin, 1977, p. 211). Rising anti-Semitism and consequent restrictions on Jewish upward mobility during the 1930s also resulted in an attraction of Jews to the left (A. Liebman, 1979, pp. 420ff, 507) at a time when in the Soviet Union anti-Semitism was outlawed and many Jews had achieved elite status there (Slezkine, 2004; MacDonald, 2005b).

It will be apparent in Chapter 2 that the cultural determinism of the Boasian school of anthropology functioned to combat anti-Semitism by combating racialist thinking and eugenic programs advocated mainly by gentiles. Psychoanalysis (Ch. 5) and the Frankfurt School (Ch. 6) have also been instrumental in developing and propagating theories attributing anti-Semitism to irrational projections of gentiles. In the case of the Frankfurt School, the theory also functioned to pathologize gentile group allegiances as a symptom of a psychiatric disorder while ignoring Jewish group allegiances.

Second, Jewish involvement in social criticism may be influenced by social identity processes independent of any practical goal such as ending anti-Semitism. Research in social identity processes finds a tendency for displacement of ingroup views away from outgroup norms (Hogg & D. Abrams, 1988). In the case of Jewish-gentile contact, these outgroup norms would paradigmatically represent the consensus views of the gentile society. Moreover, individuals who identify themselves as Jews would be expected to develop negative attributions regarding the outgroup, and for Jews the most salient outgroup is the gentile power structure and indeed the gentile-dominated social structure generally.

Jewish ingroup status vis-à-vis the gentile world as an outgroup would be expected to lead to a generalized negative conceptualization of the gentile outgroup and a tendency to overemphasize the negative aspects of gentile society and social structure. From the social identity perspective, the Jewish tendency to subvert the social order is thus expected to extend beyond developing ideologies and social programs that satisfy specific Jewish economic and social interests and extend to a general devaluation and critique of gentile culture—"the sheer destructive power of Jewish rationalism once it escaped the restraints of the traditional community" (P. Johnson, 1987/1988, pp. 291–292).

The social identity perspective also predicts that such negative attributions are especially likely if the gentile power structure is anti-Semitic or perceived (even falsely) to be anti-Semitic. A basic finding of social identity research is that groups attempt to subvert negative social categorizations imposed by another group (Hogg & D. Abrams, 1988). Social identity processes would therefore be intensified by Jewish perceptions that gentile culture was hostile to Jews and that Jews had often been persecuted by gentiles. Thus Feldman (1993, p. 43) finds very robust tendencies toward heightened Jewish identification and rejection of gentile culture consequent to anti-Semitism at the very beginnings of Judaism in the ancient world and throughout Jewish history. In *Lord George Bentinck: A Political Biography* (Disraeli, 1852, p. 489), the nineteenth-century racial theorist Benjamin Disraeli, who had a very strong Jewish identity despite being a baptized Christian, stated:

> [P]ersecution . . . although unjust may have reduced the modern Jews to a state almost justifying malignant vengeance. They may have become so odious and so hostile to mankind, as to merit for their present conduct, no matter how occasioned, the obloquy and ill-treatment of the communities in which they dwell and with which they are scarcely permitted to mingle.

The result, according to Disraeli (1852, pp. 497–498), is that Jews would perceive gentile society in extremely negative terms and may attempt to overthrow the existing social order:

> But existing society has chosen to persecute this race which should furnish its choice allies, and what have been the consequences?
> They may be traced in the last outbreak of the destructive principle in Europe [i.e., the revolutions of 1848]. An insurrection takes place against tradition and aristocracy, against religion and property. Destruction of the Semitic principle, extirpation of the Jewish religion, whether in the Mosaic or in the Christian form, the natural equality of man and the abrogation of property, are proclaimed by the secret societies who form provisional governments, and men of Jewish race are found at the head of every

one of them.[27] The people of God co-operate with atheists; the most skilful accumulators of property ally themselves with communists; the peculiar and chosen race touch the hand of all the scum and low castes of Europe! And all this because they wish to destroy that ungrateful Christendom which owes to them even its name, and whose tyranny they can no longer endure.[28]

Indeed, Theodor Herzl espoused socialism in the 1890s as a Jewish response to continuing anti-Semitism, not because of its political goal of economic leveling, but because it would destroy the anti-Semitic gentile power structure:

> From outcasts of society they [Jews] will become enemies of society. Ah, they are not protected in their civic honor, they are permitted to be insulted, scorned and on occasion also a bit plundered and maimed—what prevents them from going over to the side of anarchy? [Jews] no longer have a stake in the state. They will join the revolutionary parties, supplying or sharpening their weapons. They want to turn the Jews over to the mob—good, they themselves will go over to the people. Beware, they are at their limit; do not go too far. (in Kornberg, 1993, p. 122)

Similarly, Sammons (1979, p. 263) describes the basis of the mutual attraction between Heinrich Heine and Karl Marx by noting that "they were not reformers, but haters, and this was very likely their most fundamental bond with one another." The suggestion, consistent with social identity theory, is that a fundamental motivation of Jewish intellectuals involved in social criticism has simply been hatred of the gentile-dominated power structure which is perceived as anti-Semitic. This deep antipathy toward the non-Jewish world can also be seen in sociologist and New York Intellectual Michael Walzer's (1994, pp. 6-7) comment on the "pathologies of Jewish life," particularly "the sense that 'all the world is against us,' the resulting fear, resentment, and hatred of the *goy*, the secret dreams of reversal and triumph." Such "secret dreams of reversal and triumph" are a theme of the treatment of Jewish radicals in Chapter 3 and of Freud and the psychoanalytic movement discussed in Chapter 5.

---

[27] Rather (1986) notes that anti-Semites who believed in Jewish conspiracies often cited this passage as well as the *Protocols* in support of their theories. He also points out, citing J. M. Roberts (1972), that Disraeli's view that events were controlled by vast international conspiracies was commonplace in the nineteenth century. Rather links these beliefs with the secret society at the center of the psychoanalytic movement (see Ch. 5) as well as with a secret society named "the sons of Moshe" organized by the Zionist Ahad Ha'am (Asher Ginsberg), whose work is discussed in *SAID* (Ch. 5).

[28] This passage was invoked by Lucien Wolf, secretary of the Conjoint Foreign Committee of the Board of Deputies and the Anglo-Jewish Association, to rationalize Jewish support for Russian revolutionary movements (see Szajkowski, 1967, p. 9).

Indeed, intense hatred of perceived enemies appears to be an important psychological characteristic of Jews. It is remarkable that Schatz (1991, p. 113) finds that while all Polish communists in the interwar period hated their enemies, Jewish communists had more perceived enemies and hated them more intensely. As described more fully in Chapter 3, these communist groups were actually highly cohesive ingroups entirely analogous to traditional Jewish groups in their structure and psychological orientation. The proposal that Jewish communists had more intensely negative feelings toward their enemies is highly compatible with the material in PTSDA (Ch. 8) and SAID (Ch. 1) indicating that Jews may be viewed as having exaggerated social identity systems and a greater proneness toward collectivist social structures; it is also compatible with the comments on Jews as high on affect intensity, as noted in the Preface. The greater intensity of Jewish hatred toward outgroups and perceived enemies may be simply an emotional manifestation of these tendencies. Indeed, in PTSDA (Ch. 7) I reviewed evidence indicating that Jews were highly compartmentalized in their emotional lives—prone to alternations between positive social interactions (paradigmatically directed toward members of a perceived ingroup) and intense interpersonal hostility (paradigmatically directed toward members of a perceived outgroup).

An article by Meir Y. Soloveichik (2003), aptly titled "The Virtue of Hate," amplifies this theme of normative Jewish fanatical hatred: "Judaism believes that while forgiveness is often a virtue, hate can be virtuous when one is dealing with the frightfully wicked. Rather than forgive, we can wish ill; rather than hope for repentance, we can instead hope that our enemies experience the wrath of God." Soloveichik notes that the Old Testament is replete with descriptions of horribly violent deaths inflicted on the enemies of the Israelites—the desire not only for revenge but for revenge in the bloodiest, most degrading manner imaginable: "The Hebrew prophets not only hated their enemies, but rather reveled in their suffering, finding in it a fitting justice." In the Book of Esther, after the Jews kill the ten sons of Haman, their persecutor, Esther asks that they be hanged on gallows.

Social identity theory also predicts that Jewish intellectual activity will be directed at developing ideologies that affirm their own social identity in the face of the social categories developed by anti-Semites. Historically this has been a common theme in Jewish religious apologia (see SAID, Ch. 7), but it also occurs among Jewish secular writers. Castro (1954, p. 558) describes attempts by New Christian intellectuals to "defend the Hebrew lineage" from anti-Semitic slurs during the period of the Spanish Inquisition. The converso bishop of Burgos stated, "Do not think you can insult me by calling my forefathers Jews. They are, to be sure, and I am glad that it is so; for if great age is nobility, who can go back so far?" The Jew, descended from the Maccabees and the Levites, is "noble by birth." Castro (p. 559) also notes that a theme of the New

Christian literature of the period was that of "esteem for [the] socially inferior man marginally situated in society." The category in which Jews see themselves is regarded in a positive light.

Interestingly, the converso humanist ideology stressed individual merit in opposition to the corporate nature of gentile Christian society in which people discriminated on the basis of group status (Faur, 1992, p. 35).[29] Reflecting the salience of Jewish-gentile group conflict during the period, Old Christians viewed religious affiliation (i.e., group identity) as important in judging individual merit: "In the sixteenth century the scale of values became ever more unbalanced, resulting in the concept that it was more important to establish *who* the person was rather than evaluate his capacity for work or thought" (Castro, 1971, p. 581; italics in text). The ideology of individual merit as the basis of value promoted by the converso intellectuals may thus be seen not only as benefiting Jews because of Jewish traits such as intelligence that facilitate individual merit, but also as an instance of combating categories of social identity in which one is devalued.[30]

The other side of the coin is that Jews have often reacted quite negatively to Jewish writers who portray Jewish characters as having negative or disapproved traits. For example, Philip Roth has been extensively criticized by Jews and Jewish organizations for portraying such characters (e.g., the sex-obsessed Portnoy in *Portnoy's Complaint*), or at least for portraying such characters in America, where his work could be read by anti-Semites (see Roth, 1963). While the ostensible reason for this concern was the possibility that such portrayals might lead to anti-Semitism, Roth also suggests that "what is really objected to, what is immediately painful . . . is its direct effect upon certain Jews. 'You have hurt a lot of people's feelings because you have revealed something they are ashamed of.'" The implication of Roth's critics is that the ingroup should be portrayed in positive terms; and indeed, the most common type of Jewish literary activity has portrayed Jews as having positive traits (Alter, 1965, p. 72). Roth's quote also reflects the discussion of Jewish self-deception in SAID

---

[29] The New Christian ideology implies that members of a highly cohesive, economically successful group are seeking to be judged as individuals rather than as members of a group by the surrounding society. It is of interest that the moral imperative of judging on the basis of individual merit was also a theme in the work of nineteenth-century Jewish writer Michael Beer (see Kahn, 1985, p. 122) and is a major theme of the contemporary neoconservative movement of Jewish intellectuals (see Ch. 4). Beer was forced to disguise the identity of his protagonist (as a lower-caste Hindu) because his audience was unlikely to view an explicitly Jewish protagonist positively.

[30] Castro's thesis is that economic and intellectual backwardness was the heavy price Spain paid for its successful resistance to the ideology of individual merit. As noted in SAID (Ch. 1), maladaptive ideologies can develop in the context of group conflict because they provide a positive social identity in opposition to an outgroup. Thus Spain was unlikely to move toward an individualist, post-Enlightenment society when the advocates of individualism were viewed as covertly having allegiance to a highly cohesive group.

(Ch. 8): the shame resulting from awareness of actual Jewish behavior is only half-conscious, and any challenge to this self-deception results in a great deal of psychological conflict.

The importance of social identity processes in Jewish intellectual activity was recognized some time ago by Thorstein Veblen (1934). Veblen described the preeminence of Jewish scholars and scientists in Europe and noted their tendency to be iconoclasts. He noted that while the Enlightenment had destroyed the ability of Jewish intellectuals to find comfort in the identity provided by religion, they do not simply accept uncritically the intellectual structures of gentile society. By engaging in iconoclasm, Veblen (p. 229) suggests, Jews are in fact subjecting to criticism the basic social categorization system of the gentile world—a categorization system with which the gentile, but not the Jew, is comfortable:

> [The Jew] is not ... invested with the gentile's peculiar heritage of conventional preconceptions which have stood over, by inertia of habit, out of the gentile past, which go, on the one hand, to make the safe and sane gentile conservative and complacent, and which conduce also, on the other hand, to blur the safe and sane gentile's intellectual vision, and to leave him intellectually sessile.[31]

Indeed, Jewish social scientists have at least sometimes been aware of these linkages. Peter Gay (1987, p. 137) quotes the following from a 1926 letter written by Sigmund Freud, whose antipathy to Western culture is described in Chapter 5: "Because I was a Jew, I found myself free from many prejudices

---

[31] Paul Johnson (1987/1988, p. 408) takes the view that Jewish iconoclasm simply sped up "changes that were coming anyway. The Jews were natural iconoclasts. Like the prophets, they set about smiting and overturning all the idols of the conventional modes with skill and ferocious glee." Because it essentially trivializes the ultimate effects of Jewish intellectual efforts, such a view is inconsistent with Johnson's claim that the emergence of Jews into the mainstream of Western intellectual discourse was "an event of shattering importance to world history" (pp. 340–341). Johnson offers no evidence for his view that the changes advocated by Jewish intellectuals were inevitable. Surely traditional Judaism did not encourage iconoclasm within the Jewish community—witness Spinoza's fate and the generally authoritarian nature of community controls in traditional Jewish society (PTSDA, Ch. 8)—nor did traditional Jewish scholarship encourage iconoclasm. Although Talmudic studies definitely encouraged argumentation (pilpul; see PTSDA, Ch. 7), these discussions were performed within a very narrowly prescribed range in which the basic assumptions were not questioned. In the post-Enlightenment world, Jewish iconoclasm has clearly been much more directed at gentile culture than at Judaism, and evidence provided here and in the following chapters indicates that the iconoclasm was often motivated by hostility toward gentile culture. By Johnson's own account, both Marxism and psychoanalysis are unlikely to have arisen from gentiles, since they both contain strong overtones of Jewish religious thinking, and I would argue that psychoanalysis especially is unlikely to have arisen except as a tool in the war on gentile culture. The results are much more plausibly due to the generally higher verbal IQ among Jews and their ability to form cohesive groups now directed at critiquing gentile culture rather than at comprehending the Torah and thereby achieving status within the Jewish community.

which limited others in the employment of their intellects, and as a Jew I was prepared to go into opposition and to do without the agreement of the 'compact majority.'" In another letter, Freud stated that to accept psychoanalysis "called for a certain measure of readiness to accept a situation of solitary opposition—a situation with which nobody is more familiar than a Jew" (in p. 146).[32]

There is a profound sense of alienation vis-à-vis the surrounding society. The Jewish intellectual, in the words of New York Intellectual and political radical Irving Howe (1978, p. 106), tends "to feel at some distance from society; to assume, almost as a birthright, a critical stance toward received dogmas, to recognize oneself as not quite at home in the world." John Murray Cuddihy (1974, p. 68) notes (see Preface) the hostility of Jewish intellectuals to Western culture and institutions: "This wonder, this anger, and the vindictive objectivity of the marginal nonmember are recidivist; they continue unabated into our own time be-cause Jewish Emancipation continues into our own time."

Although intellectual criticism resulting from social identity processes need not be functional in attaining any concrete goal of Judaism, this body of theory is highly compatible with supposing that Jewish intellectual activity may be directed at influencing social categorization processes in a manner that benefits Jews. Evidence will be provided in later chapters that Jewish intellectual movements have advocated universalist ideologies for the entire society in which the Jew-gentile social category is reduced in salience and is of no theoretical importance. Thus, for example, within a Marxist analysis social conflict is theorized to result solely from economically based conflict between social classes in which resource competition between ethnic groups is irrelevant. Social identity research predicts that the acceptance of such a theory would lessen anti-Semitism because within the universalist ideology the Jew-gentile social categorization is not salient.

Finally, there is good reason to suppose that minority perspectives are able to have a strong influence on the attitudes of the majority (e.g., Pérez & Mugny, 1990). Social identity research indicates that a minority viewpoint, especially when possessing a high degree of internal consistency, is able to have an impact,

> because it introduces the possibility of an alternative to the taken-for-granted, unquestioned, consensual majority perspective. Suddenly people can discern cracks in the façade of majority consensus. New issues,

---

[32] The comment referring to "solitary opposition" is disingenuous, since psychoanalysis from its origins was characterized by a strong group consciousness emanating from a committed core of members. Psychoanalysis itself energetically cultivated the image of Freud as a solitary hero-scientist battling for truth against a biased, hostile intellectual establishment. See Chapter 5.

problems, and questions arise which demand attention. The status quo is no longer passively accepted as an immutable and stable entity which is the sole legitimate arbiter of the nature of things. People are free to change their beliefs, views, customs, and so forth. And where do they turn? One direction is to the active minority. It (by definition and design) furnishes a conceptually coherent and elegantly simple resolution of the very issues which, due to its activities, now plague the public conscious-ness. In the language of "ideology" . . . active minorities seek to replace the dominant ideology with a new one. (Hogg & D. Abrams, 1988, p. 181)

A critical component of minority group influence is intellectual con-sistency (Moscovici, 1976), and an important theme in the following will be that Jewish-dominated intellectual movements have had a high degree of internal group cohesion and have often expelled dissenters. And they have often been typified by high levels of ingroup-outgroup thinking—a traditional aspect of Judaism. However, because these movements were intended to appeal to gen-tiles, they were forced to minimize any overt indication that Jewish group identity or Jewish group interests were important to the participants.

Such a result is also highly compatible with social identity theory: the ex-tent to which individuals are willing to be influenced depends on their willing-ness to accept the social category from which the divergent opinion derives. For Jews intent on influencing the wider society, overt Jewish group identity and overtly stated Jewish interests could only detract from the ability of these movements to influence their intended targets. As a result, Jewish involvement in these movements was often actively concealed, and the intellectual struc-tures themselves were phrased in universalist terms to minimize the im-portance of the social category of Jew-gentile.

Moreover, since one's willingness to accept influence depends on one's willingness to identify with the stereotypical qualities of an ingroup, the move-ments were not only conceptualized in terms of universalism, rather than Jew-ish particularism, but were also depicted as motivated only by the highest moral and ethical standards. As Cuddihy (1974, p. 66n) notes, Jewish intellectu-als developed a sense that Judaism had a "mission to the West" in which cor-rupt Western civilization would be confronted by a specifically Jewish sense of morality. To a considerable extent these movements constitute concrete ex-amples of the ancient and recurrent Jewish self-conceptualization as a "light of the nations," reviewed extensively in SAID (Ch. 7). This rhetoric of moral con-demnation of the outgroup thus represents a secular version of the central pose of post-Enlightenment Jewish intellectuals, that Judaism represents a moral beacon to the rest of humanity; but to exert their influence, they were forced to deny the importance of specifically Jewish identity and interests at the heart of the movement.

Such appeals to virtue are particularly effective if the virtue-signaling group has power in the media and academic world—as Jews certainly do (see Preface)—and such appeals are particularly effective in Western societies because of Western individualism. Western societies are uniquely based on moral communities rather than kinship, and moral communities are created in a top-down process emanating from media and academic elites in which Jews are highly overrepresented (*Individualism*, especially Ch. 8).

The high degree of internal group cohesion characteristic of the movements considered in this volume was accompanied by the development of theories that not only possessed a great deal of internal intellectual consistency but also, as in the case of psychoanalysis and radical political theory, could take the form of hermeneutic systems able to accommodate any and all events into their interpretive schemas. And although these movements sought the veneer of science, they inevitably controverted the fundamental principles of science as an individualistic inquiry into the nature of reality (see Ch. 7). Although the extent to which these intellectual and political movements influenced gentile society cannot be assessed with certainty, the material presented in the following chapters is highly compatible with supposing that Jewish-dominated intellectual movements were a critical factor (i.e., a necessary condition) for the triumph of the intellectual left in late twentieth-century Western societies.

CONCLUSION

No evolutionist should be surprised at the implicit theory in all this, namely that intellectual activities of all types may at bottom involve ethnic warfare, any more than one should be surprised at the fact that political and religious ideologies typically reflect the interests of those holding them. The truly doubtful proposition for an evolutionist is whether real social science as a disinterested attempt to understand human behavior is at all possible.

This does not imply that all strongly identified Jewish social scientists participated in the movements discussed in the following chapters. It implies only that Jewish identification and perceived Jewish interests were a powerful motivating force among those who led these movements and among many of their followers. As I will attempt to show, these scientist-activists had very strong Jewish identities. They were very concerned with anti-Semitism and self-consciously developed theories aimed at showing that Jewish behavior was irrelevant to anti-Semitism while at same time (in the case of psychoanalysis and the Frankfurt School) showing that gentile ethnocentrism and participation in cohesive anti-Semitic movements were indications of psychopathology.

Collectively, these movements have called into question the fundamental moral, political, cultural, and economic foundations of Western society. It will be apparent that these movements have served various Jewish interests quite well. It will also become apparent, however, that these movements have often conflicted with the cultural and ultimately genetic interests of important sectors of the non-Jewish, European-derived peoples of late twentieth-century European and North American societies.

2

THE BOASIAN SCHOOL OF ANTHROPOLOGY AND THE DECLINE OF DARWINISM IN THE SOCIAL SCIENCES

If . . . we were to treat Margaret Mead's Coming of Age in Samoa *as utopia, not as ethnography, then we would understand it better and save a lot of pointless debate.*

— Robin Fox, 1989, p. 3

Several writers have commented on the "radical changes" that occurred in the goals and methods of the social sciences consequent to the entry of Jews to these fields (C. Liebman, 1973, p. 213; see also Degler, 1991; Hollinger, 1996; I. L. Horowitz, 1993, p. 75; Rothman & Lichter, 1982/1996). Degler (1991, pp. 187ff) notes that the shift away from Darwinism as the fundamental paradigm of the social sciences resulted from an ideological shift rather than from the emergence of any new empirical data:

As we have seen in regard to the shift in outlook among anthropologists and sociologists, professional or scientific attitudes were not the full explanation. One needs to look beyond professionalism and standard science; for the change in outlook was too fundamental, too radical to be accounted for on those grounds alone. After all, we are not dealing here with a long-held, well-substantiated theory (that is, race) which new and conclusive evidence had unambiguously disproved and overturned. Rather we

31

see essentially the substitution of one unproved (though strongly held) assumption by another. (p. 187)

Degler (1991, p. 200) also notes that Jewish intellectuals have been instrumental in the decline of Darwinism and other biological perspectives in American social science since the 1930s. The opposition of Jewish intellectuals to Darwinism has long been noticed (e.g., Lenz, 1931, p. 674; see also the comments of John Maynard Smith in Lewin, 1992, p. 43).[33]

In sociology, the advent of Jewish intellectuals in the pre-World War II period resulted in "a level of politicization unknown to sociology's founding fathers. It is not only that the names of Marx, Weber, and Durkheim replaced those of Charles Darwin and Herbert Spencer, but also that the sense of America as a consensual experience gave way to a sense of America as a series of conflicting definitions" (I. L. Horowitz, 1993, p. 75). In the post-World War II period, sociology "became populated by Jews to such a degree that jokes abounded: one did not need the synagogue, the *minyan* [i.e., the minimum number of Jews required for a communal religious service] was to be found in sociology departments; or, one did not need a sociology of Jewish life, since the two had become synonymous" (p. 77). Indeed, the ethnic conflict within American sociology parallels to a remarkable degree the ethnic conflict in American anthropology, a theme of this chapter. Here the conflict was played out between leftist Jewish social scientists and an old-line, empirically oriented Protestant establishment that was eventually eclipsed:

---

[33] Lenz (1931, p. 675) notes the historical association between Jewish intellectuals and Lamarckism in Germany and its political overtones. Lenz cites an "extremely characteristic" statement of a Jewish intellectual: "The denial of the racial importance of acquired characters favours race hatred." The obvious interpretation of such sentiments is that Jewish intellectuals opposed the theory of natural selection because of its possible negative political implications. The suggestion is that these intellectuals were well aware of ethnic differences between Jews and Germans but wished to deny their importance for political reasons—an example of deception as an aspect of Judaism as an evolutionary strategy (SAID, Chs. 6–8). Indeed, Lenz notes that the Lamarckian Paul Kammerer, who was a Jew, committed suicide when exposed as a scientific fraud in an article in the prestigious British journal *Nature*. (The black spots on frogs, which were supposed to prove the theory of Lamarckism, were in fact the result of injections of ink.) Lenz states that many of his Jewish acquaintances accept Lamarckism because they wish to believe that they could become "transformed into genuine Teutons." Such a belief may be an example of deception, since it fosters the idea that Jews can become "genuine Teutons" simply by "writing books about Goethe," in the words of one commentator, despite retaining their genetic separatism. In a note (p. 674n), Lenz chides both the anti-Semites and the Jews of his day, the former for not accepting a greater influence of Judaism on modern civilization, and the latter for condemning any discussion of Judaism in terms of race. Lenz states that the Jewish opposition to discussion of race "inevitably arouses the impression that they must have some reason for fighting shy of any exposition of racial questions." Lenz notes that Lamarckism became less common among Jews when the theory was completely discredited; nevertheless, two very prominent and influential Jewish intellectuals, Franz Boas (D. Freeman, 1983, p. 28) and Sigmund Freud (see Ch. 5), continued to accept it.

American sociology has struggled with the contrary claims of those afflicted with physics envy and researchers ... more engaged in the dilemmas of society. In that struggle, midwestern Protestant mandarins of positivist science often came into conflict with East Coast Jews who in turn wrestled with their own Marxist commitments; great quantitative researchers from abroad, like Paul Lazarsfeld at Columbia, sought to disrupt the complacency of native bean counters. (Sennett, 1995, p. 43)

This chapter will emphasize the ethnopolitical agenda of Franz Boas, but it is worth mentioning the work of Franco-Jewish structuralist anthropologist Claude Lévi-Strauss because he appears to have been similarly motivated, although the French structuralist movement as a whole cannot be viewed as a Jewish intellectual movement. Lévi-Strauss interacted extensively with Boas and acknowledged his influence (Dosse, 1997 I, pp. 15, 16). In turn, Lévi-Strauss was very influential in France, Dosse (p. xxi) describing him as "the common father" of Michel Foucault, Louis Althusser, Roland Barthes, and Jacques Lacan. He had a strong Jewish identity and a deep concern with anti-Semitism (Cuddihy, 1974, pp. 151ff). In response to an assertion that he was "the very picture of a Jewish intellectual," Lévi-Strauss stated,

[C]ertain mental attitudes are perhaps more common among Jews than elsewhere. . . . Attitudes that come from the profound feeling of belonging to a national community, all the while knowing that in the midst of this community there are people—fewer and fewer of them, I admit—who reject you. One keeps one's sensitivity attuned, accompanied by the irrational feeling that in all circumstances one has to do a bit more than other people to disarm potential critics. (Lévi-Strauss & Eribon, 1991, pp. 155–156)

Like many Jewish intellectuals discussed here, Lévi-Strauss's writings were aimed at enshrining cultural differences and subverting the universalist Western approaches to science, a position that validates the position of Judaism as a non-assimilating group. Like Boas, Lévi-Strauss rejected biological and evolutionary theories. He theorized that cultures, like languages, were arbitrary collections of symbols with no natural relationships to their referents. Lévi-Strauss rejected Western modernization theory in favor of the idea that there were no superior societies. The role of the anthropologist was to be a "natural subversive or convinced opponent of traditional usage" (in Cuddihy, 1974, p. 155) in Western societies, while respecting and even romanticizing the virtues of non-Western societies (see Dosse, 1997 II, p. 30). Western universalism and ideas of human rights were viewed as masks for ethnocentrism, colonialism, and genocide:

Lévi-Strauss's most significant works were all published during the breakup of the French colonial empire and contributed enormously to the way it was understood by intellectuals. . . . [H]is elegant writings worked an aesthetic transformation on his readers, who were subtly made to feel ashamed to be Europeans. . . . [H]e evoked the beauty, dignity, and irreducible strangeness of Third World cultures that were simply trying to preserve their difference. . . . [H]is writings would soon feed the suspicion among the new left . . . that all the universal ideas to which Europe claimed allegiance—reason, science, progress, liberal democracy—were culturally specific weapons fashioned to rob the non-European Other of his difference. (Lilla, 1998)

PART I: BOASIAN ANTHROPOLOGY AS A JEWISH INTELLECTUAL MOVEMENT

Carl Degler (1991, p. 61) emphasizes the role of Franz Boas in the anti-Darwinian transformation of American social science: "Boas's influence upon American social scientists in matters of race can hardly be exaggerated." Boas engaged in a "life-long assault on the idea that race was a primary source of the differences to be found in the mental or social capabilities of human groups. He accomplished his mission largely through his ceaseless, almost relentless articulation of the concept of culture" (p. 61), and "Boas, almost single-handedly, developed in America the concept of culture, which, like a powerful solvent, would in time expunge race from the literature of social science" (p. 71). Degler (pp. 82–83) goes on to write:

Boas did not arrive at that position from a disinterested, scientific inquiry into a vexed if controversial question. . . . There is no doubt that he had a deep interest in collecting evidence and designing arguments that would rebut or refute an ideological outlook—racism—which he considered restrictive upon individuals and undesirable for society. . . . Much evidence does come to light in [his] correspondence to suggest a persistent interest in pressing his social values upon the profession and the public.

As Gelya Frank (1997, p. 731) points out, "The preponderance of Jewish intellectuals in the early years of Boasian anthropology and the Jewish identities of anthropologists in subsequent generations has been downplayed in standard histories of the discipline." Jewish identifications and the pursuit of perceived Jewish interests, particularly in advocating an ideology of cultural pluralism as a model for Western societies, has been the "invisible subject" of American anthropology—invisible because the ethnic identifications and ethnic interests of its advocates have been masked by a language of science in which such identifications and interests were publicly illegitimate. Indeed,

Gershenhorn (2004, p. 20) notes that "Boas was influenced by his liberal philosophy, his strict attachment to scientific accuracy, and perhaps most important, his Jewish identity," despite the obvious fact that a strong ethnic identity might well interfere with scientific objectivity. And as noted, Boas's views were not the result of "disinterested, scientific inquiry" (Degler, 1991, p. 82).

Franz Boas as Jewish Academic Activist

Boas was reared in a "Jewish-liberal" family in which the revolutionary ideals of 1848 remained influential—e.g., his mother established a Froebel kindergarten which was a "a highly contested left-liberal innovation" (Frank, 1997, p. 733). He developed a "left-liberal posture which . . . is at once scientific and political" (Stocking, 1968, p. 149). Boas was intensely concerned with anti-Semitism from an early period in his life (L. White, 1966, p. 16); for example, he was aware that his chances for a university professorship in geography in Germany were likely to be limited, as he stated in letters, because of his Jewish origins and his outspokenness. "His writings from 1882 to 1884 indicate that he felt alienated from the Germany of his day" (Stocking, p. 150), a reality that motivated him and his non-Jewish wife Marie Krackowizer, the daughter of a revolutionary socialist from Vienna, to move to America. Alfred Kroeber (1943, p. 8) recounted a story,

> which [Boas] is said to have revealed confidentially but which cannot be vouched for, . . . that on hearing an anti-Semitic insult in a public café, he threw the speaker out of doors, and was challenged. Next morning his adversary offered to apologize; but Boas insisted that the duel be gone through with. Apocryphal or not, the tale absolutely fits the character of the man as we know him in America.

Anti-Jewish attitudes were becoming increasingly common in the Germany of Boas's youth, an era when anti-Jewish writers and organizers achieved prominence. People like Wilhelm Marr (author of *The Victory of Jewry over Germandom*), Christian populist organizer Adolf Stoecker, and prominent academic Heinrich von Treitschke voiced concerns about eventual Jewish domination of the economy, the stock exchanges, and the newspapers. Although there were ups and downs in the intensity of anti-Semitism, the general trend over the course of the nineteenth and early twentieth centuries was that calls for assimilation were increasingly replaced by calls for cohesive, collectivist gentile groups that would enable Germans to compete with Jews and even exclude them entirely from German economic and social life (see SAID, Ch. 5).

Despite Jewish declarations and appearances of assimilation (e.g., the movement of Reform Judaism designed to remove overt signs of Jewish separatism), Jews continued to "move in social and occupational circles that were disproportionately Jewish" (Glick, 1982, p. 548). To quote a passage from Chapter 5 of SAID (pp. 166–167):

In addition to a very visible group of Orthodox immigrants from Eastern Europe, Reform Jews generally opposed intermarriage, and secular Jews developed a wide range of institutions that effectively cut them off from socializing with gentiles. "What secular Jews remained attached to was not easy to define, but neither, for the Jews involved, was it easy to let go of: there were family ties, economic interests, and perhaps above all sentiments and habits of mind which could not be measured and could not be eradicated" (Katz 1996, 33). Moreover, a substantial minority of German Jews, especially in rural areas and in certain geographical regions (especially Bavaria) remained Orthodox well into the 20th century (Lowenstein 1992, 18). Vestiges of traditional separatist practices, such as Yiddish words, continued throughout this period.

Intermarriage between Jews and Germans was negligible in the 19th century. Even though intermarriage increased later, these individuals and their children "almost always" were lost to the Jewish community (Katz 1985, 86; see also Levenson 1989, 321n). "Opposition to intermarriage did constitute the bottom line of Jewish assimilation" (G. Mosse 1985, 9). These patterns of endogamy and within-group association constituted the most obvious signs of continued Jewish group separatism in German society for the entire period prior to the rise of National Socialism. Levenson (1989, 321) notes that Jewish defences of endogamy during this period "invariably appeared to hostile non-Jews as being misanthropic and ungrateful," another indication that Jewish endogamy was an important ingredient of the anti-Semitism of the period.

Moreover, Jewish converts would typically marry other Jewish converts and continue to live among and associate with Jews (Levenson 1989, 321n), in effect behaving as crypto-Jews. The importance of genealogy rather than surface religion can also be seen in that, while baptized Jews of the *haute bourgeoisie* were viewed as acceptable marriage partners by the Jewish *haute bourgeoisie*, gentiles of the *haute bourgeoisie* were not ([W. E.] Mosse 1989, 335). These patterns may well have fed into the perception among Germans that even overt signs of assimilation were little more than window dressing masking a strong sense of Jewish ethnic identity and a desire for endogamy. Indeed, the general pattern was that complete loss of Jewishness was confined to females from a "handful" of families who had married into the gentile aristocracy ([W. E.] Mosse 1989, 181).

Boas experienced anti-Semitism at his university: "The correspondence repeatedly shows how central this problem [anti-Semitism] was in Boas's formative years. A letter from October 6, 1870 records a poignant incident. His

letters from Kiel are particularly full of accounts of unpleasant activities and gross personal behavior" (Kluckhohn & Prufer, 1959, pp. 10–11). Glick (1982, p. 553) notes that during Boas's university years, "Volkish ideology and anti-Semitism were a pervasive feature of life, something that no Jewish student could ignore. . . . Thus it's not surprising that many Jews, Franz Boas among them, departed for America."

Volkish anti-Semitism was based on an ideology of opposing ethnic interests, that the rise of a Jewish economic and media elite compromised the interests of Germans as a people, resulting, as noted above, in increasing calls for Germans to cohere into collectivist groups to compete with Jews. But Boas publicly claimed that Jews were only a religious group, thus avoiding issues related to ethnic conflicts of interest: "He did not acknowledge a specifically Jewish cultural or ethnic identity. . . . To the extent that Jews were possessed of a culture, it was . . . strictly a matter of religious adherence" (Glick, 1982, p. 554). Nevertheless, his Jewish identity was central to his scientific work: "Boas's primary self-definition as a scientist came in response to being Jewish, not to being 'white'" (Liss, 1998, p. 153). But although their Jewish identification was central to the work of Jewish intellectuals during this period, it was never framed as specifically Jewish. Liss (p. 153) continues:

> As David Hollinger has argued for a somewhat later time period, Jews transformed the academy, particularly the sciences, with their "cosmopolitan, enlightenment-inspired" outlook and refusal "to be Jewish parochials" (1996:19). Similarly, in his time, Boas also persisted in the belief that science could offer a cosmopolitan answer to the particularism of prejudice. This different self-concept encouraged Boas to continue his faith in science by separating the cultural self from the intellectual problems he addressed, to evade, in effect, a racialized view of self.

After leaving Germany because of anti-Semitism, Boas immigrated to the United States "where he endured outsider status as an immigrant and a Jew. By attacking racist science, which concluded that blacks were inferior to whites, Boas was also able to mount an indirect challenge to the anti-Semitic belief that Jews were an inferior race" (Gershenhorn, 2004, p. 20). Ignoring Gershenhorn's negative comments on the racial science of the day, this clearly shows that Boas's research was motivated at least in part by his sense of Jewish interests. Boas was thus an example of David L. Lewis's observation that Jews supported civil rights for Blacks and attacked racial science in order to "fight anti-Semitism by remote control."

> By assisting in the crusade to prove that Afro-Americans could be decent, conformist, cultured human beings, the civil rights Jews were, in a sense,

spared some of the necessity of directly rebutting anti-Semitic stereotypes; for if blacks could make good citizens, clearly, most white Americans believed, all other groups could make better ones. (D. L. Lewis, 1992,
p. 31)

D. L. Lewis (1984, p. 84) notes that the Jewish press often compared the
situation of Jews to the situation of Blacks, e.g., comparing the 1917 race riot in
East St. Louis to the 1903 Kishinev pogrom in Russia; and *Forward* editor Abraham Cahan commenting on the Pulitzer Prize-winning play *The Green Pastures*
(1930, the first Broadway play with an all-Black cast) that, "In this play [pre-
senting Old Testament stories from a Black perspective], the souls of two nations are woven together." According to D. L. Lewis (p. 85), even prior to the
1920s,

> the NAACP had something of the aspect of an adjunct of B'nai B'rith and
> the American Jewish Committee, with the brothers Joel and Arthur
> Spingarn serving as board chairman and chief legal counsel respectively;
> Herbert Lehman on the executive committee; Lillian Wald and Walter
> Sachs on the board . . . ; and Jacob Schiff and Paul Warburg [the latter two
> of whom supported Boas's research financially; see below] as financial an-
> gels.

Boas himself was one of the Jews "closely connected with the NAACP and
the Urban League" (D. L. Lewis, 1984, p. 91). Further, "upper-crust Jews established the Kehillah and other defense organizations, and mobilized the formidable scholarship of Franz Boas and Alexander Goldenweiser" (p. 88).

Similarly, David S. Koffman (2019, p. 176) has documented how Jewish anthropologists advocated for the cause of Native Americans because of their
Jewish identity, while at the same time "they assumed that their own Jewishness would remain an invisible and insignificant force in shaping the ideas they
would use to shape ideas about others." He continues:

> This chapter argues that the Jewishness of so many of this first generation
> of professional anthropologists mattered; Jewishness shaped the profes-
> sion's engagement with its principal object of study, the American Indian,
> just as it steered the intellectual agenda of American anthropology. It de-
> scribes anthropology's antiracism agenda and considers how Jews' ef-
> forts— presented as the efforts of science itself—to salvage, collect, and
> preserve disappearing American Indian culture was a form of ventrilo-
> quism. Anthropologists like Edward Sapir, Paul Radin, Sol Tax, Leslie Spier,
> Ruth Leah Bunzel, Edgar Siskin, and many more focused on Native Amer-
> ican families, religions, languages, and cultures. These foci dovetailed with
> the concerns that preoccupied American Jewry in the 1930s through the

1950s. Jewish anthropologists devoted portions of their extraprofessional energies to both Jewish and Native American causes. (Koffman, 2019, p. 18)

They strongly identified as Jews:

Boas and his fellow Jewish immigrant students Edward Sapir, Paul Radin, and Robert Lowie, along with dozens of their students, recorded, classified, and analyzed the cultures of "disappearing" Native worlds. Most of these anthropologists came of age in New York in the 1920s, and more than half of them trained at Columbia University under Boas. They either descended from eastern or central European Jewish immigrants or had immigrated themselves. These Jews tended to marry other Jews, be buried in Jewish cemeteries, and socialize with fellow Jews, all core features of Jewish ethnicity, though they conceived of themselves as agents of science and enlightenment, not Jewish activists. (Koffman, 2019, pp. 180–181)

And they worked for Jewish causes:

In addition to the fieldwork, ethnographies, and public and scholarly writings that they produced about American Indians, many American Jewish anthropologists also devoted considerable time and attention to Jewish causes both in their professional print life and in private. Political action formed a part of many anthropologists' sense of the intellectual mission of the field. Their findings, and the framings of distinct cultures, each worthy of careful attention in its own right, mattered to social existence in the United States. Their scholarship on Native American cultures and languages developed alongside their personal and political work on behalf of Jewish causes, though Jewish anthropologists neither conceived of themselves as a group per se nor interacted in intentional concert with one another. (Koffman, 2019, p. 170)

For example, Koffman (2019, p. 183) discusses Melville Jacobs:

As a political actor on behalf of Jewish issues, Jacobs worked with the Academic Friends of Hebrew University, the Conference of Christians and Jews, the Hillel Foundation, the B'nai B'rith, the Anti-Defamation League (ADL), and YIVO [Institute for Jewish Research]. He scrawled marginalia on the ADL bulletins to which he subscribed on matters of Jewish concern, including Nazism and the fate of Jewish communists. Dozens of items in his personal archives make clear that Jacobs keenly read about Jewish issues and felt them sharply in the 1930s and 1940s.

And Edward Sapir:

He learned Hebrew, engaged in the study of Torah, and excluded shellfish and pork from his diet, though he did not observe Jewish holidays. His first marriage was to a Jewish woman, Florence Delson, his cousin, and his second, to Jean Victoria McClenaghan, was said to have endured rough patches on account of his Jewish background. . . .

Indeed, Sapir's Jewish background continuously influenced and intersected with his scholarship on American Indians. Sapir's biography shows a fascinating parallel preoccupation with both Native and Jewish social issues. These tracks run side by side, concerned as both were with parallel questions about ethnic survival, adaptability, dignity, cultural autonomy, and ethnicity. . . . While working to repeal an antipotlach law in Canada, for example, he was writing his "Notes on Judeo-German Phonology." . . .

While at the University of Chicago between 1926 and 1931, Sapir thrived in the social milieu of Chicago Jewish intelligentsia as a frequent guest at the homes of Louis Wirth, Henry Schultz, Jacob Viner, Morris Swadesh, Max Radin, Paul Radin, and Ralph Linton. Through ethnomusicologist George Herzog's wife Betsy, Sapir was introduced to wealthy Chicago Jewry with whom he socialized. In 1931, Sapir moved to Yale, where, according to his biographer Regna Darnell, he became "more and more engrossed in and concerned with the problems of being a Jew and with the turmoil of modern events." His personal experience with anti-Semitism at Yale, combined with the growth of anti-Semitism worldwide, seems to have profoundly impacted his Jewish identification. Jews, he concluded, were stuck in a conflict between cultures that was "perpetually insoluble," a predicament with which he himself must have certainly identified. In New Haven, he also befriended Maurice Zigmond, a nonpracticing orthodox rabbi and Yale Semitics PhD, with whom he discussed Talmud. He also struck up a friendship and talked at length about Jewish matters with Edgar Siskin, another rabbi cum graduate student at Yale (in anthropology). Sapir sat on YIVO's honorary committee with some of the most prominent Jewish intellectuals of the twentieth century: Salo Baron, Horrace Kallen, Simon Dubnow, Albert Einstein, Sigmund Freud, Moses Gaster, Berhard Wachsein, and Chaim Zhitlovsky. Sapir wrote to colleagues on behalf of YIVO in 1933 about a project that he, Boas, Wirth, and Weinreich hoped to undertake for an "extensive study of personality of the eastern European Jew under conditions of rapid social change." He established the American Intra-University Committee on Jewish Social Science with Leonard Bloomfield, Melville Herskovits, Max Radin, Henry Schultz, and Louis Wirth. "I cannot imagine a more exalted and a more practical way for bringing the Jewish masses of Eastern Europe and America into strong contact with the world culture," he wrote, "than forging a language [i.e., Yiddish] held in scorn into an instrument of a magnificent, clear, creative expression." Sapir was one of the founders of the Conference on Jewish Social Studies, which launched the journal *Jewish Social*

Studies in 1939, served as its vice president until his death, and helped organize the Conference on Jewish Relations, a national committee of eminent Jewish scholars interested in the scientific evaluation of social trends affecting Jews. "In conversation," recalled one of his Jewish students, Sapir "would occasionally tell how profoundly Judaism had affected his life." He wrote of "the necessity of having a cultural background if one is to be oneself." He grew a sizable library of Judaica, read the Bible in Hebrew, and acquired several sets of the Talmud. He agonized over Hitler's rise to power. As president of the American Anthropological Association, Sapir wrote to Boas about drafting a protest statement against the Nazi government and its treatment of the Jews; Boas, along with 13,000 distinguished signatories, published a letter in Nature magazine denouncing Nazism.

Sapir used the tools of social science, motivated by the spirit of relativism and liberalism, to promote ethnic Jewish identity as well as the social and economic health of Jewish communal, urban, cultural, and even religious life. . . .

These and still other Jewish anthropologists took to the study of American Indian life with an explicit, progressive, antirace agenda. As scholars and as Jews, they provided a dual service: to a liberalism that promoted ethically grounded, limited intellectual relativism on the one hand and to these scholars' sense of how liberalism would best serve different peoples' needs on the other. They studied Native American cultures and understood this effort as a contribution to building a more multiethnic America. Their work was simultaneously ethnographic and social-justice oriented. (Koffman, 2019, pp. 184–187)

Paul Radin was less explicitly Jewish. However:

Alongside the American Zionist leader and founder of Hadassah, the Women's Zionist Organization of America, Henrietta Szold, Radin helped translate Louis Ginzberg's *The Legends of the Jews*. He addressed the Jewish Historical Society of England on the topic of monotheism among primitive peoples in 1924. He was, in other words, hardly devoid of or divorced from the influences of his Jewish milieu. (Koffman, 2019, p. 184)

Some Jewish anthropologists avoided referencing Jewishness in their professional writing. Some even avoided using Jewish examples to illustrate more general points in their scholarly publications and in their writings for public audiences in newspapers, popular journals, pamphlets writing on race, or in other public forums. This absence is certainly remarkable, but to focus on scholars' scholarly writing alone misses an important point—namely, that many Jewish anthropologists and other social scientists maintained some measure of existential filiation with their Jewishness, irrespective of how they construed this Jewishness. They kept abreast of American and international Jewish news and issues, subscribed to Jewish papers, sat on the boards of Jewish organizations, and maintained correspondences with Jewish communal agencies, even if they avoided Jewish matters in print. . . . They often socialized in Jewish circles and ritually marked their own lives with Jewish rite of passage rituals (like weddings and funerals). Some Jewish anthropologists married one another: Erna Gunther and Leslie Spier, and Gene Weltfish and Alexander Lesser. David Mandelbaum's classmate and fellow rabbi, Edgar Siskin, found him a job and introduced him to his future wife, Ruth Weiss. Maurice Zigmond, their Yale classmate and fellow rabbi, married the two. These Jewish scholars were engaged with Jewish questions, in other words, if inconsistently and unevenly, even as they avoided writing about Jews or Jewish subjects. . . . They wanted to be seen as motivated only by science and liberalism, not ethnic investment. (Koffman, 2019, pp. 191–193)

Finding power and influence in the federal government for the first time in America under the Roosevelt Administration, a handful of Jews took to advancing a range of pro-Indian issues with zeal. They helped build the organizational infrastructure and intellectual foundations of the Indian civil rights movement that blossomed in Indian hands after World War II, particularly the Association on American Indian Affairs (AAIA) with the financial backing of quasi-Jewish bodies like the Robert Marshall Trust and the American Civil Liberties Union (ACLU). Within the government itself, William Zimmerman, Nathan Margold, and Felix S. Cohen played fundamental roles in drafting, passing, and implementing the 1934 IRA, consolidating federal case law on Indian affairs, and promoting Indian cultural, economic, health, education, and political interests. The Jews who worked for the Department of the Interior, particularly the Bureau of Indian Affairs (BIA), consistently linked Indian uplift with an articulation of minority rights and cultural pluralism within the United States and on international stages that went beyond Indian paternalism. Jewish activism on behalf of minority rights and cultural autonomy, in rhetoric and in policy, was, simply put, "good for the Jews." Jewish enlightened self-interest impacted the course of American Indian life in the middle of the twentieth century. (Koffman, 2019, p. 18)

Cohen's biographer Dalia Mitchell (2007, p. 32) points out that Cohen's generation of young Jewish lawyers "viewed the study of law as providing tools with which they could challenge the authority of the Anglo-Saxon elite in American life." For Cohen, this involved the "personal hope that American law could remedy wrongs against Jews, specifically forced exclusion" (p. 7)—a reference to the Immigration Act of 1924 which favored Northwest Europeans (see Ch. 8). As Andrew Joyce (2021b, p. 84) notes, "The primary weapon in this fight would be the promotion of pluralism within American law, both by expanding the concept of citizenship and weakening America's borders."

Both Cohen and Margold benefited from Jewish ethnic nepotism:

> Cohen's big break came thanks to FDR's momentous decision to nominate Felix Frankfurter to the Supreme Court. Previously reluctant to hire Jews, the legal establishment in Washington was thereafter inundated thanks to a wave of ethnic nepotism ushered in by Frankfurter. Cohen biographer Alice Kehoe [2014, p. 46] remarks that "Frankfurter unabashedly recommended young Jewish lawyers for federal positions to the point that newspapers wrote of the unprecedented number of Jews hired and of fears that a 'Jewish cabal' was taking over America." Frankfurter was a close personal friend of [Felix Cohen's father and philosopher] Morris Cohen (the pair were also close friends with Horace Kallen), and when Frankfurter hired the family's neighbor Nathan Margold to oversee the legal team at Department of the Interior, it was a foregone conclusion that Margold would in turn hire Felix Cohen to join the team. Like the Cohens, Nathan Margold . . . was an early activist for multiculturalism and author of the 1933 "Margold Report" commissioned by the National Association for the Advancement of Colored People to provide a legal strategy to combat the "separate but equal" theory underlying segregation; he was also a member of the Modern Forum of the League for Peace and Democracy which was named as a Communist front organization by the House Un-American Activities Committee in 1938. . . .
>
> Together at the Interior, Margold and Cohen initially decided to promote pluralism by focusing on the position of Indians/Native Americans in American law. The approach was thought particularly suitable because Cohen's wife, Lucy Kramer, was an anthropologist working alongside Franz Boas (also a friend of Morris Cohen) at Columbia, where she focused on promoting culturally relativistic understandings of Native American life. At one point, for example, Kramer wrote a manuscript titled "Red Man's Gifts to Modern America," which was so overblown and unrealistic that it was rejected by her editor with the comment: "Sounds too much as though ballyhooing. Something which she wants to believe" [Washburn, 2009, p. 604]. . . .
>
> [Cohen] was strident in his insistence, echoing . . . Horace Kallen [see below and Ch. 8], that Jews should be able to continue their separate existence within the 'Melting Pot," viewing Jewish assimilation as "cultural death," [Washburn, 2009, p. 587], and telling one colleague that he would "punch . . . in the nose" anyone who suggested Jews "ought to be beneficially assimilated into the Anglo-Saxon Protestant mainstream of American life" [p. 604]. (Joyce, 2021b, pp. 85, 87)

Gershenhorn (2004, p. 21) notes that "it is no coincidence that many of the scholars who joined with Boas to attack racial hierarchy were also Jewish, including Otto Klineberg, Ashley Montagu, Alexander Goldenweiser, and [Melville] Herskovits. Boas acknowledged this fact in a 1934 speech, noting that much of the important research on race was 'the product of Jewish students and scholars.'" However, he never explains exactly why this non-coincidence might occur, although clearly it has something to do with Jewish identity. In this regard, it is interesting to contrast the attitudes of Boas with a prominent non-Jewish student of his, Alfred Kroeber:

> Whereas Boas's attack on race was intimately connected with his personal and ideological commitment to opportunities for blacks in American society, Kroeber's interest in the concept of culture was almost entirely theoretical and professional. Neither his private nor his public writings reflect the attention to public policy questions regarding blacks or the general question of race in American life that are so conspicuous in Boas's professional correspondence and publications. Kroeber rejected race as an analytical category as forthrightly and thoroughly as Boas, but he reached that position primarily through theory rather than ideology. (Degler, 1991, p. 90).

Kroeber argued that "our business is to promote anthropology rather than to wage battles on behalf of tolerance in other fields" (in Stocking, 1968, p. 286). Nevertheless, although Kroeber did not have a self-conscious political agenda, his education in a leftist-Jewish environment may have had a lasting influence. Frank (1997, p. 734) notes that Kroeber was educated in schools linked to the Ethical Culture movement, "an offshoot of Reform Judaism" linked with leftist educational programs and characterized by an ideology of a humanistic faith that embraced all humanity.

Another non-Jew who has been linked to Boas is Rudolf Virchow, a German scientist who opposed Darwinist explanations of behavior and the idea of superior and inferior races. However, this may well be because Virchow was also a staunch opponent of anti-Semitism: "It seems evident that one of the many things that made Virchow as much of an 'idol' as Boas ever permitted himself was Virchow's stalwart opposition to all forms of anti-Semitism" (Kluckhohn & Prufer, 1959, p. 10).

Nevertheless, the social context of Boas's research was heavily Jewish. As Frank (1997, p. 739) notes, Boas carried out his research within the German-Jewish milieu of New York, and doubtless—given the support for anti-restriction among wealthy German Jews of the period (Okrent, 2019; see Ch. 8)—his views corresponded to those of the wider Jewish community whose views were quite out of step with broader American opinion:

Context is critical . . . to understanding Franz Boas's life and work in relation to being Jewish. Although Boas experienced anti-Semitism in Germany and discrimination as a German immigrant in America, he was able to establish powerful connections and a thriving discipline in the academic mainstream. Many of his contacts and much of his support came, however, from the cosmopolitan New York world in which Jewish Germans were well-established and active. Boas's championing of race equality and racial justice took place in a peculiarly American context: Jews were threatening to nativists who dominated America's institutions, but seemingly less so than other "racial" groups such as blacks, Japanese, and Mexicans.

The following quote is a further indication of the Jewish milieu of Boas's life in America:

> Boas was not a practicing Jew; most likely, he was an atheist. In New York, he became a member of the Society for Ethical Culture, a nondenominational offshoot of Reform Judaism. The Ethical Culture movement was inaugurated in 1876 by [Reform rabbi] Felix Adler, an educator, social activist, and, later, professor of political and social ethics at Columbia University. (Frank, 1997, p. 734)

Glick (1982, p. 556) notes that the Society of Ethical Culture was "heavily and probably predominantly composed of cultivated German Jews for whom it gave organizational legitimacy to the very same values that Boas summarized as 'the ideals of the revolution of 1848.'"

Boas's German Identity. Despite the anti-Semitism he experienced in Germany, it is often said that Boas had a deep fondness for Germany and German culture, as indicated by his involvement with a German-American cultural society and a letter he wrote to *The New York Times* in 1916 opposing the vilification of Germany during World War I. Regarding the former, the Germanistic Society of America had a great many Jewish members at its inception including: Boas, who was the secretary; his cousin Emil Boas, treasurer; and his uncle Abraham Jacobi, who was a financial supporter, a communist friend of Marx and Engels, and later the president of the society (Germanistic Society of America, 1917). By 1910 the roster included wealthy Jewish activists Felix and Paul Warburg and Jacob and Mortimer Schiff (see Germanistic Society of America, 1910), all of whom were associated with Kuhn, Loeb & Co. investment bankers. Felix Warburg, his brother Max, and Jacob Schiff supported Boas's research. This is not to deny that the main goal of the society was to foster appreciation of Germany and its culture in America; the point here is that membership was compatible with Jewish activism.

For example, Felix Warburg was the head of the American Jewish Joint Distribution Committee (AJJDC), which raised millions of dollars for European Jews during this period (twenty-two million dollars in 1919–1920 according to the Felix Warburg entry on *Wikipedia*), and he carried on an extensive correspondence with Boas from 1908 to 1937 (H. S. Lewis, 2020). Jacob Schiff, the head of Kuhn, Loeb & Co., was a major donor to the AJJDC and the premier Jewish activist of the era:

> From his base on Wall Street, he was the foremost Jewish leader from 1880 to 1920 in what later became known as the "Schiff era," grappling with all major Jewish issues and problems of the day, including the plight of Russian Jews under the Tsar, American and international anti-semitism, care of needy Jewish immigrants, and the rise of Zionism. (N. W. Cohen, 1999, book jacket)

Schiff was vice-president of the Baron de Hirsch Fund, which assisted Jews to settle and find work in America, and he sponsored the Anglo-Jewish Association and the Alliance Israélite Universelle to do likewise in Britain and France. As a leading member of the AJCommittee, he lobbied to sever American trade with Russia. He also (with the Rothschilds and Warburgs) financed Japan's war against Russia in 1905, attempted to finance Germany in World War I, and maintained a boycott on lending to the Russian Empire following the Kishinev riots of 1903 and lifted it when Emperor Nicholas abdicated in February 1917. Schiff was closely involved with Boas:

> There are 38 letters from Boas to Schiff from 1904 to 1917 and 27 from Schiff to Boas from 1902. Franz Boas often turned to Jacob Schiff for help with his plans for developing anthropology at the AMNH [American Museum of Natural History], or Columbia, or anywhere that he could further the cause of understanding other cultures. (H. S. Lewis, 2020).

These efforts at times involved ethnic networking. At Boas's request, Schiff contributed money for Berthold Laufer, a Jewish sinologist whose research at the AMNH was supported by Schiff, in an effort to obtain a professorship at Columbia. Besides a variety of liberal-leaning Jews and non-Jews, "the other category [of contributors to a 1906 *festschrift*] consisted of really rich Jewish bankers . . . [who] were also dedicated to Jewish causes" (Schiff to Boas, 1906). (One is impressed by the degree of intermarriage among these banking families—too extensive to go into here.)

Moreover, in 1939 Boas was deeply engaged in attempting to obtain financing for publication and translation for a book on Jewish contributions to German culture authored by Karl Georg Wendinger and "based on the judgement of eminent Germans." Boas thought that such a book would "exert a wholesome influence in Germany," but for obvious reasons that would have to "wait until political conditions change" (Boas to Wendinger, 1939).

Boas and World War I. Given the anti-Semitism of the period and the necessity of posing as a detached, disinterested scientist, it is not surprising that, like most German Jews of his generation, Boas sought to be identified foremost as a German and as little as possible as a Jew—despite his close associations with the Jewish activist community. "He was determined not to be classified as a Jew" (Glick, 1982, p. 554). He portrayed himself as "an autonomous individual," "determined not to be classified as a member of any group" (p. 557).

It is sometimes argued that a letter from 1916 decrying criticism of Germans during World War I shows the predominance of Boas's German identity. However, it should be pointed out that by far the most prominent attitude of Diaspora Jewish communities was to oppose Czarist Russia because of its perceived anti-Semitism and thus support the German war effort. For example, immigrant Jews in the U.K. overwhelmingly refused to be drafted into military service because Germany was fighting Russia (Alderman, 1992, p. 236). As I noted in Chapter 2 of SAID (p. 74):

> It is revealing that the immigrant German-American-Jewish leaders of the American Jewish Committee also favored Germany in World War I, but only until the success of the Bolshevik Revolution. They adopted this position not because of their ties with Germany but rather because of their ties with Russian Jews whom they believed were being oppressed by the czar, and because Germany was at war with Russia.

Moreover, the above-mentioned Jacob Schiff—perhaps the most effective and powerful activist of his era—was a staunch opponent of Russia, attempted to finance Germany in World War I, and did finance the Bolsheviks before and after the fall of the czar.

Thus Boas's attitudes toward Germany in 1916 coincided with those of the main Jewish activist organization in the U.S.

Boas's Writing on Jews. When writing specifically about Jews, Boas limited his focus exclusively to fighting invidious stereotypes. Ironically, he did so by ruling out a cultural approach, which could have included issues that have often been linked to anti-Semitism—issues such as the traditional Jewish commitment to endogamy, ethnic nepotism, and separation from and economic competition with the surrounding society—instead emphasizing the irrelevant issue that Jews vary in their physical features too much to be considered a single racial type. This comment was made in an era prior to recent population genetic research confirming substantial genetic commonality among widely dispersed Jewish groups, such as the Ashkenazi and Sephardic Jews (e.g., Behar et al., 2010). Glick (1982, p. 557) suggests that Boas was being less than candid in his analysis:

> Paradoxically, by concentrating in this manner on physical anthropology, to the virtual exclusion of the historical, economic, and cultural factors that shaped European Jewish identity over nearly two millennia, Boas was employing the very principle to which he was most fundamentally opposed, that "racial" type is the fundamental consideration in national identity, in order to reach conclusions precisely opposite to those of his racist antagonists [in the U.S.] and in Germany. Had he carried his analyses one essential step further and given serious consideration to European Jewish history and culture (including its distinguished German variant), he might have reached more penetrating conclusions on assimilation and related questions. But to have done so would have required more candid examination of Jewish identity than he was ever prepared to undertake.

As a result, Boas avoided the idea that "being Jewish might in itself operate as a formative element in a social environment" (Glick 1982, 557)—that being reared in a left-liberal Jewish environment and being subjected to anti-Semitism may have affected his attitudes toward non-Jewish society. Quite clearly, a discussion of Jewish history and culture would also have raised issues about the role of Jews and Jewish culture in provoking anti-Semitism, as discussed throughout SAID.

In pursuing his activism, Boas had no compunctions about associating with others despite wildly disparate views. For example, during the mid-1920s Boas corresponded with Louis Marshall—a founder of the AJCommittee and the most prominent Jewish opponent to the Immigration Act of 1924 (see Ch. 8)—in support of a project proposed by Ignaz Zollschan, the prominent Zionist race scientist who subscribed to a Lamarckian theory of Jewish history as shaped by the inheritance of characteristics Jews acquired during the diaspora. In his early writing, Zollschan was motivated by a perceived need to end Jewish intermarriage and preserve Jewish racial purity (Efron, 1994). Indeed, Zollschan was a Jewish racial supremacist: in an October 31st, 1935 letter to Albert Einstein, Boas complained that "[Zollschan's] whole attitude is to set up the Jews as a particularly gifted and excellent group as over against other groups." Zollschan's book on the Jewish racial question went through five editions beginning in 1910 and was well known to both Jewish and gentile anthropologists (Efron, p. 155). In this book Zollschan criticized other race scientists, not for claiming that Jews were a race, but for criticizing Jewish culture and lack of creative accomplishments, and for claiming that Germans were a superior race. He advocated Zionism as the only way to retain Jewish racial purity from the threat of mixed marriages and assimilation (Gilman, 1993, p. 109).

Nevertheless, Boas supported Zollschan's proposed research on condition that it would be "worked in with a general plan of showing the fallacy of modern race theory" (Boas to Marshall, 1925). In fact, in 1926, Zollschan used a proposal drawn up by Boas as a basis for lobbying in Europe to refute anti-Semitic racism (Weindling, 2007, p. 270). This plan apparently came to fruition in Zollschan's 1942 *Racialism Against Civilization*, with a preface by British evolutionary biologist Julian Huxley. Huxley (p. 7) wrote, "Zollschan has done a service to the world by demonstrating that Nazi race-theory is not, as many academic scientists assumed, merely an intellectual rationalization, but an attempt to build up an anti-rational, anti-ethical and anti-humanist theory of life as a basis for the German state." Clearly Boas was well-connected to the Jewish activist community of the day, whatever their views.

Boas on Jewish Assimilation. Regarding Boas's position on Jewish assimilation, the following quote is often cited (e.g., in Glick, 1982, p. 557; in D. L. Lewis, 1984, p. 97), as indicating that he favored complete Jewish cultural and genetic assimilation to the point of disappearance:

> Thus it would seem that man being what he is, the Negro problem will not disappear in America until the Negro blood has been so much diluted that it will no longer be recognized just as anti-Semitism will not disappear until the last vestige of Jew as a Jew has disappeared. (Boas, 1921b)

However, this is simply an allegation of fact, a claim that because human nature is what it is, hostility toward Blacks and Jews will only end when they disappear completely. It is not, at least explicitly, a recommendation that either group ought to disappear. Boas's activism was clearly aimed at promoting the idea that all cultures are equal, and as Frank (1997, p. 731) emphasizes, the effect of his movement has been to promote cultural pluralism and tolerance and acceptance of diverse cultures and peoples as a model for American society. This was also the view of Horace Kallen (1933), a prominent intellectual who corresponded with Boas on combatting National Socialist views on race. Kallen's views were opposed to genetic and cultural homogenization and were vastly influential in the wider American Jewish community of the period and thereafter (see below and Ch. 8). He was a staunch Zionist and saw Judaism in terms of race and nationality, noting although "men may change their clothes. . . . They cannot change their grandfathers" (Kallen, 1915, p. 220).

Given that Jewish immigration during the decades preceding the Immigration Act of 1924 included a substantial portion of Orthodox and Hasidic Jews dedicated to creating their own ghetto-like communities and actively resisting intermarriage—a phenomenon that continues today—Boas likely realized that a program of complete Jewish submergence into the surrounding society was not realistic, and indeed Jewish intermarriage remained at very low levels until well after Boas died in 1942. Maurice Samuel's well-known and highly ethnocentric *You Gentiles* (1924/2022), written partly as a hostile response to the Immigration Act of 1924 (see Ch. 8), includes a detailed discussion showing that the idea of complete Jewish disappearance via intermarriage would be unlikely in the extreme.

Nevertheless, in a February 6th, 1921 review for *The New York Times*, after reviewing putative cases where genetic and cultural assimilation occurred (e.g., the gradual racial transition from Europe to China; and the many invasions of Spain resulting in "the blood of practically all European types run[ning] in the veins of the Spanish people"), Boas condemns attempts to prevent immigrant groups from retaining their own language and culture, because doing so will only delay the inevitability of assimilation:

> Assimilation is thus as inevitable as it is desirable; it is impossible for the immigrants we receive to remain permanently in separate groups. Through point after point of contact, as they find situations in America intelligible to them in the light of old knowledge and experience, they identify themselves with us. We can delay or hasten this development. We cannot stop it. If we give the immigrants a favorable milieu, if we tolerate their strangeness during their period of adjustment, if we give them freedom to make their own connections between old and new experiences, if we help them to find points of contact, then we hasten their assimilation.

Here Boas claims the inevitability *and* desirability of assimilation. Nevertheless, Boas was not entirely consistent on these issues. Messer (1986, p. 140n16) notes that "Boas was … surprisingly willing to romanticize the value and decry the loss of native American communities, being forced to assimilate to more 'universal' and 'civilized' American values, which would seem to contradict his views on assimilation for Jews and Negroes."

Moreover, given Kallen's and Samuel's writings during this period, Boas's support for a thoroughgoing assimilation by blood and culture, as in his comments on Spain, was far from universal within the wider Jewish community, and indeed, his disciple Melville Herskovits moved from an assimilationist point of view to the view that each group should have pride in their culture and accomplishments (see below). It's noteworthy that Boas did not mention any examples where Jews underwent complete assimilation by blood and culture in their two-millennia-long sojourn in the West, so one wonders if he actually believed that it would happen—when he wrote in 1921, it should have been apparent that assimilation of immigrant Jews was not happening to any appreciable extent. Using his example of Spain, Jews never assimilated in this blood-and-culture manner: after repeated attempts at forced conversions from the fifth century to the pogroms of 1391, Jews were expelled in 1492, apart from a substantial group that became crypto-Jews for centuries thereafter, marrying among themselves and only superficially assimilating to Spanish culture (SAID, Ch. 4). This hardly speaks to inevitability of Jewish assimilation.

In any case, despite the history of Jewish non-assimilation, Boas is claiming the inevitability of radical assimilation by blood and culture and advocating tolerating different cultures until the inevitability of assimilation is achieved.

Although Jewish intermarriage is indeed quite high at present, Jews marry other Jews at well above random levels (Philips, 2013), and a major rationale for Zionism has been to avoid intermarriage, which has been successfully accomplished by the establishment of Israel. When it comes to culture, the mainstream activist Jewish community remains attached to the pursuit of Jewish interests a century after Boas encouraged Jewish support for Israel despite its immigration policies (while promoting non-White immigration to the West).

Boasian Anthropology and Cultural Critique. As has been common among Jewish intellectuals in several historical eras, Boas was deeply alienated from and hostile toward gentile culture, particularly the cultural ideal of the Prussian aristocracy (Degler, 1991, p. 200; Stocking, 1968, p. 150).

> Whatever their individual origin, the Boasians felt deeply estranged from mainstream American society and the male WASP elites they were displacing in anthropology. Gene Weltfish, another student of Boas, epitomized this sense of alienation when she said she felt that her generation had only three choices—go live in Paris, sell *The Daily Worker* (the U.S. Communist Party newspaper) [an indication that communist affiliation was a mainstream view in the Jewish community of the period] on street corners, or study anthropology at Columbia. The Boasians shared an outgroup sensibility, a commitment to a common viewpoint and a program to dominate the institutional structure of anthropology. Through it they successfully dethroned "the moral and political monopoly of an elite which had justified its rule with the claim that their superior virtue was the outcome of the evolutionary process." The cultural determinism of the Boasians served as a corrective to the genetic determinism of racial anthropology, emphasizing the variation within races, the overlap between them, and the plasticity of human behavior. The price, however, was divorcing the science of man from the science of life in general. The evolutionary perspective was abandoned, and anthropology began its slide into the abyss of deconstructionism. (Sarich & Miele, 2018, pp. 90–91)

As another example, when Margaret Mead wanted to persuade Boas to allow her to pursue her research in the South Sea islands:

She hit upon a sure way of getting him to change his mind. "I knew there was one thing that mattered more to Boas than the direction taken by anthropological research. . . . This was that he should behave like a liberal, democratic, modern man, not like a Prussian autocrat." The ploy worked for Mead because she had indeed uncovered the heart of his personal values. (Degler, 1991, p. 73)

Boas's Links to the Jewish Activist Community. I conclude that Boas had a strong Jewish identification and that he was deeply concerned about anti-Semitism and other issues favored by the wider Jewish community, such as immigration, biological theories of race, and combatting anti-Black attitudes. It's thus no accident that the AJCommittee "for years . . . supported liberally my work on race," although AJCommittee support ended when Boas refused to support "the political principles of Russia," presumably because he did not want his work to be seen as political (Boas to M. Warburg, 1942a). In a follow-up letter to Max Warburg, Boas (1942b) writes:

I quite understand that the [American] Jewish Committee cannot spend its funds on general educational work as a foundation may properly do but that it must conserve its funds primarily for Jewish defense and public relations and that is exactly the kind of work that I am doing. Specifically, I have been working all these years on the question of how far it is possible to claim that the members of a race have uniform characteristics which are biologically so determined that every member of the race must exhibit them in some way or other [at best a tendentious description of the racial science of the day which was fully aware that there was within-race variation in physical characteristics].

In an earlier letter to Felix Warburg, Boas (1935b) writes, "I think it would be well worthwhile for the various Jewish Committees to consider the importance of this question." Commenting on this, George Stocking (1992, pp. 108–109) notes:

Privately [Boas] acknowledged that the methods the Soviets used to achieve the socialist ideal of "equal rights for every member of humanity" had "much in common" with those of fascist totalitarianism. . . . Publicly, however, his posture was that of the "united front"—even in the period of the Nazi-Soviet pact and even to the jeopardy of funding that the American Jewish Committee had been providing for his research on race. Boas rationalized his position on the grounds that he could not "influence foreign countries"—though in other contexts he had attempted just that—and that in this country the real danger was not radical totalitarianism but "the spread of fascist ideology." . . . So long as people agreed with him "in regard to one specific problem on which we wish to cooperate," their views on other matters were irrelevant.

Clearly Boas's research fit into the general thrust of Jewish activism of the period. However, he was quite conscious of the need to not present his research as motivated by Jewish interests and often attempted to recruit non-Jews to endorse his efforts: "As in all the other investigations it seemed important to show the general applicability of the results to all races both from the scientific point of view and in order to avoid the impression that this is a purely Jewish undertaking" (Boas to F. Warburg, 1935b). Warburg agrees with this perspective:

> You are right, however, that such investigation [on the relevance of racial purity], if made at all, should not be made under Jewish auspices and I therefore would feel that any meeting called together for that purpose probably would give the signal to the Nazi spies who are abounding in this country just now that this is not a scientific piece of research but a counter-propaganda scheme backed by Jews. . . . If you have any students in the Anthropology Department who might want to use such an inquiry as a doctor's dissertation or something like that, they could use the material available in the Lushan collection and elsewhere, under the guidance of a professor who would be a recognized authority on such things, but the latter should not be a Jew. (Warburg to Boas, 1933)

Regarding another appeal to Felix Warburg, Boas writes:

> I am perfectly clear in my mind that work of this kind, even if made accessible to the general public as quickly as possible, will take time to have striking results but I feel that it is the only way in which the situation can be combatted. . . . I might say, that the plan as conceived would be to have a committee consisting largely of non-Jews heading the investigation. I have the promise of Professor MacIver of Barnard and of Professor Carlton Hayes of Columbia University to join such a small committee. (Boas to F. Warburg, 1933).

And again, during the same period:

> [Boas] launched a research program aimed at providing data to "attack the racial craze" by "undermining its alleged scientific basis" and creating opportunities to combat racist fallacies in an educational campaign. Boas recognized that he would be considered a partisan in conducting an investigation on racial questions, specifically if it involved the Jewish question, and therefore organized a committee which consisted largely of non-

Jews. Financial support, however, was mostly Jewish since non-Jews had declined solicitations. . . . The committee was largely a facade for the work of Boas and his students. For some time the [C]ouncil [of Research of the Social Sciences at Columbia University] had been supporting the research of [Boas protégé] Otto Klineberg, who demonstrated the predominant role of environment in determining the mental characteristics of American blacks. (Barkan, 1992, p. 283)

On the basis of the foregoing, it is reasonable to suppose that his concern with Jewish issues and a perceived need to conceal Jewish involvement was a major influence in the development of American anthropology.

Boas and the Battle to Dominate American Academic Anthropology. Indeed, it is difficult to avoid the conclusion that ethnic conflict played a major role in the development of American anthropology. Boas's views conflicted with the then-prevalent idea that cultures had evolved in a series of developmental stages labeled savagery, barbarism, and civilization. The stages were associated with racial differences, and modern European culture—and most especially, I suppose, the hated Prussian aristocracy—was at the highest level of this gradation. Wolf (1990, p. 168) describes the attack of the Boasians as calling into question "the moral and political monopoly of a [gentile] elite which had justified its rule with the claim that their superior virtue was the outcome of the evolutionary process." Boas's theories were also meant to counter the racialist theories of Houston Stewart Chamberlain (see SAID, Ch. 5) and American eugenicists like Madison Grant, whose book, *The Passing of the Great Race* (1921, p. 17), was highly critical of Boas's research on the environmental influences on skull size. The result was that "in message and purpose, [Boas's anthropology] was an explicitly antiracist science" (Frank, 1997, p. 741).

Grant (1921, pp. 16, 91) characterized Jewish immigrants as ruthlessly self-interested whereas American Nordics were committing racial suicide and allowing themselves to be "elbowed out" of their own land. Grant (pp. xxxi–xxxii) also believed Jews were engaged in a campaign to discredit racial research:

It is well-nigh impossible to publish in the American newspapers any reflection upon certain religions or races which are hysterically sensitive even when mentioned by name. . . . Abroad, conditions are fully as bad, and we have the authority of one of the most eminent anthropologists in France that the collection of anthropological measurements and data among French recruits at the outbreak of the Great War was prevented by Jewish influence, which aimed to suppress any suggestion of racial differentiation in France.

An important technique of the Boasian school was to cast doubt on general theories of human evolution, such as those implying developmental sequences with Western culture at the pinnacle, by emphasizing the vast diversity and chaotic minutiae of human behavior, as well as the relativism of standards of cultural evaluation. The Boasians argued that general theories of cultural evolution must await a detailed cataloguing of cultural diversity, but in fact no general theories emerged from this body of research in the ensuing half century of its dominance of the profession (Stocking, 1968, p. 210). Leslie White, an evolutionary anthropologist and therefore someone whose professional opportunities within anthropology were limited because of his theoretical orientation, noted that because of its rejection of fundamental scientific activities such as generalization and classification, Boasian anthropology should be characterized more as an anti-theory than a theory of human culture (L. White, 1966, p. 15). For example, in 1930, Boas advocated an anthropology focused on the study of individuals rather than "abstractions":

> It is only since the development of the evolutional theory that it became clear that the object of study is the individual, not abstractions from the individual under observation. . . . An error of modern anthropology, as I see it, lies in the overemphasis on historical reconstruction, the importance of which should not be minimized, as against a penetrating study of the individual under the stress of the culture in which he lives. (in Kluckhohn & Prufer, 1959, p. 20).

Boas (1928, pp. xiii–xiv) elaborates on this theme in his Foreword to Margaret Mead's *Coming of Age in Samoa:*

> Some anthropologists even hope that the comparative study will reveal some tendencies of development that recur so often that significant generalisations regarding the processes of cultural growth [presumably a reference to the cultural gradations theory, with Western culture at the pinnacle] will be discovered. To the lay reader these studies are interesting on account of the strangeness of the scene, the peculiar attitudes characteristic of foreign cultures that set off in strong light our own achievements and behaviour. However, a systematic description of human activities gives us very little insight into the mental attitudes of the individual. His thoughts and actions appear merely as expressions of rigidly defined cultural forms. We learn little about his rational thinking, about his friendships and conflicts with his fellowmen. The personal side of the life of the individual is almost eliminated in the systematic presentation of the cultural life of the people. The picture is standardised, like a collection of laws that tell us how we should behave, and not how we behave; like rules set down defining the style of art, but not the way in which the artist

elaborates his ideas of beauty; like a list of inventions, and not the way in which the individual overcomes technical difficulties that present themselves. And yet the way in which the personality reacts to culture is a matter that should concern us deeply and that makes the studies of foreign cultures a fruitful and useful field of research.

Boas's views imply that research should focus on individuals, not the general characteristics of a culture. Boas's "continuing efforts to discredit scientifically all forms of racial prejudice, religious bias, and nationalistic chauvinism illustrate a man for whom the cult of the individual was not only a philosophical but a practical personal imperative" (Messer, 1986, p. 132). Applied to Judaism, such a perspective would preclude any generalizations about Jews or Jewish culture, but only research on how individual Jews interact with the cultures around them. Another version:

The habit of identifying an individual with a class, owing to his bodily appearance, language, or manners has always seemed to me a survival of barbaric, or rather of primitive habits of mind. Groups, as they exist among us, are all too often subjective constructions, because those who are assigned to that group do not feel themselves as members of the groups and the injustice done them is one of the blots of our civilization. There are too few among us who are willing to forget completely that a particular person is a Negro, a Jew, or a member of some nationality for which we have no sympathy, and to judge him as an individual. (in Messer, 1986, p. 131)

Boas also opposed research in human genetics—what Derek Freeman (1991, p. 198) terms his "obscurantist antipathy to genetics," and what Kluckhohn and Prufer (1959, p. 22) describe as "his relative lack of interest in Darwinian evolution and his skepticism about Mendelian heredity."

It is of critical importance to note that Boas and his students were intensely concerned with pushing an ideological agenda within the American anthropological profession (Degler, 1991; D. Freeman, 1991; Torrey, 1992)—the antithesis of science as an open-ended pursuit of truth by individuals (see Ch. 7). Boas and his associates had a sense of group identity, a commitment to a common viewpoint, and an agenda to dominate the institutional structure of anthropology (Stocking, 1968, pp. 279–280). They were a compact group with a clear intellectual and political agenda rather than individualist seekers of disinterested truth. The defeat of the Darwinians "had not happened without considerable exhortation of 'every mother's son' standing for the 'Right.' Nor had it been accomplished without some rather strong pressure applied both to staunch friends and to the 'weaker brethren'—often by the sheer force of

Boas's personality" (Stocking, p. 286). Such a phenomenon has no place in real science.

By 1915 the Boasians controlled the American Anthropological Association and held a two-thirds majority on its executive board (Stocking, 1968, p. 285). In 1919 Boas could state that "most of the anthropological work done at the present time in the United States" was done by his students at Columbia (in Stocking, 1968, p. 296). By 1926 every major department of anthropology was headed by Boas's students, the majority of whom were Jewish. His protégé Melville Herskovits (1953, p. 23) noted:

> [T]he four decades of the tenure of [Boas's] professorship at Columbia gave a continuity to his teaching that permitted him to develop students who eventually made up the greater part of the significant professional core of American anthropologists, and who came to man and direct most of the major departments of anthropology in the United States. In their turn, they trained the students who ... have continued the tradition in which their teachers were trained.

Moreover, this continuity continued long after Boas's death:

> Intersections between Jewish anthropologists and Native Americans continued among a number of Sol Tax's students and their students' students in turn as they had with Boas, his students, and his students' students and with Sapir, his students, and his students' students. There is a certain intergenerational transfer among anthropologists who "happened to be Jews" in evidence (though, of course, the profession was by no means an exclusively or explicitly Jewish one). ... While this legacy has not been fully assessed, there can be little doubt that dozens of Jewish anthropologists taught at dozens of universities, for dozens of years each, and would have made some meaningful impact on countless numbers of university students. (Koffman, 2019, pp. 209–210)

According to Leslie White (1966, p. 26), Boas's most influential students were Ruth Benedict, Alexander Goldenweiser, Melville Herskovits, Alfred Kroeber, Robert Lowie, Margaret Mead, Paul Radin, Edward Sapir, and Leslie Spier. Every member of this "small, compact group of scholars ... gathered about their leader" (p. 26) were Jews with the exception of Kroeber, Benedict, and Mead. Frank (1997, p. 732) also mentions several other prominent, first-generation Jewish students of Boas besides the influential Melville Herskovits, including Alexander Lesser, Ruth Bunzel, Gene (Regina) Weltfish, Esther Schiff Goldfrank, and Ruth Landes. (Especially later in his career, Boas had a significant number of non-Jewish students, but, as discussed above, any Jew intent on establishing an influential movement in a situation where Jews are a small minority is well advised to recruit non-Jews—a recurrent theme in this volume.)

It's noteworthy that Sapir's family fled the pogroms in Russia for New York, where Yiddish was his first language. Although not religious, he took an increasing interest in Jewish topics early in his career and later became engaged in Jewish activism, particularly in establishing a prominent center for Jewish learning in Lithuania (Frank, 1997, p. 735). Ruth Landes's background also shows the ethnic nexus of the Boasian movement. Her family was prominent in the Jewish leftist subculture of Brooklyn, and she was introduced to Boas by Alexander Goldenweiser, a close friend of her father and another of Boas's prominent students (p. 736).

Melville Herskovits as Jewish Academic Activist

I focus on Melville Herskovits because of the availability of Jerry Gershenhorn's extensive biography, appropriately titled *Melville J. Herskovits and the Racial Politics of Knowledge*. Herskovits was an early student of Boas and, like Boas, his career illustrates the problems of a Jewish social scientist attempting to present his views as completely objective and scientific—to the point that, despite his own activism on behalf of Black issues (which were pursued outside of his publishing in scholarly journals), he has been accused of "using the rhetoric of 'objectivity' to exclude black scholars" whom he regarded as too overtly engaged in political activism (Editorial Introduction to Gershenhorn, 2004, p. xiii). Like other Boasians, he "promulgated the principle that all cultures deserve respect" and "sought to undermine the racial and cultural hierarchy throughout his career" (Gershenhorn, pp. 3–4). Gershenhorn (pp. 4–6) continues:

> Herskovits challenged the biological definition of race and helped steer scholars toward a more modern conception of race as a sociological category. By doing so, he undercut the notion that race determined behavior. Instead, he substituted environment and culture for race as the explanation of behavioral and intellectual differences between individuals. In this way he attacked racial hierarchy and demonstrated the falsity of intellectual rankings based on race. . . . At a time when most white Americans assumed black Americans to be inferior as a race and a culture, Herskovits' establishment of the strength and complexity of American and African-influenced cultures was a great intellectual achievement. . . . He laid the foundation for a dynamic view of cultural change that emphasized cultural diversity and cultural pluralism. At the same time, by providing evidence of the diverse influences on American culture, Herskovits helped transform notions of American identity from exclusive and unitary (white Anglo-Saxon Protestant) to inclusive and pluralist.

Despite his aversion to the older race science based on gradations of culture from peoples with different evolutionary histories, Herskovits accepted that races (Mongoloid, Caucasian, African) and subraces existed. However, like Richard Lewontin (see below) he argued that there was more variability in physical measurements within a race than between races; he claimed that races are "categories based on outer appearance as reflected in scientific measurements or observations that permit us to make convenient classifications of human materials" (in Gershenhorn, 2004, pp. 55)—a comment indicating his position that race is only "skin deep" and not a useful category for finding between-population differences in traits not visible in outer appearance, such as IQ. Nevertheless, he accepted the idea that ultimately research on race would be based on genetics and that such research would reveal that races were simply family trees, thus marking him as a "transitional figure" to the "race-is-a-social-construct" view that is common today (p. 55). It can be suspected that, given his activism for leftist causes (see below), Herskovits, along with the vast majority of contemporary social scientists, would reject the idea that genetic research would ultimately lead to findings indicating that genetically-based racial differences would be linked to traits like IQ and personality. For Herskovits, the issue of American identity was personal:

> His experience as the son of Jewish immigrants as one who had taken up and then rejected rabbinical studies, as one who had experienced anti-Semitism, as a war veteran, and as an advocate of leftist politics made the question of identity a very personal one. (Gershenhorn, 2004, p. 61).

As discussed in Chapter 8 and above, Horace Kallen, a Jewish philosopher and Zionist, developed a theoretical approach that rejected Jewish assimilation. This view was influential with Herskovits (Gershenhorn, 2004, p. 67), pushing him in the direction of non-assimilation, in contrast to his earlier views discounting differences between Black and White American culture, and "moving from a universalist one-sided emphasis on assimilation to a particularist emphasis on diversity" (p. 92). A staunch Zionist, Kallen's views were shaped by his desire to avoid Jewish assimilation in the U.S. He developed the ideology that different ethnic groups would maintain their separate identities while contributing to a harmonious, conflict-free future, using the analogy of different sections of a symphony orchestra, each contributing something unique while in harmony with the other sections—an early version of the current "diversity is our greatest strength" mantra. As John Higham (1984, p. 209) noted, "Kallen lifted his eyes above the strife that swirled around him to an ideal realm where diversity and harmony coexist."

As with Boas, cultivating the appearance of scientific objectivity was critically important for Herskovits as a Jewish scholar in an America still dominated by a White, Protestant elite:

> As a Jewish scholar in an academic environment dominated by white Protestants—many of whom were anti-Semitic—Herskovits tried to deflect their tendency to devalue the scholarship on race produced by Jews, who were assumed to have a 'subjective, minority agenda.' Thus Herskovits emphasized his professional legitimacy by wrapping himself in the mantle of science. ... Herskovits—like other Boasian anthropologists—emphasized objectivity to discredit social scientists who supported the status quo in race relations or advocated reactionary policies designed to control non-whites or minority groups. Thus despite his avowed support for objectivity and detached scholarship, Herskovits's own strongly held egalitarian values influenced his work in physical and cultural anthropology. He believed that by shedding light on the diverse cultures of the world, anthropologists "documented the essential dignity of all human cultures" [Herskovits, 1947, p. 653]. (Gershenhorn, 2004, pp. 127–128)

As with Boas, Herskovits's attitudes reflected the leftist attitudes that were mainstream within the Jewish community at the time. He also became an activist for Black causes and attacked the applied anthropology of European scholars who used anthropology to support imperialism. When not writing in scholarly publications where the appearance of objectivity was required, Herskovits "spoke out against racism, imperialism, and injustice" (Gershenhorn, 2004, p. 130), and in 1934 he joined the Conference on Jewish Relations which was formed to "dispel the various myths that people invent to justify race prejudice" (p. 131). Cementing his leftist credentials, he joined the radical Industrial Workers of the World, the American Civil Liberties Union, and a variety of other progressive organizations (p. 131). David S. Koffman (2019, pp. 196–197) further elaborates on Herskovits's Jewish activism:

> Though he occupies a slim place on the American Jewish history bookshelf, Herskovits maintained a steady interest in Jewish affairs from the 1920s until his death, actively engaging with the B'nai B'rith of Cincinnati, its Hillel Foundation, magazine, and orphanage, the Conference on Jewish Relations, the National Conference of Jews and Christians, the Jewish Bibliographic Bureau, Chicago's Jewish People's Institute, the Jewish Charities of Chicago, the Council of Jewish Federations, and the Welfare Funds of the Bureau of Jewish Social Research. He helped Jewish scholars flee from German occupied territory in the 1930s and early 1940s, arranged assistance, coordinated with foreign diplomats, raised money, and located American jobs. He distributed anti-Nazi pamphlets to refute Nazi

propaganda and wrote and lectured widely on the scientific distortions of racial difference, on racism as the spearhead of fascism, and on racism as an infection of American life. The effects of racism, Herskovits noted, impacted "the Negro, the Oriental, the Mexican, the Indian" as a matter of physical characteristics and as a matter of cultural and linguistic peculiarity, as is the case of various immigrant groups, including Jews, about whom he wrote, "As in the case of the Jew, it may be a combination of all these factors." He delivered antiracism lectures to Jewish audiences too. He spoke at a Temple Men's Club and a Chicago Roundtable National Conference of Christians and Jews for Chicago teachers and maintained relationships throughout the 1930s and 1940s with YIVO, Louis Finkelstein of the Jewish Theological Seminary, the Hebrew Union College, and Rabbi Bertram W. Korn, the Reform rabbi in Philadelphia and historian of American Jewry.

In a revealing comment indicating his opposition to the then-dominant White male Protestant elite, a Black female graduate student noted that "Herskovits had two special places in his heart: one for students who were African American, and another for students who were women" (in Gershenhorn, 2004, p. 139). He also became active in opposing the colonial regimes of the West: "Herskovits lobbied the U.S. government to support the independence of Africa and to bring an end to white supremacy regimes on the continent" (p. 6). As suggested by David L. Lewis's (1992, p. 31) comment that Jews fought anti-Semitism "by remote control" by supporting Black causes, Herskovits's ethnic identity was a factor in his motivation: "Herskovits's interpretation of black cultures was grounded in his ethnographic research, his ethnic identity, the influence of Harlem Renaissance writers, and the influence of his mentor, Franz Boas." D. L. Lewis (p. 21) goes on: "Like his mentor [Boas], Herskovits's Jewish heritage made him sensitive to his own outsider status and that of African Americans. . . . As a Jew who grew up in predominantly Christian small towns, Herskovits felt this outsider status with keen intensity." Herskovits thus "sought to employ the authority of scientific objectivity and detached scholarship to counter pseudoscientific racism and advance black studies by empowering the subjects of his research—black people—as creators of their own culture" (p. 9). Gershenhorn's thesis is "that Herskovits's work on Africans and African Americans is inextricably connected by his embrace of cultural relativism, his attack on racial and cultural hierarchy, and his conceptualization of Negro studies" (p. 9). "Through his research, writing, and teaching, he dignified the lives and struggles of people of African descent on both sides of the Atlantic" (p. 10).

However, Herskovits never acknowledged that his ethnic identity had anything to do with his activism on behalf of Blacks. He wrote that "neither in training, in tradition, in religious beliefs, nor in culture am I what may be termed a person any more Jewish than any American born and raised in a typical Middle Western milieu" (in Gershenhorn, 2004, p. 13)—a comment that Gershenhorn notes was made "during a period of historically high anti-Semitism in the United States [1927]," and seeming to imply the obvious: that there was an element of deception in the statement. Indeed, Gershenhorn goes on to note that "Herskovits's attempts to minimize the significance of his Jewishness do not square with his youthful experience"—he was a former rabbinical student and regularly attended synagogue as a child (p. 13); and he married within his ethnic group (p. 16)—clearly not indications of a childhood spent in a "typical Middle Western milieu." Nevertheless, "Jewish identity, argued Herskovits, was a matter of personal and very subjective choice, neither ethnicity or religious belief is relevant: 'A person is a Jew if he calls himself a Jew or if he is called a Jew by others.'" (W. A. Jackson, 1986, p. 101). According to Koffman (2019, p. 197), "Herskovits was not the only Jewish scholar of Indian life or language to have worked toward a rabbinic degree, earned one, or actually practiced from the pulpit. Bernard Stern, Melford Spiro, Maurice Zigmond, and David Mandelbaum all trained as both anthropologists and rabbis." Koffman then describes their continuing connections to Judaism throughout their professional careers.

Moreover, after dropping out of rabbinical school, Herskovits became a political radical at the University of Chicago, at a time when there was a very mainstream and widespread Jewish subculture of political radicalism (see Ch. 3). While still at the university, he wrote a letter condemning a social club for wanting to hold separate dances for Jewish and non-Jewish students. He continued his radical associations after moving to New York; besides joining the Industrial Workers of the World, he "befriended a group of like-minded individuals [including Margaret Mead] who were interested in art, music, and literature, and who embraced gender and racial equality and radical politics" (Gershenhorn, 2004, p. 16).

Other Boasians

Ashley Montagu was another influential student of Boas (see Shipman, 1994, pp. 159ff). Montagu, whose original name was Israel Ehrenberg, was a highly visible crusader in favor of the idea of race as a social construct and against racial differences in mental capacities. He was also highly conscious of being Jewish, stating on one occasion that "if you are brought up a Jew, you know that all non-Jews are anti-Semitic. . . . I think it is a good working hypothesis" (in Shipman, p. 166). Moreover, he proposed that humans are innately cooperative (but not innately aggressive) and that there is a universal brotherhood among humans—a highly problematic idea in the wake of the carnage of World War II.

Mention should also be made of Otto Klineberg, a professor of psychology at Columbia. Klineberg was "tireless" and "ingenious" in his arguments against the reality of racial differences. He came under the influence of Boas at Columbia and dedicated his 1935 book *Race Differences* to him. Klineberg "made it his business to do for psychology what his friend and colleague at Columbia [Boas] had done for anthropology: to rid his discipline of racial explanations for human social differences" (Degler, 1991, p. 179). As noted above, Klineberg was a member of the solidary core of influential Jews surrounding Boas.

[The Executive Director of the Association of American Indian Affairs], Alexander Lesser, was a trained anthropologist, and its field research initiatives, government relations efforts, and leadership all the way up to the executive level deployed and employed anthropologists, including a large number of fellow Jewish anthropologists including Frank Speck, Otto Kleinberg [sic], Gene Weltfish, and many others. (Koffman, 2019, p. 204)

It is interesting in this regard that the members of the Boasian school who achieved the greatest public renown were two gentiles, Ruth Benedict and Margaret Mead.[34] As noted above, Boas often attempted to persuade non-Jewish scientists to endorse his projects, and in several other prominent historical cases (see Chs. 3–5; SAID, Ch. 6), gentiles became the publicly visible spokespersons for a movement dominated by Jews. Indeed, like Freud, Boas in the later years of his tenure at Columbia recruited gentiles out of concern "that his Jewishness would make his science appear partisan and thus compromised" (Efron, 1994, p. 180). Again, Jews as a small minority have often recruited sympathetic non-Jews to their intellectual and political causes.

Boas devised Margaret Mead's classic study on adolescence in Samoa with an eye to its usefulness in the nature-nurture debate raging at the time (D. Freeman, 1983, pp. 60–61, 75). The result of this research was *Coming of Age in Samoa* (1928), a book that pushed American anthropology in the direction of radical environmentalism. Its success stemmed ultimately from its promotion by Boas's students in departments of anthropology at prominent American universities (D. Freeman, 1991). This work and Ruth Benedict's *Patterns of Culture* (1934) were also widely influential among other social scientists, psychiatrists, and the public at large, so that "by the middle of the twentieth century,

---

[34] Torrey (1992, pp. 60ff) argues cogently that the cultural criticism of Benedict and Mead and their commitment to cultural determinism were motivated by their attempts to develop self-esteem as lesbians. As indicated in Chapter 1, any number of reasons explain why gentile intellectuals may be attracted to intellectual movements dominated by Jews, including the identity politics of other ethnic groups or, in this case, sexual nonconformity. Sarich and Miele (2018, p. 90) concur: "Their sexual preferences are relevant, because developing a critique of traditional American values was as much a part of the Boasian program in anthropology as was their attack on eugenics and nativism."

it was a commonplace for educated Americans to refer to human differences in cultural terms, and to say that 'modern science has shown that all human races are equal'" (Stocking, 1968, p. 306).

Reflecting the ingroup-outgroup perspective of his movement, Boas rarely cited works of people outside his group except to disparage them, whereas he strenuously promoted and cited the work of people within the ingroup, such as Mead and Benedict. Similarly, Herskovits "blocked from the means of production (publication and research funding) those not indebted to him or not supporting his positions (and position of primacy) during the period when area studies was heavily funded by the U.S. government and foundations (particularly the Ford Foundation)" (Editorial Introduction to Gershenhorn, 2004, p. xii). The Boasian school of anthropology thus came to resemble in microcosm key features of Judaism as a highly collectivist group evolutionary strategy: a high level of ingroup identification, exclusionary policies, and cohesiveness in pursuit of common interests—a stance that is completely foreign to the scientific spirit.

The Guru Phenomenon in Boasian Anthropology. A theme in later chapters is that Jewish intellectual and political movements tend to center around guru-like charismatic figures who are slavishly admired by their followers. This phenomenon has strong roots in Jewish history and can still be seen today among Hasidic and Orthodox Jewish leaders such as Rebbe Menachem Schneerson, "a towering charismatic figure in the Jewish world" (Keinon, 2020). Twenty-six years after Schneerson's death in 1994, Rabbi Adin Steinsaltz wrote, "For Hasidic movements . . . the death of any Rebbe is a disaster, almost like the death of a father. Because of the particularly close bond that existed between the Rebbe and his hassidim, that trauma was multiplied many times" (in Keinon). The following is an account of a service at a synagogue in Galicia in 1903:

> There were no benches, and several thousand Jews were standing closely packed together, swaying in prayer like the corn in the wind. When the rabbi appeared the service began. Everybody tried to get as close to him as possible. The rabbi led the prayers in a thin, weeping voice. It seemed to arouse a sort of ecstasy in the listeners. They closed their eyes, violently swaying. The loud praying sounded like a gale. Anyone seeing these Jews in prayer would have concluded that they were the most religious people on earth. (Ruppin, 1971, p. 69)

At the end of the service, those closest to the rabbi were intensely eager to eat any food touched by him, and the fish bones were preserved by his followers as relics. Another account notes that "devotees hoping to catch a spark from this holy fire run to receive him" (R. Mahler, 1985, p. 8).

Boasian anthropology, at least during Boas's lifetime, was highly authoritarian and intolerant of dissent, and it was centered around a charismatic figure who served as an unquestioned leader. As in the case of Freud (see Ch. 5), Boas was a patriarchal father figure, strongly supporting those who agreed with him and excluding those who did not. Alfred Kroeber regarded Boas as "a true patriarch" who "functioned as a powerful father figure, cherishing and supporting those with whom he identified in the degree that he felt they were genuinely identifying with him, but, as regards others, aloof and probably fundamentally indifferent, coldly hostile if the occasion demanded it" (in Stocking, 1968, pp. 305–306). "Boas has all the attributes of the head of a cult, a revered charismatic teacher and master, 'literally worshipped' by disciples whose 'permanent loyalty' has been 'effectively established'" (L. White, 1966, pp. 25–26).

As in the case of Freud, in the eyes of his disciples, virtually everything Boas did was of monumental importance and justified, placing him among the intellectual giants of all time. Like Freud, Boas did not tolerate theoretical or ideological differences with his students. Individuals who disagreed with the leader or had personality clashes with him, such as Clark Wissler and Ralph Linton, were simply excluded from the movement. Paul Radin, mentioned above as an influential member of the core group of Boas's students, claimed that Boas was a "powerful figure who did not tolerate theoretical or ideological differences in his students" (in Darnell, 2001, p. 35). Essentially, he made a generation of students an extension of himself and his ideas.

L. White (1966, pp. 26–27) represents the exclusion of Wissler and Linton as having ethnic overtones, as both were gentiles. Wissler was a member of the Galton Society (founded by eugenicist scientist Charles Davenport and Nordicist writer Madison Grant), which promoted eugenics and accepted the theory that there is a gradation of cultures from lower forms to higher forms, with Western civilization at the top (Gershenhorn, 2004, p. 23), so his exclusion is not surprising. However, White (pp. 26–27) also suggests that George A. Dorsey's status as a gentile was relevant to his exclusion from the Boas group despite Dorsey's intensive efforts to be a member. Kroeber (1956, p. 26) notes that Dorsey, "an American-born gentile and a Ph.D. from Harvard, tried to gain admittance to the select group but failed." (It should be noted that the very idea of a "select group" in a supposedly scientific enterprise contradicts the entire idea of a science; see Ch. 7). As an aspect of this exclusionary authoritarianism, Boas was instrumental in completely suppressing evolutionary theory in anthropology (D. Freeman, 1990, p. 197). Group solidarity within the Boasians has also drawn this comment from anthropologist Regna Darnell (2001, p. 35): they "shared a heady sense of solidarity, viewing themselves as rewriting the history of anthropology, creating a professionally respectable and scientifically rigorous discipline whose practitioners were loyal to a common enterprise"—a testament to a sense of group commitment that is antithetical to scientific research (see Ch. 7).

Boas as Pseudoscientist. Boas was the quintessential skeptic and an ardent defender of methodological rigor when it came to theories of cultural evolution and genetic influences on individual differences, yet "the burden of proof rested lightly upon Boas's own shoulders" (L. White, 1966, p. 12). Although Boas (like Freud; see Ch. 5) made his conjectures in a very dogmatic manner, his "historical reconstructions are inferences, guesses, and unsupported assertions [ranging] from the possible to the preposterous. Almost none is verifiable" (p. 13). An unrelenting foe of generalization and theory construction (such as the cultural gradation theory that previously dominated anthropology), Boas nevertheless completely accepted the "absolute generalization at which [Margaret] Mead had arrived after probing for a few months into adolescent behavior on Samoa," even though Mead's results were contrary to previous research in the area (D. Freeman, 1983, p. 291). Moreover, Boas uncritically allowed Ruth Benedict to distort his own data on the Kwakiutl (see Torrey, 1992, p. 83).

This suggests that Boas might even go so far as to fudge his data or inflate their significance in order to support his political attitudes. Boas's famous study purporting to show that skull shape changed as a result of immigration from Europe to America was a very effective propaganda weapon in the cause of the anti-racialists and against those who wanted to restrict immigration. As noted in Chapter 1, Boas was greatly motivated by the immigration issue. Indeed, it was likely intended as propaganda and has been highly successful in that regard, having been "cited innumerable times by writers of textbooks and anyone wishing to make the point that the cranium is plastic" (Sparks & Jantz, 2003, p. 334). Boas was far more concerned with showing that the cranial measurements of Eastern European Jews had altered toward the American (i.e., northwest European) type than showing similar results among Italians, writing in 1909, "The composition of the Italian types in the schools proved to be so complex that no safe inference could be drawn in regard to the stability of the type" (in Sparks & Jantz, p. 334). Quite possibly this emphasis on showing the malleability of Jewish skulls reflected Boas's ethnic affinity to this group as well as the fact that Eastern European Jews were seen as particularly unassimilable at the time (see Ch. 8).

Based on their reanalysis of Boas's data, physical anthropologists Corey Sparks and Richard Jantz (2002) do not accuse Boas of scientific fraud, but they do find that his data do not show any significant environmental effects on cranial form as a result of immigration. Moreover, Boas made inflated claims about the results: very minor changes in cranial index were described as changes of "type" so that Boas was claiming that within one generation immigrants developed the long-headed type characteristic of northwest Europeans (Sparks &

Jantz, 2003, p. 334). As Sparks and Jantz (2003) note, several modern studies show that cranial shape is under strong genetic influence, including a study showing that, while both American Blacks and Whites have altered their cranial measurements over the last 150 years, these changes have occurred in parallel and have not resulted in convergence. Their reanalysis of Boas's data indicated that no more than one percent of the variation between groups could be ascribed to the environmental effects of immigration, with the remainder due to variation between ethnic groups.

Sparks and Jantz (2003, p. 335) also claim that Boas may well have been motivated by a desire to end racialist views in anthropology:

> While Boas [like Herskovits] never stated explicitly that he had based any conclusions on anything but the data themselves, it is obvious that he had a personal agenda in the displacement of the eugenics movement in the United States. In order to do this, any differences observed between European- and U.S.-born individuals will be used to its fullest extent to prove his point.

Conclusion

The entire Boasian enterprise may thus be characterized as a highly authoritarian political movement centered around a charismatic leader. The results were extraordinarily successful: "The profession as a whole was united within a single national organization of academically oriented anthropologists. By and large, they shared a common understanding of the fundamental significance of the historically conditioned variety of human cultures in the determination of human behavior" (Stocking, 1968, p. 296). Research on racial differences ceased, and the profession completely excluded eugenicists and racial theorists like Madison Grant and Charles Davenport.

By the mid-1930s the Boasian view of the cultural determination of human behavior had a strong influence on social scientists generally (Stocking, 1968, p. 300). The followers of Boas also eventually became some of the most influential academic supporters of another Jewish-dominated movement, psychoanalysis (see Ch. 5). Marvin Harris (1968, p. 431) notes that psychoanalysis was adopted by the Boasian school because of its utility as a critique of Euro-American culture, and, indeed, as we shall see in later chapters, psychoanalysis is an ideal vehicle of cultural critique. In the hands of the Boasian school, psychoanalysis was completely stripped of its evolutionary associations, and there was a much greater accommodation to the importance of cultural variables (p. 433).[35]

Cultural critique was also an important aspect of the Boasian school. Stocking (1989, pp. 215–216) shows that several prominent Boasians, including Robert Lowie and Edward Sapir, were involved in the cultural criticism of the 1920s, which centered around the perception of American culture as overly homogeneous, hypocritical, and emotionally and aesthetically repressive (especially with regard to sexuality). Central to this program was creating ethnographies of idyllic cultures that were free of the negatively perceived traits that were attributed to Western culture. Among these Boasians, cultural criticism crystallized as an ideology of "romantic primitivism" in which certain non-Western cultures epitomized the approved characteristics Western societies should emulate.

Cultural criticism was a central feature of the two most well-known Boasian ethnographies, *Coming of Age in Samoa* and *Patterns of Culture*. These works are not only offered as critiques of Western civilization, but often systematically misrepresent key issues related to evolutionary perspectives on human behavior. For example, Benedict's Zuni were described as being free of war, homicide, and concern with accumulation of wealth. Children were not disciplined. Sex was casual, with little concern for virginity, sexual possessiveness, or paternity confidence. Contemporary Western societies are, of course, the opposite of these idyllic paradises, and Benedict suggests that we should study such cultures in order "to pass judgment on the dominant traits of our own civilization" (Benedict, 1934, p. 179). Mead's similar portrayal of the Samoans ignored her own evidence contrary to her thesis (Orans, 1996, p. 155). Negatively perceived behaviors of Mead's Samoans, such as rape and concern for virginity, were attributed to Western influence (Stocking, 1989, p. 245).

Both of these ethnographic accounts have been subjected to devastating criticisms. The picture of these societies that has emerged is far more compatible with evolutionary expectations than the societies depicted by Benedict and Mead (see Caton, 1990; D. Freeman, 1983; Orans, 1996; Stocking, 1989). In the controversy surrounding Mead's work, some defenders of Mead have pointed to possible negative political implications of the demythologization of her work (see, e.g., the summary in Caton, pp. 226–227).

---

[35] Although Freud is often viewed as a "biologist of the mind" (Sulloway, 1979a), and although he was clearly influenced by Darwin and proposed a universal human nature, psychoanalysis is highly compatible with environmental influences and the cultural relativism championed by the Boasian school. Freud viewed mental disorder as the result of environmental influences, particularly the repression of sexuality so apparent in the Western culture of his day. For Freud, the biological was universal, whereas individual differences were the result of environmental influences. Gay (1988, pp. 122–124) notes that until Freud, psychiatry was dominated by a biological model in which mental disorder had direct physical (e.g., genetic) causes.

Indeed, one consequence of the triumph of the Boasians was that there was almost no research on warfare and violence among the peoples studied by anthropologists (Keegan, 1993, pp. 90–94). Warfare and warriors were ignored, and cultures were perceived as consisting merely of myth-makers and gift-givers. (Orans, 1996, p. 120 shows that Mead systematically ignored cases of competition, violence, rape, and revolution in her account of Samoa.) Only five articles on the anthropology of warfare appeared during the 1950s. Revealingly, when Harry Holbert Turney-High published his volume *Primitive War* in 1949 documenting the universality of warfare and its oftentimes awesome savagery, the book was completely ignored by the anthropological profession— another example of the exclusionary tactics used against dissenters among the Boasians and characteristic of the other intellectual movements reviewed in this volume as well. Turney-High's massive data on non-Western peoples conflicted with the image of them favored by a highly politicized profession whose members simply excluded these data entirely from intellectual discourse. The result was a "pacified past" (Keeley, 1996, pp. 163ff) and an "attitude of self-reproach" (p. 179) in which the behavior of primitive peoples was bowdlerized while the behavior of European peoples was not only excoriated as uniquely evil but also as responsible for all extant examples of warfare among primitive peoples. From this perspective, it is only the fundamental inadequacy of European culture that prevents an idyllic world free from between-group conflict. Of course, these trends have been exacerbated in recent decades far beyond anything envisioned by Benedict or Mead.

The reality, of course, is far different. Warfare was and remains a recurrent phenomenon among pre-state societies; indeed, evolutionary biologist Richard Alexander (1979) and others have argued that warfare was a critical force in human evolution, selecting for greater intelligence and a suite of other human characteristics. Surveys indicate over 90 percent of societies engage in warfare, the great majority engaging in military activities at least once per year (Keeley, 1996, pp. 27–32). Moreover, "whenever modern humans appear on the scene, definitive evidence of homicidal violence becomes more common, given a sufficient sample of burials" (p. 37). Because of its frequency and the seriousness of its consequences, primitive warfare was more deadly than civilized warfare. Most adult males in primitive and prehistoric societies engaged in warfare and "saw combat repeatedly in a lifetime" (p. 174).

PART II: BEYOND BOAS: RECENT EXAMPLES OF JEWISH POLITICAL
AGENDAS INFLUENCING SOCIAL SCIENCE RESEARCH

Jewish influence on the social sciences has extended far beyond Boas and
the American Anthropological Association. As stated in the Preface, Hollinger
(1996, p. 4) notes "the transformation of the ethnoreligious demography of
American academic life by Jews" in the period from the 1930s to the 1960s, as
well as the Jewish influence on trends toward the secularization of American
society and in advancing an ideal of cosmopolitanism (p. 11). As early as the
early 1940s, this transformation resulted in "a secular, increasingly Jewish, decidedly left-of-center intelligentsia based largely but not exclusively in the disciplinary communities of philosophy and the social sciences" (p. 160). By 1968,
Jews constituted 20 percent of the faculty of elite American colleges and universities and 30 percent of the "most liberal" faculty. At this time, Jews, representing less than 3 percent of the population, constituted 25 percent of the
social sciences faculty at elite universities and 40 percent of liberal faculty who
published most (see Rothman & Lichter, 1982/1996, p. 103). Jewish academics
were also far more likely to support "progressive" or communist parties from
the 1930s to the 1950s. In 1948, approximately 30 percent of Jewish faculty
voted for the Progressive Party, compared to less than 5 percent of gentile faculty (p. 101).

Boas, who was a socialist, is a good example of the leftist bent of Jewish
social scientists, and many of his followers were political radicals (Torrey, 1992,
p. 57; see also above), including Melville Herskovits, as noted above.[36] Similar
associations are apparent in the psychoanalytic movement and the Frankfurt
School of Social Research (see Chs. 5–6) as well as among several critics of sociobiology mentioned in this chapter. The attraction of Jewish intellectuals to
the left is a general phenomenon and has typically co-occurred with a strong
Jewish identity and sense of pursuing specifically Jewish interests (see Ch. 3).

Stephen Jay Gould and Leon Kamin are good examples of these trends.
Gould (1992), whose perspective on social influences on evolutionary theory
was mentioned in SAID (Ch. 5), would appear to be a prime example of this
conflation of personal and ethnopolitical interests in the construction of science. Gould has been an ardent, highly publicized opponent of evolutionary
approaches to human behavior. Like many of the other prominent, left-leaning
critics of sociobiology (e.g., Jerry Hirsch, Leon Kamin, R. C. Lewontin, and

---

[36] Stocking (1968, pp. 273ff) recounts Boas's declaration of war on a group of anthropologists
who had contributed to the war effort in World War I. Boas's letter, printed in the leftist periodical The Nation, referred to President Wilson as a hypocrite and to American democracy as
a sham. The group responded with "outraged patriotism" (Stocking, p. 275), although the conflict also reflected the deep schism between the Boasian school and the rest of the profession.

Steven Rose; see Myers, 1990), Gould is Jewish. Michael Ruse (1989, p. 203) notes that a very prominent theme of Gould's (1996c) *The Mismeasure of Man* was how hereditarian views on intelligence had been used by "Teutonic supremacists" to discriminate against Jews early in the century. Gould's views on the IQ debates of the 1920s and their link to the immigration issue and eventually the Holocaust bear scrutiny. They illustrate how skill as a propagandist and ethnic activist can be combined with a highly visible and prestigious academic position to have a major influence on public attitudes in an area of research with important implications for public policy.

Ruse points out that Gould's book was very passionately written and was "widely criticized" by historians of psychology, suggesting that Gould had allowed his feelings about anti-Semitism to color his scientific writings on genetic influences on individual differences in intelligence. Ruse (1989, p. 203) goes on as follows:

> It does not seem to me entirely implausible to suggest that Gould's passion against human sociobiology was linked to the fear that it was yet another tool which could be used for anti-semitic purposes. I did ask Gould about this once. . . . He did not entirely repudiate the idea, but inclined to think that the opposition stemmed more from Marxism, and as it so contingently happens, most American Marxists are from Eastern European Jewish families. Perhaps both factors were involved.

Gould's comments highlight the fact that the role of Jewish academics in opposing Darwinian approaches to human behavior has often co-occurred with a strong commitment to a leftist political agenda. Indeed, Gould has acknowledged that his theory of evolution as punctuated equilibria was attractive to him as a Marxist because it posited periodic revolutionary upheavals in evolution rather than conservative, gradualist change. Gould learned his Marxism "at his Daddy's knee" (see Gould, 1996c, p. 39), indicating that he grew up as part of the Jewish-Marxist subculture discussed in Chapter 3. Gould (1996b) reminisces fondly about *The Forward*, a politically radical but also ethnically conscious Yiddish newspaper (see Ch. 3), stating that he recalls that many of his relatives bought the newspaper daily. As Arthur Hertzberg (1989, pp. 211–212) notes, "Those who read the *Forward* knew that the commitment of Jews to remain Jewish was beyond question and discussion."

Although Gould's family did not practice Jewish religious rituals, his family "embraced Jewish culture" (J. Mahler, 1996). A common ingredient in Jewish culture is a sense of the historical prevalence of anti-Semitism (see SAID, Ch. 6). Gould's sense of the historical oppression of Jews comes out in his review of *The Bell Curve* (Gould, 1994a), in which he rejects Herrnstein and Murray's (1994) vision of a socially cohesive society where everyone has a valued role to play: "They [Herrnstein and Murray] have forgotten about the town Jew and the dwellers on the other side of the tracks in many of these idyllic villages." Clearly Gould is blaming historical Western societies for failing to include Jews in their social structures despite the long history and ideology of Jewish separateness. Moreover, Gould's antipathy toward the people and culture of the West can been seen in the following article in *The Forward*:

> The Holocaust was not a remote historical tragedy [for Gould]. In *I Have Landed*, he observes: "I need hardly mention the searing events of my parents' generation to remind everyone that current acceptance [of Jews in society] should breed no complacency." Although he was a music lover and a fan of Johann Sebastian Bach, Gould notes, "I recoil from Bach's anti-Semitic Passion texts because they express the worst aspects of our common nature, and because these words have wreaked actual death and havoc." In another recently reprinted book, *Leonardo's Mountain of Clams and the Diet of Worms*, Gould asks how it is possible that throughout European history, cultivated Germans could "promote such iniquity [of anti-Semitism] of their own free will (and with apparent moral calm and intensity of supposed purpose)?" (Ivry, 2012)

Kamin and Gould have quite similar backgrounds in the leftist Jewish subculture described more fully in Chapter 3, and they share with many American Jews a strong personal animosity to the immigration legislation of the 1920s (see Ch. 8). Kamin was the son of an immigrant rabbi from Poland, and "the experience of growing up Jewish in a small and predominantly Christian town strongly sensitized him to the power of the social environment in shaping personality" (Fancher, 1985, p. 201)—a comment that also suggests that Kamin grew up with a strong Jewish identity. While at Harvard, Kamin joined the Communist Party USA and became the New England editor of the party's newspaper. After resigning from the party, he became a target of Joseph McCarthy's Senate Subcommittee Hearings in 1953. Kamin was charged and acquitted on technical grounds of charges of criminal contempt of Congress for failing to answer all the questions of the subcommittee. Fancher describes Kamin's work on IQ as having "little pretense to 'objectivity'" (p. 212) and suggests a link between Kamin's background and his position on IQ: "No doubt reflecting that his own middle-European family [and supposedly other Jews] could have been excluded by the restrictive immigration laws, Kamin concluded that an arrogant and unfounded assumption of IQ heritability had helped produce an unjust social policy in the 1920s" (p. 208).

L. J. Kamin (1974a; 1974b) and Gould (1996c) have been in the forefront of spreading disinformation about the role of IQ testing in the immigration debates of the 1920s. Snyderman and Herrnstein (1983; see also Samelson, 1982) show that Kamin and Gould misrepresented Henry H. Goddard's (1917) study of the IQ of Jewish immigrants as indicating that "83 percent of the Jews, 80 percent of the Hungarians, 79 percent of the Italians, and 87 percent of the Russians were 'feeble-minded'" (L. J. Kamin, 1974a, p. 16). As Snyderman and Herrnstein (p. 987) note:

> The "fact" that is most often cited as evidence of IQ's nativistic bias was not based on IQ scores, not taken even by its discoverer as accurately representative of immigrants or as a clean measure of inherited abilities, and it used a test that was known at the time to exaggerate feeblemindedness in adult populations of all sorts.

Indeed, Goddard (1917, p. 270) noted that "we have no data on this point, but indirectly we may argue that it is far more probable that their condition is due to environment than it is due to heredity," and he cited his own work indicating that immigrants accounted for only 4.5 percent of inmates in institutions for the feebleminded.

Degler (1991) finds that Gould engaged in a "single-minded pursuit" of Goddard (p. 39), presenting a false picture of Goddard as a "rigid hereditarian or elitist" (p. 40). Gould ignored Goddard's explicit doubts and qualifications as well as his statements on the importance of the environment. There can be little doubt that Gould was engaging in scholarly fraud in this endeavor: Degler (p. 354n16) notes that Gould quoted Goddard just prior to the following passage and was thus aware that Goddard was far from rigid in his beliefs on the nature of feeblemindedness: "Even now we are far from believing the case [on whether feeblemindedness is a unitary character] settled. The problem is too deep to be thus easily disposed of." Nevertheless, Gould chose to ignore the passage. Gould also ignored Degler's comments in his 1996 revision of *The Mismeasure of Man* described more fully below.

Moreover, Kamin and Gould present a highly exaggerated and largely false account of the general attitudes of the testing community on the subject of ethnic group differences in intelligence, as well as the role of IQ testing in the congressional debates of the period (Degler, 1991, p. 52; Samelson, 1975, p. 473; Snyderman & Herrnstein, 1983)—the latter point confirmed in my own reading of the debates. Indeed, IQ testing was never mentioned in either the House Majority Report or the Minority Report. (The Minority Report was written and signed by the two Jewish congressmen, Representatives Dickstein and Sabath, who led the battle against restrictionism.) Contrary to Gould's (1981, p. 232) claim that "Congressional debates leading to passage of the Immigration Restriction Act of 1924 continually invoke the army [IQ] test data," Snyderman and Herrnstein (p. 994) note:

[T]here is no mention of intelligence testing in the Act; test results on immigrants appear only briefly in the committee hearings and are then largely ignored or criticized, and they are brought up only once in over 600 pages of congressional floor debate, where they are subjected to further criticism without rejoinder. None of the major contemporary figures in testing . . . were called to testify, nor were their writings inserted into the legislative record.

Also, as Samelson (1975) points out, the drive to restrict immigration originated long before IQ testing came into existence, and restriction was favored by a variety of groups, including organized labor, for reasons other than those related to race and IQ, including especially the fairness of maintaining the ethnic status quo in the United States (see Ch. 8).

Samelson (1975) describes several other areas of Kamin's scholarly malfeasance, most notably his defamatory discussions of Goddard,[37] Lewis M. Terman, and Robert M. Yerkes in which these pioneers of mental testing are portrayed as allowing political beliefs to color their data. Terman, for example, found that Asians were not inferior to Caucasians, results he reasonably interpreted as indicating the inadequacy of cultural explanations; these findings are compatible with contemporary data (Lynn, 1987; Rushton, 1995). Jews were also overrepresented in Terman's study of gifted children, a result that was trumpeted in the Jewish press at the time (e.g., *The American Hebrew*, July 13th, 1923, p. 177) and is compatible with contemporary data (PTSDA, Ch. 7). Both findings are contrary to the theory of Nordic superiority.

L. J. Kamin (1974a, p. 27) also concluded that "the use of the 1890 census had only one purpose, acknowledged by the bill's supporters. The 'New Immigration' had begun after 1890, and the law was designed to exclude the biologically inferior . . . peoples of southeastern Europe." This is a very tendentious interpretation of the motives of the restrictionists. As discussed in Chapter 8, the 1890 census of the foreign born was used because the percentages of foreign-born ethnic groups in 1890 approximated the proportions of these groups in the general population as of 1920. The principal argument of the restrictionists was that use of the 1890 census was fair to all ethnic groups.

This false picture of the 1920s immigration debates was then used by Kamin, Gould, and others to argue that the "overtly racist immigration act" of 1924 (L. J. Kamin, 1982, p. 98) was passed because of racist bias emanating from the IQ-testing community and that this law was a primary cause of the death of Jews in the Holocaust. Thus L. J. Kamin (1974a, p. 27) concluded that "the law, for which the science of mental testing may claim substantial credit, resulted in the deaths of literally hundreds of thousands of victims of the Nazi biological

---

[37] See also Gelb (1986) for a revealing discussion of H. H. Goddard's involvement in testing immigrants.

theorists. The victims were denied admission to the United States because the 'German quota' was filled." Kamin's portrayal of early-twentieth-century intelligence testing became received wisdom, appearing repeatedly in newspapers, popular magazines, court decisions, and occasionally even scholarly publications. My own introduction to Kamin's ideas came from reading a popular textbook on developmental psychology I was using in my teaching.

Similarly, Gould proposes a link between hereditarian views on IQ and the U.S. Immigration Act of 1924 which restricted immigration from Eastern and Southern Europe and biased immigration in favor of the peoples of Northwestern Europe. The Immigration Act of 1924 is then linked to the Holocaust:

> The quotas . . . slowed immigration from southern and eastern Europe to a trickle. Throughout the 1930s, Jewish refugees, anticipating the Holocaust, sought to emigrate, but were not admitted. The legal quotas, and continuing eugenical propaganda, barred them even in years when inflated quotas for western and northern European nations were not filled. Chase (1977) has estimated that the quotas barred up to 6 million southern, central, and eastern Europeans between 1924 and the outbreak of World War II (assuming that immigration had continued at its pre-1924 rate). We know what happened to many who wished to leave but had nowhere to go. The paths to destruction are often indirect, but ideas can be agents as sure as guns and bombs. (Gould, 1981, p. 233; see also Gould, 1998)

Indeed, although there is no evidence that IQ testing or eugenic theories had anything more than a trivial influence on the Immigration Act of 1924, there is evidence that the law was perceived by Jews as directed against them (see Ch. 8). Moreover, concerns about Jews and their ultimate effect on American society may well have been a motive of some of the gentiles favoring immigration restriction, including, among the intellectuals, Madison Grant and Charles Davenport.

Because of his desire to counteract the publicity given to *The Bell Curve* (see Gould, 1996c, p. 31), Gould reissued *The Mismeasure of Man* in 1996 with a new introduction in which he states, "May I end up next to Judas Iscariot, Brutus, and Cassius in the devil's mouth at the center of hell if I ever fail to present my most honest assessment and best judgment of the evidence for empirical truth" (p. 39). Despite this (rather self-consciously defensive) pledge of scholarly objectivity, Gould took no steps to deal with the objections of his critics— exactly the type of behavior one expects from a propagandist rather than a scholar (see Rushton, 1997). The Snyderman and Herrnstein article, Samelson's work, and Degler's book are not cited at all, and Gould does not retract his statement that IQ testing was a prominent feature of the congressional immigration debates of the 1920s.

Perhaps most egregiously of all, Gould (1996c, p. 22) makes the amazing argument that he will continue to ignore all recent scholarship on IQ in favor of the older "classical" research because of the "transient and ephemeral" nature of contemporary scholarship. The argument is that there is no progress in IQ research but only a repetition of the same bad arguments—an argument that I doubt Gould would apply to any other area of science. Thus Gould continues to denigrate studies linking brain size with IQ, despite a great deal of contrary research both prior to and especially since his 1981 edition (see summary below). Using magnetic resonance imaging to get a more accurate measure of brain size, modern research vindicates the discoveries of nineteenth-century pioneers like Paul Broca, Sir Francis Galton, and Samuel George Morton who are systematically defamed by Gould. However, as Rushton (1997) notes, Gould's revised edition apparently omitted his 1981 discussion of Arthur Jensen's research on the brain size-IQ correlation because of his realization that the contemporary data are unequivocal in their support of a moderate ($r > .40$) association. Instead, in the 1996 edition Gould reprints his approval of a 1971 review of the literature that concluded that there was no relationship. Gould's revision thus ignores twenty-five years of research, including van Valen's (1974) paper on which Jensen's ideas were based.

In his revision, Gould also does not discuss an article by J. S. Michael (1988) that shows that, contrary to Gould's claim, Samuel George Morton did not fudge his data on race differences in skull size, intentionally or otherwise. Moreover, although Morton's research "was conducted with integrity" (Michael, p. 253), it included an error that actually favored a non-Caucasian group—an error that Gould failed to mention while at the same time Gould himself made systematic errors and used arbitrarily chosen procedures in his calculations. Additionally, Gould did so in a manner that favored his own hypothesis that there are no racial differences in cranial capacity.

Michael's research was replicated and extended in a 2011 study by Jason Lewis et al. which found that Morton did not selectively choose which data to report and did not manipulate his samples in order to show that the cranial capacities of American Indians were lower. Critically, a remeasuring of 308 skulls (Gould never actually measured any of Morton's skulls) showed that Morton's errors were random with respect to the group measured.

> Our analysis of Gould's claims reveals that most of Gould's criticisms are poorly supported or falsified. It is doubtful that Morton equated cranial capacity and intelligence calling into question his motivation for manipulating capacity averages. ... Of the approximately seven minor errors in Morton's work identified by Gould, only two appear to be actual errors, and their overall impact confounds rather than supports Morton's presumed a priori rankings. ... [O]ur results falsify Gould's hypothesis that

Morton manipulated his data to conform with his a priori views. The data on cranial capacity gathered by Morton are generally reliable, and he reported them fully. Overall, we find that Morton's initial reputation as the objectivist of his era was well-deserved. (J. E. Lewis et al., 2011, p. 5–6)

Ralph L. Holloway, a physical anthropologist and co-author of the study stated, "I just didn't trust Gould. . . . I had the feeling that his ideological stance was supreme. When the 1996 version of 'The Mismeasure of Man' came and he never even bothered to mention Michael's study, I just felt he was a charlatan" (in Wade, 2011). Indeed, failure to respond to the criticism is a sure sign of academic dishonesty.

Gould also failed to retract his defamation of Goddard in which he claimed that Goddard (1912) had doctored photographs of the famous Kallikak family to make them look mentally retarded and menacing. (In his book, Goddard had compared the Kallikaks, who were the descendants of a tavern maid and an upstanding citizen, with the descendants of the same man and his wife.) A subsequent study by Glenn and Ellis (1988) appearing well before the revised edition concluded, however, that these photographs are judged as appearing "kind." To put it charitably, Gould's presuppositions about the malicious intentions of IQ researchers result in his overattributing bias to others.

Finally, in the 1996 revision Gould failed to rebut arguments against his claim that g (i.e., general intelligence) was nothing more than a statistical artifact (see, e.g., J. B. Carroll, 1995; Hunt, 1995; Jensen & Weng, 1994). This is noteworthy because in his introduction to the 1996 edition, Gould is clearly apologetic about his lack of expertise as a historian of science or as a psychologist, but he does claim to be an expert in factor analysis. His failure to mount a defense against his scholarly critics is therefore another example of his intellectual dishonesty in the service of his ethnopolitical agenda. As the review of the 1996 edition by Rushton (1997) indicates, a great many other errors of commission and omission abound in *The Mismeasure of Man*, all having to do with politically sensitive issues involving racial differences and sex differences in cognitive abilities.

Gould has also strongly opposed the idea that there is progress in evolution, quite possibly because of his belief that such ideas among German evolutionists contributed to the rise of National Socialism (see Robert Richards's comments in Lewin, 1992, p. 143). As recounted by Lewin (p. 144), Gould acknowledges an ideological influence on his beliefs but reiterates his belief that the trends toward greater intelligence and larger brain size are not important in the overall scheme of evolution.[38] However, Gould acknowledges

---

[38] The idea that advances in complexity are important to evolution continues to draw a great deal of support (Bonner, 1988; Russell, 1983, 1989; E. O. Wilson, see Miele, 1998, p. 83).

that there is a deeper issue at stake than whether all animal groups show this tendency. At the basis of this perspective is Gould's assertion that human consciousness, intelligence, and the general trend toward larger brain size in human evolution are mere accidents and did not contribute to Darwinian fitness or to the solution of adaptive problems in ancestral environments (see Lewin, pp. 145–146).[39] His perspective is thus meant to be a skirmish in the nature-nurture debate over intelligence.[40]

In addition, Dennett's (1993, 1995) devastating analysis of the rhetorical devices used by Gould in his war against adaptationism leaves little doubt regarding the fundamental intellectual dishonesty of Gould's writings. Dennett implies that a non-scientific agenda motivates Gould but stops short of attempting to analyze the reasons for this agenda. Gould (1993, p. 317) himself recounts an incident in which the British biologist Arthur Cain, referring to Gould and Lewontin's (1979) famous anti-adaptationist paper "The Spandrels of San Marco and the Panglossian Paradigm: A Critique of the Adaptationist Programme," accused him of having "betrayed the norms of science and intellectual decency by denying something that we knew to be true (adaptationism) because he so disliked the political implications of an argument (sociobiology) based upon it."

The verdict must be that Gould has indeed forfeited his membership in the "ancient and universal company of scholars" and will spend his afterlife in the devil's mouth at the center of hell. However, it is noteworthy that despite

---

[39] More recently, Gould (1997) accepts the idea that the human brain became large as a result of natural selection. Nevertheless, he states that most of our mental abilities and potentials may be spandrels. This is presumably an example of one of Alcock's (1997) principles of Gouldian rhetoric, specifically that of protecting his own position by making illusory concessions to give the appearance of fair-mindedness in an attempt to restrict debate. Here Gould concedes that the brain must have evolved as a set of adaptations but concludes, without any evidence, that the result is mostly a collection of spandrels. Gould never lists even one example of a human mental or behavioral adaptation, even going so far as describing as "guesswork" the proposal that the human preference for sweets is innate. There is in fact an enormous body of research on many mammals showing that preference for sweets is innate (prenatal rats and sheep will increase their rate of swallowing shortly after the mother is injected with sweets; human neonates are attracted to sweet-tasting solutions). In addition, brain modules and chromosomal loci related to preference for sweets have been located (Glayde Whitney, personal communication).

[40] As indicated below, a substantial body of research links brain size with IQ. Within Gould's perspective, one could accept this research but still deny that intelligence has been an important aspect of human adaptation. It is interesting to note that Gould's proposal is incompatible with two basic theses of this project: (1) a fundamental aspect of the Jewish group evolutionary strategy has been a conscious effort to engage in eugenic practices directed at producing a highly intelligent elite and raising the mean intelligence of the Jewish population above the levels of gentile populations; and (2) intelligence has been a major aspect of Jewish adaptation throughout its history (see PTSDA, Ch. 7). Gould's views on the importance of intelligence for human adaptation thus clearly conflict with the views and practices of his ancestors—views clearly articulated in the Talmud and in practices that were carried out for centuries. These practices are undoubtedly directly implicated in Gould's success as an articulate, highly productive professor at Harvard.

the widespread belief that Gould has a highly politicized agenda and is dishonest and self-serving as a scholar, the prominent evolutionary biologist John Maynard Smith (1995, p. 46) notes:

> [Gould] has come to be seen by non-biologists as the pre-eminent evolutionary theorist. In contrast, the evolutionary biologists with whom I have discussed his work tend to see him as a man whose ideas are so confused as to be hardly worth bothering with. . . . All this would not matter were it not that he is giving non-biologists a largely false picture of the state of evolutionary theory.

Similarly, Steven Pinker (1997), a prominent linguist and a major figure in the evolutionary psychology movement, labels Gould's ideas on adaptationism as "misguided" and "uninformed." He also takes Gould to task for failing to properly cite the widely known work of G. C. Williams and Donald Symons in which these authors have proposed non-adaptive explanations for some human behaviors while nevertheless adopting an adaptationist perspective on human behavior generally. Gould has thus dishonestly taken credit for others' ideas while utilizing them in a wholly inappropriate manner to discredit the adaptationist program generally.

In an article entitled "*Homo deceptus*: Never Trust Stephen Jay Gould," journalist Robert Wright (1996), author of *The Moral Animal* (1994), makes the same charge in a debate over a flagrantly dishonest interpretation by Gould (1996a) of the evolutionary psychology of sex differences. Wright notes that Gould "has convinced the public he is not merely a great writer, but a great theorist of evolution. Yet among top-flight evolutionary biologists, Gould is considered a pest—not just a lightweight but an actively muddled man who has warped the public's understanding of Darwinism." A false picture perhaps, but one that is not without its usefulness in satisfying political and, I suppose, ethnic agendas.

Another prominent biologist, John Alcock (1997), provides an extended and, I think, accurate analysis of several aspects of Gould's rhetorical style: demonstrations of erudition—foreign phrases, poetry—irrelevant to the intellectual arguments but widely regarded even by his critics; branding the opposition with denigrating labels, such as "pop science," "pop psychology," "cardboard Darwinism," or "fundamentalist Darwinians" (similarly, Pinker, 1997 decries Gould's hyperbolic rhetoric, including his description of the ideas of evolutionary psychology as "'fatuous,' 'pathetic,' and 'egregiously simplistic' and his use of some twenty-five synonyms for 'fanatical'"); oversimplifying his opponents' positions in order to set up straw man arguments, the classic being labeling his opponents as "genetic determinists"; protecting his own position by making illusory concessions to give the appearance of fair-mindedness in the attempt to restrict debate; claiming the moral high ground; ignoring relevant data known to all in the scientific community; proposing nonadaptationist alternatives without attempting to test them and ignoring data supporting adaptationist interpretations; and arguing that proximate explanations (i.e., explanations of how a trait works at the neurophysiological level) render ultimate explanations (i.e., the adaptive function of the trait) unnecessary.

The comments of Maynard Smith, Wright, and Alcock highlight the important issue that despite the scholarly community's widespread recognition of Gould's intellectual dishonesty, Gould has been highly publicized as a public spokesperson on issues related to evolution and intelligence. As Alcock (1997) notes, Gould, as a widely published Harvard professor, makes it respectable to be an anti-adaptationist, and I have noticed this effect not only among the educated public but also among many academics outside the biological sciences. He has had access to highly prestigious intellectual forums, including a regular column in *Natural History*, and, along with Richard C. Lewontin (another scholar-activist whose works are discussed here), he is often featured as a book reviewer in *The New York Review of Books* (NYRB). The NYRB has long been a bastion of the intellectual left. In Chapter 5, I discuss the role of the NYRB in promulgating psychoanalysis, and in Chapter 7 the NYRB is listed among the journals of the New York Intellectuals, a predominantly Jewish coterie that dominated intellectual discourse in the post-World War II era. The point here is that Gould's career of intellectual dishonesty has not existed in a vacuum but has been part and parcel of a wide-ranging movement that has dominated the most prestigious intellectual arenas in the United States and the West—a movement that is here conceptualized as a facet of Judaism as a group evolutionary strategy.

On a more personal level, I clearly recall that one of my first noteworthy experiences in graduate school in the behavioral sciences was being exposed to the great "instinct" debate between the Austrian ethologists Konrad Lorenz and Irenäus Eibl-Eibesfeldt and several, predominantly Jewish, American developmental psychobiologists (Daniel S. Lehrman, Jay S. Rosenblatt, T. C. Schneirla, Howard Moltz, Gilbert Gottlieb, and Ethel Tobach). Lorenz's connections to National Socialism (see R. M. Lerner, 1992, pp. 59ff) were a barely concealed aspect of this debate, and I remember feeling that I was witnessing some sort of ethnic warfare rather than a dispassionate scientific debate of the evidence. Indeed, the intense, extra-scientific passions these issues raised in some participants were openly admitted toward the end of this extraordinary conflict. In a 1970 article, Lehrman (p. 22) stated:

> I should not point out irrational, emotion-laden elements in Lorenz's reaction to criticism without acknowledging that, when I look over my 1953 critique of his theory, I perceive elements of hostility to which its target

would have been bound to react. My critique does not now read to me like an analysis of a scientific problem, with an evaluation of the contribution of a particular point of view, but rather like an assault upon a theoretical point of view, the writer of which assault was not interested in pointing out what positive contributions that point of view had made.

More recently, as the debate has shifted away from opposing human ethology toward attacks on human sociobiology, several of these developmental psychobiologists have also become prominent critics of sociobiology (see Myers, 1990, p. 225).

This is not, of course, to deny the very important contributions of these developmental psychobiologists and their emphasis on the role of the environment in behavioral development—a tradition that remains influential within developmental psychology in the writings of several theorists, including Alan Fogel, Richard Lerner, Arnold Sameroff, and Esther Thelen. Moreover, it must be recognized that several Jews have been important contributors to evolutionary thinking as it applies to humans as well as human behavior genetics, including Daniel G. Freedman, Richard J. Herrnstein, Seymour Itzkoff, Irwin Silverman, Nancy Segal, Lionel Tiger, and Glenn Weisfeld. Of course, non-Jews have been counted among the critics of evolutionary-biological thinking. Nevertheless, the entire episode clearly indicates that there are often important human interests that involve Jewish identity and that influence scientific debate. The suggestion here is that one consequence of Judaism as a group evolutionary strategy has been to skew these debates in a manner that has impeded progress in the biological and social sciences.

Barry Mehler, a protégé of Jerry Hirsch, is explicit in linking race science and eugenics with anti-Semitism. Although not a prominent academic, Mehler has been an effective publicist against race science in leftist intellectual media and as head of the Institute for the Study of Academic Racism at Ferris State University (see Mehler, 1984a, 1984b). Mehler graduated from Yeshiva University and has a long history of working in collaboration with the Anti-Defamation League. Mehler's strong Jewish identification—further indicated by the fact that as of 2019 he is faculty advisor to Jewish students at Ferris State University—has informed his crusade against race science: Mehler "immediately saw parallels between the far-right network of intellectuals and the rapid, devastating way in which eugenics research had been used in Nazi Germany, terrifying him with the possibility that the brutal atrocities of the past could happen once more" (Saini, 2019).

Richard Lerner (1992) in his *Final Solutions: Biology, Prejudice, and Genocide* is perhaps the most egregious example of a scientist motivated to discredit evolutionary-biological thinking because of putative links with anti-Semitism. Lerner is a prominent developmental psychologist—a recipient of several lifetime achievement awards from the American Psychological Association. His book indicates an intense personal involvement directed at combating anti-Semitism by influencing theory in the behavioral sciences. Prior to discussing the explicit links between Lerner's theoretical perspective and his attempt to combat anti-Semitism, I will describe his theory and illustrate the type of strained thinking with which he has attempted to discredit the application of evolutionary thinking to human behavior. Central to this program is Lerner's rejection of biological determinism in favor of a developmental contextualist approach to human development. Lerner also rejects environmental determinism, but there is little discussion of the latter view because environmental determinism is "perhaps less often socially pernicious" (p. xx). In this regard, Lerner is surely wrong. A theory that there is no human nature would imply that humans could easily be programmed to accept all manner of exploitation, including slavery. From a radical environmentalist perspective, it should not matter how societies are constructed, since people should be able to learn to accept any type of social structure. Women could easily be programmed to accept rape, and ethnic groups could be programmed to accept their own domination by other ethnic groups. The view that radical environmentalism is not socially pernicious also ignores the fact that the communist government of the Soviet Union murdered millions of its citizens and later engaged in officially sponsored anti-Semitism while committed to an ideology of radical environmentalism.[41]

Lerner's developmental contextualism pays lip service to biological influences while actually rendering them inconsequential and unanalyzable. This theory has strong roots in the developmental psychobiological tradition described above, and there are numerous references to these writers. The developmental contextualist perspective conceptualizes development as a dialectical interaction between organism and environment. Biological influences are viewed as a reality, but they are ultimately unanalyzable, since they are viewed as being inextricably fused with environmental influences. The most notable conclusion is that any attempt to study genetic variation as an independently analyzable influence on individual differences (the program of the science of quantitative behavior genetics) is rejected. Many of the critics of sociobiology have also been strong opponents of behavior genetic research (e.g., Gould, Hirsch, Kamin, Lewontin, and Rose). For a particularly egregious example

---

[41] After noting the tens of millions of deaths resulting from Soviet communism, Richard Pipes (1993, p. 511) states, "Communism failed because it proceeded from the erroneous doctrine of the Enlightenment, perhaps the most pernicious idea in the history of thought, that man is merely a material compound, devoid of either soul or innate ideas, and as such a passive product of an infinitely malleable social environment." Although there is much to disagree with in this statement, it captures the idea that radical environmentalism is eminently capable of serving as an ideology underlying political regimes that carry out mass murder.

embodying practically every possible misunderstanding of basic behavior genetic concepts, see Gould (1998).

It bears mentioning that developmental contextualism and its emphasis on the dialectical interaction between organism and environment bear more than a passing resemblance to Marxism. The foreword of Lerner's book was written by R. C. Lewontin, the Harvard population biologist who has engaged in a high-profile attempt to fuse science, leftist politics, and opposition to evolutionary and biological theorizing about human behavior (e.g., Levins & Lewontin, 1985; see also E. O. Wilson, 1994). Lewontin (with Steven Rose and Leon Kamin) was the first author of *Not in Our Genes: Biology, Ideology, and Human Nature* (1984), a book that begins with a statement of the authors' commitment to socialism (p. ix) and, among a great many other intellectual sins, continues the disinformation regarding the role of IQ testing in the immigration debates of the 1920s and its putative links to the Holocaust (p. 27). Indeed, E. O. Wilson (1994, p. 344), whose synthetic volume *Sociobiology: The New Synthesis* (1975) inaugurated the field of sociobiology, notes that "without Lewontin, the [sociobiology] controversy would not have been so intense or attracted such widespread attention." In his foreword to R. M. Lerner's (1992, p. ix) book, Lewontin states:

> [Developmental contextualism] is the alternative to biological and cultural determinism. It is the statement of the developmental contextual view that is the important central point of *Final Solutions*, and it is the full elaboration of that point of view that is a pressing program for social theory. Nowhere has this world view been put more succinctly than in Marx's third Thesis on Feuerbach."

Lewontin goes on to quote a passage from Marx that does indeed express something like the fundamental idea of developmental contextualism. Gould (1987, p. 153) has also endorsed a Marxist dialectical perspective in the social sciences.

Lerner devotes much of his book to showing that developmental contextualism, because of its emphasis on plasticity, provides a politically acceptable perspective on racial and sexual differences, as well as promising a hope for ending anti-Semitism. This type of messianic, redemptionist attempt to develop a universalist theoretical framework within which Jewish-gentile group differences are submerged in importance is a common feature of other predominantly Jewish movements in the twentieth century, including radical political theories and psychoanalysis (see Chs. 3, 5). The common theme is that these ideologies have been consistently promoted by individuals who, like Lerner, are self-consciously pursuing a Jewish ethnic and political agenda. (Recall also Gould's tendency to seize the moral high ground.) However, the ideologies are advocated because of their universalist promise to lead humanity to a higher level of morality—a level of morality in which there is continuity of Jewish group identity but an eradication of anti-Semitism. As such, developmental contextualism can be seen as one of many post-Enlightenment attempts to reconcile Judaism with the modern world.

There is no question that Lerner strongly believes in the moral imperative of his position, but his moral crusade has led him well beyond science in his attempts to discredit biological theories in the interest of combating anti-Semitism.[42] Lerner coauthored an article in the journal *Human Development* (R. M. Lerner & von Eye, 1992) directed at combating the influence of biological thinking in research on human development. My edited volume (*Sociobiological Perspectives on Human Development*, MacDonald, 1988b) is prominently cited as an example of an evolutionary approach deriving from E. O. Wilson's work and as a point of view that has "found support and application" (R. M. Lerner & von Eye, p. 13). As their example of how this point of view has been supported and applied, Lerner and von Eye cite the work of J. Philippe Rushton on racial differences in r/K reproductive styles. The implication would appear to be that my edited volume was somehow a basis of Rushton's work. This is inaccurate, since (1) the volume never mentioned Black-White differences in intelligence or any other phenotype, and (2) the book was published after Rushton had already published his work on the r/K theory of racial differences. However, the association between this book and Rushton is highly effective in producing a negative evaluation of the book because of Rushton's current *persona non grata status* as a theorist of racial differences (see Gross, 1990).

---

[42] I should note that I have had considerable professional contact with Lerner and at one time he was a major influence on my thinking. Early in my career Richard Lerner wrote letters of recommendation for me, both when I was applying for academic positions and during the tenure review process after I was employed. The rejection of biological determinism is clearly central to the theoretical basis of my work in this volume and has been characteristic of my writing in the area of developmental psychology as well. Indeed, I have gone out of my way to cite Lerner's work on developmental plasticity in my writings, and he cited some of my work on developmental plasticity in his *On the Nature of Human Plasticity*. I have also contributed to two books coedited by Lerner (*Biological and Psychosocial Interactions in Early Adolescence*, 1987 and *Encyclopedia of Adolescence*, 1991).

Moreover, I have also been strongly influenced by the contextualist perspective in developmental psychology associated with Urie Bronfenbrenner and Richard Lerner and have several times cited Lerner in this regard; see my *Social and Personality Development: An Evolutionary Synthesis* (MacDonald, 1988a, Ch. 9) and *Sociobiological Perspectives in Human Development* (MacDonald, 1988b). As a result of this influence, I made a major effort to reconcile contextualism with an evolutionary approach. Within this perspective, social structure is underdetermined by evolutionary theory, with the result that human development is also underdetermined by biological influences. (Indeed, in Chapter 9 of *Social and Personality Development*, I show how National Socialism affected the socialization of German children, including indoctrination with anti-Semitism.) This theoretical perspective remains central to my worldview and is described in some detail in PTSDA (Ch. 1).

The next section of the Lerner and von Eye (1992) article is entitled "Genetic Determinism as Sociobiology's Key to Interdisciplinary Integration." Implicit in this juxtaposition is the implication that the authors in my edited volume accept the thesis of genetic determinism, and indeed, at the end of the section, Lerner and von Eye lump my edited volume together with the work of a number of other sociobiological writers who are said to believe that anatomy is destiny, that environmental influences are fictional, and that "the social world does not interact with humans' genes" (p. 18).

Scholars connected to evolutionary perspectives on human behavior or behavior genetics have commonly been branded genetic determinists in this highly politicized literature. Such accusations are a staple of Gouldian rhetoric and are a major theme of Lewontin, Rose, and Kamin's (1984) overtly political *Not in Our Genes*. I rather doubt that any of the writers discussed in this section of Lerner and von Eye's article can be accurately described as genetic determinists (see the reply to Lerner & von Eye's article by Burgess & Molenaar, 1993). Indeed, Degler (1991, p. 310) accurately summarizes recent evolutionary thinking in the social sciences as characterized by "a full recognition of the power and influence of environment or culture." However, I would like to stress here that this is a completely inaccurate characterization of my writings and that it is difficult to suppose that Lerner was unaware of this. Two of my contributions to the edited volume are greatly concerned with environmental and cultural influences on behavior and the underdetermination of behavior by the genes. In particular, my theoretical perspective, as described in Chapter 1 of the edited volume (MacDonald, 1988b), takes a strong position supporting the importance of developmental plasticity and affirming the importance of contextual influences on human development. In both of these sections of my paper I cite Richard Lerner's work. However, Lerner and von Eye are seemingly careful to avoid actually describing what I have written. Instead, their strategy is that of innuendo and guilt by association: by placing my edited book at the end of a section devoted to writers who are supposedly genetic determinists, they manage to imply that all of the writers in the volume are genetic determinists. Unfortunately, such innuendos are typical in attacks on evolutionary perspectives on human behavior.

The point here is that there is every reason to suppose that a major impetus for these attacks is an attempt to combat anti-Semitism. R. M. Lerner (1992) begins his preface to *Final Solutions* with a heart-wrenching portrait of his childhood surrounded by stories of Nazi atrocities. "As a Jewish boy growing up in Brooklyn in the late 1940s and early 1950s I could not escape Hitler. He, Nazis, the Gestapo, Auschwitz were everywhere" (p. xv). Lerner re-creates a conversation with his grandmother describing the fate of some of his relatives at the hands of the Nazis. He asks why the Nazis hated the Jews, and his grandmother responds by saying, "Just because" (p. xvi). Lerner states (p. xvii):

In the time that has passed since that afternoon in my grandmother's apartment I have learned—and increasingly so as the years go by—how deeply I was affected by these early lessons about Nazi genocide. I now understand that much of my life has been shaped by my attempts to go beyond the answer of "Just because."

Lerner explains that he chose to study developmental psychology because the nature-nurture issue is central to this field and therefore central to his attempt to combat anti-Semitism. Lerner thus apparently actually chose his career in an effort to advance Jewish interests in the social sciences. In the preface, Lerner cites as intellectual influences virtually the entire list of predominantly Jewish developmental psychobiologists and anti-sociobiologists mentioned above, including Gottlieb, Gould, Kamin, Lewontin, Rose, Schneirla (who was not Jewish), and Tobach. As is common among Jewish historians (see SAID, Ch. 7), Lerner dedicates the book to his family: "To all my relatives. . . . Your lives will not be forgotten" (1992, p. xxii). Clearly there is no pretense that this book is a dispassionate scientific endeavor to develop a theory of behavioral development or to come to grips with ethnically based social conflict.

The central message of Lerner's book is that there is a possible causal chain linking Darwinism to an ideology of genetic determinism, to the legitimization of the status quo as a biological imperative, to negatively evaluating individuals with "inferior" genotypes, to eugenics, and finally to destruction of those with inferior genes. This story line is said to have been played out in several historical instances, including the massacres of Native Americans, the Ottoman genocide of Armenians, and most particularly in the Holocaust. It is nowhere mentioned that an ideology of genetic determinism is hardly a necessary condition for genocide, since there are a great many historical examples of genocide in societies where Darwin was unknown, including the annihilation of the Amorites and Midianites by the Israelites described in the Tanakh (see PTSDA, Ch. 3)—examples that are ignored by Lerner. Nor is there evidence that, for example, the Ottoman Turks were acquainted with Darwin or had views, scientific or otherwise, about the genetic determination of behavior.

Lerner's agenda is to discredit evolutionary thinking because of its association with Nazism. The logic is as follows (R. M. Lerner, 1992, pp. 17–19): although Lerner acknowledges that genetic determinists need not be "racists" and that they may even have "enlightened" political views, he states that genetic determinism is an ideology that can be used to give scientific credence to their viewpoint—that it "provides fertile ground for co-optation by racist and/or fascist political movements." Sociobiology, as the most recent incarnation of the scientific justification of genetic determinism, must be intellectually discredited:

Contemporary sociobiologists are certainly not neo-Nazis. They do not in any way advocate genocide and may not even espouse conservative political views. Nevertheless, the correspondence between their ideas (especially regarding women) and those of the Nazi theorists is more than striking. (R. M. Lerner, 1992, p. 20)

R. M. Lerner (1992, p. 17) correctly describes Nazi ideology as essentially an ideology of group impermeability:

the belief that the world . . . may be divided unequivocally into two major groups: an "in-group" comprising those possessing the best human characteristics, and an "out-group" comprising the worst features of human existence. There can be no crossing-over between these groups, because blood, or genes, divides them.

Similarly, Lewontin, in his foreword to R. M. Lerner's (1992, p. viii) book, states:

But whatever the generating forces that keep nationalism alive . . . they must, in the end, assert the unchanging and unchangeable nature of social identity. . . . Exploiters and exploited alike share in the consciousness of a cultural and biological heritage that marks out indelible group boundaries that transcend human historical development.

Lerner and Lewontin condemn sociobiology because they suppose that sociobiology could be used to justify such a result. However, the evolutionary theory of social identity processes developed in SAID (Ch. 1) as the basis of the theory of anti-Semitism implies just the opposite: although humans appear to be biologically predisposed toward ingroup-outgroup conflict, there is no reason whatever to suppose that group membership or group permeability itself is genetically determined; that is, there is no reason to suppose that there is a genetic imperative that societies *must* be organized around impermeable groups, and indeed, prototypical Western societies have not been organized in this manner. Social identity research indicates that hostility toward outgroups also occurs in randomly composed groups and even in the absence of between-group competition. The outstanding feature of Judaism has been that it has steadfastly raised barriers between Jews as an ingroup and the surrounding society as an outgroup. But, even though it is reasonable to suppose that Jews are genetically more prone to ethnocentrism than Western peoples (see PTSDA, Ch. 8; SAID, Ch. 1), the erection of cultural barriers between Jews and gentiles is a critical aspect of Judaism as a culture.

Moreover, a salient point here is that there is no appreciation by either Lerner or Lewontin of the great extent to which Jews have themselves created impermeable groups in which biological descent was of the highest importance, in which there were hierarchies of racial purity, and in which genetic and cultural assimilation were viewed as anathema (see PTSDA, *passim*). Judaism as a group evolutionary strategy has resulted in societies torn apart by internal conflict between impermeable, competing ethnic groups (see SAID, Chs. 2–5). Nevertheless, Jewish cultural practices are at least a necessary condition for the group impermeability that has been so central to Judaism as a group evolutionary strategy. It is thus a supreme irony that Lerner and Lewontin should be attempting to combat anti-Semitism by saying that ethnic identification and the permeability of groups are not genetically determined.

There are good reasons to suppose that group permeability is not genetically determined, and the evidence reviewed in PTSDA indicates that Jews have been exquisitely aware of this since the origins of Judaism as a group evolutionary strategy. At times Jewish groups have endeavored to foster an illusion of group permeability in order to minimize anti-Semitism (see SAID, Ch. 6). Although Jews may well be genetically predisposed to form impermeable ethnic groups and resist genetic and cultural assimilation, there is little reason to suppose that this is genetically determined. Indeed, the evidence reviewed in PTSDA (Chs. 7–8) indicates the central importance of several cultural and environmental factors for the success of Judaism as a relatively impermeable group evolutionary strategy: intensive socialization for a Jewish ingroup identity and group allegiance; the great variety of mechanisms of separation (clothes, language, hairstyles, etc.); and the cultural invention of the hereditary priestly and Levitical classes. As a result, in the contemporary Western world Jewish groups often go to great lengths to discourage intermarriage and to develop greater Jewish consciousness and commitment among Jews. This attempt to reestablish the cultural supports for Jewish identification and non-assimilation often involves the suggestion of a return to Jewish religious belief and ritual as the only way to stave off the long-term assimilative pressures of contemporary Western societies (see SAID, Ch. 9).

Conclusion

A common thread of this chapter has been that scientific skepticism and what one might term "scientific obscurantism" have been useful tools in combating scientific theories one dislikes for deeper reasons. Thus, the Boasian demand for the highest standards of proof for generalizations about culture and for establishing a role for genetic variation in the development of individual differences coincided with the acceptance of an "anti-theory" of culture that was fundamentally in opposition to attempts to develop classifications and generalizations in the field.[43] Similarly, the developmental contextualist theoretical perspective, though rejecting behavior genetics and evolutionary theorizing about human development as failing to meet scientific standards of proof, has proposed a theory of development in which the relation between genes and environment is an extremely complex and ultimately unanalyzable fusion. Moreover, a major theme of Chapter 6 is that the radical skepticism of the Frankfurt School of Social Research was self-consciously directed at deconstructing universalist, assimilatory theories of society as a homogeneous, harmonious whole.

Scientific skepticism regarding politically sensitive issues has also been a powerful trend in the writings of S. J. Gould (1987, *passim*; 1991). Carl Degler (1991, p. 322) writes that "an opponent of sociobiology like Gould does indeed emphasize that interaction [between biology and environment], yet at the same time, he persistently resists investigations of the role of each of the interacting elements." Jensen (1982, p. 124) states of Gould's work on intelligence testing, "I believe that he has succeeded brilliantly in obfuscating all the important open questions that actually concern today's scientists." This type of intellectual work is aimed at precluding the development of general theories of human behavior in which genetic variation plays an independently analyzable causative role in producing adaptive behavior.

We have seen how R. C. Lewontin has linked theories of behavioral development with Marxist political ideology. As do Lerner and Gould, Lewontin advocates theories proposing that nature consists of extremely complex dialectical interactions between organism and environment. Lewontin rejects reductionistic scientific methods, such as quantitative behavior genetics or the use of analysis of variance procedures, because they inevitably oversimplify real processes in their use of averages (Segerstråle, 1986, 2000). The result is a hyper-purism that settles for nothing less than absolute certainty and absolutely correct methodology, epistemology, and ontology. In developmental psychology such a program would ultimately lead to rejection of all generalizations, including those relating to the average effects of environments. Because each individual has a unique set of genes and is constantly developing in a unique and constantly changing environment, God himself would probably have difficulty providing a deterministic account of individual development,

---

[43] Anti-theoretical perspectives are far from dead in anthropology. For example, the very influential Clifford Geertz (1973) has carried on the Boasian particularist tradition in anthropology in his rejection of attempts to find generalizations or laws of human culture in favor of interpretive, hermeneutic inquiries into the subjective, symbolic meaning systems unique to each culture. Applied to the present project, such a theoretical perspective would, for example, probe the subjective religious meanings to Jews of the Pentateuchal commandment to be fruitful and multiply and their fear of exogamy rather than attempt to describe the effects of fulfilling these commands on group and individual fitness, the genetic structure of Jewish populations, anti-Semitism, and so on.

and in any case such an account must necessarily, like a Boasian theory of culture, be deferred long into the future.

By adopting this philosophy of science, Lewontin is able to discredit attempts by scientists to develop theories and generalizations and thus, in the name of scientific rigor, avoid the possibility of any politically unacceptable scientific findings. Segerstråle notes that, while using this theory as a weapon against biological views in the social sciences, Lewontin's own empirical research in population biology has remained firmly within the reductionistic tradition.

Gould and Lewontin's (1979) critique of adaptationism may also be viewed as an exemplar of the skeptical thrust of Jewish intellectual activity. Acknowledging the existence of adaptations, the argument effectively problematizes the status of any putative adaptation. Gould (e.g., 1994b) then goes from the possibility that any putative adaptation may simply be a "spandrel" that, like the architectural form from which its name derives, results from structural constraints imposed by true adaptations, to the absurd suggestion that the human mind be viewed as a collection of such nonfunctional spandrels. As noted above, Gould's larger agenda is to convince his audience that the human brain has not evolved to solve adaptive problems—a view anthropologist Vincent Sarich (1995) has termed "behavioral creationism." (For mainstream views on adaptationism, see Boyd & Richerson, 1985, p. 282; Dennett, 1995; Hull, 1988, pp. 424–426; G. C. Williams, 1985.) Indeed, fascination with the slippery rhetoric of the Gould and Lewontin "spandrels" article has resulted in an entire volume of essays dedicated to dissecting its writing style (Selzer, 1993; see especially Fahnestock, 1993; see also comments on the deceptiveness of Lewontin's rhetorical style in J. Carroll, 1995, pp. 449ff).

Scientific skepticism is a powerful approach, since a very basic feature of science is an openness to criticism and a requirement that arguments be supported with evidence. As E. O. Wilson (1994, p. 345) notes, "By adopting a narrow criterion of publishable research, Lewontin freed himself to pursue a political agenda unencumbered by science. He adopted the relativist view that accepted truth, unless based on ineluctable fact, is no more than a reflection of dominant ideology and political power."[44] Similar themes with similar

---

[44] It is interesting in this regard that the proto-Nazi racial theorist Houston Stewart Chamberlain mounted an attempt to discredit science because of its perceived incompatibility with his political and cultural aims. In a move that long antedated the anti-science ideology of the Frankfurt School and contemporary postmodernism (see Ch. 6), Chamberlain argued that science was a social construction and the scientist was like an artist who was engaged in developing a symbolic representation of reality. "So strong was his insistence upon the mythical nature of scientific theory that he removed any real possibility of choosing between one concept and another, thus opening the door wide to subjective arbitrariness" (Field, 1981, p. 296). In what I believe is a mirror image of the motivations of many in the current anti-science movement, Chamberlain's subjectivism was motivated by his belief that recent scientific

motivations characterize the ideologies of the Frankfurt School and postmodernism discussed in Chapter 6.

Nevertheless, Lewontin (1994a) portrays his ideologically inspired efforts as deriving from a concern for scientific rigor: "We demand certain canons of evidence and argument that are formal and without reference to empirical content . . . the logic of statistical inference; the power of replicating experiments; the distinction between observations and causal claims." The result is a thoroughgoing skepticism; for example, all theories of the origins of the sexual division of labor are said to be "speculative." Similarly, Gould rejects all accounts of the empirical data in the area of intelligence testing but provides no alternatives. As Jensen (1982, p. 131) notes, "Gould offers no alternative ideas to account for all of these well-established observations. His mission in this area appears entirely nihilistic." Similarly, Buss et al. (1998) note that whereas the adaptationist perspective in psychology has resulted in a rich body of theoretical predictions and in numerous confirmatory empirical studies, Gould's ideas of spandrels and exaptations (the latter is a term variously used by Gould, but perhaps most often referring to mechanisms that have new biological functions that are not the ones that caused the original selection of the mechanism) have resulted in no theoretical predictions and no empirical research. Again, the mission seems to be what one might term nihilistic anti-science.

As with Boas, Lewontin holds biologically oriented research on humans to an extremely rigorous standard but is remarkably lenient in the standards required to prove biology has very little influence. Lewontin claims, for example, that "nearly all the biology of gender is bad science" (Lewontin, 1994a), but on the following page he states as an obvious truth that "the human being is the nexus of a large number of weakly acting causes." And Lewontin states without argument or reference that "no one has ever found a correlation between cognitive ability and brain size." As of 1998, there have been at least twenty-six published studies on thirty-nine independent samples showing a correlation of approximately 0.20 between head circumference and IQ (see Wickett et al., 1994); there have also been at least six published studies showing a correlation of approximately 0.40 between brain size and IQ using the more accurate technique of magnetic resonance imaging to directly scan the brain (Andreasen et al., 1993; Egan et al., 1994; Harvey et al., 1994; Raz et al., 1993; Wickett et al.,

---

investigations did not support his racialist theories of human differences. When science conflicts with political agendas, the best move is to discredit science. As noted in SAID (Ch. 5), Chamberlain was also very hostile toward evolutionary theory for political reasons. Amazingly, Chamberlain developed anti-selectionist arguments in opposition to Darwinism that predate similar arguments of modern critics of adaptationism such as Richard Lewontin and Stephen Jay Gould reviewed in this chapter: Chamberlain viewed Darwin's emphasis on competition and natural selection as aspects of the evolutionary process as simply an anthropocentric version of the nineteenth-century "dogma of progress and perfectibility adapted to biology" (Field, p. 298).

1994; Willerman et al., 1991). Given this body of findings, it is at least misleading to make such a statement, although Lewontin (1994b) would presumably argue that none of these studies reach acceptable levels of scientific proof.

Franz Boas would be proud.

3

Jews and the Left

I could never understand what Judaism had to do with Marxism, and why questioning the latter was tantamount to being disloyal to the God of Abraham, Isaac, and Jacob.

— Ralph de Toledano, 1996, p. 50,
discussing his experiences with Eastern European Jewish intellectuals

Socialism, for many immigrant Jews, was not merely politics or an idea, it was an encompassing culture, a style of perceiving and judging through which to structure their lives.

— Irving Howe, 1982, p. 9

The association between Jews and the political left has been widely noticed and commented on beginning in the nineteenth century. "Whatever their situation . . . in almost every country about which we have information, a segment of the Jewish community played a very vital role in movements designed to undermine the existing order" (Rothman & Lichter, 1982/1996, p. 110).

The disproportionate historical contribution of Jews to the political Left has been well documented. Both as individual theorists and activists of the stature of Marx, Trotsky, Rosa Luxemburg, Léon Blum and Emma Goldman, and as organized mass labor movements in, for example, revolutionary Russia and early-mid 20th century Warsaw, Amsterdam, Paris, Toronto, Buenos Aires, New York and London, Jews have been conspicuous for their socialist and communist affiliations. (Mendes, 2014, p. viii)

On the surface at least, Jewish involvement in radical political activity may seem surprising. Marxism, at least as envisaged by Marx, is the very antithesis of Judaism. Marxism is an exemplar of a universalist ideology in which ethnic barriers within the society and nationalist barriers between societies are eventually removed in the interests of social harmony and a sense of communal interest. Moreover, Marx himself, though born of two ethnically Jewish parents, has been viewed by many as an anti-Semite. His critique of Judaism, "On the Jewish Question" (Marx, 1843/1975), conceptualized Judaism as fundamentally concerned with egoistic money seeking; it had achieved world domination by making both man and nature into saleable objects. Marx viewed Judaism as an abstract principle of human greed that would end in the communist society of the future.

However, there is continuing controversy over whether Marx's "On the Jewish Question" implies that he was an anti-Semite. For example, Shlomo Avineri (2019) argues that the most likely explanation for Marx's anti-Jewish remarks is that he strongly backed Jewish emancipation and was opposed to Bruno Bauer's demand that Jews be forced to convert to Christianity before being granted legal equality. Marx "had to bend over backward and distance himself as much as possible from Jews and Judaism so as not to be accused of supporting Jewish rights because of his own Jewish background" (p. 48). This at least suggests a Jewish identity and concern for Jewish interests.[45]

---

[45] Other comments on the controversy over Marx's Jewishness: Marx associated with both practicing Jews and individuals of Jewish ancestry throughout his life. Moreover, he was considered by others as Jewish and was continually reminded of his Jewishness by his opponents (see Carlebach, 1978, pp. 310ff; Meyer, 1989). As indicated below, such externally imposed Jewish identity may have been common among Jewish radicals and surely implies that Marx remained conscious of being Jewish. Like many other Jewish intellectuals reviewed here, Marx had an antipathy toward gentile society which may well have been due to his Jewish background. Sammons (1979, p. 263) describes the basis of the mutual attraction between Heinrich Heine and Karl Marx by noting that "they were not reformers, but haters, and this was very likely their most fundamental bond with one another." Deception may also be involved: Carlebach (p. 357) suggests that Marx may have viewed his Jewishness as a liability, and Otto Rühle (1929/1935, p. 377) suggests that Marx (like Freud; see Ch. 5) went to elaborate lengths to deny his Jewishness in order to prevent criticism of his writings. Many writers have emphasized Marx's Jewishness and professed to find Jewish elements (e.g., messianism, social justice) in his writing. A theme of anti-Semitic writing (most notably, perhaps, in Hitler's writings) has been to propose that Marx had a specifically Jewish agenda in advocating a world society dominated by Jews in which gentile nationalism, gentile ethnic consciousness, and traditional gentile elites would be eliminated (see review in Carlebach, pp. 318ff).

Moreover, as discussed in the section "Universalism and the Blurring of Group Boundaries" below, Marxism often functioned to render Jewish identity irrelevant because it explained society solely in terms of class conflict.

However, the entire issue of Marx's attitude toward Judaism is unimportant for evaluating the role of Jews in leftist political movements in the twentieth century up to about 1970, the topic of this volume, since Marx died in 1883.

Whatever Marx's views on the subject, a critical question in the following is whether acceptance of radical, universalist ideologies and participation in radical, universalist movements are compatible with Jewish identification. Does the adoption of such an ideology essentially remove one from the Jewish community and its traditional commitment to separatism and Jewish nationhood? Or, to rephrase this question in terms of my perspective, could the advocacy of radical, universalist ideologies and actions be compatible with continued participation in Judaism as a group evolutionary strategy?

Notice that this question is different from the question of whether Jews as a group can be adequately characterized as advocating radical political solutions for gentile societies. There is no implication that Judaism constitutes a unified movement or that all segments of the Jewish community have the same beliefs or attitudes toward the gentile community (see Ch. 1). Jews may constitute a predominant or necessary element in radical political movements and Jewish identification may be highly compatible with or facilitate involvement in radical political movements without most Jews being involved in these movements and even if Jews are a numerical minority within these movements. Even in the nineteenth and early twentieth centuries, Jews, while also assuming a leading role in various non-socialist movements, had a special role as leaders of Marxist-oriented movements. "The adaptability and intellectual vivacity of the Jews do not suffice to explain the qualitative and quantitative predominance of persons of Hebrew race in the party of the workers" (Michels, 1911/1915, p. 259), particularly in Germany where the first leaders were Marx, Ferdinand Lassalle, and Moses Hess, the latter a friend of Marx who is best known as a proto-Zionist (SAID, Ch. 6).

RADICALISM AND JEWISH IDENTIFICATION

The hypothesis that Jewish radicalism is compatible with Judaism as a group evolutionary strategy implies that radical Jews continue to identify as Jews. Solzhenitsyn (2002/2011, Ch. 15) notes that "As for the Jewish authors, those who denied the Jews' share in the revolution as well as those who have always recognised it, all agree that these Jews were not Jews by spirit, they were renegades." Nevertheless, there is little doubt that the vast majority of the Jews who advocated leftist causes beginning in the late nineteenth century were strongly self-identified as Jews and saw no conflict between Judaism and radicalism (Levin, 1977, p. 65; 1988, I, p. 4–5; Marcus, 1983, pp. 280ff; Mendes, 2014, p. 3; Mishkinsky, 1968, pp. 290–291; Rothman & Lichter, 1982/1996, pp. 92–93; Sorin, 1985, *passim*). Indeed, the largest Jewish radical movements in both Russia and Poland were the Jewish Bunds which had an exclusively Jewish membership and a very clear program of pursuing specifically Jewish interests. The proletarianism of the Polish Bund was really part of an attempt to preserve their national identity as Jews (Marcus, p. 282). Fraternity with the non-Jewish working class was intended to facilitate their specifically Jewish aims, and a similar statement can be made for the Russian Jewish Bund (A. Liebman, 1979, p. 111ff). Since the Bunds comprised by far the majority of the Jewish radical movement in these areas, the vast majority of Jews participating in radical movements in this period were strongly identified as Jews.

Moreover, many Jewish members of the Communist Party of the Soviet Union appear to have been intent on establishing a form of secular Judaism rather than ending Jewish group continuity. The postrevolutionary Soviet government and the Jewish socialist movements struggled over the issue of the preservation of national identity (Levin, 1988; Pinkus, 1988). Despite an official ideology in which nationalism and ethnic separatism were viewed as reactionary, the Soviet government was forced to come to grips with the reality of very strong ethnic and national identifications within the Soviet Union. As a result, a Jewish section of the Communist Party (Evsektsiya) was created.

> [Evsektsiya] fought hard against the Zionist-Socialist Parties, against democratic Jewish communities, against the Jewish faith and against Hebrew culture. It had, however, succeeded in shaping a secular life pattern based on Yiddish as the recognized national language of the Jewish nationality; in fighting for Jewish national survival in the 1920s; and in working in the 1930s to slow down the assimilatory process of the Sovietization of Jewish language and culture. (Pinkus, 1988, p. 62).

Similarly, Levin (1988, I, p. 280) notes that some Evsektsiya activists clearly envisaged themselves as promoting Jewish nationalism as compatible with existence within the Soviet Union:

> It can even be argued that the Evsektsiya prolonged Jewish activity and certain levels of Jewish consciousness by their very efforts to wrench a new concept of a badly battered and traumatized Jewry . . . though at incalculable cost.

The cost was borne by the older Orthodox Jews who did not move to the cities and maintained their traditional way of life in the shtetls:

> If we look at life of regular, not "commanding", Jewish folk, we see desolation and despair in formerly vibrant and thriving shtetls. *Jewish Tribune* reproduced a report by a special official who inspected towns and shtetls in the south-west of Russia in 1923, indicating that as the most active inhabitants moved into cities, the remaining population of elders and families with many children lived to large extent by relying on humanitarian and financial aid from America. (Solzhenitsyn 2002/2011, Ch. 17).

The result of these efforts was the development of a state-sponsored separatist Yiddish subculture, including Yiddish schools and even Yiddish soviets. This separatist culture was very aggressively sponsored by the Evsektsiya. Reluctant Jewish parents were forced "by terror" to send their children to these culturally separatist schools rather than schools where the children would not have to relearn their subjects in the Russian language in order to pass entrance examinations (Gitelman, 1991, p. 12). The themes of the prominent and officially honored Soviet Jewish writers in the 1930s also bespeak the importance of ethnic identity: "The thrust of their prose, poetry and drama boiled down to one idea—the limitations on their rights under tsarism and the flowering of once-oppressed Jews under the sun of the Lenin-Stalin constitution" (Vaksberg, 1994, p. 115).

Further, beginning in 1942, the government-sponsored Jewish Anti-Fascist Committee (JAC) served to promote Jewish cultural and political interests (including an attempt to establish a Jewish republic in the Crimea) until it was dissolved in 1948 by the government amid charges of Jewish nationalism, resistance to assimilation, and Zionist sympathies (Kostyrchenko, 1995, pp. 30ff; Vaksberg, 1994, pp. 112ff). The leaders of the JAC strongly identified as Jews. The following comments of JAC leader Itsik Fefer on his attitudes during the war indicate a powerful sense of Jewish peoplehood extending backward in historical time:

> I [said] that I love my people. But who doesn't love one's own people? . . . My interests in regard to the Crimea and Birobidzhan [an area of the Soviet Union designated for Jewish settlement] had been dictated by this. It seemed to me that only Stalin could rectify that historical injustice, which had been created by the Roman emperors. It seemed to me that only the Soviet government could rectify this injustice, by creating a Jewish nation. (in Kostyrchenko, 1995, p. 39)

Thus, despite their complete lack of identification with Judaism as a religion and despite their battles against some of the more salient signs of Jewish group separatism, membership in the Soviet Communist Party by these Jewish activists was not incompatible with developing mechanisms designed to ensure Jewish group continuity as a secular entity. In the event, apart from the offspring of interethnic marriages, very few Jews lost their Jewish identity during the entire Soviet era (Gitelman, 1991, p. 5), and the post-World War II years saw a powerful strengthening of Jewish culture and Zionism in the Soviet Union. Beginning with the dissolution of the JAC, the Soviet government initiated a campaign of repression against all manifestations of Jewish nationalism and Jewish culture, including closing Jewish theaters and museums and disbanding Jewish writers' unions. And yet, a secret survey published in *The New York Times* in 1981 (Shipler) on data from 1977 indicated that 78 percent of Soviet Jews said they would have "an aversion to a close relative marrying a non-Jew," and 85 percent "wanted their children or grandchildren to learn Yiddish or Hebrew." Other results indicate a continuing strong desire for Jewish culture in the Soviet Union: 86 percent of Jews wanted their children to go to Jewish schools, and 82 percent advocated establishing a Russian-language periodical on Jewish subjects.

The issue of the Jewish identification of prominent Bolsheviks who were Jews by birth is difficult. R. Pipes (1993, pp. 102–104) asserts that Bolsheviks of Jewish background in the czarist period did not identify as Jews, although they were perceived by gentiles as acting on behalf of Jewish interests and were subjected to anti-Semitism. For example, Leon Trotsky, the most important Bolshevik after Lenin, took great pains to avoid the appearance that he had any Jewish identity or that he had any interest in Jewish issues at all. As noted in Chapters 1 and 2, Jews often avoid overt indications of Jewish identity if a Jewish identity would result in anti-Semitism or damage their credibility as a scientist or, in the case of Jewish radicals, being an advocate of Marxist universalism based on social class differences, not ethnic or racial differences.

Nevertheless, while Trotsky claimed his Jewish origins did not influence his attraction to Bolshevism, he "was a Jew in spite of himself," who "gravitated to Jews wherever he lived," "spent a good deal of his adult life among Jews in London, Paris, Vienna, New York, and Russia itself," and "never abided physical attacks on Jews, and often intervened to denounce such violence and organize a defense" (J. Rubenstein, 2013, pp. 67, 78, 114, 52), most notably his outrage and disgust at the trial of Mendel Beilis for ritual murder in 1911. Just prior to leaving for Russia in 1917 after the March Revolution, Trotsky was interviewed by and wrote four columns for the Yiddish newspaper *Forverts* (J. Rubenstein, p. 78). As leader of the Red Army during the Civil War, he "successfully recruited Jews for the Red Army because they were eager to avenge pogrom attacks"; however, he was unsuccessful in forming Jewish military units in order to refute the charge that Jews avoided military service. At the same time, he "voiced his concern over the high number of Jews in the Cheka, knowing that their presence could only provoke hatred towards Jews as a group" (p. 113). Nevertheless, Rubenstein claims that Trotsky regarded Jews as "just another small, persecuted minority," and that he had love for the Jewish people or attachment to Jewish continuity (p. 114). In any case, Trotsky was well known to be ethnically Jewish and Stalin eventually used "anti-Jewish prejudice" (p. 141) in his competition with Trotsky for leadership of the party.

> "Is it true," Trotsky asked [Nicholai] Bukharin, "is it possible that in our party, in Moscow, in workers' cells, anti-Semitic agitation should be carried out with impunity?" ... The revolution had triumphed, the autocracy and its prejudices had been discarded, yet Trotsky could not rid himself of the handicap of being a Jew. (J. Rubenstein, 2013, p. 141)

The Stalinist faction came out with allusions to their enemies' "exotic" origins and drew on chauvinist prejudices that remained anchored in the consciousness of Soviet workers (Brossat & Klingberg, 1983/2016, p. 211). Solzhenitsyn's (2002/2011, Ch. 17) take:

> In 1926 Zinoviev and Kamenev, deceived by Stalin, united with Trotsky ("the United Opposition")—that is, three of the most visible Jewish leaders turned out on one side. Not surprisingly, many of the lower rank Trotskyites were Jewish. (Agursky cites A. Chiliga, exiled with Trotskyites in the Urals: "indeed the Trotskyites were young Jewish intellectuals and technicians," particularly from Left Bundists.
>
> "The opposition was viewed as principally Jewish" and this greatly alarmed Trotsky. In March of 1924 he complained to Bukharin that among the workers it is openly stated: "The kikes are rebelling!" and he claimed to have received hundreds of letters on the topic. Bukharin dismissed it as trivial. Then "Trotsky tried to bring the question of anti-Semitism to a Politburo session but no one supported him." More than anything, Trotsky feared that Stalin would use popular anti-Semitism against him in their battle for power. And such was partially the case according to Uglanov, then secretary of the Moscow Committee of the [Communist Party]. "Anti-Semitic cries were heard" during Uglanov's dispersal of a pro-Trotsky demonstration in Moscow November 7, 1927.

The conflict in the 1920s between Stalin and the Left Opposition, led by Trotsky, Grigory Zinoviev, Lev Kamenev, and Grigory Sokolnikov (all of whom were ethnic Jews), thus had strong overtones of a Jewish-gentile group conflict: "The obvious 'alienness' allegedly uniting an entire bloc of candidates was a glaring circumstance" (Vaksberg, 1994, p. 19; see also Ginsberg, 1993, p. 53; Lindemann, 1997, p. 452; Pinkus, 1988, pp. 85–86; Rapoport, 1990, p. 38; Rothman & Lichter, 1982/1996, p. 94). For all of the participants, the Jewish or gentile backgrounds of their adversaries was highly salient, and indeed Sidney Hook (1949, p. 464) notes that non-Jewish Stalinists used anti-Semitic arguments against the Trotskyists. Vaksberg (1994) quotes Vyacheslav Molotov (Minister of Foreign Affairs and the second most prominent Soviet leader at the time) as saying that Stalin passed over Kamenev because he wanted a non-Jew to head that bureau. Moreover, the internationalism of the Jewish bloc compared to the nationalism implicit in the Stalinist position (Lindemann, 1997, pp. 449–450) is more congruent with Jewish interests and certainly reflects a common theme of Jewish attitudes in post-Enlightenment societies generally. Throughout this period into the 1930s, "for the Kremlin and the Lubyanka [a reference to the Soviet secret police] it was not religion but blood that determined Jewishness" (Vaksberg, 1994, p. 64). Indeed, the secret police used ethnic outsiders (e.g., Jews in the traditionally anti-Semitic Ukraine) as agents because they would have less sympathy with the natives (Lindemann, 1997, p. 443)—a policy that makes excellent evolutionary sense.

Shafarevich (1989, p. 34) notes that Trotsky had a Jewish deputy and that Jewish writers have tended to idolize him. He cites a biography of Trotsky as noting:

> From every indication, the rationalistic approach to the Jewish question that the Marxism he professed demanded of him in no way expressed his genuine feelings. It even seems that he was in his own way "obsessed" with that question; he wrote about it almost more than did any other revolutionary.

Shafarevich (1989, p. 34) also describes several other examples of Jewish communists and leftists who had very pronounced tendencies toward Jewish nationalism. For example, Charles Rappoport, later a leader of the French Communist Party, is quoted as declaring that "The Jewish people [are] the bearer of all the great ideas of unity and human community in history. . . . The disappearance of the Jewish people would signify the death of humankind, the final transformation of man into a wild beast." Chapter 7 describes the attraction of the anti-Stalinist proto-neocons to Trotsky.

It is difficult to believe that these radicals were wholly without a Jewish identity, given that they were regarded as Jews by others and were the target of anti-Semites. In general, anti-Semitism increases Jewish identification (SAID, Ch. 6; see also below).

Jewish ethnic background was thus important not only to gentiles, but was also subjectively important to Jews as well. When the secret police wanted to investigate a Jewish agent, they recruited a "pure Jewish maiden" to develop an intimate relationship with him—implicitly assuming that the operation would work better if the relationship was intraethnic (Vaksberg, 1994, p. 44n).

Similarly, there has been a pronounced tendency for leftist Jews to idolize other Jews such as Trotsky and Rosa Luxemburg rather than leftist gentiles, as in Poland (Schatz, 1991, pp. 62, 89), even though some scholars have serious doubts about the Jewish identifications of these two revolutionaries. Indeed, Hook (1949, p. 465) finds a perception among leftists that there was an ethnic basis for the attraction of Jewish intellectuals to Trotsky. In the words of one, "It is not by accident that three quarters of the Trotskyist leaders are Jews."

There is, then, considerable evidence that Jewish Bolsheviks generally retained at least a residual Jewish identity. In some cases, this Jewish identity may indeed have been "reactive" (i.e., resulting from others' perceptions). For example, Rosa Luxemburg may have had a reactive Jewish identity, since she was perceived as a Jew despite the fact that she "was the most critical of her own people, descending at times to merciless abuse of other Jews" (Shepherd, 1993, p. 118). Nevertheless, Luxemburg's only important sexual relationship was with a Jew, and she continued to maintain ties to her family. Lindemann (1997, p. 178) comments that the conflict between Luxemburg's revolutionary left and the social-democratic reformists in Germany had overtones of German-Jewish ethnic conflict, given the large percentage and high visibility of Jews among the former. By World War I:

> Luxemburg's dwindling friendships within the party had become more exclusively Jewish, whereas her contempt for the (mostly non-Jewish) leaders of the party became more open and vitriolic. Her references to the leadership were often laced with characteristically Jewish phrases: The leaders were "shabbesgoyim of the bourgeoisie." For many right-wing Germans, Luxemburg became the most detested of all revolutionaries, the personification of the destructive Jewish alien. (Lindemann, 1997, p. 402).

Given these findings, the possibilities that Luxemburg was in fact a crypto-Jew or that she was engaged in self-deception regarding her Jewish identity—the latter a common enough occurrence among Jewish radicals (see below)—seem to be at least as likely as supposing that she did not identify as a Jew at all.

In terms of social identity theory, anti-Semitism would make it difficult to adopt the identity of the surrounding culture. Traditional Jewish separatist practices combined with economic competition tend to result in anti-Semitism, but anti-Semitism in turn makes Jewish assimilation more difficult because it becomes more difficult for Jews to accept a non-Jewish identity. Thus in the interwar period in Poland, Jewish cultural assimilation increased substantially; by 1939 one-half of Jewish high school students identified Polish as their native language. However, the continuation of traditional Jewish culture among a substantial proportion of Jews and its correlative anti-Semitism resulted in a barrier for Jews in adopting a Polish identification (Schatz, 1991, pp. 34–35).

From the standpoint of non-Jews, however, anti-Semitic reactions to individuals like Luxemburg and other outwardly assimilating Jews may be viewed as resulting from an attempt to prevent deception by erring on the side of caution by exaggerating the extent to which people who are ethnically Jews identify as Jews and are consciously or unconsciously attempting to advance specifically Jewish interests (see SAID, Ch. 1). Such perceptions of secular Jews and Jews who converted to Christianity have been a common feature of anti-Semitism in the post-Enlightenment world, and indeed, such Jews often maintained informal social and business networks that resulted in marriages with other baptized Jews and Jewish families who had not changed their surface religion (see SAID, Chs. 5–6).

As a general point, several factors favor the supposition that Jewish identification occurred in a substantial percentage of ethnic Jews: (1) People were classified as Jews depending on their ethnic background at least partly because of residual anti-Semitism; this would tend to impose a Jewish identity on these individuals and make it difficult to assume an exclusive identity as a member of a larger, more inclusive political group. (2) Many Jewish Bolsheviks, such as those in the Evsektsiya and the JAC, aggressively sought to establish a secular Jewish subculture. (3) Very few Jews on the left envisioned a postrevolutionary society without a continuation of Judaism as a group; indeed, the predominant ideology among Jewish leftists was that postrevolutionary society would end anti-Semitism because it would end class conflict and the peculiar Jewish occupational profile. (4) The behavior of American communists shows that Jewish identity and the primacy of Jewish interests over communist interests were commonplace among individuals who were ethnically Jewish communists (see below).

(5) Jewish identity may emerge among Jews without a conscious Jewish identity as a result of a perceived threat to Jews, as during the 1967 Arab-Israeli war or the rise of National Socialism. Jewish identification is a complex area where surface declarations may be deceptive. Jews may not consciously know how strongly they identify with Judaism. Silberman (1985, p. 184), for example, notes that around the time of the 1967 Arab-Israeli war, many Jews could identify with the statement of Rabbi Abraham Joshua Heschel that "I had not known how Jewish I was" (emphasis original). Silberman comments, "This was the response, not of some newcomer to Judaism or casual devotee but of the man whom many, myself included, consider the greatest Jewish spiritual leader of our time." Many others made the same surprising discovery about themselves. For example, as stated in the Preface, Arthur Hertzberg (1979, p. 210) wrote:

The immediate reaction of American Jewry to the crisis was far more intense and widespread than anyone could have foreseen. Many Jews would never have believed that grave danger to Israel could dominate their thoughts and emotions to the exclusion of everything else.

The point is that the Jewish identity of even a highly assimilated Jew, and even one who has subjectively rejected a Jewish identity, may surface at times of crisis to the group or when Jewish identification conflicts with any other identity that a Jew might have, including identification as a political radical.

As a result, assertions regarding Jewish identification that fail to take account of perceived threats to Judaism may seriously underestimate the extent of Jewish commitment. Surface declarations of a lack of Jewish identity may be highly misleading. Consider the following comment on Heinrich Heine, who was baptized but remained strongly identified as a Jew: "Whenever Jews were threatened—whether in Hamburg during the Hep-Hep riots [in 1819 in Germany] or in Damascus at the time of the ritual murder accusation [1840]— Heine at once felt solidarity with his people" (Prawer, 1983, p. 762).

Consider also the case of Vitaly Rubin, a prominent philosopher and an ethnic Jew, who recounted his career at a top Moscow school in the 1930s where over half the students were Jewish:

> Understandably, the Jewish question did not arise there. Not only did it not arise in the form of anti-Semitism; it did not arise at all. All the Jews knew themselves to be Jews but considered everything to do with Jewishness a thing of the past. I remember thinking of my father's stories about his childhood, heder [Jewish elementary school], and traditional Jewish upbringing as something consigned to oblivion. None of that had anything to do with me. There was no active desire to renounce one's Jewishness. The problem simply did not exist. (Slezkine, 2004, pp. 253–254)

These Jews clearly have a Jewish identity, but they have been removed from traditional Jewish religious and cultural forms. In such a predominantly Jewish milieu, there was no need to renounce their Jewish identity and no need to push aggressively for Jewish interests, because they had achieved elite status.

However, just prior to World War II, as Russians started replacing Jews among the political elite and National Socialism emerged as an officially anti-Jewish ideology, overt Jewish identity reemerged. Following World War II, Israel began exerting its gravitational pull on Jews, much to the chagrin of a suspicious Stalin. The visit of Golda Meir, who was Israel's plenipotentiary minister to the USSR in 1948, resulted in an outpouring of Jewish support for Zionism and was a watershed event for Soviet Jewry. Stalin reacted to it by initiating a campaign against leaders of the Jewish community and Yiddish culture. As Solzhenitsyn noted, although only 21 percent were found to speak Yiddish in 1959 compared to 72 percent in 1926, in general Jews did not lose their Jewish identity during the Soviet period. In 1966 an official source claimed that "even assimilated Russian-speaking Jews still retain their unique character, distinct from any other segment of the population" (in Solzhenitsyn, 2002/2011, Ch. 23).

(6) As a final factor, the existence of Jewish crypsis in other times and places, as well as the possibility of self-deception, identificatory flexibility, and identificatory ambivalence, are important components of Judaism as a group evolutionary strategy (see SAID, Ch. 8). The best evidence that individuals have really ceased to have a Jewish identity is if they choose a political option that they perceive as clearly not in the interests of Jews as a group. In the absence of a clearly perceived conflict with Jewish interests, it remains possible that different political choices among ethnic Jews are only differences in tactics for how best to achieve Jewish interests. In the case of the Jewish members of the Communist Party USA (CPUSA) reviewed below, the best evidence that ethnically Jewish members continued to have a Jewish identity is that in general their support for the CPUSA waxed and waned depending on whether Soviet policies were perceived as violating specific Jewish interests, such as support for Israel or opposition to National Socialist Germany.

Consider the case of Polina Zhemchuzhina, who was the wife of Vyacheslav Molotov (premier of the USSR during the 1930s), a prominent revolutionary who joined the Communist Party in 1918, and a member of the Party Central Committee, among other accomplishments. When Golda Meir visited the Soviet Union in 1948, Zhemchuzhina repeatedly uttered the phrase "Ich bin a Yiddishe tochter" (I am a daughter of the Jewish people) when Meir asked how she spoke Yiddish so well (J. Rubenstein, 1996, p. 262). "She parted from the [Israeli delegation] with tears in her eyes, saying 'I wish all will go well for you there and then it will be good for all the Jews'" (p. 262). Vaksberg (1994, p. 192) describes her as "an iron Stalinist whose fanaticism did not keep her from being a 'good Jewish daughter.'"

Consider also the identificatory complexities of Ilya Ehrenburg, the prominent Soviet journalist and anti-fascist propagandist for the Soviet Union whose life is described in a book whose title, *Tangled Loyalties* (J. Rubenstein, 1996), refers to this complexity. Ehrenburg was a loyal Stalinist, supporting the Soviet line on Zionism and refusing to condemn Soviet anti-Jewish actions. Nevertheless, Ehrenburg held Zionist views, maintained Jewish associational patterns, believed in the uniqueness of the Jewish people, and was deeply concerned about anti-Semitism and the Holocaust. Ehrenburg was an organizing member of the JAC, which advocated Jewish cultural revival and greater contact with Jews abroad. A writer friend described him as "first of all a Jew. . . .

Ehrenburg had rejected his origins with all his being, disguised himself in the West, smoking Dutch tobacco and making his travel plans at Cook's. . . . But he did not erase the Jew" (p. 204). "Ehrenburg never denied his Jewish origins and near the end of his life often repeated the defiant conviction that he would consider himself a Jew 'as long as there was a single anti-Semite left on earth'" (p. 13). In a famous article, he cited a statement that "blood exists in two forms; the blood that flows inside the veins and the blood that flows out of the veins. . . . Why do I say, 'We Jews'? Because of blood" (p. 259). Indeed, his intense loyalty to Stalin's regime and his silence about Soviet brutalities involving the murder of millions of its citizens during the 1930s may have been motivated largely by his view that the Soviet Union was a bulwark against fascism (pp. 143–145). "No transgression angered him more than anti-Semitism" (p. 313).

Another example is Georg Lukács, as described by Yuri Slezkine, author of *The Jewish Century* (2004). Lukács was the son of a prominent Jewish capitalist who rejected his father's way of life but also expressed his hatred for "the whole of official Hungary," extending his unhappiness with his father to "cover the whole of Magyar life, Magyar history, and Magyar literature indiscriminately (save for Petőfi [1823–1849, a Hungarian poet and liberal revolutionary])" (p. 97). All else—the people and the culture—would have to go. Lazar Kaganovich, the most prolific Jewish mass murderer of the Stalinist era, is pictured at the end of his life reading Pushkin, Tolstoy, and Turgenev (pp. 97–98). But rather than see this as an aspect of traditional Jewish alienation from non-Jews and their culture rationalized with a veneer of Marxism, Slezkine depicts these radicals as enlightened modernists who wished to destroy the old culture except for a few classics of modern literature. At least Shakespeare would have survived the revolution.

Consider also Lev Kopelev, a Soviet writer who witnessed and rationalized the Ukrainian famine as "historical necessity" (Slezkine, 2004, p. 230). Slezkine states categorically that Kopelev did not identify as a Jew, but his own material indicates the complexity of the matter. Kopelev identified himself on Soviet documents as "Jewish" but claimed that was only because he did not want to be seen as a "'cowardly apostate,' and—after World War II—because he did not want to renounce those who had been murdered for being Jewish" (p. 241). To the external world, Kopelev was a proud Jew, but to his close associates—in his "heart of hearts"—he was only a communist and Soviet patriot. But of course many of his close associates were ethnic Jews, and he shed no tears for the Ukrainian and Russian peasants and nationalists who were murdered in the name of international socialism even as he mourned the loss of Jews murdered because they were Jews. By World War II he had become one of the "leading ideologues of Russian patriotism" (p. 279), developing "an acute sense of hurt and injustice on behalf of Russia, Russian history, and the Russian word" (p. 280) as he attempted to rally the Russians to do battle with the Germans.

Russian patriotism had suddenly become useful—much as, I would argue, harnessing the patriotism and high regard for military service among Americans has been useful for Jewish neoconservatives eager to rearrange the politics of the Middle East in the interests of Israel (see Ch. 4). Patriotism is a wonderfully effective instrument in the service of deception (or self-deception).

Ethnic Networking as Reflecting Jewish Identification

It is interesting that the leading Soviet spokesmen on anti-Semitism were both ethnic Jews with non-Jewish-sounding names, Emilian Yaroslavsky (Gubelman) and Yuri Larin (Lurie). Both referred to Jews in the third person (Slezkine, 2004, p. 245), as if they themselves were not Jews. But when Larin tried to explain the embarrassing fact that Jews were "preeminent, overabundant, dominant, and so on" (p. 251) among the elite in the Soviet Union, he mentioned the "unusually strong sense of solidarity and a predisposition toward mutual help and support" (p. 252)—ethnic networking by any other name. Obviously, "mutual help and support" require that Jews recognize each other as Jews. Jewish identity may not have been much discussed, but it operated nonetheless, even if subconsciously, in the rarefied circles at the top of Soviet society.

Another example appears in a report of 1950 to the Central Committee of the Soviet Communist Party on Jewish activities at an aircraft production facility:

> In a number of extremely important departments of the Central Aero-Hy-drodynamic Institute there are workers due to be substituted for political reasons. They gather around themselves people of the same nationality, impose the habit of praising one another (while making others erroneously believe that they are indispensable), and force their protégés through to high posts. (in Kostyrchenko, 1995, p. 237)

Indeed, there is no other way to explain the extraordinary percentages of Jews throughout elite institutions in the USSR prior to the late 1940s when the purges began. High IQ and achievement motivation can only go so far, and cannot explain why, for example, in the late 1940s Jews made up 80 percent of the Soviet Academy of Sciences' Institute of Russian Literature (the Pushkin House), 42 percent of the directors of Moscow theaters, over half of Soviet circus directors (Slezkine, 2004, p. 302), or eight of the top ten directors of the Bolshoi Theater (Kostyrchenko, 1995, p. 15). In the case of the Pushkin House, the opponents of the dominant clique stated that it had been forged "by long-lasting relationships of families and friends, mutual protection, homogeneous

(Jewish) national composition, and anti-patriotic (anti-Russian) tendencies" (in Kostyrchenko, p. 171).

Conclusion: The Complexity of Jewish Identification Among Bolsheviks

Jewish identity always becomes more salient when Jews feel threatened or feel that their interests as Jews are at stake, but Jewish identity becomes submerged when Jewish interests coincide with other interests and identities. This is a human universal; e.g., there has been an increase in White identification consequent to high-profile examples of anti-White hatred in the mainstream media and demographic changes in which Whites are projected to become a minority in the United States within the coming decades (*Individualism*, Ch. 8). The relative submergence of Jewish identity within the Jewish milieu in elite circles of the Soviet Union during the 1920s and 1930s is thus a poor indicator of whether or not these people identified as Jews or would do so in later years when Jewish and Soviet identities began to diverge, when National Socialism reemphasized Jewish identity, or when Israel emerged as a beacon for Jewish identity and loyalty. The emergence of Israel tended to bring Jewish identity to the surface:

> It seemed that all Jews, regardless of age, profession, or social status, felt responsible for the distant little state that had become a symbol of national revival. Even the Soviet Jews who had seemed irrevocably assimilated were now under the spell of the Middle Eastern miracle. Yekaterina Davidovna (Golda Gorbman) was a fanatic Bolshevik internationalist and wife of Marshal Kliment Voroshilov, and in her youth she had been excommunicated as an unbeliever; but now she struck her relatives dumb by saying, "Now at last we have our motherland, too." (Kostyrchenko, 1995, p. 102)

Moreover, there is good evidence that both in the czarist period and in the Bolshevik period, Jewish Bolsheviks perceived their activities as entirely congruent with Jewish interests. The Revolution ended the czarist government—seen by Jews as anti-Semitic—and, although popular anti-Semitism continued in the postrevolutionary period, the government officially outlawed anti-Semitism. Jews were highly overrepresented in positions of economic and political power as well as cultural influence in the USSR at least into the late 1940s. It was also a government that aggressively attempted to destroy all vestiges of Christianity as a socially unifying force within the Soviet Union, while at the same time it established a secular Jewish subculture so that Judaism would not lose its group continuity or its unifying mechanisms, such as the Yiddish language.

It is doubtful, therefore, that Soviet Jewish Bolsheviks ever had to choose between a Jewish identity and a Bolshevik identity, at least in the prerevolutionary period and well into the 1940s. Given this congruence of what one might term "identificatory self-interest," it is quite possible that individual Jewish Bolsheviks would deny or ignore their Jewish identities—perhaps aided by mechanisms of self-deception—while they nevertheless may well have retained a Jewish identity that would have surfaced only if a clear conflict between Jewish interests and communist policies occurred or the establishment of Israel brought out submerged Jewish identities.

JEWS AS ELITE IN THE USSR

In many times and places, Jews have been willing agents of exploitative elites, not only in Western societies, but also in the Muslim world (PTSDA, Ch. 5; SAID, Ch. 2). This is an overarching generalization that one can make about Jewish economic behavior over the ages. Their frequent role went far beyond performing tasks deemed inappropriate for the natives for religious reasons; rather, they performed tasks at which the natives would be relatively less ruthless than Jews, such as tax farming. This resulted in a common theme of traditional anti-Semitism, beginning in the fifth century BC, that blamed ruling elites for exploitative alliances with Jews (SAID, Ch. 2).

> It was primarily because of the functions of the Jews as the king's revenue gatherers in the urban areas that the cities saw the Jews as the monarch's agents, who treated them as objects of massive exploitation. By serving as they did the interests of the kings, the Jews seemed to be working against the interests of the cities; and thus we touch again on the phenomenon we have referred to: the fundamental conflict between the kings and their people—a conflict not limited to financial matters, but one that embraced all spheres of government that had a bearing on the people's life. It was in part thanks to this conflict of interests that the Jews could survive the harsh climate of the Middle Ages, and it is hard to believe that they did not discern it when they came to resettle in Christian Europe. Indeed, their requests, since the days of the Carolingians, for assurances of protection before they settled in a place show (a) that they realized that the kings' positions on many issues differed from those of the common people and (b) that the kings were prepared, for the sake of their interests, to make common cause with the "alien" Jews against the clear wishes of their Christian subjects. In a sense, therefore, the Jews' agreements with the kings in the Middle Ages resembled the understandings they had reached with foreign conquerors in the ancient world. (Netanyahu, 1995, pp. 71–72)

This was also the case in Eastern Europe in the nineteenth century, where economic arrangements such as tax farming, estate management, and monopolies on retail liquor distribution lasted far longer than in the West:

> In this way, the Jewish arendator became the master of life and death over the population of entire districts, and having nothing but a short-term and purely financial interest in the relationship, was faced with the irresistible temptation to pare his temporary subjects to the bone. On the noble estates he tended to put his relatives and co-religionists in charge of the flour-mill, the brewery, and in particular of the lord's taverns where by custom the peasants were obliged to drink. On the church estates, he became the collector of all ecclesiastical dues, standing by the church door for his payment from tithe-payers, baptized infants, newly-weds, and mourners. On the [royal] estates . . . , he became in effect the Crown Agent, farming out the tolls, taxes, and courts, and adorning his oppressions with all the dignity of royal authority. (Davies, 1981, p. 444)

Jewish involvement in the communist elite of the USSR can be seen as a variation on this ancient theme in Jewish culture, instead of a new one sprung from the special circumstances of the Bolshevik Revolution. Rather than being the willing agents of exploitative non-Jewish elites who were clearly separated from both the Jews and the people they ruled, Jews became an entrenched part of an exploitative, oppressive, and indeed murderous elite in which group boundaries were blurred. This blurring of boundaries was aided by several processes: shedding overt Jewish identities in favor of a veneer of international socialism in which Jewish identity and ethnic networking were relatively less visible; adopting Slavic names; and engaging in a limited amount of intermarriage with non-Jewish elites (Lindemann, 1997; Slezkine, 2004). Indeed, the "plethora of Jewish wives" among non-Jewish leaders (Vaksberg, 1994, p. 49), doubtless heightened the Jewish atmosphere at the top levels of the Soviet government, given that, as noted, everyone, especially Stalin, appears to have been quite conscious of ethnicity. For their part, anti-Semites have accused Jews of having "*implanted those of their own category as wives and husbands for influential figures and officials*" (in Kostyrchenko, 1995, p. 272; emphasis original).

As part of the context of the elite status of Jews in the USSR, Yuri Slezkine provides statistics of Jewish domination only dimly hinted at in the following examples from Europe in the late nineteenth century to the rise of National Socialism: in Austria, all but one bank in *fin de siècle* Vienna was administered by Jews, and Jews constituted 70 percent of the stock exchange council; in Hungary, between 50 and 90 percent of all industry was controlled by Jewish banking families, and 71 percent of the wealthiest taxpayers were Jews; in

Germany, Jews were overrepresented among the economic elite by a factor of 33. Similar massive overrepresentation was also to be found in educational attainment and among professionals (e.g., Jews constituted 62 percent of the lawyers in Vienna in 1900, 25 percent in Prussia in 1925, 34 percent in Poland, and 51 percent in Hungary). Indeed, "the universities, 'free' professions, salons, coffeehouses, concert halls, and art galleries in Berlin, Vienna, and Budapest became so heavily Jewish that liberalism and Jewishness became almost indistinguishable" (Slezkine, 2004, p. 63).

Jewish competition had suppressed the formation of a native middle class in Eastern Europe. (This has also occurred throughout Southeast Asia, because of competition from the Overseas Chinese.) When Jews won the economic competition in early modern Poland, the result was that the great majority of Poles were reduced to the status of agricultural laborers supervised by Jewish estate managers in an economy in which trade, manufacturing, and artisanry were in large part controlled by Jews (PTSDA, Ch. 5). On the other hand, in most of Western Europe Jews had been expelled in the Middle Ages. As a result, when modernization occurred, it was accomplished with an indigenous middle class. If, as in Eastern Europe, Jews had won the economic competition in most of these professions, there would not have been a non-Jewish middle class in England. Whatever one imagines might have been the fortunes and character of England with predominantly Jewish artisans, merchants, and manufacturers, it seems reasonable to suppose that the Christian taxpayers of England made a good investment in their own future when they agreed to pay King Edward I a massive tax of 116,346 pounds (worth over 85 million pounds as of 2017) in return for expelling two thousand Jews in 1290 (Mundill, 1998, pp. 249ff).

The rise of the Jews in the USSR came at the expense of the Germans as a middleman minority in Russia prior to the Revolution. (The vast majority of Jews were excluded from traditional Russia apart from the Pale of Settlement, which included Ukraine, Lithuania, Byelorussia, Crimea, and part of Poland.) Germans manned the imperial bureaucracy, formed a large percentage of professionals, entrepreneurs, and artisans, were more literate than the Russians, and had a sense of cultural superiority and ethnic solidarity:

> And so they were, mutatis mutandis, head to the Russian heart, mind to the Russian soul, conscientiousness to Russian spontaneity. They stood for calculation, efficiency, and discipline; cleanliness, fastidiousness, and sobriety; pushiness, tactlessness, and energy; sentimentality, love of family, and unmanliness (or absurdly exaggerated manliness).... Perhaps paradoxically in light of what would happen in the twentieth century, Germans were, occupationally and conceptually, the Jews of ethnic Russia (as well as much of Eastern Europe). Or rather, the Russian Germans were to

Russia what the German Jews were to Germany—only much more so. So fundamental were the German Mercurians [i.e., urban, mobile, literate, articulate, and intellectually sophisticated] to Russia's view of itself that both their existence and their complete and abrupt disappearance have been routinely taken for granted. (Slezkine, 2004, pp. 113–114)

Although the replacement of Germans by Jews was well under way by the time of the Bolshevik Revolution, a key consequence of the Revolution was furthering this replacement. The difference between the Jews and the Germans was that the Jews had a longstanding visceral antipathy, out of past historical grievances, both real and imagined, toward the people and culture they came to administer. Indeed, Russians on the nationalist right admired the Germans, at least up to World War I. For example, a statute of one nationalist organization, Michael the Archangel Russian People's Union, expressed "particular trust in the German population of the Empire" (in Kellogg, 2005, p. 41), while its leader, Vladimir Purishkevich, accused the Jews of "irreconcilable hatred of Russia and everything Russian" (p. 37). Jews disliked the Christian religion of the vast majority of Russians because of the antagonistic relationship between Judaism and Christianity over the ages; Jews distrusted the peasants, who experienced a "fall from grace" (Slezkine, 2004, p. 140) with the intelligentsia after the numerous anti-Jewish pogroms, especially after 1880; and Jews blamed the Czar for not doing enough to keep the peasants in check and for imposing the various quotas on Jewish advancement that went into place, also beginning in the 1880s—quotas that slowed down but by no means halted Jewish overrepresentation in the universities and the professions. In this respect, the Germans were far more like the Overseas Chinese, in that they became an elite without having an aggressively hostile attitude toward the people and culture they administered to and dominated economically. Thus when Jews achieved power in Russia, it was as a hostile elite with a deep sense of historic grievance. As a result, they became willing executioners of both the people and cultures they came to rule, including the Germans.

After the Revolution, not only were the Germans replaced, but also all establishment figures of the older order *and their descendants* were actively suppressed. Jews have always shown a tendency to rise because of their natural abilities (e.g., high intelligence) and powerful ethnic networking, but here they also benefited from "antibourgeois" quotas in educational institutions and other forms of discrimination against the middle class and aristocratic elements of the old regime that would have provided more competition with Jews. In a letter intercepted by the secret police, the father of a student wrote that his son and their friends were about to be purged from the university because of their class origins: "[I]t's clear that only the Jerusalem academics and the Communists, Party members generally, are going to stay" (Slezkine, 2004, p.

243). The bourgeois elements from the previous regime, including the ethnic Germans, would have no future. Thus the mass murder of peasants and nationalists was combined with the systematic exclusion of the previously existing non-Jewish middle class. The wife of a Leningrad University professor noted, "[I]n all the institutions, only workers and Israelites are admitted; the life of the intelligentsia is very hard" (p. 243). Even at the end of the 1930s, prior to the Russification that accompanied World War II, "the Russian Federation . . . was still doing penance for its imperial past while also serving as an example of an ethnicity-free society" (p. 276). While all other nationalities, including Jews, were allowed and encouraged to keep their ethnic identities, the Revolution remained an anti-majoritarian movement.

The Bolshevik Revolution as Ethnic Warfare

Jews were prominently involved in the Bolshevik Revolution and formed an elite group in the Soviet Union well into the post–World War II era. It is interesting that a great many of the non-Jewish Bolsheviks were members of non-Russian ethnic groups. It was a common perception during the early stages of the Soviet Union that the government was dominated by "a small knot of foreigners" (Szajkowski, 1977, p. 55). Stalin, Lavrentiy Beria (deputy premier and head of the Soviet secret police), Sergo Ordzhonikidze (prominent in the Bolshevik Revolution and the subsequent Civil War) were Georgians; Dzerzhinsky, the ruthless head of the Cheka and the OGPU during the 1920s, was a Pole with strong pro-Jewish attitudes—three of Dzerzhinsky's four assistants were Jews: G. Yagoda, V. L. Gerson, and M. M. Lutsky (Solzhenitsyn 2002/2011, Ch. 18). The original Cheka was made up largely of non-Russians, and the Russians in the Cheka tended to be sadistic psychopaths and criminals (Werth, 1999, p. 62; Wolin & Slusser, 1957, p. 6)—people who are unlikely to have any allegiance to or identification with their people. Solzhenitsyn (2002/2011, Ch. 18) cites research indicating that from the "Red Terror" (1918–1922) to the mid-1920s, non-Russians in the OGPU declined from 50 percent to 30–35 percent, and non-Russians in leadership positions declined from 70 percent to 40–45 percent, but that Jewish representation actually increased.

The Bolshevik Revolution therefore had a pronounced ethnic angle: to a very great extent, Jews and other non-Russians ruled over the Russian people, with disastrous consequences for the Russians and other ethnic groups that were not able to become part of the power structure. For example, when Stalin decided to deport the Chechens, he placed an Ossetian—a group from which he himself was partly derived and a historic enemy of the Chechens—in charge of the deportation. Ossetians and Georgians, Stalin's own ancestral groups, were allowed to expand at the expense of other ethnic groups.

While Stalin favored the Georgians, Jews had their own ethnic scores to settle. It seems likely that at least some of the Bolshevik mass murder and terror was motivated by revenge against peoples that had historically been anti-Jewish. Several historians have suggested that Jews were motivated to join the security forces to get revenge for their treatment under the Czar (Rapoport, 1990, p. 31; Baron, 1975, p. 170). Similarly, Jews were placed in charge of security in Ukraine, which had a long history of anti-Semitism (Lindemann, 1997, p. 443) and became a scene of mass murder in the 1930s.

As noted, many of the non-Jewish elite in the USSR had Jewish wives, suggesting philosemitism. Additionally, there were philosemites like writer Maxim Gorky who, as Albert Lindemann (1997, p. 433) phrased it, were "jewified non-Jews,"

> a term, freed of its ugly connotations, [that] might be used to underline an often overlooked point: Even in Russia there were some non-Jews, whether Bolsheviks or not, who respected Jews, praised them abundantly, imitated them, cared about their welfare, and established intimate friendships or romantic liaisons with them.

For example, Gorky's love for the Jews was boundless. Gorky saw Jews as possessors of "heroic" idealism, "all-probing, all-scrutinizing"; "this idealism, which expresses itself in their tireless striving to remake the world according to new principles of equality and justice, is the main, and possibly the only, reason for the hostility toward Jews" (in Slezkine, 2004, p. 164). What united the Jews and philosemites was their hatred for what Lenin (who had a Jewish grandfather) called "the thick-skulled, boorish, inert, and bearishly savage Russian or Ukrainian peasant"—the same peasant Gorky described as "savage, somnolent, and glued to his pile of manure" (Slezkine, 2004, p. 163). It was attitudes like these that created the climate that justified the slaughter of many millions of peasants in the name of creating the new "Soviet man." Philosemites continued to be common among the non-Jewish elite in the USSR, even into the 1950s, when Jews began to be targeted as Jews. One such philosemite was Pavel Sudoplatov, a Slav married to a Jew and with many Jewish friends; Sudoplatov was a high-ranking secret police official with a great deal of blood on his hands. The only murder he unequivocally condemned in his memoirs was that of Paul Mikhoels, a Jewish ethnic activist associated with the Jewish Anti-Fascist Committee.

Figures like Gorky and Sudoplatov were critical to the success of Jews in the Soviet Union. This is a general principle of Jewish political activity in a diaspora situation: because Jews tend to constitute a tiny percentage of a society, they need to make alliances with non-Jews whose perceived interests dovetail with theirs. As indicated in Chapter 4 on neoconservatism, non-Jews have a variety of reasons for being associated with Jewish interests, including career advancement, close personal relationships or admiration for individual Jews, and deeply held personal convictions.

Jewish Dominance of Bolshevism

Yuri Slezkine (2004) has summarized previously available data indicating Jewish dominance of the revolutionary movements before 1917 and of Soviet society thereafter. (Oddly, he makes only a passing reference to Albert Lindemann's important 1997 *Esau's Tears*, which makes many of the same points.) Not only were Jews vastly overrepresented among revolutionaries, but they were also "particularly well represented at the top, among theoreticians, journalists, and leaders" (p. 155). Radical Jews, like other Jews, were very talented, highly intelligent, hardworking, and in addition dedicated to creating effective ethnic networks. These traits propelled them to the top of radical organizations and made the organizations themselves more effective (MacDonald, 2023d).

Although most Jews were not Bolsheviks before the Revolution, Jews were prominent among the Bolsheviks, and once the Revolution was under way, the vast majority of Russian Jews became sympathizers and active participants. Jews were particularly visible in the cities and as leaders in the army and in the revolutionary councils and committees. For example, there were twenty-three Jews among the sixty-two Bolsheviks in the All-Russian Central Executive Committee elected at the Second Congress of Soviets in October 1917. Jews were the leaders of the movement, and to a great extent they were its public face. Slezkine (2004, p. 176) quotes historian Mikhail Beizer who notes, commenting on the situation in Leningrad, that "Jewish names were constantly popping up in newspapers. Jews spoke relatively more often than others at rallies, conferences, and meetings of all kinds." In general, Jews were deployed in supervisory positions rather than positions that placed them in physical danger. In a Politburo meeting on April 18th, 1919, Trotsky urged that Jews be redeployed because there were relatively few Jews in frontline combat units, while Jews constituted a "vast percentage" of the Cheka at the front and in the Executive Committees at the front and at the rear. This pattern had caused "chauvinist agitation" in the Red Army (p. 187).

Citing Paul Johnson's (1987/1988) important work, Lindemann (1997, p. 448) notes Trotsky's "paramount" role in planning and leading the Bolshevik uprising and his role as a "brilliant military leader" in establishing the Red Army as a military force; moreover, many of Trotsky's personality traits are stereotypically Jewish:

If one accepts that anti-Semitism was most potently driven by anxiety and fear, as distinguished from contempt, then the extent to which Trotsky became a source of preoccupation for anti-Semites is significant. Here, too, Johnson's words are suggestive: He writes of Trotsky's "demonic power"—the same term, revealingly, used repeatedly by others in referring to Zinoviev's oratory or Uritsky's ruthlessness [Lev Zinoviev was known for his skill as an orator and his brutality toward counterrevolutionaries; he was a close associate of Lenin and held a number of highly visible posts in the Soviet government; Moisei Solomonovich Uritsky was the notoriously brutal Cheka chief for Petrograd]. Trotsky's boundless self-confidence, his notorious arrogance, and sense of superiority were other traits often associated with Jews. Fantasies there were about Trotsky and other Bolsheviks, but there were also realities around which the fantasies grew.

The high profile of Jews led to popular anti-Semitism:

Any revolution releases a flood of obscenity, envy, and anger from the people. The same happened among the Russian people, with their weakened Christian spirituality. And so the Jews—many of whom had ascended to the top, to visibility, and, what is more, who had not concealed their revolutionary jubilation, nor waited in the miserable lines—increasingly became a target of popular resentment.

Many instances of such resentment were documented in 1917 newspapers. . . . [E.g.:] Newspaper *Russkaya Volya* (*Russian Freedom*) reported: "Right in front of our eyes, anti-Semitism, in its most primitive form . . . re-arises and spreads. . . . It is enough to hear to conversations streetcars [in Petrograd] or in waiting lines to various shops, or in the countless fleeting rallies at every corner and crossroad. . . . They accuse Jews of political stranglehold, of seizing parties and soviets, and even of ruining the army . . . of looting and hoarding goods." (Solzhenitsyn, 2002/2011, Ch. 14)

Solzhenitsyn (2002/2011, Ch. 15) does not blame the Jews for the October 1917 coup:

It is necessary to state explicitly that the October coup was not carried out by Jews (though it was under the general command of Trotsky and with energetic actions of young Grigory Chudnovsky during the arrest of the Provisional Government and the massacre of the defenders of the Winter Palace). Broadly speaking, the common rebuke, that the 170 million people could not be pushed into Bolshevism by a small Jewish minority, is justified. Indeed, we had ourselves sealed our fate in 1917, through our foolishness from February to October–December.

Nevertheless, Solzhenitsyn (2002/2011, Ch. 15) also notes:

[A]t the "historic meeting" in Karpovka Street, in the apartment of Him-
mer and Flaksermann, on 10 October 1917, when the decision to launch the
Bolshevik coup was taken, among the twelve participants were Trotsky,
Zinoviev, Kamenev, [Yakov] Sverdlov, Uritsky, [Grigory] Sokolnikov. It was
there that the first 'Politburo' was elected which was to have such a brilliant future, and among its seven members, always the same: Trotsky, Zinoviev, Kamenev, Sokolnikov.

Moreover, the following document describes a meeting of the Political Bureau of the Central Committee of the All-Russian Communist Party of Bolsheviks dated April 18th, 1919, obtained from the Trotsky archive at Columbia University:

Attended cc.[comrades] Lenin, Krestinsky, Stalin, Trotsky. . . .
     Statement of c.[comrade] Trotsky that Jews and Latvians constitute a
huge percentage of officials in the front-line Chekas, front-line and rear
area executive commissions and central Soviet agencies, and that their
percentage in the front-line troops is relatively small, and that because of
this, strong chauvinist agitation is conducted among the Red Army sol-
diers with certain success, and that, according to c. Trotsky's opinion, it is
necessary to redistribute the Party personnel to achieve a more uniform
representation of officials of all nationalities between front-line and rear
areas. (Solzhenitsyn, 2002/2011, Ch. 16)

Jewish representation at the top levels of the Cheka, the OGPU, and NKVD
(the acronyms by which the secret police were known in different periods) has
often been the focus of those stressing Jewish involvement in the Revolution
and its aftermath. Solzhenitsyn (2002/2011, Ch. 16) quotes a Russian contemporary researcher who found:

"[A]t the initial stage of activity of the punitive agencies, during the 'Red
Terror,' national minorities constituted approximately 50% of the central
Cheka apparatus, with their representation on the major posts reaching
70%." The author provides September 25, 1918 statistical data: among the
ethnic minorities—numerous Latvians and fairly numerous Poles. "The
Jews are quite noticeable, especially among 'major and active Cheka officials,' i.e., commissars and investigators. For instance, among the 'investigators of the Department of Counter-Revolutionary Activities—the most
important Cheka department—half were Jews.'" . . .
     Materials produced by the *Special Investigative Commission in the
South of Russia* provide insights into the Kiev Cheka and its command personnel (based on the testimony of a captured Cheka interrogator): "The
headcount of the 'Cheka' staff varied between 150 and 300 . . . percentage-

wise, there was 75% Jews and 25% others, and those in charge were almost exclusively Jews." Out of twenty members of the Commission, i.e., the top brass who determined people's destinies, fourteen were Jews.

Further:

Zinoviev "gathered many Jews around himself in the Petersburg leadership." . . . By 1921 the preponderance of Jews in Petrograd CP organization . . . "was apparently so odious that the Politburo, reflecting on the lessons of Kronshtadt [a failed rebellion with anti-Jewish overtones] and the anti-Semitic mood of Petrograd, decided to send several ethnic Russian communists to Petrograd, though entirely for publicity purposes." So Uglanov took the place of Zorin-Homberg as head of Gubkom; Komarov replaced Trilisser and Semyonov went to the Cheka. But Zinoviev "objected to the decision of Politboro and fought the new group"—and as a result Uglanov was recalled from Petrograd and "a purely Russian opposition group formed spontaneously in the Petrograd organization," a group, "forced to counter the rest of the organization whose tone was set by Jews." . . .

At the first diplomatic conferences with Soviets in Geneva and the Hague in 1922, Europe could not help but notice that Soviet delegations and their staff were mostly Jewish. . . . In 1922 Gorky told the academic Ipatiev that 98% of the Soviet trade mission in Berlin was Jewish and this probably was not much of an exaggeration. (Solzhenitsyn, 2002/2011, Ch. 18)

Slezkine (2004, p. 177) provides statistics on Jewish overrepresentation in several organizations, especially in supervisory roles. During the 1930s the secret police, then known as the NKVD, "was one of the most Jewish of all Soviet institutions" (p. 254), with forty-two of its 111 top officials being Jewish. At this time, twelve of the twenty NKVD directorates were headed by ethnic Jews, including those in charge of state security, police, labor camps, and resettlement (i.e., deportation). The Gulag was headed by ethnic Jews from its beginning in 1930 until the end of 1938, a period that encompasses the worst excesses of the Great Terror (1936–1938). One might call them "Stalin's willing executioners."

Jews also "abounded at the lower levels of the party machinery," particularly in the secret police (Schapiro, 1961, p. 165). The special role of Jews in the Bolshevik government was not lost on Russians:

For the most prominent and colourful figure after Lenin was Trotsky, in Petrograd the dominant and hated figure was Zinoviev, while anyone who had the misfortune to fall into the hands of the *Cheka* stood a very good chance of finding himself confronted with, and possibly shot by, a Jewish investigator. (Schapiro, 1961, p. 165; cited also by Solzhenitsyn, 2002/2011, and Slezkine, 2004).

Beginning in 1917 it was common for Russians to associate Jews with the Revolution (Werth, 1999, p. 86). Even after the German invasion in 1941, many Russians hoped for German victory to rid the country of "Jews and Bolsheviks"—until the brutality of the invaders became apparent (p. 215).

In addition to many lower-ranking security personnel, prominent Jews included Matvei Berman and Naftali Frenkel, who developed the slave labor system which resulted in hundreds of thousands of deaths. (The construction of a canal between the Baltic Sea and the White Sea claimed many thousands of lives. The six overseers of the project were Jews: Firin, Berman, Frenkel, Kogan, Rappoport, and Zhuk.) Other Jews who were prominent in carrying out the Red Terror included Genrikh Yagoda (head of the secret police), Aron Soltz (a prominent early Bolshevist but an opponent of the Great Purge of the 1930s), Lev Inzhir (chief accountant of the Gulag Archipelago), M. I. Gay (head of a special secret police department), A. A. Slutsky and his deputy Boris Berman (in charge of terror abroad), K. V. Pauker (secret police Chief of Operations), and Lazar Kaganovich (most powerful government official behind Stalin during the 1930s and prominently involved in the mass murders that took place during that period) (Rapoport, 1990, pp. 44–50).

The Soviet government murdered over twenty million of its own citizens, the vast majority in the first twenty-five years of its existence during the height of Jewish power. It was "a state against its people" (Werth, 1999), mounting murderous campaigns of collective punishment (usually involving deportation or forced starvation) against a great many ethnic groups, including Great Russian peasants, Ukrainians, Cossacks, Chechens, Crimean Tatars, Volga Germans, Moldavians, Kalmyks, Karachai, Balkars, Ingush, Greeks, Bulgars, Crimean Armenians, Meskhetian Turks, Kurds, and Khemshins as groups (Courtois et al, 1999, p. 10; Werth, 1999, pp. 219ff). Although individual Jews were caught up in the Bolshevik violence, there was never any violence directed at Jews as a group, and indeed, anti-Semitism was outlawed.

The Bolsheviks continued to apologize for Jewish overrepresentation until the topic became taboo in the 1930s, and it was not until the late 1930s that there was a rise in visibility and assertiveness of "anti-Semites, ethnic nationalists, and advocates of proportional representation" (Slezkine, 2004, p. 188). By this time the worst of the slaughters in the Gulag, the purges, and the contrived famines had been completed.

The belief in the prominence of Jews in the Revolution and its aftermath was common among influential figures in the West, such as Winston Churchill (1920), who wrote that the role of Jews in the Revolution "is certainly a very great one; it probably outweighs all others." Indeed, conservatives throughout

Europe and the United States believed that Jews were responsible for communism and the Bolshevik Revolution (Bendersky, 2000; A. Mayer, 1988; Nolte, 1965). Slezkine (2004, p. 181, emphasis original) highlights similar comments from a book published in 1927 by V. V. Shulgin, a Russian nationalist, who experienced firsthand the murderous acts of the Bolsheviks in his native Kiev in 1919:

> We do not like the fact that this whole terrible thing was done *on the Russian back* and that it has cost us unutterable losses. We do not like the fact that you, Jews, a relatively small group within the Russian population, participated in this vile deed *out of all proportion to your numbers*.

Slezkine (2004, p. 180) does not disagree with this assessment, but argues that Jews were hardly the only revolutionaries. This is certainly true but does not affect the argument that Jewish involvement was a necessary condition, not a sufficient condition, for the success of the Bolshevik Revolution and its bloody aftermath (see also below).

Overall, Slezkine's account clearly supports the Jews-as-necessary-condition claim, especially because of his emphasis on the leadership role of Jews. Indeed, in *Lenin in Zurich* "Solzhenitsyn offers tantalizing evidence that the October Revolution would not have occurred (or would not have been successful) without actions carried out by Jews at its most critical moments" (S. J. Quinn, 2021, p. 47). Jews were overrepresented in the October Revolution and subsequent governments: six of the twelve conspirators and, according to mass murderer Lazar Kaganovich, "the vast majority of the presidium at the table were Jews," as well as at least half of Lenin's first Soviet Politburo (p. 103). However, much like Slezkine, Solzhenitsyn portrays the 1930s as the height of Jewish power in the USSR:

> Despite offering the caveat that Jews never constituted all of these powerful organizations, Solzhenitsyn goes on for pages detailing the Jewish dominance of Soviet economics, diplomacy, culture, and politics during the 1930s. . . . And this was occurring while Stalin was supposedly purging Jews from the Party. (S. J. Quinn, 2021, pp. 119–120)

American Jews rarely criticized the USSR until there were signs that Jews were being persecuted in the USSR. Indeed, the origins of the neoconservative movement can be traced to the 1950s when reports began to trickle in that Jews were being removed from positions of power (see Ch. 4).

However, the claim that Jewish involvement was a necessary condition is itself an understatement because, as Shulgin noted, the effectiveness of Jewish revolutionaries was far out of proportion to the number of Jews. A claim that a group constituting a large proportion of the population was necessary to the success of a movement would be unexceptional. But the critical importance of Jews occurred even though Jews constituted approximately 5 percent of the Russian population around the time of the Revolution, and they were much less represented in the major urban areas of Moscow and Leningrad prior to the Revolution because they were prevented from living there by the Pale of Settlement laws. Slezkine is correct that Jews were not the only revolutionaries, but his point only underscores the importance of Jewish personality traits underlying the intensity and effectiveness of Jewish activism (see Preface), as noted above by Lindemann (1997), and the alliances Jews typically make with non-Jews in diaspora situations in order to advance their perceived interests as a small minority.

In 1923, several Jewish intellectuals published a collection of essays admitting the "bitter sin" of Jewish complicity in the crimes of the Revolution. In the words of a contributor, I. L. Bikerman, "it goes without saying that not all Jews are Bolsheviks and not all Bolsheviks are Jews, but what is equally obvious is that disproportionate and immeasurably fervent Jewish participation in the torment of half-dead Russia by the Bolsheviks" (in Slezkine, 2004, p. 183).

Vaksberg (1994, p. 20) has a particularly interesting presentation. He notes, for example, that in a photomontage of the Bolshevik leaders taken in 1920, twenty-two of the sixty-one leaders were Jews, "and the picture did not include Kaganovich, Pyatnitsky, Goloshchekin, and many others who were part of the ruling circle, and whose presence on that album page would have raised the percentage of Jews even higher." Recall that, as noted above, anti-Semites accused Jews of having "*implanted those of their own category as wives and husbands for influential figures and officials*" (in Kostyrchenko, 1995, p. 272, emphasis original). This point fits well with Lindemann's description of gentile Bolsheviks as "jewified non-Jews," as also noted above.

Among gentile Russians there was a widespread perception that "whereas everybody else had lost from the Revolution, the Jews, and they alone, had benefited from it" (R. Pipes, 1993, p. 101), as indicated, for example, by official Soviet government efforts against anti-Semitism. As in the case of post-World War II Poland, Jews were considered trustworthy supporters of the regime because of the very great change in their status brought about by the Revolution (Vaksberg, 1994, p. 60). As a result, the immediate postrevolutionary period was characterized by intense anti-Semitism, including the numerous pogroms carried out by the White Army. However, Stalin "decided to destroy the 'myth' of the decisive role of the Jews in the planning, organization, and realization of the revolution" and to emphasize the role of Russians (p. 82). Just as do contemporary Jewish apologists, Stalin had an interest in deemphasizing the role of Jews in the Revolution, but for different reasons.

Jews were highly overrepresented among the political and cultural elite in the Soviet Union throughout the 1920s (Ginsberg, 1993, p. 53; I. L. Horowitz, 1993, p. 83; R. Pipes, 1993, p. 112) and, indeed, into the 1950s era during purges of Jews from the economic and cultural elite (Kostyrchenko, 1995). I interpret Vaksberg's (1994) thesis regarding Stalin as implying that Stalin was an anti-Semite from very early on, but that because of the powerful presence of Jews at the top reaches of the government and other areas of Soviet society as well as the need to appeal to Western governments, his efforts to remove Jews from top levels of government developed only slowly, and he was forced to engage in considerable deception. Thus Stalin mixed his measures against Jews with overt expressions of philo-Semitism and often included a few non-Jews to mask the anti-Jewish intent. For example, just prior to a series of trials in which eleven of the sixteen defendants were Jewish, there was a widely publicized trial of two non-Jews on charges of anti-Semitism (p. 77). In the trials of the Jews, no mention was made of Jewish ethnic background, and, with one exception, the defendants were referred to only by their (non-Jewish-sounding) party pseudonyms rather than their Jewish names. Stalin continued to give honors and awards to Jewish artists during the 1930s even while he was removing the top Jewish political leaders and replacing them with gentiles (see also J. Rubenstein, 1996, p. 272).

Jewish overrepresentation in the Bolshevik Revolution has been a potent source of anti-Semitism ever since the Revolution and was prominent in National Socialist writing about Jews (e.g., *Mein Kampf*). In his *Russophobia*, originally distributed as Samizdat in 1982 and officially published in 1989, Igor Shafarevich, a mathematician and member of the prestigious U.S. National Academy of Sciences (NAS), argued that Jews bore considerable responsibility for the Bolshevik Revolution (see R. Stone, 1992, p. 743; Spector, 1992). Shafarevich argued that Jews occupied many top leadership positions during the Revolution and that their activities during this period and later were motivated by hostility to Russians and their culture. Shafarevich claimed that Jews were critically involved in actions that destroyed traditional Russian institutions, particularly in their role in dominating the secret police. He stresses the Jewish role in liquidating Russian nationalists and undermining Russian patriotism, murdering the Czar and his family, dispossessing the kulaks, and destroying the Orthodox Church. He views Jewish "Russophobia" not as a unique phenomenon, but as resulting from traditional Jewish hostility toward the gentile world considered as *tref* (unclean) and toward gentiles themselves considered as sub-human and as worthy of destruction—another example of the separatist and misanthropic themes of anti-Semitism (SAID, Ch. 2). Shafarevich reviewed Jewish literary works during the Soviet and post-Soviet period indicating hatred toward Russia and its culture mixed with a powerful desire for revenge. Reflecting the cultural domination theme of anti-Semitism, Shafarevich claimed that Jews have had more influence on Russia than perhaps any other country, but that discussion of the role of Jews either in contemporary Russia or even in the theoretically more open United States results in intense hostility and reprisals. Indeed, in a comment that is quite similar to neoconservative claims that the interests of the U.S. and Israel dovetail completely (see Ch. 4), Shafarevich stated that any possibility that Jewish interests conflict with the interests of others cannot even be proposed as a hypothesis.

The NAS asked Shafarevich to resign from his position in the academy, but he refused. *Russophobia* was followed by a deluge of charges of anti-Semitism, the vast majority from Jewish writers, as well as condemnation from throughout the Western academic and popular media, including *Newsweek, The Washington Post, The Boston Globe,* and *The New Republic* (S. J. Quinn, 2022a,b; see also Berglund, 2012).

The Transformation of Jews After the Bolshevik Revolution

Many of the commentators on Jewish Bolsheviks noted the "transformation" of Jews. In the words of a Jewish commentator, G. A. Landau, "cruelty, sadism, and violence had seemed alien to a nation so far removed from physical activity." Another commentator, I. A. Bromberg (also Jewish), noted:

[T]he formerly oppressed lover of liberty had turned into a tyrant of "unheard-of-despotic arbitrariness." . . . The convinced and unconditional opponent of the death penalty not just for political crimes but for the most heinous offenses, who could not, as it were, watch a chicken being killed, has been transformed outwardly into a leather-clad person with a revolver and, in fact, lost all human likeness. (in Slezkine, 2004, pp. 183–184)

This psychological "transformation" of Russian Jews was probably not all that surprising to the Russians themselves, given Gorky's finding that Russians prior to the Revolution saw Jews as possessed of "cruel egoism" and that they were concerned about becoming slaves of the Jews. Gorky himself remained a philosemite to the end, although in 1922 he complained that there were too many Jews in the government (Solzhenitsyn, 2002/2011, Ch. 18); he also commented:

[T]he reason for the current anti-Semitism in Russia is the tactlessness of the Jewish Bolsheviks. The Jewish Bolsheviks, not all of them but some irresponsible boys, are taking part in the defiling of the holy sites of the Russian people. They have turned churches into movie theaters and reading rooms without considering the feelings of the Russian people. [However, Gorky did not blame the Jews for this.] The fact that the Bolsheviks sent the Jews, the helpless and irresponsible Jewish youths, to do these things, does smack of provocation, of course. But the Jews should have refrained. (in Slezkine, 2004, p. 186)

From Solzhenitsyn (2002/2011, Ch. 17):

We have not forgotten how it looked at the height of the decade [1920s]: Russian patriotism was abolished forever. But the feelings of the people will not be forgotten. Not how it felt to see the Church of the Redeemer blown up by the engineer Dzhevalkin and that the main mover behind this was Kaganovich who wanted to destroy St. Basil's cathedral as well. Russian Orthodoxy was publicly harassed by "warrior atheists" led by Gubelman-Yaroslavsky. It is truthfully noted: "That Jewish communists took part in the destruction of churches was particularly offensive. . . . No matter how offensive the participation of sons of Russian peasants in the persecution of the church, the part played by each non-Russian was even more offensive."

Further, Solzhenitsyn (2002/2011, Ch. 18) quotes an author, S.S. Maslov, who emigrated in 1922:

Maslov tries to understand "the cause of the widespread and bitter hatred of Jews in modern Russia" and it seems to him to be the "identification throughout society of Soviet power and Jewish power."
   "The expression 'Yid Power' is often used in Russia and particularly in Ukraine and in the former Pale of Settlement not as a polemic, but as a completely objective definition of power, its content and its politics." "Soviet power in the first place answers the wishes and interests of Jews and they are its ardent supporters and in the second place, power resides in Jewish hands."

Those who carried out the mass murder and dispossession of the Russian peasants saw themselves, at least in their public pronouncements, as doing what was necessary in pursuit of the greater good. This was the official view not only of the Soviet Union, where Jews formed a dominant elite, but also the "more or less official view" among Jewish intellectuals in the United States (Slezkine, 2004, p. 215) and elsewhere. (It is still far more common for leftist intellectuals to bemoan McCarthyism than the horrors of the USSR; see below.)

It is for the sake of creating a perfect human being . . . that Levinson steels himself for doing what is "necessary," including the requisitioning of a weeping farmer's last pig and the killing of a wounded comrade too weak to be evacuated. . . . The greater the personal responsibility for acts ordinarily considered evil, the more visible the signs of election and the inner strength they bespoke. Demonic as well as Promethean, Bolshevik commissars "carried within them" the pain of historical necessity. (in Slezkine, 2004, p. 194)

Levinson, a character in A. Fadeyev's *The Rout* (1926)—a prominent example of socialist realism in the early Soviet period—is not ideologically Jewish, "but there is little doubt that for reasons of both aesthetic and sociological verisimilitude, canonical Jewishness seemed an appropriate expression of the Bolshevik vision of disembodied consciousness triumphing over [peasant] inertia" (Slezkine, 2004, p. 193). So it is not surprising that Gorky's mild rebuke of Jewish anti-Christian zealotry was too much for Esther Frumkin, a leader of the Party's Jewish section. Frumkin accused Gorky of attacking "Jewish Communists for their selfless struggle against darkness and fanaticism" (p. 187). In their self-perceptions, Jews are selflessly altruistic even when acting out ancient hatreds.

RADICALISM AND JEWISH IDENTIFICATION IN THE UNITED STATES AND ENGLAND

Jews and the Old Left

A strong sense of Jewish identification also characterized American Jewish radicals, from their origins in the late nineteenth century—e.g., the Union of Hebrew Trades and the Jewish Socialist Federation (see Levin, 1977; A. Liebman, 1979). In Sorin's (1985) study of Jewish radicals who immigrated to the United States early in the twentieth century, only 7 percent were hostile to any form of Jewish separatism, while over 70 percent "were imbued with positive Jewish consciousness. The great majority were significantly caught up in a web of overlapping institutions, affiliations, and Jewish social formations" (p. 119). Moreover, "at the very most" twenty-six of ninety-five radicals were in Sorin's "hostile, ambivalent, or assimilationist" categories, but "in some if not all of the cases, these were persons struggling, often creatively, to synthesize new identities" (p. 115). A major theme of this chapter is that a great many avowedly "deracinated" Jewish radicals had self-deceptive images of their lack of Jewish identification.

The following comment about Emma Goldman, a very prominent American Jewish radical, illustrates the general trend:

The pages of the magazine *Mother Earth* that Emma Goldman edited from 1906 to 1917 are filled with Yiddish stories, tales from the Talmud, and translations of Morris Rosenfeld's poetry. Moreover, her commitment to

anarchism did not divert her from speaking and writing, openly and frequently, about the *particular* burdens Jews faced in a world in which anti-
semitism was a living enemy. Apparently, Emma Goldman's faith in anarchism, with its emphasis on *universalism*, did not result from and was not
dependent on a casting off of Jewish identity. (Sorin, 1985, p. 8; emphasis
original)

Twentieth-century American Jewish radicalism was a specifically Jewish
subculture, or "contraculture" to use Arthur Liebman's (1979, p. 26) term. The
American Jewish left never removed itself from the wider Jewish community,
and, indeed, membership of Jews in the movement fluctuated depending on
whether these movements clashed with specifically Jewish interests.

Similarly in England, the short-lived Hebrew Socialist Union was established in London in 1876 as a specifically Jewish association. Alderman (1992, p.
171) comments:

[The Hebrew Socialist Union] threw into sharp relief the problem that was
to face all succeeding Jewish socialist organs and all subsequent Jewish
trade unions: whether their task was simply to act as a channel through
which Jewish workers would enter the English working-class movements—the Anglicization of the Anglo-Jewish proletariat—or whether
there was a specifically Jewish (and Anglo-Jewish) form of labour organization and of socialist philosophy that demanded a separate and autonomous articulation.

Eventually a Yiddish-speaking Jewish trade union movement was established, and in cases where Jews joined previously existing unions, they formed
specifically Jewish subgroups within the unions.

Fundamentally, the Jewish Old Left, including the unions, the leftist press,
and the leftist fraternal orders—which were often associated with a synagogue
(A. Liebman, 1979, p. 284)—were part of the wider Jewish community. And when
the Jewish working class and the importance of radical political beliefs declined, specifically Jewish concerns and identity gained increasing prominence. This tendency for Jewish members of leftist organizations to concern
themselves with specifically Jewish affairs increased after 1930 primarily because of recurring gaps between specific Jewish interests and universalist leftist causes at that time. This phenomenon occurred within the entire spectrum
of leftist organizations, including the CPUSA and the Socialist Party, whose
membership also included gentiles (pp. 267ff).

Jewish separatism in leftist movements was facilitated by a very traditional aspect: the use of an ingroup language. Yiddish eventually became highly
valued for its unifying effect on the Jewish labor movement and its ability to

cement ties with the wider Jewish community (Levin, 1977, p. 210; A. Liebman, 1979, pp. 259–260).

> The *landsmanshaften* [Jewish social clubs], the Yiddish press and theatre, East Side socialist cafés, literary societies and *fereyns*, which were so much a part of Jewish socialist culture, created an unmistakable Jewish milieu, which the shop, union, or Socialist party could not possibly duplicate. Even the class enemy—the Jewish employer—spoke Yiddish. (Levin, 1977, p. 210).

Indeed, the socialist educational program of the Workmen's Circle (the largest Jewish labor fraternal order in the early twentieth century) failed at first (prior to 1916) because of the absence of Yiddish and Jewish content: "Even radical Jewish parents wanted their children to learn Yiddish and know something about their people" (A. Liebman, 1979, p. 292). These schools succeeded when they began including a Jewish curriculum with a stress on Jewish peoplehood. They persisted through the 1940s as Jewish schools with a socialist ideology which stressed the idea that a concern for social justice was the key to Jewish survival in the modern world. Clearly, socialism and liberal politics had become a form of secular Judaism. The organization had been transformed over its history "from a radical labor fraternal order with Jewish members into a Jewish fraternal order with liberal sentiments and a socialist heritage" (p. 295).

Similarly, the communist-oriented Jewish subculture, including organizations such as the International Workers Order (IWO), included Yiddish-speaking sections. One such section, the Jewish Peoples Fraternal Order (JPFO), was an affiliate of the American Jewish Congress (AJCongress)—the largest Jewish organization in America—and was listed as a subversive organization by the U.S. Attorney General. The JPFO had fifty thousand members and was the financial and organizational "bulwark" of the CPUSA after World War II; it also provided critical funding for the *Daily Worker* and the *Morgen Freiheit*, both affiliated with the CPUSA (Svonkin, 1997, p. 166). Consistent with the present emphasis on the compatibility of communism, radical politics, and Jewish identity, it funded children's educational programs that promulgated a strong relationship between Jewish identity and radical concerns. The IWO Yiddish schools and summer camps, which continued into the 1960s, stressed Jewish culture and even reinterpreted Marxism not as a theory of class struggle but as a theory of struggle for Jewish freedom from oppression. Although the AJCongress eventually severed its ties with the JPFO during the Cold War period and stated that communism was a threat, it was "at best a reluctant and unenthusiastic participant" (Svonkin, 1997, p. 132) in the Jewish effort to develop a public image of anti-communism—a position reflecting the sympathies of many among its predominantly second- and third-generation Eastern European immigrant membership.

David Horowitz (1997, p. 42) describes the world of his parents who had joined a "shul" run by the CPUSA in which Jewish holidays were given a political interpretation. Psychologically these people might as well have been in eighteenth-century Poland:

> What my parents had done in joining the Communist Party and moving to Sunnyside was to return to the ghetto. There was the same shared private language, the same hermetically sealed universe, the same dual posturing revealing one face to the outer world and another to the tribe. More importantly, there was the same conviction of being marked for persecution and specially ordained, the sense of moral superiority toward the stronger and more numerous *goyim* outside. And there was the same fear of expulsion for heretical thoughts, which was the fear that riveted the chosen to the faith.

A strong sense of Jewish peoplehood was also characteristic of the leftist Yiddish press. Thus a letter writer to the radical *Jewish Daily Forward* complained that his nonreligious parents were upset because he wanted to marry a non-Jew:

> He wrote to the *Forward* on the presumption that he would find sympathy, only to discover that the socialist and freethinking editors of the paper insisted . . . that it was imperative that he marry a Jew and that he continue to identify with the Jewish community. . . . [T]hose who read the Forward knew that the commitment of Jews to remain Jewish was beyond question and discussion. (Hertzberg, 1989, pp. 211–212).

The *Forward* had the largest circulation of any Jewish periodical in the world into the 1930s and maintained close ties to the Socialist Party.

Werner Cohn (1958, p. 621) describes the general milieu of the immigrant Jewish community from 1886 to 1920 as "one big radical debating society":

> By 1886 the Jewish community in New York had become conspicuous for its support of the third-party (United Labor) candidacy of Henry George, the theoretician of the Single Tax. From then on Jewish districts in New York and elsewhere were famous for their radical voting habits. The Lower East Side repeatedly picked as its congressman Meyer London, the only New York Socialist ever to be elected to Congress. And many Socialists went to the State Assembly in Albany from Jewish districts. In the 1917 mayoralty campaign in New York City, the Socialist and anti-war candidacy of Morris Hillquit was supported by the most authoritative voices of

the Jewish Lower East Side: The United Hebrew Trades, the International Ladies' Garment Workers' Union, and most importantly, the very popular Yiddish *Daily Forward*. This was the period in which extreme radicals—like Alexander Berkman and Emma Goldman—were giants in the Jewish community, and when almost all the Jewish giants—among them Abraham Cahan, Morris Hillquit, and the young Morris R. Cohen—were radicals. Even Samuel Gompers, when speaking before Jewish audiences, felt it necessary to use radical phrases.

Jews and the CPUSA

The *Morgen Freiheit*, an unofficial organ of the CPUSA from the 1920s to the 1950s, "stood at the center of Yiddish proletarian institutions and subculture ... [which offered] identity, meaning, friendship, and understanding" (A. Liebman, 1979, pp. 349–350). The newspaper lost considerable support in the Jewish community in 1929 when it took the Communist Party position in opposition to Zionism, and by the 1950s it essentially had to choose between satisfying its Jewish soul or its status as a communist organ. Choosing the former, by the late 1960s it was justifying not returning the Israeli-occupied territories in opposition to the line of the CPUSA.

The relationship of Jews and the CPUSA is particularly interesting because the party often adopted positions opposed by the rest of the Jewish community, especially because of its close association with the Soviet Union. Beginning in the late 1920s Jews played a very prominent role in the CPUSA (Klehr, 1978, pp. 37ff). As always, merely citing percentages of Jewish leaders does not adequately indicate the extent of Jewish influence because it fails to take account of the personal characteristics of Jewish radicals as a talented, educated, and ambitious group (Sorin, 1985, pp. 121–122)—as well as capable of producing charismatic leaders like Trotsky, as noted above. Efforts were made to recruit gentiles as "window dressing" to conceal the extent of Jewish dominance (Klehr, 1978, p. 40; Rothman & Lichter, 1982/1996, p. 99). Lyons (1982, p. 81) quotes a gentile communist who said that many working-class gentiles felt that they were recruited in order to "diversify the Party's ethnic composition"; the informant recounts his experience as a gentile representative at a communist-sponsored youth conference:

> It became increasingly apparent to most participants that virtually all of the speakers were Jewish New Yorkers. Speakers with thick New York accents would identify themselves as "the delegate from the Lower East Side" or "the comrade from Brownsville." Finally the national leadership called a recess to discuss what was becoming an embarrassment. How could a supposedly national student organization be so totally dominated by New York Jews? Finally, they resolved to intervene and remedy the

situation by asking the New York caucus to give "out-of-towners" a chance to speak. The convention was held in Wisconsin.

Klehr (1978, p. 40) estimates that from 1921 to 1961, Jews constituted 33.5 percent of the CPUSA Central Committee members, and the representation of Jews was often above 40 percent (p. 46). Jews were the only native-born ethnic group from which the party was able to recruit. Glazer (1969, p. 129) states that at least half of the CPUSA membership of around fifty thousand were Jews into the 1950s and that the rate of turnover was very high; thus perhaps ten times that number of individuals were involved in the party, and there were "an equal or larger number who were Socialists of one kind or another." Writing of the 1920s, Buhle (1980/1991, p. 89) notes that "most of those favorable to the party and the *Freiheit* simply did not join—no more than a few thousand out of a following of a hundred times that large."

Ethel and Julius Rosenberg, who were convicted of spying for the Soviet Union, exemplify the powerful sense of Jewish identification among many Jews on the left. Svonkin (1997, p. 158) shows that they viewed themselves as Jewish martyrs. Like many other Jewish leftists, they perceived a strong link between Judaism and their communist sympathies. Their prison correspondence, in the words of one reviewer, was filled with a "continual display of Judaism and Jewishness," including the comment that "in a couple of days, the Passover celebration of our people's search for freedom will be here. This cultural heritage has an added meaning for us, who are imprisoned away from each other and our loved ones by the modern Pharaohs" (pp. 158–159).

Embarrassed by the self-perceptions of the Rosenbergs as Jewish martyrs, the Anti-Defamation League (ADL) interpreted Julius Rosenberg's professions of Jewishness as an attempt to obtain "every possible shred of advantage from the faith that he had repudiated" (Svonkin, 1997, p. 159)—another example of the many apologetic attempts, some recounted in this chapter, to render incompatible Jewish identification and political radicalism, and thus completely obscure an important chapter of Jewish history.

As in the case of the Soviet Union in the early decades, the CPUSA had separate sections for different ethnic groups, including a Yiddish-speaking Jewish Federation.[46] When these were abolished in 1925 in the interests of developing a party that would appeal to native Americans (who tended to have a low level of ethnic consciousness), there was a mass exodus of Jews from the party, and many of those who remained continued to participate in an unofficial Yiddish subculture within the party.

In the following years Jewish support for the CPUSA rose and fell depending on party support for specific Jewish issues. During the 1930s the CPUSA

---

[46] The following discussion is based on A. Liebman (1979, pp. 492ff).

changed its position and took great pains to appeal to specific Jewish interests, including a primary focus against anti-Semitism, supporting Zionism and eventually Israel, and advocating the importance of maintaining Jewish cultural traditions. As in Poland during this period, "The American radical movement glorified the development of Jewish life in the Soviet Union. . . . The Soviet Union was living proof that under socialism the Jewish question could be solved" (Kann, 1981, pp. 152–153). Communism was thus perceived as "good for Jews." Despite temporary problems caused by the Soviet-German nonaggression pact of 1939, the result was an end to the CPUSA's isolation from the Jewish community during World War II and the immediate postwar years.

Interestingly, the Jews who remained within the party during the period of the nonaggression pact faced a difficult conflict between divided loyalties, indicating that Jewish identity was still important to these individuals. The nonaggression pact provoked a great deal of rationalization on the part of Jewish CPUSA members, often involving an attempt to interpret the Soviet Union's actions as actually benefiting Jewish interests—clearly an indication that these individuals had not given up their Jewish identities. Others continued to be members but silently opposed the party's line because of their Jewish loyalties. Of great concern for all of these individuals was that the nonaggression pact was destroying their relationship with the wider Jewish community.

At the time of the creation of Israel in 1948, part of the CPUSA's appeal to Jews was due to its support for Israel at a time when President Truman was waffling on the issue. In 1946 the CPUSA even adopted a resolution advocating the continuation of the Jewish people as an ethnic entity within socialist societies. Arthur Liebman describes CPUSA members during the period as being elated because of the congruity of their Jewish interests and membership in the party. Feelings of commonality with the wider Jewish community were expressed, and there was an enhanced feeling of Jewishness resulting from interactions with other Jews within the CPUSA. During the early postwar years:

> Communist Jews were expected and encouraged to be Jews, to relate to Jews, and to think of the Jewish people and the Jewish culture in a positive light. At the same time, non-Communist Jews, with some notable exceptions [in the non-communist Jewish left] accepted their Jewish credentials and agreed to work with them in an all-Jewish context. (A. Liebman, 1979, p. 514)

As has happened so often in Jewish history, this upsurge in Jewish self-identity was facilitated by the persecution of Jews, in this case the Holocaust.

This period of easy compatibility of Jewish interests with CPUSA interests evaporated after 1948, especially because of the altered Soviet position on Israel and revelations of state-sponsored anti-Semitism in the Soviet Union and

Eastern Europe. Many Jews abandoned the CPUSA as a result. Once again, those who remained in the CPUSA tended to rationalize Soviet anti-Semitism in a way that allowed them to maintain their Jewish identification. Some viewed the persecutions as an aberration and the result of individual pathology rather than the fault of the communist system itself, or the West was blamed as being indirectly responsible. Moreover, the reasons for remaining in the CPUSA appear to have typically involved a desire to remain in its self-contained Yiddish communist subculture. A. Liebman (1979, p. 522) describes an individual who finally resigned when the evidence on Soviet anti-Semitism became overwhelming: "In 1958, after more than 25 years with the Communist party, this leader resigned and developed a strong Jewish identity which encompassed a fierce loyalty to Israel." Alternatively, Jewish CPUSA members simply failed to adopt the Soviet party line, as occurred on the issue of support for Israel during the 1967 and 1973 wars. Eventually, there was virtually a complete severing of Jews from the CPUSA.

Lyons's (1982, p. 180) description of a Jewish-communist club in Philadelphia reveals the ambivalence and self-deception that occurred when Jewish interests clashed with communist sympathies:

> The club . . . faced rising tension over Jewishness, especially as it related to Israel. In the mid-sixties conflict erupted over the club's decision to criticize Soviet treatment of Jews. Some orthodox pro-Soviet club members resigned; others disagreed but stayed. Meanwhile the club continued to change, becoming less Marxist and more Zionist. During the 1967 Middle East War, "we got dogmatic, for one week," as Ben Green, a club leader, puts it. They allowed no discussion on the merits of supporting Israel, but simply raised funds to show their full support. Nevertheless, several members insist that the club is not Zionist and engages in "critical support" of Israel.

As in the case of Poland, there is every reason to suppose that American Jewish communists regarded the USSR as generally satisfying Jewish interests at least until well into the post-World War II era. Beginning in the 1920s the CPUSA was financially supported by the Soviet Union, adhered closely to its positions, and engaged in a successful espionage effort against the United States on behalf of the Soviet Union, including stealing atomic secrets (Klehr et al., 1995).[47] In the 1930s Jews "constituted a substantial majority of known

---

[47] The American businessman Armand Hammer had very close ties with the Soviet Union and served as a courier bringing money from the USSR for the support of communist espionage in the United States. Hammer is illustrative of the complexities of the Jewish identifications of communists and communist sympathizers. For most of his life he denied his Jewish background, but when near death he returned to Judaism and scheduled an elaborate bar mitzvah

members of the Soviet underground apparatus in the United States" and almost half of the Communist leaders prosecuted under the Smith Act of 1947 (Rothman & Lichter, 1982/1996, p. 100).

> Although all party functionaries may not have known the details of the special relationship with the Soviet Union, "special work" [i.e., espionage] was part and parcel of the Communist mission in the United States, and this was well known and discussed openly in the CPUSA's Political Bureau. ... [I]t was these ordinary Communists whose lives demonstrate that some rank-and-file members were willing to serve the USSR by spying on their own country. There but for the grace of not being asked went other American Communists. The CPUSA showered hosannas on the USSR as the promised land. In Communist propaganda the survival of the Soviet Union as the one bright, shining star of humankind was a constant refrain, as in the 1934 American Communist poem that described the Soviet Union as "a heaven . . . brought to earth in Russia." (Klehr et al., 1995, p. 324)

Klehr et al. (1995, p. 325) suggest that the CPUSA had important effects on U.S. history. Without excusing the excesses of the anti-communist movement, they note that "the peculiar and particular edge to American anticommunism cannot be severed from the CPUSA's allegiance to the Soviet Union; the belief that American communists were disloyal is what made the communist issue so powerful and at times poisonous."

> Communists lied to and deceived the New Dealers with whom they were allied. Those liberals who believed the denials then denounced as mudslingers those anti-Communists who complained of concealed Communist activity. Furious at denials of what they knew to be true, anti-Communists then suspected that those who denied the Communist presence were themselves dishonest. The Communists' duplicity poisoned normal political relationships and contributed to the harshness of the anti-Communist reaction of the late 1940s and 1950s. (Klehr et al., 1995, p. 106)

The liberal defense of communism during the Cold War era also raises issues related to this volume. Nicholas von Hoffman (1996) notes the role of the liberal defenders of communism during this period, such as the editors of *The New Republic* and Harvard historian Richard Hofstadter (1965), who attributed the contemporary concern with communist infiltration of the U.S. government

---

(E. J. Epstein, 1996). Were his surface denials of his Jewish heritage to be taken at face value at the time they were made? (Hammer also portrayed himself as a Unitarian in dealing with Muslims.) Or was Hammer a crypto-Jew his entire life until openly embracing Judaism at the end?

to the "paranoid style in American politics."[48] The official liberal version was that American communists were *sui generis* and unconnected to the Soviet Union, so there was no domestic communist threat. The liberals had seized the intellectual and moral high ground during this period, while supporters of Joseph McCarthy were viewed as intellectual and cultural primitives:

> In the ongoing *kulturkampf* dividing the society, the elites of Hollywood, Cambridge, and liberal think-tankery had little sympathy for bow-legged men with their American Legion caps and their fat wives, their yapping about Yalta and the Katyn Forest. Catholic and kitsch, looking out of their picture windows at their flock of pink plastic flamingos, the lower middles and their foreign policy anguish were too *infra dig* to be taken seriously. (von Hoffman, 1996).

However, besides poisoning the atmosphere of domestic politics, communist espionage had effects on foreign policy as well:

> It is difficult to overstate the importance of Soviet atomic espionage in shaping the history of the Cold War. World War II had ended with Americans confident that the atomic bomb gave them a monopoly on the ultimate weapon, a monopoly expected to last ten to twenty years. The Soviet explosion of a nuclear bomb in 1949 destroyed this sense of physical security. America had fought in two world wars without suffering serious civilian deaths or destruction. Now it faced an enemy led by a ruthless dictator who could wipe out any American city with a single bomb.
>
> Had the American nuclear monopoly lasted longer, Stalin might have refused to allow North Korean Communists to launch the Korean War, or the Chinese Communists might have hesitated to intervene in the war. Had the American nuclear monopoly lasted until Stalin's death, the restraint on Soviet aggressiveness might have alleviated the most dangerous years of the Cold War. (Klehr et al., 1995, p. 106)

American Jewish Radicals: Rationalization and Apologia

The horrific consequences of Bolshevism for millions of non-Jewish Soviet citizens do not seem to have been an issue for Jewish leftists in the U.S. During the 1930s, when millions of Soviet citizens were being murdered by the Soviet government, the CPUSA took great pains to appeal to specific Jewish interests, including opposing anti-Semitism, supporting Zionism, and advocating the importance of maintaining Jewish cultural traditions. During this period, "the

---

[48] Rothman and Lichter (1982/1996, p. 105) include *The New Republic* as among a group of liberal and radical publications with a large presence of Jewish writers and editors; regarding Hofstadter, see also Ch. 6.

American radical movement glorified the development of Jewish life in the Soviet Union.... The Soviet Union was living proof that under socialism the Jewish question could be solved" (Kann, 1981, pp. 152–153). Communism was perceived as "good for the Jews." Radical Jews—a substantial percentage of the
entire Jewish community at that time—saw the world through Jewish lenses.

Peter Novick's 1999 book, *The Holocaust in American Life*, shows that Jewish organizations in the United States were well aware of Jewish involvement
in communism, but they argued that only a minority of Jews were involved and
downplayed the fact that a majority of communists were Jews, that an even
greater majority of communist leaders were Jews, that the great majority of
those called up by the House Un-American Activities Committee in the 1940s
and 1950s were Jews, and that most of those prosecuted for spying for the Soviet Union were Jews (see also SAID, Ch. 6). Indeed, the proposal that leftist
radicalism represented a minority of the American Jewish community in the
decades from 1920 to 1950 is far from obvious. Leftist sympathies were widespread in the AJCongress—by far the largest organization of American Jews
during this period—and communist-oriented groups were affiliated with the
AJCongress until they were reluctantly purged during the McCarthy era (Svonkin, 1997, pp. 132, 166). Novick notes that Jewish organizations made sure that
Hollywood movies did not show any communist characters with Jewish names.
Newspapers and magazines such as *Time* and *Life*, which were at that time
controlled by non-Jews, agreed not to publish letters on the Jewishness of accused American communists at the behest of a staff member of the AJCommittee (Novick, 1999, p. 95).

Novick also notes that Jewish communists often used the Holocaust as a
rhetorical device at a time when mainstream Jewish organizations were trying
to keep a low profile, clearly indicating strong Jewish identification among the
vast majority of Jewish communists. Invocations of the Holocaust "became the
dominant argument, at least in Jewish circles, for opposition to Cold War mobilization" (Novick, 1999, p. 93). Julius and Ethel Rosenberg, convicted of spying
for the Soviet Union, often invoked the Holocaust in rationalizing their actions.
Julius testified that the USSR "contributed a major share in destroying the Hitler beast who killed 6,000,000 of my co-religionists" (in p. 94). Public demonstrations of support for the Rosenbergs often invoked the Holocaust.

Although Bendersky (2000) presents an apologetic account in which Jewish involvement in radical leftism is seen as nothing more than the paranoia of
racist military officers, he shows that U.S. military intelligence had confirmation of this involvement from multiple independent sources, including information on financial support of revolutionary activity provided by wealthy Jews
like Jacob Schiff and the Warburg family. These sources included not only its
own agents, but also the British government and the U.S. State Department's
Division of Russian Affairs. These sources asserted that Jews dominated the

Bolshevik governments of the Soviet Union and Hungary and that Jews in other countries were sympathetic to Bolshevism. Similarly, Szajkowski (1977) shows that the view that Jews dominated the Bolshevik government was very widespread among Russians and foreigners in the Soviet Union, including American and British military and diplomatic personnel and administrators of relief agencies. He also shows that sympathy for the Bolshevik government was the norm within the Eastern European immigrant Jewish community in the United States in the period from 1918 to 1920, but that the older German-Jewish establishment (whose numbers were dwarfed by the more recent immigrants from Eastern Europe) opposed Bolshevism during this period.

While ignoring Soviet mass murder, American Jews were furious at Stalin's efforts against a relative handful of high-ranking Jewish communists during the purges of the 1930s. Stalin moved very cautiously and used deception to downplay the Jewish identity of the victims. Throughout the 1920s and the 1930s, the Soviet Union accepted aid for Soviet Jews from foreign Jewish organizations, especially the American Jewish Joint Distribution Committee, which was funded by wealthy American Jews (Warburg, Schiff, Kuhn, Loeb, Lehman, Marshall). Another revealing incident occurred when Stalin ordered the murder of two Jewish leaders of the international socialist movement, Henryk Ehrlich and Victor Alter. These murders created an international incident, and there were protests by leftists around the world (Rapoport, 1990, p. 68). The furor did not die down until the Soviets established a Jewish organization, the Jewish Anti-Fascist Committee (JAC), dedicated to winning the favor of American Jews. American Jewish leaders, such as Nahum Goldmann of the World Jewish Congress and Rabbi Stephen S. Wise of the AJCongress, helped quell the uproar over the incident and shore up positive views of the Soviet Union among American Jews. They, along with a wide range of American Jewish radicals, warmly greeted JAC representatives in New York during World War II.

Again, the contrast is striking. The Soviet government killed millions of Ukrainian and Russian peasants during the 1920s and 1930s, executed hundreds of thousands of people who were purged from their positions in the party and throughout the economy, imprisoned hundreds of thousands of people in appalling conditions that produced incredibly high mortality and without any meaningful due process, drafted hundreds of thousands of people into forced labor with enormous loss of life, and ordered the collective punishment and deportation of Cossacks and other ethnic groups, resulting in mass murder of these groups. At the same time, actions against a handful of Jewish communists were taken cautiously and performed with reassurances that the government still had very positive views of Jews and Judaism.

While the Jewish Holocaust has become a moral touchstone and premier cultural icon in Western societies, this blind spot about the horrors of

Bolshevism continues into the present time. Jewish media figures who were blacklisted because of their communist affiliations in the 1940s are now heroes who are honored by the film industry, praised in newspapers, and have their work exhibited in museums. For example, an event commemorating the blacklist was held at the Academy of Motion Picture Arts and Sciences in October 1997. Organized by the four guilds—American Federation of Television and Radio Artists (AFTRA), Directors Guild of America (DGA), Screen Actors Guild (SAG), and Writers Guild of America West (WGAW)—the event honored the lives and careers of the blacklisted writers and condemned the guilds' lack of response fifty years earlier. At the same time, the Writers Guild of America has been restoring dozens of credits to movies written by screenwriters who wrote under pseudonyms while blacklisted. Movies on the topic paint a picture of innocent Jewish idealists hounded by a ruthless, oppressive government, and critics like Bernheimer (1998, pp. 163–166) clearly approve this assessment. In the same vein, the 1983 movie *Daniel*, based on a novel by E. L. Doctorow and directed by Sydney Lumet, portrayed the conviction of the Rosenbergs as "a matter of political expediency. The persecution is presented as a nightmarish vision of Jewish victimization, senseless and brutal" (p. 178).

A nostalgic and exculpatory attitude toward the Jewish Old Left is apparent in recent accounts of the children of "red diaper babies," including those who have come to reject their leftist commitments. For example, Ronald Radosh's (2001a) *Commies* describes the all-encompassing world of Jewish radicalism of his youth. His father belonged to a classic Communist Party front organization called the Trade Union Unity League. Radosh was a dutiful son, throwing himself fervently into every cause that bore the Party's stamp of approval, attending a Party-inspired summer camp and a New York City red diaper high school (known as "the Little Red Schoolhouse for little Reds"), and participating in youth festivals modeled on Soviet extravaganzas. It says a lot about the Jewish milieu of the Party that a common joke was: "What Jewish holidays do you celebrate?" "Paul Robeson's birthday and May Day." Radosh only questioned the leftist faith when he was rejected and blackballed by his leftist comrades for publishing a book that established the guilt of Julius Rosenberg. Radosh shows that academic departments of history remain a bastion of apologia for the far left. Many academic historians shunned Radosh because of his findings, including Eric Foner, another red diaper baby, who was a president of the American Historical Association. Radosh writes of the "reflexive hatred of the American system" that pervades the left. It was indeed a "reflexive hatred"—a hatred that was due far more to their strong Jewish identifications than to anything objectively wrong with American society. Nevertheless, despite his reservations about the leftism of his past, he presents the motivations of Jewish communists as idealistic even as they provided "the ideological arguments meant to rationalize Soviet crimes and gain the support by Americans for Soviet foreign policy" (Radosh, 2001b).

Despite the massive evidence for a very large Jewish involvement in these movements, there are no apologies from Jewish organizations and very few *mea culpas* from Jewish intellectuals. If anything, the opposite is true, given the idealization of blacklisted writers and the continuing tendency to portray U.S. communists as idealists who were crushed by repressive McCarthyism. Because many communist societies eventually developed anti-Jewish movements, Jewish organizations portray Jews as victims of communism, not as critical to its rise to power, as deeply involved in the murderous reigns of terror unleashed by these regimes, and as apologists for the Soviet Union in the West. Forgotten in this history are the millions of deaths, the forced labor, the suppression of all dissent that occurred during the height of Jewish power in the Soviet Union. Remembered are the anti-Jewish trends of late communism.[49]

---

[49] A fascinating case study of an American Jewish radical who extolled the virtues of the Soviet Union is Joe Rapoport (Kann, 1981, pp. 20–42, 109–125), but his example merits closer examination. Rapoport joined a Jewish detachment of the Red Army that was fighting the Ukrainian nationalists in the Civil War that followed the Bolshevik Revolution in 1917. Like many other Jews, he chose the Red Army because it opposed the anti-Jewish actions of Ukrainian nationalists. Like the vast majority of Russian Jews, he greeted the Revolution because it improved the lives of the Jews.

After immigrating to the United States, Rapoport visited Ukraine in November 1934, less than one year after the famine created by Soviet government actions that killed four million Ukrainian peasants (Werth, 1999, pp. 159ff). The peasants had resisted being forced to join collective farms and were aided by local Ukrainian authorities. The response of the central government was to arrest farmers and confiscate all grain, including reserves to be used for next year's harvest. Since they had no food, the peasants attempted to leave for the cities but were prevented from doing so by the government. The peasants starved by the millions. Parents abandoned starving children before starving themselves; cannibalism was rampant; remaining workers were tortured to force them to hand over any remaining food. Methods of torture included "the 'cold' method where the victim [was] stripped bare and left out in the cold, stark naked in a hangar. Sometimes whole brigades of collective workers [were] treated in this fashion. In the 'hot' method, the feet and the bottom of the skirt of female workers [were] doused with gasoline and then set alight. The flames [were] put out, and the process [was] repeated" (in Werth, 1999, p. 166). During the period when the famine claimed a total of six million lives throughout the country, the government exported eighteen million hundredweight (1.8 billion pounds) of grain in order to obtain money for industrialization.

These horrors are unmentioned by Rapoport in his account of his 1934 visit. Instead, he paints a very positive portrait of life in Ukraine under the Soviets. Life is good for the Jews. He is pleased that Yiddish culture is accepted not only by Jews but by non-Jews as well. (For example, he recounts an incident in which a Ukrainian worker read a story in Yiddish to the other workers, Jews and non-Jews alike.) Young Jews were taking advantage of new opportunities not only in Yiddish culture but also "in the economy, in the government, in participation in the general life of the country" (Kann, 1981, p. 120). Older Jews complained that the government was anti-religious, and young Jews complained that Leon Trotsky, "the national pride of the Jewish people," had been removed. But the message to American radicals was upbeat: "It was sufficient to learn that the Jewish young people were in higher positions and embraced the Soviet system" (Kann, 1981, p. 122). Rapoport sees the world through Jewish-only eyes. The

Joe McCarthy and the Jews

The Jewish "contraculture" continued to sustain a radical, specifically Jewish subculture into the 1950s—long after the great majority of Jews were no longer in the working class (A. Liebman, 1979, pp. 206, 289ff). Weingarten (2008, pp. 6, 9) points to a "hard core of Jews" who continued to support the Communist Party into the 1950s and continued to have a "decisive role" in shaping the policies of the CPUSA. She notes that unlike other communists, Jewish communists continued to have an ethnic identity and often participated in the wider Jewish community. This history of Jewish involvement in communism and sympathy toward communism was now combined with the new situation of the Cold War in which the Soviet Union had become the mortal enemy of the United States.

I suppose that in the ideal Jewish world of 1950, Jewish organizations and the great majority of Jews would have smoothly transitioned to a world of what became mainstream liberal politics: the movements for civil rights, for non-European immigration, and for removing any sense that the United States had a European, Christian identity. But, as Weingarten's (2008) book makes clear, Senator Joseph McCarthy made this transition a delicate matter because McCarthy's investigations into communist infiltration of the government often targeted Jews—not because they were Jews but because Jews were highly overrepresented among communists. And, Jewish defendants accused of communist affiliations were typically represented by Jewish attorneys. The result was that Jewish organizations were terrified that the public would be reinforced with the stereotype of Jewish communists.

Such fears were well-founded. A survey by the AJCommittee in 1948 found that 21 percent of Americans answered affirmatively to the question, "Do you think most Jews are Communists?" And an informal survey showed that more than half the people mentioned Jews in responding to the question, "What do you think of the atom [spy] stories in the newspapers?," even though the question didn't mention Jews (Weingarten, 2008, p. 34).

The matter was compounded by the fact that many of the causes championed by Jewish organizations in the area of civil rights, immigration, and globalist internationalism were also championed by the CPUSA. And throughout

---

massive suffering in which a total of nearly twenty million Soviet citizens had already died because of government actions is irrelevant. When he looks back on his life as an American Jewish radical, his only ambivalence and regrets are about supporting Soviet actions he saw as not in Jewish interests, such as its non-aggression pact with Germany and its failure to consistently support Israel. Rapoport was thus an exemplar of the many defenders of communism in the U.S. media and intellectual circles.

the period, the CPUSA viewed Jews as a group that was particularly susceptible to communist messages and recruitment and therefore actively courted them.

In particular, the CPUSA and pro-communist sympathizers continually tried to paint as anti-Semitism any targeting of Jews as communists, no matter how well founded. A paradigmatic case was the espionage trial of Ethel and Julius Rosenberg. The CPUSA-inspired National Committee to Secure Justice in the Rosenberg Trial held meetings defending the Rosenbergs in Jewish community buildings. "Headlines in the *Daily Worker* in the form of 'Anti-Semitism and the Rosenbergs' were an inseparable part of this campaign" (Weingarten, 2008, p. 32)—a view that the Rosenbergs themselves promoted. Indeed, as noted, the Rosenbergs saw themselves as Jewish martyrs and viewed their political radicalism as intimately bound up with their Jewish identification (Svonkin, 1997, pp. 158–159).

The strategy pursued by the organized Jewish community under these circumstances had several facets:

(1) Education within the Jewish community aimed at decreasing sympathy for communism. The main organizations here were the ADL and the AJCommittee, with the AJCongress conspicuous by its absence due to its far-left proclivities. A main tactic was to point out the anti-Semitism in the Soviet Union after World War II—a tactic that assumed (correctly) that Jewish communists had a Jewish identity and would be motivated by it. The ADL and the AJCommittee also fought against Jews who cooperated with high-profile communist campaigns, such as the defense of Ethel and Julius Rosenberg who were convicted of spying for the Soviet Union and executed. In 1954 the ADL advocated continuing old programs begun in 1950 and established new programs, indicating that they saw a continuing need for anti-communist work within the Jewish community. For example, there was great embarrassment in 1953 when a person who invoked the Fifth Amendment when questioned by the House Un-American Activities Committee turned out to be a member of the Council for Jewish Community Centers in Cleveland.

(2) Public condemnations of communism by Jewish organizations and Jewish leaders, such as Senator Herbert Lehman (D-NY). However, the established Jewish organizations rejected the American Jewish League Against Communism (AJLAC), a Jewish organization that supported McCarthy and took a strong stand in favor of ridding the Jewish community of communism. They were worried that the AJLAC would bring too much attention to the Jews-as-communists concerns of the mainstream Jewish organizations.

(3) Intellectual work rationalizing the political goals of Jewish organizations in the areas of civil rights and immigration as fulfilling American ideals rather than communist ideals. Here Weingarten credits the "mostly Jewish" New York Intellectuals as developing a left-liberal anti-communist perspective that left an "indelible mark" on American intellectual life (see Ch. 7).

Weingarten highlights the role of the intellectual journal *Commentary* (published by the AJCommittee) as publicizing anti-Semitism in the USSR and Eastern European countries. *Commentary* also published articles on the incompatibility of Judaism and communism. Throughout the entire period the organized Jewish community continued to engage in propaganda campaigns designed to reeducate the American public along liberal lines. Both the ADL and the AJCommittee financially supported academic research by the Frankfurt School and the New York Intellectuals designed to promote civil rights, end the European bias of US immigration laws, and promote the idea of the United States as a proposition nation with no ethnic or cultural core. It bears emphasizing that although the intellectuals associated with these movements began their careers as Marxists and continued to promote anti-White policies in areas such as immigration reform, they framed their ideas in language that was more acceptable to an American audience and often appealed to American ideals of democracy and freedom (see MacDonald, 2019b).

And, (4) strong opposition to McCarthy himself.

But why exactly were these Jewish organizations and the vast majority of individual Jews so opposed to McCarthy? One might think that the Jewish organizations could simply cooperate with McCarthy to rid the Jewish community of hard-core communists.

One reason was that the atmosphere created by McCarthy was not conducive to the liberal-left political agenda that the Jewish organizations were actively pursuing in the areas of civil rights and immigration policy. The McCarthy era produced an upsurge of patriotism in the United States at a time when patriotism had strong overtones of supporting the traditional people and culture of America. Everything linked to communism came under suspicion. And since the CPUSA supported the domestic political agenda of Jewish organizations—an agenda entirely at odds with traditional conceptions of America—Jewish organizations had an obvious motive to end McCarthyism as soon as possible.

Moreover, McCarthy fanned the passions of anti-communism and, because of the strong association of Jews and communism, these passions often had anti-Jewish overtones. A well-known example was the so-called Peekskill riots of 1949 in which demonstrators yelled out anti-communist and anti-Jewish epithets at people attending a performance by Black baritone and political radical Paul Robeson. Most of the concertgoers were Jewish radicals from New York City.

Jews were also vastly overrepresented in high-profile cases among those invoking the Fifth Amendment right not to incriminate oneself, so that public hearings like McCarthy's inevitably highlighted the Jewish role in communism. For example, in 1952, of 124 people questioned by the Senate Committee on Homeland Security and Government Affairs, Weingarten (2008) identifies seventy-nine Jews, thirty-two non-Jews, and thirteen of unknown ethnicity. All invoked the Fifth Amendment.

Even more remarkably, of the forty-two people who were dismissed from their positions at the Fort Monmouth Laboratories in New Jersey on suspicion of constituting a spy ring (the same one that Julius Rosenberg belonged to), thirty-nine were Jews and one other was married to a Jewish woman. M. Stanton Evans (2007) has an excellent chapter on the Monmouth case in his *Blacklisted by History*—by far the best and most exhaustive survey of McCarthy's battles. Evans shows how many of the Fort Monmouth accused invoked the Fifth Amendment under questioning by McCarthy, and he exposes the incredibly lax security procedures at the facility. For example, one employee "had signed out at one time or another for more than 2,700 documents (not a typo)" (Evans, 2007, p. 519). Two-thirds were still missing after an investigation, but when the employee was brought up on security charges, all of this was omitted from the record on orders from above.

Evans (2007, p. 510) also quotes the post-McCarthy testimony of a Soviet scientist that "in the 1940s secret U.S. material involving radar had turned up in Russia in vast amounts, and that literally 'thousands' of these had been identified on their face as having come from Monmouth." Other evidence indicated that the Monmouth spying continued into the 1950s at the time of McCarthy's hearings. In the end, the Fort Monmouth battle proved pivotal for McCarthy, "provoking a constitutional showdown of epic nature between McCarthy and executive branch officials" (p. 510).

I also suspect there was a visceral solidarity with the Jewish left which made it very difficult for the organized Jewish community to simply cooperate with McCarthy. Again, the AJCongress was by far the largest Jewish organization during this period, and its membership was sympathetic to the left even when not explicitly pro-communist, including, as noted, its affiliate, the overtly communist JPFO.

The organized Jewish community consistently opposed measures intended to make it more difficult for communists to operate within the American system even as it officially opposed communism. For example, Jewish organizations objected to any infringements of civil liberties or academic freedom enacted to strengthen national security. Weingarten (2008, p. 66) attributes this stand to a principled Jewish respect for human rights, particularly on the part of the AJCongress, the Jewish organization most closely identified with the far left.

But it can be easily seen that Jews and Jewish organizations have not consistently been on the side of civil liberties and academic freedom. During the 1920s and 1930s mainstream Jewish organizations and Jewish intellectuals rationalized Soviet despotism and turned a blind eye to Soviet mass murder during a period when Jews were an elite within the Soviet Union. And in the present era, Jewish organizations, most notably the ADL, have been prime advocates of "hate crime" legislation aimed at penalizing beliefs and ideas (MacDonald, 2009a) and censoring social media (see Preface). Jewish organizations have also attacked the academic freedom of professors who have been critical of Israel (*Indybay Collective*, 2009). Additionally, the ADL cooperated with the Southern Poverty Law Center (which is financially dependent on Jewish donations) in an effort to get me fired from my position at California State University–Long Beach, and has engaged in public denunciations of my writing (MacDonald, n.d.). In general, Jewish behavior is better predicted by understanding their perceived interests in particular situations than by general principles.

Finally, another reason the organized Jewish community opposed McCarthy was that even though Joe McCarthy surrounded himself with Jews and did his best to ingratiate himself with the Jewish community, some of his supporters and associates were well known to be anti-Jewish. Most of these people are little known now, perhaps with the exception of Gerald L. K. Smith. Weingarten interprets these associations as McCarthy using these people for his own ends, not as indicating that McCarthy was anti-Jewish.

Indeed, some of McCarthy's closest associates were Jews, including Roy Cohn, chief counsel of McCarthy's Permanent Subcommittee on Investigations, and Cohn's protégé David Schine. Cohn is portrayed as a strongly identified Jew who felt that Jewish organizations did not do enough to support Jews who were in the front lines opposing communism. Cohn was remembered by college friends as "reacting almost violently to any Jew suspected of pro-communist leanings," and a TV producer claimed that Cohn had said that "not all Jews are Communists, but all Communists are Jews" (Weingarten, 2008, p. 92).

Another Jew close to McCarthy was George Sokolsky, a journalist for the Hearst newspapers, who was associated with the "China Lobby," a group devoted to Chiang Kai-shek and a non-communist China. Sokolsky was the Hearst newspapers' liaison with McCarthy and set up McCarthy's relationship with Cohn. Sokolsky also set up a meeting of McCarthy with the ADL. There are varying accounts of this meeting, but nothing positive came of it. One observer claimed that a drunken McCarthy stated, "You just write what my credo ought to be and I'll sign it" (Weingarten, 2008, p. 108), but the offer was turned down by the ADL representatives.

Alfred Kohlberg, a businessman associated with the China Lobby, was also a close friend of McCarthy, and Kohlberg, Sokolsky, and Cohn were all associated with the AJLAC. As Weingarten notes, "the fact of their being Jews and anti-communists was made full use of by McCarthy, who wanted to expand his circle of support, while doing his best to free himself of any hint of anti-Semitism" (Weingarten, 2008, p. 100). McCarthy also attempted to get Cohn appointed to a position on the ADL executive council, presumably, as Weingarten suggests, in order to dampen the animosity of these organizations toward him.

Indeed, McCarthy seems to have done everything he could to curry favor with Jews. Jewish historian Lucy Dawidowicz wrote that in the early 1950s,

> for anyone in public life [anti-Semitism] is the sign of Cain. So overwhelming is the disrepute of anti-Semitism that an unrestrained demagogue like McCarthy has studiously avoided the Communist provocation and has, as a matter of fact, tried to establish himself as a philo-Semite. (in Weingarten, 2008, p. 128)

The fact that McCarthy attempted to gain Jewish allies and did his best not to offend the Jews shows quite clearly that Jews were very powerful in 1950s America. In retrospect, the campaign of the organized Jewish community and their allies in the media and the intellectual world was quite successful in containing the threat posed by McCarthy to the general public policy positions pursued by the organized Jewish community during this period: civil rights for African Americans, non-White immigration, and the idea that America is a proposition nation with no ethnic or religious identity. All these campaigns were carried on in the teeth of McCarthyism and despite the fact that these same ideas were promulgated by communists.

In the long run, these public policy positions were far more important than the national security threat posed by pro-Soviet Jewish leftists. The general climate created by McCarthy quite possibly delayed the triumph of these policies but could not ultimately hold them back. At least part of the problem was that McCarthy was not concerned with challenging the policy positions of the Jewish organizations related to civil rights, immigration, and the proposition nation, but focused exclusively on containing the internal security threat. The liberal nexus among elites in politics, the intellectual world, and the media was not threatened by McCarthy or his allies in the moribund conservative movement of the period. Indeed, this elite ultimately caused his downfall.

Jews and the New Left

The fundamentally Jewish institutions and families that constituted the Old Left then fed into the New Left (A. Liebman, 1979, pp. 536ff). The original impetus of the 1960s student protest movement "almost necessarily began with the scions of the relatively well-to-do, liberal-to-left, disproportionately Jewish intelligentsia—the largest pool of those ideologically disposed to sympathize with radical student action in the population" (Lipset, 1971, p. 83; see also Glazer, 1969). Flacks (1967, p. 64) found that 40 percent of students involved in a protest at the University of Chicago were Jewish, but his original sample was "'adjusted' to obtain better balance" (Rothman & Lichter, 1982/1996, p. 82; see Mendes, 2014 for similar data). Jews constituted 80 percent of the students signing a petition to end ROTC at Harvard and 30–50 percent of the Students for a Democratic Society (SDS)—the central organization of student radicals. A. Adelson (1972) found that 90 percent of his sample of radical students at the University of Michigan were Jewish, and it would appear that a similar rate of participation is likely to have occurred at other universities, such as Wisconsin and Minnesota. Braungart (1979) found that 43 percent of the SDS membership in his sample of ten universities had at least one Jewish parent and an additional 20 percent had no religious affiliation. The latter are most likely to be predominantly Jewish: Rothman and Lichter (1982/1996, p. 82) found that the "overwhelming majority" of the radical students who claimed that their parents were atheists had Jewish backgrounds.

Jews also tended to be the most publicized leaders of campus protests (Sachar, 1992, p. 804). Abbie Hoffman, Jerry Rubin, and Rennie Davis achieved national fame as members of the "Chicago Seven" group convicted of crossing state lines with intent to incite a riot at the 1968 Democratic National Convention. Cuddihy (1974, p. 193ff) notes the overtly ethnic subplot of the trial, particularly the infighting between defendant Abbie Hoffman and Judge Julius Hoffman, the former representing the children of the Eastern European immigrant generation that tended toward political radicalism, and the latter representing the older, more assimilated German-Jewish establishment. During the trial Abbie Hoffman ridiculed Judge Hoffman in Yiddish as "Shande fur de Goyim" (disgrace for the gentiles)—translated by Abbie Hoffman as "Front man for the WASP power elite." Clearly Hoffman and Rubin (who spent time on a kibbutz in Israel) had strong Jewish identifications and antipathy to the White Protestant establishment. Cuddihy (1974, pp. 191–192) also credits the origins of the Yippie movement to the activities of the underground journalist Paul Krassner (publisher of *The Realist*, a "daring, scatological, curiously apolitical" journal of "irreverent satire and impolite reportage") and the countercultural sensibility of comedian Lenny Bruce.

As a group, radical students came from relatively well-to-do families, whereas conservative students tended to come from less affluent families (Gottfried, 1993, p. 53). The movement was therefore initiated and led by an elite, but it was not aimed at advancing the interests of the unionized lower middle class. Indeed, the New Left regarded the working class as "fat, contented, and conservative, and their trade unions reflected them" (Glazer, 1969, p. 123)—the people with "pink plastic flamingos" in their front yards (von Hoffman, 1996).

Moreover, although mild forms of Jewish anti-Semitism and rebellion against parental hypocrisy did occur among Jewish New Left radicals, the predominant pattern was a continuity with parental ideology (Flacks, 1967; Glazer,

1969, p. 12; Lipset, 1968/1988, p. 393; Rothman & Lichter, 1982/1996, p. 82).[50] Many of these "red diaper babies" came from,

> families which around the breakfast table, day after day, in Scarsdale, Newton, Great Neck, and Beverly Hills have discussed what an awful, corrupt, immoral, undemocratic, racist society the United States is. Many Jewish parents live in the lily-white suburbs, go to Miami Beach in the winter, belong to expensive country clubs, arrange Bar Mitzvahs costing thousands of dollars—all the while espousing a left-liberal ideology. (Lipset, 1968/1988, p. 393)

As mentioned above, Glazer (1969) estimates that approximately one million Jews were members of the CPUSA or were socialists prior to 1950. The result was that among Jews there was "a substantial reservoir of present-day parents for whose children to be radical is not something shocking and strange but may well be seen as a means of fulfilling the best drives of their parents" (p. 129).

Moreover, the "American Jewish establishment never really distanced itself from these young Jews" (Hertzberg, 1989, p. 369). Indeed, establishment Jewish organizations, including the AJCongress, the Union of American Hebrew Congregations (a lay Reform group), and the Synagogue Council of America (Winston, 1978), were prominent early opponents of the war in Vietnam. The anti-war attitudes of official Jewish organizations may have resulted in some anti-Semitism. President Lyndon Johnson was reported to have been "disturbed by the lack of support for the Vietnam war in the American Jewish community at a time when he [was] taking new steps to aid Israel" (in Winston, p. 198), and the ADL took steps to deal with an anti-Jewish backlash they expected to occur as a result of Jews tending to be hawks on military matters related to Israel and doves on military matters related to Vietnam (Winston).

As with the Old Left, many of the Jewish New Left strongly identified as Jews (A. Liebman, 1979, pp. 536ff). A Hanukah service was held and the "Hatikvah" (the Israeli national anthem) was sung during an important sit-in at Berkeley (Rothman & Lichter, 1982/1996, p. 81). The New Left lost Jewish members when it advocated positions incompatible with specific Jewish interests (especially regarding Israel) and attracted Jewish members when its positions coincided with these interests (A. Liebman, pp. 527ff). Jewish New Left leaders often spent time at kibbutzim in Israel, and there is some indication that New Leftists consciously attempted to minimize the more overt signs of Jewish

---

[50] Similarly, during the Weimar period the Frankfurt School radicals rejected their parents' commercial values but did not personally reject their family. Indeed, their families tended to provide moral and financial support for them in their radical political activities (Cuddihy, 1974, p. 154).

identity and to minimize discussion of issues on which Jewish and non-Jewish New Leftists would disagree, particularly Israel. Eventually the incompatibility of Jewish interests and the New Left resulted in most Jews abandoning the New Left, with many going to Israel to join kibbutzim, becoming involved in more traditional Jewish religious observances, or becoming involved in leftist organizations with a specifically Jewish identity. After the 1967 Six-Day War, the most important issue for the Jewish New Left was Israel, but the movement also worked on behalf of Soviet Jews and demanded Jewish studies programs at universities (E. S. Shapiro, 1992, p. 225). As SDS activist Jay Rosenberg wrote:

> From this point on I shall join no movement that does not accept and support my people's struggle. If I must choose between the Jewish cause and a "progressive" anti-Israel SDS, I shall choose the Jewish cause. If barricades are erected, I will fight as a Jew. (in Sachar, 1992, p. 808)

Paul Gottfried (1996, pp. 9–10), a Jewish conservative, commenting on his graduate student days at Yale in the 1960s:

> All my Jewish colleagues in graduate school, noisy anti-anti-Communists, opposed American capitalist imperialism, but then became enthusiastic warmongers during the Arab-Israeli War in 1967. One Jewish Marxist acquaintance went into a rage that the Israelis did not demand the entire Mideast at the end of that war. Another, though a feminist, lamented that the Israeli soldiers did not rape more Arab women. It would be no exaggeration to say that my graduate school days resounded with Jewish hysterics at an institution where WASPs seemed to count only for decoration.

Jews were also a critical component of the public acceptance of the New Left. Jews were overrepresented among radicals and their supporters in the media, universities, and the wider intellectual community, and Jewish leftist social scientists were instrumental in conducting research that portrayed student radicalism in a positive light (Rothman & Lichter, 1982/1996, p. 104). However, in their review of the literature on the New Left, Rothman and Lichter (pp. ix, xiii) note a continuing tendency to ignore the role of Jews in the movement and that when the Jewish role is mentioned, it is attributed to Jewish idealism or other positively valued traits. Cuddihy (1974, p. 194n) notes that the media almost completely ignored the Jewish infighting that occurred during the Chicago Seven trial. He also describes several evaluations of the trial written by Jews in the media (The New York Times, New York Post, The Village Voice) that excused the behavior of the defendants and praised their radical Jewish lawyer, William Kunstler.

Finally, a similar ebb and flow of Jewish attraction to communism depending on its convergence with specifically Jewish interests occurred also in England. During the 1930s the Communist Party appealed to Jews partly because it was the only political movement that was stridently anti-fascist. There was no conflict at all between a strong Jewish ethnic identity and being a member of the Communist Party: "Communist sympathy among Jews of that generation had about it some of the qualities of a group identification, a means, perhaps, of ethnic self-assertion" (Alderman, 1992, pp. 317–318). In the post-World War II period, virtually all the successful communist political candidates represented Jewish wards. However, Jewish support for communism declined with the revelation of Stalin's anti-Semitism, and many Jews left the Communist Party after the Middle East crisis of 1967 when the USSR broke off diplomatic relations with Israel (Alderman, 1983, p. 162).

The conclusion must be that Jewish identity was often perceived to be highly compatible with radical politics. When radical politics came in conflict with specific Jewish interests, Jews eventually ceased being radical, although there were often instances of ambivalence and rationalization.

My Personal Experiences With the New Left at the University of Wisconsin

As a personal note from when I was a student and then graduate student in philosophy at the University of Wisconsin in the 1960s, the overrepresentation of Jews in the New Left, especially during the early stages of protest to the Vietnam War, was rather obvious to everyone. I experienced it personally for the first time as a reporter for the student newspaper covering a meeting of a group called the Ad Hoc Committee to End the War in Vietnam. Later, after moving in with Jewish roommates I became immersed in Madison's radical subculture, although more as a fringe observer than an active participant—so much so that during a "teach-in" on the war held during the 1960s, I was recruited to give a talk in which I was to explain how an ex-Catholic from a small town in Wisconsin had come to be converted to the cause. The geographical (East Coast) and family origins (Jewish) of the vast majority of the movement were apparently a source of concern. The practice of having gentile spokespersons for movements dominated by Jews is noted in several sections of this volume and is also a common tactic against anti-Semitism (SAID, Ch. 6). Rothman and Lichter (1982/1996, p. 81) quote another observer of the New Left scene at the University of Wisconsin as follows: "I am struck by the lack of Wisconsin-born people and the massive preponderance of New York Jews. The situation at the University of Minnesota is similar." His correspondent replied, "As you perceived, the Madison left is built on New York Jews."

My personal experience at Wisconsin during the 1960s was that the student protest movement was originated and dominated by Jews and that a great many of them were "red diaper babies" whose parents had been radicals. The intellectual atmosphere of the movement closely resembled the atmosphere in the Polish communist movement described by Schatz (1991, p. 117; see below)—intensely verbal *pilpul*-like discussions in which one's reputation as a leftist was related to one's ability in Marxist intellectual analysis and familiarity with Marxist scholarship, both of which required a great deal of study. There was also a great deal of hostility to Western cultural institutions as politically and sexually oppressive combined with an ever-present sense of danger and imminent destruction by the forces of repression—an ingroup bunker mentality discussed in PTSDA Chapter 7 that I now believe is a fundamental characteristic of Jewish social forms. There was an attitude of moral and intellectual superiority and even contempt toward traditional American culture, particularly rural America and most particularly the South—attitudes that are hallmarks of several of the intellectual movements reviewed here (e.g., the attitudes of Polish-Jewish communists toward traditional Polish culture; see also Chs. 7–8 on Jewish attitudes toward populism). There was also a strong desire for bloody, apocalyptic revenge against the entire social structure viewed as having victimized not only Jews but non-elite gentiles as well—reflecting the revenge theme of many commenters on Jewish motivation.

These students had very positive attitudes toward Judaism as well as negative attitudes toward Christianity, but perhaps surprisingly, the most salient contrast between Judaism and Christianity in their minds was in attitudes toward sexuality. In line with the very large Freudian influence of the period, the general tendency was to contrast a putative sexual permissiveness of Judaism with the sexual repression and prudery of Christianity, and this contrast was then linked with psychoanalytic analyses that attributed various forms of psychopathology and even capitalism, racism, and other forms of political oppression to Christian sexual attitudes. (See Chs. 5–6 for discussions of the wider context of this type of analysis.) The powerful Jewish identification of these anti-Vietnam War radicals was clearly highlighted by their intense concern and eventual euphoria surrounding Israel's Six-Day War of 1967, also noted by Paul Gottfried (see above).

It is also noteworthy that at Wisconsin the student movement idolized iconic Jewish activists of the left, especially Trotsky, Luxemburg, and the Frankfurt School's Herbert Marcuse. They also hero-worshipped certain Jewish professors at Wisconsin, particularly the charismatic social historian Harvey Goldberg, whose lectures presenting his Marxist view of European social history enthralled a very large following in the largest lecture hall on campus. (The tendency for Jewish intellectual movements to become centered around highly charismatic Jewish figures is apparent in this chapter and is summarized as a general phenomenon in Chapter 7.) They adopted an attitude of condescension toward another well-known liberal historian, George Mosse.

Mosse's Jewishness was quite salient to them, but he was viewed as insufficiently radical.

EXPLAINING JEWISH RADICALISM:
SOCIAL IDENTITY PROCESSES AND PERCEIVED JEWISH GROUP INTERESTS

Jewish Radicals Are on a Moral Mission

One view of Jewish radicalism emphasizes the moral basis of Judaism. This is yet another example of the attempt to portray Judaism as a universalist, morally superior movement—the "light of the nations" theme that has repeatedly emerged as an aspect of Jewish self-identity since antiquity and especially since the Enlightenment (SAID, Ch. 7). Thus Fuchs (1956, pp. 190–191) suggests that the Jewish involvement in liberal causes stems from the unique moral nature of Judaism in inculcating charity toward the poor and needy. Involvement in these causes is viewed as simply an extension of traditional Jewish religious practices. Similarly, Hertzberg (1985) writes of "the echo of a unique moral sensibility, a willingness to act in disregard of economic interest when the cause seems just."

As indicated in PTSDA Chapters 5 and 6, there is every indication that traditional Jewish concern for the poor and needy was confined within Jewish groups, and in fact Jews have often served oppressive ruling elites in traditional societies and in post-World War II Eastern Europe (see also critiques of Fuchs by A. Liebman, 1979, pp. 5–11; C. Liebman, 1973, p. 140; and Rothman & Lichter, 1982/1996, p. 112). Ginsberg (1993, p. 140) describes these putative humanistic motivations as "a bit fanciful," and notes that in different contexts (notably in the postrevolutionary Soviet Union) Jews have organized "ruthless agencies of coercion and terror," including especially a very prominent involvement in the Soviet secret police from the postrevolutionary period into the 1930s (see also Baron, 1975, p. 170; Lincoln, 1989; Rapoport, 1990, pp. 30–31). Similarly, Jews were very prominent in the internal security forces in Poland (see Schatz, 1991, pp. 223–228) and Hungary (Rothman & Lichter, 1982/1996, p. 89).

Mendes (2014, p. 56) views Jewish involvement in communism as motivated by idealistic utopian visions of the future—the militancy of Jewish communists "was always messianic, optimistic, oriented to the Good." As Brenton Sanderson (2019, p. 77) notes:

> Free discussion of the Jewish role in communist crimes undermines Jewish pretentions to moral authority grounded in their self-designated status as history's preeminent victims. In contemporary academia there are,

in addition, strong personal and professional disincentives for highlighting the Jewish role in communist crimes, and it is, therefore, not surprising that non-Jewish historians and intellectuals are equally reluctant to recognize the Jewish backgrounds of many revolutionaries and to explore how their Jewish identity influenced their beliefs and actions.

Anti-Semitism as a Cause of Jewish Radicalism

As a variation on the theme of radical Jews engaging in a moral crusade, several authors have proposed anti-Semitism as a cause of Jewish radicalism, although without a serious examination of the morally tinged attitudes linked to anti-Jewish sentiment, such as Jewish monopolization of entire industries (including the sale of liquor to peasants on credit), predatory moneylending, and radical political agitation (Sanderson, 2018, pp. 72–73). For example, Brossat and Klingberg (1983/2016, p. 85) claim that the Jewish involvement in Bolshevism was "morally justified ethnic self-defense," insisting that anti-Semitism was "an insidious poison hovering in the air of the time" that comprised "the sinister background music to the action of the Yiddishland revolutionaries." Rather than seeing Jewish communist militants as willing agents of ethnically motivated oppression and mass murder, the authors depict them as noble victims who tragically "linked their fate to the grand narrative of working-class emancipation, fraternity between peoples, socialist egalitarianism" (Brossat & Klingberg, p. ix).

> Determined to absolve their co-ethnics of any culpability for communist crimes, Brossat and Klingberg assure us that the militancy of their informants "was always messianic, optimistic, oriented to the Good—a fundamental and irreducible difference from that of the fascists with which some people have been tempted to compare it, on the pretext that one 'militant ideal' is equivalent to any other" [Brossat & Klingberg, 1983/2016, p. 56]. In other words, tens of millions may have died as a result of the actions of Jewish communist militants, but their hearts were pure. (Sanderson, 2018, pp. 72–73)

Similarly, for Mendes (2014, p. 16), the extensive Jewish involvement in communism was a defensive and morally justified response to the European persecution of Jews, noting that "many if not most of these Jewish activists were almost certainly influenced towards their radicalism by their Jewish origins and upbringing, and particularly by their personal experiences of anti-Semitism"—a recurrent theme of this volume. While this influence was "downplayed later on in response to the assimilationist atmosphere of the movement," a "surprising" number of radical Jews expressed,

concern about specifically Jewish issues, and solidarity with Jewish victims of anti-Semitism at particular points of their careers. They included
Anna Kulichev, Rosalie Bograd, Charles Rappoport, Julius Martov, Pavel
Axelrod and Henri Polak. Even committed internationalists such as Leon
Trotsky and Emma Goldman still demonstrated considerable sensitivity
to, and interest in, the question of anti-Semitism. Other radicals such as
the German revolutionaries Kurt Eisner, Erich Mühsam, Gustav Landauer
and Ernst Toller also demonstrated considerable Jewish consciousness.
(Mendes, 2014, p. 16)

Jewish Radicals as Reflecting Jewish Intelligence and Upward Mobility

R. Pipes (1993, p. 112) theorizes that although it is "undeniable" that Jews
were overrepresented in the Bolshevik party and the early Soviet government
as well as communist revolutionary activities in Hungary, Germany, and Austria in the period from 1918 to 1923, Jews were also overrepresented in a variety
of other areas, including business, art, literature, and science. As a result, Pipes
argues that their disproportionate representation in communist political
movements should not be an issue. Pipes couples this argument with the assertion that Jewish Bolsheviks did not identify as Jews—"they did not speak for
the Jews because they had broken with them long before the revolution. They
spoke for no one but themselves" (p. 113)—an assertion that, as we have seen,
is questionable at best.

However, even assuming that these ethnically Jewish communists did not
identify as Jews, such an argument fails to explain why such "de-ethnicized"
Jews (as well as Jewish businessmen, artists, writers, and scientists) should
have typically been overrepresented in leftist movements and underrepresented in nationalist, populist, and other types of rightist political movements.[51] Even if nationalist movements are anti-Semitic, as has often been the
case, anti-Semitism should be irrelevant if these individuals are indeed completely "de-ethnicized" as Pipes proposes. Jewish prominence in occupations
requiring high intelligence is no argument for understanding their very prominent role in communist and other leftist movements and their relative un-
derrepresentation in nationalist movements. And, as noted in the Preface,
non-Jewish Whites outnumber Jews at every level of IQ, yet White were far
from being overrepresented in communism and the left.

---

[51] As detailed in Chapter 4, American neoconservatism is a specifically Jewish conservative political movement but is not relevant to Pipes's argument as it applies to the Bolsheviks because
its proponents have an overt Jewish identity and the movement is directed at achieving perceived Jewish interests, for example, with regard to Israel, affirmative action, and immigration
policy.

Social Identity Theory and Jewish Radicalism

Social identity theory provides a quite different perspective on Jewish radicalism. It stresses that perceived Jewish group interests are fundamental to Jewish political behavior, and that these perceived group interests are importantly influenced by social identity processes. If indeed radical politics resulted in a strong sense of identification with a Jewish ingroup, then Jewish involvement in these movements would be associated with very negative and exaggerated conceptions of the wider gentile society, and particularly the most powerful elements of that society, as an outgroup. In conformity with this expectation, A. Liebman (1979, p. 26) uses the term "contraculture" to describe the American Jewish left because "conflict with or antagonism toward society is a central feature of this subculture and ... many of its values and cultural patterns are contradictions of those existing in the surrounding society." For example, the New Left was fundamentally involved in radical social criticism in which all elements that contributed to the cohesive social fabric of mid-twentieth-century America were regarded as oppressive and in need of radical alteration.

The emphasis here on social identity processes is compatible with Jewish radicalism serving particular perceived Jewish group interests. Anti-Semitism and Jewish economic interests were undoubtedly important motivating factors for Jewish leftism in czarist Russia. Jewish leaders in Western societies, many of whom were wealthy capitalists, proudly acknowledged Jewish overrepresentation in the Russian revolutionary movement; they also provided financial and political support for these movements by, for example, attempting to influence U.S. foreign policy (Szajkowski, 1967). Representative of this attitude is financier Jacob Schiff's statement:

> [T]he claim that among the ranks of those who in Russia are seeking to undermine governmental authority there are a considerable number of Jews may perhaps be true. In fact, it would be rather surprising if some of those so terribly afflicted by persecution and exceptional laws should not at last have turned against their merciless oppressors. (in Szajkowski, 1967, p. 10)

The moral-idealistic case for Jewish involvement in communism and the left as justified by Russian oppression has also been made by Brossat and Klingberg (1983/2016), much of it based on exaggerated accounts of Russian oppression of Jews in the nineteenth century (Joyce, 2012).

However, when Jews have been relatively well off, they have often still tended toward radicalism. As noted above, Jews associated with the New Left in the U.S. were often middle-class and better off than more conservative students. And in Hungary, "The prominence of Jews in the Hungarian Soviet Republic [of 1919] is all the more striking when one considers that the Jews of Hungary were richer than their coreligionists in eastern Europe and remarkably successful in attaining positions of status" (Muller, 2010, p. 153). Although only 5 percent of the population, on the eve of World War I Jews made up almost half the doctors, lawyers, and journalists in Hungary (p. 154). Despite this, of the forty-nine commissars who governed Béla Kun's short-lived Hungarian Soviet Republic, thirty-one were Jewish (p. 154). Kun's government attempted to destroy all elements of traditional Hungarian culture:

> Statues of Hungarian kings and national heroes were torn down, the national anthem was banned, and the display of the national colors was made a punishable offense. . . . Radical agitators were dispatched to the countryside, where they ridiculed the institution of the family and threatened to turn churches into movie theatres. . . . Antipathy soon enough focused on the Jews. Young revolutionaries of Jewish origin had been sent to the countryside to administer the newly collectivized agricultural estates; their radicalism was exceeded only by their incompetence, reinforcing peasant anti-Semitism. The Jesuits, for their part, interpreted the revolution as Jewish and anti-Christian in essence. . . . Rumors abounded that the revolutionaries were everywhere desecrating the Host. In Budapest as in the countryside, opposition to the regime, defense of the church, and anti-Semitism went hand in hand. (Muller, 2010, pp. 156–157)

Reflecting on this history in 2017, Zsolt Bayer, co-founder of Hungary's ruling Fidesz Party, asked:

> Why are we surprised that the simple peasant whose determinant experience was that the Jews broke into his village, beat his priest to death, threatened to convert his church into a movie theatre—why do we find it shocking that twenty years later he watched without pity as the gendarmes dragged the Jews away from his village? (in Liphshiz, 2017)

Economic Self-Interest and Jewish Radicalism

At the risk of oversimplification and acknowledging that economic explanations are inadequate in several important contexts, it is nevertheless the case that economic adversity for many Jews in the Pale and their constructions of the causes of anti-Semitism combined with the Jewish demographic explosion in Eastern Europe were of critical importance for producing the sheer number of disaffected Jewish radicals and therefore the ultimate influence of Jewish radicalism in Europe and its spillover into the United States. Despite

the immigration of close to two million Jews to the United States and elsewhere, many Eastern European Jews were impoverished, at least partly because of their high birth rate. Jewish populations in Eastern Europe had the
highest rate of natural increase of any European population in the nineteenth
century, with a natural increase of 120,000 per year in the 1880s and an overall
increase within the Russian Empire from one to six million in the course of the
nineteenth century (Alderman, 1992, p. 112; Frankel, 1981, p. 103; Lindemann,
1991, pp. 28–29, 133–135).

Despite periodic restrictions and outbursts of hostility, Jews came to
dominate the entire economy from agricultural labor up to the nobility. Jews
had an advantage in the competition of trade and artisanry because they were
able to control the trade in raw materials and therefore sell at lower prices (see
PTSDA). This increasing economic domination went along with a great increase in the population of Jews. Jews not only made up large percentages of
urban populations, but they also increasingly migrated to small towns and rural areas.

In short, Jews had overshot their economic niche: the economy was unable
to support this burgeoning Jewish population in the sorts of positions that
Jews had traditionally filled, with the result that a large percentage of the Jewish population became mired in poverty. The result was a cauldron of ethnic
hostility, with the government placing various restrictions on Jewish economic
activity; rampant anti-Jewish attitudes; and increasing Jewish anger and des-
peration. The main Jewish response to this situation was an upsurge of fundamentalist extremism that coalesced in the Hasidic movement and, later in the
nineteenth century, into political radicalism and Zionism as solutions to Jewish
problems. Anti-Semitism and the exploding Jewish population, combined with
economic adversity, were of critical importance for producing the sheer number of disaffected Jews who dreamed of deliverance through various messianic
movements—the ethnocentric mysticism of the Kabbala, Zionism, or the
dream of a Marxist political revolution and the end of anti-Semitism. Religious
fanaticism and messianic expectations have been a typical Jewish response to
hard times throughout history (e.g., PTSDA, Ch. 3; Scholem, 1971).

As a result, a great many Jews were attracted to radical political solutions
that would transform the economic and political basis of society and would
also be consistent with the continuity of Judaism. Within Russian Jewish communities, the acceptance of radical political ideology often coexisted with
messianic forms of Zionism as well as intense commitment to Jewish nationalism and religious and cultural separatism, and many individuals held various
and often rapidly changing combinations of these ideas (see Frankel, 1981).

Indeed, one might propose that messianic forms of political radicalism
may be viewed as secular forms of this Jewish response to perceived anti-Semitism, different from traditional forms only in that they also promise a utopian

future for gentiles as well. The overall picture is reminiscent of the situation in the late Ottoman Empire, where by the mid-eighteenth century until the intervention of the European powers in the twentieth century there was "an unmistakable picture of grinding poverty, ignorance, and insecurity" (B. Lewis, 1984, p. 164) in the context of high levels of anti-Semitism that effectively prevented Jewish upward mobility. These phenomena were accompanied by the prevalence of mysticism and a high-fertility, low-investment parenting style among Jews. In the long run the community became too poor to provide for the education of most children, with the result that most were illiterate and pursued occupations requiring only limited intelligence and training.

However, when presented with opportunities for upward social mobility, the strategy quickly changes to a low-fertility, high-investment reproductive strategy. In nineteenth-century Germany, for example, the Jews were the first group to enter the demographic transition and take advantage of opportunities for upward social mobility by having fewer children (e.g., A. Goldstein, 1981; Knode, 1974). At the same time, poor Jews in Eastern Europe with no hope of upward mobility married earlier than their Western European counterparts, who delayed marriage in order to be financially better prepared (Efron, 1994, p. 77). And the resurgence of Ottoman Jewry in the nineteenth century resulting from patronage and protection from Western European Jews brought with it a flowering of a highly literate culture, including secular schools based on Western models (see Shaw, 1991, pp. 143ff, 175–176). Similarly, when the oppressed Eastern European Jews immigrated to the United States, they developed a low-fertility, high-investment culture that took advantage of opportunities for upward mobility. The suggestion is that the overall pattern of the Jewish response to lack of opportunity for upward mobility and anti-Semitism is to facultatively adopt a high-fertility, low-investment style of reproduction combined at the ideological level with various forms of messianism, including, in the modern era, radical political ideology.

Ultimately this population explosion in the context of poverty and politically imposed restrictions on Jews was responsible for the generally destabilizing effects of Jewish radicalism on Russia up to the Revolution. These conditions also had spillover effects in Germany, where the negative attitudes toward the immigrant Ostjuden contributed to the anti-Semitism of the period (Aschheim, 1982). In the United States, a main point of this chapter is that a high level of inertia characterized the radical political beliefs held by a great many Jewish immigrants and their descendants in the sense that radical political beliefs persisted even in the absence of oppressive economic and political conditions. In Sorin's (1985, p. 46) study of immigrant Jewish radical activists in America, over half had been involved in radical politics in Europe before immigrating, and for those immigrating after 1900, the percentage rose to 69 percent. Glazer (1961, p. 21) notes that the biographies of almost all radical leaders show that they first came into contact with radical political ideas in Europe. The persistence of these beliefs influenced the general political sensibility of the Jewish community and had a destabilizing effect on American society, ranging from the paranoia of the McCarthy era, to the triumph of the 1960s countercultural revolution, to the contemporary institutional dominance of the left.

The immigration of Eastern European Jews into England after 1880 had a similarly transformative effect on the political attitudes of British Jewry in the direction of socialism, trade unionism, and Zionism, often combined with religious orthodoxy and devotion to a highly separatist traditional lifestyle (Alderman, 1983, pp. 47ff).

> Far more significant than the handful of publicity-seeking Jewish socialists, both in Russia and England, who organized ham-sandwich picnics on the fast of Yom Kippur, the Day of Atonement, were the mass of working-class Jews who experienced no inner conflict when they repaired to the synagogue for religious services three times each day, and then used the same premises to discuss socialist principles and organize industrial stoppages. (Alderman, 1983, p. 54)[52]

As in the United States, the immigrant Eastern European Jews demographically swamped the previously existing Jewish community, and the older community reacted to this influx with considerable trepidation because of the possibility of increased anti-Semitism. And as in the United States, attempts were made by the established Jewish community to misrepresent the prevalence of radical political ideas among the immigrants (Alderman, 1983, p. 60; SAID, Ch. 8).

Nevertheless, economic interests are not the whole story. While the origin of widespread political radicalism among Jews can be characterized as a typical Jewish response to the political and economic adversity of late-nineteenth-century Eastern Europe, radical political ideology became dissociated from the usual demographic variables not long after arrival in the United States, and it is this phenomenon that requires another type of explanation. For the most part, American Jews had far less reason than other ethnic groups to wish for an overthrow of capitalism because they tended to be relatively economically privileged and successful in a capitalist system. Surveys from the 1960s and 1970s indicated that middle-class Jews were more radical than working-class

---

[52] Religious orthodoxy was also compatible with attraction to anarchism: Alderman (1983, p. 64) quotes a contemporary writer to the effect that "the anarchists had achieved such popularity that they became almost respectable. A sympathizer could lay on his *tefillin* (phylacteries) on the morning of an Anarchist-sponsored strike, bless Rocker [a gentile anarchist leader], and still go off to evening service as an orthodox Jew."

Jews—a pattern opposite to that of non-Jewish radical students (Rothman & Lichter, 1982/1996, pp. 117, 219;[53] Levey, 1996, p. 375). Lower percentages of Jews than members of other religions believed that supporting a Democratic candidate would further their economic interests, but Jews nevertheless tended overwhelmingly to vote Democratic (C. Liebman, 1973, pp. 136–137).

The gap between economic interests and political ideology dates at least from the 1920s (A. Liebman, 1979, pp. 290ff). Indeed, for the entire period from 1921 to 1961, Jews on the Central Committee of the CPUSA were much more likely to have middle-class, professional backgrounds and tended to have more education than their gentile colleagues (Klehr, 1978, pp. 42ff). They were also much more likely to have joined prior to the economic difficulties of the Great Depression. Further, as indicated above, New Left radical students came disproportionately from highly educated and affluent families (see also C. Liebman, 1973, p. 210).

Even successful Jewish capitalists have tended to adopt political beliefs to the left of the beliefs of their gentile counterparts. For example, German-Jewish capitalists in the nineteenth century "tended to take up positions distinctly to the 'left' of their Gentile peers and thus to place themselves in isolation from them" (W. E. Mosse, 1989, p. 225). Although as a group they tended to be to the right of the Jewish population as a whole, a few even supported the Social Democratic Party and its socialist program. Among the plausible reasons for this state of affairs suggested by Mosse is that anti-Semitism tended to be associated with the German right. Consistent with social identity theory, Jewish capitalists did not identify with groups that perceived them negatively and identified with groups that opposed an outgroup perceived as hostile. Social identity processes and their influence on perception of ethnic (group) interests rather than economic self-interest appears to be paramount here.

The association between Jews and liberal political attitudes is therefore independent of the usual demographic associations. In a passage that shows that Jewish cultural and ethnic estrangement and hostility to White America often supersedes economic interests in explaining Jewish political behavior, Silberman (1985, pp. 347–348) comments on the attraction of Jews to,

> the Democratic party . . . with its traditional hospitality to non-WASP ethnic groups. . . . A distinguished economist who strongly disagreed with [presidential candidate Walter] Mondale's economic policies voted for him

---

[53] In Rothman and Lichter's (1982/1996, p. 217) study, radicalism among American Jews was inversely related to religious orthodoxy. Moreover, there was a major gap between the fairly homogeneous set of mean radicalism scores of students from homes affiliated with a Jewish religious denomination (Orthodox, Conservative, or Reform) compared to the higher radicalism scores of those from homes without Jewish religious affiliation. These results again suggest that radicalism functioned as a form of secular Judaism among this latter group.

nonetheless. "I watched the conventions on television," he explained, "and the Republicans did not look like my kind of people." That same reaction led many Jews to vote for Carter in 1980 despite their dislike of him; "I'd rather live in a country governed by the faces I saw at the Democratic convention than by those I saw at the Republican convention," a well-known author told me.

The suggestion is that in general Jewish political motivation is influenced by non-economic issues related to perceived Jewish group interests, the latter influenced by social identity processes. Similarly, in the politically charged area of cultural attitudes, Silberman (1985, p. 350) notes:

American Jews are committed to cultural tolerance because of their be-lief—one firmly rooted in history—that Jews are safe only in a society ac-ceptant of a wide range of attitudes and behaviors, as well as a diversity of religious and ethnic groups. It is this belief, for example, not approval of homosexuality, that leads an overwhelming majority of American Jews to endorse "gay rights" and to take a liberal stance on most other so-called "social" issues.

A perceived Jewish group interest in cultural pluralism transcends nega-tive personal attitudes regarding the behavior in question.

Silberman's comment that Jewish attitudes are "firmly rooted in history" is particularly relevant: a consistent tendency has been for Jews to be perse-cuted as a minority group within a culturally or ethnically homogeneous soci-ety. A discussion of the political, religious, and cultural pluralism as a very ra-tional motivation for American Jews will be highlighted in Chapter 8, which discusses Jewish involvement in shaping U.S. immigration policy. The point here is that the perceived Jewish group interest in developing a pluralistic so-ciety is of far more importance than mere economic self-interest in determin-ing Jewish political behavior. Similarly, Earl Raab (1996, p. 44) explains Jewish political behavior in terms of security issues related in part to a long memory of the Republican Party as linked to Christian fundamentalism and its history of being "resolutely nativist and anti-immigrant." The pattern of supporting the Democratic Party is therefore an aspect of ethnic conflict between Jews and sectors of the European-derived White population in the United States, not economic issues. Indeed, economic issues appear to have no relevance at all, since support for the Democratic Party among Jews does not differ by so-cial status (Raab, 1996, p. 45).

Nevertheless, there is evidence that Jewish voting behavior increasingly separates the traditional economic left-liberalism from issues related to cul-tural pluralism, immigration, and church-state separation. Polls and data on

Jewish voting patterns indicate that Jews continue to view the right wing of the Republican Party as "a threat to American cosmopolitanism" because it is perceived as advocating a homogeneous Christian culture and is opposed to immigration (Beinart, 1997, p. 25). I suspect this remains true. The Pew Research Center (2021) found that Jews generally voted for Democrats (71 percent Democrat-leaning), despite being "a relatively high-income group, with roughly half saying their annual household income is at least $100,000—much higher than the percentage of all U.S. households at that level." And in the same survey, Jews disapproved of President Trump (73 percent) in general and his performance on immigration in particular (14 percent rating it excellent, and 7 percent good), while nearly three-quarters called it only fair (7 percent) or poor (67 percent).

In addition to the pursuit of specific group interests, however, social identity processes appear to make an independent contribution to explaining Jewish political behavior. Social identity processes appear to be necessary for explaining why the Jewish labor movement was far more radical than the rest of the American labor movement in the early decades of the twentieth century. In a passage that indicates Jewish radicals' profound sense of Jewish identity and separatism as well as complete antipathy to the entire gentile social order, Levin (1977, p. 213) notes:

> [T]heir socialist ideas ... created a gulf between themselves and other American workers who were not interested in radical changes in the social order. Although Jewish trade unions joined the AFL, they never felt ideologically at home there, for the AFL did not seek a radical transformation of society, nor was it internationalist in outlook.

We have also noted that the New Left completely abandoned the aims and interests of the lower-middle working class once that group had essentially achieved its social aims with the success of the trade union movement.

Antipathy Toward the Gentile Social Order: Revenge, Displacement, and Domination

Again, there is the strong suggestion that social criticism and feelings of cultural estrangement among Jews have deep psychological roots that reach far beyond particular economic or political interests. As indicated in Chapter 1, a critical psychological component appears to involve a very deep antipathy to the entire gentile-dominated social order, which is viewed as anti-Semitic—the desire for "malignant vengeance" that Disraeli asserted made many Jews "odious and so hostile to mankind." Recall Lipset's (1968/1988, p. 393) description of the many Jewish "families which around the breakfast table, day after day, in Scarsdale, Newton, Great Neck, and Beverly Hills have discussed what an awful, corrupt, immoral, undemocratic, racist society the United States is." These families clearly perceive themselves as separate from the wider culture of the United States; they also view conservative forces as attempting to maintain this malignant culture. As in the case of traditional Judaism vis-à-vis gentile society, the traditional culture of the United States—and particularly the political basis of cultural conservatism that has historically been associated with anti-Semitism—is perceived as a manifestation of a negatively evaluated outgroup, and as such it warrants a motive of revenge.

As noted above in the example of Jews in the communist security forces in post-World War II Poland, this antipathy toward gentile-dominated society was often accompanied by a powerful desire to avenge the evils of the old social order. Norman Cantor (1996, p. 364):

> The Bolshevik Revolution and some of its aftermath represented, from one perspective, Jewish revenge. During the heyday of the Cold War, American Jewish publicists spent a lot of time denying that—as 1930s anti-Semites claimed—Jews played a disproportionately important role in Soviet and world Communism. The truth is until the early 1950s Jews did play such a role, and there is nothing to be ashamed of. In time Jews will learn to take pride in the record of the Jewish Communists in the Soviet Union and elsewhere. It was a species of striking back.

A leading Jewish communist and founder of the Mensheviks Yuli Martov, who became a close associate of Lenin and Trotsky, made a point of recalling his childhood experiences of Russian and Ukrainian anti-Semitism. The 1881 Odessa pogrom was his "first taste of primitive Russian anti-Semitism," and Martov was "shaken to the depths of his being by the pogromist barbarity of Tsarist Russia" (Wistrich, 1976, p. 178). The event left a "permanent mark on his impressionable mind," and he later underlined the connection between this experience and his subsequent revolutionary career, posing the question:

> Would I have become what I became if the Russian reality had not imprinted her coarse fingers on my plastic, youthful soul in that memorable night and carefully planted under the cover of that burning pity which she aroused in my childlike heart, the seeds of a redeeming hatred [a hatred that justified the murder of millions]? (Wistrich, 1976, p. 178)

Similarly, for many Jewish New Leftists, "the revolution promises to avenge the sufferings and to right the wrongs which have, for so long, been inflicted on Jews with the permission or encouragement, or even at the command of, the authorities in prerevolutionary societies" (P. S. Cohen, 1980, p.

208). Interviews with New Left Jewish radicals revealed that many had destructive fantasies in which the Revolution would result in "humiliation, dispossession, imprisonment or execution of the oppressors" (p. 208) combined with the belief in their own omnipotence and ability to create a nonoppressive social order—findings that are reminiscent of the motivating role of revenge for anti-Semitism among the Jewish-dominated security forces in communist Poland discussed above. These findings are also entirely consistent with my experience among Jewish New Left activists at the University of Wisconsin in the 1960s (see above) and with Mark Rudd's (2005) "Why Were There So Many Jews in the SDS? Or, The Ordeal of Civility":

> But World War II and the holocaust were our fixed reference points. This was only twenty years after the end of the war. We often talked about the moral imperative to not be Good Germans. Many of my older comrades had mobilized for the civil rights movement; we were all anti-racists. We saw American racism as akin to German racism toward the Jews. As we learned more about the war, we discovered that killing Vietnamese en masse was of no moral consequence to American war planners. So we started describing the war as racist genocide, reflecting the genocide of the holocaust. American imperialist goals around the world were to us little different from the Nazi goal of global conquest. If you really didn't like somebody—and we loathed President Lyndon B. Johnson—you might call him a fascist.

Ultimately, in Jewish radicalism, whether in the post-1917 Soviet Union or the English faculty at Columbia, there is a strong element of a desire for displacement and domination. The displacement of what Rudd called "the air of genteel civility" at Columbia—and the institutional structure of the United States—since the 1960s is largely complete. Recall the Jewish radicals who fled the shtetls of Eastern Europe and, instead of going to Ellis Island, became the dominant elite in the USSR after the success of the Bolshevik Revolution. These Jewish radicals were able to actually carry out in the USSR the fantasies of the New Left Jewish radicals in the US—i.e., the "humiliation, dispossession, imprisonment or execution of the oppressors" mentioned above. Since the 2020 election we are seeing increasing calls for limiting speech, including calls for canceling mainstream conservative outlets like Fox News, and the Department of Homeland Security has declared that the most important threat facing America is "domestic extremism," and in particular, "white supremacists" (Miroff, 2021).

Radicalism and Positive Attitudes Toward the Jewish Ingroup

The social identity perspective predicts that generalized negative attributions of the outgroup would be accompanied by positive attributions regarding the Jewish ingroup. Both Jewish communists in Poland and Jewish New Left radicals had a powerful feeling of cultural superiority that was continuous with traditional Jewish conceptions of the superiority of their ingroup (P. S. Cohen, 1980, p. 212; Schatz, 1991, p. 119). Jewish self-conceptualizations of their activity in developing an adversarial culture in the United States tended to emphasize either the Jew as the historical victim of gentile anti-Semitism or the Jew as the moral hero, but "in both cases the portrait is the obverse of that of the anti-Semite. Jews lack warts. Their motives are pure, their idealism genuine" (Rothman & Lichter, 1982/1996, p. 112). Studies of Jewish radicals by Jewish social scientists have tended to gratuitously attribute Jewish radicalism to a "free choice of a gifted minority" (p. 118) when economic explanations failed—yet another example where Jewish group status appears to affect social science research in a manner that serves Jewish group interests.

Moreover, a universalist utopian ideology such as Marxism is an ideal vehicle for serving Jewish attempts to develop a positive self-identity while still retaining their positive identity as Jews and their negative evaluation of gentile power structures. First, the utopian nature of radical ideology in contrast to existing gentile-dominated social systems (which are inevitably less than perfect) facilitates development of a positive identity for the ingroup. Radical ideology thus facilitates positive group identity and a sense of moral rectitude because of its advocacy of universalist ethical principles. Psychologists have found that a sense of moral rectitude is an important component of self-esteem (e.g., Harter, 1983), and self-esteem has been proposed as a motivating factor in social identity processes (SAID, Ch. 1). The moral veneer of leftist movements is particularly effective in individualist Western cultures because Western cultures tend toward individualism (*Individualism*). Rather than being based on kinship, the social glue of Western cultures is membership in a moral community. Hence movements claiming the moral high ground are particularly effective in recruiting Europeans to their point of view.

As was also true of psychoanalysis, leftist political movements developed redemptive-messianic overtones highly conducive to ingroup pride and loyalty. Members of the Russian Jewish Bund and their progeny in the United States had intense personal pride and a powerful sense that they were "part of a moral and political vanguard for great historical change. They had a mission that inspired them and people who believed in them" (A. Liebman, 1979, p. 133).

This sense of ingroup pride and messianic fervor is undoubtedly a critical ingredient of Judaism in all historical eras. As Schatz (1991, p. 105) notes in his description of the underground Jewish communist revolutionaries in Poland during the interwar period:

> The movement was ... part of a worldwide, international struggle for nothing less than the fundamental change of the very foundations of human society. The joint effect of this situation was a specific sense of revolutionary loneliness and mission, an intense cohesion, a feeling of brotherhood, and a readiness for personal sacrifice on the altar of struggle.

What distinguished Jewish communists from other communists was not only their desire for a postrevolutionary world without anti-Semitism, but also their "distinct [emotional] intensity with roots in messianic longings" (Schatz, 1991, p. 140). As one respondent said, "I believed in Stalin and in the party as my father believed in the Messiah" (in p. 140).

Reflecting traditional Jewish social structure, these Jewish radical groups were hierarchical and highly authoritarian, and they developed their own private language (Schatz, 1991, pp. 109–112). As in traditional Judaism, continuing study and self-education were viewed as very important features of the movement: "To study was a point of honor and an obligation" (p. 117). The discussions replicated the traditional methods of Torah study: memorization of long passages of text combined with analysis and interpretation carried out in an atmosphere of intense intellectual competition quite analogous to the traditional *pilpul*. In the words of a novice to these discussions, "We behaved like *yeshiva bukhers* [students] and they [the more experienced intellectual mentors] like rabbis" (p. 139). I experienced a similar phenomenon among Jewish 1960s radicals at the University of Wisconsin (see above).

As expected on the basis of social identity theory, there was also a high level of ingroup-outgroup thinking characterized by a lofty sense of moral rectitude among the ingroup combined with an implacable hostility and rejection of the outgroup. In the period after World War II, for example, the Polish-Jewish communists viewed the new economic plan "in truly mystical terms. [It was] a scientifically conceived, infallible scheme that would totally restructure societal relations and prepare the country for socialism" (Schatz, 1991, p. 249). The economic difficulties that befell the people merely resulted in transferring their hopes to the future, while at the same time they developed,

> an uncompromising attitude toward those who might not be willing to accept the hardships of the present and a merciless hostility toward those perceived as the enemy. Thus the burning will to produce general harmony and happiness was married to distrust and suspiciousness regarding its objects and a hatred toward its actual, potential, or imagined opponents. (Schatz, 1991, p. 250)

Clearly, to be a communist revolutionary was to develop an intense commitment to a cohesive authoritarian group that valued intellectual accomplishments and exhibited intense hatred against enemies and outgroups while having very positive feelings toward an ingroup viewed as morally and intellectually superior. These groups operated as embattled minorities that viewed the surrounding society as hostile and threatening. Being a member of such a group required a great deal of personal sacrifice and even altruism. All these attributes can be found as defining features of more traditional Jewish groups.

Universalism and the Blurring of Group Boundaries

Further evidence of the importance of social identity processes may be found in Charles Liebman's (1973, pp. 153ff) suggestion that leftist universalist ideology allows Jews to subvert traditional social categorizations in which Jews are viewed in negative terms. The adoption of such ideologies by Jews is an attempt to overcome Jewish feelings of alienation "from the roots and the traditions of [gentile] society" (p. 153).

> The Jew continues his search for an ethic or ethos which is not only universal or capable of universality, but which provides a cutting edge against the older traditions of the society, a search whose intensity is compounded and reinforced by the Gentile's treatment of the Jew. (C. Liebman, 1973, p. 157)

Such attempts at subverting negative social categorizations imposed by an outgroup are a central aspect of social identity theory (Hogg & D. Abrams, 1988; see SAID, Ch. 1).

The universalist ideology thus functions as a secular form of Judaism. Sectarian forms of Judaism are rejected as a "survival strategy" (C. Liebman, 1973, p. 157) because of their tendency to produce anti-Semitism, their lack of intellectual appeal in the post-Enlightenment world, and their ineffectiveness in appealing to gentiles and thereby altering the gentile social world in a manner that furthers Jewish group interests. Indeed, while the universalist ideology is formally congruent with Enlightenment ideals, the retention of traditional Jewish separatism and patterns of association among those espousing the ideology suggest an element of deception or self-deception:

> Jews prefer to get together with other Jews to promote ostensibly non-Jewish enterprises (which assist Jewish acceptance), and then to pretend the whole matter has nothing to do with being Jewish. But this type of activity is most prevalent among Jews who are the most estranged from their own traditions and hence most concerned with finding a value that

supports Jewish acceptance without overtly destroying Jewish group ties.
(C. Liebman, 1973, p. 159)

The universalist ideology therefore allows Jews to escape their alienation
or estrangement from gentile society while nevertheless allowing for the retention of a strong Jewish identity and rationalizing displacement of previous
non-Jewish elites. Institutions that promote group ties among gentiles (such
as nationalism and traditional gentile religious associations) are actively opposed and subverted, while the structural integrity of Jewish separatism is
maintained. A consistent thread of radical theorizing since Marx has been a
fear that nationalism could serve as a social cement that would result in a compromise between the social classes and result in a highly unified social order
based on hierarchical but harmonious relationships between existing social
classes. It is only this type of highly cohesive gentile social organization that is
fundamentally at odds with Judaism as a group evolutionary strategy (see Ch.
6; SAID, Ch. 5). Both the Old Left and the New Left, as noted, actively attempted
to subvert the cohesiveness of gentile social structure, including especially the
modus vivendi achieved between business and labor by the 1960s. And, as discussed in the Appendix to this chapter, the Jewish-dominated Polish communist government campaigned actively against Polish nationalism, and
against the political and cultural power of the Catholic Church, the main force
of social cohesion in traditional Polish society.

Finally, as emphasized by Rothman and Lichter (1982/1996, p. 119), Marxism is particularly attractive as the basis for an ideology that subverts the negative social categorizations of the gentile outgroup because within such an
ideology the Jewish-gentile categorization becomes less salient while Jewish
group cohesion and separatism may nevertheless persist:

> By adopting variants of Marxist ideology, Jews deny the reality of cultural
> or religious differences between Jews and Christians. These differences
> become "epiphenomenal," compared to the more fundamental opposition
> of workers and capitalists. Thus Jews and non-Jews are really brothers
> under the skin. Even when not adopting a Marxist position, many Jews
> have tended toward radical environmentalist positions, which serve a
> similar function.

Similarly, as indicated in Chapters 5 and 6, both psychoanalysis and the
ideology of the Frankfurt School downplay the importance of ethnic and cultural differences, engage in radical criticism of gentile culture, and simultaneously allow for the continuity of Jewish identification. Rothman and Isenberg
(1974b, p. 75) note that the theme of combining hostility to gentile culture with

accepting a universalist culture can be seen in Philip Roth's *Portnoy's Complaint*:

> Portnoy considers himself something of a radical and despises his parents for their parochial Jewishness and their hatred of Christians. He supposedly identifies with the poor and the downtrodden, but his tirade to his analyst makes it clear that this identification is based partly on his own feelings of inferiority and partly on his desire to "screw" the "goyim."

Such a strategy makes excellent sense from the standpoint of social identity theory: a consistent finding in research on intergroup contact is that making the social categories that define groups in less salient terms would lessen intergroup differentiation and would facilitate positive social interactions between members from different groups (Brewer & Miller, 1984; Doise & Sinclair, 1973; Miller et al., 1985). At the extreme, acceptance of a universalist ideology by gentiles would result in gentiles not perceiving Jews as in a different social category at all, while nonetheless Jews would be able to maintain a strong personal identity as Jews.

These features of Jewish radicalism together constitute a very compelling analysis of the role of social identity processes in this phenomenon. The last mechanism is particularly interesting as an analysis of both the tendency for Jewish political overrepresentation in radical causes and the Jewish tendency to adopt radical environmentalist ideologies noted as a common characteristic of Jewish social scientists in Chapter 2. The analysis implies that the Jews involved in these intellectual movements are engaged in a subtle process of deception of gentiles (and, perhaps, self-deception), and that these movements essentially function as a form of crypto-Judaism.

In the language of social identity theory, an ideology is created in which the social categorization of Jew-gentile is minimized in importance, and there are no negative attributions regarding Jewish group membership. The importance of ethnic group membership is minimized as a social category, and, because of its lack of importance, ethnic self-interest among gentiles is analyzed as fundamentally misguided because it does not recognize the priority of class conflict among gentiles. Jews can remain Jews because being a Jew is no longer important. At the same time, traditional institutions of social cohesiveness within gentile society are subverted, and gentile society itself is viewed as permeated by conflicts of interest between social classes, rather than by commonalities of interest and feelings of social solidarity among different social classes.

Rothman and Lichter (1982/1996, pp. 119ff) support their argument by noting that the adoption of universalist ideologies is a common technique among minority groups in a wide range of cultures around the world. Despite the veneer of universalism, these movements are most definitely not assimilation-ist, and in fact Rothman and Lichter view assimilation, defined as complete absorption and loss of minority group identity, as an alternative to the adop-tion of universalist political movements. Universalist ideologies may be smokescreens that actually facilitate the continued existence of group strate-gies while promoting the denial of their importance by ingroup and outgroup members alike. Judaism as a cohesive, ethnically based group strategy is able to continue to exist, but in a cryptic or semi-cryptic state.

Corroborating this perspective, Levin (1977, p. 105) states, "Marx's analysis [of Judaism as a caste] gave socialist thinkers an easy way out—to ignore or minimize the Jewish problem." In Poland, the Jewish-dominated Communist Party decried worker and peasant participation in anti-Semitic pogroms dur-ing the 1930s because such individuals were not acting on behalf of their class interests (Schatz, 1991, p. 99), an interpretation in which ethnic conflicts result from capitalism and will end after the communist revolution. One reason little anti-Semitism existed within the Social Democratic movement in late nine-teenth-century Germany was that Marxist theory explained all social phenom-ena; Social Democrats "did not need anti-Semitism, another all-embracing theory, to explain the events of their lives" (Dawidowicz, 1975, p. 42). The Social Democrats (and Marx) analyzed Judaism as a religious and economic commu-nity, not as a nation or as an ethnic group (Pulzer, 1964, p. 269).

In theory, therefore, anti-Semitism and other ethnic conflicts would dis-appear with the advent of a socialist society. It is possible that such an inter-pretation actually served to lower anti-Semitism in some cases. Levy (1975, p. 190) suggests that anti-Semitism was minimized among the gentile working-class constituency of the German Social Democrats by the activities of party leaders and socialist theoreticians who framed the political and economic problems of this group in terms of class conflict rather than Jewish-gentile conflict and actively opposed any cooperation with anti-Semitic parties.

Trotsky and other Jews in the Russian Social Democratic Labor Party con-sidered themselves as representing the Jewish proletariat within the wider so-cialist movement (see above), but they were opposed to the separatist, nation-alist program of the Russian Jewish Bund. Arthur Liebman (1979, pp. 122–123) suggests that these assimilationist socialists consciously conceptualized a postrevolutionary society in which Judaism would exist, but with a lessened social salience:

> For them, the ultimate solution of the Jewish problem would be an inter-nationalist socialist society that paid no heed to distinctions between Jews and non-Jews. To hasten the establishment of such a society, it became necessary, in the view of these assimilationist socialists, for Jews to

consider ethnic and religious distinctions between them and non-Jews as irrelevant.

Similarly, after the Revolution:

Having abandoned their own origins and identity, yet not finding, or sharing, or being fully admitted to Russian life (except in the world of the party), the Jewish Bolsheviks found their ideological home in revolutionary universalism. They dreamt of a classless and stateless society supported by Marxist faith and doctrine that transcended the particularities and burdens of Jewish existence. (Levin, 1988 I, p. 49).

These individuals, along with many highly nationalist ex-Bundists, ended up administrating programs related to Jewish national life in the Soviet Union. Apparently, although they rejected the radical Jewish separatism of either the Bundists or the Zionists, they envisioned the continuity of secular Jewish national life in the Soviet Union (e.g., Levin, 1988 I, p. 52).

This belief in the invisibility of Judaism in a socialist society can also be found among American Jewish radicals. American Jewish socialists of the 1890s, for example, envisioned a society in which race played no part (Rogoff, 1930, p. 115), apparently a proposal in which Jews and non-Jews would remain in their separate spheres in a class-based workers movement. In the event, even this level of assimilation was not attained; these organizers worked in a completely Jewish milieu and retained strong ties with the Jewish community. "Their actions continued to be at variance with their ideology. The more deeply they moved into the field of organizing Jewish workers, the more loudly they insisted on their socialist universalism" (A. Liebman, 1979, p. 256–257).

The gap between rhetoric and reality strongly suggests the importance of deception and self-deception in these phenomena. Indeed, these socialist labor organizers never abandoned their universalistic rhetoric, but actively resisted incorporating their unions into the wider American labor movement even after the decline of Yiddish among their members left them without any excuses for failing to do so. Within the unions they engaged in ethnic politics aimed at keeping their own ethnic group in power (A. Liebman, 1979, pp. 270ff), actions obviously at odds with socialist rhetoric. In the end, the attachment of many of these individuals to socialism declined and was replaced by a strong sense of Jewish ethnicity and peoplehood (p. 270).

The result was that the veneer of universalism covered up a continued separatism of radical Jewish intellectuals and political organizers:

[Gentile intellectuals] really are not totally accepted into even the secularist humanist liberal company of their quondam Jewish friends. Jews continue to insist in indirect and often inexplicable ways on their own uniqueness. Jewish universalism in relations between Jews and non-Jews has an empty ring. . . . Still, we have the anomaly of Jewish secularists and atheists writing their own prayer books. We find Jewish political reformers breaking with their local parties which stress an ethnic style of politics, and ostensibly pressing for universal political goals—while organizing their own political clubs which are so Jewish in style and manner that non-Jews often feel unwelcome. (C. Liebman, 1973, p. 158)

Universalism may thus be viewed as a mechanism for Jewish continuity via crypsis or semi-crypsis. The Jewish radical is invisible to the gentile as a Jew and thereby avoids anti-Semitism while at the same time covertly retains his or her Jewish identity. Lyons (1982, p. 73) finds:

[M]ost Jewish Communists wear their Jewishness very casually but experience it deeply. It is not a religious or even an institutional Jewishness for most; nevertheless, it is rooted in a subculture of identity, style, language, and social network. . . . In fact, this second-generation Jewishness was antiethnic and yet the height of ethnicity. The emperor believed that he was clothed in transethnic, American garb, but Gentiles saw the nuances and details of his naked ethnicity.

These remarks indicate an element of crypsis—a self-deceptive disjunction between private and public personas—"a dual posturing revealing one face to the outer world and another to the tribe" (D. Horowitz, 1997, p. 42). But this pose has a cost. As Albert Memmi (1966, p. 236) notes:

The Jew-of-the-Left must pay for this protection by his modesty and anonymity, his apparent lack of concern for all that relates to his own people. . . . Like the poor man who enters a middle-class family, they demand that he at least have the good taste to make himself invisible.

Because of the nature of their own ideology, Jews on the left were forced to deemphasize specifically Jewish issues, such as the Holocaust and Israel, despite their strong identification as Jews (Wisse, 1987). It is precisely this feature of the Jewish leftist intellectual movements that is most repellent to ethnically committed Jews (see, e.g., Wisse, 1987).

Ethnic identification was often unconscious, suggesting self-deception. Among his sample of Jewish American communists, Lyons (1982, p. 74) finds:

[E]vidence of the importance of ethnicity in general and Jewishness in particular permeates the available record. Many Communists, for example, state that they could never have married a spouse who was not a leftist. When Jews were asked if they could have married Gentiles, many hesitated, surprised by the question, and found it difficult to answer. Upon reflection, many concluded that they had always taken marriage to some-one Jewish for granted. The alternative was never really considered, par-ticularly among Jewish men.

Moreover, there were conscious attempts at deception directed at making Jewish involvement in radical political movements invisible by placing an American face on what was in reality largely a Jewish movement (A. Liebman, 1979, pp. 527ff). Both the Socialist Party and the CPUSA took pains to have gen-tiles prominently displayed as leaders, and the CPUSA actively encouraged Jewish members to take gentile-sounding names. (As noted elsewhere in this chapter, this phenomenon also occurred in Poland and the Soviet Union.) De-spite representing over half the membership in both the Socialist Party and the CPUSA during some periods, neither party ever had Jews as presidential candidates and no Jew held the top position in the CPUSA after 1929. Gentiles were brought from long distances and given highly visible staff positions in Jewish-dominated socialist organizations in New York. Jewish domination of these organizations not uncommonly led gentiles to leave when they became aware of their role as window dressing in a fundamentally Jewish organization.

A. Liebman (1979, pp. 560–561) notes that New Left radicals often took pains to ignore Jewish issues entirely. The New Left deemphasized ethnicity and religion in its ideology while emphasizing social categories and political issues such as the Vietnam War and discrimination against Blacks, which were very divisive among White gentiles but for which Jewish identity was irrele-vant; moreover, these issues did not threaten Jewish middle-class interests, especially Zionism. Jewish identity, though salient to the participants, was publicly submerged. And as noted above, when the New Left began adopting positions incompatible with Jewish interests, Jews tended to sever their ties with the movement.

In a remarkable illustration of the perceived invisibility of the group dy-namics of Jewish involvement in radical political movements, C. Liebman (1973, p. 167) describes 1960s student activists as completely unaware that their ac-tions could lead to anti-Semitism because Jews were overrepresented among the activists. (Liebman shows that in fact other Jews were concerned that their actions could lead to anti-Semitism.) From their own perspective, they were successfully engaging in crypsis: they supposed that their Jewishness was completely invisible to the outside world while at the same time it retained a great deal of subjective salience to themselves. At a theoretical level, this is a classic case of self-deception, considered in SAID (Ch. 8) as an essential feature of Jewish religious ideology and reactions to anti-Semitism.

In the event, the deception appears to have generally failed, if not for the New Left, at least for the Old Left. There was a general lack of rapport between Jewish radical intellectuals and non-Jewish intellectuals within Old Left radical organizations (C. Liebman, 1973, pp. 158–159). Some gentile intellectuals found the movement attractive *because* of its Jewish dominance, but for the most part the essentially Jewish milieu was a barrier (A. Liebman, 1979, pp. 530ff). The Jewish commitment of these radicals, their desire to remain within a Jewish milieu, and their negative attitudes toward Christian gentile culture prevented them from being effective recruiters among the gentile working class. As David Horowitz's (1997, p. 29) communist father wrote while on a trip through Colorado in the 1930s:

> I've had a feeling . . . that I'm in a foreign land. And it strikes me that unless we learn the people of this country so thoroughly so that we won't feel that way, we won't get anywhere. I'm afraid that most of us aren't really "patriotic," I mean at bottom deeply fond of the country and people.

Similarly, former communist Sidney Hook (1987, p. 188) noted, "it was as if [Jewish members of the CPUSA] had no roots in, or knowledge of, the American society they wanted to transform." A similar situation occurred in Poland, where the efforts of even the most "de-ethnicized" Jewish communists were inhibited by the traditional Jewish attitudes of superiority toward and estrangement from traditional Polish culture (Schatz, 1991, p. 119).

And once in the party, many non-Jews were repelled by its highly intellectual atmosphere and dropped out. As expected on the basis of social identity theory on the hypothesis that radicalism was fundamentally a form of secular Judaism, there are indications of an anti-gentile atmosphere within these organizations: "There was also present among Jewish intellectuals and leftists a mixture of hostility and superiority toward Gentiles" (A. Liebman, 1979, p. 534). There was also an ethnic divide between Jewish and Black Communist Party workers resulting at least partly from "a missionary and patronizing attitude" of the Jewish organizers (Lyons, 1982, p. 80).

> Encounters between Blacks and Jews always seemed to involve Jews reaching out and "helping" Blacks, "teaching" them, "guiding" them. Many Black intellectuals ended their flirtation with the Communist Party bitter not only at the communists but at Jews they felt had treated them condescendingly. "How can the average public-school Negro be expected to understand the exigencies of the capitalist system as it applies to both Jew and Gentile in America . . . since both groups act strangely like Hitlerian Aryans . . . when it comes to colored folks?" asked Langston Hughes, bitter after a feud with Jewish communists. (J. Kaufman, 1997, p. 110)

CONCLUSION

The twentieth century in Europe and the Western world, like the fifteenth century in Spain, was a Jewish century because Jews and Jewish organizations were intimately and decisively involved in all of the important events. If I am correct in asserting that Jewish participation was a necessary condition for the Bolshevik Revolution and its murderous aftermath, one could also argue that Jews thereby had a massive influence on later events. The following is an "alternative history"; i.e., a history of what might have happened if certain events had not happened. For example, in his *The Pity of War* (1999), Niall Ferguson makes a plausible case that if England had not entered World War I, Germany would have defeated France and Russia and would have become the dominant power in Europe. The Czar's government may well have collapsed, but the changes would have led to a constitutional government instead of the Bolshevik regime. Hitler would not have come to power because Germans would have already achieved their national aspirations. World War II would not have happened, and there would have been no Cold War.

But of course, these things did happen. In the same way, one can then also ask what might have happened in the absence of Jewish involvement in the Bolshevik Revolution. The argument would go as follows:

(1) Given that World War I did occur and that the Czar's government was drastically weakened, it seems reasonable that there would have been major changes in Russia. However, without Jewish involvement, the changes in Russia would likely have resulted in a constitutional monarchy, a representative republic, or even a nationalist military junta that enjoyed broad popular support among the Great Russian majority instead of a dictatorship dominated by ethnic outsiders, especially Jews and "jewified non-Jews," to use Lindemann's (1997, p. 433) term. It would not have been an explicitly Marxist revolution, and therefore it would not have had a blueprint for a society that sanctioned war against its own people and their traditional culture. The ideology of the Bolshevik Revolution sanctioned the elimination of whole classes of people, and indeed mass murder has been a characteristic of communism wherever it has come to power (Courtois et al., 1999). These massacres were made all the easier because the Bolshevik Revolution was led by ethnic outsiders with little or no sympathy for the Russians or other peoples who suffered the most.

(2) Conservatives throughout Europe and the United States believed that Jews were responsible for communism and the Bolshevik Revolution (Bendersky, 2000; A. Mayer, 1988; Nolte, 1965). The Jewish role in leftist political movements was a common source of anti-Jewish attitudes among the National Socialists in Germany as well as among a great many non-Jewish intellectuals. Writing in 1920, Winston Churchill typified the perception that Jews were

behind what he termed a "world-wide conspiracy for the overthrow of civilization." Churchill noted the predominance of Jews among Bolshevik leaders (Trotsky, Zinoviev, Litvinov, Krassin, Radek) and among those responsible for "the system of [state] terrorism." Churchill also noted that Jews were prominent in revolutionary movements in Hungary, Germany, and the United States. The identification of Jews with revolutionary radicalism became a major concern of military and political leaders throughout Europe and the United States (Bendersky, 2000).

(3) In Germany, the identification of Jews and Bolshevism was common in the middle classes and was a critical part of the National Socialist view of the world. For middle-class Germans, "the experience of the Bolshevik revolution in Germany was so immediate, so close to home, and so disquieting, and statistics seemed to prove the overwhelming participation of Jewish ringleaders so irrefutably," that even many liberals believed in Jewish responsibility (Nolte, 1965, p. 331). Hitler was also well aware of the predominance of Jews in the short-lived revolutions in Hungary and in the German province of Bavaria in 1919. He had personally experienced the Jewish involvement in the Bavarian revolution, and this may well have been a decisive moment in the development of his anti-Jewish ideas (Lindemann, 1997, p. 90).

Jewish involvement in the horrors of communism was therefore an important ingredient in Hitler's determination to destroy the USSR and in the anti-Jewish actions of the German National Socialist government. Ernst Nolte and several other historians have argued that the Jewish role in the Bolshevik Revolution was an important cause of the Holocaust. Hitler and the National Socialists certainly believed that Jews were critical to the success of the Bolshevik Revolution. They likened the Soviet Union to a man with a Slavic body and a Jewish-Bolshevik brain (Nolte, 1965, pp. 357–358), and they attributed the mass murders of communism—"the most radical form of Jewish genocide ever known"—to the Jewish-Bolshevik brain (p. 393). The National Socialists were well aware that the Soviet government committed mass murder against its enemies and that it was intent on promoting a world revolution in which many more millions of people would be murdered. As early as 1918 a prominent Jewish Bolshevik, Grigory Zinoviev, spoke publicly about the need to eliminate ten million Russians—an underestimate by half, as it turned out. Seizing upon this background, Hitler (1943/1992, p. 296) wrote:

> Now begins the great last revolution. In gaining political power the Jew casts off the few cloaks that he stills wears. The democratic people's Jew becomes the blood-Jew and tyrant over peoples. In a few years he tries to exterminate the national intelligentsia and by robbing the peoples of their natural intellectual leadership makes them ripe for the slave's lot of permanent subjugation.

The most frightful example of this kind is offered by Russia, where he killed or starved about thirty million people with positively fanatical savagery, in part amid inhuman tortures, in order to give a gang of Jewish journalists and stock exchange bandits domination over a great people.

This line of reasoning does not imply that there were no other critical factors. If World War I had not occurred and if the Czar hadn't entered that war, then the Czar could have stayed in power much longer. Russia might have been transformed gradually into a modern Western state rather than be subjected to the horrors of communism. In the same way, Hitler might not have come to power if there had been no Great Depression or if Germany had won World War I.

(4) The victory over National Socialism then set the stage for the tremendous increase in Jewish power in the post–World War II Western world. This newfound power facilitated the establishment of Israel, the transformation of the United States and other Western nations in the direction of multiracial, multicultural societies via large-scale non-White immigration, and the consequent decline in European demographic and cultural preeminence.

The Long-Term Fate of Jews Under Communism

It is of some interest to attempt to understand the ultimate fate of Judaism in situations where society became organized according to a politically radical universalist ideology. The campaign to remove Jews from administrative positions in the cultural establishment in the USSR began as early as 1942, again accompanied by prizes and awards to prominent Jewish scientists and artists to deflect charges of anti-Semitism. Full-blown state-sponsored anti-Semitism emerged in the post–World War II era, complete with quotas on Jewish admission to universities that were harsher than in czarist times. However, it was not merely Stalin's personal anti-Semitism that was involved; rather, anti-Semitism was motivated by very traditional concerns about Jews relating to economic and cultural domination and loyalty. Kostyrchenko (1995) shows that ethnic Russians seeking to dislodge Jews from dominant positions among the Soviet elite were an important source of pressure on Stalin. Purges of disproportionately Jewish elites were made in the areas of journalism, the arts, academic departments of history, pedagogy, philosophy, economics, medicine, and psychiatry, and scientific research institutes in all areas of the natural sciences. There were also widespread purges of Jews at the top levels of management and engineering throughout the economy. Jewish intellectuals were characterized as "rootless cosmopolitans" who lacked sympathy with Russian national culture, and they were regarded as disloyal because of their open enthusiasm for Israel and their close ties to American Jews.

Solzhenitsyn (2002/2011, Ch. 25, emphasis original) observed that Jews later rejected communism but in general refused to accept any responsibility for the horrors of the early decades of the USSR:

In the 1920s and 1930s, the fusion of the Soviet Jewry and Bolshevism seemed permanent. Then suddenly, they diverge? What a joy!

Of course, as is always true for both individuals and nations, it is unreasonable to expect words of remorse from Jews regarding their past involvement. But I absolutely could not expect that the Jews, while deserting Bolshevism, rather than expressing even a sign of repentance or at least some embarrassment, instead angrily turned on the Russian people: it is the *Russians* who had ruined democracy in Russia (i.e., in February 1917), it is the *Russians* who are guilty of support of this regime from 1918 on.

Sure, they claim, it is we (the Russian people) who are the guilty! Actually, it was earlier than 1918—the dirty scenes of the *radiant* February Revolution were tale-telling. Yet the neophyte anti-communists were uncompromising—from now on everyone must accept that they have always fought against this regime, and no one should recall that it used to be their favorite and should not mention how well they had once served this tyranny. Because it was the "natives" who created, nurtured and cared for it:

"The leaders of the October Coup . . . were the followers rather than the leaders. [Really? The New Iron Party was made up of the "followers"?] They simply voiced the dormant wishes of the masses and worked to implement them. They did not break with the grassroots." "The October coup was a disaster for Russia. The country could evolve differently. . . . Then [in the stormy anarchy of the February Revolution] Russia saw the signs of law, freedom and respect for human dignity by the state, but they all were swept away by the people's wrath."

Jews were also highly overrepresented as leaders among the other communist governments in Eastern Europe as well as in communist revolutionary movements in Germany and Austria from 1918 to 1923. In the short-lived communist government in Hungary in 1919, 95 percent of the leading figures of Béla Kun's government were Jews (R. Pipes, 1993, p. 112). This government energetically liquidated predominantly gentile counterrevolutionaries, and the ensuing struggle led by Admiral Horthy eventuated in the execution of most of the Jewish leadership of the communist government—a struggle with clear anti-Semitic overtones.

Jews thus achieved leading positions in these societies in the early stages, but in the long run, anti-Semitism in the Soviet Union and other Eastern European communist societies became a well-known phenomenon and an important political cause among American Jews (Sachar, 1992; Woocher, 1986). As we have seen, Stalin gradually reduced the power of Jews in the Soviet Union, and anti-Semitism was an important factor in the decline of Jews in leadership positions in Eastern European communist governments. The same phenomenon occurred in Poland, culminating in the 1968 purges of Jews (see above).

The case of Hungary is entirely analogous to Poland both in the origins of the triumph of communist Jews and in their eventual defeat by an anti-Semitic movement. Stalin installed Jewish communists as leaders of his effort to dominate Hungary after World War II. The government was "completely dominated" by Jews (Rothman & Lichter, 1982/1996, p. 89), a common perception among the Hungarian people (see also: Irving, 1981, pp. 47ff; Mendes, 2014, pp. 144). "The wags of Budapest explained the presence of a lone gentile in the party leadership on the grounds that a 'goy' was needed to turn on the lights on Saturday" (Rothman & Lichter, p. 89). The Hungarian Communist Party, with the backing of the Red Army, tortured, imprisoned, and executed opposition political leaders and other dissidents and effectively harnessed Hungary's economy in the service of the Soviet Union. They thus created a situation similar to that in Poland: Jews were installed by their Russian masters as the ideal middleman minority between an exploitative alien ruling elite and a subject native population. Jews were seen as having engineered the communist revolution and as having benefited most from the revolution. Jews constituted nearly all of the party's elite, held the top positions in the security police, and dominated managerial positions throughout the economy. Not only were Jewish Communist Party functionaries and economic managers economically dominant, but they also appear to have had fairly unrestricted access to gentile females working under them—partly as a result of the poverty to which the vast majority of the population had descended, and partly because of specific government policies designed to undermine traditional sexual mores by, for example, paying women to have illegitimate children (see Irving, p. 111). The domination of the Hungarian communist-Jewish bureaucracy thus appears to have had overtones of sexual and reproductive domination of gentiles in which Jewish males were able to have disproportionate sexual access to gentile females.

As an indication of the gulf between ruler and ruled in Hungary, a student commented:

> Take Hungary: Who was the enemy? For Rákosi [the Jewish leader of the Hungarian Communist Party] and his gang the enemy was us, the Hungarian people. They believed that Hungarians were innately fascist. This was the attitude of the Jewish communists, the Moscow group. They had nothing but contempt for the people. (in Irving, 1981, p. 146)

The comment illustrates a theme of the loyalty issue discussed in SAID (Ch. 2): Jewish disloyalty to the people among whom they have lived is often exacerbated by anti-Semitism, which itself is linked to the other common sources of anti-Semitism. Similarly, Mendes (2014, p. 247) notes:

> [T]hese Jews were loyal communists who could be relied on to introduce unpopular policies and defend Soviet interests amidst hostility from the nationalist intelligentsia. They were often highly educated and able to speak foreign languages, which made them valuable assets in areas such as propaganda, education, and foreign affairs and trade.

Moreover, ethnicity continued to be a prominent factor in the post-revolutionary period despite its theoretical unimportance. When Jewish functionaries wanted to penalize a farmer who failed to meet his quota, gypsies were sent to strip the farmer's property because other townspeople would not cooperate in the destruction of one of their own (Irving, 1981, p. 132). Here the party functionaries were taking advantage of the same principle Stalin and other alien rulers have recognized when they used Jews as an exploitative middleman minority between themselves and a subject native population: foreign ethnics are more willing to exploit the natives. It is not surprising, therefore, that the Hungarian uprising of 1956 included elements of a traditional anti-Semitic pogrom, as indicated by anti-Jewish attitudes among the refugees of the period. In this regard, the uprising was not unlike many anti-Semitic pogroms that occurred in traditional societies when the power of the alien ruling elite who supported the Jews diminished (see SAID, Ch. 2; PTSDA, Ch. 5).

As with all experiments in living, leftist universalist ideology and political structure may not achieve the results desired by their Jewish proponents.[54] On the basis of the data presented here, the eventual failure of political radicalism to guarantee Jewish interests has been a prime factor in Jews' abandoning radical movements or attempting to combine radicalism with an overt Jewish identity and commitment to Jewish interests. In the long run, it would appear that ideologies of universalism in the presence of continued group cohesion and identity may not be an effective mechanism for combating anti-Semitism.

In retrospect, Jewish advocacy of highly collectivist social structure represented by socialism and communism has been a poor long-term strategy for Judaism as a group evolutionary strategy. Judaism and bureaucratic, statist socialism are not obviously incompatible, and we have seen that Jews were able to develop a predominant political and cultural position in socialist societies, as they have in more individualistic societies. However, the highly

---

[54] Similarly, Himmelstrand (1969) notes that the Ibo in Nigeria were the strongest supporters of a nationalist government constituting all tribes. However, when they were disproportionately successful in this new, nontribal form of social organization, there was a violent backlash against them, and they then attempted to abandon the national government in favor of establishing their own tribal homeland.

authoritarian, collectivist structure of these societies also results in the highly efficient institutionalization of anti-Semitism in the event that Jewish predominance within the society, despite a great deal of crypsis, comes to be viewed negatively, particularly if there is an upsurge in nationalism among the natives, as happened, for example, in Russia, Hungary, and Poland, as described in this chapter.

Moreover, the tendency for such societies to develop a political monoculture implies that Judaism can survive only by engaging in semi-crypsis. As I. L. Horowitz (1993, p. 86) notes:

> Jewish life is diminished when the creative opposition of the sacred and the secular, or the church and the state, are seen as having to yield to a higher set of political values. Jews suffer, their numbers decline, and immigration becomes a survival solution when the state demands integration into a national mainstream, a religious universal defined by a state religion or a near-state religion.

In the long run, radical individualism among gentiles, the fragmentation of gentile culture, and opportunities for Jews to ascend to elite status in media, academia, and political involvement offer a superior environment for Judaism as a group evolutionary strategy, and this is indeed an important direction of current Jewish intellectual and political activity, as exemplified by the writing of Leo Strauss (see Chs. 4, 6).

In this regard it is interesting that many neoconservative Jewish intellectuals discussed in Chapter 4 have rejected corporate, statist ideologies as a direct consequence of the recognition that these ideologies have resulted in corporate, state-sponsored anti-Semitism. Indeed, the beginnings of the neoconservative movement can be traced to the Moscow Trials of the 1930s in which many of the old Jewish Bolsheviks, including Trotsky, were convicted of treason. The result was the development of the New York Intellectuals as an anti-Stalinist leftist movement, parts of which gradually evolved into neoconservatism (see Ch. 4). The neoconservative movement has been fervently anti-communist and has opposed ethnic quotas and affirmative action policies in the United States—policies that would clearly preclude free competition between Jews and gentiles. Part of the attraction neoconservatism held for Jewish intellectuals was its compatibility with support for Israel at a time when Third World countries supported by most American leftists were strongly anti-Zionist (Rothman & Lichter, 1982/1996, pp. 105–106). Many neoconservative intellectuals had previously been ardent leftists, and the split between these previous allies resulted in an intense internecine feud.

Similarly, there was a trend toward libertarian and individualist perspectives by converso intellectuals consequent to corporate, state-sponsored anti-

Semitism during the period of the Inquisition. Castro (1971, pp. 327ff) emphasizes the libertarian, anarchist, individualistic, and anti-corporate strand of converso thought and attributes it to the fact that the conversos were being oppressed by an anti-libertarian, corporate state. These intellectuals, oppressed by the purity of blood laws and the Inquisition itself, argued that "God did not distinguish between one Christian and another" (p. 333).

When an experiment in ideology and political structure fails, another experiment is launched. Since the Enlightenment, Judaism has not been a unified, monolithic movement. Judaism is a series of experiments in living, and since the Enlightenment there have been a variety of Jewish experiments in living. There has clearly been a great deal of disagreement among Jews as how best to attain their interests during this period, and certainly the interests of Jewish radicals conflicted at times with the interests of wealthy Jews—often their Jewish employers (Levin, 1977, p. 210). The voluntary nature of Jewish association since the Enlightenment has resulted in relative fractionation of Judaism, with individual Jews drawn to different "experiments in Jewish living." In this sense, Jewish radicalism must be viewed as one of several solutions to the problem of developing a viable Judaism in the post-Enlightenment period, along with Zionism, neo-Orthodoxy, Conservative Judaism, Reform Judaism, neoconservatism, psychoanalysis, and Judaism as a civil religion.

APPENDIX: COMMUNISM AND JEWISH IDENTIFICATION IN POLAND

Schatz's (1991) work on the group of Jewish communists who came to power in Poland after World War II (termed by Schatz "the generation") is important because it sheds light on the identificatory processes of an entire generation of communist Jews in Eastern Europe. Unlike the situation in the Soviet Union where the predominantly Jewish faction led by Trotsky was defeated, it is possible to trace the activities and identifications of a Jewish communist elite that actually obtained political power and held it for a significant period.

> The great majority of this group were socialized in very traditional Jewish families whose inner life, customs and folklore, religious traditions, leisure time, contacts between generations, and ways of socializing were, despite variations, essentially permeated by traditional Jewish values and norms of conduct. . . . The core of cultural heritage was handed down to them through formal religious education and practice, through holiday celebrations, tales, and songs, through the stories told by parents and grandparents, through listening to discussions among their elders. . . . The result was a deep core of their identity, values, norms, and attitudes with

which they entered the rebellious period of their youth and adulthood. *This core was to be transformed in the processes of acculturation, secularization, and radicalization sometimes even to the point of explicit denial. However, it was through this deep layer that all later perceptions were filtered.* (Schatz, 1991, pp. 37–38; emphasis mine)

Note the implication that self-deceptive processes were at work here: members of the generation denied the effects of a pervasive, typically Orthodox socialization experience that colored all of their subsequent perceptions, so that in a very real sense, they did not know how Jewish they were. Most of these individuals spoke Yiddish in their daily lives and had only a poor command of Polish even after joining the party (Schatz, 1991, p. 54). They socialized entirely with other Jews whom they met in the Jewish world of work, neighborhood, and Jewish social and political organizations. After they became communists, they dated and married among themselves, and their social gatherings were conducted in Yiddish (p. 116). As is the case for all of the Jewish intellectual and political movements discussed in this volume, their mentors and principal influences were other ethnic Jews, including especially Luxemburg and Trotsky (pp. 62, 89), and when they recalled personal heroes, they were mostly Jews whose exploits achieved semi-mythical proportions (p. 112).

Jews who joined the communist movement did not first reject their ethnic identity, and there were many who "cherished Jewish culture ... [and] dreamed of a society in which Jews would be equal as Jews" (Schatz, 1991, p. 48). Indeed, it was common for individuals to combine a strong Jewish identity with Marxism as well as various combinations of Zionism and Bundism. While the older generation tended to reject these movements, for the many Jewish youth who supported revolution, including communists, "their commitment to the movement was not a sign of forgetting or denying their identity; they participated in it as Jews, drawing Jewish workers into the great movement of universal emancipation" (Brossat & Klingberg, 1983/2016, p. 51). Brossat and Klingberg's informants' accounts of their transition from the closed world of religion to the open world of modernity was "not expressed in terms of violent rupture, rather of evolution, reconciliation between the deep identity of Judaism and the rationalist, enlightened aspiration of a just and humane world" (p. 47). The testimony of their informants revealed "the plasticity, capacity for evolution and basic internal dynamism of the Jewish world of Eastern Europe" (p. 46). One informant noted (p. 61):

There was such a high proportion of Jewish youth in the communist movement here that you could almost say it was a Jewish national movement. In any case, the question of stifling or denial of Jewish national identity absolutely didn't arise. The majority of Jewish young people joined it with a Jewish national consciousness.

Moreover, the attraction of Polish Jews to communism was greatly facilitated by their knowledge that Jews had attained high-level positions of power and influence in the Soviet Union and that the Soviet government had established a system of Jewish education and culture (Schatz, 1991, p. 60). In both the Soviet Union and Poland, and throughout the Jewish world at the time, communism was seen as opposing anti-Semitism. In marked contrast, during the 1930s the Polish government developed policies in which Jews were excluded from public-sector employment, quotas were placed on Jewish representation in universities and the professions, and government-organized boycotts of Jewish businesses and artisans were staged (Hagen, 1996). Clearly, Jews perceived communism as good for Jews: it was a movement that did not threaten Jewish group continuity, and it held the promise of power and influence for Jews and the end of state-sponsored anti-Semitism.

At one end of the spectrum of Jewish identification were communists who began their career in the Bund or in Zionist organizations, spoke Yiddish, and worked entirely within a Jewish milieu. Jewish and communist identities were completely sincere, without ambivalence or perceived conflict between these two sources of identity. At the other end of the spectrum of Jewish identification, some Jewish communists may have intended to establish a "de-ethnicized" state without Jewish group continuity, although the evidence for this is less than compelling. In the prewar period even the most "de-ethnicized" Jews only outwardly assimilated by dressing like gentiles, taking gentile-sounding names (suggesting deception), and learning their languages. They attempted to recruit gentiles into the movement but did not assimilate or attempt to assimilate into Polish culture; they retained traditional Jewish "disdainful and supercilious attitudes" toward what, as Marxists, they viewed as a "retarded" Polish peasant culture (Schatz, 1991, p. 119). Even the most highly assimilated Jewish communists working in urban areas with non-Jews were upset by the Soviet-German nonaggression pact but were relieved when the German-Soviet war finally broke out (p. 121)—a clear indication that Jewish personal identity remained quite close to the surface (see also Brossat & Klingberg, 1983/2016, pp. 139–141). The Communist Party of Poland (KPP) also retained a sense of promoting specifically Jewish interests rather than blind allegiance to the Soviet Union. Indeed, Schatz (1991, p. 102) suggests that Stalin dissolved the KPP in 1938 because of the presence of Trotskyists within the KPP and because the Soviet leadership expected the KPP to be opposed to the alliance with Nazi Germany.

In SAID (Ch. 8) it was noted that identificatory ambivalence has been a consistent feature of Judaism since the Enlightenment. It is interesting that

Polish Jewish activists showed a great deal of identificatory ambivalence stemming ultimately from the contradiction between,

> the belief in some kind of Jewish collective existence and, at the same time, a rejection of such an ethnic communion, as it was thought incompatible with class divisions and harmful to the general political struggle; striving to maintain a specific kind of Jewish culture and, at the same time, a view of this as a mere ethnic form of the communist message, instrumental in incorporating Jews into the Polish Socialist community; and maintaining separate Jewish institutions while at the same time desiring to eliminate Jewish separateness as such. (Schatz, 1991, p. 234)

It will be apparent in the following that the Jews, including Jewish communists at the highest levels of the government, continued as a cohesive, identifiable group. However, although they themselves appear not to have noticed the Jewish collective nature of their experience (Schatz, 1991, p. 240), it was observable to others—a clear example of self-deception also evident in the case of American Jewish leftists, as noted above.

These Jewish communists were also engaged in elaborate rationalizations and self-deceptions related to the role of the communist movement in Poland, so that one cannot take the lack of evidence for overt Jewish ethnic identity as strong evidence of a lack of a Jewish identity.

> Cognitive and emotional anomalies—unfree, mutilated, and distorted thoughts and emotions—became the price for retaining their beliefs unchanged. ... Adjusting their experiences to their beliefs was achieved through mechanisms of interpreting, suppressing, justifying, or explaining away. . . .
>
> As much as they were able to skillfully apply their critical thinking to penetrative analyses of the sociopolitical system they rejected, as much were they blocked when it came to applying the same rules of critical analysis to the system they regarded as the future of all mankind. (Schatz, 1991, pp. 191–192).

This combination of self-deceptive rationalization as well as considerable evidence of a Jewish identity can be seen in the comments of Jakub Berman, one of the most prominent leaders of the postwar era. (Two of the three communist leaders who dominated Poland between 1948 and 1956, Berman and Hilary Minc, were Jews, the third being Bolesław Bierut.) Regarding the purges and murders of thousands of communists, including many Jews, in the Soviet Union in the 1930s, Berman states:

I tried as best I could to explain what was happening; to clarify the background, the situations full of conflict and internal contradictions in which Stalin had probably found himself and which forced him to act as he did; and to exaggerate the mistakes of the opposition, which assumed grotesque proportions in the subsequent charges against them and were further blown up by Soviet propaganda. You had to have a great deal of endurance and dedication to the cause then in order to accept what was happening despite all the distortions, injuries and torments. (in Toranska, 1987, p. 207)

As to his Jewish identity, Berman responded as follows when asked about his plans after the war:

I didn't have any particular plans. But I was aware of the fact that as a Jew I either shouldn't or wouldn't be able to fill any of the highest posts. Besides, I didn't mind not being in the front ranks: not because I'm particularly humble by nature, but because it's not at all the case that you have to project yourself into a position of prominence in order to wield real power. The important thing to me was to exert my influence, leave my stamp on the complicated government formation, which was being created, but without projecting myself. Naturally, this required a certain agility. (in Toranska, 1987, p. 237)

Clearly Berman identifies as a Jew and is well aware that others perceive him as a Jew and that therefore he must deceptively lower his public profile. Berman also notes that he was under suspicion as a Jew during the Soviet anti-"cosmopolite" campaign beginning in the late 1940s. His brother, an activist in the Central Committee of Polish Jews (the organization for establishing a secular Jewish culture in communist Poland), immigrated to Israel in 1950 to avoid the consequences of the Soviet-inspired anti-Semitic policies in Poland. Berman comments that he did not follow his brother to Israel even though his brother strongly urged him to do so: "I was, of course, interested in what was going on in Israel, especially since I was quite familiar with the people there" (in Toranska, 1987, p. 322). Obviously, Berman's brother viewed Berman not as a non-Jew but, rather, as a Jew who should immigrate to Israel because of incipient anti-Semitism. The close ties of family and friendship between a very high official in the Polish communist government and an activist in the organization promoting Jewish secular culture in Poland also strongly suggest that there was no perceived incompatibility with identifying both as a Jew and a communist even among the most assimilated Polish communists of the period.

While Jewish members saw the KPP as beneficial to Jewish interests, the party was perceived by gentile Poles even before the war as "pro-Soviet, anti-patriotic, and ethnically 'not truly Polish'" (Schatz, 1991, pp. 82). This perception of lack of patriotism was the main source of popular hostility to the KPP (p. 91).

> On the one hand, for much of its existence the KPP had been at war not only with the Polish State, but with its entire body politic, including the legal opposition parties of the Left. On the other hand, in the eyes of the great majority of Poles, the KPP was a foreign, subversive agency of Moscow, bent on the destruction of Poland's hard-won independence and the incorporation of Poland into the Soviet Union. Labeled a "Soviet agency" or the "Jew-Commune," it was viewed as a dangerous and fundamentally un-Polish conspiracy dedicated to undermining national sovereignty and restoring, in a new guise, Russian domination. (Coutouvidis & Reynolds, 1986, p. 115)

The KPP backed the Soviet Union in the Polish-Soviet war of 1919–1920 and in the Soviet invasion of 1939. It also accepted the 1939 border with the USSR and was relatively unconcerned with the Soviet massacre of Polish prisoners of war during World War II, whereas the Polish government in exile in London held nationalist views on these matters. The Soviet army and its Polish allies, "led by cold-blooded political calculation, military necessities, or both," allowed the uprising of the Home Army (which was faithful to the noncommunist Polish government in exile) to be defeated by the Germans, resulting in two hundred thousand dead, thus wiping out "the cream of the anti- and non-communist activist elite" (Schatz, 1991, p. 188). The Soviets also arrested surviving noncommunist resistance leaders immediately after the war.

Moreover, as was the case with the CPUSA, actual Jewish leadership and involvement in Polish communism was much greater than surface appearances; ethnic Poles were recruited and promoted to high positions in order to lessen the perception that the KPP was a Jewish movement (Schatz, 1991, p. 97). This attempt to deceptively lower the Jewish profile of the communist movement was also apparent in the ZPP (and in the U.S.; see above). (The ZPP refers to the Union of Polish Patriots—an Orwellian-named communist front organization created by the Soviet Union to occupy Poland after the war.) Apart from members of the generation whose political loyalties could be counted on and who formed the leadership core of the group, Jews were often discouraged from joining the movement out of fear that the movement would appear too Jewish. However, Jews who could physically pass as Poles were allowed to join and were encouraged to state they were ethnic Poles and to change their names to Polish-sounding names. "Not everyone was approached [to engage in deception], and some were spared such proposals because nothing could be done with them: they just looked too Jewish" (p. 185).

When this group came to power after the war, they advanced Soviet political, economic, and cultural interests in Poland while aggressively pursuing specifically Jewish interests, including the destruction of the nationalist political opposition whose openly expressed anti-Semitism derived at least partly from the fact that Jews were (correctly) perceived as generally favoring Soviet domination.[55] The purge of Władysław Gomułka's group shortly after the war resulted in the promotion of Jews and the complete banning of anti-Semitism. Moreover, the general opposition between the Jewish-dominated Polish communist government supported by the Soviets and the nationalist, anti-Semitic underground helped forge the allegiance of the great majority of the Jewish population to the communist government while the great majority of non-Jewish Poles favored the anti-Soviet parties (Schatz, 1991, pp. 204–205). The result was widespread anti-Semitism: by the summer of 1947, approximately 1,500 Jews had been killed in incidents at 155 localities. In the words of Cardinal Hlond in 1946, commenting on an incident in which forty-one Jews were killed, the pogrom was "due to the Jews who today occupy leading positions in Poland's government and endeavor to introduce a governmental structure that the majority of the Poles do not wish to have" (in p. 107).

The Jewish-dominated communist government actively sought to revive and perpetuate Jewish life in Poland (Schatz, 1991, p. 208) so that, as in the case of the Soviet Union, there was no expectation that Judaism would wither away under a communist regime. Jewish activists had an "ethnopolitical vision" in which Jewish secular culture would continue in Poland with the cooperation and approval of the government (p. 230). Thus while the government campaigned actively against the political and cultural power of the Catholic Church, collective Jewish life flourished in the postwar period. Yiddish- and Hebrew-language schools and publications were established, as well as a great variety of cultural and social welfare organizations for Jews. A substantial percentage of the Jewish population was employed in Jewish economic cooperatives.

Moreover, the Jewish-dominated government regarded the Jewish population, many of whom had not previously been communists, as,

> a reservoir that could be trusted and enlisted in its efforts to rebuild the country. Although not old, "tested" comrades, they were not rooted in the social networks of the anti-communist society, they were outsiders with

---

[55] The cultural changes included the suppression of science in favor of political interests and the canonization of the works of Lysenko and Pavlov. Whereas Pavlov's scientific work remains interesting, an evolutionist, of course, is struck by the elevation of Lysenkoism to the status of dogma. Lysenkoism is a politically inspired Lamarckism useful to communism because of the implication that people could be biologically changed by changing the environment. As indicated in Chapter 2 (see footnote 34), Jewish intellectuals were strongly attracted to Lamarckism because of its political usefulness.

regard to its historically shaped traditions, without connections to the
Catholic Church, and hated by those who hated the regime.[56] Thus they
could be depended on and used to fill the required positions. (Schatz, 1991,
pp. 212–213)

Jewish ethnic background was particularly important in recruiting for the
internal security service: the generation of Jewish communists realized that
their power derived entirely from the Soviet Union and that they would have
to resort to coercion in order to control a fundamentally hostile noncommunist society (Schatz, 1991, p. 262). The core members of the security service
came from the Jewish communists who had been communists before the establishment of the Polish communist government, but these were joined by
other Jews sympathetic to the government and alienated from the wider society. This in turn reinforced the popular image of Jews as servants of foreign
interests and enemies of ethnic Poles (p. 225).

Jewish members of the internal security force often appear to have been
motivated by personal rage and a desire for revenge related to their Jewish
identity:

> Their families had been murdered and the anti-Communist underground
> was, in their perception, a continuation of essentially the same anti-Se-
> mitic and anti-Communist tradition. They hated those who had collabo-
> rated with the Nazis and those who opposed the new order with almost
> the same intensity and knew that as Communists, or as both Communists
> and Jews, they were hated at least in the same way. In their eyes, the en-
> emy was essentially the same. The old evil deeds had to be punished and
> new ones prevented and a merciless struggle was necessary before a bet-
> ter world could be built. (Schatz, 1991, p. 226)

The utopian end thus justified the means, no matter how vicious.

As in the case of post-World War II Hungary (see above), Poland became
polarized between a predominantly Jewish ruling and administrative class
supported by the rest of the Jewish population and by Soviet military power,
arrayed against the great majority of the native non-Jewish population. The
situation was exactly analogous to the many instances in traditional societies
where Jews formed a middle layer between an alien ruling elite, in this case
the Soviets, and the gentile native population (see PTSDA, Ch. 5). However, this
intermediary role made the former outsiders into an elite group in Poland, and
the former champions of social justice went to great lengths to protect their

---

[56] The "tested" comrades constituted an underground Jewish communist group in prewar Poland. When they came to power following the war, they allied themselves with other Jews who
had not been communists prior to the war.

own personal prerogatives, including a great deal of rationalization and self-deception (Schatz, 1991, p. 261). Indeed, when a defector's accounts of the elite's lavish lifestyle—e.g., Bolesław Bierut had four villas and the use of five others (Toranska, 1987, p. 28)—their corruption, as well as their role as Soviet agents became known in 1954, it resulted in shock waves throughout the lower levels of the party (Schatz, p. 266). Clearly, the sense of moral superiority and the altruistic motivations of this group were entirely in their own self-deceptions.

Although attempts were made to place a Polish face on what was in reality a Jewish-dominated government, such attempts were limited by the lack of trustworthy Poles able to fill positions in the Communist Party, government administration, the military, and the internal security forces. Jews who had severed formal ties with the Jewish community, or who had changed their names to Polish-sounding names, or who could pass as Poles because of their physical appearance or lack of a Jewish accent were favored in promotions (Schatz, 1991, p. 214). Whatever the subjective personal identities of the individuals recruited into these government positions, the recruiters were clearly acting on the perceived ethnic background of the individual as a cue to dependability, and the result was that the situation resembled the many instances in traditional societies where Jews and crypto-Jews developed economic and political networks of coreligionists:

> Besides a group of influential politicians, too small to be called a category, there were the soldiers; the apparatchiks and the administrators; the intellectuals and ideologists; the policemen; the diplomats; and finally, the activists in the Jewish sector. There also existed the mass of common people—clerks, craftsmen, and workers—whose common denominator with the others was a shared ideological vision, a past history, and the essentially similar mode of ethnic aspiration. (Schatz, 1991, p. 226)

The End of Jewish Domination of Post-War Communism in Poland

It is revealing that when Jewish economic and political domination gradually decreased in the mid- to late 1950s, many of these individuals began working in the Jewish economic cooperatives, and Jews purged from the internal security service were aided by Jewish organizations funded ultimately by American Jews. There can be little doubt of their continuing Jewish identity and Jewish economic and cultural separatism. Indeed, after the collapse of the communist regime in Poland, "numerous Jews, some of them children and grandchildren of former communists, came 'out of the closet'" (Porat, 1995, p. 115), openly adopting a Jewish identity and reinforcing the idea that many Jewish communists were in fact crypto-Jews.

When the anti-Zionism and anti-Semitism in the Soviet Union filtered down to Poland following the Soviet policy change toward Israel in the late 1940s, there was another crisis of identity resulting from the belief that anti-Semitism and communism were incompatible. One response was to engage in "ethnic self-abnegation" by making statements denying the existence of a Jewish identity; another advised Jews to adopt a low profile. Because of the very strong identification with the system among Jews, the general tendency was to rationalize even their own persecution during the period when Jews were gradually being purged from important positions:

> Even when the methods grew surprisingly painful and harsh, when the goal of forcing one to admit uncommitted crimes and to frame others became clear, and when the perception of being unjustly treated by methods that contradicted communist ethos came forth, the basic ideological convictions stayed untouched. Thus the holy madness triumphed, even in the prison cells. (Schatz, 1991, p. 260)

In the end, an important ingredient in the anti-Jewish campaign of the 1960s was the assertion that the communist Jews of the generation opposed the Soviet Union's Mideast policy favoring the Arabs.

Wlodzimierz Rozenbaum (1973) provides a general treatment of the period from 1949 to 1968 that generally corroborates Schatz, noting that Jews were targeted because they were seen as overrepresented in the government. Even in 1947 Deputy Prime Minister Władysław Gomułka, who was eventually removed due to "nationalist deviation," approved a request by the Minister of Public Security (secret police) to replace Jewish personnel with "true" Poles, a policy Gomułka claimed had been approved by Stalin; however, there is no indication that this was carried out. Many Jewish communists had joined the government in the immediate aftermath of the war, as Schatz also notes, but beginning in 1949 they began to be "systematically eliminated from important positions in the Party apparatus, the administration, and in the armed forces" (p. 76). These trends paralleled trends in the Soviet Union at the time and accelerated after Stalin's death—e.g., Nikita Khrushchev's remark that "you have already too many Abramoviches" (in Schatz, 1991, p. 272).

From 1955 to 1957 this continued, with Jews who had held powerful positions in the post-war period being targeted by Stalinists who blamed them for abuses during this period and appealed to popular hatred for "Jewish rule" to rally public opinion against liberalizing tendencies (favored by Jews). After a spate of emigration, by 1957 only twenty-five thousand Jews remained in Poland, but the trend to remove Jews from positions of power continued, followed by "the all-out purge of 1967–1968" (Rozenbaum, 1973, p. 83). At the end,

Jews were targeted because of or, more likely, on the pretext of their Zionist sympathies in the context of the 1967 Arab-Israeli war.

Thus Jews were increasingly victimized by the government and security forces from 1949–1968 because of their prominent positions in the government—an account in agreement with Schatz (1991). If there is one thing Jews have learned, it's that no system of government is guaranteed to be resistant to anti-Jewish attitudes. The main storyline is the gradual triumph of Polish nationalism at the expense of Jewish power. Similarly, after being a dominant elite in the Soviet Union beginning with the Bolshevik Revolution and extending at least well into the 1930s (and really until after World War II), Jewish power declined, Jews were purged from positions of power, and Jews ultimately became leaders of the refusenik movement aimed at being able to emigrate from the USSR.

As with Jewish groups throughout the ages (see PTSDA, Ch. 3), the anti-Jewish purges did not result in Jews abandoning their group commitment even when the purges were unjust. Instead, they resulted in increased commitment,

> unswerving ideological discipline, and obedience to the point of self-deception. . . . They regarded the party as the collective personification of the progressive forces of history and, regarding themselves as its servants, expressed a specific kind of teleological-deductive dogmatism, revolutionary haughtiness, and moral ambiguity. (Schatz, 1991, pp. 260–261)

Indeed, there is some indication that group cohesiveness increased as the fortunes of the generation declined (Schatz, 1991, p. 301). As their position was gradually eroded by a nascent anti-Semitic Polish nationalism, they became ever more conscious of their "groupness." After their final defeat they quickly lost any Polish identity they might have had and quickly assumed overtly Jewish identities, especially in Israel, the destination of most Polish Jews. They came to see their former anti-Zionism as a mistake and now became strong supporters of Israel (p. 314).

Anti-Semitism increased dramatically toward the end of the 1960s. Jews were gradually downgraded in status, and Jewish communists were blamed for Poland's misfortunes. The Protocols of the Elders of Zion circulated widely among party activists, students, and army personnel. The security force, which had been dominated by Jews and directed toward suppressing Polish nationalism, was now dominated by Poles who viewed Jews "as a group in need of close and constant surveillance" (Schatz, 1991, p. 290). Jews were removed from important positions in the government, the military, and the media. Extensive files were maintained on Jews, including the crypto-Jews who had changed their names and adopted non-Jewish external identities. As the Jews had done earlier, the anti-Jewish faction developed networks that promoted their own people throughout the government and the media. Jews now became dissidents and defectors, where before they had dominated the state forces of orthodoxy.

The "earthquake" finally erupted in 1968 with an anti-Semitic campaign consequent to outpourings of joy among Jews over Israel's victory in the Six-Day War. Israel's victory occurred despite Soviet bloc support for the Arabs, and President Gomułka condemned the Jewish "fifth column" in the country. Extensive purges of Jews swept the country, and secular Jewish life (e.g., Yiddish magazines and Jewish schools and day camps) was essentially dissolved. This hatred toward Jews clearly resulted from the role Jews played in postwar Poland. As one intellectual described it, Poland's problems resulted essentially from ethnic conflict between Poles and Jews in which the Jews were supported by the Russians. The problems were due to, "the arrival in our country . . . of certain politicians dressed in officer's uniforms, who later presumed that only they—the Zambrowskis, the Radkiewiczes, the Bermans—had the right to leadership, a monopoly over deciding what was right for the Polish nation" (in Schatz, 1991, p. 306). The solution would come when the "abnormal ethnic composition" of the government was corrected (in p. 307). The remaining Jews "both as a collective and as individuals . . . were singled out, slandered, ostracized, degraded, threatened, and intimidated with breathtaking intensity and . . . malignance" (p. 308). Most left Poland for Israel, and all were forced to renounce their Polish citizenship. They left behind only a few thousand mostly aged Jews.

Conclusion

In conclusion, the Polish-Jewish communists who came to power after World War II and their ethnically Jewish supporters must be considered as a historic Jewish group. The evidence indicates that this group pursued specifically Jewish interests, including especially their interest in securing Jewish group continuity in Poland while at the same time attempting to destroy institutions like the Catholic Church and other manifestations of Polish nationalism that promoted social cohesion among Poles. The communist government also combated anti-Semitism, and it promoted Jewish economic and political interests. While the extent of subjective Jewish identity among this group undoubtedly varied, the evidence indicates submerged and self-deceptive levels of Jewish identity even among the most assimilated. The entire episode illustrates the complexity of Jewish identification, and it exemplifies the importance of self-deception and rationalization as central aspects of Judaism as a group evolutionary strategy (see SAID, Chs. 7–8). There was massive self-deception and rationalization regarding the role of the Jewish-dominated government and its Jewish supporters in eliminating gentile nationalist elites, of their role in opposing Polish national culture and the Catholic Church while building up a secular Jewish culture, of their role as agents of Soviet domination of Poland, and of their own privileged position as administrators of Poland's economy which was designed to meet Soviet interests while demanding sacrifices from the Poles.

4

Neoconservatism as a Jewish Movement[57]

Neoconservatism received only scant mention in *CofC*, either in the 1998 hardback or the 2002 reprint. However, in the lead up to the Iraq War, I became aware of their power in the foreign policy establishment, their fealty to Israel, and the fact that a great many of them were strongly identified Jews.

In recent years, there has been a torrent of articles on neoconservatism raising (usually implicitly) some difficult issues: Are neoconservatives different from other conservatives? Is neoconservatism a Jewish movement? Is it "anti-Semitic" to say so?

The thesis presented here is that neoconservatism is indeed a Jewish intellectual and political movement. Jacob Heilbrunn (2008, pp. 10–11) is quite clear about the role of Jewishness in neoconservatism. After dismissing other views of what neoconservatism is, he states flatly that neoconservatism,

> is about a mindset, one that has been decisively shaped by the Jewish immigrant experience, by the Holocaust, and by the twentieth-century struggle against totalitarianism. . . . Indeed, as much as they may deny it,

[57] This chapter has been modified from a paper published in *The Occidental Quarterly* (Mac-Donald, 2004b). I thank the late Sam Francis for his very helpful comments on the original version of this paper. I am also grateful to an expert on Leo Strauss for his comments, many of which have been incorporated into the section on Strauss. Unfortunately, at his request, he must remain anonymous.

neoconservatism is in a decisive respect a Jewish phenomenon, reflecting a subset of Jewish concerns.

The neoconservatives exemplify the characteristic background traits of Jewish activism: ethnocentrism, intelligence, psychological intensity, and aggressiveness (MacDonald, 2003a). The ethnocentrism of the neocons has enabled them to create highly organized, cohesive, and effective ethnic networks. Neoconservatives have also exhibited the high intelligence necessary for attaining eminence in the academic world, the elite media and think tanks, and at the highest levels of government. As described below, they have aggressively pursued their goals, not only in purging more traditional conservatives from positions of power and influence, but also in reorienting U.S. foreign policy in the direction of hegemony and empire—and unquestioned support for Israel.

Neocons are also psychologically intense. Heilbrunn (2008, p. 13) describes the psychological profile of the neocons: they have "an uncompromising temperament who use (and treat) ideas as weapons in a moral struggle." Neocons "always believe what they are saying with the utmost intensity; it's in their nature as prophetic personalities" (p. 29). Writing of the neocons of the Reagan administration, Winik (1988, p. 136) notes "The neoconservatives served with an intensity and a commitment rarely found in government." Heilbrunn (2008, p. 25) gets at the passion of Jewish involvement in political causes, tracing it back to traditional Jewish attitudes in Eastern Europe: "As one Yiddish newspaper put it, 'with hatred, with a threefold curse, we must weave the shroud for the Russian autocratic government, for the entire anti-Semitic criminal gang.'" Regarding Max Shachtman, an early neocon follower of Trotsky discussed extensively below, "his father transmitted his hatred of the Russian, German, and Austro-Hungarian empires to him" (p. 29). The proto-neocons of the 1930s "reveled in their hatred of capitalism and their snobbish alienation from American society" (p. 43), the "social exclusion and WASP snobbery that their fathers experienced in the early part of the twentieth century—an attitude they carried with them through the debates of the cold war and into the halls of power after 9/11" (pp. 11–12). When George H. W. Bush became president, "the eastern establishment Republicans brought in by Bush, men like James Baker and Brent Scowcroft, represented everything the neocons despised" (p. 194).

Although not typical of all Jews, neocons exemplify the aggressive aspect of Jewish activism. Ron Unz (2018b) comments on the "sharp elbows" and "sheer ferocity" of neocons attacking their enemies:

I've . . . sometimes suggested to people that one under-emphasized aspect of a Jewish population, greatly magnifying its problematical character, is the existence of what might be considered a biological sub-morph of exceptionally fanatical individuals, always on hair-trigger alert to launch verbal and sometimes physical attacks of unprecedented fury against anyone they regard as insufficiently friendly towards Jewish interests. Every now and then, a particularly brave or foolhardy public figure challenges some off-limits topic and is almost always overwhelmed and destroyed by a veritable swarm of these fanatical Jewish attackers. Just as the painful stings of the self-sacrificing warrior caste of an ant colony can quickly teach large predators to go elsewhere, fears of provoking these "Jewish berserkers" can often severely intimidate writers or politicians, causing them to choose their words very carefully or even completely avoid discussing certain controversial subjects, thereby greatly benefiting Jewish interests as a whole. And the more such influential people are thus intimidated into avoiding a particular topic, the more that topic is perceived as strictly taboo, and avoided by everyone else as well.

Another trait typical of Jewish movements in general: the self-image of an embattled ingroup engaged in a "moral struggle" (Heilbrunn, 2008, p. 13) and fighting against overwhelming odds—in short, a bunker mentality that is entirely typical of traditional Jews (PTSDA, Ch. 7) and Jewish intellectual and political movements reviewed here (e.g., Jewish involvement in leftist politics and psychoanalysis; see Chs. 3, 5). As Jay Winik (1997, p. 55) describe the neocons:

> In their eyes, the inhabitants of the Bunker were the beleaguered few, fighting the lonely war against the left-wing forces of darkness, always on the precipice, about to be overwhelmed. [Richard] Perle constantly talked about lonely battles, the isolation, the attacks on himself and his colleagues.[58]

When the war in Iraq went badly and they were attacked by the left and the right, a "prominent New York neoconservative" stated that being "beleaguered plays into all the old psychological reflexes. Everyone's decided the neocons are wrong. That's vindication" (Heilbrunn, 2008, p. 280). There is obviously a healthy dose of self-deception in this sort of rhetoric—another common facet of Jewish intellectual activity (SAID, Ch. 8). Despite being ensconced in well-funded think tanks and eventually in the corridors of power in Washington, they think of themselves as besieged outsiders—outsiders with "seething rage at the government bureaucracy and social elites" (Heilbrunn, p. 124). The double standards apparent in Jewish moral posturing noted above also strongly suggest deception or self-deception.

In addition to these psychological traits, another motivation is hatred of the existing social order as anti-Jewish, coupled with psychological intensity.

---

[58] Freud had a similar sense of being under attack; see Ch. 5.

Indeed, Heilbrunn (2008, p. 77) contrasts William Buckley with the passionate intensity of Norman Podhoretz:

> The contrast with a Tory conservative such as William F. Buckley Jr. is striking. Buckley didn't have ex-friends. He never saw political differences as tantamount to personal betrayal. He was best friends, for example, with the legendary journalist Murray Kempton, who was at the other end of the political pole. This is not necessarily to Podhoretz's discredit. There is something to be said for the almost willful, naïve ferocity of his political passions.

In addition to these psychological traits, neoconservatism reflects many of the characteristics of Jewish intellectual and political movements studied throughout this volume (see Table 2).

1.	A deep concern with furthering specific Jewish interests, such as helping Israel or promoting immigration.
2.	Issues are framed in a rhetoric of universalism rather than Jewish particularism.
3.	Issues are framed in moral terms that appeal to the individualistic peoples of the West (*Individualism*); an attitude of moral superiority pervades the movement.
4.	Movements are centered around charismatic leaders (e.g., Bill Kristol, Richard Perle, Leo Strauss).
5.	Jews form a cohesive, mutually reinforcing core.
6.	Non-Jews often appear in highly visible roles, often as spokespersons for the movement.
7.	There is a pronounced ingroup-outgroup atmosphere within the movement—dissenters are portrayed not simply as wrong, but as the personification of evil and are expunged from the movement.
8.	The movement is irrational in the sense that it is fundamentally concerned with using available intellectual resources to advance a political cause.
9.	The movement is associated with the most prestigious academic institutions in the society.
10.	Access to prestigious and mainstream media sources, partly as a result of Jewish influence on the media.
11.	Active involvement of the wider Jewish community in financially supporting the movement.

Table 2: Characteristics of Jewish Intellectual and Political Movements

However, neoconservatism also presents several problems to any analysis, the main one being that the history of neoconservatism is relatively convoluted and complex compared to other Jewish intellectual and political movements. To an unusual extent, the history of neoconservatism presents a zigzag of positions and alliances, and a multiplicity of influences. This is perhaps inevitable in a fundamentally political movement needing to adjust to changing circumstances and attempting to influence the very large, complex political culture of the United States. The main changes neoconservatives have been forced to confront have been their loss of influence in the Democratic Party during the presidency of Jimmy Carter, the fall of the Soviet Union, and their present-day influence throughout the mainstream political spectrum. Although there is a remarkable continuity in Jewish neoconservatives' interests as Jews—the prime one being the safety and prosperity of Israel—these upheavals required new political alliances and produced a need for new work designed to reinvent the intellectual foundation of American foreign policy.

Neoconservatism also raises difficult problems of labeling. As described in the following, neoconservatism as a movement derives from the long association of Jews with the left. But contemporary neoconservatism is not simply a term for former liberals or leftists. Rather, neoconservatism represents a fundamentally new version of American conservatism, if it can be properly termed conservative at all. By displacing traditional forms of conservatism, neoconservatism has actually solidified the hold of the left on political and cultural discourse in the United States. The deep and continuing chasm between neocons and more traditional American conservatives—a topic of this chapter—indicates that this problem is far from being resolved.

The multiplicity of influences among neoconservatives requires some comment. Neoconservatives have at times been described as Trotskyists. As will be seen, in some cases the intellectual influences of neoconservatives can be traced to Trotsky, but Trotskyism cannot be seen as a current influence within the movement. And although the political philosopher Leo Strauss is indeed a guru for some neoconservatives, his influence is by no means pervasive, and in any case provides only a very broad guide for what the neoconservatives advocate in the area of public policy. Indeed, by far the best predictor of neoconservative attitudes on foreign policy is what the political right in Israel deems to be in Israel's best interests.

Neoconservatism is a complex, interlocking, professional and family-based network centered around Jewish publicists and organizers flexibly deployed to recruit the sympathies of both Jews and non-Jews in harnessing the wealth and power of the United States in the service of Israel. As such, neoconservatism should be considered a semi-covert branch of the massive and highly effective pro-Israel Lobby, which includes organizations like the American Israel Public Affairs Committee (AIPAC)—the most powerful lobbying group in Washington—and the Zionist Organization of America (ZOA).

In their *The Israel Lobby and U.S. Foreign Policy*, John Mearsheimer and Stephen Walt (2007) show that the interests of the Israel Lobby are not at all the same as the interests of the U.S. Quoting from my own previous review of the book (MacDonald, 2007b):

(1) Palestinian terrorism is not at all directed against the United States but against Israel because of its policies; it has no known links to al Qaeda.

(2) Terrorism is a legitimate tool used by those without other options. It is often used in state creation, and indeed, prominent Israeli leaders (Begin, Shamir) were themselves terrorists during Israel's formative years.

(3) Most importantly, "the United States has a terrorism problem in good part because it has long been so supportive of Israel" (p. 64) Exhibit A is Osama bin Laden himself. Mearsheimer and Walt provide an excellent account showing that bin Laden "has been deeply sympathetic to the Palestinian cause ever since he was a young man and that he has long been angry at the United States for backing Israel so strongly" (p. 66).

(4) The proliferation of weapons of mass destruction (WMDs) in the region is not a real strategic threat to the United States. This is particularly important given that a rationale for the invasion of Iraq and the impending invasion of Iran is their possession of such weapons: "If the United States could live with a nuclear Soviet Union or a nuclear China . . . and if it can tolerate a nuclear Pakistan and embrace a nuclear India, then it could live (however reluctantly) with a nuclear Iran as well" (p. 73). Moreover, the U.S. relationship with Israel makes it harder, not easier, to deal with these threats.

(5) Israel is not the loyal ally it is often made out to be. Mearsheimer and Walt provide a long list of cases where Israel has openly flouted U.S. interests, ranging from the Lavon affair of 1954 (a false flag operation in which Israeli agents blew up U.S. offices in Egypt in order to provoke a U.S.–Egypt crisis), to espionage, to selling weapons and technology.

As discussed below, prominent neoconservatives have been associated with such overtly pro-Israel organizations as JINSA, WINEP, and ZOA. (Acronyms of the main neoconservative and pro-Israel activist organizations used in this chapter are provided in Table 3.)

Compared with their deep and emotionally intense commitment to Israel, neoconservative attitudes on domestic policy reflect the attitudes of the mainstream liberal-left Jewish community in the U.S. In general, neoconservatives advocate maintaining the social welfare, immigration, and civil rights policies typical of liberalism (and the wider Jewish community) up to about 1970. Some of these policies represent clear examples of Jewish ethnic strategizing—in particular, the role of the entire Jewish political spectrum and the entire organized Jewish community as the moving force behind the Immigration and Nationality Act of 1965, which opened the floodgates to non-White immigration (Ch. 8). Since the neocons have developed a decisive influence in the mainstream conservative movement (at least until the rise of Donald Trump), their support for large-scale, multiracial immigration policies has likely had more significance for the future of the United States than their support for Israel.

Acronym	Name	Description and Website
AEI	American Enterprise Institute	A neoconservative think tank; produces and disseminates books and articles on foreign and domestic policy: aei.org
AIPAC	American Israel Public Affairs Committee	The main pro-Israel lobbying organization in the United States, specializing in influencing the U.S. Congress: aipac.org
CSP	Center for Security Policy	Neoconservative think tank specializing in defense policy; the CSP is strongly pro-Israel and favors a strong U.S. military: centerforsecuritypolicy.org
FDD	Foundation for Defense of Democracies	Neoconservative think tank whose initial documents to achieve tax-exempt status described its mission as to "provide education to enhance Israel's image in North America and the public's understanding of issues affecting Israeli-Arab relations"[59]: fdd.org
JINSA	Jewish Institute for National Security of America (formerly Affairs)	Pro-Israel think tank specializing in promoting military cooperation between the United States and Israel: jinsa.org
MEF	Middle East Forum	The MEF is a pro-Israel advocacy organization overlapping with the WINEP but generally more strident: meforum.org
PNAC	Project for the New American Century	Founded in 1997 but disbanded in 2006, the PNAC issued letters and statements signed mainly by prominent neocons and designed to influence public policy: newamericancentury.org
SD/U.S.A.	Social Democrats/U.S.A.	"Left-neoconservative" political organization advocating pro-labor social policy and pro-Israel, anticommunist foreign policy: socialdemocrats.org
WINEP	Washington Institute for Near East Policy	Pro-Israel think tank specializing in producing and disseminating pro-Israel media material: washingtoninstitute.org
ZOA	Zionist Organization of America	Pro-Israel lobbying organization associated with the more fanatical end of the pro-Israel spectrum in America: zoa.org

Table 3: *Acronyms of Neoconservative and Pro-Israel Activist Organizations Used Here*

---

[59] FDD's CEO Mark Dubowitz and President Clifford May are both Jews; donations to FDD have been dominated by wealthy Jews, including Sheldon Adelson, Roland Arnall, Leonard Abramson, Bernard Marcus, Paul Singer, Michael Steinhardt, Bernard Marcus, Edgar and Charles Bronfman, Jennifer Laszlo Mizrahi, Haim Saban, and Douglas Feith ("Foundation for Defense of Democracies," 2025.)

However, as discussed below, since the presidential campaign of Donald Trump in 2016, many neocons who formerly promoted at least some conservative perspectives within the Republican Party (e.g., opposition to gay marriage) have switched to supporting the entire program of the progressive elements of the Democratic Party.

As always, when discussing Jewish involvement in intellectual movements, there is no implication that all or even most Jews are involved in these movements. As discussed below, the organized Jewish community shares the neocon commitment to the government of Israel no matter what its policies are. However, neoconservatism has never been a majority viewpoint in the American Jewish community, at least if being a neoconservative implies voting for the Republican Party, since in recent years 70–80 percent of Jews support the Democrats. But the critical issue is not to determine what percentage of Jews support neoconservatism but rather to determine the extent to which Jews dominate the movement and are a critical component of its success. One must then document the fact that the Jews involved in the movement have a Jewish identity and are motivated by it—that is, that they see their participation as aimed at achieving specific Jewish goals. In the case of neoconservatives, an important line of evidence is their deep connections to Israel—their "passionate attachment to a nation not their own," as Patrick Buchanan (2004) termed it.

I reject the sort of arguments made by Richard Perle, who responded to charges that neoconservatives were predominantly Jews by noting that Jews always tend to be disproportionately involved in intellectual undertakings, like Nathan Cofnas (see MacDonald, 2022a), and that many Jews oppose the neoconservatives.[60] While this is often indeed the case, it leaves open the question

---

[60] See Ben Wattenberg's (2002) interview of Richard Perle. The entire relevant passage from the interview follows. Note Perle's odd argument that it was not in Israel's interest that the United States invade Iraq because Saddam Hussein posed a much greater threat to Israel than the United States:

Ben Wattenberg: As this argument has gotten rancorous, there is also an undertone that says that these neoconservative hawks, that so many of them are Jewish. Is that valid and how do you handle that?
Richard Perle: Well, a number are. I see Trent Lott there and maybe that's Newt Gingrich, I'm not sure, but by no means uniformly.
Ben Wattenberg: Well, and of course the people who are executing policy, President Bush, Vice President Cheney, Don Rumsfeld, Colin Powell, Connie Rice, they are not Jewish at last report.
Richard Perle: No, they're not. Well, you're going to find a disproportionate number of Jews in any sort of intellectual undertaking.
Ben Wattenberg: On both sides.
Richard Perle: On both sides. Jews gravitate toward that and I'll tell you if you balance out the hawkish Jews against the dovish ones, then we are badly outnumbered, badly outnumbered. But look, there's clearly an undertone of anti-Semitism about it. There's no doubt.

of whether neoconservative Jews perceive their ideas as advancing Jewish interests and whether they have a dominant role in formulating and enacting policy (see MacDonald, 2022a). Rather than attempting to determine percentages of Jews on each side, the methodology used here analyzes where Jewish power was directed during specific historical eras on particular issues. As presented in Chapter 1, the contrast been these two perspectives can be illustrated as follows: imagine a scenario in which the major Jewish activist organizations, Jewish donors, and Jewish activists are on one side of an issue, but on the other side of the issue are Jews who collectively represent more than 3 percent of the membership but without any major Jewish financial, organizational, media, and activist networks behind them. Obviously, although Jewish representation on either side is of interest, it is far more valuable to document the role of major Jewish activist organizations, Jewish donors, and Jewish activists.

THE MORAL NEXUS OF NEOCONSERVATISM

Heilbrunn notes the tendency for neocons to frame issues in moral terms—a theme prominent throughout this volume. (Moral messages are very effective in the West. My book, *Individualism and the Western Liberal Tradition*, 2019, Ch. 8, describes individualistic Western societies as based on moral communities where dissenters from a moral consensus are punished, whereas elsewhere morality depends critically on kinship distance; in the contemporary West, the elite media and academic culture are able to create moral communities.) When Podhoretz became editor of *Commentary*, he greeted the New Left with enthusiasm: "This left movement will be a moral criticism of all existing social institutions" (Heilbrunn, 2008, p. 78). The neocons, while decamping from the far left, never strayed from framing issues in moral terms. Winik (1988, p. 137), wrote that the neocons of the Reagan administration "embraced the view that the cold war is a Manichaean struggle [i.e., a struggle between

---

Ben Wattenberg: Well, and the linkage is that this war on Iraq if it comes about would help Israel and that that's the hidden agenda, and that's sort of the way that works.

Richard Perle: Well, sometimes there's an out-and-out accusation that if you take the view that I take and some others take towards Saddam Hussein, we are somehow motivated not by the best interest of the United States but by Israel's best interest. There's not a logical argument underpinning that. In fact, Israel is probably more exposed and vulnerable in the context of a war with Saddam than we are because they're right next door. Weapons that Saddam cannot today deliver against us could potentially be delivered against Israel. And for a long time, the Israelis themselves were very reluctant to take on Saddam Hussein. I've argued this issue with Israelis. But it's a nasty line of argument to suggest that somehow we're confused about where our loyalties are.

Ben Wattenberg: It's the old dual loyalty argument.

good and evil], perhaps temporarily to be managed through nuclear deterrence or balance-of-power theories, but ultimately to be won."

Nevertheless, they have never allowed themselves to be swayed by moral crusades that are against their interests. Prime examples of this are the demonization of Jimmy Carter and the defense of Israeli genocide against the Palestinians in Gaza post-October 7th, 2023. Regarding the former, Carter's emphasis on human rights and his appointment of Andrew Young as UN Ambassador infuriated the neocons because Carter saw the Palestinians' grievances against Israel in moral terms. Carter (2006) continued his moral criticism of Israel, for example, with his book, *Palestine: Peace Not Apartheid*, and he has been routinely labeled an anti-Semite by the neocons and other activist Jews. Perhaps the most rabid example of this rather extensive genre is *Jimmy Carter's War Against the Jews*, written by Jacob Laskin (2007) and published by the David Horowitz Freedom Center. On the other hand, using moral arguments against the USSR became stock-in-trade for the neocons, and after the fall of the USSR, they shifted smoothly to framing the proper role for U.S. foreign policy in the Middle East as a moral crusade for democracy and human rights in the Muslim world. This double standard on moral crusades is also reflected in neocons' support for the war against Serbia. While Israel's expansion of its territory is enshrined as a moral imperative and while many of the neocons (e.g., Douglas Feith) have close associations with the settler movement in Israel, the neocons supported the use of force against Serbia's attempt to retain its historic territory against the invading Kosovars (Heilbrunn, 2008, p. 208).

NON-JEWISH PARTICIPATION IN NEOCONSERVATISM

As with other Jewish intellectual and political movements, non-Jews have been welcomed into the movement and often given highly visible roles as the public face of the movement. This of course lessens the perception that the movement is indeed a Jewish movement, and it makes excellent psychological sense to have the spokespersons for any movement resemble the people they are trying to influence. That's why Ahmed Chalabi (a Shiite Iraqi, a student of early neocon theorist Albert Wohlstetter, and a close personal associate of prominent neocons, including Richard Perle) was the neocons' choice to lead postwar Iraq.[61] There are many more examples, including Freud's famous comments on needing a non-Jew to represent psychoanalysis (see Ch. 5). Margaret Mead and Ruth Benedict were the most publicly recognized Boasian

---

[61] Chalabi's status with the neocons was in flux because of doubts about his true allegiances. See Dizard, 2004.

anthropologists (Ch. 2), and there were a great many non-Jewish leftists and pro-immigration advocates who were promoted to visible positions in Jewish-dominated movements—and sometimes resented their role.[62] As noted in Chapter 3, Albert Lindemann (1997, p. 433) describes non-Jews among the leaders of the Bolshevik Revolution as "jewified non-Jews." There was also a smattering of non-Jews among the New York Intellectuals, who, as members of the anti-Stalinist left in the 1940s, were forerunners of the neoconservatives (see Ch. 7).

This need for the involvement of non-Jews is especially acute for neoconservatism as a political movement: because neoconservative Jews constitute a tiny percentage of the electorate, they need to make alliances with non-Jews whose perceived interests dovetail with theirs. Non-Jews have a variety of reasons for being associated with Jewish interests, including career advancement, close personal relationships or admiration for individual Jews, and deeply held personal convictions. For example, as described below, Senator Henry Jackson, whose political ambitions were intimately bound up with the neoconservatives, was a strong philo-Semite due partly to his experiences in childhood and as a young adult; his alliance with neoconservatives also stemmed from his belief that the United States and the Soviet Union were engaged in a deadly conflict and his belief that Israel was a valuable ally in that struggle. Because neoconservatives command a large and lucrative presence in the media, think tanks, and political culture generally, it is hardly surprising that complex blends of opportunism and personal conviction characterize participating non-Jews.

UNIVERSITY AND MEDIA INVOLVEMENT

An important feature of the Jewish intellectual and political movements has been their association with prestigious universities and media. The university most closely associated with the original crop of neoconservatives was the University of Chicago, the academic home not only of Leo Strauss, but also of Albert Wohlstetter, a mathematician turned foreign policy strategist, who was mentor to Richard Perle and Paul Wolfowitz, both of whom achieved power and influence in the administration of George W. Bush. The University of Chicago was also home to Strauss disciple Allan Bloom, sociologist Edward Shils, and novelist Saul Bellow among the earlier generation of neoconservatives.

---

[62] See Chs. 3, 7; Klehr, 1978, p. 40; A. Liebman, 1979, pp. 527ff; Neuringer, 1971/1980, p. 92; Rothman & Lichter, 1982/1996, p. 99; Svonkin, 1997, pp. 45, 51, 65, 71–72.

Another important academic home for the neocons has been the School of Advanced International Studies (SAIS) at Johns Hopkins University. Wolfowitz spent most of the Clinton years as a professor at SAIS; the director of the Strategic Studies Program at SAIS at the time of the 2004 version of this chapter was Eliot Cohen, who remains a dean in the program and has been a signatory to a number of PNAC's statements and letters, including the April 2002 letter to President Bush on Israel and Iraq (see below). Cohen is also an adviser for Frank Gaffney's CSP, an important neocon think tank, and he is a strong advocate for a Russian defeat in the Ukraine war (E. A. Cohen, 2023). Cohen is famous for labeling the war against terrorism "World War IV." His book, *Supreme Command*, argues that civilian leaders should make the important decisions and not defer to military leaders. This message was understood by Dick Cheney and Paul Wolfowitz as underscoring the need to prevent the military from having too much influence, as in the aftermath of the 1991 Gulf War when Colin Powell as chairman of the Joint Chiefs of Staff had been influential in opposing the removal of Saddam Hussein (Mann, 2004, p. 197).

Unlike other Jewish intellectual movements, the neoconservatives have been forced to deal with major opposition from within the academy, especially from Arabs and leftists in academic departments of Middle East studies. As a result, neoconservative activist groups, especially the WINEP and the MEF's Campus Watch, have monitored academic discourse and course content and organized protests against professors, and they were behind congressional legislation mandating U.S. government monitoring of programs in Middle East studies (see below).

Jewish intellectual and political movements also have typically had ready access to prestigious mainstream media outlets, and this is certainly true for the neocons. Most notable are *The Wall Street Journal*, *Commentary*, *The Public Interest*, *The Atlantic*, Basic Books (book publishing), and the media empires of Conrad Black and Rupert Murdoch. Murdoch's company owns the Fox News Channel, the *New York Post*, and *The Wall Street Journal*, and was the main source of funding for Bill Kristol's *Weekly Standard*—all major neocon outlets. (*Weekly Standard* ceased publication in 2018, most likely due to the divergence between its pro-Trump readership and neocon hostility toward Trump.)

Prior to the invasion of Iraq, *The New York Times* was deeply involved in spreading deception about Iraqi weapons of mass destruction and ties to terrorist organizations. The front-page articles by Judith Miller (who is Jewish) were based on information from Iraqi defectors well known to be untrustworthy because of their own interest in toppling Saddam (J. C. Moore, 2004). Many of these sources, including Ahmed Chalabi, were also touted by the Office of Special Plans of the Department of Defense, which is associated with many of the most prominent Bush administration neocons (see below). Miller's indiscretions might be chalked up to incompetence were it not for her close connections to prominent neocon organizations, in particular Daniel Pipes's MEF, which avidly sought the war in Iraq. The MEF lists Miller as an author; she has published articles in MEF media, including the *Middle East Quarterly* and the *MEF Wire*. The MEF also threw a launch party for her book on Islamic fundamentalism, *God Has Ninety-Nine Names*. Miller, whose father is ethnically Jewish, has a strong Jewish consciousness: her book *One by One: Facing the Holocaust* "tried to . . . show how each [European] country that I lived and worked in, was suppressing or distorting or politically manipulating the memory of the Holocaust" (in Lamb, 1990).

The *New York Times* has apologized for "coverage that was not as rigorous as it should have been" but did not single out Miller's stories as worthy of special censure (NYT Editors, 2004).[63] Indeed, the *Times*'s failure goes well beyond Miller, as noted in 2004 by Daniel Okrent, public editor of *The New York Times*:

> Some of the *Times*'s coverage in the months leading up to the invasion of Iraq was credulous; much of it was inappropriately italicized by lavish front-page display and heavy-breathing headlines; and several fine articles by David Johnston, James Risen and others that provided perspective or challenged information in the faulty stories were played as quietly as a lullaby. Especially notable among these was Risen's "C.I.A. Aides Feel Pressure in Preparing Iraqi Reports," which was completed several days before the invasion and unaccountably held for a week. It didn't appear until three days after the war's start, and even then was interred on Page B10.

As is well known, *The New York Times* is Jewish-owned and has often been accused of slanting its coverage on issues of importance to Jews (see Preface). It is perhaps another example of the legacy of Jacob Schiff, the Jewish activist-philanthropist who backed Adolph Ochs's purchase of *The New York Times* in 1896 because he believed he "could be of great service to the Jews generally" (Tifft & Jones, 1999, p. 38).

INVOLVEMENT OF THE WIDER JEWISH COMMUNITY

Another common theme of Jewish intellectual and political movements has been the involvement and clout of the wider Jewish community. While the prominent neoconservatives represent a small fraction of the American Jewish community, there is little doubt that the organized Jewish community shares their commitment to the Israeli right and, one might reasonably infer, its

---

[63] Okrent (2004) notes that the story was effectively buried by printing it on p. A10.

desire to see the United States conquer and effectively control virtually all of Israel's enemies (MacDonald, 2003b; M. Massing, 2002). For example:

> The power of AIPAC over members of Congress is literally awesome, although not in a good way. Has anyone ever seen so many members of Congress, of both parties, running to the microphones and sending out press releases to denounce one first-termer [Ilhan Omar] for criticizing the power of . . . a lobby? [AIPAC] is designated by virtually all the mainstream Jewish organizations as their official lobby, and they invariably jump when AIPAC tells them to. (Rosenberg, 2019)[64]

Since the 1980s AIPAC has leaned toward the right and only reluctantly went along with the Labor government of the 1990s (M. Massing, 2002). Months before the Iraq War, in October 2002, the Conference of Presidents of Major American Jewish Organizations issued a declaration of support for disarming the Iraqi regime (Cockburn, 2003). Jack Rosen, the president of the AJCongress, noted that "the final statement ought to be crystal clear in backing the President having to take unilateral action if necessary against Iraq to eliminate weapons of mass destruction" (Cockburn).

The organized Jewish community also plays the role of credential validator, especially for non-Jews. For example, the neocon choice for the leader of Iran following regime change was Reza Pahlavi, son of the former Shah. As is the case with Ahmed Chalabi, who was promoted by the neocons as the leader of post-Saddam Iraq, Pahlavi has proven his commitment to Jewish causes and the wider Jewish community. He has addressed the board of JINSA, given a public speech at the Simon Wiesenthal Center's Museum of Tolerance in Los Angeles, met with American Jewish communal leaders, and is on friendly terms with Likud party officials in Israel (M. Massing, 2002).

Most importantly, the main Jewish activist organizations have been quick to condemn those who have noted the Jewish commitments of the neoconservative activists in the Bush administration or seen the hand of the Jewish community in pushing for war against Iraq and other Arab countries. For example, the ADL's Abraham Foxman (2003) singled out Pat Buchanan, Joe Sobran, Representative James Moran, Chris Matthews of MSNBC, James O.

---

[64] Similarly, in the U.K. (M. S. Smith, 2023): "The possibility of Corbyn being elected terrified the British right and the British elite, who deeply distrust democracy. There is a parallel here with the fate of Bernie Sanders, who was opposed by the entire Democratic party establishment. The lobby's campaign against Corbyn got help from the Israeli government, British intelligence, and the entire British media, including the liberal *Guardian* newspaper, the BBC, the right wing of the Labour Party, and even the CIA. Corbyn and the socialists in the Labour Party in England were crushed by the massive campaign. Labeling Corbyn as an antisemite was a preposterous charge, but it has stuck. The Labour Party now has reverted to the way it was when Tony Blair, a supporter of austerity and America's war in Iraq, was the head of what was called 'New Labour.'"

Goldsborough (a columnist for the *San Diego Union-Tribune*), columnist Robert Novak, and writer Ian Buruma as subscribers to,

> a canard that America's going to war has little to do with disarming Saddam, but everything to do with Jews, the "Jewish lobby" and the hawkish Jewish members of the Bush Administration who, according to this chorus, will favor any war that benefits Israel.

Similarly, when Senator Ernest F. Hollings (D-SC) made a speech in the U.S. Senate and wrote a newspaper op-ed piece which claimed the war in Iraq was motivated by "President Bush's policy to secure Israel" and advanced by a handful of Jewish officials and opinion leaders, Foxman stated, "when the debate veers into anti-Jewish stereotyping, it is tantamount to scapegoating and an appeal to ethnic hatred. . . . This is reminiscent of age-old, anti-Semitic canards about a Jewish conspiracy to control and manipulate government" (in ADL, 2004).[65] (Foxman does not offer a serious analysis of Jews in the Bush administration; he correctly regards a simple assertion that this is a negative stereotype of Jews as enough to end such talk.) Despite negative comments from Jewish activist organizations and a great deal of coverage in the American Jewish press, there were no articles on this story in any of the major U.S. national newspapers.[66]

Mearsheimer and Walt (2007, p. 231) discuss the role of the Israel Lobby in the origins of the Iraq War: "We argue that the war was motivated at least in good part by a desire to make Israel more secure." They note that "some Israeli leaders" actually favored a war with Iran but were mollified by assurances that war with Iran would come later. The originators of the plan for the war with Iraq were Jewish-American neoconservatives "who conceived the idea and were principally responsible for pushing it forward in the wake of September 11" (p. 234). Israel then chimed in to do its part, chiefly by providing false intelligence and by having its leaders join the public chorus in America in favor of the war.

---

[65] These sentiments were shortly followed by a similar assessment by the American Board of Rabbis which "drafted a resolution demanding that Senator Hollings immediately resign his position in the Senate, and further demanded that the Democratic Party condemn Hollings' blatant and overt anti-Semitism, as well" (USA *Today*, May 24th, 2004); the American Board of Rabbis is an Orthodox Jewish group that regards Sharon's policies as too lenient and advocates assassination of all PLO leaders.

[66] Daily Google News searches from May 6th–29th, 2004. During this period, several articles on the topic appeared in *The Forward*, and there were articles in the *Baltimore Jewish Times* and the *Jewish Telegraphic Agency*. Summary articles written in *The Jerusalem Post* and *Haaretz* more than three weeks after the incident focused on anxiety among American Jews that Jews would be blamed for the Iraq War (Zacharia, 2004; Guttman, 2004). There were no articles on this topic in Hollinger-owned media in the United States.

These mainstream media and political figures stand accused of anti-Semitism—the most deadly charge that can be imagined in the contemporary world—by the most powerful Jewish activist organization in the United States. The Simon Wiesenthal Center (SWC) has also charged Buchanan and Moran with anti-Semitism for their comments on this issue (2003). While Foxman feels no need to provide any argument at all, the SWC feels it is sufficient to note that Jews have varying opinions on the war. This of course is a non-issue. The real issue is whether it is legitimate to open up to debate the question of the degree to which the neocon activists in the Bush administration are motivated by their long ties to the Israeli right and whether the organized Jewish community in the United States similarly supports the Israeli right and its desire to enmesh the United States in wars that are in Israel's interest. (There's not much doubt about how the SWC viewed the war with Iraq; Defense Secretary Donald Rumsfeld invited Rabbi Marvin Hier, dean of the Center, to briefings on the war; Morris, 2003).

Of course, neocons in the media—most notably David Frum, Max Boot, Lawrence F. Kaplan, Jonah Goldberg, and Alan Wald (J. Goldberg, 2003; L. F. Kaplan, 2003; Lind, 2003; Wald, 2003)—have also been busy labeling their opponents "anti-Semites." An early example concerned a 1988 speech given by Russell Kirk at the Heritage Foundation in which he remarked that "not seldom it has seemed as if some eminent neoconservatives mistook Tel Aviv for the capital of United States"—what Sam Francis (2004, p. 9) characterizes as "a wisecrack about the slavishly pro-Israel sympathies among neoconservatives." Midge Decter, a prominent neocon writer and wife of *Commentary* editor Norman Podhoretz, labeled the comment "a bloody outrage, a piece of anti-Semitism by Kirk that impugns the loyalty of neoconservatives" (in Francis, p. 9).

Accusations of anti-Semitism became a common response to suggestions that neoconservatives have promoted the war in Iraq for the benefit of Israel (Buchanan, 2003). For example, Joshua Muravchik (2003), whose ties to the neocons are elaborated below, authored an apologetic article in *Commentary* aimed at denying that neoconservative foreign policy prescriptions are tailored to benefit Israel and that imputations to that effect amount to "anti-Semitism." These accusations are notable for uniformly failing to seriously address the Jewish motivations and commitments of neoconservatives.

Finally, the wider Jewish community provides financial support for intellectual and political movements, as in the case of psychoanalysis, where the Jewish community signed on as patients and as consumers of psychoanalytic literature (Ch. 5). This has also been the case with neoconservatism, as noted by Gary North (2003):

> With respect to the close connection between Jews and neoconservatism, it is worth citing [Robert] Nisbet's assessment of the revival of his

academic career after 1965. His only book, *The Quest for Community* (Oxford University Press, 1953), had come back into print in paperback in 1962 as *Community and Power*. He then began to write for the neoconservative journals. Immediately, there were contracts for him to write a series of books on conservatism, history, and culture, beginning with *The Sociological Tradition*, published in 1966 by Basic Books, the newly created neoconservative publishing house. Sometime in the late 1960's, he told me: "I became an in-house sociologist for the *Commentary-Public Interest* crowd. Jews buy lots of academic books in America." Some things are obvious but unstated. He could follow the money: book royalties. So could his publishers.

The support of the wider Jewish community and the elaborate neoconservative infrastructure in the media and think tanks provide irresistible professional opportunities for Jews and non-Jews alike. I am not claiming that people like Nisbet don't believe what they write for neoconservative publications, but simply that having opinions that are attractive to neoconservatives can be very lucrative and professionally rewarding.

Similarly, the Jewish campaign to get the UK into war with Germany after the rise of Hitler was lavishly funded and actively recruited non-Jews. The main Jewish activist group was the Focus (Focus in Defence of Freedom and Peace) which was administered by Robert Waley Cohen, vice-president of the Board of Deputies of British Jews.[67] As Robert Henriques (1966, p. 361) describes, "Bob" was one of the leaders of Anglo-Jewry, for whom there was a need,

> to find a platform which would enlist the whole-hearted support of the greatest possible number of Gentile friends. . . . Every week Bob and a few other leaders of Anglo-Jewry met at New Court to plan a form of defence against anti-Semitic propaganda. In June, Bob, and several others had an interview with the Home Secretary and returned with the assurance that the Government would do everything in its power to arrest what it acknowledged to be "a growing evil."[68]

Further, describing Churchill:

> He enlisted many eminent men in his "Defence of Freedom and Peace" movement, and this formed a nucleus of sympathetic, liberal, non-Jewish

---

[67] The following on the Focus is based on Horus, 2024.

[68] Cohen was a director of Royal Dutch Shell, a company created with Rothschild finance; New Court was the business premises of N. M. Rothschild. Natty Cohen, Robert's father, was on the Russo-Jewish Committee (Henriques, 1966, pp. 42–43). In the tradition of the Anglo-Jewish Cousinhood, Cohen and his wife Alice were first cousins (see Joyce, 2022).

opinion with which the Anglo-Jewish leaders could co-operate. While
Jewish Defence was continued by the Board of Deputies with direct propaganda which probably did more to reassure British Jews than to combat
the infiltration of Nazi doctrine, it was decided at New Court to raise a
secret fund, initially of £50,000, which would work with the sympathetic
non-Jewish organisations as well as with the Jewish Telegraph Agency, the
latter providing the hard facts of Nazi atrocities which were so seldom
reported in the press. Bob agreed to raise, control and administer this
fund. It was started with a dinner party at Caen Wood Towers on 22nd July
[1936], from which over £25,000 was immediately subscribed, and the balance promised. Bob insisted from the start that the Jewish defence movement must concentrate on attacking Nazi philosophy and its denial of human rights, rather than on the direct refutation of anti-Semitic propaganda. . . . [H]e insisted that propaganda should be directed against "pursuing peace without caring for freedom and justice"—a summary of the
British policy of appeasement. (Henriques, 1966, pp. 362–363)[69]

David Irving (1987, p. 64) notes that 50,000 pounds "was a colossal sum for
such an organisation to butter around in 1936—five times the annual budget of
the British Council," and it was only "initially" 50,000 pounds.[70] Cohen, thanks
in part to his wealth, took charge of the Focus, as Henriques (1966, p. 363) describes:

[T]he "Defence of Freedom and Peace" movement was publishing a series
of pamphlets explaining what Nazi-ism meant and refuting the belief in
the country that it had its legitimate aspects. Each pamphlet was read in
manuscript by Bob and usually edited and amended profusely. Even Winston Churchill was not exempt; and one of his articles entitled "The Better
Way," which he sent to Bob in draft, was returned to its author with copi-
ous alterations, all of which were accepted. Soon the "Defence of Freedom
and Peace" movement, whose secretary was AH Richards, began publication of a journal known as *Focus* on which [journalist] Wickham Steed and
Bob [Cohen]—the latter described as "the veritable dynamic force of Focus"—were Churchill's main lieutenants.

Regarding Churchill, Patrick Cleburne (2024) describes how Sir Henry
Strakosch, another wealthy Jew, rescued Churchill from bankruptcy beginning
in the mid-1930s and extending well into World War II:

The simple fact is that Sir Henry Strakosch had Churchill by his financial
throat. Had he wished, he could probably have ruined Churchill financially

---

[69] See also R. Hawkins, 2007, p. 46; Spier, 1963, p. 9.
[70] About the British Council's budget, see P. Taylor, 1978.

and certainly have shattered his public reputation. This was not simply a matter of being a hired hand: Churchill could not easily have resigned.

The implication is that advocating for Jewish interests in opposing Hitler was profitable. This is not to say that Churchill did not sincerely believe what he advocated, but it's a good example of how non-Jews can benefit by advocating for Jewish interests.

In the remainder of this chapter, I will first trace the historical roots of neoconservatism, followed by portraits of several important neoconservatives that focus on their Jewish identities and their connections to pro-Israel activism.

HISTORICAL ROOTS OF NEOCONSERVATISM: COMING TO NEOCONSERVATISM FROM THE FAR LEFT

Like their radical cousins, the early neocons,

> sought . . . to overturn the old order in America. . . . After all, no matter how hard they worked, there were still quotas at the Ivy League universities. Then there were the fancy clubs, the legal and financial firms that saw Jews as interlopers who would soil their proud escutcheons and were to be kept at bay. Smarting with unsurpassed social resentment, the young Jews viewed themselves as liberators, proclaiming a new faith. (Heilbrunn, 2008, p. 28)

Heilbrunn (2008, p. 73) mentions,

> the snobbery of the Columbia English department, where Jews were seen as cultural interlopers. This attitude, which also prevailed on Wall Street and at the State Department, produced a lifelong antipathy toward the patrician class among the neocons and prompted them to create their own parallel establishment.

The result, as Norman Podhoretz phrased it, was to proclaim a war against the "WASP patriciate" (in Heilbrunn, 2008, p. 83).

All twentieth-century Jewish intellectual and political movements stem from the deep involvement of Jews with the left. However, beginning in the late 1920s, when the followers of Leon Trotsky broke off from the mainstream communist movement, the Jewish left has not been unified. By all accounts, the major figure linking Trotsky and the neoconservative movement is Max Shachtman, a Jew born in Poland in 1904 but brought to the United States as an infant. Like other leftists during the 1920s, Shachtman was enthusiastic about the Soviet Union, writing in 1923 that it was "a brilliant red light in the darkness of capitalist gloom" (in Drucker, 1994, p. 25). Shachtman began as a follower of James P. Cannon,[71] who became converted to Trotsky's view that the Soviet Union should actively foment "permanent revolution," i.e., revolution in other countries besides the USSR.

The Trotskyist movement was a heavily Jewish milieu, as Shachtman attracted young Jewish disciples—the familiar rabbi-disciple model of Jewish intellectual movements: "Youngsters around Shachtman made little effort to hide their New York background or intellectual skills and tastes. Years later they could still hear Shachtman's voice in one another's speeches" (Drucker, 1994, p. 43).[72] To a much greater extent than the Communist Party U.S.A., which was much larger and was committed to following the Soviet line, the Trotskyists survived as a small group centered around charismatic leaders like Shachtman, who paid homage to the famous Trotsky, who lurked in the background as an exile from the USSR living in Mexico. In the Jewish milieu of the movement, Shachtman was much admired as a speaker because of his ability in debate and polemics. He became the quintessential Hasidic guru—the leader of a close, psychologically intense group: "He would hug them and kiss [his followers]. He would pinch both their cheeks, hard, in a habit that some felt blended sadism and affection" (in Drucker, p. 43).

Trotskyists took seriously the Marxist idea that the proletarian socialist revolution should occur first in the economically advanced societies of the West rather than in backward Russia or China. They also thought that a revolution only in Russia was doomed to failure because the success of socialism in Russia depended inevitably on the world economy. The conclusion of this line of logic was that Marxists should advocate a permanent revolution that would sweep away capitalism completely, rather than concentrate on building socialism in the Soviet Union.

Shachtman broke with Trotsky over the latter's defense of the Soviet Union in World War II, setting out to develop his own brand of "third camp Marxism" that followed James Burnham in stressing internal democracy and analyzing the USSR as "bureaucratic collectivism." In 1939–1941, Shachtman battled leftist intellectuals like Sidney Hook, Max Eastman, and Dwight Macdonald, who rejected not only Stalinism but also Trotskyism as insufficiently open and democratic; they also saw Trotsky himself as guilty of some of the worst excesses of the early Bolshevik regime, especially his banning of opposition parties and his actions in crushing the Kronstadt sailors who had called for democracy. Shachtman defended a more open, democratic version of Marxism

[71] Cannon was not Jewish but lived in a very Jewish milieu, and he was married to Rose Karsner.
[72] "A younger, Jewish Trotskyist milieu began to form around him in New York" (p. 35).

but was concerned that his critics were abandoning socialism—throwing out the baby with the bathwater.

Hook, Eastman, Burnham, and Macdonald therefore constituted a "rightist" force within the anti-Stalinist left; it is this force that may with greater accuracy be labeled as one of the immediate intellectual ancestors of neoconservatism. By 1940, Macdonald was Shachtman's only link to the *Partisan Review* crowd of the New York Intellectuals (see Ch. 7), and the link became tenuous. James Burnham also broke with Shachtman in 1940. By 1941 Burnham rejected Stalinism, fascism, and even the New Deal as bureaucratic menaces, staking out a position characterized by "juridical defense, his criticism of managerial political tendencies, and his own defense of liberty" (Francis, 1984/1999, p. 52), eventually becoming a fixture at *National Review* in the decades before it became a neoconservative journal.

Shachtman himself became a Cold Warrior and social democrat in the late 1940s, attempting to build an all-inclusive left while his erstwhile Trotskyist allies in the Fourth International were bent on continuing their isolation in separate factions on the left. During this period, Shachtman saw the Stalinist takeover in Eastern Europe as a far greater threat than U.S. power, a prelude to his support for the Bay of Pigs invasion of Cuba and the U.S. role in Vietnam. By the 1950s he rejected revolutionary socialism and stopped calling himself a Trotskyist (Drucker, 1994, p. 219). During the 1960s he saw the Democratic Party as the path to social democracy, while nevertheless retaining some commitment to Marxism and socialism.

> Though he would insist for the rest of his life that he had found the keys to Marxism in his era, he was recutting the keys as he went along. In the early 1950s he had spoken, written, and acted as a left-wing, though no longer revolutionary, socialist. By the late 1950s he moved into the mainstream of U.S. social democracy. (Drucker, 1994, p. 261)

And this with a strategy of pushing big business and White Southerners out of the Democratic Party (the converse of Nixon's "Southern strategy" for the Republican Party). In the 1960s "he suggested more openly than ever before that U.S. power could be used to promote democracy in the Third World" (Drucker, 1994, p. 179)—a view that aligns him with later neoconservatives.

In the 1960s, Michael Harrington, author of the influential *The Other America*, became the best-known Shachtmanite, but they diverged when Harrington showed more sympathy toward the emerging multiculturalist, antiwar, feminist, "New Politics" influence in the Democratic Party while Shachtman remained committed to the Democrats as the party of organized labor and anti-communism (Drucker, 1994, p. 288). Shachtman became an enemy of the New Left, which he saw as overly apologetic toward the Soviet Union. "As I watch the New Left, I simply weep. If somebody set out to take the errors and stupidities of the Old Left and multiplied them to the nth degree, you would have the New Left of today" (in p. 305). This was linked to disagreements with Irving Howe, editor of *Dissent*, who published a wide range of authors, including Harrington, although Shachtman followers Carl Gershman and Tom Kahn remained on the editorial board of *Dissent* until 1971–1972.

The main link between Shachtman and the political mainstream was the influence he and his followers had on the AFL-CIO. In 1972, shortly before his death, Shachtman, "as an open anti-communist and supporter of both the Vietnam War and Zionism" (Vann, 2003), backed Senator Henry Jackson in the Democratic presidential primary. Jackson was a strong supporter of Israel (see below), and by this time support for Israel had become a litmus test for Shachtmanites.[73] Jackson, who was closely associated with the AFL-CIO, hired Tom Kahn, who had become a follower of Shachtman in the 1950s. Kahn was executive secretary of the Shachtmanite League for Industrial Democracy, headed at the time by Tom Harrington, and he was also the head of the Department of International Affairs of the AFL-CIO, where he was an "obsessive promoter of Israel" (Brenner, 1997) to the point that the AFL-CIO became the world's largest non-Jewish holder of Israel bonds. His department had a budget of around forty million dollars, most of which was provided by the federally funded National Endowment for Democracy (NED) (M. Massing, 1987). During the Reagan administration, the AFL-CIO received approximately 40 percent of available funding from the NED, while no other funded group received more than 10 percent. That imbalance has prompted speculation that NED was effectively in the hands of SD/U.S.A.—Shachtman's political legacy (see below). Carl Gershman was executive director of SD/U.S.A. from 1975 to 1980 and president of NED from 1984 to 2012.

In 1972, under the leadership of Gershman and the Shachtmanites, the Socialist Party of America changed its name to Social Democrats, U.S.A.[74] Working with Henry Jackson, SD/U.S.A.'s members achieved little political power because of the dominance of the New Politics wing of the Democratic Party, with its strong New Left influence from the 1960s. With the election of Ronald Reagan in 1980, however, key figures from SD/U.S.A. achieved positions of power and influence both in the labor movement and in the government. Among the latter were Reagan-era appointees such as U.S. Ambassador to the UN Jeane Kirkpatrick, Assistant Secretary of State for Inter-American Affairs

---

[73] As with everything else, there was an evolution of the Shachtmanites' views on Zionism. The Shachtmanite journal, *The New International*, published two articles by Hal Draper (1956, 1957) that were quite critical of Israel; this journal ceased publication in 1958 when the Shachtmanites merged with the Socialist Party of America.

[74] This led to the resignations of many and the eventual reconstruction of the Socialist Party U.S.A. with the left wing of the former organization.

Elliott Abrams (son-in-law of Norman Podhoretz and Midge Decter), Geneva arms talks negotiator Max Kampelman (aide to Hubert Humphrey and founding member of JINSA; he remained on its advisory board until his death in 2020), and Gershman, who was an aide to Kirkpatrick and head of the NED (Sims, 1992, pp. 46ff; M. Massing, 1987). Other Shachtmanites in the Reagan administration included Joshua Muravchik, a member of SD/U.S.A.'s National Committee, who wrote articles defending Reagan's foreign policy, and Penn Kemble, an SD/U.S.A. vice-chairman, who headed Prodemca, an influential lobbying group for the Contra opponents of the leftist Sandinistas in Nicaragua. Abrams and Muravchik continued to play an important role in neocon circles in the George W. Bush administration (see below).

In addition to being associated with SD/U.S.A. (Sims, 1992, p. 46), Kirkpatrick had strong neocon credentials. She was on the JINSA board of directors and was a senior fellow at the AEI. She also received several awards from Jewish organizations, including the Defender of Israel Award (New York), given to non-Jews who stand up for the Jewish people (other neocon recipients include Henry Jackson and Bayard Rustin), the Humanitarian Award of B'nai B'rith, and the 50th Anniversary Friend of Zion Award from the prime minister of Israel in 1998 (AEI, 2005). Kirkpatrick's husband Evron was a promoter of Hubert Humphrey and a long-time collaborator of neocon godfather Irving Kristol.

During the Reagan administration, Lane Kirkland, the head of the AFL-CIO from 1979 to 1995, was also a Shachtmanite and an officer of the SD/U.S.A. As secretary-treasurer of the AFL-CIO during the 1970s, Kirkland was a member of the Committee on the Present Danger, a group of neoconservatives in which "prominent Jackson supporters, advisers, and admirers from both sides of the aisle predominated" (R. G. Kaufman, 2000, p. 296). Kirkland gave a eulogy at Henry Jackson's funeral. Kirkland was not a Jew but was married to a Jew and, like Jackson, had very close ties to Jews:

> Throughout his career Kirkland maintained a special affection for the struggle of the Jews. It may be the result of his marriage to Irena [née Neumann in 1973—his second marriage], a Czech survivor of the Holocaust and an inspiring figure in her own right. Or it may be because he recognized . . . that the cause of the Jews and the cause of labor have been inseparable. (*The Forward*, August 20th, 1999).

Carl Gershman's NED supported the U.S.-led invasion and nation-building effort in Iraq (Gershman, 2004). The general line of the NED is that Arab countries should "get over" the Arab-Israeli conflict and embrace democracy, Israel, and the United States. In reporting on talks with representatives of the Jewish community in Turkey, Gershman (2003) framed the issues in terms of ending anti-Semitism in Turkey by destroying Al Qaeda; there is no criticism of the role of Israel and its policies in producing hatred throughout the region. During the 1980s, NED supported nonviolent strategies to end apartheid in South Africa in association with the A. Philip Randolph Institute, headed by longtime civil rights activist and SD/U.S.A. neocon Bayard Rustin (M. Massing, 1987). Critics of the NED, such as Representative Ron Paul (2003) (R-Tex), have complained that the NED "is nothing more than a costly program that takes U.S. taxpayer funds to promote favored politicians and political parties abroad." Paul suggested that the NED's support of former communists reflects Gershman's leftist background.

SD/U.S.A. continues to exist, maintaining a website and holding conventions. In 2003 SD/U.S.A. passed a resolution stating that the main conflict in the world was not between Islam and the West but between democratic and non-democratic governments, with Israel being the only democracy in the Middle East. A resolution of 2010 that remains on their website states:

> We are unconditional advocates of Israel's right to exist, but we are sometimes critical of its governmental policies. We support Israeli democratic ideals and those who work for them. Whenever those ideals are compromised, we will vigorously protest, because we are pro-Israel. (Hacker, 2010)

SD/U.S.A. strongly supported the democratic nation-building project that was the Iraq War, but the 2010 resolution distances itself from its former neoconservative attitudes: "We reject the lurch toward neo-conservatism and militarism of the old SDU.S.A."

Joshua Muravchik was a prominent neocon member of SD/U.S.A. and a member of their National Advisory Council. He has also been a member of the advisory board of JINSA, a resident scholar at the AEI, and an adjunct scholar at WINEP. Muravchik's (2002) book *Heaven on Earth: The Rise and Fall of Socialism* views socialism critically, but advocates a reformist social democracy that falls short of socialism; he views socialism as a failed religion that is relatively poor at creating wealth and is incompatible with very powerful human desires for private ownership.

Another prominent member of SD/U.S.A. was Max Kampelman (1920–2013), whose article "Trust the United Nations?" posted on the SD/U.S.A. website makes the standard neoconservative complaints about the UN dating from the 1970s, especially regarding its treatment of Israel:

> Since 1964 . . . the U.N. Security Council has passed 88 resolutions against Israel—the only democracy in the area—and the General Assembly has passed more than 400 such resolutions, including one in 1975 declaring "Zionism is a form of racism." When the terrorist leader of the Palestinians,

Arafat, spoke in 1974 to the General Assembly, he did so wearing a pistol on his hip and received a standing ovation. While totalitarian and repressive regimes are eligible and do serve on the U.N. Security Council, democratic Israel is barred by U.N. rules from serving in that senior body. (Kampelman, n.d.)[75]

NEOCONSERVATISM AS A CONTINUATION OF COLD WAR LIBERALISM'S "VITAL CENTER"

The other strand that merged into neoconservatism stems from Cold War liberalism, which became dominant within the Democratic Party during the Truman administration. It remained dominant until the rise of the New Politics influence in the party during the 1960s, culminating in the presidential nomination of George McGovern in 1972 (Ehrman, 1995). In the late 1940s, a key organization was Americans for Democratic Action, associated with such figures as Reinhold Niebuhr, Hubert Humphrey, and Arthur M. Schlesinger, Jr. (1947, p. 256), whose book *The Vital Center* distilled a liberal anticommunist perspective which combined vigorous containment of communism with "the struggle within our country against oppression and stagnation." This general perspective was also evident in the Congress for Cultural Freedom, whose central figure was New York Intellectual Sidney Hook (see Ch. 7; Hook, 1987, p. 432–460; Ehrman, p. 47). The CCF was a group of anticommunist intellectuals organized in 1950 and funded by the CIA, and it included a number of prominent liberals, such as Schlesinger.

A new wrinkle, in comparison to earlier Jewish intellectual and political movements discussed in *CofC*, has been that the central figures, Norman Podhoretz and Irving Kristol, have operated not so much as intellectual gurus in the manner of Freud or Boas or even Shachtman, but more as promoters and publicists of views which they saw as advancing Jewish interests. Podhoretz's *Commentary* (published by the AJCommittee) and Kristol's *The Public Interest* became clearinghouses for neoconservative ideas, but many of the articles were written by people with strong academic credentials. For example, in the area of foreign policy Robert W. Tucker and Walter Laqueur appeared in these journals as critics of liberal foreign policy (Ehrman, 1995, p. 50). Their work updated the anticommunist tradition of the "vital center" by taking account of Western weakness apparent in the New Politics liberalism of the Democratic

---

[75] The article has the following description of Kampelman: "Max M. Kampelman was Counselor of the State Department; U.S. Ambassador to the Conference on Security and Cooperation in Europe; and Ambassador and U.S. negotiator with the Soviet Union on Nuclear and Space Arms. He is now Chairman Emeritus of Freedom House; the American Academy of Diplomacy; and the Georgetown University Institute for the Study of Diplomacy."

Party and the American left, as well as the anti-Western posturing of the Third World.[76]

This "vital center" intellectual framework typified key neoconservatives at the origin of the movement in the late 1960s, including the two most pivotal figures, Irving Kristol and Norman Podhoretz. In the area of foreign policy, a primary concern of Jewish neoconservatives from the 1960s to the 1980s was the safety and prosperity of Israel, at a time when the Soviet Union was seen as hostile to Jews within its borders and was making alliances with Arab regimes against Israel.

> As they saw it, the world was gravely threatened by a totalitarian Soviet Union with aggressive outposts around the world and a Third World corrupted by vicious anti-Semitism. .... A major project of Moynihan, Kirkpatrick, and other neoconservatives in and out of government was the defense of Israel. .... By the mid-1970s, Israel was also under fire from the Soviet Union and the Third World and much of the West. The United States was the one exception, and the neoconservatives—stressing that Israel was a just, democratic state constantly threatened by vicious and aggressive neighbors—sought to deepen and strengthen this support. (Gerson, 1996, pp. 161–162)

Irving Kristol (2003) is quite frank in his view that the United States should support Israel even if it is not in its national interest to do so:

> Large nations, whose identity is ideological, like the Soviet Union of yesteryear and the United States of today, inevitably have ideological interests in addition to more material concerns. .... That is why we feel it necessary to defend Israel today, when its survival is threatened. No complicated geopolitical calculations of national interest are necessary.

A watershed event in neoconservatism was the statement of November 10th, 1975 by U.S. Ambassador to the UN Daniel P. Moynihan in response to the UN resolution of 1975 equating Zionism with racism (in Gerson, 1996, pp. 93–99). Moynihan, whose work in the UN made him a neocon icon and soon a senator from New York,[77] argued against the "discredited" notion that "there are significant biological differences among clearly identifiable groups, and that these differences establish, in effect, different levels of humanity" (p. 95). (In

---

[76] R. W. Tucker (1999) later argued that the United States should avoid the temptations of dominion in a unipolar world. It should attempt to spread democracy by example rather than force, and should achieve broad coalitions for its foreign policy endeavors.

[77] See Ehrman, 1995, p. 63–96. Moynihan was especially close to Norman Podhoretz, editor of *Commentary*, who was Moynihan's "unofficial advisor and writer" during his stint as UN ambassador (p. 84).

this regard Moynihan may not have been entirely candid, since he appears to have been much impressed by Arthur Jensen's research on race differences in intelligence. As an adviser to President Nixon on domestic affairs, one of Moynihan's jobs was to keep Nixon abreast of Jensen's research; Miele, 2002, p. 36–38.) In his UN speech, Moynihan ascribed the idea that Jews are a race to theorists like Houston Stewart Chamberlain, whose motivation was to find "new justifications . . . for excluding and persecuting Jews" in an era in which religious ideology was losing its power to do so. Moynihan (p. 96) describes Zionism as a "national liberation movement," but one with no genetic basis: "Zionists defined themselves merely as Jews, and declared to be Jewish anyone born of a Jewish mother or—and this is the absolutely crucial fact—anyone who converted to Judaism." Moynihan describes the Zionist movement as composed of a wide range of "racial stocks" (quotation marks in original)—"black Jews, brown Jews, white Jews, Jews from the Orient and Jews from the West."

Obviously, there is much to disagree with in these ideas. Jewish racial theorists, among them Zionists like Arthur Ruppin and Vladimir Jabotinsky (the hero of the Likud party throughout its history), were in the forefront of racial theorizing about Jews from the late nineteenth century onwards, and some had theories of Jewish racial superiority and opposed intermarriage, with Zionism being seen as a way to avoid intermarriage in the diaspora of the West (SAID, Ch. 5). And there is a great deal of evidence that Jews, including most notably Orthodox and Conservative Jews and much of the settler movement that constitutes the vanguard of Zionism in Israel today, have been and continue to be vitally interested in maintaining their ethnic integrity (SAID, Ch. 5). (Indeed, as discussed below, Elliott Abrams has been a prominent neoconservative voice in favor of Jews marrying Jews and retaining their ethnic cohesion.)

Nevertheless, Moynihan's speech is revealing in its depiction of the Jewish community as unconcerned about its ethnic cohesion, and for its denial of the biological reality of race. In general, neoconservatives have been staunch promoters of the racial *zeitgeist* of post-World War II liberal America. Indeed, as typical Cold War liberals up to the end of the 1960s, many of the older neocons were in the forefront of the racial revolution in the United States. It is also noteworthy that Moynihan's UN speech is typical of the large apologetic literature by Jewish activists and intellectuals in response to the UN's "Zionism is racism" resolution, of which *The Myth of the Jewish Race* by Raphael Patai and Jennifer Patai (1989) is perhaps the best-known example (see SAID, Ch. 7).

The flagship neoconservative magazine *Commentary*, under the editorship of Norman Podhoretz, has published many articles defending Israel. Harvard professor Ruth Wisse's 1981 *Commentary* article "The Delegitimation of Israel" (reprinted in Gerson, 1996, pp. 190–206) is described by Mark Gerson (p. 162) as "perhaps the best expression" of the neoconservative view that Israel "was a just, democratic state constantly threatened by vicious and aggressive neighbors." Wisse viewed hostility toward Israel as another example of the long history of anti-Jewish attitudes that seeks to delegitimize Judaism (in Gerson). This tradition is said to have begun with the Christian belief that Jews ought to be relegated to an inferior position because they had rejected Christ. It culminated in twentieth-century Europe in hatred directed at secular Jews because of their failure to assimilate completely to European culture. The result was the Holocaust, which was "from the standpoint of its perpetrators and collaborators successful beyond belief" (in p. 192). Israel, then, is an attempt at normalization in which Jews would be just another country fending for itself and seeking stability; it "should [also] have been the end of anti-Semitism, and the Jews may in any case be pardoned for feeling that they had earned a moment of rest in history" (in p. 193). But the Arab countries never accepted the legitimacy of Israel, not only with their wars against the Jewish state, but also by the "Zionism is racism" UN resolution, which "institutionalized anti-Semitism in international politics" (in p. 193). Wisse criticizes New York Times columnist Anthony Lewis for criticizing Israeli policies while failing to similarly criticize Arab states that fail to embody Western ideals of freedom of expression and respect for minority rights. Wisse also faults certain American Jewish organizations and liberal Jews for criticizing the policies of the government of Menachem Begin.[78]

The article stands out for its cartoonish view that the behavior and attitudes of Jews are completely irrelevant for understanding the history of anti-Semitism. The message of the article is that Jews as innocent victims of the irrational hatred of Europeans have a claim for "a respite" from history that Arabs are bound to honor by allowing the dispossession of the Palestinians. The article is also a testimony to the sea change among American Jews in their support for the Likud party and its expansionist policies in Israel. Since Wisse's article appeared in 1981, the positive attitudes toward the Likud party characteristic of the neoconservatives have become the mainstream view of the organized American Jewish community, and the liberal Jewish critics attacked by Wisse have been relegated to the fringe of the American Jewish community (MacDonald, 2003b).

---

[78] Wisse singles out Arthur Hertzberg as an example of an American Jew critical of Begin's government. Hertzberg continues to be a critic of Israeli policies, especially of the settlement movement. In The New York Times, Hertzberg (2003) urges the United States to cease funding the expansion of Jewish settlements while also preventing the Palestinians' access to foreign funds used for violence against Israel: "The United States must act now to disarm each side of the nasty things that they can do to each other. We must end the threat of the settlements to a Palestinian state of the future. The Palestinian militants must be forced to stop threatening the lives of Israelis, wherever they may be. A grand settlement is not in sight, but the United States can lead both parties to a more livable, untidy accommodation."

In the area of domestic policy, Jewish neoconservatives were motivated by concerns that the radicalism of the New Left (many of whom were Jews) compromised Jewish interests as a highly intelligent, upwardly mobile group. Although Jews were major allies of Blacks in the civil rights movement, by the late 1960s many Jews bitterly opposed Black efforts at community control of schools in New York because they threatened Jewish hegemony in the educational system, including the teachers' union (see M. Friedman, 1995, pp. 257ff). Black-Jewish interests also diverged when affirmative action and quotas for Black college admission became a divisive issue in the 1970s (p. 72). It was not only neoconservatives who worried about affirmative action: the main Jewish activist groups—the AJCommittee, the AJCongress, and the ADL—sided with Allan P. Bakke in a landmark case on racial quota systems in the University of California–Davis medical school, thereby promoting meritocracy, which serves the interests of highly intelligent, upwardly-mobile minorities.[79] However, in the 2023 Supreme Court ruling on affirmative action in which Asians were the plaintiffs, the ADL sided with Harvard, claiming there was no evidence of quotas at Harvard (ADL, 2023). Interestingly, Ron Unz (2023a) has shown that, although the representation of non-Jewish Whites has declined as a result of affirmative action for Blacks and Latinos, this has not been the case for Jewish representation despite lower academic performance as measured by scores on the National Merit Scholarship Qualifying Test. A similar 2012 paper from Unz was cited by the plaintiffs in the case (Pilkington, 2023).

Indeed, some neoconservatives, despite their record of youthful radicalism and support for the civil rights movement, began to see Jewish interests as bound up with those of the middle class. As Nathan Glazer (1969, p. 36) noted, commenting on Black anti-Semitism and the murderous urges of the New Left toward the middle class:

> Anti-Semitism is only part of this whole syndrome, for if the members of the middle class do not deserve to hold on to their property, their positions, or even their lives, then certainly the Jews, the most middle-class of all, are going to be placed at the head of the column marked for liquidation.

The New Left also tended to have negative attitudes toward Israel, with the result that many Jewish radicals eventually abandoned the left. In the late 1960s, the Student Nonviolent Coordinating Committee, which advocated for Black causes, described Zionism as "racist colonialism" (M. Friedman, 1995, p. 230) which massacred and oppressed Arabs. In Jewish eyes, a great many Black

---

[79] See MacDonald, 2006. In recent years mainstream Jewish groups such as the AJCommittee have supported some forms of affirmative action, as in the 2003 University of Michigan case.

leaders, including Stokely Carmichael (Kwame Touré), Jesse Jackson, Louis Far-rakhan, and Andrew Young, were seen as overly pro-Palestinian. (Young lost his position as U.S. Ambassador to the UN because he engaged in a secret meeting with the Palestinian representative to the UN.) During the 1960s, ex-pressions of solidarity with the Palestinians by radical Blacks, some of whom had adopted Islam, became a focus of neoconservative ire and resulted in many Jewish New Leftists leaving the movement (A. Liebman, 1979, p. 561; see also Ch. 3). Besides radical Blacks, other New Left figures, such as I. F. Stone and Noam Chomsky (both Jews), also criticized Israel and were perceived by neo-cons as taking a pro-Soviet line (Ehrman, 1995, p. 38). The origins of neocon-servatism as a Jewish movement are thus linked to the fact that the left, in-cluding the Soviet Union and leftist radicals in the United States, had become anti-Zionist—a problem for the Israel Lobby that has increased in recent years with the rise of an anti-Israel left within the Democratic Party (Lerer & Medina, 2021; McGreal, 2022; Judah, 2023).

In 1970 Podhoretz transformed *Commentary* into a weapon against the New Left (Ehrman, 1995, p. 43). In December of that year *National Review* be-gan, warily at first, to welcome neocons into the conservative tent, stating in 1971, "We will be delighted when the new realism manifested in these articles is applied by *Commentary* to the full range of national and international issues" (Ehrman, p. 46). Irving Kristol supported Nixon in 1972 and became a Republi-can about ten years before most neocons made the switch—until many left the Republican Party with the nomination of Donald Trump in 2016 over his non-interventionist statements on foreign policy and likely his comments on im-migration (MacDonald, 2016a). Nevertheless, even in the 1990s the neocons "continued to be distinct from traditional Midwestern and Southern conserva-tives for their Northeastern roots, combative style, and secularism" (Ehrman, p. 174)—all ways of saying that neoconservatism retained its fundamentally Jewish character.

The fault lines between neoconservatives and paleoconservatives were apparent during the Reagan administration in the battle over the appointment of the head of the National Endowment for the Humanities, eventually won by the neoconservative Bill Bennett. The campaign featured smear tactics and in-nuendo aimed at M. E. Bradford, an academic literary critic and defender of Southern agrarian culture who was favored by traditional conservatives. After neocons accused him of being a "virulent racist" and an admirer of Hitler, Brad-ford was eventually rejected as a potential liability to the administration (Fran-cis, 2004, p. 7).

The entry of the neoconservatives into the conservative mainstream did not, therefore, proceed without a struggle. Samuel Francis witnessed much of the early infighting among conservatives, won eventually by the neocons. Francis (2004, p. 9) recounts the "catalog of neoconservative efforts not merely to debate, criticize, and refute the ideas of traditional conservatism but to denounce, vilify, and harm the careers of those Old Right figures and institutions they have targeted." Continuing for Francis (pp. 11–12):

> There are countless stories of how neoconservatives have succeeded in entering conservative institutions, forcing out or demoting traditional conservatives, and changing the positions and philosophy of such institutions in neoconservative directions. . . . Writers like M. E. Bradford, Joseph Sobran, Pat Buchanan, and Russell Kirk, and institutions like *Chronicles*, the Rockford Institute, the Philadelphia Society, and the Intercollegiate Studies Institute have been among the most respected and distinguished names in American conservatism. The dedication of their neoconservative enemies to driving them out of the movement they have taken over and demonizing them as marginal and dangerous figures has no legitimate basis in reality. It is clear evidence of the ulterior aspirations of those behind neoconservatism to dominate and subvert American conservatism from its original purposes and agenda and turn it to other purposes. . . . What neoconservatives really dislike about their "allies" among traditional conservatives is simply the fact that the conservatives are conservatives at all—that they support "this notion of a Christian civilization," as Midge Decter put it, that they oppose mass immigration, that they criticize Martin Luther King and reject the racial dispossession of white Western culture, that they support or approve of Joe McCarthy, that they entertain doubts or strong disagreement over American foreign policy in the Middle East, that they oppose reckless involvement in foreign wars and foreign entanglements, and that, in company with the Founding Fathers of the United States, they reject the concept of a pure democracy and the belief that the United States is or should evolve toward it.

Most notably, neoconservatives have been staunch supporters of arguably the most destructive force associated with the left in the twentieth century—massive non-European immigration. Support for massive non-European immigration has spanned the Jewish political spectrum throughout the twentieth century to the present (see Ch. 8). A principal motivation of the organized Jewish community for encouraging such immigration has involved a deeply felt animosity toward the people and culture responsible for the Immigration Act of 1924 conceptualized as intended to ensure that the United States would remain a White, Christian nation—Midge Decter's "notion of a Christian civilization" (see Preface, Ch. 8). As neoconservative Ben Wattenberg (1984, p. 84) has famously written, "The non-Europeanization of America is heartening news of an almost transcendental quality."[80] The only exception—thus far without any influence—is that since 9/11 some Jewish activists, including neoconservative Daniel Pipes, head of the MEF, and Stephen Steinlight, senior fellow of the AJCommittee, have opposed Muslim—and only Muslim—immigration because of possible effects on pro-Israel sentiment in the United States (D. Pipes, 2001; Steinlight, 2001, 2004),[81] which is only getting stronger with the election of Muslims to the U.S. Congress and the general rise of criticism of Israel on the left and its non-White base.

The general impression one gets is that the neocons adopted positions on domestic policies in order to win influence within the Republican Party and then used their influence to further their foreign policy agenda. As a result, domestic policies were never the focus of the intense pressure that neocons were able to muster for their foreign policy initiatives. For example, Heilbrunn (2008, p. 213) notes:

> [Bill Kristol] made it a particular point to attack homosexuality, even participating in a conference at Georgetown University about "curing" gays of their supposed pathology. It is hard to imagine that Kristol himself harbors any real prejudice against gays. Politically, however, it remained a highly effective wedge issue.

---

[80] Scott McConnell, a former columnist for the *New York Post* and the founding editor of *The American Conservative*, commented on the intense commitment to open immigration among Jewish neoconservatives on an email discussion list (September 30th, 2001). Responding to someone who doubted the neoconservative commitment on this issue, McConnell notes (emphasis original): "Read some of Norman Podhoretz's writing, particularly his recent book—the *only* polemics against anyone right of center are directed against immigration restrictionists. Several years ago, I was at a party talking to Norman, and Abe Rosenthal came over, and Norman introduced us with the words, 'Scott is very solid on all the issues, except immigration.' The very first words out of his mouth. This was when we were ostensibly on very good terms, and I held a job which required important people to talk to me. There is a complicated history between the neo-cons and *National Review* [NR], which John O'Sullivan could tell better than I, but it involved neo-con attacks on NR using language that equated modern-day immigration restrictionism with the effort to send Jews back to Nazi death camps, a tone so vicious that [it] was really strange among ostensible Reaganite allies in 1995. . . . The *Forward*, a neo-connish Jewish weekly, used to run articles trying to link FAIR, an immigration restriction group headed by former [Colorado governor] Richard Lamm, with neo-nazism, using the kind of crude smear techniques many on this list are aware of. None of my neo-con friends (at a time when *all* my friends were Jewish neo-cons) thought there was anything wrong with this. . . . Read the *Weekly Standard*, read Ben Wattenberg. Read the [Podhoretzes]. Or don't. But if you were engaged on the issue, you couldn't help but being struck by this, particularly because it came as such a shock. One doesn't like to name names, because no one on the right wants to get on the bad side of the neo-cons, but I can think of one young scholar, who writes very temperately on immigration-related issues who trained at Harvard under a leading neo-con sociologist told me he was just amazed at the neo-cons' attachment to high immigration—it seemed to go against every principle of valuing balance and order in a society, and being aware of social vulnerabilities, that they seemed to advocate. Perhaps it's worth some time, writing a lengthy article on all this, on how the American right lost its way after the Cold War."

[81] See also Pipes' Middle East Forum website: meforum.org.

Similarly, although not mentioned by Heilbrunn, the neocons jumped on the bandwagon when illegal immigration became an issue, although they certainly did not originate this issue. As John O'Sullivan (2007) noted regarding Kristol's activism on an amnesty bill:

> Kristol, representing many neoconservatives disposed to favor the bill, came out against it. He did so in part because it had serious drafting defects but, more importantly, because it was creating a bitter gulf between rank-and-file Republicans and the party leadership. That in turn was imperiling Republican objectives in other areas, notably Iraq.

Peter Brimelow (2007) says it best: "Kristol will return to immigration enthusiasm once he has helped persuade Bush to attack Iran."

In general, neoconservatives have been far more attached to Jewish interests, and especially the interests of Israel, than to any other identifiable interest. It is revealing that as the war in Iraq has become an expensive quagmire in both lives and money, Bill Kristol has become willing to abandon the neoconservatives' alliance with traditional conservatives by allying with John Kerry and the Democratic Party. This is because Kerry has promised to increase troop strength and retain the commitment to Iraq, and because Kerry has declared that he has "a 100 percent record—not a 99, a 100 percent record—of sustaining the special relationship and friendship that we have with Israel" (in Buchanan, 2004). As Pat Buchanan notes, the fact that John Kerry "backs partial birth abortion, quotas, raising taxes, homosexual unions, liberals on the Supreme Court and has a voting record to the left of Teddy Kennedy" is less important than his stand on the fundamental issue of a foreign policy that is in the interest of Israel.

As noted, in 2016 Kristol supported Hillary Clinton, who voted for the Iraq War and was instrumental in the disaster in Libya (Becker & Shane, 2016). She supported sending arms to Syrian rebels and likened Russia's president, Vladimir Putin, to Hitler (Rucker, 2014). She wholeheartedly backs Israel and had her own set of rabidly pro-Israel foreign policy advisers, especially neocon Robert Kagan (discussed below) who advocates military intervention and democracy creation throughout the Middle East as a moral imperative—exactly the ideology that led the U.S. into the disastrous Iraq War. Clinton's main donor was Haim Saban, a rabid Zionist who has said that his only issue is Israel (see, e.g., MacDonald, 2009d). She has also firmly supported the war in Ukraine (Clinton & Schwerin, 2022).

THE FALL OF HENRY JACKSON AND THE RISE OF
NEOCONSERVATISM IN THE REPUBLICAN PARTY

The neoconservative takeover of the Republican Party and of American conservatism in general would have been unnecessary had not the Democratic Party shifted markedly to the left in the late 1960s. Henry Jackson is the pivotal figure in the defection of the neocons from the Democratic Party to the Republican Party—the person whose political fortunes most determined the later trajectory of neoconservatism. Jackson embodied the political attitudes and ambitions of a Jewish political network that saw Jewish interests as combining traditionally liberal social policies of the civil rights and Great Society era (but stopping short of advocating quota-type affirmative action policies or minority ethnic nationalism) with a Cold War posture that was at once aggressively pro-Israel and anticommunist at a time when the Soviet Union was perceived as the most powerful enemy of Israel. This "Cold War liberal" faction was dominant in the Democratic Party until 1972 and the nomination of George McGovern. After the defeat of McGovern, the neoconservatives founded the Committee for a Democratic Majority, whose attempt to resuscitate the Cold War coalition of the Democratic Party had a strong representation of Shachtmanite labor leaders as well as people centered around Norman Podhoretz's *Commentary*: Podhoretz; the above-mentioned Ben Wattenberg (who wrote speeches for Hubert Humphrey and was an aide to Jackson); Midge Decter; Max Kampelman; Penn Kemble of the SD/U.S.A.; Jeane Kirkpatrick (who began writing for *Commentary* during this period); sociologists Daniel Bell, Nathan Glazer, and Seymour Martin Lipset; Michael Novak; Soviet expert Richard Pipes; and Albert Shanker, president of the American Federation of Teachers. Nevertheless:

> [B]y the end of 1974, the neoconservatives appeared to have reached a political dead end. As guardians of vital center liberalism, they had become a minority faction within the Democratic Party, unable to do more than protest the party's leftward drift. (Ehrman, 1995, p. 62)

The basic storyline is that after failing again in 1976 and 1980 to gain the presidential nomination for a Democratic candidate who represented their views, this largely Jewish faction of political activists—now known as neoconservatives—switched allegiance to the Republican Party. The neocons had considerable influence in the Reagan years but less in the George H. W. Bush administration, only to become a critically important force in the foreign policy of the George W. Bush administration where, in the absence of a threat from the Soviet Union, neoconservatives have attempted to use the power of the United States to fundamentally alter the political landscape of the Middle East.

Henry Jackson was an ideal vehicle for this role as champion of Jewish interests. He was a very conscious philo-Semite: "My mother was a Christian who believed in a strong Judaism. She taught me to respect the Jews, help the Jews! It was a lesson I never forgot" (in R. G. Kaufman, 2000, p. 13). Jackson also had very positive personal experiences with Jews during his youth. During his college years he was the beneficiary of generosity from a Jew who allowed him to use a car to commute to college, and he developed lifelong friendships with two Jews, Stan Golub and Paul Friedlander. He was also horrified after seeing Buchenwald, the World War II German concentration camp, an experience that made him more determined to help Israel and Jews.

Entering Congress in 1940, Jackson was a strong supporter of Israel from its beginnings in 1948. By the 1970s he was widely viewed as Israel's best friend in Congress: "Jackson's devotion to Israel made Nixon and Kissinger's look tepid" (R. G. Kaufman, 2000, p. 263). The Jackson-Vanik Amendment linking U.S.-Soviet trade to the ability of Jews to emigrate from the Soviet Union was passed over strenuous opposition from the Nixon administration. And despite developing a reputation as the "Senator from Boeing," Jackson opposed the sale of Boeing-made AWACS surveillance aircraft to Saudi Arabia because of the possibility that they might harm the interests of Israel.

Jackson's experience of the Great Depression made him a liberal, deeply empathetic toward the suffering that was so common during the period. He defined himself as "vigilantly internationalist and anticommunist abroad but statist at home, committed to realizing the New Deal-Fair Deal vision of a strong, active federal government presiding over the economy, preserving and enhancing welfare protection, and extending civil rights" (R. G. Kaufman, 2000, p. 47). These attitudes of Jackson, and particularly his attitudes on foreign policy, brought him into the orbit of Jewish neoconservatives who held similar attitudes on domestic issues and whose attitudes on foreign policy stemmed fundamentally from their devotion to the cause of Israel:

> Jackson's visceral anticommunism and antitotalitarianism . . . brought him into the orbit of Jewish neoconservatives despite the subtle but important distinction in their outlook. The senator viewed the threat to Israel as a manifestation of the totalitarian threat he considered paramount. Some neoconservatives viewed Soviet totalitarianism as the threat to Israel they considered paramount. (R. G. Kaufman, 2000, p. 295)[82]

---

[82] R. G. Kaufman footnotes the last assertion with a reference to an interview with Daniel Patrick Moynihan on July 28th, 1996.

Jackson had developed close ties with a number of neocons who would later become important. Richard Perle was Jackson's most important national security adviser between 1969 and 1979, and Jackson maintained close relations with Paul Wolfowitz, who began his career in Washington working with Perle in Jackson's office. Jackson employed Perle even after credible evidence surfaced that he had spied for Israel: an FBI wiretap on the Israeli Embassy revealed Perle discussing classified information that had been supplied to him by someone on the National Security Council staff, presumably Helmut ("Hal") Sonnenfeldt. Sonnenfeldt, who was Jewish, "was known from previous wiretaps to have close ties to the Israelis as well as to Perle. . . . [He] had been repeatedly investigated by the FBI for other suspected leaks early in his career" (Hersh, 1982). As indicated below, several prominent neocons have been investigated on credible charges of spying for Israel: Perle, Wolfowitz, Stephen Bryen, Douglas Feith, and Michael Ledeen. Neocon Frank Gaffney, the non-Jewish president of the CSP, a neocon think tank, was also a Jackson aide. And Jackson was close to Bernard Lewis of Princeton University; Lewis is a Jewish expert on the Middle East who has had an important influence on the neocons in the George W. Bush administration as well as close ties to Israel (see below; R. G. Kaufman, 2000, p. 172; Waldman, 2004).

In the 1970s Jackson was involved with two of the most important neocon groups of the period. In 1976 he convened Team B, headed by Richard Pipes (a Harvard University Soviet expert), and including Paul Nitze, Wolfowitz, and Seymour Weiss (former director of the State Department's Bureau of Political-Military Affairs). Albert Wohlstetter, who was Wolfowitz's Ph.D. adviser at the University of Chicago, was a major catalyst for Team B. Jackson was also close to the Committee on the Present Danger (CPD). Formed in November 1976, CPD was a who's who of Jackson supporters, advisers, confidants, and admirers from both the Democratic and Republican parties, and included several members associated with the SD/U.S.A.: Paul Nitze, Eugene Rostow, Jeane Kirkpatrick, Admiral Elmo Zumwalt, Max Kampelman, Lane Kirkland, Richard Pipes, Seymour Martin Lipset, Bayard Rustin, and Norman Podhoretz. CPD was a sort of halfway house for Democratic neocons sliding toward the Republican Party.

The result was that all the important neocons backed Jackson for president in 1972 and 1976. Jackson commanded a great deal of financial support from the Jewish community in Hollywood and elsewhere because of his strong support for Israel, but he failed to win the 1976 Democratic nomination, despite having more money than his rivals. After Jackson's defeat and the ascendance of the leftist tendencies of the Carter administration, many of Jackson's allies went to work for Reagan with Jackson's tacit approval, with the result that they were frozen out of the Democratic Party once Carter was defeated (Zbigniew Brzezinski, in R. G. Kaufman, 2000, p. 351).

A large part of the disillusionment of Jackson and his coterie stemmed from the Carter administration's attitude toward Israel. Carter alienated American Jews by his proposals for a more evenhanded policy toward Israel, in which Israel would return to its 1967 borders in exchange for peace with the Arabs. Jews were also concerned because of the Andrew Young incident mentioned above—that he had been fired from his position as U.S. Ambassador to the UN after failing to disclose to the State Department details of his unauthorized meeting with representatives of the Palestinians. Blacks charged that Jews were responsible for Young's firing.

In October 1977 the Carter administration, in a joint communiqué with the Soviet Union, suggested Israel pull back to the 1967 borders:

> Jackson joined the ferocious attack on the administration that ensued from devotees of Kissinger's incremental approach and from Israel's supporters in the United States. He continued to regard unswerving U.S. support for Israel as not only a moral but a strategic imperative, and to insist that the maintenance of a strong, secure, militarily powerful Israel impeded rather than facilitated Soviet penetration of the Middle East. (R. G. Kaufman, 2000, p. 374)[83]

Jackson was particularly fond of pointing to maps of Israel showing how narrow Israel's borders had been before its 1967 conquests. For his part, Carter threatened to ask the American people "to choose between those who supported the national interest and those who supported a foreign interest such as Israel" (R. G. Kaufman, 2000, p. 375).

There was one last attempt to mend relations between the neocons and the Democrats: a 1980 White House meeting between Carter and major neocons, including Jeane Kirkpatrick, Norman Podhoretz, Midge Decter, Ben Wattenberg, Elliott Abrams (aide to neocon favorite Daniel P. Moynihan),[84] Max Kampelman, and Penn Kemble. The meeting, which discussed policy toward the USSR, did not go well, and "henceforth, their disdain for Carter and dislike of Kennedy would impel the neoconservatives to turn away from the Democratic Party and vote for Reagan" (R. G. Kaufman, 2000, p. 308).

> They had hoped to find a new Truman to rally around, a Democrat to promote their liberal ideas at home while fighting the cold war abroad. Not

---

[83] Despite his strong support for Israel, Jackson drew the line at support for the Likud party, which came into power in 1977 with the election of Menachem Begin. Whereas the Likud policy has been to seize as much of the West Bank as possible and relegate the Palestinians to isolated, impotent Bantustan-like enclaves, Jackson favored full sovereignty for the Palestinians on the West Bank, except for national security and foreign policy.

[84] Moynihan was expelled from the movement in 1984 because he softened his foreign policy line; Ehrman, 1995, p. 170.

finding one, they embraced the Republican party and Ronald Reagan as the best alternative. (Ehrman, 1995, p. 95)

Perle left Jackson's office in March 1980 to go into business with John F. Lehman. (Secretary of the Navy during the Reagan administration and, as of 2004, a member of the panel investigating the events of 9/11). Quite a few neocons assumed positions in the Reagan administration in the area of defense and foreign policy: Kirkpatrick as UN ambassador (Kirkpatrick hired Joshua Muravchik, Kenneth Adelman, and Carl Gershman as deputies); Perle as Assistant Secretary of Defense for International Security Policy (Perle hired Frank Gaffney and Douglas Feith); Elliott Abrams as Assistant Secretary of State for Human Rights Affairs; Max Kampelman as U.S. ambassador to the Helsinki Human Rights Conference and later as chief U.S. arms negotiator; Wolfowitz as Assistant Secretary of State for East Asian affairs. Another Jewish neocon, Richard Pipes, was influential in putting together a paper on grand strategy toward the USSR. Nevertheless, Reagan kept the neocons at arm's length and ceased heeding their advice. He favored developing trust and confidence with Soviet leaders rather than escalating tensions by threats of aggressive action (Diggins, 2004).

Bill Clinton courted neocons who had defected to Reagan. Perle, Kirkpatrick, and Abrams remained Republicans, but thirty-three "moderate and neoconservative foreign policy experts" endorsed Clinton in 1992, including Nitze, Kemble, and Muravchik, although Muravchik and several others later repudiated their endorsement, saying that Clinton had returned to the left-liberal foreign policy of the Democrats since McGovern (R. G. Kaufman, 2000, p. 446). Ben Wattenberg and Robert Strauss remained Democrats "who have not written off the Jackson tradition in their own party" (p. 446). Senator Joseph Lieberman, the Democratic 2000 vice-presidential nominee, is an heir to this tradition.

RESPONDING TO THE FALL OF THE SOVIET UNION

With the end of the Cold War, neoconservatives at first advocated a reduced role for the United States, but this stance switched gradually to the view that U.S. interests required the vigorous promotion of democracy in the rest of the world.[85] This aggressively pro-democracy theme, which appears first in the writings of Charles Krauthammer and then those of Elliott Abrams (Ehrman, 1995, p. 181), eventually became an incessant drumbeat in the campaign

---

[85] It's interesting that *Commentary* continued to write of a Soviet threat even after the fall of the Soviet Union, presumably because they feared a unipolar world in which Israel could not be portrayed as a vital ally of the United States (Ehrman, 1995, pp. 175–176).

for the war in Iraq. Krauthammer also broached the now familiar themes of unilateral intervention, and he emphasized the danger that smaller states could develop weapons of mass destruction which could be used to threaten world security (p. 182).

A cynic would argue that this newfound interest in democracy was tailor-made as a program for advancing the interests of Israel. After all, Israel is advertised as the only democracy in the Middle East, and democracy has a certain emotional appeal for the United States, which has at times engaged in an idealistic foreign policy aimed at furthering the cause of human rights and democracy in other countries. It is ironic that during the Cold War the standard neocon criticism of President Carter's foreign policy was that it was overly sensitive to human rights abuses in countries that were opposed to the Soviet Union and insufficiently condemnatory of the human rights abuses of the Soviet Union. The classic expression of this view was Jeane Kirkpatrick's 1979 *Commentary* article, "Dictatorships and Double Standards" (in Gerson, 1996, pp. 163–189). In an essay that would have been excellent reading prior to the invasion of Iraq, Kirkpatrick noted that in many countries political power is tied to complex family and kinship networks resistant to modernization. Nevertheless, "no idea holds greater sway in the mind of educated Americans than the belief that it is possible to democratize governments, anytime, anywhere, under any circumstances" (p. 169). Democracies are said to make heavy demands on citizens in terms of participation and restraint, and developing democracies is the work of "decades, if not centuries" (p. 171). My view is that democracy is a component of the uniquely Western suite of traits deriving from the evolution of Western peoples and their cultural history: Faustian aristocratic culture (with the gradual decline of aristocratic institutions and the rise of what I call egalitarian individualism rooted in the peoples of northwest Europe); individual rights against the state; representative government; moral universalism; and science (*Individualism*). This social structure cannot easily be exported to other societies, and particularly to Middle Eastern societies whose traditional cultures exhibit traits opposite to these.

It is revealing that, while neocons generally lost interest in Africa, Latin America, and Eastern Europe after these areas were no longer points of contention in the Cold War, there was no lessening of interest in the Middle East (Ehrman, 1995, p. 192). Indeed, neoconservatives and Jews in general failed to support President George H. W. Bush when, in the aftermath of the 1991 Gulf War, his administration pressured Israel to make concessions to the Palestinians and resisted a proposal for ten billion dollars in loan guarantees for Israel. This occurred in the context of Secretary of State James A. Baker's famous comment, "Fuck the Jews. They didn't vote for us" (p. 197).

NEOCONSERVATIVE PORTRAITS

Like members of other Jewish intellectual and political movements, neo-conservatives have a history of mutual admiration, close, mutually supportive personal, professional, and familial relationships, and focused cooperation in pursuit of common goals.

Leo Strauss (1899–1973)

Leo Strauss is an important influence on several prominent neoconservatives, particularly Irving Kristol and Bill Kristol. Strauss was a classicist and political philosopher at the University of Chicago, had a very strong Jewish identity, and viewed his philosophy as a means of ensuring Jewish survival in the Diaspora. As Strauss (1962/1994) himself noted, "I believe I can say, without any exaggeration, that since a very, very early time the main theme of my reflections has been what is called the 'Jewish Question.'"

Much of Strauss's early writing was on Jewish issues, and a constant theme in his writing was the idea that Western civilization was the product of the "energizing tension" between Athens and Jerusalem—Greek rationalism and the Jewish emphasis on faith, revelation, and religious intensity (Dannhauser, 1996, p. 160). Although Strauss believed that religion had effects on non-Jews that benefited Jews, there is little doubt that Strauss viewed religious fervor as an indispensable element of Jewish commitment and group loyalty—ethno-centrism by any other name:

> Some great love and loyalty to the Jewish people are in evidence in the life and works of Strauss. . . . Strauss *was* a good Jew. He knew the dignity and worth of love of one's own. Love of the good, which is the same as love of the truth, is higher than love of one's own, but there is only one road to the truth, and it leads through love of one's own. Strauss showed his loyalty to things Jewish in a way he was uniquely qualified to do, by showing generations of students how to treat Jewish texts with the utmost care and devotion. In this way he turned a number of his Jewish students in the direction of becoming better Jews. (Dannhauser, 1996, pp. 169–170, emphasis original)[86]

---

[86] Dannhauser concludes the passage by noting, "I know for I am one of them." Dannhauser poses the Athens/Jerusalem dichotomy as a choice between "the flatland of modern science, especially social science, and the fanaticism in the *Mea Shaarim* section of Jerusalem (incidentally, I would prefer the latter)" (p. 160).

Strauss believed that liberal, individualistic, modern Western societies were best for Jews because the illiberal alternative of the right (National Socialism) was anti-Jewish and the illiberal alternative of the left (communism) had eventually turned on the Jews. (By the 1950s, anti-Semitism had become an important force in the Soviet Union.) However, Strauss believed that liberal societies were not ideal because they tended to break down group loyalties and group distinctiveness—both qualities essential to the survival of the Jewish community. And he thought that there is a danger that, like the Weimar Republic, liberal societies could give way to fascism, especially if traditional religious and cultural forms were overturned; hence the neoconservative attitude that traditional religious forms among non-Jews are good for Jews (Strauss, 1962/1994; Tarcov & Pangle, 1987; Holmes, 1993, pp. 61–87). (Although Strauss believed in the importance of Israel for Jewish survival, his philosophy is not a defense of Israel but rather a blueprint for Jewish survival as a diaspora in Western societies.)

The fate of the Weimar Republic, combined with the emergence of anti-Semitism in the Soviet Union, had a formative influence on his thinking. As Stephen Holmes writes, "Strauss made his young Jewish-American students gulp by informing them that toleration [i.e., secular humanism] was dangerous and that the Enlightenment—rather than the failure of the Enlightenment—led directly to Adolf Hitler" (Holmes, 1993, p. 63). Hitler was also at the center of Strauss's admiration for Churchill—hence the roots of the neocon cult of Churchill: "The tyrant stood at the pinnacle of his power. The contrast between the indomitable and magnanimous statesman and the insane tyrant—this spectacle in its clear simplicity was one of the greatest lessons which men can learn, at any time" (in Jaffa, 1999, p. 44). I suspect that, given Strauss's strong Jewish identity, a very large part of his admiration of Churchill was not that Churchill opposed tyrants, but that he went to war against an anti-Jewish tyrant at enormous cost to his own people and nation while allied with another tyrant, Joseph Stalin, who had by 1939 already murdered far more people than Hitler ever would.

Strauss has become a cult figure—the quintessential rabbinical guru, with devoted disciples such as Allan Bloom. "There are many excellent teachers. They have students. Strauss had disciples" (M. Himmelfarb, 1974). "This group has the trappings of a cult. After all, there is a secret teaching and the extreme seriousness of those who are 'initiates'" (Levine, 1994, p. 354; see also Easton, 2000, p. 38; Drury, 1997, p. 2). Strauss (1952, p. 36) relished his role as a guru to worshiping disciples, once writing of "the love of the mature philosopher for the puppies of his race, by whom he wants to be loved in turn." Strauss was also a disciple of Hermann Cohen, a philosopher at the University of Marburg, who ended his career teaching in a rabbinical school; Cohen was a central figure in the Marburg school of neo-Kantian intellectuals whose main concern was to rationalize Jewish non-assimilation into German society.

Strauss understood that inequalities among humans were inevitable and advocated rule by an aristocratic elite of philosopher kings forced to pay lip service to the traditional religious and political beliefs of the masses while not believing them (Drury, 1997; Holmes, 1993; Tarcov & Pangle, 1987, p. 915). This elite should pursue its vision of the common good but must reach out to others using deception and manipulation to achieve its goals. As Bill Kristol has described it, elites have the duty to guide public opinion, but "one of the main teachings [of Strauss] is that all politics are limited and none of them is really based on the truth" (Easton, 2000, pp. 45, 183). A more cynical characterization is provided by Stephen Holmes (p. 74): "The good society, on this model, consists of the sedated masses, the gentlemen rulers, the promising puppies, and the philosophers who pursue knowledge, manipulate the gentlemen, anesthetize the people, and housebreak the most talented young"—a comment that is an alarmingly accurate description of the present situation in the United States and elsewhere in the Western world. Given Strauss's central concern that an acceptable political order be compatible with Jewish survival, it is reasonable to assume that Strauss believed that the aristocracy would have a considerable Jewish component (which it does) and thus be compatible with Jewish interests.

Strauss's philosophy is not really conservative. The rule by an aristocratic elite would require a complete political transformation in order to create a society that was "as just as possible":

> Nothing short of a *total transformation* of imbedded custom must be undertaken. To secure this inversion of the traditional hierarchies, the political, social, and educational system must be subjected to a radical reformation. For justice to be possible the founders have to "wipe clean the dispositions of men," that is, justice is possible only if the city and its citizens are *not* what they *are*: the weakest [i.e., the philosophic elite] is supposed to rule the strongest [the masses], the irrational is supposed to submit to the rule of the rational. (Levine, 1994, p. 366, emphasis original)

This emphasis on control by an intellectual elite clearly plays into Jewish strengths and fits well with the anti-populist strand of Jewish thinking discussed in Chapter 6.

Strauss (1952, Ch. 2) described the need for an external *exoteric* language directed at outsiders and an internal *esoteric* language directed at insiders. A general feature of the Jewish intellectual movements I have studied is that this Straussian prescription has been followed: issues are framed in language that appeals to non-Jews rather than explicitly in terms of Jewish interests, although Jewish interests are evident if one cares to look a little deeper. The most common rhetoric used by Jewish intellectual and political movements has been the language of moral universalism and the language of science—languages that appeal to the educated elites of the modern Western world. But beneath the rhetoric it is easy to find statements describing the Jewish agendas of the principal actors. And the language of moral universalism (e.g., advocating democracy as a universal moral imperative) goes hand in hand with a narrow Jewish moral particularism (e.g., overthrowing governments that represent a danger to Israel).

It is noteworthy in this respect that the split between the leftist critics of Strauss like Shadia Drury and Stephen Holmes versus Strauss's disciples like Allan Bloom and Harry V. Jaffa comes down to whether Strauss is properly seen as a universalist. The leftist critics claim that the moral universalism espoused by Strauss's disciples is nothing more than a veneer for his vision of a hierarchical society based on manipulation of the masses. As noted above, the use of a universalist rhetoric to mask particularist causes has a long history among Jewish intellectual and political movements, and it fits well with Strauss's famous emphasis on esoteric messages embedded in the texts of great thinkers. Moreover, there is at least some textual support for the leftist critique, although there can never be certainty because of the intentionally enigmatic nature of Strauss's writings.

I am merely adding to the leftist critique the idea that Strauss crafted his vision of an aristocratic elite manipulating the masses as a Jewish survival strategy. In doing so, I am taking seriously Strauss's own characterization of his work as centrally motivated by "the Jewish question" and by the excellent evidence for his strong commitment to the continuity of the Jewish people. At a fundamental level, based on my scholarship on Jewish intellectual and political movements, one cannot understand Strauss's well-attested standing as a Jewish guru—as an exemplar of the familiar pattern of an intellectual leader in the manner of Boas or Freud surrounded by devoted Jewish disciples—*unless he had a specifically Jewish message.*

The simple logic is as follows: based on the data presented here, it is quite clear that Strauss understood that neither communism nor fascism was good for Jews in the long run. But democracy cannot be trusted given that Weimar ended with Hitler. A solution is to advocate democracy and the trappings of traditional religious culture, but managed by an elite able to manipulate the masses via control of the media and academic discourse. Jews have a long history as an elite in Western societies, so it is not in the least surprising that Strauss would advocate an ideal society in which Jews would be a central component of the elite. In my view, this is Strauss's esoteric message. The exoteric message is the universalist veneer promulgated by Strauss's disciples—a common enough pattern among Jewish intellectual and political movements.

On the other hand, if one accepts at face value the view of Strauss's disciples that he should be understood as a theorist of egalitarianism and democracy, then Strauss's legacy becomes just another form of leftism, and a rather undistinguished one at that. In this version, the United States is seen as a "proposition nation" committed only to the ideals of democracy and egalitarianism—an ideology that originated with Jewish leftist intellectuals like Horace Kallen (see Ch. 8). Such an ideology not only fails to protect the ethnic interests of European-Americans in maintaining their culture and their demographic dominance, but it also fails as an adequate survival strategy for Jews because of the possibility that, like Weimar Germany, the United States could be democratically transformed into a state that self-consciously opposes the ethnic interests of Jews.

The most reasonable interpretation is that neocons see Strauss's moral universalism as a powerful exoteric ideology, particularly among non-Jews because of the strong roots of democracy and egalitarianism in American history and in the history of the West; it is attractive to Jews because it has no ethnic content and is therefore useful in combating the ethnic interests of European Americans—its function for the Jewish left throughout the twentieth century as noted throughout this volume. But without the esoteric message that the proposition nation must be managed and manipulated by a covert, Jewish-dominated elite, such an ideology is inherently unstable and cannot be guaranteed to meet the long-term interests of Jews.

And one must remember that the neocons' public commitment to egalitarianism belies their own status as an elite who were educated at elite academic institutions and created an elite network at the highest levels of the government. They form an elite that is deeply involved in deception, manipulation, and espionage on issues related to Israel and the war in Iraq. They also established the massive neocon infrastructure in the elite media and think tanks, and they have often become wealthy in the process. Their public pronouncements advocating a democratic, egalitarian ideology have not prevented them from having strong ethnic identities and a strong sense of their own ethnic interests; nor have their public pronouncements supporting the Enlightenment ideals of egalitarianism and democracy prevented them from having a thoroughly anti-Enlightenment, ethnic particularist commitment to the most nationalistic, aggressive, racialist elements within Israel—the Likud party, the settler movement, and the religious fanatics. At the end of the day, the only alternative to the existence of an esoteric Straussian message along the lines described here is massive self-deception.

Sidney Hook (1902–1989)

Sidney Hook was an important leader of the anti-Stalinist, non-Trotskyist left. Hook's career is interesting because he illustrates an evolution toward neoconservatism that was in many ways parallel to the Shachtmanites. Indeed, Hook ended up as honorary chairman of the SD/U.S.A. during the 1980s (M. Massing, 1987). Hook (1987, p. 46) became a socialist at a time when virtually all socialists supported the Bolshevik Revolution as the only alternative to what Jews tended to see as the anti-Jewish government of the Czar. As a professional philosopher, he saw his role as an attempt to develop an intellectually respectable Marxism strengthened with Dewey's ideas. But, until the Moscow Trials of the 1930s, he was blind to the violence and oppression in the USSR. During a visit to the USSR in 1929:

> I was completely oblivious at the time to the systematic repressions that were then going on against noncommunist elements and altogether ignorant of the liquidation of the so-called kulaks that had already begun that summer. I was not even curious enough to probe and pry, possibly for fear of what I would discover. (Hook, 1987, p. 123).

During the 1930s, when the Communist Party U.S.A. exercised a dominant cultural influence on the leftist-radical subculture in the United States, "the fear of fascism helped to blur our vision and blunt our hearing to the reports that kept trickling out of the Soviet Union" (Hook, 1987, p. 179). Even the Moscow Trials were dismissed by large sectors of liberal opinion. It was the time of the Popular Front, where the fundamental principle was the defense of the Soviet Union. Liberal journals like *The New Republic* did not support inquiries into the trials, citing disgraced *New York Times* reporter Walter Duranty as an authority who reported that the confessions were true (NYT Co, n.d.).

Unlike the Shachtmanites, Hook (1987, p. 244) never accepted Trotsky because of his record of defending "every act of the Soviet regime, until he himself lost power."

> To the very end Trotsky remained a blind, pitiless (even when pitiable) giant, defending the right of the minority vanguard of the proletariat—the Party—to exercise its dictatorship over "the backward layers of the proletariat"—i.e., those who disagreed with the self-designated vanguard. (Hook, 1987, p. 246)

Hook became a leader of the anti-Stalinist left in the 1930s and during the Cold War, usually with John Dewey as the most visible public persona in various organizations dedicated to opposing intellectual thought control. His main issue came to be openness versus totalitarianism, rather than capitalism versus socialism. Like other neoconservatives, from the 1960s on, he opposed the excesses of the New Left, including affirmative action. Hook received the Presidential Medal of Freedom from Ronald Reagan. Like many neoconservatives, he never abandoned many of his leftist views: in his acceptance speech, Hook (1987, p. 598) stated that he was "an unreconstructed believer in the welfare state, steeply progressive income tax, a secular humanist," and pro-choice on abortion. Sounding much like SD/U.S.A. stalwart Joshua Muravchik (2002), Hook (p. 600) noted that socialists like him "never took the problem of incentives seriously enough."

Like Strauss, Hook's advocacy of the open society stemmed from his belief that such societies were far better for Jews than either the totalitarian left or right. Hook (1989) had a strong Jewish identification: he was a Zionist, a strong supporter of Israel, and an advocate of Jewish education for Jewish children. Hook developed an elaborate apologia for Jews and against anti-Semitism in the modern world (see Ch. 7), and he was deeply concerned about the emergence of anti-Semitism in the USSR (Hook, 1987, p. 420).[87] His ideal society was culturally and ethnically diverse and democratic:

> No philosophy of Jewish life is required except one—identical with the democratic way of life—which enables Jews who for any reason at all accept their existence as Jews to lead a dignified and significant life, a life in which together with their fellowmen they strive collectively to improve the quality of democratic, secular cultures and thus encourage a maximum of cultural diversity, both Jewish and non-Jewish. (Hook, 1987, pp. 480–481)

Stephen Bryen (1942–)

Despite his low profile in the George W. Bush administration, Stephen Bryen is an important neocon. Bryen served as executive director of JINSA from 1979 to 1981 and remains on its advisory board. He is also affiliated with the AEI and the CSP. Richard Perle hired Bryen as Deputy Assistant Secretary of Defense during the Reagan administration. At the Pentagon, Perle and Bryen led an effort to extend and strengthen the Export Administration Act to grant the Pentagon a major role in technology transfer policy. This policy worked to the benefit of Israel at the expense of Europe, as Israel alone had access to the most secret technology designs (Saba, 1984). In 1988 Bryen and Perle

---

[87] Anti-Semitism in the USSR "had a sobering effect upon intellectuals of Jewish extraction, who had been disproportionately represented among dissidents and radicals."

temporarily received permission to export sensitive klystron technology, used in antiballistic missiles, to Israel.

> Two senior colleagues in [the Department of Defense] who wish to remain anonymous have confirmed that this attempt by Bryen to obtain klystrons for his friends was not unusual, and was in fact "standard operating procedure" for him, recalling numerous instances when U.S. companies were denied licenses to export sensitive technology, only to learn later that Israeli companies subsequently exported similar (U.S.-derived) weapons and technology to the intended customers/governments. (S. Green, 2004)

It is surprising that Perle was able to hire Bryen at all given that, beginning in 1978, Bryen was investigated for offering classified documents to the Mossad station chief of the Israeli embassy in the presence of an AIPAC representative (Saba, 1984; S. Green, 2004). Bryen's fingerprints were found on the documents in question despite his denials that he had ever had the documents in his possession. (Bryen refused to take a polygraph test.) The Bryen investigation was ultimately shut down because of the failure of the Senate Foreign Relations Committee to grant the Justice Department access to files important to the investigation, and because of the decision by Philip Heymann, the chief of the Justice Department's Criminal Division and later Deputy Attorney General in the Clinton administration, to drop the case.

Heymann is Jewish and had a close relationship with Bryen's lawyer, Nathan Lewin. Heymann's Jewish consciousness can be seen from the fact that he participated in the campaign to free Jonathan Pollard (an American citizen who was convicted of spying for Israel) and expunge his record—a major effort by a great many Jewish organizations and Jewish activists such as Alan Dershowitz. There were reports that Heymann was attempting to bypass Attorney General Janet Reno by preparing a Justice Department recommendation for presidential clemency, and that Heymann's behavior may have been a factor in his resignation shortly thereafter (Dershowitz, 1994; N. Jones, 1996).

Despite this history of overt and covert pro-Israeli activism, in 2001 Bryen was appointed, at the urging of Paul Wolfowitz, to the China Commission, which monitors illicit technology transfers to China, a position that requires top secret security clearance (S. Green, 2004). Many of the illicit technology transfers investigated by the commission are thought to have occurred via Israel.

Charles Krauthammer (1950–2018)

In his 1995 book, *The Rise of Neoconservatism: Intellectuals and Foreign Affairs, 1945–1994*, John Ehrman regards Charles Krauthammer as a key neoconservative foreign policy analyst because Krauthammer was on the cutting edge of neocon thinking on how to respond to the unipolar world created by the collapse of the Soviet Union. Krauthammer has consistently urged that the United States pursue a policy to remake the entire Middle East—a view that represents the "party line" among neoconservatives, e.g., Michael Ledeen, Norman Podhoretz, Bill Kristol, David Frum, and Richard Perle (Frum & Perle, 2003). In a speech to the AEI in February 2004, Krauthammer argued for a unilateral confrontation with the entire Arab-Muslim world (and nowhere else) in the interests of "democratic globalism." He advocated a U.S. foreign policy that is not "tied down" by "multilateralism":

> The whole point of the multilateral enterprise: To reduce American freedom of action by making it subservient to, dependent on, constricted by the will—and interests—of other nations. To tie down Gulliver with a thousand strings. To domesticate the most undomesticated, most outsized, national interest on the planet—ours. (Krauthammer, 2004a)

Democratic globalism is aimed at winning the struggle with the Arab-Muslim world:

> Beyond power. Beyond interest. Beyond interest defined as power. That is the credo of democratic globalism. Which explains its political appeal: America is a nation uniquely built not on blood, race or consanguinity, but on a proposition—to which its sacred honor has been pledged for two centuries.... Today, post-9/11, we find ourselves in an ... existential struggle but with a different enemy: not Soviet communism, but Arab-Islamic totalitarianism, both secular and religious.... [D]emocratic globalism is an improvement over realism. What it can teach realism is that the spread of democracy is not just an end but a means, an indispensable means for securing American interests. The reason is simple. Democracies are inherently more friendly to the United States, less belligerent to their neighbors, and generally more inclined to peace. Realists are right that to protect your interests you often have to go around the world bashing bad guys over the head. But that technique, no matter how satisfying, has its limits. At some point, you have to implant something, something organic and self-developing. And that something is democracy. But where? The danger of democratic globalism is its universalism, its open-ended commitment to human freedom, its temptation to plant the flag of democracy

everywhere. It must learn to say no. And indeed, it does say no. But when it says no to Liberia, or Congo, or Burma, or countenances alliances with authoritarian rulers in places like Pakistan or, for that matter, Russia, it stands accused of hypocrisy. Which is why we must articulate criteria for saying yes. . . . I propose a single criterion: where it counts. . . . And this is its axiom: *We will support democracy everywhere, but we will commit blood and treasure only in places where there is a strategic necessity—meaning, places central to the larger war against the existential enemy, the enemy that poses a global mortal threat to freedom.*

Where does it count today? Where the overthrow of radicalism and the beginnings of democracy can have a decisive effect in the war against the new global threat to freedom, the new existential enemy, the Arab-Islamic totalitarianism that has threatened us in both its secular and religious forms for the quarter-century since the Khomeini revolution of 1979 . . . There is not a single, remotely plausible, alternative strategy for attacking the monster behind 9/11. It's not Osama bin Laden; it is the cauldron of political oppression, religious intolerance, and social ruin in the Arab-Islamic world—oppression transmuted and deflected by regimes with no legitimacy into virulent, murderous anti-Americanism. It's not one man; it is a condition. (Krauthammer, 2004a)

Krauthammer's Jewish identification and pro-Israel motivation are typical of Jewish neoconservatives, as is his obeisance to the idea that America is a proposition nation, rather than a nation founded by a particular ethnic group—an ethno-cultural creation of Western Europe that should attempt to preserve this heritage. The same attitude can be seen in Irving Kristol's comment that the United States is an "ideological nation" committed to defend Israel independent of national interest. This ideology was the creation of leftist Jewish intellectuals attempting to rationalize a multicultural America in which European Americans were just one of many cultural/ethnic groups (see Chs. 7–8).

Krauthammer was a regular columnist for *The Jerusalem Post* and has written extensively in support of hardline policies in Israel and on what he interprets as a rise in age-old anti-Jewish attitudes in Europe. In 2002 Krauthammer was presented with Bar-Ilan University's annual Guardian of Zion Award at the King David Hotel in Jerusalem. His acceptance speech reveals him to have been an observant Jew who is steeped in Jewish history and the Hebrew tradition. He described the 1993 Oslo Accords as "the most catastrophic and self-inflicted wound by any state in modern history"; this disastrous policy was based on "an extreme expression of post-Zionistic messianism" (Krauthammer, 2002a). Krauthammer rejected the "secular messianism" of Shimon Peres as more dangerous than the religious messianism of Gush Emunim (a prominent settler group with a message of Jewish racialism and a vision of a "Greater Israel" encompassing the lands promised to Abraham in Genesis—from the Nile to the Euphrates; see MacDonald, 2003a,b) or of certain followers of the Lubavitcher Rebbe because of its impact on shaping contemporary Jewish history.

Krauthammer (2002b) was also deeply concerned with anti-Semitism:

> What is odd is not the anti-Semitism of today [in Europe], but its relative absence during the last half-century. That was the historical anomaly. Holocaust shame kept the demon corked for that half-century. But now the atonement is passed. The genie is out again. This time, however, it is more sophisticated. It is not a blanket hatred of Jews. Jews can be tolerated, even accepted, but they must know their place. Jews are fine so long as they are powerless, passive and picturesque. What is intolerable is Jewish assertiveness, the Jewish refusal to accept victimhood. And nothing so embodies that as the Jewish state.

Another barometer of Krauthammer's Jewish identification was his take on Mel Gibson's *The Passion of the Christ*. In sentiments similar to those of many other Jewish activists and writers, he termed it a "blood libel," "a singular act of interreligious aggression," a "spectacularly vicious" personal interpretation. Gibson's interpretations "point overwhelmingly in a single direction—to the villainy and culpability of the Jews." The crucifixion is "a history of centuries of relentless, and at times savage, persecution of Jews in Christian lands" (Krauthammer, 2004b). One gets the impression of a writer searching as best he can to find the most extreme terms possible to express his loathing of Gibson's account of the Christian gospels.

Paul Wolfowitz (1943–)

Wolfowitz's background indicates a strong Jewish identity. His father Jacob was a committed Zionist throughout his life and in his later years organized protests against Soviet treatment of Jews (Mann, 2004, p. 23). Jacob was deeply concerned about the Holocaust (Hirsh, 2003), and, in his own reminiscences of his teenage years, Paul recalls reading books about the Holocaust and traveling to Israel when his father was a visiting professor at an Israeli university. Wolfowitz reads Hebrew, and his sister married an Israeli and lives in Israel (Mann, pp. 23, 30). All the professors mentioned in his account of his period at the University of Chicago are Jews (Tannenhaus, 2003): Albert Wohlstetter, his Ph.D. adviser; Leo Strauss (Wolfowitz's original intent when enrolling at the University of Chicago was to study with Strauss, and he ended up taking two courses from him); Strauss's disciple Allan Bloom, whose book, *Closing of the American Mind: How Higher Education Has Failed Democracy and Impoverished the Souls of Today's Students* (1987), is a neocon classic; and Saul Bellow, the novelist.

Also indicative of a strong Jewish identity is a conversation Wolfowitz had with Natan Sharansky—who was an Israeli cabinet minister in several Israeli governments and leader of a right-wing, pro-settlement political party—at a conference on Middle East policy in Aspen, Colorado, in 2002. The conference was arranged by Richard Perle under the auspices of the AEI. Wolfowitz and Sharansky walked to a reception, because the latter, as an observant Jew, could not drive on the Sabbath. Sharansky noted that the walk "gave us a chance to talk about everything—Arafat, international terrorism, Iraq and Iran and, of course, Jewish history, our roots and so on" (Ephron & Lipper, 2002). Wolfowitz is married to Clare Selgin, and they have three children, Sara, David, and Rachel (Curtiss, 2003).

Ravelstein (2000) is Saul Bellow's fictionalized but essentially accurate description of Allan Bloom and his circle at the University of Chicago (Locke, 2002). It is of some interest because it recreates the Jewish atmosphere of Wolfowitz's academic environment. Wolfowitz was a member of Bloom's circle at Cornell University and for his graduate training chose the University of Chicago, most likely at the urging of Bloom, because of the presence there of Leo Strauss. Wolfowitz and Bloom maintained a close relationship after Bloom moved to the University of Chicago and during Wolfowitz's later career in the government. Wolfowitz was one of the "favored students" of Bloom described in Robert Locke's (2002) comment that "favored students of the usually haughty Bloom were gradually introduced to greater and greater intimacies with the master, culminating in exclusive dinner parties with him and Saul [Bellow] in Bloom's lavishly furnished million-dollar apartment."

As depicted by Bellow (2000, p. 27), Bloom personifies the Jewish-guru theme of this volume, surrounded by disciples—a "father" who attempts not only to direct his disciples' careers but also their personal lives as well. His disciples are described as "clones who dressed as he did, smoked the same Marlboros"; they were heading toward "the Promised Land of the intellect toward which Ravelstein, their Moses and their Socrates, led them" (p. 56). "To be cut off from his informants in Washington and Paris, from his students, the people he had trained, the band of brothers, the initiates, the happy few made him extremely uncomfortable" (p. 103).

Bloom in turn is depicted as a "disciple" of the Strauss character, Felix Davarr: "Ravelstein talked so much about him that in the end I was obliged to read some of his books. It had to be done if I was to understand what [Ravelstein] was all about" (Bellow, 2000, p. 101).

Bloom's Ravelstein is depicted as very self-consciously Jewish. One theme is the contrast between "crude" Jewish behavior and genteel WASP behavior (Bellow, 2000, pp. 57–58)—a theme described beautifully and authoritatively in the writings of John Murray Cuddihy (1974). And there is the acute consciousness of who is a Jew and who isn't; all of Ravelstein's close friends are Jews.

There is an intense interest in whether non-Jews dislike Jews or have connections to fascism. And there is a fixation on the Holocaust and when it will happen again: "They kill more than half of the European Jews . . . There's no telling which corner it will come from next" (Bellow, p. 174). Ravelstein thought of Jews as displacing WASPs: "[He] liked to think of living in one of the tony flat buildings formerly occupied by the exclusively WASP faculty" (p. 61).

Following Strauss, Bloom thought of Western civilization as the product of Athens and Jerusalem, and is said to have preferred the former, at least until the end of his life, when Jerusalem loomed large. Bellow's (2000, pp. 178–179) narrator writes, "I could see that [Ravelstein/Bloom] was following a trail of Jewish ideas or Jewish essences. It was unusual for him these days, in any conversation, to mention even Plato or Thucydides. He was full of Scripture now"—all connected to "the great evil," the belief during the World War II era "that almost everybody agreed that the Jews had no right to live . . . a vast collective agreement that the world would be improved by their disappearance and their extinction." Ravelstein's conclusion is that "it is impossible to get rid of one's origins, it is impossible not to remain a Jew. The Jews, Ravelstein . . . thought, following the line laid down by [his] teacher Davarr [Strauss], were historically witnesses to the absence of redemption" (p. 179).

Ravelstein recounts a conversation with the Wolfowitz character, Philip Gorman, which reflects Wolfowitz's well-known desire to invade Iraq in 1991:

> Colin Powell and Baker have advised the President not to send the troops all the way to Baghdad. Bush will announce it tomorrow. They're afraid of a few casualties. They send out a terrific army and give a demonstration of up-to-date high-tech warfare that flesh and blood can't stand up to. But then they leave the dictatorship in place and steal away. (Bellow, 2000, p. 58)

Wolfowitz has had a close relationship with Richard Perle beginning with their service in the office of Senator Henry Jackson (Keller, 2002). Heilbrunn (2008, p. 230) recalls that "In August 1999 an excited Wolfowitz told me over lunch . . . that [George W.] Bush had the ability to penetrate the dense fog of foreign policy expertise to ask a simple question. 'Tell me what I need to know? [sic]' Bush, Wolfowitz said, was 'another Scoop Jackson'"—a comment that certainly doesn't reflect well on Jackson.

Wolfowitz has a long record of pro-Israel advocacy. In 1973 he was appointed to the Arms Control and Disarmament Agency (ACDA); Stephen Green (2004) notes that "Wolfowitz . . . brought to ACDA a strong attachment to Israel's security, and a certain confusion about his obligation to U.S. national security." In 1978, he was investigated for providing a classified document to the Israeli government through an AIPAC intermediary, but the investigation ended without indictment. As Paul Findley shows, leakage of classified information to Israel by American Jews is routine within the Departments of State and Defense—so routine that it is accepted as a part of life in these departments, and investigations of the sources of leaks are seldom performed (S. Green). Later, in 1992, the Department of Defense discovered that Wolfowitz, as Undersecretary of Defense for Policy, was promoting the export to Israel of advanced AIM-9M air-to-air missiles. The sale was canceled because Israel had been caught selling the previous version to the Chinese. Until his appointment as Deputy Secretary of Defense in the Bush administration, Wolfowitz was on the Advisory Board of WINEP and was a patron of Dennis Ross, who was Ambassador to Israel in the Clinton administration before becoming Director of Policy and Strategic Planning at WINEP.

Wolfowitz wrote a 1997 *Weekly Standard* article advocating the removal of Saddam Hussein, and he signed the public letter to President Clinton organized by Bill Kristol's Project for the New American Century urging a regime change in Iraq. Within the George H. W. Bush administration, Wolfowitz was "the intellectual godfather and fiercest advocate for toppling Saddam" (Woodward, 2004, p. 21). Wolfowitz became famous as a key advocate for war with Iraq rather than Afghanistan in the immediate aftermath of September 11th (Mann, 2004, p. 302). Richard Clarke recounts an incident on September 12th, 2001, in which President Bush asked a group at the White House for any information that Saddam Hussein was involved in the September 11th attacks. After Bush left, a staffer "stared at [Bush] with her mouth open. 'Wolfowitz got to him'" (Clarke, 2004, p. 32).

Former CIA political analysts Kathleen and Bill Christison (2002) note that "One source inside the administration has described [Wolfowitz] frankly as 'over-the-top crazy when it comes to Israel.'" Although they find such an assessment insufficiently nuanced, they acknowledge that zealotry for Israel is a prime motivator for Wolfowitz. Writing in 2002, Bill Keller, a *New York Times* columnist at the time, is much more cautious:

> You hear from some of Wolfowitz's critics, always off the record, that Israel exercises a powerful gravitational pull on the man. They may not know that as a teenager he spent his father's sabbatical semester in Israel or that his sister is married to an Israeli, but they certainly know that he is friendly with Israel's generals and diplomats and that he is something of a hero to the heavily Jewish neoconservative movement. Those who know him well say this—leaving aside the offensive suggestion of dual loyalty— is looking at Wolfowitz through the wrong end of the telescope. As the Sadat story illustrates, he has generally been less excited by the security of Israel than by the promise of a more moderate Islam.

This is a remarkable statement. "The Sadat story" refers to Wolfowitz's very positive reaction to Egypt's President Anwar Sadat's speech to the Knesset as part of the peace process between Israel and Egypt. Obviously, it is silly to suppose that this event shows Wolfowitz's relative disinterest in Israel's security. Moreover, statements linking Wolfowitz to Israel are always off the record, presumably because people fear retaliation for stating the obvious. Thus Bill Keller coyly manages to document the associations between Wolfowitz and Israel while finding assertions of dual loyalty "offensive" rather than a well-grounded probability.

One of Joshua Muravchik's (2003) apologetic claims is that "in fact the careers of leading neoconservatives have rarely involved work on Middle East issues." This is false (see also the following discussion of Richard Perle). For example, Wolfowitz wrote his Ph.D. dissertation on nuclear proliferation in the Middle East. During the Carter administration, he prepared the Limited Contingency Study, which emphasized the "Iraqi threat" to the region; during the Reagan administration he lobbied against selling AWACS surveillance aircraft to Saudi Arabia and against negotiating with the Palestinians; and during the George H. W. Bush administration he was Undersecretary of Defense for Policy, a position where he "would once again have responsibility for arms control, the Middle East and the Persian Gulf, the areas to which he had devoted the early years of his career" (Mann, 2004, p. 170, see also pp. 79–81, 113).

Richard Perle (1941–)

As with Wolfowitz and the Strauss-Bloom nexus at the University of Chicago, so it is with Perle from an interview on BBC's *Panorama*:

> [T]he defining moment in our history was certainly the Holocaust. . . . It was the destruction, the genocide of a whole people, and it was the failure to respond in a timely fashion to a threat that was clearly gathering. . . . We don't want that to happen again . . . when we have the ability to stop totalitarian regimes we should do so, because when we fail to do so, the results are catastrophic. (in Lobe, 2003c)

Richard Perle first came into prominence in Washington as Senator Henry Jackson's chief aide on foreign policy. He organized Congressional support for the 1974 Jackson-Vanik Amendment, which angered the Soviet Union by linking bilateral trade issues to freedom of emigration, primarily of Jews from the Soviet Union to Israel and the United States. In 1970 Perle was recorded by the FBI discussing classified information with the Israeli embassy. In 1981 he was on the payroll of an Israeli defense contractor shortly before being appointed Assistant Secretary of Defense for International Security Policy, a position responsible for monitoring U.S. defense technology exports (Findley, 1989, p. 160; S. Green, 2004). During his tenure in the Reagan administration, Perle recommended purchase of an artillery shell made by Soltan, an Israeli munitions manufacturer. After leaving his position in the Defense Department in 1987, he assumed a position with Soltan. Like many other former government officials, he has also used his reputation and contacts in the government to develop a highly lucrative business career. For example, although he did not personally register as a lobbyist, he became a paid consultant to a firm headed by Douglas Feith that was established to lobby on behalf of Turkey (Hilzenrath, 2004). He was also a close personal friend of Israel Prime Minister Ariel Sharon (Brownfield, 2003). According to Jay Winik (1988, pp. 135–136):

> The history of the neoconservatives in the Reagan era will record the following: As assistant secretary of defense for international security policy, Richard Perle became the most effective player in that department. He was successful in staving off a precipitous rush to arms control agreements for the better part of 6 years and helped to curb the flow of sensitive technology to the East bloc. Eugene Rostow and Kenneth Adelman, successive heads of the Arms Control and Disarmament Agency, departed from the post's traditional role to advocate a military build-up as a prerequisite for successful arms reductions and stable U.S.-Soviet relations. Max Kampelman, the head of the U.S. delegation to the negotiations on nuclear and space arms with the Soviet Union, became one of the administration's few elder statesmen. Elliott Abrams, assistant secretary of state for inter-American affairs, never wavered in the battle to secure aid for the *contras* in their war against the Sandinista regime in Nicaragua. And Jeane Kirkpatrick, as U.S. chief representative to the United Nations, set the world on notice that all countries, large and small, would be accountable for their behavior toward America in that organization.

Perle was the "Study Group Leader" of a 1996 report titled "A Clean Break: A New Strategy for Securing the Realm" published by the Institute for Advanced Strategic and Political Studies (IASPS), an Israeli think tank. The membership of the study group illustrates the overlap between Israeli think tanks close to the Israeli government, American policy makers and government officials, and pro-Israel activists working in the United States. Other members of this group who accepted positions in the George W. Bush administration or in pro-Israel activist organizations in the United States include Douglas Feith (Deputy Undersecretary of Defense for Policy), David Wurmser (member of IASPS, a protégé of Perle at AEI, and senior adviser in the State Department), Meyrav Wurmser (head of the Hudson Institute, a neocon think tank), James Colbert (JINSA), and Jonathan Torop (WINEP).

Despite Joshua Muravchik's (2003) apologetic claims, the "Clean Break" report was clearly intended as advice for another of Perle's personal friends (Hilzenrath, 2004), Benjamin Netanyahu, who was then the new prime minister of Israel; there is no indication that it was an effort to further U.S. interests in the region. The purpose was to "forge a peace process and strategy based on an entirely *new intellectual foundation*, one that restores strategic initiative and provides the nation the room to engage every possible energy on rebuilding Zionism" (IASPS, 1996, emphasis original). Indeed, the report advises the United States to avoid pressure on the Israelis to give land for peace, a strategy "which required funneling American money to repressive and aggressive regimes, was risky, expensive, and very costly for both the United States and Israel, and placed the United States in roles it should neither have nor want." The authors of the report speak as Jews and Israelis, not as U.S. citizens: "Our claim to the land—to which we have clung for hope for 2,000 years—is legitimate and noble." Much of the focus is on removing the threat of Syria, and it is in this context that the report notes, "This effort can focus on removing Saddam Hussein from power in Iraq—an important Israeli strategic objective in its own right—as a means of foiling Syria's regional ambitions." The ultimate result of this has been the 2003–2011 Iraq War and ultimately the Syrian civil war that began in 2011 and ended with the overthrow of President Assad in 2024. The Iraq War brought great devastation to the country: hundreds of thousands of Iraqis were killed, and over 4,400 Americans were killed and almost 32,000 wounded ("Casualties of the Iraq War," 2025). The Syrian civil war became part of the ongoing conflict between Russia and its allies against the West, with Iran and Russia siding with Assad, while Israel and the United States, along with other Western countries, have supported the rebels—essentially the same forces arrayed against each other in the Ukraine war.

Proposals for regime change, such as found in "A Clean Break," have a long history in Israeli thought. For example, in 1982 Israeli strategist Oded Yinon echoed a long line of Israeli strategists who argued that Israel should attempt to dissolve all the existing Arab states into smaller, less potentially powerful states. These states would then become clients of Israel as a regional imperial power. Neocons advertised the war in Iraq as a crusade for a democratic, secular, Western-oriented, pro-Israel Iraq—a dream that has a great deal of appeal in the West, for obvious reasons. However, it is quite possible that the long-term result is that Iraq would fracture along ethnic and religious lines (Sunnis, Shiites, Kurds). This would also be in Israel's interests, because the resulting states would pose less of a threat than the Iraqi regime of Saddam Hussein. As Yinon (1982) noted:

> Iraq, rich in oil on the one hand and internally torn on the other, *is guaranteed as a candidate for Israel's targets.* Its dissolution is even more

important for us than that of Syria. Iraq is stronger than Syria. In the short run it is Iraqi power which constitutes the greatest threat to Israel.

Former Ambassador Joseph C. Wilson (2004, p. 484) has suggested that the dissolution of Iraq may well have been a motive for the war:

> A more cynical reading of the agenda of certain Bush advisers could con-clude that the Balkanization of Iraq was always an acceptable outcome, because Israel would then find itself surrounded by small Arab countries worried about each other instead of forming a solid bloc against Israel. After all, Iraq was an artificial country that had always had a troublesome history.[88]

As the Iraqi insurgency achieved momentum, there is evidence that Israeli military and intelligence units were operating in Kurdish regions of Iraq and that Israel was encouraging the Kurds to form their own state (Hersh, 2004). There is little doubt that an independent Kurdish state would have major re-percussions for Syria, Iran, and Turkey, and would lead to continuing instabil-ity in the Middle East. A senior Turkish official noted:

> If you end up with a divided Iraq, it will bring more blood, tears, and pain to the Middle East, and [the United States] will be blamed.... From Mexico to Russia, everybody will claim that the United States had a secret agenda in Iraq: you came there to break up Iraq. If Iraq is divided, America cannot explain this to the world. (in Hersh, 2004)

In the wake of the war, the Kurds have solidified their autonomous region; the government of Iraq is dysfunctional because of corruption, incompetence, and continuing sectarian divisions—certainly an acceptable outcome for the neocons.

Elliott Abrams (1948–)

Some of Elliott Abrams' neoconservative family and professional associa-tions have been described above. In December 2002 Abrams became President Bush's top Middle East adviser. He is closely associated with the Likud party in Israel and with prominent neocons (Richard Perle, Bill Kristol, Reuel Marc Gerecht, Michael Ledeen, Jeane Kirkpatrick, Paul Wolfowitz) and neocon think tanks (PNAC, AEI, CSP, JINSA) (Lobe, 2002b). Because of his reputation as a

---

[88] Wilson suggests that Scooter Libby or Elliott Abrams revealed that Wilson's wife, Valerie Plame, was a CIA agent in retaliation for Wilson's failure to find evidence supporting purchase of material for nuclear weapons by Iraq.

strongly identified Jew, Abrams was tapped for the role of rallying Jews in support of Reagan in the 1980 campaign (Ehrman, 1995, p. 139).

Abrams is also an activist on behalf of Jewish continuity. The purpose of his book *Faith or Fear: How Jews Can Survive in Christian America* (1997) is to ensure Jewish continuity by strengthening Jewish religious identification, opposing secularization, and discouraging intermarriage. In this regard it is interesting that other prominent neocons have advocated interracial marriage between Whites and Blacks in the United States. For example, Douglas J. Besharov, a resident scholar at the AEI, has written that the offspring of interracial marriages "are the best hope for the future of American race relations" (Besharov & Sullivan, 1996, p. 21).[89]

In *Faith or Fear*, Abrams (1997, p. ix) notes his own deep immersion in the Yiddish-speaking culture of his parents and grandparents. In his grandparents' generation, "all their children married Jews, and [they] kept Kosher homes." Abrams acknowledges that the mainstream Jewish community "clings to what is at bottom a dark vision of America, as a land permeated with anti-Semitism and always on the verge of anti-Semitic outbursts." The result is that Jews have taken the lead in secularizing America, but that has not been a good strategy for Jews because Jews themselves have become less religious and therefore less inclined to marry other Jews. (This "dark vision of America" is a critical motive of the "culture of critique" promoted by Jewish intellectual and political movements; it is also a major reason why the Jewish community has been united in favor of large-scale non-White immigration to the United States: diluting the White majority and lessening their power is seen as preventing an anti-Jewish outburst; see Ch. 8). Following Strauss, therefore, Abrams (p. 188) thinks that a strong role for Christianity in America is good for Jews:

> In this century we have seen two gigantic experiments at post-religious societies where the traditional restraints of religion and morality were entirely removed: Communism and Nazism. In both cases Jews became the special targets, but there was evil enough even without the scourge of anti-Semitism. For when the transcendental inhibition against evil is removed, when society becomes so purely secular that the restraints imposed by God on man are truly eradicated, minorities are but the earliest victims.

---

[89] Besharov apparently did not take a position as moderator of a debate between Elliott Abrams and Seymour Martin Lipset on whether the American Jewish community could survive only as a religious community (*The Diamondback*, student newspaper at the University of Maryland, College Park, December 9th, 1997). Another prominent neocon, Ben Wattenberg (2001), who is a senior fellow at AEI, is very upbeat about interracial marriage and immigration generally—the better to create a "universal nation." Wattenberg's article notes, with no apparent concern, that Jews have high rates of intermarriage as well.

Douglas Feith (1953–)

Feith has a strong Jewish identity that motivates his activism. Heilbrunn (2008, p. 12) writes that Feith "told me in an interview that because of his family history [i.e., decimated by the Holocaust] he understands the true nature of foreign policy, unlike the 'WASPs' in the State Department." Feith sees foreign policy from a Jewish, Holocaust-centric perspective that the WASPs can never understand. He was at the center of power during recent American history, but he sees himself as an outsider, and his enemies are the evil WASPs whose fathers didn't allow Jews into their country clubs. Feith is typical in his hatred for the WASPs for formerly dominating the State Department and not being enthusiastically pro-Israel. They assume an almost legendary role in the demonology of neoconservatism—consigned to the lowest reaches of hell. Their unforgiveable sin was to fail to see the world fundamentally in terms of Jewish interests, beginning with their opposition to recognizing Israel during the Truman administration. As Howard Sachar (1992, p. 597) notes in his history of Jews in America, Truman's defense secretary, James Forrestal, "was all but obsessed by the threat to [American interests] he discerned in Zionist ambitions. His concern was shared by the State Department and specifically by the Near East Desk." Former U.S. Undersecretary of State George Ball, whose co-authored 1992 book, *The Passionate Attachment*, was critical of Israel and the Israel Lobby, is the prototype of a hated State Department WASP. (Notice that the title of Ball's excellent book reflects the theme of psychological intensity among neocons and Jewish activists generally.)

Like most of his cronies, Feith has been suspected of spying for Israel. In 1972 Feith was fired from a position with the National Security Council because of an investigation into whether he had provided documents to the Israeli embassy. Nevertheless, Perle, who was Assistant Secretary for International Security Policy, hired him as his "special counsel" and then as his deputy. Feith worked for Perle until 1986, when he left government service to form a law firm, Feith & Zell, which was originally based in Israel and is best known for obtaining a pardon for the notorious Marc Rich during the final days of the Clinton administration (Joyce, 2013). In 2001, Douglas Feith returned to the Department of Defense as Donald Rumsfeld's Undersecretary for Policy, and it was in his office that Abram Shulsky's Office of Special Plans (OSP) was created. It was OSP that originated much of the fraudulent intelligence that Bush, Cheney, and Rumsfeld used to justify the invasion of Iraq. A key member of OSP was David Wurmser who, as indicated above, is a protégé of Richard Perle (Risen, 2004).

Retired army officer Karen Kwiatkowski (2004a) described Feith as knowing little about the Pentagon and paying little attention to any issues except those relating to Israel and Iraq. As Kwiatkowski escorted a group of Israeli generals into the Pentagon,

> the leader of the pack surged ahead, his colleagues in close formation, leaving us to double-time behind the group as they sped to Undersecretary Feith's office on the fourth floor. . . . Once in Feith's waiting room, the leader continued at speed to Feith's closed door. An alert secretary saw this coming and had leapt from her desk to block the door. "Mr. Feith has a visitor. It will only be a few more minutes." The leader craned his neck to look around the secretary's head as he demanded, "Who is in there with him?"

Unlike the usual practice, the Israeli generals did not have to sign in, so there are no official records of their visits (Kwiatkowski, 2004b). Kwiatkowski describes the anti-Arab, pro-Israel sentiment that pervaded the neocon network at the Department of Defense. Career military officers who failed to go along with these attitudes were simply replaced.

Feith has a strong Jewish identity and has been an activist on behalf of Israel. While in law school he collaborated with Joseph Churba, an associate and friend of Rabbi Meir Kahane, founder of the anti-Western and racialist Jewish Defense League. During the late 1980s to early 1990s he wrote pro-Likud op-ed pieces in Israeli newspapers, arguing that the West Bank is part of Israel, that the Palestinians belong in Jordan, and that there should be regime change in Iraq. He also headed the CSP and was a founding member of One Jerusalem, an Israeli organization "determined to prevent any compromise with the Palestinians over the fate of any part of Jerusalem" (Bamford, 2004, p. 279).

He has served as an officer of the Foundation for Jewish Studies, which is "dedicated to fostering Jewish learning and building communities of educated and committed Jews who are conscious of and faithful to the high ideals of Judaism," according to their website. In 1997 Feith and his father (a member of Betar, the Zionist youth movement founded by Vladimir Jabotinsky) were given awards from the ZOA because of their work as pro-Israel activists. The ZOA is a staunch supporter of the most extreme elements within Israel. Feith's law partner, L. Marc Zell of the firm's Tel Aviv office, was a spokesman for the settler movement in Israel, and the firm itself was deeply involved in legal issues related to the reconstruction of Iraq, a situation that has raised eyebrows because Feith is head of reconstruction in Iraq (Kamen, 2003).

Zell was one of many neocons close to Ahmed Chalabi but abandoned his support because Chalabi had not come through on his prewar pledges regarding Israel—further evidence that aiding Israel was an important motive for the neocons. According to Zell, Chalabi "said he would end Iraq's boycott of trade with Israel, and would allow Israeli companies to do business there. He said [the new Iraqi government] would agree to rebuild the pipeline from Mosul [in the northern Iraqi oil fields] to Haifa [the Israeli port, and the location of a major refinery]" (Dizard, 2004).[90] Another partner in the law firm of Feith & Zell is Salem Chalabi, Ahmed Chalabi's nephew. In 2003 Salem Chalabi was appointed General Director of the Iraqi Special Tribunal in charge of the trial of Saddam Hussein and other members of his government (TAC, 2004).

Abram Shulsky (1942–)

Shulsky was a student of Leo Strauss, a close friend of Paul Wolfowitz both at Cornell and the University of Chicago (Mann, 2004, p. 75), and yet another protégé of Richard Perle. He was an aide to neocon Senators Henry Jackson (along with Perle and Elliott Abrams) and Daniel Patrick Moynihan, and he worked in the Department of Defense in the Reagan administration. During the George W. Bush administration, he was appointed head of the Office of Special Plans (OSP) under Feith and Wolfowitz. The OSP became more influential on Iraq policy than the CIA or the Defense Intelligence Agency (Kwiatkowski, 2004a),[91] but it is widely viewed by retired intelligence operatives as having manipulated intelligence data on Iraq in order to influence policy (Lobe, 2003c). Reports suggest that the OSP worked closely with Israeli intelligence to paint an exaggerated picture of Iraqi capabilities in unconventional weapons.[92] It is tempting to link the actions of the OSP under Shulsky with Strauss's idea of a "noble lie" carried out by an elite to manipulate the masses, but one doesn't really need Strauss to understand the importance of lying in order to manipulate public opinion on behalf of Israel.

The OSP included other neocons with no professional qualifications in intelligence but long records of service in neoconservative think tanks and pro-Israel activist organizations, especially WINEP. Examples include Michael Rubin, who is affiliated with AEI and is an adjunct scholar at WINEP, David

---

[90] Dizard notes: "Why did the neocons put such enormous faith in Ahmed Chalabi, an exile with a shady past and no standing with Iraqis? One word: Israel. They saw the invasion of Iraq as the precondition for a reorganization of the Middle East that would solve Israel's strategic problems, without the need for an accommodation with either the Palestinians or the existing Arab states. Chalabi assured them that the Iraqi democracy he would build would develop diplomatic and trade ties with Israel, and eschew Arab nationalism. Now some influential allies believe those assurances were part of an elaborate con, and that Chalabi has betrayed his promises on Israel while cozying up to Iranian Shia leaders."

[91] Hersh, 2003: "'They [the CIA] see themselves as outsiders,' a former C.I.A. expert who spent the past decade immersed in Iraqi-exile affairs said of the Special Plans people."

[92] Marshall, 2004: "Shlomo Brom, a former Israeli intelligence officer now at the Jaffe Center for Strategic Studies at Tel Aviv University, has confirmed that Israeli intelligence played a major role in bolstering the administration's case for attacking Iraq. The problem, Brom maintains, is that the information was not reliable."

Schenker, who has written books and articles on Middle East issues published by WINEP and the *Middle East Quarterly* (published by Daniel Pipes' MEF, another pro-Israel activist organization), Elliott Abrams, David Wurmser, and Michael Ledeen. The OSP relied heavily on Iraqi defectors associated with Ahmed Chalabi, who, as indicated above, had a close personal relationship with Wolfowitz, Perle, and other neocons (see Hersh, 2003; Bamford, 2004).

Michael Ledeen (1941–2025)

Ledeen's career illustrates the interconnectedness of the neoconservative network. Ledeen was the first executive director of JINSA (1977–1979) and continued on its board of advisers at least until 2011. He was hired by Richard Perle in the Defense Department during the Reagan years, and during the same period he was hired as special adviser by Wolfowitz in his role as head of the State Department Policy Planning Staff. Along with Stephen Bryen, Ledeen became a member of the China Commission during the George W. Bush administration. He was also a consultant to Abram Shulsky's OSP, the Defense Department organization most closely linked with the manufacture of fraudulent intelligence leading up to the Iraq War. The OSP was created by Douglas Feith, who in turn reports to Paul Wolfowitz.

Ledeen has been suspected of spying for Israel (see S. Green, 2004). During the Reagan years, he was regarded by the CIA as "an agent of influence of a foreign government: Israel," and he was suspected of spying for Israel by his immediate superior at the Department of Defense, Noel Koch (S. Green, 2004). While working for the White House in 1984, Ledeen was also accused by National Security Adviser Robert C. McFarlane of participating in an unauthorized meeting with Israeli Prime Minister Shimon Peres that led to the proposal to funnel arms through Israel to Iran in order to free U.S. hostages being held in Lebanon—the origins of the Iran-Contra affair (Milstein, 1991).

Ledeen has been a major propagandist for forcing change on the entire Arab world. Ledeen's revolutionary ideology stems not from Marx or Trotsky, but from his favorable view of Italian fascism as a universalist (nonracial) revolutionary movement (Laughland, 2003). His book, *The War Against the Terror Masters* (2002), is a program for the complete restructuring of the Middle East by the United States couched in the rhetoric of universalism and moral concern, not for Israel, but for the Arab peoples who would benefit from regime change. Ledeen (pp. 216–217) is committed to "creative destruction" of the old social order:

> Behind all the anti-American venom from the secular radicals in Baghdad, the religious fanatics in Tehran, the minority regime in Damascus, and the multicultural kleptomaniacs in the Palestinian Authority is the knowledge

that they are hated by their own people. Their power rests on terror, recently directed against us, but always, first and foremost, against their own citizens. Given the chance to express themselves freely, the Iraqi, Iranian, Syrian, Lebanese, and Palestinian people would oust their current oppressors. Properly waged, our revolutionary war will give them a chance. . . .

Creative destruction is our middle name, both within our own society and abroad. We tear down the old order every day, from business to science, literature, art, architecture, and cinema to politics and the law. Our enemies have always hated this whirlwind of energy and creativity, which menaces their traditions (whatever they may be) and shames them for their inability to keep pace. Seeing America undo traditional societies, they fear us, for they do not wish to be undone. They cannot feel secure so long as we are there, for our very existence—our existence, not our politics—threatens their legitimacy. They must attack us in order to survive, just as we must destroy them to advance our historic mission.

Bernard Lewis (1916–2018)

Lewis was perhaps the main intellectual source for imposing democracy on the Arab world during the run-up to the Iraq War. A Princeton University historian, he argued that Muslim cultures have an inferiority complex stemming from their decline relative to the West over the last three hundred years. (Such arguments minimize the role of Israel and U.S. support for Israel as a source of Arab malaise. However, there is good evidence that the motives of Osama bin Laden and the 9/11 conspirators derived much more from U.S. support for Israel than a general anti-Western animus; see Bamford, 2004, pp. 96–101, 138–145.) Lewis contended that Arab societies with their antiquated, kinship-based structure can only be changed by forcing democracy on them (Waldman, 2004). Wolfowitz has used Lewis as the intellectual underpinning of the invasion of Iraq: "Bernard has taught how to understand the complex and important history of the Middle East, and use it to guide us where we will go next to build a better world for generations to come" (Waldman). During the 1970s Lewis was invited by Richard Perle to give a talk to Henry Jackson's group, and, as Perle notes, "Lewis became Jackson's guru, more or less." Lewis also established ties with Daniel Patrick Moynihan and with Jackson's other aides, including Wolfowitz, Abrams, and Gaffney. One of Lewis's main arguments was that the Palestinians have no historical claim to a state because they were not a state before the British Mandate in 1918.

Lewis also argued that Arabs have a long history of consensus government, if not democracy, and that a modicum of outside force should be sufficient to democratize the area—a view that runs counter to the huge cultural differences between the Middle East and the West that stem ultimately from very different evolutionary pressures and have persisted ever since the ancient world when Greek and Roman domination failed to leave any lasting imprint (*Individualism*, Ch. 4). Lewis, as a cultural historian, was in a poor position to understand the deep structure of the cultural differences between Europe and the Middle East. He seemed completely unaware of the differences in family and kinship structure between Europe and the Middle East, and he regarded the difference in attitudes toward women as a mere cultural difference rather than as a marker for an entirely different social structure (MacDonald, 2002c).

Lewis's flawed beliefs about the Middle East have nevertheless been quite useful to Israel—reflecting the theme that Jewish intellectual movements have often used available intellectual resources to advance a political cause. Not only did he provide an important intellectual rationale for the war against Iraq, but he was also very close to governmental and academic circles in Israel—the confidant of successive Israeli prime ministers from Golda Meir to Ariel Sharon (Waldman, 2004). As Stephen Green (2004) notes:

> If one looks at the outcomes of the Iraq war and following quagmire in terms of the objectives of the Sharon administration in Israel, there's been little but success. Israel has not had to pay for the cost of the invasion and its results: attention has been diverted from Sharon's trashing of the Middle East peace process; America has adopted Sharon's policy of unilateral military intervention and his attitude toward the UN and international human rights organizations; and the largest single military threat to the State of Israel has been eliminated. It's fair to ask, then, whose interests were being advanced by these individuals?

Dick Cheney (1941–)

By several accounts, Vice President Cheney had a "fever" to invade Iraq and transform the politics of the Middle East and was the leading force within the administration convincing President Bush of the need to do so (Woodward, 2004, p. 416). However, as Ron Unz (2018a) suggests:

> [T]he entire demonization of Cheney and Rumsfeld in anti-Iraq War circles has seemed somewhat suspicious to me. I always wondered whether the heavily Jewish liberal media had focused its wrath upon those two individuals in order to deflect culpability from the Jews.

In other words, Cheney and Rumsfeld were part of a neocon network and have a long history of support for Jewish causes.

As with the other Jewish intellectual and political movements I have reviewed, non-Jews have been welcomed into the movement and often given highly visible roles as the movement's public face. Among the current crop in this intellectual lineage, the most important non-Jews are Dick Cheney and Donald Rumsfeld, both of whom have close professional and personal relationships with neoconservatives that long predate their power and visibility. During the George W. Bush administration both Cheney and Rumsfeld have been associated with Bill Kristol's PNAC—which advocated a unilateral war for regime change in Iraq at least as early as 1998 (PNAC, 1998a,b)—and the CSP, two neocon think tanks; Cheney was presented with the ADL's Distinguished Statesman Award in 1993 and was described by Abraham Foxman as "sensitive to Jewish concerns" (Samber, 2000). When Cheney was a congressman during the early 1980s, he attended lunches hosted for Republican Jewish leaders by the House leadership. Cheney was described by Marshall Breger, a senior official in the Reagan and George H. W. Bush administrations as "very interested in outreach and engaging the Jewish community" (Samber). He was also a member of JINSA, the major pro-Israel activist organization, until assuming his office as vice president in 2001.

Cheney has also had a close involvement with leading Israeli politicians, especially Natan Sharansky (see above), a prime architect of the ideology that the key to peace between Israel and the Arab world, including the Palestinians, is Arab acceptance of democracy. President Bush articulated the importance of Palestinian democracy for his plan for a Middle East "roadmap for peace" in his June 2002 policy speech. The links to Sharansky were obvious:

> Sharansky could have written the speech himself, and, for that matter, may have had a direct hand in its drafting. The weekend prior to the speech, he spent long hours at a conference [organized by Richard Perle and] sponsored by the AEI in Aspen secluded together with Vice President Cheney and Deputy Secretary of Defense Paul Wolfowitz. The Bush speech clearly represented a triumph for the Cheney-Rumsfeld-Wolfowitz axis in the administration over the State Department, which was eager to offer the Palestinians a provisional state immediately. (Rosenblum, 2002)[93]

---

[93] See also Milbank, 2002. In a later column, Rosenblum (2003) noted: "Now [Sharansky] delivered the same message to Cheney: No matter how many conditions Bush placed on the creation of a Palestinian state under Arafat, any such announcement would constitute a reward for two years of non-stop terror against Israeli civilians. The normally laconic Cheney shot to attention when he heard these words. 'But your own government has already signed off on this,' he told Sharansky, confirming the latter's worst suspicions. Sharansky nevertheless repeated, as Cheney scribbled notes, that without the removal of Arafat and the entire junta from Tunis, the creation of an atmosphere in which Palestinians could express themselves without fear of reprisal, and the cessation of incitement against Israel in the Palestinian schools and media peace is impossible. President Bush's upcoming speech had already undergone 30 drafts at that point. It was about to undergo another crucial shift based on Sharansky's conversation with Cheney. Two days later, on June 24, 2002, President Bush announced at the outset, 'Peace requires a new and different Palestinian leadership.' He did not mention Yasir Arafat once."

Both Cheney and Rumsfeld had close personal relationships with Kenneth Adelman, a former Ford and Reagan administration official (Drew, 2003). Adelman wrote op-ed pieces in *The Washington Post* and *The Wall Street Journal* in the period leading up to the war, and he, along with Wolfowitz and Irving Lewis "Scooter" Libby (Cheney's chief of staff), were guests of Cheney for a victory celebration in the immediate aftermath of the war on April 13th, 2003 (Woodward, 2004, pp. 409–412). Adelman has excellent neocon credentials. He was a member of the Committee on the Present Danger in the 1970s and was Deputy UN Ambassador during the Reagan administration; he also worked under Donald Rumsfeld on three different occasions. He was a signatory to the April 3rd, 2002, letter of PNAC to President Bush calling for Saddam Hussein's ouster and increased support for Israel. The letter stated, "Israel is targeted in part because it is our friend, and in part because it is an island of liberal, democratic principles—American principles—in a sea of tyranny, intolerance, and hatred." The advocacy of war with Iraq was linked to advancing Israeli interests:

> If we do not move against Saddam Hussein and his regime, the damage our Israeli friends and we have suffered until now may someday appear but a prelude to much greater horrors. . . . Israel's fight against terrorism is our fight. Israel's victory is an important part of our victory. For reasons both moral and strategic, we need to stand with Israel in its fight against terrorism. (PNAC, 2002)[94]

Adelman's wife, Carol, is affiliated with the Hudson Institute, a neoconservative think tank.

Cheney's role in the ascendancy of the neocons in the Bush administration is particularly important: as head of the transition team, he and Libby were able to staff the subcabinet levels of the State Department (John Bolton) and the Defense Department (Wolfowitz, Feith) with key supporters of the neocon agenda. Libby was a close personal friend of Cheney, whose views "echo many of Wolfowitz's policies"; he "is considered a hawk among hawks and was an early supporter of military action against terrorism and particularly against Iraq" (Chicago Model United Nations, 2001, p. 11). He is Jewish and has a long history of involvement in Zionist causes and as the attorney for Marc Rich. Libby and Cheney were involved in pressuring the CIA to color intelligence

---

[94] Other signatories include William Kristol, Gary Bauer, Jeffrey Bell, William J. Bennett, Ellen Bork, Linda Chavez, Eliot Cohen, Midge Decter, Thomas Donnelly, Nicholas Eberstadt, Hillel Fradkin, Frank Gaffney, Jeffrey Gedmin, Reuel Marc Gerecht, Charles Hill, Bruce P. Jackson, Donald Kagan, Robert Kagan, John Lehman, Tod Lindberg, Rich Lowry, Clifford May, Joshua Muravchik, Martin Peretz, Richard Perle, Daniel Pipes, Norman Podhoretz, Stephen P. Rosen, Randy Scheunemann, Gary Schmitt, William Schneider, Jr., Marshall Wittmann, and R. James Woolsey.

reports to fit with their desire for a war with Iraq (Pincus & Priest, 2003; Bamford, 2004, pp. 368–370). Libby entered the neocon orbit when he was "captivated" while taking a political science course from Wolfowitz at Yale, and he worked under Wolfowitz in the Reagan and the George H. W. Bush administrations (Keller, 2002; see also Woodward, 2004, p. 48). He was the coauthor (with Wolfowitz) of the ill-fated draft of the Defense Planning Guidance document of 1992, which advocated U.S. dominance over all of Eurasia and urged preventing any other country from even contemplating challenging U.S. hegemony (Lobe, 2002a; Mann, 2004, pp. 208–210). (Cheney was Secretary of Defense at that time.) After an uproar, the document was radically altered, but this blueprint for U.S. hegemony remains central to neocon attitudes since the collapse of the Soviet Union.

Donald Rumsfeld (1932–2021)

As noted above, Rumsfeld had deep links with neoconservative think tanks and individual Jews such as Kenneth Adelman, who began his career working for Rumsfeld when he headed the Office of Economic Opportunity in the Nixon administration. Another close associate is Robert A. Goldwin, a student of Leo Strauss and Rumsfeld's deputy both at NATO and at the Gerald Ford White House; Goldwin was also a resident scholar at the AEI.

Rumsfeld also has a long history of appealing to Jewish and Israeli causes. In his 1964 campaign for reelection to Congress as representative from a district on the North Shore of Chicago with an important Jewish constituency, he emphasized Soviet persecution of Jews and introduced a bill on this topic in the House. After the 1967 Six-Day War, he urged the United States not to demand that Israel withdraw to its previous borders and he criticized delays in sending U.S. military hardware to Israel (Decter, 2003, pp. 41–43). More recently, as Secretary of Defense in the George W. Bush administration, Rumsfeld was praised by the ZOA for distancing himself from the phrase "occupied territories," referring to them as the "so-called occupied territories" (ZOA, 2002).[95] Rumsfeld was apparently nonplussed at Mossad dominating the U.S. Defense Department during his tenure there, reportedly stating, "I don't run this building. Mossad does" (in Wilkerson, 2025).

Despite these links with neoconservatives and Jewish causes (likely motivated by his career aspirations), Rumsfeld emerges as less an ideologue and less a passionate advocate for war with Iraq than Cheney. Bob Woodward

---

[95] ZOA National President Morton A. Klein said: "Israel has the greater historical, legal, and moral right to Judea, Samaria, and Gaza. At the very least, those areas should be called disputed territories, not occupied territories, since the term 'occupied' clearly suggests that the 'occupier' has no right to be there. We strongly applaud Secretary Rumsfeld's courageous and principled stance in distancing himself from the 'occupied territory' fallacy."

(2004, p. 416) describes him as lacking the feverish intensity of Cheney, as a dispassionate "defense technocrat" who, unlike Cheney, Wolfowitz, and Feith, would have been content if the United States had not gone to war with Iraq.

Daniel Pipes (1949–)

Many neoconservatives work mainly as lobbyists and propagandists. Rather than attempt to describe this massive infrastructure in its entirety, I profile Daniel Pipes as a prototypical example of the highly competent Jewish lobbyist. Pipes is the son of Richard Pipes, the Harvard professor who, as noted above, was an early neocon and an expert on the Soviet Union. He is the director of MEF, a columnist at the *New York Post* and *The Jerusalem Post*, and has appeared on the Fox News Channel. Pipes is described as "An authoritative commentator on the Middle East" by *The Wall Street Journal*, according to the masthead of his website.[96] A former official in the Departments of State and Defense, he has taught at the University of Chicago, Harvard University, and the U.S. Naval War College. He is the author of numerous books on the Middle East, Islam, and other political topics; his book *Militant Islam Reaches America* (2002), was a polemic against political Islam, arguing that militant Islam is the greatest threat to the West since the Cold War. He served on the "Special Task Force on Terrorism and Technology" at the Department of Defense, has testified before many congressional committees, and has served on four presidential campaigns.

The MEF issues a quasi-academic publication, the *Middle East Quarterly*. A 2002 MEQ article on weapons of mass destruction claimed that Syria "has more destructive capabilities" than Iraq or Iran. The *Middle East Intelligence Bulletin* "specializes in covering the seamy side of Lebanese and Syrian politics" (Whitaker, 2002), an effort aimed at depicting these regimes as worthy of forcible change by the U.S. or Israeli military.

Martin Kramer is "senior and past editor" of the *Middle East Quarterly*. Kramer is also affiliated with Tel Aviv University's Moshe Dayan Center for Middle Eastern and African Studies. His book, *Ivory Towers on Sand: The Failure of Middle Eastern Studies in America* (2001), has been a major impetus behind the recent effort to prevent criticism of Israel on college campuses. The book was warmly reviewed in the *Weekly Standard*, whose editor, Bill Kristol, is a member of the MEF along with Kramer. Kristol wrote that "Kramer has performed a crucial service by exposing intellectual rot in a scholarly field of capital importance to national wellbeing" (in Whitaker, 2002).

The MEF also targets universities through its campus speakers bureau, seeking to correct "inaccurate Middle Eastern curricula in American

---

[96] www.danielpipes.org

education," by addressing "biases" and "basic errors" and providing "better information" than students can get from the many "irresponsible" professors that it believes lurk in U.S. universities.

The MEF is behind Campus Watch, an organization responsible for repressing academic discussion of Middle East issues at U.S. universities. Campus Watch (n.d.) compiles profiles on recommended professors, professors to avoid, supporters and opponents of the Boycott, Divestment and Sanction movement, and professors who declared solidarity with the Palestinians.

Pipes is also on the Advisory Board of Endowment for Middle East Truth, which describes itself on its website as a "think tank and policy center with an unabashedly pro-America and pro-Israel stance. EMET (which means truth in Hebrew) prides itself on challenging the falsehoods and misrepresentations that abound in U.S. Middle East policy." Its mission is "to educate policy-makers by providing pertinent information to senators and representatives to make informed decisions that will improve American security and the security of America's ally, Israel."

Jewish Institute for National Security of America (JINSA)[97]

Rather than profile all of the many neoconservative think tanks and lobbying groups, I will describe JINSA as a prototypical example. In 2025 JINSA describes itself as follows on their website:

> [JINSA] is dedicated to advancing U.S. national security interests in the Middle East, of which a critical pillar is a robust U.S.-Israel security relationship. JINSA believes that Israel is the most capable and critical U.S. security partner in the 21st century and that a strong America is the best guarantor of Western civilization.

Typical of Jewish intellectual movements is that Jewish interests are submerged in a rhetoric of American interests and ethical universalism—in this case, the idea that Israel is a beacon of democracy.

In addition to a core of prominent neoconservative Jews mentioned above, JINSA's advisory board includes and has included a bevy of non-Jewish retired U.S. military officers, a variety of non-Jewish political figures, and foreign policy analysts with access to the media who are staunch supporters of Israel. As is typical of Jewish intellectual movements, JINSA is well funded and has succeeded in bringing in high-profile non-Jews who often act on behalf of its policies. For example, the former head of the Iraq occupation government and recipient of JINSA's Flag and General Officers Trip to Israel, General Jay

---

[97] Formerly the Jewish Institute for National Security *Affairs*, from its founding in 1976 to 2017.

Garner, signed an October 2000 JINSA statement saying that "the Israel Defense Forces have exercised remarkable restraint in the face of lethal violence orchestrated by the leadership of [the] Palestinian Authority." One would have to be completely subservient to the Israel Lobby to say something similar in the wake of the Gaza genocide.

JINSA reflects the recent trend of American Jewish activist groups not simply to support Israeli policies but to support the Israeli right wing. For JINSA:

> "[R]egime change" by any means necessary in Iraq, Iran, Syria, Saudi Arabia, and the Palestinian Authority is an urgent imperative. Anyone who dissents—be it Colin Powell's State Department, the CIA or career military officers—is committing heresy against articles of faith that effectively hold there is no difference between U.S. and Israeli national security interests, and that the only way to assure continued safety and prosperity for both countries is through hegemony in the Middle East—a hegemony achieved with the traditional Cold War recipe of feints, force, clientism and covert action. (Vest, 2002)

Note the exclusionary, us-versus-them attitude typical of the Jewish intellectual and political movements covered in *CofC*.

Part of JINSA's effectiveness comes from recruiting non-Jews who gain from increased defense spending or are willing to be spokesmen in return for fees and travel to Israel. The bulk of JINSA's budget is spent on taking a host of retired U.S. generals and admirals to Israel, where JINSA facilitates meetings between Israeli officials and retired but still-influential U.S. flag officers. These officers then write op-ed pieces and sign letters and advertisements championing JINSA's positions. In one such statement (from October 2000, mentioned above), issued soon after the outbreak of the latest intifada, twenty-six JINSAns of retired flag rank, including many from the advisory board, struck a moralizing tone, characterizing Palestinian violence as a "perversion of military ethics" and holding that "America's role as facilitator in this process should never yield to America's responsibility as a friend to Israel," because "friends don't leave friends on the battlefield" (Vest, 2002). Sowing seeds for the future, JINSA also takes U.S. service academy cadets to Israel each summer and sponsors a lecture series at the Army, Navy, and Air Force academies.

JINSA also patronizes companies in the defense industry that stand to gain from the drive for total war. "Almost every retired officer who sits on JINSA's board of advisers or has participated in its Israel trips or signed a JINSA letter works or has worked with military contractors who do business with the Pentagon and Israel" (Vest, 2002). For example, JINSA advisory board members Admiral Leon Edney, Admiral David Jeremiah, and Lieutenant General Charles

May, all retired, have served Northrop Grumman or its subsidiaries as either consultants or board members. Northrop Grumman has built ships for the Israeli Navy and sold F-16 avionics and E-2C Hawkeye planes to the Israeli Air Force, as well as the Longbow radar system to the Israeli Army for use in its attack helicopters. It also works with Tamam, a subsidiary of Israeli Aircraft Industries, to produce drones.

JINSA is supported not only by defense contractor money but also by deeply committed Zionists, notably Irving Moscowitz (1928–2016), the California bingo magnate who also provided financial support to the AEI. Moscowitz not only sent millions of dollars a year to far-right Israeli West Bank settler groups like Ateret Cohanim, but he has also funded land purchases in key Arab areas around Jerusalem. Moscowitz provided the money that enabled the 1996 reopening of a tunnel under the Temple Mount/Haram al-Sharif, which resulted in seventy deaths due to rioting. Also involved in funding JINSA is New York investment banker Lawrence Kadish, who also contributes to Republican causes. Again, we see the effects of the most committed Jews. People like Moscowitz have an enormous effect because they use their wealth to advance their people's interests, a very common pattern among wealthy Jews (MacDonald, 2003a).

The integration of JINSA with the U.S. defense establishment can be seen in the program for its 2001 Jackson Award Dinner, an annual event named after Senator Henry Jackson that draws an "A-list" group of politicians and defense celebrities. At the dinner were representatives of U.S. defense industries (the dinner was sponsored by Boeing), as well as the following Defense Department personnel: Under Secretary of Defense Paul Wolfowitz; Under Secretary of Defense Dov Zakheim (an ordained rabbi); Assistant Secretary of the Navy John Young; Dr. William Schneider, Jr., the Chairman of the Defense Science Board; the Honorable Mark Rosenker, Senior Military Advisor to the President; Admiral William Fallon, Vice Chief of Naval Operations; General John Keane, Vice Chief of Staff of the Army; General Michael Williams, Vice Commandant of the Marines; Lieutenant General Lance Lord, Assistant Vice Chief of Staff of the Air Force. Also present were a large number of U.S. flag and general officers who were alumni of JINSA trips to Israel, as well as assorted congressmen, a U.S. senator, and a variety of Israeli military and political figures. The 2002 Jackson Award Dinner, sponsored by Northrop Grumman, honored Paul Wolfowitz. Dick Cheney was a previous recipient of the award.

The 2019 Award Dinner featured Senator Lindsey Graham, recipient of the Henry M. "Scoop" Jackson Distinguished Service Award. It was attended by many U.S. military officers and sponsored by prominent defense contractors, including Raytheon, Boeing, Lockheed Martin, Pratt Whitney, and General Dynamics.

The activities of JINSA are a good illustration of the point that whatever the deeply held beliefs of the non-Jews who are involved in the neoconservative movement, financial motives and military careerism are also of considerable importance—a testimony to the extent to which neoconservatism has permeated the political and military establishments of the United States. A similar statement could be made about the deep influence of neoconservatism among intellectuals generally.

NEOCON FAMILY TIES—AND THE UKRAINE WAR

Intertwined Jewish power families are an important aspect of Jewish history, cementing business relationships by creating networks of close relatives who married only among themselves. Paul Johnson (1987/1988, p. 257) notes that the Court Jews of seventeenth- and eighteenth-century Europe married exclusively among themselves and developed a large network of financial families whose resources could be organized to support particular goals. For example, Samuel Oppenheimer (1630–1703) was able to organize the resources of a "vast network" of such families, virtually all of whom were interrelated. "It became rare for Court Jews to marry any other kind," so that they in effect became a separate endogamous class within the Jewish community. In particular, S. Stern (1950, p. 28) notes that Oppenheimer's son served as his general representative in the Empire and that his two sons-in-law were stationed in the important trading center of Frankfurt; his brother Moses was the principal agent in Heidelberg, and, in Hanover, he was represented by another close relative (Leffmann Behrends) and his son; in Italy, his interests were supervised by his grandson, and, in Amsterdam and Cleves, his relatives, the Gumpertz family, were in charge.

We see echoes of that in the contemporary world, including among the neocons. As with the other Jewish intellectual movements I have studied, neoconservatives have a history of mutual admiration, close, mutually supportive personal, professional, and familial relationships, as well as focused cooperation in pursuit of common goals. For example, Norman Podhoretz, the former editor of *Commentary*, is the father of John Podhoretz, a neoconservative editor and columnist. Norman Podhoretz is also the father-in-law of Elliott Abrams whose neocon credentials are described here. Norman's wife, Midge Decter, published a hagiographic biography of Secretary of Defense Donald Rumsfeld in 2003, whose number-two and number-three deputies at the Pentagon, respectively, were Wolfowitz and Feith (Lobe, 2003a). He originally helped Wolfowitz obtain a job with the Arms Control and Disarmament Agency in 1973. In 1982, Perle, as Deputy Secretary of Defense for International Security Policy, hired Feith for a position as his Special Counsel, and then as

Deputy Assistant Secretary for Negotiations Policy. In 2001, Deputy Secretary of Defense Wolfowitz helped Feith obtain an appointment as Undersecretary for Policy. Feith then appointed Perle as chairman of the Defense Policy Board. This is only the tip of a very large iceberg.

Ethnic networking and ties cemented by marriage were on display in the 2014 U.S.-supported coup that overthrew the government of Ukraine in favor of a government aligned with the West. U.S. involvement was led by Assistant Secretary of State Victoria Nuland whose phone conversation with Geoffrey Pyatt, U.S. Ambassador to Ukraine, made clear her preferences for the new leader of Ukraine. Nuland was the principal foreign policy adviser to Vice President Dick Cheney during the George W. Bush administration. Since then, she has served in both the Obama and Biden administrations. She was most recently (2021–2024) the Under Secretary of State for Political Affairs and was deeply involved in promoting the U.S. involvement in the Ukraine war which began in 2022 as a direct consequence of the coup of 2014 and pressure thereafter to make Ukraine a member of NATO, a red line for Russian president Vladimir Putin.

Nuland is married to Robert Kagan, a prominent neocon linked to liberal politics—he supported Hillary Clinton in 2016. The Kagan family is another Jewish neocon family tree, beginning with Robert's father, Donald Kagan, a Yale historian whose history of the Peloponnesian War has been used by neocons as a rationale for invasions of countries in the Middle East. Donald Kagan was also a signatory to a 2002 letter to George W. Bush distributed by Bill Kristol's PNAC equating threats to Israel from Middle Eastern countries with threats to the U.S.

Donald Kagan's sons, Frederick Kagan (the conservative AEI) and Robert Kagan (the liberal Brookings Institution) are neocon stalwarts and ensconced on both sides of the American political spectrum. For example, Donald, Robert, and Frederick are all signatories to the neocon manifesto, *Rebuilding America's Defenses* (2000), put out by PNAC ("Frederick Kagan," 2024). They and their wives are all graduates of elite universities and well entrenched in the neocon think tank/government infrastructure. Frederick's wife Kimberly (née Kessler) is the founder and head of the Institute for the Study of War and has published op-eds in major U.S. media and university presses (Harvard, University of Michigan) ("Kimberly Kagan," 2024).

Although U.S. policy toward Ukraine likely stems from other issues besides the neocon hostility toward Russia (the latter due to issues such as Putin's crackdown on the oligarchs, Russia's support of Israel's enemies, Iran and Syria, and perhaps the long history of anti-Semitism in Russia; see MacDonald, 2008b), there can be little doubt that neocon support for the Ukraine war is well represented on both sides of the political aisle in the U.S.

CONCLUSION

To bring this up to date, since writing my 2004 paper the wars in Iraq and Afghanistan have been concluded, with the general consensus that they were disastrous mistakes, and now the U.S. is engaging in a dangerous and costly proxy war with Russia in Ukraine that has the possibility of a full-scale U.S.-Russia war. The neocons remain dominant in U.S. foreign policy, whether in the Democrat or Republican parties (O. Williams, 2023). As Ron Unz (2023b) notes:

> Despite the unprecedented strategic disaster of the Iraq War, the Neocons fully retained their hold on the Republican Party's foreign policy, while their Democratic counterparts achieved the same success across the political aisle. Thus, when the manifest failures of the Bush Administration led to the overwhelming victory of Barack Obama in 2008, Bush Neocons were merely replaced by Obama Neocons. Donald Trump's unexpected triumph in 2016 brought to power the Trump Neocons such as Mike Pompeo and John Bolton, who were then succeeded in 2020 by Biden Neocons Antony Blinken and Victoria Nuland.

In the wake of the U.S. attack on Iran in 2025, John Mearsheimer stated that the neocons had triumphed in the second Trump administration despite Trump's antiwar rhetoric and previous neocon animosity toward Trump (Mearsheimer, 2025b). To be sure, several prominent neocons have apologized for their promoting the Iraq War. In his *Corrosion of Conservatism: Why I Left the Right*, Max Boot (2018, p. 54) writes, "I regret advocating the invasion and feel guilty about all the lives lost. It was a chastening lesson in the limits of American power." But, like the neocons in general, he shows he is a liberal on social issues and complains that the Republicans are too committed to isolationism (p. 165). He now writes for liberal publications and is a fervent supporter of the U.S.'s proxy war in Ukraine. Other contemporary neocons who supported the Iraq War have also repented, including David Frum ("a grave and costly error") and Robert Kagan (2023) ("It didn't go exactly the way we wanted it to, certainly to say the least"). But all have returned to their liberal roots on social issues despite never abandoning their views on foreign policy (O. Williams, 2023).

The neocon interest in destroying the Arab-Muslim world intersects with their interest in destroying Russia via victory in the Ukraine war. As noted, Russia has supported both Iran and Syria, both of which, especially Iran, are seen as enemies of Israel. It is thus no surprise that today's neocons (including veteran neocon Bill Kristol) were furious when Florida governor Ron DeSantis (along with the much-hated Donald Trump—who can forget neocon "Never Trump" hysteria in the 2016 election campaign when comparisons to Hitler abounded; see MacDonald, 2016b) stated in 2023 that the dispute between Russia and Ukraine will bring Russia and China into closer ties and should be thought of as a simple territorial dispute and not relevant to U.S. national interests (Wulfsohn, 2023). In the mainstream media, former Fox News host Tucker Carlson has also championed such views, a likely reason he lost his position at the network.

*   *   *

The rapid rise and immense influence of the neoconservatives make them a remarkable example of Jewish organization and influence. Individuals with strong Jewish identities maintain close ties to Israeli politicians and military figures and to Jewish activist organizations and pro-Israeli lobbying groups while occupying influential policy-making positions in the defense and foreign policy establishment. Despite having no substantial constituency within the electorate, these same individuals, as well as a chorus of other prominent Jews, have routine access to the most prestigious media outlets in the United States. People who criticize Israel, however, are routinely vilified and subjected to professional and personal abuse (Findley, 1989; MacDonald, 2003a).

Perhaps the most telling feature of this entire state of affairs is the surreal fact that in this discourse Jewish identity and affiliations of the main figures are rarely mentioned, and never by their supporters. When Charles Krauthammer, Bill Kristol, Max Boot, Jennifer Rubin, or the legions of other prominent media figures write their reflexively pro-Israel pieces in *The New York Times*, *The Wall Street Journal*, or opine on the Fox News Network of MSNBC, there is never any mention that they are Jewish Americans who have an intense ethnic interest in Israel. When Richard Perle authors a report for an Israeli think tank; is on the board of directors of an Israeli newspaper; maintains close personal ties with prominent Israelis, especially those associated with the Israeli right; has worked for an Israeli defense company; and, according to credible reports, was discovered by the FBI passing classified information to Israel—when, despite all of this, he is a central figure in the network of those pushing for wars to rearrange the entire politics of the Middle East in Israel's favor, and with nary a soul having the courage to mention the obvious overriding Jewish loyalty apparent in Perle's actions, that is indeed a breathtaking display of power.

In this chapter I have provided a small glimpse of the incredible array of Jewish pro-Israel activist organizations, their funding, their access to the media, and their power over the political process. Taken as a whole, neoconservatism is an excellent illustration of the key traits behind the success of Jewish activism: ethnocentrism, intelligence and wealth, psychological intensity, and aggressiveness (MacDonald, 2003a). Now imagine a similar level of organization, commitment, and funding directed toward changing the U.S. immigration system put into law in 1924 and 1952, or inaugurating the revolution in civil rights, or the post-1965 countercultural revolution. In the case of the immigration laws we see the same use of prominent non-Jews to attain Jewish goals, the same access to the major media, and the same ability to have a decisive influence on the political process by establishing lobbying organizations, recruiting non-Jews as important players, funneling financial and media support to political candidates who agree with their point of view, and providing effective leadership in government (see Ch. 8). Given this state of affairs, one can easily see how Jews, despite being a tiny minority of the U.S. population, have been able to transform the country to serve their interests. It's a story that has been played out many times in Western history, but the possible effects now seem enormous, not only for Europeans but literally for everyone on the planet, as Israel and its hegemonic ally restructure the politics of the world.

5

JEWISH INVOLVEMENT IN THE PSYCHOANALYTIC MOVEMENT

The familiar caricature of the bearded and monocled Freudian analyst probing his reclining patient for memories of toilet training gone awry and parentally directed lust is now an anachronism, as is the professional practice of that mostly empty and confabulatory art. How such an elaborate theory could have become so widely accepted—on the basis of no systematic evidence or critical experiments, and in the face of chronic failures of therapeutic intervention in all of the major classes of mental illness (schizophrenia, mania, and depression)—is something that sociologists of science and popular culture have yet to fully explain.

— Paul Churchland, 1995, p. 181

The thesis of this chapter is that it is impossible to understand psychoanalysis as a "science," or more properly as a political movement, without taking into account the role of Judaism. Sigmund Freud is a prime example of a Jewish social scientist whose writings were influenced by his Jewish identity and his negative attributions regarding gentile culture as the source of anti-Semitism.

The discussion of Jewish involvement in the psychoanalytic movement was until recently, "as though by tacit agreement, beyond the pale" (Yerushalmi, 1991, p. 98). Nevertheless, the Jewish involvement in psychoanalysis—

the "Jewish science"—has been apparent to those inside and outside the movement since its inception (p. 98):

> History made psychoanalysis a "Jewish science." It continued to be attacked as such. It was destroyed in Germany, Italy, and Austria and exiled to the four winds, as such. It continues even now to be perceived as such by enemies and friends alike. Of course there are by now distinguished analysts who are not Jews. . . . But the vanguard of the movement over the last fifty years has remained predominantly Jewish, as it was from the beginning.

In addition to constituting the core of the leadership and the intellectual vanguard of the movement, Jews have also constituted the majority of the movement's members. In 1906 all seventeen members of the movement were Jewish, and they strongly identified as Jews (Klein, 1981, p. 32). A 1971 study found that 62.1 percent of their sample of American psychoanalysts identified themselves as having a Jewish cultural affinity, compared with only 16.7 percent indicating a Protestant affinity and 2.6 percent a Catholic affinity. An additional 18.6 percent indicated no cultural affinity, a percentage considerably higher than the other categories of mental health professionals and suggesting that the percentage of psychoanalysts with a Jewish background was even higher than 62 percent (Henry et al., 1971, p. 27).[98]

The Budapest School of Psychoanalysis

Psychoanalysis in Hungary presents a similar picture. The Hungarian Psychoanalytical Society (later the Budapest School of Psychoanalysis) was established in 1913 by five Jews (Sándor Ferenczi, Lajos Lévy, István Hollós, Hugo Ignotus, and Sándor Radó) and became quite influential in psychoanalysis generally and in intellectual circles in Hungary in particular; in Hungary it had a decisive influence on culture generally, including medicine, the social sciences, painting, literature, and literary criticism (Mészáros, 2014, p. 27). Psychoanalysts were almost exclusively Jews and politically on the left in Hungary during the early twentieth century: "The vast majority of the first psychoanalysts—regardless of gender and geographic location—were of Jewish origin" (Borgos, 2006).

The most prominent was Sándor Ferenczi, a disciple of Freud. Ferenczi wrote in 1909 to Freud about a lecture to the Galileo Circle, the vanguard of

---

[98] A 2024 search indicated that the ethnic composition of the editorial board of *The Psychoanalytic Quarterly* continues to have a large representation of Jewish names, indicating that psychoanalysis remains fundamentally an ethnic movement.

Bolshevism in Hungary—"the core of the progressive, radical and socialist elite that played a crucial role in the revolutionary movements and events in 1918 and 1919" (Erős, 2019, p. 6):

> So, today was the lecture about "Everyday Life." I was happy that I could speak before approximately three hundred young and enthusiastic medical students, who listened to my (or, that is to say, your) words with bated breath. . . . The medical students surrounded me and wanted me to promise them, at any price, to tell them more about these things. I asked for time to think it over. Budapest seems, after all, not to be such an absolutely bad place. The audience was naturally composed of nine tenths Jews! (Brabant et al., 1993, p. 91–92, in Erős, 2019, p. 7)

Ferenczi was refused a position at Budapest University in 1913 and 1918 but, along with several other professors of Jewish origin (e.g., Géza Révész, Imre Hermann, Sándor Radó) was provided a professorship in 1919 after the Béla Kun-led communist revolution despite "the faculty's vehement resistance" (Erős, 2019, p. 13).

> As a matter of fact, quite a few psychoanalysts, future analysts, and sympathisers (e.g., Jenő Hárnik, Sándor Radó, Géza Róheim, Imre Hermann, Sándor Varjas, Jenő Varga) co-operated—more or less actively—with the Communist government. There is an element of truth in the exaggerated statement of the sociologist Oszkár Jászi, the leading theorist and politician of the bourgeois radicalism, who wrote in his 1920 book *Hungarian Calvary—Hungarian Resurrection*: "During the revolutions . . . Freudianism was the idol of Communist youth." (Erős, 2018, p. 44)

> After 1919 the gates of the university became more closed than ever before. A numerus clausus was introduced in 1920 which seriously limited the number of Jewish students who could be admitted to Hungarian higher education institutions. In fact, Hungary was the first country in Central Europe which introduced anti-Jewish laws, already several years before the Nazi takeover in Germany [Kovács, 1994]. Furthermore, the number of women admissible to universities was also radically restricted, mostly under pressure from right-wing, conservative medical professors, such as . . . Professor Jendrassik.
>
> None of the members of Ferenczi's psychoanalytic circle remained in their positions after August 1919 [when the Béla Kun regime was toppled]. Radó, Alexander and Hárnik emigrated to Berlin, joining the Berlin association and institute, thus founding the core of the Hungarian psychoanalytic diaspora there. (Erős, 2019, p. 16)

Ferenczi's professorship was thus short-lived. In a letter to Freud (August 1919) he was clearly oblivious to the reasons why Hungarians would resent the actions of the Kun government against Hungarian culture and single out Jews as responsible despite the vast overrepresentation of Jews in the Kun government:

> [T]he ruthless clerical-anti-Semitic spirit seems to have eked out a victory. If everything does not deceive, we Hungarian Jews are now facing a period of brutal persecution of Jews. They will, I think, have cured us in a very short time of the illusion with which we were brought up, namely, that we are 'Hungarians of Jewish faith.' I picture Hungarian anti-Semitism commensurate with the national character—to be more brutal than the petty-hateful type of the Austrians. . . . Personally, one will have to take this trauma as an occasion to abandon certain prejudices brought along from the nursery and to come to terms with the bitter truth of being, as a Jew, really without a country. (in Erős, 2019, p. 17)

In a manner quite similar to that of the Frankfurt School discussed in the following chapter, Ferenczi presents anti-Semitism as due to tendencies apparent in other religions, whereas Judaism is depicted (falsely) as fostering intellectual freedom:

> The Jewish ritual reduces religiosity to keeping certain rules (prayers, ten commandments, fasting), that is to say it moulds religion into "compelled actions"—but beyond these, it permits total intellectual freedom and freedom of action. The Jews use this freedom to the full, and are more audacious, more unabashed and more egotistic, primarily in the material, but also in the moral sphere. On the other hand, Buddhism and Christianity bring with them an enormous *verdrangung* (dominating instinct not through *understanding*, but via infantile repression and *self-denial*). It is the Jews who, for Christians, represent their own unconscious "guilty" and audacious inclinations. It is the case that man "loathes his sins," [I detest him like I detest my sins—says the Hungarian proverb]. So he detests the Jew. (in Keve, 2012, p. 103)

Ferenczi founded the International Psychoanalytic Association and the Hungarian Psychoanalytic Association; his legacy is carried on by the International Sándor Ferenczi Network which holds conferences and publishes collections of Ferenczi's works. His work continues to be part of the curriculum of the most prestigious university in Hungary, ELTE University. As noted, almost all of the Budapest School members were Jews and politically on the left, and psychoanalysis in Hungary continues to be largely Jewish (Borgos, 2021, Chs. 1-2, 5). Ferenczi was buried with Jewish rites in a Jewish cemetery.

"Numerous figures from our medical, literary and artistic establishments were in attendance. Also present were Anna Freud, Martin Freud, Paul Federn and Helene Deutsch" (Szekacs-Weisz & Keve, 2012, p. 2).

PSYCHOANALYSIS AND SUBVERSION OF CULTURE

We have seen that a common component of Jewish intellectual activity since the Enlightenment has been to subject gentile culture to negative critiques—to place the culture of the outgroup on the couch, so to speak. Freud's ideas have often been labeled as subversive. Indeed,

> [Freud] was convinced that it was in the very nature of psychoanalytic doctrine to appear shocking and subversive. On board ship to America, he did not feel that he was bringing that country a new panacea. With his typically dry wit he told his traveling companions, "We are bringing them the plague." (Mannoni, 1971, p. 168)

And a plague it has been.

Peter Gay labels Freud's work generally as "subversive" (1987, p. 140), his sexual ideology in particular as "deeply subversive for his time" (1988, p. 149), and he describes his *Totem and Taboo* as containing "subversive conjectures" (1988, p. 327) in its analysis of culture. "While the implications of Darwin's views were threatening and unsettling, they were not quite so directly abrasive, not quite so unrespectable, as Freud's views on infantile sexuality, the ubiquity of perversions, and the dynamic power of unconscious urges" (1987, p. 144).

There was a general perception among many anti-Semites that Jewish intellectuals were subverting German culture in the period prior to 1933 (SAID, Ch. 2), and psychoanalysis was a major aspect of this concern. A great deal of hostility to psychoanalysis centered around the perceived threat of psychoanalysis to Christian sexual ethics, including the acceptance of masturbation and premarital sex (Kurzweil, 1989, p. 18). Psychoanalysis became a target of gentiles decrying the Jewish subversion of culture—"the decadent influence of Judaism," as one writer termed it (see Klein, 1981, p. 144). In 1928 Carl Christian Clemen, a professor of ethnology at the University of Bonn, reacted strongly to *The Future of an Illusion*, Freud's analysis of religious belief in terms of infantile needs. Clemen decried the psychoanalytic tendency to find sex everywhere, a tendency he attributed to the Jewish composition of the movement: "One could explain this by the particular circles from which its advocates and perhaps, too, the patients it treats, principally hail" (in Gay, 1988, p. 537). Freud's books were burned in the May 1933 book burnings in Germany, and when the Germans entered Vienna in 1938, they ordered Freud to leave and abolished the Internationaler Psychoanalytischer Verlag (International Psychoanalytic Publishing).

In Hungary a professor of zoology remarked on the negative effects of psychoanalysis from an evolutionary perspective:

> István Apáthy, professor of zoology in Kolozsvár, who founded a eugenics section within the Hungarian Social Sciences Association in 1914, expressed his opinion on psychoanalysis at the inaugural meeting of the section: "This sensual, erotic trend, which is unrestrainedly sensual in sexual matters, is always ready to sacrifice the interests of the community and the guarantees of healthy species development [the focus of eugenics] for the benefit or pleasure of the individual. This erotic tendency has most recently been recruited in particular by a thoroughly silly and unscientific Viennese school, the school of Siegmund [sic] Freud, which, under the guise of the scientific method of psychoanalysis, spreads a corrupting world view, which is very conspicuously marked by one of the most characteristic badges of our time, the desire for pleasure at all costs." (Erős, 2015, p. 71n6)

Interestingly, Ferenczi advocated non-discrimination against homosexuals and transgendered people on the grounds that they did not reproduce and thus did not threaten society (Mészáros, 2014, pp. 18–19). And he theorized that pedophilic actions resulted in trauma only because "guilt-ridden" adults disapproved and wanted such acts punished (Ferenczi & Dupont, 1995, p. 178). He was an advocate for Freud's sexual repression concept as causing a wide range of societal ills; he considered it key to the social sciences.

In the United States, by the second decade of the twentieth century Freud was firmly associated with the movement for sexual freedom and social reform, and had become the target of social conservatives (Torrey, 1992, pp. 16ff). As late as 1956 a psychiatrist writing in *The American Journal of Psychiatry* complained, "Is it possible that we are developing the equivalent of a secular church, supported by government monies, staffed by a genital-level apostolate unwittingly dispensing a broth of existential atheism, hedonism, and other dubious religio-philosophical ingredients?" (H. Johnson, 1956, p. 40).

The continuing role of psychoanalysis in the movement toward sexual liberation can be seen in a 1994 debate over teenage sexuality. An article in the *Los Angeles Times* (Granberry, 1994) noted the opposition of the American Civil Liberties Union and Planned Parenthood to a school program that advocated teenage celibacy. Sheldon Zablow, a psychiatrist and spokesperson for this perspective, stated, "Repeated studies show that if you try to repress sexual feelings, they may come out later in far more dangerous ways—sexual abuse, rape." This psychoanalytic fantasy was compounded by Zablow's claim that sexual abstinence has never worked in all of human history—a claim that indicates his lack of awareness of historical data on sexual behavior in the West (including Jewish sexual behavior), at least from the Middle Ages until the twentieth century (e.g., Le Roy Ladurie, 1977/1987). I am not aware of any stratified traditional human society (and certainly not Muslim societies) that has taken the view that it is impossible and undesirable to prevent teenage sexual activity, especially by girls. As J. J. Goldberg (1996, p. 46) notes, "within the world of liberal organizations like the ACLU . . . Jewish influence is so profound that non-Jews sometimes blur the distinction between them and the formal Jewish community."

FREUD'S JEWISH IDENTITY

Although he rejected religion, Freud himself had a very strong Jewish identity. In a 1931 letter he described himself as "a fanatical Jew," and on another occasion he wrote that he found "the attraction of Judaism and of Jews so irresistible, many dark emotional powers, all the mightier the less they let themselves be grasped in words, as well as the clear consciousness of inner identity, the secrecy of the same mental construction" (in Gay, 1988, p. 601). On another occasion he wrote of "strange secret longings" related to his Jewish identity (in p. 601). At least by 1930 Freud had also become sympathetic to Zionism (at a time when the mainstream Jewish community, at least in the U.S., had rejected Zionism because of worries about accusations of dual loyalty):

> Freud did not take a stance that in principle rejects, utterly, territorial Jewish nationalism. On the contrary, he cites pragmatic considerations regarding the Jewish settlement project in Palestine. He objected not to Jewish nationalism per se, but to the revived Jewish nationalism in Palestine. The point he made is, at base, both practical and psychological: it relates to the "historical burden" that Palestine bears on its shoulders, and the expected refusal of the Christian and Muslim communities to place their holy sites in Jewish hands. (Rolnik & Watzman, 2012, p. 68)

His sons Ernst and Martin were also Zionists, and none of Freud's six children converted to Christianity or married gentiles.

As expected by social identity theory, Freud's strong sense of Jewish identity involved a deep estrangement from gentiles. Yerushalmi (1991, p. 39) notes:

> We find in Freud a sense of otherness vis-à-vis non-Jews which cannot be explained merely as a reaction to anti-Semitism. Though anti-Semitism would periodically reinforce or modify it, this feeling seems to have been

primal, inherited from his family and early milieu, and it remained with him throughout his life.

In a revealing comment, Freud stated, "I have often felt as though I inherited all the obstinacy and all the passions of our ancestors when they defended their temple, as though I could throw away my life with joy for a great moment" (in Gay, 1988, p. 604). His identity as a Jew was thus associated with a self-concept in which he selflessly does battle with the enemies of the group, dying in an act of heroic altruism defending group interests—a mirror-image Jewish version of the grand finale of Wagner's *Nibelungenlied* that was an ingredient in National Socialist ideology and corroborates the view that Judaism may be seen as a mirror image of National Socialism (see SAID, Ch. 5). In terms of social identity theory, Freud thus had a very powerful sense of ingroup membership and a sense of duty to work altruistically for the interests of the group.

Gay (1988, p. 601) interprets Freud as having the belief that his identity as a Jew was the result of his phylogenetic inheritance. As Yerushalmi (1991, p. 30) notes, his psycho-Lamarckism was "neither casual nor circumstantial." Freud grasped what Yerushalmi (p. 31) terms the "subjective dimension" of Lamarckism, that is, the feeling of a powerful tie to the Jewish past as shaped by Jewish culture, the feeling that one cannot escape being a Jew, and "that often what one feels most deeply and obscurely is a trilling wire in the blood." In the following passage from *Moses and Monotheism*, the Jews are proposed to have fashioned themselves to become a morally and intellectually superior people:

> The preference which through two thousand years the Jews have given to spiritual endeavour has, of course, had its effect; it has helped to build a dike against brutality and the inclination to violence which are usually found where athletic development becomes the ideal of the people. The harmonious development of spiritual and bodily activity, as achieved by the Greeks, was denied to the Jews. In this conflict their decision was at least made in favour of what is culturally the more important. (Freud, 1939/1955, p. 147)

Such a statement ignores violent Jewish behavior in the early decades of the Soviet Union (Ch. 3) and the contemporary Israeli genocide of the Gazan Palestinians.

Freud's sense of Jewish superiority can also be seen in a diary entry by Joseph Wortis based on an interview with Freud in 1935: Freud commented that he viewed gentiles as prone to "ruthless egoism," whereas Jews had a superior family and intellectual life. Wortis then asked Freud if he viewed Jews as a superior people. Freud replied: "I think nowadays they are. . . . When one thinks that 10 or 12 of the Nobel winners are Jews, and when one thinks of their other great achievements in the sciences and in the arts, one has every reason to think them superior" (in Cuddihy, 1974, p. 36).

Further, Freud viewed these differences as unchangeable. In a 1933 letter Freud decried the upsurge in anti-Semitism: "My judgment of human nature, especially the Christian-Aryan variety, has had little reason to change" (in Yerushalmi, 1991, p. 48). Nor, in Freud's opinion, would the Jewish character change. In *Moses and Monotheism*, Freud (1939/1955, p. 51n) in reference to the concern with racial purity apparent in the Books of Ezra and Nehemiah (see PTSDA, Ch. 2), "It is historically certain that the Jewish type was finally fixed as a result of the reforms of Ezra and Nehemiah in the fifth century before Christ." "Freud was thoroughly convinced that once the Jewish character was created in ancient times it had remained constant, immutable, its quintessential qualities indelible" (Yerushalmi, 1991, p. 52).

The obvious racialism and the clear statement of Jewish ethical, spiritual, and intellectual superiority contained in Freud's last work, *Moses and Monotheism*, must be seen not as an aberration of Freud's thinking but as central to his attitudes, if not his published work, dating from a much earlier period. In SAID (Ch. 5) I noted that prior to the rise of National Socialism, an important set of Jewish intellectuals had a strong racial sense of Jewish peoplehood and felt racial estrangement from gentiles; they also made statements that can only be interpreted as indicating a sense of Jewish racial superiority. The psychoanalytic movement was an important example of these tendencies. It was characterized by ideas of "Jewish intellectual superiority, racial opposition, national pride, and Jewish solidarity" (Klein, 1981, p. 143). Freud and his colleagues felt a sense of "racial kinship" with their Jewish colleagues and a "racial strangeness" toward others (Klein, 1981, p. 142; see also Gilman, 1993, pp. 12ff). Commenting on Ernest Jones, one of his disciples, Freud wrote, "The racial mixture in our band is very interesting to me. He [Jones] is a Celt and hence not quite accessible to us, the Teuton [C. G. Jung] and the Mediterranean man [himself as a Jew]" (in Gay, 1988, p. 186).

Freud and other early psychoanalysts frequently distinguished themselves as Jews on the basis of race and referred to non-Jews as Aryans, instead of as Germans or Christians (Klein, 1981, p. 142). He wrote to C. G. Jung that Ernest Jones gave him a feeling of "racial strangeness" (p. 142). During the 1920s Jones was viewed as a gentile outsider even by the other members of the secret Committee of Freud's loyalists and even though he had married a Jewish woman.

In the eyes of all of [the Jewish members of the Committee], Jones was a Gentile. . . . [T]he others always seized every opportunity to make him aware that he could never belong. His fantasy of penetrating the inner circle by creating the Committee was an illusion, because he would forever be an unattractive little man with his ferret face pressed imploringly against the glass. (Grosskurth, 1991, p. 137)

Early in their relationship Freud also had suspicions about Jung, the result of "worries about Jung's inherited Christian and even anti-Jewish biases, indeed his very ability as a non-Jew to fully understand and accept psychoanalysis itself" (Yerushalmi, 1991, p. 42). Before their rupture, Freud described Jung as a "strong, independent personality, as a Teuton" (in Gay, 1988, p. 201). After Jung was made head of the International Psychoanalytical Association, a colleague of Freud was concerned because "taken as a race," Jung and his gentile colleagues were "completely different from us Viennese" (in Gay, 1988, p. 219). In 1908 Freud wrote a letter to the psychoanalyst Karl Abraham in which Abraham is described as keen while Jung is described as having a great deal of *élan*—a description that, as Yerushalmi (1991, p. 43) notes, indicates a tendency to stereotype individuals on the basis of group membership (the intellectually sharp Jew and the energetic Aryan). Whereas Jung was inherently suspect because of his genetic background, Abraham was not. Freud, after delicately inquiring about whether Abraham was a Jew, wrote that it was easier for Abraham to understand psychoanalysis because he had a racial kinship (*Rassenverwandschaft*) to Freud (Yerushalmi, 1991, p. 42).

Jung has increasingly become the focus of condemnation, deconstruction, and criticism in recent years. In the recently-published *Anti-Semitism and Analytical Psychology: Jung, Politics and Culture*, Jewish academic Daniel Burston (2021) cites Thomas B. Kirsch (2000, p. 132) who notes:

> In today's world of psychotherapy, one cannot be a Jungian without having to answer the charge that Jung was both a Nazi and anti-Semitic. . . . His statements on the over-materialistic values of Jewish psychology, and its corrosive effects on the spiritual nature of the psyche, were made in the 1930s. . . . Psychoanalysts have used it as a reason not to study Jung; other intellectuals use it as a reason to discredit Jung.

Freud's powerful racial sense of ingroup-outgroup barriers between Jews and gentiles may also be seen in the personal dynamics of the psychoanalytic movement. We have seen that Jews were numerically dominant within psychoanalysis, especially in the early stages when all the members were Jews. "The fact that these were Jews was certainly not accidental. I also think that in a profound though unacknowledged sense Freud wanted it that way" (Yerushalmi, 1991, p. 41). As in other forms of Judaism, there was a sense of being an ingroup within a specifically Jewish milieu.

Whatever the reasons—historical, sociological—group bonds did provide a warm shelter from the outside world. In social relations with other Jews, informality and familiarity formed a kind of inner security, a "we-feeling," illustrated even by the selection of jokes and stories recounted within the group. (Grollman, 1965, p. 41)

Also adding to the Jewish milieu of the movement was the fact that Freud was idolized by Jews generally. Freud himself noted in his letters that "from all sides and places, the Jews have enthusiastically seized me for themselves." "He was embarrassed by the way they treated him, as if he were 'a God-fearing Chief Rabbi,' or 'a national hero,'" and by the way they viewed his work as "genuinely Jewish" (in Klein, 1981, pp. 85–86; see also Gay, 1988, p. 599).

Similarly for female psychoanalysts:

For many of the Europeans, Jewishness was certainly a more salient self-categorization, and this was a characteristic shared with men. Participation in psychoanalytic families and couples, in a psychoanalytic social world, and in the radical social movement that was psychoanalysis itself, being a lay analyst in medical psychoanalytic America, socialist youth movement membership, and participation in other avant-garde movements or social groups like Bloomsbury also created identities, all held in common with some male psychoanalysts, that modulated the salience of gender identity. (Chodorow, 1989, p. 214)

As in the case of several Jewish intellectual and political movements reviewed here (see also SAID, Ch. 6), Freud took great pains to ensure that a gentile, Jung, would be the head of his psychoanalytic movement—a move that infuriated his Jewish colleagues in Vienna, but one that was clearly intended to deemphasize the very large overrepresentation of Jews in the movement during this period. To persuade his Jewish colleagues of the need for Jung to head the International Psychoanalytical Association, he argued, "Most of you are Jews, and therefore you are incompetent to win friends for the new teaching. Jews must be content with the modest role of preparing the ground. It is absolutely essential that I should form ties in the world of science" (in Gay, 1988, p. 218). As Yerushalmi (1991, p. 41) notes, "To put it very crudely, Freud needed a goy, and not just any goy but one of genuine intellectual stature and influence." Later, when the movement was reconstituted after World War I, another gentile, the sycophantic and submissive Ernest Jones, became president of the International Psychoanalytical Association.

Interestingly, although recent scholarship is unanimous that Freud had a very strong Jewish identity, Freud took pains to conceal this identity from others because of a concern that his psychoanalytic movement would be viewed as a specifically Jewish movement and thus be the focus of anti-Semitism.

Whereas his private correspondence is filled with a strong sense of Jewish ethnic identity, his public statements and writings exhibited a "generally guarded, distanced tone" (Yerushalmi, 1991, p. 42), indicating an effort at deception. Freud also attempted to downplay in public the extent to which Judaism pervaded his family environment while growing up, his religious education, and his knowledge of Hebrew, Yiddish, and Jewish religious traditions (Goodnick, 1993; E. Rice, 1990; Yerushalmi, 1991, pp. 61ff). Also suggesting deception is that two of the Jewish members of Freud's secret Committee (Otto Rank and Sándor Ferenczi) had altered their names to appear non-Jewish (Grosskurth, 1991, p. 17).

Deception is also indicated by the evidence that Freud felt that one reason psychoanalysis needed highly visible gentiles was because he viewed psychoanalysis as subverting gentile culture. Before publishing *Little Hans* in 1909, he wrote to Karl Abraham that the book would create an uproar: "German ideals threatened again! Our Aryan comrades are really completely indispensable to us, otherwise psychoanalysis would succumb to anti-Semitism" (in Yerushalmi, 1991, p. 43).

Social identity theory emphasizes the importance of positive attributions regarding the ingroup and negative attributions regarding the outgroup. Freud's strong sense of Jewish identity was accompanied by feelings of intellectual superiority to gentiles (Klein, 1981, p. 61). In an early letter to his future wife, Freud stated, "In the future, for the remainder of my apprenticeship in the hospital, I think I shall try to live more like the gentiles—modestly, learning and practicing the usual things and not striving after discoveries or delving too deep" (in Yerushalmi, 1991, p. 39). Freud used the word *goyim* to refer to gentiles in this passage, and Yerushalmi comments, "The hand is the hand of Sigmund; the voice is the voice of Jakob [Freud's religiously observant father]" (p. 39). It is the voice of separation and estrangement.

An attitude of Jewish superiority to gentiles not only characterized Freud but pervaded the entire movement. Ernest Jones (1959, p. 211) mentioned "the Jewish belief, which they often impose on other people too, concerning the superiority of their intellectual powers." As in the case of radical intellectual circles dominated by Jews (see Ch. 3), "The feeling of Jewish superiority alienated many non-Jews within the movement and encouraged many outside the movement to dismiss as hypocritical the humanitarian claims of the psychoanalysts" (Klein, 1981, p. 143)—a comment suggesting self-deception among psychoanalysts regarding their motives.

Freud's estrangement from gentiles also involved positive views of Judaism and negative views of gentile culture, the latter viewed as something to be conquered in the interest of leading humanity to a higher moral level and ending anti-Semitism. Freud had a sense of "Jewish moral superiority to the injustices of an intolerant, inhumane—indeed, anti-Semitic—society" (Klein, 1981, p.

86). Freud "supported those in the Jewish society [B'nai B'rith] who urged Jews to regard themselves as mankind's champions of democratic and fraternal ideals" (p. 86). He wrote of his messianic hope to achieve the "integration of Jews and anti-Semites on the soil of [psychoanalysis]" (in Gay, 1988, p. 231), a quote clearly indicating that psychoanalysis was viewed by its founder as a mechanism for ending anti-Semitism.

> [Freud] was proud of his enemies—the persecuting Roman Catholic Church, the hypocritical bourgeoisie, the obtuse psychiatric establishment, the materialistic Americans—so proud, indeed, that they grew in his mind into potent specters far more malevolent and far less divided than they were in reality. He likened himself to Hannibal, to Ahasuerus, to Joseph, to Moses, all men with historic missions, potent adversaries, and difficult fates. (Gay, 1988, p. 604)

This comment is an excellent example of the consequences of a strong sense of social identity: Freud's powerful sense of Jewish group identity resulted in negative stereotypical thinking regarding the gentile outgroup. Gentile society, and particularly the most salient institutions of gentile culture, were viewed stereotypically as evil. These institutions were not only viewed negatively, but the accentuation effect (see SAID, Ch. 1) also came into play and resulted in a general attribution of homogeneity to the outgroup, so that these institutions were seen as much less divided than they actually were.

Consider also Sulloway's (1979b) description of the genesis of Freud's self-concept as a hero dating from his childhood and inculcated by his family. Attesting to the intensity of Freud's Jewish identification and his self-concept as a Jewish hero, all of Freud's childhood heroes were related to Judaism: Hannibal, the Semitic combatant against Rome; Cromwell, who allowed the Jews to enter England; and Napoleon, who gave Jews civil rights. Early on he described himself as a "conquistador" rather than as a man of science.

This type of messianic thought was common in *fin de siècle* Vienna among Jewish intellectuals who were attempting to bring about a "supranational, supraethnic world" (Klein, 1981, p. 29), a characterization that, as seen in Chapter 3, would also apply to Jewish involvement in radical political movements. These intellectuals "frequently expressed their humanitarianism in terms of their renewed Jewish self-conception. . . . [They had] a shared belief that Jews were responsible for the fate of humanity in the twentieth century" (p. 31).

Many early proponents viewed psychoanalysis as a redemptive messianic movement that would end anti-Semitism by freeing the world of neuroses produced by sexually repressive Western civilization. Klein shows that some of Freud's closest associates had a very clearly articulated conception of psychoanalysis as a Jewish mission to the gentiles—what one might view as a uniquely modern version of the ancient "light of the nations" theme of Jewish religious thought very common among intellectual apologists of Reform Judaism during the same period.

Thus for Otto Rank, who developed a close father-son relationship with Freud, Jews were uniquely qualified to cure neuroses and act as the healers of humanity (Klein, 1981, p. 129). Developing a variant of the perspective Freud used in *Totem and Taboo* and *Civilization and Its Discontents*, Rank argued that whereas other human cultures had repressed their primitive sexuality in the ascent to civilization, "Jews possessed special creative powers since they had been able to maintain a 'direct relation to "nature," to primitive sexuality'" (Klein, 1981, p. 6)—an argument reminiscent of Adorno and Horkheimer's argument in *Dialectic of Enlightenment* (see Ch. 6).[99] Within this perspective, anti-Semitism results from the denial of sexuality, and the role of the Jewish mission of psychoanalysis was to end anti-Semitism by freeing humanity of its sexual repressions. A theoretical basis for this perspective was provided by Freud's *Three Essays on the Theory of Sexuality*, in which aggression was linked with the frustration of drives.

Klein shows that this conceptualization of psychoanalysis as a redemptive "light of the nations" was common among other Jewish intimates of Freud. Thus Fritz Wittels advocated complete freedom of sexual expression and wrote, "Some of us believed that psychoanalysis would change the surface of the earth . . . [and introduce] a golden age in which there would be no room for neuroses any more. We felt like great men. . . . Some people have a mission in their life" (in Klein, 1981, pp. 138–139). Jews were viewed as having the responsibility to lead the gentiles toward truth and nobility of behavior. "The tendency to place the Jew and the non-Jew in a relationship of fundamental opposition imbued even the expressions of redemption with an adversary quality" (p. 142). Gentile culture was something to be conquered in battle by the morally superior, redemptive Jew: "The spirit of the Jews will conquer the world" (Wittels, in Klein, p. 142). Coincident with Wittels's belief that the mission of psychoanalysis was to achieve a positive Jewish self-identity, he described the convert Jew as characterized by the "psychological disability of

---

[99] Rank had a very strong Jewish identity, viewing the pressures of assimilation emanating from German society during this period in very negative terms—as "morally and spiritually destructive" (Klein, 1981, p. 130). Rank also had a positive attitude toward anti-Semitism and pressures to assimilate because they promoted the development of Jewish redemptive movements such as psychoanalysis: "Rank believed that the reaction of Jews to the threats of external and internal repression prompted them to preserve their relationship with nature and, in the process, to gain consciousness of this special relationship" (p. 131). Rank, whose original name was Rosenfeld, appears to have been a crypto-Jew during part of his life. He adopted a non-Jewish name and converted to Catholicism in 1908 when entering the University of Vienna. In 1918, he converted back to Judaism in order to enter into a Jewish marriage.

hypocrisy" (p. 139). Ferenczi also believed in the redemptive power of psycho-analysis, writing to Freud:

> Once society has gone beyond the infantile, then hitherto completely un-imagined possibilities for social and political life are opened up. Just think what it would mean if one could *tell everyone the truth*, one's father, teacher, neighbor, and even the king. All fabricated, imposed authority would go to the devil—what is *rightful* would remain natural. The eradica-tion of lies from private and public life would necessarily *have* to bring about better conditions; if reason and not dogmas (to which I add the word "morality") prevail, a more purposeful, less costly, and in every respect more economical reconciliation of individual interests with the common good would ensue. (The opposition between the two will not be removed from the world—nor should it be.) I do not think that the Ψα [psychoana-lytic] worldview leads to democratic egalitarianism; the *intellectual elite of humanity* should maintain its hegemony; I believe Plato desired something similar. (Brabant et al., 1993, p. 130; emphasis original)

Given the preponderance of Jews in psychoanalysis—well known and com-mented on by Ferenczi—this is clearly a call for a Jewish intellectual elite to dominate society. It is also an example of the anti-populist strain of Jewish intellectuals discussed in Chapter 7.

The cure for the aggression characteristic of anti-Semitism was therefore believed to lie in freeing gentiles from their sexual repressions. Although Freud himself eventually developed the idea of a death instinct to explain aggression, a consistent theme of the Freudian critique of Western culture, as exemplified for example by Wilhelm Reich, Herbert Marcuse, and Norman O. Brown, has been that the liberation of sexual repressions would lead to lowered aggression and usher in an era of universal love.

It is therefore of interest that when Jung and Alfred Adler were expelled from the movement for heresy, the issue that appears to have been most im-portant to Freud was their rejection of the interrelated ideas of the sexual eti-ology of neurosis, the Oedipal complex, and childhood sexuality.[100] Jung's case

---

[100] Adler "openly questioned Freud's fundamental thesis that early sexual development is deci-sive for the making of character" (Gay, 1988, pp. 216–217) and neglected the Oedipal complex, infantile sexuality, the unconscious, and the sexual etiology of neuroses. Instead, Adler devel-oped his ideas on "organ inferiority" and the hereditary etiology of "anal" character traits. Ad-ler was an avid Marxist and actively attempted to create a theoretical synthesis in which psy-chological theory served utopian social goals (Kurzweil, 1989, p. 84). Nevertheless, Freud termed Adler's views "reactionary and retrograde" (Gay, p. 222), presumably because from Freud's view, the social revolution envisioned by psychoanalysis depended on these con-structs. Freud's actions regarding Adler are entirely comprehensible on the supposition that his acceptance of Adler's "watered-down" version of psychoanalysis would destroy Freud's version of psychoanalysis as a radical critique of Western culture.

is particularly interesting. Jung was expelled from the movement when he developed ideas that denigrated the centrality of sexual repression in Freud's theory.

> Jung's most besetting disagreement with Freud, which runs through the whole sequence of his letters like an ominous subtext, involved what he once gently called his inability to define libido—which meant, translated, that he was unwilling to accept Freud's definition. Jung steadily attempted to widen the meaning of Freud's term, to make it stand not just for the sexual drives, but for a general mental energy. (Gay, 1988, p. 226; see also Grosskurth, 1991, p. 43)

Like Adler, Jung rejected the sexual etiology of neuroses, childhood sexuality, and the Oedipal complex; and like Adler's ideas and unlike these fundamental Freudian doctrines, the idea of libido as restricted to sexual desire is of little use in developing a radical critique of Western culture, because Freud's theory, as described below, depends on the conflation of sexual desire and love.

However, in addition, Jung developed a view that religious experience was a vital component of mental health: Freud, in contrast, remained hostile to religious belief—indeed, Gay (1988, p. 331) writes of Freud's "pugilistic atheism." As indicated elsewhere in this chapter, central to what one might term Freud's pathologization of Christianity is his view that religious belief is nothing more than a reaction formation to avoid guilt feelings consequent to a primeval Oedipal event or, as developed in *The Future of an Illusion*, merely childish feelings of helplessness. Thus a central function of *Totem and Taboo* appears to have been to combat "everything that is Aryan-religious" (in Gay, p. 331), a comment that at once illustrates Freud's agenda of discrediting not just religion but gentile religion in particular and is another indication of the extent to which he viewed his work as an aspect of competition between ethnic groups.

Sexual repression in Western societies during this period was highly salient and undeniable. Freud's theory may thus be viewed as an invention whose utility in the assault on Western culture derived from the intuitive plausibility of supposing that the liberation of sexual urges would result in major changes in behavior that could possibly have psychotherapeutic effects. Moreover, the concept of the Oedipal complex proved to be critical to Freud's thesis for the centrality of sexual repression in *Totem and Taboo*—what Gay (1988, p. 329) terms some of Freud's "most subversive conjectures" and discussed in more detail below.

This belief in the curative powers of sexual freedom coincided with a leftist political agenda common to the vast majority of Jewish intellectuals of the period and reviewed throughout this book. This leftist political agenda proved to be a recurrent theme throughout the history of psychoanalysis. Support for radical and Marxist ideals was common among Freud's early followers, and leftist attitudes were common in later years among psychoanalysts (Hale, 1995, p. 31; Kurzweil, 1989, pp. 36, 46–47, 284; Torrey, 1992, pp. 33, 93ff, 122–123), as well as in Freudian-inspired theorists such as Erich Fromm, Wilhelm Reich (see below), and Alfred Adler. (Kurzweil, 1989, pp. 286–287 terms Adler the leader of "far left" psychoanalysis, noting that Adler wanted to immediately politicize teachers as radicals rather than wait for the perfection of psychoanalysis to do so.) The apex of the association between Marxism and psychoanalysis came in the 1920s in the Soviet Union, where all the top psychoanalysts were Bolsheviks, Trotsky supporters, and among the most powerful political figures in the country (see Chamberlain, 1995). (Trotsky himself was an ardent enthusiast of psychoanalysis.) This group organized a government-sponsored State Psychoanalytical Institute and developed a program of "pedology" aimed at producing the "new Soviet man" on the basis of psychoanalytic principles applied to the education of children. The program, which encouraged sexual precocity in children, was put into practice in state-run schools. However, "once it became clear that 'Freudian man' was devoid of any utopian yearnings, revolutionary discourse in its Soviet version turned away from Freud's teachings and psychoanalysis was officially removed from the party's ideological armamentarium" (Rolnik & Watzman, 2012, p. 20).

There is also evidence that Freud conceptualized himself as a leader in a war on gentile culture. We have seen that Freud had a great deal of hostility to Western culture, especially the Catholic Church and its ally, the Austrian Habsburg monarchy (Gay, 1988; McGrath, 1974; Rothman & Isenberg, 1974b).[101] In a remarkable passage from The Interpretation of Dreams, Freud, in attempting to understand why he has been unable to set foot in Rome, proposes that he has been retracing the footsteps of Hannibal, the Semitic leader of Carthage against Rome during the Punic Wars:

> Hannibal . . . had been the favourite hero of my later school days. . . . And when in the higher classes I began to understand for the first time what it meant to belong to an alien race . . . the figure of the semitic general rose still higher in my esteem. To my youthful mind Hannibal and Rome symbolized the conflict between the tenacity of Jewry and the organisation of the Catholic Church. (Freud, 1932/1969; in Rothman & Isenberg, 1974b, p. 64)

---

[101] It is noteworthy that an early member of the psychoanalytic movement, Ludwig Braun, believed that Freud was "genuinely Jewish," and that to be Jewish meant, among other things, that one had a "courageous determination to combat or oppose the rest of society, his enemy" (Klein, 1981, p. 85).

The passage clearly indicates that Freud identified himself as a member of "an alien race" at war with Rome and its daughter institution, the Catholic Church, a central institution of Western culture. Gay (1988, p. 132) states, "A charged and ambivalent symbol, Rome stood for Freud's most potent concealed erotic, and only slightly less concealed aggressive wishes."[102] Rome was a "supreme prize and incomprehensible menace" (p. 132). Freud himself described this "Hannibal fantasy" as "one of the driving forces of [my] mental life" (in McGrath, 1974, p. 35).

A strong connection exists between anti-Semitism and Freud's hostility to Rome. Freud's conscious identification with Hannibal occurred following an anti-Semitic incident involving his father in which his father behaved passively. Freud's response to the incident was to visualize "the scene in which Hannibal's father, Hamilcar Barca, made his boy swear before the household altar to take vengeance on the Romans. Ever since that time Hannibal had . . . a place in my phantasies" (in McGrath, 1974, p. 35). "Rome was the center of Christian civilization. To conquer Rome would certainly be to avenge his father and his people" (Rothman & Isenberg, 1974b, p. 62). Cuddihy (1974, p. 54) makes the same point:

> Like Hamilcar's son Hannibal, he will storm Rome seeking vengeance. He will control his anger, as his father had done, but he will use it to probe relentlessly beneath the beautiful surface of the diaspora to the murderous rage and lust coiled beneath its so-called civilities.

FREUD'S ANTI-CHRISTIAN WRITING

Rothman and Isenberg (1974b) convincingly argue that Freud actually viewed *The Interpretation of Dreams* as a victory against the Catholic Church and that he viewed *Totem and Taboo* as a successful attempt to analyze the Christian religion in terms of defense mechanisms and primitive drives. Regarding *Totem and Taboo*, Freud told a colleague that it would "serve to make a sharp division between us and all Aryan religiosity" (in Rothman & Isenberg, p. 63; see also Gay, 1988, p. 326). They also suggest that Freud consciously attempted to conceal his subversive motivation; a central aspect of Freud's theory of dreams is that rebellion against a powerful authority must often be carried on with deception: "According to the strength . . . of the censorship, [the authority-defying individual] finds himself compelled . . . to speak in allusions

---

[102] As a psychoanalyst himself, Gay imagines an erotic message underlying the surface meaning of aggression and hostility toward Western culture.

... or he must conceal his objection beneath some apparently innocent disguise" (Freud, 1932/1969; in Rothman & Isenberg, p. 64).

The bizarre argument of Freud's (1939) *Moses and Monotheism* is quite clearly an attempt to show the moral superiority of Judaism compared to Christianity. Freud's hostility to the Catholic Church is apparent in this work: "The Catholic Church, which so far has been the implacable enemy of all freedom of thought and has resolutely opposed any idea of this world being governed by advance towards the recognition of truth!" (p. 67). Freud also reiterates his conviction that religion is nothing more than neurotic symptomatology—a view first developed in his *Totem and Taboo* (1912).

All religions may be symptoms of neurosis, but Freud clearly believed that Judaism is an ethically and intellectually superior form of neurosis. According to Freud (1939/1955, p. 109), the Jewish religion,

> formed their [the Jews'] character for good through the disdaining of magic and mysticism and encouraging them to progress in spirituality and sublimations. The people, happy in their conviction of possessing the truth, overcome by the consciousness of being the chosen, came to value highly all intellectual and ethical achievements.

The proposal that Jews avoided magic and mysticism flies in the face of the powerful strain of mysticism apparent in Jewish writings, such as the Kabbala:

> It was in this atmosphere [of poverty and anti-Semitism] that Hasidism rose to dominance in Eastern Europe. The Hasidim passionately rejected all the assimilatory pressures coming from the government. They so cherished the Yiddish language that well into the twentieth century the vast majority of Eastern European Jews could not speak the languages of the non-Jews living around them [Vital, 1975, p. 46]. They turned to the Kabbala (the writings of Jewish mystics), superstition, and anti-rationalism, believing in "magical remedies, amulets, exorcisms, demonic possession (dybbuks), ghosts, devils, and teasing, mischievous genies [R. Mahler, 1985, p. 16]." (MacDonald, 2003b)

In contrast, Freud (1939/1955, p. 112) claims that "The Christian religion did not keep to the lofty heights of spirituality to which the Jewish religion had soared." Freud argues that in Judaism the repressed memory of killing the Mosaic father figure lifts Judaism to a very high ethical level, whereas in Christianity the unrepressed memory of killing a father figure eventually results in a reversion to Egyptian paganism. Indeed, Freud's formulation of Judaism might even be termed reactionary, since it retains the traditional idea of Jews as a chosen people (Yerushalmi, 1991, p. 34).

Freud's psychoanalytic reinterpretation may be viewed as an attempt to reinterpret Judaism in a "scientific" manner: the creation of a secular, "scientific" Jewish theology. The only substantial difference from the traditional account is that Moses replaces God as the central figure of Jewish history. In this regard, it is interesting that from an early period Freud strongly identified with Moses (Klein, 1981, p. 94; E. Rice, 1990, pp. 123ff), suggesting an identification in which he viewed himself as a leader who would guide his people through a dangerous time. Given Freud's intense identification with Moses, the following passage from *Moses and Monotheism* (1939/1952, pp. 141–142), ostensibly referring to the ancient prophets who came after Moses, may be taken to apply to Freud himself:

> Monotheism had failed to take root in Egypt. The same thing might have happened in Israel after the people had thrown off the inconvenient and pretentious religion imposed on them. From the mass of the Jewish people, however, there arose again and again men who lent new colour to the fading tradition, renewed the admonishments and demands of Moses, and did not rest until the lost cause was once more regained.

Moses and Monotheism also links monotheism with the superiority of Jewish ethics, but nowhere does Freud make clear how an ideology of monotheism could possibly result in a higher sense of ethics. As indicated in PTSDA (Ch. 3), Jewish monotheism is closely linked to ethnocentrism and fear of exogamy. Also, as indicated in PTSDA (Ch. 6), Jewish ethics is fundamentally a tribalistic ethics in which there are major differences in how individuals are treated depending on whether or not they are Jews. Christian ethics on the other hand are universalist, and universalist ethics are deeply ingrained in Western philosophy (e.g., Kant's categorical imperative).

As I have noted, perceived anti-Semitism would be expected to exacerbate the tendency to subject gentile culture to radical criticism. There is excellent evidence that Freud was intensely concerned with anti-Semitism, perhaps dating from the anti-Semitic incident involving his father (e.g., E. Rice, 1990; Rothman & Isenberg, 1974a,b; Yerushalmi, 1991). Indeed, as expected on the basis of social identity theory, Gay (1987, p. 138) notes that Freud's Jewish identity was most intense "when times were hardest for Jews"—a common phenomenon among Jews, as during the wars of 1967, 1973, and the Gaza war of 2023–present (MacDonald, 2023a).

Freud's theory of anti-Semitism in *Moses and Monotheism* (Freud, 1939/1955, pp. 114–117) contains several assertions that anti-Semitism is fundamentally a pathological gentile reaction to Jewish ethical superiority. Freud dismisses several surface causes of anti-Semitism, although he gives some credence to the view that anti-Semitism is caused by Jewish defiance of oppression (obviously a cause in which Judaism is portrayed in a positive light).

But *Moses and Monotheism* traces the deeper causes of anti-Semitism to the unconscious: "The jealousy which the Jews evoked in other peoples by maintaining that they were the first-born, favourite child of God the Father has not yet been overcome by those others, just as if the latter had given credence to the assumption" (Freud, 1939/1955, p. 116). Further, the Jewish ceremony of circumcision is said to remind gentiles of "the dreaded castration idea and of things in their primeval past which they would fain forget" (p. 116). And finally, anti-Semitism is said to result from the fact that many Christians have become Christians only recently as the result of forced conversion from even more barbarically polytheistic folk religions than Christianity itself is. Because of the violence of their forced conversions, these barbarians "have not yet overcome their grudge against the new religion which was forced upon them, and they have projected it on to the source from which Christianity came to them [i.e., the Jews]" (p. 117).

Freud (1939/1955, p. 117) describes Christians as having been forced to convert from pagan attitudes that never really disappeared: "One might say that they have remained 'Badly Christened'; under the thin veneer of Christianity, they have remained what their ancestors were, barbarically polytheistic." This is a claim to Jewish ethical superiority given that Freud attributes Jewish ethical superiority ultimately to their belief in monotheism (p. 173):

> In a new transport of moral asceticism the Jews imposed on themselves constantly increasing instinctual renunciation and thereby reached—at least in doctrine and precepts—ethical heights that had remained inaccessible to the other peoples of antiquity. . . . Our investigation is intended to show how it [i.e., ethical heights] is connected . . . with the conception of the one and only God.

Thus, their hatred toward Judaism stems from the fact that at heart they are still barbarians who resent the ethical superiority Judaism achieved long ago by accepting monotheism. Even the phrase "barbarically polytheistic" has the connotation that these barbarians are inferior to refined Jewish monotheists. Indeed, the word "barbarian" has very negative connotations: "a person from an alien land, culture, or group believed to be inferior, uncivilized, or violent—used chiefly in historical references; a person in a savage, primitive state; uncivilized person" (Merriam-Webster definition).

A more self-serving, far-fetched theory of anti-Semitism is difficult to imagine.[103] The general scholarly community has tended to regard *Moses and Monotheism* as "recklessly fanciful" (McGrath, 1991), but this is certainly not the case for Freud's other works. In this regard, it is interesting to note that Freud's highly influential (and equally speculative) *Totem and Taboo* and *Civilization and Its Discontents* present the view that the repression of sex, so apparent as an aspect of Western culture during Freud's life, is the source of art, love, and even civilization itself. However, neurosis and unhappiness are the price to be paid for these traits because neurosis and unhappiness are the inevitable result of repressing sexual urges. As Herbert Marcuse (1955/1974, p. 17) writes concerning this aspect of Freud's thought:

> The notion that a non-repressive civilization is impossible is a cornerstone of Freudian theory. However, his theory contains elements that break through this rationalization; they shatter the predominant tradition of Western thought and even suggest its reversal. His work is characterized by an uncompromising insistence on showing the repressive content of the highest values and achievements of culture.

Western culture has been placed on the couch, and the role of psychoanalysis is to help the patient adjust somewhat to a sick, psychopathology-inducing society:

> While psychoanalytic theory recognizes that the sickness of the individual is ultimately caused and sustained by the sickness of his civilization, psychoanalytic therapy aims at curing the individual so that he can continue to function as part of a sick civilization without surrendering to it altogether. (Marcuse, 1955/1974, p. 245)

As was the case with some of Freud's close associates described above, Freud viewed himself as a sexual reformer against this most Western of cultural practices, the suppression of sexuality. Freud wrote in 1915: "Sexual morality—as society, in its extreme form, the American, defines it—seems to me very contemptible. I advocate an incomparably freer sexual life" (in Gay, 1988,

---

[103] Other psychoanalytic interpretations of anti-Semitism as a pathological gentile reaction to Jewish superiority occurred during the period. In 1938 Jakob Meitlis, a psychoanalyst of the Yiddish Institute of Science (YIVO), stated: "We Jews have always known how to respect spiritual values. We preserved our unity through ideas, and because of them we survived to this day. Once again our people is faced with dark times requiring us to gather all our strength to preserve unharmed all culture and science during the present harsh storms" (in Yerushalmi, 1991, p. 52). Anti-Semitism is here conceptualized as the price to be paid by Jews for bearing the burden of being the originators and defenders of science and culture. (Several other psychoanalytic theories of anti-Semitism are discussed below and in Chapter 6 on the Frankfurt School.)

p. 143). As Gay (p. 149) notes, it was an ideology which "was deeply subversive for his time."

THE SCIENTIFIC STATUS OF PSYCHOANALYSIS

Nathan of Gaza [a seventeenth-century intellectual associated with the ill-fated Shabbetean messianic movement] was an outstanding example of a highly imaginative and dangerous Jewish archetype which was to become of world importance when the Jewish intellect became secularized. He could construct a system of explanations and predictions of phenomena which was both highly plausible and at the same time sufficiently imprecise and flexible to accommodate new—and often highly inconvenient—events when they occurred. And he had the gift of presenting his protean-type theory ... with tremendous conviction and aplomb. Marx and Freud were to exploit a similar capacity.

— Paul Johnson, 1987/1988, pp. 267–268

There is a long history of well-argued claims that psychoanalysis is a pseudoscience. Even ignoring the longstanding objections of experimentally inclined researchers in mainstream psychology, there is a distinguished pedigree of highly critical accounts of psychoanalysis that began appearing in the 1970s by scholars such as Henri Ellenberger (1970), Frank Sulloway (1979a), Adolf Grünbaum (1984), Frank Cioffi (1969, 1970, 1972), Hans Eysenck (1990), Malcolm Macmillan (1991), E. Fuller Torrey (1992), and perhaps most famously, Frederick Crews (1993; Crews et al., 1995). The following passages sum up this tradition of scholarship:

> Should we therefore conclude that psychoanalysis is a science? My evaluation shows that at none of the different stages through which it evolved was Freud's theory one from which adequate explanations could be generated. From the beginning, much of what passed as theory was found to be description, and poor description at that. ... In every one of the later key developmental theses, Freud assumed what had to be explained. ...
>
> None of his followers, including his revisionist critics who are themselves psychoanalysts, have probed any deeper than did Freud into the assumptions underlying their practise, particularly the assumptions underlying "the basic method"—free association. None question whether those assumptions hold in the therapeutic situation; none has attempted to break out of the circle. (Macmillan, 1991, pp. 610–612)

What passes today for Freud bashing is simply the long-postponed exposure of Freudian ideas to the same standards of noncontradiction, clarity, testability, cogency, and parsimonious explanatory power that prevail in empirical discourse at large. Step by step, we are learning that Freud has been the most overrated figure in the entire history of science and medicine—one who wrought immense harm through the propagation of false etiologies, mistaken diagnoses, and fruitless lines of inquiry.

Still, the legend dies hard, and those who challenge it continue to be greeted like rabid dogs. (Crews et al., 1995, pp. 298–299)

Even those within the psychoanalytic camp have often noted the lack of scientific rigor of the early psychoanalysts, and indeed, lack of scientific rigor is a continuing concern within psychoanalytic circles (e.g., Cooper, 1990; R. Michaels, 1988; Orgel, 1990; Reiser, 1989). Gay (1988, p. 235), who clearly regards psychoanalysis as a science, states of the first-generation psychoanalysts that they,

fearlessly interpreted one another's dreams; fell on the others' slips of tongue or pen; freely, much too freely, employed diagnostic terms like "paranoid" and "homosexual" to characterize their associates and indeed themselves. They all practiced in their circle the kind of wild analysis they decried in outsiders as tactless, unscientific, and counterproductive.

Gay (1988, p. 543) calls *Civilization and Its Discontents* "one of [Freud's] most influential writings." It now seems apparent that the theory Freud developed in *Civilization and Its Discontents* and his earlier work, *Totem and Taboo*, rests on a number of extremely naive, prescientific conceptualizations of human sexual behavior and its relation to culture. It is noteworthy that in arriving at his views Freud was forced to summarily reject Edvard Westermarck's theory of incest (i.e., that incest avoidance evolved because it resulted in fewer deleterious genetic mutations), which is the basis of modern scientific theories of incest (see MacDonald, 1986).

However, by means of these speculative leaps, Freud managed to diagnose Western culture as essentially neurotic while apparently, on the basis of the argument in *Moses and Monotheism*, holding the view that Judaism represents the epitome of mental health and moral and intellectual superiority. Freud appears to have been well aware that his highly subversive conjectures in *Totem and Taboo* were entirely speculative. When the book was called a "just-so story" by a British anthropologist in 1920, Freud was "amused" and stated only that his critic "was deficient in phantasy" (Gay, 1988, p. 327), apparently a concession that the work was fanciful. Freud stated, "It would be nonsensical to strive for exactitude with this material, as it would be unreasonable to demand certainty" (in p. 330). Similarly, Freud described *Civilization and Its Discontents* as "an essentially dilettantish foundation" on which "rises a thinly tapered analytic investigation" (in p. 543).

Peter Gay (1988, p. 331) terms Freud's proposal of the Lamarckian inheritance of guilt, which runs through these works, as "sheer extravagance, piled upon the earlier extravagance of the claim that the primal murder had been an historical event." However, even this assessment fails to get at the incredible rejection of the scientific spirit apparent in these writings. It was more than extravagance. Freud was accepting a genetic theory, the inheritance of acquired characteristics, which had, at least by the time *Civilization and Its Discontents* reaffirmed the doctrine, been completely rejected by the scientific community. This was a self-consciously speculative theory, but Freud's speculations clearly had an agenda. Rather than provide speculations that reaffirmed the moral and intellectual basis of the culture of his day, his speculations were an integral part of his war on gentile culture—so much so that he viewed *Totem and Taboo* as a victory over Rome and the Catholic Church.

Similarly, Freud's *Future of an Illusion* is a strong attack on religion in the name of science. Freud himself acknowledged that the scientific content was weak, stating, "the analytic content of the work is very thin" (in Gay, 1988, p. 524). Gay (p. 537) finds that it "fell short of his self-imposed standards," which, as we have already seen, were hardly averse to speculation in the service of a political agenda. Again, however, Freud engages in scientific speculation in the service of an agenda of subverting the institutions of gentile society. This type of posturing was typical of Freud. For example, Crews (1993) notes that Freud advanced his theory that Dostoevsky was not an epileptic but a hysteric suffering from having witnessed a primal scene "with a typically guileful show of tentativeness; but then, just as typically, he goes on to treat it as firmly settled." Dostoevsky was in fact an epileptic.

The theory of the Oedipal complex, childhood sexuality, and the sexual etiology of the neuroses—the three central doctrines that underlie Freud's radical critique of gentile culture—play absolutely no role in contemporary mainstream developmental psychology. From the standpoint of evolutionary theory, the idea that children would have a specifically sexual attraction to their opposite-sex parent is highly implausible, since such an incestuous relationship would result in inbreeding depression and be more likely to result in disorders caused by recessive genes (see MacDonald, 1986). The proposal that boys desire to kill their fathers conflicts with the general importance of paternal provisioning of resources in understanding the evolution of the family (MacDonald, 1988a, 1992): boys who had succeeded in killing their fathers and having sex with their mothers would not only be left with genetically inferior offspring, but also be deprived of paternal support and protection. Modern developmental studies indicate that many fathers and sons have very close, reciprocated affectional relationships beginning in infancy, and the normative pattern is for mothers and sons to have very intimate and affectionate, but decidedly nonsexual, relationships.

The continued life of these concepts in psychoanalytic circles is testimony to the continuing unscientific nature of the entire enterprise. Indeed, Kurzweil (1989, p. 89) notes:

> In the beginning, the Freudians tried to "prove" the universality of the Oedipus complex; later on, they took it for granted. Ultimately, they no longer spelled out the reasons for the pervasiveness of childhood sexuality and its consequences in the cultural monographs: they all accepted it.[104]

What started out as a speculation in need of empirical support ended up as a fundamental *a priori* assumption.

Research inspired by these basic Freudian tenets ceased long ago and in a sense never started: fundamentally, psychoanalysis has not inspired any significant research on these three basic Freudian constructs. Interestingly, there is evidence that Freud fraudulently portrayed the data underlying these concepts. Esterson (1992, pp. 25ff; see also Crews, 1994) convincingly argues that Freud's patients did not volunteer any information on seduction or primal scenes at all. The seduction stories that provide the empirical basis of the Oedipal complex were a construction by Freud, who then interpreted his patients' distress on hearing his constructions as proof of the theory. Freud then engaged in deception to obscure the fact that his patients' stories were reconstructions and interpretations based on an *a priori* theory. Freud also retroactively changed the identity of the fancied seducers from nonfamily members (such as servants) because the Oedipal story required fathers. Esterson provides numerous other examples of deception (and self-deception) and notes that they were typically couched in Freud's brilliant and highly convincing rhetorical style. Both Esterson and Lakoff and Coyne (1993, pp. 83–86) show that Freud's famous analysis of the teenage Dora (in which her rejection of the pedophilic sexual advances of an older married man is attributed to hysteria and sexual repression) was based entirely on preconceived ideas and circular reasoning in which the patient's negative emotional response to the psychoanalytic hypothesis is construed as evidence for the hypothesis. Freud engaged in similar deceptive reconstructions in an earlier phase of his theory construction when he believed that seductions had actually occurred (Powell & Boer, 1994). It was a methodology that could produce any desired result.

---

[104] Similarly, in the French psychoanalytic movement of the mid-1960s, "The propositions of 'linguistic' psychoanalysis became assumptions. Soon, no one any longer questioned whether a self-assured disposition really could hide a vulnerable unconscious structure ... : most French intellectuals accepted that both conscious and unconscious thought were organized in accordance with linguistic structures" (Kurzweil, 1989, pp. 244–245).

A particularly egregious tendency is to interpret patient resistance and distress as an indication of the truth of psychoanalytic claims. Of course, patients were not the only ones who resisted psychoanalysis, and all other forms of resistance were similarly an indication of the truth of psychoanalysis. As Freud himself noted, "I am met with hostility and live in such isolation that one must suppose I had discovered the greatest truths" (in Bonaparte et al., 1957, p. 163). As we shall see, resistance to psychoanalytic "truth" on the part of patients, deviating psychoanalysts, and even entire cultures were viewed as a sure sign of the truth of psychoanalysis and the pathology of those who resisted.

Because of this reconstructive, interpretive manner of theory construction, the authority of the psychoanalyst became the only criterion of the truth of psychoanalytic claims—a situation that leads quite naturally to the expectation that the movement, in order to be successful, would *necessarily* be highly authoritarian. As indicated below, the movement was authoritarian from the beginning and has remained so throughout its history.

Notice that the interpretive, hermeneutic basis of theory construction in psychoanalysis is formally identical to the procedures of Talmudic and Midrashic commentaries on scripture (Hartung, 1995; see PTSDA, Ch. 7). Psychoanalysts have tended to suppose that consistency with observable facts is an adequate criterion for a scientifically acceptable causal explanation. Psychoanalysts "inhabit a kind of scientific preschool in which no one divulges the grown-up secret that successful causal explanation must be *differential*, establishing the *superiority* of a given hypothesis to all of its extant rivals" (Crews, 1994; emphasis original). As indicated in Chapter 7, the development of consensual theories consistent with observable reality but without any scientific content is a hallmark of twentieth-century Jewish intellectual movements.

Any theorist on the contemporary scientific scene who proposed that children are normally sexually attracted to their opposite-sex parent would be ostracized for providing a psychological basis for supposing that children would seek such contact. A glaring mistake that persists throughout Freud's writings is the systematic conflation of sexual desire and love (see MacDonald, 1986): "From the very first, in psychoanalysis, it has seemed better to speak of these love impulses as sexual impulses" (in Wittels, 1924, p. 141)—a comment that suggests the self-conscious nature of this conflation as well as indicates the casual manner in which psychoanalysts have framed their hypotheses. Indeed, Freud conflated all types of pleasure as fundamentally different manifestations of an underlying and unitary but infinitely transformable sexual pleasure, including the oral gratification resulting from breastfeeding, anal gratification resulting from defecation, sexual gratification, and love. Contemporary researchers have often proposed that affectional ties between parents and children are developmentally important and that children actively seek these ties. However, modern theory and data, and certainly an evolutionary approach, provide absolutely no support for identifying affectional ties with sexual desire or with supposing that affectional ties are sublimated or redirected sexual desire. Modern approaches support instead a discrete systems perspective in which sexual desire and affection (and other sources of pleasure) involve quite separate, independent systems. From an evolutionary perspective, the powerful affectional (love) relationships between spouses and between parents and children function as a source of social cohesiveness whose ultimate purpose is to provide a high level of support for children (see MacDonald, 1992, 2012b).

This conflation between sexual desire and love is also apparent in many of Freud's psychoanalytic successors, including Wilhelm Reich, Herbert Marcuse, and Norman O. Brown, whose works are reviewed below. The common thread of their writings is that if society could somehow rid itself of sexual repressions, human relations could be based on love and affection. This is an extremely naive and socially destructive viewpoint, given the current research in the field. Psychoanalytic assertions to the contrary were never any more than speculations in the service of waging a war on gentile culture.

In his insightful ruminations on Freud, Cuddihy (1974, p. 71) traces Freud's views in this matter to the fact that for Jews, marriage was completely utilitarian (see PTSDA, Ch. 7). Theodor Reik, a disciple of Freud, stated that the older generation of Jews held the conviction that "love is to be found only in novels and plays." "Love or romance had no place in the Judengasse [Jewish quarter]." Love was therefore viewed by Freud as an invention of the alien gentile culture and thus morally suspect. Its true hypocritical nature as a veneer for and really only a sublimation of the sexual instinct would be unmasked by psychoanalysis. As described more fully below, it was a devastating analysis— an analysis with important consequences for the social fabric of hypersexualized Western societies in the late twentieth century and beyond.

Finally, another general mistake, and one that illustrates the political nature of Freud's entire agenda, is that sexual urges are viewed as having a powerful biological basis (the id), while traits such as responsibility, dependability, orderliness, guilt, and delay of gratification (i.e., the conscientiousness system of personality theory; MacDonald, 2008a, 2012b) are imposed by a repressive, pathology-inducing society. In a comment indicating the usefulness of these psychoanalytic notions in the war on gentile culture, James Q. Wilson (1993b, p. 104) correctly states that the belief that conscience "is the result of repression is a useful thing to believe if you would like to free yourself of the constraints of conscience—conscience becomes a 'hang-up' that prevents you from 'realizing yourself.'" In fact, conscientiousness is a critical biological system (MacDonald, 2008a, 2012b)—a system that has been under intensive eugenic selection within the Jewish community (see PTSDA, Ch. 7). An evolutionary perspective implies, rather, that both systems have a powerful biological basis and both serve critical adaptive functions. No animal and certainly no human has ever been able to be devoted entirely to self-gratification, and there is no reason whatever to suppose that our biology would solely be directed toward obtaining immediate gratification and pleasure. In the real world, achieving evolutionary goals demands that attention be paid to details, careful plans be made, and gratification be deferred.

The continued life of these notions within the psychoanalytic community testifies to the vitality of psychoanalysis as a political movement. The continued self-imposed separation of psychoanalysis from the mainstream science of developmental psychology, as indicated by separate organizations, separate journals, and a largely nonoverlapping membership, is a further indication that the fundamental structure of psychoanalysis as a closed intellectual movement continues into the present era. Indeed, the self-segregation of psychoanalysis conforms well to the traditional structure of Judaism vis-à-vis gentile society: parallel universes of discourse on human psychology—two incompatible worldviews quite analogous to the differences in religious discourse that have separated Jews from their gentile neighbors over the ages.

PSYCHOANALYSIS AS A POLITICAL MOVEMENT

While Darwin was satisfied with revising his work after further reflection and absorbing palpable hits by rational critics, while he trusted the passage of time and the weight of his argumentation, Freud orchestrated his wooing of the public mind through a loyal cadre of adherents, founded periodicals and wrote popularizations that would spread the authorized word, dominated international congresses of analysts until he felt too frail to attend them and after that through surrogates like his daughter Anna.

— Peter Gay, 1987, p. 144

Scholars have recognized that this self-consciously oppositional, subversive stance characteristic of psychoanalysis was maintained by methods that are completely contrary to the scientific spirit. The really incredible thing about the history of psychoanalysis is that Freud should be the object of such intense adulatory emotions long after his death and well over one hundred years after the birth of psychoanalysis—another indication that the entire subject must carry us well beyond science into the realm of politics and religion. What Grosskurth (1991, p. 219) says about herself is the only important scientific issue: "I am ... fascinated by the fact that thousands of people continue to idealize and defend [Freud] without really knowing anything about him as a person." It is the continuation of this movement and the veneration of its founder, not the pseudoscientific content of the theory, that is of interest.

I have already noted the self-consciously speculative nature of these subversive doctrines, but another important aspect of this phenomenon is the
structure of the movement and the manner in which dissent was handled
within the movement. Psychoanalysis "conducted itself less like a scientific-
medical enterprise than like a politburo bent upon snuffing out deviationism"
(Crews, 1994). It is not surprising, therefore, that observers such as Sulloway
(1979b) have described the "cultlike" aura of religion that has permeated psychoanalysis. Psychoanalysis has often been compared to a religion by outsiders
as well as by insiders. Gay (1988, p. 175) notes the "persistent charge that Freud
had founded a secular religion." Although Gay disputes the charge, he also uses
words such as "movement" (p. 180, *passim*), "conversion" (p. 184), and "the
Cause" (p. 201) in describing psychoanalysis; and he uses "strayed disciple" (p.
485) to describe a defector (Otto Rank) and "recruit" (p. 540) to describe Prin-
cess Marie Bonaparte. Similarly, Yerushalmi (1991, p. 41) speaks of Freud as be-
stowing on Jung "the mantle of apostolic succession." And I can't help noting
that Freud's staunch disciple Fritz Wittels (1924, p. 138) reports that during the
period when Freud and Jung were close, Freud often said of Jung, "This is my
beloved son in whom I am well pleased."

Wittels (1924) also decried the "suppression of free criticism within the
Society. . . . Freud is treated as a demigod, or even as a god. No criticism of his
utterances is permitted." Wittels (pp. 142–143, 134) tells us that Freud's *Three
Essays on the Theory of Sexuality* is,

> the psychoanalyst's Bible. This is no mere figure of speech. The faithful
> disciples regard one another's books as of no account. They recognize no
> authority but Freud's; they rarely read or quote one another. When they
> quote, it is from the Master, that they may give the pure milk of the word.

> [Freud] had little desire that [his] associates should be persons of strong
> individuality, and that they should be critical and ambitious collaborators.
> The realm of psychoanalysis was his idea and his will, and he welcomed
> anyone who accepted his views.

The authoritarianism of the movement repelled some. The influential
Swiss psychiatrist Eugen Bleuler left the movement in 1911, telling Freud that
"this 'who is not for us is against us,' this 'all or nothing,' is necessary for religious communities and useful for political parties. I can therefore understand
the principle as such, but for science I consider it harmful" (in Gay, 1987, p. 145).

Other independent thinkers were simply expelled. There were emotionally charged, highly politicized scenes when Adler and Jung were expelled from
the movement. As indicated above, both individuals had developed perspectives that clashed with those aspects of psychoanalytic orthodoxy that were

crucial to developing a radical critique of Western culture, and the result was a bitter schism. In the case of Adler, although some members in the movement and Adler himself attempted to minimize his differences with Freudian orthodoxy by, for example, depicting his ideas as extensions of Freud rather than as contradictions, "Freud was not interested in such forced compromises" (Gay, 1988, p. 222). Indeed, Jung stated in 1925 that Freud's attitude toward him was "the bitterness of the person who is entirely misunderstood, and his manners always seemed to say: 'If they do not understand, they must be stamped into hell'" (in Ellenberger, 1970, p. 462). After his schism with Freud, Jung stated: "I criticize in Freudian psychology a certain narrowness and bias and, in 'Freudians,' a certain unfree, sectarian spirit of intolerance and fanaticism" (in Gay, 1988, p. 238).

The defections/expulsions of Jung and Adler were an early indication of the inability to tolerate any form of dissent from fundamental doctrines. Otto Rank defected in the mid-1920s, and again the problem was disagreement with the importance of a fundamental Freudian doctrine, the Oedipal complex. This defection was accompanied by a great deal of character assassination, often consisting of attempts to show that Rank's behavior was an indication of psychopathology.

Jung gradually developed highly critical attitudes toward Jews, likely leading to the common charge among Jewish intellectuals that he was an anti-Semite and Nazi sympathizer (e.g., Burston, 2021). Andrew Joyce (2024a) comments:

> Jung's professional and private writings contain a significant amount of material about Jews, and the content is most often highly critical. It is therefore not surprising that Jews should see Jung as a formidable opponent. . . . In 1934 Jung received much criticism for an article he published titled *The State of Psychotherapy Today*, in which he wrote that psychoanalysis was "a Jewish psychology." Defending himself against accusations of racism for suggesting that Jews and Europeans have a different psychology, Jung explained:
>
> "Psychological differences obtain between all nations and races, and even between the inhabitants of Zurich, Basel, and Bern. (Where else would all the good jokes come from?) There are in fact differences between families and between individuals. That is why I attack every levelling psychology when it raises a claim to universal validity, as for instance the Freudian and the Adlerian. . . . All branches of mankind unite in one stem—yes, but what is a stem without separate branches? Why this ridiculous touchiness when anybody dares to say anything about the psychological difference between Jews and Christians? Every child knows that differences exist."

Jung believed that Jews, like all peoples, have a characteristic personality, and he stressed the need to take this personality into account. In his own sphere of expertise, Jung warned that "Freud and Adler's psychologies were specifically Jewish, and therefore not legitimate for Aryans." [B. Cohen, 2012, p. 59] For Jung, a formative factor in the Jewish personality was the rootlessness of the Jews and the persistence of the Diaspora. Jung argued that Jews lacked a "chthonic quality," meaning "the Jew . . . is badly at a loss for that quality in man which roots him to the earth and draws new strength from below." [p. 58] Jung penned these words in 1918, but they retain significance even after the founding of the State of Israel, since vastly more Jews live outside Israel than within it. Jews remain a Diaspora people, and many continue to see their Diaspora status as a strength. Because they are scattered and rootless, however, Jung argued that Jews developed methods of getting on in the world that are built on exploiting weakness in others rather than expressing explicit strength. In Jung's phrasing, "the Jews have this particularity in common with women; being physically weaker, they have to aim at the chinks in the armour of their adversary." [p. 58]

Jung also believed . . . that there was a certain psychological aggressiveness in Jews, which was partly a result of the internal mechanics of Judaism. In a remarkably prescient set of observations in the 1950s, Jung expressed distaste for the behavior of Jewish women and essentially predicted the rise of feminism as a symptom of the pathological Jewess. Jung believed that Jewish men were "brides of Yahweh," rendering Jewish women more or less obsolete within Judaism. In reaction, argued Jung, Jewish women in the early twentieth century began aggressively venting their frustrations against the male-centric nature of Judaism (and against the host society as a whole) while still conforming to the characteristic Jewish psychology and its related strategies. Writing to Martha Bernays, Freud's wife, he once remarked of Jewish women that "so many of them are loud, aren't they?" [Kirsch, 2016, p. 174]

Jeffrey Masson was expelled from the movement because he questioned the Freudian doctrine that patients' reports of sexual abuse were fantasies. As with the other dissenters, such a view entails a radical critique of Freud, since it entails the rejection of the Oedipal complex. As with Talmudic discussions, one could question Freud, but the questioning had to be done "within a certain framework and within the guild. Stepping outside of the framework, being willing to question the very foundations of psychoanalysis, is unthinkable for most analysts" (Masson, 1990, p. 211). Masson's expulsion was characterized not by scientific debate about the accuracy of his claims but by a Stalinist show trial complete with character assassination.

In the history of psychoanalysis, character assassination typically involves analyzing scientific disagreement as an indication of neurosis. Freud himself "never tired of repeating the now notorious contention that the opposition to psychoanalysis stemmed from 'resistances'" arising from emotional sources (Esterson, 1992, p. 216). For example, Freud attributed Jung's defection to "strong neurotic and egotistic motives" (in Gay, 1988, p. 481).

Such imputations of egotistic motives are particularly interesting. As discussed in Chapter 7, all of the Jewish intellectual movements reviewed in this volume are fundamentally collectivist movements that demand authoritarian submission to hierarchical authority. Egotistic motives are therefore incompatible with these movements: such movements thrive on the submergence of self-interest to the goals of the group. In that chapter I argue that science is inherently an individualistic enterprise in which there is minimal loyalty to an ingroup.

Gay (1988, p. 481) comments:

These ventures into character assassination are instances of the kind of aggressive analysis that psychoanalysts, Freud in the vanguard, at once deplored and practiced. This . . . was the way that analysts thought about others, and about themselves. . . . [The practice was] endemic among analysts, a common professional deformation.

One might also note the similarity of these phenomena to the Soviet practice of committing dissenters to mental hospitals. This tradition lives on. Frederick Crews's (1995, p. 293) critique of psychoanalysis has been portrayed by psychoanalysts as "composed in a state of bitter anger by a malcontent with a vicious disposition." Crews's behavior was explained in terms of botched transferences and Oedipal complexes gone awry.

Perhaps the most astonishing case is Otto Rank's letter of 1924 in which he attributes his heretical actions to his own neurotic unconscious conflicts, promises to "see things more objectively after the removal of my affective resistance," and notes that Freud "found my explanations satisfactory and has forgiven me personally" (in Grosskurth, 1991, p. 166). In this matter, "Freud seems to have acted as the Grand Inquisitor, and Rank's groveling 'confession' could have served as a model for the Russian show trials of the 1930s" (p. 167). Freud viewed the entire episode as a success; Rank had been cured of his neurosis "just as if he had gone through a proper analysis" (in p. 168). Clearly, we are dealing with no ordinary science here, but rather with a religio-political movement in which psychoanalysis is a form of thought control and an instrument of domination and interpersonal aggression.

The apex of this authoritarian aspect of the movement was the creation of the Committee, "a tight, small organization of loyalists" whose main task was to prevent departures from orthodoxy (Gay, 1988, pp. 229–230). When Ernest Jones proposed its creation, Freud accepted the idea with enthusiasm:

> What took hold of my imagination immediately, is your [Jones's] idea of a secret council composed of the best and most trustworthy among our men to take care of the further development of [psychoanalysis] and defend the cause against personalities and accidents when I am no more.... [The Committee would] make living and dying easier for me. ... [T]his committee had to be *strictly secret*. (Freud, in Gay, 1988, p. 230; emphasis original)[105]

The workings of the Committee have been extensively documented by Grosskurth (1991, p. 15; emphasis original), who notes:

> By insisting that the Committee must be *absolutely secret*, Freud enshrined the principle of confidentiality. The various psychoanalytic societies that emerged from the Committee were like Communist cells, in which the members vowed eternal obedience to their leader. Psychoanalysis became institutionalized by the founding of journals and the training of candidates; in short, an extraordinarily effective political entity.

There were repeated admonitions for the Committee to present a "united front" against all opposition, for "maintaining control over the whole organization," for "keeping the troops in line," and for "reporting to the commander" (Grosskurth, 1991, p. 97). These are not the workings of a scientific organization, but rather of an authoritarian, religious-political, and quasi-military movement—something resembling the Spanish Inquisition or Stalinism far more than anything resembling what we usually think of as science.

The authoritarian nature of the psychoanalytic movement is exemplified by the personalities of the members of the Committee, all of whom appear to have had extremely submissive personalities and absolute devotion to Freud. Indeed, the members appear to have self-consciously viewed themselves as loyal sons to Freud the father figure (complete with sibling rivalry as the "brothers" jockeyed for position as the "father's" favorite), while Freud viewed his close followers as his children, with power to interfere in their personal lives (Grosskurth, 1991, p. 123; Hale, 1995, p. 29). To the loyalists, the truth of

---

[105] Fritz Wittels (1924, p. 137) dates the desire for a "strict organization" to discussions among Freud, Ferenczi, and Jung that occurred during the 1909 voyage to the United States: "I think there is good reason to suppose that they discussed the need for a strict organization of the psychoanalytical movement. Henceforward, Freud no longer treated psychoanalysis as a branch of pure science. The politics of psychoanalysis had begun. The three travelers took vows of mutual fidelity, agreeing to join forces in the defense of the doctrine against all danger."

psychoanalysis was far less important than their psychological need to be appreciated by Freud (Deutsch, 1940).

These relationships went far beyond mere loyalty, however. "[Ernest] Jones had grasped the fact that to be a friend of Freud's meant being a sycophant. It meant opening oneself up completely to him, to be willing to pour out all one's confidences to him" (Groskurth, 1991, p. 48). "Jones believed that to disagree with Freud (the father) was tantamount to patricide (father murder)," so that when Sándor Ferenczi disagreed with Freud on the reality of childhood sexual abuse, Jones called him a "homicidal maniac" (Masson, 1990, p. 152).

Regarding Ferenczi, Groskurth (1991) notes, "The thought of a disagreement with Freud was unbearable" (p. 141); "there were occasions when he [Ferenczi] rebelled against his dependency, but always he returned, repentant and submissive" (pp. 53–54). The situation was similar for Kurt Eissler, the closest confidant of Anna Freud's inner circle in the 1960s: "What he felt for Freud seemed to border on worship" (Masson, 1990, p. 121). "He held one thing sacred, and hence beyond criticism: Freud" (p. 122). It was common among the disciples to imitate Freud's personal mannerisms, and even among analysts who did not know Freud personally there were "intense feelings, fantasies, transferences, identifications" (Hale, 1995, p. 30).

This authoritarian aspect of the movement continued long after the dissolution of the secret Committee and long after Freud's death. Anna Freud received a ring from her father and kept a "special group" around her whose existence was not public knowledge (Masson, 1990, p. 113). "Psychoanalysis always was, from the moment Freud found disciples, a semisecret society. This secrecy has never disappeared" (p. 209).

The tendency to stifle dissent continued in psychoanalysis long after the well-documented tendencies of the founding father and his disciples (Orgel, 1990). "Psychoanalysis demanded loyalty that could not be questioned, the blind acceptance of unexamined 'wisdom'" (Masson, 1990, p. 209). "Success as a psychoanalyst meant being a team player and not questioning the work of other analysts on one's team" (p. 70). Intellectual dissent was stifled with statements by superiors that doubters had a further need for analysis or simply by removing dissenters from training programs.

Further evidence for the essentially political character of psychoanalysis is the unique role of disciples able to trace themselves back to Freud in a direct line of descent. "The idea of being a chosen disciple, privileged to have direct contact with the master, has survived and is continued in the procedures of many of the training programs of the institutes" (Arlow & Brenner, 1988, p. 5; see also Masson, 1990, pp. 55, 123).

The intensely filial relationships to Freud of the first generation were gradually replaced by highly emotional relationships to a fantasied Freud, still the primal founder, but also to organizations, to peers, to superiors in the institute hierarchy—above all—to the training analyst, the training analyst's analyst, and, if possible, back to Freud and his circle became a determinant of psychoanalytic prestige. (Hale, 1995, p. 32)

Unlike in a real science, in psychoanalysis there is a continuing role for what one might term the sacred texts of the movement, Freud's writings, both in teaching and in the current psychoanalytic literature. *Studies of Hysteria* and *The Interpretation of Dreams* are well over one hundred years old but remain standard texts in psychoanalytic training programs. There is a "recurrent appearance in the analytic literature of articles redoing, extending, deepening, and modifying Freud's early case histories" (Arlow & Brenner, 1988, p. 5). Indeed, it is remarkable to simply scan psychoanalytic journal articles and find that a large number of references are to Freud's work performed one hundred years ago. The 1997 volume of *The Psychoanalytic Quarterly* had seventy-seven references to Freud in twenty-four articles. Only five articles had no references to Freud, and of these, one had no references at all. (In keeping with psychoanalytic tradition, there were no empirical studies.) There thus appears to be a continuing tendency noted by Wittels (1924, p. 143) long ago: "The faithful disciples regard one another's books as of no account. They recognize no authority but Freud's; they rarely read or quote one another. When they quote it is from the Master, that they may give the pure milk of the word."

The continued use of Freud's texts in instruction and the continuing references to Freud's work are simply not conceivable in a real science. In this regard, although Darwin is venerated for his scientific work as the founder of the modern science of evolutionary biology, studies in evolutionary biology only infrequently refer to Darwin's writings because the field has moved so far beyond his work. *On the Origin of Species* and Darwin's other works are important texts in the history of science, but they are not used for current instruction. Moreover, central features of Darwin's account of evolution, such as his views on inheritance, have been completely rejected by modern evolutionary biologists. With Freud, however, there is continuing fealty to the master, at least within an important subset of the movement.

One rationalization for the authoritarian character of the movement was that it was necessary because of the irrational hostility psychoanalysis aroused in the scientific and lay communities (e.g., Gay, 1987). However, Sulloway (1979a, p. 448; see also Ellenberger, 1970, pp. 418–420; Esterson, 1992, pp. 172–173; Kiell, 1988) finds the supposedly hostile reception of Freud's theories to be "one of the most well-entrenched legends" of psychoanalytic history. Moreover, one might note that Darwin's theory also provoked intense hostility during Darwin's life, and recently there has been a great deal of public hostility directed at recent elaborations of Darwin's theory as it pertains to human behavior.

Nevertheless, these theoretical perspectives have not developed the authoritarian, separatist traits of psychoanalysis. Indeed, evolutionists and behavioral geneticists have attempted to influence mainstream research in anthropology, psychology, sociology, and other fields by publishing data in mainstream journals and often by using mainstream methodologies. Controversy and hostility by itself need not lead to orthodoxy or to separation from the realm of empirical science. In the world of science, controversy leads to experimentation and rational argumentation. In the world of psychoanalysis, it leads to expulsion of the nonorthodox and to splendid isolation from scientific psychology.

Indeed, in works such as Grosskurth's *The Secret Ring* (1991) and Peter Gay's *Freud: A Life for Our Time* (1988) biography of Freud, much comment is made on the authoritarian nature of the movement, but discussions of the need for authoritarianism as resulting from external pressures on psychoanalysis are extremely vague and almost completely absent. Instead, the drive for orthodoxy comes from within the movement as the direct result of the personalities of a small group of loyalists and their absolute commitment to their master's cause.

Reflecting the utility of psychoanalysis as an instrument of psychological domination and thought control, Freud himself refused to be analyzed. Freud's refusal resulted in difficulties with Jung (1961) and, much later, with Ferenczi, who commented that the refusal was an example of Freud's arrogance (Grosskurth, 1991, pp. 210–211). In contrast, Freud used psychoanalysis to sexually humiliate two of his most fervent disciples, Ferenczi and Jones. Freud's analysis of the women involved in relationships with Ferenczi and Jones resulted in the women leaving the men but remaining on friendly terms with Freud (see Grosskurth, p. 65). Grosskurth suggests that Freud's actions were a test of his disciples' loyalty, and the fact that Jones continued in the movement after this humiliation indicates the extent to which Freud's followers showed unquestioned obedience to their master.

An ethologist observing these events would conclude that Freud had behaved like the quintessential dominant male, which Freud mythologized in *Totem and Taboo*, but only symbolically, since Freud did not apparently have sexual relationships with the women—although he was "captivated" by Jones's gentile female friend (Grosskurth, 1991, p. 65). To have refrained from killing the father under these circumstances was to have successfully passed through the Oedipal situation—an acknowledgment of fealty to Freud the father figure.

Besides controlling his male underlings, Freud used psychoanalysis to pathologize female resistance to male sexual advances. This is apparent in the famous analysis of the teenage Dora, who rejected the advances of an older married man. Dora's father sent her to Freud because he wanted her to accede to the man's advances as an appeasement gesture because the father was having an affair with the man's wife. Freud obligingly attributed Dora's rejection to repressing amorous desires toward the man. The message is that fourteen-year-old girls who reject the sexual advances of older married men are behaving hysterically. An evolutionist would interpret her behavior as an understandable (and adaptive) consequence of her evolved psychology. Reflecting the generally positive accounts of Freud in the popular media of the 1950s, Donald Kaplan (1967), a lay analyst writing in *Harper's*, wrote that Freud had "exercised his finest ingenuity" in the case of Dora: "Three months with Freud may have been the only experience with unimpeachable integrity in her long, unhappy life." Lakoff and Coyne (1993) conclude their discussion of Dora by arguing that in general psychoanalysis was characterized by thought control, manipulation, and debasement of the analysand. Crews (1993) also describes a "scarcely believable" case in which Freud manipulated Horace Frink, president of the New York Psychoanalytic Society, into a disastrous divorce and remarriage to an heiress, the latter event to be accompanied by a sizable financial contribution to the psychoanalytic movement. Frink's second wife later divorced him. Both divorces were accompanied by episodes of manic depression.

An important corollary of these findings is that psychoanalysis has many features in common with brainwashing (Bailey, 1961, 1965; Salter, 1998a). During training sessions, any objection by the future psychoanalyst is viewed as a resistance to be overcome (Sulloway, 1979b). Many contemporary analysands feel that their analysts behaved aggressively toward them, turning them into passive and devoted followers of their highly idealized analyst, a role facilitated by the "unquestioned authority" of the analyst (Orgel, 1990, p. 14). Masson (1990, p. 86) describes his training analysis as "like growing up with a despotic parent," since the qualities it requires in the prospective analysts are meekness and abject obedience.

I suggest that the inculcation of passive and devoted followers via the aggression and thought control represented by psychoanalysis has always been an important aspect of the entire project. At a deep level, the fundamentally pseudoscientific structure of psychoanalysis implies that disputes cannot be resolved in a scientific manner, with the result that, as J. Kerr (1992) notes, the only means of resolving disputes involves the exercise of personal power. The result was that the movement was doomed to develop into a mainstream orthodoxy punctuated by numerous sectarian deviations originated by individuals who were expelled from the movement. These offshoots then replicated the fundamental structure of all psychoanalysis-inspired movements: "Each major disagreement over theory or therapy seemed to require a new validating social group, a psychoanalytic tradition that recent splits within Freudian institutes seem only to confirm" (Hale, 1995, p. 26). Whereas real science is individualistic at its core, psychoanalysis in all its manifestations is fundamentally a set of cohesive, authoritarian groups centered around a charismatic leader—what I have termed the "guru phenomenon" typical of all Jewish-dominated movements, as noted in other chapters of this volume.

Despite the complete lack of support by a body of scientific research and the authoritarian, highly politicized atmosphere of the movement, psychoanalysis has at least until recently "maintained a considerable place of honor within residency and medical student curricula and teaching." The American Psychiatric Association (APA) "over many years has been led primarily by medical psychoanalysts, both as medical director in the person of Dr. Melvin Sabshin and through a succession of psychoanalyst presidents" (Cooper, 1990, p. 182). The APA has supported the American Psychoanalytic Society in many ways, directly and indirectly. The intellectual credibility of psychoanalysis within the wider psychiatric community and a considerable portion of its financial resources have therefore been achieved not by developing a body of scientific research or even being open to alternative perspectives, but by political influence within the APA.

Another source of financial support for psychoanalysis derived from its acceptance within the Jewish community. Jews have been vastly overrepresented as patients seeking psychoanalytic treatments and account for 60 percent of the applicants to psychoanalytic clinics in the 1960s (Kadushin, 1969). Indeed, Glazer and Moynihan (1963/1970, p. 163) describe a Jewish subculture in New York in mid-twentieth-century America in which psychoanalysis was a central cultural institution that filled some of the same functions as traditional religious affiliation.

> Psychoanalysis in America is a peculiarly Jewish product.... [Psychoanalysis] was a scientific form of soul-rebuilding to make them whole and hardy, and it was divorced, at least on the surface, from mysticism, will, religion, and all those other romantic and obscure trends that their rational minds rejected. (Glazer & Moynihan, 1963/1970, p. 175)

Patients and analysts alike were participating in a secular movement that retained the critical psychological features of traditional Judaism as a separatist, authoritarian, and collectivist cultlike movement.

Jews in general seem to be drawn to cult-like movements. In *Deadly Cults: The Crimes of True Believers*, Robert L. Snow (2003, p. 135) comments:

> Interestingly, studies have also found that cults are more appealing to certain groups of people. For example, research has shown that the percentage of Jews in cults is far higher than the number of Jews in the general population. Estimates of the proportion of Jews in cults range from 20 percent to 50 percent.

Similar data showing disproportionate Jewish involvement in cults was also reviewed in Chapter 1 of SAID.

Finally, it is reasonable to conclude that Freud's real analysand was gentile culture, and that psychoanalysis was fundamentally an act of aggression toward that culture. The methodology and institutional structure of psychoanalysis may be viewed as attempts to brainwash gentiles into passively accepting the radical criticism of their culture entailed by the fundamental postulates of psychoanalysis. Draped in scientific jargon, the authority of the analyst depended ultimately on a highly authoritarian movement in which dissent resulted in expulsion and elaborate rationalizations in which such behavior was pathologized.

Indeed, the following passage, written to Karl Abraham, shows that Freud thought that in order to accept psychoanalysis, gentiles had to overcome "inner resistances" resulting from their racial origins. Comparing Abraham to Jung, Freud wrote, "You are closer to my intellectual constitution because of racial kinship [Rassenverwandschaft], while he as a Christian and a pastor's son finds his way to me only against great inner resistances" (in Yerushalmi, 1991, p. 42).

Gentiles accepting psychoanalysis would thus, in a sense, represent the Jews conquering the "innate" tendencies of the Christians—the victory of the Semitic general against his hated adversaries, gentiles and their culture. Indeed, Kurzweil (1989) shows that the tendency to pathologize disagreement not only occurred within the movement and in reference to defectors but was also often applied to whole countries where psychoanalysis failed to take root. Thus the early lack of a positive reception for psychoanalysis in France was ascribed to "irrational defenses" (p. 30), and a similar situation in Austria was attributed to a "general resistance" to psychoanalysis (p. 245), where "resistance" was used with psychoanalytic connotations.

PSYCHOANALYSIS AS A TOOL IN THE RADICAL CRITICISM OF WESTERN CULTURE:
THE WIDER CULTURAL INFLUENCE OF FREUD'S THEORY

Because Freud's ideology was self-consciously subversive and, in particular, because it tended to undermine Western institutions surrounding sex and marriage, it is of some interest to consider the effects of these practices from an evolutionary perspective. Western marriage has long been monogamous and exogamous, and these features contrast strongly with features of other stratified societies, especially societies from the Near East, such as ancient Israel (MacDonald, 1999; PTSDA, Ch. 8).

Freud's views in Totem and Taboo and Civilization and Its Discontents represent a failure to grasp the uniqueness of Roman and later Christian institutions of marriage and the role of Christian religious practices in pro-ducing the uniquely egalitarian mating systems characteristic of Western Europe. In Western Europe the repression of sexual behavior has fundamentally served to support socially imposed monogamy, a mating system in which differences in male wealth are much less associated with access to females and reproductive success than in traditional non-Western civilizations where polygyny has been the norm. Polygyny implies sexual competition among males, with wealthy males having access to vastly disproportionate numbers of women and lower-status men often being unable to mate at all. This type of marriage system is very common among the traditional stratified human societies of the world, such as classical China, India, Muslim societies, and ancient Israel (Betzig, 1986; Dickemann, 1979). While poor males cannot find a mate in such a system, women are often reduced to chattel and are typically purchased as concubines by wealthy males. Socially imposed monogamy thus represents a relatively egalitarian mating system for men.

Moreover, because of higher levels of sexual competition among males, the status of women in non-Western societies is immeasurably lower than in Western societies where monogamy is the norm (MacDonald, 1988a, pp. 227–228; 2019a; J. Q. Wilson, 1993b). It is no accident that the recent movement toward women's rights developed in Western societies rather than in the other stratified societies of the world. The massive confusion characteristic of psychoanalysis is also apparent in Freud's close colleague, Fritz Wittels. Wittels expected an era of liberation and sexual freedom to be ushered in by a group of Jewish psychoanalytic messianists, but his expectation was based on a profound misunderstanding of sex and human psychology. Wittels condemned "our contemporary goddamned culture" for forcing women into "the cage of monogamy" (in Gay, 1988, p. 512), a comment that completely misunderstands the effects of inter-male sexual competition as represented by polygyny.

This failure to comprehend the egalitarian nature of Western sexual customs was also apparent in German-Jewish poet Heinrich Heine's vigorous opposition to the bourgeois sexual morality of the nineteenth century. As did Freud, Heine viewed sexual emancipation as a matter of liberation from the constraints imposed by an oppressive and overly spiritual Western culture. Sammons (1979, p. 199) notes, however:

> [I]n the middle-class public, sexual license had long been regarded as a characteristic vice of the aristocracy, while sexual discipline and respect for feminine virtue were associated with bourgeois virtue. In driving so roughly across the grain of these tabus, Heine was running his familiar risk of being perceived, not as an emancipator, but as temperamentally an aristocrat, and the resistance he generated was by no means restricted to the conservative public.

Indeed, lower- and middle-status males' concern with controlling aristocratic sexual behavior was a prominent feature of nineteenth-century discourse about sex (see MacDonald, 1995a,c). Wealthy individuals stand to benefit far more than their inferiors from the relaxation of traditional Western sexual mores—possibly a motive for Jews as an elite, particularly in the contemporary world where sexual license has essentially triumphed and wealthy men have greater access to females and are very attractive to females for well-established reasons that fit with the evolutionary psychology of sex (see, e.g., Buss, 2019).

There are sound reasons for supposing that monogamy was a necessary condition for the peculiarly European "low-pressure" demographic profile described by Wrigley and Schofield (1981). This demographic profile results from late marriage and celibacy of large percentages of females during times of economic scarcity. The theoretical connection with monogamy is that monogamous marriage results in a situation where the poor of both sexes are unable to mate, whereas in polygynous systems an excess of poor females merely lowers the price of concubines for wealthy males. Thus, for example, at the end of the seventeenth century approximately 23 percent of individuals of both sexes remained unmarried between ages forty and forty-four, but, as a result of altered economic opportunities, this percentage dropped at the beginning of the eighteenth century to 9 percent, and there was a corresponding decline in age of marriage (Wrigley & Schofield). Like monogamy, this pattern was unique among the stratified societies of Eurasia (Hajnal, 1965, 1983; Macfarlane, 1986; R. Wall, 1983; Wrigley & Schofield).

In turn, the low-pressure demographic profile appears to have had economic consequences. Not only was marriage rate the main damper on population growth, but, especially in England, this response had a tendency to lag well behind favorable economic changes so that there was a tendency for capital accumulation during good times rather than a constant pressure of population on food supply:

> The fact that the rolling adjustment between economic and demographic fluctuations took place in such a leisurely fashion, tending to produce large if gradual swings in real wages, represented an opportunity to break clear from the low-level income trap which is sometimes supposed to have inhibited all pre-industrial nations. A long period of rising real wages, by changing the structure of demand, will tend to give a disproportionately strong boost to demand for commodities other than the basic necessities of life, and so to sectors of the economy whose growth is especially important if an industrial revolution is to occur. (Wrigley & Schofield, 1981, p. 439; see also Hajnal, 1965; Macfarlane, 1986)

There is thus some reason to suppose that monogamy, by resulting in a low-pressure demographic profile, was a necessary condition for industrialization. This argument suggests that socially imposed monogamy—embedded in the religious and cultural framework of Western societies—may indeed be a central aspect of the architecture of Western modernization.

Another important effect of Western institutions of sex and marriage was to facilitate high-investment parenting. As already indicated, perhaps the most basic mistake Freud made was the systematic conflation of sex and love. This was also his most subversive mistake, and one cannot overemphasize the absolutely disastrous consequences of accepting the Freudian view that sexual liberation would have salutary effects on society.

Contrary to the psychoanalytic perspective, evolutionary theory is compatible with a discrete systems perspective in which there are at least two independent systems influencing reproductive behavior (MacDonald, 1988a, 1992, 1995b, 2012b; MacDonald et al., 2016): One system is a pair-bonding system that facilitates stable pair bonds and high-investment parenting. This system essentially brings the father into the family as a provider of resources for children by providing a basis for close affectional ties (romantic love) between men and women. There is good evidence for such a system both in attachment research and personality psychology.

The second system may be characterized as a sexual attraction-mating system that facilitates mating and short-term sexual relationships. This system is psychometrically associated with extraversion, sensation seeking, aggression, and other appetitive systems, not Love/Nurturance. Psychological research supports the hypothesis that individuals who are high on these systems tend to have more sexual partners and relatively disinhibited sexual behavior. Highest in young adult males, this system underlies a low-investment style of mating behavior in which the male's role is simply to inseminate females rather than provide continuing investment in the children. Many human societies have been characterized by intense sexual competition among males to control large numbers of females (e.g., Betzig, 1986; Dickemann, 1979; MacDonald, 1983). This male pursuit of large numbers of mates and sexual relationships has nothing to do with love. It is the defining characteristic of Western culture to have significantly inhibited this male tendency while at the same time providing cultural supports for pair bonding and companionate marriage. The result has been a relatively egalitarian, high-investment mating system.

The psychoanalytic emphasis on legitimizing extramarital and premarital sex, which often result in women rearing children without male investment, is therefore fundamentally a program that promotes low-investment parenting styles, especially in contexts where such parenting is supported by a generous welfare system. Low-investment parenting is associated with precocious sexuality, early reproduction, lack of impulse control, and unstable pair bonds

(Belsky et al., 1991). Ecologically, high-investment parenting is associated with the need to produce competitive offspring, and we have seen that one aspect of Judaism as a group evolutionary strategy has been a strong emphasis on high-investment parenting (PTSDA, Ch. 7). Applied to gentile culture, the subversive program of psychoanalysis would have the expected effect of resulting in less competitive children; in the long term, gentile culture would be increasingly characterized by low-investment parenting, and, as indicated below, there is evidence that the sexual revolution inaugurated, or at least greatly facilitated, by psychoanalysis has indeed had this effect.

In this regard, it is interesting to note that an important aspect of the social imposition of monogamy in Western Europe has been the development of companionate marriage. One of the peculiar features of Western marriage is that there has been a trend toward companionate marriage based on affection, companionship, and consent between partners (e.g., Brundage, 1987; Hanawalt, 1986; Macfarlane, 1986; L. Stone, 1977, 1990; Westermarck, 1922). Although dating this affective revolution in the various social strata remains controversial (R. Phillips, 1988), several historians have noted the prevalence and psychological importance of affectionate parent-child and husband-wife relations in Western Europe since the Middle Ages (Hanawalt; Macfarlane; Pollack, 1983), or at least since the seventeenth century (e.g., R. Phillips; L. Stone), and likely before (Individualism). L. Stone (1990, p. 60) notes that by the end of the eighteenth century "even in great aristocratic households, mutual affection was regarded as the essential prerequisite for matrimony."

In view of Freud's animosity toward Western culture and the Catholic Church in particular, it is interesting that the Church's policy on marriage included a largely successful attempt to emphasize consent and affection between partners as normative features of marriage (Brundage, 1975, 1987; Duby, 1983; Hanawalt, 1986; Herlihy, 1985; Macfarlane, 1986; Noonan, 1967, 1973; Quaife, 1979; Rouche, 1987; Sheehan, 1978; reviewed in Individualism). Anti-hedonism and the idealization of romantic love as the basis of monogamous marriage have also periodically characterized Western secular intellectual movements (Brundage, 1987), such as late-antiquity Stoicism (e.g., P. Brown, 1987; Veyne, 1987) and nineteenth-century Romanticism (e.g., Corbin, 1990; Porter, 1982).

From an evolutionary perspective, consent frees individuals to pursue their own interests in marriage, among which may be compatibility and conjugal affection. Although affection can certainly occur in the context of arranged marriages—and this has been emphasized by some historians of Republican Rome (e.g., Dixon, 1985)—all things equal, free consent to marriage is more likely to result in affection being one criterion of importance.

Indeed, one sees in these findings a fundamental difference between Judaism as a collectivist group strategy, in which individual decisions are submerged to the interests of the group, versus Western institutions based on individualism. Recall the material reviewed in PTSDA (Ch. 7) indicating that until after World War I arranged marriages were the rule among Jews because the economic basis of marriage was too important to leave to the vagaries of romantic love (P. E. Hyman, 1989). Although high-investment parenting was an important aspect of Judaism as a group evolutionary strategy, conjugal affection was not viewed as central to marriage, with the result that, as Cuddihy (1974) noted, a long line of Jewish intellectuals regarded it as a highly suspect product of an alien culture. Jews also continued to practice consanguineous marriages—a practice that highlights the fundamentally biological agenda of Judaism (see PTSDA, Ch. 8)—well into the twentieth century whereas, as we have seen, the Church successfully opposed consanguinity as a basis of marriage beginning in the Middle Ages. Judaism thus continued to emphasize the collectivist mechanism of the social control of individual behavior in conformity to family and group interests centuries after the control of marriage in the West passed from family and clan to individuals. In contrast to Jewish emphasis on group mechanisms, Western culture has thus uniquely emphasized individualist mechanisms of personal attraction and free consent (see PTSDA, Ch. 8; Individualism).

I conclude that Western religious and secular institutions have resulted in a highly egalitarian mating system that is associated with high-investment parenting. These institutions provided a central role for pair bonding, conjugality, and companionship as the basis of marriage. However, when these institutions were subjected to the radical critique presented by psychoanalysis, they came to be seen as engendering neurosis and anti-Semitism, and Western society itself was viewed as pathogenic. Freud's writings on this issue (see Kurzweil, 1989, p. 85, passim) are replete with assertions on the need for greater sexual freedom to overcome debilitating neurosis. As we shall see, later psychoanalytic critiques of gentile culture pointed to the repression of sexuality as leading to anti-Semitism and a host of other modern ills.

PSYCHOANALYSIS AND THE CRITIQUE OF WESTERN CULTURE

Psychoanalysis has proved to be a veritable treasure trove of ideas for those intent on developing radical critiques of Western culture. Psychoanalysis has influenced thought in a wide range of areas, including sociology, child rearing, criminology, anthropology, literary criticism, art, literature, and the popular media. Kurzweil (1989, p. 102) notes that "something like a culture of psychoanalysis was being established." Torrey (1992) describes in some detail the spread of the movement in the United States, originally through the actions of a small group of predominantly Jewish activists with access to the popular media, the academic world, and the arts, to a pervasive influence in the 1950s: "It is a long road from a beachhead among New York intellectuals to a widespread influence in almost every phase of American life" (p. 37)—what Torrey terms an "assault on American culture" (p. 127).

And as E. S. Shapiro (1989, p. 292) points out, the vast majority of the New York Intellectuals not only had Jewish backgrounds but also strongly identified as Jews:

> The surprising thing about the Jewish intellectuals is not that their expressions of Jewish identity were so pale but that they rejected the easy path of assimilation. That supposedly "cosmopolitan" intellectuals should concern themselves with such a parochial matter as Jewish identity reveals the hold which Jewishness has had on even the most acculturated.

As indicated in Chapter 7, the New York Intellectuals were politically radical and deeply alienated from American political and cultural institutions.

Psychoanalysis was a major component of the *Weltanschauung* of these intellectuals. Torrey's (1992) study indicates a strong overlap among psychoanalysis, liberal-radical politics, and Jewish identification among the American intellectual elite since the 1930s. Torrey (p. 95) describes Dwight Macdonald as "one of the few *goyim* among the New York intelligentsia" involved in this movement, which was centered around the journal *Partisan Review* (see Ch. 7). Given this association of psychoanalysis and the left, it is not surprising that Frederick Crews's (1993; Crews et al., 1995) critique of psychoanalysis has been analyzed as an attack on the left. Writing in *Tikkun*, a publication that combines liberal-radical politics with Jewish activism and is regarded as a journal of the New York Intellectuals (see Ch. 7), Eli Zaretsky (1994, p. 67) remarked that critiques like that of Crews "are continuous with the attack on the Left that began with the election of Richard Nixon in 1968. . . . They continue the repudiation of the revolutionary and utopian possibilities glimpsed in the 1960s." Psychoanalysis was an integral component of the countercultural movement of the 1960s; attacks on it are tantamount to attacking a cornerstone of liberal-radical political culture.

Moreover, the material reviewed by Torrey indicates that the preponderance of psychoanalytically inclined Jews among the intellectual elite continued in the post-World War II era. Torrey studied twenty-one elite American intellectuals identified originally by Kadushin (1974) on the basis of peer ratings as being the most influential. Of the twenty-one, fifteen were Jewish, and questionnaires and analysis of the writings of these fifteen indicated that eleven had been "significantly influenced by Freudian theory at some point in their careers" (p. 185). (This includes intellectuals for whom the writings of Wilhelm Reich, a leading figure of the Freudian left, were more influential than those of

Freud: Saul Bellow, Paul Goodman, and Norman Mailer.) In addition, ten of these eleven (Saul Bellow excepted) were identified as having liberal or radical political beliefs at some period of their career.[106]

The link between psychoanalysis and the political left, as well as the critical role of Jewish-controlled media in the propagation of psychoanalysis, can be seen in the recent uproar of Frederick Crews's critiques of the culture of psychoanalysis. The original articles were published in *The New York Review of Books* (NYRB)—a journal that, along with *Partisan Review* and *Commentary*, is associated with the New York Intellectuals (see Ch. 7). In publishing these articles, the editors of the NYRB "appeared almost like pet owners who had negligently or maliciously consigned their parakeet to the mercies of an ever-lurking cat" (Crews et al., 1995, p. 288). The implication is that publications like the NYRB and the other journals associated with the New York Intellectuals have been instrumental in propagating psychoanalytic and similar doctrines as scientifically and intellectually reputable for decades, and it also suggests that had Crews published his articles in a less visible and less politicized medium, they could have been safely ignored, as has commonly been the practice throughout the long history of psychoanalysis.

Several prominent Freudian critiques of culture remained fairly true to Freud's original premises. For example, Norman O. Brown's influential *Life against Death: The Psychoanalytical Meaning of History* (1959/1985) completely accepts Freud's analysis of culture as delineated in *Civilization and Its Discontents*. Brown finds the most important Freudian doctrine to be the repression of human nature, particularly the repression of pleasure seeking. This repression-caused neurosis is a universal characteristic of humans, but Brown claims that the intellectual history of repression originated in Western philosophy and Western religion. In terms highly reminiscent of some of Freud's early associates, Brown points to a utopian future in which there is a "resurrection of the body" and a complete freeing of the human spirit.

Herbert Marcuse, a countercultural guru of the 1960s, was a member of the first generation of the Frankfurt School whose activities are discussed extensively in Chapter 6. In *Eros and Civilization* Marcuse (1955/1974) accepts Freud's theory that Western culture is pathogenic as a result of the repression of sexual urges, paying homage to Freud, who "recognized the work of repression in the highest values of Western civilization—which presuppose and perpetuate unfreedom and suffering" (p. 240). Marcuse approvingly cites Wilhelm

---

[106] The four elite Jewish intellectuals in this study who were apparently not influenced by Freud were Hannah Arendt, Noam Chomsky, Richard Hofstadter, and Irving Kristol. Of these, only Noam Chomsky could possibly be regarded as someone whose writings were not highly influenced by their Jewish identity and specifically Jewish interests. The findings taken together indicate that the American intellectual scene has been significantly dominated by specifically Jewish interests and that psychoanalysis has been an important tool in advancing these interests.

Reich's early work as an exemplar of the "leftist" wing of Freud's legacy. Reich "emphasized the extent to which sexual repression is enforced by the interests of domination and exploitation, and the extent to which these interests are in turn reinforced and reproduced by sexual repression" (p. 239). Like Freud, Marcuse points the way to a nonexploitative utopian civilization that would result from the complete end of sexual repression, but Marcuse goes beyond Freud's ideas in *Civilization and Its Discontents* only in his even greater optimism regarding the beneficial effects of ending sexual repression.

Indeed, Marcuse ends the book with a ringing defense of the fundamental importance of sexual repression in opposition to several "neo-Freudian revisionist" theorists such as Erich Fromm, Karen Horney, and Henry Stack Sullivan. Interestingly, Marcuse (1955/1974, pp. 238–239) proposes that neo-Freudianism arose because of the belief that orthodox Freudian sexual repression theory would suggest that socialism was unattainable. These neo-Freudian revisionists must thus be seen as continuing the psychoanalytic critique of culture, but in a manner that deemphasizes the exclusive concern with sexual repression. These theorists—particularly Fromm, who had a very strong Jewish identity (Marcus & Tarr, 1986, pp. 348–350; Wiggershaus, 1994, pp. 52ff) and very self-consciously attempted to use psychoanalysis to further a radical political agenda—can be viewed as optimistic-utopian.

Like Marcuse, Fromm was a member of the first generation of the Frankfurt School. A cornerstone of his approach was to view contemporary society as pathogenic and the development of socialism as ushering in a new era of loving human relationships. These writers were highly influential. For example, "A whole generation of college-educated Americans was deeply influenced by Erich Fromm's argument, in *Escape from Freedom*, that National Socialism was the natural outcome of the interplay between a Protestant sensibility and the contradictions inherent in capitalism" (Rothman & Lichter, 1982/1996, p. 87). Fromm (1941) essentially viewed authoritarianism as resulting from an unconscious fear of freedom and a consequent need to seek certainty by joining fascist movements—an example of the tendency among Jewish intellectuals to develop theories in which anti-Semitism is fundamentally the result of the individual or social pathology of gentiles. Fromm (p. 272), like the other Frankfurt School theorists reviewed in Chapter 6, developed a view in which psychological health was epitomized by individualists who achieved their potentials without relying on membership in collectivist groups: "Progress for democracy lies in enhancing the actual freedom, initiative, and spontaneity of the individual, not only in certain private and spiritual matters, but above all in the activity fundamental to every man's existence, his work." As indicated in Chapter 5, radical individualism among gentiles is an excellent prescription for the continuation of Judaism as a cohesive group. The irony (hypocrisy?) is that Fromm and the other members of the Frankfurt School, as individuals who strongly identified with a highly collectivist group (Judaism), advocated radical individ-ualism for the society as a whole—also emphasized by the Frankfurt School (Ch. 6).

John Murray Cuddihy emphasizes that a common theme of psychoanalytic critiques of Western culture is to suppose that Western civility is a thin veneer overlying anti-Semitism and other forms of psychopathology. Wilhelm Reich is an exemplar of this trend—"the violent encounter of the 'tribal' society of the *shtetl* with the 'civil' society of the West" (Cuddihy, 1974, p. 111). In his book *The Function of the Orgasm: Sex-Economic Problems of Biological Energy*, W. Reich (1942/1961, pp. 206–207; emphasis original) wrote:

[T]he forces which had been kept in check for so long by the superficial veneer of good breeding and artificial self-control now borne by the very multitudes that were striving for freedom, broke through into action: In concentration camps, in the persecution of the Jews. . . . In Fascism, the psychic mass disease revealed itself in an *undisguised* form.

For Reich, the "character armor" that ultimately results from repressing sexual orgasms begins in civilized discourse and ends at Auschwitz. Cuddihy notes Reich's very wide influence from the 1940s into the 1970s (I knew some Reichians in college in the 1960s), including anarchist Paul Goodman, poet Karl Shapiro, novelists Stanley Elkin, Isaac Rosenfeld, and Saul Bellow, and psycho-therapists "Fritz" Perls of the Esalen Institute and Arthur Janov (author of *Primal Scream*). Goodman (1960), who, along with Rosenfeld and Bellow, is grouped among the New York Intellectuals discussed in Chapter 7, wrote *Growing Up Absurd: Problems of Youth in the Organized Society*, a highly influ-ential indictment of society as thwarting instinctual urges by its insistence on conformity and repression. For Goodman, the utopian society was to be ush-ered in by a revolutionary vanguard of students, and indeed a 1965 survey of the leaders of the radical Students for a Democratic Society, the most promi-nent radical student organization of the period, found that over half had read Goodman and Marcuse, a much higher percentage than had read Marx, Lenin, or Trotsky (Sale, 1973, p. 205). In an article published in *Commentary*—pub-lished by the American Jewish Committee (an indication of the extent to which psychoanalytic social criticism had penetrated Jewish intellectual circles), Goodman (1961; emphasis original) asks, "*What if the censorship itself, part of a general repressive anti-sexuality, causes the evil, creates the need for sadistic pornography sold at a criminal profit?*" Without adducing any evidence what-ever that sadistic urges result from repressing sexuality, Goodman manages to suggest in typical psychoanalytic style that if only society would cease at-tempting to control sexuality, all would be well.

The disastrous conflation of sex and love in the writings of Freud and his disciples is also apparent in the literary world. Using the example of Leslie Fiedler, Cuddihy (1974, p. 71) emphasized the fascination of Jewish intellectuals with cultural criticism emanating from Freud and Marx—whichever one seemed to work best for a particular author at a particular time. Courtly love was unmasked as sublimation—a ritualized attempt to avoid the coarseness of sexual intercourse with a female. And Dickstein (1977, p. 52) notes regarding Norman Mailer:

> Gradually, like the rest of America, he shifted from a Marxian to a Freudian terrain. Like other fifties radicals he was most effective, and most pro- phetic in the psychosexual sphere rather than in the old political one. . . . Where repression was, let liberation be: this was the message not only of Mailer but of a whole new line of Freudian (or Reichian) radicalism, which did so much to undermine the intellectual consensus of the cold war pe- riod.

Although the works of Marcuse, Goodman, Fiedler, and Mailer are illustra- tive of the deeply subversive cultural critiques emanating from psychoanalysis, these works are only one aspect of an incredibly broad program. Kurzweil (1989) has provided a comprehensive overview of the influence of psychoanal- ysis on cultural critique in all Western societies. A consistent thread in this literature is a concern for developing theories that entail radical critiques of society. The followers of Jacques Lacan, the French literary critic, for example, rejected a biological interpretation of drive theory but were nevertheless "as eager as their German colleagues to restore the radical stance of psychoanal- ysis" (p. 78). As expected in a nonscience, psychoanalytic influence has resulted in a veritable tower of Babel of theories in the area of literary studies: "In America, not even the contributors could agree on what their activities ulti- mately were proving or what they amounted to; they all had their own preju- dices" (p. 195). Lacan's movement splintered into numerous groups after his death, each group claiming legitimate descent from the master. Lacanian psy- choanalysis continued to be a tool in the radical cultural critiques of the Marx- ist Louis Althusser, as well as the highly influential Michel Foucault and Roland Barthes. All of these intellectuals, including Lacan, were disciples of Claude Lévi-Strauss (see Ch. 2), who in turn was influenced by Freud (and Marx) (Dosse, 1997 I, pp. 14, 112–113).

The central role of psychoanalysis in the culture of critique can also be seen in its role in Germany after World War II. T. W. Adorno, first author of The Authoritarian Personality, is an excellent example of a social scientist who uti- lized the language of social science in the service of combating anti-Semitism, pathologizing gentile culture, and rationalizing Jewish separatism (see Ch. 6).

Returning to Germany after World War II, Adorno expressed his fears that psychoanalysis would become "a beauty no longer able to disturb the sleep of humanity" (in Kurzweil, 1989, p. 253). Eventually psychoanalysis became state-supported in Germany, with every German citizen eligible for up to three hundred hours of psychoanalysis (more in severe cases). In 1983 the government of Hesse sought empirical data on the success of psychoanalysis in return for funding a psychoanalytic institute. The response of the offended analysts is a revealing reminder of two central aspects of the psychoanalytic agenda, the pathologization of enemies and the centrality of social criticism: "They rose to the defense of psychoanalysis as a social critique. [They attacked the] unconscious lies of (unnamed but recognizable) psychoanalysts, their unhappy relationship to power, and their frequent neglect of the countertransference." The result was a reinvigoration of psychoanalysis as a social critique and the production of a book that "enlarged their critiques to every political topic" (Kurzweil, p. 315). Kurzweil describes a project in which a full-time staff of twenty psychoanalysts failed to alter the antisocial tendencies of ten hardened criminals through a permissive rehabilitation program. The failure of the program was attributed to the difficulty of reversing the effects of early experiences, and there were calls for preventive psychoanalysis for all German children. The message was that psychoanalysis was justified solely by its usefulness in cultural criticism independent of data on its effectiveness in therapy.

The most influential psychoanalyst in post-World War II Germany was the leftist Alexander Mitscherlich, who viewed psychoanalysis as necessary to humanize Germans and "defend against the inhumanities of civilization" (in Kurzweil, 1989, p. 234). Regarding the necessity to transform Germans in the wake of the Nazi era, Mitscherlich believed that only psychoanalysis held out the hope of redemption for the German people: "Each German had to face this past individually via a more or less 'pragmatic' Freudian analysis" (p. 275). His journal *Psyche* adopted a generally adversarial stance toward German culture, combining Marxist and psychoanalytic perspectives in an attempt to further "antifascist thinking" (p. 236). The "Bernfeld circle" of leftist psychoanalysts emphasizing the "social-critical elements of psychoanalysis" was also active in Germany during this period (p. 234).

In 1962 Mitscherlich organized a conference entitled "The Psychological and Social Assumptions of Anti-Semitism: Analysis of the Psychodynamics of a Prejudice," which offered several highly imaginative psychoanalytic theories in which anti-Semitism was analyzed as essentially a social and individual pathology of gentiles. For example, in his contribution Mitscherlich proposed that children developed hostility when required to obey teachers, and that this then led to identification with the aggressor and ultimately to a glorification of war. Mitscherlich believed that German anti-Semitism was "just one more manifestation of German infantile authoritarianism" (Kurzweil, 1989, p. 295–

296). Béla Grunberger concluded that "oedipal ambivalence toward the father and anal-sadistic relations in early childhood are the anti-Semite's irrevocable inheritance" (p. 296). Martin Wangh analyzed Nazi anti-Semitism as resulting from enhanced Oedipal complexes resulting from father absence during World War I: "Longing for the father ... had strengthened childish homosexual wishes which later projected onto the Jews" (p. 297).

CONCLUSION

We begin to grasp that the deviser of psychoanalysis was at bottom a visionary but endlessly calculating artist, engaged in casting himself as the hero of a multivolume fictional opus that is part epic, part detective story, and part satire on human self-interestedness and animality. This scientifically deflating realization ... is what the Freudian community needs to challenge if it can.

— Crews et al., 1995, p. 12–13

I conclude that psychoanalysis has fundamentally been a political movement of the left that has been dominated throughout its history by individuals who strongly identified as Jews. A consistent theme has been that psychoanalysis has been characterized by intense personal involvement. The intense level of emotional commitment to psychoanalytic doctrines and the intense personal identification with Freud himself as well as with others in the direct line of descent from Freud suggest that for many of its practitioners, participation in the psychoanalytic movement satisfied deep psychological needs related to being a member of a highly cohesive, authoritarian movement.

It is also not surprising, given the clear sense of Jewish intellectual, moral, and, indeed, racial superiority to gentiles that pervaded the early phases of the movement, that outsiders have proposed that psychoanalysis not only had powerful religious overtones but also was directed at achieving specific Jewish interests (Klein, 1981, p. 146). The view that psychoanalysis is a "special interest" movement has continued into the contemporary era (p. 150).

I have noted that Jewish intellectual activity involving the radical critique of gentile culture need not be conceptualized as directed at attaining specific economic or social goals of Judaism. From this perspective, the psychoanalytic subversion of the moral and intellectual basis of Western culture may simply result from social identity processes in which the culture of the outgroup is negatively valued. This does not appear to be the whole story, however.

One way in which psychoanalysis has served specific Jewish interests is the development of theories of anti-Semitism that bear the mantle of science but deemphasize the importance of conflicts of interest between Jews and gentiles, although these theories vary greatly in detail—and, as typical of psychoanalytic theories generally, there is no way to empirically decide among them. Within this body of theory, anti-Semitism is viewed as a form of gentile psychopathology resulting from projections, repressions, and reaction formations stemming ultimately from a pathology-inducing society. The psychoanalysts who emigrated from Europe to the United States during the National Socialist era expected to make psychoanalysis "into the ultimate weapon against fascism, anti-Semitism, and every other antiliberal bias" (Kurzweil, 1989, p. 294). The most influential such attempts, deriving from the Frankfurt School, will be discussed in the following chapter, but such theories continue to appear (e.g., Bergmann, 1995; Ostow, 1995; Young-Bruehl, 1996). Katz (1983), in discussing two examples of this genre, notes that "this sort of theory is as irrefutable as it is undemonstrable"—a description that has, as we have seen, always been a hallmark of psychoanalytic theorizing whatever the subject matter. In both cases there is no link whatever between the historical narrative of anti-Semitism and psychoanalytic theory, and Katz concludes that "the fact that such analogies [between anti-Semitism and certain clinical case histories of obsessive behavior] are far-fetched does not seem to disturb those who interpret all human affairs in psychoanalytic terms."

However, beyond this overt agenda in pathologizing anti-Semitism, it is noteworthy that within psychoanalytic theory, Jewish identity is irrelevant to understanding human behavior. As in the case of radical political ideology, psychoanalysis is a messianic universalist ideology that attempts to subvert traditional gentile social categories as well as the Jewish-gentile distinction itself (Ch. 3), yet it allows for the possibility of a continuation of Jewish group cohesion, though in a cryptic or semi-cryptic state. As with radical political ideology, the Jew-gentile social categorization is of diminished salience and of no theoretical significance. As in the case of psychoanalytic theories of anti-Semitism, to the extent that psychoanalysis becomes part of the worldview of gentiles, social identity theory predicts that anti-Semitism would be minimized.

Gilman (1993, pp. 115, 122, 124) suggests that Freud—as well as several other Jewish scientists of the period—developed theories of hysteria as a reaction to the view that Jews as a "race" were biologically predisposed to hysteria. In contrast to this racially based argument, Freud proposed a universal human nature—"the common basis of human life" (Klein, 1981, p. 71)—and then theorized that all individual differences resulted from environmental influences emanating ultimately from a repressive, inhumane society. Thus although Freud himself believed that Jewish intellectual and moral superiority resulted from Lamarckian inheritance and were thus genetically based, psychoanalysis officially denied the importance of biologically based ethnic differences or indeed the theoretical primacy of ethnic differences or ethnic conflict of any kind. Ethnic conflict, especially anti-Semitism, came to be viewed within psychoanalytic theory as a secondary phenomenon resulting from irrational repressions, projections, and reaction formations—and as an indication of gentile pathology rather than as a reaction to actual behavior.

I have noted that there was often an overlap between psychoanalysis and radical political beliefs among Jews. This is not at all surprising. Both phenomena are essentially Jewish responses to the Enlightenment and its denigration of religious belief as the basis for developing an intellectually legitimate sense of group or individual identity. Both movements are compatible with a strong personal sense of Jewish identity and with some form of group continuity of Judaism; indeed, Yerushalmi (1991, pp. 81ff) argues persuasively that Freud saw himself as a leader of the Jewish people and that his "science" provided a secular interpretation of fundamental Jewish religious themes.

The similarities between these movements are far deeper, however. Both psychoanalysis and radical political ideology present critiques in which the traditional institutions and socio-religious categorizations of gentile society are negatively evaluated. Both movements, and especially psychoanalysis, present their intellectual critiques in the language of science and rationality, the *lingua franca* of post-Enlightenment intellectual discourse. However, both movements have a pronounced political (and ethnic) atmosphere despite their scientific veneer. Such a result is perhaps scarcely surprising in the case of Marxist political ideology, although even Marxism has often been touted by its proponents as "scientific socialism." Psychoanalysis has from the beginning been burdened in its quest for scientific respectability by the clear overtones of its being a sectarian political movement masquerading as science.

Both psychoanalysis and radical political ideology often resulted in a sense of a personal messianic mission to gentile society promising a utopian world free of class struggle, ethnic conflict, and debilitating neuroses. Both movements characteristically developed conceptions of Jewish group identity as leading gentiles to a utopian society of the future, the familiar "light of the nations" concept represented here in wholly secular and "scientific" terms. The social categorizations advocated by these movements completely obliterated the social categorization of Jew-gentile, and both movements developed ideologies in which anti-Semitism was fundamentally the result of factors entirely extraneous to Jewish identity, Jewish group continuity, and Jewish-gentile resource competition. In the promised utopian societies of the future, the category of Jew-gentile would be of no theoretical importance, but Jews could continue to identify as Jews and there could be continuation of Jewish group identity while at the same time a principal source of gentile identity—religion and its concomitant supports for high-investment parenting—would be conceptualized as infantile aberrations. The universalist ideologies of Marxism and psychoanalysis thus were highly compatible with the continuation of Jewish particularism.

As in the case of the other movements discussed here, psychoanalysis was thus a hyper-aggressive attack on Europeans and their culture by a tiny minority. Psychoanalysis denigrated their culture and religion in the service of a social and political transformation that would conform to Jewish interests and utterly compromise the legitimate interests of gentiles.

Effects of the Culture of Psychoanalysis on Gentiles

Besides these functions, the cultural influence of psychoanalysis may actually have benefited Judaism by increasing Jewish-gentile differences in resource competition ability, although there is no reason to suppose that this was consciously intended by the leaders of the movement. Given the psychometrically significant mean differences between Jews and gentiles in intelligence and tendencies toward high-investment parenting, there is every reason to suppose that Jews and gentiles have very different interests in the construction of culture. Jews suffer to a lesser extent than gentiles from the erosion of cultural supports for high-investment parenting, and Jews benefit from the decline in religious belief among gentiles. As Podhoretz (1995) notes, it is in fact the case that Jewish intellectuals, Jewish organizations like the AJCongress, and Jewish-dominated organizations such as the American Civil Liberties Union (see above) have ridiculed Christian religious beliefs, attempted to undermine the public strength of Christianity, and have led the fight for unrestricted pornography, resulting, as noted above, in the hyper-sexualization of Western culture. The evidence of this chapter indicates that psychoanalysis as a Jewish-dominated intellectual movement has been a central component of this war on gentile cultural supports for high-investment parenting.

It is interesting in this regard that Freud held the view that Judaism as a religion was no longer necessary because it had already performed its function of creating the intellectually, spiritually, and morally superior Jewish character: "Having forged the character of the Jews, Judaism as a religion had performed its vital task and could now be dispensed with" (Yerushalmi, 1991, p. 52). The data summarized in this chapter indicate that Freud viewed Jewish intellectual, spiritual, and moral superiority as genetically determined and that gentiles were genetically prone to being slaves of their senses and prone to brutality. The superior Jewish character was genetically determined via Lamarckian inheritance acting for generations as a result of the unique Jewish experience. The data reviewed in PTSDA (Ch. 7) indicate that there is indeed very good evidence for the view that there is a genetic basis for Jewish-gentile differences in IQ and high-investment parenting brought about ultimately by Jewish religious practices over historical time (but via eugenic practices, not via Lamarckian inheritance).

Given that the differences between Jews and gentiles are genetically mediated, Jews would not be as dependent on the preservation of cultural supports for high-investment parenting as would be the case among gentiles. Freud's war on gentile culture through facilitation of the pursuit of sexual gratification, low-investment parenting, and elimination of social controls on sexual behavior may therefore be expected to affect Jews and gentiles differently, with the result that the competitive difference between Jews and gentiles, already significant on the basis of the material reviewed in PTSDA (Chs. 5, 7), would be exacerbated. There is evidence, for example, that more intelligent, affluent, and educated adolescents mature sexually at a relatively slow rate (Belsky et al., 1991; Rushton, 1995). Such adolescents are more likely to abstain from sexual intercourse, so that sexual freedom and the legitimization of nonmarital sex are less likely to result in early marriage, single parenting, and other types of low-investment parenting in this group. Greater intelligence is also associated with later age of marriage, lower levels of illegitimacy, and lower levels of divorce (Herrnstein & Murray, 1994). P. E. Hyman (1989) notes that Jewish families in contemporary America have a lower divorce rate (see also S. M. Cohen, 1986; Waxman, 1989), later age of first marriage, and greater investment in education than non-Jewish families. Recent findings indicate that the age of first sexual intercourse for Jewish adolescents is higher and the rate of unwed teenage pregnancy lower than for any other ethnic or religious group in the United States. Moreover, since Jews are disproportionately economically affluent, the negative effects of divorce and single parenting on children are undoubtedly much attenuated among Jews because the economic stresses typically accompanying divorce and single parenting are much lessened (McLanahan & Booth, 1989; Wallerstein & Kelly, 1980).

These data indicate that Jews have been relatively insulated from the trends toward hyper-sexualization and low-investment parenting characteristic of American society generally since the countercultural revolution of the 1960s. This finding is compatible with data reviewed by Herrnstein and Murray (1994) indicating overwhelming evidence that the negative effects of the shifts that have taken place in Western practices related to sex and marriage in the last several decades have been disproportionately felt at the lower end of the IQ and socioeconomic class distributions and have therefore included relatively few Jews. For example, only 2 percent of the White women in Herrnstein and Murray's top category of cognitive ability (IQ minimum of 125) and 4 percent of the White women in the second category of cognitive ability (IQ between 110 and 125) gave birth to illegitimate children, compared to 23 percent in the fourth class of cognitive ability (IQ between 75 and 90) and 42 percent in the fifth class of cognitive ability (IQ less than 75). Even controlling for poverty fails to remove the influence of IQ: high-IQ women living in poverty are seven times less likely to give birth to an illegitimate child than are low-IQ women living in poverty. Moreover, in the period from 1960 to 1991, illegitimacy among Blacks rose from 24 percent to 68 percent, while illegitimacy among Whites rose from 2 percent to 18 percent. Since the mean Jewish IQ in the United States is approximately 111 and verbal IQ even higher (Lynn, 2011), this finding is compatible with supposing that only a very small percentage of Jewish women would give birth to illegitimate babies, and those who do are undoubtedly much more likely to be economically viable, intelligent, and nurturing than the typical single mother from the lower cognitive classes.

The sexual revolution has thus had little effect on parental investment among people in the highest categories of cognitive ability. These results are highly compatible with the findings of Dunne et al. (1997) that the heritability of age of first sexual intercourse has increased since the 1960s. In their younger cohort (born between 1952 and 1965), genetic factors accounted for 49 percent of the variance among females and 72 percent of the variance among males, and there were no shared environmental influences. In the older cohort (born between 1922 and 1952), genetic influences accounted for 32 percent of the variance for females and none of the variance among males, and there was a significant shared environmental component for both sexes. These data indicate that the erosion of traditional Western controls on sexuality have had far more effect on those who are genetically inclined toward precocious sexuality and, in conjunction with the data presented above, indicate gentiles have been far more affected by these changes than have Jews.

Although other factors are undoubtedly involved, it is remarkable that the increasing trend toward low-investment parenting in the United States largely coincides with the rise of Jews to elite status in American society and the triumph of the psychoanalytic and radical critiques of American culture represented by the political and cultural success of the countercultural movement of the 1960s (Ch. 3). From 1970 to 1991 the rate of single parenting has increased from one in ten families to one in three families (Norton & Miller, 1992), and there have been dramatic increases in teenage sexual activity and teenage childbearing without marriage (Furstenberg, 1991). There is excellent evidence for an association among teenage single parenting, poverty, lack of education, and poor developmental outcomes for children (e.g., Dornbusch & Gray, 1988; Furstenberg & Brooks-Gunn, 1989; McLanahan & Booth, 1989; J. Q. Wilson, 1993a).

Indeed, all the negative trends related to the family show very large increases that developed in the mid-1960s coincident with the countercultural revolution, with its very large Jewish component (Ch. 3) (Herrnstein & Murray, 1994, pp. 168ff; see also W. J. Bennett, 1994; Kaus, 1995; Magnet, 1993), including increases in trends toward lower rates of marriage, "cataclysmic" increases in divorce rates (Herrnstein & Murray, p. 172), and increases in rates of illegitimacy. In the case of divorce and illegitimacy rates, the data indicate a major shift upward during the 1960s from previously existing trend lines, with the upward trend lines established during that period continuing into the present.

The 1960s cultural shift was thus a watershed period in American cultural history, a view that is compatible with Rothman and Lichter's (1982/1996, pp. xviii ff) interpretation of the shift during the 1960s in the direction of "expressive individualism" among cultural elites and the decline of external controls on behavior that had been the cornerstone of the formerly dominant Protestant culture. They note the influence of the New Left in producing these changes, and I have emphasized here the close connections between psychoanalysis and the New Left. Both movements were led and dominated by Jews (see Ch. 3 on the New Left).

The sexual revolution is "the most obvious culprit" underlying the decline in the importance of marriage (Herrnstein & Murray, 1994, p. 544) and its concomitant increase in low-investment parenting:

> What is striking about the 1960s "sexual revolution," as it has properly been called, is how revolutionary it was, in sensibility as well as reality. In 1965, 69 percent of American women and 65 percent of men under the age of thirty said that premarital sex was always or almost always wrong; by 1972, these figures had plummeted to 24 percent and 21 percent. . . . In 1990, only 6 percent of British men and women under the age of thirty-four believed that it was always or almost always wrong. (G. Himmelfarb, 1995, p. 236)

Thus, although there is little reason to suppose that the battle for sexual freedom so central to psychoanalysis had the intention of benefiting the average resource competition ability of Jews vis-à-vis gentiles, the psychoanalytic intellectual war on gentile culture may indeed have resulted in an increased competitive advantage for Jews beyond merely lessening the theoretical importance of the Jew-gentile distinction and providing a "scientific" rationale for pathologizing anti-Semitism. It is also a war that has resulted in a society increasingly split between a disproportionately Jewish cognitive elite and a growing mass of individuals who are intellectually incompetent, irresponsible as parents, prone to criminal behavior, psychiatric disorders, and substance abuse, and who require public assistance. Indeed, the radical changes in the welfare system originating during the 1960s made it easier for women to get by without male investment, with dramatic effects on sexual behavior of both men and women.

Although psychoanalysis is in decline now, especially in the United States, the historical record suggests that other ideological structures will attempt to accomplish some of the same goals psychoanalysis attempted to achieve—the transgender movement, pioneered by Magnus Hirschfield in the 1920s (Joyce,

2021c) and now an integral part of the culture of the left, comes to mind. As it has done throughout its history, Judaism continues to show extraordinary ideological flexibility in achieving the goal of legitimizing the continuation of Jewish group identity and genetic separatism. As indicated in Chapter 2, many Jewish social scientists continue to fashion a social science that serves the interests of Judaism and to develop powerful critiques of theories perceived as antithetical to those interests. The relative disrepute of psychoanalysis as a weapon in these battles will be of little long-term importance in this effort.

6

THE FRANKFURT SCHOOL OF SOCIAL RESEARCH AND THE PATHOLOGIZATION OF GENTILE GROUP ALLEGIANCES

To write poetry after Auschwitz is barbaric.

— Theodor W. Adorno, 1967, p. 34

Chapters 2–5 reviewed several strands of theory and research by Jewish social scientists-ethnic activists that appear to have been influenced by specifically Jewish interests. This theme is continued in the present chapter with a discussion of the main figures of the Frankfurt Institute of Social Research and contains a review of their most influential work, *The Authoritarian Personality* (TAP). This classic work in social psychology was sponsored by the Department of Scientific Research of the American Jewish Committee (AJCommittee) in a series entitled *Studies in Prejudice*. The AJCommittee funded the Institute's research, and funds were also solicited from other activist Jewish organizations (Adorno & Horkheimer, 2004, pp. 345–346). After World War II, the Institute "returned to Germany with great fanfare, it received the generous support of HICOG [the U.S. High Commissioner in Occupied Germany] and the Rockefeller Foundation, ... and its staff was viewed as a living bridge to the past" (Wheatland, 2009, p. 261).

The first generation of the Frankfurt School were all Jews by ethnic background, and the Institute of Social Research itself was founded in 1923 by Carl Grünberg, a Jewish professor of law; it was funded by Felix Weil, a Jewish millionaire (Wiggershaus, 1994, p. 13) during the Weimar period in Germany. Weil's efforts as a "patron of the left" were extraordinarily successful: by the early 1930s the University of Frankfurt had become a bastion of the academic left and "the place where all the thinking of interest in the area of social theory was concentrated" (p. 112). During this period sociology was referred to as a "Jewish science," and the National Socialists came to view Frankfurt itself as a "New Jerusalem on the Franconian Jordan" (p. 112–113).

The National Socialists correctly perceived the Institute of Social Research as a Marxist-oriented organization and closed it within six weeks of Hitler's ascent to power because it had "encouraged activities hostile to the state" (in Wiggershaus, 1994, p. 128). Even after the immigration of the leading members of the Institute to the United States, it was widely perceived as a communist front organization with a dogmatic and biased Marxist perspective, and there was a constant balancing act to attempt not to betray the left "while simultaneously defending themselves against corresponding suspicions" (Wiggershaus, 1994, p. 251, see also p. 255).[107]

Gershom Scholem, the Israeli theologian and documentarian of Jewish mysticism (kabbala), termed the Frankfurt School a "Jewish sect," and there is good evidence for very strong Jewish identifications of the core members.

> Gershon Scholem . . . once quipped that the Institute, in the era during which it was headed by Max Horkheimer, was one of "the three most remarkable 'Jewish sects' that German Jewry produced" [Scholem, 1980, p. 131]. He also recognized that certain members of the Institute would by no means appreciate this designation. But whether (like [Leo] Lowenthal, [Erich] Fromm, and Horkheimer), the members of the Horkheimer circle eventually admitted the impact of their Jewish origins on their life paths and thought, or whether (like [Felix] Weil), they strenuously denied it throughout their lives, Scholem's quip appears to have been on target. . . . In the brief period between Horkheimer's installation as the Institute's Director and the emigration from Germany of most of those associated with the Institute, all of the individuals formally and closely involved with the Institute of Social Research on a full-time basis—Horkheimer, Lowenthal, [Henryk] Grossmann, Fromm, and [Friedrich] Pollock—were Jewish. The members of the Institute of Social Research, to be sure, arrived at the Institute via somewhat different paths. Fromm and Lowenthal arrived via intense involvement with Judaism and Zionism. Grossmann arrived via Bundism [a socialist Jewish labor movement]. Horkheimer and Pollock

---

[107] Part of this balancing act was a conscious practice of self-censorship in an effort to remove Marxist language from their publications, so that, for example, "Marxism" was replaced with "socialism," and "means of production" was replaced by "industrial apparatus" (Wiggershaus, 1994, p. 366). The Marxist substance remained, but by means of this deception the Institute could attempt to defuse accusations of political dogmatism.

arrived via rebellion against the lives, aspirations, and values of their wealthy Jewish fathers. But however different the paths that led all of these men to the Institute, it remains true that they all traveled to it down recognizably Jewish roads. (Jacobs, 2015, p. 42)

Paul W. Massing, who was not Jewish, began his dissertation under Institute Director Carl Grünberg in 1927 (Jacobs, 2015, p. 3); in his discussion of the "small number" of non-Jews affiliated with the Institute, Jacobs notes:

Massing for one came to feel that his non-Jewish background was a factor preventing him from being fully accepted by what ultimately became the inner circle of Institute members. The preponderance of men of Jewish origin at the Institute of Social Research became particularly noticeable after 1930. . . . While members were definitely not chosen on the basis of their family backgrounds, all of the full members of the Institute in residence in Frankfurt and actively involved in its affairs in the period immediately preceding its relocation out of Germany (Horkheimer, Pollack, Grossman, Fromm, and Lowenthal) were Jews. The leftist intellectuals attracted to the Institute had an elective affinity for people like themselves. . . . The differences in the families of Horkheimer, Pollack, Grossman, Fromm, and Lowenthal notwithstanding, all five of these men had Jewish life paths.

Jacobs adds that all arrived at the Institute via "recognizably Jewish roads"—meaning that Jews during that period did not suddenly become individualists but followed one (or more than one) path that was common among Jews, such as Zionism, political radicalism, religion (ranging from Orthodox to Reform), and assimilation with continuing substantial Jewish social and cultural affinities. Moreover, the Institute became centrally concerned with anti-Semitism:

Both *Dialectic of Enlightenment* and *The Authoritarian Personality*—arguably the most important works of the Institute and written while they were in America—are deeply colored by the desire to elucidate and confront hatred of Jews. Indeed, neither of these classic works can be understood without understanding of how and why Horkheimer and Adorno . . . came to believe that explaining antisemitism was a crucial task. A growing fear that anti-Jewish sentiment was both dangerously strong in the United States and might grow stronger, and a dawning comprehension of the nature and implications of Nazi antisemitism—both of which were affected by their family backgrounds and experiences—shaped the ideas of Horkheimer and Adorno during this period, and led to major alterations in their ideas. In addition, [the half-Jewish] Adorno, who had not been involved in

Jewish life in Germany, seems to have come, eventually, to think of himself as a Holocaust survivor and even, to some extent, as a Jew. Though raised without a positive Jewish identity, Adorno's Jewish roots ultimately impacted his sense of self and his analysis of the world in which he lived. (Jacobs, 2015, p. 4)

As discussed below, the "major alterations in their ideas" mainly involved a shift from orthodox Marxism to a fundamental concern with pathologizing White ethnocentrism in an attempt to prevent anti-Semitism and, in particular, a racially conscious anti-Jewish movement like National Socialism.

THE JEWISH IDENTITIES AND SENSE OF JEWISH INTERESTS AMONG THE CORE MEMBERS OF THE FRANKFURT SCHOOL

Max Horkheimer and Theodor Adorno were the central figures in the development of both *Dialectic of Enlightenment* (*DofE*) and TAP.

Max Horkheimer (1895–1973)

Jacobs (2015) notes that Horkheimer's family was Jewishly observant and "strongly attached" to the Jewish community; he was bar mitzvahed. His father Moses was a prominent businessman and actively involved in B'nai B'rith. "Max once asserted that his father's affiliation with B'nai B'rith was a 'contributing determinant' of Max's youth" (p. 8). "Horkheimer's serious involvement with a non-Jewish woman, and the tension that this involvement caused with his parents ... should not be taken as indicating that Horkheimer ceased to worry about matters affecting the Jewish community after 1916" (p. 10). Jacobs attributes Horkheimer's concern with anti-Semitism to his experience in the military where, for example, he wrote after returning from a leave, "I was regarded with spiteful apprehension because I am Jewish" (p. 10); this concern was reflected in his early fictional writings where, for example, he portrays an anti-Jewish agitator rhetorically asking for whom those in the crowd and their families sacrificed during the war. The character states, "Not even people of our own clan, not even people of our own faith, not Germans, not Christians. *Jews* are responsible for everything. *Jews* pocket the profit from our wounds; the same villains who struck down our Lord on the cross—Down with the Jews" (p. 10; emphasis original).

Horkheimer, writing in 1944, noted:

As early as 1930 when I was still in Frankfurt, I became aware of the gravity of the problem of anti-Semitism which even then was a real menace for

Germany and the rest of the world. At that time, I tried to convince outstanding leaders of the community in Germany, in France, and in other
countries of its seriousness. (in Jacobs, 2015, pp. 11–12).

After immigrating to the U.S.,

Horkheimer's sense that antisemitism was a very serious problem that
needed to be addressed increased markedly and led him to devote substantial portions of the Institute's resources to that issue. Significantly,
Horkheimer's analysis of antisemitism in his American years ... which
suggested that the phenomenon had irrational, political, and religious
roots, echoed themes already apparent in his early works of fiction. (Jacobs, 2015, p. 12)

His writing did not include specifically Jewish ideas, "but no less a commentator than Leo Lowenthal has stressed that 'in his thinking [Horkheimer]
was always conscious of his Jewish heritage'" (Jacobs, 2015, p. 12). Horkheimer
"believed that antisemitism needed to be fought, not merely studied, and
hoped that the work done by the Frankfurt School would contribute to this
fight" (p. 107). World War II brought out this concern. On November 17th, 1942,
Horkheimer wrote to Lowenthal, "These days are days of sadness. The extermination of the Jewish people has reached dimensions greater than at any time
in history. I think that the night after these events will be very long and may
devour humanity" (in Jacobs, p. 64).

Moreover, Horkheimer was strongly connected to the Jewish community
in the post-World War II era and deeply concerned with anti-Semitism not
only in Germany, writing in 1954 that he saw Jews as "endangered everywhere
today" (in Jacobs, 2015, p. 134).

In Frankfurt am Main he supported the reconstruction of the Jewish community, of which he became a member in February 1951. Later, together
with his wife Maidon, who had already approached Judaism in emigration,
he belonged to the Jewish religious community in Bern. On holidays, the
couple attended the synagogue.

In addition to his academic activities, Horkheimer moved in Jewish
contexts as a matter of course. He remained a member of the B'nai B'rith
lodge, to which his father had already belonged, and maintained contacts
with the Central Council of Jews, paid a regular contribution to several
Israeli national funds, and supported the founding of the Association of
Friends and Sponsors of the Leo Baeck Institute in the Federal Republic as
well as the Society for Christian-Jewish Cooperation. He was a member of
the Commission for Research into the History of the Jews of Frankfurt.
Beginning in 1956, on Horkheimer's initiative, the Loeb Lectures, a series

of guest lectures on the history, religion, and science of Judaism, were held at Frankfurt's Goethe University, with Leo Baeck giving the opening lecture. The lecture series, which lasted for more than ten years, also laid the foundation for the Seminar for Jewish Studies at Goethe University, which was founded in 1969. (Boll, 2011, pp. 115–116)

Moreover, Horkheimer viewed the Institute's research as Jewish activism intended to combat anti-Semitism. Writing to John Slawson of the AJCommittee on February 14th, 1946 (in Jacobs, 2015, p. 11) he noted:

The period which lies before us is indeed crucial for our work. Whether the results which our long-range studies are going to yield will become useful in our fight is a problem with many aspects. Our findings must be transferred from the medium of scientific techniques into one more practically applicable to our actual task; they must be employed as a basis for drafting new types of educational material, which in turn must be tested out and eventually recommended for use. In connection with these practical experiments the studies which are yielding the results should be carried even further in the direction which seems most promising. Only insofar as we succeed in this decisive stage of our work, will the intellectual and financial effort already put forth, be rewarded.

Horkheimer was quite aware that the AJCommittee, as an activist organization, was only interested in research that would further their activist goals. In a 1940 fundraising appeal addressed to Edward S. Greenbaum, a prominent attorney associated with the AJCommittee, Horkheimer (June 18th, 1940) wrote:

Of all the research we propose to initiate, this project on anti-Semitism ... lies closest to our hearts. It is both our own peculiar problem and at the same time one of the most burning problems for humanity today. We believe that the time is ripe to attack this problem with all the means which modern science places at its disposal.

In a 1946 draft of the Institute's proposal to the AJCommittee, Horkheimer (1946a) emphasized practical aspects of fighting anti-Semitism:

4th Draft
March 4, 1946
FRAME OF REFERENCE FOR THE DEPARTMENT OF SCIENTIFIC
RESEARCH AND PROGRAM EVALUATION
Plan of Work for 1946

> This Department has been founded to serve a practical purpose. The study of anti-Semitism is, for the American Jewish Committee, not a question of academic interest; it is subordinated to the purpose of all the Committee's activities, to fight anti-Semitism in the United States. Ultimately, therefore, the Committee expects that the results of scientific study will provide a type of insight into anti-Semitism that will lend itself to a translation into defensive or preventive action.
>
> This practical purpose is the reason for the Department's existence; the relevance of a project to this purpose is the ultimate criterion for its adoption or rejection.

Horkheimer was also positive about Israel, stating in 1957 that it was a refuge from anti-Semitism; he only rarely criticized Israel, and at times he defended it, although he continued to believe that Israel had departed from the Jewish religious tradition (Jacobs, 2015, p. 142).

Finally, Horkheimer had a sense of Jewish superiority:

> The Jews have been the pioneers of civilization. Their recent history is deeply interconnected with the progress of industry, commerce and science. Their existence is a constant challenge to those who want to be lazy. The Jews are the competitors par excellence. (Horkheimer to Adorno, October 11th, 1945)

Theodor Wiesengrund Adorno (1903–1969)

T. W. Adorno was born to a Catholic mother and an ethnically Jewish father who converted to Protestantism when Theodor was seven. He was apparently not influenced by anti-Semitism as a youth, but there was some taunting. In September 1933, Adorno lost his official permission to teach because he was a "non-Aryan." Jacobs (2015, p. 57) notes that, "Adorno did not think of himself as Jewish during the Weimar years or at the beginning of the Nazi era, and that his self-understanding was linked to German culture far, far more than to his father's Jewish roots." Nevertheless, writing to a young Austrian scholar in 1988, Leo Lowenthal discussed matters relevant to Adorno's relationship to Jewishness and explicitly declared "in conversations, although he was half Jewish, he always identified himself as a Jew, and ascribed an 'aristocratic' significance to this state of affairs" (Jacobs, p. 109), a comment indicating pride in his Jewish heritage. In any case, by the time TAP was written (late 1940s), Adorno clearly had a strong Jewish identity.

Adorno, first author of the famous Berkeley studies of authoritarian personality reviewed here, was a director of the Institute, and he had a very close professional relationship with Institute Director Max Horkheimer to the point that Horkheimer (1947, p. vii) wrote of their work, "It would be difficult to say which of the ideas originated in his mind and which in my own; our philosophy is one." Nevertheless, I interpret the following as indicating that Adorno was mainly responsible for the Institute's shift from an orthodox Marxist interpretation of anti-Semitism to the perspective of TAP that emphasized a psychoanalytically based interpretation of White ethnocentrism. Horkheimer was not credited as an author of TAP.

Jewish themes became increasingly prominent in Adorno's writings beginning in 1940 as a reaction to National Socialist anti-Semitism. Indeed, much of Adorno's later work may be viewed as a reaction to the Holocaust, as typified by his famous comment that "to write poetry after Auschwitz is barbaric" (Adorno, 1967, p. 34) and his question "whether after Auschwitz you can go on living—especially whether one who escaped by accident, one who by rights should have been killed" (Adorno, 1973, p. 363). Tarr (1977, p. 158) notes that the point of the former comment is that "no study of sociology could be possible without reflecting on Auschwitz and without concerning oneself with preventing new Auschwitzes"—clearly a mandate that sociology be based on an activist discipline based on a moral commitment rather than science. "The experience of Auschwitz was turned into an absolute historical and sociological category" (Tarr, p. 165). Clearly there was an intense Jewish consciousness and commitment to Judaism among those most responsible for the works reviewed here.

Adorno's (2006) letters to his parents from 1939–1951 indicate a strong Jewish identity and sense of Jewish interests.

> The anti-Semitism project [which resulted in TAP] is a true blessing. Incidentally, I agree entirely with WK [Oscar Wiesengrund, Adorno's ethnically Jewish father] that abolishing the racial distinction would be the only right thing to do, and God knows our study espouses no less. But: the others do not want to. And at a time when millions of Jews are being murdered, it would not be so appropriate to reproach those people for isolating themselves. The problem lies with the Christians. I hope with all my heart that we really can do something—however modest—to help. (March 29th, 1943; Adorno, 2006, p. 131)

This quote indicates Adorno's activist intent to "abolish the racial distinction," a program that, along with Boasian anthropology, eradicated the influence of racial Darwinism and now dominates social science in the West, where race is widely seen as a social construction divorced from biology. As indicated below, a major thrust of TAP was to combat White ethnocentrism which naturally implies a privileging of one's racial or ethnic group. And, as argued in TAP and as Adorno and Horkheimer argued in DofE, anti-Semitism is a psychological problem among non-Jews and has nothing to do with the characteristics of Jews. Here it's interesting that Adorno blames Christianity for anti-Semitism and mentions (and rejects) Jewish isolation as contributing to anti-Semitism—a major theme of my book *Separation and Its Discontents* (SAID) which emphasizes that Jewish isolation from the surrounding society (leading to invidious ingroup-outgroup dynamics) combined with competition and even exploitation of elements of the non-Jewish population (e.g., the common pattern of Jewish alliances with exploitative non-Jewish elites rationalized by Jewish particularist ethics as described in canonical Jewish religious texts, such as the Talmud or the Shulchan Aruch) was a major cause of historical anti-Semitism.

Regarding Adorno's Jewish identity and his feeling separate from "Aryans"—a racial rather than a religious label which feeds into the program of the Institute to focus on White ethnocentrism: "I am totally Jewified, i.e., have nothing but anti-Semitism on my mind. It is hard to find anything new because Jews are so clever—'Jews know everything'! Yesterday I hired an (Aryan) assistant, I hope it will work out" (April 15th, 1943; Adorno, 2006, p. 132).

Adorno's social circle during the war was entirely Jewish: "We are seeing very few people except a few Jewish bigwigs, who correspond roughly to what one in Germany so charmingly used to term 'business friends'" (November 11th, 1943; Adorno, 2006, p. 157).

When the outcome of the war was clear, Adorno expressed his hatred and desire for revenge toward the "Boches"—a pejorative reference to Germans—and the fulfilment of his wish that ordinary Germans (hence the names "Inges," "Hansjürgens," and "Ute") would die by the millions. One can certainly understand Jewish hatred in this context, but it clearly indicates Adorno's overriding passion against fascism and, given the focus of TAP on fascism, it is certainly reasonable to suppose that this hatred influenced his writing.

> I think that, in military terms, Germany's fate is sealed—even now, before the power of the Allies has reached its pinnacle, and one must almost hope that it does not happen too quickly: that there is not a political collapse which would spare the Germans an open military defeat instead of making them feel themselves what they have done, to prevent them from hatching any new mischief and infecting the world, which is so open to infection. But in any case, I would not even give them another year, and thus solemnly wish for you and for all of us that we might witness the fall of Hitler and the revenge within the next 12 months. For I have nothing against revenge as such, even if I do not wish to be its executor—I object only to its rationalization as justice and law. So: may the little Horst Günthers revel in their own blood, and the Inges be handed over to the Polish brothels, with extra vouchers for Jews. And may they return to us, as to the others, what they have stolen: for there is about as much similarity between organized theft by the oppressors and socialism as there is between heaven and hell. (September 26th, 1943; Adorno, 2006, p. 149)

Nonetheless, there can no longer be any doubt as to the genuine defeat of the Boches—after I had still thought, until a few days ago, that they were drawing back in order to strain the Allied connecting lines and then, as in December, further postpone the end through a counter-offensive. But no, they could not go on any longer, and everything one has been wishing for all these years has taken place: the country reduced to rubble, millions of Hansjürgens and Utes dead, the neck of the German people probably broken in such a way that it will disappear from history as the Carthaginians did after the Second Punic War. Only one cannot be nearly as happy about it as one would think. I at least cannot shake off the feeling of 'too late'— in truth, the Germans have pulled the whole of civilization down with them, and what we are now witnessing is precisely that downfall which could have been prevented if Germany's defeat had been 10 years ago. It is as if that yearning had consumed itself, and now that it has been fulfilled it lacks the ability to feel any joy. All the more so because there is every reason to believe that the principle upheld by the Nazis will outlast them— on a broader economic basis, and therefore all the more horrifically. In the face of the historical tendency, I do not feel able to hope for any more than breathing spaces and loopholes. I am nonetheless deeply grateful that you can experience this moment—for you in particular there is an element of that justice which cannot bring us nearly as much joy, and ultimately one has to say that, in reality, Hitler is the most dreadful thing there ever was, in relation to which everything else was a form of fear and expectation, but not yet real—so one can certainly be happy that it has ended. (May 1st, 1945; Adorno, 2006, p. 217)

Victory in World War II therefore did not diminish the need for prophy-laxes against anti-Semitism given that the world is "so open to infection"—us-ing the analogy to a virus which has become a common way of speaking about anti-Semitism. Reflecting the lack of concern about Jewish behavior as con-tributing to anti-Semitism, Adorno was unwilling to criticize any behavior of groups of Jews in the wake of World War II, no matter how antisocial:

I am reluctant to correspond with you about the Jews, as that is not good for both our more or less broken hearts. After 6 million have been mur-dered, it goes against my instincts to dwell on the manners of those few who survived, whom I incidentally do not need to like [a reference to the manners of an insular Jewish community in Brooklyn described by his cor-respondent as "Practically mediaeval. These people are openly hostile to those outside of their own circles."]. In addition to that, the 50% goy in me feels somehow responsible for the Jewish persecution, so I am therefore quite especially allergic to everything that is said against the chosen peo-ple, e.g., also by Max [Horkheimer], whose anti-Semitism more or less matches that of WK, though he has the excuse of having spent a year working for the American Jewish Committee. *Commentary*, the journal of 'our' (anti-Zionist) committee, is a revolting, lying gutter-rag, and I only sent you the issue because of the passage about Bavaria [a reference to compensation to Jews by the Bavarian government for events before and during the war]. (November 3rd, 1946; Adorno, 2006, p. 248)

Adorno thus feels the "50% goy" in him is responsible for anti-Jewish persecution, suggesting a racial interpretation of anti-Semitism and that he believes that anti-Jewish persecution is inherent in non-Jews, not just Germans (see also below). The passage does not imply that his father (i.e., WK) and Horkheimer were in any ordinary sense anti-Semites. Horkheimer was unhappy with how he was treated by the AJCommittee, but that is certainly compatible with his own strong sense of Jewish identity and interests. And Adorno seems clearly aware that the clannishness and hostility toward outsiders seen among Orthodox Jews provokes a hostile reaction among others (including other Jews), but he is unwilling to blame any Jews for their behavior in the wake of World War II—clearly indicating that he did not view Jewish issues dispassionately—so it is not surprising that *TAP* (or *DofE*) failed to consider Jewish behavior as contributing to anti-Semitism.

Adorno's comments on the AJCommittee-sponsored *Commentary* magazine would seem to imply he was a Zionist at a time when many in the Jewish community—likely a majority—opposed Zionism, typically believing that Zionist commitments by American Jews would lead to charges of disloyalty, a common enough anti-Jewish theme historically (see SAID, Ch. 2). On the other hand, Horkheimer wrote the following in 1946 in corresponding with Elliot Cohen, editor of *Commentary*:

I am following the development of *Commentary* with great interest and enthusiasm. The February issue is a model of how pertinent questions of the various fields of culture can be treated on a high literary level and still make good and easy reading. The Jewish viewpoint makes itself felt as a principle which keeps the diversity of articles from tilting over into mere plurality. Also it is handled with true finesse. Yet, this may be one of the reasons why we feel that the Jewish idea can still be very much alive. (in Wheatland, 2009, p. 154)

Horkheimer likely believed that reaching out to *Commentary* was in the interests of the Institute because it could be a vehicle for the Institute's ideas:

Horkheimer was determined to use the anti-Semitism project as a springboard for the reputation of his Institute and the work of its members. By seeking allies from the masthead of *Commentary*, Horkheimer not only hoped to recruit some potentially powerful allies within the world of the

[AJCommittee], but also to gain some much-needed publicity for his group and its work. . . . *Commentary* helped build an audience for *Studies in Prejudice* by reporting on some of the findings that later appeared in all five of the books. Although Elliot Cohen, *Commentary's* editor, was legitimately intrigued by Horkheimer and the Institute's research regarding anti-Semitism, it is also clear that his public support of the Frankfurt School and its members may have represented an instance in which Cohen was able to gain favor with his sponsors at the [AJCommittee]. . . . Regardless of motives, however, Cohen continually encouraged members of the Institute for Social Research to contribute articles to *Commentary*, and the magazine eventually became one of the significant places where the views of the Institute for Social Research gained access to a broader American audience. (Wheatland, 2009, pp. 155–156)

And they reached out to prominent Jews for support:

Members of the Institute, following the director's example, thus sought the support of prominent American Jews, such as Supreme Court Justice Louis Brandeis, as well as scholars, such as Paul Oppenheim, who had close ties to influential Jewish figures in the United States. . . . In the interim, the Institute impatiently sought other allies from the private sector—most significantly, from America's psychoanalytic establishment. (Wheatland, 2009, p. 223)

Adorno's Jewish activism is mentioned throughout the letters to his parents (2006). He often refers to "Jewish project(s)" in reference to his works and meetings with, or speeches, or lectures given to Jews or Jewish groups. For example:

Next week I have to speak in a highly official capacity, together with a professor from the university here [the editors suggest it was Leonard Bloom, a sociologist], at an executive dinner held by the local branch of the American Jewish Committee; in general, a great deal of Jewish stuff. (April 28th, 1948; Adorno, 2006, p. 323)

The editors note that the talk was "with the purpose of inaugurating a new project towards the 'Re-education of the Germans.'"

Adorno held the view that something very much like what happened in Germany could happen in the United States and that in general, all Europeans were potential fascists. This is important because TAP was clearly aimed at preventing the rise of a fascist movement in the United States by undermining White ethnocentrism. For example:

Fascism in Germany, which is inseparable from anti-Semitism, is no psychological anomaly of the German national character. It is a universal tendency and has an economic basis. . . . The conditions for it—and I mean all of them, not only the economic but also the mass psychological ones—are at least as present here as in Germany, however, and the barbaric semi-civilization of this country will spawn forms no less terrible than those in Germany (we shall send you the novel *It Can't Happen Here* by Sinclair Lewis [a 1935 novel depicting the rise of a Hitler-like dictator in the U.S.], which should be of interest to you; moreover, it is no coincidence that Jack London's *Iron Heel* [a 1908 novel depicting the rise of a conservative dictatorship as a reaction to a rising radical socialist movement], with its prediction of fascism, was written in America). . . . Essentially, I am convinced that one is hopelessly trapped, regardless of where one may be. And it was this conviction that was the root of my resistance against emigration. . . . If one is definitely going to be struck dead, I thought, then at least in the place where one belongs most, according to one's whole nature and the character of one's insights. The only chance to survive the horror, and by no means one that I rate highly, is for fascism to collapse in Germany before it breaks out here. (February 12th, 1940; Adorno, 2006, pp. 40–41)

Indeed, all the Western democracies and Russia are seen as potentially fascist, indicating a problem of Europeans generally as TAP conceived it; hence the need to combat White ethnocentrism. Adorno:

In my opinion, the true reason for the débâcle is that the so-called democracies essentially thirst for fascism, and have virtually invoked the disaster themselves. I found a hundred examples of this in England, and those are actually what make me so suspicious of all things English. . . . As far as America is concerned, we think that the chances have improved a little through [Republican Wendell] Willkie's nomination. While [Senator Arthur] Vandenberg or [Senator Robert] Taft [both of whom were isolationists until after the Pearl Harbor attack] would no doubt have proved all too amenable to some sort of fascist efforts along the lines of [Charles] Lindbergh [see below] or [Father Charles] Coughlin [the anti-Jewish radio personality whose show was cancelled by the Roosevelt administration in 1939], Willkie is the most democratic, anti-fascist and pro-Allies of all the Republican candidates. One can assume, admittedly, that America will be forced to adopt significant elements of fascism—such as the replacement of unemployment benefit with some open or concealed form of labour service for the arms industry—but Willkie at least offers the best guarantee that the next four years will be free of all terror and racial persecution, and what will happen after four years really cannot be predicted. At any rate, I should think that there will be a certain breathing space. If fascism truly does succeed on the largest scale, it is still not out of the question that some territorial solution for the Jewish question will be found after all. I do not share the hopes held by many regarding the supposedly anti-German policies of Russia. The Russian industry is probably already 'organized' by the Germans to such a degree that the Russians no longer have any liberty of action anyway, even if they wanted to. I do not even think they want it, but rather that they are themselves 3 /4 fascist. (June 30th, 1940; Adorno, 2006, p. 58)

In *Minima Moralia* Adorno condemns all of European civilization:

The idea that after this war life will continue 'normally' or even that culture might be 'rebuilt'—as if the rebuilding of culture were not already its negation is idiotic. Millions of Jews have been murdered, and this is to be seen as an interlude and not the catastrophe itself. What more is this culture waiting for? And even if countless people still have time to wait, is it conceivable that what happened in Europe will have no consequences, that the quantity of victims will not be transformed into a new quality of society at large, barbarism? (Adorno, 1951/1974, p. 55; originally written 1944–1947)

Similarly, in a book titled *Towards a New Manifesto* (Adorno & Horkheimer, 2011, pp. 64–65), Horkheimer stated in the mid-1950s—a time when Jews were being pushed out of elite positions in the Soviet Union (a major concern of the New York Intellectuals; see Ch. 7): "The Russians are already halfway towards fascism." Adorno agreed: "If German hearts warm more towards the Russians, that is not just a negative fact. They think the Russians stand for socialism. People are as yet unaware that the Russians are fascists, especially ordinary people."

Horkheimer, writing to a correspondent on Adorno's funeral in 1969:

I am telling you this in order to help you understand the complicated attitude of the deceased to religion and to a specific faith. On the other hand, I may say that Critical Theory, which we both developed, has its roots in Judaism. It derives from the idea that thou shalt make no image of God. That Adorno identified with the persecuted is proven by his declaration that no poem should be created after what happened in Auschwitz. Had he lived longer, and had we spoken about the funeral before he died, it is not impossible that the funeral would have been conducted in the [Jewish] manner suggested in your letter. (in Jacobs, 2015, p. 109)

As noted, in his letter of June 30th, 1940, Adorno mentioned Charles Lindbergh, the famed aviator and a spokesman for the America First Committee that opposed American entry into World War II until after Pearl Harbor.

Adorno's letter implies that Lindbergh would attempt to establish fascism in America; it was written prior to Lindbergh's famous Des Moines speech of September 1941 in which he claimed, correctly, that the Jewish community was one of the influences promoting U.S. entry into the war, along with the British government and the Roosevelt administration (see Preface).

After Lindbergh's Des Moines speech, in a letter to Horkheimer dated September 23rd, 1941, Adorno suggested forming a committee funded by Marshall Field, a wealthy non-Jew, and including other non-Jews: "I therefore think that there must now be a central interest in the anti-Semitism complex among government agencies, and that it is not impossible for us to get something serious from the non-Jewish side, while the Jews are too cowardly" (Adorno & Horkheimer, 2004, p. 248). As noted throughout this volume, Jews as a small minority have often attempted to recruit non-Jews for their causes.

Adorno is quite clear that authoritarianism linked to fascism occupied his interests rather than authoritarianism linked to communism. Rather than developing a general theory of authoritarianism, their main work, TAP, was exclusively concerned with fascism because of what the authors saw as their interests at the time ("National Socialists were our enemies"). Writing in 1953, he noted:

> The fact that less attention was given in the volume to the authoritarian communist party-line than to the potential fascist is solely due to the historical situation. At the time the questionnaire and interview schedule were set up and the material was gathered (1944–1945), the National Socialists were our enemies and Russians our allies. In the atmosphere then prevailing, the common denominator of anti-Nazism did not yet allow the difference between autonomous thinking and its perversion by the communist dictatorship to crystallize as clearly as later on. . . . [E]ven today a large percentage of non-authoritarian persons may be attracted by communism simply because they have not yet learned that communism has turned into a 'rightist party' . . . and has become thoroughly identified with Russian imperialism. (in Jacobs, 2015, p. 93)

This quite possibly reflects his idea that Russians were "3/4 fascists" (see above). Similarly, Horkheimer (2007, pp. 173–174), in a letter to British Marxist political theorist and economist Harold Laski (March 10th, 1941) wrote that he saw fascism as an attempt to retain traditional social structures: "I visualize the authoritarianism as a universal system of repressive domination, aimed fundamentally to preserve obsolescent forms of society by ruthlessly keeping down all their inherent antagonisms." In using the phrase "obsolescent forms of society"—presumably forms such as the pre-1917 government of Russia or traditional American culture dominated by Protestant religions and capitalism—he seems to be looking forward to a revolutionary alteration such as the Bolshevik project of creating "the New Soviet Man."

In a letter to Horkheimer (August 5th, 1940) Adorno gives the first hints of rejecting the Marxist analysis of the proletariat, a view that eventually led the Institute to focus on White ethnocentrism:

> I am beginning to feel, particularly under the influence of the latest news from Germany, that I cannot stop thinking about the fate of the Jews any more. It often seems to me that everything that we used to see from the point of view of the proletariat has been concentrated today with frightful force upon the Jews. No matter what happens to the project, I ask myself whether we should not say what we want to say in connection with the Jews, who are now at the opposite pole to the concentration of power. (in Jacobs, 2015, p. 59)

This was the beginning of the shift from an emphasis on Marxist-oriented economic explanations of anti-Semitism, apparent in Horkheimer's 1939 essay "Juden und Europa," to a psychological perspective. In their 1941 formal proposal for a project on anti-Semitism, the Institute explicitly emphasized psychological issues, while stating that economic factors rooted in Marxism were partly correct (Jacobs 2015, pp. 44, 60). Jacobs suggests that Adorno's influence is likely the reason for the shift (p. 60), and, commenting on a letter to Horkheimer dated October 2nd, 1941, he writes (p. 61):

> Adorno's continuing desire to write on antisemitism was sparked not by Benjamin's death per se, but by a deeper sense that, as he put it in this letter, antisemitism had become the contemporary world's "central injustice," and that it was the task of Critical Theory to "attend to the world where it shows its face at its most gruesome."

Horkheimer's identity as a Jew was important to the development of the anti-Semitism project:

> Horkheimer's desire that the Institute conduct a research project on antisemitism was fed by a number of streams. Horkheimer's Jewish family background, which led him to identify himself as Jewish when speaking to American audiences in the 1940s, was among these streams, and ultimately sensitized him to the general issue of Jew hatred. In a speech on antisemitism delivered on April 16, 1943, Horkheimer told his audience that "[o]ur interest as Jews which leads us to engage in such a work is identical with our task as laborers for the future of mankind." It is altogether possible that Horkheimer was inclined to make such statements by his belief that he would be telling American Jews what they wanted to

hear, and thus increasing the level of support he could obtain from American Jewish organizations. However, there were more heart-felt reasons for Horkheimer to make declarations of this kind. (Jacobs, 2015, pp. 61–62)

Jacobs (2015, p. 63) reviews the general phenomenon of anti-Jewish sentiment in the U.S. from 1920–1940 as also influencing the Institute to focus on anti-Semitism: quotas on Jewish enrolment in higher education, exclusion from hiring and social clubs, restrictive covenants in housing, popular anti-Jewish figures like Father Coughlin, etc.:

> Pollsters found, on the eve of American entry into the Second World War, that ever higher proportions of the American population replied affirmatively to the question, "Do you think Jews have too much power in the United States?" Forty one percent of those polled responded affirmatively to this question in March 1938. Forty three percent responded positively in April 1940. The proportion rose to 45 percent in February 1941, and to 48 percent in October 1941. [Such polls were influential in the [AJCommittee]'s funding of the project (Jacobs, 2015, p. 67).] Leo Lowenthal later noted that it was not until he and his colleagues had come to the United States that they "suddenly discovered that something like a real everyday antisemitism did exist here and that as a Jew one couldn't freely take part in all social spheres. That hotels and clubs, even whole professions, were simply closed to Jews—that didn't yet exist in Germany to such an extent" in the formative years of the members of the Institute. There is no doubt whatsoever that the members of the Frankfurt School also became aware, at some point during their American years, of figures like Father Coughlin. . . .
>
> The Institute's pressing financial needs . . . certainly played a major role in Horkheimer's decision to have his associates seek large-scale grants for a series of projects related to antisemitism. However, it was not, in the last analysis, the need for funds that best explains why Horkheimer himself chose to write on antisemitism, but rather Adorno's premonition of the destruction of European Jewry, Adorno's repeated suggestions that he and Horkheimer write on antisemitism, and a growing sense on the part of both Horkheimer and Adorno of the significance of continuing Jew hatred. By 1941, Horkheimer . . . had come to believe, as he wrote in a letter to Harold Laski, that "society itself can be properly understood only through Antisemitism."

An AJCommittee-sponsored conference of May 1944 attended by Horkheimer and Adorno was motivated not only by a "desire to evaluate the findings" of the studies that had been submitted by the Institute to the AJCommittee but also by "the urgent need of validating the premises of a sound [Jewish] defense program'" (Jacobs, 2015, p. 82)—in other words, to link the Institute's research to Jewish activism. "The consensus view was that the defense program 'should not be limited to a rational approach and that strong emphasis be placed upon latent anti-Semitism and upon the intrinsic relationship between anti-Semitism and anti-democratic values" (p. 83), and there was concern that there would be an upsurge of anti-Semitism after the war. As a result, Horkheimer was appointed "research consultant in its domestic defense program" (p. 83), thus explicitly linking Horkheimer to activist research appealing to emotion rather than rationality; this included work on the anti-Semitism scale eventually used in TAP (p. 84).

Herbert Marcuse (1898–1979)

Marcuse's parents "maintained affiliations, observed Jewish religious traditions, and evinced a set of prejudices, quite typical for German Jews of their time, place, and class" (Jacobs, 2015, p. 112). He received a "rudimentary" Jewish education and was bar mitzvahed, but never developed a theory for the treatment of Jews in World War II. "This fact should not be taken as suggesting that Marcuse was altogether indifferent to antisemitism. In 1971, Marcuse reportedly signed a cable to Aleksei N. Kosygin, Premier of the Soviet Union, which deplored the treatment of Jews in that country" (p. 114–115). He claimed he was Jewish "by tradition and culture, but if culture includes dietary laws and the Bible as holy writ then I can't be classified in that way. I've always defined myself as a Jew when Jews were unjustly attacked. In Germany, being Jewish in the face of overt anti-semitism was being on the left" (p. 116). However, "he was not altogether devoid of Jewish consciousness. Peter Marcuse [his son] notes, 'I remember at home hearing Jewish jokes, a smattering of Yiddish, Jewish friends, a Jewish intellectual circle'" (p. 117). In 1979 Marcuse hosted a seder in his home.

Marcuse supported Israel in the 1967 war and reacted as follows in the aftermath of the war:

> You will understand that I have personal, though not only personal, feelings of solidarity and identification with Israel. Though I have always stressed that emotions, moral concepts and sentiments belong to politics and even to science, and that you cannot motivate either politics or science without emotions, I must see more than a personal prejudice in this solidarity. I cannot forget that for centuries the Jews belonged to the persecuted and oppressed; that not too long ago six million of them were annihilated. . . . When finally a place is to be created for these people where they will not need to fear persecution and oppression that is a goal with which I must declare my sympathy. . . . I agree with Jean-Paul Sartre, who

has said that under all circumstances a new war of annihilation against Israel must be prevented. (Jacobs, 2015, p. 118).

In 1970 Marcuse reiterated his support for Israel as a safe haven for Jews and expressed dismay at Israel's behavior toward the Palestinians: "But it seems to me now, that the Israeli policy, far from preventing the recurrence of such conditions, may very well work toward their recurrence, unless the policies towards the Arabs radically change" (Jacobs, 2015, p. 118). Similarly, during a lecture tour of Israel in 1971 he met many top Israeli leaders (p. 119) but continued to criticize Israeli behavior: "I have a Jewish identity in the context of the expected dangers of the persecution of Jews. I have a difficult time identifying myself with them when they are the persecutors" (p. 121–122).

Leo Lowenthal (1900–1993)

Jacobs (2015, p. 12) comments that Lowenthal was "far more intimately involved in Jewish affairs in the period immediately preceding his initial involvement with the Institute than Horkheimer had ever been." He became a Zionist in the early 1920s and advocated fusing Zionism with traditional Jewish learning at a time when Zionism was deeply divisive within the Jewish community, likely as a rebellion against his more mainstream anti-Zionist father (p. 19). He became involved with what Jacobs (p. 21) labels a "cult community" centered around a charismatic "Torah true" rabbi, Nehemiah Anton Nobel, along with other Jewish intellectuals of the period, including Erich Fromm, Ernst Simon, Martin Buber, Franz Rosenzweig, and Siegfried Kracauer—an example of the "guru phenomenon" that is a recurrent theme of this book. He married Golde Ginsburg who was a Zionist from a "relatively orthodox" Jewish family (p. 22), and he accepted a position with a Jewish organization, the goal of which was to help mainly Orthodox *Ostjuden* settle in Germany. He also co-edited and wrote for an Orthodox-oriented publication, the *Jüdisches Wochenblatt*. Later he joined another cult, this one centered around Frieda Reichmann, a psychoanalyst. Jacobs (p. 29) quotes another member of this cult, Ernst Simon:

> The Jewish "rhythm of life" was an integral part of the intellectual atmosphere of the community, which was purely Jewish. At meals, there were prayers and readings from traditional Jewish scriptures. The Sabbath and Jewish holidays were carefully observed.

Lowenthal described this latter cult as follows:

> The sanatorium was a kind of Jewish-psychoanalytic boarding school and hotel. An almost cultlike atmosphere prevailed there. . . . The sanatorium

adhered to Jewish religious laws: the meals were kosher, and all religious holidays were observed. The Judeo-religious atmosphere intermingled with the interest in psychoanalysis. Somehow, in my recollection I sometimes link this syncretic coupling of the Jewish and the psychoanalytic traditions with our later "marriage" of Marxist theory and psychoanalysis in the Institute, which was to play such a great role in my intellectual life. (in Jacobs, 2015, p. 29)

Noteworthy here is the point that the Institute's orientation of combining Marx and Freud was influenced by this cult-like experience. Gershon Scholem wrote that in the cult, "the Torah and therapy were cultivated on a Freudian foundation." Lowenthal eventually moved away from Orthodox Judaism but continued to write for Jewish publications after joining the Institute in 1926, stopping only after accepting a full-time position in 1930. Much later he acknowledged in 1979, without explicitly specifying the period of the Institute's history but apparently thinking about the Weimar era, "[N]ow, years later and after mature consideration, I must admit to a certain influence of Jewish tradition, which was codeterminative in the development of Critical Theory" (Jacobs, 2015, p. 32).

Wheatland (2009, p. 158) notes Lowenthal's resonance to nineteenth-century German-Jewish poet Heinrich Heine who converted to Christianity but continued to be strongly Jewishly identified:

Thus through Heine was Lowenthal able to discover a distinctly Jewish identity consistent with Critical Theory and the prewar political impulses that gathered the Horkheimer Circle together. For the readers of *Commentary*, a similar revelation was offered. Judaism provided the same vision that the New York Intellectuals had glimpsed in the fusion of radicalism and modernism that they had imagined [i.e., he "had sacrificed his Jewish traditions in order to embrace the same ideal of cosmopolitanism— embodied by the Enlightenment and the French Revolution"; see also Ch. 7 on the New York Intellectuals].

Regarding Israel, Lowenthal took a supportive but critical position much like that of Marcuse described above, except that his support "linked him to his attitude towards Jewish messianism, and stemmed, in part from his (continued) strong sympathy for the prophetic tradition" (Jacobs, 2015, p. 147).

Erich Fromm (1900–1980)

Jacobs (2015, p. 36) notes that Fromm was immersed in Judaism springing from his Orthodox background, and that for five to six years from 1919 or 1920 he studied the Talmud, the philosopher Maimonides, The Book of Tanya (written by the founder of Chabad-Lubavitch Hasidism, essentially a philosophy of his movement), and Jewish history with Orthodox rabbis. He was thus "even more deeply involved in Jewish life before he became associated with the Institute of Social Research than was Lowenthal" (p. 32). He joined a Zionist youth organization, remaining "strictly observant" (p. 33). He drifted away from Orthodoxy after marrying Reichmann in 1926, assuming a more leftist orientation. Around 1926, he published an article in *Imago*, a psychoanalytic publication, attempting to explain Judaism within a psychoanalytic perspective. After being introduced by Lowenthal, who had been involved with him in the Nobel group and Zionist circles, he became a full-time member of the Institute in 1930 (p. 35).

Much later, Fromm notes the continuity between his later views and his early experiences in an intensely Jewish environment:

> In *You Shall be as Gods*, published in 1966, Fromm, referring explicitly to Kraus, Nobel, and Rabinkow [his teachers in Jewish studies], notes that while he no longer practices or believes in religious Judaism, "yet my views have grown out of their teaching, and it is my conviction that at no point has the continuity between their teaching and my own views been interrupted." (Jacobs, 2015, p. 36)

Fromm was a strong critic of Israel while remaining strongly identified as a Jew:

> Fromm, who had been a religiously observant Jew throughout his childhood and young adult years, and who had engaged in deep and sustained study of Jewish texts, retained strong emotional affinities for some portions of the Jewish religious tradition long after he stopped practicing Judaism. It was precisely these affinities, and his interpretations of Judaism, which explain the tenor of his condemnation of Israeli policies, and his continuing disavowal of the notion of a Jewish state in Palestine. (Jacobs, 2015, p. 132)

Wheatland (2009) presents evidence that the Institute separated themselves from Fromm because of his revisionist views on psychoanalysis. Nevertheless, the separation was more tactical than real. Both Fromm and his former Frankfurt colleagues developed a similar intellectual rationale for radical individualism among Whites—mainly because they viewed it as effective in combating anti-Semitism. Prototypical individualists such as libertarians are much less prone to enmeshing themselves in cohesive groups—especially mass movements of ethnic defense. They have no allegiance to their race, their culture, or even their family. The following is a famous passage from Fromm's *Escape from Freedom* (1941, p. 35):

There is only one possible, productive solution for the relationship of individualized man with the world: his active solidarity with all men and his spontaneous activity, love and work, which unite him again with the world, not by primary ties [e.g., family, religion, ethnic group, and race] but as a free and independent individual. . . . However, if the economic, social and political conditions . . . do not offer a basis for the realization of individuality in the sense just mentioned, while at the same time people have lost those ties which gave them security, this lag makes freedom an unbearable burden. It then becomes identical with doubt, with a kind of life which lacks meaning and direction. Powerful tendencies arise to escape from this kind of freedom into submission or some kind of relationship to man and the world which promises relief from uncertainty, even if it deprives the individual of his freedom.

In other words, psychologically healthy people have no psychological ties to anything except their "active solidarity" with all of humanity. This lack of ethnic commitment is what defines freedom.

Friedrich Pollock (1894–1970)

Pollock was raised to "disdain Judaism" (Jacobs, 2015, p. 9), but his career followed a recognizably Jewish trajectory.

Pollock . . . kept Jewish affairs of all kinds at arm's length throughout the period of the Republic. Yet Pollock's life path is as Jewish as is that of his colleagues, albeit in a different sense. For Pollock's assimilatory perspective was *more* typical for German Jews than were the explicitly Jewish stances taken early on by Fromm or Lowenthal. A significant proportion of German Jews of Pollock's generation were highly acculturated, uninvolved in Jewish affairs, and not particularly interested in Judaism, Zionism, or related matters. . . .

Pollock's involvement in German (non-Jewish) leftist intellectual life is similar to and parallels the involvement of countless of his German Jewish counterparts in a range of left-wing political and cultural movements. Acculturated German Jews played visible roles among intellectuals in the Social Democratic party and (in its earliest years) in the Communist party, in such periodicals as the *Weltbühne*, and in left-wing cultural circles. The young German Jews involved in these institutions may well have had no interest in Judaism or Jewishness, but spent much of their time in a milieu in which Jews were present in far greater numbers than their presence in the general population could explain. Unlike Horkheimer, Fromm, Lowenthal, and Grossmann (all of whom, as we have seen, were associated, at various points in their early years, with Jewish institutions) Pollock was a "non-Jewish Jew." But non-Jewish Jews, by definition, are also Jewish.

Jewish identity was not important to Pollock. There can be no doubt, however, that the larger, non-Jewish, world tended to relate to Pollock and to other individuals of Jewish origin active on the left or in German cultural life as Jews [as also commonly occurred on the left in general; see Ch. 3]. The Jewish origins of the active members of the Institute meant that much of the population of the country in which they were born and raised perceived these men as separate from Germans and Germanness. Jewishness, Istvan Deak [1968, p. 24] reminds us, "was a publicly imposed condition" in Weimar Germany: "A significant minority of those whom the German public considered Jews were not aware of their Jewishness or, rather, denied this awareness." The career choices of German Jews remained circumscribed in the 1920s and early 1930s not only by their own abilities and inclinations, but also by continuing anti-Jewish prejudice. (Jacobs, 2015, pp. 40–41, emphasis original)

Walter Benjamin (1892–1940)

Benjamin, who committed suicide in 1940, also had a strong Jewish identification: "Benjamin was interested in Judaism, and influenced by Jewish ideas. He discussed messianism, Jewish mysticism, Zionism, and the nature of his Jewishness, among other topics, at different points in his life. However, he did not devote sustained study to antisemitism per se" (Jacobs, 2015, p. 49).

Writing on Benjamin, Lowenthal noted:

Here we come . . . to the third element . . . which joins the messianic and the political: the Jewish. Some of us long denied its essential role in our development. In retrospect, this must be corrected. . . . The utopian-messianic motif, which is deeply rooted in Jewish metaphysics and mysticism, played a significant role for Benjamin, surely also for Ernst Bloch and Herbert Marcuse, and for myself. In his later years, when he ventured—a bit too far for my taste—into concrete religious symbolism, Horkheimer frequently said (and on this point I agree with him completely) that the Jewish doctrine that the name of God may not be spoken or even written should be adhered to. The name of God is not yet fulfilled, and perhaps it will never be fulfilled; nor is it for us to determine if, when, and how it will be fulfilled for those who come after us. . . . The notion of something perhaps unattainable, perhaps unnameable, but which holds the messianic hope of fulfillment—I suppose this idea is very Jewish; it is certainly a motif in my thinking. (in Jacobs, 2015, pp. 246–247)

BACKGROUND TO THE AUTHORITARIAN PERSONALITY

In Chapter 1 it was noted that since the Enlightenment many Jewish intellectuals have participated in the radical criticism of gentile culture. Max Horkheimer, head of the Institute, very self-consciously perceived an intimate link between Jewish assimilation and the critique of gentile society, stating on one occasion that "assimilation and criticism are but two moments in the same process of emancipation" (Horkheimer, 1974, p. 108). A consistent theme of Horkheimer and Theodor Adorno's Critical Theory was the transformation of society according to moral principles (Tarr, 1977). From the beginning there was a rejection of value-free social science research ("the fetishism of facts") in favor of the fundamental priority of a moral perspective in which present societies, including capitalist, fascist, and eventually Stalinist societies, were to be transformed into utopias of cultural and ethnic pluralism.

Indeed, long before *Studies in Prejudice*, Critical Theorists developed the idea that positivistic (i.e., empirically oriented) social science was an aspect of domination and oppression. Horkheimer wrote in 1937:

> [I]f science as a whole follows the lead of empiricism and the intellect renounces its insistent and confident probing of the tangled brush of observations in order to unearth more about the world than even our well-meaning daily press, it will be participating passively in the maintenance of universal injustice. (in Wiggershaus, 1994, p. 184)

The social scientist must therefore be a critic of culture and adopt an attitude of resistance toward contemporary societies. Presumably this is a stance that would be mitigated in societies where the cultural and political values of the left had substantially triumphed, as, e.g., throughout the contemporary West where Jews are substantially overrepresented among the elite, and journalists and academics commonly defend elite culture and the current political establishment.

The unscientific nature of the enterprise can also be seen in its handling of dissent within the ranks of the Institute. Writing approvingly of Walter Benjamin's work, Adorno stated, "I have come to be convinced that his work will contain *nothing* which could not be defended from the point of view of dialectical materialism" (in Wiggershaus, 1994, p. 161; emphasis original). On the other hand, Erich Fromm was excised from the Institute in the 1930s because his leftist humanism (which indicted the authoritarian nature of the psychoanalyst-patient relationship) was not compatible with the leftist authoritarianism that was an integral part of the current Horkheimer-Adorno line:

[Fromm] takes the easy way out with the concept of authority, without which, after all, neither Lenin's avant-garde nor dictatorship can be conceived of. I would strongly advise him to read Lenin. . . . I must tell you that I see a real threat in this article to the line which the journal takes. (Adorno, in Wiggershaus, 1994, p. 266)

Fromm was excised from the Institute despite the fact that his position was among the most radically leftist to emerge from the psychoanalytic camp. Throughout his career, Fromm remained the embodiment of the psychoanalytic left and its view that bourgeois-capitalist society and fascism resulted from (and reliably reproduced) gross distortions of human nature (see Ch. 5).

Similarly, Marcuse was excluded when his orthodox Marxist views began to diverge from the evolving ideology of Horkheimer and Adorno (see Wiggershaus, 1994, pp. 391–392). Marcuse remained an ardent communist after Adorno and Horkheimer abandoned communism. In an internal document of the Institute from 1947, Marcuse wrote, "The Communist Parties are, and will remain, the sole anti-fascist power. Denunciation of them must be purely theoretical. Such denunciation is conscious of the fact that the realization of the theory is only possible through the Communist Parties" (in Wiggershaus, p. 391). In the same document Marcuse advocated anarchy as a mechanism for achieving the revolution. Yet, Marcuse and Horkheimer never ceased contact, and Horkheimer was an admirer of Marcuse's *Eros and Civilization* (Wiggershaus, p. 470) as reflecting the Institute's view that sexual repression resulted in domination over nature and that ending sexual repression would weaken destructive tendencies.

These exclusionary trends are also apparent in the aborted plans to reinstitute the Institute's journal in the 1950s. It was decided that there were too few contributors supporting the Horkheimer-Adorno line to support a journal and the plans foundered (Wiggershaus, 1994, p. 471). Throughout its history, to be a member of the Institute was to adopt a certain viewpoint and to submit to heavy editing and even censorship of one's works to ensure conformity to a clearly articulated ideological position—reminiscent of elite opposition to free speech and intellectual diversity that is now pervasive throughout the West.

Thus it is not surprising that the Institute developed a reputation as politically motivated and intensely networked. In a letter to Adorno dated June 23rd, 1941, Horkheimer (2007, p. 177) paraphrased someone on the board of the Rockefeller Foundation objecting to a grant for the Frankfurt School; after citing a negative evaluation from 1929, this objector noted:

We know these people from their time in Europe. . . . But what's the record of these people in this country anyway? It only confirms the old testimony that we're dealing with a group of friends who don't want anyone else to

see their cards and have little to do with genuine science. They have provided neither proof that they truly pursue social research nor that they
want to fit in with life here. One doesn't know how or for what purposes
money is spent here; one can only guess based on the mind-set of these
gentlemen.

The Frankfurt School as Self-Conscious Propaganda

In a letter to Adorno dated November 24th, 1944, Horkheimer advocated
disseminating anti-anti-Jewish propaganda via a top-down approach to Jewish
activism:

> The way to do this is not to approach the individuals from the outside, to
> appeal to the masses. This would rather correspond to a mechanistic,
> summative, abstract thought. The change of the group atmosphere is
> achieved by training the leaders, who will train the sub-leaders who will
> in turn train the members. Such concrete thinking ... conquered all
> branches of advanced social psychology. ... And why shouldn't we use
> such psychology to shut the mouths that say bad things about Jews. We
> simply experiment with intercultural groups, then train the leaders, sub-
> leaders and members, and eventually achieve that the less desirable [writ-
> ten in English] sorts of people are consumed more pleasurably. This is the
> dark path of humanity. (Adorno & Horkheimer, 2004, p. 370; trans. from
> the German)

Such a top-down approach is entirely compatible with TAP's being directed toward an academic audience. Further, Horkheimer expresses his belief
that people are manipulable by propaganda:

> The view propagated from the left that one must distinguish between Na-
> zis and Germans belongs to the open transition from the class to the
> racket phase of society. The meaning of this slogan is no other than that
> the peoples are simply herds of cattle, which naturally run after any leader
> or: to put it more modernly, on the basis of experience in psychological
> methods of management, can be brought to anything to which one wants
> them. The Russians, who of course have every reason to do so, are adver-
> tising this fact by entering the Romanian cities with regiments formed of
> Romanian prisoners of war. The people in arms need only be exposed to a
> few months of scientifically based propaganda to go to their deaths for the
> opposite clique instead of one. Basically, the same is true for France, which
> passed from Herriot-Weygand to Laval-Petain and from there to de
> Gaulle, each time shedding its revolutionary blood in the name of la
> grande France. From the same spirit springs the propaganda of the Free
> Germans and their inevitable Dorothy Thompson. Who will blame the

Germans for the Nazis: we know perfectly well that they go over to Stalin or the General Motors with the same enthusiasm! And that's what we need! (November 24th, 1944; Adorno & Horkheimer, 2004, p. 369)

Further indicating a propagandistic thrust and envisioning their top-down program of propagandizing the masses:

As for the Berkeley Project, I would also like to recall that its immediate value to the Committee is in proving the link between anti-Semitism, fascism, and destructive character. If we could provide experimental proof of the threatening nature of anti-Semitism to democratic civilization, we would have already delivered almost more than we promised. In this way, the Committee could indeed gain powerful allies, especially persons and agencies that would take action in the army and the civilian population. (Horkheimer to Adorno, December 9th, 1944; Adorno & Horkheimer, 2004, p. 382)

Opposing what they consider anti-Jewish stereotypes by pressure on the media:

As part of the project on indirect anti-Semitic propaganda, it should be envisaged that, on the basis of the results, the film and radio industry, as far as it is sympathetic to us, should be made aware of the stereotypical configurations that we have identified as indirectly anti-Semitic (a fictitious example: a psychoanalyst in a women serial who destroys women through demonic forces, or deceitful and slick advocates or bankers in those films that glorify the common man). If we could prove the anti-Semitic implication of such imagines, or at least make it somewhat plausible, we could certainly work to eradicate them. (Adorno to Horkheimer, December 30th, 1944; Adorno & Horkheimer, 2004, p. 416)

As discussed below, Samuel Flowerman, who was closely associated with the Frankfurt School, led a campaign to influence the mass media staffed by people with expertise in influencing public opinion in the direction of disseminating such propaganda.

The Moral and Political Agenda of the Frankfurt School

As might be expected from a highly authoritarian political movement, the result was a speculative, philosophical body of work that ultimately had no influence on empirically oriented sociology, although, as indicated below, it has had a profound influence on theory in the humanities. (TAP is not included in this statement; it was very influential but had a faulty and inadequate empirical basis based on psychoanalysis, as described below—a simulacrum of empirical science.) This body of work does not qualify as science because of its rejection of experimentation, quantification, and verification, and because of the priority of moral and political concerns over the investigation of the nature of human social psychology.

The priority of the moral and political agenda of Critical Theory is essential to understanding the Frankfurt School and its influence. Horkheimer and Adorno eventually rejected the classical Marxist perspective on the importance of class struggle for the development of fascism in favor of a perspective in which both fascism and capitalism were fundamentally conceptualized as deriving from supposed psychological deficiencies resulting in domination and authoritarianism. Further, they developed a psychoanalytically based theory that disturbed parent-child relations involving the suppression of human nature were a necessary condition for domination and authoritarianism—and White ethnocentrism.

Indeed psychoanalysis was a fundamental influence on their thinking. Adorno made clear the relation between psychoanalysis and TAP in a 1948 paper (Adorno, 1948/2016), writing that TAP as a whole "is in full harmony with psychoanalysis in its more orthodox, Freudian version." Although he does not reject economic factors as irrelevant, he looks forward to combining these two approaches.

Virtually from the beginning, psychoanalysis had a respected position within the Institute for Social Research, particularly under the influence of Erich Fromm. Fromm held positions at the Frankfurt Psychoanalytic Institute as well as at the Institute for Social Research, and along with other "left-Freudians" such as Wilhelm Reich and eventually Marcuse, he developed theories that incorporated both Marxism and psychoanalysis essentially by developing a theoretical link between the repression of instincts in the context of family relationships (or, as in the case of Fromm, the development of "sadomasochistic" and "anal" personality traits within the family) and the development of oppressive social and economic structures.

It is interesting that although the Horkheimer group developed a very strong hostility to empirical science and the positivistic philosophy of science, they felt no need to abandon psychoanalysis. Indeed, psychoanalysis was "a central factor in giving Horkheimer and the most important of his fellow theoreticians the sense that important insights could also be achieved—or even better achieved—by skipping over the specialized disciplines" (Wiggershaus, 1994, p. 186). We shall see that psychoanalysis as a nonempirically based hermeneutic structure (which nevertheless masqueraded as a science) was an infinitely plastic tool in the hands of those constructing a theory aimed at achieving purely political objectives.

For Horkheimer and Adorno, *the fundamental shift from a Marxist sociological level to the psychological level that occurred during the 1940s was motivated by the fact that in Germany the proletariat had succumbed to fascism and in the Soviet Union socialism had not prevented the development of an authoritarian government that failed to guarantee individual autonomy or Jewish group interests* (see Tarr, 1977, p. 80; Wiggershaus, 1994, pp. 137ff, 391ff). Within the new perspective, authoritarianism was viewed as the fundamental problem, its origin traceable to family interactions and ultimately to the suppression of human nature (Tarr, pp. 87–88). Nevertheless, suggesting that the empirical work was aimed at confirming an a priori theory, the formal outline of the theory can be seen in philosophical form in the earlier work *Studien über Autorität und Familie* (*Studies on Authority and the Family*) of 1936, a work that presented Fromm's psychoanalytic theory of authoritarian "sadomasochistic" family relationships and their putative linkages with bourgeois capitalism and fascism.

Unlike Fromm (see above), the Frankfurt School retained an orthodox view of psychoanalysis. This had a major payoff for the Frankfurt School because it was able to ally itself with Ernst Simmel's Psychoanalytic Institute. Simmel, a powerful and well-connected psychoanalyst of Jewish background, had direct ties to Freud—the gold standard of psychoanalytic royalty. (Those with direct ties to the master enjoyed a privileged position within psychoanalysis—a sure sign, among many others, that we are dealing with a cult rather than a scientific movement.) "Among the followers of Freud, of the early as well as of the later years, none was more loyal, more devoted, more meticulous in adhering to basic principles in psychoanalysis than Ernst Simmel" (Deri & Brunswick, 1964). Simmel then promoted the Frankfurt School's work and used his position to promote research on anti-Semitism within the American Psychiatric Association (APA) at a time when psychoanalysis used its political muscle to dominate the APA (Wheatland, 2009, p. 325). Simmel also sought funding for the Frankfurt School from wealthy, presumably Jewish, benefactors of psychoanalysis.

The entire episode is a wonderful example of Jewish ethnic networking that had the effect of subverting scientific psychiatry. Psychoanalysis is clearly a Jewish intellectual movement, as indicated not only by the ethnic background of the leading lights of the field, but also by the support it received from the wider Jewish community (see Ch. 5). Fortunately, the rise of scientific psychiatry has resulted in the more or less complete eradication of psychoanalysis within mainstream psychiatry. Ultimately this was due mainly to the rise of biological psychiatry as well as the usefulness of cognitive and learning perspectives derived from mainstream psychology. During its heyday, however, psychoanalysts like Simmel used their power within the APA to promote psychoanalysis and psychoanalytic theories of anti-Semitism—an effort that had the effect of retarding scientific research in psychiatry while propagating apologetic, scientifically worthless theories of anti-Jewish attitudes.

In the event, the Institute received funding for its *Studies in Prejudice* project (including TAP) from the AJCommittee. Wheatland (2009) shows that the ADL was enthusiastic about the project. The Institute's successful funding proposal argued that modern anti-Semitism,

> aims not only at exterminating the Jews, but also at annihilating liberty and democracy. It has become the spearhead of the totalitarian order. . . . The attacks on the Jews are not primarily aimed at the Jews but at large sections of modern society, especially the free middle classes, which appear as an obstacle to the establishment of totalitarianism. (in Wheatland, 2009, p. 236)

In other words, the war on anti-Semitism was framed as a war against those who would destroy democracy, freedom, and the middle classes—clearly an attempt to appeal to mainstream Americans rather than solely to Jewish interests.

Particularly interesting is that prior to the publication of the *Studies in Prejudice* series, *Commentary*, published by the AJCommittee, developed a public relations campaign to promote the books. "From the very first issue [in 1945], the magazine began to publish a series of [uniformly uncritical] articles that brought the work of the Horkheimer Circle to the attention of American readers" (Wheatland, 2009, p. 253).

After the Frankfurt School received funding from the AJCommittee, Horkheimer's office and *Commentary* were housed in the same building. Nathan Glazer, a prominent New York Intellectual, got his job at *Commentary* because he was already working for Horkheimer. There was an obvious congruence between the views of the AJCommittee and the Frankfurt School:

> Rather than simply fulfilling Jewish aims that had been dramatically highlighted by the Holocaust, the Studies in Prejudice were envisioned to be a broader contribution to American society and culture—efforts consistent with the AJC's [AJCommittee's] desire to promote pluralism and Jewish cultural interests within the United States. . . . Unlike Partisan Review which self-consciously promoted an ideal of cosmopolitan universalism that was framed by the influences of Marxism and modernism, *Commentary* . . . was envisioned to be a distinctly Jewish magazine. (Wheatland, 2009, p. 154)

Indeed, despite a carefully crafted public image of *Commentary* as completely independent of the AJCommittee, in fact its "autonomy may have been more of an illusion than a reality" (Wheatland, 2009, p. 155). Wheatland cites evidence that Elliot Cohen (the editor of *Commentary* from 1945–1959) was occasionally reprimanded by the AJCommittee executive board and at other times was pressured to promote projects advocated by the AJCommittee. Significantly, Cohen encouraged members of the Frankfurt School to write for *Commentary*, and the AJCommittee had become the main financial support for the Frankfurt School. Wheatland shows that *Commentary* played a major role in promoting the Frankfurt School's *Studies in Prejudice* series, including TAP. The Institute also appealed to the wider Jewish community, publicizing their work "through public lectures at Jewish colleges and local temples" (p. 251) as well as other public venues.

An example of Frankfurt School writing in *Commentary* is Leo Lowenthal's 1947 article on Heinrich Heine, the nineteenth-century Jewish poet who converted to Christianity early in his career but later renounced his conversion. Lowenthal's article "Heine's Religion" is interesting because, as Wheatland notes, it reflects not only Heine's attitudes but also the attitudes of the New York Intellectuals and the other members of the Frankfurt School.

> Heine ... sacrificed his Jewish traditions in order to embrace the same ideal of cosmopolitanism—embodied by the Enlightenment and the French Revolution—that the Frankfurt School and the prewar writers for *Partisan Review* adopted. ... For both groups [i.e., the Frankfurt School and the New York Intellectuals] Marxism embodied the yearning for a repaired and redeemed humanity—a world in which racial prejudice and socioeconomic injustice were overcome. (Wheatland, 2009, p. 157).

Eventually, however, Heine and Lowenthal (and the rest of the Frankfurt coterie as well as the New York Intellectuals) abandoned the Enlightenment and reverted to Jewish patriotism. Heine wrote:

> My preference for Greece has since declined. I see now that the Greeks were merely handsome youths, while the Jews were, and still are, grown men, mighty, indomitable men, despite eighteen centuries of persecution and misery. I have learned to rate them at their true value. (in Wheatland, 2009, p. 158)

Lowenthal concurred, as Wheatland (2009, p. 158) writes, acknowledging that "Judaism was a tradition that need not be transcended in the name of loftier ideals."

In other words, Jews could advocate cosmopolitan universalism for Whites while at the same time retaining their particularist Jewish commitments. This is perhaps the fundamental intellectual stance of Diaspora Jewish intellectuals since the Enlightenment (and strikingly absent in Israel which has opted for strongly ethnonationalist governments at least since the 1970s). Wheatland doesn't comment on the obvious contradiction here. White

Christians are to give up their ethnic and religious attachments as outmoded and "anti-democratic," while Jews fashion an ethnic identity that wears the mask of cosmopolitan universalism.

Dialectic of Enlightenment. Horkheimer and Adorno's (1944/1990) *Dialectic of Enlightenment (DofE)* developed a philosophical-speculative theory of anti-Semitism.[108] In addition to being highly abstract and written in what might be termed a Hegelian manner, the style of writing is assertional: statements about anti-Semitism are simply asserted with no attempt to provide any empirical justification.[109] As Jacob Katz (1983) notes, the Frankfurt School has "not been notable for the accuracy of its evaluation of the Jewish situation either before the advent of Nazism or afterward." However, many of the ideas simply asserted there in a philosophical, speculative manner are identical to the theories of anti-Semitism contained in TAP. Indeed, the authors viewed the chapter on anti-Semitism as a theoretical study for their anticipated empirical study of anti-Semitism (Wiggershaus, 1994, p. 324). TAP may thus be viewed as an attempt to provide these philosophical theories of anti-Semitism with empirical support, but the theory itself was fundamentally an *a priori* philosophical theory and was not viewed by its authors as subject to either verification or falsification:

> Horkheimer seemed to consider the dialectics project and the anti-Semitism project as two distinct items relating to one another in the way that an abstract theory relates to its application to a concrete topic, or in the way that Hegel's logic relates to the Hegelian philosophies of history, law or aesthetics. Was this not turning a distinction within the theoretical and empirical research process into a distinction which silently gave the theory the dignity of speculation and made it independent of the empiricism appropriate to science? And was empirical research not thus being denied

---

[108] The general thesis of *DofE* is that the Enlightenment reflected the Western attempt to dominate nature and suppress human nature. Fascism was then viewed as the ultimate embodiment of the Enlightenment, since it represented the apotheosis of domination and the use of science as an instrument of oppression. In this perspective fascist collectivism is the logical outgrowth of Western individualism—a perspective that is fanciful to say the least. As discussed in *Individualism and the Western Liberal Tradition*, the collectivist nature of fascism has not been characteristic of Western political organizations. To a much greater extent than any other world cultural group, Western cultures have instead tended toward individualism beginning with the Greco-Roman world of antiquity; Judaism, in contrast, is a paradigm of a collectivist, group-oriented culture. As Charles Liebman (1973, p. 157) points out, it was the Jews who "sought the options of the Enlightenment but rejected its consequences," by (in my terms) retaining a strong sense of group identity in a society nominally committed to individualism. And as argued in SAID (Chs. 3–5), there is good reason to suppose that the presence of Jews as a highly salient and successful group evolutionary strategy was a necessary condition for the development of prominent Western examples of collectivism.

[109] Adorno's philosophical style is virtually impenetrable. See Karl Popper's (1984) humorous (and valid) dissection of the vacuity and pretentiousness of Adorno's language. Piccone (1993) proposes that Adorno's difficult prose was necessary to camouflage his revolutionary intent.

its status as a dimension of reflected experience, and degraded into a means of illustrating the theory? . . . A further open question was whether their enthusiasm for the theory, and their contemptuous remarks about research in specific scientific disciplines, in fact represented more than mere evidence of personal values and moods; whether these did not have an influence on the way in which their scholarly work was carried out and on its results—particularly when external influences were forcing them to take both dimensions seriously. (Wiggershaus, 1994, pp. 320–321; see also Jay, 1973, pp. 240, 251)

The non-empirical nature of the theory of anti-Semitism was quite clear to Adorno as well:

> [W]e never regarded the theory simply as a set of hypotheses but as in some sense standing on its own feet, and therefore did not intend to prove or disprove the theory through our findings but only to derive from it concrete questions for investigation, which must then be judged on their own merit and demonstrate certain prevalent socio-psychological structures. (Adorno, 1969a, p. 363)

The findings do indeed have to be judged on their own merit, and as indicated below, there is reason to suppose that the procedures used to verify the theory went well beyond the bounds of normal scientific practice.

Fundamentally, the TAP studies resulted from a felt need to develop an empirical program of research that would support a politically and intellectually satisfying *a priori* theory of anti-Semitism in order to influence an American academic audience. As Horkheimer stated in 1943:

> When we became aware that a few of our American friends expected of an Institute of Social Sciences that it engage in studies on pertinent social problems, fieldwork and other empirical investigations, we tried to satisfy these demands as well as we could, but our heart was set on individual studies in the sense of *Geisteswissenschaften* [i.e., the humanities] and the philosophical analysis of culture. (in Wiggershaus, 1994, p. 252).

The Frankfurt School was thus a neophyte in the area of empirical research. Indeed, the goal of producing political propaganda by using the methods of social science was self-consciously articulated by Horkheimer. Thus Horkheimer reacted with enthusiasm to the idea of including criminals in the study:

> Research would be able here to transform itself *directly* into propaganda, i.e., if it could be reliably established that a particularly high percentage of

criminals were extreme anti-Semites, the result would as such already be propaganda. I would also like to try to examine psychopaths in mental hospitals. (Adorno to Horkheimer, October 26th, 1944; Adorno & Hork-heimer, 2004, p. 332, emphasis original; see also Wiggershaus, 1994, p. 375)

Both groups were eventually included in the study.

A general theme in *DofE* is that anti-Semitism is the result of "the will to destroy born of a false social order" (p. 168). The ideology that Jews possess a variety of negative traits is simply a projection resulting in a self-portrait of the anti-Semite: anti-Semites accuse the Jews of wanting power, but in reality the anti-Semites "long for total possession and unlimited power, at any price. They transfer their guilt for this to the Jews" (p. 169).

There is a recognition that anti-Semitism is associated with gentile move-ments for national cohesiveness (*DofE*, pp. 169–170). The anti-Semitism arising along with such movements is interpreted as resulting from the "urge to de-stroy" carried out by "covetous mobs" that are ultimately manipulated by rul-ing gentile elites to conceal their own economic domination. Anti-Semitism is without function except to serve as a means of discharging the anger of those who are frustrated economically and sexually (p. 171).

Horkheimer and Adorno propose that modern fascism is basically the same as traditional Christianity because both involve opposition to and subju-gation of nature. While Judaism remained a "natural religion" concerned with national life and self-preservation, Christianity turned toward domination and a rejection of all that is natural. In an argument reminiscent of Freud's argu-ment in *Moses and Monotheism* (see Ch. 5), religious anti-Semitism then arises because of hatred of those "who did not make the dull sacrifice of reason. . . . The adherents of the religion of the Father are hated by those who support the religion of the Son—hated as those who know better" (*DofE*, p. 179).

This tendency to interpret anti-Semitism as fundamentally deriving from suppressing nature is central to *Studies in Prejudice*, and particularly TAP.[110]

---

[110] The theme that all modern ills, including National Socialism, collectivism, adolescent rebel-lion, mental illness, and criminality are due to the suppression of nature, including human nature, is also prominent in Horkheimer's (1947, pp. 92ff) *Eclipse of Reason*. In a passage that directly conforms to the psychoanalytic perspectives discussed in Chapter 5, the suppression of nature characteristic of civilization is said to begin at birth: "Each human being experiences the domineering aspect of civilization from his birth. To the child, the father's power seems overwhelming, supernatural in the literal sense of the word. The father's command is reason exempt from nature, an inexorable spiritual force. The child suffers in submitting to this force. It is almost impossible for an adult to remember all the pangs he experienced as a child in heeding innumerable parental admonitions not to stick his tongue out, not to mimic others, not to be untidy or forget to wash behind his ears. In these demands, the child is confronted by the fundamental postulates of civilization. He is forced to resist the immediate pressure of his urges, to differentiate between himself and the environment, to be efficient—in short, to borrow Freud's terminology, to adopt a superego embodying all the so-called principles that his father and other father-like figures hold up to him" (pp. 109–110).

Suppression of nature results in projection of qualities of self onto the environment and particularly onto the Jews. "Impulses which the subject will not admit as his own even though they are most assuredly so, are attributed to the object—the prospective victim" (DofE, p. 187). Particularly important for this projection process are sexual impulses: "The same sexual impulses which the human species suppressed have survived and prevailed—in individuals and in nations—by way of the mental conversion of the ambient world into a diabolical system" (p. 187). Christian self-denial and, in particular, the suppression of sex result in evil and anti-Semitism via projection.[111]

Psychoanalytic theory is invoked as an explanation of this process in a manner that, in its emphasis on suppressed hatred for the father, also anticipates the theory utilized in TAP. Aggressive urges originating in the id are projected onto the external world by actions of the superego.

> The forbidden action which is converted into aggression is generally homosexual in nature. Through fear of castration, obedience to the father is taken to the extreme of an anticipation of castration in conscious emotional approximation to the nature of a small girl, and actual hatred to the father is suppressed. (DofE, p. 192)

Forbidden actions underlain by powerful instincts are thus turned into aggression, which is then projected onto victims in the external world, with the result that "he attacks other individuals in envy or persecution just as the repressed bestialist hunts or torments an animal" (DofE, p. 192). A later passage decries the "suppression of animal nature into scientific methods of controlling nature" (p. 193). Domination of nature, viewed as central to Christianity and fascism, thus derives ultimately from suppressing our animal nature.

Horkheimer and Adorno then attempt to explain the role of conformity in fascism. They argue that cohesive gentile group strategies are fundamentally based on a distortion of human nature—a central theme of TAP. They posit a natural, nonconforming, reflective self in opposition to society that has been corrupted by capitalism or fascism. The development of large industrial interests and the culture industry of late capitalism have destroyed in most people the inner-directed, reflective power that can produce "self-comprehending guilt" (DofE, p. 198), which could oppose the forces leading to anti-Semitism. This inner-directed reflection was "emancipated" from society and even

---

[111] In a comment that predates the thesis of TAP that anti-Semites are not introspective, Horkheimer and Adorno state that anti-Semitism is not simply projection, but projection in the absence of reflection. Anti-Semites have no inner life and therefore tend to project their hatreds, desires, and inadequacies onto the environment: "It invests the outer world with its own content" (p. 190).

directed against society (p. 198), but under the above-mentioned forces, it conforms blindly to the values of the external society.

Thus humans are portrayed as naturally opposed to the conformity demanded by a highly cohesive society. As indicated below, a consistent theme of TAP is the idea that gentile participation in cohesive groups with high levels of social conformity is pathological, whereas similar behavior of Jews with respect to the group cohesiveness characteristic of Judaism is ignored: indeed, we have seen that Judaism is portrayed in *DofE* as morally superior to Christianity.

The gentile elite is then said to take advantage of the situation by directing the projected hostility of the masses into anti-Semitism. Jews are an ideal target for this projected hostility because they represent all that is antithetical to totalitarianism:

> Happiness without power, wages without work, a home without frontiers, religion without myth. These characteristics are hated by the rulers because the ruled secretly long to possess them. The rulers are only safe as long as the people they rule turn their longed-for goals into hated forms of evil. (*DofE*, p. 199)

The conclusion is that if the rulers in fact allowed the ruled to be like the Jews, there would be a fundamental turning point of history:

> By overcoming that sickness of the mind which thrives on the ground of self-assertion untainted by reflective thought, mankind would develop from a set of opposing races to the species which, even in nature, is more than mere nature. Individual and social emancipation from domination is the countermovement to false projection, and no Jew would then resemble the senseless evil visited upon him as upon all persecuted beings, be they animals or men. (*DofE*, p. 200)

The end of anti-Semitism is thus viewed as a precondition for the development of a utopian society and the liberation of humanity—perhaps the closest that the Frankfurt School ever came to defining utopia. Such a position not only indicates the self-conscious Jewish identifications of the Frankfurt School, but has also been interpreted in order to explain the refusal of Frankfurt theorists to "name the other" to their following the traditional Jewish taboo on naming God or describing paradise (see Jay, 1980, p. 139). The envisioned utopian society is one in which Judaism can continue as a cohesive group but in which cohesive, nationalistic, corporate, gentile groups based on conformity to group norms have been abolished as manifestations of psychopathology.

Horkheimer and Adorno developed the view that the unique role of Judaism in world history was to vindicate the concept of difference against the homogenizing forces thought to represent the essence of Western civilization: "The Jews became the metaphoric equivalent of that remnant of society preserving negation and the non-identical" (Jay, 1980, p. 148). Judaism thus represents the antithesis of Western universalism. The continuation and acceptance of Jewish particularism becomes a precondition for the development of a utopian society of the future.

Within this perspective, the roots of anti-Semitism are therefore to be sought in individual psychopathology, not in the behavior of Jews. Nevertheless, there is some acknowledgment that the actual characteristics of Jews may be involved in historical anti-Semitism, but Horkheimer and Adorno theorize that the Jewish characteristics that have led to anti-Semitism were forced upon Jews. Jews are said to have incurred the wrath of the lower classes because Jews were the originators of capitalism:

> For the sake of economic progress which is now proving their downfall, the Jews were always a thorn in the side of the craftsmen and peasants who were declassed by capitalism. They are now experiencing to their own cost the exclusive, particularist character of capitalism. (*DofE*, p. 175)

However, this Jewish role is viewed as forced on the Jews who were completely dependent on gentile elites for their rights even into the nineteenth century. Under these circumstances, "Commerce is not their vocation, it is their fate" (*DofE*, p. 175). The success of the Jews then constituted a trauma to the gentile bourgeoisie, "who had to pretend to be creative" (p. 175); their anti-Semitism is thus "self-hatred, the bad conscience of the parasite" (p. 176).

There are indications that the original anti-Semitism project envisioned a more elaborate discussion of "Jewish character traits" that led to anti-Semitism along with suggested methods for overcoming them. However:

> The topic never became part of the Institute's programme, perhaps partly out of consideration for the sensitivity of most Jews towards this topic, and partly to avoid exposing the Institute to the accusation that it was turning the problem of anti-Semitism into a Jewish problem. (Wiggershaus, 1994, p. 366)

Indeed, the Institute was well aware of a 1945 Jewish Labor Committee (JLC) survey of working-class Americans in which the latter complained of Jewish behaviors related to the types of actual dealings working-class individuals would be likely to have with Jews (see *SAID*, Ch. 2). Adorno appears to have believed that these attitudes were "less irrational" than the anti-Semitism of other social classes (see Wiggershaus, 1994, p. 369), and, likely as a result, he rejected the idea of publishing the JLC's results as part of the *Studies in Prejudice* series published by the Institute (Jacobs, 2015, pp. 81–83).

Invisibility as a Solution to Anti-Semitism. It's interesting that a project to understand Jewish psychology was abandoned, perhaps because they realized that Jewish exclusion of non-Jews was an important aspect of anti-Jewish attitudes; hence, perhaps, the idea that making Jewishness invisible to counter anti-Semitism:

> The decisive factor here is the progressive-enlightenment self-image of the authors [Adorno and Horkheimer], which in some aspects remains astonishingly undialectical and on the other hand leads to distortions in the perception of Jewishness. It is closely linked to a logic of making the Jewish invisible, to which all reflections on Judaism are indirectly related. This applies equally to the chapter on "Elements of Anti-Semitism" in *Dialectic of Enlightenment* and to the empirical research projects of the early 1940s. The new social research was conceived in such a way that with it another, supposedly fundamentally superior affiliation took the place of a possible Jewish affiliation; this new affiliation was supposed to dissolve any remnants of a Jewish affiliation in a critical consciousness and make all external signs of Jewishness invisible. This normative claim was not abandoned even with the end of the project of "Jewish psychology." It shifted to various progressive projects of the postwar period, among them the studies on the rural population and on education after Auschwitz. (von Wussow, 2014, p. 174)

It seems, however, that Adorno's proposal triggered deeply hidden considerations in Horkheimer. In his letter to Adorno on November 13th, 1944, he vigorously pursued the parallelization of the fascist exclusion of Jews with the Jewish exclusion of non-Jews in the Weimar Republic: "There were whole branches in intellectual and extra-intellectual districts in which one was simply lost without Jewish connections." From the Weimar conditions, the gaze immediately moved on to the immediate present in America: "Think, furthermore, of certain circles in Washington today, which, while not exactly excluding all Christians, do exclude all those who do not belong to a rather narrowly defined Jewish-progressive clique" (von Wussow, 2014, pp. 198–199).

> The real vanishing point of the passage—and at the same time its normative content—is, however, the prospective advice to the emigrants on how they could "avoid provocation." The assumption that to do so they should above all not become visible as Jews is consistent with the well-known fact that Horkheimer did not want the Institute for Social Research in America to become recognizable as a "Jewish" institute. Numerous later

statements, especially by Leo Löwenthal in his late autobiographical re-flections, also support the assumption that the relationship of the Insti-tute's members to Judaism was to a large extent characterized by a logic of invisibility. The invisibility of Jewishness was the correlate of the "lib-erated society" in which the differences between Jews and non-Jews would be abolished, perhaps even the price that critical Jews had to pay for their participation in the idea of the liberated society. But while the liberated society receded into ever greater distance, the invisibilization of Jewishness was a task that could be accomplished by critical social re-search already in the here and now of the "anti-Semitic society." (von Wussow, 2014, p. 206)

This strategy of Jewish invisibility seems to be ongoing in the contempo-rary West in some areas but not others. On the one hand, Jews are typically classified as Whites in discussions, say, of media ownership or other aspects of elite influence, such as in the arts, academia, or as contributors to political campaigns, even though the attitudes of Jews tend to diverge strongly from other European-descended Whites. Studies of the ethnic composition of American elites that separate out Jews are essentially non-existent in main-stream academic literature. On the other hand, Jewish organizations such as the ADL have adopted a high-profile image as aggressive advocates for the po-litical priorities of the left: not restricting abortion, restricting gun ownership, and favoring immigration, multiculturalism, and LGBTQ+ advocacy through-out the media and the educational system.

Jewish Opposition to Collectivism Among Gentiles. I have noted that a powerful tendency in both radical politics and psychoanalysis has been a thor-oughgoing critique of gentile society. An important theme here is that *Studies in Prejudice* and, especially, TAP attempt to show that gentile group affiliations, and particularly membership in Christian religious sects, gentile nationalism, and close family relationships among gentiles, are an indication of psychiatric disorder. At a deep level the work of the Frankfurt School was aimed at altering Western societies in an attempt to make them resistant to anti-Semitism by pathologizing gentile group affiliations down to the level of the family. And be-cause this effort ultimately eschews the leftist solutions that have attracted so many twentieth-century Jewish intellectuals, it is an effort that remains highly relevant to the current post-communist intellectual and political context.

The opposition of Jewish intellectuals to cohesive gentile groups and a ho-mogeneous gentile culture has perhaps not been sufficiently emphasized. I have noted in Chapter 1 that the conversos were vastly overrepresented among the humanist thinkers in fifteenth- and sixteenth-century Spain who opposed the corporate nature of Spanish society centered around the Catholic religion. I have also noted that a central thrust of Freud's work was to continue to strongly identify as a Jew while at the same time developing a theory of Christian religious affiliation in which the latter is conceptualized as fulfilling infantile needs.

Similarly, another way of conceptualizing the Jewish advocacy of radical political movements consistent with the discussion of the Jewish left in Chapter 3 is that these political movements may be understood as simultaneously undermining gentile intrasocietal group affiliations, such as Christianity and nationalism, while at the same time allowing for the continuation of Jewish identification. For example, Jewish communists consistently opposed Polish nationalist aspirations, and after they came to power in the post-World War II era, they liquidated Polish nationalists and undermined the role of the Catholic Church while simultaneously establishing secular Jewish economic and social structures.

It is of some historical interest to note that an important feature of the rhetoric of German anti-Semites (e.g., Paul de Lagarde; see F. Stern, 1961, pp. 60, 65) throughout the nineteenth century into the Weimar period was that Jews advocated political forms such as liberalism, which opposed structuring society as a highly cohesive group, while at the same time Jews themselves retained an extraordinary group cohesiveness that enabled them to dominate Germans. During the Weimar period the Nazi theoretician Alfred Rosenberg complained that Jews advocated a completely atomized society while at the same time exempting themselves from this process. Whereas the rest of society was to be prevented from participating in highly cohesive groups, the Jews "would retain their international cohesiveness, blood ties, and spiritual unity" (Aschheim, 1985, p. 239). In *Mein Kampf*, Hitler (1943/1992, p. 315) clearly believed that Jewish advocacy of liberal attitudes was a deception overlaying a commitment to racialism and a highly cohesive group strategy: "While he [the Jew] seems to overflow with 'enlightenment,' 'progress,' 'freedom,' 'humanity,' etc., he himself practices the severest segregation of his race." The conflict between Jewish advocacy of Enlightenment ideals and actual Jewish behavior was also noted by Klein (1981, p. 146):

> Annoyed by the parochial attachments of other people, and unreceptive to the idea of a pluralistic state, many non-Jews interpreted the Jewish assertion of pride as a subversion of the "enlightened" or egalitarian state. The Jewish stress on national or racial pride reinforced the non-Jewish perception of the Jew as a disruptive social force.

F. K. Ringer (1983, p. 7) also notes that a common component of anti-Semitism among academics during the Weimar period was a perception that Jews attempted to undermine patriotic commitment and the social cohesion of society. Indeed, the perception that Jewish critical analysis of gentile society was aimed at dissolving the bonds of cohesiveness within the society was common among educated gentile Germans, including university professors. One academic referred to the Jews as "the classic party of national decomposition" (in p. 7).

In the event, National Socialism developed as a cohesive gentile group strategy in opposition to Judaism, a strategy that completely rejected the Enlightenment ideal of an atomized society based on individual rights in opposition to the state. As I have argued in SAID (Ch. 5) based on research on social identity, in this regard National Socialism was very much like Judaism, which has been throughout its history fundamentally a group phenomenon in which the rights of the individual are subordinated to the interests of the group.

As evident in the material reviewed here and in the previous chapters, at least some influential Jewish social scientists and intellectuals have attempted to undermine gentile group strategies while leaving open the possibility that Judaism continue as a highly cohesive group strategy. This theme is highly compatible with the Frankfurt School's consistent rejection of all forms of nationalism (Tarr, 1977, p. 20). The result is that in the end the ideology of the Frankfurt School may be described as a form of radical individualism that nevertheless despised capitalism—an individualism in which all forms of gentile collectivism are condemned as an indication of social or individual pathology.[112] Thus in Horkheimer's (1974) essay on German Jews, the true enemy of the Jews is gentile collectivism of any kind, especially nationalism. Although no mention is made of the collectivist nature of Judaism, Zionism, or Israeli ethnonationalism, the collectivist tendencies of modern gentile society are deplored, especially fascism and communism. The prescription for gentile society is radical individualism and the acceptance of pluralism. People have an inherent right to be different from others and to be accepted by others as different—a program that now goes under the ubiquitous and powerful banner of Diversity, Equity, and Inclusion. Indeed, to become differentiated from others is to achieve the highest level of humanity. The result is that "no party and no movement, neither the Old Left nor the New, indeed no collectivity of any sort was on the side of truth. . . . [T]he residue of the forces of true change was located in the critical individual alone" (Maier, 1984, p. 45).

As a corollary of this thesis, Adorno adopted the idea that the basic role of philosophy is the negative role of resisting attempts to endow the world with any "universality," "objectivity," or "totality," that is, with a single organizing

---

[112] The Frankfurt theorists inherited a strong opposition to capitalism from their previously held radical beliefs. Irving Louis Horowitz (1987, p. 118) notes that the Critical Theorists were "caught between the Charybdis of capitalism—which they despised as a system of exploitation (whose fruits they nonetheless enjoyed), and the Scylla of communism—which they despised as a system of worse exploitation (whose bitter fruits they often escaped, unlike their Russian-Jewish counterparts)."

principle for society that would homogenize society because it applied to all humans (see especially Adorno's *Negative Dialectics*, 1973; see also the review of Adorno's ideas on this concept in Jay, 1984, pp. 241–275). In *Negative Dialectics* the main example attacked by Adorno is Hegel's idea of universal history (also a stalking horse for Jacques Derrida; see below), but a similar argument applies to any ideology, such as nationalism, that results in a sense of national or pan-human universality. For example, the principle of exchange characteristic of capitalism is rejected because through it all humans become commensurable and thus lose their unique particularity. Science is also condemned because of its tendency to seek universal principles of reality (including human nature) and its tendency to look for quantitative, commensurable differences between humans rather than qualitative differences. Each object "should be respected in its ungeneralized historical uniqueness" (Landmann, 1984, p. 123). Or, as Adorno (1951/1974, p. 17) himself noted in *Minima Moralia*: "In the face of the totalitarian unison with which the eradication of difference is proclaimed as a purpose in itself, even part of the social force of liberation may have temporarily withdrawn to the individual sphere." In the end, the only criterion for a better society was that it be one in which "one can be different without fear" (p. 131). The former communist had become an advocate of radical individualism, at least for the gentiles. As discussed in Chapter 5, Erich Fromm (1941) also recognized the utility of individualism as a prescription for gentile society while nevertheless remaining strongly identified as a Jew.

Congruent with this stress on individualism and the glorification of difference, Adorno embraced a radical form of philosophical skepticism which is completely incompatible with the entire social science enterprise of TAP. Indeed, Adorno rejected even the possibility of ontology ("reification") because he viewed the contrary positions as ultimately supporting totalitarianism. Given Adorno's preoccupation with Jewish issues and strong Jewish identity, it is reasonable to suppose that these ideological structures are intended to serve as a justification of Jewish particularism. In this view, Judaism, like any other historically particular entity, must remain beyond the reach of science, forever incomprehensible in its uniqueness and forever in opposition to all attempts to develop homogeneous social structures in the society as a whole. However, its continued existence is guaranteed as an *a priori* moral imperative.

The prescription that gentile society adopt a social organization based on radical individualism is indeed an excellent strategy for the continuation of Judaism as a cohesive, collectivist group strategy. Research summarized by *Individualism* (Ch. 8) and Triandis (1990, 1991) on cross-cultural differences in individualism and collectivism indicates that anti-Semitism would be lowest in individualist societies rather than societies that are collectivist and homogeneous apart from Jews. European societies (with the notable exceptions of the National Socialist era in Germany and the medieval period of Christian religious hegemony—both periods of intense anti-Semitism) have been unique among the economically advanced traditional and modern cultures of the world in their commitment to individualism (Henrich, 2020; *Individualism*). As I have argued in SAID (Chs. 3–5), the presence of Judaism as a highly successful and salient group strategy provokes anti-individualist responses from gentile societies.

Collectivist cultures—and Triandis (1990, p. 57) explicitly includes Judaism in this category—place a much greater emphasis on the goals and needs of the ingroup rather than on individual rights and interests. Collectivist cultures develop an "unquestioned attachment" to the ingroup, including "the perception that ingroup norms are universally valid (a form of ethnocentrism), automatic obedience to ingroup authorities, and willingness to fight and die for the ingroup. These characteristics are usually associated with distrust of and unwillingness to cooperate with outgroups" (p. 55). In collectivist cultures morality is conceptualized as that which benefits the group, and aggression and exploitation of outgroups are acceptable (p. 90).

People in individualist cultures, in contrast, show little emotional attachment to ingroups. Personal goals are paramount, and socialization emphasizes the importance of self-reliance, independence, individual responsibility, and "finding yourself" (Triandis, 1991, p. 82). Individualists have more positive attitudes toward strangers and outgroup members and are more likely to behave in a prosocial, altruistic manner to strangers. Because they are less aware of ingroup-outgroup boundaries, people in individualist cultures are less likely to have negative attitudes toward outgroup members (p. 80). They often disagree with ingroup policy, show little emotional commitment or loyalty to ingroups, and do not have a sense of common fate with other ingroup members. Opposition to outgroups occurs in individualist societies, but the opposition is more "rational" in the sense that there is less of a tendency to suppose that all of the outgroup members are culpable for the misdeeds of a few. Individualists form mild attachments to many groups, whereas collectivists have an intense attachment and identification to a few ingroups (Triandis, 1990, p. 61).

The expectation is that individualists will tend to be less predisposed to anti-Semitism and more likely to blame any offensive Jewish behavior as resulting from transgressions by individual Jews rather than stereotypically true of all Jews. However, Jews, as members of a collectivist subculture living in an individualistic society, are themselves more likely to view the Jewish-gentile distinction as extremely salient and to develop stereotypically negative views about gentiles.

In Triandis's terms, then, the fundamental intellectual difficulty presented by TAP is that Judaism itself is a highly collectivist subculture in which authoritarianism and obedience to ingroup norms and the suppression of individual interests in favor of the common good have been of vital importance throughout its history (SAID, Chs. 6, 8). Such attributes in gentiles tend to re-sult in anti-Semitism because of social identity processes. Jews may, as a re-sult, perceive themselves to have a vital interest in advocating a highly indi-vidualist, atomized gentile culture while simultaneously maintaining their own highly elaborated collectivist subculture, as noted here mainly in the tendency of the intellectuals and activists discussed here for ethnic networking and so-cializing with co-ethnics, even among non-religious Jews. This advocacy of in-dividualist, atomized gentile cultures and societies is the perspective devel-oped by the Frankfurt School and apparent throughout *Studies in Prejudice*.

However, as discussed in the appendix to this chapter, TAP extends be-yond the attempt to pathologize cohesive gentile groups and attempts to pathologize adaptive gentile behavior in general. The principal intellectual dif-ficulty is that behavior that is critical to Judaism as a successful group evolu-tionary strategy is conceptualized as pathological in gentiles.

THE FRANKFURT SCHOOL AND THE CRITIQUE OF MASS CULTURE

The Frankfurt School viewed contemporary Western societies of the 1930s and '40s as "soft authoritarianism." From their point of view, the basic problem, once again, was to explain the lack of revolutionary fervor in Western societies. Quite clearly, orthodox Marxism was wrong.

This lack of fervor was particularly problematic in Western societies where there was a considerable degree of personal freedom: theoretically at least, people had the freedom to be revolutionary, but instead they passively accepted their lot in the putatively evil, exploitative system of capitalism.

These intellectuals developed the theory that control had shifted from ob-vious forms of external control (such as the gulags in the USSR) to control via the media—"secondary emanations of authority . . . namely newspapers, ad-vertising, radio, etc." (Wheatland, 2009, p. 79). Because the media was an ex-pression of "late capitalism," it prevented people from seeing the world as good leftists should, and as a result they were unable to "break the cycle of injustice and domination" (p. 79) The solution essentially was to advocate for Jewish-owned media outlets to spread the messages of the left on race, anti-Semitism, etc.—an ongoing effort now compromised to some extent by the decline of the legacy media and the rise of podcasts and social media (see Ch. 9).

Early on, Erich Fromm gathered survey data showing that working-class Germans were not interested in revolution but were passive and prone to es-capism. The passivity and escapism of the working class were viewed as due to the failure of the culture, and particularly the media, to properly foment rev-olutionary consciousness. For example, during the 1930s, Herbert Marcuse wrote attacking "all bourgeois culture for its escapism, repression, and concealment of capitalism's harsh realities" (Wheatland, 2009, p. 160).

Eventually, there was a general understanding among both the Frankfurt School and the New York Intellectuals that mass culture—whether in the USSR, National Socialist Germany, or bourgeois United States—promoted conformism and escape from harsh political realities; it "offered false pleasure, reaffirmed the status quo, and promoted a pervasive conformity that stripped the masses of their individuality and subjectivity" (Wheatland, 2009, p. 175). Obviously this fits well with the Frankfurt School ideas on the family: again, there is a plea for individualists free from family and ethnic ties and in favor of nonconformity with the status quo. Ironically perhaps, this is exactly the critique of the media that is now made by dissident intellectuals of the right. What has changed, of course, is that the mainstream media is now in the hands of the liberal-left, much of it Jewish-owned (see Preface); the status quo is buttressed by the universities and mainstream media which are controlled by the left.[113]

These intellectuals promoted modernism in art at least partly because of its compatibility with expressive individualism, but also because they believed that it effectively opposed the culture of capitalism. Modernism was thus seen as capable of alienating people from modern Western societies. To be modern was, in their eyes, to be alienated from the society of capitalism. The alienation of the New York Intellectuals is legendary. As noted in Chapter 7, Norman Podhoretz (1979, p. 283) was famously asked by a *New Yorker* editor in the 1950s "whether there was a special typewriter at *Partisan Review* with the word 'alienation' on a single key." In short, they were trying to make all of America as alienated and opposed to the mainstream Protestant-dominated culture of America as these Jewish intellectuals were.

Both the New York Intellectuals and the Frankfurt School had nothing but disdain for traditional art. Adorno (2002, p. 609), who was a prolific music critic, wrote that they sought "the end of the order that bore the sonata"—the end of European high culture. The New York Intellectuals strongly opposed regionalism in American art, typified by Thomas Hart Benton with its inclusion of American farmers and railroad workers (see Ch. 7). And if the audience failed

---

[113] In reading the views of the Frankfurt School on the importance of cultural control, it struck me that those of us attempting to preserve the traditional peoples and culture of the West are in a similar situation to the Frankfurt School and the New York Intellectuals before around 1965, but now the roles are reversed. Whereas the New York Intellectuals and the Frankfurt School felt alienated from the culture of the West, now White advocates are the ones with feelings of alienation—dismayed at the failure of the media to properly address White interests or even to allow expressions of White identity to be seen or heard in the mainstream media. And when there is a failure of media self-censorship—e.g., when a prominent scientist like James Watson (2007) publicly declares his belief in racial differences in intelligence, or when Andrew Fraser noted the role of Jewish organizations in advocating a multi-racial Australia (MacDonald, 2009c)—there are powerful campaigns to punish the guilty parties and to get them to recant.

to appreciate modernism, it was their fault. For example, Adorno wrote that the failure of the audience to appreciate Arnold Schoenberg's abstract, dissonant music "pointed to widespread alienation and irrationalism that were pervasive in society" (Wheatland, 2009, p. 29). Only the revolution would make people psychologically whole again and in tune with a genuine aesthetic sense.

The view that modernism would ultimately usher in the revolution eventually faded when it became obvious that it would never be popular with the great mass of people. The view that, say, Schoenberg could ever have become popular with the great mass of people can only be described as amazingly naive. However, just as the Frankfurt School noted, the West has come under the control of soft totalitarianism. But now the shoe is on the other foot: it is the soft totalitarianism of the multicultural, multi-racial left that has the power, and the escapism promoted by the media functions to take people's minds off the existential threat of demographic displacement occurring in all Western nations.

It's interesting that the Frankfurt School critics of the media and mass culture completely ignored the actual mechanisms of cultural control that were in place during the period when they were writing. The controls on culture during the period from approximately the late-1920s to the mid-1960s had nothing whatever to do with the culture of "late capitalism." Instead, the traditional Anglo-American culture managed to retain its primacy during this period because of political activism on the part of White Americans, often quite self-consciously directed against Jewish influence in the media.

Jewish influence on the media, especially Hollywood movies, weighed heavily on the minds of people like Henry Ford early in the twentieth century. An article in Ford's *The International Jew* stated:

> Not only the "legitimate" stage, so-called, but the motion picture industry—the fifth greatest of all the great industries—is also Jew-controlled, not in spots only, not 50 per cent merely, but entirely; with the natural consequence that the world is in arms against the trivializing and demoralizing influences of that form of entertainment as at present managed. As soon as the Jew got control of American Liquor, we had a liquor problem with drastic consequences. As soon as the Jew gained control of the "movies," we had a movie problem, the consequences of which are not yet visible. It is the genius of the race to create problems in whatever business they achieve a majority. . . . Millions of Americans every day place themselves voluntarily within range of Jewish ideas of life, love and labor; within range of Jewish propaganda, sometimes cleverly, sometimes cunningly concealed. (January 1st, 1921; reviewed in MacDonald, 2002a)

Public outrage at the content of Hollywood movies led to more or less successful controls on the moral and political content of movies until around the mid-1960s. During the McCarthy era, there was concern that the entertainment industry would influence American culture by, in the words of an overt anti-Semite, Congressman John R. Rankin of Mississippi, "insidiously trying to spread subversive propaganda, poison the minds of your children, distort the history of our country and discredit Christianity" (Sachar, 1992, p. 624).

> The great majority of those stigmatized by the Un-American Activities Committee of the House of Representatives (HUAC) were Jews, many of them in the entertainment industry. . . . A belief that "Jewish Hollywood" was promoting subversive ideas, including leftist political beliefs, was a common component of anti-Semitism in the post-World War II period, and indeed the push for the HUAC investigation was led by such well-known anti-Semites as Gerald L. K. Smith and Congressman Rankin. . . . For example, Smith stated that "there is a general belief that Russian Jews control too much of Hollywood propaganda and they are trying to popularize Russian Communism in America through that instrumentality. Personally, I believe that is the case." (Platt, 1977/1978)

The substantive basis of the opinion of Rankin and others was that beginning in the 1930s Hollywood screenwriters were predominantly Jewish and politically liberal or radical (Gabler, 1988, pp. 322ff)—a general association that has been typical of Jewish intellectual history in the twentieth century. The American Communist Party (CPUSA), which was under Soviet control during the period, sent V. J. Jerome and Stanley Lawrence, both Jews, to Hollywood to organize the writers and take advantage of their political sentiments. Jerome argued that "agitprop propaganda was actually better drama because Marxists better understood the forces that shaped human beings, and could therefore write better characters" (p. 329). Writers responded by self-consciously viewing themselves as contributing to "the Cause" by their script writing. "But as much as the Hollywood Communist party was a writers' party, it was also . . . a Jewish party. (Indeed, to be the former meant to be the latter as well)" (p. 330).

Nevertheless, during this period the radical writers were able to have little influence on the ultimate product, although there is good evidence that they did their best to influence movie content in the direction of their political views (Ceplair & Englund, 1980; D. B. Jones, 1956/1972, pp. 196–304). Their failure was at least partly because of pressures brought to bear on Hollywood by conservative, predominantly non-Jewish political forces, resulting in a great deal of self-censorship by the movie industry. The Motion Picture Producers and Distributors of America, headed by Will H. Hays, was created in 1922 in response to movements in over thirty state legislatures to enact strict censorship laws, and the Production Code Administration, headed by Joseph I. Breen, was launched in response to a campaign by the National Catholic Legion of Decency. The result was that producers were forced to develop projects "along the lines of a standard Hollywood genre while steering clear of both the Hays and Breen offices and the radical writer who may have been assigned to the project" (Ceplair & Englund, pp. 303–304).

In addition, the HUAC investigations of the late 1940s and early 1950s and the active campaigning of religious (National Catholic Legion of Decency; Knights of Columbus), patriotic (Daughters of the American Revolution—DAR), and educational (Parent Teacher Association) groups influenced movie content well into the 1950s, including a great many anti-communist films made as a rather direct response to the HUAC investigations. The result was, in the words of one studio executive, that "I now read scripts through the eyes of the DAR, whereas formerly I read them through the eyes of my boss" (Ceplair & Englund, 1980, p. 340). Particular mention should be made of the American Legion, described as "the prime mover" in attempting to eradicate "communist influence" in the movie industry during the 1950s. The list of sixty-six movie personalities said to be associated with communism published in the *American Legion Magazine* caused panic in Hollywood and a prolonged series of investigations, firings, and blacklistings.

Thus there were strong controls emanating from religious and cultural traditionalists that limited Jewish influence on culture through the 1950s— doubtless much to the chagrin of the Frankfurt School and the New York Intellectuals.

This all ended when the culture of the left finally triumphed in the 1960s, as discussed in Chapter 3. At that point, when the multicultural, anti-White left had seized the high ground in the cultural wars, they had far less reason to engage in the types of cultural criticism so apparent in the writings of the Frankfurt School and the New York Intellectuals. Hollywood and the rest of the American media were unleashed, and it must have become apparent to many that escapism and conformity could be used to prevent a counter-revolution.

What would have surprised these intellectuals is that the culture of the left could co-exist with capitalism, as we see now with the explosion of "woke" corporations and Environmental, Social, Governance (ESG) pressures from companies like BlackRock, headed by CEO Larry Fink, with around 11.6 trillion dollars in assets under management as of the end of 2024 (BlackRock, 2025). BlackRock is able to use these assets to invest in companies in order to pressure management in the direction of their leftist political goals, resulting in pushback from conservative states (Guynn, 2022). As Marxists at heart for most of their existence, the Frankfurt School intellectuals typically felt that it was necessary to get rid of capitalism in order to usher in a revolution in culture that would affect the great mass of people.

THE INFLUENCE OF THE FRANKFURT SCHOOL

Although it is difficult to assess the effect of works like TAP on gentile culture, there can be little question that the thrust of the radical critique of gentile culture in this work, as well as other works inspired by psychoanalysis and its derivatives, was to pathologize high-investment parenting and upward social mobility, as well as pride in family, religion, and country, among gentiles (see appendix to this chapter). Certainly many of the central attitudes of the largely successful 1960s countercultural revolution find expression in TAP, including idealizing rebellion against parents, low-investment sexual relationships, and scorn for upward social mobility, social status, family pride, the Christian religion, and patriotism.

We have seen that despite this antagonistic perspective on American culture, Jewish 1960s radicals continued to identify with their parents and with Judaism (see Ch. 3). The countercultural revolution was in a very deep sense a mission to the gentiles in which adaptive behavior and group identifications among gentiles were pathologized while Jewish group identification, ingroup pride, family pride, upward social mobility, and group continuity retained their psychological importance and positive moral evaluation. In this regard, the behavior of these radicals was exactly analogous to that of the authors of TAP and to Jewish involvement in psychoanalysis and radical politics generally: gentile culture and gentile group strategies are fundamentally pathological and are to be anathematized in the interests of making the world safe for Judaism as a group evolutionary strategy.

As with political radicalism, only a rarified cultural elite could attain the extremely high level of mental health epitomized by the true liberal:

> The replacement of moral and political argument by reckless psychologizing not only enabled Adorno and his collaborators to dismiss unacceptable political opinions on medical grounds; it led them to set up an impossible standard of political health—one that only members of a self-constituted cultural vanguard could consistently meet. In order to establish their emotional "autonomy," the subjects of their research had to hold the right opinions and also to hold them deeply and spontaneously. (Lasch, 1991, pp. 453–454)

In the post-World War II era TAP became an ideological weapon against historical American populist movements, especially McCarthyism (Gottfried, 1998; Lasch, 1991, pp. 455ff). "[T]he people as a whole had little understanding of liberal democracy and ... important questions of public policy should be decided by educated elites, not submitted to a popular vote" (Lasch, p. 455). As discussed in Chapter 8, this was indeed the case with the nation-transforming Immigration and Nationality Act of 1965, enacted at a time when public sentiment was decidedly against it.

These trends are exemplified in *The Politics of Unreason: Right-Wing Extremism in America, 1790–1970*, a volume in the *Patterns of American Prejudice* series funded by the ADL and written by Seymour Martin Lipset and Earl Raab (1970). (Raab and Lipset also wrote *Prejudice and Society*, published by the ADL in 1959. Again, as in the *Studies in Prejudice* series, funded by the AJCommittee, there is a link between academic research on ethnic relations and Jewish activist organizations. Raab's career has combined academic scholarship with deep involvement as a Jewish ethnic activist; see Ch. 8, footnote 143.)

As indicated by the title, *The Politics of Unreason* analyzes political and ideological expressions of ethnocentrism by European-derived peoples as irrational and as being unrelated to legitimate ethnic interests in retaining political power. "Right-wing extremist" movements aim at retaining or restoring the power of the European-derived majority of the United States, but "extremist politics is the politics of despair" (Lipset & Raab, 1970, p. 3). For Lipset and Raab, tolerance of cultural and ethnic pluralism is a defining feature of democracy, so that groups that oppose cultural and ethnic pluralism are by definition extremist and anti-democratic. Indeed, citing New York Intellectual Edward A. Shils (1956, p. 154), they conceptualize pluralism as implying multiple centers of power without domination by any one group—a view in which the self-interest of ethnic groups in retaining and expanding their power is conceptualized as fundamentally anti-democratic. Attempts by majorities to resist the increase in the power and influence of other groups are therefore contrary to "the fixed spiritual center of the democratic political process" (Lipset & Raab, p. 5). "Extremism is anti-pluralism. . . . And the operational heart of extremism is the repression of difference and dissent" (p. 6; emphasis original).

Such proposals are obviously in the interests of Jews as a minority group and oppose the interests of the White, Christian majority to retain its cultural and demographic power. Right-wing extremism is condemned for its moralism—an ironic move given the centrality of a sense of moral superiority that pervades the Jewish-dominated intellectual movements reviewed here, not to mention Lipset and Raab's (1970, p. 4) own analysis in which right-wing extremism is labeled "an absolute political evil" because of its links with authoritarianism and totalitarianism. Right-wing extremism is also condemned for its tendency to advocate simple solutions to complex problems, which, as noted by Lasch (1991), is a plea that solutions to social problems should be formulated by an intellectual elite. And finally, right-wing extremism is condemned because of its tendency to distrust institutions that intervene between the people and their direct exercise of power, an anti-populist plea for the power of elites: "Populism identifies the will of the people with justice and morality"

(Lipset & Raab, p. 13). The conclusion of this analysis is that democracy is identified not with the power of the people to pursue their perceived interests; rather, democracy is conceptualized as guaranteeing that majorities will not resist the expansion of power of minorities even if that means a decline in their own power.

Viewed at its most abstract level, a fundamental agenda is thus to influence the European-derived peoples of the United States to view concern about their own demographic and cultural eclipse as irrational, evil, and an indication of psychopathology.

Adorno's concept of the "pseudo-conservative" was used by influential intellectuals such as Harvard historian Richard Hofstadter to condemn departures from liberal orthodoxy in terms of the psychopathology of "status anxiety." Hofstadter developed the "consensus" approach to history, characterized by Nugent (1963, p. 22) as having "a querulous view of popular movements, which seem to threaten the leadership of an urbanized, often academic, intelligentsia or elite, and the use of concepts that originated in the behavioral sciences." In terms derived entirely from the TAP studies, pseudo-conservatism is diagnosed as "among other things a disorder in relation to authority, characterized by an inability to find other modes for human relationship than those of more or less complete domination or submission" (Hofstadter, 1965, p. 58). As Nugent (p. 26) points out, this perspective largely ignored the "concrete economic and political reality involved in populism and therefore left it to be viewed fundamentally in terms of the psychopathological and irrational." This is precisely the method of TAP: real conflicts of interest between ethnic groups are conceptualized as nothing more than the irrational projections of the inadequate personalities of majority group members.

Lasch also focuses on the work of Leslie Fiedler, Daniel Bell, and Seymour Martin Lipset as representing similar tendencies. (In a collection of essays edited by Daniel Bell in 1955 entitled *The New American Right*, both Hofstadter and Lipset refer approvingly to TAP as a way of understanding right-wing political attitudes and behavior.) Nugent (1963, pp. 7ff) mentions an overlapping set of individuals who were not historians and whose views were based mostly on impressions without any attempt at detailed study, including Victor Ferkiss, David Riesman, Nathan Glazer, Seymour Martin Lipset, Edward A. Shils, and Peter Viereck. However, this group also included historians who "were among the luminaries of the historical profession" (p. 13), including Hofstadter, Oscar Handlin, and Max Lerner—all of whom were involved in intellectual activity in opposition to restrictionist immigration policies (see Ch. 8). A common theme was what Nugent (p. 15) terms "undue stress" on the image of the populist as an anti-Semite—an image that exaggerated and oversimplified the populist movement but was sufficient to render the movement as morally repugnant. Novick (1988, p. 341) is more explicit in finding that Jewish identification was an important ingredient in this analysis, attributing the negative view of American populism held by some American Jewish historians (Hofstadter, Bell, and Lipset) to the fact that "they were one generation removed from the Eastern European *shtetl* [small Eastern European Jewish town], where insurgent gentile peasants meant pogrom."

There may be some truth in the latter comment, but I rather doubt that the interpretations of these Jewish historians were simply an irrational legacy left over from European anti-Semitism. There were also real conflicts of interest involved. On one side were Jewish intellectuals advancing their interests as an urbanized intellectual elite bent on ending Protestant, Anglo-Saxon demographic and cultural predominance. On the other side were what Higham (1984, p. 49) terms "the common people of the South and West" who were battling to maintain their own cultural and demographic dominance. (The struggle between these groups is the theme of the discussion of Jewish involvement in shaping U.S. immigration policy in Chapter 8 as well as the discussion of the New York Intellectuals in Chapter 7. Several of the intellectuals mentioned here are regarded as members of the New York Intellectuals—Bell, Glazer, Lipset, Riesman, and Shils—while others, such as Hofstadter and Handlin, may be regarded as peripheral members.)

As the vanguard of an urbanized Jewish intellectual elite, this group of intellectuals was also contemptuous of the lower middle class generally. From the perspective of these intellectuals, this class,

> clung to outworn folkways—conventional religiosity, hearth and home, the sentimental cult of motherhood—and obsolete modes of production. It looked back to a mythical golden age in the past. It resented social classes more highly placed but internalized their standards, lording it over the poor instead of joining them in a common struggle against oppression. It was haunted by the fear of slipping farther down the social scale and clutched the shreds of respectability that distinguished it from the class of manual workers. Fiercely committed to a work ethic, it believed that anyone who wanted a job could find one and that those who refused to work should starve. Lacking liberal culture, it fell easy prey to all sorts of nostrums and political fads. (Lasch, 1991, p. 458)

Recall also Nicholas von Hoffman's (1996) comment on the attitude of cultural superiority to the lower middle class held by the liberal defenders of communism during this period, such as Hofstadter and the editors of *The New Republic*:

> In the ongoing *kulturkampf* dividing the society, the elites of Hollywood, Cambridge, and liberal think-tankery had little sympathy for bow-legged men with their American Legion caps and their fat wives, their yapping

about Yalta and the Katyn Forest. Catholic and kitsch, looking out of their picture windows at their flock of pink plastic flamingos, the lower middles and their foreign policy anguish were too *infra dig* to be taken seriously.

Another good example of this intellectual onslaught on the lower middle class associated with the Frankfurt School is Erich Fromm's (1941) *Escape from Freedom*, in which the lower middle class is regarded as highly prone to developing "sadomasochistic" reaction formations as indicated by participating in authoritarian groups as a response to their economic and social status frustrations. It is not surprising that the lower-middle-class target of this intellectual onslaught—including, one might add, the *Mittelstand* of Wilhelmine German politics—has historically been prone to anti-Semitism as an explanation of their downward social mobility and their frustrated attempts to achieve upward social mobility. This group has also been prone to joining cohesive authoritarian groups as a means of attaining their political goals. But within the context of TAP, the desire for upward social mobility and the concern with downward social mobility characteristic of many supporters of populist movements are signs of a specific psychiatric disorder—pathetic results of inappropriate socialization that would disappear in the liberalized utopian society of the future.

Although Critical Theory ceased to be a guide for protest movements by the early 1970s (Wiggershaus, 1994, p. 656), it has retained a very large influence in the intellectual world generally. In the 1970s, the Frankfurt School intellectuals continued to draw the fire of German conservatives, who characterized them as the "intellectual foster-parents" of terrorists and as fomenters of "cultural revolution to destroy the traditions of the Christian West" (p. 657). "The inseparability of concepts such as Frankfurt School, Critical Theory and neo-Marxism indicates that, from the 1930s onwards, theoretically productive left-wing ideas in German-speaking countries had focused on Horkheimer, Adorno and the Institute of Social Research" (p. 658).

However, the influence of the Frankfurt School has gone well beyond the German-speaking world, and not only due to the TAP studies, the writings of Erich Fromm, and the enormously influential work of Herbert Marcuse as a countercultural guru to the New Left. In the contemporary intellectual world, there are several journals devoted to this legacy, including *New German Critique, Cultural Critique,* and *Theory, Culture and Society: Explorations in Critical Social Science*; books focusing on the Frankfurt School, some of which are cited here, continue to appear. The influence of the Frankfurt School increased greatly following the success of the New Left countercultural movement of the 1960s (Piccone, 1993, p. xii). A search on Google Scholar for "Frankfurt School" listed around 57,000 items between 1998 and June 2023.

SAMUEL H. FLOWERMAN: PATHOLOGIZING WHITE ETHNOCENTRISM IN THE MASS MEDIA

We have seen that the Frankfurt School advocated a top-down approach to propagandizing their ideas—an approach that, given its focus on anti-Semitism, assumes that opposition to anti-Semitism should become entrenched among opinion-influencing elites in the media and academic world. The person most responsible for disseminating such propaganda in the mass media was Samuel H. Flowerman who was closely associated with the Frankfurt School. He was Research Director for the AJCommittee and co-editor with Horkheimer of the *Studies in Prejudice* series published by the AJCommittee. Flowerman was based in New York at a time when Adorno and Horkheimer were located in southern California. Despite their general affinities, there was a "decidedly cool" relationship between Horkheimer and Flowerman basically resulting from a personal dispute over control of the Institute's work (Jacobs, 2015, p. 88). Flowerman's attempt to disseminate these ideas in the mass media occurred at a time when all the Hollywood studios, the three major television networks, and influential newspapers, such as *The New York Times* and *The Washington Post*, were owned by Jews, and, as indicated below, individuals familiar with research on influencing opinion discussed here were employed by the major television networks.

Joyce (2019c) describes what was in effect,

> a series of interlinked battalions of Jewish psychologists and sociologists [including Flowerman] operating with a kind of religious fervor in the fields of "prejudice studies," opinion-shaping, and mass communications between the 1930s and 1950s, all with the goal of "unlocking" the White mind and opening it to "tolerance." In a remarkable invasion (and creation) of disciplines similar to the Jewish flood into the medical and race sciences in the 1920s and 1930s, Jews also flooded, and then dominated, the fields of opinion research and mass communications—areas of research that overlapped so often under Jewish scholars like Flowerman that they were practically indistinguishable. . . .
>
> [O]f the four academics considered the "founding fathers" of mass communication research in America, two (Vienna-born Paul Lazarsfeld and Kurt Lewin) were Jews [Jeřábek, 2017, p. 17]. Of the two European-American founding fathers, most of Harold Lasswell's graduate students were Jewish [Oren, 2003, p. 13] (e.g., Daniel Lerner, Abraham Kaplan, Gabriel Almond, Morris Janowitz, Edward Shils, and Nathan Leites), and he also sponsored the Institute for Social Research's project on anti-Semitism [Wheatland, 2009, p. 384]. The fourth, Carl Hoveland, had an equally Jewish coterie around him at Yale, where he operated a team of researchers along with Milton Rosenberg and Robert Abelson. . . . Hynek Jeřábek

[2017, p. 18] notes that Lazarsfeld's influence in particular can't be understated; by 1983, seven years after his death, "the directors of social research at the three largest media networks in the United States, CBS, ABC, and NBC were all his former students." Another Jew, Jay Blumler, has been called "a founding father of British media studies" [Curran, 2015]. . . .

Despite some superficial differences in the titles of "opinion research," "prejudice studies," and "mass communications," these academics all worked with each other to some degree, if not directly (in organizations or in co-written studies or papers) then via mutual associations. For example, in addition to two of the four founding fathers of mass communications research being Jews, three of them (including gentile Harold Lasswell) were also very intimately involved with the Frankfurt School and the broader Jewish agenda to "adapt" public opinion. Paul Lazarsfeld and Kurt Lewin, the two gurus of mass communication, together attended a 1944 conference on anti-Semitism organized by the research department of the American Jewish Committee (headed by Samuel H. Flowerman) and the Berkeley faction of the Frankfurt School in exile (headed by Theodor Adorno) [J. P. Jackson & Weidman, 2005, p. 176]. David Kettler and Gerhard Lauer also point out that Lazarsfeld was in regular communication with Max Horkheimer, was "strongly supportive of the Horkheimer Circle and its work," and even furnished the latter with "notes and recommendations for the Horkheimer Circle's unpublished 'Anti-Semitism Among American Labor'" [Kettler & Lauer, 2005, p. 184]. He was also a colleague at Columbia with, and close confidante of, Leo Lowenthal [J. Schmidt, 2007, p. 47]. By the late 1940s, Lazarsfeld's ex-wife and mother of his child, Marie Jahoda, had even come to act as an American Jewish Committee liaison between Horkheimer and Samuel H. Flowerman, and co-wrote a number of articles on "prejudice" with Flowerman in *Commentary*. One should by now begin to see clear connections forming between the American Jewish Committee, the Frankfurt School, "prejudice studies," Jewish dominance of the academic field of "mass communications," and, finally, the flow of influence from this field into the mass media (most clearly in the positions at CBS, ABC, and NBC quickly obtained by Lazarsfeld's students). . . .

A reasonable working hypothesis for such a sudden concentration of mutually networking Jews (often from different countries) in these areas of research would be that Jewish identity and Jewish interests played a significant part in their career choices, and that the trend was then accelerated by ethnic nepotism and promotion from within the group. Jeřábek appears to concur when he states that "Paul Lazarsfeld's Jewish background, or the fact that many people around him in Vienna were Jewish, can help to explain his future affinities, friendships, or decisions" [Jeřábek, 2017, p. 23]. Setting aside the deep historical context of conflict between Jews and Europeans, a contingent and contemporary explanation might be that Jews were moved to enter into fields involving mass opinion and perceptions of prejudice because they were deeply disturbed by the rise of National Socialism and continuing anti-Semitism in Western countries like the United States.

Jeřábek (2017, p. 13) notes that, despite his criticism of Adorno's lack of concern with proper methodology noted above, Lazarsfeld had "extensive co-operation" with the Frankfurt School from 1933–1936, and well after the publication of TAP, he "lavished praise on Horkheimer and extended his hopes for future collaborations between the Institute and his Bureau of Applied Social Research" (Wheatland, 2009, p. 248). It's interesting therefore that there is consensus that Lazarsfeld was a rigorous researcher and pioneer in applying quantitative methods to sociology. Lazarsfeld and Robert K. Merton (the latter an important sociologist and also Jewish) noted the following in an influential co-authored 1948 paper on the effects of the mass media: (1) it confers social status (e.g., people are seen as having higher social status if they are given positive coverage in the media or, I would argue, if their views conform to the elite media, such as The New York Times); (2) it articulates current social norms (e.g., the current social norms related to race, multiculturalism, gender, etc.); (3) it provides a social-narcotic function (e.g., anesthetizing audiences by flooding them with information, resulting in apathy—seen as dysfunctional by Lazarsfeld and Merton, but likely seen as positive in today's political climate). These three social consequences are described as occurring under certain circumstances: (a) the media are monopolized to take just one view, one perspective, of an event (e.g., the Holocaust) or phenomenon (White racism as the cause of Black underachievement); (b) the force of the media is combined with a "channelled" change, i.e., a small, specific change is achieved instead of a larger, general change; and (c) when the effect of the mass media is purposefully accompanied by face-to-face communication (e.g., when people exposed to ideas in the media discuss them with their acquaintances).

Of these, the importance of monopolistic control is particularly interesting given that throughout the present-day West, there is a virtual uniformity in the mainstream media on matters related to race, multiculturalism, immigration, gender, etc., combined with ever-increasing censorship and other penalties (e.g., loss of job, ostracism) directed at those with alternate perspectives, not only among academics and mainstream media figures who say or write things opposing established narratives, but also in social media, spearheaded by organizations like the ADL (e.g., I was permanently banned from Twitter, after it was acquired by Elon Musk, without explanation; I have since been reinstated under a different handle). As Lazarsfeld and Merton (1948, p. 573) note, "the effectiveness of these morale-building efforts [during World War II] was in large measure due to the virtually complete absence of counterpropaganda."

Monopolistic control of information was already within reach in 1949, as noted in a report to the AJCommittee titled "The Use of the Mass Media in Combating Anti-Semitism":

> Because we are able to present anti-Semitism and other inter-group tensions as an American rather than a strictly Jewish interest, we are able, not only to enlist the cooperation of the vast majority of those engaged in supplying the American people with this flow of news, facts, entertainment and ideas, but to enlist them with all their prestige and influence—the Eleanor Roosevelts, the Fred Allens, the Frank Sinatras, and the rest. Such allies are not available for the selling of commercial products. . . . For the fact is that the overwhelming majority of editors, writers, cartoonists, radio directors, station managers, actors and movie executives are on our side in this matter of combatting bigotry and discrimination. And we should certainly be remiss if we failed to utilize them to the fullest. (Rothschild, 1949, pp. 4–5)

Like artificial intelligence today, "It is widely felt that the mass media comprise a powerful instrument which may be used for good or for ill and that, in the absence of adequate controls, the latter possibility is on the whole more likely" (Lazarsfeld & Merton, 1948, p. 554). Under the heading "The Structure of Ownership and Operation," the authors note only that the media in the U.S. is owned by private companies—thus no analysis of Jewish ownership of media which was very considerable at that time, as noted above. But of course, the heavy Jewish involvement in media makes a difference (see Preface), so that, for example, the opinions and slants of the mainstream media reflect the views of the wider Jewish community and are often quite different from the views of the wider culture. As leftists, the authors are concerned that the media is not sufficiently progressive—that it tends to reinforce the status quo:

> For these media not only continue to affirm the status quo but, in the same measure, they fail to raise essential questions about the structure of society. Hence, by leading toward *conformism* and by providing little basis for a critical appraisal of society, the commercially sponsored mass media indirectly but effectively restrain the cogent development of a genuinely critical outlook. . . . Minor tokens of "progressive" views are of slight importance since they are included only by the grace of the sponsors and only on the condition that they be sufficiently acceptable as not to alienate any appreciable part of the audience. (Lazarsfeld & Merton, 1948, p. 567, emphasis original)

However, since the left has achieved establishment status in the culture and increasingly in the political arena, this is a problem that no longer exists (see, e.g., the above comments on BlackRock's ability to steer public corporations in a progressive direction).

Lazarsfeld and Merton (1948, p. 575) highlight the difference between advertising that simply tries to get people to choose a certain brand versus propaganda intended to alter deep-seated beliefs:

> But mass propaganda typically meets a more complex situation. It may seek objectives which are at odds with deep-lying attitudes. It may seek to reshape rather than to canalize current systems of values. And the successes of advertising may only highlight the failures of propaganda. Much of the current propaganda which is aimed at abolishing deep-seated ethnic and racial prejudices, for example, seems to have had little effectiveness. Media of mass communication, then, have been effectively used to canalize basic attitudes, but there is little evidence of their having served to change these attitudes.

This may have been true in 1948, but seems very unlikely in the intervening seventy-five years of essentially monopolistic messages related to "deep-seated ethnic and racial prejudices" which have emanated from the mainstream media and the educational system from kindergarten through university.

Flowerman, writing in 1947 (p. 429), notes that already "Millions of leaflets, pamphlets, cartoons, comic books, articles—and more recently radio and movie scripts—have been produced and disseminated in the propaganda war," and that this "war" has the following aims: (1) "The restructuring of the attitudes of prejudiced individuals, or at least their neutralization"; (2) "The restructuring of group values toward intolerance;" (3) "The reinforcement of attitudes of those already committed to a democratic ideology perhaps by creating an illusion of universality or victory"; (4) "The continued neutralization of those whose attitudes are yet unstructured and who are deemed "safer" if they remain immune to symbols of bias"; (5) "Off-setting the counter-symbols of intolerance."

Flowerman (1947) is thus aiming at the "successful mass persuasion in the field of intergroup relations" (p. 429), seen as requiring first and foremost the "control by pro-tolerance groups or individuals of the channels of mass communication" (p. 430). Since "control" in Flowerman's phrasing is not qualified, he is implying that there can be no "leakage" in which some channels opposed to the pro-tolerance propaganda remain popularly accessible. Such total control is to be achieved via "force, commercial monopoly, and/or crisis (designed or accidental)" (p. 430)—his use of "force" implying that this goal should be achieved by any means necessary. Only then would "pro-tolerance" forces be able to use "the persuasive devices and techniques of the elite playing upon the susceptibilities of the manipulated" (p. 430)—clearly an acknowledgement that this revolution in attitudes would be top-down and essentially manipulative, as recommended by Adorno and Horkheimer (see above). Citing Erich Fromm's *Escape from Freedom* (1941), he also notes that people in general have "a desire to be controlled."

Thus the recommendation is top-down control of a population that will willingly accept the control. As Flowerman noted in a 1949 article (pp. 105–106):

> Adherents of the theory of prejudice by tradition frequently say that they hope to make such forms of prejudice as anti-Semitism "unstylish" through mass propaganda. But unless such mass propaganda can reach and modify the behavior of those key individuals in our culture from whom influence flows to other members of our culture—and who can set the style—we cannot hope to expect individuals who are members of groups in which certain forms of prejudice are the accepted way of life to change these traditions spontaneously as a result of propaganda.

And indicating his dissatisfaction with the state of research at the time, Flowerman (1949, p. 107) noted:

> We must first thoroughly understand group structure, relationships between leaders and followers, etc., as well as group needs before we can hope to profit from a study of techniques for change. Techniques must derive from group needs and not from armchairs or the advertising office.

Thus, unlike TAP which was directed at pathologizing the family structure and attitudes of White gentiles using an essentially fraudulent interpretation of their data (see appendix of this chapter), this body of research was attempting to build on a solid empirical basis in order to be able to alter public opinion in a manner favored by the AJCommittee—an effort greatly facilitated by Jewish ownership and other involvement (e.g., as screenwriters) in the mass media.

A concrete example of Jewish activism in the media involving Frankfurt School intellectuals, media experts, and the staff of Jewish activist organizations concerned the 1947 film *Crossfire* in which a Jew is gratuitously murdered by an anti-Semite. The potential release of the film ignited an intense debate within the activist Jewish community about strategies to combat anti-Semitism via the media, with the AJCommittee opposed to releasing a film produced by a Jewish producer, Dore Schary, because of its general view that Americans were prone to fascism and would identify with the murderer.

> Though most of the [AJCommittee] leadership had seen *Crossfire* on May 8 [1947] at a special New York screening arranged by Schary, they prevailed upon him to run the film again on June 19 for a panel of "experts" chaired

by New York psychiatrist David M. Levy. The expert audience was hand-picked by the [AJCommittee], and included leading academics—sociologists, psychologists, psychiatrists, and even anthropologist Margaret Mead—as well as key figures in the field of mass-media studies, most notably Paul Lazar[s]feld, Leo Lowenthal, Robert K. Merton, and Sigfried Kracauer, author of *From Caligari to Hitler* [a study of cinema in the Weimar Republic]. [AJCommittee staff members] John Slawson and Richard Rothschild also attended, as well as Dr. Samuel Flowerman and Dr. Marie Jahoda of the Scientific Research Department, and Elliott E. Cohen, executive editor of the [AJCommittee]-funded journal *Commentary*. The only ADL representative in attendance was Frank Trager. . . .

The discussion was organized around a number of rather leading questions: "Is [such a film] worth trying?" "Can the conflict between propaganda and entertainment in *Crossfire* be resolved?" "Will it intensify antisemitic feelings, even inflame smouldering feelings into active hostility among those already antisemitic? In other words, is *Crossfire* a dangerous movie?" "Can a group like ours . . . predict the response of the general public?" Or, "Are [such] considerations merely arm-chair strategy—nothing but hunches and abstract theories that make interesting conversations, but [are] completely irrelevant?" Following the screening, the experts filled out a questionnaire rating their own psychological identification with key characters in the film and speculating on the psychological identification of a "typical" movie audience. The experts' responses strikingly reveal their abiding faith in the efficacy of applying social-science techniques to the problem of prejudice, as well as an equally deep-seated lack of faith in both the intuitive responses and the intellectual capacities of ordinary Americans. Though they were not necessarily averse to the liberal propaganda in *Crossfire*, they were extremely concerned that average moviegoers might be easily "duped" by "dangerous" propaganda. In the specific instance of *Crossfire*, however, the experts were more concerned with psychological mechanisms than with overt propaganda; like Horkheimer, they believed that unconscious psychological identification would most likely invalidate the film's liberal message. ...

Significantly, the experts assumed that the average moviegoer, and particularly the average anti-Semite, was male. Thus, for some, Monty was the most troubling character in *Crossfire*. Though a few (particularly those with "experience with GIs") believed that Monty's bullying tendency would make him "feared more than admired," many felt that he was "too attractive, too virile" and thus, would be too appealing to the average moviegoer. (Langdon, 2008, Ch. 7)

Thus masculine White males were seen as the problem—perhaps portending the more recent cultural messages condemning "toxic masculinity." As noted above, both Adorno and Horkheimer believed that Americans had a strong tendency toward fascism.

There was also concern about the depiction of the Jew, with some concerned that he was portrayed as sexually ambiguous (perhaps bisexual in the view of some, such as *Commentary*'s Elliott Cohen). Moreover, Cohen saw in Samuels a "composite of many of the anti-Semitic stereotypes of the Jew": "[S]oft-handed, flashily dressed, suave, artistic, intellectual, moralizing, comfortably berthed in a cushy bachelor apartment during the war, with a bosomy Gentile mistress, self-assured, pushing in where he is not wanted" (Langdon, 2008, Ch. 7).

In any case, the episode illustrates the deep concern about portrayals related to Jews and anti-Semitism in the media. Indeed, Cohen and many of the experts criticized Schary for not having consulted experts prior to filming. In the event, *Crossfire* received five Academy Award nominations including for Best Picture, losing to Best Picture winner, *Gentleman's Agreement*, another anti-anti-Semitic film.

THE FRANKFURT SCHOOL AND POSTMODERNISM

Reflecting the congruence between the Frankfurt School and contemporary postmodernism, the enormously influential postmodernist Michel Foucault stated:

> If I had known about the Frankfurt School in time, I would have been saved a great deal of work. I would not have said a certain amount of nonsense and would not have taken so many false trails trying not to get lost, when the Frankfurt School had already cleared the way. (in Wiggershaus, 1994, p. 4)

Whereas the strategy of the Frankfurt School was to deconstruct universalist, scientific thinking by the use of "critical reason," postmodernism has opted for complete relativism and the lack of objective standards of any kind in the interests of preventing any general theories of society or universally valid philosophical or moral systems (Norris, 1993, pp. 287ff).[114]

---

[114] Consider the influential postmodernist Jean-François Lyotard (1984, p. 8), who states that "the right to decide what is true is not independent of the right to decide what is just." In the best tradition of the Frankfurt School, Lyotard rejects scientific accounts as totalitarian because they replace traditional accounts of culture with scientifically derived universals. As with Derrida, Lyotard's solution is to legitimize all narratives, but the main project is to attempt to prevent what Berman (1989, p. 8) terms the development of "an institutionalized master narrative"—the same deconstructive project that originated with the Frankfurt School. It

Contemporary postmodernism and multiculturalist ideology (see, e.g., Gless & Smith, 1992) have adopted several central pillars of the Frankfurt School: the fundamental priority of ethics and values in approaching education and the social sciences; empirical science as oppressive and an aspect of social domination; a rejection of the possibility of shared values or any sense of universalism or national culture (see also Jacoby, 1995, p. 35, a discussion of "postcolonial theory," another intellectual descendant of the Frankfurt School); a "hermeneutics of suspicion" in which any attempt to construct such universals or a national culture is energetically resisted and "deconstructed"—essentially the same activity that Adorno termed "negative dialectics" and likely an attempt to inoculate the culture against a hegemonic culture of the right, such as National Socialism. There is an implicit acceptance of a Balkanized model of society in which certain groups and their interests have *a priori* moral value and there is no possibility of developing a scientific, rational theory of any particular group, much less a theory of pan-human universals. Both the Frankfurt School and postmodernism implicitly accept a model in which there is competition among antagonistic groups and no rational way of reaching consensus, although there is also an implicit double standard in which cohesive groups formed by majorities are viewed as pathological and subject to radical critique.

Jacques Derrida (1930–2004)

It is immensely ironic that this onslaught against Western universalism effectively rationalizes minority group ethnocentrism while undercutting the intellectual basis of ethnocentrism. Intellectually one wonders how one could be a postmodernist and a committed Jew at the same time. Intellectual consistency would seem to require that all personal identifications be subjected to the same deconstructing logic, unless, of course, personal identity itself involves deep ambiguities, deception, and self-deception. This in fact appears to be the case for Jacques Derrida, the premier philosopher of deconstruction, whose philosophy shows the deep connections between the intellectual agendas of postmodernism and the Frankfurt School.[115] Derrida had a complex and

---

goes without saying that the rejection of science is entirely *a priori*—in the best tradition of the Frankfurt School.

[115] I noted briefly the anti-Western ideology of Claude Lévi-Strauss in Chapter 2. It is interesting that Derrida "deconstructed" Lévi-Strauss by accusing him of reactivating Rousseau's romantic views of non-Western cultures and thereby making a whole series of essentialist assumptions that are not warranted within the framework of Derrida's radical skepticism. "In response to Lévi-Strauss's criticisms of philosophers of consciousness, Derrida answered that none of them . . . would have been as naive as Lévi-Strauss had been to conclude so hastily in favor of the innocence and original goodness of the Nambikwara [an African tribe]. Derrida saw Lévi-Strauss's ostensibly ethnocentric-free viewpoint as a reverse ethnocentrism with

ambiguous Jewish identity despite being "a leftist Parisian intellectual, a secularist and an atheist" (Caputo, 1997, p. xxiii). Derrida was born into a Sephardic Jewish family that immigrated to Algeria from Spain in the nineteenth century. His family were thus crypto-Jews who retained their religious-ethnic identity for four hundred years in Spain during the period of the Inquisition.

Derrida (1993a, p. 81) identifies himself as a crypto-Jew: "Marranos that we are, Marranos in any case whether we want to be or not, whether we know it or not"—perhaps a confession of the complexity, ambivalence, and self-deception often involved in post-Enlightenment forms of Jewish identity. In his notebooks, Derrida (1993b, p. 70) writes of the centrality that Jewish issues have held in his writing: "Circumcision, that's all I've ever talked about." In the same passage (pp. 72–730), he writes that he has always taken,

> the most careful account, in anamnesis, of the fact that in my family and among the Algerian Jews, one scarcely ever said "circumcision" but "baptism," not Bar Mitzvah but "communion," with the consequences of softening, dulling, through fearful acculturation, that I've always suffered from more or less consciously.

This is an allusion to the continuation of crypto-Jewish practices among the Algerian Jews and a clear indication that Jewish identification and the need to hide it have remained psychologically salient to Derrida. Significantly, he (1993b, p. 73) identifies his mother as Esther, the biblical heroine who "had not made known her people nor her kindred" (Est. 2:10) and who was an inspiration to generations of crypto-Jews. Derrida was deeply attached to his mother and stated as she neared death, "I can be sure that you will not understand much of what you will nonetheless have dictated to me, inspired me with, asked of me, ordered from me." Like his mother (who spoke of baptism and communion rather than circumcision and bar mitzvah), Derrida thus has an inward Jewish identity while outwardly assimilating to the French Catholic culture of Algeria. For Derrida (p. 170), however, there are indications of ambivalence for both identities: "I am one of those *marranes* who no longer say they are Jews even in the secret of their own hearts" (see also Caputo, 1997, p. 304).

Derrida's experience with anti-Semitism during World War II in Algeria was traumatic and inevitably resulted in a deep consciousness of his own Jewishness. Derrida (1993b, p. 58) was expelled from school at age thirteen under

---

ethnic-political positions accusing the West of being initially responsible, through writing, for the death of innocent speech" (Dosse, 1997 II, p. 30). These comments are symptomatic of the changes inaugurated by postmodernism into the current intellectual *zeitgeist*. While the earlier critiques of the West by the Boasians and the structuralists romanticized non-Western cultures and vilified the West, the more recent trend is to express a pervasive skepticism regarding knowledge of any kind, motivated, I suppose, by the reasons outlined in this chapter and Chapter 7.

the Vichy government because of the *numerus clausus*, a self-described "little black and very Arab Jew who understood nothing about it, to whom no one ever gave the slightest reason, neither his parents nor his friends."

> The persecutions, which were unlike those of Europe, were all the same unleashed in the absence of any German occupier. . . . It is an experience that leaves nothing intact, an atmosphere that one goes on breathing forever. Jewish children expulsed from school. The principal's office: You are going to go home, your parents will explain. Then the Allies landed, it was the period of the so-called two-headed government (de Gaulle-Giraud): racial laws maintained for almost six months, under a "free" French government. Friends who no longer knew you, insults, the Jewish high school with its expulsed teachers and never a whisper of protest from their colleagues. . . . From that moment, I felt—how to put it?—just as out-of-place in a closed Jewish community as I did on the other side (we called them "the Catholics"). In France, the suffering subsided. I naively thought that anti-Semitism had disappeared. . . . But during adolescence, it was *the* tragedy, it was present in everything else. . . . Paradoxical effect, perhaps, of this brutalization: a desire for integration in the non-Jewish community, a fascinated but painful and suspicious desire, nervously vigilant, an exhausting aptitude to detect signs of racism, in its most discreet configurations or its noisiest disavowals. (Derrida, 1995b, pp. 120–121; emphasis original)

Bennington (1993, p. 326) proposes that the expulsion from school and its aftermath were,

> no doubt . . . the years during which the singular character of J.D.'s "belonging" to Judaism is imprinted on him: wound, certainly, painful and practiced sensitivity to antisemitism and any racism, "raw" response to xenophobia, but also impatience with gregarious identification, with the militancy of belonging in general, even if it is Jewish. . . . I believe that this difficulty with belonging, one would almost say of identification, affects the whole of J.D.'s oeuvre, and it seems to me that "the deconstruction of the proper" is the very thought of this, its thinking affection.

Indeed, Derrida says as much. He (1993b, p. 289) recalls just before his bar mitzvah (which he again notes was termed "communion" by the Algerian Jewish community), when the Vichy government expelled him from school and withdrew his citizenship:

> I became the outside, try as they might to come close to me they'll never touch me again. . . . I did my "communion" by fleeing the prison of all

languages, the sacred one they tried to lock me up in without opening me to it [i.e., Hebrew], the secular [i.e., French] they made clear would never be mine.

As with many Jews seeking a semi-cryptic pose in a largely non-Jewish environment, Derrida (1995b, p. 344) altered his name to Jacques:

By choosing what was in some way, to be sure, a semi-pseudonym but also very French, Christian, simple, I must have erased more things than I could say in a few words (one would have to analyze the conditions in which a certain community—the Jewish community in Algeria—in the '30s sometimes chose American names.

Changing his name is thus a form of crypsis as practiced by the Algerian Jewish community, a way of outwardly conforming to the French, Christian culture while secretly remaining Jewish.

Derrida's Jewish political agenda is identical to that of the Frankfurt School:

The idea behind deconstruction is to deconstruct the workings of strong nation-states with powerful immigration policies, to deconstruct the rhetoric of nationalism, the politics of place, the metaphysics of native land and native tongue. . . . The idea is to disarm the bombs . . . of identity that nation-states build to defend themselves against the stranger, against Jews and Arabs and immigrants, . . . all of whom . . . are wholly other. Contrary to the claims of Derrida's more careless critics, the passion of deconstruction is deeply political, for deconstruction is a relentless, if sometimes indirect, discourse on democracy, on a democracy to come. Derrida's democracy is a radically pluralistic polity that resists the terror of an organic, ethnic, spiritual unity, of the natural, native bonds of the nation (natus, natio), which grind to dust everything that is not a kin of the ruling kind and genus (Geschlecht). He dreams of a nation without nationalist or nativist closure, of a community without identity, of a non–identical community that cannot say I or we, for, after all, the very idea of a community is to fortify (munis, muneris) ourselves in common against the other. His work is driven by a sense of the consummate danger of an identitarian community, of the spirit of the "we" of "Christian Europe," or of a "Christian politics," lethal compounds that spell death for Arabs and Jews, for Africans and Asians, for anything other. The heaving and sighing of this Christian European spirit is a lethal air for Jews and Arabs, for all les juifs [i.e., Jews as prototypical others], even if they go back to father Abraham, a way of gassing them according to both the letter and the spirit. (Caputo, 1997, pp. 231–232)

Derrida sees undeconstructed architecture as reinforcing a sense of community which sees its architecture as its natural environment that closes the community off against "the other." Vitale (2010, pp. 217–218) comments on Derrida's views on architecture:

> I would like to explain that deconstruction of architecture implies rather the deconstruction of the political and that it can be put into effect only through the actual deconstruction of the architectural structure which the Western tradition of the political has embodied itself into.
>
> The tradition that is itself based on the link which strengthens the identity—of the individual and the community—to a supposed original space, to the stability of the frontiers separating it from the otherness in general, from what is therefore conceived of, simultaneously or alternately, as external, foreign, stranger or strange. . . .
>
> In the Western tradition the (individual and collective) identity is thought of as an internal, permanent, stable space, autonomous and independent from the other in general, which is represented as external, stranger and, thus, is experienced as a possible threat.
>
> To do space for the other, to give a place for that relation is the task of deconstruction of the political. The achievement of this task necessarily requires deconstruction of the architecture which provides such axiomatics with a concrete and durable form, with a form imposing itself upon our experience as if it were our natural environment.

Derrida's analysis is the diametric opposite to Richard Wagner's (1850/1869/2022, pp. 13, 16) analysis of music in which he proposes that the musical works of Jews cannot resonate with the German spirit and cannot,

> rise, even by accident, to the ardor of a higher, heartfelt expression. . . .
> The true poet, no matter in what branch of art, still gains his stimulus from nothing but a faithful, loving contemplation of instinctive life, of that life that only greets his sight among the Folk.

Thus architecture as an art form should resonate with the spirit of the people living in the area and reflect their natural tendencies—an evolutionary aesthetics in which architecture springs naturally from the biological tendencies of the people. Derrida's deconstruction of architecture opposes any attempt for architecture to create a natural environment; it is thus aimed at creating an environment that would weaken the sense of a natural community because such a community might erect barriers between itself and "the other."

Derrida published a pamphlet advocating immigration of non-Europeans into France (see Lilla, 1998). As with the Frankfurt School, the radical skepticism of the deconstructionist movement is in the service of preventing the development of hegemonic, universalist ideologies and other foundations of gentile group allegiance in the name of the *tout autre*, i.e., the "wholly other." Caputo ascribes Derrida's motivation for his deconstruction of Hegel to the latter's conceptualization of Judaism as morally and spiritually inferior to Christianity because of its legalism and tribalistic exclusivism, whereas Christianity is the religion of love and assimilation, a product of the Greek, not the Jewish, spirit. These Hegelian interpretations are remarkably congruent with Christian self-conceptualizations and Christian conceptions of Judaism originating in antiquity (see SAID, Ch. 3), and such a conceptualization fits well with the evolutionary analysis of Judaism developed in PTSDA. Reinterpretations and refutations of Hegel were common among nineteenth-century Jewish intellectuals (see SAID, Ch. 6), and we have seen that in *Negative Dialectics* Adorno was concerned with refuting the Hegelian idea of universal history for similar reasons.

> Hegel's searing, hateful portrait of the Jew ... seem[s] to haunt all of Derrida's work; ... by presenting in the most loyal and literal way just what Hegel says, Derrida shows ... that Hegel's denunciations of the Jew's castrated heart is a heartless, hateful castration of the other. (Caputo, 1997, pp. 234, 243)

As with the Frankfurt School, Derrida posits that the messianic future is unknown because to say otherwise would lead to the possibility of imposed uniformity, "a systematic whole with infinite warrant" (Caputo, 1997, p. 246), a triumphal and dangerous truth in which Jews as exemplars of the *tout autre* would necessarily suffer. The human condition is conceptualized as "a blindness that cannot be remedied, a radical, structural condition in virtue of which everyone is blind from birth" (p. 313).

As with the Frankfurt School, the exemplars of otherness have *a priori* moral value.

> In deconstruction love is extricated from the polemic against the Jews by being rethought in terms of the other, of *les juifs*. ... If this organic Hegelian Christian-European community is defined as making a common (*com*) defense (*munis*) against the other, Derrida advances the idea of laying down his arms, *rendre les armes*, surrendering to the other. (Caputo, 1997, p. 248)

From this perspective, acknowledging the possibility of truth is dangerous because of the possibility that truth could be used against the other. The best strategy, therefore, is to open up "a salutary competition among interpretations, a certain salutary radical hermeneuticizing, in which we dream with passion of something unforeseeable and impossible" (Caputo, 1997, p. 277). To the conflicting views of differing religions and ideologies, Derrida,

> opposes a community, if it is one, of the blind[;] . . . of the blind leading the blind. Blindness makes for good communities, provided we all admit that we do not see, that in the crucial matters we are all stone blind and without privileged access, adrift in the same boat without a lighthouse to show the other shore. (Caputo, 1997, pp. 313–314)

Such a world is safe for Judaism, the prototypical other, and provides no warrant for the universalizing tendencies of Western civilization (Caputo, 1997, p. 335)—one might term deconstruction as de-Hellenization or de-Westernization. Minority group ethnic consciousness is thus validated not in the sense that it is known to be based on some sort of psychological truth, but in the sense that it can't be proved untrue. On the other hand, the cultural and ethnic interests of majorities are "hermeneuticized" and thus rendered impotent—impotent because they cannot serve as the basis for a mass ethnic movement that would conflict with the interests of other groups.

Ironically from the standpoint of the theory of Judaism developed here, Derrida (who has thought a great deal about his own circumcision in his "Circumfession," 1993b) realizes that circumcision, which he likens to a *shibboleth* because of its usefulness as a mechanism of ingroup demarcation (i.e., as a mark of Jewish exclusiveness and "otherness"), is a two-edged sword. Commenting on the work of Holocaust poet Paul Celan, Derrida (1994, pp. 67–68, emphasis original) states:

> [T]he mark of a covenant or alliance, it also *intervenes*, it interdicts, it signifies the sentence of exclusion, of discrimination, indeed of extermination. One may, thanks to the *shibboleth*, recognize and be recognized by one's own, for better and for worse, in the cleaving of partaking: on the one hand, for the sake of the partaking and the ring of the covenant, but also, on the other hand, for the purpose of denying the other, of denying him passage or life. . . . Because of the *shibboleth* and exactly to the extent that one may make use of it, one may see it turned against oneself: then it is the circumcised who are proscribed or held at the border, excluded from the community, put to death, or reduced to ashes.

Despite the dangers of circumcision as a two-edged sword, Derrida (1994, p. 68) concludes that "there must be circumcision," a conclusion that Caputo (1997, p. 252) interprets as an assertion of an irreducible and undeniable human demand "for a differentiating mark, for a mark of difference." Derrida thus subscribes to the inevitability (possibly innateness) of group demarcations, but, amazingly and apologetically, he manages to conceptualize circumcision not as a sign of tribal exclusivism, but as "the cut that opens the space for the incoming of the *tout autre*" (Caputo, p. 250)—a remarkable move because, as we have seen, Derrida seems quite aware that circumcision results in separatism, the erection of ingroup-outgroup barriers, and the possibility of between-group conflict and even extermination. But in Derrida's gloss, "spiritually we are all Jews, all called and chosen to welcome the other" (Caputo, p. 262), so that Judaism turns out to be a universalist ideology where marks of separatism are interpreted as openness to the other. In Derrida's view, "if circumcision is Jewish it is only in the sense that all poets are Jews. . . . Everyone ought to have a circumcised heart; this ought to form a universal religion" (Caputo, p. 262). Similarly, in a discussion of James Joyce, Derrida contrasts Joyce and Hegel (as prototypical Western thinkers) who "close the circle of the same" with "Abrahamic [i.e., Jewish] circumcision, which cuts the cord of the same in order to be open to the other, circumcision as saying yes . . . to the other" (Caputo, p. 257). Thus in the end, Derrida develops yet another in the age-old conceptualizations of Judaism as a morally superior group, while ideologies of sameness and universality that might underlie ideologies of social homogeneity and group consciousness among European gentiles are deconstructed and rendered as morally inferior.

DADA, DERRIDA, AND DECONSTRUCTION

[Frankfurt School intellectual Walter] Benjamin speaks of Dada's moral shock effects as anticipating the technical effects of film in the way that they "assail the spectator."

— Leah Dickerman, 2005, p. 9

Dada was an artistic movement that began in the context of World War I and has been linked by several scholars to the general thrust of the Frankfurt School. Brenton Sanderson (2023, p. 3):

A prominent example of a cultural movement from this time with important Jewish involvement was Dada. The Dadaists challenged the very foundations of Western civilization which they regarded, in the context of the destruction of World War One and continuing anti-Semitism throughout Europe, as pathological. The artists and intellectuals of Dada responded to this socio-political diagnosis with assorted acts of cultural subversion. Dada was a movement that was destructive and nihilistic, irrational and absurdist, and which preached the overturning of every cultural tradition of the European past, including rationality itself. . . . While there were many non-Jews involved in Dada, the Jewish contribution was fundamental to shaping its intellectual tenor as a movement, for Dada was as much an attitude and way of thinking as a mode of artistic output.

Sanderson explores the relationship between Dada, Derrida, the Frankfurt School, and Jewishness. For example, the intellectual and spiritual background of Tristan Tzara, a founder of Dada, was infused with the Yiddish and Hassidic subcultures of his early-twentieth-century Moldavian homeland, and this cultural milieu was critically important in producing the revolutionary zeitgeist as the leader of Dada (Sandqvist, 2006). Sandqvist thus links Tzara's revolt against European culture directly to his Jewish identity, and his perception of the Jewish population of Romania (and particularly of his native Moldavia) as cruelly oppressed by anti-Semitism.

Sanderson (2023, pp. 23–26) notes that Dada's "anti-rationalism prefigured Jacques Derrida's deconstruction as a Jewish intellectual movement arrayed against Western civilization":

> The parallels between Dada and Deconstruction have been noted by numerous scholars. Robert Wicks observes how strongly Dada resonates "with the definitively poststructuralist conception of deconstruction advanced by Jacques Derrida in the 1960s" [Wicks, 2007, p. 11]. Pegrum likewise notes the "strong link between Dada and postmodern artistic theory, the most obvious point of contact being with the work of Derrida" [Pegrum, 2000, p. 269]. Richard Sheppard regards the poststructuralists "as more introverted, less politicized, and less carnivalesque descendants of their Dada daddies" [Sheppard, 1999, p. 365].
>
> For the Dadaists, European civilization consisted of "an alienation-generating amalgam of rationalistic thinking, science, and technology that adhered to the preservation of order, systematicity, and methodicality." They believed firmly that "European cultural values were not worth preserving" [Wicks, 2007, pp. 9–10]. Tzara once stated that "logic is always false," and a core concept in his thought was "as long as we do things the way we think we once did them, we will be unable to achieve any kind of livable society" [Beitchman, 1988, p. 29]. The Dadaists famously "spat in the eye of the world," replacing logic and sense with absurdity and defiance [Unger & Unger, 2006, p. 354]. Even the word Dada itself, suggesting basic drives and childlike behavior, was self-consciously absurd, even self-mocking, and a subversive anthem of resistance to more fully instrumentalized speech and disciplined rationality, and ridiculed Western confidence in the "autonomy of the rational ego and the efficacy of reason." They denounced the post-Renaissance Western conception of reality which "assumed that the world was organized according to humanly intelligible laws," and "condemned 'bourgeois cultures' deadening determination to stabilize and categorize all phenomena" [Short, 1994, p. 12]. . . .

In order to deconstruct Western culture, Derrida had to identify a fundamental fault with it—which he decided was its "logocentrism." By this he meant Western culture privileged speech over the written word (a dubious assertion), and that it is founded on the false belief that the world really is as our concepts describe it (i.e., on philosophical realism). Like Barthes and Foucault, Derrida used nominalism (the view that concepts are nothing more than human constructions with no necessary relationship to the real world) to deconstruct and subvert Western realism. In doing so, he mimicked the approach of the Dadaists: "It followed from their rejection of the belief in progress, in tamable nature and rational man, that the Dadas should cast doubt on the power of language, literature and art to represent reality. The information which the senses communicated to men was misleading, even the ideas of the individual 'personality' and the external world were elusive and incoherent. How then could language, by definition an instrument of public communication, do other than deform and betray life's authentic character as a discontinuous sequence of immediate experiences? The Dadas answered that words were mere fictions and that there was no correspondence between the structures of language and those of reality. Thus the belief in order which the power of a common, inherited language inculcated was illusory" [Short, 1994, p. 17].

In order to attack Western realism Derrida and the Dadaists borrowed from the Swiss linguist Ferdinand de Saussure the notion of "*différence*"—which Saussure used to denote the arbitrary nature of language signs. It does not matter what signs we use to mean "night" and "day;" what matters is that we use signs to signal a certain difference, and this structural property was, for Saussure, the true carrier of meaning. The French *différer* also means to defer, in the sense of put off, and on this coincidental etymological basis Derrida decided that that Saussure had definitively proven that meaning is always deferred by the text.

The consequence is that the process of meaning is something that never gets started: or rather, if and when meaning starts is an arbitrary human decision. Texts do not have a single authoritative meaning: rather, there is a "free play of meaning" and anything goes. Consequently, we are *liberated* from meaning. Moreover, the text is "emancipated from authorship." Once written, the author disappears and a text becomes a public artifact. It is for us to decide what the text means, and we are free to decide as we please; and since "all interpretation is misinterpretation," no particular reading is privileged [Scruton, 1994, pp. 478–79]. Sheppard [1999, p. 363] notes that: "Derrida, dynamizing Saussure's model of the sign, sees humanity caught in an endless flow of textuality where signifieds and signifiers perpetually fracture and recombine anew. Consequently, he concludes that there is nothing outside the text." Under Derrida's deconstruction "a new text thus gradually begins to emerge, but this text too is at subtle variance with itself, and the deconstruction continues in what could be an infinite regress of dialectical readings" [Poole, 2000, p. 203]. . . .

Furthermore, he took his crypto-Judaism to the grave: "When Derrida was buried, his elder brother, René, wore a tallit at the suburban French cemetery and recited the Kaddish to himself inwardly, since Jacques had asked for no public prayers. This discreet, highly personal, yet emotionally and spiritually meaningful approach to recognizing Derrida's Judaism seems emblematic of this complex, imperfect, yet valuably nuanced thinker" [Ivry, 2010]. . . .

Derrida's sociological preoccupations (and suggested solutions) replicated those of Tristan Tzara. Sandqvist links Tzara's profound revolt against European social constraints directly to his Jewish identity, and his anger at the persistence of anti-Semitism. For Sandqvist, the treatment of Jews in Romania fueled the Dada leader's revolt against Western civilization. Bodenheimer [2017] notes that:

"As a Jew, Tzara had many reasons to call into question the so-called disastrous truths and rationalizations of European thinking, one result of which was the First World War—with the discrimination of Jews for centuries being another. . . . He came from a background in which jingoistic and anti-Semitic arguments had long reproached Jews for using impure, falsified language, from early examples in the sixteenth century . . . all the way to the arguments of the Romanian intellectuals in Tzara's time, who attacked Jews as 'foreigners' importing 'diseased ideas' into Romanian literature and culture. [Tzara consequently] seeks to unmask language itself as a construction that draws its value, and sometimes its claim to superiority, from an equally constructed concept of identities and values. In themselves, all languages are equal, but equal in their differences. This claim to the right of equality while upholding difference is the basic Jewish claim to a secular society. But the European peoples, be it first for religious or later for nationalist reasons, have never managed to actually understand this right, let alone grant it to minority societies."

One of the catalysts for the dissolution of Dada in Paris was Surrealist leader André Breton's concern that Dada's nihilism posed a threat to the "process of intellectual sanitation" that became necessary with the rise of fascism [Haslam, 1978, p. p. 93]. Boime [2010, p. 102] likewise claims the Dadaists in their "assault on the Enlightenment and bourgeois liberalism in Zurich and then in Berlin eventually played into the hands of the Fascists and right-wing nationalists. Although these latter groups condemned Dadaist spectacle and modernist thinking, Dada's rejection of parliamentary politics and democratic institutions helped pave the way for Nazism's direct assault on humanitarian ideals."

Derrida has been similarly criticized by some Jews because his writings "lead to 'nihilism,' which threatens, in their denial of the notion of objective truth, to 'efface many of the essential differences between

Nazism and non-Nazism'" [Ivry, 2010]. However, Derrida's writings have certainly not had any effect on the power of the Holocaust Industry, and indeed, some of Derrida's biggest backers were intellectual Holocaust activists. This strange state of affairs may be explained by the fact that for some Jews, like Derrida, acknowledging the possibility of objective truth is dangerous because of the possibility that truth could be arrayed against the "other." Similarly, for the Dadaists, the principles of Western rationality "were held to be highly problematic, because of its instrumental connections to social repressions and domination" [Biro, 2009, p. 154]. Consequently, a world where truth had been deconstructed is very much a desirable world. . . .

When the Frankfurt School established itself in the United States, it made a conscious effort to give its Jewish intellectual activism a "scientific" veneer by gathering "empirical data" (such as that which formed the basis for *The Authoritarian Personality*) in order to challenge existing scientific theories seen as inimical to Jewish interests (such as Darwinian anthropology). Derrida and the poststructuralists instead sought (like the Jews within Dada) to discredit threatening concepts by undermining the notion of objective truth underpinning *all* Western thought. Like the Dadaists, the poststructuralists decided, if you dislike the prevailing power, then strive to ruin its concepts. Dada used nonsense and absurdity to achieve this goal, while Derrida developed his methodology of deconstruction.

APPENDIX: REVIEW OF THE AUTHORITARIAN PERSONALITY

TAP (Adorno, Frenkel-Brunswik, Levinson, & Sanford, 1950) is a true classic of research in social psychology. It has generated thousands of studies, and references continue to appear in textbooks, although there has been no absence of criticism of the personality approach to intergroup prejudice and hostility. Nathan Glazer (1954) noted, "No volume published since [World War II] in the field of social psychology has had a greater impact on the direction of the actual empirical work being carried on in the universities today." Despite its influence, from the beginning it has been common to point out technical problems with the construction of the scales and the conduct and interpretation of the interviews (see Altemeyer, 1981, pp. 33–51; 1988, pp. 52–54; Billings et al., 1993; R. Brown, 1965, pp. 509ff; Collier et al., 1991, p. 196; H. H. Hyman & Sheatsley, 1954). The result is that TAP has become something of a textbook example of how *not* to do social science research.

Indeed, Paul Lazarsfeld, a prominent Jewish sociologist and champion of rigorous empirical research in sociology, complained to Adorno about his scholarship in a lengthy letter from September 1938:

You know that I have an unchanging respect for your ideas and that I am sure our project will profit greatly by your cooperation. But you also know that I have great objections against the way you present your ideas and against your disregard of evidence and systematic empirical research. . . . Just because you express new and aggressive ideas you have to be especially careful not to be open yourself to justified attacks, and I am sorry to say that in many parts your memorandum is definitely below the Standards of intellectual cleanliness, discipline and responsibility which have to be requested from any one active in academic work. (Adorno & Horkheimer, 2004, pp. 436–437)

It's fascinating that after the publication of TAP, Adorno embarked on a series of articles completely repudiating the entire concept of empirical research (Wheatland, 2009).

Nevertheless, despite technical problems with the original scale construction, there is no question that there is such a thing as psychological authoritarianism, in the sense that it is possible to construct a reliable psychometric scale that measures such a construct. Whereas the F-scale from the original TAP studies is plagued with an acquiescent response set bias, more recent versions of the scale have managed to avoid this difficulty while retaining substantially the same correlates with other scales.

In any case, my treatment will emphasize two aspects of TAP that are central to the political program of the Frankfurt School: (1) I will emphasize the double standard in which gentile behavior inferred from high scores on the F-Scale or the Ethnocentrism Scale is viewed as an indication of psychopathology, whereas precisely the same behavior is central to Judaism as a group evolutionary strategy; (2) I will also criticize the psychodynamic mechanisms involving disturbed parent-child relationships proposed to underlie authoritarianism. These proposed psychodynamic mechanisms are responsible for the highly subversive nature of the book considered as political propaganda; not coincidentally, it is this strand of the project that has often struck commentators as highly questionable. Thus Altemeyer (1988, p. 53) notes that despite the "unconvincing" nature of the scientific evidence supporting it, the basic idea that anti-Semitism is the result of disturbed parent-child relationships has "spread so widely through our culture that it has become a stereotype." Moreover, much of the incredible success of the TAP studies occurred because of the book's widespread acceptance among Jewish social scientists, who by the 1950s had assumed a prominent role in the American academic community and were very concerned with anti-Semitism (Higham, 1984, p. 154; see also below and Preface).

The politicized nature of TAP has long been apparent to mainstream psychologists. Roger Brown (1965, pp. 479, 544) noted:

The study called *The Authoritarian Personality* has affected American life: the theory of prejudice it propounded has become a part of popular culture and a force against racial discrimination. Is it also true? You must be the judge. ... The Berkeley study of authoritarian personality does not leave many people indifferent. Cool objectivity has not been the hallmark of this tradition. Most of those who have participated have cared deeply about the social issues involved.

The last part of Brown's comment reflects the feeling many readers have had, namely that the beliefs and goals of the authors were important in conceptualizing and interpreting the research.

A good example of one such reader is Christopher Lasch (1991, pp. 445ff), who noted:

The purpose and design of *Studies in Prejudice* dictated the conclusion that prejudice, a psychological disorder rooted in the "authoritarian" personality structure, could be eradicated only by subjecting the American people to what amounted to collective psychotherapy—by treating them as inmates of an insane asylum.

From the beginning, this was social science with a political agenda:

By identifying the "liberal personality" as the antithesis of the authoritarian personality, they equated mental health with an approved political position. They defended liberalism ... on the grounds that other positions had their roots in personal pathology. (Lasch, 1991, p. 453)

TAP begins by acknowledging Freud as a general influence, and especially his role in making the intellectual world "more and more aware of the connection between the suppression of children (both within the home and outside) and society's usually naive ignorance of the psychological dynamics of the life of the child and the adult alike" (p. x). In congruence with this general perspective, Adorno and his colleagues, "in common with most social scientists, hold the view that anti-Semitism is based more largely upon factors in the subject and in his total situation than upon actual characteristics of Jews" (p. 2). The roots of anti-Semitism are therefore to be sought in individual psychopathology—"the deep-lying needs of the personality" (p. 9)—and not in the behavior of Jews.

Chapter II (by R. Nevitt Sanford) consists of interview material from two individuals, one high on anti-Semitism (Mack), the other low on anti-Semitism (Larry). Mack is quite ethnocentric and tends to see people in terms of ingroup-outgroup relationships in which the outgroup is characterized in a stereotypically negative manner. As predicted for such a person on the basis of social identity theory (Hogg & D. Abrams, 1988), his own group, the Irish, has approved traits, and outgroups are seen as homogeneous and threatening. Whereas Mack is strongly conscious of groups as units of social categorization, Larry does not think in terms of groups at all.

Although Mack's ethnocentrism is clearly viewed as pathological, there is no thought given to the possibility that Jews also have analogously ethnocentric thought processes as a result of the extreme salience of ingroup-outgroup relationships as an aspect of Jewish socialization. Indeed, in SAID (Ch. 1) I noted that Jews would be more likely than gentiles to have negative stereotypes about outgroups and to view the world as composed fundamentally of homogeneous, competing, threatening, and negatively stereotyped outgroups. Moreover, there is excellent evidence, summarized throughout this volume, that Jews have often held negative views of gentile (i.e., outgroup) culture. Nevertheless, as we shall see, the agenda of TAP is that similar ethnocentric attitudes among gentiles are traceable to pathological early influences on personality.

Further, a consistent theme in Chapters 2–5 is that a major thrust of Jewish intellectual movements since the nineteenth century has been to devise theories that minimize the importance of the social category Jew-gentile while allowing for the continuation of a very strong sense of Jewish identity—the "logic of invisibility" tactic noted above as characteristic of the Frankfurt School intellectuals. Larry's tendency not to see the social environment in terms of groups is linked with an absence of anti-Semitism, whereas Mack's anti-Semitism is necessarily linked to the importance of groups as a social category.

These themes and their influence on scale construction can be seen in Chapters III and IV (by Daniel J. Levinson). Levinson notes that anti-Semites tend to see Jews as members of groups rather than as individuals, and he suggests that the effects of individual experience with Jews (e.g., a negative encounter with an individual Jew generalized as reflecting on all Jews or most Jews), "would seem to depend in large part on the individual's *capacity for individuated experience*" (p. 95, emphasis original).[116] Levinson also notes that

---

[116] An interesting feature of the material in this section of TAP is an attempt to demonstrate the irrationality of anti-Semitism by showing that anti-Semites have contradictory beliefs about Jews. As noted in SAID (Ch. 1), anti-Semitic beliefs are not expected to necessarily be true or, I suppose, even logically consistent. However, TAP exaggerates the self-contradictory nature of anti-Semitic beliefs in the service of emphasizing the irrational, projective nature of anti-Semitism. Thus Levinson states that it is contradictory for individuals to believe both that Jews are clannish and aloof as well as to believe that Jews should be segregated and restricted (p. 76). Similarly, in another volume of the *Studies in Prejudice* series, Ackerman and Jahoda (1950, p. 58) propose that anti-Semitic attitudes that Jews are clannish and intrusive are contradictory.

individuals who themselves belong to groups with a strong ingroup ideology, such as sororities, are more likely to be anti-Semitic (p. 104). Again, the implication is that strong ingroup ideologies should be reserved for Jews and are dangerous in others. Recall Adorno's (2006, p. 248) comment, quoted above, that "After 6 million have been murdered, it goes against my instincts to dwell on the manners of those few who survived, whom I incidentally do not need to like," referring to the hostile attitudes of a Jewish community toward outsiders that reflected the traditional, pre-Enlightenment insularity of Jewish groups throughout Europe. These findings fit well with the discussion of individualist versus collectivist societies at the beginning of this chapter: Jews, as a highly cohesive group, have an interest in advocating a completely atomistic,

---

Agreement with such items is not self-contradictory. Such attitudes are probably a common component of the reactive processes discussed in SAID (Chs. 3–5). Jews are viewed by these anti-Semites as members of a strongly cohesive group who attempt to penetrate gentile circles of power and high social status, perhaps even undermining the cohesiveness of these gentile groups, while retaining their own separatism and clannishness. The belief that Jews should be restricted is certainly consistent with this attitude. Moreover, contradictory negative stereotypes of Jews, such as their being capitalist and communist (Ackerman & Jahoda, 1950, p. 58), may be applied by anti-Semites to different groups of Jews, and these stereotyping processes may have a significant degree of truth: Jews may be overrepresented among successful capitalists and among radical political leaders. As noted in SAID (Ch. 2), there was indeed some truth to the idea that Jews were disproportionately likely to be political radicals and successful capitalists. "From emancipation onwards, the Jews were blamed both for seeking to ingratiate themselves with established society, enter in and dominate it; and, at the same time, for trying to destroy it utterly. Both charges had an element of truth" (P. Johnson, 1987/1988, p. 345).

Levinson also notes that the "Seclusive" scale includes statements such as "Jewish millionaires may do a certain amount to help their own people, but little of their money goes into worthwhile American causes," whereas the "Intrusive" scale includes contradictory items such as "When Jews create large funds for educational or scientific research (Rosenwald, Heller, etc.), it is mainly due to a desire for fame and public notice rather than a really sincere scientific interest." Again, one could easily affirm the first statement as a general rule and consistently believe that the exceptions result from Jewish self-interest. Nevertheless, Levinson concludes, "One major characteristic of anti-Semites is a relatively blind hostility which is reflected in the stereotypy, self-contradiction, and destructiveness of their thinking about Jews" (p. 76).

Anti-Semites are also said to oppose Jewish clannishness and Jewish assimilation. They demand that Jews "liquidate themselves, that they lose entirely their cultural identity and adhere instead to the prevailing cultural ways"; at the same time, "Jews who attempt to assimilate are apparently even more suspect than the others. Accusations of 'prying,' 'power-seeking,' and 'imitation' are made, and seemingly generous acts by Jews are attributed to hidden selfish motives. . . . There is no logical basis for urging on the one hand that Jews become like everyone else, and on the other hand, that Jews be limited and excluded in the most important areas of social life" (p. 97).

This is a strange interpretation of the data. One could easily advocate that an outgroup assimilate but at the same time have negative attitudes regarding the present clannish, power-seeking behavior of outgroup members. Again, social identity research and evolutionary theory do not predict that individuals will hold true or self-consistent beliefs about an outgroup such as the Jews. Levinson, however, is clearly going far beyond the data in an attempt to portray anti-Semitism as entirely irrational.

individualistic society in which ingroup-outgroup distinctions are not salient to gentiles.

The Ethnocentrism Scale has three subscales, one involving attitudes toward African Americans, one involving attitudes toward minorities in general, and one involving patriotism. Although the presentation of the Ethnocentrism Scale leads one to believe that the researchers are studying ethnocentrism in general, in fact the scale items are exclusively concerned with ethnocentrism among the White Christian population. Those high in ethnocentrism according to this scale have negative attitudes toward African Americans and Jews and positive attitudes toward White, Christian dominance. For example, one item on the Ethnocentrism Scale is "In view of the present national emergency [World War II], it is highly important to limit responsible government jobs to native, white, Christian Americans." The result of including such items is that a strongly identified Jew, for whom the ingroup-outgroup distinction is salient, would have a low score on Levinson's Ethnocentrism Scale.

Items on the Anti-Semitism Scale appear to imply that an aspect of anti-Semitism is the gentile view that Jews constitute a distinctive group. For example, one of the items is "The trouble with letting Jews into a nice neighborhood is that they gradually give it a typical Jewish atmosphere." R. Brown (1965, p. 483) comments, "How could it be otherwise? Surely Jews will produce a Jewish atmosphere. They will at any rate do so if one thinks of Jews as 'categorically different from non-Jews.' However, it is just this saliency of 'Jewishness' which the authors consider the beginning of anti-Semitism." Here the implicit assumption is that awareness of the Jewish-gentile social categorization signals anti-Semitism in gentiles and therefore indicates disturbed parent-child relations—another indication that Institute intellectuals regarded Jewish invisibility as a desirable goal. Nevertheless, among Jews such a social categorization process is critical for the continuation of Judaism as a group evolutionary strategy.

Similarly ironic as an aspect of the Anti-Semitism Scale is the inclusion of the items "I can hardly imagine myself marrying a Jew" and "It is wrong for Jews and Gentiles to intermarry." Such attitudes apparently result from disturbed parent-child relationships among gentiles and the suppression of human nature, yet an abhorrence of intermarriage was typical of traditional Jewish communities and that taboo remained strong at the time TAP was written, although it has relaxed considerably in recent decades (see MacDonald, 2022a). However, a 1957 survey published by the AJCommittee noted that the taboo was quite strong at that time:

> About one-eighth [17 percent of fathers, 8 percent of mothers] either refused to contemplate the possibility [of intermarriage], or said they would reject the child. [One father: "'I'd kill her if she ever married a goy,' he

shouted, slamming his fist on the table. 'I'd absolutely kill her. No daughter of mine is going to marry a goy. There are plenty of Jews around.'" (p. 34)] At the other extreme, 2 per cent replied that they would accept the situation completely. Most parents, however, would try first to prevent or discourage the marriage, and, failing that, accept it. . . .

Many special organizations, institutions and clubs have been set up to help ensure that young Jews meet each other, rather than Christians. Parents are thus hoping to keep two somewhat disparate values from coming into conflict. On the one hand, they want love and marital happiness for their children. But on the other hand, the deep urge to preserve Jewish identity compels them to keep their sons and daughters from the kind of association with Gentile children which might lead to marriage. Fear of intermarriage thus becomes one of the most important determinants of Jewish-non-Jewish friendship. (Sklare & Vosk, 1957, p. 33)

Other items reflecting aspects of Judaism as a group evolutionary strategy in fact have substantial empirical support. For example, several items are concerned with perceptions of Jewish clannishness and its effect on residential patterns and business practices.[117] Other items are concerned with perceptions that Jews engage in cultural separatism and with perceptions that Jews have power, money, and influence out of proportion to their numbers in the population. There is an item that reflects the overrepresentation of Jews in leftist and radical political causes: "There seems to be some revolutionary streak in the Jewish make-up as shown by the fact that there are so many Jewish Communists and agitators." However, data reviewed in this volume, SAID, and PTSDA indicate that in fact there is considerable truth in all these generalizations. Being high on the Anti-Semitism Scale may therefore simply mean that one has access to more information rather than a sign of a disturbed childhood.

Particularly interesting is the Patriotism Scale, designed to tap attitudes involving "blind attachment to certain national cultural values, uncritical conformity with the prevailing group ways, and rejection of other nations as outgroups" (p. 107). Again, strong attachment to group interests among the majority group is considered pathological, whereas no mention is made of analogous group attachments among Jews. An advocacy of strong discipline and conformity within the majority group is an important indicator of this pathology: one scale item reads, "Minor forms of military training, obedience, and

---

[117] See also the discussion in SAID (Ch. 6) of ADL strategies to combat anti-Semitism by turning true statements about Jews into exemplars of anti-Semitic attitudes. E. Mayer (1979, p. 84) notes that Orthodox Jews are highly concerned about living in an area which has a sufficiently high concentration of Jews, and Lowenstein (1983) shows that Jews continued to live in concentrated areas in Germany well after emancipation. See also Glazer and Moynihan (1963/1970) for similar data for American Jews.

discipline, such as drill, marching, and simple commands, should be made a part of the elementary school educational program." However, no mention is made of discipline, conformity, and the socialization of group cohesiveness as important ideals within minority group strategies. As indicated in PTSDA (Ch. 7), traditional Jewish socialization practices have placed strong emphasis on discipline within the group and psychological acceptance of group goals (i.e., conformity).

These results are of interest because an important aspect of this entire effort is to pathologize positive attitudes toward creating a highly cohesive, well-disciplined group strategy among gentiles, but nevertheless failing to censure such attitudes among Jews—a program that continues throughout the West today where only White ethnocentrism is condemned by Jewish groups but not among the myriad non-European-derived groups that now inhabit the West. Individuals high on the Ethnocentrism Scale as well as the Anti-Semitism Scale are undoubtedly people who are very group-conscious. They see themselves as members of cohesive groups, including, in some cases, their own ethnic group and, at the highest level, the nation—which, in the 1940s was generally thought of as a White, Christian nation—and such people have relatively negative views of outgroups and individuals in the ingroup who deviate from group goals and group norms. In Chapter III Levinson states that anti-Semites want power for their own groups and value clannishness in their own groups while condemning similar Jewish behavior (p. 97). Conversely, the data reviewed in this volume are highly compatible with the proposition that many Jews want power for their own group and value clannishness in their own group but condemn such behavior in gentiles. Similarly, in the present, it's common to see non-Whites in the myriad of ethnic groups now living in the West valuing their own group's power and accomplishments while condemning any such attitudes among Whites.

From the standpoint of the authors of TAP, group consciousness in the majority is viewed as pathological because it tends necessarily to be opposed to Jews as a separate group—a group represented by powerful, well-funded activist organizations like the ADL and well-represented in the corridors of power in Washington. *Viewed from this perspective, the central agenda of The Authoritarian Personality is to pathologize gentile group strategies while nevertheless leaving open the possibility of Judaism as a minority group strategy.*

In his discussion, Levinson views ethnocentrism as fundamentally concerned with ingroup-outgroup perceptions, a perspective that is congruent with social identity theory which I have proposed as the best candidate for developing a viable theory of anti-Semitism (see SAID, Ch. 1). Levinson concludes, "*Ethnocentrism is based on a pervasive and rigid ingroup-outgroup distinction; it involves stereotyped negative imagery and hostile attitudes regarding outgroups, stereotyped positive imagery and submissive attitudes regarding ingroups, and a hierarchical, authoritarian view of group interaction in which ingroups are rightly dominant, outgroups subordinate*" (p. 150; emphasis original).

Further, Levinson notes, "The ethnocentric 'need for an outgroup' prevents that identification with humanity as a whole which is found in anti-ethnocentrism" (p. 148). Levinson clearly believes that ethnocentrism is a sign of psychiatric disorder and that identification with humanity is the epitome of mental health, but he never draws the obvious inference that Jews themselves are unlikely to identify with humanity, given the importance of ingroup-outgroup distinctions so central to Judaism. Moreover, Levinson describes the anti-Semite Mack's demand that Jews assimilate as a demand that Jews "liquidate themselves, that they lose entirely their cultural identity and adhere instead to the prevailing cultural ways" (p. 97). Levinson sees the demand that Jews assimilate, and thus abandon rigid ingroup-outgroup social categorization processes, as an aspect of Mack's anti-Semitic psychopathology; at the same time, Levinson is perfectly willing to advocate that the anti-Semite identify with humanity and abandon ingroup-outgroup social categorization processes. Clearly ethnocentrism and its concomitant salience of ingroup-outgroup social categorization is to be reserved for Jews and pathologized as an aspect of gentile behavior.

The material reviewed throughout this volume indicates that a major thrust of Jewish intellectual activity has been to promote liberal-radical political beliefs among gentiles. Here Levinson links ethnocentrism with conservative economic and political views, with the implication that these attitudes are part of a pervasive social pathology stemming ultimately from disturbed parent-child relationships. Levinson finds associations among political conservatism, economic conservatism (support of prevailing politico-economic ideology and authority), and ethnocentrism (stigmatization of outgroups).[118] Moreover, "The further development of liberal-radical views is ordinarily based on imagery and attitudes identical to those underlying anti-ethnocentric ideology: opposition to hierarchy and to dominance-submission, removal of class and group barriers, emphasis on equalitarian interaction, and so on" (p. 181).

---

[118] Political conservatism and ethnocentrism are said to be difficult to separate, as indicated by the following item from the Political and Economic Conservatism Scale (PEC): "America may not be perfect, but the American Way has brought us about as close as human beings can get to a perfect society." Levinson comments, "To support this idea is, it would seem, to express politico-economic conservatism and the ingroup idealization so characteristic of ethnocentrism" (p. 181). Here, as in the case of the discussion of the Ethnocentrism Scale itself, individuals who identify strongly with a dominant majority group and its interests are viewed as pathological. In fact, the PEC scale was not as highly correlated with the F-Scale as was the Ethnocentrism Scale (E-Scale), a finding that Adorno tendentiously interpreted not as indicating that these concepts were not highly related but as indicating that "we are living in potentially fascist times" (p. 656)! As indicated in the conclusion of this chapter, the high correlation between the F-Scale and the E-Scale was a matter of design rather than an empirical finding.

Given the overwhelming evidence that diaspora Jews in the West support liberal or radical political programs and continue to have a strong Jewish identification (see Ch. 3), I conclude that the results are another confirmation of the analysis presented there: leftism among Jews has functioned as a means of deemphasizing the importance of the Jewish-gentile distinction among gentiles while nevertheless allowing for its continuation among Jews.

Levinson then proceeds to a section of the analysis with far-reaching repercussions, providing data showing that individuals with different political party preferences than their fathers have lower ethnocentrism scores. He then proposes that rebelling against the father is an important predictor of lack of ethnocentrism: "Ethnocentrists tend to be submissive to ingroup authority, anti-ethnocentrists to be critical and rebellious, and . . . the family is the first and prototypic ingroup" (p. 192).

Levinson asks the reader to consider a two-generation situation in which the first generation tends to be relatively high on ethnocentrism and political conservatism; that is, they identify with their ethnic group and its perceived economic and political interests. Prediction of whether children will similarly identify with their ethnic group and its perceived interests depends on whether children rebel against their parents' values. The conclusion of this syllogism, given the values implicit in the study, is that rebelling against parental values is psychologically healthy because it results in lower ethnocentrism scores. Conversely, lack of rebellion against parents is viewed as pathological. These ideas are expanded in later sections of TAP and indeed constitute a central aspect of the entire project.

One wonders if these social scientists would similarly advocate that Jewish children should reject their families as the prototypical ingroup. The transmission of Judaism over the generations has required that children accept parental values. In Chapter 3 it was noted that during the 1960s radical Jewish students, but not radical gentile students, identified strongly with their parents and with Judaism. I have also discussed extensive socialization practices whereby Jewish children were socialized to accept community interests over individual interests. These practices function to produce strong ingroup loyalty among Jews (see PTSDA, Chs. 7–8). Again, there is an implicit double standard: rebellion against parents and the complete abandonment of all ingroup designations is the epitome of mental health for gentiles, whereas Jews are implicitly allowed to continue with a strong sense of ingroup identity and to follow in their parents' footsteps.

Similarly with regard to religious affiliation, R. Nevitt Sanford (Chapter VI) finds that affiliation with various Christian religious sects is associated with ethnocentrism, and that individuals who have rebelled against their parents and adopted another religion or abandoned religion altogether are lower on ethnocentrism. These relationships are explained as due to the fact that acceptance of a Christian religion is associated with "conformity, convention-alism, authoritarian submission, determination by external pressures, thinking in ingroup-outgroup terms and the like vs. nonconformity, independence, in-ternalization of values, and so forth" (p. 220). Again, individuals identifying strongly with the ideology of a majority group are viewed as suffering from psychopathology, yet Judaism as a viable religion would necessarily be associ-ated with these same psychological processes. Indeed, Sirkin and Grellong (1988) found that rebellion and negative parent-child relationships during ad-olescence were associated with Jewish young people's abandoning Judaism to join religious cults. Negative parent-child relationships predict lack of ac-ceptance of parents' religious group membership, whatever the religion in-volved.

Psychoanalysis as a Tool Aimed at Pathologizing
Adaptive Families Among Gentiles

Adorno wrote in 1948 that TAP "is in full harmony with psychoanalysis in its more orthodox, Freudian version" (in Jacobs, 2015, p. 90). Psychoanalytic interpretations were indeed central to the subversive agenda of TAP because they created a false, upside-down portrait of family relationships and their connection to authoritarianism and ethnic hostility. Part II consists of five chapters by Else Frenkel-Brunswik presenting interview data from a subset of the subjects studied in Part I. Although there are pervasive methodological dif-ficulties with these data, they provide a fairly consistent, theoretically intelli-gible contrast in the family relationships between high scorers and low scorers on the Ethnocentrism Scale.[119] However, the picture presented is quite

---

[119] Frenkel-Brunswik's interview data have been shown to suffer from serious methodological difficulties "from beginning to end" (Altemeyer, 1981, p. 37; see also R. Brown, 1965, pp. 514ff). There are problems of generalization since fully 40 percent of the high-scoring male inter-viewees (eight out of twenty) were inmates at San Quentin prison and two were patients at a psychiatric hospital at the time of the interviews. (Three of the twenty low scorers were from San Quentin, and two were from the psychiatric clinic.) As Altemeyer (1981, p. 37) notes, this type of sample obviously presents problems of generalization even granting the possibility that high scorers are more likely to be in prison. This problem is much less apparent in the interviews from the women, however, where the high scorers were mainly students and health workers, although three of the twenty-five were psychiatric patients.

Nevertheless, Altemeyer (1988, p. 37) notes that the San Quentin interviewees were "the backbone" of the statistically significant results separating the high and low scorers. Besides this method of inflating the level of statistical significance by including highly unrepresenta-tive subjects, there was also a strong tendency to discuss results as if they were based on statistically significant differences when in fact the differences were not significant (p. 38).

It has also been shown that scores on the Ethnocentrism Scale are negatively associated with IQ, education, and socioeconomic status to a much greater extent than found by the Berkeley group (H. H. Hyman & Sheatsley, 1954). Lower socioeconomic status and its correla-tive lower IQ and education may result in ethnocentrism because such individuals have not

different from that which the authors of TAP intend to convey. In conjunction with the material from the projective questions in Chapter XV, the data strongly suggest that high scorers on the Ethnocentrism Scale tend to come from very functional, adaptive, competent, and concerned families. These individuals identify with their families as a prototypical ingroup and appear intent on replicating that family structure in their own lives. Low scorers appear to have ambivalent, rebellious relationships with their families and to identify minimally with their family as an ingroup.

Frenkel-Brunswik first discusses differences in attitudes toward parents and conceptions of the family. Prejudiced individuals "glorify" their parents and view their family as an ingroup.[120] Low-scoring individuals, in contrast, are said to have an "objective" view of their parents combined with genuine affection. To make these claims plausible, Frenkel-Brunswik must show that the very positive attitudes shown by high scorers are not genuine affection but are simply masks for repressed hostility. However, as Altemeyer (1981, p. 43) notes, "It is at least possible ... that [the parents of the high scorers] really were a little better than most, and that the small relationships found have a perfectly factual, nonpsychodynamic explanation." I would go further than Altemeyer and claim that the parents and families of the high scorers were almost certainly quite a bit "better" than the parents and families of the low scorers.

Frenkel-Brunswik's only example of genuine affection on the part of a low scorer involves a female subject who recounted her despair at being abandoned by her father. (It would appear from data discussed below that abandonment and ambivalence are generally more common among the low scorers.) This subject, F63, makes the following comment: "But I remember when my father left, [my mother] came to my room and said, 'You'll never see your Daddy again.' Those were her exact words. I was crazy with grief and felt it was her fault. I threw things, emptied drawers out of the window, pulled the spreads off the bed, then threw things at the wall" (p. 346). The example does indeed show a strong attachment between father and daughter, but the point clearly is that the relationship is one of abandonment, not affection. Moreover, Frenkel-Brunswik mentions that some of the low scorers appear to have

---

been socialized in a university environment and because economic pressures (i.e., resource competition) are more likely to result in group identifications within the lower social classes. The latter perspective fits well with social identity research and with the general findings of another volume in the *Studies in Prejudice* series, *Prophets of Deceit* (Lowenthal & Guterman, 1970).

[120] Excerpts indicate that these individuals had very positive attitudes about their parents. A high-scoring female describes her mother as follows: "Mother—she amazes me—millions of activities—had two maids in ——— years ago, but never since—such calmness—never sick, *never*—beautiful woman she really is" (p. 340; emphasis original). Another, F24, describes her father as follows: "Father—he is wonderful; couldn't make him better. He is always willing to do anything for you. He is about ——— years old, six feet tall, has dark brown hair, slim build, young-looking face, good-looking, dark green eyes" (p. 342).

"blocked affect" regarding their parents; that is, the low scorers have no emotional response at all toward them (p. 347). One wonders, then, in what sense the low scorers can be said to have genuinely positive emotional relationships with their parents. As we shall see, the data as a whole indicate very high levels of hostility and ambivalence among the low scorers.

In contrast, high-scoring women are said to perceive themselves as "victimized" by their parents. The word "victimized" has negative connotations, and my own reading of the published interview material suggests that the subjects are expressing negative feelings toward parental discipline or unfairness within the context of an overall positive relationship. Parent-child relationships, like any relationship, may be viewed as consisting of positive and negative attributes from the standpoint of the child—much like an account ledger. Relationships in general are not likely to be perfect from the standpoint of all parties because people's interests conflict. The result is that a perfect relationship from one person's standpoint may seem like exploitation to the other person in the relationship. So it is in parent-child relationships (MacDonald, 1988a, pp. 166–169). A perfect relationship from the standpoint of the child would be highly unbalanced against the parent—what is usually termed a permissive or indulgent parent-child relationship.

My interpretation of the research on parent-child interaction (and this is a mainstream point of view) is that children will accept high levels of parental control if the relationship with the parents is positive overall (MacDonald, 1988a, 1992a, 1997). Developmental psychologists use the term "authoritative parenting" to refer to parenting in which the child accepts parental control within the context of a generally positive relationship (Baumrind, 1971; Maccoby & Martin, 1983). Although children of authoritative parents undoubtedly may not always enjoy parental discipline and restrictions, this style of parenting is associated with well-adjusted children.

A child may therefore resent some activities of the parent within the context of an overall positive relationship, and there is no psychological difficulty with supposing that the child could accept having to perform unpleasant work or even being discriminated against as a female while nevertheless having a very positive overall view of the parent-child relationship. Frenkel-Brunswik's examples of girls who have very positive views of their parents but also complain about situations in which they were made to do housework or were treated less well than their brothers need not be interpreted as indicating suppressed hostility.

Frenkel-Brunswik states that these resentments are not "ego-accepted" by the girls, a comment I interpret as indicating that the girls did not view the resentment as completely compromising the relationship. Her example of such non-ego-accepted resentment is as follows, from F39: Mother was "terribly strict with me about learning to keep house. . . . I am glad now, but I resented it then." It is only by accepting a psychodynamic interpretation in which normal resentments about being required to work are a sign of powerful suppressed hostilities and rigid defense mechanisms that we can view these women as in any sense pathological.[121] This is important because it is ultimately the proposed repressed hostility engendered by parental discipline that results in anti-Semitism: "The displacement of a repressed antagonism toward authority may be one of the sources, and perhaps the principal source, of . . . antagonism toward outgroups" (p. 482).

Whereas the negative feelings high scorers had toward their parents tend to derive from parental efforts to discipline the child or get the child to do household chores, the negative feelings of the low scorers are the result of feelings of desertion and loss of affection (p. 349). However, in the case of the low scorers, Frenkel-Brunswik emphasizes that the desertions and loss of love are frankly accepted, and this acceptance, in her view, precludes psychopathology. I have already discussed F63, whose father abandoned her; another low-scoring subject, M55, states, "For example, he would take a delicacy like candy, pretend to offer us some and then eat it himself and laugh uproariously. . . . Makes him seem sort of a monster, though he's not really" (p. 350). It is not surprising that such egregious examples of parental insensitivity are vividly recalled by the subject. However, in the upside-down world of TAP, their being recalled is viewed as a sign of mental health in the subjects, whereas the overtly positive relationships of the high scorers are a sign of deep, unconscious layers of psychopathology.

Contemporary developmental research on authoritative parenting and parent-child warmth also indicates that authoritative parents are more successful in transmitting cultural values to their children (e.g., MacDonald, 1988a, 1992, 1997a). In reading the interview material, one is struck by the fact that low scorers have rather negative views of their parents, whereas high scorers have quite positive views. It is reasonable to suppose that the low scorers would be more rebellious against parental values, and this is indeed what the study concluded.

Part of the deception of TAP, however, is that low scorers' resentment directed toward their parents is interpreted as a sign that parental discipline is not overpowering. "Since typical low scorers do not really see their parents as

---

[121] Other examples of proposed resentment against parents by high-scoring subjects clearly suggest a parent who has strict rules and enforces them within the context of a relationship that is viewed positively overall. Thus a high-scoring subject says about her father, "Can't say I don't like him . . . but he wouldn't let me date at 16. I had to stay home" (p. 348). The interview material of a high-scoring female, F78, shows that "[h]er parents definitely approve of the engagement. Subject wouldn't even go with anyone if they didn't like him" (p. 351). Again, these subjects are labeled as victimized by their parents. The supposition seems to be that any parental strictures on children's behavior, no matter how reasonable, are bound to result in enormously high levels of suppressed hostility and aggression in children.

... too overpowering or frightening, they can afford to express their feelings of resentment more readily" (p. 346). The meager signs of affection in the children of low scorers and the obvious signs of resentment are thus interpreted by Frenkel-Brunswik as genuine affection, whereas the very positive perceptions of their parents held by the high scorers are viewed as the result of extreme parental authoritarianism resulting in repressions and denial of parental faults.

These results are an excellent example of the ideological biases characteristic of this entire project. A developmental psychologist looking at these data is impressed by the fact that the parents of the high scorers manage to inculcate a very positive perception of family life in their children while managing to discipline them nonetheless. As indicated above, contemporary researchers label this type of parent as authoritative, and the research supports the general proposal that children from such families will have close relationships with their parents and accept parental values and group identifications. Thus if the parents accept religious identifications, the child from such a family is more likely to accept them as well. And if parents hold up education as a value, the children are also likely to accept the importance of doing well in school. These authoritative parents set standards for their children's behavior and monitor compliance with these standards. The warmth of the parent-child relationship motivates the child to conform to these standards and to regulate his or her behavior so as to avoid violating ingroup (i.e., family) norms of behavior.

The deeply subversive agenda of TAP is to pathologize this type of family among gentiles. However, since parental affection is viewed positively according to the theory, evidence for parental affection among the high scorers must be interpreted as a mask for parental hostility, and the low scorers had to be interpreted as having affectionate parents despite surface appearances to the contrary. Rebellion against parents by the low scorers is then conceptualized as the normal outcome of affectionate child rearing—a ridiculous view at best.[122]

---

[122] This idea that rebellion against parental values and authority is a sign of mental health can also be seen in the theory of the half-Jewish (on his mother's side) psychoanalyst Erik Homburger Erikson (1968). Erikson proposed that the most important developmental issue of adolescence was the identity crisis and that going through an identity crisis was a necessary prerequisite for healthy adult psychological functioning. The evidence indicates, however, that adolescence is not normatively a time of rebellion against parents, but rebellion against parents is associated with hostile, rejecting parent-child relationships.

The interesting point here is that research on identity processes during adolescence does not support the idea that adolescents who accept adult values show signs of psychopathology. The subjects who most resemble those viewed as pathological in TAP are termed "foreclosure" subjects by Marcia (1966, 1967). These subjects have not experienced an identity crisis but have made commitments which they have accepted from other individuals, usually parents, without question. The families of foreclosure subjects tend to be child-centered and conformist (Adams et al., 1994). Matteson (1974) found that foreclosures participated in a "love affair" with

Fundamentally, then, the political agenda of TAP is to undercut gentile family structure, but the ultimate aim is to subvert the entire social categorization scheme underlying gentile society. The authors of TAP are studying a society in which variation in families can be seen as ranging from families that essentially replicate current social structure to families that produce rebellion and change in social structure. The former families are highly cohesive, and children within these families have a strong sense of ingroup feeling toward their families. The children also fundamentally accept the social categorization structure of their parents as the social categories expand to include church, community, and nation.

This relatively strong sense of ingroup thinking then tends, as expected by social identity research, to result in negative attitudes to individuals from different religions, communities, and nations. From the standpoint of the authors of TAP, this type of family must be established as pathological, despite the fact that this is exactly the type of family necessary for the continuation of a strong sense of Jewish identity: Jewish children must accept the social categorization system of their parents; they must view their families as ingroups and ultimately accept the ingroup represented by Judaism. Again, the fundamental intellectual difficulty that runs throughout the entire book is that its agenda must inevitably pathologize in gentiles what is critical to the maintenance of Judaism.

The success of the families of high scorers in transmitting parental values is illustrated by the fact that children of the high scorers feel a sense of obligation and duty toward their parents. Note particularly the response of F78, about whom it was said, "Her parents definitely approve of the engagement. Subject wouldn't even go with anyone if they didn't like him" (p. 351). Here a woman who intends to marry someone approved by her parents and who takes account of the views of her parents in dating is viewed as having a psychiatric

---

their families, and Muuss (1988) summarizes evidence indicating that foreclosures are very close to and feel highly valued by their parents. Degree of control is intermediate, neither too harsh nor too limited, and such individuals perceive parents as accepting and supportive. The parent-child relationships of these individuals appear to be the authoritative parent-child relationships commonly viewed by developmental psychologists as producing optimal child development. Marcia and Friedman (1970) found that foreclosure women had high self-esteem and were low in anxiety, and Marcia (1980) summarizes several studies showing that the foreclosure females are well adjusted. There is thus no reason to suppose that adolescents who accept parental values are in any sense suffering from psychopathology.

On the contrary, individuals who have very poor parent-child relationships tend to be in the "identity-diffused" category, namely individuals who completely fail to develop an identity. Very negative parent-child relationships are characteristic of such identity-diffused subjects (Adams et al., 1994), and they appear to lead to minimal identification with the values and ideologies of the parents. Parents of such individuals are described as "detached, distant, uninvolved, and unconcerned" (Muuss, 1988, p. 79; see also Marcia, 1980) and such individuals appear not to accept the values of their parents. There is even evidence that identity-diffused individuals are at risk for psychopathology.

disorder. One wonders if Frenkel-Brunswik would similarly analyze such a response in a Jewish subject.

Another indication of the overwhelmingly positive family experiences of the high scorers is that they often comment that their parents were very solicitous toward them. Within Frenkel-Brunswik's worldview, this is another sign of pathology among the high scorers that is variously labeled "ego-alien dependence" (p. 353) and "blatant opportunism" (p. 354).

Consider, for example, the following response from a high scorer, F68: "I always say my mother is still taking care of me. You should see my closets—stacked with fruits, jams, pickles. . . . She just loves to do things for people" (p. 354).[123] To categorize such an expression of parental solicitude as part of a pathological syndrome is truly astonishing. Similarly, Frenkel-Brunswik terms the following comment by a high-scoring woman, F71, as illustrative of the "blatant opportunism" (p. 354) characteristic of high scorers: "Father was extremely devoted to family—will work his fingers to the bone for them—never has done any drinking" (p. 365). Another high scorer, F24 , in describing how "wonderful" her father is, says, "He is always willing to do anything for you" (p. 365).

An evolutionist would interpret these comments as indicating that the parents of high scorers invest greatly in their families and make the welfare of their families their first priority. They insist on appropriate behavior from their children and are not reticent about using physical punishment to control their children's behavior. Data summarized in PTSDA (Ch. 7) indicate that this is exactly the type of parenting characteristic of Jews in traditional Eastern European *shtetl* societies. In these societies high-investment parenting and conformity to parental practices, especially religious belief, were very important. Jewish mothers in these communities are said to be characterized by an "unremitting solicitude" regarding their children (Zborowski & Herzog, 1952, p. 193). They engage in "boundless suffering and sacrifice. Parents 'kill themselves' for the sake of their children" (p. 294). At the same time, there is a strong

---

[123] Other examples: F71: "Right now, I'm [father's] favorite. . . . [H]e'll do anything for me—takes me to school and calls for me" (p. 354). M47: "Well, I guess her [mother] being so good and friendly to everybody, especially me. (For example?) Well, always trying to do everything for me. Very seldom go uptown without bringing something back for me" (p. 354). M13: "Mostly [father's] attention to us kids was very admirable. He's very honest, so much so that he won't condone charge accounts. He's known throughout the country as a man whose word is as good as his bond. His greatest contribution was denying himself pleasure to take care of us kids" (p. 354).

In the section "Image of the Mother: Sacrifice, Moralism, Restrictiveness," mothers of high scorers are individuals who are highly self-sacrificing on behalf of their children and also have a strong sense of appropriate behavior which they attempt to inculcate in their children. M57: "She was a hard-working lady, took care of us kids; she never did mistreat us in any way" (p. 366). M13: "Mother was sick in bed a great deal of the time. She devoted her last strength to us kids" (p. 366). M47: "She always taught me the difference between right and wrong, the things I should do and shouldn't" (p. 367).

degree of parental control over children, including anger directed at the child and considerable use of physical punishment performed in anger (pp. 336–337). Patterns of highly intrusive, solicitous, dependency-producing, and authoritarian parenting continue among traditional Ashkenazi communities, including contemporary Hasidic Jews (Mintz, 1992, pp. 176ff).

This style of high-investment parenting in which high levels of solicitude are combined with powerful controls over children's behavior is effective in getting children to identify with parental values in traditional Jewish societies. Supreme among these values is accepting parents' religious commitments and the necessity of choosing a marriage partner suitable to the parents and especially to avoid marrying a gentile. To have a child marry a gentile is a horrifying, catastrophic event that indicates that "something must be wrong with the parents" (Zborowski & Herzog, 1952, p. 231). For Frenkel-Brunswik, however, parental solicitude, accepting parental values, and parental influence on marriage decisions are a sign of pathology—a forerunner of fascism. For gentiles, but apparently not for Jews, rebellion against parental values is the epitome of mental health.

The interview data on the family as an ingroup are particularly interesting in this regard. High-scoring subjects are proud of their families, their accomplishments, and their traditions. With typical rhetorical *chutzpah*, Frenkel-Brunswik calls these expressions of family pride "a setting off of a homogeneous totalitarian family against the rest of the world" (p. 356). For example, a high scorer, F68, states of her father, "His folks were pioneers—gold settlers and quite wealthy. Everyone knows the ———'s of ——— County up that way" (p. 356). Pride in oneself and one's family is an indicator of psychiatric disorder.

Further evidence that the family relationships of high scorers are more positive comes from the data on parental conflict. The following comment is described as typical by the high-scoring men as a response to being asked how their parents got along together. M41: "Fine, never did hear no quarreling."[124] In contrast, rather severe parental conflict is quite apparent in the records of the low scorers. M59: "Well, just the usual family quarrels. Maybe raise her voice a bit. (What bones of contention?) Well, the fact that in the first ten years of my mother's married life, my dad used to get drunk quite often and he would beat her physically and later on, as the children were growing up, she resented my

---

[124] Other typical comments of high scorers are as follows: M58: "If there were any conflicts between mother and father, I didn't know" (p. 369). F24: "Parents get along swell—never quarrel—hardly ever. Just over nonsense if they do. They quarrelled once after drinking wine over who got the last. Silly stuff like that" (p. 370). F31: "My parents get along very well with each other, so far—knock on wood. They have their arguments, but they're never serious because of my mother's easy-going personality" (p. 370).

father's influence, though he contributed to our support. . . . He used to come about twice a week, sometimes oftener" (p. 369).[125]

This picture of conflict in the families of low scorers receives the following interpretation by Frenkel-Brunswik: "The foregoing records illustrate the frankness and the greater insight into the marital conflicts of the parents" (p. 369). The assumption seems to be that all families are characterized by alcoholism, desertion, physical abuse, quarreling, and narcissistic preoccupation with one's own pleasures rather than family needs. Mental health in the low scorers is indicated by their being aware of familial psychopathology, whereas the pathological high scorers simply fail to recognize these phenomena in their families and persist in their delusions that their parents are self-sacrificing, loving disciplinarians.

This is a good example of the usefulness of psychodynamic theory in creating a politically effective "reality." Behavior that conflicts with one's theory can be ascribed to repression of deep conflicts, and truly pathological behavior becomes the essence of sanity because the subject recognizes it as such. Frenkel-Brunswik invents the term "denial of conflict" as a description of the "pathology" of the high-scoring families (p. 369), a term that is reminiscent of "ego-alien dependence" and "victimization" mentioned earlier. My reading of these protocols would lead me to label the relationships as "lack of conflict," but in the upside-down world of TAP, lack of apparent conflict is a sure sign of the denial of extremely severe conflict.[126]

The same picture is presented in sibling relationships. Sibling relationships described in very positive terms by high-scoring subjects are pathologized as "conventional idealization" or "glorification of siblings" (p. 377), whereas the very negative relationships of low scorers are described as "objective appraisal" (p. 378). The following description of a brother from a high scorer illustrates how Frenkel-Brunswik manages to pathologize highly cohesive, self-sacrificing family life among gentiles. M52: "Well, he's a wonderful kid. . . . Has been wonderful to my parents. . . . Now 21. Always lived at home. . . . Gives most of his earnings to my parents" (p. 378). The assumption seems

---

[125] Other typical comments of the low scorers are as follows: M15: "Mother accuses father of 'keeping her down.' She talks about her ambitions too much. Mother thinks of herself first. She doesn't want to settle down in any church. Keeps suspecting father lets another singer get ahead of her. There are many quarrels between them, which upset me. Father sometimes threatened to leave" (p. 369). M50: "Father was temperamental and father and mother had considerable domestic strife" (p. 369). M55: "Mother went along with him on all the moralizing, though not as harsh as he was, not really a very good marriage. Mother should have married someone a lot more human and she probably would have been a lot better off . . . well, it's hard to imagine him with anyone with whom he would get along" (p. 369)

[126] Similarly, when a subject reports no aggression against his father on the Thematic Apperception Test, the results are interpreted as indicating suppressed aggression against the father because the only aggression in the stories is done by characters the subject rejects. Aggressive imagery unrelated to the father is evidence for suppressed aggression against the father.

to be that this description could not conceivably be accurate and is therefore an example of pathological "glorification of siblings."

Frenkel-Brunswik also attempts to pathologize gentile concern with social class and upward social mobility. High scorers are portrayed as "status-concerned" and therefore pathological for such statements as the following: M57, on being asked why his parents disciplined him, replies, "Well, they didn't want me to run with some kind of people—slummy women—always wanted me to associate with the higher class of people" (p. 383).[127]

A concern with social status is thus viewed as pathological. An evolutionary perspective, in contrast to Frenkel-Brunswik's view, emphasizes the adaptive significance of social-class status. An evolutionist would find the behavior of the parents to be quite adaptive, since they want their son to be concerned about upward social mobility and want a respectable woman for a daughter-in-law, if only to assure that their grandchildren are genetically related to them. The parents are concerned about social status, and an evolutionist would note that such a concern has been of critical evolutionary importance in stratified societies over historical time (see PTSDA, Ch. 7).

The other example of concern with social status presented by Frenkel-Brunswik is an individual who is concerned with having biological heirs. A high scorer, M51, says, "I want a home and I want to get married, not because I want a wife, but because I want a child. I want the child because I want someone to pass my things on to—I suddenly have become very conscious of my background that I forget about. (How do you mean?) Family background" (p. 383). Again, biologically adaptive gentile behavior is pathologized, and one wonders if the authors would consider the official, religiously based concern with reproductive success, biological relatedness, and control of resources among traditional Jews as similarly pathological.

In her summary and discussion of the family interview data, Frenkel-Brunswik (pp. 384–389) then chooses to ignore the obvious signs of conflict, hostility, and ambivalence in the families of low scorers and characterizes them as retaining a "love-dependent nurturance-succorance attitude toward women which is not easily satisfied" (p. 388) and as exhibiting "free-flowing affection" (p. 386). These families produce children with a "greater richness

---

[127] Another example of concern for social status among high scorers is the following from F79, who comes from a wealthy family that owns a lumber mill, a logging camp, and other business interests: "It's a medium-sized mill but I have no idea of his [father's] income. Of course, we children have always been to private schools and lived in exclusive residential section. In —— — we had tennis courts and horses. We had more or less to start over again when we came to this country. We lived in a nice house but really couldn't afford it. It was quite an effort to get into social circles. In ——— we felt secure and fitted in. Back here, we have lived at the same level but with anxiety about it. Mother and daddy have climbed socially . . . and I don't care so much" (p. 384). Since the subject seems not so concerned about social status, one might wonder why the protocol was scored as it was.

and liberation of emotional life" (p. 388), and the children exhibit a successful "sublimation of instinctual tendencies" (p. 388). Obvious signs of cohesiveness, affection, harmony, discipline, and successful transmission of family values in the families of high scorers are interpreted as an "orientation toward power and ... contempt for the allegedly inferior and weak" (p. 387). These families are characterized by "fearful subservience to the demands of the parents and by an early suppression of impulses not acceptable to them" (p. 385).

This inversion of reality continues in the chapter entitled "Sex, People, and Self as Seen Through the Interviews." High-scoring males appear as more sexually successful and as having high self-conceptions of their masculinity; high-scoring females are described as popular with boys. Low-scoring males appear as sexually inadequate and low-scoring females as uninterested in men or unable to attract men. The low-scoring pattern is then interpreted as "open admission" of sexual inadequacy and therefore a sign of psychological health (p. 391), and the high-scoring pattern is labeled as "status-concerned " (p. 382) and seen as pathological. The assumption is that psychopathology is indicated by overt social adjustment and feelings of self-esteem, while mental health is indicated by feelings of inadequacy and open admissions of sexual insufficiency.

Frenkel-Brunswik then attempts to show that high scorers are characterized by "anti-id moralism" (p. 395). The protocols indicate that the men are attracted to and fall in love with women who are not particularly interested in sex. For example, M45: "We didn't get on too good sexually because she was kind of on the frigid line, but still in all I was in love with her and I still am. I'd like nothing more than to go back to her" (p. 396). High-scoring males appear to value sexual decorum in females they intend to marry; M20: "Yes, I went through high school with one girl. . . . Very religious. . . . She was more or less what I was looking for. Very religious" (p. 397).[128]

An evolutionist looking at these protocols is impressed by the fact that the high-scoring males appear as individuals who wish to enter a marriage in which they have a high degree of paternity confidence. They want a woman with high moral standards who is unlikely to be sexually attracted to other males, and they seek women with conventional moral values. High-scoring females seem intent on being exactly this sort of woman. They project the image

---

[128] The examples of "anti-id moralism" among the high-scoring women include the following. F22: "Sex isn't uppermost in my mind by any means. . . . I'm more for having a good time with the exclusion of sex interest" (p. 396). F31: "I think a girl should be friendly, but I don't like necking in the back of a show. A boy and girl should be just friends" (p. 396).

Further examples that high-scoring males appear to value sexual decorum in females they intend to marry are the following. M6: "I like a girl who is level-headed and can talk on several topics. I don't like the Maizie and Flo type or the sex boxes" (p. 397). M14: "I want a girl whose sole interest is in the home" (p. 397).

of having very high standards of sexual decorum and wish to maintain a reputation as nonpromiscuous.

Further, the high-scoring females want males who are "hard-working, 'go-getting', energetic, 'a good personality', (conventionally) moral, 'clean-cut', deferent toward women" (p. 401).[129] An evolutionist would expect this type of sexual behavior and discrimination of marriage partners to be characteristic of those entering "high-investment" marriages characterized by sexual fidelity for the female and by high levels of paternal involvement. This highly adaptive tendency of high-scoring females to seek investment from males Frenkel-Brunswik labels "opportunistic" (p. 401).

Conventional attitudes toward marriage are also an aspect of the "pathological" attitudes of high scorers. High scorers "tend to place a great deal of emphasis on socioeconomic status, church membership, and conformity with conventional values" (p. 402). For example, F74: "(Desirable traits?) Boyfriend should be about the same socioeconomic status. They should enjoy doing the same things and get along without too many quarrels" (p. 403).[130] This woman is highly discriminating in her choice of mate. She is very concerned to marry someone who is responsible, reliable, and will invest in a long-term relationship. For Frenkel-Brunswik, however, these attitudes are a sign of opportunistic behavior. Despite obvious signs of strong affection in F78 and the clear indication that F74 desires a relationship characterized by harmony and mutual attraction and interests, Frenkel-Brunswik summarizes the results as

---

[129] Other examples of adaptive female mate discrimination behavior among the high scorers deemed pathological by Frenkel-Brunswik are the following. F71: "Fine boy. Father a writer; grandfather secretary of ——— Canal; very wealthy family but he doesn't have the drive and ambition that I want; I just have to have more drive; somebody who doesn't have to lean on me. I had the feeling that if I walked away he would collapse. . . . Another boy here has everything except that he isn't thoughtful like. . . . I've got to have someone who isn't selfish" (p. 401). F22: "I'm going to look (among other things) for the fellow's views on supporting me. I'd like to marry someone, for instance, who is going into a profession—maybe a doctor" (p. 401).

[130] The other two examples given of such "pathological" attitudes among females are the following:

"F32: 'Well, I think that because of the society in which we live, young people miss a great deal by not being married in the church of their faith. They lose the reverence for marriage and don't learn the true meaning of the marriage vows, when it is done so commercially (in a public office). I think that when people are married in church—by that I don't mean a large wedding necessarily—they have one of the most beautiful experiences of their lives. . . . The thing which the church can teach youth is "to choose." By this, she means principally the choice between right and wrong, but also to choose one's friends. 'In a church group one meets the right kind of young people; not the kind who hang around the lake shore at night.'" (pp. 402–403)

"F78: 'It was just love at first sight. He has brown hair, brown eyes, white teeth, not handsome, but good clean-cut looking; beautiful smile; mixes well, easy to get along with but has a will of his own. He's lots of fun, interested in everything. He's a high school graduate, now a mechanic in the ground crew of the Naval Air Transport. He wants to get into something in the mechanical line. Before the war he was an apprentice in the auto industry. . . .' The vocation of her husband really wouldn't matter. She thinks boy friend has good chances of getting along, definitely. She would like a profession—'sort of middle class.'" (p. 403)

indicating a "lack of individuation and of real object relationship" and a "paucity of affection" (p. 404).

Again, psychodynamic theory allows the author to ascribe surface admiration and affection to underlying hostility, whereas the surface problems of the low scorers are a sign of mental health: "Some of the records of low-scoring subjects . . . reveal a great deal of conflict in this area. Such subjects refer rather frankly to their inadequacies, inhibitions, and failures in sex adjustment. There also is evidence of ambivalence toward one's own sex role and toward the opposite sex although this ambivalence is of a different, more internalized kind from the combination of overt admiration and underlying disrespect characteristic of high scorers" (p. 405). We may not see this underlying disrespect and thus have no evidence for its existence, but psychodynamic theory allows Frenkel-Brunswik to infer its existence nonetheless.

The tendency to pathologize behaviors related to adaptive functioning can also be seen in the discussion of self-concept. High scorers are found to have a very positive self-image, whereas low scorers are filled with insecurity, self-condemnation, and even "morbid" self-accusations (pp. 423ff)—results interpreted as due to the repressions of the high-scorers and the objectivity of the low scorers.[131]

In a later section, "Conformity of Self and Ideal," Frenkel-Brunswik finds that for high scorers there is little gap between present self and ideal self. Thus high-scoring men describe themselves in a "pseudo-masculine" manner and idealize this type of behavior. Part of their supposed pathology is to have famous American heroes whom they admire and wish to emulate, such as Douglas MacArthur, Andrew Carnegie, and George Patton. Low scorers, however, perceive a gap between their present and ideal selves—a gap Frenkel-Brunswik interprets thus: "Being basically more secure, it seems, they can more easily afford to see a discrepancy between ego-ideal and actual reality" (p. 431). "As adults, low scorers often continue to manifest open anxieties and feelings of

---

[131] The high scorers are said to engage in "self-glorification" for saying such things as the following. F71: "Child—nervous because of mastoid operations . . . terrible time getting started in school . . . afraid of kids . . . this in first half of kindergarten . . . by second half I was a leader. Think one of my best assets is my poise—learned from moving around so much" (p. 425). F38, commenting on overcoming infantile paralysis: "I have always had a happy disposition, and I've always been honest with my family. I appreciate what they did for me. I've always tried to find a way so that I wouldn't be a burden to them. I've never wanted to be a cripple. I was always dependable in a pinch. I've always been cheerful and I'm sure I've never made anyone feel bad because of my handicap. Maybe one of the reasons I have been cheerful is because of my handicap. I wore a cast on my leg until I was 4 years old" (p. 425). (Subject goes on to describe her marital fidelity, happy married life, and good relationships with her family.) Only an extremely perverse interpretation of these data—an interpretation made possible by psychodynamic theory—could result in supposing that these individuals are anything less than heroic in their ability to overcome their disabilities and lead fulfilling, productive lives.

depression, due perhaps at least in part to their greater capacity of facing insecurity and conflict" (p. 441).

Again, psychodynamic theory comes to the rescue. Low-scoring subjects appear on the surface as deeply insecure and self-abnegating, and they are unsatisfied with their present selves. But this behavior is interpreted as a sign of greater security than that of the high scorers, who on the surface appear to be self-confident and proud of themselves. In another inversion of reality, Frenkel-Brunswik summarizes her data on self-concept as indicating that "unprejudiced individuals seem to be on better terms with themselves, due perhaps to the fact that they have been more loved and accepted by their parents. Thus they are more ready to admit falling short of their ideals and of the roles they are expected to play by our culture" (p. 441).

Gentiles' striving after success is also pathologized. In addition to being more likely to seek higher social status and have highly successful American heroes as role models, high scorers appear to want material resources (pp. 433ff). Whereas low scorers describe themselves as isolated during childhood, high scorers are socially popular, hold offices in schools and social organizations, and have many friends. The latter attributes are termed "gang-sociability" by Frenkel-Brunswik (p. 439)—another rhetorical flourish intended to pathologize the behavior of socially successful gentiles.

In fact, one might infer that a prominent aspect of this material is the attempt to pathologize adaptive gentile behavior in general. Gentiles who value high-investment marital relationships and cohesive families, who are upwardly mobile and seek material resources, who are proud of their families and identify with their parents, who have high self-concepts, who believe that Christianity is a positive moral force (p. 408) and a spiritual consolation (p. 450), who strongly identify as males or females (but not both!), and who are socially successful and wish to emulate paragons of social success (e.g., American heroes) are viewed as having a psychiatric disorder.

It is highly ironic that a publication of a major Jewish organization would include a concern with social status and material resources, high-investment parenting, identifying with parents, and having pride in one's family among the signs of psychiatric disorder in gentiles given the extent to which all these attributes characterize Jews. Indeed, Daniel J. Levinson makes the remarkable conclusion, "We are led to suspect, on the basis of results in numerous areas, that upward class mobility and identification with the *status quo* correlate positively with ethnocentrism, and that downward class mobility and identification go with anti-ethnocentrism" (p. 204).

Again, the proposed indicators of gentile pathology have been and continue to be critical to the success of Judaism as a group evolutionary strategy. There has always been intense social pressure for upward mobility and resource acquisition in the Jewish community emanating partly from parents, and Jews have in fact been extraordinarily upwardly mobile. Indeed, Herz and Rosen (1982, p. 368) note, "Success is so vitally important to the Jewish family ethos that we can hardly overemphasize it. . . . We cannot hope to understand the Jewish family without understanding the place that success for men (and recently women) plays in the system." And in PTSDA (Ch. 7) it was noted that social class status has been strongly linked with reproductive success in Jewish communities in traditional societies.

Yet, gentiles who are socially isolated, who have negative and rebellious attitudes toward their families, who are ambivalent and insecure in their sexual identities, who have low self-esteem and are filled with debilitating insecurities and conflicts (including insecurities regarding parental affection), who are moving downward in social status, and who have negative attitudes toward high social status and acquisition of material resources are viewed as the epitome of psychological health.[132]

In all this material much is made of the fact that low scorers often seem to seek affection in their relationships. A reasonable interpretation of the findings on affection-striving is that the low scorers have had much more rejecting, ambivalent parent-child relationships compared to the high scorers, with the result that they seek such warm, affectionate relationships in others. There is much evidence in the interview material that the actual parent-child relationships of the low scorers were ambivalent and hostile, and often characterized by desertion and even abuse (see above). The expected consequence of such a situation is that the child will be rebellious against the parents, not identify with the family or larger social categories accepted by the family, and be preoccupied with seeking affection (MacDonald, 1992a, 1997a).

The positive family experiences of the high scorers, in contrast, provide them with a powerful sense of emotional security in their personal relationships, with the result that in the projective testing they are "externally oriented" (pp. 563, 565) and concentrate to a much greater extent on instrumental values important in attaining social status and accomplishing other socially approved tasks, such as accumulating resources—"work-ambition-activity" (p. 575). Levinson pathologizes this external orientation by saying that "individuals giving these responses seem afraid to look inward at all, for fear of what they will find" (p. 565). Their worries center around failing and letting down the group, especially the family. They seem intensely motivated to succeed and to make their families proud.

---

[132] These tendencies are confirmed in the projective material in Chapter XV. Low scorers again appear to be highly conflicted, anxious, and guilt-ridden (pp. 550, 562). They "identify with the underdog" (p. 566) and have a "strong sense of failure, of self-blame, of helplessness or impotence" (p. 562). They strive after close relationships and at the same time attribute feelings of hostility and exploitiveness to others (p. 551).

However, this does not mean that the high scorers are unable to develop affectional relationships or that love and affection are unimportant to them. We have already seen that high scorers are attracted to high-investment relationships in which sex is a relatively minor concern, and these individuals appear to accept the primacy of other qualities, including love and common interests, as the basis of marriage. For the high scorers the achievement of emotional security does not become a "holy grail" quest; they do not look for it everywhere. The low scorers, though, seem to be engaged in a rather pathetic search for love and affection that was presumably missing from their early relationships. As Frenkel-Brunswik comments in summarizing the interview data on sexual orientation, "Ambivalence toward the other sex seems in low scorers often to be the consequence of an overly intense search for love that is not easily satisfied" (p. 405).

Like securely attached children in the presence of an attachment object, high scorers are free to explore the world and engage in adaptive, externally directed behavior without constantly worrying about the status of their attachment with their mothers (Ainsworth et al., 1978). Low scorers, in contrast, like insecurely attached children, seem preoccupied with security and affection needs. Since these needs have not been met within their families, they seek affection in all their relationships; at the same time, they are preoccupied with their own failures, have diffuse hostility toward others, and are rebellious against anything their parents valued.

FINAL THOUGHTS ON THE AUTHORITARIAN PERSONALITY

In a remarkable admission, Adorno, responding to his critics in a private letter to Marie Jahoda, one of the contributors to TAP, wrote:

> I have stated the partly speculative nature of my interpretations quite frankly and my critics accept this statement—why then, do they blame me when they find that I actually do speculate? To argue pragmatically, I am pretty certain that, if Freud had been subjected to such a "control," the whole bulk of psychodynamic theory would never have been evolved, which would mean, among other things, there would be no controversy about the Authoritarian Personality. (Jacobs, 2015, p. 93)

This, of course, is quite true, for both psychoanalysis and TAP—which means they should never have been presented as scientific works.

The perspective developed here inverts the psychodynamic perspective of TAP because it essentially accepts the data at their face value. Because of their fundamentally political program of indicting gentile culture and especially gentiles who represent the most successful and culturally approved members of their society, the authors of TAP were forced to adopt a psychodynamic perspective in which all of the relationships were inverted. Surface insecurity becomes a sign of deep-felt security and a realistic perspective on life. Surface security and self-confidence become signs of deep insecurities and unresolved hostilities symptomatic of a fear of "looking inside."

Another fundamental mistake is to suppose that any inhibition of children's desires produces hostility and submerged aggression toward the parent. That the parents of the high scorers discipline their children but their children still admire them and, indeed, "glorify" them is thus, from the intellectual perspective of TAP, ipso facto evidence that there is suppressed hostility and aggression toward the parents (see especially p. 357).

It should be apparent from the above discussion, however, that the "victimization" and the underlying hostility are entirely inferred. They are theoretical constructs for which there is not a shred of evidence. There is no reason whatever to suppose that disciplining children leads to suppressed hostility when it is done in the context of a generally positive relationship.

Psychoanalysis was obviously an ideal vehicle for creating this upside-down world. Both R. Brown (1965) and especially Altemeyer (1988) note the arbitrariness of the psychodynamic explanations found in TAP. Thus Altemeyer (p. 54) notes that statements of praise for one's parents in high scorers are a sign of "over-glorification" and repression of aggression, whereas statements of hostility are taken at face value. Statements alluding to both praise and hostility are taken as a combination of over-glorification and accurate recollection.

Psychoanalysis essentially allowed the authors to make up any story they wanted. If the family relationships of high scorers were very positive on the surface, one could propose that the surface happiness and affection masked deep, unconscious hostilities. Any shred of negative feelings high scorers felt toward their parents then became a lever to be used to create an imaginary world of suppressed hostility masked by surface affection. Yet when, in another volume of the *Studies in Prejudice* series, Bettelheim and Janowitz (1950) found that anti-Semites described poor relationships with their parents, the results were taken at face value. The result was not science, but it was effective in achieving its political goals.

It is noteworthy that all five volumes of the *Studies in Prejudice* series utilize psychoanalysis to produce theories in which anti-Semitism is attributed to intrapsychic conflict, sexual repressions, and troubled parent-child relationships while also denying the importance of cultural separatism and the reality of group-based competition for resources (other examples, including Freud's theory in his *Moses and Monotheism*, are reviewed in Chapter 5). Psychoanalytic interpretations of anti-Semitism continue to appear (e.g., Klafter,

2020; Strosberg, 2022). There is a sort of family resemblance to the theories in that much use is made of projections and the development of complicated psychodynamic formulations, although the actual dynamics are not at all identical. At times, as in another volume in the *Studies in Prejudice* series (*Anti-Semitism and Emotional Disorder* by Ackerman and Jahoda, 1950), there seems to be no comprehensible general theory of anti-Semitism, but rather a set of *ad hoc* psychodynamic proposals whose only similarity is that anti-Semitism involves the projection of some sort of intrapsychic conflict. So far as I know, there has been no attempt to subject these different psychodynamic theories to empirical tests that would distinguish among them.

It may appear disturbing to accept the alternative picture developed here. I am essentially saying that the families of the high scorers were adaptive. They combined warmth and affection with a sense of responsibility and discipline, and the children appear to have been ambitious and interested in upholding the values of family and country. The family functioned as an ingroup, as Frenkel-Brunswik and Levinson propose, and the successful transmission of cultural values may well have included negative attributions toward individuals from other groups of which the family was not a member. The high scorers then accepted the ingroup-outgroup biases of their parents, just as they accepted many other parental values. High scorers are thus socially connected and feel a responsibility to ingroup (family) norms. In Triandis's (1990, p. 55) terms, these individuals are "allocentric" people living in an individualist society; that is, they are people who are socially integrated and receive high levels of social support. They identify strongly with ingroup (family) norms.

The perspective developed here emphasizes identificatory processes as underlying the transmission of family attitudes (MacDonald, 1992a, 1997a). As Aronson (1992, pp. 320–321) notes, all of the studies connecting prejudice with parent-child relationships inspired by TAP are correlational, and the results can be equally well explained as due to identificatory processes. Similarly, Billig (1976, pp. 116–117) argues that competent families may be prejudiced and that prejudices may be transmitted within families in the same manner as any number of other beliefs are transmitted. Thus Pettigrew (1958) found high levels of anti-Black prejudice among South African Whites, but their personalities were rather normal and they were not high on the F-scale measuring authoritarianism.

The high scorers studied in TAP accept the ingroup-outgroup biases of their parents and other parental values, but this does not explain the origins of parental values themselves. The data provided here show how competent families can be instrumental in transmitting such values between generations. Contemporary developmental psychology provides no reason to suppose that competent, affectionate families would necessarily produce children with no negative attributions regarding outgroups.

Another major theme here is that whereas allegiance to ingroups indicates psychopathology in gentiles, the epitome of psychological health for the authors of TAP is the individualist who is completely detached from all ingroups, including his or her family. As indicated above, research on individualism-collectivism indicates that such individualists would be less prone to anti-Semitism. It is interesting that for Adorno the most laudable type of low scorer is the "genuine liberal," whose "views regarding minorities are guided by the idea of the individual" (p. 782).[133] The exemplar of a genuine liberal discussed in the text, F515, believes that anti-Semitism is due to jealousy because Jews are smarter. This person is quite willing to allow completely free competition between Jews and gentiles: "We don't want any competition. If they [Jews] want it they should have it. I don't know if they are more intelligent, but if they are they should have it" (p. 782).[134]

According to Adorno, then, psychologically healthy gentiles are unconcerned about being outcompeted by Jews and declining in social status. They are complete individualists with a strong sense of personal autonomy and independence, and they conceptualize Jews as individuals completely independent of their group affiliation. While gentiles are censured for not being individualists, Adorno does not censure Jews who identify strongly with a group that historically has functioned to facilitate resource competition with gentiles (PTSDA, Chs. 5–6) and remains a powerful influence in several highly contentious areas of public policy, including immigration, church-state separation, abortion rights, and civil liberties (J. J. Goldberg, 1996, p. 5). Indeed, social identity theory predicts that Jews would be more likely to have stereotyped, negative conceptualizations of gentiles than the reverse (SAID, Ch. 1).

The personality approach to outgroup prejudice has been criticized in the years since the publication of TAP. Social identity research suggests that variation in outgroup hostility is independent of variation in personality or in parent-child relationships. This research indicates that although there are individual differences in attraction to ingroups (and, indeed, Jews are very high on ethnocentrism), attitudes toward outgroups reflect universal adaptations (see SAID, Ch. 1). Within the social identity perspective, much of the variation in outgroup hostility can be explained by situational variables such as the perceived permeability of the outgroup and whether the ingroup and outgroup are engaged in resource competition.

---

[133] In keeping with his generally unscientific approach to the data, Adorno provides no information on how these types were arrived at or what proportion of the subjects fit into the various categories. In the case of the "genuine liberal," there is a discussion of only one subject.
[134] Interestingly, immediately after expressing the moral legitimacy of free competition between Jews and gentiles, the "genuine liberal" states, "Maybe if the Jews get in power, they would liquidate the majority! That's not smart. Because we would fight back" (p. 782). This subject clearly views Jews not as individuals but as a potentially menacing, cohesive group.

Consistent with this perspective, Billig (1976, p. 119–120) notes that the exclusive focus on personality (i.e., the unchanging traits of individuals) fails to take into account the role of self-interest in ethnic conflict. Moreover, studies such as that of Pettigrew (1958) indicate that one can easily be a racist without having an authoritarian personality; these studies also suggest a role for local norms which may themselves be influenced by perceived resource competition between groups.

Conversely, Altemeyer (1981, p. 28) notes that fascist, authoritarian governments are not necessarily hostile toward minorities, as in the case of Fascist Italy. Indeed, the role of traditional norms is well illustrated by this example. Jews were prominent members of early Italian Fascist governments and active thereafter (P. Johnson, 1987/1988, p. 501). Italian society during the period was, however, highly authoritarian, and there was a corporate, highly cohesive group structure to the society as a whole. The government was highly popular, but anti-Semitism was not important until Germany forced the issue. Because anti-Semitism was not an official component of the Italian Fascist corporate state, authoritarianism occurred without anti-Semitism.

Altemeyer (1981, pp. 238–239) also reports finding much lower correlations between authoritarianism and ethnic prejudice in his studies than were found by Adorno et al. Moreover, Altemeyer notes that the data are consistent with the proposal that authoritarian individuals are ethnocentric only to the extent that other ethnic groups are conventional targets of discrimination by groups with which the authoritarian individual identifies. Similarly, "intrinsically" religious people tend to be hostile toward outgroups only where the religion itself does not proscribe such hostility (Batson & Burris, 1994). The defining feature of authoritarian individuals in this view is simply their adoption of the social conventions and norms of the group, some of which may involve negative attitudes toward outgroups. This proposal is highly compatible with the present approach to group identification and group conflict.

In addition, Billig (1976) found that many fascists failed to conform to the rigid, inhibited stereotype portrayed by the authors of TAP. Such a portrayal is implicit in the psychoanalytic theory that liberation of sexual urges would lead to an end to anti-Semitism, but these fascists were uninhibited, violent, and anti-authoritarian.[135] Personality trait theory also fails to explain short-term changes in attitudes toward Jews, such as found by P. W. Massing (1949), which could not possibly have been caused by changes in parent-child relationships or patterns of sexual repression. One might also mention the very rapid changes in American attitudes toward the Japanese before, during, and after

---

[135] Similarly, in another volume of the *Studies in Prejudice* series, Bettelheim and Janowitz (1950) found that some of their anti-Semitic subjects were rebellious and uninhibited.

World War II, or the rapid decline in anti-Semitism in the United States following World War II.

A prominent aspect of *The Authoritarian Personality* program of research was the conflation of two rather separate concepts: hostility toward other ethnic groups; and authoritarianism. It is interesting in this regard that authoritarianism in personality would appear to involve susceptibility to submitting to group goals, and that the groups themselves may or may not be hostile toward other ethnic groups. Altemeyer (1988, p. 2) defines "right-wing authoritarianism" as involving three central attributes: submission to legitimate social authority; aggression toward individuals that is sanctioned by the authorities; and adherence to social conventions.

Clearly, individuals high on these traits would be ideal members of cohesive human group evolutionary strategies. Indeed, such attributes would define the ideal Jew in traditional societies: submissive to the *kehilla* authorities, strongly adherent to within-group social conventions such as the observance of Jewish religious law, and characterized by negative attitudes toward gentile society and culture seen as manifestations of an outgroup. Consistent with this formulation, high scorers on the Right-Wing Authoritarianism Scale (RWA) tend to be highly religious; they tend to be the most orthodox and committed members of their denomination; they strongly value group cohesiveness, group loyalty, and identify strongly with ingroups (Altemeyer, 1994, p. 134; 1996, p. 84). Without question, traditional Jewish society and contemporary Jewish Orthodox and fundamentalist groups are highly authoritarian by any measure. Indeed, G. Rubenstein (1996) found that Orthodox Jews had higher scores on the RWA than "traditional Jews," and both of these groups were higher than secular Jews.

A primary motivation of the Berkeley group can therefore be seen as an attempt to pathologize this powerful sense of group orientation among gentiles partly by forging a largely illusory (or at least highly contingent) link between these "group-cohesiveness" promoting traits and anti-Semitism. The Berkeley group succeeded in disseminating the ideology that there was a "deep," structural connection between anti-Semitism and this powerful sense of group orientation. By providing a unitary account of authoritarianism and hostility toward outgroups and by locating the origins of this syndrome in disturbed parent-child relations, the Berkeley group had effectively developed a powerful weapon in the war against anti-Semitism.

The present theoretical perspective is thus compatible with the research results indicating that ethnic hostility and anti-Semitism are only tangentially related to authoritarianism. Indeed, recently there has been an upsurge of left-wing violence directed at censoring opinions they disagree with. For example, even mainstream conservative voices have been prevented from speaking at college campuses, or their presence as speakers results in protests and even violence: a speech by Riley Gaines, an opponent of biological males competing as transgender females in women's sports, was greeted with a riotous demonstration, and she claimed physical assault, at a speech she was to give at San Francisco State University (Chen & Mossberg, 2023); and Kyle Duncan, a conservative U.S. Circuit Court judge, was unable to give his talk after being shouted down by law students at Stanford University (Ward, 2023). Recent research has implicated left-wing authoritarianism as involving positive attitudes toward censorship and "anti-hierarchical aggression," with the "drive to use force against those in power and who endorse conservative values" linked to "antagonistic narcissism," "demonstrating manipulative and exploitative behaviors, indulging in self-perceived entitlement, arrogance, reactive anger, distrust, lack of empathy, and thrill-seeking" but not dispositional altruism or social justice commitment (Krispenz & Bertrams, 2024). A second study in the same paper indicated an association between anti-hierarchical aggression and psychopathy, including items such as "I'll do anything to get what I want" and a general disregard for social norms; along with the two other traits of the so-called "dark triad" (Machiavellianism, narcissism), such individuals are "self-promoting, emotionally callous, and have a tendency to manipulate others to take advantage of them." In general, "individuals who strongly endorse antihierarchical aggression to overthrow conservatives are narcissistic individuals with psychopathic attributes and thus driven by ego-focused motives." Such individuals may favor left-wing or right-wing causes depending on their perceived self-interest. Hostility toward minority groups may or may not be a focus of their ingroups.

It has been noted that authoritarianism refers to a set of traits that predispose individuals to strongly identify with highly cohesive groups that impose uniform standards of behavior on group members. Since authoritarian individuals are highly prone to submerging themselves within the group, conforming to group conventions, and accepting group goals, there will indeed be a tendency toward anti-Semitism when the ingroup itself is anti-Semitic; there will also be a tendency toward ethnocentrism and devaluation of—or even hostility toward—outgroups when the group membership itself is based on advancing the interests of a particular ethnic group.

This is essentially the position of Altemeyer (1981, p. 238), since he proposes that the fairly weak associations usually found between authoritarianism and hostility toward outgroups reflect conventional hostility toward outgroups. From this perspective, these concepts may be empirically associated in particular samples, but there is no structural connection between them. The association simply reflects the authoritarian tendency to adopt social conventions and norms of the group, including negative attitudes toward particular outgroups. This perspective would account for the significant but modest correlations (0.30–0.50) Altemeyer (1994) finds between authoritarianism and ethnocentrism.

Moreover, from the standpoint of social identity research, there is no empirical or logical requirement that powerful, cohesive groups need necessarily be based on ethnicity as an organizing principle. As argued in Chapter 1 of SAID, whether the group itself is anti-Semitic seems to depend crucially on whether Jews are perceived as a highly salient, powerful group within the larger society and whether they are perceived as having conflicts of interest with gentiles. There is a great deal of evidence that perceptions of group competition with Jews have often not been *illusory* (SAID, *passim*). Social identity theory proposes that as between-group competition becomes more salient, there will be an increasing tendency for people to join cohesive, authoritarian groups arrayed against perceived outgroups.

Conclusion

I have no doubt that, apart from the data on family dynamics, many of the results of studies on authoritarianism, including TAP, can be integrated with contemporary psychological data. However, I would suggest that developing a body of scientific knowledge was never an important consideration in these studies. The agenda is to develop an ideology of anti-Semitism that rallies ingroup loyalties to Judaism and attempts to alter gentile culture in a manner that benefits Judaism by portraying gentile group loyalties (including nationalism, Christian religious affiliation, close family relationships, high-investment parenting, and concern with social and material success) as indicators of psychiatric disorder. Within these writings the nature of Judaism is completely irrelevant to anti-Semitism; Judaism is conceptualized, as Ackerman and Jahoda (1950, p. 74) suggest in another volume of *Studies in Prejudice*, as a Rorschach inkblot in which the pathology of anti-Semites is revealed. These theories serve the same functions that Jewish religious ideology has always served: the rationalization of the continuation of Judaism both to ingroup members and to gentiles combined with very negative views of gentile culture.

As in the case of psychoanalysis generally, the results of scientific investigation appear to be largely unrelated to the dissemination and persistence of the idea that authoritarianism or certain types of parent-child relationships are linked to hostility toward other groups. A consistent thread of Altemeyer's (1981) review of TAP literature is that these ideas persist within the wider culture and even within textbooks in college psychology courses despite the absence of scientific support:[136]

> The reader familiar with the matter knows that most of these criticisms are over 25 years old, and now they might be considered little more than flaying a dead horse. Unfortunately the flaying is necessary, for the horse is not dead, but still trotting around—in various introductory psychology and developmental psychology textbooks, for example. Methodological criticisms seem to travel a shorter circuit and die a much quicker death than "scientific breakthroughs." In conclusion then, no matter how often it is stated that the Berkeley investigators [i.e., Adorno et al.] discovered the childhood origins of authoritarianism, the facts of the matter are anything but convincing. (Altemeyer, 1988, p. 38)[137]

In this regard it is interesting that in addition to the failure to replicate the Berkeley group's central empirical finding of a strong association between authoritarianism and hostility toward other ethnic groups, TAP also suffers from severe methodological shortcomings, some of which suggest conscious attempts at deception. Besides the "response set" difficulty pervading the construction of all the scales, perhaps simply reflecting naivety in scale construction, Altemeyer (1981, pp. 27–28) notes that the F-scale measuring authoritarianism was constructed by retaining items that correlated well with anti-Semitism. Altemeyer notes, for example, that the item "Books and movies ought not to deal so much with the sordid and seamy side of life; they ought to concentrate on themes that are entertaining and uplifting" appeared on earlier versions of the F-scale and was highly discriminating. However, it did not correlate highly with the Anti-Semitism Scale and was dropped from later versions. Altemeyer (pp. 27–28) notes:

> Despite the statement . . . that the most discriminating items on the initial form were carried over to the next model "in the same or slightly revised form," the "books and movies" item simply disappeared, forever. It is not hard to construct a scale which will correlate highly with another if you eliminate items that are insufficiently related with the target.

---

[136] Gottfredson (1994) likewise notes that in the media and public opinion there persists the idea that intelligence tests are culturally biased and have nothing to do with performance in life—long after these ideas have been shown to be false by researchers on intelligence. In the contemporary U.S., this ideology has resulted in eradicating requirements for using IQ-linked tests for admission to many universities, including graduate programs in law and medicine.

[137] The same might be said about Margaret Mead's work discussed in Chapter 2. Despite the fact that at this point any reasonable person must assume that the work is at least highly questionable, her work continues to appear prominently in many college textbooks. Mead was on the advisory board of the Institute's anti-Semitism project, which produced TAP.

The suggestion is that highly discriminating items were dropped if they did not correlate with anti-Semitism, despite assurances to the contrary. In fact, Wiggershaus (1994, pp. 372ff) shows quite clearly that Adorno placed a high priority on developing the F-scale as an indirect means of measuring anti-Semitism, that he was little concerned about following normal scientific procedures in achieving this goal, and that his procedure was exactly as Altemeyer describes:

> In Berkeley, we then developed the F-scale with a freedom which differed considerably from the idea of a pedantic science which has to justify each of its steps. The reason for this was probably what, over there, might have been termed the "psychoanalytic background" of the four of us who were leading the project, particularly our familiarity with the method of free association. I emphasize this because a work like *The Authoritarian Personality* . . . was produced in a manner which does not correspond at all to the usual image of positivism in social science. . . . We spent hours waiting for ideas to occur to us, not just for entire dimensions, "variables" and syndromes, but also for individual items for the questionnaire. The less their relation to the main topic was visible, the prouder we were of them, while we expected for theoretical reasons to find correlations between ethnocentrism, anti-Semitism and reactionary views in the political and economic sphere. We then checked these items in constant "pre-tests," using these both to restrict the questionnaire to a reasonable size, which was technically necessary, and to exclude those items which proved not to be sufficiently selective. (Adorno; in Wiggershaus, 1994, p. 373)

It is not difficult to suppose that the entire program of research for TAP involved deception from beginning to end. This is suggested by the authors' clear political agenda and the pervasive double standard in which gentile ethnocentrism and gentile involvement in cohesive groups are seen as symptoms of psychopathology, whereas Jews are simply viewed as victims of irrational gentile pathologies with no mention of Jewish ethnocentrism or allegiance to cohesive groups. There was also a double standard in which left-wing authoritarianism was completely ignored whereas right-wing authoritarianism was "found" to be a psychiatric disorder.[138] As indicated above, deception is also

---

[138] Several authors have found evidence for a general authoritarianism dimension in which attitudes toward authority are divorced from the ethnocentrism often included in measures of right-wing authoritarianism (e.g., Bhushan, 1982; Ray, 1972). Altemeyer (1994) notes that authoritarian individuals in North America and in the Soviet Union under communism had mirror-image authoritarian attitudes, with the latter supporting "hard-line" authoritarian communism. In *Studies on Authority and the Family* (the earlier attempt of the Frankfurt School to link family relationships and authoritarianism), it was impossible for an individual to be classified as authoritarian if he or she stated that socialism would improve the world situation and

suggested by the fact that the basic theory of the role of parent-child relations in producing ethnocentrism and hostility toward outgroups was developed as a philosophical theory conceptualized by the authors as not subject to empirical verification or falsification. Indeed, the entire thrust of the Frankfurt School's view of science rejects the idea that science should attempt to understand reality, in favor of the ideology that science ought to serve moral (i.e., political) interests. Further, it is suggested by the fact that the anti-democratic leanings of Adorno and Horkheimer and their radical critique of the mass culture of capitalism were not apparent in this work intended for an American audience (Jay, 1973, p. 248). Similarly, Horkheimer tended to portray Critical Theory as a form of radicalism to his "Marxist friends" while representing it "as a form of faithfulness to the European tradition in the humanities and philosophy" when discussing it with "official university people" (Wiggershaus, 1994, p. 252).

Finally, there were a host of well-recognized methodological difficulties, including the use of unrepresentative subjects in the interview data, the very incomplete and misleading information on the reliability of the measures, and the discussion of insignificant relationships as if they were significant (Altemeyer, 1981). I have also pointed out the extremely strained, *ad hoc*, and counterintuitive interpretations that characterize the study (see also Lasch, 1991, p. 453). Particularly egregious is the consistent use of psychodynamic thinking to produce any desired interpretive outcome.

Of course, deception may not be as important here as self-deception—a common enough feature of Jewish intellectual history (see SAID, Chs. 7–8). In any case, the result was excellent political propaganda and a potent weapon in the war on anti-Semitism.

---

that capitalism caused hyperinflation. "The possibility that someone could remain loyal to the Communist Party or to its programme and nevertheless be authoritarian was thus excluded" (Wiggershaus, 1994, p. 174).

THE NEW YORK INTELLECTUALS AND SOME GENERAL
COMMENTS ON JEWISH CRITIQUES OF GENTILE CULTURE

THE NEW YORK INTELLECTUALS AS A JEWISH INTELLECTUAL MOVEMENT:
THEIR RISE TO ELITE STATUS IN THE 1950S

The New York Intellectuals were a highly influential movement beginning in the 1930s firmly on the left as devotees of Trotsky, but morphing toward neoconservatism motivated by their perceptions of anti-Semitism in the Soviet Union.

The highly influential left-wing journal *Partisan Review* (PR) was a principal showcase of the New York Intellectuals, a group dominated by editors and contributors with a Jewish ethnic identity and a deep alienation from American political and cultural institutions (Cooney, 1986, pp. 225ff; E. S. Shapiro, 1989; Wisse, 1987). Clement Greenberg, an influential art critic whose work helped establish the Abstract Expressionist movement in the 1940s, was a prototypical member of this group. He made his reputation entirely within what one might term a Jewish intellectual milieu. Greenberg was a writer for PR, managing editor of *Contemporary Jewish Record* (the forerunner of *Commentary*), and long-time editor of *Commentary* under Elliot Cohen, as well as art critic for *The Nation*, a leftist publication.

There was thus an overlap between official Jewish publications and the secular intellectual journals associated with the New York Intellectuals. Indeed, *Commentary*, published by the AJCommittee, became the most widely known journal of the New York Intellectuals, serving to introduce a wider, educated audience to their ideas while also dealing with Jewish issues. Several New York Intellectuals had editorial positions at *Commentary*, including, besides Greenberg, Robert Warshow, Nathan Glazer, Irving Kristol, Sidney Hook, and Norman Podhoretz; PR editor Philip Rahv also served as managing editor for *Contemporary Jewish Record*. Because of the overlap among the contributors and editors, the following are considered the magazines associated with the New York Intellectuals (Jumonville, 1991, pp. 8, 234): PR, *Commentary*, *The Menorah Journal*, *Dissent*, *The Nation*, *Politics*, *Encounter*, *The New Leader*, *The New York Review of Books*, *The Public Interest*, *The New Criterion*, *The National Interest*, and *Tikkun*. Like other Jewish movements, the New York Intellectuals developed an elaborate intellectual infrastructure that was attractive to Jews and non-Jews alike so long as they were able to fit into the intellectual milieu favored by the media outlets.

PR originated as an offshoot of the Communist Party USA, its central figures all Marxists and admirers of Trotsky. There was, however, an increasingly heavy dose of psychoanalysis beginning in the 1940s—Lionel Trilling, for example, wrote of his much greater allegiance to Freud relative to Marx (Jumonville, 1991, p. 126). There was also a great deal of influence and cross-fertilization between the New York Intellectuals and the Frankfurt School (p. 66; see also Ch. 5). The New York Intellectuals gradually evolved away from advocacy of socialist revolution toward a shared commitment to anti-nationalism and cosmopolitanism, "a broad and inclusive culture" in which cultural differences were esteemed (Cooney, 1986, p. 233)—a perspective that virtually defines the American Jewish mainstream and clearly fits with Jewish interests as a minority group in what was then an overwhelmingly White, Christian society while completely ignoring or demeaning the interests of White Americans in a more homogeneous society both ethnically and culturally. (As noted in Chapter 8, *Commentary* published articles during the 1950s favoring multiculturalism and high levels of immigration of all racial and national groups into the United States.)

The New York Intellectuals conceived themselves as alienated, marginalized figures—a modern version of traditional Jewish separateness and alienation from gentile culture. "*They did not feel that they belonged to America or that America belonged to them*" (Podhoretz, 1967, p. 117; emphasis original). Indeed, as noted in Chapter 6, Podhoretz (1979, p. 283) was asked by a *New Yorker* editor in the 1950s "whether there was a special typewriter key at *Partisan Review* with the word 'alienation' on a single key." They also advocated a secular humanist perspective and opposed religious values at least partly because of the past association between anti-Semitism and Christian religious ideology. The result was, a continuity of perspective in the work of the New York Intellectuals running through the 1930s and 1940s. . . . [T]he New York Intellectuals embraced cosmopolitan values. . . . [T]heir loyalty to those values was intensified by their consciousness of being Jewish, and [that] consciousness helped to make the *Partisan Review* variant of cosmopolitanism a discrete intellectual position. (Cooney, 1986, p. 245)

It would be difficult to overestimate the New York Intellectuals' influence on American high culture in the 1940s and 1950s, particularly in the areas of literary criticism, art criticism, sociology, and "intellectual high journalism" (Jumonville, 1991, p. 9). Irving Kristol (1983, p. 10) writes of PR's "intimidating presence" among his college friends. In the words of art critic Hilton Kramer (1996, p. 43):

For certain writers and intellectuals of my generation . . . drawn to PR in the late forties and early fifties . . . it was more than a magazine, it was an essential part of our education, as much a part of that education as the books we read, the visits we made to the museums, the concerts we attended, and the records we bought. It gave us an entrée to modern cultural life—to its gravity and complexity and combative character—that few of our teachers could match. . . . It conferred upon every subject it encompassed—art, literature, politics, history, and current affairs—an air of intellectual urgency that made us, as readers, feel implicated and called upon to respond.

Greenberg grew up in the Yiddish-speaking radical subculture of New York. "Everyone his family knew was a socialist. As a small boy he thought *socialist* meant *Jewish*" (Rubenfeld, 1997, p. 60). Like the other New York Intellectuals, Greenberg had a strong Jewish identity that ultimately influenced his work. "I believe that a quality of Jewishness is present in every word I write, as it is in almost every word of every other contemporary American Jewish writer" (in p. 89). As editor of *Contemporary Jewish Record*, Greenberg published an article that openly referred to Henry Adams's anti-Semitism, a taboo at the time. He was also a major promoter of the work of Franz Kafka, whom he regarded as a quintessentially Jewish voice in literature:

The revolutionary and hypnotic effect of the works of Franz Kafka . . . upon the literary avant-garde of the world has been without parallel. . . . Kafka seems to initiate a new [age of fiction] single-handed, pointing a way beyond most of the cardinal assumptions upon which Western fiction has rested until now. Kafka's writings represent, moreover, perhaps the first time that an essentially and uniquely Jewish notion of reality, expressed hitherto nowhere but in religious forms, has found a secular voice. (in Rubenfeld, 1997, pp. 92–93)

In a review in PR of a militantly Zionist book by Arthur Koestler denigrating European Jews and praising the Zionists who were colonizing Palestine, Greenberg (1946, p. 582) exhibited a sense of Jewish superiority, noting: "It is possible, I want to suggest, to adopt standards of evaluation other than those of Western Europe. It is possible that by 'world-historical' standards the European Jew represents a higher type than any yet achieved in history." In 1949 a conflict broke out between this nascent Jewish intellectual establishment and the older, predominantly gentile literary establishment over the issue of an award to Ezra Pound, whose poetry reflected his fascist sympathies and his anti-Semitism. Greenberg (1949, p. 515, emphasis original) emphasized the priority of the moral over the aesthetic, writing:

[L]ife includes and is more important than art and it judges things by their consequences. ... As a Jew, I myself cannot help being offended by the matter of Pound's latest poetry; and since 1943 things like that make me feel *physically* afraid too.

Philosopher Sidney Hook also had a strong Jewish identification; he was a Zionist, a strong supporter of Israel, and an advocate of Jewish education for Jewish children (see Hook, 1989). Hook played a decisive leadership role among the New York Intellectuals (Jumonville, 1991, p. 28), and, as indicated above, he had an editorial position at *Commentary*. In his "Reflections on the Jewish Question" he wrote, "the causes of antisemitism are not to be found in the behavior of Jews" (Hook, 1949, p. 465). Rather, the sources of anti-Semitism are to be found "in the beliefs and habits and culture of the non-Jews" (p. 468), particularly Christianity. Anti-Semitism "is endemic to every Christian culture whose religions made Jews the eternal villain in the Christian drama of salvation" (pp. 471–472).

Hook developed an elaborate apologia for Judaism in the modern world. Being a Jew is simply a social category with no ethnic implications: "*A Jew is anyone who for any reason calls himself such or is called such in any community whose practices take note of the distinction*" (Hook, 1949, p. 475; emphasis original). According to Hook, there are no Jewish intellectual movements except those, like Zionism and Hasidism, that are explainable "by the social and cultural pressures of Western Christendom." Jewish intellectuals are said to be influenced much more by gentile intellectuals than by their status as Jews. Indeed, Hook asserts an extreme philosophical nominalism completely at odds with the entire history of Judaism: Jews do not exist as a group at all. Judaism is a completely atomistic voluntary concatenation of individuals whose only biological ties are within the nuclear family: "Only individuals exist" (p. 481).

Moreover, Hook (1949, p. 479) felt that one had a moral obligation to remain a Jew:

> [For most Jews] escape [from being Jewish] was practically impossible, that where it was possible the psychological costs were usually too burdensome, and that morally it was intrinsically degrading to capitulate to irrational prejudice and deny kinship with their own fathers and mothers who, often against heroic odds, had courageously kept their integrity and faith whatever it was.

Like many leftists, Hook (1949, p. 481) approved of the dream of human universalism, but the dream,

> overlooks the fact that human beings live as Jews and non-Jews here and now and will continue to do so for a long time to come; that the dream itself is based upon the acceptance of differences among men and not on the hope of an undifferentiated unity; and that the microbes of antisemitism infect even movements which do not officially allow for its existence.

(Hook was highly sensitive to anti-Semitism on the left, beginning with the Trotsky-Stalin conflict during the 1920s; see Ch. 3.) Jews would thus continue to exist as Jews long after Hook's utopia of democratic socialism had been created. For Hook (1949, pp. 480–481), leftist universalism properly understood implies an acceptance of cultural diversity as not only central to a philosophy of Judaism but also central to the idea of democracy itself:

> No philosophy of Jewish life is required except one—identical with the democratic way of life—which enables Jews who for any reason at all accept their existence as Jews to lead a dignified and significant life, a life in which together with their fellowmen they strive collectively to improve the quality of democratic, secular cultures and thus encourage a maximum of cultural diversity, both Jewish and non-Jewish. ... If it is pruned of its Utopianism and its failure to understand that the ethics of democracy presupposes not an equality of sameness or identity but an equality of differences, much of the universalist view still has a large measure of validity.

For Hook (1948, pp. 201–202):

> [D]iversity of experience [including ethnic and cultural diversity], direct or indirect, is immediately enjoyable. ... It safeguards us against

provincialism and the tyranny of the familiar, whose hold may sometimes be so strong as to incapacitate us from making new responses necessary for survival. . . . Growth in maturity consists largely in learning to appreciate differences.

Hook thus expresses the fundamental Jewish interest in cultural and ethnic diversity that is a central theme of Chapter 8 on Jewish involvement in U.S. immigration policy without attempting a serious analysis of how these values are in the interests of non-Jewish Americans; as noted below, the New York Intellectuals in general were highly critical of the American culture of the period.

The New York Intellectuals included the following prominent Jewish participants, classified roughly according to main area of involvement, although they tended to be generalists rather than specialists: Elliot Cohen (editor of *The Menorah Journal* and founding editor of *Commentary*); Sidney Hook and Hannah Arendt (political philosophy, political and intellectual journalism); William Phillips and Philip Rahv (editors of PR; literary criticism, intellectual journalism); Lionel Trilling, Diana Trilling, Leslie Fiedler, Alfred Kazin, and Susan Sontag (literary criticism); Robert Warshow (film criticism and cultural criticism); Isaac Rosenfeld, Delmore Schwartz, Paul Goodman, Saul Bellow, and Norman Mailer (fiction and poetry, literary criticism); Irving Howe (political journalism, literary criticism); Melvin J. Lasky, Norman Podhoretz, and Irving Kristol (political journalism); Nathan Glazer, Seymour Martin Lipset, Daniel Bell, Edward Shils, David Riesman, and Michael Walzer (sociology); Lionel Abel, Clement Greenberg, George L. K. Morris, Meyer Schapiro, and Harold Rosenberg (art criticism).

The New York Intellectuals spent their careers within an almost entirely Jewish social and intellectual milieu. When Rubenfeld (1997, p. 97) lists people Greenberg invited to social occasions at his apartment in New York, the only gentile mentioned is artist Willem de Kooning. Revealingly, Michael Wreszin (1994, p. 33) refers to Dwight Macdonald, another Trotskyist contributor to PR, as "a distinguished goy among the Partisanskies." Another non-Jew was writer James T. Farrell, but his diary records a virtually all-Jewish social milieu in which a large part of his life was spent in virtual non-stop social interaction with other New York Intellectuals (Cooney, 1986, p. 248). Indeed, Podhoretz (1967, pp. 246–248) refers to the New York Intellectuals as a "family" who, when they attended a party, arrived at the same time and socialized among their in-group.

Cultural critique was central to the work of the New York Intellectuals. To Philip Rahv (1978, pp. 305–306), modernist culture was important because of its potential for cultural critique. Modernism encouraged "the creation of moral and aesthetic values running counter to and often violently critical of the bourgeois spirit. . . . What is modern literature if not a vindictive, neurotic, and continually renewed dispute with the modern world?" Such pronouncements on the critical potential of even the most abstract art reflected the views of Frankfurt School theorists Adorno and Horkheimer, the latter of whom noted that "An element of resistance is inherent in the most aloof art" (Horkheimer, 1941, p. 291).

The New York Intellectuals exemplified the tendency to exude a sense of moral and intellectual superiority combined with a very *realpolitik* ability to promote and consolidate the power of the ingroup—both characteristics which are typical of the movements reviewed in this volume. In their own self-conception, the New York Intellectuals "combined genuine loyalty to values under siege with the cultivation of an image—the image of a detached and alienated intelligentsia holding the line against corruptions of mind and spirit" (Cooney, 1986, p. 200). I have noted that Clement Greenberg emphasized the priority of the moral over the aesthetic. Similarly, Lionel Trilling viewed literary criticism as centrally concerned with "the quality that life does not have but should have" (in Jumonville, 1991, p. 123). In the political arena, issues were portrayed as,

> a struggle between good and evil. . . . The emphatic, emotion-charged, often moralistic positions that the New York Intellectuals established, and the tendency to identify their own views with fundamental intellectual integrity, worked against the commitment to openness and free thought proclaimed in their public statements and implicit in their attachment to cosmopolitan values. (Cooney, 1986, p. 265).

> The elitism in [the New York Intellectuals'] outlook was not a socioeconomic sort dependent on upper-class privileges, of course, but rather an intellectual elitism—a Jeffersonian aristocracy of talent, ability, intelligence, and critical acuity. They were worried about maintaining the intellectual vocation and its values. Further, they were the elite as the vanguard, the principled, minority, avant-garde intellectual cadre—as well as elite in the sense of being the elect or chosen [an ancient Jewish conceit]. But all these types of elitism had some connection: they were ways of conserving power for one group, and they resulted in a patronizing condescension toward the lower orders of society. (Jumonville, 1991, p. 169)

This condescension and failure to respect others' ideas are particularly obvious in the New York Intellectuals' attitudes toward traditional American culture, especially the culture of rural America. There is a large overlap between the New York Intellectuals and the anti-populist forces who, as discussed in Chapter 6, used *The Authoritarian Personality* (TAP) to pathologize the ethnic identifications and behavior of gentile Americans and particularly the lower middle class. The New York Intellectuals were cultural elitists who abhorred cultural democracy and feared the masses while nevertheless remaining consistently left-of-center politically. The movement espoused "a leftist elitism—a leftist conservatism, we might say—that slowly evolved into . . . neoconservatism" (Jumonville, 1991, p. 185). The New York Intellectuals associated rural America with,

> nativism, anti-Semitism, nationalism, and fascism as well as with anti-intellectualism and provincialism; the urban was associated antithetically with ethnic and cultural tolerance, with internationalism, and with advanced ideas. . . . The New York Intellectuals simply *began* with the assumption that the rural—with which they associated much of American tradition and most of the territory beyond New York—had little to contribute to a cosmopolitan culture. . . . By interpreting cultural and political issues through the urban-rural lens, writers could even mask assertions of superiority and expressions of anti-democratic sentiments as the judgments of an objective expertise. (Cooney, 1986, pp. 267–268; emphasis original)

In Chapter 8 the battle between this urbanized intellectual and political establishment and rural America is joined over the issue of immigration, in this case with the pro-immigration side supported by all of the mainstream Jewish political organizations.

PR also had an ingroup-outgroup mentality that is entirely consistent with the other Jewish-dominated intellectual movements reviewed here. Norman Podhoretz (1967, pp. 115–116, emphasis original) describes the PR crowd as a "family" that derived an "elitism,"

> out of the feeling of beleaguered isolation shared with the masters of the modernist movement themselves . . . —the conviction that *others* were not worth taking into consideration except to attack, and need not be addressed in one's writing; out of that feeling as well, a sense of hopelessness as to the fate of American culture at large and the correlative conviction that integrity and standards were only possible among "us."

It was an insular world in which the only people who even existed were ingroup members: "[T]he family paid virtually no heed to anyone outside it except kissing cousins. . . . To be adopted into the family was a mark of great distinction: it meant you were good enough, that you *existed* as a writer and an intellectual" (Podhoretz, 1967, p. 151; emphasis original).

Like the other intellectual movements reviewed in this volume, PR had a sense of community and groupness, "a sense of common purpose and group support around the magazine"; the basic question about a prospective writer was whether he was "'our' kind of writer" (Cooney, 1986, pp. 225, 249). Among this self-described alienated and marginalized group there was also an atmosphere of social support that undoubtedly functioned as had traditional Jewish ingroup solidarity arrayed against a morally and intellectually inferior outside world. They perceived themselves as "rebel intellectuals defending a minority position and upholding the best traditions of radicalism" (p. 265). PR provided "a haven and support" and a sense of social identity; it "served to assure many of its members that they were not alone in the world, that sympathetic intellectuals existed in sufficient number to provide them with social and professional moorings" (p. 249). There was thus a great deal of continuity to this "coherent, distinguishable group" of intellectuals "who mainly began their careers as revolutionary communists in the 1930s [to] become an institutionalized and even hegemonic component of American culture during the conservative 1950s while maintaining a high degree of collective continuity" (Wald, 1987, pp. 12, 10).

Consistent with the multiple overlapping alliances generated by this Jewish intellectual milieu, there were charges that a Jewish literary establishment was able to determine success in the literary world and that it advanced the careers of Jewish writers. Jewish group cohesiveness was implied by Truman Capote and Gore Vidal, who complained about the ability of Jewish intellectuals to determine success in the literary world and their tendency to promote Jewish writers (see Podhoretz, 1986). Capote described a "Jewish mafia" in the literary world as a,

> clique of New York-oriented writers who control much of the literary scene through the influence of the quarterlies and intellectual magazines. All of these publications are Jewish-dominated and this particular coterie employs them to make or break writers by advancing or withholding attention. (in Podhoretz, 1986)

SOME GENERAL COMMENTS ON JEWISH CRITIQUES OF GENTILE CULTURE

Do you remember, he asked me, what Lueger, the anti-Semitic mayor of Vienna, once said to the municipality of Vienna when a subsidy for the natural sciences was asked for? "Science? That is what one Jew cribs from another." That is what I say about Ideengeschichte, history of ideas.

— Isaiah Berlin, in Efron, 1994, p. 13,
reflecting on a conversation with Lewis Namier

The material in the previous six chapters indicates that individuals who strongly identified as Jews have been the main motivating force behind several highly influential intellectual movements that have simultaneously subjected gentile culture to radical criticism and allowed for the continuity of Jewish identification. Together these movements comprise the intellectual and political left of the twentieth century continuing into the present, and they are the direct intellectual ancestors of current leftist intellectual and political movements, particularly postmodernism and multiculturalism.

Collectively, these movements have called into question the fundamental moral, political, and economic foundations of Western society. They are thus highly aggressive moves against the people and culture of the West and, as discussed in the following chapter, they have been critical for altering the intellectual context of immigration that now threatens to relegate Europeans to minority status—and likely a beleaguered, persecuted minority—in nations they have dominated for centuries. In rejecting the idea of racially based genetic influences on culture in favor of race-as-social-construct, Boasian anthropology undercut intellectual defenses of nativism and any sense of racial identity or pride. Leftist social and political movements have subjected every aspect of traditional Western culture, including religion, economics, race, and now gender, to radical critique. Psychoanalysis portrayed the Christian religion as based on infantile needs and Christian sexual mores as repressive, thus undercutting marriage and family, particularly for lower-IQ people. Psychoanalysis also provided the Frankfurt School with a highly pliable theoretical structure that it used to pathologize White ethnocentrism as resulting from disturbed parent-child relationships. Neoconservatism pledged its allegiance to the basic institutions of the West (capitalism, democracy) with the understanding that Jews as an elite with strong influence in the media, academia, and finance would be able to best achieve their interests within that context compared to either communism or fascism, with support for Israel being the most prominent example.

A critical feature of these movements is that they have been top-down movements in the sense that they were originated and dominated by members of a highly intelligent and highly educated group. These movements have been advocated with great intellectual passion and moral fervor and with a very high level of theoretical sophistication. Each movement promised its own often overlapping and complementary version of utopia: a society composed of people with the same biological potential for accomplishment and able to be easily molded by culture into ideal citizens as imagined by a morally and intellectually superior elite; a classless society in which there would be no conflicts of interest and people would altruistically work for the good of the group; a society in which people would be free of neuroses and aggression toward outgroups and in tune with their biological urges; a multicultural paradise in which different racial and ethnic groups would live in harmony and cooperation—a utopian dream that also occupies center stage in the discussion of

Jewish involvement in shaping U.S. immigration policy in Chapter 8. Each of these utopias is profoundly problematic from an evolutionary perspective, a theme that will be returned to in the concluding chapter.

The originators of these movements were all vitally concerned with anti-Semitism, and all of the utopias envisioned by these intellectual and political movements would end anti-Semitism while allowing for Jewish group continuity. A generation of Jewish radicals averted their eyes from the mass murder and oppression that characterized the early decades of the Soviet Union, seeing it as an idyllic place where Jews could rise to positions of preeminence and where anti-Semitism was officially outlawed while Jewish national life flourished. The psychoanalytic movement and the Frankfurt School looked forward to the day when gentiles would be inoculated against anti-Semitism by a clinical priesthood that could heal the personal inadequacies and the frustrations at loss of status that gentiles murderously projected onto the Jews. And the Boasians and the Frankfurt School and their descendants would prevent the development of anti-Semitic ideologies of majoritarian ethnocentrism. Neoconservatism would take advantage of Jewish talents to secure the interests of Israel within Western social and political forms.

A palpable sense of intellectual and moral superiority of those participating in these movements is another characteristic feature. This sense of intellectual superiority and hostility to gentiles and their culture were recurrent themes of the leftist movements discussed in Chapter 3. I have also documented a profound sense of intellectual superiority and estrangement from gentile culture that characterized not only Freud but also the entire psychoanalytic movement. The sense of superiority on the part of a "self-constituted cultural vanguard" (Lasch, 1991, p. 453) of Jewish intellectuals toward lower-middle-class mores and attitudes was a theme of Chapter 6, and quite clearly, lower- and middle-class Whites have been the biggest losers in this cultural transformation.

Regarding moral superiority, the central pose of post-Enlightenment Jewish intellectuals is a sense that Judaism represents a moral beacon to the rest of humanity. These movements thus constitute concrete examples of the ancient and recurrent Jewish self-conceptualization as a "light of the nations," reviewed extensively in SAID (Ch. 7) and existing uncomfortably with actual Jewish behavior, as in the early decades of the Soviet Union and in Israeli dispossession and even genocide of the Palestinians. Moral indictments of their opponents are a prominent theme in the writings of political radicals and those opposing biological perspectives on individual and group differences in IQ. A sense of moral superiority was also prevalent in the psychoanalytic movement, and we have seen that the Frankfurt School developed a moral perspective in which the existence of Judaism was viewed as an *a priori* moral absolute and in which social science was to be judged by moral criteria.

As noted in Chapter 1, current psychological theory and data are highly compatible with supposing that viewpoints advocated by minorities are able to influence attitudes held by the majority, especially when possessing a high degree of internal consistency and especially when they are disseminated from the most prestigious academic and media institutions in the society. Although the influence on gentile societies of Jewish involvement in these intellectual and political movements cannot be assessed with mathematical certainty, the material presented here strongly suggests that Jewish involvement was a critical factor in the triumph of the intellectual left in late-twentieth-century Western societies.

Several features of these intellectual movements can be viewed as serving Jewish interests. The greatest danger for a minority group strategy is the development of a highly cohesive, sectarian majority group that views the minority group as a negatively evaluated outgroup, as happened in Germany in the 1930s. In combating this potential threat, one type of strategy has been to actively promote universalist ideologies within the larger society in which the Jewish-gentile social categorization is of minimal importance. Judaism as a cohesive, ethnically based group strategy continues to exist, but in a cryptic or semi-cryptic state. The exemplar of this strategy is leftist political ideology; however, psychoanalysis and even forms of Judaism that minimize phenotypic differentiation between Jews and gentiles, such as Reform Judaism (see SAID, Ch. 6), adopt a similar strategy.

Jewish interests are also served by facilitating radical individualism (social atomization) among gentiles while retaining a powerful sense of group cohesion among Jews—the agenda of the Frankfurt School. Gentile group identifications are regarded as an indication of psychopathology, with the obvious exception that Jewish group affiliations are ignored or even regarded as pure, morally superior, and inviolate. An important component of this strategy is the deconstruction of majoritarian intellectual movements that are incompatible with the continuation of Judaism. These majoritarian intellectual movements may range from radical assimilationism (e.g., the forced conversions to Christianity) to exclusivist majority group strategies based on majority group ethnocentrism (e.g., National Socialism).

Jewish interests are also served by the Frankfurt School ideology that gentile concerns about losing social status and being eclipsed economically, socially, and demographically by other groups are an indication of psychopathology. As an exceptionally upwardly mobile group, Jews and their interests are served by this ideology by defusing gentile concerns about their downward mobility and demographic swamping, and we shall see in Chapter 8 that Jewish organizations and Jewish intellectuals have been at the forefront of the movement to eclipse the demographic and cultural dominance of European-derived peoples in Western societies.

Several themes common to these Jewish intellectual movements bear mentioning. An important thread apparent in the discussions of psychoanalysis, Boasian anthropology, the Frankfurt School, and radical intellectual and political circles has been that Jewish intellectuals have formed highly cohesive groups whose influence derives to a great extent from the solidarity and cohesiveness of the group. The influence of minority ideologies is augmented to the extent that there is a high degree of consensus and internal intellectual consistency among those adopting the minority position (see Ch. 1). Intellectual activity is like any other human endeavor: cohesive groups outcompete individualist strategies. Indeed, the fundamental truth of this axiom has been central to the success of Judaism throughout its history (PTSDA, Ch. 5).

Indeed, Jewish associational patterns in science go well beyond the cohesive intellectual movements discussed here. Greenwald and Schuh (1994) demonstrated a pattern of ethnic discrimination in scientific citations whereby Jewish authors were 40 percent more likely to cite Jewish authors than were non-Jewish authors. Jewish first authors of scientific papers were also approximately three times more likely to have Jewish coauthors than were non-Jewish first authors. Although the methods used in the study did not allow determination of the direction of discrimination, the findings reported throughout this volume strongly suggest that a large proportion of the discrimination originates with Jewish scientists. This is also suggested by the disproportionate representation of Jewish coauthors, presumably the result of Jewish ingroup associational patterns both as mentors and colleagues. Moreover, where there are proportionate differences in group size, individuals in minority groups are generally more prone to ingroup bias than are majority group members (Mullen, 1991), suggesting that Jews would be more strongly inclined toward ethnic discrimination than gentiles.

Citation by other scientists is an important indication of scholarly accomplishment and is often a key measure used in tenure decisions by universities. As a result, ethnocentric biases in citation patterns are not merely an index of ingroup bias among Jewish scientists; these patterns also have the effect of promoting the careers and reputation of other Jewish scientists. Providing further evidence in this regard, the studies by Kadushin (1974), E. S. Shapiro (1989, 1992), and Torrey (1992) of twentieth-century American intellectuals indicate not only a strong overlap among Jewish background, Jewish ethnic identification, Jewish associational patterns, radical political beliefs, and psychoanalytic influence, but also a pattern of mutual citation and admiration. In Kadushin's study, almost half of the complete sample of elite American intellectuals were Jewish (Kadushin, 1974, p. 23). The sample was based on the most frequent contributors to leading intellectual journals, followed by interviews in which the intellectuals "voted" for another intellectual whom he or she considered most influential in their thinking. Over 40 percent of the Jews in the sample received six or more votes as being most influential, compared to only 15 percent of non-Jews (p. 32).

Jews have also been greatly overrepresented as editors, publishers, and contributors to a variety of radical and liberal periodicals, including *The Nation*, *The New Republic*, *Ramparts*, and *The Progressive* (Rothman & Lichter, 1982/1996, p. 105). In 1974 *The New Republic* (TNR) was purchased by Martin Peretz, son of a "devoted Labor Zionist and right-wing Jabotinskyist" (Alterman, 1992, p. 185) and himself a leftist student activist before moving in the direction of neoconservatism.[139] The only consistent theme in Peretz's career is a devotion to Jewish causes, particularly Israel. He reflects a major theme of Chapter 3 in that he abandoned the New Left when some in the movement condemned Israel as racist and imperialist. During the 1967 Arab-Israeli war, he told Henry Kissinger that his "dovishness stopped at the delicatessen door" (p. 185), and many among his staff feared that all issues would be decided on the basis of what was "good for the Jews" (p. 186). Indeed, one editor was instructed to obtain material from the Israeli embassy for use in TNR editorials. "It is not enough to say that TNR's owner is merely obsessed with Israel; he says so himself. But more importantly, Peretz is obsessed with Israel's critics, Israel's would-be critics, and people who never heard of Israel, but might one day know someone who might someday become a critic" (p. 195).

PSYCHOLOGY OF JEWISH INTELLECTUAL MOVEMENTS

I suppose that in addition to whatever conscious feelings of Jewishness underlie the associational patterns of the New York Intellectuals, there is also an unconscious solidarity that Jews have with other Jews and that facilitates the overlapping alliances and mutual citation patterns discussed here. Greenwald and Schuh (1994) argue that the discrimination effects found in their study of Jewish scientists are unconscious, partly because they find the pattern of Jewish ethnic discrimination among scientists involved in research on prejudice, who, it is plausible to suppose, would not themselves consciously adopt a pattern of ethnic discrimination. In fact, a large body of research indicates unconscious prejudice among people who qualify as unprejudiced on the basis of apparently honest self-reports (Crosby et al., 1980; Gaertner & Dovidio, 1986). These findings fit well with the importance of self-deception as an aspect of Judaism (SAID, Ch. 8): Jewish scientists who perceive themselves to be entirely unprejudiced unconsciously favor ingroup members.

---

[139] Vladimir Jabotinsky (1880–1940) was a radical Zionist prior to the establishment of Israel. He is much admired by the dominant ethnonationalist right in Israel.

Several examples of such deep feelings of Jewish solidarity were given in SAID (Ch. 1), and these feelings were found to be characteristic of Freud in Chapter 5. They are exemplified by the following comments of Clinton administration Secretary of Labor Robert Reich (1997, p. 79) on his first face-to-face meeting with Federal Reserve Board Chairman Alan Greenspan:

> We have never met before, but I instantly know him. One look, one phrase, and I know where he grew up, how he grew up, where he got his drive and his sense of humor. He is New York. He is Jewish. He looks like my uncle Louis, his voice is my uncle Sam. I feel we've been together at countless weddings, bar mitzvahs, and funerals. I know his genetic structure. I'm certain that within the last five hundred years—perhaps even more recently—we shared the same ancestor.

As New York Intellectual Daniel Bell (1961) notes:

> I was born in *galut* [exile] and I accept—now gladly, though once in pain—the double burden and the double pleasure of my self-consciousness, the outward life of an American and the inward secret of the Jew. I walk with this sign as a frontlet between my eyes, and it is as visible to some secret others as their sign is to me.

Theologian Eugene Borowitz (1973, p. 136) writes that Jews seek each other out in social situations and feel "far more at home" after they have discovered who is Jewish.[140] Moreover, "most Jews claim to be equipped with an interpersonal friend-or-foe sensing device that enables them to detect the presence of another Jew, despite heavy camouflage." These deep and typically unconscious ties of genetic similarity (Rushton, 1989) and sense of common fate as members of the same ingroup lead to the powerful group ties among Jewish intellectual and political activists studied throughout this volume.

The theory of individual differences in individualism-collectivism developed in SAID (Ch. 1; see also *Individualism*) predicts that Jews, because of a greater genetic and environmental push toward collectivism, would be especially attracted to such groups. Sulloway (1979b) describes the "cultlike" aura of religion that has permeated psychoanalysis—a characterization that fits well with the evidence that Jews are overrepresented in participating in religious cults (see SAID, Ch. 1). The parallels between traditional Judaism and psychoanalysis as an authoritarian, cohesive ingroup that enforces conformity on

---

[140] I became aware of Borowitz's (1973) interesting account of Jewish self-deception, *The Mask Jews Wear: The Self-Deceptions of American Jewry*, too late for inclusion in Chapter 8 of SAID. It is a good treatment of the complexities of Jewish identity in the post-Enlightenment world, albeit with some self-deceptions of its own, such as its equation of Jewish ethnocentrism with applied morality.

group members thus go well beyond the formal structure of the movement to include a deep sense of personal involvement that satisfies similar psychological needs. From the standpoint of the theory developed in SAID, it is not in the least surprising that the secular organizations developed and dominated by Jews, including radical political movements and Boasian anthropology, would end up appealing to the same psychological systems as did traditional Judaism. At a basic level, Judaism involves a commitment to an exclusionary group that actively maintains barriers between the ingroup and the rest of the world.

This group cohesion is particularly striking in situations where Jewish intellectuals have continued to function as cohesive groups even after anti-Semitism during the National Socialist era forced them to emigrate. This occurred with psychoanalysis and the Frankfurt School. A similar pattern was evident in the highly influential Vienna Circle in philosophy (I. L. Horowitz, 1987).

In the intellectual world, group cohesiveness has facilitated the advocacy of particular viewpoints within academic professional associations (e.g., the Boasian program within the American Anthropological Association; psychoanalysis within the American Psychiatric Association). Sachar (1992, p. 804) notes that the Caucus for a New Politics within the American Political Science Association was "overwhelmingly Jewish" and that the Union of Radical Political Economists was initially disproportionately Jewish. Moreover, as Higham (1984, p. 154) notes, the incredible success of the TAP studies was facilitated by the "extraordinary ascent" of Jews concerned with anti-Semitism in academic social science departments in the post–World War II era.[141]

Rothman and Lichter (1982/1996, pp. 104–105) note that Jews formed and dominated cohesive subgroups with a radical political agenda in several academic societies in the 1960s, including professional associations in economics, political science, sociology, history, education, and literature (e.g., in the Modern Language Association). They also suggest a broad political agenda of Jewish social scientists during this period (p. 104):

> We have already pointed out the weaknesses of some of these studies [on Jewish involvement in radical political movements]. We suspect that many of the "truths" established in other areas of the social sciences during this period suffer from similar weaknesses. Their widespread acceptance . . . may have had as much to do with the changing ethnic and ideological characteristics of those who dominated the social science community as they did with any real advance in knowledge.

It is well known that there is a replication crisis in social psychology, an area that Jewish psychologists have been particularly attracted to. Prof. Lee

---

[141] This is reminiscent of the Galileo Circle discussed in conjunction with the Budapest School of Psychoanalysis discussed in Chapter 5.

Jussim's (2014) *Social Perception and Social Reality: Why Accuracy Dominates Bias and Self-Fulfilling Prophecy* describes several examples of non-replicable findings that have become hugely influential in the field. For example, a study claimed to show 100+ point improvements in IQ scores as the result of expectancy effects, placing these individuals in the top 99.9999999987th percentile; others assumed stereotypes were always wrong and only held by bigoted people. Stereotypes are wrongly believed by many social psychologists to have massive effects that are impervious to individuating information on particular people.

Once an organization becomes dominated by a particular intellectual perspective, there is enormous intellectual inertia created by the fact that the informal networks dominating elite universities serve as gatekeepers for the next generation of scholars. Aspiring intellectuals, whether Jewish or gentile, are subjected to a high level of indoctrination at the undergraduate and graduate levels; there is tremendous psychological pressure to adopt the fundamental intellectual assumptions that lie at the center of the power hierarchy of the discipline. As discussed in Chapter 1, once a Jewish-dominated intellectual movement attains intellectual predominance, it is not surprising that gentiles would be attracted to Jewish intellectuals as members of a socially dominant and prestigious group and as dispensers of valued resources.

Group cohesiveness can also be seen in the development of worshipful cults that have lionized the achievements of group leaders (e.g., Boasian anthropology and psychoanalysis). Similarly, Whitfield (1988, p. 32) summarizes the "ludicrous overpraise" of Zionist scholar Gershom Scholem. Daniel Bell, a Harvard sociologist and leading member of the New York Intellectuals, labeled Scholem's *Sabbatai Sevi: The Mystical Messiah* the most important book of the post-World War II era. Novelist Cynthia Ozick proclaimed:

> There are certain magisterial works of the human mind that alter ordinary comprehension so unpredictably and on so prodigious a scale that culture is set awry and nothing can ever be seen again except in the strange light of that new knowledge . . . an accretion of fundamental insight [that] takes on the power of a natural force. Gershom Scholem's oeuvre has such a force; and its massive keystone, *Sabbatai Sevi*, presses down on the grasping consciousness with the strength not simply of its invulnerable, almost tidal, scholarship, but of its singular instruction in the nature of man. (in Whitfield, 1988, p. 32)

Whitfield (1988, p. 32) comments that "by the time Ozick was done, even Aristotle began to look like an underachiever; even Freud was confined to 'a peephole into a dark chamber,' while Scholem had become elevated into 'a radio telescope monitoring the universe.'"

Apart from ethnic boosterism, perhaps Scholem was viewed as of universal importance because he deliberately downplayed Jewish particularism in his work (see Preface).

Other Examples of Cohesive Groups of Jewish Intellectuals

It is interesting to note other examples of cohesive groups of Jewish intellectuals besides those considered in the previous chapters. In sixteenth-century Spain a concentrated group of converso intellectuals were intimately involved in making the University of Alcalá a bastion of nominalism—a doctrine widely viewed as subversive of religion (González, 1989). George Mosse (1970, p. 172) describes a group of predominantly Jewish leftist intellectuals in the Weimar period that "attained a certain cohesion through the journals it made its own." Similarly, Irving Louis Horowitz (1987, p. 123) describes an "organic group" of Austrian Marxist intellectuals during the pre-World War II period who "shared in common Jewish ancestry if not Zionist persuasions." I. L. Horowitz (p. 124) notes that the Austrian Marxist group and the Frankfurt School had "shared ethnic and religious backgrounds . . . not to mention overlapping networks and cohorts" resulting ultimately from the unity of prewar European German Jewish life.

Another interesting example is a highly cohesive group of neo-Kantian Jewish intellectuals centered at the University of Marburg under the leadership of Hermann Cohen in late nineteenth-century Germany (Schwarzschild, 1979, p. 136). Cohen (1842–1918), who ended his career teaching at a rabbinical seminary, rejected the historicism of the Hegelians and the *völkisch* thinkers in favor of an idealistic version of Kantian rationalism. A primary intellectual goal was to suppose that the ideal Germany must be defined in universal moral terms that rationalized the continued existence of Jewish particularism:

> A Germanism that might demand of me that I surrender my religion and my religious inheritance, I would not acknowledge as an ideal peoplehood in which the power and dignity of the state inhere. . . . [A] Germanism that might demand such a surrender of religious selfhood, or that could even approve of and project it, simply contradicts the world-historical impulsion of Germanism. (in Schwarzschild, 1979, p. 143)

As with the Frankfurt School, there is an absolute ethical imperative that Judaism exist and that Germany not be defined in ethnic terms that would exclude Jews: in Cohen's philosophical utopia, different "socio-historical entities will not so much merge into one as live peaceably and creatively with one another" (Schwarzschild, 1979, p. 145), a version of Horace Kallen's influential model of cultural pluralism reviewed in Chapter 8. Cohen's group was viewed by anti-Semites as having an ethnic agenda, and Schwarzschild (p. 140) notes that "the spirit of Marburg neo-Kantianism was in fact largely determined by the Jewishness of its adherents." A common criticism was that the Marburg School engaged in highly creative reinterpretations of historical texts, notably including interpretations of Judaism and such notoriously ethnocentric Jewish thinkers as Maimonides as representing a universalistic ethical imperative. Suggesting deception or self-deception, there was a tension between Cohen's avowed German nationalism and his pronouncements of great concern for the suffering of Jews in other countries and his urging of other Jews to look to German Jews for guidance (Rather, 1990, pp. 182–183).

During the 1920s, there was "a distinct coterie" of Jewish intellectuals (Lionel Trilling, Herbert Solow, Henry Rosenthal, Tess Slesinger, Felix Morrow, Clifton Fadiman, Anita Brenner) centered around *The Menorah Journal* under the leadership of Elliot Cohen (later the founding editor of *Commentary*) (Wald, 1987, p. 32). This group, which later overlapped a great deal with the New York Intellectuals, was devoted to promoting the ideas of cultural pluralism. (Horace Kallen, the originator of cultural pluralism as a model for the United States—see Ch. 8—was a founder of the Menorah Society.) Reflecting its fundamentally Jewish political agenda, during the 1930s this group gravitated to the Communist Party USA and its auxiliary organizations, believing (at a time when Jews held a dominant position in the Soviet Union) that, in the words of one observer, "the socialist revolution and its extension held out the only realistic hope of saving the Jews, among others, from destruction" (in Wald, 1987, p. 43). Further, while adopting an ideology of revolutionary internationalism, the group "shared with cultural pluralism a hostility to assimilation by the dominant culture" (p. 43)—another indication of the compatibility of leftist universalism and Jewish non-assimilation that is a theme of Chapter 3.

Beginning in the early 1950s there was a group centered around Irving Howe, including Stanley Plastrik, Emanuel Geltman, and Lewis Coser, who organized the magazine *Dissent* as the PR coterie moved steadily away from revolutionary socialism (Bulik, 1993, p. 18). In addition to leftist social criticism, Howe wrote extensively about Yiddish literature and Jewish history; his *World of Our Fathers* records his nostalgic appreciation of the Yiddish-socialist subculture of his youth. *Dissent* was greatly influenced by the Frankfurt School in the area of cultural criticism, particularly the work of Adorno and Horkheimer, and it published work by Erich Fromm and Herbert Marcuse based on their syntheses of Freud and Marx. Finally, in the New Left era, the radical Institute for Policy Studies was centered around a group of Jewish intellectuals (Sachar, 1992, p. 805).

Dedication to Jewish Gurus

As one would expect in a cultlike situation, these movements tended to center around a charismatic leader with a powerful moral, intellectual, and social vision, and the followers of these leaders had an intense devotion toward them. There was an intense psychological sense of missionary zeal and moral fervor. This phenomenon occurred in the case of psychoanalysis and the Boasian movement, and (with massive irony) this was also the case with Critical Theory:

> The theory which filled Adorno and Marcuse with a sense of mission both before and after the war was a theory of a special sort: in the midst of doubts, it was still inspiring, in the midst of pessimism it still spurred them on towards a kind of salvation through knowledge and discovery. The promise was neither fulfilled nor betrayed—it was kept alive. (Wiggershaus, 1994, p. 6)

Jewish communists tended to have Jewish mentors and idealized other Jews, especially Trotsky, who were leaders or martyrs of the cause (see Ch. 3).

Like Freud, Horkheimer inspired intense loyalty in his followers combined with personal insecurity—at least partly because of his control over the budget of the Institute for Social Research (Wiggershaus, 1994, pp. 161–162)—so that his underlings at the Institute, like Adorno, became fixated on him and intensely jealous of their rivals for their master's favors. Adorno "was prepared to identify himself completely with the great cause of the Institute, measuring everything by that standard" (p. 160). When fellow Institute member Leo Lowenthal complained that "Adorno showed a sense of zealousness not far removed from a sense of resentment," Horkheimer commented that this is what he valued in Adorno:

> For [Horkheimer], all that mattered was that [Adorno's] zealous aggressiveness, which was able to detect concessions to the bourgeois academic system in the work of Lowenthal, Marcuse, Fromm, and even more so in the work of others, should be channelled along the right lines, namely those with significance for social theory. (Wiggershaus, 1994, p. 163)

Rallying around charismatic leaders (Leon Trotsky, Rosa Luxemburg, Emma Goldman) has also been apparent among Jewish radicals (see Ch. 3), and the neoconservative movement has sought intellectual inspiration from Leo Strauss rather than from gentile conservative intellectuals such as Edmund Burke, Russell Kirk, or James Burnham (Gottfried, 1993, p. 88). For Strauss as a highly committed Jew, liberalism is only the best of several alternatives that are even more unacceptable (i.e., the extreme left or right). Strauss complains of the assimilatory tendencies in liberal society and its tendencies to break down the group loyalty so central to Judaism and to replace it with "membership in a nonexistent universal human society" (Tarcov & Pangle, 1987, p. 909). Strauss's political philosophy of democratic liberalism was fashioned as an instrument of achieving Jewish group survival in the post-Enlightenment political world (see pp. 909–910). Finally, prior to their abandoning Trotskyism, J. J. Goldberg (1996, p. 160) notes that many future neoconservatives were disciples of Trotskyist theoretician Max Shachtman, also a Jew and a prominent member of the New York Intellectuals (see also Ch. 4; Irving Kristol, 1983, "Memoirs of a Trotskyist," pp. 3–13).

The New York Intellectuals may be an exception because they were relatively decentralized and quite querulous and competitive with each other, with no one rising to the preeminent status of a Freud or Boas. However, like many Jewish leftists, they tended to idolize Trotsky at least early on, and, as we have seen, Sidney Hook played a decisive leadership role in the group (Jumonville, 1991, p. 28). They also constituted a distinct coterie centered around the "little magazines" whose editors wielded great power and influence over the careers of would-be group members. Elliot Cohen, despite his lack of presence as a writer, had a charismatic influence on those who wrote for him as editor of *The Menorah Journal* and *Commentary*. Lionel Trilling labeled him a "tormented 'genius'" (in Jumonville, p. 117), a leader who influenced many, including Trilling himself, in their journey from Stalinism to anti-Stalinism and finally toward the beginning phase of neoconservatism. Prospective members of the ingroup typically idolized ingroup members as cultural icons. Norman Podhoretz (1967, p. 147) writes of his "wide-eyed worshipful fascination" with the PR crowd at the beginning of his career. Ingroup members paid "rapt attention" to others in the group (Cooney, 1986, p. 249). Like different branches of psychoanalysis, there were offshoots of these magazines initiated by people with somewhat different aesthetic or political visions, such as the circle around *Dissent*, whose central figure was Irving Howe.

This tendency to rally around a charismatic leader is also a characteristic of traditional Jewish groups. These groups are extremely collectivist in Triandis's (1990, 1991) sense. The authoritarian nature of these groups and the central role of a charismatic rabbi are particularly striking:

> The haredim's blind obeisance to rabbis is one of the most striking characteristics of haredism in the eyes of the outside world, both Jewish and Gentile. . . . A haredi . . . will consult his rabbi or hasidic rebbe on every aspect of his life, and will obey the advice he receives as though it were an halachic ruling. (Landau, 1993, pp. 45, 47)

Famous rebbes are revered in an almost godlike manner (*tzaddikism*, or cult of personality), and indeed there was a recent controversy over whether the Lubavitcher Rebbe Menachem Mendel Schneerson claimed to be the Messiah. Many of his followers believed that he was; Mintz (1992, pp. 348ff) points out that it is common for Hasidic Jews to view their rebbe as the Messiah.

This intensity of group feeling centered around a charismatic leader is reminiscent of that found among traditional Eastern European Jews who were the immediate ancestors of many of these intellectuals. Zionist leader Arthur Ruppin (1971, p. 69) recounts his visit to a synagogue in Galicia (Poland) in 1903:

> There were no benches, and several thousand Jews were standing closely packed together, swaying in prayer like the corn in the wind. When the rabbi appeared, the service began. Everybody tried to get as close to him as possible. The rabbi led the prayers in a thin, weeping voice. It seemed to arouse a sort of ecstasy in the listeners. They closed their eyes, violently swaying. The loud praying sounded like a gale. Anyone seeing these Jews in prayer would have concluded that they were the most religious people on earth.

Later those closest to the rabbi were intensely eager to eat any food touched by the rabbi, and the fish bones were preserved by his followers as relics.

The Authoritarianism of Jewish Intellectual Movements

In the cases of psychoanalysis and the Frankfurt School, and to a lesser extent Boasian anthropology, we have seen that these cohesive groups typically had strong overtones of authoritarianism, and like traditional Judaism itself, they were highly exclusionary and intolerant of dissent. Cuddihy (1974, p. 106) points out that Wilhelm Reich had the distinction of being expelled from both the German Communist Party (for his "incorrect" view of the causes of fascism) and the psychoanalytic movement (for his political fanaticism): "Reich's attempt to 'marry' two of the Diaspora ideologues, Freud and Marx, ended in his separation from the two movements speaking in their names." Recall also David Horowitz's (1997, p. 42) description of the world of his parents who had joined a "shul" run by the CPUSA; note the ingroup-outgroup mentality, the sense of moral superiority, the sense of being a minority persecuted by the *goyim*, and the powerful overtones of authoritarianism and intolerance of dissent:

> What my parents had done in joining the Communist Party and moving to Sunnyside was to return to the ghetto. There was the same shared private

language, the same hermetically sealed universe, the same dual posturing revealing one face to the outer world and another to the tribe. More importantly, there was the same conviction of being marked for persecution and specially ordained, the sense of moral superiority toward the stronger and more numerous *goyim* outside. And there was the same fear of expulsion for heretical thoughts, which was the fear that riveted the chosen to the faith.

An ingroup-outgroup orientation, noted above as a characteristic of the PR coterie, was apparent also in leftist political groups which were also predominantly Jewish during this period. In the words of PR editor William Phillips (1983, p. 41):

> The Communists were experts at maintaining a fraternal atmosphere that distinguished sharply between insider and outsider. One couldn't just leave; one had to be expelled. And expulsion from the tribe brought into motion a machinery calculated to make the expelled one a complete pariah. Party members were forbidden to talk to the ex-Communist, and a campaign of vilification was unleashed whose intensity varied according to the importance of the expelled person.

We have seen that psychoanalysis dealt with its dissenters in a similar manner.

The Sense of Moral and Intellectual Superiority

As expected on the basis of social identity theory, all these movements appear to have had a strong sense of belonging to an ingroup viewed as intellectually and morally superior and fighting against outgroups seen as morally depraved and as intellectually inferior (e.g., Horkheimer's constant admonition that they were among the "chosen few" destined to develop Critical Theory). Within the ingroup, disagreement was channeled into a narrowly confined intellectual space, and those who overstepped the boundaries were simply excised from the movement. The comments of Eugen Bleuler to Freud when he left the psychoanalytic movement in 1911 are worth quoting again because they describe a central feature of psychoanalysis and the other movements reviewed in this volume: "[T]his 'who is not for us is against us,' this 'all or nothing,' is necessary for religious communities and useful for political parties. I can therefore understand the principle as such, but for science I consider it harmful" (in Gay, 1987, p. 145). All these features are central to traditional Judaism as well and are compatible with proposing that a basic feature of all manifestations of Judaism is a proneness to developing highly collectivist social structures with a strong sense of ingroup-outgroup barriers (see PTSDA, Ch. 8).

The Psychopathology of Dissenters

Another important theme is that psychoanalysis and the TAP studies showed strong overtones of indoctrination: theories were developed in which behavior that did not conform to politically acceptable standards was conceptualized as an indication of psychopathology. This is apparent in the tendency for psychoanalysis to attribute rejection of psychoanalysis itself to various forms of psychopathology, as well as in its general perspective that a pathology-inducing gentile culture was the source of all forms of psychiatric disorder and that anti-Semitism was the sign of a disturbed personality. The TAP studies built on this tradition with their "discovery" that the failure to develop a "liberal personality" and to deeply and sincerely accept liberal political beliefs was a sign of psychopathology resulting from disturbed parent-child relationships.

Indeed, one might note that a common theme of all these movements of cultural criticism is that gentile-dominated social structures are pathogenic. From the psychoanalytic perspective, including the Frankfurt School, human societies fail to meet human needs that are rooted in human nature, with the result that humans develop a variety of psychiatric disorders as a response to abandoning naturalness and harmony with nature. Or, humans are seen as a blank slate on which Western capitalist culture has written greed, gentile ethnocentrism, and other supposed psychiatric disorders (Marxism, Boasian anthropology).

Connections to the Wider Jewish Community

Group cohesion can also be seen in the support these movements have obtained from the wider Jewish community. In Chapter 3 I noted the importance Jewish radicals placed on maintaining ties with the wider Jewish community. The wider Jewish community also provided economic support for psychoanalysis as the preferred form of psychotherapy among Jews (Glazer & Moynihan, 1963/1970), and it provided philanthropic support for institutes of psychoanalysis.

Jews also provided the great majority of the financial support of the University of Frankfurt as a haven for German-Jewish intellectuals beginning in the Wilhelmine period (see W. E. Mosse, 1989, pp. 318ff), and the Institute for Social Research at the University of Frankfurt was established by a Jewish millionaire, Felix Weil, with a specific intellectual-political mission that eventually developed into Critical Theory (Wiggershaus, 1994). In the United States, foundations such as the Stern Family Fund, the Rabinowitz Fund, and the Rubin Foundation provided money for radical underground publications during the 1960s (Sachar, 1992, p. 804). Much earlier, American Jewish capitalists like Jacob Schiff financed Russian radical movements directed at overthrowing the Czar, leading to the period of Jewish dominance in the USSR, and may well have had considerable impact (J. Goldstein, 1990, pp. 26–27; Szajkowski, 1967). Schiff and Paul and Felix Warburg also financially supported the research of Franz Boas (see Ch. 2).

Moreover, Jewish influence in the popular media was an important source of favorable coverage of Jewish intellectual movements, particularly psychoanalysis and 1960s political radicalism (Rothman & Lichter, 1982/1996). Favorable media depictions of psychoanalysis were common during the 1950s, peaking in the mid-1960s when psychoanalysis was at the apex of its influence in the United States (Hale, 1995, p. 289). "Popular images of Freud revealed him as a painstaking observer, a tenacious worker, a great healer, a truly original explorer, a paragon of domestic virtue, the discoverer of personal energy, and a genius" (p. 289). Psychiatrists were portrayed in movies as "humane and effective. The number of Hollywood stars, directors, and producers who were 'in analysis' was legion" (p. 289). An important aspect of this process has been the establishment of journals directed not only at a closed community of academic specialists but also at a wide audience of educated readers and other consumers of the counterculture.

The support of the wider Jewish community can also be seen in the associations between these intellectual movements and Jewish-owned publishing houses, as in the case of the association between the Frankfurt School and the Hirschfeld Publishing Company (Wiggershaus, 1994, p. 2). Similarly, the Straussian neoconservative movement developed access to the mainstream intellectual media. Disciples of Leo Strauss have developed their own publishing and reviewing network, including neoconservative periodicals, Basic Books, and the university presses at Cornell University, Johns Hopkins University, and the University of Chicago (Gottfried, 1993, p. 73).

The Elite Status of Jewish Intellectual Movements

These ideologies were promulgated by the most prestigious institutions, and especially by elite universities and the mainstream media, as the essence of scientific objectivity. The New York Intellectuals, for example, developed ties with elite universities, particularly Harvard, Columbia, the University of Chicago, and the University of California–Berkeley, while psychoanalysis and Boasian anthropology became well entrenched throughout academia. The moral and intellectual elite established by these movements dominated intellectual discourse during a critical period after World War II and leading into the countercultural revolution of the 1960s. These movements dominated intellectual discourse by the time of the sea change in immigration policy in the 1960s (see Ch. 8).

The implication is that individuals receiving a college education during this period were powerfully socialized to adopt liberal-radical cultural and political beliefs. The ideology that ethnocentrism was a form of psychopathology was promulgated by a group that over its long history had arguably been the most ethnocentric group among all the cultures of the world. This ideology was promulgated by strongly identified members of a group whose right to continue to exist as cohesive groups ideally suited to maximizing their own political, economic, and cultural power was never a subject of discussion. However, the failure to adopt these beliefs on the part of gentiles was viewed as an admission of personal inadequacy and an acknowledgment that one was suffering from a condition that would benefit from psychiatric counseling.

The Irrationality of the Jewish Intellectual Movements Reviewed Here

Scientific and intellectual respectability was thus a critical feature of the movements reviewed here. Nevertheless, these intellectual movements have been fundamentally irrational—an irrationality that is most apparent in the entire conduct of psychoanalysis as an authoritarian, quasi-scientific enterprise and in the explicit depiction of science as an instrument of social domination by the Frankfurt School. It is also apparent in the structure of psychoanalysis and radical political ideology, which are, like traditional Jewish religious ideology, essentially hermeneutic theories in the sense that the theory is derived in an *a priori* manner and is constructed so that any event is interpretable within the theory. The paradigm is shifted from a scientific perspective that emphasizes the selective retention of theoretical variants (Campbell, 1987; Hull, 1988; Popper, 1963) to a hermeneutic exercise in which any and all events can be interpreted within the context of the theory. In the case of Critical Theory and, to a considerable extent, psychoanalysis, the actual content of the theory continually changed and there was divergence among its practitioners, but the function of the theory as a tool of leftist social criticism remained intact.

Despite the fundamental irrationality of these movements, they have often masqueraded as the essence of scientific or philosophical objectivity. They have all sought the aura of science. Hollinger (1996, p. 160) described what he termed "a secular, increasingly Jewish, decidedly left-of-center intelligentsia based largely but not exclusively in the disciplinary communities of philosophy and the social sciences."

[S]cience offered itself to [Harvard historian Richard] Hofstadter [see Ch. 6] and to many of his secular contemporaries as a magnificent ideological resource. Or, to put the point more sharply, these men and women selected from the available inventory those images of science most useful to them, those serving to connect the adjective *scientific* with public rather than private knowledge, with open rather than closed discourses, with universal rather than local standards of warrant, with democratic rather than aristocratic models of authority). Harvard sociologist Nathan Glazer included himself and the other New York Intellectuals in his statement that "sociology is still for many socialists and sociologists the pursuit of politics through academic means." (in Jumonville, 1991, p. 89).

Jumonville (1991, p. 90) comments:

Part of the impact of the New York group on American intellectual life is that they dignified that outlook of political pursuit. They were never embarrassed to admit the political content of their work, and in fact brought into the intellectual mainstream the idea that all strong work had ideological and political overtones.

Even the Frankfurt School, which developed an ideology in which science, politics, and morality were systematically conflated, presented TAP as a scientifically based, empirically grounded study of human behavior because of a perceived need to appeal to an American audience of empirically oriented social scientists. Moreover, the rhetoric of the Institute for Social Research never failed to emphasize the scientific nature of its undertaking. Carl Grünberg, the first director of the Institute, very self-consciously attempted to dispel the suspicion that the Institute was committed to a dogmatic, political form of Marxism. It was committed, he maintained, to a clearly articulated scientific research methodology:

I need not emphasize the fact that when I speak of Marxism here I do not mean it in a party-political sense, but in a purely scientific one, as a term for an economic system complete in itself, for a particular ideology and for a clearly delineated research methodology. (in Wiggershaus, 1994, p. 26)

Similarly, the PR group portrayed itself as being on the side of science, as exemplified by PR editor William Phillips, whose list of "scientists" included Marx, Lenin, and Trotsky (Cooney, 1986, pp. 155, 194).

Philosophical Skepticism Aimed at Combatting Theories
and Data Disliked for Political/Ethnic Reasons

Particularly important in this general endeavor has been the use of a rationally argued, philosophical skepticism as a tool in combating scientific universalism. Skepticism in the interest of combating scientific theories one dislikes for political or ethnic reasons has been a prominent aspect of twentieth-century Jewish intellectual activity, apparent not only as a defining feature of Boasian anthropology but also in much anti-evolutionary theorizing and in the developmental contextualist view of behavioral development discussed in Chapter 2. In general this skepticism has been aimed at precluding the development of general theories of human behavior in which genetic variation plays a causative role in producing behavioral or psychological variation or in which adaptationist processes play an important role in the development of the human mind. The apotheosis of radical skepticism can be seen in the "negative dialectics" of the Frankfurt School and in Jacques Derrida's philosophy of deconstruction, both of which are directed at deconstructing universalist, assimilatory theories of society as a homogeneous, harmonious whole on the grounds that such a society might be incompatible with the continuity of Judaism. As in the case of Jewish political activity described in Chapter 8 on Jewish involvement in promoting immigration, the effort is aimed at preventing the development of mass movements of solidary groups of gentiles and a repetition of the Holocaust.

The fundamental insight of the Frankfurt School and its recent postmodernist offshoots, as well as the Boasian school of anthropology and much of the criticism of biological and evolutionary perspectives in the social sciences reviewed in Chapter 2, is that a thoroughgoing skepticism and its consequent fragmentation of intellectual discourse within the society as a whole is an excellent prescription for the continuity of collectivist minority group strategies. Within the intellectual world, the greatest potential danger for a collectivist minority group strategy is that science itself as an individualist enterprise conducted in an atomistic universe of discourse could in fact coalesce around a set of universalist propositions about human behavior, propositions that would call into question the moral and intellectual bases of collectivist minority group strategies such as Judaism. One way to prevent this is for science itself to be problematized and replaced by a pervasive skepticism about the structure of all reality.

The intended effect of such movements (and to a considerable extent their actual effect) has been to impose a medieval, anti-scientific orthodoxy on much of the contemporary intellectual world. Unlike the Christian medieval orthodoxy which was fundamentally anti-Semitic, it is an orthodoxy that simultaneously facilitates the continuation of Judaism as a group evolutionary strategy, deemphasizes Judaism as an intellectual or social category, and deconstructs the intellectual basis for the development of majoritarian gentile group strategies.

Real Science as an Individualist Undertaking

None of this should be surprising to an evolutionist. Intellectual activity in the service of evolutionary goals has been a characteristic of Judaism dating from the ancient world (see SAID, Ch. 7). In this regard it is no accident that science has developed uniquely in Western individualistic societies (*Individualism*). Science is fundamentally an individualistic phenomenon incompatible with high levels of the ingroup-outgroup thinking that have characterized the Jewish intellectual movements discussed in these chapters and indeed have come to characterize much of what currently passes as intellectual discourse in the West—especially postmodernism and the currently fashionable multicultural movement and critical race theory.

Scientific groups do not have essences in the sense that there are no essential group members and no essential propositions one must subscribe to in order to be a group member (Hull, 1988, p. 512). In the movements reviewed here, however, both of these essentialist propositions appear to be true. For example, whereas, as Hull suggests, even Darwin could have absented himself or been ejected from scientific studies of evolution without the evolutionary program losing its identity, I rather doubt that Freud could have been similarly ejected from the psychoanalytic movement without fundamentally changing the focus of the movement. In a comment that indicates the fundamentally individualist nature of scientific communities, Hull notes that although each individual scientist has his or her own view of the essential nature of the conceptual system, the adoption of such an essentialist perspective by the community as a whole could only prevent the conceptual growth characteristic of real science.

This individualistic conceptualization of science is highly compatible with work in the philosophy of science. A fundamental issue in the philosophy of science is to describe the type of discourse community that promotes scientific thinking in any area of endeavor. As phrased by Donald Campbell (1993, p. 97), the question is "which social systems of belief revision and belief retention would be most likely to improve the competence-of-reference of beliefs to their presumed referents?" I propose that a minimal requirement of a scientific social system is that science not be conducted from an ingroup-outgroup perspective. Scientific progress (Campbell's "competence-of-reference") depends on an individualistic, atomistic universe of discourse in which each individual sees himself or herself not as a member of a larger political or cultural entity advancing a particular point of view but as an independent agent endeavoring to evaluate evidence and discover the structure of reality. As Campbell (1986, pp. 121–122) notes, a critical feature of science as it evolved in the seventeenth century was that individuals were independent agents who could each replicate scientific findings for themselves. Scientific opinion certainly coalesces around certain propositions in real science (e.g., the structure of DNA, the mechanisms of reinforcement), but this scientific consensus is highly prone to defection in the event new data cast doubt on presently held theories. Thus Barker and Gholson (1984) show that the long rivalry between cognitivist and behaviorist positions in psychology essentially hinged on the results of key experiments that resulted in defection or recruitment to these positions within the psychological community. Arthur Jensen (1982, p. 124) summarizes this view well when he notes that "when many individual scientists . . . are all able to think as they please and do their research unfettered by collectivist or totalitarian constraints, science is a self-correcting process."

Each individual participant in a real science must view himself or herself as a free agent who is continually evaluating the available evidence to arrive at the best possible current understanding of reality. A variety of extra-scientific influences may affect individual scientists in conducting and evaluating research results, such as the need not to offend one's superior or give comfort to a rival research group (Campbell, 1993). A real scientist, however, must self-consciously attempt to remove at least the influence of personal relationships, group ties, gender, social class, political and moral agendas, and even career advancement possibilities. Real scientists change their beliefs based on evidence and are willing to abandon presently held beliefs if they conflict with the evidence (Hull, 1988, p. 19).

The assumption is that by honestly endeavoring to remove these influences, scientific consensus increasingly coalesces around propositions in which the referents of scientific propositions have an important role in the creation of scientific belief. As Stove (1982, p. 3) notes, despite resistance to the proposition in a large part of the intellectual world, there has been an enormous growth of knowledge in the past four hundred years. Nevertheless, consensual progress in the social sciences has not occurred, and as noted above, there is a replication crisis in psychology, particularly in politically sensitive areas. I doubt that consensual progress will occur until research ceases to be conducted from an ingroup-outgroup perspective.

In the movements reviewed here, intellectual endeavor had strong overtones of social group solidarity, as individual participants could always count on others to hold similar views and to present a united front against any unwelcome data. One consequence of the group conflict in the Iberian Peninsula during the period of the Inquisition was that science became impossible (Castro, 1971, p. 576; Haliczer, 1989). The ideology supporting the Inquisition, including theologically derived views of the nature of physical reality, became an aspect of a collectivist worldview in which any deviation from the established ideology was viewed as treason to the group. Science requires the possibility and intellectual respectability of committing treason; or rather, it requires the impossibility of treason because there is an implicit understanding that one's views of reality are not a function of group allegiance but of one's independent (individualistic) evaluation of the available evidence.

In a real science the fundamental structure of reality cannot be decided *a priori* and protected from empirical disconfirmation, as is the case whenever groups develop a political stake in a particular interpretation of reality. Yet this is precisely what occurred during the Inquisition and the period of medieval Christian religious orthodoxy, and it has been the case in all the intellectual movements reviewed here (as well as in much of the Jewish historiography reviewed in SAID, Ch. 7). Because the movements reviewed here have had an underlying Jewish political agenda, the essential doctrines and the direction of research were developed *a priori* to conform to those interests. And because of the fundamental irrationality of the ideologies involved, the only form these movements could take was that of an authoritarian ingroup that would simply excise dissenters from the group. Within these movements the route to a successful career involved—as a necessary condition—authoritarian submission to the fundamental tenets of the intellectual movement.

Nevertheless, at times the situation is more complicated, and even participation in a real scientific culture can also be used to advance Jewish ethnic interests. In Chapter 2 it was noted that the empirical research of Harvard population biologist R. C. Lewontin uses methods condemned by the extreme methodological purism with which he has opposed several evolutionary and biological approaches to human behavior. It is interesting in this regard that Lewontin (1994a) appears to be aware that participation in a truly scientific culture creates a "bank account of legitimacy which we can then spend on our political and humanist pursuits." Lewontin has therefore established a reputation in a real scientific community (population genetics) and then used that reputation to advance his ethnic agenda, part of which is to insist on a methodological rigor that is incompatible with social science. Even real science can be converted into political currency.

Conflating Truth and Consensus

At a deeper level, I suppose, a fundamental aspect of Jewish intellectual history has been the realization that there is no demonstrable difference between truth and consensus. Within traditional Jewish religious discourse, "truth" was the prerogative of a privileged interpretive elite that in traditional societies consisted of the scholarly class within the Jewish community. Within this community, "truth" and "reality" were nothing more (and were undoubtedly perceived as nothing more) than consensus within a sufficiently large portion of the interpretive community.

> Without the community we cannot ascribe any real meaning to notions like the word of God or holiness. Canonization of Holy Scripture takes place only in the context of the understanding of those scriptures by a community. Nor can scripture be holy for an individual alone without a community. The holiness of writ depends upon a meaning that is "really there" in the text. Only the communal reading-understanding of the texts makes their meaning, the meaning that is capable of being called holy, as real as the community itself. (Agus, 1997, p. 34)

As we have seen in SAID (Ch. 7), Jewish religious ideology was an infinitely plastic set of propositions that could rationalize and interpret any event in a manner compatible with serving the interests of the community. Authority within the Jewish intellectual community was always understood to be based entirely on what recognized (i.e., consensual) scholars had said. It never occurred to the members of this discourse community to seek confirmation of their views from outside the discourse community itself, either from other (gentile) discourse communities or by trying to understand the nature of reality itself. Reality was whatever the group decided it should be, and any dissent from this socially constructed reality would have to be performed within a narrow intellectual space that would not endanger the overall goals of the group or risk expulsion.

Acceptance of the Jewish canon, like membership in the intellectual movements reviewed here, was essentially an act of authoritarian submission. The basic genius of the Jewish intellectual activity reviewed in these chapters is the realization that hermeneutic communities based solely on intellectual consensus within a committed group are possible even within the post-Enlightenment world of intellectual discourse and may even be successfully disseminated within the wider gentile community to facilitate specific Jewish political interests.

The difference from the pre-Enlightenment world, of course, is that these intellectual discourses were forced to develop a façade of science in order to appeal to gentiles. Or, in the case of the skeptical thrust of Derrida's philosophy of deconstruction and the Frankfurt School Critical Theory (but not involvement in activities such as TAP), it was necessary to defend the viability of philosophical skepticism. The scientific veneer and philosophical respectability sought by these movements then functioned to portray these intellectual movements as the result of individualistic free choice based on rational appraisals of the evidence. This in turn necessitated that great efforts were required to mask Jewish involvement and domination of the movements, as well as the extent to which the movements sought to attain specific Jewish political interests.

Such efforts at deemphasizing Jewish involvement have been most apparent in radical political movements and psychoanalysis, but they are also apparent in Boasian anthropology. Although the Jewish political agenda of the Frankfurt School was far less camouflaged, even here an important aspect of the program was the development of a body of theory applicable to any universalist conception of society and not in any way dependent on the articulation of a specifically Jewish political agenda. As a result, this ideological perspective and its postmodern descendants have been enthusiastically embraced by non-Jewish minority group intellectuals with their own political agendas.

The phenomenon is a good example of the susceptibility of Western individualist societies to invasion by cohesive collectivist groups of any kind. I have noted a strong historical tendency for Judaism to prosper in Western individualist societies and to decline in Eastern or Western collectivist societies (see SAID, Chs. 3–5; PTSDA, Ch. 8). Jews benefit greatly from open, individualistic societies in which barriers to upward mobility are absent and in which intellectual discourse is not prescribed by gentile-dominated institutions like the Catholic Church. But, as Charles Liebman (1973, p. 157) points out, Jews "sought the options of the Enlightenment but rejected its consequences" by (in my terms) retaining a strong sense of group identity in a society nominally committed to individualism. Individualist societies develop republican political institutions and institutions of scientific inquiry that assume that groups are maximally permeable and highly subject to defection when individual needs are not being met. Individualists have little loyalty to ingroups and tend not to see the world in terms of ingroups and outgroups. There is a strong tendency to see others as individuals and evaluate them as individuals, even when the others are acting as part of a collectivist group (Triandis, 1995).

As a result, intellectual movements that are highly collectivist may come to be regarded by outsiders in individualistic societies as the result of individualistic, rational choice of free agents. Evidence suggests that Jews have been concerned to portray Jewish intellectual movements as the result of enlightened free choice. Thus Jewish social scientists were instrumental in portraying Jewish involvement in radical political causes as "the free choice of a gifted minority" (Rothman & Lichter, 1982/1996, p. 118), and I have noted the role of the media in portraying Freud as a tireless seeker of truth. Yet because of their collective, highly focused efforts and energy, these groups can be much more influential than the atomized, fragmented efforts of individuals. The efforts of individualists can easily be ignored, marginalized, or anathematized; in contrast, the collectivity continues to dominate intellectual discourse because of its cohesiveness and its control of the means of intellectual production. In the long run, however, there is reason to believe that the Western commitment to individualism depends on the absence of powerful and cohesive collectivist groups acting within society (SAID, Chs. 3–5).

It is of some importance that none of the post-Enlightenment intellectual movements reviewed here developed a specific positive rationale for continued Jewish identification. The material reviewed in this volume indicates that such an ideological rationale will not be forthcoming because, in a very basic sense, Judaism represents the antithesis of the Enlightenment values of individualism and its correlative scientific intellectual discourse. In the economic and social sphere, Judaism represents the possibility of a powerful, cohesive group ethnic strategy that provokes anti-individualist reactions in gentile outgroups and threatens the viability of individualist political and social institutions. In the intellectual sphere, Judaism has resulted in collectivist enterprises that have systematically impeded inquiry in the social sciences in the interests of developing and disseminating theories directed at achieving specific political and social interests.

It is thus not surprising that although these movements were directed at achieving specific Jewish interests in the manipulation of culture, they "could not tell their name"; that is, they were forced to minimize any overt indication that Jewish group identity or Jewish group interests were involved, and they could not develop a specific rationale for Judaism acceptable within a post-Enlightenment intellectual context. In SAID (Ch. 2) I noted that the Jewish contribution to the wider gentile culture in nineteenth-century Germany was accomplished from a highly particularistic perspective in which Jewish group identity continued to be of paramount subjective importance despite its "invisibility." Similarly, because of the need for invisibility, the theories and movements discussed here were forced to deemphasize Judaism as a social category—a form of crypsis discussed extensively in SAID (Ch. 6) as a common Jewish technique in combating anti-Semitism. In the case of the Frankfurt School, "What strikes the current observer is the intensity with which many of the Institute's members denied, and in some cases still deny, any meaning at all to their Jewish identities" (Jay, 1973, p. 32). The originators and practitioners of these theories attempted to conceal their Jewish identities, as in the case of Freud, and to engage in massive self-deception, as appears to have been common among many Jewish political radicals. Recall the Jewish radicals who believed in their own invisibility as Jews while nevertheless appearing as the quintessential ethnics to outside observers and at the same time taking steps to ensure that gentiles would have highly visible positions in the movement (Ch. 3). The technique of having gentiles as highly visible exemplars of Jewish-dominated movements has been commonly used by Jewish groups attempting to appeal to gentiles on a wide range of Jewish issues (SAID, Ch. 6) and is apparent in the discussion of Jewish involvement in influencing immigration policy in the following chapter. As an additional example, Irving Louis Horowitz (1993, p. 91) contrasts the "high-profile," special interest pleading of the new ethnic and sexual minorities within sociology with the Jewish tendency toward a low-profile strategy. Although Jews dominated American sociology beginning in the 1930s, specifically Jewish interests and political agendas were never made salient.

Given this history, it is highly ironic that Jewish neoconservative intellectuals have been in the forefront demanding that social science accept a scientific paradigm rather than the subjectivist, anti-science racialist ideologies typical of recent multiculturalist ideologues. Thus I. L. Horowitz (1993) shows that Jews dominated American sociology beginning in the 1930s and were instrumental in the decline of Darwinian paradigms and the rise of conflict models of society based on radical political theory. I. L. Horowitz notes, however, that this Jewish domination of sociology is now threatened by affirmative action hiring policies that place a cap on the number of Jews admitted to the profession as well as by the anti-Semitism and the politically motivated research agendas of these new ethnic minorities that increasingly influence the profession. Faced with this state of affairs, I. L. Horowitz (p. 92) makes a plea for a scientific, individualist sociology: "Jewish survival and growth are best served in a democratic polity and by a scientific community."

Evolution and Culture

The material reviewed here is highly relevant to developing a theory of how human evolved psychology interfaces with cultural messages. Evolutionists have shown considerable interest in cultural evolution and its relation to organic evolution.[142] Dawkins (1976), for example, developed the idea of "memes" as replicating cultural units transmitted within societies. Memes may be adaptive or maladaptive for the individuals or the societies that adopt them. In terms of the present undertaking, the Jewish intellectual and political movements reviewed here may be viewed as propagating memes designed to facilitate the continued existence of Judaism as a group evolutionary strategy; their adaptiveness for gentiles who adopt them is highly questionable, however, and, indeed, it is unlikely that a gentile who believes that, for example, anti-Semitism is necessarily a sign of a pathological personality is behaving adaptively.

The question is, what evolved features of the human mind make people likely to adopt memes that are inimical to their own interests? On the basis of the material reviewed here, one critical component appears to be that these

---

[142] For example, the Cultural Evolution Society was established in 2015; in addition to the theory embedded in *CofC*, I have written scholarly papers in the area: see MacDonald, 2009b, 2010.

memes are promulgated from highly prestigious sources, suggesting that one feature of our evolved psychology is a greater proneness to adopt cultural messages deriving from people and individuals with high social status. Social learning theory has long been aware of the tendency for models to be more effective if they have prestige and high status, and this tendency fits well with an evolutionary perspective in which seeking high social status is a universal feature of the human mind (MacDonald, 1988a). Like other modeling influences, therefore, maladaptive memes are best promulgated by individuals and institutions with high social status, and we have seen that a consistent thread of the Jewish intellectual movements reviewed here has been that they have been promulgated by individuals representing society's most prestigious intellectual and media institutions, and that they have attempted to cloak themselves with the mantle of science because of the high status of science. Individuals such as Freud have become cultural icons—true cultural heroes. The memes emanating from his thought, therefore, have a much greater opportunity to take root in the culture as a whole.

Also relevant is that the movements reviewed here typically operated in an atmosphere of Jewish crypsis or semi-crypsis in the sense that the Jewish political agenda was not an aspect of their theories and the theories themselves had no overt Jewish content. Gentile intellectuals approaching these theories were therefore unlikely to view them as aspects of Jewish-gentile cultural competition or as an aspect of a specifically Jewish political agenda; to the contrary, they were more likely to view the promulgators of these theories as "just like themselves"—as individualists seeking scientifically grounded truth about humans and their societies. Viewing others as "just like themselves" appears to be a particular conceit of the individualist cultures of the West, apparent, for example, in nineteenth-century American Protestants who thought that people of different religions and even different races would eventually become proper Protestants like themselves (see *Individualism*, Ch. 6).

Social psychological theory has long known that similarity is highly conducive to liking, and this phenomenon is susceptible to an evolutionary analysis (Rushton, 1989). The proposal is that if these theories had been promulgated by traditionally Orthodox Jews, with their different modes of dress and patterns of speech, they never would have had the cultural impact that they in fact had. From this perspective, Jewish crypsis and semi-crypsis are essential to the success of Judaism in post-Enlightenment societies—a theme discussed in SAID (Ch. 9).

Evolved mechanisms that facilitate the acceptance of maladaptive ideologies among gentiles are not the whole story, however. In SAID (Ch. 8) I noted a general tendency for self-deception among Jews as a robust pattern apparent in several historical eras and touching on a wide range of issues, including personal identity, the causes and extent of anti-Semitism, the characteristics of

Jews (e.g., economic success), and the role of Jews in the political and cultural process in traditional and contemporary societies. Self-deception may well be important in facilitating Jewish involvement in the movements discussed here. I have noted evidence for this in the case of Jewish political radicals (see Ch. 3), and Greenwald and Schuh (1994) persuasively argue that the ingroup ethnic bias exhibited by their sample of researchers on prejudice is not conscious. Many of the Jews involved in the movements reviewed here may sincerely believe that these movements are really divorced from specifically Jewish interests or are in the best interests of other groups as well as Jews. They may sincerely believe that they are not biased in their associational patterns or in their patterns of citation in scientific articles, but as Trivers (1985) notes, the best deceivers are those who are self-deceived.

Finally, theories of social influence deriving from social psychology are also relevant and may yield to an evolutionary analysis. I have suggested that the memes generated by these Jewish intellectual movements achieve their influence, at least at first, because of the processes of minority group influence. The issue of whether this aspect of social psychology may be viewed as part of the evolved design features of the human mind remains to be researched.

8

Jewish Involvement in Shaping U.S. Immigration Policy

Today, . . . the immigrants—above all the Jewish immigrants—seem more Ameri-
can than [the WASP] does. They are the faces and voices and inflections of thought
that seem most familiar to us, literally second nature. [The WASP] is the odd ball,
the stranger, the fossil. We glance at him, a bit startled and say to ourselves,
"Where did he go?" We remember him: pale, poised, neatly dressed, briskly sure
of himself. And we see him as an outsider, an outlander, a reasonably noble breed
in the act of vanishing. . . . He has stopped being representative, and we didn't
notice it until this minute. Not so emphatically, anyway.

What has happened since World War II is that the American sensibility has
become part Jewish, perhaps as much Jewish as it is anything else. . . . The literate
American mind has come in some measure to think Jewishly. It has been taught
to, and it was ready to. After the entertainers and novelists came the Jewish crit-
ics, politicians, theologians. Critics and politicians and theologians are by pro-
fession molders; they form ways of seeing.

— Walter Kerr, 1968, pp. D1, D3

Immigration policy is a paradigmatic example of conflicts of interest between ethnic groups because immigration policy determines the future demographic composition of the nation. Ethnic groups unable to influence immigration policy in their own interests will eventually be displaced by groups able

481

to accomplish this goal. Immigration policy is thus of fundamental interest to an evolutionist.

This chapter discusses ethnic conflict between Jews and gentiles in the area of immigration policy. Immigration policy is, however, only one aspect of conflicts of interest between Jews and gentiles in the United States. The skirmishes between Jews and the gentile power structure beginning in the late nineteenth century always had strong overtones of anti-Semitism. These battles involved issues of Jewish upward mobility, quotas on Jewish representation in elite universities beginning in the nineteenth century and peaking in the 1920s and 1930s, and the anti-communist crusades in the post-World War II era, as well as the very powerful concern with the cultural influences of the major media, extending from Henry Ford's writings in the 1920s to the Hollywood inquisitions of the McCarthy era and into the contemporary era (SAID, Ch. 2). That anti-Semitism was involved in these issues can be seen by the fact that historians of Judaism (e.g., Sachar, 1992, pp. 620ff) feel compelled to include accounts of these events as important to the history of Jews in the United States, by the anti-Semitic pronouncements of many of the gentile participants, and by the self-conscious understanding of Jewish participants and observers.

The Jewish involvement in influencing immigration policy in the United States is especially noteworthy as an aspect of ethnic conflict. Jewish involvement in influencing immigration policy has had certain unique qualities that have distinguished Jewish interests from the interests of other groups favoring liberal immigration policies. Throughout much of the period from 1881 to 1965, one Jewish interest in liberal immigration policies stemmed from a desire to provide a sanctuary for Jews fleeing from anti-Semitic persecutions in Europe and elsewhere. Anti-Semitic persecutions have been a recurrent phenomenon in the modern world beginning with the Russian pogroms of 1881 and continuing into the post-World War II era in the Soviet Union and Eastern Europe. As a result, liberal immigration has been a Jewish interest because "survival often dictated that Jews seek refuge in other lands" (N. W. Cohen, 1972, p. 341). For a similar reason, Jews have consistently advocated an internationalist foreign policy because "an internationally-minded America was likely to be more sensitive to the problems of foreign Jewries" (p. 342).

There is also evidence that Jews, much more than any other European-derived ethnic group in the United States, have viewed liberal immigration policies as a mechanism of ensuring that the United States would be a pluralistic rather than a unitary, homogeneous society (e.g., N. W. Cohen, 1972). Pluralism serves both internal (within-group) and external (between-group) Jewish interests. Pluralism serves internal Jewish interests because it legitimizes the internal Jewish interest in rationalizing and openly advocating an interest in overt   rather   than   semi-cryptic   Jewish   group   commitment   and nonassimilation, what Howard Sachar (1992, p. 427) terms its function in "legitimizing the preservation of a minority culture in the midst of a majority's host society." Both Neusner (1993) and Ellman (1987) suggest that the increased sense of ethnic consciousness seen in Jewish circles has been influenced by this general movement within American society toward the legitimization of cultural pluralism and minority group ethnocentrism. This trend toward overt rather than the semi-cryptic forms that have characterized Judaism in twentieth-century Western societies is viewed by many as critical to the continuity of Judaism (e.g., E. Abrams, 1997; Dershowitz, 1997; see SAID, Ch. 8). A 1998 conference of Reform rabbis emphasized that the upsurge in traditionalism is partly the result of the increasing legitimacy of ethnic consciousness in general (Schrader, 1998).

Ethnic and religious pluralism also serve external Jewish interests because Jews become just one of many ethnic groups. This results in the diffusion of political and cultural influence among the various ethnic and religious groups, and it becomes difficult or impossible to develop unified, cohesive groups of gentiles united in their opposition to Judaism. Historically, major anti-Semitic movements have tended to erupt in societies that have been, apart from the Jews, religiously or ethnically homogeneous (see SAID). Conversely, one reason for the relative lack of anti-Semitism in the United States compared to Europe was that "Jews did not stand out as a solitary group of [religious] non-conformists" (Higham, 1984, p. 156). Although ethnic and cultural pluralism are certainly not guaranteed to satisfy Jewish interests (see Ch. 9), it is nonetheless the case that ethnically and religiously pluralistic societies have been perceived by Jews as more likely to satisfy Jewish interests than are societies characterized by ethnic and religious homogeneity among gentiles.

Indeed, at a basic level, the motivation for all of the Jewish intellectual and political activity reviewed throughout this volume is intimately linked to fears of anti-Semitism. Svonkin (1997, pp. 8ff) shows that a sense of "uneasiness" and insecurity pervaded American Jewry in the wake of World War II even in the face of evidence that anti-Semitism had declined to the point that it had become a marginal phenomenon. As a direct result, "The primary objective of the Jewish intergroup relations agencies [i.e., the AJCommittee, the AJCongress, and the ADL] after 1945 was ... to prevent the emergence of an anti-Semitic reactionary mass movement in the United States" (Svonkin, 1997, p. 8).

Writing in the 1970s, Isaacs (1974, pp. 14ff) describes the pervasive insecurity of American Jews and their hypersensitivity to anything that might be deemed anti-Semitic. Interviewing "noted public men" on the subject of anti-Semitism in the early 1970s, Isaacs asked, "Do you think it could happen here?"

Never was it necessary to define "it." In almost every case, the reply was approximately the same: "If you know history at all, you have to presume not that it could happen, but that it probably will," or "It's not a matter of if; it's a matter of when." (Isaacs, 1974, p. 15)

Isaacs, correctly in my view, attributes the intensity of Jewish involvement in politics to this fear of anti-Semitism. Jewish activism on immigration is merely one aspect of a multipronged movement directed at preventing the development of a mass movement of anti-Semitism in Western societies. Other aspects of this program are briefly reviewed below.

Explicit statements linking immigration policy to a Jewish interest in cultural pluralism can be found among prominent Jewish social scientists and political activists. In his review of Horace Kallen's (1956) *Cultural Pluralism and the American Idea* appearing in *Congress Weekly* (published by the AJCongress), Joseph L. Blau (1958, p. 15) noted that "Kallen's view is needed to serve the cause of minority groups and minority cultures in this nation without a permanent majority"—the implication being that Kallen's ideology of multiculturalism opposes the interests of any ethnic group in dominating the United States. The well-known author and prominent Zionist Maurice Samuel (1924/2022, p. 215), writing partly as a negative reaction to the Immigration Act of 1924, wrote:

If, then, the struggle between us [i.e., Jews and gentiles] is ever to be lifted beyond the physical, your democracies will have to alter their demands for racial, spiritual and cultural homogeneity within the State. But it would be foolish to regard this as a possibility, for the tendency of this civilization is in the opposite direction. There is a steady approach toward the identification of government with race, instead of with the political State.

Samuel (1924/2022, pp. 218–220) deplored the Immigration Act of 1924 as violating his conceptualization of the United States as a purely political entity with no ethnic implications:

We have just witnessed, in America, the repetition, in the peculiar form adapted to this country, of the evil farce to which the experience of many centuries has not yet quite accustomed us. If America had any meaning at all, it lay in the peculiar attempt to rise above the trend of our present civilization—the identification of race with State. . . . America was therefore the New World in this vital respect—that the State was purely an ideal, and nationality was identical only with acceptance of the ideal. But it seems now that the entire point of view was a mistaken one, that America was incapable of rising above her origins, and the semblance of an ideal-nationalism was only a stage in the proper development of the universal gentile spirit. . . . To-day, with race triumphant over ideal, anti-Semitism uncovers its fangs, and to the heartless refusal of the most elementary human right, the right of asylum, is added cowardly insult. We are not only

excluded, but we are told, in the unmistakable language of the immigration laws, that we are an "inferior" people. Without the moral courage to
stand up squarely to its evil instincts, the country prepared itself, through
its journalists, by a long draught of vilification of the Jew, and, when sufficiently inspired by the popular and "scientific" potions, committed the
act.

A congruent opinion is expressed by prominent Jewish social scientist and
ethnic activist Earl Raab, who remarks very positively on the success of American immigration policy in altering the ethnic composition of the United States
since 1965.[143] Raab notes that the Jewish community has taken a leadership role
in changing the Northwestern European bias of American immigration policy
(1993a), and he has also maintained that one factor inhibiting anti-Semitism in
the contemporary United States is that "an increasing ethnic heterogeneity, as
a result of immigration, has made it even more difficult for a political party or
mass movement of bigotry to develop" (1995, p. 91). Or more colorfully:

> The Census Bureau has just reported that about half of the American pop-
> ulation will soon be non-white or non-European. And they will all be
> American citizens. We have tipped beyond the point where a Nazi-Aryan
> party will be able to prevail in this country.
>
> We [Jews] have been nourishing the American climate of opposition
> to bigotry for about half a century. That climate has not yet been per-
> fected, but the heterogeneous nature of our population tends to make it
> irreversible—and makes our constitutional constraints against bigotry
> more practical than ever. (Raab, 1993b)

Boston Globe writer S. I. Rosenbaum claimed in 2019 that the main lesson
of "the Holocaust" is "that white supremacy could turn on us at any moment"
and that the strategy of appealing to the White majority "has never worked for
us. It didn't protect us in Spain, or England, or France, or Germany. There's no
reason to think it will work now." The central question of Jewish political engagement in Western societies, Rosenbaum insisted, is "how we survive as a
minority population," where the one great advantage American Jewry enjoys is
that "unlike other places where ethno-nationalism has flourished, the U.S. is
fast approaching a plurality of minorities." Presiding over a coalition of non-

---

[143] Raab was associated with the ADL and was executive director emeritus of the Perlmutter
Institute for Jewish Advocacy at Brandeis University. He was also a columnist for the San Francisco *Jewish Bulletin*. Among other works, he has co-authored, with Seymour Martin Lipset,
The Politics of Unreason: Right-Wing Extremism in America, 1790–1970 (1970), a volume in a
series of books on anti-Semitism in the United States sponsored by the ADL and discussed in
Chapter 6. Lipset is regarded as a member of the New York Intellectuals discussed in Chapter
7.

White groups to actively oppose White interests is the new Jewish ethno-political imperative: "If Jews are going to survive in the future, we will have to stand with people of color for our mutual benefit."

The "diversity-as-safety" argument was made by Leonard S. Glickman, president and CEO of the Hebrew Immigrant Aid Society (HIAS), a Jewish group that has advocated open immigration to the United States for over a century. Glickman stated, "The more diverse American society is the safer [Jews] are" (in Cattan, 2002). At the present time, HIAS is deeply involved in recruiting refugees from Africa to immigrate to the US.

Positive attitudes toward cultural diversity have also appeared in other statements on immigration by Jewish authors and leaders. Charles Silberman (1985, p. 350) notes:

> American Jews are committed to cultural tolerance because of their belief—one firmly rooted in history—that Jews are safe only in a society acceptant of a wide range of attitudes and behaviors, as well as a diversity of religious and ethnic groups. It is this belief, for example, not approval of homosexuality, that leads an overwhelming majority of U.S. Jews to endorse "gay rights" and to take a liberal stance on most other so-called "social" issues.[144]

Similarly, in listing the positive benefits of immigration, the director of the Washington Action Office of the Council of Jewish Federations stated that immigration "is about diversity, cultural enrichment and economic opportunity for the immigrants" (in *The Forward*, March 8, 1996, p. 5). And in summarizing Jewish involvement in the 1996 legislative battles over immigration, James Besser (1996) stated, "Jewish groups failed to kill a number of provisions that reflect the kind of political expediency that they regard as a direct attack on American pluralism."

Because liberal immigration policies are a vital Jewish interest, it is not surprising that support for liberal immigration policies spans the Jewish political spectrum. We have seen that Sidney Hook, who along with the other New York Intellectuals may be viewed as an intellectual precursor of neoconservatism, identified democracy with the equality of differences and with the

---

[144] Moreover, a deep concern that an ethnically and culturally homogeneous America would compromise Jewish interests can be seen in Silberman's (1985, pp. 347–348) comments on the attraction of Jews to "the Democratic party . . . with its traditional hospitality to non-WASP ethnic groups. . . . A distinguished economist who strongly disagreed with Mondale's economic policies voted for him nonetheless. 'I watched the conventions on television,' he explained, 'and the Republicans did not look like my kind of people.' That same reaction led many Jews to vote for Carter in 1980 despite their dislike of him; 'I'd rather live in a country governed by the faces I saw at the Democratic convention than by those I saw at the Republican convention,' a well-known author told me."

maximization of cultural diversity (see Ch. 7). Neoconservatives have been strong advocates of liberal immigration policies, and there has been a conflict between predominantly Jewish neoconservatives and predominantly gentile paleoconservatives over the issue of Third World immigration into the United States (see also Ch. 4). Neoconservative Norman Podhoretz reacted very negatively to an article by a paleoconservative concerned that such immigration would eventually lead to the United States being dominated by such immigrants (see Judis, 1990). Other examples are neoconservatives Julian Simon (1990) and Ben Wattenberg (1991), both of whom advocate very high levels of immigration from all parts of the world, so that the United States will become what Wattenberg describes as the world's first "universal nation." Fetzer (1996) reported that Jews remain far more favorable to immigration to the United States than any other ethnic group or religion.

It should be noted as a general point that the effectiveness of Jewish organizations in influencing U.S. immigration policy has been facilitated by certain characteristics of American Jewry that are directly linked with Judaism as a group evolutionary strategy, and particularly an IQ that is at least one standard deviation above the Caucasian mean (PTSDA, Ch. 7). High IQ is associated with success in a broad range of activities in contemporary societies, including especially wealth and social status (Herrnstein & Murray, 1994). As Neuringer (1971/1980, p. 87) notes, Jewish influence on immigration policy was facilitated by Jewish wealth, education, and social status. Reflecting its general disproportionate representation in markers of economic success and political influence, Jewish organizations have been able to have a vastly disproportionate effect on U.S. immigration policy because Jews as a group are highly organized, highly intelligent, politically astute, and able to command a high level of financial, political, and intellectual resources in pursuing their political aims (see also the Preface, "Background Traits for Jewish Influence"). Similarly, Hollinger (1996, p. 19) notes that Jews were more influential in the decline of a homogeneous Protestant Christian culture in the United States than Catholics because of their greater wealth, social standing, and technical skill in the intellectual arena. In the area of immigration policy, the main Jewish activist organization influencing immigration policy, the AJCommittee, was characterized by "strong leadership [particularly that of Louis Marshall], internal cohesion, well-funded programs, sophisticated lobbying techniques, well-chosen non-Jewish allies, and good timing" (J. Goldstein, 1990, p. 333). Writing in 1996, J. J. Goldberg (pp. 38–39) noted that there were approximately three hundred national Jewish organizations in the United States with a combined budget estimated in the range of six billion dollars—a sum, as he noted, greater than the gross national product of half the members of the United Nations.

The Jewish effort toward transforming the United States into a pluralistic society has been waged on several fronts. In addition to discussing legislative and lobbying activities related to immigration policy, mention will also be made of Jewish efforts in influencing the wider cultural context of the post-World War II immigration debates, including the intellectual-academic arena, the area of church-state relationships, and organizing African Americans as a political and cultural force.

(1) Intellectual-Academic Efforts

Hollinger (1996, p. 4) notes "the transformation of the ethnoreligious demography of American academic life by Jews" in the period from the 1930s to the 1960s, as well as the Jewish influence on trends toward the secularization of American society and in advancing an ideal of cosmopolitanism (p. 11). The pace of this influence was very likely influenced by the immigration battles of the 1920s. Hollinger notes (p. 22):

> The old Protestant establishment's influence persisted until the 1960s in large measure because of the Immigration Act of 1924: had massive immigration of Catholics and Jews continued at pre-1924 levels, the course of U.S. history would have been different in many ways, including, one may reasonably speculate, a more rapid diminution of Protestant cultural hegemony. Immigration restriction gave that hegemony a new lease of life.

It is reasonable to suppose, therefore, that the immigration battles from 1881 to 1965 have been of momentous historical importance in shaping the contours of American culture in the late twentieth century.

Of particular interest here is the ideology that the United States ought to be an ethnically and culturally pluralistic society. Beginning with Horace Kallen, Jewish intellectuals have been at the forefront in developing models of the United States as a culturally and ethnically pluralistic society. Reflecting the utility of cultural pluralism in serving Jewish group interests in maintaining cultural separatism, Kallen personally combined his ideology of cultural pluralism with a deep immersion in Jewish history and literature, a commitment to Zionism, and political activity on behalf of Jews in Eastern Europe (Sachar, 1992, pp. 425ff; Frommer, 1978).

Kallen (1915, 1924) developed a "polycentric" ideal for American ethnic relationships. Kallen defined ethnicity as deriving from one's biological endowment, implying that Jews should be able to remain a genetically and culturally cohesive group while participating in American democratic institutions. This conception that the United States should be organized as a set of separate ethnic-cultural groups was accompanied by an ideology that relationships between groups would be cooperative and benign: "Kallen lifted his eyes above the strife that swirled around him to an ideal realm where diversity and harmony coexist" (Higham, 1984, p. 209). Similarly in Germany, the Jewish leader Moritz Lazarus argued in opposition to the views of the German intellectual Heinrich von Treitschke that the continued separateness of diverse ethnic groups contributed to the richness of German culture (Schorsch, 1972, p. 63). Lazarus also developed the doctrine of dual loyalty, which became a cornerstone of the Zionist movement. Already in 1862 Moses Hess had developed the view that Judaism would lead the world to an era of universal harmony in which each ethnic group retained its separate existence but no group controlled any area of land (see SAID, Ch. 5).

Kallen wrote his 1915 article partly in reaction to the ideas of Edward A. Ross (1914). Ross was a Darwinian sociologist who believed that the existence of clearly demarcated groups would tend to result in between-group competition for resources—clearly a perspective that is highly congruent with the theory and data presented in SAID. Higham's comment is interesting because it shows that Kallen's romantic views of group coexistence were massively contradicted by the reality of between-group competition in his own day. Indeed, it is noteworthy that Kallen was a prominent leader of the AJCongress. During the 1920s and 1930s the AJCongress championed group economic and political rights for Jews in Eastern Europe at a time when there was widespread ethnic tensions and persecution of Jews, and despite the fears of many that such activism would merely exacerbate current tensions. The AJCongress demanded that Jews be allowed proportional political representation as well as the ability to organize their own communities and preserve an autonomous Jewish national culture. The treaties with Eastern European countries and Turkey included provisions that the state provide instruction in minority languages and that Jews have the right to refuse to attend courts or other public functions on the Sabbath (Frommer, 1978, p. 162).

Kallen's idea of cultural pluralism as a model for the United States was popularized among gentile intellectuals by John Dewey (Higham, 1984, p. 209), who in turn was promoted by Jewish intellectuals:

> If lapsed Congregationalists like Dewey did not need immigrants to inspire them to press against the boundaries of even the most liberal of Protestant sensibilities, Dewey's kind were resoundingly encouraged in that direction by the Jewish intellectuals they encountered in urban academic and literary communities. . . .
>
> One force in this [culture war of the 1940s] was a secular, increasingly Jewish, decidedly left-of-center intelligentsia based largely . . . in the disciplinary communities of philosophy and the social sciences. . . . The presiding spirit was the aging John Dewey himself, still contributing occasional articles and addresses to the cause. (Hollinger, 1996, pp. 24, 160)

The editors of *Partisan Review* (W. Phillips & Rahv, 1946, p. 608), the principal journal of the New York Intellectuals, published work by Dewey and called him "America's leading philosopher." Dewey's student, New York Intellectual Sidney Hook (1987, p. 82), was also unsparing in his praise of Dewey, terming him "the intellectual leader of the liberal community in the United States" and "a sort of intellectual tribune of progressive causes."

Dewey, as the leading American secularist, was allied with a group of Jewish intellectuals opposed to "specifically Christian formulations of American democracy" (Hollinger, 1996, p. 158). Dewey had close links with the New York Intellectuals, many of whom were Trotskyists, and he headed the Dewey Commission that exonerated Trotsky of charges brought against him in the Moscow Trials of 1936. Dewey was highly influential with the public at large. Henry Steele Commager described Dewey as "the guide, the mentor, and the conscience of the American people; it is scarcely an exaggeration to say that for a generation no issue was clarified until Dewey had spoken" (in Sandel, 1996). Dewey was the foremost advocate of "progressive education" and helped establish the New School for Social Research and the American Civil Liberties Union (ACLU), both essentially Jewish organizations (J. J. Goldberg, 1996, pp. 46, 131). As with several other gentiles discussed in this volume, Dewey, whose "lack of presence as a writer, speaker, or personality makes his popular appeal something of a mystery" (Sandel), thus represented the public face of a movement dominated by Jewish intellectuals.

Kallen's ideas have been very influential in producing Jewish self-conceptualizations of their status in America. This influence was apparent as early as 1915 among American Zionists, such as Louis D. Brandeis.[145] Brandeis viewed

---

[145] The American Zionist Maurice Samuel, although condemning the Immigration Act of 1924 as racist (see above), had well-developed racialist ideas of his own. Samuel wrote a well-known work, *You Gentiles* (1924/2022), that contains a very clear statement of biological differences creating an unbridgeable gulf between Jews and gentiles:

- "Though you and we were to agree on all fundamental principles . . . yet we should remain fundamentally different. The language of our external expression is alike, but the language of our internal meaning is different. . . . Instinct endures for glacial ages; religions revolve with civilizations." (pp. 28–29)
- "The difference between us is abysmal." (p. 30)
- "This difference in behavior and reaction springs from something much more earnest and significant than a difference in beliefs: it springs from a difference in our biologic equipment." (p. 34)
- "These are two ways of life, each utterly alien to the other. Each has its place in the world—but they cannot flourish in the same soil, they cannot remain in contact without antagonism. Though to life itself each way is a perfect utterance, to each other they are enemies." (pp. 36–37)

The prominent and influential American Jewish pro-immigration activist Louis Marshall also had a strong attachment to Judaism which he viewed as a race. He stated that "As you know, I am not a Zionist, certainly not a Nationalist. I am . . . one who takes a pride in the literature, the history, the traditions, and the spiritual and intellectual contributions which Judaism has made to the world, and as I grow older, the feelings of love and reverence for the

the United States as composed of different nationalities whose free development would "spiritually enrich the United States and would make it a democracy *par excellence*" (Gal, 1989, p. 70). These views became "a hallmark of mainstream American Zionism, secular and religious alike" (p. 70). Cultural pluralism was also a hallmark of the Jewish-dominated intergroup relations movement following World War II, although these intellectuals sometimes couched these ideas in terms of "unity in diversity" or "cultural democracy" in an effort to remove the connotation that the United States should literally be a federation of different national groups as the AJCongress advocated in the case of Eastern Europe and elsewhere (Svonkin, 1997, p. 22). Kallen's influence extended really to all educated Jews:

> Legitimizing the preservation of a minority culture in the midst of a majority's host society, pluralism functioned as intellectual anchorage for an educated Jewish second generation, sustained its cohesiveness and its most tenacious communal endeavors through the rigors of the Depression and revived anti-semitism, through the shock of Nazism and the Holocaust, until the emergence of Zionism in the post-World War II years swept through American Jewry with a climactic redemptionist fervor of its own. (Sachar, 1992, p. 427)

As David Petegorsky, executive director of the AJCongress, stated in an address to the biennial convention of the AJCongress in 1948:

> We are profoundly convinced that Jewish survival will depend on Jewish statehood in Palestine, on the one hand, and on the existence of a creative, conscious and well-adjusted Jewish *community* in this country on the other. Such a creative community can exist only within the framework of a progressive and expanding democratic society, which through its institutions and public policies gives full expression to the concept of cultural pluralism. (in Svonkin, 1997, p. 82; emphasis original)

Besides the ideology of ethnic and cultural pluralism, the ultimate success of Jewish attitudes and lobbying efforts on immigration was also influenced by intellectual movements reviewed in Chapters 2–7. These movements, and particularly the work of Franz Boas, collectively resulted in the decline of evolutionary and biological thinking in the academic world. Although playing virtually no role in the restrictionist position in the congressional debates on immigration (which focused mainly on the fairness of maintaining the ethnic

---

cradle of our race increase in intensity" (in N. W. Cohen, 1972, p. 107). The comment is another example of Jewish identification and group commitment increasing with age (see PTSDA, Ch. 7, note 27).

status quo; see below), a component of the intellectual *zeitgeist* of the 1920s was the prevalence of evolutionary theories of race and ethnicity (Singerman, 1986), particularly the theories of Madison Grant. In *The Passing of the Great Race*, Grant (1921) argued that the American colonial stock was derived from superior Nordic racial elements and that immigration of other races would lower the competence level of the society as a whole as well as threaten democratic and republican institutions. Grant's ideas were popularized in the media at the time of the immigration debates (see Divine, 1957, pp. 12ff) and often provoked negative comments in Jewish publications such as *The American Hebrew* (e.g., March 21, 1924, pp. 554, 625).

Grant's letter to the House Committee on Immigration and Naturalization emphasized the principal argument of the restrictionists, that is, that the use of the 1890 census of the foreign born as the basis of the immigration law was fair to all ethnic groups currently in the country, and that the use of the 1910 census discriminated against the "native Americans whose ancestors were in this country before its independence." He also argued in favor of quotas restricting immigration from Western Hemisphere nations because these countries,

> in some cases furnish very undesirable immigrants. The Mexicans who come into the United States are overwhelmingly of Indian blood, and the recent intelligence tests have shown their very low intellectual status. We have already got too many of them in our Southwestern States, and a check should be put on their increase. (*Restriction of Immigration*, 1924, p. 571)

Grant was also concerned about the unassimilability of recent immigrants. He included with his letter a *Chicago Tribune* editorial commenting on a situation in Hamtramck, Michigan, in which recent immigrants were described as demanding "Polish rule," the expulsion of non-Poles, and use of only the Polish language by federal officials. Grant also argued that differential fertility would result in displacement of groups that delayed marriage and had fewer children—a comment that reflects ethnic differences in life history strategy (Rushton, 1995) and clearly indicating a concern that as a result of immigration his ethnic group would be displaced by ethnic groups with a higher rate of natural increase. Reflecting his concerns about immigrants from Mexico. Recent data indicate continuing racial/ethnic differences in fertility, with Hispanic women's fertility higher than Black women's fertility, and both above White women's fertility. Asian-American women have the lowest fertility rate for American women (Migiro, 2020). Moreover, Latino activists have a clearly articulated policy of "reconquering" the United States via immigration and high birth rates (see CCIR, 1997).

In Chapter 2 I showed that Stephen Jay Gould and Leon Kamin have presented a highly exaggerated and largely false account of the role of the IQ debates of the 1920s in passing immigration restriction legislation. It is also very easy to overemphasize the importance of theories of Nordic superiority as an ingredient of popular and congressional restrictionist sentiment. As Singerman (1986, pp. 118–119) points out, "racial anti-Semitism" was employed by only "a handful of writers"; moreover "the Jewish 'problem' . . . was a minor preoccupation even among such widely published authors as Madison Grant or T. Lothrop Stoddard, and none of the individuals examined [in Singerman's review] could be regarded as professional Jew-baiters or full-time propagandists against Jews, domestic or foreign." As indicated below, arguments related to Nordic superiority, including supposed Nordic intellectual superiority, played remarkably little role in congressional debates over immigration in the 1920s, the common argument of the restrictionists being that immigration policy should reflect equally the interests of all ethnic groups currently in the country. There is even evidence that the Nordic superiority argument had little favor with the public: a member of the Immigration Restriction League stated in 1924 that "the country is somewhat fed up on high-brow Nordic superiority stuff" (in Samelson, 1979, p. 136).

Nevertheless, it is probable that the decline in evolutionary and biological theories of race and ethnicity facilitated the sea change in immigration policy brought about by the 1965 law. As Higham (1984) notes, by the time of the final victory in 1965, which removed national origins and racial ancestry from immigration policy and opened up immigration to all human groups, the Boasian perspective of cultural determinism and anti-biologism had become standard academic wisdom. The result was that "it became intellectually fashionable to discount the very existence of persistent ethnic differences. The whole reaction deprived popular race feelings of a powerful ideological weapon" (pp. 58–59).

Jewish intellectuals were prominently involved in the movement to eradicate the racialist ideas of Grant and others (Degler, 1991, pp. 200–201). Indeed, even during the earlier debates leading up to the Immigration Acts of 1921 and 1924, restrictionists perceived themselves to be under attack from Jewish intellectuals. In 1918 Prescott F. Hall, secretary of the Immigration Restriction League, wrote to Grant:

> What I wanted . . . was the names of a few anthropologists of note who have declared in favor of the inequality of the races. . . . I am up against the Jews all the time in the equality argument and thought perhaps you might be able offhand to name a few (besides [Henry Fairfield] Osborn) whom I could quote in support. (in Samelson, 1975, p. 467)

Grant also believed that Jews were engaged in a campaign to discredit racial research. In the introduction to the 1921 edition of *The Passing of the Great Race*, Grant (pp. xxxi–xxxii) complained:

> [I]t is well-nigh impossible to publish in the American newspapers any reflection upon certain religions or races which are hysterically sensitive even when mentioned by name. The underlying idea seems to be that if publication can be suppressed the facts themselves will ultimately disappear. Abroad, conditions are fully as bad, and we have the authority of one of the most eminent anthropologists in France that the collection of anthropological measurements and data among French recruits at the outbreak of the Great War was prevented by Jewish influence, which aimed to suppress any suggestion of racial differentiation in France.

Boas was greatly motivated by the immigration issue as it developed early in the century. Carl Degler (1991, p. 74) notes that Boas's professional correspondence "reveals that an important motive behind his famous head-measuring project in 1910 was his strong personal interest in keeping the United States diverse in population." The study, whose conclusions were placed into the Congressional Record by Representative Emanuel Celler during the debate on immigration restriction (65 Cong. Rec., 1924, pp. 5915–5916), concluded that the environmental differences consequent to immigration caused differences in head shape. (At the time, head shape as determined by the cephalic index was the main measurement used by scientists involved in racial differences research.) The two men thus cooperated on immigration policy. In a letter (May 26th, 1927) Boas tells Celler, "I wish very much that an amendment to allow Hindues to come here could go through," arguing that higher caste Indians are basically European. "The difficulty at present lies with the definition of what is a white person and Caucasian race."

Boas argued that his research showed that all foreign groups living in favorable social circumstances had become assimilated to the United States in the sense that their physical measurements converged on the American type. Although he was considerably more circumspect regarding his conclusions in the body of his report (see also Stocking, 1968, pp. 178–179), Boas (1911, p. 5) stated in his introduction that "all fear of an unfavorable influence of South European immigration upon the body of our people should be dismissed." As a further indication of Boas's ideological commitment to the immigration issue, Degler (1994, p. 75) makes the following comment regarding one of Boas's environmentalist explanations for mental differences between immigrant and native children: "Why Boas chose to advance such an ad hoc interpretation is hard to understand until one recognizes his desire to explain in a favorable way the apparent mental backwardness of the immigrant children."

The ideology of racial equality was an important weapon on behalf of opening immigration up to all human groups. For example, in a 1951 statement to Congress (*Revision of Immigration*, 1951, p. 391), the AJCongress stated, "The findings of science must force even the most prejudiced among us to accept, as unqualifiedly as we do the law of gravity, that intelligence, morality and character, bear no relationship whatever to geography or place of birth." The statement went on to cite some of Boas's popular writings on the subject as well as the writings of Boas's protégé Ashley Montagu, perhaps the most visible opponent of the concept of race during this period (pp. 402–403). Montagu, whose original name was Israel Ehrenberg, theorized in the period immediately following World War II that humans are innately cooperative, but not innately aggressive, and that there is a universal brotherhood among humans (see Shipman, 1994, pp. 159ff). In 1952 another Boas protégé, Margaret Mead, testified before the President's Commission on Immigration and Naturalization (PCIN, 1953/1971, p. 92) that "all human beings from all groups of people have the same potentialities.... Our best anthropological evidence today suggests that the people of every group have about the same distribution of potentialities." Another witness stated that the executive board of the American Anthropological Association had unanimously endorsed the proposition that "[a]ll scientific evidence indicates that all peoples are inherently capable of acquiring or adapting to our civilization" (p. 93) (see Ch. 2 for a discussion of the success of the political efforts of the Boasians to dominate the American Anthropological Association). By 1965 Senator Jacob Javits (111 Cong. Rec., 1965, p. 24469) could confidently announce to the Senate during the debate on the immigration bill that,

> both the dictates of our consciences as well as the precepts of sociologists tell us that immigration, as it exists in the national origins quota system, is wrong and without any basis in reason or fact for we know better than to say that one man is better than another because of the color of his skin.

The intellectual revolution and its translation into public policy had been completed.

(2) Church-State Relationships

One aspect of the Jewish interest in cultural pluralism in the United States has been that Jews have a perceived interest that the United States not be a homogeneous Christian culture. As Ivers (1995, p. 2) notes, "Jewish civil rights organizations have had an historic role in the postwar development of American church-state law and policy." In this case the main Jewish effort began only after World War II, although Jews opposed linkages between the state and the

Protestant religion much earlier. For example, Jewish publications were unanimous in their opposition to Tennessee's law that resulted in the 1925 Scopes trial in which Darwinism was pitted against religious fundamentalism (Goldfarb, 1984, p. 43).

> It matters not whether evolution is or is not true. What matters is that there are certain forces in this country who insist that the Government shall see to it that nothing is taught in this country which will in any way cast a doubt on the *infallibility* of the Bible. There you have the whole issue boiled down. In other words, it is a deliberate *un-American* attempt to unite Church and State. . . . And we go even further than that and assert that it is an attempt to unite *State* with *Protestant Church*. (Joseph, 1925, p. 18; emphasis original)

The Jewish effort in this case was well funded and was the focus of well-organized, highly dedicated Jewish civil service organizations, including the AJCommittee, the AJCongress, and the ADL. It involved keen legal expertise not only in the actual litigation but also in influencing legal opinion via articles in law journals and other forums of intellectual debate, including the popular media. It also involved a highly charismatic and effective leadership, particularly Leo Pfeffer of the AJCongress:

> No other lawyer exercised such complete intellectual dominance over a chosen area of law for so extensive a period—as an author, scholar, public citizen, and above all, legal advocate who harnessed his multiple and formidable talents into a single force capable of satisfying all that an institution needs for a successful constitutional reform movement. . . . That Pfeffer, through an enviable combination of skill, determination, and persistence, was able in such a short period of time to make church-state reform the foremost cause with which rival organizations associated the AJCongress illustrates well the impact that individual lawyers endowed with exceptional skills can have on the character and life of the organizations for which they work. . . . As if to confirm the extent to which Pfeffer is associated with post-*Everson* [i.e., post-1946] constitutional development, even the major critics of the Court's church-state jurisprudence during this period and the modern doctrine of separationism rarely fail to make reference to Pfeffer as the central force responsible for what they lament as the lost meaning of the establishment clause. (Ivers, 1995, pp. 222–224)

Similarly, Jews in nineteenth-century France and Germany attempted to remove education from the control of the Catholic and Lutheran churches respectively, while for many gentiles Christianity was an important part of national identity (Lindemann, 1997, p. 214). Because of such activities, anti-Semites commonly viewed Jews as destroyers of the social fabric.

(3) Organization of African Americans and the Intergroup Relations Movement in the Post-World War II Era

Finally, Jews have also been instrumental in organizing African Americans as a political force that served Jewish interests in diluting the political and cultural hegemony of non-Jewish European Americans. Jews played a very prominent role in organizing Blacks beginning with the founding of the National Association for the Advancement of Colored People (NAACP) in 1909 and, despite increasing Black anti-Semitism, continuing into the present.

> By mid-decade [c. 1915], the NAACP had something of the aspect of an adjunct of B'nai B'rith and the American Jewish Committee, with the brothers Joel and Arthur Spingarn serving as board chairman and chief legal counsel, respectively; Herbert Lehman on the executive committee; Lillian Wald and Walter Sachs on the board (though not simultaneously); and Jacob Schiff and Paul Warburg as financial angels. By 1920, Herbert Seligman was director of public relations, and Martha Gruening served as his assistant. . . . Small wonder that a bewildered Marcus Garvey stormed out of NAACP headquarters in 1917, muttering that it was a white organization. (D. L. Lewis, 1984, p. 85)

Wealthy Jews were important contributors to the National Urban League as well: "Edwin Seligman's chairmanship, and the presence on the board of Felix Adler, Lillian Wald, Abraham Lefkowitz, and, shortly thereafter, Julius Rosenwald, principal Sears, Roebuck Company stockholder, forecast significant Jewish contributions to the League" (D. L. Lewis, 1984, p. 85). In addition to providing funding and organizational talent (the presidents of the NAACP were Jews until 1975), Jewish legal talent was harnessed on behalf of African American causes. Louis Marshall, a prominent player in the Jewish efforts on immigration (see below), was a principal NAACP attorney during the 1920s. African Americans played little role in these efforts: for example, until 1933 there were no African American lawyers in the NAACP legal department (M. Friedman, 1995, p. 106). Indeed, a theme of revisionist historians reviewed by M. Friedman is that Jews organized African Americans for their own interests rather than the best interests of African Americans. In the post-World War II period the entire gamut of Jewish civil service organizations were involved in Black issues, including the AJCommittee, the AJCongress, and the ADL: "With professionally trained personnel, fully equipped offices, and public relations know-how, they had the resources to make a difference" (M. Friedman, p. 135).

Jews contributed from two-thirds to three-quarters of the money for civil rights groups during the 1960s (J. Kaufman, 1997, p. 110). Jewish groups, particularly the AJCongress, played a leading role in drafting civil rights legislation and pursuing legal challenges related to civil rights issues mainly benefiting Blacks (Svonkin, 1997, pp. 79–112).

> Jewish support, legal and monetary, afforded the civil rights movement a string of legal victories. ... There is little exaggeration in an American Jewish Congress lawyer's claim that "many of these laws were actually written in the offices of Jewish agencies by Jewish staff people, introduced by Jewish legislators and pressured into being by Jewish voters." (D. L. Lewis, 1984, p. 94)

Harold Cruse (1967/1992) presents a particularly trenchant analysis of the Black Jewish coalition that reflects several themes of this volume. First, he notes, "Jews *know exactly what they want in America*" (p. 121; emphasis original). Jews want cultural pluralism because of their long-term policy of non-assimilation and group solidarity. Cruse notes, however, that the Jewish experience in Europe has shown them that "*two* can play this game" (i.e., develop highly nationalistic solidary groups), and "when that happens, woe be to the side that is short on numbers" (p. 122; emphasis original). Cruse is here referring to the possibility of antagonistic group strategies (and, I suppose, the reactive processes) that form the subject matter of SAID (Chs. 3–5). Correspondingly, Cruse observes that Jewish organizations view Anglo-Saxon (read Caucasian) nationalism as their greatest potential threat and that they have tended to support pro-Black integration (i.e., assimilationist, individualist) policies for Blacks in America, presumably because such policies dilute Caucasian power and lessen the possibility of a cohesive, nationalist, anti-Semitic, Caucasian majority. At the same time, Jewish organizations have opposed a Black nationalist position while pursuing an anti-assimilationist, nationalist group strategy for their own group.

Cruse also points out the asymmetry in Black-Jewish relations: while Jews have held prominent roles in Black civil rights organizations and have been actively involved in their funding and in making and implementing their policies, Blacks have been completely excluded from the inner workings and policy-making bodies in Jewish organizations. To a considerable extent, at least until quite recently, the form and goals of the Black movement in the United States should be seen as an instrument of Jewish strategy with very similar goals to those pursued in the arena of immigration legislation.

The Jewish role in African American affairs must, however, be seen as part of the broader role of what participants termed the "intergroup relations movement" that worked to "eliminate prejudice and discrimination against racial, ethnic, and religious minorities" in the period following World War II (Svonkin, 1997, p. 1). As with the other movements with strong Jewish involvement, Jewish organizations, particularly the AJCommittee, the AJCongress, and the ADL, were the leaders, and these organizations provided the major sources of funding, devised the tactics, and defined the objectives of the movement. As was also the case with the movement to shape immigration policy, its aim was the very self-interested aim of preventing the development of a mass anti-Semitic movement in the United States: Jewish activists "saw their commitment to the intergroup relations movement as a preventive measure designed to make sure 'it'—the Nazis' war of extermination against European Jewry—never happened in America" (p. 10).

This was a multifaceted effort, ranging from legal challenges to bias in housing, education, and public employment; legislative proposals and efforts to secure their passage into law in state and national legislative bodies; efforts to shape messages emanating from the media; educational programs for students and teachers; and intellectual efforts to reshape the intellectual discourse of academia. As with Jewish involvement in immigration policy and a great many other instances of Jewish political and intellectual activity in both modern and premodern times (see SAID, Ch. 6), the intergroup relations movement often worked to minimize overt Jewish involvement (e.g., Svonkin, 1997, pp. 45, 51, 65, 71–72).

As in the nineteenth-century attempt to define Jewish interests in terms of German ideals (Ragins, 1980, p. 55; H. D. Schmidt, 1959, p. 46), the rhetoric of the intergroup relations movement stressed that its goals were congruent with American self-conceptualizations, a move that stressed the Enlightenment legacy of individual rights while effectively ignoring the republican strand of American identity as a cohesive, socially homogeneous society and the "ethnocultural" strand emphasizing the importance of Anglo-Saxon ethnicity in the development and preservation of American cultural forms (R. M. Smith, 1988). Liberal cosmopolitanism and individual rights were also conceived as congruent with Jewish ideals originating with the prophets (Svonkin, 1997, pp. 7, 20), a conceptualization that ignores the negative conceptualizations of and discrimination against outgroups and a pronounced tendency toward collectivism that have been central to Judaism as a group evolutionary strategy. As Svonkin notes, Jewish rhetoric during this period relied on an illusory view of the Jewish past that was tailor-made to achieve Jewish objectives in the modern world, where the Enlightenment rhetoric of universalism and individual rights retained considerable intellectual prestige.

Of critical importance in rationalizing Jewish interests during this period were the intellectual movements discussed in this volume, particularly Boasian anthropology, psychoanalysis, and the Frankfurt School of Social Research. As also indicated in Chapter 6, Jewish organizations were involved in funding research in the social sciences (particularly social psychology), and there developed a core of predominantly Jewish academic activists who worked closely with Jewish organizations (Svonkin, 1997, p. 4). Boasian anthropology was enlisted in post-World War II propaganda efforts distributed and promoted by the AJCommittee, the AJCongress, and the ADL, as in the film *Brotherhood of Man* (1946), which depicted all human groups as having equal abilities. During the 1930s the AJCommittee financially supported Boas in his research; and in the postwar era, the Boasian ideology that there were no racial differences as well as the Boasian ideology of cultural relativism and the importance of preserving and respecting cultural differences deriving from Horace Kallen were important ingredients of educational programs sponsored by these Jewish activist organizations and widely distributed throughout the American educational system (Svonkin, 1997, pp. 63–64).

By the early 1960s an ADL official estimated that one-third of America's teachers had received ADL educational material based on these ideas (Svonkin, 1997, p. 69). The ADL was also intimately involved in staffing, developing materials, and providing financial assistance for workshops for teachers and school administrators, often with the involvement of social scientists from the academic world—an association that undoubtedly added to the scientific credibility of these exercises. It is ironic, perhaps, that this effort to influence the public school curriculum was carried on by the same groups that were endeavoring to remove overt Christian influences from the public schools.[146]

The ideology of intergroup animosity developed by the intergroup relations movement derived from the *Studies in Prejudice* series described in Chapter 6. It explicitly viewed manifestations of gentile ethnocentrism or discrimination against outgroups as a mental disease and thus literally a public health problem. The assault on intergroup animosity was likened to the medical assault on deadly infectious diseases, and people with the disease were described by activists as "infected" (Svonkin, 1997, pp. 30, 59). A consistent theme of the intellectual rationale for this body of ethnic activism emphasized the benefits to be gained by increased levels of intergroup harmony—an aspect of the idealism inherent in Horace Kallen's conceptualization of multiculturalism—without mentioning that some groups, particularly European-derived, non-Jewish groups, would lose economic and political power and decline in cultural influence (p. 5). Negative attitudes toward groups were viewed not as the result of competing group interests but rather as the result of individual psychopathology (p. 75). Finally, while gentile ethnocentrism was viewed as a

---

[146] The ADL continues to be a major promoter of diversity education through its A World of Difference Institute. From 1985 to 2023 this institute has trained annually tens of thousands of elementary and secondary school teachers in diversity education and conducted workplace diversity training programs for workers and college students in the United States. Similar teacher training programs have also been instituted by the ADL in Germany and Russia.

public health problem, the AJCongress fought against Jewish assimilation. The AJCongress "was explicitly committed to a pluralistic vision that respected group rights and group distinctiveness as a fundamental civil liberty" (p. 81).

JEWISH ANTI-RESTRICTIONIST POLITICAL ACTIVITY

Jewish Anti-Restrictionist Activity in the United States Up to 1924

Jewish involvement in altering the intellectual discussion of race and ethnicity appears to have had long-term repercussions on U.S. immigration policy, but Jewish political involvement was ultimately of much greater significance. Jews have been "the single most persistent pressure group favoring a liberal immigration policy" in the United States in the entire immigration debate beginning in 1881:

> In undertaking to sway immigration policy in a liberal direction, Jewish spokespersons and organizations demonstrated a degree of energy unsurpassed by any other interested pressure group. Immigration had constituted a prime object of concern for practically every major Jewish defense and community relations organization. Over the years, their spokespersons had assiduously attended congressional hearings, and the Jewish effort was of the utmost importance in establishing and financing such non-sectarian groups as the National Liberal Immigration League and the Citizens Committee for Displaced Persons. (Neuringer, 1971/1980, pp. 392–393)

As recounted by Nathan C. Belth (1979, p. 173) in his history of the ADL:

> In Congress, through all the years when the immigration battles were being fought, the names of Jewish legislators were in the forefront of the liberal forces: from Adolph Sabath to Samuel Dickstein and Emanuel Celler in the House and from Herbert H. Lehman to Jacob Javits in the Senate. Each in his time was a leader of the Anti-Defamation League and of major organizations concerned with democratic development.

The Jewish congressmen who are most closely identified with anti-restrictionist efforts in Congress have therefore also been leaders of the group most closely identified with Jewish ethnic political activism and self-defense.

Throughout the almost one hundred years prior to achieving success with the Immigration and Nationality Act of 1965, Jewish groups opportunistically made alliances with other groups whose interests temporarily converged with Jewish interests (e.g., a constantly changing set of ethnic groups, religious groups, pro-communists, anti-communists, the foreign policy interests of various presidents, and the political need for presidents to curry favor with groups influential in populous states in order to win national elections). Particularly noteworthy was the support of a liberal immigration policy from industrial interests wanting cheap labor, at least in the period prior to the 1924 temporary triumph of restrictionism. Within this constantly shifting set of alliances, Jewish organizations persistently pursued their goals of maximizing the number of Jewish immigrants and opening up the United States to immigration from all of the peoples of the world. As indicated in the following, the historical record supports the proposition that turning the United States into a multicultural society has been a major Jewish goal beginning in the nineteenth century.

The ultimate Jewish victory on immigration is remarkable because it was waged in different arenas against a potentially very powerful set of opponents. Beginning in the late nineteenth century, leadership of the restrictionists was provided by Eastern patricians such as Senator Henry Cabot Lodge. However, the main political basis of restrictionism from 1910 to 1952 (in addition to the relatively ineffectual labor union interests) derived from "the common people of the South and West" (Higham, 1984, p. 49) and their representatives in Congress. Fundamentally, the clashes between Jews and gentiles in the period between 1900 and 1965 were conflicts between Jews and this geographically centered group. "Jews, as a result of their intellectual energy and economic resources, constituted an advance guard of the new peoples who had no feeling for the traditions of rural America" (pp. 168–169), a theme also apparent in the discussion of the New York Intellectuals in Chapter 7 and in the discussion of Jewish involvement in political radicalism in Chapter 3.

Although often concerned that Jewish immigration would fan the flames of anti-Semitism in America, Jewish leaders fought a long and largely successful delaying action against restrictions on immigration during the period from 1891 to 1924, particularly as they affected the ability of Jews to immigrate. These efforts continued despite the fact that by 1905 there was "a polarity between Jewish and general American opinion on immigration" (Neuringer, 1971/1980, p. 83). In particular, whereas other religious groups such as Catholics and ethnic groups such as the Irish had divided and ambivalent attitudes toward immigration and were poorly organized and ineffective in influencing immigration policy, and whereas labor unions opposed immigration in their attempt to diminish the supply of cheap labor, Jewish groups engaged in an intensive and sustained effort against attempts to restrict immigration.

As recounted by N. W. Cohen (1972, pp. 40ff), the AJCommittee's efforts in opposition to immigration restriction in the early twentieth century constitute a remarkable example of the ability of Jewish organizations to influence public policy. Of all the groups affected by the immigration legislation of 1907,

Jews had the least to gain in terms of numbers of possible immigrants, but they played by far the largest role in shaping the legislation (p. 41). In the subsequent period leading up to the relatively ineffective restrictionist Immigration Act of 1917, when restrictionists again mounted an effort in Congress, "only the Jewish segment was aroused" (p. 49).

Nevertheless, because of the fear of anti-Semitism, efforts were made to prevent the perception of Jewish involvement in anti-restrictionist campaigns. In 1906 Jewish anti-restrictionist political operatives were instructed to lobby Congress without mentioning their affiliation with the AJCommittee because of "the danger that the Jews may be accused of being organized for a political purpose" (comments of Herbert Friedenwald, AJCommittee secretary; in J. Goldstein, 1990, p. 125). Beginning in the late nineteenth century, anti-restrictionist arguments developed by Jews were typically couched in terms of universalist humanitarian ideals; as part of this universalizing effort, gentiles from old-line Protestant families were recruited to act as window dressing for their efforts, and Jewish groups such as the AJCommittee funded pro-immigration groups composed of non-Jews (Neuringer, 1971/1980, p. 92).

As was the case in later pro-immigration efforts, much of the activity was behind-the-scenes personal interventions with politicians in order to minimize public perception of the Jewish role and to avoid provoking opposition (N. W. Cohen, 1972, pp. 41–42; J. Goldstein, 1990). Opposing politicians such as Henry Cabot Lodge and organizations such as the Immigration Restriction League were kept under close scrutiny and pressured by lobbyists. Lobbyists in Washington also kept a daily scorecard of voting tendencies as immigration bills wended their way through Congress and engaged in intense and successful efforts to convince Presidents Taft and Wilson to veto restrictive immigration legislation. Catholic prelates were recruited to protest the effects of restrictionist legislation on immigration from Italy and Hungary. When restrictionist arguments appeared in the media, the AJCommittee made sophisticated replies based on scholarly data and typically couched in universalist terms as benefiting the whole society. Articles favorable to immigration were published in national magazines, and letters to the editor were published in newspapers. Efforts were made to minimize the negative perceptions of immigration by distributing Jewish immigrants around the country and by getting Jewish aliens off public support. Legal proceedings were filed to prevent the deportation of Jewish aliens. Eventually mass protest meetings were organized.

Writing in 1914, the sociologist Edward A. Ross believed that liberal immigration policy was exclusively a Jewish issue. Ross quotes (p. 144) the prominent author and Zionist pioneer Israel Zangwill, who articulated the idea that the United States is an ideal place to achieve Jewish interests:

America has ample room for all the six millions of the Pale [i.e., the Pale of Settlement, home to most of Russia's Jews]; any one of her fifty states could absorb them. And next to being in a country of their own, there could be no better fate for them than to be together in a land of civil and religious liberty, of whose Constitution Christianity forms no part and where their collective votes would practically guarantee them against future persecution.

Jews therefore have a powerful interest in immigration policy:

Hence the endeavor of the Jews to control the immigration policy of the United States. Although theirs is but a seventh of our net immigration, they led the fight on the Immigration Commission's bill. The power of the million Jews in the metropolis lined up the Congressional delegation from New York in solid opposition to the literacy test. The systematic campaign in newspapers and magazines to break down all arguments for restriction and to calm nativist fears is waged by and for one race. Hebrew money is behind the National Liberal Immigration League and its numerous publications. From the paper before the commercial body or the scientific association to the heavy treatise produced with the aid of the Baron de Hirsch Fund, the literature that proves the blessings of immigration to all classes in America emanates from subtle Hebrew brains. (Ross, 1914, pp. 144–145)

Ross (1914, p. 150) also reported that immigration officials had,

become very sore over the incessant fire of false accusations to which they are subjected by the Jewish press and societies. United States senators complain that during the close of the struggle over the immigration bill they were overwhelmed with a torrent of crooked statistics and misrepresentations by the Hebrews fighting the literacy test.

Zangwill's views were well known to restrictionists in the debates over the Immigration Act of 1924 (see below). In an address reprinted in *The American Hebrew*, Zangwill (1923, p. 582) noted, "There is only one way to World Peace, and that is the absolute abolition of passports, visas, frontiers, custom houses, and all other devices that make of the population of our planet not a co-operating civilization but a mutual irritation society." His famous play, *The Melting-Pot* (1908/1914), was dedicated to Theodore Roosevelt and depicts Jewish immigrants as eager to assimilate and intermarry. The lead character describes the United States as a crucible in which all the races, including the "black and yellow" races, are being melted together.[147] However, Zangwill's views on Jewish-gentile intermarriage were ambiguous at best (Biale, 1998, pp. 22–24), and he detested Christian proselytism to Jews. Zangwill was an ardent Zionist and an admirer of his father's religious orthodoxy as a model for the preservation of Judaism. He believed Jews were a morally superior race whose moral vision had shaped Christian and Muslim societies and would eventually reform the world, although Christianity remained morally inferior to Judaism (see Leftwich, 1957, pp. 162ff). Jews would retain their racial purity if they continued to practice their religion: "So long as Judaism flourishes among Jews there is no need to talk of safeguarding race or nationality; both are automatically preserved by the religion" (in p. 161).

Despite deceptive attempts to present the pro-immigration movement as broad-based, Jewish activists were aware of the lack of enthusiasm of other ethnic and religious groups. During the fight over restrictionist legislation at the end of the Taft administration, Herbert Friedenwald, AJCommittee secretary, wrote that it was "very difficult to get any people except the Jews stirred up in this fight" (in J. Goldstein, 1990, p. 203). The AJCommittee contributed heavily to staging anti-restrictionist rallies in major American cities but allowed other ethnic groups to take credit for the events, and it organized groups of non-Jews to influence President Taft to veto restrictionist legislation (pp. 216, 227). During the Wilson administration, Louis Marshall stated, "We are practically the only ones who are fighting [the literacy test]" while a "great proportion" of the people is "indifferent to what is done" (in p. 249).

The forces of immigration restriction were temporarily successful with the Immigration Acts of 1921 and 1924, which passed despite the intense opposition of Jewish groups. Divine (1957, p. 8) notes, "Arrayed against [the restrictionist forces] in 1921 were only the spokespersons for the southeastern European immigrants, mainly Jewish leaders, whose protests were drowned out by the general cry for restriction." Similarly, during the 1924 congressional hearings on immigration, "The most prominent group of witnesses against the bill were representatives of southeastern European immigrants, particularly Jewish leaders" (p. 16).

Jewish opposition to this legislation was motivated as much by their perception that the laws were motivated by anti-Semitism and that they discriminated in favor of Northwestern Europeans as by concern that they would curtail Jewish immigration (Neuringer, 1971/1980, p. 164)—a view that is implicitly in opposition to the ethnic status quo favoring Northwestern Europeans. Opposition to biasing immigration in favor of Northwestern Europeans remained

---

[147] Although Blacks were included in the crucible described in the play, Zangwill (1908/1914) seems to have had ambiguous attitudes toward Black-White intermarriage. In an afterword he wrote that Blacks on average had lower intellect and ethics but he also looked forward to the time when superior Blacks would marry Whites.

characteristic of Jewish attitudes in the following years, but the opposition of Jewish organizations to any restrictions on immigration based on race or ethnicity can be traced back to the nineteenth century.

Thus in 1882 the Jewish press was unanimous in its condemnation of the Chinese Exclusion Act (Neuringer, 1971/1980, p. 23), even though this act had no direct bearing on Jewish immigration. In the early twentieth century the AJCommittee at times actively fought against any bill that restricted immigration to White persons or non-Asians, and only refrained from active opposition if it judged that AJCommittee support would threaten the immigration of Jews (N. W. Cohen, 1972, p. 47; J. Goldstein, 1990, p. 250). In 1920 the Central Conference of American Rabbis passed a resolution urging that "the Nation . . . keep the gates of our beloved Republic open . . . to the oppressed and distressed of all mankind in conformity with its historic role as a haven of refuge for all men and women who pledge allegiance to its laws" (in *The American Hebrew*, October 1st, 1920, p. 594). *The American Hebrew* (February 17th, 1922, p. 373), a publication that represented the German-Jewish establishment of the period, reiterated its long-standing policy that it "has always stood for the admission of worthy immigrants of all classes, irrespective of nationality." And in his testimony at the 1924 hearings before the House Committee on Immigration and Naturalization, the AJCommittee's Louis Marshall stated that the bill echoed the sentiments of the Ku Klux Klan; he characterized it as inspired by the racialist theories of Houston Stewart Chamberlain. At a time when the population of the United States was over one hundred million, Marshall stated, "[W]e have room in this country for ten times the population we have"; he advocated admission of all of the peoples of the world without quota limit, excluding only those who "were mentally, morally and physically unfit, who are enemies of organized government, and who are apt to become public charges" (*Restriction of Immigration*, 1924, pp. 309, 303). Similarly, Rabbi Stephen S. Wise, representing the AJCongress and a variety of other Jewish organizations at the House hearings, asserted "the right of every man outside of America to be considered fairly and equitably and without discrimination" (p. 341).

By prescribing that immigration be restricted to 3 percent of the foreign born as of the 1890 census, the Immigration Act of 1924 prescribed an ethnic status quo approximating the 1920 census. The House Majority Report emphasized that prior to the legislation, immigration was highly biased in favor of Eastern and Southern Europeans, and that this imbalance had been continued by the Immigration Act of 1921 in which quotas were based on the numbers of foreign born as of the 1910 census. The expressed intention was that the interests of other groups to pursue their ethnic interests by expanding their percentage of the population should be balanced against the ethnic interests of the majority in retaining their ethnic representation in the population.

The Immigration Act of 1921 gave 46 percent of quota immigration to Southern and Eastern Europe even though these areas constituted only 11.7 percent of the U.S. population as of the 1920 census. The Immigration Act of 1924 prescribed that these areas would get 15.3 percent of the quota slots—a figure actually higher than their present representation in the population.

> The use of the 1890 census is not discriminatory. It is used in an effort to preserve as nearly as possible, the racial status quo of the United States. It is hoped to guarantee as best we can at this late date, racial homogeneity in the United States. The use of a later census would discriminate against those who founded the Nation and perpetuated its institutions. (H.R. Rep. No. 350, 1924, p. 16)

After three years, quotas were derived from a national origins formula based on 1920 census data for the entire population, not only for the foreign born. No doubt this legislation represented a victory for the Northwestern European peoples of the United States, yet there was no attempt to reverse the trends in the ethnic composition of the country; rather, the efforts aimed to preserve the ethnic status quo.

Although motivated by this desire to preserve the ethnic status quo, these laws may also have been motivated partly by anti-Semitism, since during this period liberal immigration policy was perceived as mainly a Jewish issue (see above). This certainly appears to have been the perception of Jewish observers: for example, prominent Jewish writer Maurice Samuel (1924/2022, p. 217), writing in the immediate aftermath of the Immigration Act of 1924, wrote that "it is chiefly against the Jew that anti-immigration laws are passed here in America as in England and Germany," and such perceptions continue among historians of the period (e.g., Hertzberg, 1989, p. 239). This perception was not restricted to Jews. In remarks before the Senate, the anti-restrictionist Senator Reed of Missouri noted, "Attacks have likewise been made upon the Jewish people who have crowded to our shores. The spirit of intolerance has been especially active as to them" (60 Cong. Rec., 1921, p. 3463). During World War II, Secretary of War Henry L. Stimson stated that it was opposition to unrestricted immigration of Jews that resulted in the restrictive legislation of 1924 (Breitman & Kraut, 1987, p. 87).

Moreover, the House Immigration Committee Majority Report (H.R. Rep. No. 109, 1920) stated that "by far the largest percentage of immigrants [are] peoples of Jewish extraction" (p. 4), and it implied that the majority of the expected new immigrants would be Polish Jews. The report "confirmed the published statement of a commissioner of the Hebrew Sheltering and Aid Society of America made after his personal investigation in Poland, to the effect that

'If there were in existence a ship that could hold 3,000,000 human beings, the 3,000,000 Jews of Poland would board it to escape to America'" (p. 6).

The Majority Report (H.R. Rep. No. 109, 1920, p. 9) also included a report by Wilbur S. Carr, head of the United States Consular Service, which stated that the Polish Jews were,

> abnormally twisted because of (a) reaction from war strain; (b) the shock of revolutionary disorders; (c) the dullness and stultification resulting from past years of oppression and abuse. . . . Eighty-five to ninety percent lack any conception of patriotic or national spirit. And the majority of this percentage are unable to acquire it.[148]

The report also noted consular reports that warned that "many Bolshevik sympathizers are in Poland" (H.R. Rep. No. 109, 1920, p. 11). Likewise in the Senate, Senator McKellar cited the report that if there were a ship large enough, three million Poles would immigrate. He also stated:

> The Joint Distribution Committee, an American committee doing relief work among the Hebrews in Poland, distributes more than $1,000,000 per month of American money in that country alone. It is also shown that $100,000,000 a year is a conservative estimate of money sent to Poland from America through the mails, through the banks, and through the relief societies. This golden stream pouring into Poland from America makes practically every Pole wildly desirous of going to the country from which such marvelous wealth comes. (60 Cong. Rec., 1921, p. 3456)

As a further indication of the salience of Polish-Jewish immigration issues, the letter on alien visas submitted by the State Department in 1921 to Albert Johnson, chairman of the Committee on Migration and Naturalization, devoted over four times as much space to the situation in Poland as it did to any other country. The report emphasized the activities of the Polish Jewish newspaper *Der Emigrant* in promoting immigration to the United States of Polish Jews, as well as the activities of the Hebrew Sheltering and Immigrant Society and wealthy private citizens from the United States in facilitating immigration by providing financial assistance and performing the paperwork. There was indeed a large network of Jewish agents in Eastern Europe who, in violation of U.S. law, "did their best to drum up business by enticing as many emigrants as possible" (Nadell, 1984, p. 56). The report also described the condition of the prospective immigrants in negative terms:

---

[148] See Breitman & Kraut (1987, p. 12) for a discussion of Carr's anti-Semitism; in England many recent Jewish immigrants refused to be conscripted to fight the enemies of the czar during World War I.

At the present time it is only too obvious that they must be subnormal, and their normal state is of very low standard. Six years of war and confusion and famine and pestilence have racked their bodies and twisted their mentality. The elders have deteriorated to a marked degree. Minors have grown into adult years with the entire period lost in their rightful development and too frequently with the acquisition of perverted ideas which have flooded Europe since 1914 [presumably a reference to the radical political ideas that were common in this group; see below]. (61 Cong. Rec., 1921, p. 498)

In addition, the report stated that articles in the Warsaw press had reported that "propaganda favoring unrestricted immigration" is being planned, including celebrations in New York aimed at showing the contributions of immigrants to the development of the United States. The reports for Belgium (whose immigrants originated in Poland and Czechoslovakia) and Romania also highlighted the importance of Jews as prospective immigrants. In response, Representative Isaac Siegel stated that the report was "edited and doctored by certain officials"; he commented that the report did not mention countries with larger numbers of immigrants than Poland. (For example, the report did not mention Italy.) Without explicitly saying so—"I leave it to every man in the House to make his own deductions and his own inferences therefrom" (60 Cong. Rec., 1921, p. 504)—the implication was that the focus on Poland was prompted by anti-Semitism.

The House Majority Report (signed by fifteen of its seventeen members with only Representatives Dickstein and Sabath not signing) also emphasized the Jewish role in defining the intellectual battle in terms of Nordic superiority versus "American ideals" rather than in the terms of an ethnic status quo actually favored by the committee:

The cry of discrimination is, the committee believes, manufactured and built up by special representatives of racial groups, aided by aliens actually living abroad. Members of the committee have taken notice of a report in the *Jewish Tribune* (New York), February 8, 1924, of a farewell dinner to Mr. Israel Zangwill which says:

"Mr. Zangwill spoke chiefly on the immigration question, declaring that if Jews persisted in a strenuous opposition to the restricted immigration there would be no restriction. 'If you create enough fuss against this Nordic nonsense,' he said, 'you will defeat this legislation. You must make a fight against this bill; tell them they are destroying American ideals. Most fortifications are of cardboard, and if you press against them, they give way.'"

The Committee does not feel that the restriction aimed to be accomplished in this bill is directed at the Jews, for they can come within the quotas from any country in which they were born. The Committee has not dwelt on the desirability of a "Nordic" or any other particular type of immigrant, but has held steadfastly to the purpose of securing a heavy restriction, with the quota so divided that the countries from which the most came in the two decades ahead of the World War might be slowed down in order that the United States might restore its population balance. The continued charge that the Committee has built up a "Nordic" race and devoted its hearing to that end is part of a deliberately manufactured assault for as a matter of fact the committee has done nothing of the kind. (H.R. Rep. No. 350, 1924, p. 16)

Indeed, one is struck in reading the 1924 congressional debates by the rarity with which the issue of Nordic racial superiority is raised by those in favor of the legislation, whereas virtually all the anti-restrictionists raised this issue.[149] After a particularly colorful comment in opposition to the theory of Nordic racial superiority, restrictionist leader Albert Johnson remarked, "I would like very much to say on behalf of the committee that through the strenuous times of the hearings this committee undertook not to discuss the Nordic proposition or racial matters" (65 Cong. Rec., 1924, p. 5911). Earlier, during the hearings on the bill, Johnson remarked in response to the comments of Rabbi Stephen S. Wise representing the AJCongress, "I dislike to be placed continually in the attitude of assuming that there is a race prejudice, when the one thing I have tried to do for 11 years is to free myself from race prejudice, if I had it at all" (*Restriction of Immigration*, 1924, p. 351). Several restrictionists explicitly denounced the theory of Nordic superiority, including Senators Bruce (65 Cong. Rec., 1924, p. 5955) and Jones (p. 6614) and Representatives Bacon (p. 5902), Byrnes (p. 5653), Johnson (p. 5648), McLeod (pp. 5675–5676),

---

[149] For example, in the Senate debates of April 15th to 19th, 1924, Nordic superiority was not mentioned by any of the proponents of the legislation but was mentioned by the following opponents of the legislation: Senators Colt (p. 6542), Reed (p. 6468), and Walsh (p. 6355). In the House debates of April 5th, 8th, and 15th, virtually all the opponents of the legislation raised the racial inferiority issue, including Representatives Celler (pp. 5914–5915), Clancy (p. 5930), Connery (p. 5683), Dickstein (pp. 5655–5656, 5686), Gallivan (p. 5849), Jacobstein (p. 5864), James (p. 5670), Kunz (p. 5896), La Guardia (p. 5657), Mooney (pp. 5909–5910), O'Connell (p. 5836), O'Connor (p. 5648), Oliver (p. 5870), O'Sullivan (p. 5899), Perlman (p. 5651), Sabath (pp. 5651, 5662), and Tague (p. 5873). Several representatives—e.g., Representatives Dickinson (p. 6267), Garber (pp. 5689–5693), and Smith (p. 5705)—contrasted the positive characteristics of the Nordic immigrants with the negative characteristics of more recent immigrants without distinguishing genetic from environmental reasons as possible influences. They, along with several others, noted that recent immigrants had not assimilated and they tended to cluster in urban areas. Representative Allen argued that there is a "necessity for purifying and keeping pure the blood of America" (p. 5693). Representative McSwain, who argued for the need to preserve Nordic hegemony, did so not on the basis of Nordic superiority but on the basis of legitimate ethnic self-interest (pp. 5683–5685; see also comments of Representatives Lea and Miller). Representative Gasque introduced a newspaper article discussing the swamping of the race that had built America (p. 6270).

McReynolds (p. 5855), Michener (p. 5909), Miller (p. 5883), Newton (p. 6240), Rosenbloom (p. 5851), Vaile (p. 5922), Vincent (p. 6266), White (p. 5898), and Wilson (p. 5671).

Indeed, it is noteworthy that there are indications in the congressional debate that representatives from the West Coast were concerned about the competence and competitive threat presented by Japanese immigrants, and their rhetoric suggests they viewed the Japanese as racially equal or superior, not inferior. For example, Senator Jones stated, "We admit that [the Japanese] are as able as we are, that they are as progressive as we are, that they are as honest as we are, that they are as brainy as we are, and that they are equal in all that goes to make a great people and nation" (65 Cong. Rec., 1924, p. 6614); Representative MacLafferty emphasized Japanese domination of certain agricultural markets (p. 5681), and Representative Lea noted their ability to supplant "their American competitor" (p. 5697). Representative Miller described the Japanese as "a relentless and unconquerable competitor of our people wherever he places himself" (p. 5884); see also comments of Representatives Gilbert (p. 6261), Raker (p. 5892), and Free (pp. 5924ff).

Moreover, whereas the issue of Jewish-gentile resource competition was not raised during the congressional debates, quotas on Jewish admissions to Ivy League universities were a highly salient issue among Jews during this period. The quota issue was highly publicized in the Jewish media, which focused on activities of Jewish self-defense organizations such as the ADL (see, e.g., the ADL statement published in *The American Hebrew*, September 29th, 1922, p. 536). Jewish-gentile resource competition may therefore have been on the minds of some legislators. Indeed, President A. Lawrence Lowell of Harvard was the national vice-president of the Immigration Restriction League as well as a proponent of quotas on Jewish admission to Harvard (Symott, 1986, p. 238), suggesting that resource competition with an intellectually superior Jewish group was an issue for at least some prominent restrictionists.

It is probable that anti-Jewish animosity related to resource competition issues was widespread. Higham (1984, p. 141) writes of "the urgent pressure which the Jews, as an exceptionally ambitious immigrant people, put upon some of the more crowded rungs of the social ladder." Beginning in the nineteenth century, there were fairly high levels of covert and overt anti-Semitism in patrician circles resulting from the very rapid upward mobility of Jews and their competitive drive. Prior to World War I, the reaction of the gentile power structure was to construct social registers and emphasize genealogy as mechanisms of exclusion—"criteria that could not be met by money alone" (pp. 104ff, 127). During this period Edward A. Ross (1914, p. 164) described gentile resentment at "being obliged to engage in a humiliating and undignified scramble in order to keep his trade or his clients against the Jewish invader"—suggesting a rather broad-based concern with Jewish economic competition. Attempts at exclusion in a wide range of areas increased in the 1920s and reached their peak during the difficult economic situation of the Great Depression (Higham, pp. 131ff).

In the 1924 debates, however, the only congressional comments suggesting a concern with Jewish-gentile resource competition (as well as a concern that Jewish immigrants were alienated from the cultural traditions of America and tended to have a destructive influence) that I have been able to find are the following from Representative Wefald:

> I for one am not afraid of the radical ideas that some might bring with them. Ideas you can not keep out anyway, but the leadership of our intellectual life in many of its phases has come into the hands of these clever newcomers who have no sympathy with our old-time American ideals nor with those of northern Europe, who detect our weaknesses and pander to them and get wealthy through the disservices they render us.
>
> Our whole system of amusements has been taken over by men who came here on the crest of the south and east European immigration. They produce our horrible film stories, they compose and dish out to us our jazz music, they write many of the books we read, and edit our magazines and newspapers. (65 Cong. Rec., 1924, p. 6272)

The immigration debate also occurred amid discussion in the Jewish media of Thorstein Veblen's famous essay "The Intellectual Pre-eminence of Jews in Modern Europe" (serialized in *The American Hebrew* beginning September 10th, 1920). In an editorial from July 13th, 1923 (p. 177), *The American Hebrew* noted that Jews were disproportionately represented among the gifted in Lewis Terman's study of gifted children and commented that "this fact must give rise to bitter, though futile, reflection among the so-called Nordics." The editorial also noted that Jews were overrepresented among scholarship winners in competitions sponsored by the state of New York. The editorial pointedly noted that "perhaps the Nordics are too proud to try for these honors. In any event the list of names just announced by the State Department of Education at Albany as winners of these coveted scholarships is not in the least Nordic; it reads like a confirmation roster at a Temple."

There is, in fact, evidence that Jews, like East Asians, have higher IQs than Caucasians (Lynn, 1987; Rushton, 1995; PTSDA, Ch. 7). Indeed, Terman had found that Chinese were equal in IQ to Caucasians—further indication that, as Carl Degler (1991, p. 52) notes, "their [IQ] scores could not have been an excuse for the discrimination" represented by the Immigration Act of 1924. As indicated above, there is considerable evidence from the congressional debates that the exclusion of Asians was motivated at least partly by fears of competition with a highly talented, intelligent group rather than by feelings of racial superiority.

The most common argument made by those favoring the legislation, and the one reflected in the Majority Report, is the argument that in the interest of fairness to all ethnic groups, the quotas should reflect the relative ethnic composition of the entire country. Restrictionists noted that the census of 1890 was chosen because the percentages of the foreign born of different ethnic groups in that year approximated the general ethnic composition of the entire country in 1920. Senator Reed of Pennsylvania and Representative Rogers of Massachusetts proposed to achieve the same result by directly basing the quotas on the national origins of all people in the country as of the 1920 census, and this was eventually incorporated into law. Representative Rogers argued, "Gentlemen, you can not dissent from this principle, because it is fair. It does not discriminate for anybody and it does not discriminate against anybody" (65 Cong. Rec., 1924, p. 5847). Senator Reed noted, "The purpose, I think, of most of us in changing the quota basis is to cease from discriminating against the native born here and against the group of our citizens who come from northern and western Europe. I think the present system discriminates in favor of southeastern Europe" (p. 6457) (i.e., because 46 percent of the quotas under the Immigration Act of 1921 went to Eastern and Southern Europe when they constituted less than 12 percent of the U.S. population).

As an example illustrating the fundamental argument asserting a legitimate ethnic interest in maintaining an ethnic status quo without claiming racial superiority, consider the following statement from Representative William N. Vaile of Colorado, one of the most prominent restrictionists:

> Let me emphasize here that the "restrictionists" of Congress do not claim that the "Nordic" race, or even the Anglo-Saxon race, is the best race in the world. Let us concede, in all fairness, that the Czech is a more sturdy laborer, with a very low percentage of crime and insanity, that the Jew is the best business man in the world, and that the Italian has a spiritual grasp and an artistic sense which have greatly enriched the world and which have, indeed, enriched us, a spiritual exaltation and an artistic creative sense which the Nordic rarely attains. Nordics need not be vain about their own qualifications. It well behooves them to be humble. What we do claim is that the northern European, and particularly Anglo-Saxons, made this country. Oh, yes; the others helped. But that is the full statement of the case. They came to this country because it was already made as an Anglo-Saxon commonwealth. They added to it, they often enriched it, but they did not make it, and they have not yet greatly changed it. We are determined that they shall not. It is a good country. It suits us. And what we assert is that we are not going to surrender it to somebody else or allow other people, no matter what their merits, to make it something

different. If there is any changing to be done, we will do it ourselves. (65 Cong. Rec., 1924, p. 5922)

The debate in the House also illustrated the highly salient role of Jewish legislators in combating restrictionism. Representative Robison singled out Representative Sabath as the leader of anti-restrictionist efforts; he also focused on Representatives Jacobstein, Celler, and Perlman as being opposed to any restrictions on immigration (65 Cong. Rec., 1924, p. 5666). Representative Blanton, complaining of the difficulty of getting restrictionist legislation through Congress, noted, "When at least 65 per cent of the sentiment of this House, in my judgment, is in favor of the exclusion of all foreigners for five years, why do we not put that into law? Has Brother Sabath such a tremendous influence over us that he holds us down on this proposition?" (p. 5685). Representative Sabath responded, "There may be something to that." In addition, the following comments of Representative Leavitt clearly indicate the salience of Jewish congressmen to their opponents during the debate:

> The instinct for national and race preservation is not one to be condemned, as has been intimated here. No one should be better able to understand the desire of Americans to keep America American than the gentleman from Illinois [Mr. Sabath], who is leading the attack on this measure, or the gentlemen from New York, Mr. Dickstein, Mr. Jacobstein, Mr. Celler, and Mr. Perlman. They are of the one great historic people who have maintained the identity of their race throughout the centuries because they believe sincerely that they are a chosen people, with certain ideals to maintain, and knowing that the loss of racial identity means a change of ideals. That fact should make it easy for them and the majority of the most active opponents of this measure in the spoken debate to recognize and sympathize with our viewpoint, which is not so extreme as that of their own race, but only demands that the admixture of other peoples shall be only of such kind and proportions and in such quantities as will not alter racial characteristics more rapidly than there can be assimilation as to ideas of government as well as of blood. (65 Cong. Rec., 1924, pp. 6265–6266)

The view that Jews had a strong tendency to oppose genetic assimilation with surrounding groups was expressed by other observers as well and was a component of contemporary anti-Semitism (see Singerman, 1986, pp. 110–111). Jewish avoidance of exogamy certainly had a basis in reality (PTSDA, Chs. 2–4), and it is worth recalling that there was powerful opposition to intermarriage even among the more liberal segments of early twentieth-century American Judaism and certainly among the less liberal segments represented by the great majority of Orthodox immigrants from Eastern Europe who had come to constitute the great majority of American Jewry. The prominent nineteenth-century Reform leader David Einhorn, for example, was a lifelong opponent of mixed marriages and refused to officiate at such ceremonies, even when pressed to do so (Meyer, 1989). Einhorn was also a staunch opponent of conversion of gentiles to Judaism because of the effects on the "racial purity" of Judaism (Levenson, 1989, p. 331). The influential Reform intellectual Kaufman Kohler was also an ardent opponent of mixed marriage. In a view that is highly compatible with Horace Kallen's multiculturalism, Kohler (1918/1968, pp. 445–446) concluded that Israel must remain separate and avoid intermarriage until it leads humankind to an era of universal peace and brotherhood among the races. The negative attitude toward intermarriage was confirmed by survey results. A 1912 survey indicated that only seven out of one hundred Reform rabbis had officiated at a mixed marriage, and a 1909 resolution of the chief Reform group, the Central Council of American Rabbis, declared that "mixed marriages are contrary to the tradition of the Jewish religion and should be discouraged by the American Rabbinate" (Meyer). Gentile perceptions of Jewish attitudes on intermarriage, therefore, had a strong basis in reality.

Far more important than the Jewish tendency toward endogamy in engendering anti-Jewish animosity during the congressional debates of 1924 were two other prominent themes of this project: Jewish immigrants from Eastern Europe were widely perceived as unassimilable and as retaining a separate culture (see SAID, Ch. 2); they were also thought to be disproportionately involved in radical political movements (see Ch. 3).

The perception of radicalism among Jewish immigrants was common in Jewish as well as gentile publications. The American Hebrew editorialized, "[W]e must not forget the immigrants from Russia and Austria will be coming from countries infested with Bolshevism, and it will require more than a superficial effort to make good citizens out of them" (in Neuringer, 1971/1980, p. 165). The fact that Jewish immigrants from Eastern Europe were viewed as "infected with Bolshevism . . . unpatriotic, alien, unassimilable" resulted in a wave of anti-Semitism in the 1920s and contributed to the restrictive immigration legislation of the period (p. 165). In Sorin's (1985, p. 46) study of immigrant Jewish radical activists, over half had been involved in radical politics in Europe before emigrating, and for those emigrating after 1900, the percentage rose to 69 percent. Jewish publications warned of the possibilities of anti-Semitism resulting from the leftism of Jewish immigrants, and the official Jewish community engaged in "a near-desperation . . . effort to portray the Jew as one hundred per cent American" by, for example, organizing patriotic pageants on national holidays and by attempting to get the immigrants to learn English (Neuringer, p. 167).[150]

> The image of the Jew as Communist played an often-overlooked role in the history not only of Jews in America, but of the millions of Jews in Eastern Europe who would have liked to emigrate to the United States after World War I, but who were prevented from doing so by the immigration restrictions enacted in the early 1920s, culminating in the Reed-Johnson Act of 1924. For those restrictions were motivated in part by the identification of Jews with political radicalism. (Muller, 2010, pp. 161–162)

From the standpoint of the immigration debates, it is important to note that in the 1920s a majority of the members of the Socialist Party were immigrants and that an "overwhelming" (Glazer, 1961, pp. 38, 40) percentage of the CPUSA consisted of recent immigrants, a substantial percentage of whom were Jews. As late as June 1933 the national organization of the CPUSA was still 70 percent foreign born (Lyons, 1982, pp. 72–73); in Philadelphia in 1929, fully 90 percent of CPUSA members were foreign born, and 72.2 percent of the CPUSA members in Philadelphia were the children of Jewish immigrants who had come to the United States in the late nineteenth and early twentieth centuries (p. 71).

The material in the 2002 edition *CofC* on Jewish activism leading up to the Immigration Act of 1924 has been corroborated by Daniel Okrent in *The Guarded Gate* (2019). The older German-Jewish community, while expressing distaste for their rather unrefined immigrant co-ethnics, was instrumental in keeping America's open immigration system long after immigration from Eastern and Southern Europe had ceased to be popular in the population at large. Thus Senator Henry Cabot Lodge, leader of the restrictionists, wrote to a friend during the second presidency of Grover Cleveland (1893–1897), "Influences on [Cleveland] were used yesterday which I will explain to you when we meet and which were very hard to overcome"; to another he "said these other forces represented neither corporations or political factions" (p. 72). Okrent notes that they "were almost certainly members of America's moneyed and influential German Jewish community," such as Jacob Schiff "who made a personal plea to Grover Cleveland to veto the literacy test" (p. 73). (Prior to

---

[150] Similarly, the immigration of Eastern European Jews into England after 1880 had a transformative effect on the political attitudes of British Jewry in the direction of socialism, trade unionism, and Zionism, often combined with religious orthodoxy and devotion to a highly separatist traditional lifestyle (Alderman, 1983, pp. 47ff). The more established Jewish organizations fought hard to combat the well-founded image of Jewish immigrants as Zionist, religiously orthodox political radicals who refused to be conscripted into the armed forces during World War I in order to fight the enemies of the officially anti-Semitic czarist government (Alderman, 1992, pp. 237ff).

focusing on national origins, immigration restrictionists promoted a literacy test as a means of restricting immigration.)

> For a quarter of a century ... Lodge, the IRL [Immigration Restriction League], and their allies would have to contend with an array of influential organizations dominated by wealthy German Jews. ... Collectively, they composed a formidable and enduring opposition. ... The emergence in the 1890s of organized, wealthy, and well-connected Jews working on behalf of the immigrants presented Lodge and his colleagues with an opposition that few Boston Brahmins had encountered. (Okrent, 2019, pp. 72–73)

Likely because of this influence, immigration was not restricted until the 1920s, even though public opinion had turned against it at least by 1905 (Neuringer, 1971/1980, p. 83). As recounted by N. W. Cohen (1972, pp. 40ff), the AJCommittee's efforts in opposition to immigration restriction in the early twentieth century constitute a remarkable example of the ability of Jewish organizations to influence public policy—despite being composed of only a thin upper crust of the American Jewish community of the period.

Jewish Anti-Restrictionist Activity, 1924–1945

The saliency of Jewish involvement in U.S. immigration policy continued after the Immigration Act of 1924. Particularly objectionable to Jewish groups was the national origins quota system. For example, a writer for *The Jewish Tribune* stated in 1927, "[W]e ... regard all measures for regulating immigration according to nationality as illogical, unjust, and un-American" (in Neuringer, 1971/1980, p. 205). During the 1930s the most outspoken critic of further restrictions on immigration (motivated now mainly by the economic concerns that immigration would exacerbate the problems brought on by the Great Depression) was Representative Samuel Dickstein, and Dickstein's assumption of the chairmanship of the House Immigration Committee in 1931 marked the end of the ability of restrictionists to enact further reductions in quotas (Divine, 1957, pp. 79–88). Jewish groups were the primary opponents of restriction and the primary supporters of liberalized regulations during the 1930s; their opponents emphasized the economic consequences of immigration during a period of high unemployment (pp. 85–88). Between 1933 and 1938 Representative Dickstein introduced a number of bills aimed at increasing the number of refugees from Nazi Germany and supported mainly by Jewish organizations, but the restrictionists prevailed (p. 93).

During the 1930s concerns about the radicalism and unassimilability of Jewish immigrants as well as the possibility of Nazi subversion were the main factors influencing the opposition to changing the immigration laws (Breitman & Kraut, 1987). Moreover, "Charges that the Jews in America were more loyal to their tribe than to their country abounded in the United States in the 1930s" (p. 87). There was a clear perception among all parties that the public opposed any changes in immigration policy and was particularly opposed to Jewish immigration. The 1939 hearings on the proposed legislation to admit twenty thousand German refugee children therefore minimized Jewish interest in the legislation. The bill referred to people "of every race and creed suffering from conditions which compel them to seek refuge in other lands" (*Admission of German Refugee Children*, 1939, p. 1) The bill did not mention that Jews would be the main beneficiaries of the legislation, and witnesses in favor of the bill emphasized that only approximately 60 percent of the children would be Jewish. The only person identifying himself as "a member of the Jewish race" who testified in favor of the bill was "one-fourth Catholic and three-quarters Jewish," with Protestant and Catholic nieces and nephews, and from the South, a bastion of anti-immigration sentiment (p. 78).

In contrast, opponents of the bill threatened to publicize the very large percentage of Jews already being admitted under the quota system—presumably an indication of the powerful force of a "virulent and pervasive" anti-Semitism among the American public (Breitman & Kraut, 1987, p. 80). Opponents noted that the immigration permitted by the bill "would be for the most part of the Jewish race," and a witness testified "that the Jewish people will profit most by this legislation goes without saying" (in Divine, 1957, p. 100). The restrictionists argued in economic terms, for example, by frequently citing President Roosevelt's statement in his second inaugural speech, "one-third of a nation ill-housed, ill-clad, ill-nourished," and citing large numbers of needy children already in the United States. The main restrictionist concern, though, was that the bill was yet another in a long history of attempts by anti-restrictionists to develop precedents that would eventually undermine the Immigration Act of 1924. For example, Francis Kinnicutt, president of the Allied Patriotic Societies, emphasized that the Immigration Act of 1924 had been based on the idea of proportional representation based on the ethnic composition of the country. The legislation would be a precedent "for similar unscientific and favored-nation legislation in response to the pressure of foreign nationalistic or racial groups, rather than in accordance with the needs and desires of the American people" (*Admission of German Refugee Children*, 1939, p. 140).

Wilbur S. Carr and other State Department officials were important in minimizing the entry of Jewish refugees from Germany during the 1930s. Undersecretary of State William Phillips was an anti-Semite with considerable influence on immigration policy from 1933 to 1936 (Breitman & Kraut, 1987, p. 36). Throughout the period until the end of World War II attempts to promote Jewish immigration, even in the context of knowledge that the Nazis were persecuting Jews, were largely unsuccessful because of an unyielding Congress and the activities of bureaucrats, especially those in the State Department. (Indeed, the State Department remained a target of Jewish ire at least as late as the 1960s because of its opposition to U.S. support of Israel.) Public discussion in periodicals such as *The Nation* (November 19th, 1938) and *The New Republic* (November 23rd, 1938) charged that restrictionism was motivated by anti-Semitism, whereas opponents of admitting large numbers of Jews argued that admission would result in an increase in anti-Semitism. Henry Pratt Fairchild (1939, p. 344), a restrictionist highly critical of Jews in general (see Fairchild, 1947), emphasized the "powerful current of anti-foreignism and anti-Semitism that is running close to the surface of the American public mind, ready to burst out into violent eruption on relatively slight provocation." Public opinion remained steadfast against increasing the quotas for European refugees; a 1939 poll in *Fortune* (April 1939) showed that 83 percent answered no to the following question: "If you were a member of Congress would you vote yes or no on a bill to open the doors of the United States to a larger number of European refugees than now admitted under our immigration quotas?" Less than 9 percent replied yes, and the remainder had no opinion.

Jewish Anti-Restrictionist Activity, 1946–1952

Although Jewish interests were defeated by the Immigration Act of 1924, "the discriminatory character of the Reed-Johnson Act continued to rankle all sectors of American Jewish opinion" (Neuringer, 1971/1980, p. 196). During this period, an article by Will Maslow (1950) in *Congress Weekly* reiterated the belief that the restrictive immigration laws intentionally targeted Jews:

> Only one type of law, immigration legislation which relates to aliens outside the country, is not subject to constitutional guarantees, and even here hostility toward Jewish immigration has had to be disguised in an elaborate quota scheme in which eligibility was based on place of birth rather than religion.

The Jewish concern to alter the ethnic balance of the United States is apparent in the debates over immigration legislation during the post-World War II era. In 1948 the AJCommittee submitted to a Senate subcommittee a statement simultaneously denying the importance of the material interests of the United States and affirming its commitment to immigration of all races:

> Americanism is not to be measured by conformity to law, or zeal for education, or literacy, or any of these qualities in which immigrants may excel the native-born. Americanism is the spirit behind the welcome that

America has traditionally extended to people of all races, all religions, all nationalities. (in N. W. Cohen, 1972, p. 369)

In 1945 Representative Emanuel Celler introduced a bill ending Chinese exclusion by establishing token quotas for Chinese, and in 1948 the AJCommittee condemned racial quotas on Asians (Divine, 1957, p. 155). In contrast, Jewish groups showed indifference or even hostility toward immigration of non-Jews from Europe (including Southern Europe) in the post-World War II era (Neuringer, 1971/1980, pp. 356, 367–369, 383). Thus Jewish spokespersons did not testify at all during the first set of hearings on emergency legislation to allow immigration of a limited number of German, Italian, Greek, and Dutch immigrants, escapees from communism, and a small number of Poles, Asians, and Arabs. When Jewish spokespersons eventually testified (partly because a few of the escapees from communism were Jews), they took the opportunity to once again focus on their condemnation of the national origins provisions of the Immigration Act of 1924.

Jewish involvement in opposing restrictions during this period was motivated partly by attempts to establish precedents in which the quota system was bypassed and partly by attempts to increase immigration of Jews from Eastern Europe. The Citizens Committee on Displaced Persons, which advocated legislation to admit four hundred thousand refugees as nonquota immigrants over a period of four years, maintained a staff of sixty-five people and was funded mainly by the AJCommittee and other Jewish contributors (see 95 Cong. Rec., 1949, pp. 14647–14654; Neuringer, 1971/1980, p. 393). Witnesses opposing the legislation complained that the bill was an attempt to subvert the ethnic balance of the United States established by the Immigration Act of 1924 (Divine, 1957, p. 117). In the event, the bill that was reported out of the subcommittee did not satisfy Jewish interests because it established a cutoff date that excluded Jews who had migrated from Eastern Europe after World War II, including Jews fleeing Polish anti-Semitism. The Senate subcommittee "regarded the movement of Jews and other refugees from eastern Europe after 1945 as falling outside the scope of the main problem and implied that this exodus was a planned migration organized by Jewish agencies in the United States and in Europe" (S. Rep. No. 950, 1948, pp. 15–16).

Jewish representatives led the assault on the bill (Divine, 1957, p. 127), with Representative Emanuel Celler calling it "worse than no bill at all. All it does is exclude . . . Jews" (in Neuringer, 1971/1980, p. 298; see also Divine, 1957, p. 127). In reluctantly signing the bill, President Truman noted that the 1945 cutoff date "discriminates in callous fashion against displaced persons of the Jewish faith" (*Interpreter Releases* 25, July 21st, 1948, pp. 252–254). In contrast, Senator Chapman Revercomb stated that "there is no distinction, certainly no discrimination, intended between any persons because of their religion or their race, but there are differences drawn among those persons who are in fact displaced persons and have been in camp longest and have a preference" (94 Cong. Rec., 1948, p. 6793). In his analysis, Divine (1957, p. 143) concludes:

> The expressed motive of the restrictionists, to limit the program to those people displaced during the course of the war, appears to be a valid explanation for these provisions. The tendency of Jewish groups to attribute the exclusion of many of their coreligionists to anti-Semitic bias is understandable; however, the extreme charges of discrimination made during the 1948 presidential campaign lead one to suspect that the northern wing of the Democratic party was using this issue to attract votes from members of minority groups. Certainly Truman's assertion that the 1948 law was anti-Catholic, made in the face of Catholic denials, indicates that political expediency had a great deal to do with the emphasis on the discrimination issue.

In the aftermath of this bill, the Citizens Committee on Displaced Persons released a report claiming the bill was characterized by "hate and racism," and Jewish organizations were unanimous in denouncing the law (Divine, 1957, p. 131). After the 1948 elections resulted in a Democratic Congress and a sympathetic President Truman, Representative Celler introduced a bill without the 1945 cutoff date, but, after passing the House, the bill failed in the Senate because of the opposition of Senator Pat McCarran. McCarran noted that the Citizens Committee on Displaced Persons had spent over eight hundred thousand dollars (equivalent to over ten million dollars in 2024) lobbying for the bill, with the result that "there has been disseminated over the length and breadth of this nation a campaign of misrepresentation and falsehood which has misled many public-spirited and well-meaning citizens and organizations" (95 Cong. Rec., 1949, pp. 5042–5043). After defeat, the Citizens Committee on Displaced Persons increased expenditures to over one million dollars (nearly thirteen million dollars in 2024) and succeeded in passing a bill, introduced by Representative Celler, with a 1949 cutoff date that did not discriminate against Jews but largely excluded ethnic Germans who had been expelled from Eastern Europe. In an odd twist in the debate, restrictionists now accused the anti-restrictionists of ethnic bias (e.g., Senators Eastland and McCarran, 96 Cong. Rec., 1950, pp. 2737, 4743).

At a time when there were no outbreaks of anti-Semitism in other parts of the world creating an urgent need for Jewish immigration and with the presence of Israel as a safe haven for Jews, Jewish organizations still vigorously objected to the continuation of the national origins provisions of the Immigration Act of 1924 in the McCarran-Walter (Immigration and Nationality) Act of 1952 (Neuringer, 1971/1980, pp. 337ff). Indeed, when U.S. District Court of

Appeals Judge Simon H. Rifkind testified on behalf of a wide range of Jewish organizations against the McCarran-Walter bill, he noted emphatically that because of the international situation and particularly the existence of Israel as a safe haven for Jews, Jewish views on immigration legislation were not predicated on the "plight of our co-religionists but rather the impact which immigration and naturalization laws have upon the temper and quality of American life here in the United States" (AJCongress, *Revision of Immigration*, 1951, p. 565). The argument was couched in terms of "democratic principles and the cause of international amity" (N. W. Cohen, 1972, p. 368)—the implicit theory being that the principles of democracy required ethnic diversity—a view promulgated by Jewish intellectual activists such as Sidney Hook (1948, 1949; see Ch. 7) at the time—and the theory that the good will of other countries depended on American willingness to accept their citizens as immigrants.

> The enactment of [the McCarran-Walter bill] will gravely impair the national effort we are putting forth. For we are engaged in a war for the hearts and minds of men. The free nations of the world look to us for moral and spiritual reinforcement at a time when the faith which moves men is as important as the force they wield. (AJCongress, *Revision of Immigration*, 1951, p. 566)[151]

The McCarran-Walter bill explicitly included racial ancestry as a criterion in its provision that Orientals would be included in the token Oriental quotas, no matter where they were born. Herbert Lehman, a senator from New York and the most prominent senatorial opponent of immigration restriction during the 1950s (Neuringer, 1971/1980, p. 351), argued during the debates over the McCarran-Walter bill that immigrants from Jamaica of African descent should be included in the quota for England and stated that the bill would cause resentment among Asians (pp. 346, 356). Representatives Celler and Javits, the leaders of the anti-restrictionists in the House, made similar arguments (98 Cong. Rec., 1952, pp. 4306, 4219). As was also apparent in the battles dating back to the nineteenth century, the opposition to the national origins legislation went beyond its effects on Jewish immigration to advocate immigration of all the racial-ethnic groups of the world.

Reflecting a concern for maintaining the ethnic status quo as well as the salience of Jewish issues during the period, the report of the subcommittee considering the McCarran-Walter immigration bill noted that "the population of the United States has increased three-fold since 1877, while the Jewish population has increased twenty-one-fold during the same period" (S. Rep. No. 1515, 1950, pp. 2–4). The bill also included a provision that naturalized citizens

---

[151] See also statement of Rabbi Bernard J. Bamberger, President of the Synagogue Council of America; and the statement of the AJCongress, pp. 560–561.

automatically lost citizenship if they resided abroad continuously for five years. This provision was viewed by Jewish organizations as motivated by anti-Zionist attitudes: "Testimony by Government officials at the hearings . . . made it clear that the provision stemmed from a desire to dissuade naturalized American Jews from subscribing to a deeply held ideal which some officials in contravention of American policy regarded as undesirable" (Will Maslow of the AJCongress, *Revision of Immigration*, 1951, p. 394).

Reaffirming the logic of the 1920s restrictionists, the subcommittee report emphasized that a purpose of the Immigration Act of 1924 was "the restriction of immigration from southern and eastern Europe in order to preserve a pre-dominance of persons of northwestern European origin in the composition of our total population," but noted that this purpose did not imply "any theory of Nordic supremacy" (S. Rep. No. 1515, 1950, pp. 442, 445–446). The argument was mainly phrased in terms of the "similarity of cultural background" of prospec-tive immigrants, implying the rejection of theories of cultural pluralism (M. T. Bennett, 1966, p. 133). As in 1924, theories of Nordic superiority were rejected, but unlike 1924 there was no mention of the legitimate ethnic self-interest of the Northwestern European peoples, presumably a result of the effectiveness of the Boasian onslaught on this idea.

> Without giving credence to any theory of Nordic superiority, the subcom-mittee believes that the adoption of the national origins formula was a rational and logical method of numerically restricting immigration in such a manner as to best preserve the sociological and cultural balance in the population of the United States. There is no doubt that it favored the peo-ples of the countries of northern and western Europe over those of south-ern and eastern Europe, but the subcommittee holds that the peoples who had made the greatest contribution to the development of this country were fully justified in determining that the country was no longer a field for further colonization and, henceforth, further immigration would not only be restricted but directed to admit immigrants considered to be more readily assimilable because of the similarity of their cultural background to those of the principal components of our population. (S. Rep. No. 1515, 1950, p. 455)

It is important to note that Jewish spokespersons differed from other lib-eral groups in their motives for opposing restrictions on immigration during this period. In the following I emphasize the congressional testimony of Judge Simon H. Rifkind, who represented a very broad range of Jewish agencies in the hearings on the McCarran-Walter bill in 1951 (*Revision of Immigration*, 1951, p. 562–595).

(1) Immigration should come from all racial-ethnic groups:

We conceive of Americanism as the spirit behind the welcome that America has traditionally extended to people of different races, all religions, all nationalities. Americanism is a tolerant way of life that was devised by men who differed from one another vastly in religion, race background, education, and lineage, and who agreed to forget all these things and ask of a new neighbor not where he comes from but only what he can do and what is his spirit toward his fellow men. (p. 566)

(2) The total number of immigrants should be maximized within very broad economic and political constraints: "The regulation [of immigration] is the regulation of an asset, not of a liability" (p. 567). Rifkind emphasized several times that unused quotas had the effect of restricting total numbers of immigrants, and he viewed this very negatively (e.g., p. 569).

(3) Immigrants should not be viewed as economic assets and imported only to serve the present needs of the United States:

Looking at [selective immigration] from the point of view of the United States, never from the point of view of the immigrant, I say that we should, to some extent, allow for our temporary needs, but not to make our immigration problem an employment instrumentality. I do not think that we are buying economic commodities when we allow immigrants to come in. We are admitting human beings who will found families and raise children, whose children may reach the heights—at least so we hope and pray. For a small segment of the immigrant stream I think we are entitled to say, if we happen to be short of a particular talent, "Let us go out and look for them," if necessary, but let us not make that the all-pervading thought. (p. 570)

The opposition to needed skills as the basis of immigration was consistent with the prolonged Jewish attempt to delay the passage of a literacy test as a criterion for immigration beginning in the late nineteenth century until a literacy test was passed in 1917.

Although Rifkind's testimony was free of the accusation that immigration policy was based on the theory of Nordic superiority, Nordic superiority continued to be a prominent theme of other Jewish groups, particularly the AJCongress, in advocating immigration from all ethnic groups. The statement of the AJCongress focused a great deal of attention on the importance of the theory of Nordic superiority as motivating the Immigration Act of 1924. Contrary to Rifkind's surprising assertion of the traditional American openness to all ethnic groups, it noted the long history of ethnic exclusion that existed before these theories were developed, including the Chinese Exclusion Act of 1882, the gentlemen's agreement with Japan of 1907 limiting immigration of Japanese workers, and the exclusion of other Asians in 1917. The statement noted that the Immigration Act of 1924 had succeeded in preserving the ethnic balance of the United States as of the 1920 census, but it commented that "the objective is valueless. There is nothing sacrosanct about the composition of the population in 1920. It would be foolish to believe that we reached the peak of ethnic perfection in that year" (*Revision of Immigration*, 1951, p. 410). More-over, in an explicit statement of Horace Kallen's multicultural ideal, the AJCongress statement (p. 404) advocated "the thesis of cultural democracy which would guarantee to all groups 'majority and minority alike . . . the right to be different and the responsibility to make sure that their differences do not con-flict with the welfare of the American people as a whole.'"

During this period *Congress Weekly*, the journal of the AJCongress, regu-larly denounced the national origins provisions as based on the "myth of the existence of superior and inferior racial stocks" (October 17th, 1955, p. 3) and advocated immigration on the basis of "need and other criteria unrelated to race or national origin" (May 4th, 1953, p. 3). Particularly objectionable from the perspective of the AJCongress was the implication that there should be no change in the ethnic status quo prescribed by the Immigration Act of 1924 (e.g., I. Goldstein, 1952b, p. 6). The national origins formula "is outrageous now . . . when our national experience has confirmed beyond a doubt that our very strength lies in the diversity of our peoples" (I. Goldstein, 1952a, p. 5).

As indicated above, there is some evidence that the Immigration Act of 1924 and the restrictionism of the 1930s was motivated partly by anti-Semitic attitudes. Anti-Semitism and its linkage with anti-communism were also ap-parent in the immigration arguments during the 1950s preceding and follow-ing the passage of the McCarran-Walter Act. Restrictionists often pointed to evidence that over 90 percent of American communists had backgrounds link-ing them to Eastern Europe. A major thrust of restrictionist efforts was to pre-vent immigration from this area and to ease deportation procedures to prevent communist subversion. Eastern Europe was also the origin of most Jewish im-migration, and Jews were disproportionately represented among American communists, with the result that these issues became linked, and the situation lent itself to broad anti-Jewish theories about the role of Jews in U.S. politics.

For example, John Beaty, author of *Iron Curtain Over America* (1951), was a professor at Southern Methodist University and had served as a colonel in U.S. Military Intelligence in World War II. A strong anti-communist, he noted the great overrepresentation of Jews in subversive activities, a grave concern for Jewish activist organizations during the period (Unz, 2024c; Weingarten, 2008), and their threat to traditional American freedoms because of the dom-inant role of Jews in the media of the period. He also criticized the Nuremberg Trials as Jewish revenge and opposed the U.S. recognition of Israel because of its effect in alienating other groups in the Middle East.

In Congress, Representative John Rankin, a well-known anti-Semite, without making explicit reference to Jews, stated:

> They whine about discrimination. Do you know who is being discriminated against? The white Christian people of America, the ones who created this nation. . . . I am talking about the white Christian people of the North as well as the South. . . .
>
> Communism is racial. A racial minority seized control in Russia and in all her satellite countries, such as Poland, Czechoslovakia, and many other countries I could name.
>
> They have been run out of practically every country in Europe in the years gone by, and if they keep stirring race trouble in this country and trying to force their communistic program on the Christian people of America, there is no telling what will happen to them here. (98 Cong. Rec., 1952, p. 4320)

During this period mainstream Jewish organizations were deeply concerned to eradicate the stereotype of Jews as communists and to develop an image of Jews as liberal anti-communists (Svonkin, 1997). "The fight against the stereotype of Communist-Jew became a virtual obsession with Jewish leaders and opinion makers throughout America" (A. Liebman, 1979, p. 515).[152] The AJCommittee engaged in intensive efforts to change opinion within the Jewish community by arguing that Jewish interests were more compatible with advocating American democracy than Soviet communism (e.g., emphasizing Soviet anti-Semitism and support of nations opposed to Israel in the period after World War II) (N. W. Cohen, 1972, pp. 347ff).[153] Although the AJCongress acknowledged that communism was a threat, the group adopted an "anti-anti-communist" position that condemned the infringement of civil liberties contained in the anti-communist legislation of the period. It was therefore "at best a reluctant and unenthusiastic participant" (Svonkin, 1997, p. 132) in the Jewish effort to develop a strong public image of anti-communism during this period—a position that reflected the sympathies of many among its predominantly second- and third-generation Eastern European immigrant membership.

---

[152] As an indication of the extent of this stereotype, when the gentile anthropologist Eleanor Leacock was being screened for security clearance by the FBI in 1944, in an effort to document her associations with political radicals her friends were asked whether she associated with Jews (Frank, 1997, p. 738).

[153] Similarly, in England in 1887 the Federation of Minor Synagogues was created by established British Jews to moderate the radicalism of newly arrived immigrants from Eastern Europe. This organization also engaged in deception by deliberately distorting the extent to which the immigrants had radical political attitudes (Alderman, 1983, p. 60).

This radical Jewish subculture and its ties to communism were much in evidence during riots in Peekskill, New York, in 1949. Peekskill was a summer destination for approximately thirty thousand predominantly Jewish professionals associated with socialist, anarchist, and communist colonies originally established in the 1930s. The immediate cause of rioting was a concert given by avowed communist Paul Robeson and sponsored by the Civil Rights Congress, a pro-communist group branded as subversive by the U.S. attorney general. Rioters made anti-Semitic statements at a time when the linkage between Jews and communism was highly salient. The result was an image-management effort on the part of the AJCommittee in which the anti-Semitic angle of the event was minimized—an example of the quarantine method of Jewish political strategizing (see SAID, Ch. 6, n14). This strategy conflicted with other groups, such as the AJCongress and the ACLU, who endorsed a report that attributed the violence to anti-Semitic prejudice and emphasized that the victims had been deprived of their civil liberties because of their communist sympathies.

Particularly worrisome to American Jewish leaders was the arrest and conviction of Julius and Ethel Rosenberg for spying. Leftist supporters of the Rosenbergs, many of whom were Jewish, attempted to portray the event as an instance of anti-Semitism; in the words of one prominent commentator, "The lynchings of these two innocent American Jews, unless stopped by the American people, will serve as a signal for a wave of Hitler-like genocidal attacks against the Jewish people throughout the United States" (in Svonkin, 1997, p. 155). These leftist organizations actively sought to enlist mainstream Jewish opinion on the side of this interpretation (Dawidowicz, 1952). However, in doing so they made the Jewish identities of these individuals and the connection between Judaism and communism even more salient. The official Jewish community went to great lengths to alter the public stereotype of Jewish subversion and disloyalty. Similarly, in its attempt to indict communism, the AJCommittee commented on the trial of Rudolph Slansky and his Jewish colleagues in Czechoslovakia. This trial was part of the anti-Semitic purges of Jewish communist elites in Eastern Europe after World War II, completely analogous to similar events in Poland recounted by Schatz (1991) and discussed in Chapter 3. The AJCommittee stated:

> The trial of Rudolph Slansky, renegade Jew, and his colleagues, who betrayed Judaism in serving the Communist cause, should awaken everyone to the fact that anti-Semitism has become an open instrument of Communist policy. It is ironical that these men who deserted Judaism, which is inimical to Communism, are now being used as an excuse for the Communist anti-Semitic campaign. (in Svonkin, 1997, p. 282n114).

Jewish organizations cooperated fully with the House Un-American Activities Committee (HUAC), and defenders of the Rosenbergs and other communists were hounded out of mainstream Jewish organizations where they had previously been welcome. Particularly salient was the fifty-thousand-member Jewish Peoples Fraternal Order (JPFO), a subsidiary of the International Workers Order (IWO), which was listed as a subversive organization by the U.S. attorney general. The AJCommittee prevailed upon local Jewish organizations to expel the JPFO, a move staunchly resisted by the JPFO, and the AJCongress dissolved the affiliate status of the JPFO as well as another communist-dominated organization, the American Jewish Labor Council. Similarly, mainstream Jewish organizations dissociated themselves from the Social Service Employees Union, a Jewish labor union for workers in Jewish organizations. This union had previously been expelled from the Congress of Industrial Organizations because of its communist sympathies.

Jewish organizations successfully obtained a prominent role for Jews in the prosecution of the Rosenbergs, and, after the guilty verdicts, the AJCommittee and the ACLU were active in promoting public support for the verdicts (Ginsberg, 1993, p. 121; Navasky, 1980, pp. 114ff). The periodical *Commentary*, published by the AJCommittee, "was rigorously edited to ensure that nothing that appeared within it could be in any way construed as favorable to Communism" (A. Liebman, 1979, p. 516), and it even went out of its way to print extremely anti-Soviet articles.

Nevertheless, the position of mainstream Jewish organizations such as the AJCommittee, which opposed communism, often coincided with the position of the CPUSA on issues of immigration. For example, both the AJCommittee and the CPUSA condemned the McCarran-Walter Act while, on the other hand, the AJCommittee had a major role in influencing the recommendations of President Truman's Commission on Immigration and Naturalization (PCIN) for relaxing the security provisions of the McCarran-Walter Act, and these recommendations were warmly greeted by the CPUSA at a time when a prime goal of the security provisions was to exclude communists (M. T. Bennett, 1963, p. 166). (Judge Simon H. Rifkind's remarks at the Joint Hearings on the McCarran-Walter Act—see above—also condemned the security provisions of the bill.) Jews were disproportionately represented on the PCIN as well as in the organizations viewed by Congress as communist front organizations involved in immigration issues. The chairman of the PCIN was Philip B. Perlman, the staff of the commission contained a high percentage of Jews, headed by Harry N. Rosenfield (executive director) and Elliot Shirk (assistant to the executive director), and its report was wholeheartedly endorsed by the AJCongress (see *Congress Weekly*, January 12th, 1952, p. 3). The proceedings were printed as the report *Whom We Shall Welcome* with the cooperation of Representative Emanuel Celler.

In Congress, Senator McCarran accused the PCIN of containing communist sympathizers, and HUAC released a report stating:

> [S]ome two dozen Communists and many times that number with records of repeated affiliation with known Communist enterprises testified before the Commission or submitted statements for inclusion in the record of the hearings. . . . Nowhere in either the record of the hearings or in the report is there a single reference to the true background of these persons. (H.R. Rep. No. 1182, 1957, p. 47).

The report referred particularly to communists associated with the American Committee for the Protection of Foreign Born (ACPFB), headed by Abner Green. Green, who was Jewish, figured very prominently in these hearings, and Jews were generally disproportionately represented among those singled out as officers and sponsors of the ACPFB (H.R. Rep. No. 1182, 1957, pp. 13–21). HUAC provided evidence indicating that the ACPFB had close ties with the CPUSA and noted that twenty-four of the individuals associated with the ACPFB had signed statements incorporated into the printed record of the PCIN.

The AJCommittee was also heavily involved in the deliberations of the PCIN, including providing testimony and distributing data and other material to individuals and organizations testifying before the PCIN (N. W. Cohen, 1972, p. 371). All its recommendations were incorporated into the final report (p. 371), including a deemphasis on economic skills as criteria for immigration, scrapping the national origins legislation, and opening immigration to all the peoples of the world on a "first come, first served basis," the only exception being that the report recommended a lower total number of immigrants than recommended by the AJCommittee and other Jewish groups. The AJCommittee thus went beyond merely advocating the principle of immigration from all racial and ethnic groups (token quotas for Asians and Africans had already been included in the McCarran-Walter Act) to attempt to maximize the total number of immigrants from all parts of the world within the current political climate.

Indeed, the PCIN (1953/1971, p. 106) pointedly noted that the Immigration Law of 1924 had succeeded in maintaining the racial status quo and that the main barrier to changing the racial status quo was not the national origins system, because there were already high levels of nonquota immigrants and because the countries of Northern and Western Europe did not fill their quotas. Rather, the report noted that the main barrier to changing the racial status quo was the total number of immigrants. The PCIN (p. 42) thus viewed changing the racial status quo of the United States as a desirable goal, and to that end made a major point of the desirability of increasing the total number of immigrants. As M. T. Bennett (1963, p. 164) notes, in the eyes of the PCIN, the

Immigration Act of 1924 reducing the total number of immigrants "was a very bad thing because of its finding that one race is just as good as another for American citizenship or any other purpose."

Correspondingly, the defenders of the Immigration Act of 1952 (McCarran-Walter Act) conceptualized the issue as fundamentally one of ethnic warfare. Senator McCarran stated that subverting the national origins system "would, in the course of a generation or so, tend to change the ethnic and cultural composition of this nation" (in M. T. Bennett, 1963, p. 185), and Richard Arens, a congressional staff member who had a prominent role in the hearings on the McCarran-Walter bill as well as in the activities of HUAC, stated:

> These are the critics who do not like America as it is and has been. They think our people exist in unfair ethnic proportions. They prefer that we bear a greater resemblance or ethnic relationship to the foreign peoples whom they favor and for whom they are seeking disproportionately greater immigration privileges. (in M. T. Bennett, 1963, p. 186)

As Divine (1957, p. 188) notes, ethnic interests predominated on both sides. The restrictionists were implicitly advocating the ethnic status quo, while the anti-restrictionists were rather more explicit in their desire to alter the ethnic status quo in a manner that conformed to their ethnic interests, although the anti-restrictionist rhetoric was typically phrased in universalistic and moralistic terms.

The salience of Jewish involvement in immigration during this period is also apparent in several other incidents. In 1951 the representative of the AJCongress testified that the retention of the national origins system in any form would be "a political and moral catastrophe" (*Revision of Immigration*, 1951, pp. 336–337). The national origins formula implies that "persons in quest of the opportunity to live in this land are to be judged according to breed like cattle at a country fair and not on the basis of their character fitness or capacity" (*Congress Weekly* 21, 1952, pp. 3–4). Divine (1957, p. 173) characterizes the AJCongress as representing "the more militant wing" of the opposition because of its principled opposition to any form of the national origins formula, whereas other opponents merely wanted to be able to distribute unused quotas to Southern and Eastern Europe.

Representative Francis Walter noted the "propaganda drive that is being engaged in now by certain members of the American Jewish Congress opposed to the Immigration and Nationality Code" (98 Cong. Rec., 1952, p. 2283), noting particularly the activities of Rabbi Israel Goldstein, president of the AJCongress, who had been reported in *The New York Times* as having stated that the immigration and nationality law would place "a legislative seal of inferiority on all persons of other than Anglo-Saxon origin." Representative Walter then noted the special role that Jewish organizations had played in attempting to foster family reunion rather than special skills as the basis of U.S. immigration policy. After Representative Jacob Javits stated that opposition to the law was "not confined to the one group the gentleman mentioned" (p. 2284), Walter responded as follows:

> I might call your attention to the fact that Mr. Harry N. Rosenfield, Commissioner of the Displaced Persons Commission [and also the executive director of the PCIN; see above] and incidentally a brother-in-law of a lawyer who is stirring up all this agitation, in a speech recently said:
> "The proposed legislation is America's Nuremberg trial.
> "It is racious (sic) and archaic, based on a theory that people with different styles of noses should be treated differently."

Representative Walter then noted that the only two organizations hostile to the entire bill were the AJCongress and the Association of Immigration and Nationality Lawyers, the latter "represented by an attorney who is also advising and counseling the American Jewish Congress." (Israel Goldstein, 1952a, himself noted that "at the time of the Joint House-Senate hearings on the McCarran-Walter bill, the American Jewish Congress was the only civic group which dared flatly to oppose the national origins quota formula.")

Representative Emanuel Celler replied that Representative Walter "should not have overemphasized as he did the people of one particular faith who are opposing the bill" (98 Cong. Rec., 1952, p. 2285)—a declaration that avoids the more accurate idea that Jews are an ethnic group. Representative Walter agreed with Celler's comments, noting that "there are other very fine Jewish groups who endorse the bill." Nevertheless, the principal Jewish organizations, including the AJCongress, the AJCommittee, the ADL, the National Council of Jewish Women, and the Hebrew Immigrant Aid Society, did indeed oppose the bill (p. 4247), and when Judge Simon H. Rifkind testified against the bill in the joint hearings, he emphasized that he represented a very wide range of Jewish groups, "the entire body of religious opinion and lay opinion within the Jewish group, religiously speaking, from the extreme right and extreme left" (*Revision of Immigration*, 1951, p. 563). Rifkind represented a long list of national and local Jewish groups, including, in addition to the above, the Synagogue Council of America, the Jewish Labor Committee, the Jewish War Veterans of the United States, and twenty-seven local Jewish councils throughout the United States. Moreover, the fight against the bill was led by Jewish members of Congress, including especially Celler, Javits, and Lehman, all of whom, as indicated above, were prominent members of the ADL.

Albeit by indirection, Representative Walter was clearly calling attention to the special Jewish role in the immigration conflict of 1952. The special role of the AJCongress in opposing the McCarran-Walter Act was a source of pride within the group: on the verge of victory in 1965, the Congress Bi-Weekly editorialized that it was "a cause of pride" that AJCongress president Rabbi Israel Goldstein had been "singled out by Representative Walter for attack on the floor of the House of Representatives as the prime organizer of the campaign against the measures he co-sponsored" (February 1st, 1965, p. 3).

The perception that Jewish concerns were an important feature of the opposition to the McCarran-Walter Act can also be seen in the following exchange between Representative Celler and Representative Walter. Celler noted, "The national origin theory upon which our immigration law is based ... [mocks] our protestations based on a question of equality of opportunity for all peoples, regardless of race, color, or creed." Representative Walter replied, "a great menace to America lies in the fact that so many professionals, including professional Jews, are shedding crocodile tears for no reason whatsoever" (99 Cong. Rec., 1953, p. 372). And in a comment referring to the peculiarities of Jewish interests in immigration legislation, Richard Arens noted:

> One of the curious things about those who most loudly claim that the 1952 act is "discriminatory" and that it does not make allowance for a sufficient number of alleged refugees, is that they oppose admission of any of the approximately one million Arab refugees in camps where they are living in pitiful circumstances after having been driven out of Israel. (in M. T. Bennett, 1963, p. 181)

The McCarran-Walter Act passed despite President Truman's veto, and Truman's "alleged partisanship to Jews was a favorite target of anti-Semites" (N. W. Cohen, 1972, p. 377). Prior to the veto, Truman was intensively lobbied, "particularly [by] Jewish societies" opposed to the bill; government agencies, meanwhile, including the State Department (despite the anti-restrictionist argument that the bill would have catastrophic effects on U.S. foreign policy) urged Truman to sign the bill (Divine, 1957, p. 184). Moreover, individuals with openly anti-Jewish attitudes, such as John Beaty (1951), often focused on Jewish involvement in the immigration battles during this period.

Jewish Anti-Restrictionist Activity, 1953–1965

The general subject of CofC is the rise of a new, left-of-center, substantially Jewish elite in the post-World War II era, an elite centered in the media, the academic world, and political culture—the latter influenced not only by media and academic consensus, but also by political donations enabled by increasing Jewish wealth. The demise of the former White Anglo-Saxon Protestant (WASP) elite is the theme of Eric Kaufmann's (2004) The Rise and

Fall of Anglo-America (critiqued by MacDonald, 2015, basically for inappropriately downplaying Jewish influence). As noted above, Hollinger (1996) notes "the transformation of the ethnoreligious demography of American academic life by Jews" in the period from the 1930s to the 1960s (p. 4), as well as the Jewish influence on trends toward the secularization of American society and in advancing an ideal of cosmopolitanism (p. 11); also that "One force in this [culture war of the 1940s] was a secular, increasingly Jewish, decidedly left-of-center intelligentsia based largely ... in the disciplinary communities of philosophy and the social sciences" (p. 160). As noted in the Preface, Lipset and Ladd (1971), using survey data of sixty thousand academics from 1969, show that the 1960s were a critical period for the rise of Jewish academics in elite universities who were in general well to the left of non-Jewish professors.

The rise of this new elite implies that analysis cannot be restricted to only one issue, such as immigration policy, without discussing the wider context. Rather, it implies that vital issues of public policy, including immigration, the civil rights of African Americans, women's rights, religion in the public square (Hollinger's "secularization of American society"), the legitimacy of White racial identity and interests, cosmopolitanism, foreign policy in the Middle East, and many others will be affected by the attitudes and interests of this new elite. Thus, the Immigration and Nationality Act of 1965 and the civil rights movement cannot be discussed independently of academic and media perspectives on race. *CofC* discusses the role of Jewish intellectuals in the sea change in academic views related to race (Ch. 2), and this chapter discusses how Boasian ideology had become dominant in the Congressional debates of 1965 on immigration; as noted below, this racial ideology became dominant in the media during this period (Joyce, 2019c, see Ch. 6)—at a time when all the television networks and Hollywood studios were owned by Jews, and marking a huge shift from the 1920s when restrictionist arguments based on race appeared in prominent magazines and were published by mainstream book publishers. Further, Jewish influence was a major force in the civil rights movement during the critical years of 1954 to 1968 (see above), and, as discussed above, in the secularization of American culture: "Jewish civil rights organizations have had an historic role in the postwar development of American church-state law and policy" (Ivers, 1995, p. 2).

The only claim that, if true, would seriously endanger an important aspect of what Nathan Cofnas (2021) labels "the anti-Jewish narrative" is regarding the Jewish role in changing U.S. immigration policy. It's certainly legitimate for Cofnas to bring up the wider context of Hugh Davis Graham's (2002/2003) comments on the Immigration and Nationality Act of 1965, but, as elaborated above, the wider context of the law was critically influenced by other aspects of Jewish activism. Moreover, the bottom line is Graham's (p. 57) statement:

Most important for the content of immigration reform, the driving force at the core of the movement, reaching back to the 1920s, were Jewish organizations long active in opposing racial and ethnic quotas. . . . Jewish political leaders in New York, most prominently Governor Herbert Lehman, had pioneered in the 1940s in passing state antidiscrimination legislation. Importantly [because of the national origins provisions of the 1924 law giving preference to immigration from northwest Europe], these statutes and executive orders added "national origin" to race, color, and religion as impermissible grounds for discrimination.

Similarly, Otis Graham (2004, p. 67) noted:

The political core of a coalition pressing for a new, more "liberalized" policy regime was composed of ethnic lobbyists . . . claiming to speak for nationalities migrating prior to the National Origins Act of 1924, the most effective being Jews from central and eastern Europe who were deeply concerned with the rise of fascism and anti-semitism on the continent and eternally interested in haven.

Thus any critique of my treatment of immigration must consider whether Jews had important influence on the wider context discussed by Hugh Davis Graham. Cofnas ignores the role of Jewish intellectuals in the sea change in academic views related to race (see Ch. 2) and how Boasian ideology had become dominant in the Congressional immigration debates of 1965 (see below). He also ignores the material on Jewish pro-immigration activism from the 1890s to 1965 (see above), and he ignores my summary of Jewish involvement in the civil rights movement of the 1950s–1960s where Jewish activism was of critical importance (see above). As discussed extensively in Chapter 2, Jews and Jewish organizations led the intellectual effort to deny the importance of racial and ethnic differences in human affairs by dominating the American Anthropological Association since the 1920s. As discussed here, Boasian ideas on race were prominent in the immigration debates between 1945 and 1965.

Finally, as discussed in Chapter 6, Joyce (2019c) describes a campaign centered around Samuel H. Flowerman, Research Director of the AJCommittee and affiliated with the Frankfurt School's Institute for Social Research, to influence public opinion in the American media after World War II. Flowerman co-edited with Max Horkheimer (director of the Institute for Social Research) the highly influential series *Studies in Prejudice*, published by the AJCommittee. Flowerman brought together a network of Jewish intellectuals and social scientists, many with prominent positions in universities and the media (at a time when the Hollywood studios, all the American television networks, and influential newspapers—e.g., *The New York Times* and *The Washington Post*—were owned by Jews). This effort was aimed at dominating American mass communications in order to "actively reshape ingroup standards—thus reforming peer group pressures to become antagonistic to ingroup ethnocentrism"; it was "an extensive Jewish joint enterprise in which the unlocking and alteration of White American public opinion was the goal" (p. 11; see, e.g., Flowerman, 1947).

During the post-World War II period, *Congress Weekly* regularly noted the role of Jewish organizations as the vanguard of liberalized immigration laws. In its editorial of February 20th, 1956 (p. 3), for example, it congratulated President Eisenhower for his,

> unequivocal opposition to the quota system which, more than any other feature of our immigration policy, has excited the most widespread and most intense aversion among Americans. In advancing this proposal for "new guidelines and standards" in determining admissions, President Eisenhower has courageously taken a stand in advance of even many advocates of a liberal immigration policy and embraced a position which had at first been urged by the American Jewish Congress and other Jewish agencies.

Organizing Anti-Restriction. Jews and Jewish organizations organized, led, funded, and performed most of the work of the most important anti-restrictionist organizations active from 1945 to 1965, including the National Liberal Immigration League, the Citizens Committee for Displaced Persons, the National Commission on Immigration and Citizenship, the Joint Conference on Alien Legislation, the American Immigration Conference, and the PCIN.

> All these groups studied immigration laws, disseminated information to the public, presented testimony to Congress, and planned other appropriate activities. . . . There were no immediate or dramatic results; but [the AJCommittee's] dogged campaign in conjunction with like-minded organizations ultimately prodded the Kennedy and Johnson administrations to action. (N. W. Cohen, 1972, p. 373)

Regarding the PCIN, established by President Truman, recall that the AJCommittee was also heavily involved in their deliberations, including providing testimony and distributing data and other material to individuals and organizations testifying before the PCIN, with all its recommendations being incorporated into the final report (N. W. Cohen, 1972, p. 371).

Recruiting Non-Jews in These Efforts. Part of this effort was recruiting sympathetic non-Jews, especially prominent non-Jews, to these organizations. Because Jews are a small minority in Western societies, a consistent tactic for the Jewish activist community, beginning at least by the early twentieth century, has been to recruit powerful and influential non-Jews for their efforts

(SAID, Ch. 6; see also here Chs. 3–4). For example, in 1955 the AJCommittee organized a group of influential citizens as the National Commission on Immigration and Citizenship, most of whose members were non-Jews, "in order to give prestige to the campaign" (N. W. Cohen, 1972, p. 373). "To support policy change, American Jewish groups initiated an ambitious campaign to publish and widely distribute books and pamphlets and to recruit prominent politicians favoring robust immigration" (Tichenor, 2002, p. 205). An important part of this effort, according to Tichenor, was to recruit then-Senator and future President John F. Kennedy to attach his name to A *Nation of Immigrants* (1958) and to recruit Senator and future Vice-President and 1968 Democratic presidential candidate Hubert Humphrey for his *Stranger at Our Gate* (1954). Kennedy was recruited by former ADL National Director Ben Epstein (Greenblatt, 2018); the book was published by the ADL which also supplied a historian— Arthur Mann, a doctoral student of Oscar Handlin at Harvard (Ngai, 2013)—for the project (O. Graham, 2004, p. 82), and was ghost-written by Myer Feldman who was influential in the Kennedy/Johnson administration (Tichenor, p. 205).

Nevertheless, despite its clear importance to the activist Jewish community, the most prominent sponsors of the Immigration and Nationality Act of 1965,

> did their best to downplay the law's importance in public discourse. National policymakers were well aware that the general public was opposed to increases in either the volume or diversity of immigration to the United States. . . . [However,] in truth the policy departures of the mid-1960s dramatically recast immigration patterns and concomitantly the nation. Annual admissions increased sharply in the years after the law's passage. (Tichenor, 2002, p. 218)

Tichenor notes that chain migration (see below) and the ethnic diversity of the immigrants profoundly changed the United States.

Rejecting the Ethnic Status Quo Put in Place by the Immigration Acts of 1924 and 1952. Even going back to the battle over the Immigration Act of 1924, Jewish activists explicitly opposed an ethnic status quo during Congressional hearings. As stated earlier, at a time when the population of the United States was over one hundred million, Louis Marshall, influential attorney associated with the AJCommittee and leader of the anti-restrictionist lobbying forces, stated, "[W]e have room in this country for ten times the population we have"; he advocated admission of all of the peoples of the world without quota limit, excluding only those who "were mentally, morally and physically unfit, who are enemies of organized government, and who are apt to become public charges" (*Restriction of Immigration*, 1924, pp. 309, 303). Similarly, Rabbi Stephen S. Wise, representing the AJCongress and a variety of other Jewish organizations at the House hearings on the Immigration Act of 1924, asserted "the right of every man outside of America to be considered fairly and equitably and without discrimination" (p. 341).

O. Graham (2004, p. 80) notes that the Jewish lobby on immigration "was aimed not just at open doors for Jews, but also for a diversification of the immigration stream sufficient to eliminate the majority status of western Europeans so that a fascist regime in America would be more unlikely."

The fear and insecurity of the American Jewish community after World War II described above was thus the main motivation for the Jewish approach to immigration legislation.

The motivating role of fear and insecurity on the part of the activist Jewish community was thus unique and differed from other groups and individuals promoting an end to the national origins' provisions of the Immigration Acts of 1924 and 1952; such a view entailed changing the ethnic balance of the U.S.

As noted above, Rep. Emanuel Celler was involved in the publication of the report *Whom We Shall Welcome* that viewed changing the ethnic balance of the U.S. as a desirable goal. Cofnas (2021) argues against this by noting:

> Even the authors of the legislation were surprised by some of its immediate consequences. According to [H. D.] Graham [2003, pp. 94–95]: "Emanuel Celler himself, disturbed by the steep decline of European immigration, introduced a bill to allow higher immigration from Ireland, Britain, and the Scandinavian countries, which he said had suffered from 'unintentional discrimination' as a result of his own law."

However, given the substance of the PCIN report and Celler's involvement in its publication, it's difficult to believe that Celler did not advocate changing the ethnic balance of the U.S. The fact that Celler wanted to increase immigration from parts of Europe is certainly not incompatible with this. It would be far more convincing if Celler had advocated a law explicitly reaffirming the ethnic status quo, as the Immigration Acts of 1924 and 1952 had done, but, along with all the other major Jewish organizations, he vigorously opposed the ethnic status quo. Getting rid of the national origins formula was a necessary condition for changing the ethnic status quo, as Celler was well aware. All that remained was increasing the absolute numbers of immigrants, as the PCIN advocated, and that is what ultimately happened.

Chipping Away the Ethnic Status Quo Embedded in the Immigration Acts of 1924 and 1952. Regarding the "chipping away" recommended by Handlin and noted by H. D. Graham (2003) as part of the context of the Immigration and Nationality Act of 1965, most of the nonquota immigrants prior to 1965 were refugees from communism. These migrants were overwhelmingly non-Jews from Russia, Poland, and Czechoslovakia (p. 54), ethnically European groups that had taken advantage of "the 1920s law [that] gave an ethnically tense country a needed breathing space" (p. 48) to assimilate to American culture. By the 1950s these assimilated European groups were not seen as changing the demographic balance of the country, nor were these refugees from communism leftist radicals—a major concern during the 1920s and 1950s' McCarthy era, especially regarding Jewish immigrants (Ch. 3 and above). Americans also welcomed them because they were seen as affirming the superiority of American culture to communism during the Cold War; e.g., the torture and persecution of Hungarian Cardinal József Mindszenty (who lived at the American embassy in Budapest for fifteen years prior to being exiled) was very salient to Americans, especially Catholics. (I remember very clearly that the treatment of Cardinal Mindszenty was often commented on by the nuns in my Catholic grade school.)

Thus the migration that actually occurred during the 1950s was far from the profile of immigration after 1965. Although such immigration certainly did not reflect attitudes that dominated in the 1920s, the rationale was far from that of post-1965 immigration where essentially no rationale was needed—even needed skills that would benefit the country had a low priority. Indeed, a major chipping-away tactic was to allow family members to immigrate outside of quota limits. Family unification had been central to Jewish efforts on immigration going back to the 1924 debates (Neuringer, 1971/1980, p. 191), a point emphasized by Rep. Francis Walter, the leader of the restrictionist forces in the House in the 1952 debates, when he noted the special role that Jewish organizations had played in attempting to foster family reunion rather than special skills as the basis of U.S. immigration policy (98 Cong. Rec., 1952, p. 2284).

Commenting on the family unification aspects of the 1961 immigration legislation, M. T. Bennett (1963, p. 244) noted that the "relationship by blood or marriage and the principle of uniting families have become the 'open Sesame' to the immigration gates." Bennett (p. 257) also noted:

> The repeated, persistent extension of nonquota status to immigrants from countries with oversubscribed quotas and flatly discriminated against by [the McCarran-Walter Act of 1952] together with administrative waivers of inadmissibility, adjustment of status and private bills, is helping to speed and make apparently inevitable a change in the ethnic face of the nation.

The Immigration and Nationality Act of 1965 was tailor-made to increase numbers of immigrants because it allowed "chain migration" of family members (family unification) outside the quota limits. "Family preference was leverage for newcomers and left long-term residents with diminished influence over immigration streams shaping the nation's future" (O. Graham, 2004, p. 91) (i.e., because citizens with family going back more than a generation or two—and certainly founding-stock Americans—likely had few close relatives living abroad). Thus, one immigrant could bring in his immediate family and when they became citizens, they could bring in their brothers and sisters outside the quota limit, who could in turn bring in their spouses and children, etc.

Congressional and Executive Branch Leadership. Jewish politicians led anti-restrictionist efforts in Congress and were prominent in the executive branch. In Congress, the most noteworthy figures were Rep. Celler (also a leader in the anti-restrictionist forces in the 1924 Congressional debates) and Sens. Jacob Javits and Herbert Lehman, all prominent members of the ADL. After noting the leadership of Jews in Congress, H. D. Graham (2003, p. 57) notes:

> [L]ess visible, but equally important, were the efforts of key advisers on presidential and agency staffs. These included senior policy advisers such as Julius Edelson and Harry Rosenfield in the Truman administration, Maxwell Rabb in the Eisenhower White House, and presidential aide Myer Feldman [who, as noted, was the ghost writer for John F. Kennedy's *A Nation of Immigrants*], assistant secretary of state Abba Schwartz, and deputy attorney general Norbert Schlei in the Kennedy-Johnson administration.

Schlei was the head of the Department of Justice's Office of General Counsel from 1962 to 1966 and the most important figure in drafting the 1965 immigration bill (Saxon, 2003). H. D. Graham (2003, p. 88) also mentions Feldman, Schlei, and Schwarz as important figures involved in immigration-related issues during the Kennedy and Johnson administrations.

Jewish Consensus on Immigration Policy. During this period, anti-restrictionist attitudes were held by the vast majority of the organized Jewish community—"the entire body of religious opinion and lay opinion within the Jewish group, religiously speaking, from the extreme right and extreme left," in the words of Judge Simon Rifkind who testified in Congress representing a long list of national and local Jewish groups in 1948 (*Revision of Immigration*, 1951, p. 562–595). Cofnas (2021, 2023) advocates the "default hypothesis" that because of their intellectual prowess, Jews have always been highly overrepresented on both sides of various issues. This was certainly not true in the case of immigration during the critical period up to 1965 when the national origins provisions of the Immigration Acts of 1924 and 1952 were overturned—and long thereafter. I have never found any Jewish organization or prominent Jews leading the forces favoring the Immigration Acts of 1924 and 1952—or those opposed to the Immigration and Nationality Act of 1965 at the time it was enacted. Andrew Joyce (2021a) shows the continuing powerful role of Jews in pro-immigration activism in the contemporary U.S., joined now by well-organized immigrant groups dedicated to their group interests in liberal immigration policies—interests that ultimately derive from the success of the Immigration and Nationality Act of 1965 in creating a multiethnic, multicultural America.

Jewish Intellectuals Promoting Immigration. Further attesting to a Jewish consensus on immigration, prominent Jewish intellectuals, such as Harvard historian and public intellectual Oscar Handlin, published pro-immigration books—e.g., *The Uprooted* (1951/1973)—and articles. Handlin's (1952) article, "The Immigration Fight Has Only Begun," appeared in *Commentary* (published by the AJCommittee) shortly after the Democrat-controlled Congress overrode President Truman's veto of the restrictionist Immigration Act of 1952, and twenty-eight years after Jewish organizations had lost the battle over the Immigration Act of 1924. In a telling comment indicating Jewish leadership of the pro-immigration forces and reflecting the disinterest of other immigrant groups from earlier in the century (Neuringer, 1971/1980, p. 83), Handlin complained about the apathy of other "hyphenated Americans" in joining the immigration battle. "Many groups failed to see the relevance of the McCarran-Walter Bill to their own position." He suggests that these groups ought to act as groups to assert their interests: "The Italian American has the right to be heard on these issues precisely *as* an Italian American" (emphasis original). The implicit assumption is that the United States ought to be composed of cohesive subgroups with a clear sense of their group interests in opposition to the peoples deriving from Northern and Western Europe or of the United States as a whole—clearly in the interests of Jews as a minority with a strong commitment to their group interests. Also, there is the implication that Italian Americans have an interest in furthering immigration of Africans and Asians and in creating such a multiracial and multicultural society.

Handlin (1952) repeatedly used the term "we"—as in "if we cannot beat [Sen. Pat] McCarran and his cohorts with their own weapons, we can do much to destroy the efficacy of those weapons"—suggesting Handlin's belief in a unified Jewish interest in liberal immigration policy and presaging a prolonged "chipping away" of the Immigration and Nationality Act of 1952 in the ensuing years mentioned by H. D. Graham (2003) as part of the context of the Immigration and Nationality Act of 1965, and noted by Cofnas.

Handlin (1952) attempts to cast the argument in universalist terms as benefiting all Americans and as conforming to American ideals that "all men, being brothers, are equally capable of being Americans." He argues that current immigration law reflects "racist xenophobia" by its token quotas for Asians and its denial of the right of West Indian Blacks to take advantage of British quotas. Handlin ascribes the restrictionist sentiments of Pat McCarran to "the hatred of foreigners that was all about him in his youth and by the dim, recalled fear that he himself might be counted among them"—a psychoanalytic identification-with-the-aggressor argument (McCarran was of Irish Catholic ancestry).

Handlin's (1952) anti-restrictionist strategy included altering the views of social scientists to the effect "that it was possible and necessary to distinguish among the 'races' of immigrants that clamored for admission to the United States." Handlin's proposal to recruit social scientists in the immigration battles is congruent with the political agenda of the Boasian school of anthropology discussed above and in Chapter 2. As Higham (1984) notes, the ascendancy of such views was an important component of the ultimate victory over restrictionism.

Handlin (1952) presented the following highly tendentious rendering of the logic of preserving the ethnic status quo that underlay the arguments for restriction from 1921 to 1952:

> The laws are bad because they rest on the racist assumption that mankind is divided into fixed breeds, biologically and culturally separated from each other, and because, within that framework, they assume that Americans are Anglo-Saxons by origin and ought to remain so. To all other peoples, the laws say that the United States ranks them in terms of their racial proximity to our own "superior" stock; and upon the many, many millions of Americans not descended from the Anglo-Saxons, the laws cast a distinct imputation of inferiority.

Handlin developed this perspective further in a book, *Race and Nationality in American Life*, published in 1957.[154] This book is a compendium of psychoanalytic "explanations" of ethnic and class conflict deriving from *The Authoritarian Personality* studies combined with the Boasian theory that there are no biological differences between the races that influence behavior. There is also a strong strand of the belief that humans can be perfected by changing defective human institutions. Handlin advocates immigration from all areas of the world as a moral imperative. In his discussion of Israel in Chapter XII, however, there is no mention that Israel ought to be similarly inclined to view open immigration from throughout the world as a moral imperative or that Jews should not be concerned with maintaining political control of Israel. Instead, the discussion focuses on the moral compatibility of dual loyalties for American Jews to both the United States and Israel. Handlin's moral blindness regarding Jewish issues can also be seen in Albert Lindemann's (1997, p. xx) comment that

---

[154] Handlin also contributed several articles and reviews to *Partisan Review*, the flagship journal of the New York Intellectuals. Reflecting his deep-seated belief in cultural pluralism, in a 1945 book review he stated, "I simply cannot grasp a conception of 'Americanism' that rests on the notion that 'a social group constitutes a nation insofar as its members are of one mind'" (p. 269).

Handlin's book *Three Hundred Years of Jewish Life in America* failed to mention Jewish slave traders and slave owners "even while mentioning by name the 'great Jewish merchants' who made fortunes in the slave trade."

Handlin (1947) clearly rejected an ethnic status quo, arguing that it was "illusory [to expect] that the composition of American population will remain as it is." And he never addressed the stated justification used by restrictionists in the 1924 debates, describing their attitudes as follows (1951/1973, p. 257):

> The hordes of inferior breeds, even then freely pouring into the country in complete disregard for the precepts of the new racial learning [a reference to theories of racial difference common among elites and promulgated in the popular media in the 1920s], would mix promiscuously with the Anglo-Saxon and inevitably produce a deterioration of the species.

Handlin thus ignored the actual argument used by restrictionists during the Congressional debates of 1924: that the national origins formula was fair to all ethnic groups in the country because it created an ethnic status quo, with its implicit and entirely defensible assumption from an evolutionary perspective that different ethnic groups have conflicts of interest regarding immigration (e.g., conflicts between Palestinians and Jews in Israel over a Palestinian right of return).

Handlin was a critical figure in the decades leading up to the passage of the Immigration and Nationality Act of 1965. Ngai (2013, pp. 62, 65) commented on his importance:

> Handlin's thinking on immigration policy both reflected and shaped the course of reform in the postwar period. He may be credited with popularizing a new interpretation of American history—one that conceptualized immigration at the heart of American economic and democratic development. In creating this framework for immediate political reform, he founded a normative theory of immigration history—one we popularly know as "a nation of immigrants"—that endured for several generations in both scholarly and popular discourse, and arguably endures into our own time. . . .
>
> His contributions to the long reform effort to repeal the national origin quota system should not be underestimated. His writings, both scholarly and journalistic, provided an episteme for reform, a framework and a logic for critiquing old policy and for defining the contours of a new one. Handlin not only gave Euro-American ethnic groups voice and legitimacy, *as ethnics*. He also gave them a central place in the master narrative of American history and argued that pluralism and group life were pillars of American democracy. The reform agenda was thus not just a matter of immediate political interests; it was also a historical mission in the

perceived telos of American democracy and in the construction of post-World War II Americanism.

Shortly after Handlin's article, William Petersen (1955), also writing in *Commentary*, argued that pro-immigration forces should be explicit in their advocacy of a multicultural society and that the importance of this goal transcended the importance of achieving any self-interested goal of the United States, such as obtaining needed skills or improving foreign relations. In making his case he cited a group of predominantly Jewish social scientists whose works, beginning with Horace Kallen's plea for a multicultural, pluralistic society, "constitute the beginning of a scholarly legitimization of the different immigration policy that will perhaps one day become law" (p. 86), including, besides Kallen, Melville Herskovits (the Boasian anthropologist; see Ch. 2), Geoffrey Gorer, Samuel Lubell, David Riesman (a New York Intellectual; see Ch. 7), Thorsten Sellin, and Milton Konvitz.

These social scientists did indeed contribute to the immigration battles. For example, the following quotation from a scholarly book on immigration policy by Milton Konvitz of Cornell University (published by Cornell University Press) reflects the rejection of national interest as an element of U.S. immigration policy—a hallmark of the Jewish approach to immigration:

> To place so much emphasis on technological and vocational qualifications is to remove every vestige of humanitarianism from our immigration policy. We deserve small thanks from those who come here if they are admitted because we find that they are "urgently" needed, by reason of their training and experience, to advance our national interests. This is hardly immigration; it is the importation of special skills or know-how, not greatly different from the importation of coffee or rubber. It is hardly in the spirit of American ideals to disregard a man's character and promise and to look only at his education and the vocational opportunities he had the good fortune to enjoy. (Konvitz, 1953, p. 26)

Notice the reference to "American ideals"—also a tactic used by Zangwill and Handlin—rather than national interests, much less the ethnic interests of White Americans.

Other prominent social scientists who represented the anti-restrictionist perspective in their writings were Richard Hofstadter and Max Lerner. Columbia University historian Hofstadter (1955, p. 34), who did much to create the image of the populists of the West and South as irrational anti-Semites (see Ch. 6), also condemned the populists for their desire "to maintain a homogeneous Yankee civilization." He also linked populism to the immigration issue: in Hofstadter's view, populism was "in considerable part colored by the reaction to this immigrant stream among the native elements of the population" (p. 11).

In his highly acclaimed *America as a Civilization*, historian Max Lerner, who taught at several universities, including Harvard, provides an explicit link between much of the intellectual tradition covered in previous chapters and the immigration issue. Lerner (1957, p. 502) finds the United States to be a tribalistic nation with a "passionate rejection of the 'outsider,'" and he asserts that "with the passing of the [Immigration Act of 1924] quota laws racism came of age in America" (p. 504). Lerner laments the fact that these "racist" laws are still in place because of popular sentiment, "whatever the intellectuals may think." This is clearly a complaint that when it came to immigration policy, Americans were not following the lead of the predominantly Jewish urbanized intellectual elite represented by Lerner. The comment reflects the anti-democratic, anti-populist element of Jewish intellectual activity discussed in Chapter 7.

Lerner (1957) cites the work of Horace Kallen as providing a model for a multicultural, pluralistic America (p. 93), saying, for example, that he (Lerner) approves of "the existence of ethnic communities within the larger American community, each of them trying to hold on to elements of group identity and in the process enriching the total culture pattern" (p. 506). Correspondingly, while acknowledging that Jews have actively resisted exogamy (p. 510), Lerner sees immigration and interbreeding as having nothing but benign effects (p. 82):

> Although some cultural historians maintain that the dilution of native stock is followed by cultural decadence, the example of the Italian city-states, Spain, Holland, Britain, and now Russia and India as well as America indicates that the most vigorous phase may come at the height of the mingling of many stocks. The greater danger lies in closing the gates.

M. Lerner (1957, p. 83) approvingly cites Franz Boas's work on the plasticity of skull size as showing the pervasiveness of environmental influences, and on this basis he asserts that intellectual and biological differences between ethnic groups are entirely the result of environmental differences. Thus (p. 506):

> One can understand the fear of the more prolific birth rate of the minorities, but since they are largely the product of lower living standards the strategy of keeping the living standards low by enclosing the minorities in walls of caste would seem self-defeating.

And finally, M. Lerner (1957, p. 509) uses *The Authoritarian Personality* as an analytic tool in understanding ethnic conflict and anti-Semitism.

CONCLUSION

I conclude that Jews and the organized Jewish community were a necessary condition for passing the Immigration and Nationality Act of 1965. As has been typical, Jewish activism was aimed at elite institutions and political figures, with change eventually occurring in a top-down manner that did not reflect the attitudes of most Americans. As O. Graham (2004, p. 88) notes:

> There was emerging on the immigration question a pattern in public debate that could be found on many issues: elite opinion makers selected a problem and a liberal policy solution, while grassroots opinion, unfocused and marginalized, ran strongly the other way.

Handlin wrote that the McCarran-Walter Act was only a temporary setback, and he was right. Thirty years after the triumph of restrictionism, only Jewish groups remained as persistent and tenacious advocates of a multicultural America. Forty-one years after the 1924 triumph of restrictionism and the national origins provision and only thirteen years after its reaffirmation with the McCarran-Walter Act of 1952, Jewish organizations successfully supported ending the geographically based national origins basis of immigration intended to result in an ethnic status quo in what was now a radically altered intellectual and political climate.

The main victory of the restrictionists in 1965 was that Western Hemisphere nations were included in the new quota system, thus ending the possibility of unrestricted immigration from those regions. In speeches before the Senate, Senator Javits (111 Cong. Rec., 1965, p. 24469) bitterly opposed this extension of the quota system, arguing that placing any limits on immigration of all of the people of the Western Hemisphere would have severely negative effects on U.S. foreign policy. In a highly revealing discussion of the bill before the Senate, Senator Sam Ervin (pp. 24446–24451) noted that,

> those who disagree with me express no shock that Britain, in the future, can send us 10,000 fewer immigrants than she has sent on an annual average in the past. They are only shocked that British Guyana cannot send us every single citizen of that country who wishes to come.

Clearly the forces of liberal immigration really wanted unlimited immigration into the United States.

The pro-immigrationists in 1965 also failed to prevent a requirement that the secretary of labor certify that there are insufficient Americans able and willing to perform the labor that the aliens intend to perform and that the employment of such aliens will not adversely affect the wages and working conditions of American workers. Writing in the *American Jewish Year Book*, Liskofsky (1966, p. 174) noted that pro-immigration groups opposed these regulations but agreed to them in order to get a bill that ended the national origins provisions. After passage "they became intensely concerned. They voiced publicly the fear that the new, administratively cumbersome procedure might easily result in paralyzing most immigration of skilled and unskilled workers as well as of non-preference immigrants." Reflecting the long Jewish opposition to the idea that immigration policy should be in the national interest, the economic welfare of American citizens was viewed as irrelevant; securing high levels of immigration had become an end in itself.

The Immigration and Nationality Act of 1965 is having the effect that it seems reasonable to suppose had been intended by its Jewish advocates all along: the Census Bureau projects that by the year 2050, European-derived peoples will no longer be a majority of the population of the United States. Moreover, multiculturalism has already become a powerful ideological and political reality. Although the proponents of the 1965 legislation continued to insist that the bill would not affect the ethnic balance of the United States or even impact its culture, it is difficult to believe that at least some proponents were unaware of the eventual implications. Certainly, opponents quite clearly believed the legislation would indeed affect the ethnic balance of the United States. Given their intense involvement in the fine details of immigration legislation, their very negative attitudes toward the Northwestern European bias of pre-1965 U.S. immigration policy, and their very negative attitudes toward the idea of an ethnic status quo embodied, for example, in the PCIN document *Whom We Shall Welcome*, it appears unlikely to suppose that organizations like the AJCommittee and the AJCongress were unaware of the inaccuracy of the projections of the effects of this legislation that were made by its supporters. Given the clearly articulated interests in ending the ethnic status quo evident in the arguments of anti-restrictionists from 1924 through 1965, the Immigration and Nationality Act of 1965 would not have been perceived by its proponents as a victory unless they viewed it as ultimately changing the ethnic status quo. As noted, immediately after passage of the law, there was anxiety among immigration advocates to blunt the restrictive effects of administrative procedures on the number of immigrants. Revealingly, the anti-restrictionists viewed the Immigration and Nationality Act of 1965 as a victory. After regularly condemning U.S. immigration law and championing the eradication of the national origins formula precisely because it had produced an ethnic status quo, the *Congress Bi-Weekly* ceased publishing articles on this topic.

Moreover, Lawrence Auster (1990, pp. 31ff) shows that the supporters of the legislation repeatedly glossed over the distinction between quota and non-quota immigration and failed to mention the effect that the legislation would have on nonquota immigration. Projections of the number of new immigrants failed to take account of the well-known and often commented upon fact that the old quotas favoring Western European countries were not being filled. Continuing a tradition of over forty years, pro-immigration rhetoric presented the Immigration Acts of 1924 and 1952 as based on theories of racial superiority and as involving racial discrimination rather than in terms of attempting to maintain an ethnic status quo.

Finally, it is noteworthy that arguments in terms of the morality of immigration for all racial and ethnic groups were common among Jewish activists. Restrictionists were routinely called "racist" and described as not living up to "American ideals"—even though Americans had made it very clear in 1924 and 1952 that they wished to remain a Western European civilization and even though large swaths of Americans remained opposed to transformative immigration long after 1965. This continues into the present, and accounts for the success of Donald Trump's presidential campaigns of 2016 and 2024 at least in part.

These arguments framing what was intended to become massive, transformative immigration as a moral imperative and as reflecting "Jewish values" (MacDonald, 2014) were never regarded by their Jewish advocates as implying that Israel should have an immigration policy open to all the peoples of the world. However, as argued in *Individualism and the Western Liberal Tradition*, this moralistic rhetoric resonates with the individualist peoples of Western Europe where the social glue of these societies is not based on kinship but on establishing moral communities based on individual reputation and trust. Once the mainstream Jewish community had established dominance in the media and academic worlds, Westerners were inundated with messages on the morality of immigration and the evils of racism or any assertion of White identity or interests. Clearly, on the basis of this chapter, this project has been massively successful.

Even in 1952 Senator McCarran was aware of the stakes at risk in immigration policy. In a statement reminiscent of that of Representative William N. Vaile during the debates of the 1920s quoted above, McCarran stated:

> I believe that this nation is the last hope of Western civilization and if this oasis of the world shall be overrun, perverted, contaminated or destroyed, then the last flickering light of humanity will be extinguished. I take no issue with those who would praise the contributions which have been made to our society by people of many races, of varied creeds and colors. America is indeed a joining together of many streams which go to form a mighty river which we call the American way. However, we have in the United States today hard-core, indigestible blocs which have not become integrated into the American way of life, but which, on the contrary, are

its deadly enemies. Today, as never before, untold millions are storming our gates for admission and those gates are cracking under the strain. The solution of the problems of Europe and Asia will not come through a transplanting of those problems en masse to the United States. . . . I do not intend to become prophetic, but if the enemies of this legislation succeed in riddling it to pieces, or in amending it beyond recognition, they will have contributed more to promote this nation's downfall than any other group since we achieved our independence as a nation. (Senator Pat McCarran, 99 Cong. Rec., 1953, p. 1518)

APPENDIX: JEWISH PRO-IMMIGRATION EFFORTS IN OTHER WESTERN COUNTRIES

The 1998/2002 edition of *CofC* of the section on immigration in other Western counties emphasized several points:

(1) The sea changes in immigration policy occurred at approximately the same time in the United States, the United Kingdom, France, Germany, and Australia (1962–1973).

(2) The changes reflected the attitudes of elites rather than the great mass of citizens. In the United States, Britain, Canada, and Australia, public opinion polls of European-derived peoples consistently showed overwhelming rejection of immigration by non-European-derived peoples (Betts, 1988; Brimelow, 1995; F. Hawkins, 1989; Layton-Henry, 1992).

(3) Consistent themes in these changes were that immigration policies were formulated by elites with influence in the media and academia.

(4) Efforts were made by political leaders of all major parties to keep fear of immigration off the political agenda (e.g., Betts; Layton-Henry, p. 82).

(5) Jewish organizations and Jewish individuals were prominently involved in these changes.

These features continue to be found throughout the West, although the ascendance of Donald Trump has put immigration squarely in the public eye, both in Europe and America. Here I include only a portion of my previous discussion, focusing on Canada and Australia, particularly on Australia because of a recent book by Harry Richardson and Frank Salter (2023), *Anglophobia*.

It is remarkable that the sea change in immigration policy in the Western world occurred at approximately the same time (1962–1973), and in all countries the changes reflected the attitudes of elites rather than the great mass of citizens. In the United States, Britain, Canada, and Australia, public opinion polls of European-derived peoples during the period when these laws were passed and long thereafter showed overwhelming rejection of immigration by non-European-derived peoples (Betts, 1988; Brimelow, 1995; F. Hawkins, 1989; Layton-Henry, 1992). A consistent theme has been that immigration policy has been formulated by elites with control of the media and that efforts have been made by political leaders of all major parties to keep fear of immigration off the political agenda (e.g., Betts; Layton-Henry, p. 82).

For example, in Canada the decision to abandon a "White Canada" policy came from government officials, not from elected politicians. The White Canada policy was effectively killed by regulations announced in 1962, and F. Hawkins (1989, p. 39) comments:

> This very important policy change was made not as a result of parliamentary or popular demand, but because some senior officials in Canada, including Dr. [George] Davidson [Deputy Minister of Citizenship and Immigration and later a senior administrator at the United Nations], rightly saw that Canada could not operate effectively within the United Nations, or in the multiracial Commonwealth, with the millstone of a racially discriminatory immigration policy round her neck.

In neither Australia nor Canada was there ever any popular sentiment to end the older European bias of immigration policy.

> The primary and identical motivation of Canadian and Australian politicians in trying to exclude first the Chinese, then other Asian migrants, and finally all potential non-white immigrants, was the desire to build and preserve societies and political systems in their hard-won, distant lands very like those of the United Kingdom. They also wished to establish without challenge the primary role there of her founding peoples of European origin. . . . Undisputed ownership of these territories of continental size was felt to be confirmed forever, not only by the fact of possession, but by the hardships and dangers endured by the early explorers and settlers; the years of back-breaking work to build the foundations of urban and rural life. . . . The idea that other peoples, who had taken no part in these pioneering efforts, might simply arrive in large numbers to exploit important local resources, or to take advantage of these earlier settlement efforts, was anathema. (F. Hawkins, 1989, pp. 22–23)

Given the elite origins of the non-European immigration policies that emerged throughout the West during this period despite popular opposition, it is of considerable interest that very little publicity was given to certain critical events. In Canada, the Report of the Special Joint Committee of 1975 was a critical event in shaping the non-European immigration policy of the 1978 immigration law, but "sad to say, since the press failed to comment on the report and the electronic media had remained uninvolved, the Canadian public heard little of it" (F. Hawkins, 1989, p. 59–60). Further (p. 63):

Looking back on this national debate on immigration and population which lasted for six months at most, it can be said now that it was a very effective one-time consultation with the immigration world, and with those Canadian institutions and organizations to whom immigration is an important matter. It did not reach "the average Canadian" for one simple reason: The Minister and Cabinet did not trust the average Canadian to respond in a positive way on this issue, and thought this would create more trouble than it was worth. As a result of this view, they did not want to commit the funds to organize extensive public participation, and made only a minimal effort to mobilize the media on behalf of a truly national debate. The principal benefit of this approach was that the badly needed new Immigration Act was on the statute book only a little later than Mr. [Robert] Andras [Minister of Manpower and Immigration] and his colleagues [Hawkins emphasizes Andras's Deputy Minister Alan Gotlieb as the second prime mover of this legislation] originally envisaged. The principal loss was what some would regard as a golden opportunity to bring a great many individual Canadians together, to discuss the future of their vast under-populated land.

Only after the 1978 law was in effect did the government embark on a public information campaign to inform Canadians of their new immigration policy (F. Hawkins, 1989, p. 79). F. Hawkins and Betts (1988) make similar points about the changes in Australian immigration policy. In Australia the impetus for change in immigration policy came from small groups of reformers that began appearing in some Australian universities in the 1960s (F. Hawkins, p. 22). Betts (pp. 99ff) in particular emphasizes the idea that the intellectual, academic, and media elite "trained in the humanities and social sciences" (p. 100) developed a sense of being a member of a morally and intellectually superior ingroup battling against Australian parochial nonintellectuals as an outgroup. As in the United States, there is a perception among Jews that a multicultural society will be a bulwark against anti-Semitism. Miriam Faine, an editorial committee member of the *Australian Jewish Democrat* stated, "The strengthening of multicultural or diverse Australia is also our most effective insurance policy against anti-semitism. The day Australia has a Chinese Australian Governor General I would feel more confident of my freedom to live as a Jewish Australian" (in McCormack, 1994, p. 11).

As in the United States, family unification became a centerpiece of immigration policy in Canada and Australia and led to the "chaining" phenomenon mentioned above as a cornerstone of Jewish immigration in the United States. F. Hawkins (1989, p. 87) shows that in Canada, family reunion was the policy of liberal members of Parliament desiring higher levels of Third World immigration. In Australia, family reunion became increasingly important during the 1980s, which also saw a declining importance of Australian development as a criterion for immigration policy (p. 150). Reflecting these trends, the Executive Council of Australian Jewry (ECAJ) passed a resolution at its December 1st, 1996 meeting to express "its support for the proposition that Australia's long-term interests are best served by a non-discriminatory immigration policy which adopts a benevolent attitude to refugees and family reunion and gives priority to humanitarian considerations." *The Australia/Israel Review*, a publication of the ECAJ, consistently editorialized in favor of high levels of immigration of all racial and ethnic groups. It published unflattering portraits of restrictionists (e.g., Kapel, 1997) and, in an effort at punishment and intimidation, published a list of two thousand people associated with Pauline Hanson's anti-immigration One Nation party (*The Australia/Israel Review*, 1998)

Anglophobia (2023) by Harry Richardson and Frank Salter brings Jewish activism in Australia up to date. Section 18C of Australia's Racial Discrimination Act was amended in 1996 as a result of Chinese and Jewish activism in order to criminalize speech that causes someone to be offended. "Free speech has been the first casualty of multiculturalism" (p. 145)—a statement that is equally true throughout the Western world (see Preface). Originally intended mainly to combat anti-Semitism, Section 18C soon came to be used to prosecute Anglos like Andrew Bolt who criticized White-looking individuals who made dubious claims about their aboriginal ancestry to obtain benefits. "Bolt complained that at his trial he faced a Jewish prosecutor who told the Jewish judge that Bolt was like a neo-Nazi and referred repeatedly to Nazi Germany and the Holocaust" (p. 107). Similarly, when Prof. Andrew Fraser was prosecuted for his views on Black criminality,

> the prosecuting team included the president of the NSW Jewish Board of Deputies, the peak Jewish defence agency in New South Wales, that is, the organization that represented many other Jewish organizations. ... The symbolism could not have been clearer. The leader of a peak Jewish organization joined with other Jewish lawyers to sue an Anglo professor for raising a legitimate concern of ethnic and national welfare. (Richardson & Salter, 2023, p. 110)

The authors also discuss similar phenomena in America, noting the role of Noel Ignatiev in the origins of Critical Race Theory, the ADL's definition of racism in which the term is only applied to Whites, and the close relationship between the FBI and the ADL, quoting ADL head Jonathan Greenblatt:

> We're working with all the platforms by the way—Google and YouTube and Meta and Twitter and Reddit and Steam and Amazon and all these companies. That's relevant because we work with Twitter now since it was

founded. We worked with the old regime and [we're] working with the new post-Elon Musk regime. (Richardson & Salter, 2023, p. 116)

(1) The authors note similar phenomena in Sweden and the U.K., and they note that in general the Jewish community has taken a leadership role in promoting multiculturalism and immigration while making alliances with more poorly organized, less motivated ethnic groups.

The examples of Jewish activism against Anglo interests involve an intense level of motivation. . . . In Australia, Jewish organisations sometimes act as de facto peak bodies for the multicultural sector as a whole, rallying, organizing, coordinating, and supporting the actions of other minority advocates. (Richardson & Salter, 2023, p. 117)

This leadership phenomenon also occurs in the U.S., where Jewish organizations have made alliances with non-White ethnic activist organizations. For example, groups such as the AJCommittee, the Jewish Community Council of Greater Washington, and Rabbi Marc Schneir's Foundation for Ethnic Understanding have formed coalitions with organizations such as the National Council of La Raza, the League of United Latin American Citizens, the Congressional Black Caucus, the Congressional Hispanic Caucus, the Jewish Congressional Delegation, and the Congressional Asian Pacific American Caucus; the meeting was co-sponsored by the World Jewish Congress (MacDonald, 2006).

(2) In attempting to understand Jewish motivation for this, the authors note Jewish self-perceptions of ill treatment in the past (e.g., in the U.S., Jews perceived the Immigration Act of 1924 that lowered immigration and favored Northwest Europeans as hostile to Jewish immigration). However, as anti-Semitism plummeted in the wake of World War II, there was also an often-expressed concern that a homogeneous White society would eventually turn on the Jews, as happened in Germany in the 1930s (see above)—a concern that was central to the Frankfurt School's switch from orthodox Marxism to the theory that White ethnocentrism was the fundamental problem for Jews (Ch. 6). The authors have an extensive discussion of Miriam Faine, a leader of the Jewish community and editor of *The Australian Jewish Democrat*, who wrote in 1992 of the Jewish strategy to import more non-Whites and to encourage them to retain their ethnic identities as a strategy to combat anti-Semitism but also to obtain power over Anglos: "Faine's hate-filled words give us a window into explicit multicultural strategizing. She did not express vague unconscious implicit messages. This was someone intent on group domination and replacement in a very conscious and deliberate targeting of Anglo Australia" (Richardson & Salter, 2023, p. 125). She preferred a Chinese head of state because only then would she feel safe in Australia, which is quite clearly an expression of "a

preference for Anglos to be replaced in positions of power. . . . the disempow-erment of white Anglo Australians" (p. 127).

(3) Of course, Jews are not the only longstanding ethnic group in Australia with some animosity to the Anglos. The Irish have a long history of hostility toward Anglos stemming from English colonial rule over Ireland, hostilities which were transported to Australia after Irish immigration. Discussion mainly features one Greg Sheridan, a journalist since the late 1970s for *The Australian*, a Murdoch publication. Like many multiculturalism advocates in the West, he has praised other countries, like India and China, for taking steps to ensure their cultural homogeneity. Influenced by his father, as a child he refused to stand for "God Save the Queen" or any other expression of British sovereignty. However, as in America, where such multicultural activism motivated by Irish hostility toward the British is residual at best, Jewish activism and its organiz-ing influence on other imported minorities are quite clearly much greater than the residual anti-Anglo sentiments of some contemporary Irish-descended Australians. "Examples of Anglophobia can be found among Irish Catholics but that sentiment has not been general or inevitable" (Richardson & Salter, 2023, p. 141). Examples can be found, but the organizational structure, elite overrepresentation, and influence are simply not there.

It seems fair to conclude that Jewish organizations have uniformly advo-cated high levels of immigration of all racial and ethnic groups into Western societies and have also advocated a multicultural model for these societies.

9

Conclusion: Whither Judaism and the West?

This book documents several influential movements originated and dominated by strongly identified Jews acting according to their perceptions of Jewish interests. However, I don't want to be interpreted as claiming that these Jews acted in a vacuum or that their activism would work in other cultures. They acted in the context of Western individualism. Among all the cultures of the world, Western civilization is uniquely individualist (Henrich, 2020; *Individualism*). My 2019 book, *Individualism and the Western Liberal Tradition*, focuses mainly on the United States (Ch. 6),

> where a Puritan-descended elite dominated intellectual discourse and the Ivy League universities, as well as the legal, political, and commercial establishment until the rise of a Jewish elite. This new elite was influential even in the early decades of the twentieth century, but its influence expanded considerably in the post-World War II era and accelerated dramatically after 1965.

Further, in Chapter 8 of *Individualism*:

> A fundamental aspect of individualism is that group cohesion is based not on kinship but on reputation—most importantly in recent centuries, a moral reputation as capable, honest, trustworthy and fair. The moral

communities of the West have deep historical roots. . . . Christian Europe, especially in the Middle Ages, had become a moral community based on Christian religious beliefs rather than an ethnic or national identity. Moreover, the medieval moral community created by the Church, the Puritan and Quaker religious leaders of the seventeenth and eighteenth centuries, and the liberal intellectuals of the nineteenth century . . . carried on the primeval [prehistoric, genetically influenced] tendency to create moral communities as a source of identity. Moreover, . . . such moral communities have come to define the contemporary culture of the West.

These moral communities are indigenous products of the culture of the West—products of Western culture in the same way that kinship-based clans, cousin marriage and harems of elite males are products of the people of the Middle East.

Whites' greater tendency toward individualism implies that they are less likely than other peoples to make invidious distinctions between ingroups and outgroups and more likely to be open to strangers. European peoples are thus less likely to be anti-Jewish, particularly in an environment where media and the educational system are saturated with messages opposed to anti-Semitism.

As emphasized here, Jewish media and academic influence have been critical to creating what is now essentially an anti-White media and educational environment. One might say that the activist Jewish community came to realize that messages framed as moral imperatives would be able to create an anti-White moral community, and that White people could be effectively shamed into submission with messages framing replacement-level non-White immigration and ethnic and cultural diversity as morally superior policies..

ON THE POSSIBILITY OF A NON-JEWISH ELITE IN THE UNITED STATES

The rise of the new Jewish-dominated elite meant that explicit, morally framed messages (i.e., messages designed to appeal to the moral communities of the West) about race (e.g., "there's no such thing as race") and ethnocentrism (e.g., "White ethnocentrism is a sure sign of psychopathology and disturbed parent-child relationships") were being disseminated by the elite media and throughout the educational system—areas with strong Jewish influence (see Preface). In general, these intellectual and political movements with strong Jewish influence have been on the left (including neoconservatism), reflecting the political attitudes of the mainstream Jewish diaspora community in the West—and utterly opposed to the ethnonationalist attitudes that dominate Israel. The fundamental assumptions of these leftist movements, particularly as they relate to race and ethnicity, permeate intellectual and political discourse among both liberals and conservatives and define a mainstream consensus among elites in academia, the media, business, and government.

Jews ascended to the heights of American society in several stages. In the early twentieth century Henry Ford noted their prominence in a variety of fields and their hostility to Christianity.[155] Jews also had prominent roles in Franklin Roosevelt's presidency (Talmadge, 2025), but it wasn't until after World War II that anti-Jewish attitudes basically disappeared and they really entered the mainstream. Jews then led the 1960s counter-cultural revolution and became a dominant elite in the 1960s (Ch. 3); they were a necessary condition for the passage of the Immigration and Nationality Act of 1965 that eventually radically transformed the country, as well as civil rights legislation and the general ascent of the left to a position of dominance in American culture (Ch. 8). Jewish ascendency was accompanied by the decline and eventual eclipse of the previously dominant White, Anglo-Saxon Protestant East-Coast establishment (MacDonald, 2015).

The main sources of Jewish power since the 1960s have been: 1) their ownership of media and their creation of media content as writers and producers; 2) their wealth and willingness to contribute to political causes by funding political candidates and establishing nonprofit organizations and lobbying groups able to influence public policy; 3) their domination of academic culture, ultimately due to their influence in elite universities and trickling down to lower-tier universities and eventually the K-12 educational system.

This Jewish power structure is still in place, but there appear to be important changes indicating that Jewish power is not what it once was. Moreover, it's hard to believe that the organized Jewish community is able to retain its position as eternal victims and paragons of tolerance and virtue in view of Israeli actions in Gaza and the support these actions have received from the American Jewish community.

Media

When I was growing up in the 1950s, there were three television networks, all owned by Jews (ABC, CBS, NBC). These networks are still owned by Jews (see Preface). *The New York Times*, often labeled "America's newspaper of record," is still owned by a Jewish family and reflects the mainstream liberal-left Jewish community. However, the influence of these exemplars of the legacy media has declined dramatically.

---

[155] See my discussion of Henry Ford's *The International Jew* published from 1920 to 1922 in MacDonald, 2002a.

If the 2024 election shows anything, it's that the legacy mainstream media is distrusted more than ever and has been effectively replaced among wide swaths of voters, especially young voters, by alternative media, particularly podcasts and social media. Influential podcasters, such as Joe Rogan (a former liberal who supported Trump in 2024), have become increasingly conservative, and Tucker Carlson has pushed the boundaries of conservative thinking, such as with his interviews with historian/blogger Darryl Cooper questioning aspects of the sacrosanct World War II narrative (MacDonald, 2024a) and with Curt Mills touching on neoconservatism—essentially a Jewish intellectual and political movement (Ch. 4)—and America's disastrous wars in the Middle East (MacDonald, 2025). Another former liberal, Elon Musk, has become a prominent supporter of Trump in the election and was active in attempting to end the power of the Democrat-leaning federal bureaucracy.

Trump's Secretary of Defense Pete Hegseth evicted *The New York Times*, National Public Radio, NBC, and Politico from their Pentagon offices to make room for One America News Network, *The New York Post*, Breitbart News Network, and *HuffPost* (which did not ask for representation) (Terkel, 2025). All of the ones replaced are decidedly on the left, while replacements are conservative except *HuffPost*. None can be considered legacy media.

Thomas Edsall (2025) in *The New York Times* has noted that "While both Democrats and Republicans have abandoned newspapers in growing numbers, . . . the drop among Republicans accelerated much faster than it did for Democrats in 2016, the year Trump first ran for president." Legacy newspapers are thus a key source of information for Democrats but not Republicans.

Conservative media is slavishly pro-Israel even as they typically oppose liberal-left domestic political policies favored by the mainstream Jewish community, such as:

1. promoting high levels of legal non-White immigration, enabling illegal immigration, and stopping the deportation of illegals because they see them as future voters for the liberal-left and diluting the power of White Americans or at least adding to the congressional power of blue states that welcome illegals, since all residents, not just citizens, are counted in the U.S. census;
2. promoting so-called hate speech laws and other attempts to rein in free speech on racial/ethnic issues, including especially criticisms of Israel;
3. supporting Diversity, Equity, and Inclusion programs and Critical Race Theory that discriminate against and foster hatred against Whites (Sales, 2025a);
4. promoting transgenderism, gay rights, advocating easy access to abortion, etc.

Jews typically vote overwhelmingly Democrat and basically fund the Democratic Party. In the 2024 election, 71 to 79 percent of Jews voted for Harris, thus supporting the liberal-far left policies favored by the Kamala Harris campaign (MacDonald, 2024b). Even though there was some shift to more conservative voting among some groups of Jews, Jews in general are still on the left when it comes to domestic issues compared to White Americans.

Jewish neoconservatives were a longtime fixture in the Republican Party but defected with the rise of Trump because of his professed distaste for foreign wars and likely because of Trump's stated views on immigration and multiculturalism. Predictably, the neoconservatives seamlessly defected to the Democrats where their liberal-left views on domestic policy fit right in, while the Democrat establishment has continued its robust support for Israel and all that that entails (with some dissent among Democrats who disapprove of the Gaza genocide). While in the GOP, these Jewish neocons moved the party to the left on social issues while promoting pro-Israel wars in the Middle East (Ch. 4), and now they support the Ukraine war against Russia. Conservative media by and large support Trump (Thompson, 2025), and are thus anathema to most Jews.

Thus, even though conservative media are obsessively pro-Israel, they tend to oppose the attitudes and policy proposals of the mainstream liberal-left Jewish community on domestic policy.

As noted, the influence of the legacy media, a main power base of the mainstream liberal-left Jewish community, appears to be in terminal decline. Moreover, there is some indication that some legacy media outlets are becoming more conservative. For example, Jeff Bezos changed the editorial stance of *The Washington Post* away from their liberal-left positions to a more libertarian policy and refused to endorse Harris for president (Howard, 2025). Patrick Soon-Shiong, owner of the *Los Angeles Times*, also blocked the paper from endorsing Harris, stating that the paper had become too liberal, resulting in the resignation of the editor and much of the editorial board (Katzenberger, 2024). Neither Bezos nor Soon-Shiong is Jewish.

The rise of alternative media is critical. Under Elon Musk, X is clearly open to conservative views, and even anti-Jewish posts. X has become a right-leaning media outlet that attracts young people and many others who reject the legacy media.

Funding the Left

Jewish financial clout is certainly still in place, but we are seeing the rise of a very wealthy class of non-Jewish billionaires and multi-millionaires, prototypically Elon Musk, who reportedly gave Trump's campaign more than 290 million dollars (D. Wright & Leeds-Matthews, 2025). Wealthy non-Jews are thus quite willing and able to finance a competitive campaign like Trump's. As of August 14th, 2024 (L. Kamin) according to *Forbes*, of twenty-six billionaire donors to Trump (not including Musk), twenty-two were not Jewish, while four, including Bernard Marcus (who recently died) were Jewish, with only one in the top ten (pro-Israel fanatic Miriam Adelson who donated one hundred million dollars). Overall, Democrats and Democrat-affiliated groups spent 1.8 billion dollars, while Republicans and Republican-affiliated groups spent about 1.4 billion dollars (Kamisar, 2024). The Trump campaign certainly had enough money to run a credible campaign and even win despite the deluge of hate emanating from the legacy media.

Jewish money is thus not necessary to win, especially if the richest man in the world is on board. Assuming Musk gave three hundred million dollars, it was much less than 1 percent of his wealth in 2024; indeed, Musk's activism has resulted in a campaign to destroy Tesla, a main source of his wealth. But the fact remains that Musk could finance a presidential campaign all by himself—two billion dollars would be more than even the Democrats and Democrat-affiliated groups spent on the 2024 presidential campaign, but Musk could easily afford that. As the Jews have always known, money is power.

All this wealth supporting Trump 2.0 was apparent at Trump's inauguration:

> Here were America's tech tycoons, members of his court, in a pantheon at his second Inaugural Address, directly across from the former presidents and in front of Trump's presumptive cabinet. Many members of Congress, the actual elected government, were relegated to the cheaper seats.
>
> The men who control Americans' eyeballs and, often, emotions got the choicest seats; several have scarfed up big mansions in Washington to be closer to the Oval.
>
> Elon Musk sat behind the vice president's mother, pumping his arms and giving two thumbs-up when Trump said he'd put an American flag on Mars, where Musk wants to die (just not on impact).
>
> Google's Sundar Pichai was near Don Jr. and next to Jeff Bezos and Lauren Sanchez, who were near Ivanka and Jared. Shou Zi Chew, the TikTok C.E.O., sat next to Tulsi Gabbard, Trump's intended director of national intelligence. Tim Cook of Apple was close to Barron Trump. Sam Altman, the head of OpenAI, was also at the inaugural but—perhaps because of his legal duel with Elon—was in the overflow room with Ron DeSantis, Eric Adams and Conor McGregor. (Dowd, 2025)

Sam Altman is the only one of these moguls who is Jewish. Most of these tycoons were likely just trying to ingratiate themselves with the new administration, but this is a huge change from the 2017 inauguration and suggests that they are quite comfortable with at least some of the sea changes that Trump is pursuing.

Academia

The university is definitely the hardest nut to crack because hiring is rigorously policed to make sure that new faculty and administrators are on the left. Academics who fail to support the left can expect a lifetime of harassment and hostility, and, if they don't have tenure, they will certainly be fired even if their teaching and scholarship are excellent.

As in other areas, Jews ascended the heights of the academic world after World War II and especially during the 1960s (see Preface). Once they achieved prominence—and always eager as a small minority to make alliances with other groups—they promoted the establishment of academic departments essentially composed of leftist activists, such as gender studies and various ethnic studies departments for Blacks, Latinos, Asians, Jews, etc., thus expanding the liberal arts faculty and creating a critical mass of leftist activists. This structure is still in place.

Since the Israeli war in Gaza, the West Bank, Lebanon, and Syria, beginning in 2023, there have been a great many protests on campus, but Jewish power has put a rather quick end to that:

> The policies ranged from banning the erection of tents on campus grounds to limiting the times and places where students are allowed to hold demonstrations. While free speech experts agree that some time, place and manner restrictions are acceptable, they have branded some policy changes unconstitutional. (Alonso, 2024)

At UCLA, pro-Israel thugs were allowed to run amok among protesters while the police stood by:

> Even worse scenes took place at UCLA as an encampment of peaceful protesters was violently attacked and beaten by a mob of pro-Israel thugs having no university connection but armed with bars, clubs, and fireworks, resulting in some serious injuries. A professor of history described her outrage as the nearby police stood aside and did nothing while UCLA students were attacked by outsiders, then arrested some 200 of the former. (Unz, 2024a)

Obviously, these restrictions are a far cry from university responses to the Black Lives Matter riots. As Unz (2024a) noted:

I'd think that most of these students were absolutely stunned at such reactions. For decades, they and their predecessors had freely protested on
a wide range of political causes without ever encountering even a sliver of
such vicious retaliation, let alone an organized campaign that quickly
forced the resignation of two of the Ivy League presidents who had allowed their protests. Some of their student organizations were immediately banned and the future careers of the protesters were harshly threatened, but the horrifying images from Gaza continued to reach their
smartphones.

The Trump administration responded to these events by demanding one
billion dollars from UCLA in part because of supposed anti-Semitism as indicated by student protests against the Gaza war—an amount much higher than
demanded of other universities for the same reasons (e.g., Columbia University
paid 221 million dollars) (Andrews & Randazzo, 2025).

Jewish power in academia is alive and well.

The Trump administration is pushing back on the academic left but not
against Jewish power in the universities, deporting foreign students and professors involved in anti-Israel protests:

> The new attorney general, Pam Bondi, created a task force to prosecute
> antisemitic acts, including on college campuses. The president's order
> singles out last year's university protests against Israel's war in Gaza,
> which it says unleashed a barrage of discrimination against Jewish stu-
> dents. The order targets international students who participated in those
> protests with deportation. (Westervelt, 2025)

There is also a welcome campaign to end Diversity, Equity and Inclusion
programs at universities. It's long been apparent that the only way to rein in
the radical left that dominates academia is to cut their funding. Although a
Department of Education ruling of February 17th, 2025 fits with color-blind
conservative ideology, it does mention discrimination against Whites (and
Asians) and specifically targets Critical Race Theory, which is nothing but anti-
White hate. As of February 2025, the DOE has cancelled well over one billion
dollars from university grants, noting that "Review of the contracts uncovered
wasteful and ideologically driven spending not in the interest of students and
taxpayers" (R. Quinn, 2025).

Trump's attitude on foreign student protesters will put a further chill into
what has already been happening with anti-Israel protests. But fighting DEI at
universities will be an uphill struggle against an academic establishment that
has devoted huge amounts of money and hired thousands of bureaucrats to
administer DEI programs (Bradley-Dorsey, 2021). Moreover, universities will

likely find ways to continue DEI programs even if they are legally prohibited, as they have with affirmative action admissions (Poff, 2024).

However, of the three main sources of Jewish power, academic influence is least important. Students will notice that DEI jobs are drying up and notice that, if these trends continue, advocating and living the old leftist political clichés are no longer good routes to social and career success. Women in particular are likely to shift political preferences when they see a shift in the status hierarchy (Devlin, 2025), but men will also change their attitudes as they try to advance in the new hierarchy.

A Non-Jewish Elite?

Thus there is a real possibility of the rise of an essentially non-Jewish elite centered outside the traditional legacy media and with the financial resources able to mount successful political campaigns and fund compatible NGOs. Whether this could develop into an *anti*-Jewish elite is a completely different question—unlikely for the foreseeable future because of the deep personal ties and business relationships among elite Jews and non-Jews, with President Trump as an exemplar. Nevertheless, as noted, the domestic policies of the Trump administration for the most part depart dramatically from policies long favored by the mainstream liberal-left Jewish community. Already we see numerous Jewish organizations protesting an end to DEI and the deportations of illegal immigrants (Sales, 2025a, 2025b).

Although the present situation is in flux, it is quite possible that in the future the new elite described here could become far more than a possibility. This new elite may realize that Jewish support and Jewish power in American politics are not what they once were and that there is no real need to support the policies favored by the mainstream Jewish community. Indeed, this may have already happened—with the important exception of pro-Israel attitudes that also appeal to some sections of the Republican base (e.g., knee-jerk support of Israel by mainstream conservatives and Evangelicals). Some parts of this new elite may be well aware of the role Jews have played in erecting the multicultural disaster that America has become—a position that was common on the American right for decades, at least from the time of Henry Ford until neoconservatives pushed out traditional conservatives during the Reagan administration and William F. Buckley purged the conservative movement of critics of Jewish influence (MacDonald, 2004b, pp. 16, 26; S. J. Quinn, 2022c). And they may be well aware that the slavish support that America has given Israel has been enormously costly in terms of lives and treasure without really serving American interests.

Musk is a good example. He is increasingly out of step with the liberal-left mainstream in his posts on X. Deborah Lipstadt, a Holocaust activist and

United States Special Envoy for Monitoring and Combating Anti-Semitism during the Biden administration, remarked about a Musk post, "The damage was done. The endorsement of the Great Replacement theory was very harmful." Lipstadt added that she disapproved of what she saw as an attempt to "mitigate" an earlier post by Musk, noting "You can try to mitigate, but once you open the pillow, it's like chasing the feathers" (in Lapin, 2023).

> Musk was replying to a user who wrote, "Jewish communities have been pushing the exact kind of dialectical hatred against whites that they claim to want people to stop using against them. I'm deeply disinterested in giving the tiniest s--- now about western Jewish populations coming to the disturbing realization that those hordes of minorities [they] support flooding their country don't exactly like them too much." . . .
> Musk responded, "You have said the actual truth." (Lapin, 2023)

ADL head Jonathan Greenblatt and other Jewish groups, including the American Jewish Committee joined a loud chorus in condemning that post. Later in the same thread, Musk went after the ADL itself, saying the group "push[es] de facto anti-white racism" (in Lapin, 2023). He apologized for a lot of this and made the customary visits to Auschwitz and Israel, but it's hard to believe that he now rejects these ideas.

Notice that the idea of the Great Replacement is completely off limits for Jewish activists like Lipstadt. They see any claim that the Great Replacement is real as an anti-Jewish conspiracy theory no matter whether Jews are mentioned, no matter what the changing demographics indicate, and no matter what research shows was the very prominent Jewish role in promoting the transformative Immigration and Nationality Act of 1965 and their continuing promotion of non-European immigration throughout the West (Ch. 8).

As always, I am an optimist. I think that many of the figures on the right are quite aware of the deleterious effects of Jewish power and influence on formerly dominant White America. And as I noted, it's hard to believe that Musk now rejects these ideas. He likely just knows better than to continue to utter them in public.

Consider also Vice President J. D. Vance's speech at the Munich Security Conference in February 2025.[156] The fact that such ideas on immigration and

---

[156] Vice President J. D. Vance's speech at the 61st Munich Security Conference (February 18th, 2025) was attended by powerful EU leaders and opposed what has been a consensus among European elites on immigration and free speech:

"And of all the pressing challenges that the nations represented here face, I believe there is nothing more urgent than mass migration. Today, almost one in five people living in this country [Germany] moved here from abroad. That is, of course, an all-time high. It's a similar number, by the way, in the United States, also an all-time high. The number of immigrants who

free speech are being articulated at the apex of political power is a most heartening sign and suggests the possibility that a new elite can arise that would challenge Jewish power in America and throughout the West.

COSTS OF MULTICULTURALISM

Given the Jewish strategy of promoting multiculturalism and ethnic pluralism, it's relevant to discuss the costs of multiculturalism. First and foremost, multiculturalism in formerly relatively homogeneous White societies lessens the political and cultural power of Whites. We simply cannot wish away the reality that different racial and ethnic groups have different and conflicting interests.

Multiculturalism leads to "ethnic conflict sometimes leading to civil war, a loss of public trust and cooperation, reduced democracy, reduced economic growth, the emergence of ethnic criminal gangs, and psychological and social costs to majorities who become minorities" (Richardson & Salter, 2023, p. 24). The possibility of civil war has been raised by Prof. of War Studies David Betz, who has claimed that British society is "explosively configured" for mass unrest because of unchecked immigration, restrictions on free speech, and continuing lack of social cohesion—a diagnosis he applies also to other Western countries. Multiculturalism is a disaster that is,

> leading to a society that [is] ghettoized into competing communities that [have] little relation with each other. . . . [T]he financialization of the economy is essentially running out of rope.[157] . . . [W]e're considerably more

---

entered the EU from non-EU countries doubled between 2021 and 2022 alone. And of course, it's gotten much higher since.

"And we know the situation. It didn't materialize in a vacuum. It's the result of a series of conscious decisions made by politicians all over the continent, and others across the world, over the span of a decade. . . .

"I believe that dismissing people, dismissing their concerns or worse yet, shutting down media, shutting down elections or shutting people out of the political process protects nothing. In fact, it is the most surefire way to destroy democracy. Speaking up and expressing opinions isn't election interference. Even when people express views outside your own country, and even when those people are very influential. And trust me, I say this with all humor—if American democracy can survive ten years of Greta Thunberg's scolding you guys can survive a few months of Elon Musk.

"But what no democracy—American, German or European—will survive, is telling millions of voters that their thoughts and concerns, their aspirations, their pleas for relief, are invalid or unworthy of even being considered" (Full transcript in Lu, 2025).

[157] James Petras (2017) has noted the prominent role of Jews in finance and its effect on Jewish power and influence at the expense of the working class: "By the last quarter of the 20th century and especially in the 21st century, deindustrialization and the shift to financialization in the US economy increased the power and privilege of a disproportionate number of multi-

fractured as a society. We're considerably more detached from our own history; or certainly from common appreciation of the validity and acceptability of that history. We're in a period of very serious, probably persistent, structural economic decline. (Betz, 2025)

Thus a major effect of multiculturalism has been what is often termed "hyper-polarization." Many commenters on the current scene in America have noted the increased polarization and inability to communicate across the political—increasingly ethnic—divide. Opposing groups have irreconcilable world views and see the other as evil incarnate—highly reminiscent of the millenarian thinking that is a strong trend in American history (see *Individualism*, Ch. 6). As this continues to fester, the conflict is seen by all sides as irreconcilable. This results in an existential clash where fundamental values are at stake. As Hillary Clinton noted, commenting on the poisonous atmosphere of American politics in 2018, civility in American politics could only be restored if her side, the Democrats, won: "You cannot be civil with a political party that wants to destroy what you stand for, what you care about" (in Crowe, 2018).

Thus, the situation in the United States is quite similar to the U.K. as described by Betz and suggests the possibility of a civil war. (Similar dividing lines are apparent in all Western countries and in many other parts of the world.) Indeed, a 2018 *Rasmussen Reports* poll indicated 31 percent of Americans think a civil war is likely soon.

One possibility for a civil war scenario was presented by Michael Vlahos (2018), who notes that civil wars begin when "kinship groups"—a proxy for race-based groups—fractionate into opposing camps:

Just since the 2016 election, we have witnessed a rolling thunder of Blue and Red elite rhetoric—packing the Supreme Court, abolishing the electoral college, repealing the Second Amendment, wholesale state nullification of federal law, shackling of voter rights, and Deep State invocation of the 25th Amendment. These are all potential extremities of action that would not only dismantle our constitutional order, but also skew it to one side's juridical construct of virtue, thus dissolving any semblance of adherence to law by the other. Over time each party becomes emotionally invested in the lust to dismantle the old and make something new.

Hence, constitutional norms exist only conditionally, until such time as they finally be dismantled, and only as long as a precariously balanced electoral divide holds firm. A big historical tilt in favor of one party over the other would very quickly push the nation into crisis because the party

---

billionaire/millionaire Jews. This seismic shift has coincided with the pervasive impoverishment of the marginalized working class in the former 'rust belt' and central parts of the country and the incredible concentration of national wealth at the top 1%. This is a demographic shift and ethno-class apartheid of huge, but unstudied, significance."

with the new mandate would rush to enact its program. The very threat of such constitutional dismantling would be sure *casus belli*. Such tilts in the 1770s against Britain, and later in the 1850s against the slaveholding party, were the real tipping points. Not only was *Dred Scott v. Sandford* just such a tipping point in 1857, but subconsciously its legacy weighs heavily on Americans today, as they contemplate—often with hysterical passion—the dread consequences of a [Brett] Kavanaugh appointment [to the Supreme Court]. . . .

What is clear is that the two warring parties will accept nothing less from the other than submission, even though the loser will never submit. Moreover, each factional ethos is incapable of empathizing with the other.

In the U.S. the factions tend to be urban/rural and White/non-White, although of course these issues are conflated to some extent. In all Blue states, there is a divide between rural areas and the large urban centers that dominate politically, making a regional partition ineffective without very large population transfers (Badger, 2018).

Because of importing a new, liberal-leaning electorate, the left is poised to be a permanent majority within the present system. The left has shown increasingly authoritarian tendencies, and already there are prominent voices on the left that have proposed toppling much of the Constitutional order (e.g., abolishing the electoral college in favor of a popular vote, ending the practice of having two senators from each state, ending free speech, and an ideology of judicial activism in which the Constitution should be seen as malleable and open to change to accommodate new trends).

The left has shown no tolerance for dissenting voices. Indeed, dissenters are seen as the personification of evil—exactly the same as in the period prior to the Civil War. If indeed the left obtains power, the expectation would be an increase in political repression, the end of First Amendment protections for free speech, more or less official anti-White rhetoric, removal and renaming of historical monuments and place names, and increased levels of indoctrination throughout the educational system. Indeed, on several critical issues the left has changed radically from when it was out of power in the 1950s to when it achieved cultural hegemony in recent times, most particularly on the importance of free speech. Historically, of course, there is ample precedent for what happens when the left attains power, as in the Soviet Union: instituting a permanent regime of the left without the possibility of change in the power structure and suppression and even eradication of dissidents. Given that the left has already made proposals that would eradicate the Constitutional order, such a scenario is not far-fetched.

Although the left has certainly been in the forefront of curtailing the First Amendment, the Trump administration has acceded to the Jewish activist community to penalize free speech criticizing Israel at universities, particularly Israel's actions in Gaza. Neither the left nor the right have a principled commitment to the First Amendment, so one can expect that a victory by one side or the other will result in limitations on speech, the left mainly concerned with limiting speech hostile to immigration, multiculturalism, LGBTQ+ activism, and research on race differences in behavior, while the mainstream conservative movement is concerned with limiting the access of children to LGBTQ+ material and penalizing speech critical of Israel.

Around the world we see societies racked by ethnic and religious conflict. The civil war in Syria pitted Sunnis against Shiites, and within these larger groupings there are particular ethnic groups, such as Alawites, Arabs, Kurds, Druze, and Assyrians. There's also China and the Uyghurs; Israelis and Palestinians; Hindus, Christians, and Muslims in India; and the Hutu and Tutsi in Rwanda. There have also been battles between Muslim migrant-descended groups versus the police in France and the Black Lives Matter riots in the U.S. in 2020. One would think that the reality of ethnic conflict would be obvious to anyone with or without any training in evolutionary biology, but this has not stopped our pro-multicultural elites from imposing it throughout the West. It's impossible to believe that Western elites want the best possible outcomes for the West.

Regarding the above-noted loss of public trust, the problem with collectivist, kinship-based cultures is that they do not produce high trust apart from close kin, resulting in much higher levels of corruption because individuals with power have a tendency to help their relatives; in Western cultures people readily trust and cooperate with non-kin on the basis of reputation (e.g., as honest, trustworthy, and competent), not kinship connections (*Individualism*). Other examples of ethnic conflict between Jews and non-Jews have been cited throughout this book, particularly Jews versus non-Jews in communist regimes. The case of Béla Kun's heavily Jewish government in Hungary (in power for 133 days in 1919) is particularly revelatory and reflects much of the discussion in Chapter 3.

> Statues of Hungarian kings and national heroes were torn down, the national anthem was banned, and the display of the national colors was made a punishable offense. . . . Radical agitators were dispatched to the countryside, where they ridiculed the institution of the family and threatened to turn churches into movie theatres. . . . Antipathy soon enough focused on the Jews. Young revolutionaries of Jewish origin had been sent to the countryside to administer the newly collectivized agricultural estates; their radicalism was exceeded only by their incompetence, reinforcing peasant anti-Semitism. The Jesuits, for their part, interpreted the revolution as Jewish and anti-Christian in essence. . . . Rumors abounded that

the revolutionaries were everywhere desecrating the Host. In Budapest as in the countryside, opposition to the regime, defense of the church, and anti-Semitism went hand in hand. (Muller, 2010, pp. 156–157)

This example of ethnic conflict between Hungarians and Jews has not been forgotten by Hungarians. Zsolt Bayer, co-founder of Hungary's nationalist, anti-immigration Fidesz party (now led by Prime Minister Viktor Orban), wrote:

Why are we surprised that the simple peasant whose determinant experience was that the Jews broke into his village, beat his priest to death, threatened to convert his church into a movie theater—why do we find it shocking that twenty years later he watched without pity as the gendarmes dragged the Jews away from his village? (in Liphshiz, 2017)

Fidesz has not only opposed immigration in opposition to EU policy of distributing migrants among all member states but has also passed laws aimed at curtailing the influence of Western NGOs (Bayer, 2023), with George Soros being a well-publicized target, leading to charges of anti-Semitism.

George Soros and his liberal views have been a perennial target of Orban's Fidesz party over the past decade. Soros is Jewish and his central role in Fidesz propaganda has led some critics to accuse the party of antisemitism, which it denies.

"Hungarian taxpayers' money is again being used to pay for political propaganda that is deeply tainted by antisemitism," a spokesperson for the Open Society Foundations said.

Orban said those who have benefited from funds allegedly coming from George Soros and the US Democratic Party should be banned from Hungary. . . .

Orban signaled earlier this month the crackdown was coming as he praised President Donald Trump's plan to shut down the US Agency for International Development.

In late 2022, USAID launched a program to help strengthen democracy and civil society in central Europe. It included the financing of non-government organizations and independent media in Hungary. (Kasnyik, 2025)

Can Western Individualism Survive the Rise of the Jews?

The "rise of the Jews"—to use Albert Lindemann's (1997) phrase—has undoubtedly had important effects on contemporary Western societies. A major theme of the previous chapter is that high levels of immigration into Western societies conforms to a perceived Jewish interest in developing nonhomogeneous, culturally and ethnically pluralistic societies. Jewish groups have also been very active in organizing these groups in both the United States and Australia and doubtless other Western countries (Richardson & Salter, 2023; MacDonald, 2023b). It is of interest to consider the possible consequences of such a policy in the long term.

The concluding chapter of the 1998 edition of this book emphasized the divisive and destructive effects of multiculturalism that were already apparent at that time. The utopian theories of multicultural harmony originated by Horace Kallen (see Ch. 8) have given way to mainstream hatred of White America in the legacy media and elite universities; and, with the ongoing Gaza war, there is increasing hostility toward Israel, particularly among post-1965 Muslim immigrants from the Middle East, but also among leftists who see a yawning gap between the lofty moralistic sentiments that have come to define the left versus the reality of Israeli behavior and its support by Israelis, the Israel Lobby, and the vast majority of the organized Jewish community in the diaspora. Given that the Jewish community has long conflated criticism of Israel with anti-Semitism, the organized Jewish community has been activated in support of Israel by, for example, successfully pressuring authorities to put an end to public anti-Israel protests and penalizing protesters, as noted above.

Thus the increased ethnic conflict predicted in the 1998 chapter has come to pass. The importance of group-based competition cannot be overstated. I believe it is highly unlikely that Western societies based on individualism and democracy can long survive the legitimization of competition between identitarian groups in which group membership is determined by ethnicity. The discussion in SAID (Chs. 3–5) strongly suggests that ultimately group strategies are met by other group strategies, so that societies become organized around cohesive, mutually exclusionary groups. Indeed, the recent multicultural movement may be viewed as tending toward a profoundly non-Western form of social organization that has historically been much more typical of Middle Eastern segmentary societies centered around discrete homogeneous groups. However, unlike in the (utopian) multicultural ideal, in these societies there are pronounced relations of dominance and subordination. Whereas democracy is quite foreign to such societies, Western societies—uniquely among the stratified societies of the world (Henrich, 2020; *Individualism*)— have developed individualistic, democratic, and republican political institutions. Moreover, major examples of Western collectivism, including the rise of the Catholic Church in the late Roman Empire, Iberian Catholicism during the period of the Inquisition, and National Socialism from 1933 to 1945—all reactions to Jewish power (SAID, Chs. 3–5)—have been characterized by intense anti-Semitism.

There is thus a significant possibility that individualistic societies are unlikely to survive the intra-societal, group-based competition that has become increasingly common and intellectually respectable in the United States. I believe the United States is presently heading down a volatile path—a path that leads to ethnic warfare and to the development of collectivist, authoritarian, and racialist enclaves. Although ethnocentric beliefs and behavior are viewed as morally and intellectually legitimate only among ethnic minorities in the United States, the theory and the data presented in SAID (Ch. 1) and *Individualism* (Ch. 8) indicate that the development of greater ethnocentrism among European-derived peoples is a likely result of present trends, at least partly fueled by the rise of anti-White hate in elite places dominated since the 1960s by Jews.

One way of analyzing the Frankfurt School and psychoanalysis is that they have attempted with some success to erect, in the terminology of Paul Gottfried (1998) and Christopher Lasch (1991), a "therapeutic state" that pathologizes the ethnocentrism of European-derived peoples as well as their attempts to retain cultural and demographic dominance. However, ethnocentrism on the part of the European-derived majority in the United States is a likely outcome of the increasingly group-structured contemporary social and political landscape—likely because evolved psychological mechanisms in humans appear to function by making ingroup and outgroup membership more salient in situations of group-based resource competition and feelings of being under threat (see *Individualism*, Ch. 8; SAID, Ch. 1). This is occurring in a context in which there is already discrimination against Whites, especially White males, in access to jobs and university admission, a situation that affects young White males the most.

The effort to overcome these evolved inclinations thus necessitates applying to Western societies a massive "therapeutic" intervention in which manifestations of majoritarian ethnocentrism are combated at several levels, but first and foremost by promoting the ideology that such manifestations are an indication of psychopathology (the ideology of the Frankfurt School) and a cause for ostracism, shame, psychiatric intervention, and counseling. As noted in Chapter 8 of the 1998 edition:

> [O]ne may expect that as ethnic conflict continues to escalate in the United States, increasingly desperate attempts will be made to prop up the ideology of multiculturalism with sophisticated theories of the psychopathology of majority group ethnocentrism, as well as with the erection of police state controls on nonconforming thought and behavior.

This prediction has certainly panned out.

A contemporary example is Critical Race Theory which essentially pathol-ogizes Whites and their culture while blaming them for the problems of other groups. There are now dozens of textbooks and hundreds of university courses focused on the topic. The entire field is united around falsities—mainly that race is a social construct with no biological or evolutionary aspects worth not-ing and that Whites have been uniquely evil throughout history and are re-sponsible for any invidious comparisons between Whites and other races in, for example, crime statistics or academic performance. This has resulted in widespread removal of standardized tests (although there has been consider-able retrenchment as schools have realized the folly of ignoring academic po-tential), and greater leniency on crime. For example, California's Racial Justice Act of 2020 allows Black defendants to claim racial discrimination without showing any racial motivation on the part of police or prosecutors, but only that there are racial disparities in such prosecutions (Joyce, 2024b)—which of course may well be influenced by a variety of factors besides racial discrimi-nation, including the often-noted racial differences in proneness to criminal-ity.

I suppose that a major reason why some non-Jewish racial and ethnic groups adopt multiculturalism is that they are not able to compete successfully in an individualistic economic and cultural arena. As a result, multiculturalism has quickly become identified with the idea that each group ought to receive a proportional measure of economic and cultural success (thus the constant ag-itating about "equity"). As indicated above, the resulting situation may oppose Jewish interests. Because of their high intelligence, ethnic cohesiveness, and resource-acquisition ability, Jews do not benefit from affirmative action poli-cies and other group-based entitlements commonly advocated by minority groups with low social status. Jews thus come into conflict with other ethni-cally identified minority groups who use multiculturalism for their own pur-poses.

Nevertheless, because of their competitive advantage within the White, European-derived group with which they are currently classified, Jews may perceive themselves as benefiting from policies designed to dilute the power of the European-derived Americans on the assumption that they themselves would suffer much less from such policies. Indeed, despite the official opposi-tion to group-based preferences among Jewish organizations, Jews voted for an anti-affirmative action ballot measure in California in markedly lower per-centages than did other European-derived groups, and Ron Unz (2018c) has shown that, while the enrollment at elite universities of non-Jewish Whites has declined dramatically, Jewish enrollment has not declined:

> I gradually noticed that the huge and continuing increase in the enroll-ment of non-white and foreign students at our most elite universities had

caused a complete collapse in the enrollment of white American Gentiles, but oddly enough, no similar reduction in Jewish numbers. It was well-known that Jewish activists had been the primary force behind the establishment of Affirmative Action and related policies in college admissions, and I began to wonder about their true motivation, whether conscious or unconscious.

Had the goal been the stated one, of providing educational opportunities to previously excluded groups? Or had that merely been the excuse used to advance a policy that eliminated the majority of white Gentiles, their primary ethnic competitors? With the Jewish population numbering merely 2%, there was an obvious limit as to how many elite college slots they themselves could possibly fill, but if enough other groups were also brought in, then Gentile numbers could easily be reduced to low levels, despite the fact that they constituted the bulk of the national population.

Although multiculturalist ideology was invented by Jewish intellectuals to rationalize the continuation of separatism and minority-group ethnocentrism in a modern Western state, several of the recent instantiations of multiculturalism may eventually produce a monster with negative consequences for Judaism. In the 1998 edition I mentioned Irving Louis Horowitz (1993, p. 89) who noted the emergence of anti-Semitism in academic sociology as these departments are increasingly staffed by individuals who are committed to ethnic political agendas and who view Jewish domination of sociology in negative terms. There is a strong strain of anti-Semitism emanating from some multiculturalist ideologues, especially from Afrocentric ideologues (E. Alexander, 1992), and M. Cohen (1998, p. 45) finds that "multiculturalism is often identified nowadays with a segment of the left that has, to put it bluntly, a Jewish problem." The Nation of Islam, led by Louis Farrakhan, has adopted overtly anti-Semitic rhetoric. Afrocentrism is often associated with racialist ideologies, such as those of Molefi Asante (1987), in which ethnicity is viewed as the morally proper basis of self-identity and self-esteem and in which a close connection exists between ethnicity and culture. Western ideals of objectivity, universalism, individualism, rationality, and the scientific method are rejected because of their ethnic origins. Asante promotes a naive racialist theory in which Africans (the "sun people") are viewed as superior to Europeans (the "ice people").

Recent Examples of Scholarship Documenting Jewish Ethnic Networking

A recurring theme in my writing and that of other authors writing for *The Occidental Quarterly* and *The Occidental Observer* has therefore been to document Jewish ethnic networking in efforts to establish Jewish figures in positions of scientific, academic, artistic, or cultural pre-eminence. This volume discusses figures like Boas, Freud, Horkheimer, and Trotsky, and the phenomenon is also apparent with figures in philosophy such as Baruch Spinoza and Isaac La Peyrère, the beneficiaries of the efforts of Richard Popkin to credit them as critically important intellectual influences underlying the Enlightenment (Joyce, 2019a,d); such efforts also occurred in the art world, such as on behalf of Mark Rothko and Gustav Mahler, based on the work of Brenton Sanderson (see MacDonald, 2020). These efforts, although not always successful, have taken advantage of centers of Jewish power and influence described throughout this book, such as promotion in the elite media and the academic world. As Andrew Joyce (2019d) notes:

> Typically these efforts can be said to begin with the veneration by a group of Jews of a Jewish intellectual or artist, and is followed by the creation of an authoritarian cult-like aura around his or her personality. The process reaches its completion, in some cases after the death of the guru figure, in an aggressive Jewish marketing effort to convince society at large that this figure, together with his or her ideas, is or was of national or international—if not cosmic—significance. It is predominantly by this process that the notion of "Jewish Genius" is perpetuated.

The contrary process also occurs, with Jews tearing down non-Jewish figures, such as Richard Wagner, for being critical of Jews, or aiming their ire at Beethoven in an attempt to take down his towering reputation in order to show that his music was composed in the cultural context of "White supremacy," and even claiming that Beethoven was non-White (Sanderson, 2021, 2020). This has sometimes led to anti-Semitism, as for example Heinrich von Treitschke's (1881/1958, pp. 2–3) comment:

> I refer the reader to *The History of the Jews* by [Jewish nationalist historian Heinrich] Graetz. What a fanatical fury against the "arch enemy" Christianity, what deadly hatred of the purest and most powerful exponents of Germanic character, from Luther to Goethe and Fichte! And what hollow, offensive self-glorification! Here it is proved with continuous satirical invective that the nation of Kant was really educated to humanity by the Jews only, that the language of Lessing and Goethe became sensitive to beauty, spirit, and wit only through Boerne and Heine!

As is clear from the above examples, Jewish ethnic networking and promotion of other Jews is intimately connected to an exaggerated sense of Jewish ethnic pride and a desire to create a positive image of Jews among non-Jews. Andrew Joyce (2019a) provides a telling example:

Norman Lebrecht [2019], the Jewish British commentator on music and cultural affairs, published a piece at *The Spectator* titled "Do Jews Think Differently?," in which he argues that Jews possess "a common ancestral way of thinking" that has allowed them to "change the world as we know it." He insists that there exists "a way of thinking that has allowed Jews to see the world from an oblique angle," and continues: "Do Jews think differently? The moment I asked that question, there could be only one answer. . . . Some dissenting Jew, somewhere, right now, is about to change the way the world revolves." Lebrecht refers at length to his recently published *Genius & Anxiety: How Jews Changed the World, 1847–1947* (Simon & Schuster, 2019), in the course of which he profiles 36 Jews who he claims are responsible (in a positive sense) for modernity. Lebrecht is a strongly identified Jew who clearly has a high level of self-esteem at the group level. He also has a history of producing texts that have advanced Jewish self-glorification. . . .

Lebrecht's book is simply part of a steady production of texts in which Jews celebrate themselves, often with extremely tendentious claims and outlandish and misplaced self-congratulation. Lebrecht's latest text, for example, is almost a reprint of Jacques Picard's *Makers of Jewish Modernity: Thinkers, Artists, Leaders, and the World They Made* (Princeton, 1998), and this in turn is part of a tradition that includes Heinrich Graetz's 11-volume *Geschichte der Juden* (1853–1870), Cecil Roth's *The Jewish Contribution to Civilization* (1938), Fredric Bedoire's *The Jewish Contribution to Modern Architecture* (2004), and Rebecca Goldstein's *Betraying Spinoza: The Renegade Jew Who Gave Us Modernity* (2006) (see [Joyce, 2019d] for an examination of how Spinoza has been a particular focus for Jewish self-glorification).

Another example comes from Brenton Sanderson's (2011b) review of Lebrecht's *Why Mahler? How One Man and Ten Symphonies Changed the World*:

The focus here is on alerting us to fact of Mahler's towering genius, and how this genius was inextricably bound up with his identity as a Jew. Overlaying this, as ever, is the lachrymose vision of Mahler the saintly Jewish victim of gentile injustice. Lebrecht's new book is another reminder of how Jewish intellectuals have used their privileged status as self-appointed gatekeepers of Western culture to advance their group interests through the way they conceptualize the respective artistic achievements of Jews and Europeans. . . . This betokens an acknowledgement of the importance of ethnic role models in the promotion of ethnic pride and group cohesion, and how ethnocentric Jews, like Lebrecht, have hyped ethnic models in order to promote ethnic pride. This form of Jewish intellectual activity is clearly directed at influencing 'social categorization processes in a manner that benefits Jews.'

There is also an element of self-glorification among the promoters, as they bask in the reflected glory of their co-ethnics. Sanderson (2011a) comments on Mark Rothko and the role of Jewish critics in promoting him:

> For critics like [Klaus] Ottmann, Rothko's genius is indisputable and he possessed an "extraordinary talent" that enabled him to transfer his metaphysical "impulses to the canvas with a power and magnetism that stuns viewers of his work. ... In fact Rothko's skill in achieving this result—whether intentional or not—perhaps explains why he was once called "the melancholic rabbi." For prominent Jewish art historian Simon Schama, Rothko's "big vertical canvasses of contrasting bars of colour, panels of colour stacked up on top of each other" qualify Rothko as "a maker of paintings as powerful and complicated as anything by his two gods—Rembrandt and Turner." For the ethnocentric Schama, Rothko's paintings "are equivalent of these old masters. . . . Can art ever be more complete, more powerful? I don't think so."

WILL MULTICULTURALISM BACKFIRE ON JEWS?

A major point of this book is that since the Enlightenment Jewish intellectuals have been at the vanguard of secular political movements, such as the movement for cultural pluralism, intended to serve Jewish interests as well as appeal to segments of the gentile population. Also apparent is the trend for these movements to eventually fractionate, the result of anti-Semitism within the very segment of the gentile population to which the ideology attempts to appeal, and for Jews to abandon these movements and seek to pursue their interests by other means.

Thus it has been noted here that Jews have played a prominent role in the political left in this century. We have also seen that as a result of anti-Semitism among gentiles on the left, including communist governments, eventually Jews either abandoned the left or they developed their own brand of leftism in which leftist universalism was compatible with the primacy of Jewish identity and interests.[158] Thus neoconservative Jews abandoned the left mainly because the Carter administration was critical of Israel and failed to be sufficiently militaristic. The 1998 version of this section highlighted controversy already present in the 1980s in which American leftists were critical of the Israel Lobby.

---

[158] Similarly, L. C. Pogrebin (1991) describes her involvement as a major figure in the early feminist movement and her eventual disenchantment resulting from the blatant anti-Semitism of "Third World" women, which was apparent at international conferences, and the lack of zeal on the part of Western feminists in condemning these outbursts. As did many Jewish leftists, Pogrebin eventually developed a hybrid in which feminist ideas were combined with a deep commitment to Jewish culture.

For example, Gore Vidal (1986), a prominent gentile leftist intellectual, was critical of the role of neoconservative Jews in facilitating the U.S. military buildup of the 1980s and allying themselves with conservative political forces to aid Israel—charges that Norman Podhoretz (1986) construed as anti-Semitism because of the implication that American Jews place the interests of Israel above American interests. Vidal also suggests that neoconservatism is motivated by the desire of Jews to make an alliance with gentile elites as a defense against possible anti-Semitic movements emerging during times of economic crisis. The organized Jewish community has been quite aware of the need to have support from both Republicans and Democrats.

Indeed, combatting anti-Semitism on the left has been a major impetus for founding the neoconservative movement (see Ch. 4; Gottfried, 1993, p. 80) and was the final resting point of many of the New York Intellectuals whose intellectual and political evolution was discussed in Chapter 7. As Gottfried points out, the cumulative effect of neoconservatism and its current hegemony over the conservative political movement in the United States (achieved partly by its large influence on the media, think tanks, and non-profits) has been to shift the conservative movement toward the center and, in effect, to define the limits of conservative legitimacy. Clearly, these limits of conservative legitimacy are defined by whether they conflict with specific Jewish group interests in a minimally restrictive immigration policy, support for Israel, ending free speech on ethnically charged issues, and a globalism that exempts Israeli ethnonationalism and is controlled by financial, academic, and media elites with a strong representation of Jews.

As indicated in William F. Buckley's (1992) *In Search of Anti-Semitism*, however, the alliance between gentile paleoconservatives and Jewish neoconservatives in the United States is fragile, with several accusations of anti-Semitism among the paleoconservatives. This divide has increased massively with the election of Donald Trump. Neoconservatives like Bill Kristol, Max Boot, Jennifer Rubin, Bret Stephens, and many others deserted the Republican Party, likely mainly because of Trump's opposition to foreign wars and his anti-immigration rhetoric. Many decamped to the Democrats whose 2016 candidate, Hillary Clinton, had recruited prominent neocon Robert Kagan as a top foreign policy adviser. Jews continued their strong support for the Democrats in the 2016 and 2020 elections—despite Trump's strong support for Israel and the high-profile presence of his son-in-law, Orthodox Jew and pro-Israel stalwart Jared Kushner who was essentially in charge of Middle East policy.

Jennifer Rubin (2021) is a particularly egregious example of a neocon who is quite open about her hatred toward White America, commenting on a 2021 article reporting data from the U.S. Census Bureau, "a more diverse, more inclusive society. this is fabulous news. now we need to prevent minority White rule."

Bret Stephens (2016), who moved from *The Wall Street Journal* to *The New York Times* in 2017 and is routinely described as a "conservative," wrote:

> [Trumpism] is a regression to the conservatism of blood and soil, of ethnic polarization and bullying nationalism. Modern conservatives sought to bury this rubbish with a politics that strikes a balance between respect for tradition and faith in the dynamic and culture-shifting possibilities of open markets. When that balance collapses—under a Republican president, no less—it may never again be restored, at least in our lifetimes.

From Robert Kagan (2016), who abandoned the Republicans to be part of Hillary Clinton's foreign policy team:

> [Trump's] public discourse consists of attacking or ridiculing a wide range of "others"—Muslims, Hispanics, women, Chinese, Mexicans, Europeans, Arabs, immigrants, refugees—whom he depicts either as threats or as objects of derision. His program, such as it is, consists chiefly of promises to get tough with foreigners and people of nonwhite complexion. He will deport them, bar them, get them to knuckle under, make them pay up or make them shut up.

As anti-Semitism or deviation from Jewish interests develop, Jews begin to abandon the very movements for which they originally provided the intellectual impetus. This phenomenon may also occur in the case of multiculturalism. Indeed, many of the most prominent opponents of multiculturalism are Jewish neoconservatives, as well as organizations which have a large Jewish membership, such as the National Association of Scholars (NAS)—an organization of academics opposed to some of the more egregious excesses of feminism and multiculturalism in academia. It may well be the case, therefore, that the Jewish attempt to link up with secular political ideologies that appeal to gentiles is doomed in the long run.

The case of multiculturalism is particularly problematic as a Jewish strategy. In this case one might say that Jews want to have their cake and eat it too.

> Jews are often caught between fervent affirmation of the Enlightenment and criticism of it. Many Jews believe that the replacement of the Enlightenment ideal of universalism with a politics of difference and a fragmented "multiculture" would constitute a threat to Jewish achievement. At the same time, they recognize the dangers of a homogeneous "monoculture" for Jewish particularity. ... [Jews] seek to rescue the virtues of the Enlightenment from the shards of its failures and salvage an inclusive vision from multiculturalism, where fragmentation and divisiveness now reign. (Biale et al., 1998, p. 7)

Multicultural societies with their consequent fragmentation and chronic ethnic tension are unlikely to meet Jewish needs in the long run, even if they do ultimately accomplish their main goal by subverting the demographic and cultural dominance of the peoples of European origin in lands where they have been dominant. The protests surrounding the Israel-Hamas war have made this obvious.

This in turn suggests a fundamental and irresolvable friction between Judaism and prototypical Western political and social structure. Certainly, the very long history of anti-Semitism in Western societies and its recurrence time and again after periods of latency suggests such a view. The incompatibility of Judaism and Western culture can also be seen in the tendency for individualistic Western cultures to break down Jewish group cohesiveness. As Arthur Ruppin (1934/1973, p. 339) noted in the early twentieth century, all modern manifestations of Judaism, from neo-Orthodoxy to Zionism, are responses to the Enlightenment's corrosive effects on Judaism—a set of defensive structures erected against "the destructive influence of European civilization." And at a theoretical level, there is a very clear rationale for supposing that Western individualism is incompatible with the group-based resource conflict that has been the consistent consequence of the emergence of a powerful Judaism in Western societies (see SAID, Chs. 3–5).

One aspect of this friction is well articulated in Alan Ryan's (1994) discussion of the "latent contradiction" in the politics of Richard J. Herrnstein and Charles Murray, the authors of the highly controversial volume *The Bell Curve: Intelligence and Class Structure in American Life*. Ryan states:

> Herrnstein essentially wants the world in which clever Jewish kids or their equivalent make their way out of their humble backgrounds and end up running Goldman Sachs or the Harvard physics department, while Murray wants the Midwest in which he grew up—a world in which the local mechanic didn't care two cents whether he was or wasn't brighter than the local math teacher. The trouble is that the first world subverts the second, while the second feels claustrophobic to the beneficiaries of the first.[159]

Murray envisions a moderately individualistic social structure, a society that is meritocratic and hierarchical but also cohesive and culturally and

---

[159] Ryan's characterization of Herrnstein is reminiscent of Gal's (1989, p. 138) characterization of Louis Brandeis: "Brandeis worried about opportunity, about preserving a type of society in which ambitious and talented persons could, through hard work and ability, be able to make their fame and fortune." Brandeis, a Zionist leader, was instrumental in originating the use of social science research in litigating social issues, a trend that culminated in the *Brown v. Board of Education* decision (Urofsky, 1989, p. 144). P. C. Roberts and Stratton (1995) detail the unethical behavior of Supreme Court Justice Felix Frankfurter (a Brandeis protégé) and Philip Elman (a Justice Department lawyer) in bringing about this decision.

ethnically homogeneous. It is a society with harmony among the social classes and with social controls on extreme individualism among the elite.

In recent years there has been an increasing rejection among intellectuals and minority ethnic activists of the idea of creating a melting pot society based on assimilation among ethnic groups. Cultural and ethnic differences are emphasized in these writings, and ethnic assimilation and homogenization are viewed in negative terms. The tone of these writings is reminiscent of the views of many late-nineteenth- and early-twentieth-century Jewish intellectuals who rejected the assimilationist effects of Reform Judaism in favor of Zionism or a return to a more extreme form of cultural separatism such as Conservative. or Orthodox Judaism, often out of a concern that Reform would lead to intermarriage (see SAID, Ch. 5).

The movement toward ethnic separatism is of considerable interest from an evolutionary point of view. Between-group competition and monitoring of outgroups have been a characteristic of Jewish-gentile interactions not only in the West but also in Muslim societies, and there are examples of between-group competition and conflict too numerous to mention in other parts of the world. Historically, ethnic separatism, as seen in the history of Judaism, has been a divisive force within societies. It has on many occasions unleashed enormous intrasocietal hatred and distrust, ethnically based warfare, expulsions, pogroms, and attempts at genocide. Moreover, there is little reason to suppose that the future will be much different. At the present time there are ethnically based conflicts on every continent, and clearly the establishment of Israel has not ended ethnically based conflict for Jews returning from the diaspora.

Indeed, my review of the research on contact between strongly identified groups in historical societies suggests a general rule that between-group competition and monitoring of ingroup and outgroup success are the norm. These results are highly consistent with the psychological research on social identity processes reviewed in SAID (Ch. 1). From an evolutionary perspective, these results confirm the expectation that ethnic self-interest is indeed important in human affairs, and obviously ethnicity remains a common source of group identity in the contemporary world—least of all among Western peoples because of their individualism (*Individualism*), but common among the non-Western peoples that have been colonizing the West for decades and are an increasingly powerful political force in Western societies. People appear to be aware of group membership and have a general tendency to devalue and compete with outgroups. Individuals are also keenly aware of the relative standing of their own group in terms of resource control and relative reproductive success. They are also willing to take extraordinary steps to achieve and retain economic and political power in defense of these group imperatives.

Given the assumption of ethnic separatism, it is instructive to think of the circumstances that would, from an evolutionary perspective, minimize group conflict. Theorists of cultural pluralism such as Horace Kallen (1924) envision a scenario in which different ethnic groups retain their distinctive identity in the context of a level playing field economically and politically. The difficulty with this scenario from an evolutionary perspective (or even common sense) is that no provision is made for the results of competition for resources and reproductive success within the society. Indeed, the results of ethnic strife were apparent in Kallen's day, but "Kallen lifted his eyes above the strife that swirled around him to an ideal realm where diversity and harmony coexist" (Higham, 1984, p. 209).

In the best of circumstances, one might suppose that interacting ethnic groups would engage in absolute reciprocity with each other, so that there would be no differences in terms of economic exploitation of one ethnic group by the other. Moreover, there would be no differences on any measure of success in society, including social class membership, economic role (e.g., producer versus consumer; creditor versus debtor; manager versus worker), or fertility between the ethnic groups. All groups would have approximately equal numbers and equal political power; or if there were different numbers, provisions would exist to ensure that minorities would retain equitable representation in terms of the markers of social and reproductive success. Such conditions would minimize hostility between the groups because attributing one's status to the actions of the other groups would be difficult.

Given the existence of ethnic separatism, however, it would still be in the interests of each group to advance its own interests at the expense of the other groups. All things being equal, a given ethnic group would be better off if it ensured that the other groups had fewer resources, lower social status, lower fertility, and proportionately less political power than itself. The hypothesized steady state of equality therefore implies a set of balance-of-power relationships: each side constantly checking to make sure that the other is not cheating; each side constantly looking for ways to dominate and exploit by any means possible; each side willing to compromise only because of the other side's threat of retaliation; each side willing to cooperate at cost only if forced to do so by, for example, the presence of external threat. Clearly, any type of cooperation that involves true altruism toward the other group could not be expected. Historically such altruism toward minority groups has only prevailed in Western countries as a result of the dominance of a moral perspective that can only happen in individualist cultures because ethnic divisions are relatively muted and the social fabric is maintained by adherence to moral beliefs based on religion or disseminated by the media (e.g., *Individualism*, Chs. 7–8).

Thus the ideal situation of absolute equality in resource control and reproductive success would certainly require a great deal of monitoring and undoubtedly be characterized by a great deal of mutual suspicion. In the real world, however, even this rather grim ideal is highly unlikely. In the real world, ethnic groups differ in their talents and abilities (IQ being the most important); they differ in their numbers (critical in a Western-style democracy), fertility, and the extent to which they encourage parenting practices conducive to re-source acquisition; they also differ in the resources held at any point in time and in their political power. Equality or proportionate equity would be ex-tremely difficult to attain or to maintain after it has been achieved without extraordinary levels of monitoring and without extremely intense social con-trols to enforce ethnic quotas on the accumulation of wealth, admission to universities, access to high-status jobs, and so on.

Because ethnic groups have differing talents, abilities, and parenting styles, variable criteria for qualifying for jobs would be required depending on ethnic group membership, requiring affirmative action for underachieving groups and discrimination against high-achieving groups. In the Ashkenazi di-aspora in the West, achieving parity between Jews and other ethnic groups would entail a high level of discrimination against individual Jews for admis-sion to universities or access to employment opportunities and even entail a large taxation on Jews to counter the Jewish advantage in the possession of wealth, since at present Jews are vastly overrepresented among the wealthy and successful in the United States. This would especially be the case if Jews were distinguished as a separate ethnic group from gentile European Ameri-cans. Indeed, the final evolution of many of the New York Intellectuals from Trotskyism was to become neoconservatives who have been eloquent oppo-nents of affirmative action and quota mechanisms for distributing resources. Sachar (1992, pp. 818ff) mentions Daniel Bell, Sidney Hook, Irving Howe, Irving Kristol, Nathan Glazer, Charles Krauthammer, Norman Podhoretz, and Earl Raab as opposed to affirmative action, and Jewish organizations (including the ADL, the AJCommittee, and the AJCongress) have taken similar positions in the past, but this has shifted in more recent years, perhaps because Jews have not suffered from affirmative action and quotas for groups like African Americans, as, for example, in admissions to elite universities (Unz, 2018c).

In the real world, therefore, extraordinary efforts would have to be made to attain this steady state of ethnic balance of power and resources. Interest-ingly, the ideology of Jewish-gentile coexistence has sometimes included the idea that the different ethnic groups develop a similar occupational profile and implicitly control resources in proportion to their numbers. In medieval France, for example, Louis IX's ordinance of 1254 prohibited Jews from engag-ing in moneylending at interest and encouraged them to live by manual labor or trade (see Richard, 1983/1992, p. 162). The dream of German assimilationists during the nineteenth century was that the occupational profile of Jews after emancipation would mirror that of the gentiles—a "utopian expectation . . .

shared by many, Jews and non-Jews alike" (Katz, 1986, p. 67). Efforts were made to decrease the percentage of Jews involved in trade and increase the percentages involved in agriculture and artisanry. In the event, however, the result of emancipation was that Jews were vastly overrepresented among the economic and cultural elite, and this overrepresentation was a critical grievance of German anti-Semitism from 1870 to 1945 (see *SAID*, Ch. 5).

Similarly, during the 1920s when the United States was attempting to come to grips with Jewish competition at prestigious private universities, plans were proposed in which each ethnic group received a percentage of placements at Harvard reflecting the percentage of racial and national groups in the United States (Sachar, 1992, p. 329). Similar policies—uniformly denounced by Jewish organizations—developed during the same period throughout Central Europe (Hagen, 1996). Such policies certainly reflect the importance of ethnicity in human affairs, but levels of social tension are bound to be chronically high. Moreover, there is a considerable chance of ethnic warfare even if precise parity was achieved through intensive social controls: as indicated above, it is always in the interests of any ethnic group to obtain hegemony over the others.

If one adopts a cultural pluralist model involving free competition for resources and reproductive success, differences between ethnic groups are inevitable; from an evolutionary perspective, there is the very strong prediction that such differences will result in animosity from the losing groups. After emancipation there was a powerful tendency for upward mobility among Jews in Western societies, including a large overrepresentation in the professions as well as in business, politics, and the production of culture. Concomitantly there were outbreaks of anti-Semitism originating often among groups that felt left behind in this resource competition or that felt that the culture being created did not meet their interests. If the history of Judaism tells us anything, it is that self-imposed ethnic separatism tends to lead to resource competition based on group membership and consequent hatred, expulsions, and persecutions. Assuming that ethnic differences in talents and abilities exist, the supposition that ethnic separatism could be a stable situation without ethnic animosity requires either a balance-of-power situation maintained with intense social controls, as described above, or it requires that at least some ethnic groups be unconcerned that they are losing in the competition.

I regard this last possibility as unlikely in the long run. That an ethnic group would be unconcerned with its own eclipse and domination is certainly not expected by an evolutionist or, indeed, by advocates of social justice, whatever their ideology. Nevertheless, this is in fact the implicit morality of the criticism made by several historians of the behavior of the Spanish toward the Jews and Marranos during the Inquisition and the Expulsion, as, for example, in the writings of Benzion Netanyahu (1995), who at times seems openly contemptuous of the inability of the Spaniards to compete with the New Christians without resorting to the violence of the Inquisition. From this perspective, the Spaniards should have realized their inferiority and acquiesced in being economically, socially, and politically dominated by another ethnic group. Such a "morality" is unlikely to appeal to the group losing the competition, and from an evolutionary perspective, this is not in the least surprising. Goldwin Smith (1894/1972, p. 261) made a similar point a century ago:

> A community has a right to defend its territory and its national integrity against an invader whether his weapon be the sword or foreclosure. In the territories of the Italian Republics the Jews might, so far as we see, have bought land and taken to farming had they pleased. But before this they had thoroughly taken to trade. Under the falling Empire they were the great slave-traders, buying captives from barbarian invaders and probably acting as general brokers of spoils at the same time. They entered England in the train of the Norman conqueror. There was, no doubt, a perpetual struggle between their craft and the brute force of the feudal populations. But what moral prerogative has craft over force? Mr. Arnold White tells the Russians that, if they would let Jewish intelligence have free course, Jews would soon fill all high employments and places of power to the exclusion of the natives, who now hold them. Russians are bidden to acquiesce and rather to rejoice in this by philosophers, who would perhaps not relish the cup if it were commended to their own lips. The law of evolution, it is said, prescribes the survival of the fittest. To which the Russian boor may reply, that if his force beats the fine intelligence of the Jew the fittest will survive and the law of evolution will be fulfilled. It was force rather than fine intelligence which decided on the field of Zama that the Latin, not the Semite, should rule the ancient and mould the modern world.

Ironically, many intellectuals who absolutely reject evolutionary thinking and any imputation that genetic self-interest might be important in human affairs also favor policies that are rather obviously self-interestedly ethnocentric, and they often condemn the self-interested ethnocentric behavior of other groups, particularly any indication that the European-derived majority in the United States is developing a cohesive group strategy and high levels of ethnocentrism in reaction to the group strategies of others. The ideology of minority group ethnic separatism and the implicit legitimization of group competition for resources, as well as the more modern idea that ethnic group membership should be a criterion for resource acquisition, must be seen for what they are: blueprints for group evolutionary strategies. The history of the Jews must be seen as a rather tragic commentary on the results of such group strategies.

I have suggested that there is a fundamental and irresolvable friction between Judaism and prototypical Western political and social structure. The greatest mistake of the Jewish-dominated intellectual movements described in this volume is that they have attempted to establish the moral superiority of societies that embody a preconceived moral ideal (compatible with the continuation of Judaism as a group evolutionary strategy) rather than advocate for social structures based on the ethical possibilities of naturally occurring types.[160] In the twentieth century many millions of people were killed in the attempt to establish Marxist societies based on a theoretical ideal of complete economic and social leveling.

As an evolutionist, one must ask what the likely genetic consequences of this sea change in American culture are likely to be. An important consequence—and one likely to have been an underlying motivating factor in the countercultural revolution—may well be to facilitate the continued genetic distinctiveness of the Jewish gene pool in the United States. The ideology of multiculturalism may be expected to increasingly compartmentalize groups in American society, with long-term beneficial consequences for the continuation of the essential features of traditional Judaism as a group evolutionary strategy. There is increasing consensus among Jewish activists that traditional forms of Judaism are far more effective in ensuring long-term group continuity than semi-assimilationist, semi-cryptic strategies such as Reform Judaism or secular Judaism. Moreover, as discussed in several parts of this book, Jews typically perceive themselves to benefit from a nonhomogeneous culture in which they appear as only one among many ethnic groups where there is no possibility of the development of a homogeneous national culture that might exclude Jews.

In addition, there may well be negative genetic consequences for the European-derived peoples of the United States and especially for the "common people of the South and West" (Higham, 1984, p. 49)—that is, for lower-middle-class Caucasians derived from Northern and Western Europe—whose representatives desperately battled against the present immigration policy. Indeed, we have seen that a prominent theme of the New York Intellectuals as well as *The Authoritarian Personality* studies was the intellectual and moral inferiority of traditional American culture, particularly rural American culture. James

---

[160] G. L. Mosse (1970, p. 174) describes the Jewish-dominated leftist movements of the Weimar period as seeking "actively to make society correspond to a preconceived image of men and the world." And I. L. Horowitz (1993, p. 62) notes of T. W. Adorno that "the more remote real people were from his political dreams, the less regard did he show for the masses as such. . . . [Adorno] sets the stage for a culture of left-wing fascism . . . [that assumes] that what people believe is wrong and that what they ought to believe, as designed by some narrow elite stratum of the cultural apparatus, is essentially right." For their part, the *völkisch* and conservative intellectuals who advocated a society based on hierarchic harmony advocated a return to an idealized version of actually existing historical societies, particularly the Middle Ages.

Webb (1995) notes that it is the descendants of the WASPs who settled the South and West who,

> by and large did the most to lay out the infrastructure of this country, quite often suffering educational and professional regression as they tamed the wilderness, built the towns, roads and schools, and initiated a democratic way of life that later white cultures were able to take advantage of without paying the price of pioneering. Today they have the least, socioeconomically, to show for these contributions. And if one would care to check a map, they are from the areas now evincing the greatest resistance to government practices.

The war goes on, but it is easy to see who is losing.

The demographic rise of the underclass resulting from the triumph of the 1960s countercultural revolution implies that European-derived genes and gene frequencies will become less common compared to those derived from the African and the Latin American gene pools. On the other end of the IQ-reproductive strategy distribution, immigrants from East Asian countries are outcompeting Whites in gaining admission to universities and in prestigious, high-income jobs. The long-term result will be that the entire White population (not including Jews) is likely to suffer a social status decline as these new immigrants become more numerous. Jews are unlikely to suffer a major decline in social status not only because their mean IQ is well above that of East Asians but also, more importantly, because Jewish IQ is skewed toward excelling in verbal skills. The high IQ of East Asians is skewed toward performance IQ, which makes them powerful competitors in engineering and technology (see PTSDA, Ch. 7; Lynn, 1987). Jews and East Asians are thus likely to occupy different niches in contemporary societies. The United States is well on the road to being dominated by an Asian technocratic elite and a Jewish business, professional, and media elite.

Moreover, the shift to multiculturalism has coincided with an enormous growth of immigration from non-European-derived peoples beginning with the Immigration and Nationality Act of 1965, which favored immigrants from non-European countries (see Auster, 1990; Brimelow, 1995). Many of these immigrants come from non-Western countries where cultural and genetic segregation are the norm, and within the context of multicultural America, they are encouraged to retain their own languages and religions and identify strongly with their group. As indicated above, the expected result will be between-group resource and reproductive competition and increased vulnerability of democratic and republican political institutions in a context in which long-term projections indicate that European-derived peoples will no longer form a majority of the United States by the middle of this century.

Indeed, one might note that, while the Western Enlightenment has presented Judaism with its greatest challenge in all of its long history, contemporary multiculturalism in the context of high levels of immigration of peoples of all racial and ethnic groups presents the greatest challenge to Western universalism in its history. The historical record indicates that ethnic separatism among European-derived groups has a tendency to collapse within modern Western societies unless active attempts at ethnic and cultural segregation are undertaken, as has occurred among Jews. As expected from a resource-reciprocity point of view (*Individualism*), in the absence of rigid ethnic barriers, marriage in Western individualist societies tends to be importantly influenced by a wide range of phenotypic features of the prospective spouse, including not only genetic commonality but also social status, education, intelligence, personality, common interests, and financial prospects. This individualist pattern of marriage decisions has characterized Western Europe at least since the Middle Ages (e.g., *Individualism*).

The result has been a remarkable degree of ethnic assimilation in the United States among those whose ancestry derives from Europe (Alba, 1985). The long-term result of such processes is genetic homogenization, a sense of common interest, and the absence of a powerful source of intra-societal division.

To suppose that the conflict over immigration has been merely a conflict over the universalist tendencies of Western culture would, however, be disingenuous. To a great extent the immigration debate in the United States has always had powerful ethnic overtones and continues to do so even after the European-derived peoples of the United States have become assimilated into a Western universalist culture. The present immigration policy essentially places the United States and other Western societies "in play" in an evolutionary sense which does not apply to other nations of the world, where the implicit assumption is that territory is held by its historically dominant people: each racial and ethnic group in the world has an interest in expanding its demographic and political presence in Western societies and can be expected to do so if given the opportunity. Notice that the mainstream American Jewish community (e.g., the ADL; see MacDonald, 2022a) has had no interest in proposing that immigration to Israel should be similarly multiethnic, or that Israel should have an immigration policy that would threaten the hegemony of Jews. I rather doubt that Oscar Handlin (1952, p. 7) would extend his statement advocating immigration from all ethnic groups into the United States by affirming the principle that all men, being brothers, are equally capable of being Israelis. I also doubt that the Synagogue Council of America would characterize Israeli immigration law as "a gratuitous affront to the peoples of many regions of the world" (PCIN, 1953, p. 117). Indeed, the ethnic conflict within Israel indicates a failure to develop a universalist Western culture.

At present the interests of non-European-derived peoples to expand demographically and politically in the United States are widely perceived as a moral imperative, whereas the attempts of European-derived peoples to retain demographic, political, and cultural control is represented as "racist," immoral, and an indication of psychiatric disorder. From the perspective of these European-derived peoples, the prevailing ethnic morality is altruistic and self-sacrificial. It is unlikely to be viable in the long run, even in an individualistic society, and in the present context of rampant anti-White hatred, it may well lead to victimization of Whites. The viability of a morality of self-sacrifice is especially problematic in the context of a multicultural society in which everyone is conscious of group membership—including Whites.

Consider from an evolutionary perspective the status of the argument that all peoples should be allowed to immigrate to the United States. One might assert that any opposition to such a principle should not interest an evolutionist because human group genetic differences are trivial, so any psychological adaptations that make one resist such a principle are anachronisms without function in the contemporary world (much like one's appendix). A Jew maintaining this argument should, to retain intellectual consistency, agree that the traditional Jewish concern with endogamy and consanguinity has been irrational. Moreover, such a person should also believe that Jews ought not to attempt to retain political power in Israel because there is no rational reason to suppose that any particular group should have power anywhere. Nor should Jews attempt to influence the political process in the United States in such a manner as to disadvantage another group or benefit their own. And to be logically consistent, one should also apply this argument to all those who promote immigration of their own ethnic groups, the mirror image of group-based opposition to such immigration.

Indeed, if this chain of logic is pursued to its conclusion, it is irrational for anyone to claim any group interests at all. And if one also rejects the notion of individual genetic differences, it is also irrational to attempt to further individual interests, for example, by seeking to immigrate as an individual. Indeed, if one accepts these assumptions, the notion of genetic consequences and thus of the possibility of human evolution past and present becomes irrational; the idea that it is rational is merely an illusion produced perhaps by psychological adaptations that are without any meaningful evolutionary function in the contemporary world. One might note that this ideology is the final conclusion of the anti-evolutionary ideologies reviewed in this volume. These intellectual movements have asserted that scientific research shows that any important ethnic differences or individual differences are the result of environmental variation, and that genetic differences are trivial.

But there is an enormous irony in all of this: if life is truly without any evolutionary meaning, why have advocates propagated these anti-racial, anti-

Western ideologies so intensely and with such self-consciously political methods? Why have many of these same people strongly identified with their own ethnic group and its interests, and why have many of them insisted on cultural pluralism and its validation of minority group ethnocentrism as moral absolutes? By their own assumptions, it is just a meaningless game. Nobody should care who wins or loses. Of course, deception and self-deception may be involved. I have noted (see Ch. 6) that a fundamental agenda has been to make the European-derived peoples of the United States view concern about their own demographic and cultural eclipse as irrational and as an indication of psychopathology.

If one accepts that both within-group and between-group genetic variation remains and is non-trivial (i.e., if evolution is an ongoing process), then the principle of relatively unrestricted immigration, at least under the conditions of recent decades in Western societies, clearly involves altruism by some individuals and established groups. Nevertheless, although the success of the intellectual movements reviewed in this volume is an indication that people can be induced to be altruistic toward other groups, I rather doubt such altruism will continue if there are obvious signs that the status and political power of European-derived groups are decreasing while the power of other groups increases. The prediction, both on theoretical grounds and on the basis of social identity research, is that as other groups become increasingly powerful and salient in a multicultural society, the European-derived peoples of the United States will become increasingly unified; among these peoples, contemporary divisive influences, such as issues related to gender and sexual orientation, social class differences, or religious differences, will be increasingly perceived as unimportant. Eventually these groups will develop a united front and a collectivist political orientation vis-à-vis other ethnic groups. Other groups will be expelled if possible or partitions will be created, and Western societies will undergo another period of medievalism.

THE FUNDAMENTAL CONFLICT OF INTEREST BETWEEN JEWS AND NON-JEWS IN THE WEST

Jewish interests in immigration policy are a paradigmatic example of conflicts of interest between Jews and non-Jews over the construction of culture. This conflict of interests extends well beyond immigration policy. There is a growing realization that the countercultural revolution of the 1960s is a watershed event in the history of the United States. Such a conceptualization is compatible with the work of Rogers M. Smith (1988), who shows that until the triumph of the cultural pluralist model with the countercultural revolution of the 1960s, there were three competing models of American identity: the "liberal" individualist legacy of the Enlightenment based on "natural rights"; the "republican" ideal of a cohesive, socially homogeneous society; and the "eth-nocultural" strand emphasizing the importance of Anglo-Saxon ethnicity in the development and preservation of American cultural forms.

From the present perspective, no fundamental conflict exists between the latter two sources of American identity; social homogeneity may well be best and most easily achieved with an ethnically homogeneous society of peoples derived from the European cultural area. Indeed, in upholding Chinese exclu-sion in the nineteenth century, Justice Stephen J. Field noted that the Chinese were unassimilable and would destroy the republican ideal of social homoge-neity. As indicated above, the incorporation of non-European peoples, and es-pecially peoples derived from Africa and Muslim countries, into Western cul-tural forms is profoundly problematic.

As discussed at several points in this volume, the radical individualism em-bodied in the Enlightenment ideal of individual rights is especially problematic for the long-term stability of Western societies because of the danger of inva-sion and domination by group strategies such as Judaism and the possibility of the defection of gentile elites from the ideals represented in the other two models of social organization—particularly because these elites, with substan-tial Jewish representation, would likely advocate large-scale multiethnic im-migration. These developments would thus be likely to destroy the social co-hesiveness so central to Western forms of social organization. As R. M. Smith (1988, p. 245) notes, the transformations of American society in the post-Civil War era resulted from the "liberal" cultural ideal "that opposed slavery, favored immigration [from Europe], and encouraged enterprise while protecting prop-erty rights" and that posed a severe threat to the collective life at the center of American civilization.

It is this liberal legacy of American civilization that the Jewish intellectual movements reviewed in this volume have exploited in rationalizing unre-stricted immigration and the loss of social homogeneity represented by the unifying force of the Christian religion. As Israel Zangwill said in advocating a Jewish strategy for unrestricted immigration, "tell them they are destroying American ideals" (H.R. Rep. No. 350, 1924, p. 16; see Ch. 8). Western peoples are particularly susceptible to morally tinged messaging, since the social glue of Western cultures is that they are moral communities, not kinship-based com-munities (*Individualism*, Ch. 8). The effect has been to create a new American ideal that is entirely at odds with the historic sources of American identity:

> This ideal carries on the cosmopolitanism, tolerance, and respect for hu-
> man liberty of the older liberal tradition, and so it can properly be termed
> a modern version of the liberal ideal. It is novel, however, in its rejection
> of Lockean liberalism's absolutist natural law elements in favor of modern
> philosophic pragmatism and cultural relativism. And one of its chief

theoretical architects, philosopher Horace Kallen, argued that cultural pluralism better recognizes human sociality, our constitutive attachments to distinctive ethnic, religious, and cultural groups. It therefore envisions America as a "democracy of nationalities, cooperating voluntarily and autonomously through common institutions in the enterprise of self-realization through the perfection of men according to their kind" [Kallen, 1924, p. 124]. Since all groups and individuals should be guaranteed equal opportunities to pursue their own destinies, the nation's legacy of legal, racial, ethnic and gender discrimination is unacceptable according to the cultural pluralist ideal. At the same time, there must be no effort to transform equality into uniformity, to insist that all fit into a standard "Americanized" mold.

The ideal of democratic cultural pluralism finally came to predominate in American public law in the 1950s and especially the 1960s, finding expression in the 1964 Civil Rights Act, the liberalizing 1965 Immigration and Naturalization Act, the 1965 Voting Rights Act, in new programs to provide educational curricula more attuned to the nation's diverse cultural heritage, in bilingual ballots and governmental publications, and in affirmative action measures. (R. M. Smith, 1988, pp. 245–246)

Within this perspective, there is tolerance for different groups, but the result is a tendency to "deprecate the importance or even the existence of a common national identity" (R. M. Smith, 1988, p. 247, discussing Kallen). Kallen, of course, was a very strongly identified Jew and a prominent Zionist (see Ch. 8), and it is not at all surprising that his cultural ideal for the United States represents a non-Western form of social organization that conforms to Jewish interests and compromises the interests of the European-derived peoples of the United States. It is a social form that guarantees the continued existence of Judaism as a social category and as a cohesive ethnic group while at the same time, given the characteristics of Jews, guarantees Jews economic and cultural preeminence. Public policy based on this conceptualization is having the predictable long-term effect of marginalizing both culturally and demographically the European-derived peoples of the United States. Because the European-derived groups are less organized and less cohesive than Jews and because a "therapeutic state" has been erected to counter expressions of European-American ethnocentrism, it raises the distinct possibility that in the long run European Americans will be fragmented, politically powerless, subject to victimization by a hostile majority, and without an effective group identity at all.

The conflict of interest between Jews and gentiles in the construction of culture goes well beyond advocacy of the multicultural ideal. Because they are much more genetically inclined to a high-investment reproductive strategy than are gentiles, Jews are able to maintain their high-investment reproductive strategy even in the absence of traditional Western cultural supports for high-investment parenting (Ch. 5). Compared to gentiles, Jews are therefore much better able to expand their economic and cultural success without these traditional Western cultural supports. As Higham (1984, p. 173) notes, the cultural idealization of an essentially Jewish personal ethic of hedonism, anxiety, and intellectuality came at the expense of the older rural ethic of asceticism and sexual restraint.

Moreover, traditional Western supports for high-investment parenting were embedded in religious ideology and, I suppose, are difficult to achieve in a post-religious environment. Nevertheless, as Podhoretz (1995) notes, it is in fact the case that Jewish intellectuals, Jewish organizations like the AJCongress, and Jewish-funded organizations such as the ACLU have ridiculed Christian religious beliefs, attempted to undermine the public strength of Christianity, and led the fight for lifting restrictions on pornography. Further, we have seen that psychoanalysis as a Jewish-dominated intellectual movement has been a central component of this war on gentile cultural supports for high-investment parenting. Whereas Jews, because of their powerful, genetically influenced propensities for intelligence, high-investment parenting, and certain personality traits (see Preface), have been able to thrive within this cultural milieu, other sectors of the society have not; the result has been a widening gulf between the cultural success of Jews and gentiles and a disaster for society as a whole.

The countercultural revolution of the 1960s has led to a political revolution that is incompatible with traditional American freedoms. Traditional American freedoms such as freedom of speech enshrined in the First Amendment (deriving from the Enlightenment liberal strand of American identity) have enabled the Jewish activist community to fundamentally transform American society away from the cultural ideals of republicanism and ethnic and cultural homogeneity (particularly the cultural prominence of Christianity). At this time however, since the Jewish community has achieved a prominent place among the American elite, they have used their power in an ongoing effort to restrict free speech, mainly by endorsing "hate speech" laws and censoring social media accounts. These Jewish interests conflict with the possibility of constructing a cohesive society, and in fact the present multicultural political landscape in the U.S. is the most polarized in American history, with the possible exception of the Civil War era.

Given that the popular media and the current intellectual environment of universities thrive on the freedom of elites to produce socially destructive messages, the political movements attempting to restore anything remotely resembling pre-1960s American culture will undoubtedly be forced to restrict some traditional American freedoms (see, e.g., Bork, 1996)—accounting for the liberal-left mantra that the right desires to create an authoritarian state and end democracy (while ignoring the long history of leftist authoritarianism and the present reality of the American left with its efforts to restrict conservative speech and other traditional American freedoms).

The cultural supports of traditional Western societies, embedded in Christianity, have acted as external forces of social control that maximize high-investment parenting among all segments of the population, even those who for genetic or environmental reasons are relatively disinclined to engage in such practices (MacDonald, 1997a,b). Without such cultural controls, it is absolutely predictable that social disorganization will increase and society as a whole will continue to decline.

Nevertheless, the continuity of unique Western forms of social organization will remain a salient concern even if one ignores issues of ethnic competition entirely. I have emphasized that there is an inherent conflict between multiculturalism and Western universalism and individualism. Even if Western universalism were to regain its moral imperative, it remains an open question whether all of humanity is willing or able to participate in this type of culture in an age when Western countries are inundated with people from the rest of the world. Universalism is a European creation, and it is unknown whether such a culture can be continued over a long period of time in a society that is not predominantly ethnically European. When not explicitly advocating multiculturalism, the rhetoric in favor of immigration has typically assumed a radical environmentalism in which all humans are equally capable of contributing to Western societies, ignoring deeply engrained anti-Western tendencies that occur among all other human groups (Henrich, 2020; *Individualism*) as well as differences in traits that are important for upward social mobility in Western societies, prototypically IQ. Given that a great many human cultures bear a strong resemblance to the collectivist, anti-assimilatory tendencies present in Jewish culture, it is highly likely that many of our present immigrants are similarly unable or unwilling to accept the fundamental premises of a universalistic, culturally homogeneous, individualistic society. Indeed, there is considerable reason to suppose that Western tendencies toward individualism are unique (Henrich, 2020) and based on evolved psychological adaptations (see *Individualism*).

The implication is that Western societies are subject to invasion by non-Western cultures that are able to manipulate Western tendencies toward reciprocity, egalitarianism, and individual rights in a manner that results in maladaptive behavior for the European-derived peoples who remain at the core of all Western societies. Because others' interests and perspectives are viewed as legitimate, Western societies have uniquely developed a highly principled moral and religious discourse, as in the arguments against slavery characteristic of the nineteenth-century abolitionists (see *Individualism*, Ch. 7) and in the tendency for Westerners to value abstract principles of justice as opposed to the interests of one's relatives (leading to a relative lack of corruption in Western societies). Such discourse occurs in the framework of universal moral principles—that is, principles that would be viewed as fair for any rational, disinterested observer. Thus in his highly influential volume, A *Theory of Justice*, John Rawls (1971) argues that justice as objective morality can only occur behind a "veil of ignorance" in which the ethnic status of the contending parties is irrelevant to considerations of justice or morality—a perspective that is quite compatible with Kant's similarly universal categorical imperative.

It is this intellectual tradition that has been effectively manipulated by Jewish intellectual activists, such as Israel Zangwill and Oscar Handlin, who have emphasized that in developing immigration policy, Western principles of morality and fair play make it impossible to discriminate against any ethnic group or any individual. Viewed from the perspective of, say, an African native of Kenya, any policy that discriminates in favor of Northwestern Europe cannot withstand the principle that the policy be acceptable to a rational, disinterested observer, assuming that this rational, disinterested observer does not accept the liberal-left intellectual framework promoted by the Jewish intellectual movements described here. That is, they understand that there are important racial and ethnic genetic differences in IQ, proneness to criminality, proneness to ethical universalism, etc. Because Zangwill and Handlin are not constrained by Western universalism in their attitudes toward their own group, however, they are able to ignore the implications of universalistic thinking for Zionism and other expressions of Jewish particularism embedded in traditional Jewish ethics. Because of its official policy regarding the genetic and cultural background of prospective immigrants, Israel is not similarly subject to invasion by a foreign group strategy.

Indeed, one might note that despite the fact that a prominent theme of anti-Semitism has been to stress negative personality traits of Jews and their willingness to exploit gentiles deriving from traditional Jewish ethics that essentially regards non-Jews as having no moral standing (SAID, Ch. 2), a consistent theme of Jewish intellectual activity since the Enlightenment has been to cast Jewish ethnic interests and Judaism itself as embodying a unique and irreplaceable moral vision (SAID, Chs. 6–8)—terms that emphasize the unique appeal of the rhetoric of the morality of the disinterested observer among Western audiences and that fly in the face of the murderous violence seen among Bolshevik Jews in the early Soviet period (see Ch. 3) and the contemporary genocidal violence directed against the Palestinians in the war in Gaza beginning in 2023.

The result is that whether Western individualistic societies are able to defend the legitimate interests of the European-derived peoples remains questionable. A prominent theme appearing in several places in this volume and in PTSDA (Ch. 8) and SAID (Chs. 3–5) is that individualistic societies are uniquely vulnerable to invasion by cohesive groups such as has been historically represented by Judaism. Significantly, the problem of immigration of non-European peoples is not at all confined to the United States but represents a severe and increasingly contentious problem in the entire Western world and nowhere else: only European-derived peoples have opened their doors to the other peoples of the world and now stand in danger of losing control of territory occupied for hundreds or thousands of years. Western societies have traditions of individualistic humanism, which make immigration restriction difficult. In the nineteenth century, for example, the Supreme Court twice turned down Chinese exclusion acts on the basis that they legislated against a group, not an individual (Petersen, 1955, p. 78). The effort to develop an intellectual basis for immigration restriction was tortuous; by 1920 it was based on the legitimacy of the ethnic interests of Northwestern Europeans and had undertones of racialist thinking. Both these ideas were difficult to reconcile with the stated political and humanitarian ideology of a republican and democratic society in which, as Jewish pro-immigration activists such as Israel Zangwill repeatedly emphasized, racial or ethnic group membership had no official intellectual sanction. The replacement of these assertions of ethnic self-interest with an ideology of "assimilability" in the debate over the McCarran-Walter Act was perceived by its opponents as little more than a smokescreen for "racism." In the end, this intellectual tradition collapsed largely as a result of the onslaught of the intellectual movements reviewed in this volume, and so collapsed a central pillar of the defense of the ethnic interests of European-derived peoples.

The present tendencies lead one to predict that unless the ideology of individualism is abandoned not only by the multicultural minorities (who have been encouraged to affirm their ethnic and religious identities and to pursue their group interests by a generation of American intellectuals) but also by the European-derived peoples of Europe, North America, New Zealand, and Australia, the end result will be a substantial diminution of the genetic, political, and cultural influence of these peoples. It would be an unprecedented unilateral abdication of such power, and certainly an evolutionist would expect no such abdication without at least a phase of resistance by a significant segment of the population. As indicated above, European-derived peoples are expected to ultimately exhibit some of the great flexibility that Jews have shown throughout the ages in advocating particular political forms that best suit their current interests. The prediction is that segments of the European-derived peoples of the world will eventually realize that they have been and are being ill-served both by the ideologies of multiculturalism and de-ethnicized individualism.

If the analysis of anti-Semitism presented in SAID is correct, the expected reaction will emulate aspects of Judaism by adopting group-serving, collectivist ideologies and social organizations. The theoretically underdetermined nature of human group processes (PTSDA, Ch. 1; MacDonald, 1995a) disallows detailed prediction of whether the reactive strategy will be sufficient to stabilize or reverse the present decline of European peoples in the New World and, indeed, in their ancestral homelands: whether the process will degenerate into a self-destructive reactionary movement as occurred with the Spanish Inquisition; or whether it will initiate a moderate and permanent turning away from radical individualism toward a sustainable group strategy, ideally a set of institutions that promote individualism within Western societies but determined to resist the inroads of non-Western peoples by, e.g., erecting strong barriers to immigration and enforcing remigration of non-Whites.

What is certain is that the ancient dialectic between Judaism and the West will continue into the foreseeable future. It will be ironic that, whatever anti-Semitic rhetoric may be adopted by the leaders of these defensive movements, they will be constrained to emulate key elements of Judaism as a group evolutionary strategy. Such strategic mimicry will, once again, lead to a "Judaization" of Western societies not only in the sense that their social organization will become more group-oriented but also in the sense that they will be more aware of themselves as a positively evaluated ingroup and more aware of other human groups as competing, negatively evaluated outgroups. In this sense, whether the decline of the European peoples continues unabated or is arrested, it will constitute yet another profound impact of Judaism as a group evolutionary strategy on the development of Western societies.

Bibliography

Abella, I. (1990). *A Coat of Many Colours: Two Centuries of Jewish Life in Canada*. Lester & Orpen Dennys.

Abella, I., & Troper, H. E. (1981). "The Line Must Be Drawn Somewhere": Canada and Jewish Refugees, 1933–1939. In M. Weinfeld, W. Shaffir, & I. Cotler, (Eds.), *The Canadian Jewish Mosaic*. Wiley.

Abrams, D., & Hogg, M. A. (1990). *Social Identity Theory: Constructive and Critical Advances*. Springer-Verlag.

Abrams, E. (1996, March). Faith & the Holocaust. *Commentary*, 101, 68–69.

—— (1997). *Faith or Fear: How Jews Can Survive in Christian America*. Free Press.

Ackerman, N. W., & Jahoda, M. (1950). *Anti-Semitism and Emotional Disorder*, Publication No. V of The American Jewish Committee Social Studies Series. Harper & Brothers.

Adams, G. R., Gullotta, T. P., & Adams-Markstrom, C. (1994). *Adolescent Life Experiences* (3rd ed.). Brooks/Cole.

Adelson, A. (1972). SDS. Charles Scribner's Sons.

Adelson, H. L. (1999, October 1). Another Sewer Rat Appears. *The Jewish Press*.

ADL. (n.d.). *The National Strategy to Counter Antisemitism Actions*. ADL. Retrieved May 16, 2025, from https://www.adl.org/US-National-Strategy-antisemitism/actions.

—— (2004, May 14). ADL Urges Senator Hollings to Disavow Statements on Jews and the Iraq War. ADL. https://archive.ph/s5iIG.

—— (2022). Consolidated Financial Statements and Schedules, December 31, 2021 and 2020. https://tinyurl.com/bdd8k89v.

—— (2023). Brief for Anti-Defamation League as Amicus Curiae Supporting Respondent, Students for Fair Admissions, Inc., v. President and Fellows of Harvard College, No. 20-1199. (SC 2023). https://tinyurl.com/cbzubk8p.

—— (2024, April). Countering Antisemitism Act. https://tinyurl.com/55rw3abe.

Admission of German Refugee Children: Joint Hearings Before a U.S. Senate Subcommittee of the Committee on Immigration and a U.S. House of Representatives Committee on Immigration and Naturalization, 76th Cong., 1st Sess., S.J. Res. 64 and H.J. Res. 168. Joint Resolutions to Authorize the Admission to the United States of a Limited Number of German Refugee Children. (1939).

Adorno, T. W. (1967). *Prisms* (Samuel and Shierrey Weber, Trans.). MIT Press.

—— (1969a). Scientific Experiences of a European Scholar in America. In D. Fleming & B. Bailyn (Eds.), *The Intellectual Migration: Europe and America, 1930–1960*. Harvard University Press.

—— (1969b). Wissenschaftliche Erfahrungen in Amerika. In T. W. Adorno, *Stichworte*. Suhrkamp.

—— (1973). *Negative Dialectics* (E. B. Ashton, Trans.). Seabury Press.

—— (1974). *Minima Moralia: Reflections on a Damaged Life* (E. F. N. Jephcott, Trans.). Verso. (Original work published 1951.)

—— (2002). *Essays in Music*. University of California Press.

—— (2006). *Letters to His Parents 1939–1951* (W. Hoban, Trans.; C. Gödde, & H. Lonitz, Eds.). Polity Press.

—— (2016, November). Remarks on "The Authoritarian Personality" by Adorno, Frenkel-Brunswik, Levinson, Sanford. *The Platypus Review*. https://tinyurl.com/yhcntn2t. (Original work published 1948).

Adorno, T. W., Frenkel-Brunswik, E., Levinson, D. J., & Sanford, R. N. (1950). *The Authoritarian Personality*, Publication No. III of The American Jewish Committee Social Studies Series. Harper & Brothers.

Adorno, T. W., & Horkheimer, M. (2004). *Briefwechsel 1927–1969: Band II: 1938–1944 Series*. Suhrkamp Verlag AG.

—— (2011). *Towards a New Manifesto* (R. Livingstone, Trans.). Verso.

AEI. (2005, March 19). *Jeane J. Kirkpatrick: Biography*. American Enterprise Institute for Public Policy Research. https://archive.ph/UsIID#selection-839.0-839.20.

Agger, B. (1992). *The Discourse of Domination: From the Frankfurt School to Postmodernism*. Northwestern University Press.

Agus, A. R. E. (1988). *The Binding of Isaac and Messiah: Law, Martyrdom and Deliverance in Early Rabbinic Religiosity*. SUNY Press.

Ainsworth, M. D. S., Blehar, M. C., Waters, E., & Wall, S. (1978). *Patterns of Attachment*. Erlbaum.

Alba, R. D. (1985). The Twilight of Ethnicity Among Americans of European Ancestry: The Case of Italians. In R. D. Alba (Ed.), *Ethnicity and Race in the U.S.A.: Toward the Twenty-first Century*. Routledge & Kegan Paul.

Alba, R. D., & Moore, G. (1982). Ethnicity in the American Elite. *American Sociological Review*, 47(3), 373–383. https://doi.org/10.2307/2094993.

Alcock, J. (1997, June 6). Unpunctuated Equilibrium: Evolutionary Stasis in the Essays of Stephen J. Gould. Paper Presented at the Meetings of the Human Behavior and Evolution Society, Tucson, Arizona.

Alderman, G. (1983). *The Jewish Community in British Politics*. The Clarendon Press.

—— (1989). *London Jewry and London Politics 1889–1986*. Routledge.

—— (1992). *Modern British Jewry*. Clarendon Press.

Alexander, E. (1992). Multiculturalism's Jewish problem. *Academic Questions*, 5, 63–68.

Alexander, R. (1979). *Darwinism and Human Affairs*. University of Washington Press.

Alonso, J. (2024, December 19). Massive Decline in Protests from Spring to Fall. *Inside Higher Ed*. https://tinyurl.com/4vw85f7v.

Altemeyer, B. (1981). *Right-Wing Authoritarianism*. University of Manitoba Press.

—— (1988). *Enemies of Freedom: Understanding Right-Wing Authoritarianism.* Jossey-Bass.

—— (1994). Reducing prejudice in right-wing authoritarians. In M. P. Zanna, & J. M. Olson (Eds.), *The Psychology of Prejudice: The Ontario Symposium, Volume 7.* Erlbaum.

—— (1996). *The Authoritarian Specter.* Harvard University Press.

Alter, R. (1965, September). Sentimentalizing the Jews. *Commentary.* https://tinyurl.com/yufr5ak4.

Alterman, E. (1992). *Sound and Fury: The Washington Punditocracy and the Collapse of American Politics.* HarperCollins.

Altshuler, M. (1987). *Soviet Jewry Since the Second World War: Population and Social Structure.* Greenwood Press.

American Jewish Committee. (1945, November). *Anti-Semitism: A Review and Digest of Selected Publications.* https://tinyurl.com/ykmkkddm.

Amoros, R. (2018, March 19). This Graph Shows Which Political Party Corporate America Loves the Most. *Howmuch.net.* https://tinyurl.com/3r5faaws.

Anderson, M. M. (2001, October 19). German Intellectuals, Jewish Victims: A Politically Correct Solidarity. *The Chronicle of Higher Education.* https://archive.ph/X743r.

Anderson, W. L. (2001, November 17). The New York Times Missed the Wrong Missed Story. LeeRockwell. https://tinyurl.com/bdep64sf.

Andreasen, N. C., Flaum, M., Swayze, V., 2nd, O'Leary, D. S., Alliger, R., Cohen, G., Ehrhardt, J., & Yuh, W. T. (1993). Intelligence and Brain Structure in Normal Individuals. *The American Journal of Psychiatry*, 150(1), 130–134. https://doi.org/10.1176/ajp.150.1.130.

Andrews, N., & Randazzo, S. (2025, August 8). Trump Wants $1 Billion Settlement From UCLA. MSN. https://tinyurl.com/3x4ebfp3.

Antisemitism Awareness Act. H. R. 6090. 118th Cong. (2023). https://www.congress.gov/bill/118th-congress/house-bill/6090.

Archer, J. (1997). Why Do People Love Their Pets? *Evolution and Human Behavior*, 18(4), 237–259. https://doi.org/10.1016/S0162-3095(99)80001-4.

Archives of the American Jewish Committee. (1946). https://tinyurl.com/36ba87e7.

Arendt, H. (1968). *The Origins of Totalitarianism.* Harcourt, Brace & World.

—— (1969). Walter Benjamin: 1892–1940. In Walter Benjamin, *Illuminations* (H. Zohn, Trans.) (H. Arendt, Ed.). Schocken Books.

Arlow, J. A., & Brenner, C. (1988). The Future of Psychoanalysis. *Psychoanalytic Quarterly*, 57, 1–14.

Aronson, E. (1992). *The Social Animal* (6th ed.). W. H. Freeman.

Asante, M. (1987). *The Afrocentric Idea.* Temple University Press.

Aschheim, S. E. (1982). *Brothers and Strangers: The East European Jew in Germany and German Jewish Consciousness, 1800–1923.* University of Wisconsin Press.

—— (1985). "The Jew Within": The Myth of "Judaization" in Germany. In J. Reinharz & W. Schatzberg (Eds.), *The Jewish Response to German Culture: From the Enlightenment to the Second World War.* The University Press of New England for Clark University.

Associated Press. (2001, July 2). Israeli Official Calls Illegal Palestinians 'Lice.' *The Washington Post.* https://tinyurl.com/582rjbc9.

Auster, L. (1990). *The Path to National Suicide: An Essay on Immigration and Multiculturalism.* American Immigration Control Foundation.

Australia/Israel Review, The. (1998, July 8–28). Gotcha. One Nation's Secret Membership List. *The Australia/Israel Review*, 23(9).

Avineri, S. (2019). *Karl Marx: Philosophy and Revolution.* Yale University Press.

Bachrach, B. S. (1985). The Jewish community in the Later Roman Empire as seen in the Codex Theodosianus. In J. Neusner, E. S. Frerichs, & C. McCracken-Flesher (Eds.), "To See Ourselves as Others See Us": Christians, Jews, "Others" in Late Antiquity (pp. 399–421). Scholars Press.

Badger, E. (2018, May 22). Rural and Urban Americans, Equally Convinced the Rest of the Country Dislikes Them. The New York Times. https://tinyurl.com/axmdpaph.

Bailey, P. (1961). A Rigged Radio Interview: With Illustrations of Various Ego-ideals. Perspectives in Biology and Medicine, 4(2), 199–265. https://doi.org/10.1353/pbm.1961.0034.

—— (1965). Sigmund the Unserene: A Tragedy in Three Acts. Charles Thomas.

Ball, G. W., & Ball, D. B. (1992). The Passionate Attachment: America's Involvement with Israel, 1947 to the Present Norton.

Bamford, J. (2004). A Pretext for War: 9/11, Iraq, and the Abuse of America's Intelligence Agencies. Doubleday.

Bar-Tal, D., & Antebi, D. (1992). Beliefs about Negative Intentions of the World: A Study of the Israeli Siege Mentality. Political Psychology, 13(4), 633–645. https://doi.org/10.2307/3791494.

Barfield, T. J. (1993). The Nomadic Alternative. Prentice Hall.

Barkan, E. (1992). The Retreat of Scientific Racism: Changing Concepts of Race in Britain and the United States Between the World Wars. Cambridge University Press.

Barker, P., & Gholson, B. (1984). The History of the Psychology of Learning as a Rational Process: Lakatos Versus Kuhn. Advances in Child Development and Behavior, 18, 227–244. https://doi.org/10.1016/s0065-2407(08)60375-4.

Baron, S. W. (1975). The Russian Jew Under Tsars and Soviets (2nd ed.). MacMillan.

Batson, C. D., & Burris, C. T. (1994). Personal Religion: Depressant or Stimulant of Prejudice and Discrimination? In M. P. Zanna, & J. M. Olson (Eds.), The Psychology of Prejudice: The Ontario Symposium (Vol. 7). Erlbaum.

Baumeister, R. F., & Leary, M. R. (1995). The Need to Belong: Desire for Interpersonal Attachments as a Fundamental Human Motivation. Psychological Bulletin, 117(3), 497–529. https://doi.org/10.1037/0033-2909.117.3.497.

Baumrind, D. (1971). Current Patterns of Parental Authority. Developmental Psychology Monographs, 4(1, Pt. 2), 1–103. https://doi.org/10.1037/h0030372.

Bayer, L. (2023, November 13). Hungarian Plan to Target Foreign Influence Fuels NGO and Media Fears. The Guardian. https://tinyurl.com/mr3vsa9w.

Beahrs, J. O. (1996). Ritual Deception: A Window to the Hidden Determinants of Human Politics. Politics and the Life Sciences, 15(1), 3–12. https://doi.org/10.1017/S0730938400019559.

Beaty, J. (1951). The Iron Curtain Over America. Wilkinson Publishing Co.

Becker, J., & Shane, S. (2016, February 27). Hillary Clinton, 'Smart Power,' and a Dictator's Fall. The New York Times. https://tinyurl.com/4tn34ssc.

Begley, L. (1991). Wartime Lies. Knopf.

Behar, D., Yunusbayev, B., Metspalu, M. et al. (2010). The Genome-wide Structure of the Jewish people. Nature, 466, 238–242. https://doi.org/10.1038/nature09103.

Beinart, P. (1997, August 11/18). New Bedfellows: The New Latino-Jewish Alliance. The New Republic, 22–26.

Beiser, V. (1997, January 23). Slip Sliding Away. The Jerusalem Report, 33–35.

Beitchman, P. (1988). I Am a Process With No Subject. University of Florida Press.

Bell, D. (Ed.). (1955). The New American Right. Criterion Books.

—— (1961, June). Reflections of Jewish identity. Commentary. https://tinyurl.com/2b6u5cjv.

Bellow, S. (2000). Ravelstein. Viking.

Belsky, J., Steinberg, L., & Draper, P. (1991) Childhood Experience, Interpersonal Development, and Reproductive Strategy: An Evolutionary Theory of Socialization. *Child Development,* 62(4), 647–670. https://doi.org/10.2307/1131166.

Belth, N. C. (1979). *A Promise to Keep.* Anti-Defamation League of B'nai B'rith/Times Books.

Ben David, N. (2024). Building "Something That Lasts": Jewish Reactions to Persistent Nazi Antisemitism in Norway, 1945–1978. *European Journal of Jewish Studies,* 18(2), 277-300. https://doi.org/10.1163/1872471x-bja10084.

Bendersky, J. (2000). *The "Jewish Threat": Anti-Semitic Politics of the U.S. Army.* Basic Books.

Benedict, R. (1934). *Patterns of Culture.* Routledge & Kegan Paul Ltd.

Benjamin, W. (1968). *Illuminations* (H. Zohn, Trans). Harcourt, Brace & World.

Bennett, J. (2024, March 24). Judith Butler Thinks You're Overreacting. *The New York Times.* https://tinyurl.com/3x9tf4u4.

Bennett, M. T. (1963). *American Immigration Policies: A History.* Washington, DC: Public Affairs Press.

—— (1966). The Immigration and Nationality (McCarran-Walter) Act of 1952, as Amended to 1965. *The ANNALS of the American Academy of Political and Social Science,* 367(1), 127–136. https://doi.org/10.1177/000271626636700114.

Bennett, W. J. (1994). *The Index of Leading Cultural Indicators.* Simon & Schuster.

Bennington, G. (1993). Derridabase. In G. Bennington, & J. Derrida (Eds.), *Jacques Derrida* (G. Bennington, Trans.). University of Chicago Press.

Berg, A. S. (1999). *Lindbergh.* Berkley Books. (Original work published 1998).

Berglund, K. (2012). *The Vexing Case of Igor Shafarevich, a Russian Political Thinker.* Springer.

Bergman, R., & Mazzetti, M. (2024, May 16). The Unpunished: How Extremists Took Over Israel. *The New York Times Magazine.* https://tinyurl.com/47wn92wh.

Bergmann, M. S. (1995). Antisemitism and the Psychology of Prejudice. In J. A. Chanes (Ed.), *Antisemitism in America Today: Outspoken Experts Explode the Myths.* Birch Lane Press.

Berlin, I. (1980). *Personal Impressions.* Viking.

Berman, R. A. (1989). *Modern Culture and Critical Theory: Art, Politics, and the Legacy of the Frankfurt School.* University of Wisconsin Press.

Bernal, M. (1987). *Black Athena: The Afro-Asian Roots of Classical Civilization.* Free Association Press.

Bernheimer, K. (1998). *The 50 Greatest Jewish Movies: A Critic's Ranking of the Very Best.* Birch Lane Press Book.

Besharov, D. J., & T. S. Sullivan. (1996). One Flesh. *New Democrat,* 8(4), 19–21.

Besser, J. D. (1996, May 10). Compassion Seems Many Shores Away. *The Detroit Jewish News.* 124–125. https://digital.bentley.umich.edu/djnews/djn.1996.05.10.001/124.

Bettelheim, B., & Janowitz, M. (1950). *Dynamics of Prejudice: A Psychological and Sociological Study of Veterans,* Publication No. IV of the American Jewish Committee Social Studies Series. Harper & Brothers.

Betts, K. (1988). *Ideology and Immigration: Australia 1976 to 1987.* University of Melbourne Press.

Betz, D. (Guest). (2025, February 12). The Coming British Civil War (no. 124) [Audio podcast episode]. In *Maiden Mother Matriarch with Louise Perry.* YouTube. https://youtu.be/Gid48FgiHho.

Betzig, L. (1986). *Despotism and Differential Reproduction.* Aldine.

Bhushan, L. I. (1982). Validity of the California F-scale: A Review of Studies. *Indian Psychological Review,* 23(Spec Iss 1), 1–11.

Biale, D. (1998). The Melting Pot and Beyond: Jews and the Politics of American Identity. In D. Biale, M. Galchinsky, & S. Heschel (Eds.), *Insider/Outsider: American Jews and Multi-Culturalism.* University of California Press.

Biale, D., Galchinsky, M., & Heschel, S. (1998). Introduction: The Dialectic of Jewish Enlightenment. In D. Biale, M. Galchinsky, & S. Heschel (Eds.), *Insider/Outsider: American Jews and Multi-Culturalism*. University of California Press.

Billig, M. (1976). *Social Psychology and Intergroup Relations*, European Monographs in Social Psychology 9. Academic Press.

Billings, S. W., Guastello, S. J., & Rieke, M. L. (1993). A Comparative Assessment of the Construct Validity of Three Authoritarianism Measures. *Journal of Research in Personality*, 27(4), 328–348. https://doi.org/10.1006/jrpe.1993.1023.

Birnbaum, N. (1956). *The Bridge* (S. Birnbaum, Ed.). Post Publications.

Biro, M. (2009). *The Dada Cyborg: Visions of the New Human in Weimar Berlin*. University of Minnesota Press.

Black, E. C. (1988). *The Social Politics of Anglo-Jewry, 1880–1920*. Basil Blackwell.

BlackRock. (2025, January 15). BlackRock Reports Full Year 2024 Diluted EPS of $42.01, or $43.61 as Adjusted; Fourth Quarter 2024 Diluted EPS of $10.63, or $11.93 as Adjusted. https://tinyurl.com/3pkhhe87.

Blalock, H. M., Jr. (1967). *Toward a Theory of Minority-Group Relations*. John Wiley & Sons.

—— (1989). *Power and Conflict: Toward a General Theory*. Free Press.

Blau, J. L. (1958, June 16). Theory of Cultural Pluralism. *Congress Weekly*.

Boas, F. (1911). *Reports of the Immigration Commission: Changes in Bodily Form of Descendants of Immigrants*. 61st Cong., 2nd Sess., Senate Document 208. Government Printing Office.

—— (1921a, February 6, 1921). The Great Melting Pot and Its Problem. *The New York Times*. https://tinyurl.com/2y9bvedz.

—— (1921b). The Problem of the American Negro. *Yale Quarterly Review*, 10(2), 384–395.

—— (1925, May 27). Letter from Franz Boas to Louis Marshall. https://diglib.amphilsoc.org/node/101699.

—— (1927, May 26). Letter from Franz Boas to Emanuel Celler. https://diglib.amphilsoc.org/node/116198.

—— (1928). Forward to *Coming of Age in Samoa* by Margaret Mead. HarperCollins Perennial Classics.

—— (1933, November 24). Letter from Franz Boas to Felix Warburg. https://diglib.amphilsoc.org/node/128585.

—— (1935a, October 31). Letter from Franz Boas to Albert Einstein. https://diglib.amphilsoc.org/node/107687.

—— (1935b, July 15). Letter from Franz Boas to Felix Warburg. https://diglib.amphilsoc.org/node/105193.

—— (1939, October 12). Letter from Franz Boas to Karl Georg Wendinger. https://diglib.amphilsoc.org/node/123759.

—— (1942a, July 28). Letter from Franz Boas to Max Warburg. https://diglib.amphilsoc.org/node/123507.

—— (1942b, September 14). Letter from Franz Boas to Max Warburg. https://diglib.amphilsoc.org/node/105171.

Bodenheimer, A. (2017). Dada Judaism: The Avant-Garde in First World War Zurich. In M. H. Gelber, & S. Sjöberg (Eds.), *Jewish Aspects in Avant-Garde: Between Rebellion and Revelation*. De Gruyter. https://doi.org/10.1515/9783110454956.

Boime, A. (2010). Dada's Dark Secret. In R. Washton Long, M. Baigell, & M. Heyd (Eds.), *Jewish Dimensions in Modern Visual Culture: Anti-Semitism, Assimilation, Affirmation* (pp. 90–115). Brandeis University Press.

Boll, M. (2011). Konzeptionen des Judentums zwischen Säkularisierung und Marxismus: Hannah Arendt und Max Horkheimer. In L. Weissberg (Ed.), *Affinität wider Willen? Hannah Arendt, Theodor W. Adorno und die Frankfurter Schule* (pp. 103–116). Fritz Bauer Institute.

Bonaparte, M., Freud, A., & Kris, E. (Eds.). (1957). *The Origins of Psychoanalysis: Letters, Drafts, and Notes to Wilhelm Fliess, 1887–1902* (E. Mosbacher & J. Strachey, Trans.). Doubleday.

Bonner, J. T. (1988). *The Evolution of Complexity.* Princeton University Press.

Boot, M. (2018). *Corrosion of Conservatism: Why I Left the Right.* Liveright.

Borgos, A. (2006). Nők a pszichoanalízisben (Women in Psychoanalysis). *Magyar Lettre International,* 62(Fall). https://epa.oszk.hu/00000/00012/00046/borgos.html.

—— (2021). *Women in the Budapest School of Psychoanalysis: Girls of Tomorrow.* Routledge.

Bork, R. H. (1996). *Slouching Towards Gomorrah: Modern Liberalism and the American Decline.* ReganBooks/HarperCollins.

Borowitz, E. B. (1973). *The Mask Jews Wear: Self-Deceptions of American Jewry.* Simon & Schuster.

Bourhis, R. Y. (1994). Power, Gender, and Intergroup Discrimination: Some Minimal Group Experiments. In M. P. Zanna, & J. M. Olson (Eds.), *The Psychology of Prejudice: The Ontario Symposium* (Vol. 7). Erlbaum.

Boyd, R., & Richerson, P. J. (1985). *Culture and the Evolutionary Process.* University of Chicago Press.

—— (1987). The Evolution of Ethnic Markers. *Journal of Cultural Anthropology,* 2(1), 65–79. https://doi.org/10.1525/can.1987.2.1.02a00070.

—— (1992). How Microevolutionary Processes Give Rise to History. In N. H. Nitecki, & D. V. Nitecki (Eds.), *History and Evolution.* SUNY Press.

Boyle, S. S. (2001). *The Betrayal of Palestine: The Story of George Antonius.* Westview Press.

Brabant, E., Falzeder, E., Giampieri-Deutsch, P. (Eds.) (1993). *The Correspondence of Sigmund Freud and Sándor Ferenczi Volume 1, 1908-1914.* Harvard University Press.

Bradley-Dorsey, M. (2021, July 21). The Black Hole of DEI Spending at Public Universities. *Center for the Study of Partisanship and Ideology.* https://tinyurl.com/y7usws3d.

Brandeis, L. D. (1976). Your Loyalty to America Should Lead You to Support the Zionist Cause. In M. Rischin (Ed.), *Immigration and the American Tradition.* Bobbs-Merrill. (Original work published 1915).

Braungart, R. G. (1979). *Family Status, Socialization, and Student Politics.* University Microfilms International.

Breitman, R. D., & Kraut, A. M. (1986). Anti-Semitism in the State Department, 1933–44: Four case studies. In D. A. Gerber (Ed.), *Anti-Semitism in American History.* University of Illinois Press.

—— (1987). *American Refugee Policy and European Jewry, 1933–1945.* Indiana University Press.

Brenner, L. (1997, June/July). The *Forward* is Backward: New York's Unclassifiable Jewish Weekly. *Washington Report on Middle East Affairs.* https://tinyurl.com/4ud98m7w.

Brewer, M. (1993). Social Identity, Distinctiveness, and In-group Homogeneity. *Social Cognition,* 11(1), 150–164. https://doi.org/10.1521/soco.1993.11.1.150.

Brewer, M., & Miller, N. (1984). Beyond the Contact Hypothesis: Theoretical Perspectives on Desegregation. In N. Miller, & M. Brewer (Eds.), *Groups in Contact: The Psychology of Desegregation.* Academic Press.

Brewster, L. (2023, September 23). BlackRock Dissolves ESG Funds as Firm Steps Back from Label. *Yahoo! Finance.* https://tinyurl.com/39swmat5.

Brigham, C. C. (1923). *A Study of American Intelligence.* Princeton University Press.

—— (1930). Intelligence tests in immigrant groups. *Psychological Review,* 37(2), 158–165. https://doi.org/10.1037/h0072570.

Brimelow, P. (1995). *Alien Nation*. Random House.

—— (2007, August 27). Brimelow on Buckley: Making and Breaking the Conservative (And Immigration Reform) Movement. VDARE. https://tinyurl.com/pwyex8kk.

Bristow, E. J. (1983). *Prostitution and Prejudice: The Jewish Fight against White Slavery, 1870–1939*. Oxford University Press.

Bronfenbrenner, U. (1970). *Two Worlds of Childhood: U.S. and U.S.S.R.* Russell Sage.

Brossat, A. & Klingberg, S. (2016). *Revolutionary Yiddishland* (D. Fernbach, Trans.). Verso. (Original work published 1983).

Brovkin, V. N. (1994). *Behind the Front Lines of the Civil War: Political Parties and Social Movements in Russia, 1918–1922*. Princeton University Press.

Brown, M. (1987). *Jew or Juif? Jews, French Canadians, and Anglo-Canadians, 1759–1914*. Jewish Publication Society.

Brown, N. O. (1985). *Life Against Death: The Psychoanalytical Meaning of History* (2nd ed.). Wesleyan University Press. (Original work published 1959).

Brown, P. (1987). Late Antiquity. In P. Veyne (Ed.), *A History of Private Life* (Vol. 1). Harvard University Press.

Brown, R. (1965). *Social Psychology*. Collier-Macmillan.

Brownfield, A. C. (2003, May 23). Examining the Role of Israel—and Its American Friends—in Promoting War on Iraq. *Washington Report on Middle East Affairs*. https://tinyurl.com/2x8ujc7m.

Brundage, J. A. (1975). Concubinage and Marriage in Medieval Canon. *Journal of Medieval History*, 1(1): 1–17.

—— (1987). *Law, Sex, and Christian Society in Medieval Europe*. University of Chicago Press.

Buchanan, P. J. (2003, March 24). Whose War? *The American Conservative*. https://www.theamericanconservative.com/whose-war/.

—— (2004, April 23). Going Back Where They Came From. Antiwar.com. http://www.antiwar.com/pat/?articleid=2371.

Buckley, W. F. (1992). *In Search of Anti-Semitism*. Continuum.

Buhle, P. (1991). Jews and American Communism: The Cultural Question. In G. E. Pozzetta (Ed.), *Immigrant Radicals: The View from the Left*. Garland Publishing. (Reprinted from *Radical History Review*, 23, 9–33, 1980).

Bulik, L. A. (1993). *Mass Culture Criticism and Dissent*. Peter Lang.

Burgess, R. L., & Molenaar, P. C. M. (1993). Human Behavioral Biology: A Reply to R. Lerner and A. von Eye. *Human Development*, 36, 45–54.

Burton, M. L., Moore, C. C., Whiting, J. W. M., Romney, K. (1996). Regions Based on Social Structure. *Current Anthropology*, 37(1), 87–123. https://doi.org/10.1086/204474.

Burston, D. (2021). *Anti-Semitism and Analytical Psychology: Jung, Politics and Culture*. Routledge.

Buss, D. M. (1994). *The Evolution of Desire*. Basic Books.

—— (2019). *Evolutionary Psychology: The New Science of the Mind* (6th ed.). Routledge.

Buss, D. M., Haselton, M., Shackelford, T. K., Bleske, A. L., & Wakefield, J. C. (1998). Adaptations, Exaptations, and Spandrels. *American Psychologist*, 53(5), 533–548. https://doi.org/10.1037/0003-066X.53.5.533.

Butler, J. (1988). Performative Acts and Gender Constitution: An Essay in Phenomenology and Feminist Theory. *Theatre Journal*, 40(4), 519–531. https://doi.org/10.2307/3207893.

—— (2017). Foreword. In Jewish Voice for Peace, *On Antisemitism: Solidarity and the Struggle for Justice*. Haymarket Books.

Campbell, D. T. (1986). Science's Social System of Validity-Enhancing Collective Belief Change and the Problems of the Social Sciences. In D. W. Fiske, & R. A Shweder (Eds.), *Metatheory in Social Science: Pluralisms and Subjectivities*. University of Chicago Press.

—— (1987). Evolutionary Epistemology. In G. Radnitzky, & W. W. Bartley (Eds.), *Evolutionary Epistemology, Rationality, and the Sociology of Knowledge*. Open Court.

—— (1993). Plausible Coselection of Belief by Referent: All the "Objectivity" That Is Possible. *Perspectives on Science*, 1(1), 88–108.

Campus Watch. (n.d.). *Professors to Avoid*. Middle East Forum. https://tinyurl.com/4a3hus3p.

Cantor, N. (1996). *The Jewish Experience: An Illustrated History of Jewish Culture & Society*. Castle Press.

Caputo, J. D. (1997). *The Prayers and Tears of Jacques Derrida: Religion without Religion*. University of Indiana Press.

Carl, N. (2021, November 24). Did Women in Academia Cause Wokeness? *Noah's Newsletter*. https://tinyurl.com/bdfwwvxk.

Carlebach, J. (1978). *Karl Marx and the Radical Critique of Judaism*. Routledge & Kegan Paul.

Carlson, C. E. (2002). Why Judeo-Christians Support War. *Serendipity*. https://www.serendipity.li/zionism/carlson01.htm.

Carroll, F. M. (1978). *American Opinion and the Irish Question 1910–23: A Study in Opinion and Policy*. St. Martin's Press.

Carroll, J. (1995). *Evolution and Literary Theory*. University of Missouri Press.

Carroll, J. B. (1995). Reflections on Stephen Jay Gould's *The Mismeasure of Man* (1981): A Retrospective Review. *Intelligence*, 21(2), 121–134.

Carter, J. (2006). *Palestine: Peace Not Apartheid*. Simon & Schuster.

Cash, W. (1994, October 29). Kings of the Deal. *The Spectator*, 14–16.

Castro, A. (1954). *The Structure of Spanish History* (E. L. King, Trans.). Princeton University Press.

—— (1971). *The Spaniards: An Introduction to Their History* (W. F. King & S. Margaretten, Trans.). University of California Press.

Casualties of the Iraq War. (2025, February 12). In *Wikipedia*. https://en.wikipedia.org/wiki/Casualties_of_the_Iraq_War#.

Caton, H. (Ed.). (1990). *The Samoa Reader: Anthropologists Take Stock*. University Press of America.

Cattan, N. (2002, November 29). Community Questioning 'Open Door': Debate Raging on Immigration. *The Forward*.

CCIR. (1997). *Reconquista! The Takeover of America*. California Coalition for Immigration Reform.

Ceplair, L. & Englund, S. (1980). *The Inquisition in Hollywood: Politics in the Film Community 1930–1960*. Anchor Press/Doubleday.

Cesarani, D. (1994). *The Jewish Chronicle and Anglo-Jewry, 1841–1991*. Cambridge University Press.

Chafets, Z. (2007, October 14). The SY Empire. *The New York Times Magazine*. https://www.nytimes.com/2007/10/14/magazine/14syrians-t.html.

Chamberlain, L. (1995, August 25). Freud and the Eros of the Impossible. *Times Literary Supplement*, 9–10.

Chase, A. (1977). *The Legacy of Malthus*. Knopf.

Checinski, M. (1982). *Poland: Communism, Nationalism, Anti-Semitism* (T. Szafar, Trans.). Karz-Chol Publishing.

Chen, N., & Mossberg, C. (2023, April 8). Former College Swimmer Riley Gaines Claims She Was Assaulted at an Event for Opposing the Inclusion of Trans Women in Women's Sports. CNN. https://tinyurl.com/2tuvtpc5.

Chiappe, D., & MacDonald, K. (2005). The Evolution of Domain-General Mechanisms in Intelligence and Learning. *Journal of General Psychology*, 132(1), 5–40. https://doi.org/10.3200/GENP.132.1.5-40.

Chicago Model United Nations (2001, February 13). *United States National Security Background Guide.* University of Chicago. https://tinyurl.com/3fyh2sen.

Chodorow, N. J. (1989). *Feminism and Psychoanalytic Theory.* Yale University Press.

Chomsky, N. (1999). *The Fateful Triangle: The United States, Israel and the Palestinians* (2nd ed.). South End Press.

Christison, K., & Christison, B. (2002, December 13). A Rose by Another Other Name: The Bush Administration's Dual Loyalties. CounterPunch. https://archive.ph/Uk7vs.

Church of England Faith and Order Commission. (2019). *God's Unfailing Word: Theological and Practical Perspectives on Christian-Jewish Relations.* Church House Publishing. https://tinyurl.com/3vwpc6d8.

Churchill, W. (1920, February 8). Zionism Versus Bolshevism: A Struggle for the Soul of the Jewish People. *Illustrated Sunday Herald,* 5.

Churchland, P. M. (1995). *The Engine of Reason, the Seat of the Soul.* MIT Press.

Cioffi, F. (1969). Wittgenstein's Freud. In P. Winch (Ed.), *Studies in the Philosophy of Wittgenstein.* Routledge & Kegan Paul.

—— (1970). Freud and the Idea of a Pseudo-science. In R. Borger & F. Cioffi (Eds.), *Explanation in the Behavioural Sciences.* Cambridge University Press.

—— (1972). Wollheim on Freud. *Inquiry,* 15(1–4), 171–186. https://doi.org/10.1080/00201747208601672.

Clarke, R. (2004). *Against All Enemies.* Free Press.

Cleburne, P. (2023, January 31). Israel's Netanyahu to Evict ALL African Illegals. Where is America's Netanyahu? VDARE. https://tinyurl.com/3tdumwxb.

—— (2024, December 20). Why Did Churchill Have Britain Fight On after Summer 1940? It's Bad News. *The Occidental Observer.* https://tinyurl.com/yc3tswxm.

Clinton, H. R., & Schwerin, D. (2022, February 25). A State of Emergency for Democracy. *The Atlantic.* https://tinyurl.com/2erhwvnc.

Cockburn, A. (2003). My Life as an Anti-Semite. In A. Cockburn, & J. St. Clair (Eds.), *The Politics of Anti-Semitism.* Counterpunch/AK Press.

Cofnas, N. (2018). Judaism as a Group Evolutionary Strategy: A Critical Analysis of Kevin MacDonald's Theory. *Human Nature,* 29, 57436. http://dx.doi.org/10.1007/s12110-018-9310-x.

—— (2021). The Anti-Jewish Narrative. *Philosophia,* 49: 1329–1344. https://doi.org/10.1007/s11406-021-00322-w.

—— (2023). Still No Evidence for a Jewish Group Evolutionary Strategy. *Evolutionary Psychological Science,* 9, 236–259. https://doi.org/10.1007/s40806-022-00352-x.

Cogley, J. (1972). *Report on Blacklisting* (Vols. 1–2). Arno Press and *The New York Times.* (Original work published 1956).

Cohen, B. (2012). Jung's Answer to Jews. *Jung Journal: Culture and Psyche,* 6(1), 56–71. https://doi.org/10.1525/jung.2012.6.1.56.

Cohen, E. A. (1992). A Letter From Eliot A. Cohen. In W. Buckley (Ed.), *In Search of Anti-Semitism.* Continuum.

—— (2023, May 19). It's Not Enough for Ukraine to Win. Russia Has to Lose. *The Atlantic.* https://tinyurl.com/2ky9m967.

Cohen, M. (1998). In Defense of Shaatnez: A Politics for Jews in a Multicultural America. In D. Biale, M. Galchinsky, & S. Heschel (Eds.), *Insider/Outsider: American Jews and Multi-Culturalism.* University of California Press.

Cohen, N. W. (1972). *Not Free to Desist: The American Jewish Committee, 1906–1966.* Jewish Publication Society of America.

—— (1999). *Jacob H. Schiff: A Study in American Jewish Leadership.* Brandeis University Press.

Cohen, P. S. (1980). *Jewish Radicals and Radical Jews.* Academic Press.

Cohen, S. M. (1986). Vitality and Resilience in the American Jewish family. In S. M. Cohen & P. E. Hyman (Eds.), *The Jewish Family: Myths and Reality*. Holmes & Meier.

Cohen, S. M., & Liebman, C. S. (1997). American Jewish Liberalism: Unraveling the Strands. *Public Opinion Quarterly*, 61(3), 405–430. https://www.jstor.org/stable/2749579.

Cohn, W. (1958). The Politics of American Jews. In M. Sklare (Ed.), *The Jews: Social Patterns of an American Group*. Free Press.

Collier, G., Minton, H. L., & Reynolds, G. (1991). *Currents of Thought in American Social Psychology*. Oxford University Press.

Cones, J. W. (1997). *What's Really Going on in Hollywood!* Rivas Canyon Press. https://tinyurl.com/4rrhv87m.

Connelly, J. (2012, July 30). Converts Who Changed the Church. *The Forward*. https://forward.com/opinion/159955/converts-who-changed-the-church/.

Cook, J. (2016, May 9). Israel: Will Nazi Comparisons Trigger Soul Searching? *Al Jazeera*. https://tinyurl.com/2b9bafwa.

Cooklin, R., Ravindran, A., & Carney, M. (1983). The Patterns of Mental Disorder in Jewish and Non-Jewish Admissions to a District General Hospital Psychiatric Unit: Is Manic-depressive Illness a Typically Jewish Disorder? *Psychological Medicine*, 13(1), 209–212. https://doi.org/10.1017/S0033291700050236.

Coon, C. S. (1951). *Caravan: The Story of Middle East*. Henry Holt and Company.

Cooney, T. A. (1986). *The Rise of the New York Intellectuals: Partisan Review and Its Circle*. University of Wisconsin Press.

Cooper, A. M. (1990). The Future of Psychoanalysis: Challenges and Opportunities. *Psychoanalytic Quarterly*, 59(2), 177–196.

Corbin, A. (1990). Intimate Relations. In M. Perrot (Ed.), *A History of Private Life: IV. From the Fires of the Revolution to the Great War*. Harvard University Press.

Courtois, S., Werth, N., Panné, J., Paczkowski, A., Bartosek K., & Margolin, J. (1999). *The Black Book of Communism: Crimes, Terror, Repression* (J. Murphy & M. Kramer, Trans.). Harvard University Press.

Coutouvidis, J., & Reynolds, J. (1986). *Poland, 1939–1947*. Holmes & Meier.

Crews, F. (1993, November 18). The Unknown Freud. *The New York Review of Books*. https://www.nybooks.com/articles/1993/11/18/the-unknown-freud/.

—— (1994, February 3). The Unknown Freud: An Exchange. *The New York Review of Books*. https://www.nybooks.com/articles/1994/02/03/the-unknown-freud-an-exchange/.

Crews, F., et al. (1995). *The Memory Wars: Freud's Legacy in Dispute*. New York Review.

Crocker, J., Blaine, B., & Luhtanen, R. (1993). Prejudice, Intergroup Behaviour, and Self-Esteem: Enhancement and Protection Motives. In M. A. Hogg, & D. Abrams (Eds.), *Group Motivation: Social Psychological Perspectives*. Harvester Wheatsheaf.

Crosby, F., Bromley, S., & Saxe, L. (1980). Recent Unobtrusive Studies of Black and White Discrimination and Prejudice: A Literature Review. *Psychological Bulletin*, 87(3), 546–563. https://doi.org/10.1037/0033-2909.87.3.546.

Crowe, J. (2018, October 9). Hillary Clinton: 'Civility Can Start Again' When Democrats Take Congress. *National Review*. https://tinyurl.com/5frppcwj.

Cruse, H. (1992). Negroes and Jews—The Two Nationalisms and the Bloc(ked) Plurality. In J. Salzman, A. Back, & G. Sullivan Sorin (Eds.), *Bridges and Boundaries: African Americans and American Jews*. George Braziller in association with the Jewish Museum. (Reprinted from *The Crisis of the Negro Intellectual* by H. Cruse, 1967, William Morrow.)

Cuddihy, J. M. (1974). *The Ordeal of Civility: Freud, Marx, Levi-Strauss, and the Jewish Struggle with Modernity*. Basic Books.

—— (1978). *No Offense: Civil Religion and Protestant Taste*. Seabury Press.

Curran, J. (2015). Jay Blumler: A Founding Father of British Media Studies. In S. Coleman (Ed.), *Can the Media Save Democracy? Essays in Honour of Jay G. Blumler*. Palgrave.

Curtiss, R. H. (2003, April). The Pentagon's Dynamic Duo: Richard Perle and Paul Wolfowitz. *Washington Report on Middle East Affairs*. https://tinyurl.com/tkxzxhsv.

Dannhauser, W. J. (1996). Athens and Jerusalem or Jerusalem and Athens? In D. Novak (Ed.), *Leo Strauss and Judaism: Jerusalem and Athens Critically Revisited* (pp. 155–171). Rowman & Littlefield Publishers.

Darnell, R. (2001). *Creative Genealogies: A History of American Anthropology*. University of Nebraska Press.

Darwin, C. (1871). *The Descent of Man and Selection in Relation to Sex*. John Murray.

Davies, N. (1981). *God's Playground: A History of Poland* (Vols. 1–2.) Oxford University Press.

Davis, B. D. (1986). *Storm Over Biology: Essays on Science, Sentiment and Public Policy*. Prometheus Books.

Dawkins, R. (1976). *The Selfish Gene*. Oxford University Press.

Dawidowicz, L. S. (1952, July). "Anti-Semitism" and the Rosenberg Case: The Latest Communist Propaganda Trap. *Commentary*. https://tinyurl.com/4wsy7zp5.

—— (1975). *The War Against the Jews, 1933–1945*. Holt, Rinehart and Winston.

—— (1976). *A Holocaust Reader*. Behrman.

Deak, I. (1968). *Weimar Germany's Left-Wing Intellectuals*. University of California Press.

Decter, M. (1994, September). The ADL vs. the "Religious Right." *Commentary*. https://tinyurl.com/3cyjc2ff.

—— (2003). *Rumsfeld: A Personal Portrait*. Regan Books.

Degler, C. (1991). *In Search of Human Nature: The Decline and Revival of Darwinism in American Social Thought*. Oxford University Press.

Dennett, D. C. (1993, January 14). 'Confusion Over Evolution': An Exchange. *The New York Review of Books*. https://tinyurl.com/hvdyapr6.

—— (1995). *Darwin's Dangerous Idea*. Simon & Schuster.

Deri, F., & Brunswick, D. (1964). Freud's Letters to Ernst Simmel. *Journal of the American Psychoanalytic Association*, 12, 93–109. https://doi.org/10.1177/000306516401200106.

Derrida, J. (1984). Two Words for Joyce. In D. Attridge, & D. Ferrer (Eds.), *Post-structuralist Joyce: Essays from the French*. Cambridge University Press.

—— (1986). *Glas* (J. P. Leavey, Jr., & R. Rand, Trans.). University of Nebraska Press.

—— (1993a). *Aporias* (T. Dutoit, Trans.). Stanford University Press.

—— (1993b). Circumfession. In G. Bennington, & J. Derrida (Eds.), *Jacques Derrida* (G. Bennington, Trans.). University of Chicago Press.

—— (1994). Shibboleth: For Paul Celan. In A. Fioretos (Eds.), *Word Traces: Readings of Paul Celan* (J. Wilner, Trans.). Johns Hopkins University Press.

—— (1995a). Archive Fever: A Freudian Impression. *Diacritics*, 25(2), 9–63.

—— (1995b). *Points . . . Interviews, 1974–1994* (P. Kamuf et al., Trans.). Stanford University Press.

Dershowitz, A. (1994, June). The Betrayals of Jonathan Jay Pollard. *Penthouse Magazine*. https://tinyurl.com/mr49h7dd.

—— (1997). *The Vanishing American Jew: In Search of a Jewish Identity for the Next Century*. Little, Brown and Company.

—— (1999, October 1). *The Forward*.

Deutsch, H. (1940). Freud and His Pupils: A Footnote to the History of the Psychoanalytic Movement. *Psychoanalytic Quarterly*, 9, 184–194.

Devlin, F. R. (2025, March 25–26). Decadence, the Corruption of Status Hierarchies, & Female Hypergamy a Response to Rob Henderson's Article "All the Single Ladies," Parts 1 and 2. *The Occidental Observer*. https://tinyurl.com/4ytum6jb.

Diani, M. (1997). Social Movements and Social Capital: A Network Perspective on Movement Outcomes. *Mobilization: An International Quarterly*, 2(2), 129–147.

Dickerman, L. (2005). Introduction. In L. Dickerman (Ed.), *Dada: Zurich, Berlin, Hannover, Cologne, New York, Paris*. National Gallery of Art.

Dickemann, M. (1979). Female Infanticide, Reproductive Strategies, and Social Stratification: A Preliminary Model. In N. A. Chagnon & W. Irons (Eds.), *Evolutionary Biology and Human Social Behavior*. Duxbury Press.

Dickstein, M. (1977). *Gates of Eden: American Culture in the Sixties*. Basic Books.

Diggins, J. P. (2004, June 11). How Reagan Beat the Neocons. *The New York Times*. https://www.nytimes.com/2004/06/11/opinion/how-reagan-beat-the-neocons.html.

Diner, H. R. (1977). *In the Almost Promised Land: American Jews and Blacks, 1915–1935*. Greenwood Press.

Disraeli, B. (1852). *Lord George Bentinck: A Political Biography* (2nd ed.). Colburn.

Divine, R. A. (1957). *American Immigration Policy, 1924–1952*. Yale University Press.

Dixon, S. (1985). The Marriage Alliance in the Roman Elite. *Journal of Family History*, 10(4), 353–378. https://doi.org/10.1177/036319908501000402.

Dizard, J. (2004, May 4). How Ahmed Chalabi Conned the Neocons. *Salon*. https://www.salon.com/2004/05/04/chalabi_4/.

Doise, W., & Sinclair, A. (1973). The Categorization Process in Intergroup Relations. *European Journal of Social Psychology*, 3(2), 145–157. https://doi.org/10.1002/ejsp.2420030204.

Dornbusch, S. M., & Gray, K. D. (1988). Single Parent Families. In S. M. Dornbusch & M. Strober (Eds.), *Feminism, Children, and the New Families*. Guilford Press.

Dosse, F. (1997). *History of Structuralism* (Vols. 1–2) (D. Glassman, Trans.). University of Minnesota Press.

Dowd, M. (2025, January 20). Trump Has Everyone Where He Wants Them. *The New York Times*. https://tinyurl.com/4nkjv4ck.

Draper, H. (1956). Israel's Arab Minority: The Beginning of a Tragedy. *New International*, 22(2), 86–106. https://www.marxists.org/archive/draper/1956/xx/tragedy.html.

—— (1957). Israel's Arab Minority: The Great Land Robbery. *New International*, 23(1), 7–30. https://www.marxists.org/archive/draper/1957/xx/tragedy.html.

DreamWorks Pictures. (2024, February 19). In *Wikipedia*. https://en.wikipedia.org/w/index.php?title=DreamWorks_Pictures&oldid=1208885597.

Drew, E. (2003, June 12). The Neocons in Power. *The New York Review of Books*. www.nybooks.com/articles/16378.

Drucker, P. (1994). *Max Shachtman and His Left: A Socialist's Odyssey through the "American Century."* Humanities Press International.

Drury, S. (1997). *Leo Strauss and the American Right*. St. Martin's Press.

Duby, G. (1983). *The Knight, the Lady, and the Priest* (B. Bray, Trans.). Penguin Books.

Dumont, P. (1982). Jewish Communities in Turkey During the Last Decades of the Nineteenth Century in Light of the Archives of the Alliance Israélite Universelle. In B. Braude, & B. Lewis (Eds.), *Christians and Jews in the Ottoman Empire: The Functioning of a Plural Society*. Holmes & Meier Publishers.

Dunne, M. P., Martin, N. G., Statham, D. J., Slutske, W. S., Dinwiddie, S. H., Bucholz, K. K., Madden, P.A.F., & Heath, A. C. (1997). Genetic and Environmental Contributions to Variance in Age at First Sexual Intercourse. *Psychological Science*, 8(3), 211–216. https://doi.org/10.1111/j.1467-9280.1997.tb00414.x.

Easton, N. J. (2000). *Gang of Five: Leaders at the Center of the Conservative Crusade*. Simon & Schuster.

Editors of *Fortune*. (1936). *Jews in America*. Random House.

Edsall, T. B. (2025, January 21). The Right is Winning the Battle for Hearts and Minds. *The New York Times*. https://tinyurl.com/zfhxpxv8.

Efron, J. M. (1994). *Defenders of the Race: Jewish Doctors and Race Science in Fin-de-Siècle Europe*. Yale University Press.

Egan, V., Chiswick, A., Santosh, C., Naidu, K., Rimmington, J. E., & Best, J. J. K. (1994). Size Isn't Everything: A Study of Brain Volume, Intelligence and Auditory Evoked Potentials. *Personality and Individual Differences*, 17(3), 357–367. https://doi.org/10.1016/0191-8869(94)90283-6.

Ehrman, J. (1995). *The Rise of Neoconservatism: Intellectuals and Foreign Affairs 1945–1994*. Yale University Press.

Eickleman, D. F. (1981). *The Middle East: An Anthropological Approach*. Prentice-Hall.

Eksteins, M. (1975). *The Limits of Reason: The German Democratic Press and the Collapse of Weimar Democracy*. Oxford University Press.

Elazar, D. J. (1980). *Community and Polity: Organizational Dynamics of American Jewry*. Jewish Publication Society of America. (Original work published 1976).

Elder, G. (1974). *Children of the Great Depression*. University of Chicago Press.

Ellenberger, H. (1970). *The Discovery of the Unconscious*. Basic Books.

Ellensohn, R. & Putz, K. (2022). Epilogue. In R. Ellensohn, & K. Putz (Eds.), *Gut, dass wir einmal die hot potatoes ausgraben: Briefwechsel mit Theodor W.Adorno, Ernst Bloch, Max Horkheimer, Herbert Marcuse und Helmuth Plessner*. C. H. Beck.

Ellman, Y. (1987). Intermarriage in the United States: A comparative study of Jews and other ethnic and religious groups. *Jewish Social Studies*, 49, 1–26.

Elon, A. (2001, November 15). A German Requiem. *The New York Review of Books*. https://www.nybooks.com/articles/2001/11/15/a-german-requiem/.

Ephron, D., & T. Lipper. (2002, July 14). Sharansky's Quiet Role. *Newsweek*. https://www.newsweek.com/sharanskys-quiet-role-147611.

Epstein, E. J. (1996). *Dossier: The Secret History of Armand Hammer*. Random House.

Epstein, J. (1997, March 7). Dress British, Think Yiddish. *Times Literary Supplement*, 6–7.

Epstein, M. M. (1997). *Dreams of Subversion in Medieval Jewish Art and Literature*. Pennsylvania State University Press.

Erikson, E. (1968). *Identity: Youth and Crisis*. W. W. Norton.

Erős, F. (2015). A nemzetpolitikai lélektantól a tudományos fajelméletig. A magyar pszichológia történetének szürke zónája (From the Psychology of National Politics to Scientific Race Theory. The Grey Zone of The History of Hungarian Psychology). *Socio.Hu Társadalomtudományi Szemle (Social Sciences Review)*, 5(2), 67–85. https://socio.hu/index.php/so/article/view/513.

—— (2018). Some social and political issues related to Ferenczi and the Hungarian school. In A. Dimitrijević, G. Cassullo, & J. Frankel (Eds.), *Ferenczi's Influence on Contemporary Psychoanalytic Traditions: Lines of Development—Evolution of Theory and Practice over the Decades*. Routledge.

—— (2019). Sándor Ferenczi, Géza Róheim and the University of Budapest, 1918–19. *Psychoanalysis and History*, 21(1), 5–22. https://doi.org/10.3366/pah.2019.0279.

Esterson, A. (1992). *Seductive Mirage: An Exploration of the Work of Sigmund Freud*. Open Court.

Evans, M. S. (2007). *Blacklisted by History: The Untold Story of Senator Joe McCarthy and His Fight Against America's Enemies*. Crown Forum.

Eysenck, H. J. (1990). *The Decline and Fall of the Freudian Empire*. Scott-Townsend Publishers.

Fahnestock, J. (1993). Tactics of Evaluation in Gould and Lewontin's "The Spandrels of San Marco." In J. Selzer (Ed.), *Understanding Scientific Prose*. University of Wisconsin Press.

Fairchild, H. P. (1939, January 25). Should the Jews come in? *The New Republic*, 97: 344–345.

—— (1947). *Race and Nationality as Factors in American Life*. Ronald Press.

Fancher, R. E. (1985). *The Intelligence Men: Makers of the IQ Controversy*. W. W. Norton.

Farrall, L. A. (1985). *The Origins of the English Eugenics Movement, 1865–1925*. Garland Publishing.

Faur, J. (1992). *In the Shadow of History: Jews and Conversos at the Dawn of Modernity*. State University of New York Press.

Feldman, L. H. (1993). *Jew and Gentile in the Ancient World: Attitudes and Interactions from Alexander to Justinian*. Princeton University Press.

Ferenczi, S., & Dupont, J. (Ed). (1995). *The Clinical Diary of Sándor Ferenczi*. Harvard University Press.

Ferguson, N. (1999). *The Pity of War*. Basic Books.

Fetzer, J. S. (1996). Anti-immigration sentiment and nativist political movements in the United States, France and Germany: Marginality or economic self-interest? Paper presented at the 1996 Annual Meeting of the American Political Science Association, San Francisco, CA, Aug. 29–Sept. 1.

Fiedler, L. A. (1948). The State of American Writing. *Partisan Review*, 15, 870–875.

Field, G. G. (1981). *Evangelist of Race: The Germanic Vision of Houston Stewart Chamberlain*. Columbia University Press.

Findley, P. (1989). *They Dare to Speak Out: People and Institutions Confront Israel's Lobby* (2nd ed.). Lawrence Hill Books.

Finkelstein, N. G. (2000). *The Holocaust Industry: Reflections on the Exploitation of Jewish Suffering*. Verso.

—— (2001). Preface to the revised paperback edition of *The Holocaust Industry: Reflections on the Exploitation of Jewish Suffering*. Verso.

Fisher, H. E. (1992). *Anatomy of Love: The Natural History of Monogamy, Adultery, and Divorce*. W. W. Norton.

Flacks, R. (1967). The Liberated Generation: An Exploration of the Roots of Student Protest. *Journal of Social Issues*, 23(3), 52–75. https://doi.org/10.1111/j.1540-4560.1967.tb00586.x.

Flinn, M. (1997). Culture and the Evolution of Social Learning. *Evolution and Human Behavior*, 18(1), 23–67. https://doi.org/10.1016/S1090-5138(96)00046-3.

Flowerman, S. H. (1947). Mass Propaganda in the War Against Bigotry. *The Journal of Abnormal and Social Psychology*, 42: 429–439.

—— (1949). The Use of Propaganda to Reduce Prejudice: A Refutation. *International Journal of Opinion and Attitude Research*, 3, 99–108.

Fölsing, A. (1997). *Albert Einstein: A Biography* (E. Osers, Trans.). Penguin Books. (Original work published 1993).

Ford, H. (1920, March 21). The International Jew. *The Dearborn Independent*.

Foran, C., Talbot, H., & Wilson, K. (2024, May 1). House Passes Antisemitism Bill as Johnson Highlights Campus Protests. CNN. https://tinyurl.com/3runy8z3.

Foundation for Defense of Democracies. (2025, February 3). In *Wikipedia*. https://tinyurl.com/349vy66p.

Fox, R. (1989). *The Search for Society: Quest for a Biosocial Science and Morality*. Rutgers University Press.

Foxman, A. (1995). Antisemitism in America: A View From the "Defense" Agencies. In J. A. Chanes (Ed.), *Antisemitism in America Today: Outspoken Experts Explode the Myths*. Birch Lane Press.

—— (2003, May 5). Anti-Semitism, Pure and Simple. *Jerusalem Report*. https://archive.ph/lfDyh.

Foxman, A., & Wolf C. (2013). *Viral Hate: Containing Its Spread on the Internet*. St. Martin's Press.

Francis, S. (1999). *Thinkers of Our Time: James Burnham* (Rev. ed.). Claridge Press. (Original work published 1984).

—— (2004). The Neoconservative Subversion. In B. Nelson (Ed.), Neoconservatism. Occasional Papers of the Conservative Citizens' Foundation, Issue Number Six (pp. 6–12). Conservative Citizens' Foundation.

Frank, G. (1997). Jews, Multiculturalism, and Boasian Anthropology. *American Anthropologist*, 99(4), 731–745. https://doi.org/10.1525/aa.1997.99.4.731.

Frankel, J. (1981). *Prophecy and Politics: Socialism, Nationalism, and the Russian Jews, 1862–1917*. Cambridge University Press.

Fraser, A. (2022, August 11). Canada Outlaws Condoning, Denying, or Downplaying the Holocaust Mythos. *The Occidental Observer*. https://tinyurl.com/3yyc7a6j.

Frederick Kagan. (2024, December 22). In *Wikipedia*. https://en.wikipedia.org/w/index.php?title=Frederick_Kagan&oldid=1264488189.

Freeman, D. (1983). *Margaret Mead and Samoa: The Making and Unmaking of an Anthropological Myth*. Harvard University Press.

—— (1990). Historical Glosses. In H. Caton (Ed.), *The Samoan Reader: Anthropologists Take Stock*. University Press of America.

—— (1991). On Franz Boas and the Samoan Researches of Margaret Mead. *Current Anthropology*, 32(3), 322–330. https://www.jstor.org/stable/2743783.

Freeman, W. J. (1995). *Societies of Brains*. Erlbaum.

Freud, S. (1955). *Moses and Monotheism* (K. Jones, Trans.). Vintage. (Original work published 1939).

—— (1969). *The Interpretation of Dreams* (J. Strachey, Trans.). Avon Books. (Original work published 1932).

Frickel, S., & Gross, N. (2005). A General Theory of Scientific/Intellectual Movements. *American Sociological Review*, 70(2), 204–232. https://doi.org/10.1177/000312240507000202.

Friedman, M. (1995). *What Went Wrong? The Creation and Collapse of the Black-Jewish Alliance*. Free Press.

Friedman, T. L. (2023, August 15). Lebanon's Nightmare Could Become Israel's Future. *The New York Times*. https://tinyurl.com/2kf3bx2c.

Fromm, E. (1941). *Escape from Freedom*. Rinehart.

Frommer, M. (1978). The American Jewish Congress: A History, 1914–1950 (Vols. 1–2). Ph.D. Dissertation, Ohio State University.

Frum, D. (2023, March 13). The Iraq War Reconsidered. *The Atlantic*. https://tinyurl.com/49u5b5wh.

Frum, D. & R. Perle. (2003). *An End to Evil: How to Win the War on Terror*. Random House.

Fuchs, L. (1956). *The Political Behavior of American Jews*. Free Press.

Furstenberg, F. F. (1991). As the Pendulum Swings: Teenage Childbearing and Social Concern. *Family Relations*, 40(2), 127–138. https://doi.org/10.2307/585470.

Furstenberg, F. F., & Brooks-Gunn, J. (1989). Teenaged Pregnancy and Childbearing. *American Psychologist*, 44(2), 313–320. https://doi.org/10.1037/0003-066X.44.2.313.

Gabler, N. (1988). *An Empire of Their Own: How the Jews Invented Hollywood*. Crown Publishers.

Gabler, N. (1995) *Winchell: Gossip, Power, and the Culture of Celebrity*. Vintage. (Original work published 1994).

Gaertner, S. L., & Dovidio, J. F. (1986). The Aversive Form of Racism. In J. F. Dovidio & S. L. Gaertner (Eds.), *Prejudice, Racism, and Discrimination*. Academic Press.

Gal, A. (1989). Brandeis, Judaism, and Zionism. In N. L. Dawson (Ed.), *Brandeis in America*. University of Kentucky Press.

Gasman, D. (1971). *The Scientific Origins of National Socialism: Social Darwinism in Ernst Haeckel and the German Monist League*. MacDonald.

Gay, P. (1987). *A Godless Jew: Freud, Atheism, and the Making of Psychoanalysis*. Yale University Press.

—— (1988). *Freud: A Life for Our Time*. W. W. Norton.

Geary, D. C. (2005). *The Origin of Mind: Evolution of Brain, Cognition, and General Intelligence*. American Psychological Association.

Geertz, C. (1973). *The Interpretation of Cultures*. Basic Books.

Gelb, S. A. (1986). Henry H. Goddard and the Immigrants, 1910–1917: The Studies and Their Social Context. *Journal of the History of the Behavioral Sciences, 22*(4), 324–332. https://doi.org/10.1002/1520-6696(198610)22:4<324::AID-JHBS2300220404>3.0.CO;2-Y.

Gelernter, D. (1997, March). How the Intellectuals Took Over (And What to Do About It). *Commentary*. https://tinyurl.com/45ujcnk2.

Germanistic Society of America. (1910). *The Activities of the Germanistic Society of America, 1904–1910*. https://archive.org/details/activitiesofgerm00germ/page/n5/mode/2up.

—— (1917). *Annual Report*. https://archive.org/details/ldpd_11549851_002/page/n3/mode/2up.

Gershenhorn, J. (2004). *Melville Herskovits and the Racial Politics of Knowledge*. University of Nebraska Press.

Gershman, C. (2003, December 27). After the Bombings: My Visit to Turkey and Istanbul's Jewish Community. National Endowment for Democracy. https://www.ned.org/after-the-bombings/.

—— (2004, January 22). A Democracy Strategy for the Middle East. International Institute. https://international.ucla.edu/institute/article/6722.

Gershon, E., & Liebowitz, J. H. (1975). Sociocultural and Demographic Correlates of Affective Disorders in Jerusalem. *Journal of Psychiatric Research, 12*(1), 37–50. https://doi.org/10.1016/0022-3956(75)90019-9.

Gerson, M. (Ed.). (1996). *The Essential Neoconservative Reader*. Addison-Wesley Publishing Company, Inc.

Gigot, F. (1910). Judaism. In *The Catholic Encyclopedia*. Robert Appleton Company. http://www.newadvent.org/cathen/08399a.htm.

Gilman, S. L. (1993). *Freud, Race, and Gender*. Princeton University Press.

Gilson, E. (1962). *The Philosopher and Theology*. Random House.

Ginsberg, B. (1993). *The Fatal Embrace: Jews and the State*. University of Chicago Press.

Gitelman, Z. (1991). The Evolution of Jewish Culture and Identity in the Soviet Union. In Y. Ro'i, & A. Beker (Eds.), *Jewish Culture and Identity in the Soviet Union*. New York University Press.

Glazer, N. (1954, March). The Study of Man: New Light on "The Authoritarian Personality." *Commentary*. https://tinyurl.com/mtb7bb3x.

—— (1961). *The Social Basis of American Communism*. Harcourt Brace.

—— (1969). The New Left and the Jews. *Jewish Journal of Sociology, 11*(2), 121–132.

—— (1987). New Perspectives in American Jewish Sociology. *American Jewish Yearbook, 87*, 3–19. https://www.jstor.org/stable/23603942.

Glazer, N., & Moynihan, D. P. (1970). *Beyond the Melting Pot* (2nd ed.). MIT Press. (Original work published 1963).

Glenn, S. S., & Ellis, J. (1988). Do the Kallikaks Look "Menacing" or "Retarded"? *American Psychologist, 43*(9), 742–743. https://doi.org/10.1037/0003-066X.43.9.742.

Gless, D. J., & Smith, B. H. (Eds.). (1992). *The Politics of Liberal Education*. Duke University Press.

Glick, L. B. (1982). Types Distinct From Our Own: Franz Boas on Jewish Identity and Assimilation. *American Anthropologist, 84*(3), 545–565. https://doi.org/10.1525/AA.1982.84.3.02A00020.

Goddard, H. H. (1912). *The Kallikak Family: A Study in the Heredity of Feeble-Mindedness.* Macmillan.

—— The Binet Tests in Relation to Immigration. *Journal of Psycho-Asthenics, 18,* 105–110.

—— (1917). Mental Tests and the Immigrant. *Journal of Delinquency, 2,* 243–277.

Goldberg, J. (2003, March 13). Jews and War. *National Review Online.* https://tinyurl.com/39nwhf3r.

Goldberg, J. J. (1996). *Jewish Power: Inside the American Jewish Establishment.* Addison-Wesley.

Goldfarb, S. H. (1984). American Judaism and the Scopes trial. In J. R. Marcus, & A. J. Peck (Eds.), *Studies in the American Jewish Experience II.* University Press of America.

Goldschmidt, W., & Kunkel, E. J. (1971). The Structure of the Peasant Family. *American Anthropologist, 73*(5), 1058–1076. http://dx.doi.org/10.1525/aa.1971.73.5.02a00060.

Goldstein, A. (1981). Some Demographic Characteristics of Village Jews in Germany: Nonnenweier, 1800-1931. In P. Ritterband (Ed.), *Modern Jewish Fertility* (pp. 112–143). Leide Brill Publishers.

Goldstein, I. (1952a, November 3). An American Immigration Policy. *Congress Weekly,* 4.

—— (1952b, March 17). The Racist Immigration Law. *Congress Weekly, 19*(11), 6–7.

Goldstein, J. (1975). Ethnic Politics: The American Jewish Committee as Lobbyist, 1915–1917. *American Jewish Historical Quarterly, 65,* 36–58.

—— (1990). *The Politics of Ethnic Pressure: The American Jewish Committee Fight against Immigration Restriction, 1906–1917.* Garland Publishing.

Goldstein, M. (1912). Deutsch-jüdischer Parnass (German-Jewish Parnassus). *Kunstwart, 25*(11), 281–294.

González, G. (1989). The Intellectual Influence of the Conversos Luis and Antonia Coronel in Sixteenth-Century Spain. In W. D. Phillips & C. R. Phillips (Eds.), *Marginated Groups in Spanish and Portuguese History.* Society for Spanish and Portuguese Historical Studies.

Goodman, P. (1960). *Growing up Absurd: Problems of Youth in the Organized Society.* Random House.

—— (1961, March). Pornography, Art, and Censorship. *Commentary.* https://tinyurl.com/yfbhhj3f.

Goodnick, B. (1993). Jacob Freud's birthday greeting to his son Alexander. *The American Journal of Psychoanalysis, 53*(3), 255–265. https://doi.org/10.1007/BF01248336.

Gordon, S. (1984). *Hitler, Germans, and the "Jewish Question."* Princeton University Press.

Gottfredson, L. S. (1994). Egalitarian Fiction and Collective Fraud. *Society, 31,* 53–59. https://doi.org/10.1007/BF02693231.

Gottfried, P. (1993). *The Conservative Movement* (Rev. ed.). Twayne Publishers.

—— (1996). On "Being Jewish." *Rothbard-Rockwell Report, 7*(4), 7–10. https://www.unz.com/print/RothbardRockwellReport-1996apr-00007/.

—— (1998). *After Liberalism.* Princeton University Press.

—— (2000, June) A Race Apart. *Chronicles.* https://tinyurl.com/ycytuefw.

Gould, S. J. (1981). *The Mismeasure of Man.* W. W. Norton.

—— (1987). *An Urchin in the Storm: Essays about Books and Ideas.* W. W. Norton.

—— (1991, June 13). The Birth of the Two Sex World. *The New York Review of Books.* https://www.nybooks.com/articles/1991/06/13/the-birth-of-the-two-sex-world/.

—— (1992, November 19). The Confusion Over Evolution. *The New York Review of Books.* https://www.nybooks.com/articles/1992/11/19/the-confusion-over-evolution/.

—— (1993). Fulfilling the Spandrels of World and Mind. In J. Selzer (Ed.), *Understanding Scientific Prose*. University of Wisconsin Press.

—— (1994a, November 28). Curveball. *The New Yorker*, 139–149.

—— (1994b, June 30). How Can Evolutionary Theory Best Offer Insights Into Human Development? Invited Address Presented at the Meetings of the International Society for the Study of Behavioral Development, Amsterdam, The Netherlands.

—— (1996a, September). The Diet of Worms and the Defenestration of Prague. *Natural History*.

—— (1996b, November). The Dodo in the Caucus Race. *Natural History*, 105(11).

—— (1996c). *The Mismeasure of Man* (Rev. ed.). W. W. Norton.

—— (1997, June 26). Evolution: The Pleasures of Pluralism. *The New York Review of Books*. https://tinyurl.com/5f2tw29v.

—— (1998, March). The Internal Brand of the Scarlet W. *Natural History*, 107, 22–25, 70–78.

Gould, S. J., & Lewontin, R. C. (1979). The Spandrels of San Marco and the Panglossian Paradigm: A Critique of the Adaptationist Programme. *Proceedings of the Royal Society of London, Series B: Biological Sciences*, 205, 581–598. https://doi.org/10.1098/rspb.1979.0086.

Graham, H. D. (2003). *Collision Course: The Strange Coincidence of Affirmative Action and Immigration Policy in America*. Oxford University Press. (Original work published 2002).

Graham, O. (2004). *Unguarded Gates: A History of America's Immigration Crisis*. Rowman & Littlefield.

Granberry, M. (1994, February 15). Backlash to Teaching Chastity: Course in Public Schools That Proclaims Safe-Sex-Is-No-Sex Draws Fire. Backers Praise Push to Stress Morality Over Biology, But Angry Parents See Dangers in a Program They Call Inaccurate and Unrealistic. *Los Angeles Times*. https://tinyurl.com/4ymnyf6z.

Grant, M. (1921). *The Passing of the Great Race or the Racial Basis of European History* (4th ed.). Scribner.

Green, J. C. (2000). Religion and Politics in the 1990s: Confrontations and Coalitions. In M. Silk (Ed.), *Religion and American Politics: The 2000 Election in Context*. The Pew Program on Religion and the News Media, Trinity College.

Green, S. (2004, February 28). Neo-Cons, Israel and the Bush Administration. *CounterPunch*. https://tinyurl.com/56e4pd2c.

Greenberg, C. (1946). Koestler's New Novel. *Partisan Review*, 13(Nov/Dec), 580–582.

—— (1949). The Question of the Pound Award. *Partisan Review*, 16(May), 512–522.

Greenblatt, J. (2018). Foreword. In J. F. Kennedy, *A Nation of Immigrants*. Harper Perennial.

Greenwald, A. G., & Schuh, E. S. (1994). An Ethnic Bias in Scientific Citations. *European Journal of Social Psychology*, 24(6), 623–639. https://doi.org/10.1002/ejsp.2420240602.

Grollman, E. A. (1965). *Judaism in Sigmund Freud's World*. Bloch.

Gross, B. (1990). The Case of Philippe Rushton. *Academic Questions*, 3(4), 35–46.

Gross, N., & Fosse, E. (2012). Why Are Professors Liberal? *Theory and Society*, 41(2), 127–168. https://doi.org/10.1007/s11186-012-9163-y.

Grosskurth, P. (1991). *The Secret Ring: Freud's Inner Circle and the Politics of Psychoanalysis*. Addison-Wesley.

Grossman, K., Grossman, K. E., Spangler, G., Suess, G., & Unser, L. (1985). Maternal Sensitivity and Newborns' Orientation Responses as Related to Quality of Attachment in Northern Germany. *Growing Points in Attachment Theory and Research*. Monographs for the Society for Research in Child Development, 50(1/2), 233–275. https://doi.org/10.2307/3333836.

Grünbaum, A. (1984). *The Foundations of Psychoanalysis*. University of California Press.

Guttman, N. (2004, May 31). Prominent U.S. Jews, Israel Blamed for Start of Iraq War. *Haaretz*. https://tinyurl.com/5n8kahj8.

Guynn, J. (2022, December 19). GOP vs. ESG: Why Florida Gov. Ron DeSantis, Republicans Are Fighting 'Woke' ESG Investing. *USA Today*. https://tinyurl.com/bddas38z.

H.R. Rep. No. 109, 1920.

H.R. Rep. No. 1182, 1957.

H.R. Rep. No. 350, 1924.

Habermas, J. (1971). *Knowledge and Human Interests* (J. J. Shapiro, Trans.). Beacon Press. (Original work published 1968).

Hacker, D. (2010). Heritage: Learning From Our Past. *Social Currents*. https://socialistcurrents.org/?page_id=621.

Hagen, W. W. (1996). Before the "Final Solution": Toward a Comparative Analysis of Political Anti-Semitism in Interwar Germany and Poland. *Journal of Modern History*, 68:351–381.

Haidar, E. H., & Kettles, C. E. (2024, January 31). Billionaire Megadonor Ken Griffin Says He Will Stop Donations to Harvard. *The Harvard Crimson*. https://tinyurl.com/3spk43tn.

Haidt, J. (2011, January 27). The Bright Future of Post-Partisan Social Psychology. Talk given at the Annual Meeting of the Society for Personality and Social Psychology, San Antonio, TX. http://people.stern.nyu.edu/jhaidt/postpartisan.html.

Hajnal, J. (1965). European Marriage Patterns in Perspective. In D. V. Glass & D. E. C. Eversley (Eds.), *Population in History*. Aldine.

—— (1983). Two Kinds of Pre-Industrial Household Formation System. In R. Wall, J. Robin, & P. Laslett (Eds.), *Family Forms in Historic Europe*. Cambridge University Press.

Hale, N. G. (1995). *The Rise and Crisis of Psychoanalysis in the United States: Freud and the Americans, 1917–1985*. Oxford University Press.

Haliczer, S. (1989). The Outsiders: Spanish History as a History of Missed Opportunities. In W. D. Phillips, & C. R. Phillips (Eds.), *Marginated Groups in Spanish and Portuguese History*. Society for Spanish and Portuguese Historical Studies.

Halverson, C. F., & Waldrop, M. F. (1970). Maternal Behavior Toward Own and Other Preschool Children. *Developmental Psychology*, 12, 107–112.

Hamilton, D. (2000, October 3). Keeper of the Flame: A Blacklist Survivor. *Los Angeles Times*. https://www.latimes.com/archives/la-xpm-2000-oct-03-cl-30614-story.html.

Hammer, M. F., Redd, A. J., Wood, E. T., Bonner, M. R., Jarjanazi, H., Karafet, T., Santachiara-Benerecetti, S., Oppenheim, A., Jobling, M. A., Jenkins, T., Ostrer, H., & Bonné-Tamir, B. (2000). Jewish and Middle Eastern Non-Jewish Populations Share a Common Pool of Y-Chromosome Biallelic Haplotypes. *Proceedings of the National Academy of Sciences*, 97(12), 6769–6774. https://doi.org/10.1073/pnas.100115997.

Hanawalt, B. (1986). *The Ties that Bound: Peasant Families in Medieval England*. Oxford University Press.

Handlin, O. (1945). Return of the Puritans. *Partisan Review*, 12(2), 268–269.

—— (1947, January). Democracy Needs the Open Door. *Commentary*. https://tinyurl.com/2z9msyyz.

—— (1952, July). The Immigration Fight Has Only Begun: Lessons of the McCarran-Walter Setback. *Commentary*. https://tinyurl.com/5n8juh65.

—— (1957). *Race and Nationality in American Life*. Little Brown & Co.

—— (1973). *The Uprooted* (2nd ed.). Little Brown & Co. (Original work published 1951).

Hannan, K. (2000). Review of *The Culture of Critique*. *Nationalities Papers*, 28(4), 741–742.

Hapgood, N. (1916, April 15). Jews and the Immigration Bill. *Harper's Weekly*, 62.

Harris, J. F. (1994). *The People Speak! Anti-Semitism and Emancipation in Nineteenth-Century Bavaria*. University of Michigan Press.

Harris, M. (1968). *The Rise of Anthropological Theory: A History of Theories of Culture*. Thomas Y. Crowell; Harper & Row.

Harter, S. (1983). Developmental Perspectives on the Self-system. In E. M. Hetherington (Ed.), *Handbook of Child Psychology: Socialization, Personality & Social Development* (Vol. 4). Wiley.

Hartung, J. (1995). Love Thy Neighbor: The Evolution of In-Group Morality. *Skeptic*, 3(4), 86–99.

Harup, L. (1978). Class, Ethnicity, and the American Jewish Committee. In J. N. Porter (Ed.), *The Sociology of American Jews: A Critical Anthology*. University Press of America. (Original work published 1972).

Harvey, I., Persaud, R., Ron, M. A., Baker, G., & Murray, R. M. (1994). Volumetric MRI Measurements in Bipolars Compared With Schizophrenics and Healthy Controls. *Psychological Medicine*, 24(3), 689–699. https://doi.org/10.1017/s0033291700027847.

Haslam, M. (1978). *The Real World of the Surrealists*. Weidenfeld & Nicholson.

Hawkins, F. (1989). *Critical Years in Immigration: Canada and Australia Compared*. McGill-Queen's University Press.

Hawkins, R. (2007). "Hitler's Bitterest Foe": Samuel Untermyer and the Boycott of Nazi Germany, 1933–1938. *American Jewish History*, 93(1), 21–50. http://dx.doi.org/10.1353/ajh.2007.0025.

Heilbrunn, J. (1995, April 20). His Anti-Semitic Sources. *New York Review of Books*. https://www.nybooks.com/articles/1995/04/20/his-anti-semitic-sources/.

—— (2008). *They Knew They Were Right: The Rise of the Neocons*. Doubleday.

Heilman, S. (1992). *Defenders of the Faith: Inside Ultra-Orthodox Judaism*. Schocken Books.

Held, G. F. (2013, July 23). Léon de Poncins: The Problem with the Jews at the Council. *The Occidental Observer*. https://tinyurl.com/bdw5es5a.

Heller, M. (1988). *Cogs in the Wheel: The Formation of Soviet Man* (D. Floyd, Trans.). Collins Harvill.

Heller, M., & Nekrich, A. (1986). *Utopia in Power*. Summit.

Henrich, J. (2020). *The WEIRDest People in the World: How the West Became Psychologically Peculiar and Particularly Prosperous*. Farrar, Straus and Giroux.

Henriques, R. (1966). *Sir Robert Waley Cohen, 1877–1952: A Biography*. Secker & Warburg.

Henry, W. E., Sims, J. H., & Spray, S. L. (1971). *The Fifth Profession*. Jossey-Bass.

Herder, J. G. (1969). Yet Another Philosophy of History for the Enlightenment of Mankind. In *J. G. Herder on Social and Political Culture* (F. M. Barnard, Trans.). Cambridge University Press. (Original work published 1774).

Herlihy, D. (1985). *Medieval Households*. Harvard University Press.

Herrnstein, R. J., & Murray, C. (1994). *The Bell Curve: Intelligence and Class Structure in American Life*. Free Press.

Hersh, S. M. (1982, May). Kissinger and Nixon in the White House. *The Atlantic*. https://tinyurl.com/2p9kcame.

—— (2003, May 4). Selective Intelligence. *The New Yorker*. https://www.newyorker.com/magazine/2003/05/12/selective-intelligence.

—— (2004, June 20). Plan B: As June 30th Approaches, Israel Looks to the Kurds. *The New Yorker*. https://www.newyorker.com/magazine/2004/06/28/plan-b-2.

Herskovits, M. J. (1947). *Man and His Works*. Alfred A. Knopf.

—— (1953). *Franz Boas: The Science of Man in the Making*. Charles Scribner's Sons.

Hertzberg, A. (1979). *Being Jewish in America: The Modern Experience*. Schocken Books.

—— (1985, November 21). The Triumph of the Jews. *New York Review of Books*. https://www.nybooks.com/articles/1985/11/21/the-triumph-of-the-jews/.

—— (1989). *The Jews in America: Four Centuries of an Uneasy Encounter*. Simon & Schuster.

—— (1993a, September 23). 'The Great Hatred.' *New York Review of Books.*
https://www.nybooks.com/articles/1993/09/23/the-great-hatred/.

—— (1993b, June 24). Is Anti-Semitism Dying Out? *New York Review of Books.*
https://www.nybooks.com/articles/1993/06/24/is-anti-semitism-dying-out/.

—— (1995). How Jews Use Antisemitism. In J. A. Chanes (Ed.), *Antisemitism in America Today: Outspoken Experts Explode the Myths.* Birch Lane Press.

—— (2003, August 27). The Price of Not Keeping the Peace. *The New York Times.*
https://tinyurl.com/232za5ce.

Herz, F. M., & Rosen, E. J. (1982). Jewish Families. In M. McGoldrick, J. K. Pearce, & J. Giordano (Eds.), *Ethnicity and Family Therapy.* The Guilford Press.

Herzl, T. (1960). *The Complete Diaries of Theodor Herzl* (Vol. 2). Herzl Press and Thomas Yoseloff.

Higham, J. (1984). *Send These to Me: Immigrants in Urban America* (Rev. ed.). Johns Hopkins University Press.

Hilzenrath, D. S. (2004, May 24). The Ultimate Insider: Richard N. Perle's Many Business Ventures Followed His Years as a Defense Official. *The Washington Post.*
https://drugaddict.livejournal.com/493567.html.

Himmelfarb, G. (1991). A Letter to Robert Conquest. *Academic Questions,* 4(Winter), 44–48.

—— (1995). *The De-Moralization of Society: From Victorian Virtues to Modern Values.* Knopf.

Himmelfarb, M. (1974, August). On Leo Strauss. *Commentary.*
https://www.commentary.org/articles/milton-himmelfarb-2/on-leo-strauss/.

Himmelstrand, U. (1967). Tribalism, National Rank Equilibrium and Social Structure: A Theoretical Interpretation of Some Sociopolitical Processes in Southern Nigeria. *Journal of Peace Research,* 6(2), 81–102.

Hirsh, M. (2003, June 22). Neocons on the Line. *Newsweek.*
https://www.newsweek.com/neocons-line-138091.

Hitler, A. (1992). *Mein Kampf* (R. Manheim, Trans.). Pimlico. (Original work published 1943).

Hodges, W. F., Wechsler, R. C., & Ballantine, C. (1979). Divorce and the Preschool Child: Cumulative Stress. *Journal of Divorce,* 3(1), 55–67.
https://doi.org/10.1300/J279v03n01_06.

Hoffman, N. von. (1996, April 14). Was McCarthy Right About the Left? *The Washington Post.*
https://tinyurl.com/ztpzssjx.

Hofstadter, R. (1955). *The Age of Reform: From Bryan to FDR.* Vintage.

—— (1965). *The Paranoid Style in American Politics and Other Essays.* Knopf.

Hogg, M. A., & Abrams, D. (1988). *Social Identifications.* Routledge.

—— (1993). Toward a Single-process Uncertainty-reduction Model of Social Motivation in Groups. In M. A. Hogg & D. Abrams (Eds.), *Group Motivation: Social Psychological Perspectives.* Harvester Wheatsheaf.

Hollinger, D. A. (1996). *Science, Jews, and Secular Culture: Studies in Mid-Twentieth- Century American Intellectual History.* Princeton University Press.

Holmes, S. (1993). *The Anatomy of Anti-Liberalism.* Harvard University Press.

Holt, R. R. (1990, January 12). A Perestroika for Psychoanalysis: Crisis and Renewal. Paper Presented at a Meeting of Section 3, Division 39, New York University. (Cited in Richards, 1990.)

Hook, S. (1948). Why Democracy Is Better. *Commentary,* 5(March), 195–204.

—— (1949). Reflections on the Jewish question. *Partisan Review,* 16(5), 463–482.

—— (1987). *Out of Step: An Unquiet Life in the 20th Century.* Harper & Row.

—— (1989, October). On Being a Jew. *Commentary.*
https://www.commentary.org/articles/sidney-hook-2/on-being-a-jew/.

Hopkins, B. (1983). *Death and Renewal.* Harvard University Press.

Horkheimer, M. (1940, June 18). Letter from Max Horkheimer to Edward S. Greenbaum. https://sammlungen.ub.uni-frankfurt.de/horkheimer/content/pageview/3934265.

—— (1941). Art and Mass Culture. *Studies in Philosophy and Social Science*, 9(2), 290–304.

—— (1945, October 11). Letter from Max Horkheimer to Theodor Adorno. https://sammlungen.ub.uni-frankfurt.de/horkheimer/content/pageview/6322666.

—— (1946a, March 4). Frame of Reference for the Department of Scientific Research and Program Evaluation. American Jewish Committee. P. 13. https://tinyurl.com/36ba87e7.

—— (1946b, February 14). Letter from Max Horkheimer to John Slauson. American Jewish Committee. https://tinyurl.com/36ba87e7.

—— (1947). *The Eclipse of Reason*. Oxford University Press.

—— (1974). *Critique of Instrumental Reason* (M. J. O'Connell et al., Trans.). Seabury Press.

—— (2007). *A Life in Letters: Selected Correspondence* (M. & E. Jacobson, Eds. & Trans.). University of Nebraska Press.

Horkheimer, M., & Adorno, T. W. (1990). *Dialectic of Enlightenment* (J. Cumming, Trans.). Continuum. (Original work published 1944).

Horkheimer, M., & Flowerman, S. H. (1950). Foreword to Studies in Prejudice. In T. W. Adorno et al., *The Authoritarian Personality*. Harper and Brothers.

Horowitz, D. (1997). *Radical Son: A Journey Through Our Time*. Free Press.

Horowitz, E. (1998). "The Vengeance of the Jews Was Stronger Than Their Avarice": Modern Historians and the Persian Conquest of Jerusalem in 614. *Jewish Social Studies*, 4(2), 1–39.

Horowitz, I. L. (1987). Between the Charybdis of Capitalism and the Scylla of Communism: The Emigration of German Social Scientists, 1933–1945. *Social Science History*, 11, 113–138.

—— (1993). *The Decomposition of Sociology*. Oxford University Press.

Horowitz, M., Haynor, A., & Kickham, K. (2018). Sociology's Sacred Victims and the Politics of Knowledge: Moral Foundations Theory and Disciplinary Controversies. *The American Sociologist*, 49, 459–495. https://doi.org/10.1007/s12108-018-9381-5.

Horus. (2024). Champions of Judea: On the Supplanting of Pre-World War II British Foreign Policy. *The Occidental Quarterly*, 24(4), 3–33.

Howard, A. (2025, February 26). Bezos Remakes Washington Post Opinion Page in Defense of 'Personal Liberties and Free Markets.' *Politico*. https://tinyurl.com/3cwkzjes.

Howe, I. (1976). *The World of Our Fathers*. Harcourt Brace Jovanovich.

—— (1978). The East European Jews and American culture. In G. Rosen. (Ed.), *Jewish Life in America*. Institute of Human Relations Press of the American Jewish Committee.

—— (1982). *A Margin of Hope: An Intellectual Biography*. Harcourt Brace Jovanovich.

Hughes, C. (2023, November 11). Britain's Synagogues Have Never Been Fuller. *The Spectator*. https://archive.ph/fSiZr.

Hull, D. L. (1988). *Science as a Process: An Evolutionary Account of the Social and Conceptual Development of Science*. University of Chicago Press.

Hunt, E. (1995). The Role of Intelligence in Modern Society. *American Scientist*, 83(4), 356–368. https://www.jstor.org/stable/29775483.

Hutchinson, E. P. (1981). *Legislative History of American Immigration Policy 1798–1965*. University of Pennsylvania Press.

Huxley, J. (1942). Preface to *Racialism against Civilization* by Ignaz Zollschan. The New Europe Publishing Co. Ltd.

Hyman, H. H., & Sheatsley, P. B. (1954). *The Authoritarian Personality*: A Methodological Critique. In R. Christie & M. Jahoda (Eds.), *Studies in the Scope and Method of The Authoritarian Personality*. Free Press.

Hyman, P. E. (1989). The Modern Jewish Family: Image and Reality. In D. Kraemer (Ed.), *The Jewish Family*. Oxford University Press.

IASPS. (1996). *A Clean Break: A New Strategy for Securing the Realm*. Institute for Advanced Strategic and Political Studies. https://www.dougfeith.com/docs/Clean_Break.pdf.

Inbar, Y., & Lammers, J. (2012). Political Diversity in Social and Personality Psychology. *Perspectives in Psychological Science*, 7(5), 496–503. https://doi.org/10.1177/1745691612448792.

Indybay Collective. (2009, June 25). ADL Fails in Its Defamation Campaign Against UCSB Professor. *Indybay: Palestine*. https://www.indybay.org/newsitems/2009/06/25/18603971.php.

International Holocaust Remembrance Alliance. (n.d.). Working Definition of Antisemitism. Retrieved January 22, 2025 from, https://holocaustremembrance.com/resources/working-definition-antisemitism.

Irving, D. (1981). *Uprising!* Hodder and Stoughton.

—— (1987). *Churchill's War* (Vol. 1). Veritas Publishing Company.

Isaacs, S. D. (1974). *Jews and American Politics*. Doubleday.

Isaacson, W. (2023). *Elon Musk*. Simon & Schuster.

Itzkoff, S. (1991). *Human Intelligence and National Power: A Political Essay in Sociobiology*. Peter Lang.

Ivers, G. (1995). *To Build a Wall: American Jews and the Separation of Church and State*. University of Virginia Press.

Ivry, B. (2010, December 1). Sovereign or Beast? *The Forward*. https://forward.com/culture/133536/sovereign-or-beast/.

—— (2012, May 18). Evolutionary Biology After Auschwitz. *The Forward*. https://tinyurl.com/5ekphfyf.

Jackson, J. P., & Weidman, N. M. (Eds.). (2005). *Race, Racism, and Science: Social Impact and Interaction*. Rutgers University Press.

Jackson, W. A. (1986). Melville Herskovits and the Search for Afro-American Culture. In G. W. Stocking Jr. (Ed.), *Malinowski, Rivers, Benedict and Others: Essays on Culture and Personality* (pp. 195–226). University of Wisconsin Press.

Jacobs, J. (2015). *The Frankfurt School, Jewish Lives, and Anti-Semitism*. Cambridge University Press.

Jacoby, R. (1995). Marginal Returns: The Trouble With Post-Colonial Theory. *Lingua Franca*, 5(6), 30–37.

Jaffa, H. (1999). Strauss at One Hundred. In K. L. Deutsch, & J. A. Murley (Eds.), *Leo Strauss, the Straussians, and the American Regime* (pp. 41–48). Rowman & Littlefield Publishers.

Jameson, F. (1990). *Late Marxism: Adorno, or, the Persistence of the Dialectic*. Verso.

Javits, J. (1951, July 8). Let Us Open Again the Gates. *The New York Times Magazine*. https://tinyurl.com/yznr9ky5.

—— (1965). *Congressional Record* 111, 24469.

Jay, M. (1973). *The Dialectical Imagination: A History of the Frankfurt School and the Institute of Social Research, 1923–1950*. Little, Brown.

—— (1980). The Jews and the Frankfurt School: Critical Theory's Analysis of Anti-Semitism. *New German Critique*, 19(Special Issue 1), 137–149. https://doi.org/10.2307/487976.

—— (1984). *Marxism and Totality: The Adventures of a Concept from Lukács to Habermas*. University of California Press.

Jensen, A. R. (1982). The Debunking of Scientific Fossils and Straw Persons. *Contemporary Education Review*, 1(2), 121–135.

Jensen, A. R., & Weng, L. J. (1994). What Is a Good *g*? *Intelligence*, 18(3), 231–258.

Jeřábek, H. (2017). *Paul Lazarsfeld and the Origins of Communications Research*. Routledge.

Jiménez, J., & Barnes, B. (2023, May 19). What We Know about the DeSantis-Disney Dispute. *The New York Times*. https://www.nytimes.com/article/disney-florida-desantis.html.

Johnson, G. (1986). Kin Selection, Socialization, and Patriotism: An Integrating Theory. *Politics and the Life Sciences*, 4(2), 127–154.

—— (1995). The Evolutionary Origins of Government and Politics. In J. Losco & A. Somit (Eds.), *Human Nature and Politics*. JAI Press.

Johnson, H. (1956). Psychoanalysis: Some Critical Comments. *American Journal of Psychiatry*, 113(1), 36–40. https://doi.org/10.1176/ajp.113.1.36.

Johnson, P. (1988). *A History of the Jews*. Harper Perennial. (Original work published 1987).

Johnston, L., & Hewstone, M. (1990). Intergroup Contact: Social Identity and Social Cognition. In D. Abrams & M. A. Hogg (Eds.), *Social Identity Theory: Constructive and Critical Advances*. Springer-Verlag.

Jones, D. B. (1972). Communism and the Movies: A Study of Film Content. In J. Cogley (Ed.), *Report on Blacklisting* (Vol. 1: Movies) (pp. 196–304). Arno Press and *The New York Times*. (Original work published 1956).

Jones, E. (1953, 1955, 1957). *The Life and Work of Sigmund Freud*, Vols 1, 2, & 3. Basic Books.

—— (1959). *Free Associations: Memories of a Psycho-Analyst*. Basic Books.

Jones, N. (1996, October). U.S. Jewish Leaders Decry Clinton Refusal to Free Pollard. *Washington Report on Middle East Affairs*. https://tinyurl.com/2yx39eu7.

Jordan, W. C. (1989). *The French Monarchy and the Jews: From Philip Augustus to the Last Capetians*. University of Pennsylvania Press.

Joseph, C. H. (1925, July 10). Behind This Monkey Business. *The Jewish Criterion*, 66(9), 18. https://tinyurl.com/yc2pm5m4.

Joyce, A. (2009, March 3). Free Speech, Jewish Activism, and the Trial of Jez Turner. *The Occidental Observer*. https://tinyurl.com/26ntywha.

—— (2012). Revisiting the Nineteenth-Century Russian Pogroms. *The Occidental Quarterly*, 12(2), 61–87.

—— (2013, May 10). Justice Denied: Thoughts on Truth, 'Canards' and the Marc Rich Case: Part One of Two. *The Occidental Observer*. https://tinyurl.com/3vk2e3ca.

—— (2014, December 12). John Hagee: A Profile in Pathological Christian Activism. *The Occidental Observer*. https://tinyurl.com/yc4ufv5h.

—— (2019a, October 16). "Do Jews Think Differently?": Aspects of Jewish Self-Glorification. *The Occidental Observer*. https://tinyurl.com/yxyxp4jp.

—— (2019b, December 4). Jews, White Guilt, and the Death of the Church of England. *The Occidental Observer*. https://tinyurl.com/433pvxj4.

—— (2019c). "Modify the Standards of the In-Group": Jews and Mass Communication. *The Occidental Quarterly*, 19(2), 3–20.

—— (2019d, May 5). Pariah to Messiah: The Engineered Apotheosis of Baruch Spinoza. *The Occidental Observer*. https://tinyurl.com/ycyn253s.

—— (2021a, March 20). The Cofnas Problem. *The Occidental Observer*. https://tinyurl.com/ms9fx3v8.

—— (2021b). The Jewish Origins of American Legal Pluralism. *The Occidental Quarterly*, 21(3), 81–93.

—— (2021c, July 18). Magnus Hirschfeld's Racism (1934). *The Occidental Observer*. https://tinyurl.com/m22skxsy.

—— (2022, January 16). Free to Cheat: "Jewish Emancipation" and the Anglo-Jewish Cousinhood, Part 1. *The Occidental Observer*. https://tinyurl.com/mr2svfyy.

—— (2024a, June 29). Carl Jung and the Jews. *The Occidental Observer*. https://www.theoccidentalobserver.net/2024/06/29/carl-jung-and-the-jews/.

—— (2024b, June 18). Jews Are Rewarding Black Criminality. *The Occidental Observer.* https://tinyurl.com/yww6n2fh.

Judah, J. (2023, July 5). ADL CEO: The British Green Party Looks Like the Next Hub of Antisemitism in UK Politics. *Jewish Telegraphic Agency.* https://tinyurl.com/ysvxdjk3.

Judis, J. (1990, September 1). The Conservative Crackup. *The American Prospect.* https://prospect.org/power/conservative-crackup/.

Jumonville, N. (1991). *Critical Crossings: The New York Intellectuals in Postwar America.* University of California Press.

Jung, C. G. (1961). *Memories, Dreams, Reflections.* Collins.

Jussim, L. (2014). *Social Perception and Social Reality: Why Accuracy Dominates Bias and Self-Fulfilling Prophecy.* Oxford University Press.

Kadushin, C. (1969). *Why People Go to Psychiatrists.* Atherton.

—— (1974). *The American Intellectual Elite.* Little, Brown and Company.

Kagan, R. (2016, May 18). This Is How Fascism Came to America. *The Washington Post.* https://tinyurl.com/5ehm2f6n.

—— (Guest) (2023, February 24). Russia's Invasion of Ukraine: One Year Later [Audio Podcast Episode with Transcript]. *Free Expression with Gerry Baker.* The Wall Street Journal. https://tinyurl.com/9t2azam8.

Kahan, S. (1987). *The Wolf of the Kremlin.* William Morrow & Co.

Kahan Commission. (1983). *The Beirut Massacre: The Complete Kahan Commission Report.* Karz-Cohl.

Kahn, L. (1985). Heine's Jewish Writer Friends: Dilemmas of a Generation, 1817–33. In J. Reinharz & W. Schatzberg (Eds.), *The Jewish Response to German Culture: From the Enlightenment to the Second World War.* University Press of New England for Clark University.

Kallen, H. M. (1915, February 18, 25). Democracy Versus the Melting Pot. *Nation,* 100, 190–194, 217–220.

—— (1924). *Culture and Democracy in the United States.* Boni and Liveright.

—— (1933, November 21). Letter from Horace Kallen to Franz Boas. https://diglib.amphilsoc.org/node/92986.

—— (1956). *Cultural Pluralism and the American Idea.* University of Pennsylvania Press.

Kalman, G. B., Maoz, B., & Yaffe, R. (1970). Demographic Survey of an Open Psychiatric Hospital (In Hebrew). *Briut Ziburi (Public Health),* 13(67).

Kamen, A. (2003, September 10). Feith-Based Initiative. *The Washington Post.* https://tinyurl.com/4c2yuefk.

Kamin, L. (2024, August 14). Here Are Trump's Top Billionaire Donors. *Forbes.* https://tinyurl.com/5498ekcv.

Kamin, L. J. (1974a). *The Science and Politics of I.Q.* Erlbaum.

—— (1974b). The Science and Politics of I.Q. *Social Research,* 41(3), 387–425. https://pubmed.ncbi.nlm.nih.gov/11630476/.

—— (1982). Mental Testing and Immigration. *American Psychologist,* 37(1), 97–98. https://doi.org/10.1037/0003-066X.37.1.97.b.

Kamisar, B. (2024, November 8). The Final Price Tag on 2024 Political Advertising: Almost $11 Billion. NBCNews. https://tinyurl.com/3me97zzs.

Kammer, J. (2010, March 11). Immigration and the SPLC. *Center for Immigration Studies.* https://cis.org/Immigration-and-SPLC.

Kampelman, Max M. (n.d.) *Trust the United Nations?* Social Democrats. Retrieved May 9, 2008, from, https://tinyurl.com/376f44uf.

Kann, K. (1981). *Joe Rapoport: The Life of a Jewish Radical.* Temple University Press.

Kantor, K. A. (1982). *Jews on Tin Pan Alley: The Jewish Contribution to American Popular Music, 1830–1940.* KTAV Publishing.

Kapel, M., (1997, August 29–September 11). Bad Company. *Australia/Israel Review,* 22(12).

Kaplan, D. M. (1967). Freud and His Own Patients. *Harper's,* 235(December), 105–106. https://harpers.org/archive/1967/12/freud-and-his-own-patients/.

Kaplan, L. F. (2003, February 18). Toxic Talk on War. *The Washington Post.* https://tinyurl.com/3236vevc.

Karabel, J. (2005). *The Chosen: The Hidden History of Admission and Exclusion at Harvard, Yale, and Princeton.* Harper.

Kasnyik, M. (2025, February 19). Orban Orders Media and NGOs Crackdown Over Foreign Funding. *Bloomberg.* https://tinyurl.com/2wzupuwh.

Katz, J. (1983, July). Misreadings of Anti-Semitism. *Commentary.* https://www.commentary.org/articles/jacob-katz/misreadings-of-anti-semitism/.

—— (1985). German Culture and the Jews. In J. Reinharz & W. Schatzberg (Eds.), *The Jewish Response to German Culture: From the Enlightenment to the Second World War.* University Press of New England for Clark University.

—— (1986). *Jewish Emancipation and Self-Emancipation.* Jewish Publication Society of America.

—— (1996, February). Leaving the Ghetto. *Commentary.* https://www.commentary.org/articles/jacob-katz/leaving-the-ghetto/.

Katzenberger, T. (2024, October 23). LA Times editor resigns after owner blocked presidential endorsement. *Politico.* https://tinyurl.com/2efvh6h9.

Kaufman, J. (1997). Blacks and Jews: The Struggle in the Cities. In J. Salzman, & C. West (Eds.), *Struggles in the Promised Land: Toward a History of Black-Jewish Relations in the United States.* Oxford University Press.

Kaufman, R. G. (2000). *Henry M. Jackson: A Life In Politics.* University of Washington Press.

Kaufmann, E. P. (2004). *The Rise and Fall of Anglo-America.* Harvard University Press.

Kaus, M. (1995). *The End of Equality* (2nd ed.). Basic Books.

Keegan, J. (1993). *A History of Warfare.* Knopf.

Keeley, L. H. (1996). *War Before Civilization.* Oxford University Press.

Kehoe, A. B. (2014). *A Passion for the True and Just: Felix and Lucy Kramer Cohen and the Indian New Deal.* University of Arizona Press.

Keinon, H. (2020, June 18). Twenty-six Years After His Death . . . the Rebbe's Beat Goes On. *The Jerusalem Post.* https://tinyurl.com/mrxntyst.

Keller, B. (2002, September 22). The Sunshine Warrior. *The New York Times Magazine.* https://www.nytimes.com/2002/09/22/magazine/the-sunshine-warrior.html.

Kellogg, M. (2005). *The Russian Roots of Nazism: White Émigrés and the Making of National Socialism, 1917–1945.* Cambridge University Press.

Kerr, J. (1992). *A Most Dangerous Method: The Story of Jung, Freud, and Sabina Spielrein.* Knopf.

Kerr, W. (1968, April 14). Skin Deep Is Not Good Enough. *The New York Times,* D1, D3.

Kessler, J. (1999). *Poisoning the Web: Hatred Online: An ADL Report on Internet Bigotry, Extremism and Violence, Featuring 10 Frequently Asked Questions About the Law and Hate on the Internet.* Anti-Defamation League.

Kettler, D., & Lauer, G. (2005). *Exile, Science and Bildung: The Contested Legacies of German Emigre Intellectuals.* Palgrave.

Keve, T. (2012). *Ferenczi and Ortvay: Two Boys from Miskolc.* Routledge.

Kevles, D. (1985). *In the Name of Eugenics: Genetics and the Uses of Human Heredity.* Knopf.

Kiell, N. (Ed.). (1988). *Freud Without Hindsight: Reviews of His Work (1893–1939).* International Press.

Kierkegaard, E. (2024). The Politics of Sociology. Just Emil Kirkegaard Things.
    https://www.emilkirkegaard.com/p/the-politics-of-sociology.

Kiernan, T. (1986). *Citizen Murdoch*. Dodd, Mead & Company.

Kilgore, E. (2024, May 2). MTG and Matt Gaetz Manage to Smear Both Jews and Fellow
    Christians. *Intelligencer*. https://tinyurl.com/3zycaede.

Kimball, R. (1995). Farewell to the MLA. *The New Criterion*.
    https://newcriterion.com/article/farewell-to-the-mla/.

Kimberly Kagan. (2024, November 17). In *Wikipedia*.
    https://en.wikipedia.org/w/index.php?title=Kimberly_Kagan&oldid=1258021331.

Kirsch, T. B. (2000). *The Jungians: A Comparative and Historical Perspective*. Routledge.

—— (2016). Jung's Relationship with Jews and Judaism. In E. Kiehl, M. Saban, & A. Samuels
    (Eds.), *Analysis and Activism: Social and Political Contributions of Jungian Psychology*.
    Routledge.

Klafter, A. (2020). Anti-Semitism: A Psychoanalytic Perspective. In H. S. Moffic, J. R. Peteet, A.
    Hankir, & M. V. Seeman (Eds.), *Anti-Semitism and Psychiatry: Recognition, Prevention,
    and Interventions*. Springer, Cham.

Klehr, H. (1978). *Communist Cadre: The Social Background of the American Communist Party
    Elite*. Hoover Institution Press.

Klehr, H., Haynes, J. E., & Firsov, F. I. (1995). *The Secret World of American Communism* (T. D.
    Sergay, Trans.). Yale University Press.

Klein, D. B. (1981). *Jewish Origins of the Psychoanalytic Movement*. Praeger Publishers.

Klein Halevi, Y. (1996, December 26). Zionism, Phase II. *The Jerusalem Report*, 12–18.

—— (2001, February 7). Sharon Has Learned from His Mistakes. *Los Angeles Times*.
    https://www.latimes.com/archives/la-xpm-2001-feb-07-me-22176-story.html.

Kleiner, R. (1988, March 17). Archives to throw new light on Ehrenburg. *Canadian Jewish
    News*, 9.

Kline, P., & Cooper, C. (1984). A Factor Analysis of the Authoritarian Personality. *British
    Journal of Psychology, 75*(2), 171–176. https://doi.org/10.1111/j.2044-8295.1984.tb01888.x.

Kluckhohn, C., and Prufer, O. (1959). Influences During the Formative Years. In M.
    Goldschmidt (Ed.), *The Anthropology of Franz Boas* (pp. 4–28). American Anthropology
    Association.

Knode, J. (1974). *The Decline in Fertility in Germany, 1871–1979*. Princeton University Press.

Koestler, A. (1971). *The Case of the Midwife Toad*. Random House.

—— (1976). *The Thirteenth Tribe: The Khazar Empire and Its Heritage*. Random House.

Koffman, D. S. (2019). *The Jews' Indian: Colonialism, Pluralism, and Belonging in America*.
    Rutgers University Press.

Kohler, K. (1968). *Jewish Theology*. KTAV Publishing House (Original work published in 1918).

Konvitz, M. (1953). *Civil Rights in Immigration*. Cornell University Press.

—— (1978). The Quest for Equality and the Jewish Experience. In G. Rosen (Ed.), *Jewish Life in
    America*. Institute of Human Relations Press of the American Jewish Committee.

Kornberg, R. (1993). *Theodore Herzl: From Assimilation to Zionism*. Indiana University Press.

Kostyrchenko, G. (1995). *Out of the Red Shadows: Anti-Semitism in Stalin's Russia*.
    Prometheus Books.

Kotkin, J. (1993). *Tribes: How Race, Religion and Identity Determine Success in the New Global
    Economy*. Random House.

Kovács, M. M. (1994). *Liberal Professions and Illiberal Politics: Hungary from the Habsburg to
    the Holocaust*. Oxford University Press.

Kramer, H. (1996, September). Reflections on the History of *Partisan Review*. *The New
    Criterion*. https://tinyurl.com/2wze9bee.

Krauthammer, C. (2002a, June 10). He Tarries: Jewish Messianism and the Oslo Peace [Lecture Transcript]. Lecture given at Bar-Ilan University. https://www.imra.org.il/story.php?id=12456.

—— (2002b, April 29). Please Excuse the Jews for Living. *Jerusalem Post*. https://tinyurl.com/y5776rrs.

—— (2004a). *Democratic Realism: An American Foreign Policy for a Unipolar World*. The AEI Press.

—— (2004b, March 5). Gibson's Blood Libel. *The Washington Post*. https://tinyurl.com/4v7dw636.

Krispenz, A., & Bertrams, A. (2024). Understanding Left-Wing Authoritarianism: Relations to the Dark Personality Traits, Altruism, and Social Justice Commitment. *Current Psychology: A Journal for Diverse Perspectives on Diverse Psychological Issues*, 43(3), 2714–2730. https://doi.org/10.1007/s12144-023-04463-x.

Kristol, I. (1983). *Reflections of a Neoconservative*. Basic Books.

—— (1984, July). The Political Dilemma of American Jews. *Commentary*. https://tinyurl.com/4fbdf4wb.

—— (2003, August 25). The Neoconservative Persuasion. *The Weekly Standard*, 8(47), 23.

Krizman, G. (1998, January). 50 Years: SAG Remembers the Blacklist. *National Screen Actor* (Spec Iss). https://www.cobbles.com/simpp_archive/linkbackups/huac_blacklist.htm.

Kroeber, A. L. (1943). Franz Boas: The Man. *American Anthropologist*, 45(3, pt. 2).

—— (1956). The Place of Franz Boas in Anthropology. *American Anthropologist*, 58(1), 151–159. https://www.jstor.org/stable/665731.

Kurzweil, E. (1989). *The Freudians: A Comparative Perspective*. Yale University Press.

Kwiatkowski, K. (2004a, March 10). The New Pentagon Papers. *Salon*. https://www.salon.com/2004/03/10/osp_moveon/.

—— (2004b, January 19). Open Door Policy. *The American Conservative*. https://tinyurl.com/5n7jvaaj.

Lacouture, J. (1995). *Jesuits: A Multibiography* (J. Legatt, Trans.). Counterpoint.

LaFranco, R. & Peterson-Withorn, C., Eds. (2023). The Forbes 400: The Definitive Ranking of the Wealthiest Americans in 2023. *Forbes*. https://www.forbes.com/forbes-400/.

Lakoff, R. T., & Coyne, J. C. (1993). *Father Knows Best: The Use and Abuse of Power in Freud's Case of "Dora."* Teachers College Press.

Lamb, B. (1990, June 17). Judith Miller: Author of "One, By One, By One: Facing the Holocaust" [Television Broadcast Transcript]. *Booknotes*. C-SPAN. https://booknotes.c-span.org/Watch/12729-1.

Landau, D. (1993). *Piety and Power: The World of Jewish Fundamentalism*. Hill and Wang.

Landmann, M. (1984). Critique of Reason: Max Weber to Jürgen Habermas. In J. Marcus, & Z. Tarr (Eds.), *Foundations of the Frankfurt School of Social Research*. Transaction Books.

Langbert, M., Quain, A. J., & Klein, D. B. (2016). Faculty Voter Registration in Departments of Economics, History, Journalism, Law and Psychology. *Econ Journal Watch*, 13(3), 4122–451.

Langdon, J. E. (2008). *Caught in the Crossfire: Adrian Scott and the Politics of Americanism in 1940s Hollywood*. Columbia University Press.

Lapin, A. (2023, November 20). Why ADL Chief Jonathan Greenblatt Is Praising Musk as Advertisers Flee X over Antisemitism. *Jewish Telegraph Agency*. https://tinyurl.com/yc6wy25z.

Laqueur, W. (1974). *Weimar: A Cultural History 1918–1933*. Weidenfeld and Nicolson.

Larsen, R. J., & Diener, E. (1992). Problems and Promises with the Circumplex Model of Emotion. *Review of Personality and Social Psychology*, 13, 25–59.

Lasch, C. (1991). *The True and Only Heaven: Progress and Its Critics*. W. W. Norton.

Laslett, P. (1983). Family and Household as Work Group and Kin Group: Areas of Traditional Europe Compared. In R. Wall, J. Robin, & P. Laslett (Eds.), *Family Forms in Historic Europe*. Cambridge University Press.

Laskin, J. (2007). *Jimmy Carter's War against the Jews*. David Horowitz Freedom Center.

Laughland, J. (2003, June 30). Flirting with Fascism: Neocon Theorist Michael Ledeen Draws More From Italian Fascism Than From the American Right. *The American Conservative*. https://www.theamericanconservative.com/flirting-with-fascism/.

Layton-Henry, Z. (1992). *The Politics of Immigration: Immigration, "Race" and "Race" Relations in Post-War Britain*. Blackwell.

Lazarsfeld, P., & Merton, R. K. (1948). The Process and Effects of Mass Communication. In L. Bryson (Ed.), *The Communication of Ideas*, 554–578. University of Illinois Press.

Le Roy Ladurie, E. (1987). *The French Peasantry 1450–1660* (A. Sheridan, Trans.). University of California Press. (Original work published 1977).

Lebrecht, N. (2019, October 5). Do Jews Think Differently? *The Spectator*. https://www.spectator.co.uk/article/do-jews-think-differently/.

Ledeen, M. (2002). *War on the Terror Masters: Why It Happened, Where We Are Now, Why We'll Win*. St. Martin's Press.

Lefkowitz, M. R. (1993). Ethnocentric History From Aristobulus to Bernal. *Academic Questions*, 6(2), 12–20.

Leftwich, J. (1957). *Israel Zangwill*. Thomas Yoseloff.

Lehrman, D. S. (1970). Semantic and Conceptual Issues in the Nature-nurture Problem. In L. R. Aronson, E. Tobach, D. S. Lehrman, & J. S. Rosenblatt (Eds.), *The Development and Evolution of Behavior*. W. H. Freeman.

Lenz, F. (1931). The Inheritance of Intellectual Gifts. In E. Baur, E. Fischer, & F. Lenz (Eds.), *Human Heredity* (E. & C. Paul, Trans.). Macmillan.

Lerer, L., & Medina, J. (2021, May 18). Tensions Among Democrats Grow Over Israel as the Left Defends Palestinians. *The New York Times*. https://tinyurl.com/ys5cj53x.

Lerner, M. (1957). *America as a Civilization: Life and Thought in the United States Today*. Simon & Schuster.

Lerner, R., Nagai, A. K., & Rothman, S. (1996). *American Elites*. Yale University Press.

Lerner, R. M. (1992). *Final Solutions: Biology, Prejudice, and Genocide*. The Pennsylvania State University.

Lerner, R. M., & von Eye, A. (1992). Sociobiology and Human Development: Arguments and Evidence. *Human Development*, 35(1), 12–33. https://doi.org/10.1159/000277110.

Levav, I., Kohn, R., Golding, J. M., & Weissman, M. M. (1997). Vulnerability of Jews to Affective Disorders. *American Journal of Psychiatry*, 154(7), 941–947. https://doi.org/10.1176/ajp.154.7.941.

Levenson, A. (1989). Reform Attitudes, in the Past, Toward Intermarriage. *Judaism*, 38(3), 320–332.

Levey, G. B. (1996). The Liberalism of American Jews: Has It Been Explained? *British Journal of Political Science*, 26(3), 369–401. http://dx.doi.org/10.1017/S000712340000750X.

Levin, N. (1977). *While Messiah Tarried: Jewish Socialist Movements, 1871–1917*. Schocken Books.

—— (1988). *The Jews in the Soviet Union Since 1917: Paradox of Survival* (Vols. 1–2). New York University Press.

Levine, D. L. (1994). Without Malice but With Forethought. In K. L. Deutsch, & W. Nicgorski (Eds.), *Leo Strauss: Political Philosopher and Jewish Thinker*. Rowman & Littlefield Publishers, Inc.

Levins, R., & Lewontin, R. C. (1985). *The Dialectical Biologist*. Harvard University Press.

Lévi-Strauss, C., & Eribon, D. (1991). *Conversations with Claude Lévi-Strauss* (P. Wissing, Trans.). University of Chicago Press.

Levy, R. S. (1975). *The Downfall of the Anti-Semitic Political Parties in Imperial Germany*. Yale University Press.

Lewin, R. (1992). *Complexity*. MacMillan.

Lewis, B. (1984). *The Jews of Islam*. Princeton University Press.

Lewis, D. L. (1984). Shortcuts to the Mainstream: Afro-American and Jewish Notables in the 1920s and 1930s. In J. R. Washington (Ed.), *Jews in Black Perspective: A Dialogue* (pp. 83–97). Fairleigh Dickinson University; Associated University Presses.

—— (1992). Parallels and Divergences. In J. Salzman (Ed.), *Bridges and Boundaries: African Americans and American Jews: Strategies of Afro-American and Jewish Elites from 1910 to the Early 1930s* (pp. 17–35). George Brazilier.

Lewis, H. S. (2020). Who's Who in the Age of Boas: The Sponsors of Anthropological Papers Written in Honor of Franz Boas (1906). *Bérose - Encyclopédie internationale des histoires de l'anthropologie*. https://www.berose.fr/article2087.html?lang=fr.

Lewis, J. E., DeGusta, D., Meyer, M. R., Monge, J. M., Mann, A. E., Holloway, R. L. (2011). The Mismeasure of Science: Stephen Jay Gould versus Samuel George Morton on Skulls and Bias. *PLOS Biology* 9(6): e1001071. https://doi.org/10.1371/journal.pbio.1001071.

Lewontin, R. C. (1992, May 28). The Dream of the Human Genome: Doubts About the Human Genome Project. *The New York Review of Books*. https://www.nybooks.com/articles/1992/05/28/the-dream-of-the-human-genome/.

—— (1994a, April 7). Women Versus the Biologists. *The New York Review of Books*. https://www.nybooks.com/articles/1994/04/07/women-versus-the-biologists/.

—— (1994b, July 14). Women Versus the Biologists: An Exchange. *The New York Review of Books*. https://tinyurl.com/bdfyksrp.

—— (1997, October 23). The Confusion Over Cloning. *The New York Review of Books*. https://www.nybooks.com/articles/1997/10/23/the-confusion-over-cloning/.

Lewontin, R. C., & Levins, R. (1985). *The Dialectical Biologist*. Harvard University Press.

Lewontin, R. C., Rose, S. J., & Kamin, L. (1984). *Not in Our Genes: Biology, Ideology, and Human Nature*. Pantheon.

Lichter, S. R., Lichter, L. S., & Rothman, S. (1983). Hollywood and America: The Odd Couple. *Public Opinion*, 5(Dec./Jan.), 54–58.

—— (1986). *The Media Elite: America's New Powerbrokers*. Adler & Adler.

—— (1994). *Prime Time: How TV Portrays American Culture*. Regnery.

Liebman, A. (1979). *Jews and the Left*. John Wiley & Sons.

Liebman, C. (1973). *The Ambivalent American Jew: Politics, Religion, and Family in American Jewish Life*. Jewish Publication Society of America.

Lilienthal, A. M. (1978). *The Zionist Connection: What Price Peace?* Dodd, Mead.

Lilla, M. (1995, May 25). The Riddle of Walter Benjamin. *The New York Review of Books*. https://www.nybooks.com/articles/1995/05/25/the-riddle-of-walter-benjamin/.

—— (1998, June 25). The Politics of Jacques Derrida. *The New York Review of Books*. https://www.nybooks.com/articles/1998/06/25/the-politics-of-jacques-derrida/.

Lincoln, W. B. (1989). *Red Victory: A History of the Russian Civil War*. Simon and Schuster.

Lind, M. (1995a, April 20). On Pat Robertson: His Defenders. *The New York Review of Books*. https://www.nybooks.com/articles/1995/04/20/on-pat-robertson-his-defenders/.

—— (1995b, February 2). Rev. Robertson's Grand International Conspiracy Theory. *The New York Review of Books*. https://tinyurl.com/3u4afxmn.

—— (2003, June 30). I Was Smeared. *History News Network*. http://hnn.us/articles/1530.html.

Lindbergh, A. M. (1980). *War Within and Without: Diaries and Letters of Anne Morrow Lindbergh*. Harcourt Brace Jovanovich.

Lindbergh, C. A. (1939, November). Aviation, Geography, and Race. *Reader's Digest*, 35, 64–67.

Lindemann, A. S. (1991). *The Jew Accused: Three Anti-Semitic Affairs (Dreyfus, Beilis, Frank) 1894–1915*. Cambridge University Press.

—— (1997). *Esau's Tears: Modern Anti-Semitism and the Rise of the Jews*. Cambridge University Press.

Liphshiz, C. (2017, November 6). What Was the Jewish Role in the 1917 Russian Revolution: Moscow Museum Gives a Full Picture. *Jewish Telegraph Agency*. https://tinyurl.com/37up5ecw.

Lippmann, W. (1922, April 14). Public Opinion and the American Jew. *The American Hebrew*, 575.

Lipset, S. M. (1971). *Rebellion in the University*. Little, Brown.

—— (1988). *Revolution and Counterrevolution: Change and Persistence in Social Structures* (Rev. ed.). Transaction. (Original work published 1968).

Lipset, S. M., & Ladd, Jr., E. C. (1971). Jewish Academics in the United States: Their Achievements, Culture and Politics. *The American Jewish Yearbook*, 72, 89–112.

Lipset, S. M., & Raab, E. (1970). *The Politics of Unreason: Right-Wing Extremism in America, 1790–1970*. Harper & Row.

—— (1995). *Jews and the New American Scene*. Harvard University Press.

Liskofsky, S. (1966). United States Immigration Policy. *American Jewish Yearbook*, 67, 164–175. https://www.jstor.org/stable/23604995.

Liss, J. E. (1998). Diasporic Identities: The Science and Politics of Race in the Work of Franz Boas and W. E. B. Du Bois, 1894–1919. *Cultural Anthropology*, 13(2), 127–166.

List of assets owned by the Walt Disney Company. (2024, February 16). In *Wikipedia*. https://tinyurl.com/vdkhbse6.

List of assets owned by Warner Bros. Discovery. (2024, February 19). In *Wikipedia*. https://tinyurl.com/4srcdu4f.

Liukkonen, P. (2008). Ben Hecht (1893–1964). Kirjasto. https://archive.ph/dFXJz.

Lobe, J. (2002a, September 12). The Anniversary of a Neo-Imperial Moment. AlterNet.org. https://tinyurl.com/yvb2wtjk.

—— (2002b, December 19). Bush's Trusty New Mideast Point Man. *Asia Times*. https://tinyurl.com/2emzscm7.

—— (2003a, March 7). All in the Family. *Inter Press Service News Agency*. https://tinyurl.com/772jw77f.

—— (2003b, August 7). Pentagon Office Home to Neo-Con Network. *Antiwar.com*. https://www.antiwar.com/ips/lobe080703.html.

—— (2003c, August 12). What Is a Neo-Conservative Anyway? *Inter Press Service News Agency*. https://tinyurl.com/2d32zva6.

Locke, R. (2002, May 31). Leo Strauss, Conservative Mastermind. *Front Page Magazine*. https://tinyurl.com/3w9cdabs.

Loewenberg, P. (1979). Walther Rathenau and the Tensions of Wilhelmine Society. In D. Bronsen (Ed.), *Jews and Germans from 1860 to 1933: The Problematic Symbiosis*. Carl Winter Universitätsverlag.

Lowenstein, S. M. (1983). Jewish Residential Concentration in Post-Emancipation Germany. *Leo Baeck Institute Yearbook*, 28, 471–495.

—— (1992). *The Mechanics of Change: Essays in the Social History of German Jewry*. Scholars Press.

Lowenthal, L. (1947, August). Heine's Religion: The Messianic Ideals of the Poet. *Commentary*. https://tinyurl.com/bde3pd9e.

Lowenthal, L., & Guterman, N. (1970). *Prophets of Deceit: A Study of the Techniques of an American Agitator* (2nd ed.). Pacific Books. (First edition published in 1949 as Publication No. I of the American Jewish Committee Social Studies Series by Harper & Brothers).

Lu, C. (2025, February 18). The Speech That Stunned Europe. *Foreign Policy.* https://tinyurl.com/586bmjvt.

Lynn, R. (1987). The Intelligence of the Mongoloids: A Psychometric, Evolutionary and Neurological Theory. *Personality and Individual Differences*, 8(6), 813–844. https://doi.org/10.1016/0191-8869(87)90135-8.

—— (1996). *Dysgenics: Genetic Deterioration in Modern Populations.* Praeger.

—— (2011). *The Chosen People: A Study of Jewish Intelligence and Achievement.* Washington Summit Publishers.

Lyons, P. (1982). *Philadelphia Communists, 1936–1956.* Temple University Press.

Lyotard, J. F. (1984). *The Post-Modern Condition: A Report on Knowledge* (G. Bennington, & B. Mussumi, Trans.). University of Minnesota Press.

Maccoby, E., & Martin, J. (1983). Socialization in the Context of the Family. In E. M. Hetherington (Ed.), *Handbook of Child Psychology* (Vol. 4: Socialization, Personality, and Social Development). Wiley.

MacDonald, K. B. (n.d.). *Campaign Against Me by the Southern Poverty Law Center.* Kevin MacDonald. Retrieved January 27, 2025, from http://www.kevinmacdonald.net/Beirich.htm.

—— (1983). Production, Social Controls and Ideology: Toward a Sociobiology of the Phenotype. *Journal of Social and Biological Structures*, 6(4), 297–317. https://psycnet.apa.org/doi/10.1016/S0140-1750(83)90101-X.

—— (1986). Civilization and Its Discontents Revisited: Freud as an Evolutionary Biologist. *Journal of Social and Biological Structures*, 9(4), 307–318. https://doi.org/10.1016/S0140-1750(86)90177-6.

—— (1988a). *Social and Personality Development: An Evolutionary Synthesis.* Plenum.

—— (Ed.). (1988b). *Sociobiological Perspectives on Human Development.* Springer-Verlag.

—— (1989). The Plasticity of Human Social Organization and Behavior: Contextual Variables and Proximal Mechanisms. *Ethology and Sociobiology*, 10(1–3), 171–194. https://doi.org/10.1016/0162-3095(89)90018-6.

—— (1990). Mechanisms of Sexual Egalitarianism in Western Europe. *Ethology and Sociobiology*, 11(3), 195–238. http://dx.doi.org/10.1016/0162-3095(90)90010-4.

—— (1991). A Perspective on Darwinian Psychology: Domain-general Mechanisms, Plasticity, and Individual Differences. *Ethology and Sociobiology*, 12(6), 449–480. https://doi.org/10.1016/0162-3095(91)90025-L.

—— (1992). Warmth as a Developmental Construct: An Evolutionary Analysis. *Child Development*, 63(4), 753–773. https://doi.org/10.2307/1131231.

—— (1995a). The Establishment and Maintenance of Socially Imposed Monogamy in Western Europe. *Politics and Life Sciences*, 14, 3–23. http://dx.doi.org/10.1017/S0730938400011679.

—— (1995b). Evolution, the Five Factor Model, and Levels of Personality. *Journal of Personality*, 63(3), 525–567. https://doi.org/10.1111/j.1467-6494.1995.tb00505.x.

—— (1995c). Focusing on the Group: Further Issues Related to Western Monogamy. *Politics and Life Sciences*, 14(1), 38–46. https://doi.org/10.1017/S0730938400011758.

—— (1997a). The Coherence of Individual Development: An Evolutionary Perspective on Children's Internalization of Parental Values. In J. Grusec, & L. Kuczynski (Eds.), *Parenting and Children's Internalization of Values: A Handbook of Contemporary Theory.* Wiley.

—— (1997b). Life History Theory and Human Reproductive Behavior: Environmental/Contextual Influences and Heritable Variation. *Human Nature*, 8, 327–359. https://doi.org/10.1007/BF02913038.

—— (1998). Evolution, Culture, and the Five-Factor Model. *Journal of Cross-Cultural Psychology*, 29(1), 119–149. https://doi.org/10.1177/0022022198291007.

—— (2001). An Integrative Perspective on Ethnicity. *Politics and the Life Sciences*, 20(1), 67–80. https://doi.org/10.1017/S0730938400005189.

—— (2002a). Henry Ford and the Jewish Question. *The Occidental Quarterly*, 2(4), 53–77. https://www.toqonline.com/archives/v2n4/TOQv2n4MacDonald.pdf.

—— (2002b). *A People That Shall Dwell Alone: Judaism As a Group Evolutionary Strategy.* Bloomington, IN: Writers Club Press, iUniverse. (Original work published 1994).

—— (2002c) What Makes Western Culture Unique? *The Occidental Quarterly*, 2(2), 9–38. https://www.toqonline.com/archives/v2n2/TOQv2n2MacDonald.pdf.

—— (2003a). Background Traits for Jewish Activism. *The Occidental Quarterly*, 3(2), 5–37. https://www.toqonline.com/archives/v3n2/TOQv3n2MacDonald.pdf.

—— (2003b). Understanding Jewish Influence II: Zionism and the Internal Dynamics of Judaism. *The Occidental Quarterly*, 3(3), 15–44. https://www.toqonline.com/archives/v3n3/TOQv3n3MacDonald.pdf.

—— (2004a). *Separation and Its Discontents: Toward an Evolutionary Theory of Anti-Semitism.* 1st Books Library. (Original work published 1998).

—— (2004b). Understanding Jewish Influence III: Neoconservatism as a Jewish Movement. *The Occidental Quarterly*, 4(2): 7–74. https://www.toqonline.com/archives/v4n2/TOQv4n2MacDonald.pdf.

—— (2005a). Personality, Development, and Evolution. In R. Burgess & K. MacDonald (Eds.), *Evolutionary Perspectives on Human Development* (2nd ed.) (pp. 207–242). Sage Publications.

—— (2005b). Stalin's Willing Executioners: Jews as a Hostile Elite in the USSR. Review of Yuri Slezkine's The Jewish Century. *The Occidental Quarterly*, 5(3), 65–100. https://www.toqonline.com/archives/v5n3/53-km-slezkine.pdf.

—— (2006). Jews, Blacks, and Race. In S. Francis (Ed.), *Race and the American Prospect*. The Occidental Press.

—— (2007a, January 31). Mid-East Policy—Immigration Policy: Is the Other Boot About to Drop? VDARE. http://www.vdare.com/macdonald/070131_mideast.htm.

—— (2007b). The Israel Lobby: A Case Study of Jewish Influence. *The Occidental Quarterly*, 7(3), 33–58. https://www.toqonline.com/archives/v7n3/738MacDonald.pdf.

—— (2008a). Effortful Control, Explicit Processing and the Regulation of Human Evolved Predispositions. *Psychological Review*, 115(4), 1012–1031. https://doi.org/10.1037/a0013327.

—— (2008b, August 16). The Neocons Versus Russia. *The Occidental Observer*. https://www.theoccidentalobserver.net/2008/08/16/the-neocons-versus-russia/.

—— (2008c, November 21). Stalinism Lives—in the CSULB Women's Studies Department. *The Occidental Observer*. https://tinyurl.com/3pwcbvvx.

—— (2009a, December 7). The ADL: Managing White Rage. *The Occidental Observer*. https://www.theoccidentalobserver.net/2009/12/07/the-adl-managing-white-rage/.

—— (2009b). Evolution, Psychology, and a Conflict Theory of Culture. *Evolutionary Psychology*, 7(2), 208–233. http://dx.doi.org/10.1177/147470490900700206.

—— (2009c, May 11). The Hate Crimes Prevention Bill: Why Do Jewish Organizations Support It? VDARE. https://archive.ph/qYxgL.

—— (2009d, April 25). Jane Harman, Haim Saban, and AIPAC: The Disloyalty Issue in Multicultural America. *The Occidental Observer*.
https://www.theoccidentalobserver.net/2009/04/25/macdonald-harman/.

—— (2009e, March 18). Memories of Madison—My Life on the New Left. VDARE.
https://tinyurl.com/5xdxn6ma.

—— (2010a, April). Evolution and a Dual Processing Theory of Culture: Applications to Moral Idealism and Political Philosophy. *Politics and Culture*, 1.
http://www.kevinmacdonald.net/MoralDevelopment1.pdf.

—— (2010b). Why Are Professors Liberals? *The Occidental Quarterly*, 10(2), 57–84.
http://www.kevinmacdonald.net/LiberalProfessors-2020.pdf.

—— (2012a, July 31). The Role of Jewish Converts to Catholicism in Changing Traditional Catholic Teachings on Jews. *The Occidental Observer*. https://tinyurl.com/2w7mdw8v.

—— (2012b). Temperament and Evolution. In M. Zentner & R. L. Shiner (Eds.), *Handbook of Temperament* (pp. 273–296). Guilford Press.

—— (2014, April 6). Is Immigration Really a "Jewish Value"? *The Occidental Observer*.
https://www.theoccidentalobserver.net/2014/04/06/is-immigration-really-a-jewish-value/.

—— (2015). Eric Kaufmann's *The Rise and Fall of Anglo-America*. *The Occidental Quarterly*, 15(4), 3–42.

—— (2016a, March 3). Bill Kristol prefers Hillary to Trump: What happened to all those conservative principles? *The Occidental Observer*. https://tinyurl.com/4kx6va6t.

—— (2016b, March 29). Jewish Fear and Loathing of Donald Trump, #3: Hitler Comparisons Rampant—But Also, Weirdly, Signs of Second Thoughts. VDARE.
https://archive.ph/8v2IT.

—— (2019a). *Individualism and the Western Liberal Tradition: Evolutionary Origins, History, and Prospects for the Future*. CreateSpace.

—— (2019b). Joe McCarthy and the Jews. *The Occidental Quarterly*, 19(1), 97–105.

—— (2019c) Review of Thomas Wheatland's *The Frankfurt School in Exile*. *The Occidental Quarterly*, 19(2), 97–123.

—— (2020). Foreword to *Battle Lines: Essays on Western Culture, Jewish Influence, and Anti-Semitism* by Brenton Sanderson. *The Occidental Quarterly*, 20(4), 103–108.

—— (2022a). Failure of the "Default Hypothesis" of Jewish Influence: The Post-World War II Rise of a Substantially Jewish Elite in the United States and Its Influence on Immigration Policy. *The Occidental Quarterly*, 22(3): 3–53.
http://www.kevinmacdonald.net/DefaultHypothesis.pdf.

—— (2022b). The "Default Hypothesis" Fails to Explain Jewish Influence. *Philosophia*, 51, 403.
https://doi.org/10.1007/s11406-021-00439-y.

—— (2023a, October 8). The Gaza War and Jewish Identity. *The Occidental Observer*.
https://tinyurl.com/bdfp99m2.

—— (2023b). Hatred of Anglos as Central to Multiculturalism in Australia: Review of *Anglophobia: The Unrecognized Hatred*. *The Occidental Quarterly*, 23(4), 115–125.

—— (2023c). Historical Writing on Judaism and Anti-Semitism; Review of Classic Essays on the Jewish Question, 1850-1945, edited by Thomas Dalton. *The Occidental Quarterly*, 23(2), 85–112.

—— (2023d, October 3). Why Are Jews So Influential? *The Occidental Observer*.
https://www.theoccidentalobserver.net/2023/10/31/why-are-jews-so-influential/.

—— (2023e, November 7). Will the Gaza War Threaten Jewish Power in the U.S. and Their Status as Occupying the Moral High Ground? *The Occidental Observer*.
https://tinyurl.com/42ntfz3s.

—— (2024a, September 7). The Carleson-Cooper Podcast: A Major Step Forward. *The Occidental Observer*. https://tinyurl.com/25byvbxc.

—— (2024b, November 20). Trump 2.0: Harbinger of a New Elite? *The Occidental Observer*. https://tinyurl.com/yvt2vsv6.

—— (2025, February 6). Tucker Interviews Curt Mills: Pushing the Envelope on Mainstream Conservative Foreign Policy. *The Occidental Observer*. https://tinyurl.com/nk4e97e4.

MacDonald, K., & Gottfried, P. (2000, September). On The Culture of Critique. *Chronicles*. https://chroniclesmagazine.org/polemics-exchanges/on-the-culture-of-critique/.

MacDonald, K., Patch, E. A., & Figueredo, A. J. (2016). Love, Trust, and Evolution: Nurturance/Love and Trust as Two Independent Attachment Systems Underlying Intimate Relationships. *Psychology*, 7, 238–253. http://dx.doi.org/10.4236/psych.2016.72026.

Macfarlane, A. (1986). *Marriage and Love in England: Modes of Reproduction 1300–1840*. Basil Blackwell.

Macmillan, M. (1991). *Freud Evaluated: The Completed Arc*. Elsevier North Holland.

Magnet, M. (1993). *The Dream and the Nightmare: The Sixties' Legacy to the Underclass*. William Morrow.

Mahler, J. (1996, February 23). A Scientist Puts "Paleo" Back Into Liberalism. *The Forward*.

Mahler, R. (1985). *Hasidism and the Jewish Enlightenment: Their Confrontation in Galicia and Poland in the First Half of the Nineteenth Century*. Jewish Publication Society of America.

Maier, J. B. (1984). Contribution to a Critique of Critical Theory. In J. Marcus, & Z. Tarr (Eds.), *Foundations of the Frankfurt School of Social Research*. Transaction Books.

Mann, J. (2004). *Rise of the Vulcans*. Viking.

Mannoni, O. (1971). *Freud* (R. Belice, Trans.). Pantheon Books.

Marcia, J. E. (1966). Development and Validation of Ego-Identity Status. *Journal of Personality and Social Psychology*, 3(5), 551–558. https://doi.org/10.1037/h0023281.

—— (1967). Ego-Identity Status: Relationship to Change in Self-Esteem, "General Maladjustment," and Authoritarianism. *Journal of Personality*, 35(1), 119–133. https://doi.org/10.1111/j.1467-6494.1967.tb01419.x.

—— (1980). Identity in Adolescence. In J. Adelson (Ed.), *Handbook of Adolescent Psychology*. Wiley.

Marcia, J. E., & Friedman, M. L. (1970). Ego Identity in College Women. *Journal of Personality*, 38(2), 249–263. https://doi.org/10.1111/j.1467-6494.1970.tb00007.x.

Marcus. J. (1983). *Social and Political History of the Jews in Poland, 1919–1939*. Moulton Publishers.

Marcus, J., & Tarr, Z. (1986). The Judaic Elements in the Teachings of the Frankfurt School. *The Leo Baeck Institute Year Book*, 21, 339–353.

Marcus, J. R. (1993). *United States Jewry 1776–1985* (Vol. 4). Wayne State University Press.

Marcuse, H. (1964). *One-Dimensional Man: Studies in the Ideology of Advanced Industrial Society*. Beacon Press.

—— (1974). *Eros and Civilization: A Philosophical Inquiry into Freud*. Beacon Press. (Original work published 1955).

Margalit, A. (1993, November 4). Prophets With Honor. *The New York Review of Books*. https://www.nybooks.com/articles/1993/11/04/prophets-with-honor/.

Marshall, R. (2004, March 24). Sharon Offers the Palestinians a Prison Camp and Calls It Peace. *Washington Report on Middle Eastern Affairs*. https://tinyurl.com/34xs9nkm.

Martins, H. (2009, October 23). Choosing the Chosen People. *The Daily Princetonian*. https://tinyurl.com/56cptvvx.

Marx, K. (1975). On the Jewish Question. In *Karl Marx and Frederick Engels: Collected Works* (Vol. 3). International Publishers. (Original work published 1843).

Maslow, W. (1950, March 27). Is American Jewry Secure? *Congress Weekly*, 17(13), 6–9.

Massing, M. (1987, June 22). Trotsky's Orphans. *The New Republic*, 18–21.

—— (2002, March 11). Deal Breakers. *The American Prospect*. https://tinyurl.com/4277y8y4.

Massing, P. W. (1949). *Rehearsal for Destruction: A Study of Political Anti-Semitism in Imperial Germany*, Publication No. II of The American Jewish Committee Social Studies Series. Harper & Brothers.

Masson, J. M. (1984). *The Assault on Truth: Freud's Suppression of the Seduction Theory*. Farrar, Straus, & Giroux.

—— (1990). *Final Analysis: The Making and Unmaking of a Psychoanalyst*. Addison-Wesley.

Matteson, D. R. (1974). *Alienation Versus Exploration and Commitment: Personality and Family Corollaries of Adolescent Identity Statuses*. Report from the Project for Youth Research, Royal Danish School of Educational Studies, Copenhagen.

Mayer, A. (1988). *Why Did the Heavens Not Darken? The "Final Solution" in History*. Pantheon Books.

Mayer, E. (1979). *From Suburb to Shtetl: The Jews of Boro Park*. Temple University Press.

Maynard Smith, J. (1995, November 30). Genes, Memes, & Minds. *The New York Review of Books*. https://www.nybooks.com/articles/1995/11/30/genes-memes-minds/.

McConnell, S. (1988a, January). Leaving the Party: The Politics of Sterling Hayden. *The New Criterion*. https://tinyurl.com/mrxa4kvp.

—— (1988b, May 9). The New Battle Over Immigration. *Fortune*. https://fortune.com/article/the-new-battle-over-immigration-fortune-1988/.

McCormack, D. (1992, November). Immigration and Multiculturalism. Paper Presented at the Second Bureau of Immigration Research Outlook Conference, Sydney, Australia.

—— (1994). Immigration and Multiculturalism. In J. Bennett (Ed.), *Censorship Immigration and Multiculturalism*. Australian Civil Liberties Union.

McGrath, W. J. (1974). Freud as Hannibal: The Politics of the Brother Band. *Central European History*, 7, 31–57.

—— (1991, December 5). How Jewish Was Freud? *The New York Review of Books*. https://www.nybooks.com/articles/1991/12/05/how-jewish-was-freud/.

McGreal, C. (2022, July 19). Pro-Israel Hardliners Spend Millions to Transform Democratic Primaries. *The Guardian*. https://tinyurl.com/4drcut4v.

McLanahan, S., & Booth, K. (1989). Mother-Only Families: Problems, Prospects, and Politics. *Journal of Marriage and the Family*, 51(3), 557–580. https://doi.org/10.2307/352157.

Mead, M. (1928). *Coming of Age in Samoa: A Psychological Study of Primitive Youth for Western Civilization*. W. Morrow.

Mearsheimer, J. J. (Guest). (2025a, July 23). John Mearsheimer: Israel Acts Like NAZIS. [Video]. In *Katie Halper*. YouTube. https://www.youtube.com/watch?v=47lRuU7pnoo.

—— (Guest). (2025b, July 10). Prof. John Mearsheimer : Ukraine/Gaza/Iran: Is Peace Possible? [Video]. In *Judge Napolitano – Judging Freedom*. YouTube. https://www.youtube.com/watch?v=RFFzClxBmb8&t.

Mearsheimer, J. J., & Walt, S. M. (2007). *The Israel Lobby and U.S. Foreign Policy*. Farrar, Straus & Giroux.

Medding, P. Y. (1977). Towards a General Theory of Jewish Political Interests and Behavior. *Jewish Journal of Sociology*, 19, 115–144.

Medved, M. (1992). *Hollywood vs. America: Popular Culture and the War on Traditional Values*. Harper Collins.

—— (1996, August 31). Is Hollywood Too Jewish? *Moment*, 21(4), 36–42.

Mehler, B. (1984a, August 22). Eugenics: Racist Ideology Makes. *Guardian Weekly News*.

—— (1984b, Jan./Feb.). The New Eugenics: Academic Racism in the U.S.A. Today. *Israel Horizons*, 25–27.

Memmi, A. (1966). *The Liberation of the Jew* (J. Hyun, Trans.). The Viking Press.

Mendes, P. (2014). *Jews and the Left*. Palgrave MacMillan.

Messer, E. (1986). Franz Boas and Kaufmann Kohler: Anthropology and Reform Judaism. *Jewish Social Studies*, 48(2), 127–140.

Mészáros, J. (2014). *Ferenczi and Beyond: Exile of the Budapest School and Solidarity in the Psychoanalytic Movement During the Nazi Years*. Karnac Books.

Meyer, M. A. (1989, November 1). Anti-Semitism and Jewish Identity. *Commentary*. https://tinyurl.com/36pc2wva.

Michael, J. S. (1988). A New Look at Morton's Craniological Research. *Current Anthropology*, 29(2), 349–354. https://www.jstor.org/stable/2743412.

Michaels, R. (1988). The Future of Psychoanalysis. *Psychoanalytic Quarterly*, 57(2), 167–185. https://pubmed.ncbi.nlm.nih.gov/3375394/.

Michels, R. (1915). *Political Parties: A Sociological Study of the Oligarchical Tendencies of Modern Democracy* (E. & C. Paul, Trans.). Hearst's International Library. (Original work published 1911).

Miele, F. (1998). The Ionian Instauration. An Interview with E. O. Wilson on His Latest Controversial Book: *Consilience: The Unity of Knowledge*. *Skeptic*, 6(1), 76–85.

—— (2002). *Intelligence, Race, and Genetics: Conversations with Arthur Jensen*. Westview.

Migiro, G. (2020, February 13). Fertility Rates In The United States By Ethnicity. *World Atlas*. https://tinyurl.com/ycyfw7zt.

Milbank, D. (2002, July 2). A Sound Bite So Good, The President Wishes He Said It. *The Washington Post*. https://tinyurl.com/mryj66th.

Miller, N., Brewer, M., & Edwards, K. (1985). Cooperative Interaction in Desegregated Settings: A Laboratory Analogue. *Journal of Social Issues*, 41(3), 63–79. https://doi.org/10.1111/j.1540-4560.1985.tb01129.x.

Milstein, M. H. (1991, October 27). Strategic Ties or Tentacles? Institute for National Security Affairs. *Washington Report on Middle East Affairs*. https://tinyurl.com/52ft59ys.

Mintz, J. R. (1992). *Hasidic People: A Place in the New World*. Harvard University Press.

Miroff, N. (2021, February 14). The Agency Founded Because of 9/11 Is Shifting to Face the Threat of Domestic Terrorism. *The Washington Post*. https://tinyurl.com/ynxj33nc.

Mishkinsky, M. (1968). The Jewish Labor Movement and European Socialism. *Cahiers d'Histoire Mondiale*, 11, 284–296.

Mitchell, D. S. (2007). *Architect of Justice: Felix S. Cohen and the Founding of American Legal Pluralism*. Cornell University Press.

Moglia, J. (2018, December 9). Quo Vadis Vatican? Jewish Involvement in the Radical Changes of the Second Vatican Council. *The Occidental Observer*. https://tinyurl.com/3e2wf6dh.

Money, J. (1980). *Love, and Love Sickness: The Science of Sex, Gender Differences, and Pair Bonding*. Johns Hopkins University Press.

Montgomery, B. (2023, November 16). Elon Musk Agrees with Tweet Accusing Jewish People of "Hatred against Whites." *The Guardian*. https://tinyurl.com/n5nsykju.

Moore, J. C. (2004, May 27). Not Fit to Print. *Salon*. https://www.salon.com/2004/05/27/times_10/.

Moore, T. (2021, April 9). Anti-Defamation League Calls for Tucker Carlson to Be Fired. *The Hill*. https://tinyurl.com/47evrnws.

Morris, S. L. (2003, June 27–July 3). Shipwrecked: Swimming with Sharks in a Sea of Arts Funding. *LA Weekly*. https://tinyurl.com/2ar5nwxv.

Morrell, J., & Thackray, A. (1981). *Gentleman of Science*. Oxford University Press.

Moscovici, S. (1976). *Social Influence and Social Change*. Academic Press.

Mosse, G. L. (1970). *Germans and Jews: The Right, the Left, and the Search for a "Third Force" in Pre-Nazi Germany*. Howard Fertig.

—— (1985). Jewish Emancipation: Between *Bildung* and Respectability. In J. Reinharz, & W. Schatzberg (Eds.), *The Jewish Response to German Culture: From the Enlightenment to the Second World War*. University Press of New England for Clark University.

—— (1987). *Masses and Man: Nationalist and Fascist Origins of Reality*. Free Press.

Mosse, W. E. (1987). *Jews in the German Economy: The German-Jewish Economic Élite 1820–1935*. Clarendon Press.

—— (1989). *The German-Jewish Economic Élite 1820–1935: A Socio-cultural Profile*. Clarendon Press.

Mullen, B. (1991). Group Composition, Salience, and Cognitive Representations: The Phenomenology of Being in a Group. *Journal of Experimental Psychology, 27*(4), 297–323. https://doi.org/10.1016/0022-1031(91)90028-5.

Mullen, B., & Hu, L. (1989). Perceptions of In-Group and Out-Group Variability: A Meta-Analytic Integration. *Basic and Applied Social Psychology, 10*(3), 233–252. https://doi.org/10.1207/s15324834basp1003_3.

Muller, J. Z. (2010). *Capitalism and the Jews*. Princeton University Press.

Mundill, R. R. (1998). *England's Jewish Solution: Experiment and Expulsion, 1262–1290*. Cambridge University Press.

Muravchik, J. (2002). *Heaven on Earth: The Rise and Fall of Socialism*. Encounter Books.

—— (2003, September). The Neoconservative Cabal. *Commentary*. https://tinyurl.com/5sv7f4cp.

Muuss, R. E. H. (1988). *Theories of Adolescence* (5th ed.). Random House.

Myers, G. (1990). *Writing Biology: Texts in the Social Construction of Scientific Knowledge*. University of Wisconsin Press.

Nadell, P. S. (1984). From Shtetl to Border: Eastern European Jewish Emigrants and the "Agents" System, 1869–1914. In J. R. Marcus & A. J. Peck. Lanham (Eds.), *Studies in the American Jewish Experience II*. University Press of America.

Nagai, A. K., Lerner, R., & Rothman, S. (1994). *Giving for Social Change: Foundations, Public Policy, and the American Political Agenda*. Praeger.

Navasky, V. (1980). *Naming Names*. Viking.

Netanyahu, B. (1966). *The Marranos of Spain*. American Academy for Jewish Research.

—— (1995). *The Origins of the Inquisition in 15th-Century Spain*. Random House.

Neuringer, S. M. (1980). *American Jewry and United States Immigration Policy, 1881–1953*. Adorno Press. (Original work published 1971).

Neusner, J. (1993). *Conservative, American, and Jewish: I Wouldn't Have It Any Other Way*. Huntingdon House Publishers.

Ngai, M. M. (2013). Oscar Handlin and Immigration Policy Reform in the 1950s and 1960s. *Journal of American Ethnic History, 32*(3), 62–67. https://doi.org/10.5406/jamerethnhist.32.3.0062.

Niño, J. (2025, August 2). Protestant Conversos Are Important in the Evangelical Protestant Movement and Remain Strongly Pro-Israel. *The Occidental Observer*. https://tinyurl.com/34frk9mc.

Nolte, E. (1965). *Three Faces of Fascism* (L. Vennowitz, Trans.). Holt, Rinehart and Winston.

Noonan, J. T., Jr. (1967). *Contraception: A History of Its Treatment by the Theologians and Canonists*. New American Library.

—— (1973). Marriage in the Middle Ages: 1. Power to Choose. *Viator, 4*, 419–434. https://doi.org/10.1484/J.VIATOR.2.301658.

North, G. (2003, June 10). An Introduction to Neoconservatism. LewRockwell.com. www.lewrockwell.com/north/north180.html.

Norris, C. (1993). *The Truth about Postmodernism*. Blackwell.

Norton, A. J., & Miller, L. F. (1992). *Marriage, Divorce, and Remarriage in the 1990's.* U.S. Bureau of the Census Current Population Reports Special Studies P23–180.

Novick, P. (1988). *That Noble Dream: The "Objectivity Question" and the American Historical Profession.* Cambridge University Press.

—— (1999). *The Holocaust in American Life.* Houghton Mifflin.

Nugent, W. T. K. (1963). *The Tolerant Populists: Kansas Populism and Nativism.* University of Chicago Press.

NYT Co. (n.d.). New York Times Statement About 1932 Pulitzer Prize Awarded to Walter Duranty. The New York Times Company. Retrieved February 10, 2025, from https://tinyurl.com/39vh6tpr.

NYT Editors. (2004, May 26). The Times and Iraq. *The New York Times.* https://tinyurl.com/3auytdw3.

Okrent, D. (2004, May 30). Weapons of Mass Destruction? Or Mass Distraction? *The New York Times.* https://tinyurl.com/radcfre5.

—— (2019). *The Guarded Gate: Bigotry, Eugenics and the Law That Kept Two Generations of Jews, Italians, and Other European Immigrants Out of America.* Scribner.

Orans, M. (1996). *Not Even Wrong: Margaret Mead, Derek Freeman, and the Samoans.* Chandler and Sharp Publishers.

Oren, I. (2003). *Our Enemies and US: America's Rivalries and the Making of Political Science.* Cornell University Press.

Orgel, S. (1990). The Future of Psychoanalysis. *Psychoanalytic Quarterly,* 59(1), 1–20.

Osher, Y., Yaroslavsky, Y., el-Rom, R., & Belmaker, R. H. (2000). Predominant Polarity of Bipolar Patients in Israel. *Biological Psychiatry,* 1(4), 187–189. https://doi.org/10.3109/15622970009150590.

Ostow, M. (1995). *Myth and Madness: The Psychodynamics of Anti-Semitism.* Transaction Press.

Ostrovsky, V., & Hoy, C. (1990). *By Way of Deception.* St. Martin's Press.

O'Sullivan, J. (2007, July 30). Getting Immigration Right: How Conservatives Blocked the Open-Borders Establishment. *The American Conservative.* https://www.theamericanconservative.com/getting-immigration-right/.

Ozick, C. (2001, October 28). From Kafka to Babel. *Los Angeles Times Book Review.* https://www.latimes.com/archives/la-xpm-2001-oct-28-bk-62398-story.html.

Panitz, E. (1969). In Defense of the Jewish Immigrant (1891–1924). In A. J. Karp (Ed.), *The Jewish Experience in America* (Vol. 5: At Home in America). KTAV Publishing House.

Paramount Global. (2024, February 18). In *Wikipedia.* https://en.wikipedia.org/w/index.php?title=Paramount_Global&oldid=1208681007.

Patai, R., & Patai, J. (1989). *The Myth of the Jewish Race* (Rev. ed.). Wayne State University Press. (Original work published 1975).

Paul, R. (2003, October 11). National Endowment for Democracy: Paying to Make Enemies for America. *Antiwar.com.* www.antiwar.com/paul/paul79.html.

Pearl, Jonathon, & Pearl, Judith (1999). *The Chosen Image: Television's Portrayal of Jewish Themes and Characters.* McFarland & Co.

Pegrum, M. A. (2000). *Challenging Modernity: Dada between Modern and Postmodern.* Berghahn Books.

Peretz, M. (1997, September 17). The God That Did Not Fail. *The New Republic.* https://newrepublic.com/article/61283/the-god-did-not-fail.

Pérez, J. A., & Mugny, G. (1990). Minority Influence, Manifest Discrimination and Latent Influence. In D. Abrams & M. A. Hogg (Eds.), *Social Identity Theory: Constructive and Critical Advances.* Springer-Verlag.

Perman, S., Mehta S., & Masunaga, S. (2024, July 24). Hollywood power brokers pushed for Biden to step down. Now they're stepping up for Harris. *Los Angeles Times*. https://tinyurl.com/vbeup2v2.

Petersen, W. (1955, July). The "Scientific" Basis of Our Immigration Policy. *Commentary*, 20, 77–86.

Petras, J. (2017, April 17). Judeo-Centrism: Myths and Mania. *The James Petras Website*. https://petras.lahaine.org/judeo-centrism-myths-and-mania/.

Pettigrew, T. F. (1958). Personality and Sociocultural Factors in Intergroup Attitudes: A Cross-National Comparison. *Journal of Conflict Resolution*, 2(1), 29–42.

Pew Research Center. (2013, October 1). A Portrait of Jewish Americans [Report]. https://tinyurl.com/bderc2nf.

—— (2021, May 11). Jewish Americans in 2020. https://www.pewresearch.org/religion/2021/05/11/jewish-americans-in-2020/.

Philadelphia Anti-Defamation Council, The & The American Jewish Committee. (1941). *To Bigotry No Sanction: A Documented Analysis of Anti-Semitic Propaganda*. The Philadelphia Anti-Defamation Council.

Philips, B. A. (2013). New Demographic Perspectives on Studying Intermarriage in the United States. *Contemporary Jewry*, 33(1-2), 103–119. http://dx.doi.org/10.1007/s12397-013-9103-9.

Phillips, R. (1988). *Putting Asunder: A History of Divorce in Western Society*. Cambridge University Press.

Phillips, W. (1983). *A Partisan View: Five Decades of the Literary Life*. Stein and Day.

Phillips, W., & Rahv, P. (1946). The "Liberal" Fifth Column: A Discussion. *Partisan Review*, 13(5), 605–621.

Piccone, P. (1993). Introduction. In A. Arato, & E. Gebhardt (Eds.), *The Essential Frankfurt School Reader*. Continuum.

Pilkington, E. (2023, June 6). Harvard Affirmative Action Challenge Partly Based on Holocaust Denier's Work. *The Guardian*. https://tinyurl.com/364ubrfh.

Pincus, W., & D. Priest. (2003, June 4). Some Iraq Analysts Felt Pressure From Cheney Visits. *The Washington Post*. https://tinyurl.com/yc24nxue.

Pinker, S. (1997, October 9). Evolutionary Psychology: An Exchange. *The New York Review of Books*. https://tinyurl.com/82jv3aum.

Pinkus, B. (1988). *The Jews of the Soviet Union: A History of a National Minority*. Cambridge University Press.

Pipes, D. (2001, November 1). The Danger Within: Militant Islam in America. *Commentary*. https://tinyurl.com/bddc5b8j.

—— (2002). *Militant Islam Reaches America*. W. W. Norton.

Pipes, R. (1990). *The Russian Revolution*. Knopf.

—— (1993). *Russia Under the Bolshevik Regime*. Knopf.

Plagens, P. (1998, April 12). Nothing If Not Critical. *Los Angeles Times Book Review*, 12.

Platt, D. (1978). The Hollywood Witchhunt of 1947. In J. N. Porter (Ed.), *The Sociology of American Jews: A Critical Anthology*. University Press of America. (Original work published December 1977 in *Jewish Currents*).

Plitnick, M. (2023, September 9). How Democrats Learned to Defend Israel's Ethnocracy. *Mondoweiss*. https://tinyurl.com/y5s5k4pu.

PNAC. (1998, January 26). Letter to President Clinton. Project for the New American Century. https://tinyurl.com/ye86a6wj.

—— (1998b, May 29). Letter to Speaker of the House Newt Gingrich and Senate Majority Leader Trent Lott. Project for the New American Century. https://tinyurl.com/bdsa6uxt.

—— (2002, April 3). Letter to President George W. Bush. Project for a New American Century. https://tinyurl.com/3pdrj4s3.

Podhoretz, N. (1961, April). Jewishness & the Younger Intellectuals: Introduction. *Commentary*. https://tinyurl.com/52f6zwzz.

—— (1967). *Making It*. Random House.

—— (1978). The Rise and Fall of the American Jewish Novelist. In G. Rosen (Ed.), *Jewish Life in America*. Institute of Human Relations Press of the American Jewish Committee.

—— (1979). *Breaking Ranks: A Political Memoir*. Harper & Row.

—— (1985, February). The Terrible Question of Aleksandr Solzhenitsyn. *Commentary*. https://tinyurl.com/46ftkw4b.

—— (1986, November). The Hate That Dare Not Speak Its Name. *Commentary*. https://tinyurl.com/msurpjyn.

—— (1995, August). In the Matter of Pat Robertson. *Commentary*. https://tinyurl.com/an7hj5bz.

—— (2009). *Why Are Jews Liberals?* Doubleday.

Poff, J. (2024, September 25). How Universities Are Getting Around the Supreme Court's Affirmative Action Ruling. *Washington Examiner*. https://tinyurl.com/wzmmwyvx.

Pogrebin, L. C. (1991). *Deborah, Golda, and Me*. Crown Books.

Pollack, L. (1983). *Forgotten Children*. Cambridge University Press.

Poncins, Vicomte Léon de (1999), *Judaism and the Vatican: An Attempt at Spiritual Subversion*. (T. Tindal-Robertson, Trans.). Christian Book Club of America. (Original work published 1967).

Poole, R. (2000). Deconstruction. In A. Bullock, & P. Trombley (Eds.), *The New Fontana Dictionary of Modern Thought*. HarperCollins.

Popper, K. R. (1963). *Conjectures and Refutations*. Basic Books.

—— (1984). Reason or Revolution? In J. Marcus, & Z. Tarr (Eds.), *Foundations of the Frankfurt School of Social Research*. Transaction Books.

Porat, D. (Ed.). (1995). *Anti-Semitism Worldwide 1994*. Anti-Defamation League and the World Jewish Congress.

Porter, R. (1982). Mixed Feelings: The Enlightenment and Sexuality in Eighteenth-Century Britain. In P. Bouce (Ed.), *Sexuality in Eighteenth-Century Britain*. Manchester University Press.

Powell, R. A., & Boer, D. P. (1994). Did Freud Mislead Patients to Confabulate Memories of Abuse? *Psychological Reports*, 74(3, Pt 2), 1283–1298. https://doi.org/10.2466/pr0.1994.74.3c.1283.

Powers, S., Rothman, D. J., & Rothman, S. (1996). *Hollywood's America: Social and Political Themes in Motion Pictures*. Westview Press.

Pratto, F., Stallworth, L. M., & Sidanius, J. (1997). The Gender Gap: Differences in Political Attitudes and Social Dominance Orientation. *British Journal of Social Psychology*, 36(1), 49–68. https://doi.org/10.1111/j.2044-8309.1997.tb01118.x.

Prawer, S. S. (1983). *Heine's Jewish Comedy: A Study of His Portraits of Jews and Judaism*. Clarendon Press.

President's Commission on Immigration and Naturalization (PCIN). (1971). *Whom We Shall Welcome*. De Capo Press. (Original work published 1953).

Pulzer, P. (1964). *The Rise of Political Anti-Semitism in Germany and Austria*. John Wiley & Sons, Inc.

—— (1979). Jewish Participation in Wilhelmine Politics. In D. Bronsen (Ed.), *Jews and Germans from 1860 to 1933: The Problematic Symbiosis*. Carl Winter Universitätsverlag.

Quaife, G. R. (1979). *Wanton Wenches and Wayward Wives: Peasants and Illicit Sex in Early–Seventeenth-Century England*. Croom Helm.

Quinn, R. (2025, February 17). Education Department Cancels Another $350 Million in Contracts, Grants. *Inside Higher Ed.* https://tinyurl.com/57ma8xx9.

Quinn, S. J. (2021). *Solzhenitsyn and the Right.* Antelope Hill Publishing.

—— (2022a). Igor Shafarevich and the Jews. *The Occidental Quarterly*, 22(4), 79–84.

—— (2022b). On "Russophobia" and Anti-Semitism. *The Occidental Quarterly*, 22(4), 69–75.

—— (2022c, November 8). Punching Back Weakly: William F. Buckley's *In Search of Anti-Semitism*. *The Occidental Observer.* https://tinyurl.com/3624p3th.

Raab, E. (1993a, July 23). Feinstein's Immigration Reform Bill Goes Too Far. *Jewish Bulletin of Northern California*, 142(27), 17. https://tinyurl.com/vtr3yhnk.

—— (1993b, February 19). Neo-Nazis in Germany, U.S. Aren't the Same. *Jewish Bulletin of Northern California*, 142(7), 23. https://tinyurl.com/yzvv9sry.

—— (1995). Can Antisemitism Disappear? In J. A. Chanes (Ed.), *Antisemitism in America Today: Outspoken Experts Explode the Myths.* Birch Lane Press.

—— (1996). Are American Jews Still Liberals? *Commentary*, 101(2), 43–45.

Raab, E., & Lipset, S. M. (1959). *Prejudice and Society.* Anti-Defamation League.

Radosh, R. (2000, October 26). From Walter Duranty to Victor Navasky: The *New York Times'* Love Affair with Communism. *Front Page Magazine.*

—— (2001a). *Commies: A Journey Through the Old Left, the New Left and the Leftover Left.* Encounter Books.

—— (2001b, June 5). Should We Ex-Leftists Be Forgiven? *Front Page Magazine.*

Ragins, S. (1980). *Jewish Responses to Anti-Semitism in Germany, 1870–1914.* Hebrew Union College Press.

Rahv, P. (1978). Twilight of the Thirties: Passage From an Editorial. In A. Porter, & A. Dvosin (Eds.), *Essays on Literature and Politics 1932–1972.* Houghton Mifflin.

Raisin, J. S. (1953). *Gentile Reactions to Jewish Ideals.* Philosophical Library.

Rapoport, L. (1990). *Stalin's War Against the Jews: The Doctors' Plot and the Soviet Solution.* Free Press.

Rasmussen Reports. (2018, June 27). 31% Think a U.S. Civil War Likely Soon. https://tinyurl.com/2f68v4yk.

Rather, L. J. (1986). Disraeli, Freud, and Jewish Conspiracy Theories. *Journal of the History of Ideas*, 47(1), 111–131. https://doi.org/10.2307/2709598.

—— (1990). *Reading Wagner: A Study in the History of Ideas.* Louisiana State University Press.

Ratner, S. (1987). Horace M. Kallen and Cultural Pluralism. In M. R. Konvitz (Ed.), *The Legacy of Horace M. Kallen.* Herzl Press.

Rawls, J. (1971). *A Theory of Justice.* Harvard University Press.

Ray, J. J. (1972). A New Balanced F Scale and Its Relation to Social Class. *Australian Psychologist*, 7(3), 155–166. https://doi.org/10.1080/00050067208259935.

Raz, N., Torres, I. J., Spencer, W. D., Millman, D., Baertschi, J. C., & Sarpel, G. (1993). Neuroanatomical Correlates of Age-Sensitive and Age-Invariant Cognitive Abilities. *Intelligence*, 17(3), 407–422. https://doi.org/10.1016/0160-2896(93)90008-S.

Reich, R. (1997). *Locked in the Cabinet.* Scribner.

Reich, W. (1961). *The Function of the Orgasm: Sex-Economic Problems of Biological Energy* (T. P. White, Trans.). Farrar, Straus & Giroux. (Original work published 1942).

—— (1975). *The Mass Psychology of Fascism.* Penguin.

Reichmann, E. (1951). *Hostages of Civilization: The Social Sources of National Socialist Anti-Semitism.* Beacon Press.

Reiser, M. F. (1989). The Future of Psychoanalysis in Academic Psychiatry: Plain Talk. *Psychoanalytic Quarterly*, 58(2), 185–209.

Restriction of Immigration: Hearings Before the U.S. House of Representatives Committee on Immigration and Naturalization, 68th Cong., 1st Sess. (1924).

Revision of Immigration, Naturalization and Nationality Laws: Joint Hearings Before the U.S. House of Representatives Subcommittees of the Committees on the Judiciary, 82nd Cong., 1st Sess., on S. 716, H.R. 2379 and H.R. 2816. (1951).

Reynolds, V. (1991). Socioecology of Religion. In M. Maxwell (Ed.), *The Sociobiological Imagination*. SUNY Press.

Rice, E. (1990). *Freud and Moses: The Long Journey Home*. SUNY Press.

Rice, J. L. (1992). *Freud's Russia: National Identity in the Evolution of Psychoanalysis*. Transaction Press.

Richard, J. (1992). *Saint Louis: Crusader King of France* (S. Lloyd, Ed., abridged) (J. Birrell, Trans.). Cambridge University Press. (Original work published 1983).

Richards, A. D. (1990). The Future of Psychoanalysis: The Past, Present, and Future of Psychoanalytic Theory. *Psychoanalytic Quarterly*, 59(3), 347–369. https://doi.org/10.1080/21674086.1990.11927276.

Richardson, H., & Salter, F. (2023). *Anglophobia: The Unrecognized Hatred*. Social Technologies.

Richerson, P. J., & Boyd, R. (1995). The Evolution of Human Ultra-sociality. Paper Presented at the Ringberg Symposium on Ideology, Warfare, and Indoctrinability. Ringberg Castle, Germany.

Richman, J. (2005, August 19). Powerful Gun Lobby Takes Aim with First Jewish Leader. *The Forward*. https://tinyurl.com/38s2ebz4.

Ringer, B. B., & Lawless, E. R. (1989). *Race, Ethnicity and Society*. Routledge.

Ringer, F. K. (1983). Inflation, Antisemitism and the German Academic Community of the Weimar period. *Leo Baeck Institute Yearbook*, 28(1), 3–9.

Rischin, M. (1978). The Jews and Pluralism: Toward an American Freedom Symphony. In G. Rosen (Ed.), *Jewish Life in America*. Institute of Human Relations Press of the American Jewish Committee.

Risen, J. (2004, April 28). How Pair's Finding on Terror Led to Clash on Shaping Intelligence. *The New York Times*. https://tinyurl.com/mrxy4j3j.

Roberts, J. M. (1972). *The Mythology of Secret Societies*. Scribner.

Roberts, P. C., & Stratton, L. M. (1995). *The New Color Line: How Quotas and Privilege Destroy Democracy*. Regnery Publishing.

Roberts, P. M. (1984). A Conflict of Loyalties: Kuhn, Loeb and Company and the First World War, 1914–1917. In J. R. Marcus & A. J. Peck (Eds.), *Studies in the American Jewish Experience II*. University Press of America.

Robertson, P. (1991). *The New World Order*. Word Publishing.

—— (1994). *The Collected Works of Pat Robertson*. Inspirational Press.

Roddy, J., (1966, January 25). How the Jews Changed Catholic Thinking. *Look Magazine*, 30(2). https://www.fisheaters.com/jewsvaticanii.html.

Rodríguez-Puértolas, J. (1976). A Comprehensive View of Medieval Spain. In J. Rubia Barcia (Ed.), *Américo Castro and the Meaning of Spanish Civilization*. University of California Press.

Rogoff, H. (1930). *An East Side Epic: The Life and Work of Meyer London*. Vanguard Press.

Rolnik, E. J., & Watzman, H. (2012). *Freud in Zion: Psychoanalysis and the Making of Modern Jewish Identity*. Karnac Books.

Ron, J. (2001, February 5). Is Ariel Sharon Israel's Milosevic? *Los Angeles Times*. https://www.latimes.com/archives/la-xpm-2001-feb-05-me-21284-story.html.

Rosen, A. (2024, November 14). Who Won the Jewish Vote? *Tablet*. https://www.tabletmag.com/sections/news/articles/jewish-vote-elections-2024.

Rosen, E. J., & Weltman, S. F. (1982). Jewish Families. In M. McGoldrick, J. Giordano, & N. Garcia-Preto (Eds.), *Ethnicity and Family Therapy* (pp. 367–679). The Guilford Press.

Rosenbaum, S. I. (2019, March 1). A Shocking Number of Jews Have Become Willing Collaborators of White Supremacy. *Boston Globe*. https://tinyurl.com/bdhxe8ts.

Rosenberg, M. J. (2019, February 14). This Is How AIPAC Really Works. *The Nation*. https://tinyurl.com/3d4p22de.

Rosenblatt, G. (2001, October 25). Will the Jews Be Blamed for Increasing Violence? *Jewish World Review*. http://www.jewishworldreview.com/1001/be.blamed.html.

Rosenblum, J. (2002, July 5). The Power of an Idea. *Jewish Media Resources*. www.jewishmediaresources.com/article/488/.

—— (2003, June 20). A Vision in Tatters. *Jewish Media Resources*. www.jewishmediaresources.com/article/591/.

Ross, E. A. (1914). *The Old World and the New: The Significance of Past and Present Immigration to the American People*. The Century Co.

Roth, P. (1963, December). Writing About Jews. *Commentary*. https://www.commentary.org/articles/philip-roth/writing-about-jews/.

Rothman, S., & Isenberg, P. (1974a, December). Freud and Jewish Marginality. *Encounter*, 43, 46–54.

—— (1974b, March). Sigmund Freud and the Politics of Marginality. *Central European History*, 7(1), 58–78. https://doi.org/10.1017/S0008938900010475.

Rothman, S., & Lichter, S. R. (1996). *Roots of Radicalism: Jews, Christians, and the New Left*. Transaction. (Original work published 1982).

Rothschild, R. C. (1949). *The Use of the Mass Media in Combating Anti-Semitism*. American Jewish Committee. https://tinyurl.com/mwzwt34u.

Rouche, M. (1987). The Early Middle Ages in the West. In P. Veyne (Ed.), *A History of Private Life* (Vol. 1). Harvard University Press.

Rowe, D. C. (1993). *The Limits of Family Influence: Genes, Experience, and Behavior*. Guilford Press.

Rozenbaum, W. (1973). The Background of the Anti-Zionist Campaign of 1967–1968 in Poland. *Essays in History*, 17, 70–96. https://doi.org/10.25894/eih.402.

—— (1978). The Anti-Zionist Campaign in Poland, June–December 1967. *Canadian Slavonic Papers*, 20(2), 218–236. http://dx.doi.org/10.1080/00085006.1978.11091523.

Rubenfeld, F. (1997). *Clement Greenberg: A Life*. Scribner.

Rubenstein, G. (1996). Two Peoples in One Land: A Validation Study of Altemeyer's Right-Wing Authoritarianism Scale in the Palestinian and Jewish Societies in Israel. *Journal of Cross-Cultural Psychology*, 27(2), 216–230. https://doi.org/10.1177/0022022196272005.

Rubenstein, J. (1996). *Tangled Loyalties: The Life and Times of Ilya Ehrenburg*. Basic Books.

—— (2013). *Leon Trotsky: A Revolutionary's Life*. Yale University Press.

Rubenstein, W. D. (1982). *The Left, the Right, and the Jews*. Universe Books.

Rubin, B. (1995a). *Assimilation and Its Discontents*. Times Books/Random House.

—— (1995b). American Jews, Israel, and the Psychological Role of Antisemitism. In J. A. Chanes (Ed.), *Antisemitism in America Today: Outspoken Experts Explode the Myths*. Birch Lane Press.

Rubin, J. [@JRubinBlogger]. (2021, August 12). *a more diverse, more inclusive society. this is fabulous news. now we need to prevent minority White rule*. [Thumbnail with link attached] [Post]. X. https://x.com/JRubinBlogcxfxger/status/1425899248269266947.

Rucker, P. (2014, March 5). Hillary Clinton Says Putin's Actions Are Like What Hitler Did Back in the Thirties. *The Washington Post*. https://tinyurl.com/ykdutzfr.

Rudd, M. (2005) Why Were There So Many Jews in SDS? Or, The Ordeal of Civility. *Fast Capitalism*, 1(2), 55–60. https://doi.org/10.32855/fcapital.200502.008.

Rühle, O. (1935). *Karl Marx: His Life and Work* (E. & C. Paul, Trans.). The Viking Press. (Original work published 1929).

Ruppin, A. (1913). *The Jews of To-day* (M. Bentwich, Trans.). G. Bell and Sons. (Original work published 1913).

—— (1971). *Arthur Ruppin: Memoirs, Diaries, Letters* (A. Bein, Ed.) (K. Gershon, Trans.). Weidenfeld and Nicholson.

—— (1972). *The Jewish Fate and Future* (E. W. Dickes, Trans.). Greenwood Press. (Original work published 1940).

—— (1973). *The Jews in the Modern World.* Arno Press. (Original work published in 1934).

Ruse, M. (1989). Is the Theory of Punctuated Equilibria a New Paradigm? *Journal of Social and Biological Structures,* 12(2–3), 195–212. https://doi.org/10.1016/0140-1750(89)90045-6.

Rushton, J. P. (1988). Race Differences in Behavior: A Review and Evolutionary Analysis. *Personality and Individual Differences,* 9(6), 1009–1024. https://doi.org/10.1016/0191-8869(88)90135-3.

——(1989). Genetic Similarity, Human Altruism, and Group Selection. *Behavioral and Brain Sciences,* 12(3), 503–559. https://doi.org/10.1017/S0140525X00057320.

—— (1995). *Race, Evolution, and Behavior: A Life-History Perspective.* Transaction Publishers.

—— (1997). Race, Intelligence and the Brain: The Errors and Omissions of the "Revised" Edition of S. J. Gould's *The Mismeasure of Man. Personality and Individual Differences,* 23(1), 169–180. https://doi.org/10.1016/S0191-8869(97)80984-1.

Russell, D. A. (1983). Exponential Evolution: Implications for Intelligent Extraterrestrial Life. *Advances in Space Research,* 3(9), 95–103. https://doi.org/10.1016/0273-1177(83)90045-5.

—— (1989). *The Dinosaurs of North America.* University of Toronto Press.

Ryan, A. (1994, November 17). Apocalypse Now? (Review of *The Bell Curve,* by R. J. Herrnstein and Charles Murray.) *New York Review of Books.* https://www.nybooks.com/articles/1994/11/17/apocalypse-now/.

S. Rep. No. 1515. (1950).

S. Rep. No. 950. (1948).

Saba, M. P. (1984). *The Armageddon Network.* Amana Books.

Sachar, H. M. (1992). *A History of Jews in America.* Alfred A. Knopf.

Sagi, A., Lamb, M. E., Lewkowicz, K. S., Shoham, R., Dvir, R., & Estes, D. (1985). Security of Infant-Mother, -Father, -Metapelet Attachments Among Kibbutz-Reared Israeli Children. In I. Bretherton & E. Waters (Eds.), *Growing Points in Attachment Theory and Research. Monographs for the Society for Research in Child Development,* 50(1–2), 233–275.

Saini, A. (2019, May 18). Why Race Science Is on the Rise Again. *The Guardian.* https://tinyurl.com/yw86mzhu.

Sale, K. (1973). *SDS.* Random House.

Sales, B. (2025a, February 7). 34 Liberal Jewish Groups Sign a Statement Defending DEI as an 'Invaluable Tool.' *Jewish Telegraphic Agency.* https://tinyurl.com/2jxpsnay.

—— (2025b, January 27). Dozens of Jewish Groups Protest Trump's Plans for Mass Deportation. *Jewish Telegraphic Agency.* https://tinyurl.com/4yw2trcz.

Salter, F. (1998a). A Comparative Analysis of Brainwashing Techniques. In I. Eibl-Eibesfeldt & F. Salter (Eds.), *Ideology, Warfare, and Indoctrinability.* Berghahn Books.

—— (1998b). *Ethnic Infrastructures U. S. A.: An Evolutionary Analysis of Ethnic Hierarchy in a Liberal Democracy.* MS in prep., Forschungsstelle Für Humanethologie in der Max-Planck-Gesellschaft, Andechs, Germany.

—— (2000). Is MacDonald a Scholar? Review of *Culture of Critique. Human Ethology Bulletin,* 15(3), 16–22. https://ishe.org/wp-content/uploads/2019/11/HEB_2000_15_3_1-31.pdf.

—— (2006). *On Genetic Interests: Family, Ethnicity, and Humanity in an Age of Mass Migration.* Routledge.

Samber, S. (2000, July 26). Cheney Has Earned Jewish Leaders' Respect. *Jewish World Review.* http://www.jewishworldreview.com/0700/cheney.jews.html.

Samelson, F. (1975). On the Science and Politics of the IQ. *Social Research: An International Quarterly*, 42(3), 467–488. https://www.jstor.org/stable/41582845.

—— (1979). Putting Psychology on the Map: Ideology and Intelligence Testing. In A. R. Buss (Ed.), *Psychology in Social Context*. Irvington Publishers.

—— (1982). H. H. Goddard and the Immigrants. *American Psychologist*, 37, 1291–1292.

Sammons, J. L. (1979). *Heinrich Heine: A Modern Biography*. Princeton University Press.

Samuel, M. (with MacDonald, K.). (2022). *You Gentiles*. Antelope Hill Publishing. (Original work published 1924).

Sandel, M. J. (1996, May 9). Dewey Rides Again. *The New York Review of Books*. https://www.nybooks.com/articles/1996/05/09/dewey-rides-again/.

Sanderson, B. (2011a, September 21). Mark Rothko, Abstract Expressionism and the Decline of Western Art. *The Occidental Observer*. https://tinyurl.com/yc3s9bef.

—— (2011b, April 13). Why Mahler? Norman Lebrecht and the Construction of Jewish Genius. *The Occidental Observer*. https://tinyurl.com/2fyjvdnt.

—— (2014, August 8). Australian PM Caves in to Jewish Lobby. *The Occidental Observer*. https://tinyurl.com/4jbhhr2d.

—— (2018). The Genesis of the Radical Left. *The Occidental Quarterly*, 18(2), 69–101.

—— (2019). The Alliance of the Jews and the Political Left, 1870–1930. *The Occidental Quarterly*, 19(3), 75–106.

—— (2020, December 31). Triggered by Beethoven: The Cultural Politics of Racial Resentment. *The Occidental Observer*. https://tinyurl.com/3992r456.

—— (2021, November 6). Evil Genius: Constructing Wagner as Moral Pariah. *The Occidental Observer*. https://tinyurl.com/mr3vz594.

—— (2023). Tristian Tzara and the Jewish Roots of Dada. *The Occidental Quarterly*, 23(2), 3–35.

Sandqvist, T (2006). *Dada East: The Romanians of Cabaret Voltaire*. MIT Press.

Sarich, V. (1995, February 26). Paper Presented at the Skeptics Society Meetings, at the California Institute of Technology, Pasadena, CA.

Sarich, V., & Miele, F. (2018). *Race: The Reality of Human Differences*. Routledge.

Saxon, W. (2003, April 23). Norbert Schlei, 73, Legal Advisor in the Kennedy-Johnson Era. *The New York Times*. https://tinyurl.com/4ber7he7.

Schapiro, L. (1961). The Role of Jews in the Russian Revolutionary Movement. *Slavonic and East European Review*, 40, 148–167.

Schatz, J. (1991). *The Generation: The Rise and Fall of the Jewish Communists of Poland*. University of California Press.

Schechter, S. (1909 [1961]). *Aspects of Rabbinic Theology*. Schocken Books.

Schiff, J. (1906, February 15). Letter from Jacob Schiff to Franz Boas. https://diglib.amphilsoc.org/node/122540.

Schiller, M. (1996). We Are Not Alone in the World. *Tikkun*, 11(2), 59–60. https://tinyurl.com/2dewurku.

Schlesinger, A. M., Jr. (1947). *The Vital Center: The Politics of Freedom*. Houghton Mifflin.

—— (1992). *The Disuniting of America: Reflections on a Multicultural Society*. W. W. Norton.

Schmidt, H. D. (1959). Anti-Western and Anti-Jewish Tradition in German Historical Thought. In R. Weltsch (Ed.), *Leo Baeck Institute Year Book: 1959*. East and West Library.

Schmidt, J. (2007). The Eclipse of Reason and the End of the Frankfurt School in America. *New German Critique*, 34(100), 47–76. http://dx.doi.org/10.1215/0094033X-2006-018.

Scholem, G. (1971). *The Messianic Idea in Judaism*. Schocken Books.

—— (1976). Walter Benjamin. In W. J. Dannhauser (Ed.), *On Jews and Judaism in Crisis: Selected Essays*. Schocken Books. (Original work published 1965).

—— (1979). On the Social Psychology of the Jews in Germany: 1900–1933. In D. Bronsen (Ed.), *Jews and Germans from 1860 to 1933: The Problematic Symbiosis* (pp. 18–20). Carl Winter Universitätsverlag.

—— (1980). *From Berlin to Jerusalem. Memories of My Youth* (H. Zohn, Trans.). Schocken Books.

Schorsch, I. (1972). *Jewish Reactions to German Anti-Semitism, 1870–1914*. Columbia University Press.

Schrader, E. (1998, June 20). Reform Jews Seek Revival of Traditions. *Los Angeles Times*. https://www.latimes.com/archives/la-xpm-1998-jun-20-mn-61784-story.html.

Schultz, P. W., Stone, W. F., & Christie, R. (1997). Authoritarianism and Mental Rigidity: The *Einstellung* Problem Revisited. *Personality and Social Psychology Bulletin*, 23(1), 3–9. https://doi.org/10.1177/0146167297231001.

Schuster, J. K., & Finkelstein, M. J. (2006). *The American Faculty: The Restructuring of Work and Careers*. Johns Hopkins University Press.

Schwarzschild, S. S. (1979). "Germanism and Judaism"—Hermann Cohen's Normative Paradigm of the German-Jewish Symbiosis. In D. Bronsen (Ed.), *Jews and Germans from 1860 to 1933: The Problematic Symbiosis*. Carl Winter Universitätsverlag.

Scruton, R. (1994). *Modern Philosophy*. Penguin.

Segerstråle, U. (1986). Colleagues in Conflict: An "In Vivo" Analysis of the Sociobiology Controversy. *Biology and Philosophy*, 1, 53–87. https://doi.org/10.1007/BF00127089.

—— (2000). *Defenders of the Truth: The Sociobiology Debate*. Oxford University Press.

Selzer, J. (Ed.). (1993). *Understanding Scientific Prose*. University of Wisconsin Press.

Sennett, R. (1995). Untitled Letter. *New York Review of Books*, 42(9), 43.

Shafarevich, I. (1989). Russophobia. *Nash Sovremennik*, 6:167–192. Trans. in JPRS-UPA-90-115 (March 22, 1990):2–37. https://apps.dtic.mil/sti/tr/pdf/ADA335121.pdf.

Shahak, I. (1994). *Jewish History, Jewish Religion: The Weight of Three Thousand Years*. Pluto Press.

Shahak, I., & Mezvinsky, N. (1999). *Jewish Fundamentalism in Israel*. Pluto Press.

Shapiro, E. S. (1989). Jewishness and the New York Intellectuals. *Judaism*, 38(3), 282–292.

—— (1992). *A Time for Healing: American Jewry since World War II*. Johns Hopkins University Press.

Shapiro, L. (1961). The Role of the Jews in the Russian Revolutionary Movement. *Slavonic and East European Studies*, 40(94), 148–167.

Shavit, A. (1996, May 27). How Easily We Killed Them. *The New York Times*. https://archive.ph/uTrEk#selection-391.0-391.25.

Shaw, S. J. (1991). *The Jews of the Ottoman Empire and the Turkish Republic*. New York University Press.

Sheehan, M. M. (1978). Choice of Marriage Partner in the Middle Ages: Development and Mode of Application of a Theory of Marriage. *Studies in Medieval and Renaissance History*, 1, 1–33.

Shepherd, N. (1993). *A Price Before Rubies: Jewish Women as Rebels and Radicals*. Harvard University Press.

Sheppard, R. (1999). *Modernism-Dada-Postmodernism*. Northwestern University Press.

Shils, E. A. (1956). *The Torment of Secrecy*. Free Press.

Shipler, D. K. (1981, February 20). Soviet Jews Found to Retain Identity. *The New York Times*. https://tinyurl.com/35dkbudc.

Shipman, P. (1994). *The Evolution of Racism: Human Differences and the Use and Abuse of Science*. Simon & Schuster.

Short, R. (1994). *Dada and Surrealism*. Laurence King Publishing.

Silberman, C. E. (1985). *A Certain People: American Jews and Their Lives Today*. Summit Books.

Silow-Carroll, A. (2023, November 12). American Jews Are Giving Mightily to Israel. Is There Enough Left to Go Around? *Jewish Telegraph Agency.* https://tinyurl.com/46b3etz7.

Simon, J. (1990). *Population Matters: People, Resources, Environment, and Immigration.* Transaction Press.

Simon Wiesenthal Center. (2003). Buchanan: War in Iraq Fault of Israel and the Jews. Simon Wiesenthal Center. https://tinyurl.com/3h9vv8b6.

Simpson, G. E., & Yinger, J. M. (1965). *Racial and Cultural Minorities* (3rd ed.). Harper & Row.

Sims, B. (1992). *Workers of the World Undermined: American Labor's Role in U.S. Foreign Policy.* South End Press.

Singer, D. (1979, July). Living With Intermarriage. *Commentary.* https://www.commentary.org/articles/david-singer-4/living-with-intermarriage/.

Singerman, R. (1986). The Jew as Racial Alien. In D. A. Gerber (Ed.), *Anti-Semitism in American History.* University of Illinois Press.

Sirkin, M. I., & Grellong, B. A. (1988). Cult and Non-Cult Jewish Families: Factors Influencing Conversion. *Cultic Studies Journal*, 5(1), 2–22.

Sklare, M. (1972). *Conservative Judaism* (2nd ed.). Schocken Books.

Sklare, M., & Vosk, M. (1957). The Riverton Study: How Jews Look at Themselves and Their Neighbors. *American Jewish Committee.* https://tinyurl.com/bdh7zp8w.

Skorecki, K., Selig, S., Blazer, S., Bradman, R., Bradman, N., Waburton, P. J., Ismajlowicz, M., & Hammer, M. F. (1997). Y Chromosomes of Jewish Priests. *Nature*, 385(6611), 32. https://doi.org/10.1038/385032a0.

Sky Group. (2024, February 19). In *Wikipedia.* https://en.wikipedia.org/w/index.php?title=Sky_Group&oldid=1208831488.

Slezkine, Y. (2004). *The Jewish Century.* Princeton University Press.

Smith, G. (1972). *Essays on Questions of the Day* (2nd ed.). Books for Libraries Press. (Original work published 1894).

Smith, R. M. (1988). The "American Creed" and American Identity: The Limits of Liberal Citizenship in the United States. *Western Political Science Quarterly*, 41(2), 225–251. https://doi.org/10.1177/106591298804100202.

Smith, M. S. (2023, July 12). How Jeremy Corbyn Was Toppled by the Israel Lobby. *Mondoweiss.* https://tinyurl.com/58e6379c.

Smith, T. W. (1994). *Anti-Semitism in Contemporary America.* American Jewish Committee.

Smooha, S. (1990). Minority Status in an Ethnic Democracy: The Status of the Arab Minority in Israel. *Ethnic and Racial Studies*, 13(3), 389–413. https://doi.org/10.1080/01419870.1990.9993679.

Snow, R. L. (2003). *Deadly Cults: The Crimes of True Believers.* Praeger.

Snyderman, M., & Herrnstein, R. J. (1983). Intelligence Tests and the Immigration Act of 1924. *American Psychologist*, 38(9), 986–995. https://doi.org/10.1037/0003-066X.38.9.986.

Sobran, J. (1995, September). The Jewish Establishment. *Sobran's*, 2(9), 4–5. http://www.sobran.com/establishment.shtml.

—— (1996a). The Buchanan Frenzy. *Sobran's*, 3(3), 3–4.

—— (1996b, June 13). In Our Hands. *The Wanderer.* http://www.sobran.com/columns/2005/050414.shtml.

—— (1999, October 26). Smearing Buchanan. *The Wanderer.* http://www.sobran.com/columns/1999-2001/991026.shtml.

Soloveichik, M. Y. (2003, February 1). The Virtue of Hate. *First Things.* https://www.firstthings.com/article/2003/02/the-virtue-of-hate.

Solzhenitsyn, A. (2011). *200 Years Together* (Adam's Blog, Trans.). (Original work published 2002). https://200yearstogether.wordpress.com/.

Sorin, G. (1985). *The Prophetic Minority: American Jewish Immigrant Radicals, 1820–1920.* Indiana University Press.

—— (1997). *Tradition Transformed: The Jewish Experience in America.* Johns Hopkins University Press.

Sorkin, D. (1985). The Invisible Community: Emancipation, Secular Culture, and Jewish Identity in the Writings of Berthold Auerbach. In J. Reinharz & W. Schatzberg (Eds.), *The Jewish Response to German Culture: From the Enlightenment to the Second World War.* University Press of New England for Clark University.

Southwood, T. R. E. (1977). Habitat, the Templet for Ecological Strategies? *Journal of Animal Ecology,* 46(2), 337–66. https://doi.org/10.2307/3817.

—— (1981). Bionomic Strategies and Population Parameters. In R. M. May (Ed.), *Theoretical Ecology: Principles and Applications.* Sinauer Associates.

Sparks, C. S., & Jantz, R. L. (2002). A Reassessment of Human Cranial Plasticity: Boas Revisited. *Proceedings of the National Academy of Science,* 99(23), 14636–14639. https://doi.org/10.1073/pnas.222389599.

—— (2003). Changing Times, Changing Faces: Franz Boas's Immigrant Study in Modern Perspective. *American Anthropologist,* 105(2), 333–337. http://dx.doi.org/10.1525/aa.2003.105.2.333.

Spector, B. (1992, September 27) Academy Criticism of a Foreign Associate Stirs Debate Over NAS Role and Policies. *The Scientist.* https://tinyurl.com/22k67u6e.

Spier, E. (1963). *Focus: A Footnote to the History of the Thirties.* O. Wolff.

Spruiell, V. (1989). The Future of Psychoanalysis. *Psychoanalytic Quarterly,* 58, 1–28.

Stanovich, K. (1999). *Who is Rational? Studies of Individual Differences in Reasoning.* Erlbaum.

—— (2004). *The Robot's Rebellion: Finding Meaning in the Age of Darwin.* The University of Chicago Press.

Stein, B. (1976). Whatever Happened to Small-town America? *The Public Interest,* 44(Summer), 17–26.

—— (1979). *The View from Sunset Boulevard.* Basic Books.

Stein, G. J. (1987). The Biological Bases of Ethnocentrism, Racism, and Nationalism in National Socialism. In V. Reynolds, V. Falger, & I. Vine (Eds.), *The Sociobiology of Ethnocentrism.* University of Georgia Press.

Steinlight, S. (2001). *The Jewish Stake in America's Changing Demography: Reconsidering a Misguided Immigration Policy.* Center for Immigration Studies.

—— (2004. April 1). High Noon to Midnight: Why Current Immigration Policy Dooms American Jewry. Center for Immigration Studies. www.cis.org/articles/2004/back404.html#Author.

Strauss, L. (1952). *Persecution and the Art of Writing.* Greenwood.

—— (1994). Why We Remain Jews: Can Jewish Faith and History Still Speak to Us? In K. L. Deutsch, & W. Nicgorski (Eds.), *Leo Strauss: Political Philosopher and Jewish Thinker* (pp. 43–79). Rowman & Littlefield Publishers, Inc. (Reprinted from lecture at the Hillel Foundation, University of Chicago, February 4, 1962.)

Stephens, B. (2016, May 9). Hillary: The Conservative Hope. *The Wall Street Journal.* https://www.wsj.com/articles/hillary-the-conservative-hope-1462833870.

Stern, F. (1961). *The Politics of Cultural Despair: A Study in the Rise of the Germanic Ideology.* University of California Press.

Stern, S. (1950). *The Court Jew: A Contribution to the History of Absolutism in Europe* (R. Weiman, Trans.). The Jewish Publication Society of America.

Stocking, G. W. (1968). *Race, Evolution, and Culture: Essays in the History of Anthropology.* Free Press.

—— (1989). The Ethnographic Sensibility of the 1920s and the Dualism of the Anthropological Tradition. In G. W. Stocking (Ed.), *Romantic Motives: Essays on Anthropological Sensibility* (Vol. 6: History of Anthropology) (pp. 208–276). University of Wisconsin Press.

—— (1992). *The Ethnographer's Magic and Other Essays in the History of Anthropology.* University of Wisconsin Press.

Stone, L. (1977). *The Family, Sex, and Marriage in England: 1500–1800.* Harper & Row.

—— (1990). *The Road to Divorce.* Oxford University Press.

Stone, R. (1992). Random Samples. *Science,* 257(5071), 742–743. https://doi.org/10.1126/science.1496394.

Stove, D. C. (1982). *Popper and After: Four Modern Irrationalists.* Pergamon Press.

Strosberg, B. B. (2022). Critical Theory and Anti-Semitism: Implications for Politics, Education, and Psychoanalysis. In J. Mills and D. Burston (Eds.), *Critical Theory and Psychoanalysis: From the Frankfurt School to Contemporary Critique.* Routledge.

Sulloway, F. (1979a). *Freud: Biologist of the Mind.* Basic Books.

—— (1979b, August 25). Freud as Conquistador. *The New Republic,* 25–31.

Svonkin, S. (1997). *Jews Against Prejudice: American Jews and the Fight for Civil Liberties.* Columbia University Press.

Sykes, B. (2001). *The Seven Daughters of Eve.* Norton.

Symott, M. G. (1986). Anti-Semitism and American Universities: Did quotas follow the Jews? In D. A. Gerber (Ed.), *Anti-Semitism in American history.* University of Illinois Press.

Szajkowski, Z. (1967). Paul Nathan, Lucien Wolf, Jacob H. Schiff and the Jewish Revolutionary Movements in Eastern Europe. *Jewish Social Studies,* 29(1), 1–19.

—— (1977). *Kolchak, Jews and the American Intervention in Northern Russia and Siberia, 1918–1920.* S. Frydman.

Szekacs-Weisz, J., & Keve, T. (Eds.). (2012). *Ferenczi and His World: Rekindling the Spirit of the Budapest School.* Karnac Books.

TAC. (2004, May 24). Friends of Israel Are Turning Up in the Strangest Places. *The American Conservative,* 19.

Talmadge, F. (2025). The Jews and the First New Deal, 1933–1934. *The Occidental Quarterly,* 25(1), 61–108.

Tannenhaus, S. (2003, May 3). Deputy Secretary Wolfowitz Interview with Sam Tannenhaus, *Vanity Fair.* United States Department of Defense News Transcript. https://archive.ph/PkJ9f.

Tarr, Z. (1977). *The Frankfurt School: The Critical Theories of Max Horkheimer and Theodor W. Adorno.* John Wiley and Sons.

Tarcov, N., & Pangle, T. L. (1987). Epilogue: Leo Strauss and the History of Political Philosophy. In L. Strauss, & J. Cropsey (Eds.), *History of Political Philosophy* (3rd ed.). University of Chicago Press.

Taylor, S. J. (1990). *Stalin's Apologist, Walter Duranty: The New York Times's Man in Moscow.* Oxford University Press.

Taylor, P. (1978). Cultural Diplomacy and the British Council: 1934–1939. *British Journal of International Studies,* 4(3), 244–265.

Terkel, A. (2025, January 31). Pentagon Removes Major Media Outlets, Including NBC News, in New 'Rotation Program.' *NBC News.* https://tinyurl.com/4snsvj69.

Treitschke, H. von. (1958). *A Word About Our Jewry* (H. Lederer, Trans.). Reimer. (Original work published 1881).

Thernstrom, S., & Thernstrom, A. (1997). *America in Black and White: One Nation, Indivisible.* Simon & Schuster.

Thompson, S. A. (2025, February 5). In the Eyes of Right-Wing Media, Trump Just Keeps on Winning. *The New York Times.*
https://www.nytimes.com/2025/02/05/technology/trump-media-right-wing.htm.

Tichenor, D. J. (2002). *Dividing Lines: The Politics of Immigration Control in America.* Princeton University Press.

Tifft, S. E., & Jones, A. S. (1999). *The Trust: The Private and Powerful Family behind* The New York Times. Little Brown & Co.

Tobin, G. A. (1988). *Jewish Perceptions of Antisemitism.* Plenum Press.

Toledano, R. de. (1996, June). Among the Ashkenazim. *Commentary,* 101(6), 48–51.

Toranska, T. (1987). *"Them": Stalin's Polish Puppets* (A. Kolakowska, Trans.). Harper & Row.

Torrey, E. F. (1992). *Freudian Fraud: The Malignant Effect of Freud's Theory on American Thought and Culture.* HarperCollins.

Triandis, H. C. (1990). Cross-cultural Studies of Individualism and Collectivism. *Nebraska Symposium on Motivation 1989: Cross Cultural Perspectives.* University of Nebraska Press.

—— (1991). Cross-cultural Differences in Assertiveness/Competition vs. Group Loyalty/Cohesiveness. In R. A. Hinde & J. Groebel (Eds.), *Cooperation and Prosocial Behavior.* Cambridge University Press.

—— (1995). *Individualism and Collectivism.* Westview Press.

Trivers, R. (1985). *Social Evolution.* Benjamin Cummings.

—— (1991). Deceit and Self-deception: The Relationship Between Communication and Consciousness. In M. Robinson & L. Tiger (Eds.), *Man and Beast Revisited.* Smithsonian Press.

Tucker, D. M., Vannatta, K., & Rothlind, J. (1990). Arousal and Activation Systems and Primitive Adaptive Controls on Cognitive Priming. In N. L. Stein, B. Leventhal, & T. Trabasso (Eds.), *Psychological and Biological Approaches to Emotion* (pp. 145–166). Lawrence Erlbaum Associates, Inc.

Tucker, R. W. (1999, November 1). Alone or With Others: The Temptations of Post-Cold War Power. *Foreign Affairs.* https://tinyurl.com/mtaayewd.

UNESCO. (2002). Toleration and Pluralism: A Comparative Study. UNESCO Evaluation Report Request no. 9926.

Unger, I., & Unger, D. (2006). *The Guggenheims—A Family History.* Harper Perennial.

Unz, R. K. (1998, November 16). Some Minorities Are More Minor than Others. *The Wall Street Journal.* https://www.wsj.com/articles/SB910996519185599500.

—— (2012, November 28). The Myth of American Meritocracy. *The Unz Review.*
https://www.unz.com/runz/the-myth-of-american-meritocracy/.

—— (2018a, September 10). American Pravda: 9/11 Conspiracy Theories. *The Unz Review.*
https://www.unz.com/runz/american-pravda-911-conspiracy-theories/.

—— (2018b, July 16). American Pravda: Oddities of the Jewish Religion. *The Unz Review.*
https://www.unz.com/runz/american-pravda-oddities-of-the-jewish-religion/

—— (2018c, October 22). American Pravda: Racial Discrimination at Harvard. *The Unz Review.*
https://www.unz.com/runz/american-pravda-racial-discrimination-at-harvard/.

—— (2023a, July 3). Affirmative Action and the Jewish Elephant in the Room. *The Unz Review.*
https://tinyurl.com/9rpxx7wr.

—— (2023b, May 1). The Neocons and Their Rise to Power. *The Unz Review.*
https://www.unz.com/runz/the-neocons-and-their-rise-to-power/.

—— (2024a, May 6). Israel/Gaza: The Masks Come Off in American Society. *The Unz Review.*
https://www.unz.com/runz/israel-gaza-the-masks-come-off-in-american-society/.

—— (2024b, January 15). Jews and Antisemitism at Harvard University. *The Unz Review.*
https://www.unz.com/runz/jews-and-antisemitism-at-harvard-university/.

—— (2024c, January 24). Prof. John Beaty and the True Origin of the Jews. *The Unz Review.* https://www.unz.com/runz/prof-john-beaty-and-the-true-origin-of-the-jews/.

Urofsky, M. I. (1989). The Brandeis Agenda. In N. L. Dawson (Ed.), *Brandeis in America.* University of Kentucky Press.

Vaksberg, A. (1994). *Stalin Against the Jews* (A. W. Bouis, Trans.). Knopf.

van Valen, L. (1974). Brain Size and Intelligence in Man. *American Journal of Physical Anthropology,* 40(3), 417–424. https://doi.org/10.1002/ajpa.1330400314.

Vann, B. (2003, May 23). The Historical Roots of Neoconservatism: A Reply to a Slanderous Attack on Trotskyism. *World Socialist Web Site.* https://www.wsws.org/en/articles/2003/05/shac-m23.html.

Veblen, T. (1934). *Essays in Our Changing Order.* Viking Press.

Vest, J. (2002, August 15). The Men From JINSA and CSP. The Nation. https://www.thenation.com/article/archive/men-jinsa-and-csp/.

Veyne, P. (1987). The Roman Empire. In P. Veyne (Ed.), *A History of Private Life* (Vol. 1). Harvard University Press.

Vidal, G. (1986, March 22). The Empire Lovers Strike Back. *The Nation,* 242(11), 350. https://tinyurl.com/3wky75px.

Vital, D. (1975). *The Origins of Zionism.* Oxford University Press.

Vitale, F. (2010). Jacques Derrida and the Politics of Architecture. *Serbian Architectural Journal,* 2(3), 215–226. http://dx.doi.org/10.5937/SAJ1003215V.

Vlahos, M. (2018, October 29). We Were Made for Civil War. *The American Conservative.* https://www.theamericanconservative.com/articles/we-were-made-for-civil-war/.

Volkogonov, D, (1995). *Lenin: A New Biography* (H. Shukman, Ed. & Trans.). Free Press.

Wade, N. (2011, June 13). Scientists Measure the Accuracy of a Racism Claim. *The New York Times.* https://www.nytimes.com/2011/06/14/science/14skull.html.

Wagner, R. (2022). *Judaism in Music.* In T. Dalton (Ed.), *Classical Essays on the Jewish Question, 1850–1945.* Clemens & Blair. (Original work published 1850 with 1869 supplement).

Wald, A. L. (1987). *The New York Intellectuals: The Rise and Decline of the Anti-Stalinist Left from the 1930s to the 1980s.* The University of North Carolina Press.

—— (2003, June 27). Are Trotskyites Running the Pentagon? *History News Network.* https://www.historynewsnetwork.org/article/are-trotskyites-running-the-pentagon.

—— (2017). Preface to *The New York Intellectuals, Thirtieth Anniversary Edition: The Rise and Decline of the Anti-Stalinist Left from the 1930s to the 1980s.* Project Muse.

Waldman, P. (2004, February 3). An Historian's Take on Islam Steers U.S. in Terrorism Fight: Bernard Lewis' Blueprint—Sowing Arab Democracy—Is Facing a Test in Iraq. *The Wall Street Journal.* https://www.wsj.com/articles/SB107576070484918411.

Wall, R. (1983). The Household: Demographic and Economic Changes in England, 1650–1970. In R. Wall, J. Robin, & P. Laslett (Eds.), *Family Forms in Historic Europe.* Cambridge University Press.

Wallace-Wells, B. (2010, December 23). Peretz in Exile. *New York.* https://nymag.com/news/features/70310/.

Wallerstein, J., & Kelly, J. B. (1980). *Surviving the Breakup.* Basic Books.

Walzer, M. (1983). *Exodus and Revolution.* Basic Books.

—— (1994). Toward a New Realization of Jewishness. *Congress Monthly,* 61(4), 3–6.

Warburg, F. (1933, October 5). Letter from Felix Warburg to Franz Boas. https://diglib.amphilsoc.org/node/123572.

Ward, J. (2023, March 30). How a Judge's Visit to Stanford Has Changed the Debate Over Free Speech on Campus. *Yahoo News.* https://tinyurl.com/3fmvx6z5.

Washburn, K. K. (2009). Felix Cohen, Anti-Semitism, and American Indian Law. *American Indian Law Review*, 33(2), 583–605.
https://digitalcommons.law.ou.edu/cgi/viewcontent.cgi?article=1133&context=ailr.

Watson, J. (2007, October 19). To Question Genetic Intelligence Is Not Racism. *The Independent*. https://tinyurl.com/msdpr363.

Wattenberg, B. (1984). *The Good News Is the Bad News Is Wrong*. AEI Press.

—— (1991). *The First Universal Nation: Leading Indicators and Ideas about the Surge of America in the 1990s*. Free Press.

—— (2001, March 19). Melt. Melting. Melted. *Jewish World Review*.
www.jewishworldreview.com/cols/wattenberg031901.asp.

—— (2002, November 14). *Richard Perle: The Making of a Neoconservative* [Radio Broadcast Transcript]. PBS. https://www.pbs.org/thinktank/transcript1017.html.

Waxman, C. (1989). The Emancipation, the Enlightenment, and the Demography of American Jewry. *Judaism*, 38(4), 488–501.

Webb, J. (1995, June 5). In Defense of Joe Six-Pack. *The Wall Street Journal*.

Webster, R. (1995). *Why Freud Was Wrong: Sin, Science, and Psychoanalysis*. Basic Books.

Weindling, P. J. (2007). Central Europe Confronts German Racial Hygiene: Friedrich Hertz, Hugo Iltis and Ignaz Zollschan as Critics of Racial Hygiene. In M. Turda & P. J. Weindling (Eds.), *Blood and Homeland: Racism and Racial Nationalism in Central and Southeast Europe, 1900–1940* (pp. 263–280). Central European Press.

Weinfeld, M. (1993). The Ethnic Sub-Economy: Explication and Analysis of a Case Study of the Jews of Montreal. In R. J. Brym, W. Shaffir, & M. Weinfeld (Eds.), *The Jews in Canada*. Oxford University Press.

Weingarten, A. (2008). *Jewish Organizations' Response to Communism and to Senator McCarthy*. Vallentine Mitchell.

Weinstein, A., & Vassiliev, A. (1999). *The Haunted Wood: Soviet Espionage in America—The Stalin Era*. Random House.

Weiss, P. (2016, April 19). 'Forward' Columnist and Emily's List Leader Relate 'Gigantic,' 'Shocking' Role of Jewish Democratic Donors. *Mondoweiss*.
https://tinyurl.com/56r2dwr5.

Werth, N. (1999). A State Against Its People: Violence, Repression, and Terror in the Soviet Union. In Courtois, S., Werth, N., Panné, J., Paczkowski, A., Bartosek K., & Margolin, J., *The Black Book of Communism: Crimes, Terror, Repression* (J. Murphy & M. Kramer, Trans.). Harvard University Press.

Westermarck, G. (1922). *The History of Human Marriage* (5th ed.). Allerton.

Westervelt, E. (2025, February 6). Trump Executive Order Aims to Deport International Students Who Have Protested Israel. *National Public Radio*.
https://tinyurl.com/yhbfzwf3.

Weyl, N., & Marina, W. (1971). *American Statesmen on Slavery and the Negro*. Arlington House.

Wheatland, T. (2009). *The Frankfurt School in Exile*. University of Minnesota Press.

Whitaker, B. (2002, August 19). US Thinktanks Give Lessons in Foreign Policy. The Guardian.
https://www.theguardian.com/world/2002/aug/19/worlddispatch.

White, E. (2017, November 3). The Hollywood Darling Who Tanked His Career to Combat Anti-Semitism. *The Paris Review*. https://tinyurl.com/ywk7a4cd.

White, L. (1966). The Social Organization of Ethnological Theory. *Rice University Studies: Monographs in Cultural Anthropology*, 52(4), 1–66.

Whitfield, S. J. (1988). *American Space, Jewish Time*. Archon.

Wickett, J. C., Vernon, P. A., & Lee, D. H. (1994). In Vivo Brain Size, Head Perimeter, and Intelligence in a Sample of Healthy Adult Females. *Personality and Individual Differences*, 16(6), 831–838. https://doi.org/10.1016/0191-8869(94)90227-5.

Wicks, R. J. (2007). *Modern French Philosophy: From Existentialism to Postmodernism.* Oneworld.

Wiesel, E. (1985). *Against Silence: The Voice and Vision of Elie Wiesel* (Vol. 1) (I. Abrahamson, Selected and Ed.). Holocaust Library.

Wiggershaus, R. (1994). *The Frankfurt School: Its History, Theories, and Political Significance* (M. Robertson, Trans.). MIT Press.

Wilkerson, L. (Guest). (2025, July 9). COL. Lawrence Wilkerson : Does The Deep State Control Trump? In *Judge Napolitano – Judging Freedom.* YouTube. https://www.youtube.com/live/qo9JCvTbu-Q?si=7BGGAvEJgSsIsmVf.

Willerman, L., Schultz, R., Rutledge, J. N., & Bigler, E. D. (1991). *In vivo* Brain Size and Intelligence. *Intelligence, 15*(2), 223–228. https://doi.org/10.1016/0160-2896(91)90031-8.

Willets, H. (1987). Introduction to T. Trunks, "*Them*": *Stalin's Polish Puppets* (A. Kolakowska, Trans.). Harper & Row.

Williams, G. C. (1985). A Defense of Reductionism in Evolutionary Biology. In R. Dawkins, & M. Ridley (Eds.), *Oxford Surveys in Evolutionary Biology* (Vol. 2) (pp. 1–27). Oxford University Press.

Williams, O. (2023, May 2). The Extreme Center: How the Neocons Went Woke. *The Occidental Observer.* https://tinyurl.com/yfphxdm8.

Wilson, E. O. (1975). *Sociobiology: The New Synthesis.* Harvard University Press.

—— (1994). *Naturalist.* Island Press.

Wilson, J. C. (2004). *The Politics of Truth: Inside the Lies that Led to War and Betrayed My Wife's CIA Identity—A Diplomat's Memoir.* Carroll & Graf.

Wilson, J. Q. (1993a, April). The Family-Values Debate. *Commentary.* https://www.commentary.org/articles/james-wilson/the-family-values-debate/.

—— (1993b). *The Moral Sense.* Free Press.

Winik, J. (1988). The Neoconservative Reconstruction. *Foreign Policy, 73,* 135–152. https://doi.org/10.2307/1148881.

—— (1997). *On the Brink: The Dramatic Behind the Scenes Saga of the Reagan Era and the Men and Women Who Won the Cold War.* Simon & Schuster.

Winston, D. (1978). Viet Nam and the Jews. In J. N. Porter (Ed.), *The Sociology of American Jews: A Critical Anthology.* University Press of America.

Wirth, L. (1956). *The Ghetto.* University of Chicago Press.

Wisse, R. (1987, November). The New York (Jewish) Intellectuals. *Commentary.* https://tinyurl.com/y5tvtf8d.

Wistrich, R. (1976). *Revolutionary Jews from Marx to Trotsky.* George G. Harrap & Co Ltd.

Wittels, F. (1924). *Sigmund Freud: His Personality, His Teaching, & His School* (E. & C. Paul, Trans.). George Allen & Unwin.

Wolf, E. R. (1990). The Anthropology of Liberal Reform. In H. Caton (Ed.), *The Samoa Reader: Anthropologists Take Stock.* University Press of America.

Wolffsohn, M. (1993). *Eternal Guilt? Forty Years of German-Jewish-Israeli Relations* (D. Bokovoy, Trans.). Columbia University Press.

Wolin, S., & Slusser, R. M. (1957). *The Soviet Secret Police.* Praeger.

Woocher, J. S. (1986). *Sacred Survival: The Civil Religion of American Jews.* Indiana University Press.

Wood, J. L. (1974). *The Sources of American Student Activism.* Lexington Books.

Woodward, B. (2004). *Plan of Attack.* Simon & Schuster.

Wreszin, M. (1994). *A Rebel in Defense of Tradition: The Life and Politics of Dwight Macdonald.* Basic Books.

Wright, D., & Leeds-Matthews, A. (2025, February 1). Elon Musk Spent More than $290 Million on the 2024 Election, Year-End FEC Filings Show. CNN. https://tinyurl.com/5ecet3he.

Wright, R. (1990, January 29). The Intelligence Test. Review of *Wonderful Life*, by Stephen Jay Gould. *The New Republic*, 28.

—— (1996, November 28). *Homo deceptus*: Never trust Stephen Jay Gould. *Slate*. https://slate.com/news-and-politics/1996/11/homo-deceptus.html.

Wrigley, E. A., & Schofield, R. (1981). *The Population History of England, 1541–1871*. Harvard University Press.

Wulfsohn, J. F. (2023, March 13). Republican 2024 Hopefuls Respond to Tucker Carlson About Stance on Russia-Ukraine War. *Fox News*. https://tinyurl.com/ycy65a47.

Wussow, Philipp von. (2014). Horkheimer und Adorno über "jüdische Psychologie." Ein vergessenes Theorieprogramm der 1940er Jahre. *Naharaim*, 8(2), 172–209. https://doi.org/10.1515/NAHA-2014-0013.

Yeats, M. (2024, October 7). The Worldwide Holocaust Tour. *The Occidental Observer*. https://www.theoccidentalobserver.net/2024/10/07/the-worldwide-holocaust-tour/.

Yerushalmi, Y. H. (1991). *Freud's Moses: Judaism Terminable and Interminable*. Yale University Press.

Yinon, O. (1982). A *Strategy for Israel in the 1980s* (I. Shahak, Ed. & Trans.). Association of Arab-American University Graduates, Inc. https://archive.ph/n6BE6.

Yoffe, E. H. (2023, January 9). Primitive, Fanatic and Messianic: The Racist Judaism of Israel's 'Religious' Government. *Haaretz*. https://tinyurl.com/4t8susw4.

Young-Bruehl, E. (1996). *The Anatomy of Prejudices*. Harvard University Press.

Zacharia, J. (2004, May 29). Jews Fear Being Blamed for Iraq War. *The Jerusalem Post*.

Zangwill, I. (1923, October 19). *The American Hebrew*, p. 582.

—— (1914). *The Melting Pot*. In *The Works of Israel Zangwill* (Vol. 12). AMS Press. (Original work published 1908).

Zaretsky, E. (1994). The Attack on Freud. *Tikkun*, 9(May/June), 65–70.

Zaroulis, N., & Sullivan, G. (1984). *Who Spoke Up? American Protest against the War in Vietnam, 1963–1975*. Doubleday.

Zborowski, M., & Herzog, E. (1952). *Life Is with People: The Jewish Little-Town of Eastern Europe*. International Universities Press.

Zhitlowski, H. (1972). The Jewish Factor in My Socialism. In I. Howe, & E. Greenberg (Eds.), *Voices from the Yiddish: Essays, Memoirs, Diaries* (L. Dawidowicz, Trans.). University of Michigan Press.

ZOA. (2002, August 7). ZOA Strongly Praises Defense Secretary Rumsfeld for Distancing Himself From the Term "Occupied Territory." The Zionist Organization of America. https://tinyurl.com/yz92d8bn.

Zuckerman, H. (1996). *The Scientific Elite: Nobel Laureates in the United States*. Transaction. (Original work published 1977).

About the Author

Kevin MacDonald is Professor Emeritus of Psychology at California State University–Long Beach and editor of *The Occidental Quarterly* (toqonline.com) and *The Occidental Observer* (theoccidentalobserver.net). After receiving a Master's degree in evolutionary biology, he received a Ph.D. in Biobehavioral Sciences, both at the University of Connecticut. His research has focused on developing evolutionary perspectives on culture, developmental psychology and personality theory, the origins and maintenance of monogamous marriage in Western Europe, and ethnic relations (group evolutionary strategies). He is the author of more than 100 scholarly papers and reviews, and several books, most recently *Individualism and the Western Liberal Tradition: Evolutionary Origins, History, and Prospects for the Future* (2019). Besides the current new edition of *The Culture of Critique: An Evolutionary Analysis of Jewish Involvement in Twentieth-Century Intellectual and Political Movements* (originally published in 1998), he is also the author of: *Separation and Its Discontents: Toward an Evolutionary Theory of Anti-Semitism* (1998); *A People That Shall Dwell Alone: Judaism as a Group Evolutionary Strategy* (1994); and *Social and Personality Development: An Evolutionary Synthesis* (1988). *Cultural Insurrections*, a collection of essays, appeared in 2008. He has also edited three books, *Sociobiological Perspectives on Human Development* (1988), *Parent-Child Play: Descriptions and Implications* (1994), and *Evolutionary Perspectives on Human Development* (2004).

ENJOYED THIS BOOK?

TO READ MORE, VISIT US AT

ANTELOPEHILLPUBLISHING.COM